The 1988 Dow Jones-Irwin Business and Investment Almanac

The 1988 DOW JONES-IRWIN Business and Investment Almanac

Edited by

Sumner N. Levine
State University of New York
at Stony Brook
and Editor
Financial Analyst's Handbook
and
The Investment Manager's Handbook

Executive Editor
Caroline Levine

DOW JONES-IRWIN
Homewood, Illinois 60430

ISBN 1–55623–047–8

Printed in the United States of America

1 2 3 4 5 6 7 8 9 0 K 3 2 1 0 9 8 7 6

Preface

This twelfth edition of the annual *Dow Jones-Irwin Business and Investment Almanac* contains a number of new features in response to the rapidly changing business and investment scene as well as updates on our standard features.

The editor and publisher are, of course, pleased with the acceptance of the *Dow Jones-Irwin Business and Investment Almanac* as a standard and unique reference for the business and investment community. As always, we continue to invite suggestions from our readers. All suggestions should be sent to: *Dow Jones-Irwin Business and Investment Almanac*, P.O. Box D, Setauket, New York 11733.

Sumner N. Levine
Editor

References to companies, securities, and other investment information do not constitute a recommendation or endorsement.

Contents

The 1988 Dow Jones-Irwin Business and Investment Almanac

Business in Review

September 1986—September 1987

September 1986*

2 The Hunt brothers face the collapse of their family fortune following Friday's bankruptcy-court filing of Placid Oil, their flagship energy concern. Creditor banks, owed nearly $1.5 billion, are considering seeking a court trustee to run Placid, which effectively would wrest control from the Hunts and could threaten other parts of the family empire.

OPEC began observing its agreement to reduce oil production by four million barrels a day. But hopes that the accord will last depend on the course of the Iran-Iraq war and support from the oil industry.

The economy continued to move erratically over the past two months. In July, the nation's trade deficit widened to a record $18.04 billion, suggesting a worsening slump for manufacturers and farmers. But factory orders rose strongly in August, brightening prospects of an expansion.

The dollar was mostly lower in European and Asian trading, mainly in reaction to the July trade deficit. Analysts, meanwhile, urged the Fed to refrain from easing credit further despite the economy's sluggishness.

Ford and Chrysler began offering rival incentive programs after GM's plan drew a big consumer response. Their entry is likely to prevent GM from increasing its market share much from the incentives.

3 Peat Marwick Mitchell has agreed to merge with KMG Main Hurdman, sources said, creating the world's biggest accounting firm. The combination, which would eclipse No. 1 Arthur Andersen, will include various international affiliates of both companies. The accord is expected to be announced this week.

Stock and bond prices plunged amid worries of renewed inflation. The Dow Jones industrials tumbled 27.98 points, to 1870.36, while some long-term Treasury bonds skidded about 1½ points. Concern about inflation was triggered by surging precious metals and oil prices.

Factory orders jumped 2.2% during July, though analysts said a surge in military orders masked continued sluggishness in the overall economy. Construction spending rose 0.5%, indicating home building remained strong while other sectors were weak.

4 The U.S. and Britain will soon announce a framework for exchanging information on insider trading and other abuses on international securities and commodity markets.

5 Stock prices soared as the Dow Jones Industrials jumped 38.38 points to close at a record 1919.71. The rally was fueled by investor enthusiasm for energy and heavy-industry issues. It was the busiest trading day in over five months. Other stock market indexes also rose, though bonds, commodities and currencies were little changed.

U.S. car sales fell 12% in late August from the year-earlier record level, which was fueled by strong buyer incentives. But the new round of cut-rate financing boosted sales at the end of the latest period.

8 Unemployment eased in August, suggesting a slight improvement in the nation's economy. Last month's decline, to 6.8% from 6.9%, brought the civilian jobless rate to its lowest level since January. Expectations of a stronger economy, as well as surging commodity prices, have damped speculation that the Fed will push interest rates lower.

West Germany's economy grew at a strong 3.3% rate in the second quarter, making a decline in German interest rates less likely. But analysts believe the U.S. and other European nations will continue to press for a reduction in German rates.

9 Platinum and gold plunged amid heavy profit-taking, derailing the recent rally by precious metals. The decline was fueled partly by a stronger U.S. dollar,

*The cut-off date for Business in Review is usually the end of August because of our production schedule. Since the last entry in the previous Almanac was August 29, 1986, the current entry commences September 2, 1986.

which gained as the bond market slump deepened. Stock prices skidded in active trading.

Compaq Computer said it will introduce two personal computers that are at least twice as fast as IBM's PC. The new models will use Intel Corp.'s advanced microchip.

10 Delta Air Lines agreed to acquire Western Air for about $860 million. The merger will strengthen Atlanta-based Delta's position as a national carrier, giving it more Western routes and boosting its fleet 26%. The pact also signals Delta's move away from a conservative strategy of internal growth.

U.S. auto makers intend to boost production 3.7% in the fourth quarter, mainly because sales have surged in response to incentive programs. But the higher output could swell inventories again, particularly for GM.

Bond prices rebounded from a five-day slump, mainly on technical factors. The U.S. dollar finished mixed, while stock prices drifted lower. The Dow Jones industrials declined 4.50 points, to 1884.14.

Platinum prices skidded for the second day in a row, though some analysts expect the metal to rally again soon. Cobalt prices, meanwhile, have surged on reports of shortages in two big African producing nations.

Japan's economy grew at a relatively sluggish 3.6% rate in the latest quarter, as the strong yen continued to hurt exports. A Japanese official said the economy may worsen despite plans to stimulate growth.

11 Platinum prices plunged below $600 an ounce as volume hit a record in volatile trading. The metal has plummeted a total of $87.50, or 13%, in the past three days.

The trade deficit shrank slightly in the second quarter, to $36.02 billion, as imported oil prices fell. Meanwhile, Canada posted its first trade deficit in 10 years, mainly due to slower demand from the U.S.

Norway plans to trim its oil exports 10% for two months to support OPEC's effort to boost prices. The surprise move dismayed the U.S. and Britain, which had urged Norway to maintain its free-market policy.

12 Stock prices plummeted in heavy trading, pushing the Dow Jones industrials down a record 86.61 points, or 4.61%, to 1792.89. The huge sell-off, which stunned traders, was triggered by worries about higher interest rates and renewed inflation. Bond prices and precious metals also tumbled, while the dollar soared.

Rumors about a big rise in August retail sales, to be reported today, fueled the markets' decline. The latest leaks came only months after the Commerce Department tightened its control over sensitive data.

Capital spending is being cut further this year because of the energy slump and pending tax-overhaul bill, a Commerce Department poll shows. Businesses now plan to spend 2.5% less on plant and equipment, rather than 1.3% expected earlier.

Moscow soon may allow Western companies to participate in joint ventures in the Soviet Union. But American executives, who have been told of the plan by Soviet officials, have mixed feelings about the idea.

15 Reagan officials don't plan to respond with new economic initiatives in the wake of last week's stock market plunge. Meanwhile, analysts predict that some of the same factors that caused the drop are likely to fuel a rally on "triple witching" Friday. Prices on the London and Tokyo exchanges also fell steeply.

The dollar likely will decline this week amid continued confusion over the economy, analysts say. Investment managers fear the worst may yet come in the bond market.

Retail sales rose 0.8% in August after increasing a revised 0.3% in July, and producer prices were up 0.3%. The data, which refute rumors that helped drive down the financial markets last week, suggest the economy is gaining modestly and a new burst of inflation isn't in sight.

IBM announced an early retirement program aimed at cutting several thousand jobs. But some analysts said the program, IBM's biggest, won't help it avoid an earnings drop this year and doesn't trim its huge payroll and high costs enough.

Apple is introducing a new version of its Apple II in hopes of breathing new life into the product line. Separately, Apple and Northern Telecom are working together on some projects to increase their share of the U.S. office automation market.

16 Texas Air agreed to buy People Express and its Frontier Air unit for about $298 million, mostly in securities. The agreement, along with the proposed takeover of Eastern, would make

Texas Air the world's biggest airline after Aeroflot. But Texas Air faces several problems by acquiring People, including higher debt and new antitrust questions.

U.S. car sales soared 36.9% in early September because of record-low financing rates by auto makers. But the sales pace isn't expected to continue, and one analyst estimates that total 1986 auto sales may be down slightly from a year earlier.

Stock prices staged a feeble rebound, though bonds strengthened on renewed speculation of Japanese and West German interest-rate cuts. The Dow Jones industrials closed up 8.86 points, at 1767.58. The dollar weakened in lackluster trading.

Oil prices skidded to a five-week low on world markets amid a continued oversupply of refined products. The decline worsened as Indonesia's energy minister predicted that oil prices would average $15 to $16 a barrel for the rest of the decade.

Business inventories grew 0.4% in July, with retailers showing the sharpest increase. Sales rose 0.7% during the month, leaving the ratio of inventories to sales unchanged.

17 Most stocks closed lower following a jittery session, though some blue chips posted gains. The Dow Jones industrials finished up 10.96 points, at 1778.54. Bond prices rallied in the afternoon, erasing most of the sharp declines from earlier in the day.

Tokyo stocks plunged again, causing the Nikkei average to post a record drop for the second day in a row. London shares also tumbled.

Industrial output rose 0.1% during August following a revised 0.3% gain in July. The report suggested the manufacturing slump may be easing. Separately, the deficit in goods and services trade grew to a record $34.73 billion in the second quarter.

18 Housing starts rose a slight 0.4% in August from the prior month's relatively sluggish pace. Some analysts expect residential building will hold steady for the rest of this year but weaken in 1987. Separately, the industrial operating rate slipped to 79% during August.

The Farm Credit System could have a record $2.9 billion loss this year, making a federal bailout inevitable, according to a GAO report. The agency said the big farm lender could be broke by early next year.

19 Union Pacific agreed to buy Overnite Transportation for $43.25 a share, or $1.2 billion, accelerating the move by railroads into other transportation services. Union Pacific's purchase of the Virginia-based trucking firm will extend its reach into the eastern U.S. and lead to efficiencies in freight transportation.

AT&T announced a new severance package for managers it plans to lay off as part of a cost-cutting program. Speculation has been rife in the firm that up to 25,000 may be affected.

USX Corp. is attracting several corporate raiders, fueling speculation the steel and oil giant may face a takeover bid or forced restructuring. There were reports that investors Carl Icahn and Irwin Jacobs were acquiring shares in the company.

The dollar plunged as Treasury Secretary Baker stepped up pressure on West Germany and Japan to lower interest rates. The slide by the U.S. currency, which fell below two marks, sparked a sell-off in bonds.

Honeywell reorganized its controls businesses and said it may try to buy Sperry's aerospace and marine group from Burroughs. Honeywell also announced plans to lay off 4.3% of its work force by year's end.

BankAmerica's stock plunged further on continued speculation it was seeking a federal bailout. The rumors prompted SEC inquiries and have made the banking firm more vulnerable to a potential takeover bid.

GNP grew only at a 0.6% rate in the second quarter, the Commerce Department confirmed, but corporate profits were weaker than predicted. An inflation measure was lowered to 1.8%, the smallest in 19 years.

Ford Motor is tentatively boosting prices on 1987-model cars 3.2% to 9%. The increases, which seem to match GM's, come during the industry's biggest incentive program ever.

22 Congress is rushing to sell billions in federal assets to escape the threat of Gramm-Rudman spending cuts before the November elections. But some lawmakers and analysts doubt the last-ditch effort, which includes the sale of loans, will do much to shrink the deficit.

Consumer spending surged 1.1% in August, but the pace isn't expected to continue. Last month's increase, the biggest since December, mainly resulted from strong car sales buoyed by incentive programs. Personal income was up 0.4% for the month.

USX Corp.'s stock was heavily traded Friday as speculation heightened about a takeover or forced restructuring of the No. 1 steelmaker. There were rumors T. Boone Pickens had become the latest investor to acquire a large stake in USX.

23 USX Corp. moved to buy time against a possible takeover threat. The firm will study potential restructuring steps to boost the value of its stock, which analysts say is aimed at stemming shareholder defections.

Honda Motor will start making auto engines in the U.S. today, the first Japanese firm to do so. The U.S., meanwhile, wants Ottawa to abandon a program that encourages foreign auto plants in Canada.

25 U.S. car sales rose 1.7% in mid-September from a year earlier, disappointing some analysts because of the unprecedented sales incentives by auto makers. GM, which triggered the incentive programs last month, just matched its year-ago sales.

The House approved a bill to cut the deficit an estimated $15.1 billion and meet Gramm-Rudman targets. The measure authorizes a Conrail stock offering and the sale of billions of dollars in federal loans.

Fed Chairman Volcker said the dollar needn't decline much further if West Germany and Japan can step up imports. His comments, which boosted the dollar, came as the U.S. prepared to press Bonn and Tokyo on the issue during a two-day trade meeting.

BankAmerica dropped plans to buy Oregon's third-largest bank, reflecting the banking giant's financial problems. Regulatory approval was said to have been in doubt because of BankAmerica's continued losses.

U.S. computer chip makers claimed the Japanese already are violating an anti-dumping agreement signed last month. Separately, National Semiconductor signed a long-term agreement to manufacture and sell computer chips in Japan.

26 The tax-overhaul bill was approved by the House, 292–136. The measure moves today to the Senate, where it is expected to be approved and sent to Reagan, an avid supporter of the bill. The historic legislation will sharply reduce rates for businesses and individuals and eliminate dozens of tax breaks.

Stock prices tumbled as investors grew wary about the outlook for corporate profits. The Dow Jones industrials slid 34.73 points, to 1768.56. A bond rally fizzled amid uncertainty about the economy and interest rates.

Gold prices edged higher, bucking a sharp decline by other precious metals. Spot bullion rose $3 an ounce, to $434.50, on the Comex.

The British pound fell further despite continued intervention by the Bank of England. Sterling's drop diverted attention from the dollar, which was little changed. Meanwhile, West Germany again decided against lowering its interest rates.

29 The tax bill was sent to the White House after the Senate approved the landmark measure, 74–23. The bill's passage is a major victory for Reagan, but Democrats are likely to reap political benefits as well. Businesses and individuals are scrambling to prepare themselves for the sweeping tax changes.

Bertelsmann will pay over $500 million to acquire Doubleday & Co., making it the second-largest book publisher in the U.S. Some industry executives said the West German concern may be paying too much.

Economic growth picked up to a 2.3% rate in the current quarter, a Journal survey of economists shows. Separately, machine tool orders remained sluggish in August, indicating caution by durable-goods makers.

30 The Soviet Union is expected to default again on a long-term grain-purchase accord, dealing another blow to U.S. agriculture. Moscow's failure to meet its buying quota would come despite a U.S. offer of subsidies.

The dollar plunged in reaction to the Group of Seven's failure to reach an exchange-rate accord. Bond and stock prices slumped in reaction, though stocks recovered somewhat near the close of trading.

New construction contracts rose 3% in August, spurred by a 10% boost in commercial building. The rise suggests the building boom isn't over yet, an F. W. Dodge analyst said.

October 1986

1 The trade deficit shrank to $13.32 billion in August, sharply smaller than July's record level. But economists and busi-

nessmen differed on whether the report signals a turnaround in the nation's trade problems. The August trade figure, which is subject to revision, reflected a smaller deficit in manufacturing and the first surplus in farm trade since April.

Leading indicators fell 0.2% in August, the third decline in four months. The drop was attributed to sharply lower cotton prices following a cut in federal price supports. New-home sales plunged 13.4% during the month to their lowest level in two years.

Most interest rates fell as the reports signaled continued weakness in the economy. Stock prices rose and the dollar edged up, aided by continued West German intervention.

Wheat futures fell as traders abandoned hope that Moscow would make a last-minute wheat purchase before a U.S. subsidy offer expired.

Farm Credit System banks are seeking legislation to help ease their heavy debt load. The struggling banks hope to replace high-cost bonds with new debt that pays lower interest.

2 A longshoremen's strike shut ports from Maine to Virginia, catching shippers by surprise and threatening long-term damage to the Northeast ports. The walkout by about 30,000 dockworkers began early yesterday after the longshoremen's union and waterfront management broke off contract negotiations.

Factory orders fell 1.4% in August, a further sign that manufacturers remain in a slump. Construction spending surged 1.1%, though analysts predicted the strength won't last, particularly in nonresidential building.

Treasury Secretary Baker signaled willingness to soften demands for West Germany and Japan to stimulate their economies. But in a speech to the IMF, he warned the U.S. will keep pressing its case privately.

U.S. gas-mileage requirements will be lowered for 1987 and 1988 model cars to 26 miles per gallon. The DOT's decision, expected today, will save GM and Ford millions of dollars.

3 Fed governor Emmett Rice resigned unexpectedly from the board, giving Reagan another chance to appoint a supply-sider to the central bank. Rice has been among the most vocal at the Fed in warning that inflation remains a serious threat. The seven-member Fed board already has four Reagan appointees.

Humana expects a quarterly loss of as much as $111 million, mainly due to rising claims in its new medical insurance division. The company said it had underestimated the complexities of the business.

OPEC will consider extending its production-cutting accord when it begins meeting in Geneva Monday. An extension is considered crucial to keeping oil prices stable.

AT&T is revamping its strategy in the computer business amid losses that could reach $800 million this year. The company plans to deemphasize sales of computers and focus on voice and data transmission.

6 The jobless rate rose to 7% in September from 6.8%, indicating the economy remains weak and uneven. A separate report by purchasing agents showed continued growth in the industrial sector despite sluggish employment. The rise in joblessness heightened pressure on the Fed to push interest rates lower.

U.S. car sales plunged 16.7% in late September, mainly because record-low financing created a shortage of autos. The incentive programs continued to hurt sales of imports, whose U.S. market share slipped to 23.9% in September from 29.2% in August.

8 The dollar surged as several European central banks intervened to support the currency, stunning foreign-exchange markets. But traders said the dollar probably will resume falling unless the central banks combine interest rate cuts with a more sustained intervention drive.

IBM introduced a family of small computers in its boldest bid yet to stage a comeback in that market. But the long-awaited line won't be delivered until late 1987, and IBM hinted the outlook this year is worsening. The company's stock plunged.

9 General Motors is expected to post a sizable operating loss for the third quarter, which could drag down the combined profits of the Big Three as much as 36%. GM, meanwhile, is preparing to trim output to prevent further gluts of unsold cars.

Stock prices advanced on renewed hope of lower interest rates and continued takeover speculation, while bonds tumbled. The Dow Jones industrials climbed 19.40 points, to 1803.85. The dollar was little changed, with no evidence of European intervention.

Chicago Board of Trade members failed

to report nearly a third of all trades within the required half hour, the CFTC said. The agency urged the futures exchange to step up sanctions against violators of the rule.

10 Bankamerica's board is expected shortly to request the resignation of Samuel Armacost, the firm's embattled president, sources said. His ouster would come amid growing financial woes and a takeover bid by First Interstate. Possible successors are said to include former president A. W. Clausen and Bank of America unit head Thomas Cooper.

Major retailers posted modest sales gains for September, hurt by warm weather and strong auto sales. But sales of big-ticket items surged, apparently due to a recent housing boom and coming tax-law changes.

First Boston plans to sell $3.2 billion of securities backed by GM low-interest car loans. The offering, the largest ever in the U.S., could add new sophistication to the growing market in asset-backed securities.

13 Producer prices advanced 0.4% in September, the largest increase since May. The rise, caused mainly by a boost in energy prices, underscores continued inflationary pressure but doesn't suggest a lengthy acceleration is near, many economists say.

Reagan officials and private forecasters contend that stronger economic growth is just ahead, but some economists remain unconvinced. Separately, business leaders expect the economy to improve gradually.

Bankamerica named A. W. Clausen, its former top officer, to succeed Samuel Armacost as head of the troubled banking concern. Armacost relinquished the chief executive and president posts at a special directors meeting. The choice of Clausen apparently won't affect First Interstate's takeover plans.

14 Saudi Arabia joined Kuwait in opposing an extension of OPEC's production quotas, increasing the likelihood that the pact won't be renewed. The stalemate sent oil prices skidding on world markets. The quotas, which expire this month, have been credited with boosting oil prices since the summer.

IBM's profit plunged 27% in the third quarter, mainly due to slower overseas business and shrinking profit margins. The computer giant is likely to post lower earnings for the year, and analysts don't expect a rebound until the second half of 1987.

15 Coca-cola disclosed details of its plan to sell 51% of its new bottling company for $1.5 billion, the biggest initial stock offering in U.S. history. The sale will open a new front in the long rivalry with PepsiCo, as Coke takes firm control of critical markets in its bottling network.

U.S. car sales surged 22.6% in early October, buoyed by a last-minute buying rush before incentive programs ended. But the size of the increase reflected weak sales during the year-earlier period.

Eight big banking firms reported mixed quarterly results. Chase Manhattan posted a 7.4% earnings drop, while Irving Bank, J.P. Morgan and First Chicago all had higher profit. RepublicBank, the biggest bank in Texas, reported a 55% decline.

16 USX Corp. moved to sell its chemicals business to the public. The company, which is the subject of a takeover bid by Carl Icahn, hopes to raise $570 million from the offering.

Retail sales soared a record 4.6% in September, but the gain resulted almost entirely from auto sales. Many economists said the strength won't continue because auto makers have ended their incentive programs.

Stock prices spurted in the final hour of trading, lifted by buy programs, firmer bond prices and a rebound by IBM. The Dow Jones industrials rose 31.49 points, to 1831.69. Stock-index futures also rallied.

17 Industrial output rose only 0.1% in September, indicating continued weakness in that sector of the economy. The slight gain in the index—which measures production at U.S. factories, mines and utilities—reflected a rebound in auto production. Separately, business inventories were nearly unchanged in August.

The FDIC plans to sell about a third of its 80% stake in Continental Illinois back to the public by year-end. The agency could wind up with a loss of over $1 billion from its 1984 rescue of the bank holding concern.

20 Kuwait again insisted on a bigger share of OPEC's oil output, threatening a compromise production pact reached over the weekend. OPEC agreed in principle to boost output 200,000 barrels a day and extend its current production accord to year's end. But Kuwait refused to compromise on its demands for a 10% increase in its quota.

A $576 billion spending bill was signed by Reagan after Congress approved the measure for fiscal 1987. Lawmakers revamped the president's budget priorities, though they made little progress on the deficit.

Interest rates are expected to rise in the coming weeks because of the Treasury's huge borrowing needs.

Housing starts tumbled 7.6% in September, suggesting construction won't be spurring economic growth as much as it did earlier this year. Meanwhile, the operating rate at the nation's factories, mines and utilities was unchanged during the month.

21 General Motors plans to pull out of South Africa due to continued losses and growing pressure from anti-apartheid activists. The auto maker, one of South Africa's biggest employers, said it will sell its operations to a group including local GM managers. Separately, GM made further suggestions it plans major production cuts in North America.

BankAmerica is considering selling the once-sacrosanct Charles Schwab brokerage unit and Seafirst banking unit as part of a survival strategy, sources said. It also may cut as many as 5,000 jobs next year.

Stock prices tumbled amid worries about the economy and interest rates. The Dow Jones industrial average finished down 26.02 points, at 1811.02. Stock-index futures fell, while most short-term interest rates rose.

Major securities dealers plan to introduce stripped municipal bonds, where interest and principal payments are sold separately, once the new tax bill is signed into law.

All Nippon Airways is about to announce almost $1.4 billion in aircraft purchases from Boeing, sources said.

Continental Illinois declared a common dividend for the first time since its 1984 collapse. The move may help the FDIC get a higher price in its proposed sale of Continental stock.

22 A South Africa pullout was announced by IBM, the second major U.S. firm to withdraw in two days. The surprise move deals a major blow to Pretoria and to other U.S. companies hoping to remain in the country. Both IBM and GM, which announced its pullout Monday, were vocal supporters of doing business in South Africa to help end apartheid.

OPEC appears to have reached a production-sharing agreement for the rest of the year. The accord came after the group agreed to let Kuwait boost its oil output 6%, apparently ending a long and divisive session.

23 General Motors posted a 49% drop in third-quarter profit and a $338.5 million operating loss, confirming expectations. The results reflected sharply higher costs, especially from recent sales incentives. GM also announced further cost-cutting steps, including the closing of several factories in the U.S.

OPEC ministers argued about the effect of their temporary production agreement even as they left their Geneva meeting. Oil prices tumbled as world markets showed little confidence in the accord.

Reagan signed the tax bill, calling it "an historic overhaul." The president warned Congress to refrain from changing the law next year, saying he would oppose attempts to boost tax rates to shrink the budget deficit.

Two securities firms rushed to market stripped municipal bonds, which became legal under the new tax law. The bonds offer interest and principal payments separately.

GNP grew at a 2.4% rate in the third quarter, up from a dismal 0.6% the previous period but still showing a lackluster economy. The report sent bond prices higher, but had little effect on stocks or the dollar.

Four oil companies reported mixed quarterly earnings. Amoco's plunged 97% and Ashland Oil's fell 26% due to write-offs. Phillips Petroleum posted a 21% rise on one-time gains, while Hess had a 15% increase.

Two more U.S. companies plan to sell their operations in South Africa. The decisions by Honeywell and Warner Communications follow similar announcements by IBM and GM.

Tokyo stocks plummeted for the eighth straight session, resulting in a 10% drop in the Nikkei average so far this month. The market has been hurt by declining foreign investment.

Investment banking firms were invited to submit proposals for participating in the Conrail stock offering. Reagan signed the legislation requiring Conrail's sale on Tuesday.

24 Durable goods orders rose a strong 4.9% in September, the biggest increase in nearly two years. Consumer prices were up a moderate 0.3% during the month, while consumer spending gained a robust 1.6%. The favorable economic news helped spark rallies by

the dollar, stocks and bonds. The Dow Jones industrials climbed 26.93 points, to 1834.93.

Ford Motor's profit more than doubled in the third quarter and exceeded GM's net for the second consecutive period. Chrysler posted a 26% gain. Meanwhile, U.S. car sales increased 2.3% during mid-October from a weak year-earlier period.

27 Allied Stores temporarily blocked Campeau from completing the purchase of 48% of its shares. A U.S. judge will consider Allied's request to force Campeau to rescind the purchase, which was made Friday. Allied, trying to fend off a Campeau takeover, contends the buying spree was an illegal tender offer.

Texas Air's purchase of People Express and the assets of its Frontier unit was cleared by the U.S., giving Texas Air huge marketing clout with a network of carriers that controls 25% of the nation's air traffic.

Schlumberger's plan to merge its Fairchild Semiconductor unit with Fujitsu's chip business was received coolly in California's Silicon Valley. Some analysts said the merger could start a trend of Japanese firms buying U.S. semiconductor makers.

Texas Instruments reported its second consecutive quarterly profit, but a decision to eliminate 1,000 semiconductor jobs indicates the worst isn't over for chip makers.

Britain's Big Bang begins today, as barriers in the financial markets are removed. But a rocky start to deregulation appears unavoidable.

The thrift industry's commercial real estate lending practices have resulted in what could be the biggest investment debacle for the financial system since the Depression, industry and federal officials say.

28 Britain deregulated its financial markets, and the effects were immediate and sharp. Investors said commissions were eliminated on British government bonds and cut by up to 40% on trading of stocks. The London exchange overcame an early failure of its computer system.

Merrill Lynch reported that quarterly earnings more than doubled, and PaineWebber Group's profit tripled, continuing a trend of strong earnings gains in the securities industry.

Labor pacts settled in the first nine months contain an average 1.3% wage increase for the first year, compared with a 3.2% rise in previous contracts, the Labor Department said.

29 Goodyear is the target of Anglo-French financier Sir James Goldsmith, sources said. Sir James, who is rumored to own about 15% of the world's biggest tire maker, is expected to disclose his stake and intentions soon. After speculation last week of a possible bid, Goodyear said it would consider restructuring.

USX posted a net loss of $183 million for the third quarter due to a 90-day Steelworkers strike and a downturn in energy. The company, under pressure to restructure, also said it had nearly exhausted unused credit.

Beverly Enterprises said a group of its managers and investors is planning a tender offer to take the company private. The purchase of the nation's largest nursing home operator could be valued at $1.73 billion.

30 Yamani was ousted as Saudi Arabia's oil minister, after playing a leading role on the world oil scene for 24 years. A successor wasn't immediately named. Saudi Arabia's U.S. ambassador said the move carries little policy implications for oil prices and production.

Oil prices skidded amid growing skepticism of OPEC's ability to enforce its production-sharing pact. Bond prices rose sharply, while precious metals prices tumbled.

AT&T turned over production and development of its personal computer line to Ing. C. Olivetti of Italy, tacitly acknowledging its inability to repair its troubled computer business.

31 Japan is expected to cut its discount rate to 3% from 3½% today to help stimulate its flagging economy, sources said. Bond prices in the U.S. surged amid speculation the Fed may lower interest rates within weeks. Tokyo share prices soared to a record one-session point gain.

The trade deficit narrowed in September as imports of manufactured goods fell. It was the second consecutive month of improvement and many manufacturers and economists suggested a trade turnaround is emerging. The dollar rose sharply in brisk trading following the report.

November 1986

3 Tokyo agreed to U.S. demands to spur the Japanese economy, including a dis-

count-rate cut and new spending and tax-revision programs. The U.S., in return, effectively pledged to stop efforts to drive the dollar lower against the yen. But the accord, while praised in Japan, was considered by U.S. officials to be too modest to ease the trade imbalance.

The Fed has more leeway to ease credit in the U.S. following Japan's discount-rate cut on Friday, economists said. But there was disagreement on when the Fed might act.

Allied Stores agreed to be acquired by Campeau Corp. of Toronto, ending a two-month battle. The accord calls for Campeau to pay $69 a share in cash and securities for the 47% of the retailer it doesn't already own.

Occidental Petroleum was ordered to pay Coastal Corp. $724 million for breaking a contract and trying to monopolize the natural gas market in several states. The award may be one of the largest ever in a civil suit.

The Air Force narrowed the competition to build a new jet fighter to Northrop and Lockheed, the first step in an estimated $45 billion project. The Air Force also will modernize its defensive force of General Dynamics fighters, a blow to Northrop.

The economy appeared to revive in September, as leading indicators rose 0.4% and factory orders jumped 3.4%. But analysts said tax-law changes may have played a big role. A survey of purchasing agents found industrial growth slowed during October.

The U.S. savings bond rate was lowered to a minimum 6% from 7.5%, beginning with bonds issued this past Saturday. Despite the reduction, advisers said savings bonds are still attractive for small investors.

4 Stock prices advanced in response to a bond market rally and increased optimism about the economy. The Dow Jones industrials closed up 16.45 points, at 1894.26. Bonds were helped partly by a drop in oil prices.

Construction spending surged 1.4% in September, the biggest advance since April. But economists expect outlays to decline in the coming months because of overbuilding and the effects of the new tax law.

Celanese Corp. agreed to be acquired by the West German chemical giant, Hoechst AG, for $2.72 billion, or $245 a share. Hoechst's takeover, made through a U.S. unit, will be the latest in a series of foreign takeovers in the U.S. chemical industry. The trend has been aided by the weaker dollar.

Goodyear Tire placed its oil and gas operations up for sale in response to a takeover threat by a Goldsmith-led group. Analysts speculated Goodyear wants to boost its stock price, making it more costly for Goldsmith to launch a tender offer.

5 Union Carbide plans to buy back up to $2.53 billion in debt to reduce borrowing costs and give it more flexibility to sell assets and enter other businesses. The chemical company's tender offer, which begins tomorrow, will result in a fourth-quarter charge of up to $401 million and a loss for the second year in a row.

The SEC can't regulate the brokerage activities of commercial banks, a federal appeals court ruled. The decision resulted from the agency's attempt last year to require banks to form separate brokerage units.

U.S. car sales dropped 6.4% in late October from a year ago, reflecting the end of incentive programs earlier in the month. But sales for all of October were up 5.8% because of the incentives. Sales of imported cars tumbled 5.1% for the month.

Mortgage rates have dropped below 10% again, and economists expect further declines through mid-1987. The average rate on conventional, 30-year fixed-rate loans fell to 9.89% last week from 10.1% a month ago.

6 Ronald Perelman will sell back his stake in CPC International to the grocery products concern, giving him a profit estimated at up to $50 million. The move, which deflated expectations of a possible takeover bid, caused CPC's stock to fall sharply. The company denied it was paying "greenmail."

General Motors has notified the UAW that it plans to close up to nine plants in the U.S. over the next few years, sources said. The scope of the move, which may affect up to 5% of GM's hourly workers, could be one of the largest ever in auto industry.

7 Major retailers reported a moderate pickup in sales for October from a sluggish year-earlier period. Results were boosted by price-cutting, though sales of big-ticket items were hurt partly by high consumer debt.

Bond prices tumbled as the Treasury wound up its quarterly financing with the sale of $9.26 billion in bonds. Despite large Japanese purchases, U.S. investors responded coolly.

Goodyear received a takeover proposal from Sir James Goldsmith of $49 a share, or an indicated $4.71 billion. The world's biggest tire producer countered by unveiling plans to buy back 18.4% of its stock and sell up to three major units. Sir James, an Anglo-French financier, said he would allow Goodyear time to pursue its restructuring.

General Motors outlined details of its proposed plant closings. The No. 1 auto maker said it will shut 11 factories in four states, affecting about 4.6% of its work force.

10 Corporate profits rose 7% in the third quarter, helped by a somewhat stronger economy, a Wall Street Journal survey shows. It was the first time in nearly two years that earnings were above year-earlier levels. Canadian profits eased 7%.

The unemployment rate was unchanged at 7% during October, when there was a sharp gain in jobs. The Labor Department report suggests that the economy continues to perk up, though not significantly.

Canada imposed a stiff tariff on U.S. corn imports after ruling American growers are heavily subsidized. The unprecedented action prompted concern other nations may follow. Canada steelmakers, meanwhile, are worried about U.S. protectionism.

U.S. auto output is expected to be flat during the fourth quarter, though weak sales could force production cuts or a mild round of incentives. Separately, GM's planned layoffs and plant closings pose a major dilemma for the United Auto Workers.

Hopes for lower interest rates faded after the Fed said its Open Market panel voted in September to leave credit conditions unchanged. Fed members are worried about recent growth in the money supply.

A top Treasury official criticized major U.S. corporations as bloated and inefficient, setting the stage for a renewed debate about America's productivity and competitiveness.

11 Wickes is seeking to acquire Lear Siegler for $1.62 billion, its second takeover target in days. Wickes, which just agreed to buy Collins & Aikman for $1.16 billion, said it has an option to acquire AFG Partners' 9.8% stake in Lear. Wickes also is discussing a cash offer for the rest of the aerospace company.

The budget deficit could shrink to $102 billion in five years if the White House's optimistic economic forecast is accurate, a revised federal study shows. But the deficit could be as much as $180 billion if most private economic forecasts are correct.

Saudi King Fahd told Iran that he wants to cooperate with efforts to push oil prices higher. The shift in Saudi strategy comes as five key OPEC ministers prepare to meet this week on ways to boost prices.

13 The U.S. warned Japan that their recent semiconductor accord would be canceled unless Japanese makers stop "dumping" microchips in third-country markets by early December. It isn't clear, however, whether Tokyo can meet the U.S. deadline.

Eastman Kodak expects near-record operating profit next year, mainly because of current cost-control efforts. The photography company's projection appears to be well above analysts' expectations.

14 Revlon group launched a tender offer for Gillette of $65 a share, or $4.12 billion. The offer, capping weeks of speculation, represents a bold attempt by investor Ronald Perelman to combine two big brand names in personal-care products.

GAF Corp. said it owns 9.6% of Borg-Warner and may launch a tender offer for the company. Earlier, Borg-Warner said it plans to sell its financial services unit, apparently to help fend off any takeover threat.

Japan has agreed in principle to slash its exports of machine tools to the U.S., officials said. Meanwhile, a bid by Japanese firms to become primary dealers of Treasury securities is facing growing opposition from a group of U.S. lawmakers.

17 Ivan Boesky agreed to settle SEC charges of insider trading, including payment of a record $100 million in penalties. The case, which began with investment banker Dennis Levine last May, may further shake the securities industry. Boesky is said to have implicated other major Wall Street figures. The case also may hurt public confidence in securities markets and bring more regulation.

The economy remains sluggish, analysts said, though it's far stronger than some October indicators suggest. Retail sales plunged a record 5% last month, while industrial output was flat and producer prices rose 0.3%. All three figures were heavily influenced by the auto industry.

The U.S. and Japan reached a new textile-trade agreement that will slow the growth of Japanese imports in America. But the accord won't dissuade U.S. textile makers from seeking import quotas next year.

18 The SEC's probe of the Ivan Boesky insider-trading case is focusing on Drexel Burnham and its junk bond operations. The agency also is investigating at least 10 other individuals, including some of Wall Street's top professionals. The evidence is said to include wiretaps.

The junk bond market was shaken by fears that the Boesky case may hurt Drexel Burnham's ability to issue and make markets in the high-risk, high-yield bonds.

First Interstate Bancorp said it will pursue its takeover bid for BankAmerica, defying the banking giant's request to retreat. First Interstate didn't indicate its next step, but said it would continue the offer it values at $22 a share, or $3.39 billion.

Business inventories fell 0.3% in September as sales rose 2.9%, bringing the ratio to its lowest level in over 2½ years. Separately, U.S. factories operated at 79% of capacity in October, down from 79.2% in September.

Precious metals prices plunged for the second consecutive session, led by a sharp drop in platinum. The sell-off helped fuel a Treasury bond rally, though stock prices sagged in reaction to the Boesky insider-trading case.

Plans to sell the FHA to private industry apparently have been abandoned by the Reagan administration. A task force is expected to urge instead that the mortgage-insurance agency's operations be cut back.

19 Drexel Burnham is under criminal investigation for possible securities-law violations in the Ivan Boesky insider-trading case. The grand jury probe of Drexel seeks to determine whether the firm leaked information to takeover speculators of acquisitions it was financing.

Stock prices plunged, led by takeover issues, amid concern about the Drexel investigation. The Dow Jones industrials skidded 43.31 points, to 1817.21. Stock–index futures also fell, as did bond prices and junk bonds.

Gillette moved to thwart Revlon's $4.1 billion hostile offer by accusing Revlon chairman Ronald Perelman of "tipping off" traders to his takeover plans. Gillette subpoenaed records of several investment firms, including one headed by Ivan Boesky.

Congress is unlikely to impose new restrictions on corporate takeovers despite concern over the Boesky case, Democrat and GOP leaders said.

More farm banks are in trouble despite massive federal aid to farmers. Recently released Fed data show the number of farm banks with more problem loans than capital surged almost 50% in the first half.

20 An Ivan Boesky fund sold at least $440 million in securities shortly before he admitted to insider-trading charges, raising questions whether he benefited from information about his own case. The scandal has sparked big declines in takeover stocks and triggered trading losses across Wall Street. Traders are angry that Boesky was able to sell early.

Sumitomo Bank won Fed approval to buy a nonvoting stake in Goldman Sachs. But the Japanese bank agreed to limit its interest and to restrict the amount of business it does with the New York investment banking firm.

Bond prices surged amid renewed speculation the Fed will drive interest rates lower to stimulate the economy. The bond rally pushed stocks narrowly higher, though some takeover issues continued to be hurt. Precious metals and the dollar slumped.

Fed Vice Chairman Johnson suggested the central bank has more leeway to ease credit, particularly since Japan's discount-rate cut. He also said the Boesky case doesn't appear to threaten the financial system.

Third-quarter GNP was revised upward to a moderate 2.9% rate, reflecting stronger defense spending. But some analysts question whether that level of economic growth will continue. Housing starts declined to a 20-month low during October.

21 Goodyear Tire agreed to buy Sir James Goldsmith's 11.5% stake for $49.50 a share, or $618.8 million, ending a monthlong takeover threat. Goodyear also plans a tender offer for a further 36.5% for $50 a share, or $2 billion. Sir James's abrupt about-face, which stunned the financial community, will leave Goodyear heavily burdened with debt.

Stock prices soared in active trading as investors looked beyond the widening insider-trading scandal. The Dow Jones industrials closed up 34.03 points, at 1860.66. Bond prices fell amid concern about the economy and rapid growth in the money supply.

Moody's may lower its ratings on $21

billion of long-term Citicorp debt. Moody's cited concern about assets and reserves of the Citibank unit.

Consumer spending plunged 2% in October following the auto-buying spree the month before. Many economists expect heavy debt and modest income gains will continue to restrain spending. Personal income increased 0.4% during October.

24 General Motors tried recently to sell all or part of its EDS data-processing unit to AT&T. Though the talks collapsed, they highlight GM's problems with EDS since acquiring the unit for $2.5 billion two years ago in a major diversification. The attempted sale also shows how deeply GM is rethinking its future.

GM settled a strike at an Indiana parts plant, though car output will still be affected this week.

Stock prices soared Friday in robust trading, pushing the Dow Jones industrials up 32.90, to 1893.56. Bond prices and the dollar also rose.

Coca-Cola Enterprises went public at $16.50 a share, nearly one-third less than its original top target price. The bottler's $1.18 billion issue, which fell short of the U.S. record, was hurt by institutional investors' coolness.

25 Gillette blocked a $4.12 billion takeover attempt by Revlon and its chairman, Ronald Perelman, in part by paying greenmail. Gillette agreed to buy back Revlon's 13.9% stake for $558 million, giving Revlon a profit of $43.1 million. The move leaves Perelman with a bigger war chest and Gillette vulnerable to other potentially hostile bidders.

26 Carter Hawley Stores is the target of a $1.77 billion joint takeover bid planned by Limited Inc. and developer Edward DeBartolo. The $55-a-share tender offer, set to begin Monday, is the second time in 2½ years that Limited has made a hostile offer for Carter Hawley. The retailer said it will consider the bid "in the appropriate fashion."

Durable goods orders slid 6% in October, the biggest drop in 2½ years. Though the decline mostly reflected plunging defense orders, it was seen as a sign of weakness in the economy. Meanwhile, consumer prices rose a modest 0.2% during the month.

The dollar plunged, partly in response to the durable goods report. The currency's weakness sparked a drop in bond prices and gains by precious metals. Stocks finished higher following an erratic session.

New-car sales rose 6% during mid-November, but not enough to keep General Motors and AMC from announcing new incentives for some slower-selling models.

28 A $2.08 billion loss was posted by LTV Corp., one of the largest quarterly deficits ever for a U.S. firm. The loss reflected a $2.1 billion charge for pension liabilities and write-downs in its main businesses of steel, aerospace and energy products. LTV filed for Chapter 11 in July.

The nation's trade picture remains mixed even though the trade deficit narrowed to $12.06 billion in October. Oil imports declined last month, but analysts cited increased deficits with Japan and in manufactured goods.

December 1986

1 General Motors hopes to settle a bitter feud with H. Ross Perot, head of its EDS unit, by offering to buy back his GM shares for $700 million. The proposal, which also calls for Perot to leave GM's board, is expected to win board approval today. But it isn't known whether Perot, a constant critic of GM and chairman Roger Smith, will accept.

Soviet gold sales have increased significantly this year due to the country's shortage of hard currency, analysts said. The Soviet selling has been partly responsible for the recent slump in gold prices, which have fallen 12% since early October.

Japan will open an offshore banking market today, though it initially will benefit domestic banks more than foreign institutions. Foreign bankers said the problem is that Japan hasn't lifted local taxes and other duties.

The Fed won't ease credit for the rest of this year because of the dollar's recent weakness, analysts say. The currency drifted lower Friday as investors remained worried about the American economy and the furor over U.S. arms sales to Iran.

2 Construction spending surged 1.6% in October as nonresidential building rose sharply. It was the biggest gain since April, but spending is expected to weaken in the coming months due to overbuilding and tax-law changes.

General Motors cut most of its ties with H. Ross Perot, dismaying employees and stockholders. Perot agreed to sell back his stake in the auto maker for over $700 million and resign from GM's board and the EDS unit he founded. The departure of Perot, a critic of GM and chairman Roger Smith, sent GM shares tumbling in heavy trading.

3 Stocks rallied on heavy institutional buying, pushing the Dow Jones industrials up 43.03 points, to a record 1955.57. The surge, which produced the Big Board's fourth-busiest trading day, was sparked by stronger bond prices and stock-index futures. The rally grew as investors became less worried about the insider trading and Iranian arms scandals.

Leading indicators surged 0.6% in October, though analysts said it may overstate the economy's strength. Non-farm productivity rose at an anemic 0.2% rate in the third quarter. F.W. Dodge said construction contracts rebounded 7% in October.

BankAmerica's sale of assets to offset huge operating losses may only postpone a financial crisis until the second half of next year. The banking concern, whose Italian bank unit is expected to be sold today, is running out of operations to divest.

Unilever's proposed takeover of Chesebrough-Pond's for $3.1 billion would give it a long-sought expansion into the U.S. market for skin-care and related products. Chesebrough backs Unilever's $72.50-a-share bid.

4 General Motors cut car production further in an attempt to trim inventories without big sales incentives. The latest reductions indicate GM is serious about keeping output in line with sales. Though the U.S. auto industry posted higher sales for November, GM's sales declined.

A GM shareholder sued the auto maker to block its proposed $742.8 million buyout of H. Ross Perot.

New-home sales tumbled 9.6% in October to the second-lowest level this year. Many analysts expect the pace to hold steady or improve slightly through the middle of next year. Average home prices slipped 0.7% during the month, to $111,600.

5 Drexel Burnham had a major role in every transaction under investigation in the Ivan Boesky insider-trading case, an analysis shows. It also has emerged that Boesky himself was a major investor in every instance. Boesky, meanwhile, appears to have speeded up the liquidation of his operations.

Major retailers reported weak sales gains for November, underscoring the shaky financial condition of consumers. But industry executives said the results don't necessarily foreshadow poor Christmas sales.

Canada's securities industry will be opened to foreigners and Canadian financial firms on an unrestricted basis, the Ontario government said. The change likely will set off a wave of acquisitions of brokerages.

Factory orders plunged 3.6% in October, the steepest drop in over six years. Though much of the decline reflected plummeting defense orders, the report cast further doubt that the manufacturing sector is reviving.

8 The jobless rate remained at 7% for the third consecutive month. But the November employment report suggests the economy is becoming stronger and more balanced. Manufacturing jobs rose, as did the factory workweek. Still, doubts persist about a major rebound. Separately, consumer credit rose at a hefty 13.9% rate during October.

OPEC meets in Geneva later this week to fashion an oil-price strategy. Iran's dominance in the group has been enhanced by its breaking of the U.S. arms embargo. But a global surplus of oil inventories threatens OPEC's hopes of raising prices.

U.S. auto makers trimmed car-production plans slightly for the fourth quarter. There is growing speculation that more-severe reductions may be needed in the 1987 first quarter, especially by General Motors.

9 The White House revised its GNP forecast for next year, predicting a 3.2% growth rate rather than 4.2%. The less-rosy outlook reflects embarrassment about overly optimistic forecasts in the past two years. But some Reagan budget officials fear the new prediction will make it more difficult to meet Gramm-Rudman deficit targets.

Drexel Burnham's head of junk bonds, Michael Milken, is said to have hired top criminal lawyers to represent him in the Boesky investigation. Meanwhile, Drexel is drawing fire for a financing technique that may have led to leaks of takeover bids.

10 United Technologies will take a $592 million pre-tax charge for its restructuring program, resulting in a "substantial" fourth-quarter loss. The company said the reorganization, which includes shrinking its work force 6% and reducing operations, will allow it to focus on its "strong core businesses."

Goldman Sachs is considering raising additional capital, possibly through a stock offering. Despite the recent injection of $400 million from Sumitomo Bank, many at the securities firm believe Goldman must boost capital further to stay competitive.

11 The New York Fed will allow several Japanese firms to become primary dealers in U.S. government securities, sources said. But restrictions will be imposed until Tokyo makes further progress in opening up its financial markets to foreign competition. Dealerships for the Japanese have become a contentious issue on Wall Street and in Congress.

USX Corp. said it has discussed selling some of its extensive energy assets to British Petroleum as part of a major restructuring. USX also said talks continue with suitor Carl Icahn, but a quick pact isn't likely.

The trade deficit swelled 5.6% in the third quarter, to $37.67 billion, reflecting a surge of imports from Asia. The figures appear to refute White House hopes that the weaker dollar would help shrink the trade gap.

12 OPEC appeared headed toward a steep cut in oil production. The group, showing rare unity as it opened its meeting in Geneva, hopes to push oil prices up to $18 a barrel by January from the current level of $14.

U.S. oil prices rose on expectations of an OPEC agreement. Bond prices slumped partly in reaction.

Exxon plans to sell its Reliance Electric unit for $1.35 billion, pulling the plug on an investment that one analyst called an "albatross." The proposed sale, to a group including Reliance's management, will result in an after-tax gain of $275 million.

Retail sales edged up 0.5% in November as consumers boosted purchases of furniture and appliances. The modest gain followed two months of sharp sales swings due to special incentives offered by auto makers.

Three Japanese firms won permission to become primary dealers in U.S. government securities. The move came despite heated opposition in Congress and on Wall Street.

Freddie Mac and Fannie Mae increased the size limit on mortgages they buy from lenders to $153,100. The move means home buyers will be able to get bigger loans at lower rates. Mortgage rates, meanwhile, have declined to an eight-year low.

15 Westinghouse won a $4 billion contract to run the Energy Department's Hanford nuclear complex, which was ordered temporarily closed for extensive safety testing. The agency also decided to repair the plutonium facility's controversial "N" reactor, which has some design features similar to the Soviet Union's Chernobyl nuclear reactor.

Producer prices rose a modest 0.2% in November and business inventories increased a strong 0.6% in October. The figures show inflation remains in check, while the economy continues to grow moderately.

The administration has decided to seek a 3% rise, after inflation, in fiscal 1988 military spending, officials said. It would be the smallest defense increase Reagan has ever requested.

16 Chemical New York agreed to acquire Texas Commerce Bancshares for $1.19 billion, a record merger that would create the nation's fifth-biggest bank. Chemical would become the first money-center bank to purchase a Texas institution, though other big banks aren't likely to rush into the troubled market.

First Interstate Bancorp said it plans to launch its $3.23 billion bid for BankAmerica as soon as possible. First Interstate, which filed with the SEC, showed unexpected resolve to proceed with the hostile offer.

Industrial output rose a healthy 0.6% in November, suggesting manufacturers are finally pulling out of a two-year slump. But many analysts warn that the economy could be weak in the first quarter of next year, partly because of the new tax law.

U.S. car sales rose 5.2% in early December, but GM continued to post declining sales and market shares. Analysts said GM's dismal performance reflects a lack of appeal for its products and higher prices.

Twelve OPEC members agreed to cut oil production, but Iraq held up the accord by refusing to participate. Oil prices rallied amid optimism about an OPEC pact, though trading was nervous as several oil ministers made contradictory statements.

17 Housing starts slid 1.8% in November to the lowest rate in two years. Starts have fallen six out of the past seven months, mainly because of depressed apartment construction. Analysts think homebuilding may remain low through the middle of 1987.

The nation's deficit in the trade of goods

and services grew to a record $36.28 billion in the third quarter. Some analysts say the latest current-account gap may reflect the worst of America's trade woes and that the deficits may soon start shrinking.

Iraq refused again to participate in OPEC's production cuts, saying it would only accept the same oil quota as its enemy, Iran. The continued impasse in Geneva sent oil prices skidding, while bond prices edged up.

Citicorp's rating on senior debt was lowered by Moody's, which cited worries about the bank's assets and capital. The downgrade affected $21 billion of long-term debt owed by Citicorp and its main unit, Citibank.

18 The FCC proposed to sharply deregulate certain interstate telecommunications services for large business customers. The plan was viewed as a first step in fully deregulating AT&T and its former Bell concerns.

Ameritech announced a 3-for-2 stock split, a quarterly dividend increase and a 6% stock buyback.

Iraq rejected an appeal by Saudi Arabia to join in OPEC's production-cutting pact. Iraq's continued resistance is threatening the Geneva session, though members vowed to stay until a final accord is reached.

19 Cost-cutting by AT&T will result in a $3.2 billion pre-tax charge for the fourth quarter, twice the amount analysts had expected. AT&T portrayed the moves, including plant consolidations and job cuts, as a way to strengthen the company. The charge will give AT&T a big quarterly loss and a small profit for the year.

IBM said 10,000 employees signed up for its early retirement program, far more than expected. But the computer maker said it would have to take other steps to cut costs.

Consumer spending surged 1.1% in November, surprising economists and suggesting Christmas sales could be stronger than expected. Separately, capital spending is expected to grow only 0.2% next year, reflecting a conservative mood among businesses.

22 OPEC launched a major effort to regain control of world oil markets and force prices upward. Twelve of the 13 members agreed to cut output and, starting in February, refuse to sell oil at less than $18 a barrel. Analysts were split on OPEC's ability to defy the world oil market and return to fixed prices.

Consumer prices edged up 0.3% in November, suggesting inflation remains well under control. More than a third of the increase reflected higher costs for cars and auto financing. The overall inflation rate, now about 1%, is expected to be 3%–4% next year.

Christmas sales are running below the modest expectations of many retailers. The softness raises the prospect of widespread price cutting during these final shopping days.

The economy remains weak and will prompt the Fed to push interest rates lower early next year, a Wall Street Journal survey of economists says. Meanwhile, the Fed's Open Market panel left monetary policy unchanged at its Nov. 5 meeting.

23 OPEC's effort to raise oil prices may push fuel prices higher in the U.S., but not enough to revive domestic oil exploration, U.S. refiners said. The OPEC agreement sent world oil prices soaring above $17 a barrel to the highest level since February. But prices retreated somewhat later in the day on profit-taking.

24 Durable goods orders rose 5.9% in November, the biggest increase in two years. The gain reflected a rebound in military orders, which vary greatly month to month. But many economists said the report is further evidence of improvement in the manufacturing sector, which has been hard-hit by foreign competition.

Greyhound agreed to sell its domestic bus operations for $350 million, ending 73 years in the U.S. bus business. The buyer, an investor group led by Fred Currey of Dallas, will operate the buses under the Greyhound name.

The SEC charged a former librarian at a Wall Street law firm and eight of his relatives with violating insider-trading regulations.

Bankers Trust won an appeals court ruling allowing it to sell commercial paper on behalf of clients. The decision is a victory for banks, which have tried to enter the lucrative corporate paper market over the objection of securities firms.

Reagan will nominate Sen. James Abdnor of South Dakota to head the Small Business Administration. The move may reassure small-business advocates that the president no longer intends to eliminate the agency.

26 Bankers Trust got the Fed's permission to sell commercial paper through a lending subsidiary. The Fed's approval removed another barrier between commercial banking and the securities business. The Fed also will hold a rare public hearing in February on whether to allow banks to underwrite commercial paper and other types of securities.

Hitachi and Toshiba plan to begin assembly in the U.S. of one-megabit semiconductors, the largest memory chips used in commercial computers. Other Japanese firms likely will follow the move, prompted by the recent U.S.-Japan semiconductor pact.

Japan approved a draft budget for the next fiscal year with the smallest spending increase in 32 years. The meager rise prompted concern that Japan isn't doing enough to stimulate its economy.

29 Christmas sales surged in the final days of the season, allowing retailers to meet or exceed their modest forecasts. The last-minute rush, which came despite the lack of extra markdowns, saved an otherwise slow holiday shopping period. Still, retailers didn't regard the results as outstanding. Many discount chains had disappointing sales.

Machine tool orders plunged 32% in November in what is shaping up as the industry's worst year since 1983. Executives say the only bright spot next year will be U.S. restrictions on machine-tool imports, which will be a big blow to Japanese producers.

Fujitsu's bid for control of Fairchild Semiconductor has left the Pentagon divided. Some fear a takeover of the military subcontractor could hurt national security. But others say it might encourage Japan to transfer military technology to the U.S.

Japanese exports fell in November, helping to shrink the country's trade and current-account surpluses. Japanese officials said exports to the Common Market declined because of restrictions imposed to lessen trade tensions with the 12-nation group.

The dollar reached a low for the year against the West German mark in thin trading Friday. Traders expect the U.S. currency will weaken further when the markets become active again after the New Year holiday.

U.S. uranium producers are awaiting a federal appeals court decision on whether imports of uranium can be restricted. Executives say the ruling could bolster prices and production in the domestic industry, which has been battered by foreign competition.

30 The Pentagon is seeking $250 million in additional funding for the current fiscal year to begin work on a Star Wars launch vehicle. The proposal is part of $2.8 billion in supplemental funds the military will request from Congress next week. The Defense Department also will present its $312 billion proposed budget for fiscal 1988, which begins Oct. 1.

ITT and CGE of France are expected to sign a formal agreement today that will create the world's second-biggest telecommunications company, after AT&T. The joint venture will be at least 51%-owned by CGE.

New construction contracts rose 1% in November on a spurt in nonresidential building, F.W. Dodge said. The forecaster said the industry's boom hasn't been threatened yet by "tax reform and deficit reduction."

31 New York will allow state-chartered banks to form units to underwrite corporate and other types of securities, a move bankers said could challenge the Fed's prohibition against such activities. The ruling also is likely to put further pressure on the Fed to grant banks new investment-banking powers.

Leading indicators rose 1.2% in November, the sharpest increase in nearly two years. But the surge may reflect coming tax-law changes rather than strength in the economy, several analysts suggested. Meanwhile, new-home sales fell 2.2% last month.

The U.S. said it will impose 200% duties late next month on imports of certain cheese, white wine, brandy, gin and other products from Europe. But Reagan officials said they expect the EC to settle a trade dispute, which could preclude the tariffs.

McDonnell Douglas's decision to build a new jumbo jet is likely to heat up a fierce battle with Boeing and Airbus of Europe. Many analysts expect a long war that only two of the three aircraft makers may survive.

January 1987

2 The trade deficit swelled to a record $19.22 billion in November, mainly from surging imports. Though the rise was blamed on temporary factors, it still indicates a turnaround isn't under way. But U.S. officials expect the gap to shrink sharply in 1987.

Canada agreed to put a 15% tax on softwood lumber exports, settling a long trade dispute with the U.S.

Stock prices slumped on the final day of 1986 because of tax-motivated selling and worries about the dollar. The Dow Jones industrials finished at 1895.95, off 12.66 points. Bond prices drifted lower, while the dollar slid 1.4% against the German mark.

U.S. oil prices neared an 11-month high of $18 a barrel, while North Sea crude topped that mark. Prices have jumped about 11% on the New York Merc since OPEC agreed two weeks ago on an output-price strategy.

5 The U.S. economy will expand further this year, with interest rates falling in the first half and rebounding slightly in the second, a Wall Street Journal survey of 35 economists finds. Most expect the Fed to face intense pressure soon to cut rates.

Factory orders jumped 4.1% during November, the biggest gain in two years. But the surge reflected strong military and tax-related spending, suggesting only a temporary rebound. Construction spending fell 0.7% and is expected to remain weak.

The Reagan administration plans to propose a program that could pay grain farmers not to grow any crops. Officials estimate the plan, aimed at shrinking U.S. grain surpluses, could cut farm spending over 50%, to about $10.5 billion, by fiscal 1992.

6 Stock prices soared, driving the Dow Jones industrials up 44.01 points, to a record 1971.32. The broad-based rally was attributed to institutional investors, who went on a buying binge following last month's tax-related selloff. The gains were fueled by higher stock-index futures.

Bond prices surged for the second day in a row on speculation that interest rates will decline in the coming months. A stronger dollar and lower oil prices also were cited.

The dollar rebounded, helped by West German intervention that was mainly aimed at weakening the mark, dealers said. Still, the dollar is expected to remain weak and a realignment of the European Monetary System is considered inevitable.

U.S. car sales rose 27.6% in mid-December, mainly because of tax-related buying. The last-minute rush had been anticipated by auto makers and analysts and was expected to boost late December sales as well.

8 Car sales soared 16% in December, helping the industry post record sales of 11.4 million for 1986. But sales have dropped sharply since Jan. 1, and auto makers are expected to face declining sales and growing competition this year. Analysts say the industry will have to devise more creative incentives to avoid costly low-interest financing.

European central banks intervened to support the French franc, which helped the dollar rebound. France and West Germany remained at odds over measures to ease the strains within the European Monetary System.

9 The Dow Jones Industrials passed the 2000 mark for the first time, closing at 2002.25, up 8.30. The bull market has now carried the average up 1100.94 points, or 122%, since August 1982. Though yesterday's milestone was hailed on Wall Street, many professionals don't expect the index to stay above 2000 long.

Carl Icahn dropped his $7.19 billion bid for USX Corp., saying the steel and oil giant had made it "all but impossible" to complete his proposal. But investors called Icahn's failed bid the latest and biggest casualty of the Ivan Boesky insider-trading scandal.

Honda Motor plans a broad expansion of its Ohio manufacturing operations, making it the first Japanese auto company to build all major parts for its cars in the U.S.

The dollar plunged against major European currencies, worsening strains within the EMS. World oil prices surged, bolstered by a report of lower crude output by Saudi Arabia. Treasury bonds edged lower, though corporate bonds rallied.

12 The economy continued its modest pickup at the end of 1986 as inflation eased further, the latest government statistics suggest. The jobless rate fell to 6.7% in December, the lowest level since March 1980. Producer prices were unchanged, resulting in a 2.5% drop for 1986, the first annual decline in 23 years.

Common Market nations struggled to work out a realignment of the European Monetary System. The group agreed tentatively to boost the West German mark's value 3% against the French franc, sources said.

Most auto makers are boosting output this quarter, though analysts are uncertain the market can absorb all the new cars. General Motors is cutting production 8.8% because it still faces swollen inventories.

Junk bond prices have rebounded strongly from the slump triggered by the Boesky insider-trading scandal. The market has benefited partly from bargain hunting and increased institutional demand, analysts said.

OPEC has succeeded in boosting oil prices by cutting output and imposing fixed prices on new contracts. The toughest enforcer of the group's strategy has been Saudi Arabia.

13 The dollar plunged following the EMS realignment as traders focused again on the sluggish U.S. economy. The currency slid more than 1% against the West German mark and Swiss franc. Meanwhile, questions remain within the EMS whether yesterday's realignment was only a temporary solution.

U.S. bond prices slumped as the dollar's drop shocked dealers and investors. Stocks, however, continued their broad rally as the major indexes closed at record levels.

Oil prices surged above $19 a barrel for the first time in nearly a year. The gain was attributed to heavy demand for heating oil in Europe and the Soviet Union, which have been hit with a bitter cold spell.

14 OPEC received a major boost in its attempt to increase world oil prices. Four major non-OPEC producers, Norway, Mexico, the Soviet Union and Egypt, gave firm signals they will coordinate their oil policies with the cartel. Also, Saudi Arabia said its oil minister will visit Moscow despite the lack of diplomatic relations between the two countries.

The dollar plunged again despite intervention by Japan's central bank, and many traders were gloomy about the currency's outlook. The dollar's slide further depressed bond prices, while the stock rally faltered.

Three big pension plans of LTV Corp. were taken over by the government, prompting an official to warn about growing financial strains on the federal pension-insurance system.

Thrift industry profits from current operations plunged 94% in the third quarter, Bank Board data show. Thrifts also appear to be still taking big write-offs on real estate loans.

15 The dollar plunged 2.1% against the West German mark and 1.8% against the Japanese yen. Bond prices slumped as the dollar's sharp decline ignited rallies in commodities and other futures, fueling fears about inflation. Gold rose $6.90 on the Comex, to $419.20 an ounce.

Stock prices spurted in robust trading, led by technology, energy and dollar-sensitive issues. The Dow Jones industrials surged 22.07, to 2035.01, the eighth consecutive record close. Most broader indexes also hit records.

Retail sales surged 4.4% in December, another sign the economy picked up at year's end. Though much of the gain appeared to reflect tax-related buying, many economists saw some underlying strength as well.

U.S. car sales slid 38.4% in early January to the slowest pace in over four years. The plunge was expected because 1986 sales were boosted by incentives and tax considerations.

16 Stocks roared ahead as most market indexes set new highs and Big Board volume soared to a record of over 253.1 million shares. The Dow Jones industrials finished up 35.72 points, at 2070.73, the ninth record close in a row. Stock-index futures also surged in frenzied trading.

The dollar recovered slightly from its recent slide, though the currency's outlook remains bearish. The dollar's rise ended a three-day bond slump.

Ivan Boesky Corp.'s payment of $5.3 million to Drexel Burnham Lambert last March is being examined by the SEC, sources said. Boesky is said to have described the payment as "consulting fees."

19 The SEC is investigating another large payment by Ivan Boesky Corp., sources said. The agency is trying to determine whether $3 million paid to Jefferies & Co. of Los Angeles is tied to the insider-trading scandal.

Guinness admitted there was illegal stock manipulation in its takeover of Distillers last year. The disclosure heightened worries that the scandal would include big British securities firms and lead to tighter regulation of London's financial community.

Grand Metropolitan agreed to buy RJR Nabisco's Heublein unit for $1.2 billion, making it one of the world's largest wine and spirit concerns.

Industrial output surged 0.5% in December, another sign manufacturing picked up in the fourth quarter. The factory operating rate rose slightly to 79.6% of capacity.

Japan's trade surplus with the U.S. grew to a record $51.48 billion in 1986. The report heightened concern in Tokyo that Congress will enact protectionist legislation this year.

20 The dollar plunged again following another report that the White House wants the currency to drop further. Though a Treasury official denied the report, the dollar tumbled 1.6% to a record low against the Japanese yen and slid 1.8% against the West German mark. Foreign currency futures rose sharply.

Ivan Boesky's main arbitrage fund appears likely to be dissolved soon. Debenture holders are expected to be repaid at 100%, but equity investors could have substantial losses.

Stock prices rebounded from an early decline in surprisingly heavy holiday trading. The Dow Jones industrials, down about 18 points during the morning, rallied to close 25.87 points higher, at a record 2102.50.

Owens-Illinois said it would meet with Kohlberg Kravis and any other suitor to discuss a sale of the firm. Sources said directors became resigned to a takeover following Kohlberg Kravis's $3.2 billion bid.

21 The dollar rebounded on speculation about today's meeting between Treasury Secretary Baker and Japan's finance minister. The currency surged 1.6% against the German mark and 1.2% against the yen. The dollar's rise pushed bond prices higher but caused gold and other precious metals to plunge.

IBM's profit plunged 48% in the fourth quarter and 27% for the year, even worse than analysts expected. The computer giant, whose stock tumbled on the news, predicted lower earnings for the current quarter.

The Dow Jones industrials posted a record 13th consecutive gain, though an early surge was trimmed by the IBM report. Profit-taking pushed most of the broader market averages lower in heavy trading.

22 Consumer prices edged up 0.2% in December and 1.1% for all of 1986, the smallest rise in 25 years. But inflation is expected to worsen this year, partly due to the weak dollar. Separately, housing starts increased 13.7% in December and 3.7% for the year.

The FSLIC can no longer cover its guaranteed loans to ailing thrifts, Bank Board chief Edwin Gray told a Senate panel. The fund's reserves, which insure $890 billion in deposits, have dropped to $1.9 billion.

The U.S. signaled that the dollar may be falling too rapidly, but stopped short of saying it will intervene to slow the currency's slide. West Germany is expected to cut its interest rates today to try to halt the mark's surge against the dollar. The U.S. currency was mixed yesterday as traders remained bearish.

Brazil's creditor nations agreed to reschedule $4.1 billion in debt, allowing Brazil to begin talks with banks on a major new loan package.

23 Stocks roared back as the Dow Jones industrials posted a record gain of 51.60 points and closed at a high of 2145.67. Many broader market averages also hit records. Prices soared in reaction to the weak dollar and speculation about a drop in interest rates. But concern about the dollar pushed bond prices lower.

The dollar's slide continued as government efforts to stabilize the currency failed to calm the markets. A cut in West German interest rates and Baker's prediction of a smaller U.S. trade deficit had little impact.

Japanese investors may shift more new investment to other currencies. Also, the dollar's drop makes it hard for the Fed to cut interest rates.

Economic growth slowed to a lackluster 1.7% annual rate in the fourth quarter as consumer spending slowed. GNP growth for all of last year was only 2.5%, the weakest since the recession year of 1982.

AT&T plans to spend $2.5 billion this year to expand and upgrade its long-distance telephone network. Separately, MCI said it will reduce interstate phone rates an average 10% in reaction to steep cuts by AT&T.

26 The stock market's tumultuous session on Friday left Wall Street divided on whether it signaled a major downturn or brief correction. Waves of frenzied buying and selling caused a swing of 115 points, or 6% in the Dow Jones industrials. The index finally closed 44.15 points lower, at 2101.52. Big Board volume soared to a record of over 302 million shares.

The dollar's recent plunge has heightened pressure on the U.S. and its allies to take substantive steps to reduce their huge trade imbalances, analysts said. Meanwhile, West Germany's central bank hinted it was willing to support the dollar.

Personal income climbed 0.8% in December, while consumer spending surged 2%. But economists said the gains largely reflected special factors and that spending will turn sluggish in the first quarter. Separately, machine tool orders slid 22% last month.

U.S. auto sales fell 36.9% in mid-January as the market slowdown continued. GM, the only Big Three auto maker to lose market share, unveiled a program of rebates and discounts for more than half of its cars.

27 Five major oil companies reported depressed results for the fourth quarter, and analysts say the outlook for 1987 isn't much brighter. Exxon's net fell 18%, Arco's 55% and Amoco's 58%.

Japan has told the U.S. it will extend its "voluntary" export limit of 2.3 million cars a year to the U.S. for another year, through March 1988.

28 USX Corp. posted a $1.49 billion loss for the fourth quarter, the largest in the company's history, mainly due to a long steel strike and additional plant closings. Meanwhile, USX directors decided against a major restructuring. Instead, the company will continue to prune ailing steel operations and shed assets to pay for its diversification into oil.

The stock market rally revived on renewed institutional buying, pushing the Dow Jones industrials up 43.17 points, to a record 2150.45. Stock index futures also surged, while bond prices remained in a mild slump.

Short sale positions in OTC stocks tumbled 12% in the month ended Jan. 15 amid strong stock buying.

The dollar tumbled amid rising skepticism about the U.S. stance on the currency's decline. The dollar slid more than 1% against other big currencies and fell below the psychological barrier of 1.80 marks.

29 The U.S. and Japan appeared to have intervened jointly to brake the dollar's slide against the yen. The reported intervention helped push the dollar up slightly against the yen in late New York trading. But the U.S. currency fell over 1% against major European currencies.

Ivan Boesky's ex-head trader, Michael Davidoff, pleaded guilty to securities fraud and agreed to cooperate with the continuing federal probe into the insider-trading scandal.

Stocks closed higher in a session heavily influenced by program trading. The Dow Jones industrials rose 12.94 points, to a record 2163.39. Bonds edged up as the Treasury unveiled plans to sell $29 billion of debt.

February 1987

2 The trade deficit narrowed sharply in December, though the outlook remains uncertain. Analysts said the $10.66 billion gap, the smallest since March 1985, suggests the nation's trade woes haven't worsened but haven't turned around either. Meanwhile, the Big Five industrial nations decided not to meet this week to discuss trade and the dollar.

The dollar will fall further, analysts said, despite the currency's rally following Friday's trade report.

Campeau Corp. exercised an option to buy 50% of five shopping centers from Edward J. DeBartolo Corp., sources said. Also, Campeau is said to be considering selling its Brooks Brothers and Ann Taylor units.

United Air announced corporate staff cuts and wage freezes in a bid to slash costs by $100 million this year. Meanwhile, Pan Am's unions are urging it to reorganize and possibly merge with a stronger airline.

3 Fed Chairman Volcker said the dollar's slide has reached the danger point and that further declines could boost inflation. He urged other steps to ease the nation's trade woes.

Trade legislation was proposed by Senate Finance Chairman Lloyd Bentsen that emphasizes boosting exports rather than protecting U.S. firms against imports. Reagan is expected to oppose parts of the proposal.

The dollar plunged amid continued bearishness about the currency. Bonds slumped in reaction as traders braced for a big Treasury borrowing that starts today. Stocks rose solidly, pushing the Dow Jones industrials up 21.38 points, to a record 2179.42.

Nissan and Toyota began offering cash incentives to U.S. dealers in an unusual bid to spur sales of certain car models. Meanwhile, Hyundai's sales are stalling in Canada due to a surge of small-car competition.

Non-farm productivity fell at a 1.7% rate in the fourth quarter, causing a gain of only 0.7% for the year. Separately, construction spending declined 0.5% during December.

Xerox agreed to acquire 25% of VMS Realty Partners, a major real estate syndicator and investor, as part of a $200 million transaction, sources said.

The purchase is part of diversification effort by Xerox.

4 Federal investigators are focusing on secret records and other data suggesting that Ivan Boesky and some officials of Drexel Burnham Lambert engaged in a wide-ranging scheme to profit from corporate takeovers, sources said. If the government brings charges, it could represent an unprecedented crackdown on illegal takeover practices.

Merrill Lynch is revamping its arbitrage operation because of concern that insider-trading scandals have made takeover speculation too risky.

Leading indicators jumped 2.1% in December, the biggest gain in nearly four years, while factory orders rose a brisk 1.2%. Both reports indicate the economy ended 1986 on a strong note, but some economists doubt such growth will continue this quarter.

Four big oil companies agreed to long-term purchases of Saudi Arabian oil, strengthening the prospect that OPEC's new prices will hold.

Mortgage rates are continuing to fall, and analysts expect further declines in the weeks ahead. The low rates helped spark a 12.7% increase in new-home sales during December.

5 The Farm Credit System may need a federal bailout sooner than expected despite accounting changes adopted last fall to help keep the nation's big farm lender solvent.

Car sales plummeted 26% in late January despite new incentive programs, leading analysts to conclude that more production cuts are likely. Sales for the month tumbled 33% to the lowest level in four years.

USX Corp. plans to cut its steel-making capacity about 27%, less than the industry had expected. The company, which just settled a long strike, expects to regain its 17% share of the U.S. market by the third quarter.

6 Bonds surged as investors reacted enthusiastically to the Treasury's $9.3 billion bond auction. The rally, the biggest in over three months, was fueled by lower interest rates. Meanwhile, the Reagan administration said it doesn't differ with Fed Chairman Volcker on the dollar. The currency gained amid rumors the Group of Five would meet soon.

GM's profit plunged 70% in the fourth quarter, partly from the cost of plant closings and other efficiency moves. Chrysler's net jumped 51%. Meanwhile, GM Chairman Smith has launched a public-relations effort to quell criticism of his leadership.

9 The jobless rate was unchanged at 6.7% in January despite a big rise in the labor force. The report suggests the economy continued to pick up steam as the year began. Meanwhile, consumer credit grew only $105 million in December, the smallest increase in five years.

The dollar's slide probably will continue despite positive U.S. economic reports and expectations of further intervention, economists said.

Britain's takeover environment faces a test after Friday's $389 million bid by Ranks Hovis McDougall for another British food firm, Avana Group. The unfriendly offer is the largest since the Guinness scandal.

10 The U.S. has offered to help stabilize currency rates within certain target ranges if Japan and West Germany stimulate their economies. But the plan so far has been rejected by major economic allies. Reports of the U.S. offer had little effect on the dollar, which plunged after the U.S. said the Group of Five has no plans to meet.

Bond prices tumbled in reaction to the dollar's slide and an unexpected surge in short-term interest rates. Treasury bond futures and stock-index futures also plunged.

First Interstate Bancorp withdrew its takeover offer for BankAmerica, claiming the ailing banking firm's continued sale of assets had made the $3.23 billion proposal too high. But First Interstate indicated it would consider a revised offer later.

Major U.S. auto makers are resisting further production cuts during the first quarter despite bulging inventories. But unless sales rebound this month, auto companies will continue to be burdened with unsold cars.

A U.S.-Japanese accord on semiconductor sales inched closer to collapse. The U.S. industry asked Reagan to impose punitive measures against Japanese chip producers, claiming Tokyo has repeatedly violated the July trade agreement.

The Chicago Board of Trade agreed to link trading in financial futures contracts with the London International Financial Futures Exchange. The move is a major step toward internationalizing futures markets.

11 Treasury Chief Baker said the U.S. trade deficit is leveling off, so Congress

shouldn't rush to enact protectionist trade legislation. Baker also said the U.S. will continue to press West Germany and Japan to stimulate their economies. Meanwhile, the U.S. dollar rose slightly.

Most interest rates rose amid speculation the Fed may be tightening credit in order to bolster the dollar. Stock and bond prices tumbled, as did stock-index and bond futures.

OPEC appears confident that its production-price accord will hold for several more months despite cheating by some members. A main reason is that Saudi Arabia has resumed its role as OPEC's "swing" producer.

Eastern Airlines agreed to pay a $9.5 million fine for air-safety violations, the biggest civil penalty ever imposed against an airline.

More farm banks are in trouble despite massive federal subsidies, latest figures show. As of Sept. 30, the number of farm lenders with more problem loans than capital had jumped 30% from a year earlier.

12 Oil prices tumbled to about $18 a barrel on soft demand and signs of possible strains within OPEC. Recent reports of production-quota violations by some OPEC members led to sporadic selling, some analysts said.

Recent economic statistics indicate the new year may be getting off to a faster-than-expected start. The figures have prompted many economists to consider rethinking their earlier predictions of sluggish growth.

15 Gold futures plunged below $400 an ounce, leading other precious metals sharply lower. The dollar's stronger performance, weaker oil prices and technical factors were cited.

A Texas appeals-court panel affirmed $9.1 billion of Pennzoil's $11.1 billion judgment against Texaco. A jury had found that Texaco interfered with Pennzoil's merger accord with Getty. Texaco said it will appeal to the Texas Supreme Court.

Retail sales plunged 5.8% in January as auto sales plummeted 22.4% from their strong December pace. The overall sales decline, which followed a revised 4.6% increase, was the largest in 20 years.

17 Investment banker Martin Siegel pleaded guilty to two felony counts for his role in the Ivan Boesky insider-trading scandal. The expected plea came just a day after the arrest of three other top Wall Street professionals implicated in the scheme. Concern is growing that more officials of big-name firms will be charged.

Kidder Peabody could face criminal penalties from the scandal, legal specialists say, while parent GE could be the target of massive lawsuits.

Texaco and Pennzoil said prospects for a peaceful settlement have dimmed following last week's ruling affirming most of Pennzoil's $11.1 billion judgment against Texaco.

Producer prices surged 0.6% in January, but the gain resulted from a big jump in energy prices and could overstate the worsening of inflation. Industrial production rose a healthy 0.4% last month, suggesting continued improvement for manufacturers.

18 Stock prices soared on heavy foreign buying and program trading, sending the Dow Jones industrials up a record 54.14 points, to a high of 2237.49. Though most issues posted gains, brokerage stocks fell, partly in reaction to the insider trading scandal. Bond prices slumped, while the dollar was mixed.

Ford Motor's profit rose 9% in the fourth quarter, capping a year of record earnings. Quarterly sales for the No. 2 auto maker climbed 15%.

The factory operating rate climbed to 79.7% of capacity last month, the highest level in nearly a year.

19 The Farm Credit System posted a huge loss for the second year in a row, though the $1.9 billion deficit for 1986 was somewhat smaller than expected. The big farm lender's bad assets grew to $13.9 billion.

J.C. Penney reported a 13% rise in quarterly earnings and announced its entry into the electronic home shopping business. Separately, Home Shopping Network said its acquisition talks with C.O.M.B. have ended.

Japan has told its microchip producers to cut output 10% in an apparent bid to save a semiconductor trade accord with the U.S. Tokyo hopes the move will boost prices and counteract U.S. charges of "dumping."

Oil prices skidded to their lowest levels of the year amid signs OPEC's production accord is faltering. On the New York Merc, crude for March delivery fell as low as $17.26 a barrel before closing at $17.40, off 39 cents for the day. Four OPEC oil ministers plan to meet Sunday to discuss the apparent over-production by some members.

Housing starts eased 0.1% in January but

still ran at a robust annual rate. The report was viewed as a sign of strong home building, particularly of single-family homes.

20 Volcker said the Fed has abandoned growth targets for M1 because the money measure is no longer reliable for monetary policy. The Fed chairman's statement led Senate Democrats to question the legality of the move. Volcker also said the Fed hasn't tightened credit in recent weeks, as some had thought.

The dollar tumbled after Volcker warned that the mark and yen could strengthen further. The drop erased the dollar's earlier gains from the Group of Five's decision to meet.

GNP grew at only a 1.3% rate in the fourth quarter rather than 1.7% reported earlier, the government said. The revision, reflecting lower inventories, suggests the economy may pick up this quarter.

Gold rose above $400 an ounce amid concern about Brazil's ability to pay its foreign debt. The rally, which led other precious metals higher, was sparked when Volcker said Brazil was in a "grave economic crisis."

23 The U.S. and major allies signaled readiness to intervene in currency markets to help stabilize rates at "about their current levels." The statement, which declared that the dollar had fallen enough, followed a weekend meeting in Paris. In a surprise move, West Germany and Japan pledged modest but significant steps to stimulate their economies.

Brazil suspended interest payments on its commercial foreign debt. The move, announced Friday, presents international banks with one of their biggest challenges since the global debt crisis began in 1982.

Corporate profits fell 1% in the fourth quarter, reflecting huge restructuring costs and the loss of the investment tax credit, a Wall Street Journal survey says. Profits are expected to grow strongly this year.

Consumer spending plunged a record 2% in January because of a sharp drop in auto purchases. Spending is expected to grow weakly for the next few months. Machine tool orders tumbled 23% last month, and producers see little sign of an upturn.

24 OPEC's December accord to hold oil prices at about $18 a barrel is under growing pressure. More oil companies are refusing to buy the group's oil at fixed prices, while some OPEC members are continuing to violate production quotas. World oil prices plunged to two-month lows of about $17 a barrel yesterday, sparking a rally by bond prices.

Brazil's creditor banks will ask the country to agree to IMF economic measures before they lend any new money or renegotiate existing debt. But Brazil's leaders are strongly opposed to any accord with the IMF.

U.S. bank stocks skidded in reaction to Brazil's latest debt problems. The slide led the rest of the market lower, as the Dow Jones industrials closed down 18.70, at 2216.54.

Congress and the White House are moving toward an agreement to cut the fiscal 1988 deficit about $40 billion. But that target would still be more than $20 billion short of the reductions required by Gramm-Rudman.

25 Security Pacific agreed to acquire Seattle-based Rainier Bancorp. in a $1.1 billion stock swap, probably the biggest bank merger ever. The purchase reflects the growth of regional banking giants, as well as Security Pacific's push to build a major banking network in the West. But the price is likely to dilute earnings at least through 1988.

U.S. car sales tumbled 26% during mid-February, disappointing some analysts who had expected a rebound from the weak start this year. General Motors' sales plunged 38%.

World oil prices sank below $17 a barrel amid continued doubts OPEC can enforce its price-output accord. Oil prices have plunged over 10% so far this month. The slide by oil and the relative stability of the dollar fueled another credit markets rally.

IBM will buy back about four million common shares, valued at $570 million, its third such move in less than a year. Meanwhile, Matsushita Electric agreed to compensate IBM for copyright violations.

26 BankAmerica may be forced to delay or alter plans to raise up to $1 billion in capital because of a recent decline in its stock price and investor skittishness, sources said. Many potential investors are said to be backing out due to BankAmerica's huge loans to Brazil. The planned offer was considered to have helped thwart a First Interstate takeover.

Oil prices tumbled on U.S. spot and futures markets for the third consecutive day. The decline came amid signs of a continued glut in refined oil products and pessimism about OPEC's ability to prop up prices.

Brazil ordered its commercial banks not to repay any short-term loans or deposits to foreign banks. The freeze, which could affect about $15 billion, signals Brazil is hardening its stance on its foreign debt.

AT&T's ratings on $8 billion of senior debt and preferred shares were downgraded by Moody's, which cited further pressure on AT&T's profit and the possibility of more write-offs.

The Consumer Price Index is being revised to give much more weight to housing costs and less to food and transportation. The revised index will make its debut tomorrow, when the January figures are released.

27 The Chicago Merc is expected to recommend major changes soon in financial futures trading. The proposals probably will include use of block trading and automation in futures pits and limits on dual trading.

A Viacom management group submitted a "final" buyout offer of $3.1 billion and sought a shareholder vote on the bid. Separately, Viacom and Grant Broadcasting settled on payment for Viacom programs.

Major airlines backed off from a plan to sharply limit their discount fares after Texas Air, the nation's largest carrier, refused to go along. The decision leaves the industry wondering when the fare wars will end.

Durable goods orders slid 7.5% during January, damping expectations of a recovery by the manufacturing sector. Excluding military items, orders fell a record 9.9%. Analysts cautioned that the figures may be revised sharply, though many called the results disappointing.

Bond prices rose following the durables report, while the dollar drifted lower. Blue-chip stocks eased.

Volcker won't rule out tightening credit if the dollar resumes its slide. The Fed chairman told a House panel that the recent Paris accord on exchange rates has no "specific commitment about monetary policy."

World oil prices rebounded from a three-day decline. Traders cited profit-taking and sporadic buying by refiners taking advantage of lower prices. But many analysts expect oil prices to resume falling soon.

March 1987

2 Consumer prices surged 0.7% in January as the weaker dollar made imports more expensive. The rising cost of imports also helped cause the nation's trade deficit to widen to $14.78 billion during the month. Meanwhile, industrial growth slowed in February from January's strong rate, purchasing agents said.

Interest rates and the dollar are likely to move in a narrow range over the short term as the economy remains stalled, analysts said.

WPPSS may face fraud charges in connection with its $2.5 billion bond default in 1983. The SEC's enforcement staff is preparing to recommend such allegations, an official for the Washington state utility said.

Farmland taken over by agricultural banks jumped 12% during last year's third quarter, latest figures show. The report suggests farm-land prices may decline further.

Brazil received a cool response from U.S. and IMF officials as it tried again to win concessions on its foreign debt. Separately, Venezuela's foreign banks agreed in principle to restructure $20.34 billion of debt.

3 Construction spending rose 1% in January despite a sharp drop in nonresidential building. New construction contracts slid 3% during the month. Separately, non-farm productivity fell at a 2.2% rate in the fourth quarter.

Sears plans to close five of its 12 big regional warehouses and eliminate thousands of jobs over the next several years. The massive cost-cutting move reflects growing competition from discount store chains.

Exco International agreed to buy 80% of RMJ Holdings, one of the largest brokers of U.S. government securities, for about $79 million. London-based Exco is a major broker of interbank and currency deposits.

General Motors is changing the way it awards merit raises to salaried employees this year in a further effort to cut costs. The less lucrative system is likely to worsen morale among the auto maker's middle managers.

4 General Motors plans a $5.18 billion stock buyback to improve the value of its shares. The auto maker said it

will buy up to 20% of its common by 1990 and up to five million of both the Class E and Class H over an indefinite period. GM has been harshly criticized on Wall Street recently for its lackluster performance and weak returns to investors.

Oil prices rebounded sharply as Saudi Arabia stepped up efforts to hold together OPEC's fixed-price accord. Despite the rally, the biggest in four months, some analysts remained skeptical about OPEC unity.

Leading indicators slid 1% in January, but the sharp drop reflected special factors and probably overstates the economy's weakness. New-home sales tumbled 6.8%, though analysts said the overall rate is healthy.

The FSLIC ended last year technically bankrupt, a federal audit shows. Meanwhile, the Bank Board may seek Treasury funds for the first time in order to maintain confidence in the thrift insurer, sources said.

Coffee futures plunged following the collapse of talks in London to restore global export quotas. The March contract fell 16.20 cents, to $1.058 a pound, the biggest drop in 10 years.

A standard contract has been developed by dealers in interest rate and currency swaps that should make the rapidly expanding market more efficient and more liquid.

5 Bethlehem Steel is seeking legal advice on the implications of a bankruptcy-law filing. But the troubled No. 3 steelmaker stressed it hasn't any near-term plans for such a move.

Factory orders plunged 4% in January, confirming signs that manufacturing is weak. But some economists said the drop, the biggest in nearly seven years, may have been heavily influenced by tax-law changes.

Stock prices surged, triggered by GM's announcement of a huge stock buyback. The Dow Jones industrials closed up 30.93 points at a record 2257.45. Analysts, meanwhile, viewed GM's buyback as a risky gamble.

6 House Speaker Wright is working to build a consensus among House Democrats to raise taxes about $18 billion a year. Meanwhile, Interior Secretary Hodel said the U.S. should consider raising the gasoline tax.

Major retailers had stronger-than-expected sales gains in February, dispelling fears that the post-Christmas slowdown would be worse than usual. General merchandise sold well, but big-ticket items were weak.

Blue-chip stocks rallied again in heavy trading as foreign and U.S. institutions stepped up their buying. The Dow Jones industrials rose 18.98 points, to a record 2276.43. Broader indexes also set records.

Oil prices rose for the third consecutive day amid further signs that OPEC members are restraining production. Meanwhile, oil consumption in the West is expected to grow only slightly more than 1% this year, putting further pressure on OPEC.

9 The jobless rate remained at 6.7% in February, indicating the economy is stronger than recent data suggest. Friday's report sent bond prices tumbling as speculation grew that interest rates won't decline anytime soon.

The Big Board roiled London's Stock Exchange by strictly interpreting a trading rule. The New York exchange said that during its trading hours, members can't buy and sell U.S. stocks in the London market.

10 Chrysler agreed to acquire Renault's controlling stake in American Motors, paving the way for a takeover of ailing AMC that could total about $1.11 billion. The move would give Chrysler much-needed added capacity and help bolster its position in the auto market. For Renault, the sale marks the French firm's failure in the U.S. market.

11 France plans to open the Paris stock exchange to foreigners, following the lead of Tokyo and London. The proposal would allow outsiders to buy a stake in an existing brokerage and, in five years, start their own.

Nomura Securities plans to invest about $10.4 billion of its clients' cash in non-Japanese equities this year, sources said. Most of the money is expected to go into U.S. stocks.

12 The SEC charged a Merrill Lynch executive in London and a prominent Israeli businessman with masterminding a huge insider-trading scheme. The allegations against Nahum Vaskevitch and David Sofer indicate the SEC's crackdown on insider trading goes beyond the Levine-Boesky scandals, sources said.

The trade deficit swelled to a record $38.37 billion in the fourth quarter. The figure shows the stubborness of the trade imbalance, which failed to improve despite a weaker dollar.

The Dow Jones industrials will have two stocks changed in the 30-stock average, beginning today. Coca-Cola and Boeing will be included in the blue-chip indicator, replacing Owens-Illinois and Inco.

13 Retail sales jumped 4.1% in February, led by a rebound in auto sales. The gain followed a revised 7.4% decline in January. Excluding auto sales, which move erratically month to month, February retail sales rose a healthy 1.5%. Meanwhile, K mart reported stronger-than-expected quarterly profit, while Dayton Hudson posted a 32% increase.

The Senate Budget Committee will begin considering several measures next week to cut the deficit. Proposals include a 5% value-added tax, a 10% surcharge on imports and a one-year freeze on Social Security benefits.

16 Economic growth remains modest, latest figures show. Producer prices edged up 0.1% in February as energy prices rose more slowly. Industrial output increased 0.5%, led by surging auto production. Car sales fell 2.2% in early March.

Volkswagen's financial chief resigned in reaction to a currency fraud that could cost the auto maker up to $259 million. The scandal may delay the West German government's plans to sell its 20% stake in VW.

Citicorp signaled it can withstand a long showdown with Brazil over the country's suspension of interest payments. But the move could slash Citicorp's profit up to $190 million this year. Brazil, meanwhile, will present a new debt plan within two weeks.

17 The factory operating rate rose to 79.8% of capacity in February, indicating the industrial sector continued to improve modestly. Meanwhile, consumer confidence recovered last month from its January low.

Fujitsu dropped plans to buy 80% of Fairchild Semiconductor, citing "political controversy" in the U.S. over the sale. The takeover was opposed by various U.S. officials, partly due to worries that Japan eventually could dominate the computer chip industry. Disputes over U.S.-Japanese semiconductor trade also have grown recently.

Upjohn's anti-baldness drug minoxidil was recommended for approval by an FDA panel, though the advisers were skeptical about Upjohn's claims. Baldness treatments, meanwhile, are becoming a big business.

18 Fujitsu still plans several ventures with Fairchild Semiconductor despite dropping its takeover bid. Fairchild is expected to announce today plans for joint development and manufacturing of computer chips with the Japanese firm. Fairchild's management, meanwhile, is negotiating a leveraged buyout of the company from Schlumberger.

Housing starts rose 2.6% in February to the highest annual rate since April. Construction of single-family homes remained strong, though multifamily building was still weak.

Britain unveiled a cautious budget for the fiscal year beginning April 1. The budget trims income taxes, as expected, and paves the way for an immediate cut in interest rates. The pound surged over 1%, while British stocks soared to a record close.

Japan's economy grew 0.8% in the fourth quarter, making GNP growth for 1986 only 2.5%, the slowest in 12 years. Japan's export-driven economy has been hurt by the strong yen.

19 Fleet Financial Group agreed to merge with Norstar Bancorp in a $1.3 billion stock swap, the largest banking combination ever. The merger is the latest by New England regional banks, which hope to avoid takeovers by big money-center institutions.

Continental Illinois plans to classify most of its Brazilian loans as nonperforming unless there is progress in debt talks soon. Citicorp already has threatened such a move, and other major U.S. banks may follow.

Fourth-quarter GNP growth was revised to a meager 1.1% annual rate from 1.3% estimated earlier. The revision was due to weaker inventory investment, consumer spending and government outlays. Corporate profits rose a healthy 6.1% in the period.

U.S. officials warned that a Japanese proposal to limit foreign participation in a proposed telecommunications venture could violate a U.S.-Japanese trade accord and prompt congressional demands for retaliation.

American Express agreed to sell a minority stake in its Shearson Lehman unit to Nippon Life Insurance, sources said. The alliance would boost the securities firm's capital and give it entry into the important Tokyo market. Sources disputed reports that a 10% Shearson stake was sold for about $600 million, but they declined to give details.

20 American Express's board will be asked Monday to approve a share offering in the Shearson Lehman unit, sources said. Meanwhile, American Express announced its plan to sell a 13% stake in Shearson to Tokyo-based Nippon Life for $530 million.

Consumer spending jumped 1.7% in February after plunging the month before. Despite the rebound, led by higher auto sales, spending is expected to fall or change little this quarter. Meanwhile, personal income rose a healthy 0.9% last month.

Mexico is expected today to sign a $7.7 billion loan accord with most of its foreign banks. The signing was delayed for months by a dispute among banks that is likely to affect future loans to debtor nations.

The U.S. is headed for another confrontation with Latin American debtors over its plan to overhaul the Inter-American Development Bank.

Saudi Arabia has cut oil production to a near-record low in an effort to prop up oil prices, sources said. The Saudis also are leading OPEC in resisting sales of crude below the group's target of $18 a barrel.

A top SEC official proposed brief, simultaneous trading halts in stock and stock-index markets to combat excessive price volatility.

23 Friday's triple witching hour was a bit tamer than the previous quarter, and stock and futures prices climbed to records. The Dow Jones industrials closed above 2300 for the first time, rising 33.95 points to 2333.52.

Thrift regulators have been trying for months to find a buyer for Financial Corp. of America, sources said. But they add that prospects aren't good that the parent of the nation's largest thrift will be sold soon.

24 American Express said its board approved an initial stock offering of at least 18% of its Shearson Lehman Brothers securities unit. The offering would have a value of between $600 million and $700 million. The board also approved the sale of a 13% stake in Shearson to Nippon Life of Japan. American Express also announced a 2-for-1 stock split.

Japan moved to head off expected U.S. trade sanctions against Japanese microchip producers. Tokyo said it told makers to cut output of certain chips, but U.S. officials were skeptical that it would forestall sanctions.

Fannie Mae is starting a program to buy 10- and 20-year mortgages, a move that could increase the availability of those loans, officials said. Fannie Mae usually buys home loans with 15- or 30-year maturities.

The dollar plunged to a post-World War II low against the Japanese yen. The drop was triggered by Treasury Secretary Baker's comment that the U.S. doesn't have a target for the dollar's value. Bond prices slumped in reaction to the dollar's slide.

Merrill Lynch's Canadian unit is holding talks to acquire Burns Fry Corp., the parent of one of Canada's largest securities firms, sources said. Terms of the bid aren't known.

25 Durable goods orders surged 6% in February, suggesting manufacturers may have resumed a slow recovery. The jump followed a revised 9.9% decline in January. Orders data have been extremely volatile lately, mainly because of tax-law changes.

Conrail's stock offering this week is expected to raise a record total of over $1.5 billion. Investors appear eager to buy the issue, which sources believe will be priced at the high end of the $26 to $29-a-share range.

New-car sales fell 3.9% in mid-March, reflecting continued weakness in the domestic auto market. Analysts expect the industry's sluggishness to persist for some time.

26 Conrail's initial public offering was priced at $28 a share, raising a record $1.65 billion before underwriting fees. Trading in the stock begins today, and some analysts expect it to rise above the offering price.

Brazil's finance minister, Dilson Funaro, appears to have lost critical support in the country, making his future uncertain. Meanwhile, the impasse on Brazil's debt is making it more likely U.S. banks will put the loans on a nonperforming basis.

27 Reagan's top advisers recommended imposing steep tariffs on Japanese consumer electronics to retaliate for Tokyo's failure to live up to a semiconductor trade accord. U.S. officials said that the tariffs, some as high as 100%, would be applied to such products as television sets and personal computers.

House Speaker Wright indicated he backs a controversial proposal to require U.S. retaliation against countries with huge trade surpluses.

British Petroleum plans to offer $7.4 billion for the 45% of Standard Oil it doesn't already own, paving the way for further U.S. expansion. Standard Oil's stock surged to $71 a share, suggesting investors were speculating BP would raise its $70-a-share bid.

30 Japan reacted mildly to Reagan's decision to impose tariffs on certain Japanese electronics. The action, in retaliation for Japan's failure to enforce a semiconductor accord, will have little short-term impact on Japan's trade practices or the U.S. trade deficit. But it could prove to be a turning point in economic ties between the two countries.

The dollar's plunge on Friday raised questions about the effectiveness of last week's big intervention. The drop sent stock and bond prices tumbling. The Dow Jones industrials slid 36.79 points, to 2335.80.

Consumer prices rose 0.4% in February, reflecting higher energy prices and import costs. But it didn't suggest any major buildup in inflation. Meanwhile, sales of machine tools are lagging in the first quarter.

31 The dollar fell further despite continued intervention, triggering a huge sell-off in securities markets around the world. Stock and bond prices skidded in New York as the Dow Jones industrials plunged 57.39 points, the third biggest point drop ever, to 2278.41. The fall followed similar routs in London and Tokyo.

New-home sales fell 2.7% in February following a revised 8.6% drop in January. But economists expect continued low mortgage rates to spur sales in the months ahead. Several said the recent drops may reflect a shift by buyers to existing homes.

April 1987

1 The prime rate was raised by Citibank and Chase Manhattan to 7¾% from 7½%, their first increase since mid-1984. The move surprised many bankers, especially as most short-term interest rates fell yesterday. But analysts expect other banks will soon follow because of increases in their own borrowing costs and expectations of higher inflation.

The dollar recovered slightly against most currencies but fell further against the yen despite Japan's continued intervention. The stable dollar and higher bond prices helped stocks rebound. The Dow Jones industrials rose 26.28 to 2304.69.

Leading indicators rose 0.7% in February, while factory orders increased a solid 4.3%. Analysts said the gains suggest the economy may be returning to modest, steady growth after recent sharp swings that resulted from tax-law changes.

Computer chip prices are rising as fears of Japanese cutbacks cause a surge in U.S. demand. The development is making it less likely the U.S. will impose any lasting sanctions on Japanese consumer products, which are set to take effect April 17.

Farmers plan to cut plantings substantially this year in response to government incentives for idling land, a federal report shows. More farmers are expected to sign up for price and income-support programs this year.

2 Three Brazil creditors placed some of their loans to the country on a non-accural basis. BankAmerica, J.P. Morgan and Manufacturers Hanover said the decision hurt first-quarter results and may cut future profits. Other banks are expected to follow the move, which classifies Brazil as a "substandard" borrower.

More big banks raised their prime rates to 7¾% from 7½%, though most other interest rates fell and Treasury bonds rebounded slightly. Stock prices also recovered after an early sell-off. The Dow Jones industrials finished ahead 11.36 points at 2316.05.

The dollar's recovery continued in response to the prime rate increases. But many traders expect the currency will soon head for new lows.

British Petroleum launched its $7.4 billion tender offer for Standard Oil and said Standard directors tried unsuccessfully to postpone the bid.

Construction spending rose 1% in February as nonresidential building increased. The overall gain followed a revised 1% decline in January.

3 The dollar fell sharply after a U.S. official said a further drop could help cut the trade deficit. The White House disclaimed the remark, though the dollar remained lower despite U.S. intervention. Bond prices declined, while stocks edged higher.

The U.S. and economic allies face another round of critical talks next week on their growing trade imbalances. The outcome could have a major influence on the dollar.

6 Saudi Arabia is seeking to acquire a refin-

ing and marketing network outside its national borders, industry sources said. The expansion, which probably won't start soon, will challenge the international oil industry in territory that largely has been the preserve of Western oil firms.

The role of the IMF, which opens it weeklong meeting today, may change as it faces strains over the current global debt problem. Separately, major creditor nations have agreed to ease terms on debt owed by the poorest African countries.

The Dow Jones industrials rocketed a record 69.89 points Friday, to 2390.34. The bull market confounded some investors while others said expected big gains in corporate profits this year will fuel further rises.

The jobless rate declined to 6.6% in March. The employment report suggests the economy's pace slowed slightly last month despite the drop.

Car sales rose 19.3% in late March, buoyed by incentives. The figures averaged out to the strongest daily sales rate since December. Sales of imported models remained sluggish.

7 Texaco lost a key ruling in its legal battle with Pennzoil. The Supreme Court dismantled Texaco's protection against having to post a crippling $12 billion appeals bond, pushing Texaco to the brink of a Chapter 11 filing. But the court decision puts more pressure on both firms to settle the case, which stems from Texaco's 1985 takeover of Getty Oil.

General Motors slashed car production further due to continued weak sales and high inventories. The latest cutbacks, affecting four assembly plants, indicate GM has retreated from its optimistic sales outlook.

The Dow Jones industrials closed above 2400 for the first time with a modest rally by stocks. The average finished up 15.20 points, at a record 2405.54. A firmer dollar helped most bond prices edge higher, but traders said the market remains skittish.

8 Bond and stock prices tumbled amid worries about the weak dollar. Treasury bonds fell to about their lowest level this year, and some long-term issues slid about one point. A sell-off in stocks pushed the Dow Jones industrials down 44.60 points, to 2360.94. Despite bearishness about the dollar, the currency was little changed in cautious trading.

The U.S. and major allies are moving to reaffirm their currency-stabilization accord and may reinforce it with some modest changes, officials said. The indications came after Japan signaled readiness to move on an economic-stimulus plan.

Texaco moved to prevent Pennzoil from seizing its assets after losing a crucial Supreme Court ruling in their $10.3 billion legal battle. Texaco also appeared to seek face-to-face negotiations with Pennzoil representatives.

Consumer credit grew at a 3.7% annual rate in February but remained considerably lower than in recent years, the Fed said. The latest rise was fueled by a rebound in revolving credit and a pickup in auto loans.

GenCorp's hostile suitor dropped a $100-a-share bid following the tire maker's offer to buy 54% of its shares for $130 each. The suitor, led by AFG Industries and Wagner & Brown, said it couldn't compete with GenCorp's $1.6 billion stock buyback.

China placed new curbs on issuing stock and bonds, reflecting Beijing's new conservative mood and recent retreat from capitalist-type reforms.

9 The dollar retreated from an early surge after the Washington meeting of finance ministers yielded no immediate agreement. Bond and stock prices followed the dollar and wound up with small gains. The Dow Jones industrials rose 11.22 to 2372.16.

Gasoline futures prices plunged in record trading amid signs of swollen supplies, softer demand and increased output. Other oil prices also fell.

Car sales may be weaker this year than the industry expected. U.S. auto makers plan to cut output nearly 6% in the second quarter, including about 9% in April alone, sources say. Meanwhile, U.S. sales of Japanese cars are falling for the first time in years.

10 The dollar plunged amid disappointment over the Group of Seven meeting, sparking a slide by stocks and bonds and gains by precious metals and commodity futures. Interest rates soared on speculation the Fed will tighten credit soon, while Treasury bonds skidded about two points. The Dow Jones industrials closed down 32.96 points, at 2339.20.

Fears about a global recession are growing. Fed Chairman Volcker and other officials worry that the weak economies may be slowing further.

Norway will launch a global effort to stabilize oil prices at higher levels, Prime

Minister Brundtland said. In an interview, she also said Norway will continue to support OPEC by cutting its own oil production.

The Common Market said it will investigate possible Japanese dumping of computer chips in Europe. The inquiry comes as the U.S. prepares to retaliate against Japanese companies for alleged semiconductor dumping.

Major retailers reported lackluster sales gains for March, mainly due to the late Easter season. Analysts expect a big rise in April sales.

13 Texaco filed for Chapter 11 protection after it and Pennzoil were unable to settle their legal battle over ownership of Getty Oil. The two firms apparently remained at least $2 billion apart in settlement talks. The bankruptcy-court case, the biggest in history, is expected to be as unpredictable as the $10.53 billion judgment Pennzoil won against Texaco.

The Fed may be forced to push up interest rates if the dollar's slump continues, Fed officials said. The dollar is expected to come under heavy selling pressure this week, posing a critical test for the Group of Seven, which has pledged to defend its currency-stabilization accord.

TransCanada PipeLines said it offered to buy ailing Dome Petroleum for cash and stock valued at $4.3 billion (Canadian). Dome, irked by the disclosure, said it would suspend talks with TransCanada and hold discussions with other possible suitors.

Producer prices rose 0.4% in March, indicating that the dollar's decline is starting to affect domestic prices. There were big increases in such import-sensitive goods as home electronics and women's apparel.

The U.S. and Japan failed to resolve a semiconductor trade dispute, making it almost certain that the U.S. will impose tariffs on Japanese electronics imports beginning Friday.

General Motors has lowered its goal for the U.S. auto market to a 40% share from 42% set a few months ago, Chairman Roger Smith said. The new goal will allow GM to "provide maximum profitability," he said.

Japan's stock market has overtaken the U.S. as the world's largest. The change reflects Japan's huge trade surpluses and the yen's sharp rise against the dollar.

Commodity and interest-rate futures may be staging a turnaround due to the dollar's decline, some traders and analysts believe.

14 Stocks and bonds skidded in late trading as concern grew about rising interest rates and the weak dollar. Some Treasury bonds slid over 1¾ points, while the Dow Jones industrials tumbled 51.71, to 2287.07. The dollar's decline slowed as traders awaited today's report on the February U.S. trade deficit. Many expect that the trade gap narrowed.

Texaco and Pennzoil were pummeled in securities markets for pushing their $10.3 billion fight into bankruptcy court. Texaco's stock fell 11%, while Pennzoil's plunged 17%. Texaco's Chapter 11 filing, meanwhile, may limit Pennzoil's options.

Capital spending is rebounding, aided by the weaker dollar. The rise isn't expected to boost the economy much in the near term. But higher profits are expected to accelerate the investment upturn by year's end.

IBM's profit fell 23% in the first quarter, a smaller drop than analysts expected. The firm cited the first encouraging signs in its business after two years of slumping profits. IBM's stock rose $2.75, to $147.75.

15 The trade deficit grew to $15.06 billion in February, indicating the trade outlook remains bleak. The unexpected surge comes amid rising trade tensions with Japan and gives new momentum to trade legislation in Congress. The report also is a blow to Treasury Secretary Baker, who has sought a weaker dollar to curb the trade gap.

The dollar plunged to another low against the yen, sending jitters through U.S. stock and bond markets. The Dow Jones industrials closed down 34.09 points, at 2252.98.

Turmoil in the mortgage markets has caused rates for fixed-rate home loans to soar as much as two percentage points in the past month, the fastest and sharpest reversal ever. The chaos is starting to affect the availability of mortgage credit itself.

Texaco's stock rose amid speculation the Chapter 11 filing may have strengthened the firm's hand against Pennzoil. The petition, meanwhile, could raise major issues in commercial and constitutional law.

U.S. car sales fell 15% in early April, indicating continued softness in the market. Separately, a U.S. judge said GM doesn't have to recall 1980 X-cars or pay a $4 million penalty.

16 The dollar rallied after Japan indicated major industrial nations had agreed to strengthen their intervention to support the currency. The dollar's rebound helped snap a slump in bond and stock prices. Some Treasury bonds rose one point, while the Dow Jones industrials closed up 29.97 points, at 2282.95.

Industrial output fell 0.3% in March, led by a slowdown in auto production. But rising car sales pushed retail sales up a slim 0.2% for the month. Several economists said the March figures indicate the economy is continuing its sluggish growth.

Some Texaco lenders and suppliers aren't certain if it's safe to do business with the oil firm. Others denied cutting off or restricting business with Texaco, as it has claimed. Meanwhile, Pennzoil began attacking Texaco's Chapter 11 protection.

Argentina's new debt accord with foreign banks is threatening to unravel pacts with other debtor nations. The Philippines, Venezuela and possibly Chile may insist on renegotiating terms of their debt agreements.

17 The Fed's efforts to support the dollar could lead to a recession, some Reagan officials fear. Budget Director Miller said the Fed may overreact and push interest rates up too far. Economic adviser Sprinkel has voiced similar fears, sources said. Their concern comes as Treasury Secretary Baker expressed stronger support for braking the dollar's fall.

The dollar rallied after Baker's comments but eased later on profit-taking. The stronger currency again boosted stock and bond prices, though the Dow Jones industrials finished down 6.96 points, at 2275.99.

A. H. Robins filed a Chapter 11 reorganization plan to prevent a possible takeover by Rorer Group. The acquisition proposal could gain momentum if Robins and Dalkon shield claimants don't resolve disputes on a new settlement plan soon.

Housing starts fell 3.2% in March, but economists said homebuilding remains relatively strong. Separately, business inventories rose a modest 0.2% in February. The factory operating rate fell to 79.2% of capacity in March from 79.7% in February.

The SEC moved to curb excessive price markups of zero-coupon bonds. In an unusual step, the agency spelled out its markup policy on such bonds, hoping to serve notice to brokerage firms to end pricing abuses.

20 The U.S. tariffs imposed Friday on certain Japanese products will last at least through mid-June, Reagan officials said. The president decided on the duties to send a strong trade message to Japan and to convince Congress he can get tough with trading partners. According to U.S. executives, the tariffs have more political than economic importance.

Amoco agreed to buy financially ailing Dome Petroleum for $3.87 billion, outbidding Exxon and TransCanada PipeLines. The takeover, which would be Canada's largest, still must be approved by lenders, shareholders and regulators. TransCanada pledged to pursue its takeover bid.

The Fed's intervention to support the dollar has been bigger than many thought, indicating the central bank is determined to halt the currency's decline, some traders say. The dollar firmed on Friday, though trading was sparse because of the holiday.

The Big Three auto makers are expected to report lower total profits for the first quarter, mostly because of a big earnings drop at GM, according to analysts. Meanwhile, Chrysler's Iacocca received $20.6 million in compensation last year.

Money supply growth has slowed unexpectedly, touching off a debate about its significance to the economy. Fed officials said they continue to monitor the money supply, contrary to what many analysts had assumed.

21 Bond prices plunged as the weaker dollar and surging commodity prices heightened worries about inflation. Some active Treasury bonds sank 1⅞ points. The dollar slipped further in thin trading as precious metals soared, leading other commodity futures higher. Stock prices seesawed in dull trading before closing slightly lower.

Treasury Secretary Baker voiced strong support for the Fed's anti-inflation policies. His remarks seemed aimed at dispelling fears that the Reagan administration would try to block the Fed from raising interest rates to defend the dollar.

Mortgage rates exceeded 10% last week for the first time in over six months, though analysts called the rise temporary. The surge sent Financial Corp. of America scrambling to compensate for the lower value of its mortgage-backed securities.

Mellon Bank's new chairman, Nathan Pearson, asserted that he and other outside directors were "shocked and surprised" by the severity of the banking company's problem loans.

Santa Fe Southern Pacific said John Schmidt resigned as chairman and chief executive and will be succeeded temporarily by ex-chairman John S. Reed. The surprise departure comes as the company continues efforts to merge its two railroads.

22 Stock prices soared in heavy trading, pushing the Dow Jones industrials up 66.47 points, its second biggest point gain ever, to 2337.07. Analysts said the surge reflected relief that the dollar and bond market appeared to stabilize after recent weakness. Bond prices rallied after an early slump, while the dollar mostly firmed amid mild intervention.

The Fed is refraining from nudging up interest rates because it wants to keep pressure on Japan to ease credit, a senior U.S. official said. He asserted that Washington and Tokyo are engaged in a struggle over how to stabilize the dollar.

State regulation of takeovers was upheld by the Supreme Court for the first time. The justices' ruling, which backed an Indiana law challenged by the SEC, is expected to spur other states to pass takeover laws.

Citicorp's profit fell 2.2% in the first quarter, while Manufacturers Hanover's dropped 21%, after both placed loans to Brazil and Ecuador on nonaccrual status. Bankers Trust, which is less exposed to the two nations, said profit rose 7.2%.

23 Stocks tumbled in late trading, giving back most of Tuesday's gains. The Dow Jones industrials skidded 51.13 points to 2285.94. The slide was triggered by the bond market, where prices fell sharply on speculation the Fed may be tightening credit to support the dollar. The currency itself was little changed.

Durable goods orders rose 3.4% in March, mainly due to surging military orders, which move erratically. Still, the increase was bigger than expected and included widespread gains among major industries.

Hostile takeovers were set back severely by Tuesday's Supreme Court ruling upholding an Indiana takeover law, corporate raiders and others said. Many predicted that raiders may turn to waging proxy fights.

A takeover bill planned by Rep. Dingell would restrict or even outlaw greenmail payments and golden parachutes. It also would require one-share, one-vote for most securities and curb anti-takeover tactics.

24 The economy grew at a strong 4.3% rate in the first quarter, aided by a drop in imports and a rise in inventory investment. But analysts said the GNP increase, the largest in nearly three years, exaggerated the economy's strength and masked some sluggishness. Meanwhile, a GNP-based price measure showed a resurgence in inflation.

The dollar skidded 1% against other major currencies as traders ignored the GNP report. The decline, which came despite intervention by four central banks, led some traders to speculate that the currency is headed for another sharp slide.

Stock prices gyrated in volatile trading before ending lower. Silver futures jumped nearly 11%, leading a strong rally by commodities.

General Motors plans its first-ever production cut at its California joint venture with Toyota, reflecting the soft auto market. GM's profit, meanwhile, fell 23% in the first quarter. U.S. car sales rose 3.8% in mid-April, though the pace remained weak.

The personal computer industry is booming again after two years of sluggish growth. Sales of mainframe and midrange computers also are showing some signs of improvement.

27 Consumer prices rose 0.4% in March, suggesting the weak dollar is starting to push up prices for a broad range of items. There were big increases in the cost of housing, apparel and energy. Separately, personal income edged up 0.2% last month. Machine tool orders declined 23% as General Motors, a major purchaser, slashed its spending.

Tougher trade laws appear likely to be approved by Congress soon. The protectionist movement has been bolstered partly by growing corporate support. Meanwhile, Nakasone will try to ease U.S.-Japan trade tensions during talks with Reagan this week.

Interest rates may rise again soon due to the weak dollar and a wave of federal borrowing. Bond and stock prices tumbled Friday as the dollar's slide continued, raising doubts about the effectiveness of intervention.

Treasury Secretary Baker rejected

calls that the U.S. issue yen-denominated bonds to bolster the dollar.

28 The dollar rebounded after the U.S. reiterated its opposition to a further drop by the currency. The dollar's rally, helped by intervention and profit-taking, triggered a recovery by stocks and bonds but sent precious metals and other commodity futures plunging. The Dow Jones industrials, down over 40 points in the morning, closed off 4.83, at 2230.54.

U.S. investigators have uncovered substantial evidence to support criminal securities-law charges against Drexel Burnham Lambert and the head of its "junk bond" operations, Michael Milken, sources said.

The oil industry is seeing signs of stability in world petroleum markets. Though still cautious, many firms believe oil prices will stay at $18 a barrel and rise before year's end.

The U.S. proposed to continue offering vast offshore tracts for oil and gas exploration. But drilling plans for the Bering Sea may scuttle a compromise pact with conservationists.

The U.S. semiconductor market will grow 19% this year and next, faster than in Japan and Europe, according to an industry forecast.

29 Bond prices surged again as the dollar's rebound continued. Some active Treasury bonds jumped more than 1½ points, bringing the gain since Monday to over two points. The dollar was aided partly by caution ahead of Nakasone's U.S. visit. The firmer dollar and bond rally boosted stocks, but most of the gains were lost in late profit-taking.

Tokyo stock prices posted a record decline before recovering to close with only moderate losses. The rebound was triggered mainly by the stronger dollar, which also boosted shares in London and Frankfurt.

Gold prices rallied, bolstered by technical factors and a broader investor base. But silver futures continued to plunge in heavy trading, while platinum prices also weakened.

Major British banks reduced their base lending rates to 9½% from 10%, effective today. It is the first time in more than two years that the key rate has declined to single digits.

30 A trade-retaliation proposal was narrowly backed by the House, 218–214. The Gephardt amendment to the House's trade bill would force countries with big trade surpluses to reduce their imbalances by 10% a year or face U.S. retaliation. The Senate is unlikely to approve the amendment, although a variation could eventually clear Congress.

Financial markets shuddered as the House vote heightened inflation worries. Bond prices and futures plunged, as did the dollar. Stocks lost nearly half their early gains.

Merrill Lynch said it had a $250 million pre-tax loss, largely due to unauthorized mortgage-securities dealing by a senior trader. Merrill said the rest of the loss came from "subsequent market volatility," which also has hurt other firms and banks.

Ford Motor's profit more than doubled in the first quarter to a record $1.49 billion, exceeding the combined net of GM and Chrysler. The better-than-expected results triggered heavy buying of Ford's stock and led to an unusual halt in trading.

Leading indicators rose 0.4% in March, led by surging stock prices. Despite the gain, the economy isn't expected to grow as strongly as the first-quarter rate of 4.3%. New home sales eased 3.6% last month, while building contracts rebounded 10%.

May 1987

1 The U.S. and Japan are jointly adjusting their interest rates to help stem the dollar's decline. Volcker said the Fed has tightened credit slightly in recent days, while Nakasone told Reagan that Japan will cut some short-term interest rates. Both moves are intended to make dollar investments more attractive.

Bond prices soared in reaction, though the dollar recovered only slightly. Some Treasury bonds rose about 2½ points, the biggest gain in over 10 months. Stocks also rallied, but later retreated somewhat.

Factory orders rose 2.3% in March as military bookings surged. The increase, the fifth in seven months, suggests that manufacturing is continuing to improve modestly.

Commodity futures prices reached 15-month highs in a broad-based rally led by precious metal, agriculture and energy contracts.

4 The prime rate is expected to rise further in the coming weeks following Friday's increase to 8% from 7¾%. A higher

prime is predicted because the Fed may raise its discount rate soon to help support the dollar. Many economists believe the Fed's recent credit tightening, along with Japan's rate cuts, won't be enough to stem the dollar's fall.

Nakasone's visit did little to ease trade and economic tensions between the U.S. and Japan. The lack of initiatives disappointed some foreign exchange traders, who expect the dollar to decline further this week.

Japanese investors are crucial to the success of the U.S.-Japan effort to coordinate interest rates. Meanwhile, Japan's jobless rate and trade surplus hit records in the fiscal year.

The industrial sector picked up slightly in April, according to a survey of purchasing agents. New orders slowed only slightly from March, while employment growth quickened. Inventories fell modestly.

5 Bond prices tumbled as the dollar's decline heightened fears that Japanese investors will show little interest in this week's Treasury refunding. Some 30-year Treasury bonds fell nearly 1¼ points. The dollar's continued slide pushed interest rate futures lower and commodity futures higher. Stocks rebounded in late trading to close up slightly.

West Germany is considering cutting a key interest rate to help stem the dollar's decline, sources said. The possible step, viewed as largely symbolic, would complement recent rate adjustments by the U.S. and Japan.

Investing in gold has become respectable in the U.S. as bullion prices near four-year highs and inflation fears revive. Precious metals trading has been so heavy recently that an order backlog forced the Comex in New York to close early yesterday.

Non-farm productivity rose at a 1.7% rate in the first quarter following six months of declines. The rebound came as output climbed at its highest rate since early 1984.

6 Stock prices surged in reaction to a stronger bond market and dollar, causing the Dow Jones industrials to jump 51.85 points, to 2338.07. The bond rally came as the Treasury launched a huge $29 billion refinancing. Optimism that Japanese investors would participate in the auction helped bolster the dollar.

Fed Vice Chairman Manuel Johnson indicated that the Fed may avoid pushing interest rates higher, even if the dollar continues to decline.

Mortgage rates rose further last week, sowing doubts among economists whether rates will fall again soon. The average rate on 30-year, fixed-rate mortgages was 10.47%, up from 10.37% the week before.

The Japanese launched their long-awaited effort to crack the U.S. supercomputer market, introducing a three-machine line and vowing to compete head-on with U.S. rivals.

New York Comex trading continued to be disrupted by the surge in precious metal orders. Officials said a new clearing system is likely.

7 Bond prices skidded as investors in the U.S. and Japan reacted coolly to the Treasury's 10-year note sale. One analyst said interest from Japan was "virtually non-existent" due to worries about the dollar, which was little-changed yesterday. Stocks rose slightly, while the Dow Jones Transportation Average soared 18.79, to a record 964.64.

Japan's central bank began pushing interest rates lower as part of Nakasone's pledge last week to help stabilize yen-dollar exchange rates.

Three Canadian gold firms agreed to merge in a $4.03 billion stock swap, creating North America's largest gold mining company. Dome Mines, Campbell Red Lake and Placer Development produce about 25% of Canada's total gold output.

Federal tax receipts surged unexpectedly in April and may help reduce the U.S. budget deficit this year, officials said. Meanwhile, taxes are going up in many states this year as a result of the new federal tax law.

8 Bond prices revived as the Treasury ended a huge refinancing, but the gains were halved later when the auction results emerged. The 30-year bond sale drew mixed reviews and left analysts divided on the outlook for interest rates. Reports of strong Japanese interest in the bonds pushed the dollar higher. Stocks closed mixed.

Three major banks boosted rates sharply on consumer CDs, possibly signaling the start of a general rate increase for consumer deposits.

11 Corporate profits surged 11% in the first quarter, buoyed by modest economic growth and cost cutting. The gain, the biggest in three years, contrasts with a 1% drop in the 1986 fourth quarter. Most economists expect profits to strengthen the rest of this year. Canadian corporate earnings soared 55% in the quarter.

The jobless rate fell to 6.3% of the civilian work force in April, the lowest level in seven years. The decline, from a 6.6% rate in March, indicates the economy is continuing to grow steadily and may be stronger than some economists had expected.

Big New York banks are waging an interest-rate war to lure depositors, and many banks elsewhere are raising their rates.

United Airlines is talking to Europe's Airbus Industrie as well as two U.S. aircraft makers about buying as many as 190 jets for Pacific and U.S. flights, sources said. It marks the first time United has allowed Airbus to make a serious sales pitch.

The Fed may boost interest rates substantially in the coming weeks to try to keep the dollar afloat, some economists say.

South Korea plans to increase the value of its currency against the dollar in response to U.S. pressure to ease the growing trade imbalance between the two countries.

12 Inflation worries vaulted commodity prices to two-year highs, triggering sharp retreats by the bond and stock markets. The commodity gains spanned nearly every raw-material market and led to a near-record one-day advance in a widely watched price barometer.

Active 30-year Treasury bonds slid about two points. The Dow Jones industrials fell back from a big rally, closing down 15 points, at 2307.30.

Japan plans auction sales of some government bonds, suggesting Tokyo is responding to U.S. pressure to open its markets more to foreigners. An auction sale likely would give U.S. and other foreign firms a bigger role in Japan's government bond market.

Charitable contributions grew 9.4% last year to a record $87.22 billion, buoyed by the strong stock market and the new tax law, a survey said. But corporate giving seemed to have been damped by merger fever.

13 U.S. and Soviet grain crops are being threatened by bad weather, which could push up commodity prices in the coming weeks. Meanwhile, the Reagan administration appears ready to pay record subsidies for U.S. wheat sales to the Soviets, sources said.

Commodity prices retreated on profit-taking following Monday's big rally, though precious metals futures rose. The drop by commodities helped spark a bond rally, though traders said the bond market remains bearish. Stocks recovered modestly.

West Germany's central bank cut a key interest rate, as expected, as part of a coordinated effort with the U.S. and Japan to support the dollar. But currency traders said the move isn't likely to have much effect.

Italy's two biggest chemicals firms are discussing merging some operations. The move by Montedison and Enichem could result in a firm with $11.2 billion in annual revenue.

Treasury Secretary Baker warned the 24-nation OECD that the U.S. can no longer stimulate the world economy by running big deficits.

14 The dollar firmed after Tokyo urged Japanese firms to stop speculating against the U.S. currency. Traders doubted, however, that the government's appeal would have any lasting impact on the market.

U.S. oil prices rose to 16-month highs of $19.41 a barrel amid signs of tighter gasoline and fuel oil supplies. But oil-company selling later cut the gain, prompting predictions of softer oil prices in the coming days.

Japan's trade surplus with the U.S. grew to a record $5.15 billion in April, heightening Tokyo's concern about rising U.S. trade protectionism.

Airline stocks rallied on Allegis takeover speculation, pushing the Dow Jones Transportation Average up 10.62 points, to a record 967.48. Most other stock prices were little changed in moderate trading.

Retail sales rose only 0.1% in April, hurt by lower car sales. Excluding autos, sales rose 0.4% after showing no change in March. Analysts said part of the modest retail sales gains reflected higher prices, particularly for gasoline and apparel.

U.S. car sales tumbled 28.5% in early May, continuing an uneven performance that analysts say is primarily linked to incentive programs.

15 The U.S. trade deficit shrank to $13.63 billion in March as exports surged 12.9%. The deficit in merchandise trade narrowed with Japan and Canada but grew with Western Europe. Economists expect the gradual trade improvement to continue.

The dollar declined despite a favorable U.S. trade report. The weaker currency and a surge in commodity prices fueled inflation worries and helped push up interest rates. Bluechip stocks eased as the Dow Jones industrials fell 4.19 to 2325.49.

Britain will provide $755 million to help Airbus Industrie develop two new passenger jets. The pledge removes a major obstacle to Airbus's plans and puts pressure on the other European partners to assist the project.

18 Interest rates are expected to rise further in the coming weeks as the Fed attempts to keep inflation under control, analysts say. Banks boosted their prime rate to 8¼% Friday from 8%, and some analysts say the prime could rise to at least 9% this summer. Inflation fears grew with Friday's report that producer prices surged 0.7% in April.

Stocks and bonds slumped on the prime rate and producer price rises. The Dow Jones industrials slid 52.97 points to 2272.52, while some Treasury bonds sank two points. Despite the gloom in both markets, some analysts say bonds could rally soon.

OPEC is approaching its midyear conference with hopes of further increasing its revenue, either by raising crude prices or boosting production. But harmony at the June 25 parley in Vienna could founder on Iraq's campaign to expand its oil output.

19 World platinum supplies have hit record levels due to an unexpected rise in Soviet sales, Johnson Matthey of London says. But the price has been buoyed by soaring demand.

The industrial operating rate fell to 78.9% of capacity in April, the lowest level in over three years. The decline from the March rate of 79.3% was due partly to cuts in auto production.

The dollar firmed amid signs of credit-tightening by the Fed. The stronger currency and a drop in commodity prices sparked a mild bond rally and helped stocks stem early losses. The Dow Jones industrials finished down 13.86 points at 2258.66.

Fed policy is now aimed primarily at propping up the dollar, analysts say, which will keep interest rates high and could bring a recession.

20 Citicorp will add $3 billion to its foreign and domestic loan-loss reserves, resulting in a $2.5 billion loss for the second quarter. The move puts pressure on other banks to decide whether they should take the same drastic steps. Uncertainty about those banks is expected to roil world financial markets for some time.

Long-term Treasury bond yields rose to their highest levels in over a year, driven by heavy selling of financial futures and a weaker dollar. The sharp drop in bond prices and worries about the U.S. banking system sent stocks lower. The Dow Jones industrials fell 37.38, to 2221.28.

Housing starts dropped 2.9% in April, and economists expect further declines due to the recent jump in mortgage rates. Construction of multifamily homes plunged in the month, while single-family starts rose.

A federal appeals court temporarily blocked the Fed's decision to give three banking concerns limited authority to underwrite securities. The move came as the Fed gave three other banks the same powers.

21 A 6.4% stake in Texaco has been acquired by Australian financier Robert Holmes a Court, prompting speculation he will try to become a major player in Texaco's $10.3 billion legal battle with Pennzoil. Though both firms apparently haven't been contacted by Holmes a Court, Pennzoil privately speculated that he could help settle the dispute.

Big U.S. banks are expected to follow Citicorp and sharply boost reserves for doubtful foreign loans. The action could mean higher interest rates and banking fees, particularly for consumers and small businesses. BankAmerica's Clausen may find recovery efforts temporarily derailed.

Brazil reacted calmly to Citicorp's move. Britain urged its banks to boost reserves for Third World debt.

World oil prices slumped after some OPEC members indicated the group won't raise its $18-a-barrel benchmark price at its June parley. Oil prices had been rising amid expectations of an OPEC price boost.

Argentina reached an accord with the Paris Club of creditor nations to reschedule $2.1 billion of debt owed to foreign governments and receive $400 million in new loans, officials said.

22 Saudi Arabia and its closest allies in OPEC firmly rejected Iran's demands that the cartel raise oil prices, and instead called for price stability. The move implies moderate energy prices for the next few years.

Citicorp expects to cut its loans to debtor nations by as much as a third—or $5 billion—over the next three years. The strategy is an unprecedented shrinking of a big bank's portfolio of shaky foreign loans.

FDIC Chairman Seidman said banks will find it "irresistable" to follow Citicorp's recent move in boosting reserves for foreign debt.

Japan outlined a plan to make $20 billion available to aid debtor nations. The move may help boost U.S. exports and cut the trade deficit.

26 Stepped-up inflation and modest economic growth are indicated by the latest U.S. statistics. Consumer prices increased 0.4% in April as the rise in energy costs slowed and apparel prices continued to surge. Corporate profits declined 5.5% in the first quarter, while GNP growth for the period was revised to a 4.4% rate from 4.3%. Durable goods orders edged up 0.1% last month.

Three Japanese chip makers are stepping up domestic sales of custom-made computer chips, which aren't covered by the U.S.-Japan semiconductor pact. The move poses a threat to U.S. makers, which are relatively strong in specialized chips.

Machine-tool orders slid 33% in April to the lowest monthly level in four years. Machine-tool producers said some companies have big plans for investing in equipment, but are delaying a final commitment.

Japanese institutions began direct trading in U.S. and other foreign financial futures markets. Such trading is expected to grow slowly, reflecting caution by Japanese investors as well as restraints by Tokyo officials.

Some Fed members appear to have taken issue with Volcker's stand against further declines in the dollar. At the Fed's March 31 policy meeting, "a few" said a weaker dollar may be needed to ease the U.S. trade gap.

The dollar's recent stability has been tied partly to Tokyo's campaign to stop speculation against the U.S. currency. But traders doubt the effort will have any lasting effect.

27 The dollar staged its biggest one-day rally this year, sparking sharp gains by stock and bond prices. The Dow Jones industrials jumped 54.74 points, the third largest point gain ever, to 2297.94, while Treasury bond prices surged to their highest levels in almost two weeks. Precious metals and other commodities fell.

U.S. car sales tumbled 24.9% in mid-May, lower than most forecasts. Analysts said sales for the year could fall even further than expected.

Consumer spending rose a brisk 0.6% in April despite the sharpest drop in after-tax income in nearly 12 years. The increased spending and 2.4% drop in income led to a steep decline in the savings rate.

Citicorp expects to earn over $2 billion a year starting next year, an internal memo says. Some analysts said such profit growth would help the bank overcome its foreign-debt woes. But others said Citicorp still faces plenty of other problems.

28 Chase Manhattan added $1.6 billion to its loan-loss reserve, citing shaky foreign loans. The move, which will result in an estimated quarterly loss of $1.4 billion, follows Citicorp's decision last week to add $3 billion to its reserve. Chase particularly cited Brazil's suspension of interest payments on its bank debt.

Primerica Corp. agreed to acquire Smith Barney for $750 million, further consolidating the securities industry. The purchase of the old Wall Street firm is Primerica's latest expansion into financial services and represents a coup for chairman Gerald Tsai Jr.

29 Allegis's board temporarily approved a $3 billion recapitalization in another attempt to ward off takeover threats. The plan, which would pay Allegis holders $60 a share, would swell the travel company's debt to about $5.2 billion. The action follows Coniston Partners' disclosure that it owns 13% of Allegis and will seek to break up or sell the firm.

Japan is expected to unveil today a $35 billion economic stimulus plan. Analysts said the measures will spur the economy somewhat but do little to narrow Japan's trade surplus.

Bond prices rebounded on expectations of a stable dollar and signs that the Fed might not need to tighten credit soon. The mild rally pushed up stocks. The Dow Jones industrials rose 14.87 points, to 2310.68.

BankAmerica indicated it won't boost foreign loan-loss reserves by anything close to $1 billion despite pressure to match recent moves by Citicorp and Chase Manhattan. Chairman A. W. Clausen called BankAmerica's reserves "appropriate."

New loans for Argentina could be slowed by the banks' addition to reserves. The proposed $1.95 billion in loans is part of a debt restructuring.

30 A trade-retaliation proposal was narrowly backed by the House, 218–214. The Gephardt amendment to the House's trade bill would force countries with big trade surpluses to reduce their imbalances by 10% a year or face U.S. retaliation. The Senate is unlikely to approve the amendment, although a variation could eventually clear Congress.

Financial markets shuddered as the House vote heightened inflation worries. Bond prices and futures plunged, as did the dollar. Stocks lost nearly half their early gains.

Merrill Lynch said it had a $250 million pre-tax loss, largely due to unauthorized mortgage-securities dealing by a senior trader. Merrill said the rest of the loss came from "subsequent market volatility," which also has hurt other firms and banks.

Leading indicators rose 0.4% in March, led by surging stock prices. Despite the gain, the economy isn't expected to grow as strongly as the first-quarter rate of 4.3%. New home sales eased 3.6% last month, while building contracts rebounded 10%.

Ford Motor's profit more than doubled in the first quarter to a record $1.49 billion, exceeding the combined net of GM and Chrysler. The better-than-expected results triggered heavy buying of Ford's stock and led to an unusual halt in trading.

June 1987

1 SEC Chairman Shad expects major stock markets to agree in a month on a uniform voting-rights rule. The prediction came after the SEC, in a reversal, decided against requiring a one-share, one-vote standard.

Leading indicators slid 0.6% in April, but analysts said the decline exaggerated the economy's weakness. Separately, a survey of purchasing agents said the economy continued its slow but steady growth in May.

Coniston Partners plans to continue fighting for control of Allegis's board despite the travel company's proposed $3 billion recapitalization. The anti-takeover plan could result in a windfall profit for Boeing.

Japan's economic stimulus plan was unveiled Friday to generally favorable U.S. reaction. The $43 billion package of spending measures and tax cuts was bigger than expected.

The dollar and credit markets are becoming more stable amid signs of growing cooperation between the U.S. and major allies. The Fed and other central banks intervened heavily this spring to support the dollar.

2 The dollar surged to a two-month high in Tokyo trading but eased later in Europe and the U.S. The stronger dollar helped push up bond prices and fueled a continued slide by precious metals prices. Stock prices finished mixed after the rally in bonds fizzled.

U.S. semiconductor makers have made some inroads into the Japanese chip market since Washington imposed trade penalties against Tokyo in April. But the sales gains haven't signaled any major breakthrough.

Construction spending rose 0.4% in April despite weakness in the residential sector. Outlays are expected to fall soon due to rising mortgage rates. Building contracts fell slightly last month, according to F.W. Dodge.

3 Alan Greenspan was nominated Fed chairman after Paul Volcker unexpectedly declined a third term. Greenspan, a respected 61-year-old economist, is expected to pursue nearly identical policies on inflation, interest rates and economic growth. But succeeding Volcker will be a daunting task and Greenspan is expected to face political pressures as the 1988 election approaches.

The dollar and bond prices nosedived as foreign investors reacted nervously to Greenspan's nomination. Stocks were only modestly lower, apparently on speculation that Fed policies won't change much. Most commodity prices rose sharply.

Factory orders inched up 0.2% in April, but would have fallen without a big increase in military orders. The April rise, following a revised 2.6% gain in March, was viewed as sign of a sluggish economy. Meanwhile, sales of single-family homes rose 7.6%, but analysts called the surge temporary.

Non-farm productivity rose at a revised 0.5% annual rate in the first quarter, smaller than the 1.7% gain reported earlier. The rise still reflected a rebound from six months of declines, but its modest size was more in tune with the sluggish economy.

Royal Bank of Canada had a 7.2% drop in quarterly net, reflecting its classifying $971 million of loans to Brazil as non-accruing. Canada's biggest bank also plans to boost its provision for troubled foreign loans.

4 Japan will allow four U.S. banks and six other foreign firms to open securities units in Tokyo. The move is viewed as an attempt to mollify U.S. criticism that Japan unfairly limits access to its markets. Though the banks will be able to underwrite and trade in all securities, they still face stiff competition from Japanese and U.S. securities firms.

The dollar rebounded as worries faded about the change at the Fed. The currency's surge pushed up bond prices, but many economists still expect interest rates to rise. Stocks rallied, with the Dow Jones industrials gaining 42.47 points to 2320.69.

The waste disposal industry is being investigated for alleged price-fixing, bid-rigging and other criminal antitrust activities. The federal inquiry includes the two biggest waste companies, Waste Management and Browning-Ferris, sources said.

Brazil plans to propose that it pay less than half the $4.3 billion in interest it owes foreign banks this year, with the remainder being refinanced. But U.S. bankers and economists reacted skeptically to the idea.

Bank of Boston will add $300 million to its reserve for Third World loans, following similar moves by Security Pacific, Citicorp and Chase. Bank of Boston said the action will result in a quarterly loss.

5 Kidder Peabody was fined $25.3 million by the SEC to settle insider-trading and other charges. The penalty is second only to Ivan Boesky's $100 million fine last fall. The precedent-setting action makes Kidder the first major firm to settle SEC charges in the insider-trading scandal. It also allows the GE unit to escape criminal prosecution.

Major retailers reported lower-than-expected sales gains for May, indicating consumers cut back spending on general merchandise. There also were signs that rising apparel costs may damp spending later this year.

Trans World Airlines said it will boost fares soon on all flights because of soaring fuel costs. But the carrier may reconsider the move if other airlines decide not to follow.

The major stock exchanges have broken off talks on adopting uniform voting rights, sources said, forcing the SEC to move toward requiring a one-share, one-vote standard.

8 The jobless rate stayed at 6.3% in May, indicating the economy remains sluggish. Employment in manufacturing rose only slightly, with nearly all the job gains coming in the services sector. Separately, consumer credit grew at a 6.1% rate in April.

Imperial Chemical Industries agreed to buy Unilever's Stauffer Chemical group for $1.69 billion. The purchase will boost the British company's agricultural-chemicals operations, particularly in the U.S.

9 BankAmerica added $1.1 billion to its reserves for problem Third World loans, resulting in an estimated $1 billion quarterly loss and stalling the bank's turnaround efforts. Meanwhile, Manufacturers Hanover will propose to its board next Tuesday that it increase loan-loss reserves by $1.75 billion, sources said.

Reagan removed tariffs on 17% of the Japanese imports targeted in April for U.S. sanctions. But the expected action, which came at the start of the economic summit in Venice, failed to satisfy the Japanese.

The Supreme Court ruled that securities-fraud claims made under federal law must be settled by arbitration if required by the broker-investor contract. The decision will hasten the use of arbitration in such disputes.

Silver, gold and oil provided the best investment returns in the past 12 months, according to an annual tally by Salomon Brothers.

10 A new economic strategy is expected to be adopted today at the Venice summit. The plan calls for closer coordination of economic policies among the seven industrial democracies, including regular reviews and "remedial" steps if one doesn't meet its economic goals. But the seven are divided over the initiative and over expected pacts on Third World debt and farm subsidies.

The dollar fell sharply as dealers concluded that the Venice summit wouldn't bring any new agreements to support the currency. Precious metals soared in reaction, while bond prices drifted lower. Stocks rose.

BankAmerica's decision to boost loan-loss reserves won't resolve its long-term competitive problems, and that could eventually force it to merge, analysts and officials said. BankAmerica's stock fell, indicating pessimism about its prospects.

Texas thrifts are scrambling for funds to meet growing withdrawals by big and small depositors worried about the health of the state system, regulators say. The situation could turn into a liquidity crisis.

Auto makers plan to cut output 12.8% in the third quarter, but even that may not be enough to offset weak sales. Analysts said the overbuilding may reflect worries about the possibility of a strike and expectations of a new round of incentive programs.

U.S. businesses plan to spend 3.1% more on plant and equipment this year, up slightly from what they expected three months ago. Meanwhile, capital goods producers are staging a rebound.

11 The real estate industry would get a big tax break under a bill introduced yesterday to make technical corrections in last year's tax law. The legislation also would benefit the aircraft and life insurance industries.

The Venice summit ended without any new accords to stabilize the dollar, fend off a recession or curb the huge U.S. budget and trade deficits. The group's communique appeared to reflect faltering U.S. leadership of the seven major industrial democracies.

Bear Stearns introduced a security that allows investors to bet on a drop in the Japanese yen.

12 Two more big banks boosted reserves, mainly for Third World loans. Chemical New York added $1.1 billion to its reserves, while First Interstate Bancorp. raised its by $750 million. First Chicago may seek an addition of up to $800 million, sources said.

Intel Corp. purchased a big block of its shares from IBM for $361.6 million, reflecting the chip maker's return to health. IBM, whose Intel stake is now 11.5%, has been moving away from large-scale partnerships.

15 Producer prices rose a modest 0.3% in May, suggesting fears of runaway inflation have been exaggerated. Food prices surged and energy prices remained unchanged from April. Separately, the trade deficit narrowed in April, as the overall trade balance improved with Japan, Western Europe and Canada.

Bond prices rallied and the dollar strengthened Friday on the economic reports. The Dow Jones industrials rose 17.60, to close at 2377.73.

Ford is negotiating to donate most of its South African holdings to a trust for employees of its affiliate there. The No. 2 auto maker portrayed its goal as seeking an alternative to a total pull-out, which would harm employees, most of whom are black.

Pennzoil may split the company into four separate, publicly traded pieces. Its chairman said the company is considering a wide range of restructuring plans that would depend on its litigation with Texaco.

16 The dollar surged, extending the rally that followed the June 12th report of a smaller U.S. trade deficit. Speculation grew that the currency's slide may have ended, at least for the near term. The stronger dollar pushed bond and stock prices higher, though the gains were pared later as a jump in commodity prices renewed worries about inflation.

The Supreme Court ruled that federal courts can be flexible in requiring foreign firms to produce records and other evidence in U.S. lawsuits. The decision will have a big impact on international business disputes.

U.S. car sales fell 15% in early June, indicating continued sluggishness in the new-car market. The results also suggest 1987 sales may not meet analysts' previous estimates. Of the Big Three, only Ford had higher sales in the latest period.

More banks are expected to boost reserves for Third World debt, while some are considering special charges for problem domestic loans. The actions will worsen what is already the industry's most unprofitable quarter.

17 Industrial output rose a robust 0.5% in May, indicating manufacturing is recovering from years of battering by foreign competition. Housing starts slid 2.7% last month to the lowest level in nearly 2½ years, reflecting higher mortgage rates.

National Westminster Bank plans to add $759.6 million to its reserve for Third World debt, pressuring other British banks to follow. As expected, Manufacturers Hanover and Bankers Trust boosted their reserves.

The Dow Jones industrials rose to a record 2407.35, but there was little fanfare on Wall Street. The average's 15.81-point gain came in a lethargic session, and both the bond market and dollar were little changed.

18 First-quarter GNP grew at a revised 4.8% rate, up from 4.4%, reflecting a bigger-than-expected rise in exports. Though trade improved, one analyst said, the domestic economy remained "stalled." Corporate profits fell a revised 3.9% in the quarter rather than 5.5%. Also, the industrial operating rate rose to 79.6% in May from 79.4% in April.

Oil demand is rising more slowly than expected, suggesting prices will be stable the rest of the year. OPEC is expected at this month's meeting to boost output only slightly and leave its official price unchanged. Crude prices edged up again yesterday.

David S. Ruder's nomination for SEC chairman was announced by the White House. In a statement, Reagan said that Ruder, a law professor, would press ahead with the agency's campaign against insider trading.

19 Consumer spending edged up 0.1% in May, while personal income rose 0.2%. Many economists expect income gains to outpace spending in the coming months, as consumers try to pay off debts and bolster savings after strong spending last year.

Banks appear willing to lend more money to Latin America, even though many have boosted reserves sharply for loans to the region. The trend is indicated by the progress of new loans to Argentina and Colombia.

U.S. auto makers are scaling back on consumer incentives despite a continued slowdown in sales. General Motors dropped many models from its incentive program after a similar move by Ford earlier this week.

The OECD said economic growth among industrial countries will be slower than it previously predicted. The group cited the dollar's fall.

22 Friday's (June 19) triple witching session was relatively quiet, reflecting new trading procedures, fear of regulators and market conditions.

The dollar's recent stability won't last long, some analysts say, partly due to U.S. trade and budget gaps. Meanwhile, a smaller budget deficit may not buoy credit markets much.

23 The dollar rallied, reaching three-month highs against the British pound and German mark. The stronger dollar helped send commodity prices plunging and sparked gains by bond and stock prices. Bonds also were helped by heavy Japanese buying. Three big stock indexes hit highs, with the Dow Jones industrials rising 24.66, to a record 2445.51.

Britain plans to sell up to 25% of a state-owned airport operator in an innovative tender offer, but sell the rest under the fixed-price method.

The Supreme Court left intact a lower court ruling allowing banks to sell commercial paper for clients. But the case has been overshadowed by the Fed's decision to let banking units underwrite such securities.

24 Consumer prices edged up 0.3% in May, or at a 4% annual rate, easing worries about a flare-up in inflation. A surge in food prices was offset by smaller increases for energy, transportation and apparel. Meanwhile, durable goods orders fell 0.1% in May but rose a brisk 1.4% if military items are excluded.

IBM predicted record sales of its personal computers this year, moving to dispel fears that sales of its new machines are lagging. Olivetti unveiled six personal computers to compete with IBM's new models.

The dollar retreated amid growing speculation that the U.S. and major allies want to keep exchange rates within a narrow range. The dollar's slump helped dampen early rallies in the bond and stock markets.

The U.S. remained the world's biggest debtor last year as the gap in international investment more than doubled, to $263.65 billion. The widening gap reflected the need to finance the country's huge trade deficit.

The Supreme Court struck down a Washington state tax on manufacturers' and wholesalers' total sales, saying it interferes with interstate commerce. The ruling limits states' flexibility in raising revenue.

25 A Chrysler unit and two executives were charged with conspiring to sell as new more than 60,000 cars and trucks that had been allegedly used by company managers with the odometers disconnected. It is the first criminal odometer-tampering case ever brought against a major U.S. auto maker. Chrysler faces a fine of as much as $120 million.

OPEC ministers began gathering in Vienna amid general agreement to keep the group's $18-a-barrel price. Meanwhile, Kuwait's successful entry into overseas refining and marketing could herald major changes for OPEC and the global oil industry.

U.S. car sales declined 11.3% in mid-June from a year earlier but were still up from recent sluggish levels. Of the Big Three, only Ford posted higher sales for the period. General Motors' sales slid 25%.

26 OPEC's oil-price policy is being threatened by Iraq's plans to sharply increase crude exports. As OPEC opened its meeting in Vienna, members worried that Iraq's expanded output will undermine efforts to stabilize prices at $18 a barrel. Meanwhile, U.S. oil futures rose amid speculation OPEC may agree to cut fourth-quarter production quotas.

Heating oil options begin trading today on the New York Merc and are expected to attract almost as much attention as the OPEC meeting.

Two Allegis executives resigned top posts as its board approved plans for the immediate sale of the company's hotel and rental-car units. Directors also scrapped a $60-a-share payout in favor of plan that may pay holders more than that amount.

The Chicago Board of Trade and the Chicago Board Options Exchange agreed to allow members of both exchanges to trade financial futures and options contracts side by side.

29 OPEC agreed on a compromise plan that is expected to push oil prices above $18 a barrel. The accord, worked out by Iran and Saudi Arabia, calls for OPEC to boost oil output slightly, to 16.6 million barrels a day, for the rest of 1987. Despite the show of unity in Vienna, some OPEC members said many differences remained. Iraq refused to sign the new pact.

The economy is expected to grow more briskly in the next three months than it did in the second quarter, according to a Wall Street Journal survey of economists. Most added that business activity is still sluggish.

30 New-home sales plunged 14.9% in May, the sharpest drop in 5½ years, as surging mortgage rates damped buying. Though June sales are expected to have increased, economists have cut 1987 sales forecasts.

The SEC will side with Texaco on a narrow but significant issue in the company's $10.3 billion court battle with Pennzoil. The SEC's unusual move involves tender offer rules.

World oil prices surged following OPEC's weekend accord to continue restricting output. But traders said the gains were pared by profit-taking amid skepticism that OPEC members will abide by the agreement.

Big Japanese investors may step up buying of U.S. Treasury bonds despite the market's poor showing this year. But they are less bullish, reflecting worries about the weak dollar and rising U.S. interest rates.

Allis-Chalmers filed for Chapter 11 protection, citing delays in reaching an agreement with creditors on a major restructuring. One lender said there was a "cascade of problems."

July 1987

1 The ICC reaffirmed its 1986 rejection of the proposed Santa Fe-Southern Pacific merger, ending a long effort to create the nation's third-largest railroad. The agency, which continued to have strong antitrust concerns about the merger, ordered the parent corporation to sell at least one of the railroads.

Leading indicators rose a brisk 0.7% in May, suggesting the economy will strengthen in the second half. Meanwhile, factory orders were virtually unchanged in May but rose 0.8% if military items are excluded.

The Treasury's decision to terminate a 1948 tax treaty with the Netherlands Antilles sparked immediate alarm among investors as well as major U.S. corporate borrowers.

AT&T said profit rose in the second quarter due to cost-cutting and strong long-distance earnings.

Stocks fell sharply as end-of-the-quarter selling dominated the market, surprising some traders and analysts. The Dow Jones industrials tumbled 28.38 points, to 2418.53. Bond prices and the dollar eased slightly.

Big publicly traded partnerships should be subject to corporate tax, except those involving oil and gas, a Reagan official told Congress.

2 Toshiba's top officers resigned, taking responsibility for a unit's sale of militarily sensitive technology to the Soviets. The unexpected departure of Toshiba's chairman and president came amid growing criticism in the U.S. and Japan over the sale. The Pentagon said the gear will aid Soviet submarines.

The SEC may get only $87 million of the $100 million it expected from Boesky's insider-trading settlement. According to court records, one of the stocks in the portfolio Boesky turned over may be sold for $13 million less than it was thought to be worth.

3 The jobless rate fell to 6.1% in June, the lowest level in 7½ years. But the decline, from a 6.3% rate the previous month, likely exaggerates the economy's strength. Most of the improvement resulted from a drop in the labor force. Payroll employment showed only a sluggish increase of 116,000 jobs.

The Treasury will seek legislation to protect investors hurt by the termination of a U.S. tax treaty with the Netherlands Antilles. Officials were stunned by the sharp market reaction to their decision to end the pact.

6 Southland Corp.'s controlling shareholder, the Thompson family, agreed to buy the convenience-store company in a two-step transaction valued at $77 a share, or about $4 billion. The accord ends weeks of takeover speculation surrounding the Dallas-based owner of 7-Eleven stores that had pushed Southland stock from about $47 a share to near $70.

The economic expansion of the past 5½ years is expected to last at least another year, a Wall Street Journal survey of economists shows. In addition, little change is foreseen in interest rates and inflation.

Purchasing agents said the economy continued to grow in June, but at a slower pace than in May. Production rates, inventories, new orders and employment all improved.

The dollar may strengthen further over the near term, especially against the yen, some traders believe. Meanwhile, investors in U.S. stocks are expected to shift their attention from the dollar to corporate earnings, at least for the next few weeks.

London's gold market is about to undergo its own Big Bang, or deregulation. Though bullion's price will continue to be fixed by the five major gold houses, other market makers will have a bigger and more formal role in the expanding market.

7 U.S. crude oil prices surged to nearly $21 a barrel on spot and futures markets. Traders cited growing worries about tensions in the Persian Gulf as well as other factors.

A global ban on farm subsidies by the year 2000 was formally proposed by the U.S. But the idea faces such stiff opposition at home and abroad that any pact is unlikely soon.

U.S. car sales fell 13.8% in late June from a strong year-ago period. But the results represented an improvement from the weak sales pace of May and early June.

Illegal immigration is rising again after a seven-month decline, leading some U.S. officials to speculate that Latin American poverty has overpowered the eight-month-old U.S. immigration law. The officials note that the increase coincides with reports of labor shortages in U.S. farm fields and garment factories.

Mortgage rates rose slightly last week, to an average 10.36% on a 30-year, fixed-rate loan. But rates are expected to ease in coming months.

8 The dollar surged past 150 yen for the first time in 3½ months, bolstered by traders' relief that North didn't implicate Reagan in the Iran-Contra affair. The stronger U.S. currency helped push up bond prices, while North's testimony was said to have aided a rally by stocks. The Dow Jones industrials closed up 20.25 points, at 2449.78.

Genentech's British patent for a genetically engineered heart-attack drug was declared invalid by a U.K. court. If upheld, the decision could sharply limit the patent claims of biotechnology companies in Britain.

Banks are allowed to operate brokerage units that trade securities as well as give investment advice, a federal appeals court ruled. The decision will permit banks to compete more directly with the securities industry.

9 Consumer credit shrank at a 1.1% annual rate in May, suggesting that borrowers are continuing to shift funds to home-equity loans.

10 Major retailers posted modest sales gains for June, giving little evidence consumer spending is rising. Analysts still expect fiscal quarter profits to be strong. Sears's same-store sales rose 3.5%, Carter Hawley's 5.2% and Mercantile's 3.6%.

Crude oil prices surged above $21 a barrel to their highest level in 1½ years, as bond prices slumped on low volume and the dollar eased against the Japanese yen. Stocks closed mixed mostly due to profit-taking.

13 The Senate approved a measure calling for U.S. action against countries with "a consistent pattern" of import barriers. The plan, aimed at Japan, would require for the first time steps against specific nations, rather than industries, that engage in unfair trade practices.

Producer prices rose a modest 0.2% in June, or 2.9% at an annual rate, further evidence that inflation isn't increasing as quickly as feared earlier this year. Excluding often volatile food and energy prices, last month's increase was a slim 0.1%.

The Treasury will modify plans to terminate a treaty with the Netherlands Antilles. The Eurobond market has been in turmoil since plans to scrap the treaty were announced.

The Big Three auto makers may report higher combined second-quarter earnings, analysts say, despite lower sales. Ford is expected to post a profit gain of as much as 39%, which may be enough to offset expected declines at GM and Chrysler.

14 Apple Computer's profit soared 65% in the third quarter, topping its own expectations and indicating that other microcomputer makers may also post strong results. One analyst said Apple's robust showing means the industry might avoid its usual summer slowdown.

Variety will be bought from the Silverman family by Cahners Publishing. Cahners, a unit of Reed International of London, agreed to buy the bible of the entertainment industry for an undisclosed amount of cash.

Chase Manhattan posted a second-quarter loss of $1.4 billion, reflecting the impact of previously reported reserves for shaky loans to Third World nations. First Chicago reported a $698.3 million loss for the quarter.

15 Stock prices surged with the Dow Jones Industrial Average gaining 28.38 points to a record 2481.35. Strong foreign buying helped trigger the gains. Bond prices recovered some of Monday's declines, while the dollar moved higher.

Stock-index futures prices jumped amid rumors that figures to be released today would show the U.S. trade gap narrowed sharply in May.

Holmes a Court sought approval to increase his Texaco stake to as much as 15%, but company officials vowed to fight a takeover by the Australian financier, or anyone else. Texaco also said it is preparing a plan to emerge from bankruptcy-law proceedings.

Chemical New York posted a $1.1 billion second-quarter loss, reflecting increased reserves to cover troubled loans. Mellon Bank and Marine Midland also had hefty losses, while PNC Financial's profit fell 78%.

Retail sales rose 0.4% in June, but the gain was entirely due to a 1.9% increase in car purchases. Some economists said the figures suggest that consumers will no longer be the main force fueling the economy.

16 The trade deficit swelled to $14.4 billion in May from $13.32 billion in April, underscoring the tenacity of the nation's trade problem. Separately, business inventories in May jumped 0.7%, while industrial production in June rose 0.2%.

The dollar tumbled after the trade deficit report, with the U.S. currency skidding 1.6% against the Japanese yen. Bond prices also fell.

Crude oil prices surged amid continuing turbulence in the Persian Gulf, rising 57 cents a barrel to $22.15. Meanwhile, gasoline prices have been pushed higher by increased demand and rising crude prices.

U.S. auto makers plan to build 11.2% fewer cars in the third quarter than a year earlier, but they still may have to offer broad sales incentives to help trim current inventories.

The television networks are experiencing strong demand for advertising time for the 1987–88 season, analysts and industry executives said. The executives expect "upfront" prime-time ad sales to jump to about $3 billion from $2.6 billion a year ago.

Japan's major banks are discussing increasing their reserves against possible losses from foreign loans.

17 Saudi Arabia moved to curb a surge in oil demand, telling customers that they can't buy more oil in August than previously contracted for. The fresh demand was sparked by a sharp increase in spot prices this week.

Japan is making progress cutting down on the number of semiconductors sold abroad at artificially low prices, but still isn't letting enough U.S. chips into its own markets, Commerce Secretary Baldrige said.

20 Housing starts fell 0.7% in June to the lowest rate in nearly three years. But economists believe home building may be starting to recover because of recent declines in mortgage rates. Building permits, a sign of future construction activity, increased 1.4% last month.

Pennzoil is expected to propose today a $4.1 billion settlement with Texaco as part of a plan to reorganize Texaco under Chapter 11. The plan calls for all other Texaco creditors to be paid in full, a source said.

The Dow Jones industrials' rise is slowing, suggesting to some analysts a faltering bull market. The average passed 2500 for the first time Friday. Meanwhile, last week's surge in oil prices has boosted the British pound.

The U.S. banking industry's loss for the

second quarter will be at least a record $10 billion, reflecting huge increases in foreign-debt reserves. But results also were hurt by other woes, such as bond-trading losses.

21 Pennzoil unveiled its $4.1 billion settlement offer and gave Texaco three months to accept it. The proposal, which would reorganize Texaco under Chapter 11, seems aimed at pitting Texaco's shareholders and creditors against its management.

Chrysler is making its first foray into China's auto market. The company expects to sign an agreement today calling for a major transfer of engine technology to the Chinese.

22 Reagan plans to veto three major bills in Congress on banking, trade and catastrophic health insurance. Reagan strategists hope the veto fights will revive his presidency, though victory isn't certain. The banking bill, which is closest to final action, appears to have enough support to override a veto.

Fed Chairman Volcker warned his successor should keep a firm grip on credit in the next few months to prevent a serious renewal of inflation. Meanwhile, nominee Greenspan said he shares Volcker's views on credit but differs on banking regulation.

Bond prices plunged amid inflation worries. The sell-off sent the dollar and stocks skidding. The Dow Jones industrials closed off 19.77 points at 2467.95. Separately, U.S. oil prices tumbled below $22 a barrel.

Five big banking firms reported huge quarterly losses stemming from their additions to loan-loss reserves. Citicorp's loss totaled $2.59 billion, Manufacturers Hanover's $1.37 billion and Bankers Trust's $544 million.

British Petroleum plans to raise a record $2.4 billion through a stock offering in conjunction with the expected sale of the government's 32% stake.

23 General Electric agreed to sell its consumer-electronics business to French electronics giant Thomson S.A. In return, GE will get Thomson's medical equipment business and between $500 million and $1 billion in cash. The transaction will boost GE's leadership in medical equipment and make Thomson a major force in consumer electronics.

TWA plans to go private in a $1.2 billion transaction that would boost Carl Icahn's stake to 90% from 73%. The plan also would give Icahn about $440 million in cash, which he said would let him "make acquisitions without using TWA as a vehicle."

Consumer prices climbed 0.4% in June, led by a jump in energy prices. But the increase, equal to a 4.3% annual rate, likely won't rekindle fears of sharply worsening inflation.

24 General Motors posted a 3.7% drop in second-quarter earnings, while Ford's profit surged 39% to a record level. GM's results were better than expected, but they stemmed mainly from an unusually low tax rate. Meanwhile, new-car sales rose 4% during mid-July, led by relatively strong sales at Ford.

Durable goods orders rose 1.4% in June, but the gain came entirely from military items. The report was considered a further sign that the economy remains weak. But analysts say manufacturing is improving.

General Electric's agreement to acquire a French medical equipment maker is the latest shakeout in a global battle over the $4.5 billion-a-year diagnostic-imaging business.

27 Economic growth slowed to a 2.6% rate in the second quarter, though the GNP report suggests the economy is expanding more evenly. The slower GNP, from a revised 4.4% rate in the first quarter, reflected smaller inventory growth, primarily in autos. But trade improved further, and domestic demand strengthened.

Machine-tool orders rose 2.3% in June, though demand among durable goods makers remains cautious.

Brazil's debt strategy has won little support from top U.S. officials and bankers, Finance Minister Bresser Pereira indicated. Brazil is trying to get a debt accord with foreign banks before it negotiates with the IMF.

Japan's stock market could be overheating as more individuals borrow to buy stock, analysts say. Meanwhile, the Nikkei average soared a record 906.42 points Friday, but the market is expected to stay volatile.

28 Sir James Goldsmith sold most of his holdings in his main European concern, Generale Occidentale, to CGE of France for a reported $243.2 million. The financier said he was tired of managing the company.

London's stock exchange officially begins trading ADRs next week, the latest effort by Britain to boost its share of equity trading and become more competitive with the U.S.

Consumer spending surged 0.7% in June, led by a jump in auto sales. Despite the unexpected strength, economists say spending will slow soon due to sluggish income growth, rising prices and high consumer debt. Income rose 0.4% last month.

Compaq Computer's profit more than tripled in the second quarter, exceeding expectations. Sales continued to increase despite IBM's introduction of a competing computer line.

29 Boeing's stock surged over 15% in reaction to a possible takeover bid by T. Boone Pickens Jr. The jump came after Pickens's Mesa Limited Partnership got permission to buy up to 15% of the aerospace giant. Pickens, however, won't say if he plans a bid for Boeing or is trying to drive up its stock price and sell out. Boeing closed at $53.75, up $7.125.

U.S. oil prices soared above $21 a barrel amid renewed jitters about the Persian Gulf. The rise by oil and a weaker dollar cut short a bond rally. But stocks gained on the strength of a few issues. The Dow Jones industrials climbed 25.83, to a record 2519.77.

Superconductivity ventures are springing up rapidly as investors seek big profits from the new materials. Reagan, meanwhile, unveiled steps to help the private sector develop commercial uses for superconductors.

USX returned to profitability in the second quarter, rebounding from last year's steel strike and a big first-quarter loss. The firm cited strength in its energy and steel operations.

30 Boeing began seeking help from Washington state to thwart a possible hostile bid by T. Boone Pickens Jr. Boeing fell 87.5 cents, to $52.875.

Stocks and stock-index futures rose to record levels as worries about interest rates and inflation eased. The Dow Jones industrials gained 19.77 to a record 2539.54. Bonds rallied in late trading, while the dollar firmed.

31 Stocks reached highs for the third day in a row despite a weaker bond market and dollar. The Dow Jones industrials climbed 27.90 to a record 2567.44, while broader indexes also hit highs. Treasury bond prices ended lower amid heavy federal borrowing, a drop in the dollar and a jump by precious metals prices. Platinum rose to a 2½-month high.

Leading indicators surged 0.8% in June, the fifth monthly rise in a row. The gain suggests solid economic growth ahead. Meanwhile, new-home sales rose 3.5% following a revised 13.2% drop in May. Import prices climbed 4% in the second quarter.

August 1987

3 First Fidelity plans to merge with Fidelcor in a stock swap valued at $1.34 billion. The transaction, the largest bank merger to date, along with a $719 million accord between PNC and Central Bancorp., Cincinnati, attest to the rise of so-called superregionals and the growing competitive pressure they pose for money-center institutions.

The economy continued to grow in July, but employment declined after four months of expansion, a survey of buying agents said. Separately, manufactured-goods orders rose 1.7% in June, while help-wanted advertising reached a seven-year high.

4 Oil and gold prices soared on heightened Mideast tensions, renewing inflation fears and battering bond and stock prices. U.S. crude rose above $22 a barrel, though prices could collapse if Persian Gulf shipping isn't disrupted. Treasury bond yields surged above 9%, as the Dow Jones industrials fell 14.99, to 2557.08. Gold rose $13.20, to $488.30.

Construction spending fell 1.1% in June amid a continued drop in nonresidential outlays. F.W. Dodge said new construction contracts rose 9%.

Non-farm productivity rose at a 1.4% rate in the second quarter following a 0.4% gain the first period.

5 Continental Airlines is backing away from an aggressive marketing program in which it sells discount tickets at supermarkets and thrifts. The Texas Air unit fears it sold more tickets than it can guarantee.

The dollar rose on continued Mideast worries, reportedly prompting Fed intervention to calm currency markets. Profit-taking pushed crude oil below $22 a barrel, while bond and stock prices also weakened.

NEC Corp.'s stock plunged following a Japanese newspaper report that the company is being investigated by Tokyo for illegally shipping high-technology goods to the Soviet bloc.

6 General Motors is offering auto-loan rates

as low as 1.9% to help clear more than a million 1987-model cars off dealer lots. It is the third year in a row GM has resorted to a major buyer-incentive program before introducing its new models. Ford and Chrysler said they are studying the GM incentives.

Oil prices tumbled amid signs of bigger U.S. supplies and an uneasy calm in the Persian Gulf. The slide pushed precious metals lower and sparked rallies in the bond and stock markets. The dollar retreated after intervention by West Germany.

Hanson Trust of Britain agreed to acquire Kidde Inc., a consumer goods and aircraft equipment maker, for an estimated $66 to $68 a share, or $1.8 billion. The pact continues the British buying spree of U.S. companies.

7 London stocks posted record declines after major British banks increased their base lending rates to 10% from 9%. The move, reversing earlier rate cuts, heightened fears of a slowdown in Britain's economy.

Corporate profits slid 21% in the second quarter, hurt by big banks' additions to foreign-debt reserves. But profits rose 22% if big banks are excluded. Analysts expect all sectors to perform well in the second half. Canada's quarterly profits rose 40%.

Major retailers reported modest sales gains for July, indicating that consumer spending remains at the sluggish pace begun in late spring. Few analysts expect any strong pickup in sales during the third quarter.

Ford matched GM's new buyer-incentive program, offering cash rebates and financing as low as 1.9% on many 1987 and 1988 model cars.

West Germany appears to have become more firmly opposed to any new steps to stimulate its economy.

10 Unemployment fell to 6% in July, reflecting surprisingly strong job growth. The decline, from 6.1% in June, brought the jobless rate to a level once considered "full employment." But the surge in new jobs in a sluggish economy suggests that worker productivity is still growing slowly. Meanwhile, consumer credit grew at a rapid 7.6% rate in June.

Tokyo agreed to make it easier for U.S. firms to sell supercomputers in Japan. But the U.S. isn't expected to sweep that market anytime soon.

A definition of insider trading was offered by the SEC for the first time. Top officials also acknowledged that a statutory definition would strengthen the agency's enforcement program.

11 Stocks surged further as the Dow Jones industrials swept past 2600 for the first time, closing at 2635.84, up 43.84 points. The rally came despite continued worries about inflation and a weak economy. Bond prices eased despite lower oil prices and a relatively stable dollar. Precious metals soared in reaction to the miners strike in South Africa.

12 Alan Greenspan was sworn in as Fed chairman amid a mixed economic outlook. Reagan denied the Fed faces a trade-off between economic growth and inflation, but Greenspan indicated he is less sanguine.

Stocks rocketed ahead for the second day in a row, pushing market indexes to highs and continuing to puzzle traders. The Dow Jones industrials jumped 44.64 points, to a record 2680.48, while Big Board volume soared to 278 million shares, the second-busiest ever. Analysts said the rally may result from excess liquidity, foreign buying and, particularly, the fear of being left behind.

Most interest rates held steady as the Treasury launched the first part of a $28 billion quarterly financing. The huge U.S. borrowing has weighed on the bond market, which has been unable to rally with stocks.

13 The Fed agreed to allow U.S. banks to acquire up to 100% of nonfinancial companies in 33 debt-strapped developing nations. The move, which relaxes a Fed rule limiting such investments to 20%, should aid efforts by U.S. banks to swap debt for equity in big debtor countries.

14 Retail sales surged 0.8% in July, led by higher auto purchases. The June sales increase was revised upward to 1.4% from 0.4%. The gains led some economists to doubt forecasts of slower consumer spending.

Bond prices surged amid reports of heavy Japanese buying at the Treasury's quarterly bond auction. Stocks also rallied, as the Dow Jones industrials rose 22.17 points, to a record 2691.49. Precious metals tumbled, while the dollar was mixed.

Auto makers plan further cuts in third-quarter output, particularly GM. But analysts said even the latest cuts and a recent boost in sales may not avert a year-end inventory glut.

17 The trade deficit worsened in June, reflecting surging imports of oil and manufactured goods. The unexpected growth, to $15.71 billion, underscores the difficulty of shrinking the trade gap when the economy is expanding. The dollar plunged following Friday's trade report, though it recovered later.

Industrial output surged 0.8% in July, while producer prices rose a modest 0.2%. Analysts said the figures indicate that the economy is likely to continue expanding.

Union Bank of Switzerland is expected to announce a takeover offer this week for Hill Samuel Group that values the British merchant bank at as much as $1.1 billion.

18 Oil prices plunged below $20 a barrel on U.S. markets, the biggest one-day drop in nearly a year. Prices have been tumbling recently amid a growing oil glut and reports of OPEC overproduction. Analysts expect crude prices to fall further unless there is a flare-up in the Persian Gulf, though U.S. gasoline prices aren't likely to change right away.

The Dow Jones industrials closed above 2700 for the first time, ending at 2700.57, up 15.14 points. But the rally was mostly confined to blue-chip stocks. Bond prices eased as the dollar fell. Gold and silver edged up.

Chrysler tentatively plans to boost prices 4% to 8% on many 1988-model cars. But analysts doubt the steep increases will last long and that they may be followed by big discounts.

The industrial operating rate rose to 80.5% of capacity in July, the highest level in 1½ years. Improved export orders and energy-sector gains contributed to the increase.

19 The dollar plummeted in heavy trading, pulling down U.S. bond and stock prices. The currency, which slid nearly 2% against the yen and 1.4% against the mark, was battered partly by delayed reaction to the June U.S. trade gap, analysts said. The Dow Jones industrials tumbled 45.91, to 2654.66, while 30-year Treasury bonds lost nearly 1½ points.

Citicorp plans a global offering in September of 17 million shares, which is currently valued at about $1 billion. The offer would be a test of investor confidence in big U.S. banks.

Four major retailers posted mixed quarterly results, reflecting sluggish consumer spending. Dayton Hudson and Federated Department Stores had lower earnings, while Zayre and J.C. Penney reported gains.

Housing starts edged up 0.9% in July, indicating that homebuilding is recovering from last spring's jump in mortgage rates. But building permits declined 1.9% last month.

20 The dollar skidded further despite modest intervention by central banks. The currency fell 1.7% against the yen and 0.7% against the mark amid continued reaction to the huge U.S. trade deficit for June. The dollar's slide again depressed bond prices, though stocks rebounded in late trading. The Dow Jones industrials closed up 11.16, at 2665.82.

The New York Merc is considering night trading hours and links with a London-based exchange in an attempt to expand its leadership in oil futures. The exchange also will launch a propane futures contract tomorrow.

The nation's thrifts need to diversify beyond their traditional role as a mortgage lender to compete in the growing financial services industry, the Bank Board's new chairman, M. Danny Wall, said in an interview.

Major bank stocks eased following news that Citicorp plans a stock offering of up to $1 billion. Analysts said other big U.S. banks may try to boost capital by offering stock, which would dilute their shares outstanding.

21 Stock prices rallied to record levels, sparked by rebounds in the dollar and bond market. The Dow Jones industrials surged 40.97, to a record 2706.79, as other indexes hit highs. The dollar's modest recovery was fueled by signs that Tokyo may try to stem the yen's advance. Bonds were aided by the stronger dollar and falling commodity prices.

OPEC may regain control of world oil markets in the next few years because of declining production among non-OPEC nations and increasing demand for oil. But over the short term, OPEC will have difficulty getting its members to restrain output.

London stocks plunged following a report that British bank lending continued to surge last month. But share prices rose in Frankfurt and Tokyo in the wake of recent declines.

Short interest surged on the New York and American stock exchanges for the month ended Friday. The rise has spread into blue-chip stocks for the first time this year.

24 Consumer prices rose only 0.2% in July, helped by a slowdown in energy price increases and a drop in food costs. Separately, the Commerce Department cut its estimate of economic growth in the second quarter to a 2.3% annual rate from 2.6%.

The dollar continued to slide, falling 1.7% against the yen Friday. The plunge could drive interest rates higher, economists say. Separately, the Fed's policy panel expressed fear that faster economic growth could spark a dangerous inflation rise.

Citicorp aims to swap about $500 million of its Argentine debt for equity investments in various industries. Separately, Argentina signed a $34 billion debt restructuring accord with its foreign bank creditors.

25 Consumer spending jumped 0.9% for the second straight month in July, more than double the modest 0.4% rise in personal income. The pattern continued to defy economists' predictions of slower spending. Some analysts cautioned that the higher spending bodes ill for the nation's massive trade deficit.

Oil prices dipped near $18 a barrel and ended at a four-month low on reports of OPEC overproduction. Meanwhile, several big U.S. oil companies lowered the price they pay for the leading grade of domestic crude.

U.S. oil and gas drilling has risen from last year's depressed level despite lower petroleum prices.

The dollar closed mixed after Japan reportedly moved to boost the currency but failed to follow through later in the day. Worry about the dollar's slide sent the Dow Jones industrials down 12.43 to 2697.07 as bonds edged lower.

Toyota is entering the U.S. luxury car market by selling an upscale car line through a new dealer network. The auto maker faces widespread competition in the crowded field.

26 Opec moved to bolster its fragile accord, calling a series of meetings after conceding some members were violating output quotas. Some sources close to OPEC expressed skepticism the cartel would sustain any real, immediate effort to curb overproduction. The move came as Iraq launched a new price-discounting plan apparently to grab market share from Iran.

The dollar climbed 1.1% against the yen and posted smaller gains against other currencies, aided by comments by U.S., Japanese and West German officials. Some traders doubted the partial rebound from last week's slump is sustainable.

Stocks increased on the dollar's rise, with the Dow Jones industrials up 25.35 points to a record 2722.42. The bond market also showed strength.

Tobacco companies won another round in product-liability litigation. A federal appeals court reversed a finding that Liggett & Myers failed to warn consumers adequately about the dangers of cigarette smoking.

Durable goods orders fell 1.5% in July, led by a decline in bookings for military gear. But economists said they were encouraged by a 1.6% increase in non-defense orders.

Car sales jumped 18% in mid-August due to a weak year-earlier period and new financing incentives. But some dealers said sales from the latest buyer programs haven't been as strong as those from last fall.

27 IBM stock dropped $4 in heavy trading after two analysts cut their estimates for the computer maker's 1987 earnings. But other analysts are confident a profit rebound will be as strong as had been expected. The stock, which has fallen $6.625 in two days, closed at $168.

The slide sparked a broad market decline, as the Dow Jones industrials fell 20.57 points to 2701.85.

Oil prices surged amid signs OPEC will try to end above-quota output. The turnaround, which followed a three-week decline, was one of the largest one-day price rises this year. But many analysts remain skeptical the cartel can enforce its accord.

The trade deficit widened to a record $39.53 billion in the second quarter from $38.76 billion in the previous quarter. Rising imports of Japanese and South Korean automobiles accounted for much of the increase.

The dollar edged lower as the currency got a little support from statements by U.S. and Japanese officials. Most bond prices fell as the weakening dollar sparked some fear that the Fed may tighten credit soon.

Shawmut agreed to merge with Hartford National in a $2 billion stock swap. The accord, which follows a nationwide trend toward creation of super-regional banks, will result in a company with $25 billion of assets.

Construction contracts rose 1% as home building revived in July, according to the latest Dodge report.

28 Bond prices slumped on a weakening dollar and fear that the Fed is tightening credit. Yields on long-term Treasury securities surged above 9.1% to their highest level this year. Traders said the dollar's continuing fall reflected concern about the U.S. trade and budget deficits.

Stocks fell in active trading, continuing a slide that began Wednesday. The Dow Jones industrials closed at 2675.06, off 26.79 points.

Japan's economy stalled in the latest quarter, but economists expect growth to pick up. Meanwhile, West Germany's economy grew modestly, according to analysts' estimates.

31 The dollar rose slightly after European central banks intervened. But suspicion is growing that major central banks are resigned to a continuing decline, and some traders predicted the dollar will hit new lows.

Stocks dropped on concern over the dollar and speculation bond prices will fall further. The Dow Jones industrials fell 35.71 to 2639.35.

Six airlines agreed to reduce delays at four busy airports, but the extent of any service improvement is unclear. Separately, some states are preparing to crack down on the way airlines advertise discount fares.

September 1987

1 Oil prices spurted to near $20 a barrel amid renewed gulf tensions. But analysts said further gains are unlikely if supplies aren't hurt.

2 Stock prices plunged on a decline in the dollar, a tumbling bond market and other factors. The Dow Jones industrials sank 51.98 to 2610.97, the fifth-largest point drop ever. The decline, which came late in the day, was led by a $5.50 slide in IBM. The dollar's drop would have been more severe but major central banks intervened, traders said.

Leading economic indicators rose 0.5% in July, the sixth consecutive monthly rise. The gain follows an upward revised 1% increase in June and suggests healthy growth ahead. Separately, orders for factory goods and construction spending fell 0.2%.

The FDA approved Merck's cholesterol-lowering drug lovastatin. Analysts predicted the company's stock could hit new highs because of the agency's action and wide publicity.

3 Bond prices plummeted on a weakening dollar and continued fears the Fed may tighten credit. Yields on most debt securities reached their highest level in 19 months. The dollar's continuing slide came despite modest central bank intervention. The Dow Jones industrials fell 8.93 to 2602.04 after a roller-coaster stock market session.

Brazil will present bankers with a proposal later this month for an accord on its foreign commercial-bank debt. The plan will involve the conversion of half the debt into long-term, fixed-interest bonds.

Cray canceled its most advanced supercomputer project and one of the company's main designers quit. The project's scrapping leaves a gap in Cray's future product line at a time when competition is increasing.

The Chicago Merc agreed with Reuters Holdings to create an electronic trading system that will allow the exchange to trade futures and options on futures around the clock.

4 Brazil's proposal for dealing with its foreign commercial-bank debt is viewed as unacceptable by bank creditors. Conversion of half the debt into fixed-interest bonds, as proposed, would threaten to overturn other countries' debt accords and could have a severe impact on U.S. banks' earnings, bankers said.

The U.S. doesn't view the dollar's recent decline as a serious threat to February's currency-stabilization accord. But officials confirmed the Fed has intervened modestly in the past two weeks. The dollar continued its slide against most major currencies but edged up against the yen.

Car sales fell 22.5% in late August against a strong year-earlier period when buyer incentives were launched. Separately, auto makers plan to build 12.3% more cars this week than a week ago, as some plants reopen.

Japan's financial markets remained in turmoil following Tateho Chemical's disclosure Wednesday of heavy bond trading losses. But the impact on Japanese and foreign markets isn't expected to be lasting.

Industry Surveys*

The following provides information about a number of industries as well as financial data on companies in each industry. Financial Ratios are defined in the section *Investment and Financial Terms* (page 377).

EXPLANATIONS OF FINANCIAL AND STOCK MARKET INFORMATION

Revenue and Earnings

It should be noted that 12-month figures are trailing ones, calculated from figures shown in the latest interim reports and latest fiscal year reports, when appropriate. Fiscal figures are as reported by the company. Interim figures are based on cumulative data. All earnings per share figures are primary, and are reflected in all calculations. Earnings per share and total earnings figures show earnings from total operations. Earnings are before extraordinary items, but when this is not possible, special earnings footnotes are shown immediately to the right of the company name in the stock tables and these special footnotes are explained as follows:

◇—includes extraordinary gains
◆—includes extraordinary losses
□—excludes extraordinary gains
■—excludes extraordinary losses

5-Year Earnings Growth Rate The annual compound growth rate in primary earnings per share over the last five years computed by the least squares method using logarithms of the earnings per share data, brought up to date through the latest 12 months' earning per share by weighting the first and last points. The five-year earnings growth rate is calculated only for those companies which have all positive earnings per share data for each of the periods used in the calculation. An NC footnote will appear for all companies which do not have a positive earnings per share record for the five-year period. An NC footnote will appear for all companies which have an incomplete record of earnings per share for the five-year period.
Par Growth Rate Retained latest 12 months' earnings per share multiplied by latest 12 months return on common equity, as a percent of latest 12 months' earnings per share. Extra growth rate in EPS can be derived by subtracting par growth rate from 5-year EPS growth rate.

Dividends

Dividends are the latest indicated rate, and the yield is based on that amount and the latest close.
5-Year Growth Rate The figure is arrived at by the least squares method, using dividends actually paid for the first five years and the indicated rate for the sixth point.

Ratios

Profit Margin The profit margin of the company based on latest 12 months' revenue and earnings.
Asset Turnover The latest 12 months' return on total assets divided by the latest 12 months' profit margin.
Return on Common Equity The latest 12 months' earnings divided by stockholder equity from the latest balance sheet.
Return on Total Assets Based on the latest 12 months total earnings and the total asset as reported in the company's latest fiscal year balance sheet.
Leverage Ratio The latest 12 months' return on common equity divided by the latest 12 months' return on total assets.
Debt to Equity The total long-term debt of the company as a percentage of the total common equity of the company, both from the latest annual balance sheet.

Shareholdings

Market Value Latest reported shares outstanding times latest closing price per share of the common stock.
Latest Shares Outstanding Latest reported shares outstanding, adjusted for any subsequent stock splits or dividends.
Held by Banks-Funds The single figure here represents shares held by institutions with equity assets exceeding $100 million—banks, insurance companies, investment companies and managers, independent investment advisors and others. Shares held are adjusted for any stock splits or stock dividends that occur subsequent to the quarterly reporting date of the institutions covered. The data is furnished by Computer Directions Advisers, Inc.
Insider Net Trading Net change in insider holdings—purchases vs. sales—based on the latest SEC report in thousands of shares. 0 means there were no transactions or transactions netted to 0; +0 means transactions net-

* The financial data on companies in each industry come from the Media General *IndustriScope*, 301 East Grace Street, Richmond, VA 23219; June 30, 1987.

ted to purchases of fewer than 500 shares, and −0 means transactions netted to sales of fewer than 500 shares.

The most recent monthly period for insider transactions is February 11, 1987, to March 10, 1987.

Short Interest Ratio Short interest for the latest month reported, divided by average daily volume for the month corresponding to the report. The figure shows the number of days it would take to cover the short interest if the trading rate continued at the rate of the month covered by the report.

Short interest for the current issue is for the period February 13, 1987, through March 13, 1987.

GENERAL FOOTNOTES

*—As applied to beta figures, an asterisk denotes a co-efficient at least as large as its probable error (i.e., .6745 times the standard error of its mean).

G—Value calculated greater than allowed range.

L—Value calculated less than allowed range.

a—Under current dividend yield, an "a" indicates a stock dividend.

b—Indicates cash plus stock dividend when applied to dividend yield column.

NA—Item not applicable to this stock.

NE—Negative earnings invalidate calculation.

NC—Data required for calculation not available.

NS—Negative stockholder equity invalidates calculations.

NM—No meaningful figure

q—Based on first quarter information.

s—Based on second quarter information.

n—Based on third quarter information.

f—Based on fiscal year information.

*—When applied to 12-month earnings, an asterisk indicates an actual amount for an interim period, other than a quarterly multiple, resulting from a fiscal year change.

Recent Performance and Forecast: Aerospace (SIC 372,376)

(in millions of dollars except as noted)

	1984	1985[1]	1986[2]	1987[3]	Percent Change: Compound Annual 1972-84	Compound Annual 1979-84	Annual 1984-85	Annual 1985-86	Annual 1986-87
Industry Data									
Value of shipments[4]	77,826	89,745	96,576	103,524	11.5	10.0	15.3	7.6	7.2
Value of shipments (1982$)	71,700	81,635	85,010	87,902	2.9	1.4	13.9	4.1	3.4
Total employment (000)	693	746	768	782	1.2	0.3	7.8	2.9	1.8
Production workers (000)	344	370	381	387	0.5	−1.7	7.4	3.0	1.5
Average hourly earnings ($)	13.24	13.62	13.65	—	8.1	8.2	2.9	0.2	—
Product Data									
Value of shipments[5]	70,200	80,854	87,002	93,601	11.4	10.0	15.2	7.6	7.6
Value of shipments (1982$)	64,580	73,555	76,560	79,405	2.8	1.3	13.9	4.1	3.7
Shipments price index[6] (1982 = 100)	108.7	109.7	113.5	117.9	8.3	8.5	0.9	3.5	3.8

[1]Estimated except for exports and imports.
[2]Estimated.
[3]Forecast.
[4]Value of all products and services sold by the Aerospace industry.
[5]Value of products classified in the Aerospace industry produced by all industries.
[6]Developed by the Office of Aerospace Policy and Analysis, ITA.

SOURCE: U.S. Department of Commerce: Bureau of the Census, Bureau of Economic Analysis, International Trade Administration (ITA). Estimates and forecasts by ITA.

Source: *U.S. Industrial Outlook 1987*, U.S. Department of Commerce.

Company	Revenue			Earnings								Dividends						Ratio Analysis							Shareholdings					
	Pct. Change				Per Share							Current Rate			Payout															
					Last 12 Mos	Pct. Change			5-Year Growth Rate	Par Growth Rate	Date of Report			5-Year Growth Rate			Last X-Dvd Date	Pro-fit Mar-gin	Asset Turn-over	Return on Total Assets	Lever-age Ratio	Return on Equity	Debt to Eq-uity	Curr-ent Ratio	Mar-ket Value	Latest Shares Out-stndng.	Held by Banks-Funds	Insider Net Trad-ing	Short Int-erest Ratio	Fiscal Year Ends
	Last Qtr	FY to Date	Last 12 Mos	Last 12 Mos		Last Qtr	FY to Date	Last 12 Mos				Amt	Yield		Last FY	Last 5 Yrs.														
-	%	%	%	$Mil	$	%	%	%	%	%	-	$	%	%	%	%	-	π/r x	r/a =	π/a x	a/e =	π/e	%	-	$Mil	000	000	000	Days	Mo
Aerospace Manufacturing																														
Ind. Group	7.2	7.5	9.3	2,425.0	2.59	1.3	4.4	- 17.9	2	7	- - -	1.09	2.6	1	34	27	- - - -	2.6	1.62	4.2	2.74	11.5	29	1.3	39,030	927,490	459,403	- 16	1.5	- -
Boeing Co	6.7	6.7	16.5	635.0q	4.09	-20.0	-20.0	3.5	12	9	03-87	1.40	3.0	5	28	28	05-04-87	3.8	1.50	5.7	2.32	13.2	5	1.5	7,270	155,095	73,705	-9	1.0	12
Curtiss-Wright	1.7	1.7	3.7	22.5q	4.62	22.4	22.4	NE	NC	7	03-87	1.60	2.7	6	32	160	07-06-87	13.5	.56	7.5	1.52	11.4	24	4.7	289	4,863	3,528	0	1.5	12
Fairchild Ind	-7.0	-7.0	-21.0	7.9q	-3.85	NE	NE	NE	NC	29	03-87	.20	1.7	-21	NE	NE	06-23-87	1.2	1.25	1.5	18.20	27.3	449	2.0	168	14,295	5,908	+1	0.7	12
Gen Dynamics	8.9	8.9	10.4	-17.2q	-.42	49.4	49.4	-100.0	NC	-5	03-87	1.00	1.5	8	NE	20	07-13-87	-.2	2.00	-.4	3.50	-1.4	34	1.2	2,865	42,927	18,720	+4	1.5	12
Gen Motors H	NA	NA	.0	NA	NA	NA	NA	NA	NA	NC	00-00	.66	1.3	NA	NA	NA	05-08-87	NA	NC	NA	NC	NA	NA	NA	739	15,000	2,209	+8	NA	NA
Grumman Corp	3.2	3.2	11.2	79.4q	2.28	-6.3	-6.3	-4.6	-6	6	03-87	1.00	3.9	8	43	29	05-04-87	2.3	1.74	4.0	2.75	11.0	58	2.1	835	32,604	10,537	-0	2.8	12
Lockheed Corp	16.3	16.3	10.7	407.0q	6.16	-1.5	-1.5	.2	15	17	03-87	1.40	2.7	0	15	8	05-19-87	3.8	1.79	6.8	3.21	21.8	67	1.0	4,208	81,503	44,754	-10	0.9	12
Martin Marietta	5.0	5.0	7.1	200.2q	3.63	-4.8	-4.8	-23.3	NC	17	03-87	1.00	2.2	8	27	49	06-02-87	4.2	1.93	8.1	2.93	23.7	27	1.2	2,541	54,944	22,486	-17	0.9	12
McDonnel Doug	-.2	-.2	7.4	259.4q	6.41	-29.8	-29.8	-18.1	9	6	03-87	2.32	3.3	15	29	22	06-01-87	2.1	1.57	3.3	2.76	9.1	23	1.1	2,819	40,568	15,640	+1	0.0	12
Northrop Corp	7.7	7.7	8.4	42.5q	.91	2.4	2.4	-79.8	30	-1	03-87	1.20	2.9	19	135	39	05-26-87	.7	2.29	1.6	2.94	4.7	4	.7	1,921	46,578	19,980	+2	3.5	12
Rockwell Intl	3.0	3.3	4.2	650.1s	2.23	23.1	23.7	16.8	17	15	03-87	.66	2.4	6	21	28	05-13-87	5.2	1.62	8.4	2.45	20.6	20	1.1	7,770	287,776	157,630	0	1.8	09
Singer Co	15.1	15.1	11.6	94.9q	4.35	14.3	14.3	NC	NC	15	03-87	.40	1.1	0	9	7	05-20-87	5.3	1.40	7.4	2.18	16.1	53	2.0	790	20,940	11,707	+5	4.2	12
Utd Technol	12.4	12.4	8.1	43.3q	.09	-19.4	-19.4	-95.6	-40	-16	03-87	1.40	2.7	4	519	46	05-18-87	.3	1.33	.4	2.75	1.1	45	1.5	6,813	130,397	72,599	-2	1.0	12

Recent Performance and Forecast: Airlines (SIC 451)

Item	1984	1985	1986[1]	1987[2]	Percent Change				
					Compound Annual		Annual		
					1972-84	1979-84	1984-85	1985-86	1986-87
Operating revenue (billions $)	43.8	46.7	49.0	51.9	12.0	10.0	6.6	4.9	5.9
Employees (000)	345	355	359	359	1.1	0.2	2.9	1.1	0.0
Revenue passenger miles (billions)	305	336	363	385	6.0	3.1	10.2	8.0	6.1

[1]Estimate.
[2]Forecast.

SOURCE: U.S. Department of Commerce: International Trade Administration (ITA); Air Transport Association of America. Estimates and forecasts by ITA.

Source: *U.S. Industrial Outlook 1987*, U.S. Department of Commerce.

Historical Trends: Airlines (SIC 451)

Item	1972	1973	1974	1975	1976	1977	1978	1979	1980	1981	1982	1983	1984
Operating revenues (billions $)	11.2	12.4	14.7	15.4	17.5	19.9	22.9	27.2	33.7	36.7	36.4	39.0	43.8
Employees (000)	301	311	307	290	303	308	329	341	361	350	330	329	345
Revenue passenger miles (billions)	152	162	163	163	179	193	227	262	255	249	259	282	305

SOURCE: Air Transport Association of America.

Source: *U.S. Industrial Outlook 1987*, U.S. Department of Commerce.

Company	Revenue			Earnings								Dividends						Ratio Analysis							Shareholdings					
	Pct. Change				Per Share							Current Rate			Payout															
	Last Qtr	FY to Date	Last 12 Mos	Last 12 Mos	Last 12 Mos	Pct. Change Last Qtr	Pct. Change FY to Date	Pct. Change Last 12 Mos	5-Year Growth Rate	Par Growth Rate	Date of Report	Amt	Yield	5-Year Growth Rate	Last FY	Last 5 Yrs.	Last X-Dvd Date	Profit Margin	Asset Turnover	Return on Total Assets	Leverage Ratio	Return on Equity	Debt to Equity	Current Ratio	Market Value	Latest Shares Outstndng.	Held by Banks-Funds	Insider Net Trading	Short Interest Ratio	Fiscal Year Ends
-	%	%	%	$Mil	$	%	%	%	%	%	-	$	%	%	%	%	-	π/r x	r/a =	π/a x	a/e =	π/e	%	-	$Mil	000	000	000	Days	Mo
Airlines																														
Ind. Group	35.2	47.6	21.9	865.0	.80	NE	NE	.7	NC	5	- - -	.26	.8	0	18	12	- - - -	1.7	1.00	1.7	4.18	7.1	154	1.0	23,193	683,461	283,346	- 405	2.0	- -
Air Wisconsin	2.5	2.5	-8.3	3.8q	.51	-100.0	-100.0	200.0	-13	6	03-87	.00	.0	0	0	0	04-02-84	3.2	.63	2.0	2.90	5.8	121	1.8	76	7,398	2,805	0	0.0	12
Airlease Ltd	176.9	176.9	700.0	3.8q	.79	380.0	380.0	NC	NC	4	03-87	.00	.0	0	0	0	00-00-00	47.5	.08	3.7	1.16	4.3	0	.0	78	4,625	9	0	0.0	12
Alaska AirGrp	43.1	43.1	13.8	17.1q	1.40	NE	NE	-10.8	8	9	03-87	.16	.8	0	11	8	07-09-87	3.3	.76	2.5	3.88	9.7	165	.9	328	16,110	6,047	-9	0.7	12
Allegis	-87.9	-87.9	10.6	84.2q	2.12	NE	NE	NE	NC	3	03-87	1.00	1.1	0	400	27	05-11-87	1.1	1.00	1.1	4.91	5.4	169	1.0	4,477	50,092	39,905	0	0.2	12
Am West Airlns	61.2	61.2	40.6	-2.8q	-.41	NE	NE	-100.0	NC	-5	03-87	.00	.0	0	0	0	00-00-00	-.7	1.00	-.7	6.86	-4.8	441	1.8	86	10,459	1,677	+24	0.0	12
AMR Corp	3.7	3.7	-1.9	294.8q	4.93	750.0	750.0	1.4	NC	12	03-87	.00	.0	0	0	0	01-28-80	4.9	.80	3.9	3.05	11.9	97	1.1	3,481	58,747	45,206	+2	1.3	12
Atlantic SE Air	15.2	15.2	17.0	10.9q	.87	.0	.0	-7.4	38	14	03-87	.00	.0	0	0	0	08-26-85	11.4	.67	7.6	1.86	14.1	52	4.4	175	13,339	3,752	-396	0.0	12
Brit Airways □	5.4	5.4	15.3	341.4s	.48	40.0	40.0	NC	NC	48	09-86	.00	.0	0	0	0	00-00-00	7.2	1.67	12.0	4.00	48.0	65	.6	1,674	72,020	0	0	0.0	03
Comair Inc ◇	18.2	1.5	.0	-.9f	-.10	NE	-100.0	-100.0	NC	-2	03-87	.00	.0	0	0	0	08-14-85	-1.5	.93	-1.4	1.71	-2.4	52	3.2	86	9,573	2,047	-3	0.0	03
Delta Air Lines ◇	6.9	2.5	-5.5	194.4s	4.77	7525.0	460.3	21.7	NC	12	12-86	1.00	1.8	1	85	40	04-29-87	4.4	1.16	5.1	2.92	14.9	67	.8	2,643	47,199	43,119	+17	1.4	06
HAL Inc	32.9	32.9	34.4	7.1q	3.78	NE	NE	2807.7	NC	31	03-87	.15	.6	0	0	NE	03-10-87	2.9	1.76	5.1	6.29	32.1	231	1.0	47	1,879	202	0	4.9	12
KLM Airlines	465.4	132.7	132.7	301.0f	5.93	NE	89.5	153.4	57	27	03-87	.69	2.8	0	12	10	08-15-86	5.6	1.57	8.8	3.42	30.1	115	1.6	1,259	50,849	5,445	0	2.5	03
Midway Airlines	15.8	15.8	29.0	8.3q	.87	NE	NE	625.0	NC	15	03-87	.00	.0	0	0	0	00-00-00	3.1	1.77	5.5	2.71	14.9	54	1.3	161	10,274	2,417	0	0.0	12
NWA Inc	83.1	83.1	51.6	58.3q	2.71	NE	NE	13.4	60	4	03-87	.90	1.3	3	28	34	06-09-87	1.4	.93	1.3	4.08	5.3	125	.5	1,882	26,890	19,543	0	1.1	12
Pan Am Corp ◇	-12.1	-12.8	-12.7	-462.8f	-3.42	-100.0	-100.0	-100.0	NC	0	12-86	.00	.0	0	0	0	00-00-00	-15.2	1.45	-22.0	.00	NM	9393	.7	733	136,390	28,244	0	4.8	12
Pied Aviation	41.2	41.2	22.7	77.3q	4.01	NE	NE	16.6	6	9	03-87	.32	.5	10	9	8	08-10-87	4.1	1.10	4.5	2.20	9.9	40	1.2	1,285	18,551	10,060	0	0.4	12
PS Group •	5.4	14.8	14.7	-15.7f	-2.50	-100.0	-100.0	-100.0	NC	-9	12-86	.60	1.7	0	NE	275	04-21-87	-1.8	.78	-1.4	5.29	-7.4	279	1.1	262	7,593	4,159	0	1.2	12
SW Airlines	2.9	2.9	6.1	37.5q	1.17	-100.0	-100.0	-18.8	3	6	03-87	.13	.6	2	8	9	06-08-87	4.9	.71	3.5	2.09	7.3	66	1.5	653	32,254	22,013	0	0.2	12
Tex Air	298.9	298.9	190.1	-225.0q	-6.16	NE	NE	-100.0	NC	-28	03-87	.00	.0	0	0	NE	07-06-83	-3.8	.71	-2.7	10.37	-28.0	562	1.0	1,549	41,589	22,908	-44	2.2	12
Trans Wrld Air	25.5	25.5	-8.3	8.5q	-.08	NE	NE	NE	NC	6	03-87	.00	.0	0	0	0	00-00-00	.3	1.00	.3	20.00	6.0	1351	1.1	902	30,446	3,335	0	3.0	12
USAir Grp	14.3	14.3	6.4	134.8q	4.48	NE	NE	35.8	4	12	03-87	.12	.3	0	4	3	07-09-87	7.1	.89	6.3	2.03	12.8	40	1.5	1,296	27,361	20,085	+4	5.3	12
WorldCorp	25.4	25.4	-63.5	-11.0q	-2.99	NE	NE	NE	NC	0	03-87	.00	.0	0	0	0	00-00-00	-9.8	.65	-6.4	.00	NS	-168	.5	60	9,823	368	0	15.4	12

Recent Performance and Forecast: Apparel and Other Mill Products (SIC 23)

(in millions of dollars except as noted)

				Percent change			
				Compound Annual		Annual	
	1984	1985[1]	1986[2]	1972-84	1979-84	1984-85	1985-86
Industry Data							
Value of shipments[3]	57,578	57,461	59,162	6.3	6.0	−0.2	3.0
Value of shipments (1982$)	55,616	54,829	55,882	1.0	1.2	−1.4	1.9
Total employment (000)	1,152	1,142	1,133	−1.4	−2.5	−0.9	−0.7
Production workers (000)	977	967	960	−1.7	−2.9	−1.0	−0.7
Average hourly earnings ($)	5.35	—	—	6.4	6.1	—	—
Product Data							
Value of shipments[4]	50,672	50,784	53,323	6.5	6.3	0.2	3.0
Value of shipments (1982$)	49,196	48,551	49,548	1.3	1.7	−1.3	2.1
Trade Data							
Value of imports	14,001	15,711	17,744	17.8	18.9	12.2	12.9
Value of exports	1,026	991	1,102	10.8	−5.9	−3.4	11.2

[1]Estimated except for exports and imports.
[2]Estimated.
[3]Value of all products and services sold by the Apparel and Other Mill Products industry.
[4]Value of products classified in the Apparel and Other Mill Products industry produced by all industries.
SOURCE: U.S. Department of Commerce: Bureau of the Census, Bureau of Economic Analysis, International Trade Administration (ITA). Estimates and forecasts by ITA.

Source: *U.S. Industrial Outlook 1987*, U.S. Department of Commerce.

Recent Performance and Forecast: Men's and Boys' Outerwear (SIC 231,2321,2327,2328)

(in millions of dollars except as noted)

				Percent change			
				Compound Annual		Annual	
	1984	985	1986[2]	1972-84	1979-84	1984-85	1985-86
Industry Data							
Value of shipments[3]	14,401	4,191	14,512	5.0	4.3	−1.5	2.3
2311 Men/Boys' Suits/Coats	3,209	3,116	3,126	2.5	4.0	−2.9	0.3
2321 Men's Shirts/Nightwear	3,689	3,534	3,598	4.8	2.6	−4.2	1.8
2327 Men's & Boys' Trousers	2,373	2,295	2,362	2.6	3.7	−3.3	2.9
2328 Men/Boys' Work Clothes	5,130	5,246	5,426	9.4	6.2	2.3	3.4
Value of shipments (1982$)	13,799	3,405	13,551	−1.0	−0.2	−2.9	1.1
2311 Men/Boys' Suits/Coats	3,036	2,913	2,878	−3.4	−1.4	−4.1	−1.2
2321 Men's Shirts/Nightwear	3,568	3,321	3,322	−0.8	−0.2	−6.9	0.0
2327 Men's & Boys' Trousers	2,269	2,151	2,183	−2.8	−0.9	−5.2	1.5
2328 Men/Boys' Work Clothes	4,926	5,020	5,168	2.2	1.0	1.9	2.9
Total employment (000)	314	301	311	−2.4	−3.7	4.3	3.4
2311 Men/Boys' Suits/Coats	73.9	72.8	72.1	−4.3	−3.3	−1.5	−1.0
2321 Men's Shirts/Nightwear	90.9	81.1	89.4	−1.8	−5.5	−10.8	10.2
2327 Men's & Boys' Trousers	59.7	56.0	55.8	−3.5	−2.2	−6.2	−0.4
2328 Men/Boys' Work Clothes	89.6	90.8	93.5	0.0	−3.1	1.3	3.0
Production workers (000)	269	257	261	−2.7	−4.4	−4.3	1.4
2311 Men/Boys' Suits/Coats	63.9	62.5	62.0	−4.3	−3.2	−2.2	−0.8
2321 Men's Shirts/Nightwear	78.5	69.9	70.7	−2.2	−6.3	−11.0	1.1
2327 Men's & Boys' Trousers	48.1	45.0	44.9	−4.3	−3.6	−6.4	−0.2
2328 Men/Boys' Work Clothes	78.1	79.7	83.2	−0.3	−3.8	2.0	4.4

Average hourly earnings ($)	5.21	—	—	6.4	5.8	—	—
2311 Men/Boys' Suits/Coats	5.82	5.94	5.95	5.4	4.7	2.0	0.2
2321 Men's Shirts/Nightwear	5.00	5.23	5.33	7.0	6.2	4.7	1.9
2327 Men's & Boys' Trousers	5.19	5.30	5.27	7.0	6.4	2.2	−0.6
2328 Men/Boys' Work Clothes	4.94	5.15	5.34	7.1	5.7	4.3	3.7
Product Data							
Value of shipments[4]	11,198	11,004	11,433	4.9	3.7	−1.7	3.9
2311 Men/Boys' Suits/Coats	2,578	2,503	2,670	3.1	3.2	−2.9	6.7
2321 Men's Shirts/Nightwear	2,781	2,666	2,720	4.6	2.3	−4.1	2.0
2327 Men's & Boys' Trousers	1,776	1,669	1,719	1.8	4.3	−6.0	3.0
2328 Men/Boys' Work Clothes	4,064	4,116	4,324	9.1	4.8	2.5	3.8
Value of shipments (1982$)	10,797	10,457	10,733	−0.8	−0.3	−3.2	2.6
2311 Men/Boys' Suits/Coats	2,450	2,350	2,463	−2.1	−0.9	−4.1	4.8
2321 Men's Shirts/Nightwear	2,697	2,508	2,512	−1.0	−0.2	−7.0	0.2
2327 Men's & Boys' Trousers	1,762	1,636	1,664	−2.8	0.6	−7.2	1.7
2328 Men/Boys' Work Clothes	3,887	3,963	4,094	1.5	−0.2	1.9	3.3
Trade Data							
Value of imports	4,195	4,407	—	17.6	15.7	5.0	—
Value of exports	203	192	239	7.6	−9.5	−5.1	24.2

[1]Estimated except for exports and imports.
[2]Estimated.
[3]Value of all products and services sold by the Men's and Boys' Outerwear industry.

Source: *U.S. Industrial Outlook 1987*, U.S. Department of Commerce.

[4]Value of products classified in the Men's and Boys' Outerwear industry produced by all industries.

SOURCE: U.S. Department of Commerce: Bureau of the Census, Bureau of Economic Analysis, International Trade Administration (ITA). Estimates and forecasts by ITA.

Recent Performance and Forecast: Women's and Misses Outerwear (SIC 2331,2335,2337)

(in millions of dollars except as noted)

				Percent change			
				Compound Annual		Annual	
	1984	1985[1]	1986[2]	1972-84	1979-84	1984-85	1985-86
Industry Data							
Value of shipments[3]	12,814	12,521	12,652	5.6	5.5	−2.3	1.0
2331 Women's/Misses' Blouses	3,579	3,473	3,511	9.1	6.0	−3.0	1.1
2335 Women's/Misses' Dresses	4,996	4,903	4,891	2.8	4.1	−1.9	−0.2
2337 Women's Suits & Coats	4,239	4,145	4,250	7.4	6.8	−2.2	2.5
Value of shipments (1982$)	12,303	11,794	11,764	1.7	1.1	−4.1	−0.3
2331 Women's/Misses' Blouses	3,277	3,146	3,121	4.0	0.0	−4.0	−0.8
2335 Women's/Misses' Dresses	4,886	4,719	4,636	−0.9	0.4	−3.4	−1.8
2337 Women's Suits & Coats	4,140	3,929	4,007	4.3	2.9	−5.1	2.0
Total employment (000)	280	255	246	−1.9	−3.2	−8.6	−3.6
2331 Women's/Misses' Blouses	91.5	85.0	83.1	3.2	1.5	−7.1	−2.2
2335 Women's/Misses' Dresses	124	114	—	−4.3	−5.3	−8.0	−3.8
2337 Women's Suits & Coats	63.8	56.1	53.2	−1.4	−4.7	−12.1	−5.2
Production workers (000)	236	216	209	−2.1	−3.7	−8.5	−3.4
2331 Women's/Misses' Blouses	76.5	70.6	68.7	2.8	0.7	−7.7	−2.7
2335 Women's/Misses' Dresses	107	97.3	93.2	−4.5	−5.2	−9.1	−4.2
2337 Women's Suits & Coats	52.5	48.1	46.8	−1.8	−5.8	−8.4	−2.7

Average hourly earnings ($)	5.08	—	—	5.7	5.2	—	—
2331 Women's/Misses' Blouses	4.65	4.72	4.72	5.8	2.5	1.4	0.0
2335 Women's/Misses' Dresses	5.39	5.49	5.55	6.2	7.9	1.8	1.1
2337 Women's Suits & Coats	5.15	5.38	5.41	5.3	3.8	4.4	0.6
Product Data							
Value of shipments[4]	10,819	10,599	10,764	6.2	7.0	−2.0	1.6
2331 Women's/Misses' Blouses	3,269	3,174	3,206	10.3	6.0	−2.9	1.0
2335 Women's/Misses' Dresses	4,161	4,103	4,140	3.3	6.5	−1.4	0.9
2337 Women's Suits & Coats	3,390	3,322	3,418	7.4	8.8	−2.0	2.9
Value of shipments (1982$)	10,437	10,095	10,115	2.9	3.0	−3.3	0.2
2331 Women's/Misses' Blouses	2,931	2,875	2,849	5.3	−0.5	−1.9	−0.9
2335 Women's/Misses' Dresses	4,129	3,960	3,928	0.2	3.3	−4.1	−0.8
2337 Women's Suits & Coats	3,377	3,260	3,338	5.4	6.1	−3.5	2.4
Trade Data							
Value of imports	2,730	3,292	—	20.5	18.9	20.6	—
2331 Women's/Misses' Blouses	1,679	2,082	2,457	20.6	17.3	24.0	18.0
2335 Women's/Misses' Dresses	0.0	0.0	—	—	—	—	—
2337 Women's Suits & Coats	1,051	1,210	1,379	20.4	21.9	15.1	13.9
Value of exports	92.5	85.7	94.0	13.4	−2.5	−7.4	9.7
2331 Women's/Misses' Blouses	34.3	29.5	33.0	23.2	−3.1	−14.0	11.9
2335 Women's/Misses' Dresses	31.0	26.1	28.0	6.7	−4.5	−15.8	7.3
2337 Women's Suits & Coats	27.2	30.1	33.0	19.2	1.0	10.7	9.6

[1]Estimated except for exports and imports.

[2]Estimated.

[3]Value of all products and services sold by the Women's and Misses Outerwear industry.

[4]Value of products classified in the Women's and Misses Outerwear industry produced by all industries.

SOURCE: U.S. Department of Commerce: Bureau of the Census, Bureau of Economic Analysis, International Trade Administration (ITA). Estimates and forecasts by ITA.

Source: *U.S. Industrial Outlook 1987*, U.S. Department of Commerce.

Company	Revenue			Earnings								Dividends						Ratio Analysis							Shareholdings					
	Pct. Change Last Qtr	Pct. Change FY to Date	Pct. Change Last 12 Mos	Last 12 Mos	Per Share Last 12 Mos	Per Share Pct. Change Last Qtr	Per Share Pct. Change FY to Date	Per Share Pct. Change Last 12 Mos	5-Year Growth Rate	Par Growth Rate	Date of Report	Current Rate Amt	Current Rate Yield	5-Year Growth Rate	Payout Last FY	Payout Last 5 Yrs.	Last X-Dvd Date	Profit Margin	Asset Turnover	Return on Total Assets	Leverage Ratio	Return on Equity	Debt to Equity	Current Ratio	Market Value	Latest Shares Outstndng.	Held by Banks-Funds	Insider Net Trading	Short Interest Ratio	Fiscal Year Ends
-	%	%	%	$Mil	$	%	%	%	%	%	-	$	%	%	%	%	-	π/r x	r/a =	π/a x	a/e =	π/e	%	-	$Mil	000	000	000	Days	Mo
Apparel																														
Ind. Group	5.8	5.6	8.5	278.9	.99	15.9	9.5	69.8	16	14	- - -	.20	.9	1	17	19	- - - -	4.4	1.91	8.4	2.12	17.8	40	2.9	5,954	280,498	99,736	- 53	1.1	- -
Angelica	8.1	8.1	8.3	17.4q	1.86	17.9	17.9	3.9	6	8	04-87	.72	2.6	12	34	30	06-09-87	5.9	1.51	8.9	1.52	13.5	20	4.3	254	9,308	4,790	-3	0.9	01
Barco of Cal	-2.2	5.2	.0	-.7s	-.36	NE	NE	NE	NC	-6	12-86	.00	.0	0	0	144	05-07-84	-3.3	1.64	-5.4	1.19	-6.4	0	5.2	10	2,106	39	0	0.0	06
Champ Prods	34.8	34.8	22.9	5.5q	1.65	188.9	188.9	65.0	27	10	03-87	.40	1.2	0	24	53	04-29-87	3.7	1.81	6.7	1.88	12.6	30	2.5	116	3,344	1,340	+15	0.3	12
Chaus Bernard	2.7	10.2	26.2	18.7s	1.02	-38.5	-9.4	NC	NC	0	12-86	.00	.0	0	0	0	00-00-00	6.4	3.80	24.3	.00	NM	122	1.5	217	17,725	3,294	0	0.9	06
Coated Sales	104.8	67.9	66.6	7.0f	.39	33.3	62.5	62.5	NC	78	02-87	.00	.0	0	0	0	00-00-00	7.8	2.59	20.2	3.85	77.8	137	2.2	206	17,180	5,137	-105	0.0	02
Eagle Clothes	1.4	7.3	7.2	.6n	.09	NE	NE	NE	NC	3	04-87	.00	.0	0	0	0	00-00-00	.5	2.20	1.1	2.55	2.8	20	2.2	13	7,174	1,454	0	0.0	07
Farah Inc	-4.6	-3.6	1.9	1.9s	.31	32.0	-97.5	-78.8	-14	3	04-87	.00	.0	0	126	32	10-28-86	.5	1.80	.9	2.89	2.6	55	1.7	93	5,886	1,635	0	3.7	10
Garan Inc	-7.1	-2.4	-14.0	2.7s	.91	-31.4	-16.7	-23.5	-20	1	03-87	.60	2.4	1	78	42	02-13-87	2.6	1.08	2.8	1.46	4.1	13	4.1	66	2,623	1,237	0	0.1	09
Genesco Inc	-25.1	25.1	-9.3	18.0q	1.28	NE	NE	NE	NC	39	04-87	.00	.0	0	0	0	00-00-00	3.7	1.68	6.2	6.29	39.0	200	3.5	78	15,174	2,540	0	6.2	01
Hampton Ind	1.6	1.6	-.6	5.1q	1.36	.0	.0	24.8	10	11	03-87	.00	.0	0	0	0	06-10-87	3.2	1.81	5.8	1.95	11.3	59	4.3	43	3,714	382	0	0.0	12
Johnston Ind	.0	2.9	.8	8.2n	2.56	29.6	-17.9	-6.6	67	24	03-87	.00	.0	0	0	0	00-00-00	6.9	1.43	9.9	2.45	24.3	68	2.8	64	3,223	198	0	0.0	06
Kellwood Co	26.1	13.9	13.9	25.3f	2.20	3.4	8.9	8.9	23	14	04-87	.60	1.7	29	25	22	06-05-87	4.4	2.14	9.4	2.06	19.4	52	3.0	382	10,919	6,782	+11	1.7	04
Littlefield Adam	-34.8	-34.8	-13.6	-3.1q	-2.84	NE	NE	NE	NC	-45	03-87	.00	.0	0	0	NE	05-24-83	-16.3	1.20	-19.6	2.29	-44.9	70	3.3	2	1,074	57	0	2.5	12
Liz Claiborne	35.0	35.0	43.9	95.8q	1.10	37.0	37.0	41.0	52	32	03-87	.18	.5	0	12	13	06-09-87	10.8	2.65	28.6	1.35	38.7	0	3.6	3,006	86,508	44,842	+33	0.0	12
Manhattan Ind	-23.7	-23.7	-30.8	-7.8q	-1.49	-28.6	-28.6	NE	NC	-14	04-87	.20	1.4b	-3	NE	126	09-04-87	-2.5	2.28	-5.7	2.18	-12.4	41	2.0	75	5,061	3,028	0	0.7	01
Noel Industries	29.8	14.7	13.3	-.9s	-.74	NE	NE	-100.0	NC	-13	04-87	.00	.0	0	0	0	00-00-00	-2.6	2.19	-5.7	2.26	-12.9	36	2.0	2	1,134	7	0	0.0	10
Oxford Inds	13.4	1.0	1.7	11.5n	1.03	19.0	14.3	43.1	-10	5	02-87	.50	3.0	19	48	24	05-11-87	2.1	2.62	5.5	1.62	8.9	14	2.7	182	11,053	5,708	0	0.4	05
Pannill Knit	-34.3	-34.3	14.0	15.9q	1.04	-100.0	-100.0	-14.0	NC	70	03-87	.00	.0	0	0	0	00-00-00	7.0	1.00	7.0	10.06	70.4	632	2.3	174	15,000	3,976	0	0.1	12
Phil-Van Heu	8.4	8.4	-2.2	20.9q	1.32	20.8	20.8	20.0	17	10	04-87	.28	1.4	7	13	14	08-17-87	4.0	2.13	8.5	1.49	12.7	5	3.2	305	15,150	3,255	0	0.5	01
Pope Evan Rob	-10.2	5.3	-176.2	-6.4n	-.87	NE	NE	NE	NC	-28	03-87	.00	.0	0	0	0	02-01-83	-10.5	.87	-9.1	3.07	-27.9	141	2.5	14	6,817	837	0	3.1	06
Russ Togs	10.8	10.8	1.0	14.0q	2.72	7.1	7.1	23.1	6	9	04-87	.90	2.8	3	28	33	06-25-87	5.0	1.88	9.4	1.47	13.8	2	3.0	165	5,062	3,112	0	0.2	01
Salant Corp	-14.1	-14.1	-10.4	2.2q	.67	NE	NE	-38.5	NC	18	02-87	.00	.0	0	0	NE	07-30-84	1.7	1.35	2.3	7.70	17.7	2	8.9	37	3,309	530	0	1.6	11
Sanmark Star	8.6	.4	-1.6	2.2n	.35	-33.3	-6.9	-5.4	24	25	03-87	.00	.0	0	0	0	12-29-86	3.7	1.46	5.4	4.63	25.0	160	1.8	29	6,502	919	0	0.0	06
Sup Surgical	5.7	5.7	-1.0	3.7q	1.55	16.1	16.1	-7.2	9	7	03-87	.44	2.1	18	27	23	05-15-87	3.8	1.79	6.8	1.49	10.1	23	4.8	51	2,436	926	+14	0.0	12
Tultex Cp	2.0	-1.1	13.2	22.8s	1.24	-15.0	-16.7	12.7	13	15	05-87	.36	1.9	17	20	25	06-08-87	7.0	1.66	11.6	1.86	21.6	35	3.2	350	18,289	3,332	-27	2.5	11
Winter, Jack	6.5	6.5	14.2	-1.0q	-.29	-57.1	-57.1	-100.0	NC	-10	03-87	.22	4.4	0	NE	NE	04-10-87	-2.1	1.38	-2.9	1.90	-5.5	1	1.7	18	3,646	358	0	3.3	12
Wolf, Howard	.0	5.0	12.5	-.6s	-.52	.0	50.0	NE	NC	-13	11-86	.00	.0	0	0	0	08-09-84	-6.7	1.46	-9.8	1.31	-12.8	0	3.6	3	1,081	21	+10	0.0	05

Recent Performance and Forecast: Savings Institutions (SIC 603 and 612)

(in millions of dollars except as noted)

Item	1984	1985	1986[1]	1987[2]	Percent Change: Compound Annual 1972-1984	Compound Annual 1979-1984	Annual 1984-1985	Annual 1985-1986	Annual 1986-1987
Assets	1,185	1,286	1,421	1,563	11.0	10.1	8.5	10.5	10.0
Mortgages held	703	756	797	837	8.4	4.4	7.5	5.4	5.0
Mortgage-backed securities	128	134	170	207	—	32.0	4.7	26.9	21.8
Deposits	968	1,030	1,097	1,168	10.5	9.8	6.4	6.5	6.5
Net worth	49	60	71	83	6.9	2.6	22.5	18.3	16.9
Net new savings	51	-12	4	15	([3])	([3])	([3])	([3])	([3])
Mortgages made	184	211	277	249	9.3	10.2	14.7	31.3	-10.0
Number of institutions	3,550	3,603	3,600	3,525	-2.3	-4.6	1.5	0.0	-2.1
Number of offices	25,019	25,660	26,200	26,593	6.6	2.6	2.6	2.1	1.5
Employment (000)	391	428	449	472	7.5	5.2	9.5	4.9	5.1

[1]Estimated.
[2]Forecast.
[3]Changes in this series are extremely volatile, making percent changes unmeaningful.

SOURCE: Federal Home Loan Bank Board, National Council of Savings Institutions, Bureau of Labor Statistics.

Source: ***U.S. Industrial Outlook 1987,*** **U.S. Department of Commerce.**

Recent Performance and Forecast: Commercial Banking (SIC 602)

(in billions of dollars except as noted)

Item	1984	1985	1986[1]	1987[2]	Percent Change: Compound Annual 1972-84	Compound Annual 1979-84	Annual 1984-85	Annual 1985-86	Annual 1986-87
Assets	2,265	2,460	2,657	2,843	9.8	10.9	8.6	8.0	7.0
Loans	1,465	1,615	1,728	1,832	11.1	11.2	10.2	7.0	6.0
Investments	378	414	460	520	6.2	6.0	9.5	11.0	13.0
Deposits	1,633	1,764	1,887	2,000	8.5	9.6	8.0	7.0	6.0
Employment (000)	1,518	1,550	1,565	1,580	3.3	2.1	2.1	1.0	1.0

[1]Estimated.
[2]Forecast.

SOURCE: Board of Governors of the Federal Reserve System and Bureau of Labor Statistics. Estimates and forecasts by U.S. Department of Commerce, International Trade Administration.

Source: ***U.S. Industrial Outlook 1987,*** **U.S. Department of Commerce.**

Company	Revenue			Earnings								Dividends						Ratio Analysis							Shareholdings					
	Pct. Change				Per Share							Current Rate			Payout															
						Pct. Change																								
Company	Last Qtr	FY to Date	Last 12 Mos	Last 12 Mos	Last 12 Mos	Last Qtr	FY to Date	Last 12 Mos	5-Year Growth Rate	Par Growth Rate	Date of Report	Amt	Yield	5-Year Growth Rate	Last FY	Last 5 Yrs.	Last X-Dvd Date	Pro-fit Mar-gin	Asset Turn-over	Return on Total Assets	Lever-age Ratio	Return on Equity	Debt to Eq-uity	Curr-ent Ratio	Mar-ket Value	Latest Shares Out-stndng.	Held by Banks-Funds	Insider Net Trad-ing	Short Int-erest Ratio	Fiscal Year Ends
-	%	%	%	$Mil	$	%	%	%	%	%	-	$	%	%	%	%	-	π/r x	r/a =	π/a x	a/e =	π/e	%	-	$Mil	000	000	000	Days	Mo
Middle Atlantic Banks																														
Ind. Group	9.4	11.6	12.0	2,250.1	4.41	20.2	26.5	287.2	52	14	- - -	.40	1.1	1	18	25	- - - -	8.1	.10	.8	19.38	15.5	57	NC	39,438	1,118,361	130,333	+ 168	.8	- -
Balt Bancorp	6.5	6.5	12.9	10.5q	.82	.0	.0	-47.1	NC	3	03-87	.40	2.1	0	32	17	06-11-87	4.8	.08	.4	13.00	5.2	27	NA	238	12,681	7,153	+2	0.0	12
Barclays PLC □	3.4	3.4	3.3	907.6f	5.27	30.7	31.1	NC	NC	17	12-86	.00	.0	0	12	5	00-00-00	7.1	.11	.8	20.63	16.5	68	NA	25,653	691,000	0	0	0.0	12
Citzns Fst Bcp	8.2	8.2	14.6	22.7q	1.65	18.9	18.9	-50.3	44	12	03-87	.60	2.5b	14	23	29	07-16-87	13.2	.08	1.1	17.82	19.6	18	NA	319	13,167	1,538	+1	7.1	12
CoreStates Fnl	1.0	1.0	23.2	146.6q	3.57	.0	.0	20.2	12	10	03-87	1.36	3.5	11	35	34	06-01-87	10.5	.10	1.0	16.10	16.1	53	NA	1,543	39,300	16,983	+4	0.0	12
Equimark Corp	5.2	5.2	-14.7	5.2q	.06	NC	NC	-57.1	NC	4	03-87	.00	.0	0	0	0	09-04-81	2.1	.10	.2	20.00	4.0	132	NA	155	35,358	2,300	+2	1.1	12
Fidelcor Inc	52.8	52.8	72.9	105.3q	4.02	6.9	6.9	-3.8	8	12	03-87	1.52	4.1	29	35	29	04-24-87	9.4	.10	.9	21.44	19.3	35	NA	766	20,836	7,515	-2	0.0	12
Fst Fid Bcp	10.4	10.4	14.0	122.6q	4.17	4.9	4.9	13.9	5	9	03-87	1.68	3.9	9	39	38	05-29-87	9.9	.08	.8	18.88	15.1	35	NA	1,191	27,708	9,353	0	2.0	12
Fst Jersey Natl	13.0	13.0	16.8	39.2q	4.69	10.6	10.6	4.7	8	10	03-87	1.80	3.2	6	39	39	06-01-87	9.4	.10	.9	17.56	15.8	37	NA	426	7,682	2,615	0	0.0	12
Fst Penn Cp	-5.3	-5.3	-5.8	22.0q	.09	NE	NE	NE	NC	12	03-87	.00	.0	0	0	0	03-03-80	4.2	.10	.4	30.75	12.3	94	NA	411	42,722	5,667	+10	0.1	12
Horizon Bncp	3.3	3.3	5.0	35.5q	3.91	10.1	10.1	10.5	11	10	03-87	1.60	2.6	7	34	36	07-09-87	10.7	.09	1.0	17.40	17.4	4	NA	534	8,722	2,563	0	0.0	12
HUBCO Inc	-1.0	-1.0	5.4	4.9q	1.34	26.7	26.7	12.6	25	12	03-87	.44	2.5b	13	29	35	05-11-87	12.6	.09	1.1	15.73	17.3	4	NA	64	3,553	117	+53	0.0	12
Mellon Bank	4.3	7.3	7.2	183.3f	6.20	-73.2	-13.0	-13.0	-1	8	12-86	1.40	3.9	6	45	38	04-27-87	5.3	.09	.5	21.00	10.5	101	NA	980	27,497	16,434	0	0.6	12
Meridian Bcp	3.7	3.7	8.6	74.2q	2.64	36.4	36.4	11.9	12	9	03-87	1.00	4.7	18	38	35	06-09-87	10.0	.11	1.1	13.64	15.0	24	NA	576	26,955	9,655	+0	0.0	12
Midlantic Cp	47.8	47.8	67.4	167.2q	4.09	-.8	-.8	-18.2	4	11	03-87	1.36	2.9	8	31	25	06-25-87	10.5	.10	1.0	16.80	16.8	23	NA	1,687	35,999	5,198	0	0.0	12
Pennbancorp	-1.0	-1.0	30.5	29.9q	2.28	.0	.0	2.2	12	8	03-87	.88	3.0	9	35	36	03-02-87	9.6	.09	.9	15.11	13.6	22	NA	381	13,126	2,969	-11	0.0	12
PNC Financial	32.4	32.4	15.2	265.2q	4.88	11.1	11.1	20.5	14	13	03-87	1.68	3.5	12	30	33	06-01-87	12.5	.10	1.2	15.92	19.1	50	NA	3,192	65,821	27,823	0	0.0	12
SW Bancorp	26.4	26.4	35.4	1.1q	.20	-20.0	-20.0	-39.4	NC	6	03-87	.00	.0	0	0	0	00-00-00	1.7	.18	.3	21.33	6.4	41	NA	12	3,928	48	+3	4.6	12
Union Natl Cp	-6.0	-6.0	9.0	28.2q	2.80	9.1	9.1	1.4	7	6	03-87	1.32	3.9	7	42	42	05-18-87	9.8	.09	.9	12.89	11.6	12	NA	338	9,948	3,454	+100	0.0	12
Utd Jer Bk	34.9	34.9	65.1	78.9q	2.20	5.2	5.2	-.5	11	10	03-87	.86	2.9	10	37	35	06-30-87	10.5	.10	1.0	16.40	16.4	18	NA	971	32,358	8,948	+7	0.3	12

Company	Revenue Pct. Change Last Qtr	Revenue Pct. Change FY to Date	Revenue Pct. Change Last 12 Mos	Earnings Last 12 Mos	Per Share Last 12 Mos	Per Share Pct. Change Last Qtr	Per Share Pct. Change FY to Date	Per Share Pct. Change Last 12 Mos	5-Year Growth Rate	Par Growth Rate	Date of Report	Dividends Current Rate Amt	Dividends Current Rate Yield	Dividends 5-Year Growth Rate	Payout Last FY	Payout Last 5 Yrs.	Last X-Dvd Date
-	%	%	%	$Mil	$	%	%	%	%	%	-	$	%	%	%	%	-
New York Banks																	
Ind. Group	.3	1.5	.1	4,572.8	5.53	- 7.6	.0	6.2	9	10	- - -	1.82	4.0	1	30	32	- - - -
Bank of NY Co	3.0	9.8	9.7	155.2f	4.97	12.8	16.7	16.7	11	11	12-86	1.68	3.9	9	31	31	04-20-87
Bankers Tr NY	-1.2	-1.2	3.1	436.1q	6.14	7.9	7.9	8.5	12	12	03-87	1.66	3.3	10	25	26	06-24-87
Boston Five Cent	19.8	12.9	12.7	14.0f	1.97	22.4	53.9	53.9	NC	8	10-86	.48	1.8	0	14	10	03-30-87
Chase Manhttn	-5.4	-5.4	-5.5	545.8q	6.12	-31.3	-31.3	-6.7	5	8	03-87	2.16	5.2	5	31	34	04-24-87
Chem NY Cp	-3.9	-2.9	-2.8	402.4f	7.57	5.5	3.3	3.3	6	9	12-86	2.72	6.5	7	34	34	06-09-87
Citicorp •	8.8	8.8	3.7	1052.0q	6.99	-8.0	-8.0	.3	9	8	03-87	2.70	4.6	10	34	31	04-24-87
Empire of Amer	-11.6	-11.6	-.1	7.3q	.31	-87.3	-87.3	NC	NC	0	03-87	.15	3.2	0	0	0	06-24-87
Irving Bk Cp	.5	.5	-3.8	126.3q	6.72	-6.8	-6.8	6.3	7	9	03-87	2.24	4.8	6	30	34	05-26-87
KeyCorp	17.7	17.7	12.8	86.8q	3.02	13.6	13.6	11.9	17	9	03-87	1.12	4.1	12	33	33	06-24-87
Mfrs Hanover	-9.5	-9.5	-6.4	389.6q	8.34	-21.5	-21.5	.2	2	8	03-87	3.28	7.4	3	37	38	06-25-87
Marine Midland	-14.6	-10.1	-10.0	144.9f	7.19	-1.0	18.6	18.6	9	9	12-86	2.04	3.4	13	27	29	06-01-87
Matthews Wght	-42.6	-42.6	13.1	10.9q	1.93	-32.1	-32.1	NC	NC	30	03-87	.00	.0	0	0	0	00-00-00
Morgan, J.P.	-6.6	-6.6	-2.6	865.0q	4.68	-4.7	-4.7	9.9	16	12	03-87	1.36	2.8	9	26	31	06-16-87
Norstar Bncp	14.7	14.7	31.5	108.8q	2.98	16.2	16.2	12.9	7	8	03-87	1.40	4.3	8	45	45	06-04-87
Rep NY	6.5	6.5	9.4	164.6q	5.38	42.7	42.7	30.3	5	14	03-87	.16	.3	7	23	26	06-09-87
Seamen's Cp	301.0	300.5	397.5	26.8s	2.01	176.9	576.9	NC	NC	40	09-86	.40	5.5	0	0	0	07-09-87
Sterling Bncp □	-32.5	-26.2	-26.0	6.4f	1.04	-70.7	-25.7	-25.7	0	2	12-86	.80	5.0	2	77	66	06-09-87
US Trust	4.4	7.7	7.6	29.9f	3.01	-100.0	17.6	17.6	17	11	12-86	1.00	2.9	10	29	35	07-06-87
Pacific States Banks																	
Ind. Group	- 14.4	- 8.0	- 2.8	811.8	1.66	.8	2.9	3.5	- 12	3	- - -	.99	3.1	1	30	41	- - - -
Bancorp Hawaii ◇	-14.4	-14.4	-3.3	47.2q	5.14	5.6	5.6	13.2	8	11	03-87	1.60	2.9	6	29	31	05-12-87
BankAmerica □	-16.7	-16.7	-12.4	-545.0q	-3.91	-54.8	-54.8	NE	NC	-16	03-87	.00	.0	0	0	4400	11-07-85
BSD Bancorp □	2.0	2.0	.0	.2q	.06	40.0	40.0	-60.0	NC	1	03-87	.00	.0	0	0	0	00-00-00
Cap Fed	9.3	5.3	106.9	3.2s	2.38	64.9	194.6	NC	NC	11	12-86	.00	.0	0	0	0	00-00-00
City Natl ◇	10.4	10.4	8.0	33.6q	1.83	60.0	60.0	33.6	13	13	03-87	.64	2.4	12	30	34	06-24-87
Fst Hawaiian	-2.7	-2.7	1.6	31.5q	2.36	10.9	10.9	10.8	11	10	03-87	.90	3.5	9	37	38	02-23-87
Fst Intst Bcp	-99.9	-99.9	-24.4	259.0q	7.24	2.9	2.9	3.7	5	6	03-87	2.80	4.7	5	36	38	06-15-87
Grt Amer First	57.1	57.1	53.5	109.4q	4.64	58.2	58.2	64.5	NC	18	03-87	.60	3.1	0	9	9	04-30-87
La Jolla Bcp	-4.8	-4.8	-8.5	1.8q	.38	.0	.0	58.3	NC	7	03-87	.05	.6b	0	8	5	03-03-87
Rainier Bcp	.9	1.1	1.1	70.0f	3.41	9.0	4.6	4.6	11	8	12-86	1.16	2.2	10	32	32	05-30-87
Sec Pacific	27.1	27.1	12.6	413.9q	4.80	-5.4	-5.4	7.6	10	0	03-87	1.80	4.3	10	30	30	04-29-87
US Bcp	-.6	1.9	1.8	77.2f	2.56	9.5	15.3	15.3	5	8	12-86	.80	2.9	8	27	30	02-25-87
Wells Fargo	24.2	24.2	23.6	300.2q	5.26	20.4	20.4	22.3	13	11	03-87	1.56	2.9	8	28	30	06-24-87
WestAmer Bcp	6.4	6.4	5.9	9.6q	1.60	-21.9	-21.9	33.3	18	12	03-87	.40	1.7	0	21	27	07-13-87

Company	Ratio Analysis Profit Margin	Asset Turnover	Return on Total Assets	Leverage Ratio	Return on Equity	Debt to Equity	Current Ratio	Shareholdings Market Value	Latest Shares Outstndng.	Held by Banks-Funds	Insider Net Trading	Short Interest Ratio	Fiscal Year Ends
-	π/r x	r/a =	π/a x	a/e =	π/e	%	-	$Mil	000	000	000	Days	Mo
New York Banks													
Ind. Group	6.6	.11	.7	20.71	14.5	132	NC	35,200	779,839	433,569	+ 230	2.4	- -
Bank of NY Co	8.9	.08	.7	23.29	16.3	53	NA	1,305	29,994	13,129	+5	0.3	12
Bankers Tr NY	8.9	.09	.8	20.00	16.0	79	NA	3,593	70,455	48,023	+21	1.2	12
Boston Five Cent	7.2	.10	.7	14.43	10.1	140	NA	178	6,849	1,588	0	0.0	10
Chase Manhttn	5.9	.10	.6	21.33	12.8	67	NA	3,335	80,844	50,772	+2	1.1	12
Chem NY Cp	7.3	.10	.7	20.43	14.3	51	NA	2,102	50,057	31,745	0	5.2	12
Citicorp •	4.4	.11	.5	27.40	13.7	268	NA	8,119	137,615	94,562	+22	1.1	12
Empire of Amer	.7	.14	.1	.00	NM	2125	NA	71	15,000	602	0	0.3	12
Irving Bk Cp	6.5	.08	.5	25.80	12.9	61	NA	839	18,135	7,571	0	0.0	12
KeyCorp	10.1	.10	1.0	14.10	14.1	20	NA	780	28,764	3,887	0	0.1	12
Mfrs Hanover	5.0	.10	.5	25.00	12.5	236	NA	1,875	42,017	25,054	0	3.0	12
Marine Midland	6.5	.09	.6	20.67	12.4	92	NA	1,116	18,831	14,018	0	0.5	12
Matthews Wght	25.3	.17	4.2	7.02	29.5	0	NA	18	5,609	511	0	0.7	12
Morgan, J.P.	13.2	.08	1.1	16.00	17.6	47	NA	8,557	178,728	116,378	+182	0.7	12
Norstar Bncp	10.7	.09	1.0	14.80	14.8	41	NA	1,143	34,896	7,842	-9	5.5	12
Rep NY	11.5	.08	.9	16.11	14.5	106	NA	1,613	29,588	8,578	0	0.0	12
Seamen's Cp	13.5	.07	.9	55.22	49.7	46	NA	121	16,638	3,222	0	0.2	03
Sterling Bncp □	11.9	.09	1.1	9.82	10.8	17	NA	98	6,164	1,651	0	23.2	12
US Trust	9.7	.10	1.0	17.20	17.2	44	NA	338	9,655	4,436	+6	0.0	12
Pacific States Banks													
Ind. Group	2.6	.12	.3	25.00	7.5	121	NC	14,675	461,761	194,303	- 44	1.5	- -
Bancorp Hawaii ◇	10.1	.09	.9	17.22	15.5	12	NA	520	9,370	5,451	+1	0.0	12
BankAmerica □	-4.6	.11	-.5	32.80	-16.4	101	NA	1,782	154,944	31,975	-4	1.2	12
BSD Bancorp □	.5	.20	.1	12.00	1.2	31	NA	14	3,299	0	0	0.0	12
Cap Fed	3.6	.11	.4	27.00	10.8	0	NA	15	1,650	312	0	0.0	06
City Natl ◇	11.9	.09	1.1	18.09	19.9	1	NA	491	18,371	2,887	-33	0.0	12
Fst Hawaiian	10.2	.09	.9	18.67	16.8	35	NA	346	13,381	4,789	0	0.0	12
Fst Intst Bcp	6.5	.08	.5	18.80	9.4	124	NA	2,809	47,015	33,173	+16	1.5	12
Grt Amer First	7.9	.10	.8	25.13	20.1	79	NA	422	22,048	10,788	0	6.9	12
La Jolla Bcp	5.6	.09	.5	16.00	8.0	0	NA	37	4,574	3	0	0.0	12
Rainier Bcp	8.5	.09	.8	15.63	12.5	139	NA	1,110	20,852	8,770	-3	0.0	12
Sec Pacific	6.5	1.02	6.6	.00	NM	65	NA	3,252	77,437	42,505	+8	10.2	12
US Bcp	9.3	.09	.8	15.25	12.2	58	NA	843	30,114	15,362	-30	0.0	12
Wells Fargo	7.2	.10	.7	22.14	15.5	228	NA	2,918	53,662	37,778	0	0.7	12
WestAmer Bcp	7.7	.10	.8	19.75	15.8	33	NA	115	5,044	510	+1	0.0	12

Recent Performance and Forecast: Construction Materials (SIC 321,324,3251,3271-3,3275,3441,3448)

(in millions of dollars except as noted)

					Percent Change				
					Compound Annual		Annual		
	1984	1985[1]	1986[1]	1987[2]	1972-84	1979-84	1984-85	1985-86	1986-87
Industry Data									
Total value of shipments (1982$)	34,028	35,190	36,407	35,158	−0.6	−2.5	3.4	3.5	−3.4
3211 Flat Glass	2,021	2,050	2,070	2,110	1.7	0.2	1.4	1.0	1.9
3241 Hydraulic Cement	4,018	3,900	4,020	3,940	−1.1	−3.5	−2.9	3.1	−2.0
3251 Brick & Structural Tile	907	890	950	930	−2.9	−3.6	−1.8	6.7	−2.1
3271 Concrete Block & Brick	1,543	1,650	1,700	1,635	−1.8	−2.7	7.0	3.0	−3.8
3272 Concrete Products, nec	4,081	4,365	4,495	4,315	−1.0	−1.7	6.9	3.0	−4.0
3273 Ready-mixed Concrete	9,286	9,565	10,040	9,930	−0.4	−3.3	3.0	5.0	−1.1
3275 Gypsum Products	1,606	1,700	1,800	1,750	1.0	0.5	5.9	5.9	−2.8
3441 Fabr Structural Metal	8,169	8,610	8,870	8,160	−1.4	−2.3	5.4	3.0	−8.0
3448 Prefab Metal Buildings	2,398	2,460	2,462	2,388	3.2	−2.5	2.6	0.1	−3.0

[1]Estimated.
[2]Forecast.

SOURCE: U.S. Department of Commerce: Bureau of the Census, Bureau of Economic Analysis, International Trade Administration (ITA). Estimates and forecasts by ITA.

Source: *U.S. Industrial Outlook 1987*, U.S. Department of Commerce.

Recent Performance and Forecast: Hydraulic Cement (SIC 3241)

(in millions of dollars except as noted)

					Percent Change				
					Compound Annual		Annual		
	1984	1985[1]	1986[2]	1987[3]	1972-84	1979-84	1984-85	1985-86	1986-87
Industry Data									
Value of shipments[4]	4,183	4,147	4,276	—	7.3	0.8	−0.9	3.1	—
Value of shipments (1982$)	4,018	3,900	4,020	3,940	−1.1	−3.5	−2.9	3.1	−2.0
Total employment (000)	22.6	22.4	23.0	—	−2.3	−5.8	−0.9	2.7	—
Production workers (000)	17.4	17.2	17.8	—	−2.7	−6.6	−1.1	3.5	—
Average hourly earnings ($)	14.32	14.80	15.20	—	8.2	7.1	3.3	2.7	—
Product Data									
Value of shipments[5]	4,023	3,984	4,108	—	7.1	0.2	−1.0	3.1	—
Value of shipments (1982$)	3,864	3,750	3,865	3,790	−1.3	−4.1	−3.0	3.1	−1.9
Shipments price index[6] (1982 = 100)	104.1	106.3	106.3	—	8.5	4.5	2.1	0.0	—
Trade Data									
Value of imports	294	432	465	—	12.5	−0.7	46.7	7.8	—
Import/new supply ratio[7]	0.068	0.098	0.102	—	4.8	−0.9	43.4	4.1	—
Value of exports	23.9	31.5	20.0	—	16.8	−4.1	31.8	−36.5	—
Export/shipments ratio	0.006	0.008	0.005	—	9.1	−4.3	33.1	−38.4	—

[1]Estimated except for exports and imports.
[2]Estimated.
[3]Forecast.
[4]Value of all products and services sold by the Hydraulic Cement industry.
[5]Value of products classified in the Hydraulic Cement industry produced by all industries.
[6]Developed by the Office of Industry Assessment, ITA.
[7]New supply is the sum of product shipments plus imports.

SOURCE: U.S. Department of Commerce: Bureau of the Census, Bureau of Economic Analysis, International Trade Administration (ITA). Estimates and forecasts by ITA.

Source: ***U.S. Industrial Outlook 1987,*** **U.S. Department of Commerce.**

Company	Revenue Pct. Change Last Qtr	Revenue Pct. Change FY to Date	Revenue Pct. Change Last 12 Mos	Earnings Last 12 Mos	Earnings Per Share Last 12 Mos	Earnings Per Share Pct. Change Last Qtr	Earnings Per Share Pct. Change FY to Date	Earnings Per Share Pct. Change Last 12 Mos	Earnings 5-Year Growth Rate	Earnings Par Growth Rate	Earnings Date of Report	Dividends Current Rate Amt	Dividends Current Rate Yield	Dividends 5-Year Growth Rate	Dividends Payout Last FY	Dividends Payout Last 5 Yrs.	Dividends Last X-Dvd Date	Profit Margin	Asset Turnover	Return on Total Assets	Leverage Ratio	Return on Equity	Debt to Equity	Current Ratio	Market Value	Latest Shares Outstanding	Held by Banks-Funds	Insider Net Trading	Short Interest Ratio	Fiscal Year Ends
-	%	%	%	$Mil	$	%	%	%	%	%	-	$	%	%	%	%	-	π/r x	r/a =	π/a x	a/e =	π/e	%	-	$Mil	000	000	000	Days	Mo
Misc. Building Materials																														
Ind. Group	10.0	11.0	6.6	726.3	2.29	124.1	130.2	74.1	82	12	- - -	.66	2.2	0	29	31	- - - -	6.3	1.25	7.9	2.22	17.5	31	2.0	8,495	284,343	106,590	+1906	2.2	- -
Ameron Inc	-4.0	-4.0	2.2	12.2q	2.53	-100.0	-100.0	3.3	0	5	02-87	.96	2.9	3	34	36	04-20-87	3.9	1.00	3.9	2.18	8.5	42	2.0	158	4,830	1,119	+13	1.4	11
Armstrng Wrld	25.6	25.6	17.1	131.4q	2.73	39.6	39.6	24.1	32	11	03-87	.90	2.4	6	29	37	05-04-87	6.5	1.55	10.1	1.63	16.5	7	2.1	1,818	47,519	29,777	+2	0.9	12
Arundel Corp	-3.6	-3.6	9.3	4.7q	2.04	NE	NE	33.3	43	11	03-87	.00	.0	0	0	0	09-25-79	5.0	1.18	5.9	1.93	11.4	57	NA	56	2,303	1,097	+0	0.0	12
Bairnco Cp	15.3	15.3	10.9	24.6q	2.38	48.6	48.6	18.4	3	9	03-87	.70	1.8	26	30	20	06-02-87	4.1	1.44	5.9	2.24	13.2	47	1.9	397	10,174	4,305	-10	0.4	12
Bird Inc	14.1	14.1	3.8	1.3q	-.06	NE	NE	-100.0	NC	3	03-87	.00	.0	0	0	0	12-14-81	.7	1.43	1.0	2.60	2.6	71	2.3	35	4,112	1,895	0	0.0	12
Butler Mfg	17.3	17.3	16.4	5.5q	1.06	NE	NE	-42.1	NC	-1	03-87	1.32	3.9	0	186	171	06-08-87	.9	2.33	2.1	1.95	4.1	30	2.3	171	5,033	1,088	+4	0.0	12
Certain-teed	4.6	4.6	1.2	61.3q	3.23	37.5	37.5	12.2	NC	8	03-87	1.00	2.4	0	30	23	05-29-87	5.4	1.39	7.5	1.64	12.3	21	2.8	800	18,982	5,574	0	1.0	12
Custom Energy ...... ◇	-43.4	-38.8	-108.0	-6.8n	-1.74	NE	NE	NE	NC	0	03-87	.00	.0	0	0	0	00-00-00	NM	NC	NC	NC	NS	-92	.6	29	12,858	817	+1920	3.4	06
Dallas Cp	-1.2	-1.2	-.7	-.1q	-.01	-100.0	-100.0	NE	NC	-7	03-87	.66	4.8	-6	367	91	06-19-87	.0	NC	NC	NC	-.1	58	2.8	102	7,349	4,623	0	3.9	12
Elcor Cp	-4.0	4.8	-2.4	5.4n	.77	120.0	160.9	NE	NC	15	03-87	.22	1.8	5	45	NE	05-29-87	4.5	1.47	6.6	3.27	21.6	156	2.4	84	7,028	1,518	0	0.7	06
Insituform NA	19.2	19.2	55.5	2.5q	.34	20.0	20.0	78.9	NC	15	03-87	.00	.0	0	0	0	00-00-00	17.9	.59	10.5	1.43	15.0	9	4.0	107	6,480	1,298	0	0.0	12
Lawson Prods	6.1	6.1	6.9	13.0q	1.33	20.0	20.0	1.5	12	14	03-87	.28	1.0	7	18	19	06-26-87	9.4	1.47	13.8	1.33	18.3	0	5.4	285	9,827	3,572	-16	0.0	12
Manville Cp .... ◇	4.3	4.3	1.9	112.1q	3.62	533.3	533.3	NE	NC	13	03-87	.00	.0	0	0	NE	05-20-82	5.8	.81	4.7	2.72	12.8	10	2.9	93	24,001	684	0	18.2	12
Owens Corn	NA	NA	.0	NA	NA	NA	NA	NA	NA	NC	00-00	.00	.0	NA	NA	NA	00-00-00	NA	NC	NA	NC	NA	NA	NA	871	37,475	13,898	+1	NA	NA
Rep Gypsum	-21.7	-6.9	1.6	6.5n	.61	-75.0	-47.6	-32.2	53	7	03-87	.36	4.7	52	35	30	05-22-87	10.5	.96	10.1	1.72	17.4	41	3.4	79	10,318	2,593	0	2.6	06
Susquehanna	-25.8	-25.8	-36.4	-8.3q	-.61	NE	NE	NE	NC	-18	03-87	.00	.0	0	0	0	00-00-00	-12.2	1.09	-13.3	1.36	-18.1	8	3.3	36	9,590	1,318	-5	5.9	12
USG Corp	11.4	11.4	9.1	258.8q	4.38	103.7	103.7	24.1	39	33	03-87	1.12	3.3	0	29	27	05-19-87	9.3	1.39	12.9	3.43	44.3	98	1.1	1,796	52,434	24,411	-4	2.7	12
Vulcan Matls	6.1	6.1	.1	97.7q	8.87	77.0	77.0	40.1	8	12	03-87	3.40	2.3	6	35	43	05-20-87	10.1	1.16	11.7	1.65	19.3	14	2.4	1,538	10,590	6,128	0	0.1	12
Wolverine Alum	39.2	39.2	20.2	4.5q	1.34	88.9	88.9	17.5	NC	15	03-87	.16	1.4	0	12	10	06-08-87	4.2	2.26	9.5	1.76	16.7	36	3.6	40	3,440	875	0	0.0	12
Cement																														
Ind. Group	3.9	11.2	7.1	225.1	.24	NE	NE	NE	NC	1	- - -	.22	1.9	0	22	92	- - - -	5.7	.84	4.8	2.48	11.9	65	1.9	3,379	286,752	33,508	- 11	3.9	- -
Calmat Co .... ◇	89.3	89.3	55.6	73.4q	2.38	723.1	723.1	81.7	60	16	03-87	.40	1.3	-2	23	41	06-03-87	10.6	1.08	11.4	1.74	19.8	17	1.9	909	30,299	10,806	-4	0.0	12
Fla Rock Ind	-7.0	-3.3	-5.2	21.4s	2.19	-34.0	-24.8	-13.1	21	16	03-87	.50	1.9	27	18	15	06-12-87	8.4	1.57	13.2	1.61	21.2	15	2.4	239	9,273	2,986	+0	0.4	09
Giant Grp	-7.4	-7.4	8.1	14.9q	3.83	NE	NE	177.5	NC	26	03-87	.00	.0	0	0	0	00-00-00	18.6	.44	8.2	3.18	26.1	136	3.0	103	4,247	2,584	0	10.4	12
Ideal Basic .... ◇ ◆	-20.9	-20.9	-11.0	-36.9q	-1.11	NE	NE	NE	NC	0	03-87	.00	.0	0	0	NE	05-31-83	-15.3	.73	-11.2	.00	NM	809	1.6	696	174,100	2,671	0	6.2	12
Lafarge Cp	9.9	9.9	1.9	24.8q	.57	NE	NE	.0	NC	3	03-87	.20	1.7	0	34	NE	05-06-87	2.5	1.00	2.5	2.04	5.1	57	1.9	480	40,452	2,810	0	11.7	12
Lone Star Ind	-22.3	-22.3	-2.9	112.4q	7.07	NE	NE	140.5	NC	14	03-87	1.90	5.2	0	27	79	06-01-87	13.3	.58	7.7	2.55	19.6	43	1.6	603	16,570	8,505	+8	2.1	12
Puerto Rican C	29.3	29.3	19.2	8.0q	4.03	173.0	173.0	196.3	NC	14	03-87	.30	1.0	0	3	1	07-09-87	11.8	.67	7.9	1.95	15.4	48	2.7	62	1,981	62	-16	1.3	12
Slattery Grp	20.0	20.0	42.1	-.6q	-.41	NE	NE	NE	NC	-1	03-87	.00	.0	0	0	22	02-11-85	-.3	2.33	-.7	2.00	-1.4	6	1.6	34	1,503	346	0	0.1	12
Tex Ind	-19.2	-13.1	-1.6	7.7n	.73	NE	-100.0	-69.7	-11	0	02-87	.77	2.5b	0	0	27	04-27-87	1.3	.86	1.1	3.64	4.0	178	2.2	252	8,327	2,738	0	2.8	06

Recent Performance and Forecast: Chemicals and Allied Products (SIC 28)

(in millions of dollars except as noted)

					Percent Change				
					Compound Annual		Annual		
	1984	1985[1]	1986[2]	1987[3]	1972-84	1979-84	1984-85	1985-86	1986-87
Industry Data									
Value of Shipments[4]	198,233	202,438	205,858		10.9	6.1	2.1	1.7	—
Value of Shipments (1982$)	193,648	196,047	198,358	201,085	2.1	-0.0	1.2	1.2	1.4

[1]Estimated.
[2]Estimated.
[3]Forecast.

[4]Value of all products and services sold by the Chemicals and Allied Products industry.
SOURCE: U.S. Department of Commerce: Bureau of the Census, Bureau of Economic Analysis, International Trade Administration (ITA). Estimates and forecasts by ITA.

Source: *U.S. Industrial Outlook 1987*, U.S. Department of Commerce.

Recent Performance and Forecast: Petrochemicals (SIC 2821, 2822, 2824, 2843, 2865, 2869, 2873, 2895)

(in millions of dollars except as noted)

					Percent Change				
					Compound Annual		Annual		
	1984	1985[1]	1986[2]	1987[3]	1972-84	1979-84	1984-85	1985-86	1986-87
Industry Data									
Value of Shipments[4]	84,505	86,184	87,077	·	11.9	4.2	2.0	1.0	—
Value of Shipments (1982$)	83,563	86,325	88,774	90,417	2.1	-0.6	3.3	2.8	1.9

[1]Estimated.
[2]Estimated.
[3]Forecast.

[4]Value of all products and services sold by the Petrochemicals industry.
SOURCE: U.S. Departmet of Commerce: Bureau of the Census, Bureau of Economic Analysis, International Trade Administration (ITA). Estimates and forecasts by ITA.

Source: *U.S. Industrial Outlook 1987*, U.S. Department of Commerce.

Recent Performance and Forecast: Plastics Materials and Resins (SIC 2821)

(in millions of dollars except as noted)

					Percent Change				
					Compound Annual		Annual		
	1984	1985[1]	1986[2]	1987[3]	1972-84	1979-84	1984-85	1985-86	1986-87
Industry Data									
Value of shipments[4]	20,776	21,524	21,954	—	13.6	7.8	3.6	2.0	—
Value of shipments (1982$)	19,174	20,248	21,524	21,954	2.8	2.2	5.6	6.3	2.0
Total employment (000)	54.2	53.9	53.0	—	−0.1	−2.1	−0.6	−1.7	—
Production workers (000)	33.2	33.5	33.3	—	−0.4	−2.9	0.9	−0.6	—
Average hourly earnings ($)	13.33	14.00	14.60	—	8.6	8.5	5.0	4.3	—
Product Data									
Value of shipments[5]	22,730	23,550	24,000	—	14.5	6.0	3.6	1.9	—
Value of shipments (1982$)	20,794	21,970	23,365	23,830	3.3	0.4	5.7	6.3	2.0
Shipments price index[6] (1982=100)	109.3	—	—	—	10.8	5.5	—	—	—
Trade Data									
Value of imports (ITA)[7]	725	772	872	—	—	—	6.5	12.9	—
Import/new supply ratio[8]	0.031	0.032	0.035	—	—	—	2.7	10.3	—
Value of exports	2,655	2,457	2,747	—	16.2	4.0	−7.5	11.8	—
Export/shipments ratio	0.117	0.104	0.114	—	1.5	−1.9	−10.7	9.7	—

[1]Estimated except for exports and imports.
[2]Estimated.
[3]Forecast.
[4]Value of all products and services sold by the Plastics Materials and Resins industry.
[5]Value of products classified in the Plastics Materials and Resins industry produced by all industries.
[6]Developed by the Office of Industry Assessment, ITA.
[7]Import data are developed by the chapter author.
[8]New supply is the sum of product shipments plus imports.

SOURCE: U.S. Department of Commerce: Bureau of the Census, Bureau of Economic Analysis, International Trade Administration (ITA). Estimates and forecasts by ITA.

Source: *U.S. Industrial Outlook 1987*, U.S. Department of Commerce.

Recent Performance and Forecast: Synthetic Rubber (SIC 2822)

(in millions of dollars except as noted)

					Percent Change				
					Compound Annual		Annual		
	1984	1985[1]	1986[2]	1987[3]	1972-84	1979-84	1984-85	1985-86	1986-87
Industry Data									
Value of shipments[4]	3,409	3,300	3,190	—	10.0	5.3	−3.2	−3.3	—
Value of shipments (1982$)	3,528	3,445	3,375	3,425	0.7	−1.1	−2.4	−2.0	1.5
Total employment (000)	10.7	10.5	10.4	10.7	−0.8	−2.4	−1.9	−1.0	2.9
Production workers (000)	7.0	6.8	6.8	7.0	−1.3	−3.1	−2.9	0.0	2.9
Average hourly earnings ($)	15.36	—	—	—	9.0	9.0	—	—	—
Product Data									
Value of shipments[5]	3,688	3,575	3,400	—	9.2	2.7	−3.1	−4.9	—
Value of shipments (1982$)	3,837	3,745	3,670	3,725	−0.0	−3.8	−2.4	−2.0	1.5
Shipments price index[6] (1982 = 100)	96.1	95.5	92.8	—	9.2	6.8	−0.6	−2.8	—
Trade Data									
Value of imports	335	382	390	395	16.4	13.6	14.3	2.0	1.3
Import/new supply ratio[7]	0.083	0.097	0.103	—	6.2	9.9	16.2	6.5	—
Value of exports	674	628	710	730	12.1	1.6	−6.9	13.1	2.8
Export/shipments ratio	0.183	0.176	0.209	—	2.7	−1.1	−4.0	19.0	—

[1]Estimated except for exports and imports.
[2]Estimated.
[3]Forecast.
[4]Value of all products and services sold by the Synthetic Rubber industry.
[5]Value of products classified in the Synthetic Rubber industry produced by all industries.
[6]Developed by the Office of Industry Assessment, ITA.
[7]New supply is the sum of product shipments plus imports.

SOURCE: U.S. Department of Commerce: Bureau of the Census, Bureau of Economic Analysis, International Trade Administration (ITA). Estimates and forecasts by ITA.

Source: *U.S. Industrial Outlook 1987*, U.S. Department of Commerce.

Recent Performance and Forecast: Tires and Inner Tubes (SIC 3011)

(in millions of dollars except as noted)

					Percent Change				
					Compound Annual		Annual		
	1984	1985[1]	1986[2]	1987[3]	1972-84	1979-84	1984-85	1985-86	1986-87
Industry Data									
Value of shipments[4]	10,723	10,325	9,975	—	5.3	2.4	−3.7	−3.4	—
Value of shipments (1982$)	11,230	10,700	10,500	10,660	−1.5	−1.2	−4.7	−1.9	1.5
Total employment (000)	70.4	66.0	62.0	—	−3.5	−7.4	−6.2	−6.1	—
Production workers (000)	56.3	52.0	49.0	—	−3.2	−7.0	−7.6	−5.8	—
Average hourly earnings ($)	14.18	14.20	15.0	—	8.4	8.3	0.1	5.6	—
Product Data									
Value of shipments[5]	10,281	9,900	9,560	—	6.4	2.8	−3.7	−3.4	—
Value of shipments (1982$)	10,767	10,260	10,050	10,200	−0.5	−0.8	−4.7	−2.0	1.5
Shipments price index[6] (1982 = 100)	95.5	96.5	95.1	—	6.9	3.6	1.0	−1.5	—
Trade Data									
Value of imports	1,792	1,872	1,750	1,775	13.8	9.8	4.5	−6.5	1.4
Import/new supply ratio[7]	0.154	0.165	0.161	—	6.2	5.8	7.1	−2.7	—
Value of exports	419	369	300	350	12.6	3.5	−11.9	−18.7	16.7
Export/shipments ratio	0.041	0.037	0.031	—	5.9	0.7	−8.5	−15.8	—

[1]Estimated except for exports and imports.
[2]Estimated.
[3]Forecast.
[4]Value of all products and services sold by the Tires and Inner Tubes industry.
[5]Value of products classified in the Tires and Inner Tubes industry produced by all industries.
[6]Developed by the Office of Industry Assessment, ITA.
[7]New supply is the sum of product shipments plus imports.

SOURCE: U.S. Department of Commerce: Bureau of the Census, Bureau of Economic Analysis, International Trade Administration (ITA). Estimates and forecasts by ITA.

Source: *U.S. Industrial Outlook 1987*, U.S. Department of Commerce.

Company	Revenue Pct. Change Last Qtr	Revenue Pct. Change FY to Date	Revenue Pct. Change Last 12 Mos	Earnings Last 12 Mos	Earnings Per Share Last 12 Mos	Earnings Per Share Pct. Change Last Qtr	Earnings Per Share Pct. Change FY to Date	Earnings Per Share Pct. Change Last 12 Mos	Earnings 5-Year Growth Rate	Earnings Par Growth Rate	Earnings Date of Report	Dividends Current Rate Amt	Dividends Current Rate Yield	Dividends 5-Year Growth Rate	Dividends Payout Last FY	Dividends Payout Last 5 Yrs.	Dividends Last X-Dvd Date	Ratio Analysis Profit Margin	Ratio Analysis Asset Turnover	Ratio Analysis Return on Total Assets	Ratio Analysis Leverage Ratio	Ratio Analysis Return on Equity	Ratio Analysis Debt to Equity	Ratio Analysis Current Ratio	Shareholdings Market Value	Shareholdings Latest Shares Outstndng.	Shareholdings Held by Banks-Funds	Shareholdings Insider Net Trading	Shareholdings Short Interest Ratio	Shareholdings Fiscal Year Ends
-	%	%	%	$Mil	$	%	%	%	%	%	-	$	%	%	%	%	-	π/r x	r/a =	π/a x	a/e =	π/e	%	-	$Mil	000	000	000	Days	Mo
Chemicals and Synthetics																														
Ind. Group	10.9	3.5	- 5.3	4,669.5	3.16	12.2	9.0	75.1	7	5	- - -	1.83	2.7	1	38	55	- - - -	5.1	1.00	5.1	2.33	11.9	47	1.7	98,505	1,471,482	678,276	-2917	1.1	- -
Air Pd & Chem ◆	3.6	7.7	7.1	7.6s	.18	10.6	8.0	-92.9	-40	-3	03-87	1.00	2.1	14	950	32	06-26-87	.4	.75	.3	2.33	.7	64	1.5	2,692	57,280	36,819	+1	1.6	09
Am Cyanamid	10.5	10.5	9.5	214.9q	2.32	26.4	26.4	66.9	4	7	03-87	1.05	2.1	3	44	52	06-12-87	5.5	1.07	5.9	2.12	12.5	34	1.7	4,505	91,938	57,474	+13	0.4	12
Aristech/Chem	11.2	11.2	310.6	46.6q	1.81	26.2	26.2	NC	NC	14	03-87	.18	.6	0	0	0	04-27-87	6.0	1.63	9.8	1.53	15.0	19	1.9	624	22,500	18,173	0	0.0	12
Ausimont Comp	25.3	25.3	67.5	49.5q	1.70	16.7	16.7	39.3	NC	14	03-87	.32	1.5	0	9	6	06-08-87	7.1	1.04	7.4	2.31	17.1	25	1.7	595	28,354	4,552	0	0.0	12
Cabot Corp	-2.6	-9.3	-10.8	67.7s	2.43	11.1	-8.7	20.9	-4	7	03-87	.92	2.6	1	36	38	05-15-87	5.4	.83	4.5	2.56	11.5	72	2.0	980	27,810	16,012	-26	1.1	09
Dow Chemical	10.2	10.2	-1.0	812.0q	4.23	39.1	39.1	550.8	-3	8	03-87	2.20	2.6	0	47	88	06-24-87	7.1	.93	6.6	2.38	15.7	66	1.6	16,491	191,477	100,328	+11	1.1	12
Dupont	-.6	-.6	-7.9	1525.0q	6.30	-3.6	-3.6	10.5	5	6	03-87	3.20	2.7	4	48	55	05-11-87	5.6	1.02	5.7	2.04	11.6	25	1.6	28,793	239,943	94,669	+37	1.4	12
Essex Chemical	-6.3	-6.3	3.5	8.3q	1.34	-23.8	-23.8	-5.6	7	8	03-87	.60	2.4	11	40	41	04-06-87	4.1	1.24	5.1	2.75	14.0	62	1.5	151	5,987	1,849	0	3.0	12
Ethyl Corp	2.9	2.9	2.7	192.1q	1.52	48.0	48.0	60.0	20	15	03-87	.40	1.5	11	23	27	06-09-87	12.1	.93	11.2	1.82	20.4	43	2.2	3,373	126,093	44,055	-2997	1.6	12
Genex Cp	-66.7	-66.7	-75.0	-13.5q	-1.05	NE	NE	NE	NC	0	03-87	.00	.0	0	0	0	00-00-00	NM	NC	NC	NC	NM	7	.8	16	12,819	1,036	0	0.0	12
Grace W R ◇	-23.0	-23.0	-50.3	-429.9q	-10.34	NE	NE	-100.0	NC	-42	03-87	2.80	4.4	2	NE	347	05-01-87	-12.5	.84	-10.5	3.14	-33.0	84	1.3	2,670	41,549	25,053	-1	1.5	12
Hercules Inc	1.5	1.5	.8	313.4q	5.53	186.4	186.4	116.0	10	13	03-87	1.76	2.8	6	43	53	06-01-87	11.9	.91	10.8	1.70	18.4	32	2.6	3,463	54,751	36,882	-49	1.4	12
Imperial Chem	77.0	11.2	11.2	817.0f	5.11	-34.7	-9.7	2.4	23	7	12-86	2.81	3.0	6	33	44	08-20-86	5.1	1.33	6.8	2.38	16.2	37	1.7	15,329	162,000	21,850	0	0.7	12
Intl Flav Frag	20.9	20.9	23.4	91.2q	2.43	23.7	23.7	21.5	5	9	03-87	1.24	2.6	4	51	56	06-17-87	14.0	.97	13.6	1.29	17.5	0	4.7	1,801	37,041	20,773	0	0.0	12
Koppers Co	3.8	3.8	7.4	60.8q	2.06	NE	NE	NE	NC	8	03-87	.80	2.0	-12	38	NE	05-11-87	4.3	1.40	6.0	2.12	12.7	25	1.6	1,207	29,900	16,393	-1	0.6	12
Monsanto Co	7.2	7.2	1.9	453.0q	5.79	15.8	15.8	NE	NC	6	03-87	2.80	3.3	7	46	63	05-06-87	6.5	.86	5.5	2.18	12.0	43	1.6	6,494	77,659	51,837	+4	1.1	12
Pennwalt Corp	3.5	3.5	8.1	51.3q	3.60	-4.4	-4.4	NE	NC	5	03-87	2.20	3.5	0	60	108	06-26-87	4.6	1.11	5.1	2.71	13.8	51	2.1	704	11,214	6,684	+7	2.7	12
Portage Ind	-17.9	-17.9	5.0	.9q	.73	-21.1	-21.1	NC	NC	35	03-87	.00	.0	0	0	0	00-00-00	4.3	1.72	7.4	4.68	34.6	4	.4	8	1,133	0	0	0.0	12
Publicker Ind	-22.0	-22.0	-43.4	-.6q	-.06	NE	NE	NE	NC	-4	03-87	.00	.0	0	0	0	00-00-00	-4.6	.24	-1.1	3.73	-4.1	195	7.8	38	12,521	806	0	0.0	12
Regal Intl	35.3	35.3	-33.3	-5.3q	-.51	NE	NE	NE	NC	-86	03-87	.00	.0	0	0	0	00-00-00	-88.3	.63	-55.2	1.55	-85.5	2	2.4	13	10,264	476	0	0.0	12
Reichhold Chm	-12.4	-12.4	-12.6	18.2q	2.45	228.6	228.6	NE	NC	6	03-87	.80	1.3	13	38	66	05-05-87	2.5	1.60	4.0	2.33	9.3	47	1.6	452	7,438	4,897	+0	1.5	12
Rohm & Haas	-1.4	-1.4	.9	157.1q	2.28	48.2	48.2	13.4	14	10	03-87	.80	1.7	13	39	34	05-11-87	7.6	1.12	8.5	1.85	15.7	28	2.2	3,267	68,960	31,532	+13	1.2	12
Stepan Co	3.7	3.7	7.8	8.2q	2.73	28.6	28.6	17.7	9	11	03-87	.80	1.7	7	29	35	05-21-87	3.1	1.74	5.4	2.76	14.9	63	1.6	138	2,898	412	0	4.6	12
Union Carbide	-2.2	-2.2	-27.4	158.0q	1.43	34.2	34.2	NE	NC	-1	03-87	1.50	5.1	61	2423	1396	05-01-87	2.5	.84	2.1	7.48	15.7	356	1.3	3,783	127,695	72,384	+69	2.0	12
Witco Chemical	-2.8	-2.8	-5.7	66.0q	2.95	3.2	3.2	9.3	14	9	03-87	1.12	2.7	6	36	38	06-15-87	4.9	1.65	8.1	1.75	14.2	21	2.5	918	22,258	13,330	+0	1.0	12

Company	Revenue: Pct. Change Last Qtr	Revenue: Pct. Change FY to Date	Revenue: Pct. Change Last 12 Mos	Revenue: Last 12 Mos	Earnings: Per Share Last 12 Mos	Earnings: Per Share Pct. Change Last Qtr	Earnings: Per Share Pct. Change FY to Date	Earnings: Per Share Pct. Change Last 12 Mos	Earnings: 5-Year Growth Rate	Earnings: Par Growth Rate	Earnings: Date of Report	Dividends: Current Rate Amt	Dividends: Current Rate Yield	Dividends: 5-Year Growth Rate	Dividends: Payout Last FY	Dividends: Payout Last 5 Yrs.	Dividends: Last X-Dvd Date	Ratio Analysis: Profit Margin	Ratio Analysis: Asset Turnover	Ratio Analysis: Return on Total Assets	Ratio Analysis: Leverage Ratio	Ratio Analysis: Return on Equity	Ratio Analysis: Debt to Equity	Ratio Analysis: Current Ratio	Shareholdings: Market Value	Shareholdings: Latest Shares Outstndng.	Shareholdings: Held by Banks-Funds	Shareholdings: Insider Net Trading	Shareholdings: Short Interest Ratio	Fiscal Year Ends
-	%	%	%	$Mil	$	%	%	%	%	%	-	$	%	%	%	%	-	π/r x	r/a =	π/a x	a/e =	π/e	%	-	$Mil	000	000	000	Days	Mo
Specialty Chemicals																														
Ind. Group	13.6	16.5	9.2	673.0	1.84	17.0	11.3	37.7	9	9	- - -	.79	2.2	1	40	45	- - - -	6.3	1.37	8.6	1.83	15.7	24	2.2	13,050	357,538	183,524	- 166	.5	- -
Betz Laboratories	5.7	5.7	7.0	35.7q	2.25	3.3	3.3	-3.8	4	6	03-87	1.52	3.1	15	61	50	07-24-87	10.2	1.29	13.2	1.33	17.5	0	2.5	772	15,750	10,450	-41	0.0	12
Bio Rad Lab	25.0	25.0	24.0	6.7q	.89	20.0	20.0	21.9	50	16	03-87	.00	.0	0	0	0	00-00-00	5.0	1.32	6.6	2.35	15.5	49	1.9	135	5,563	568	0	0.6	12
Chemed Cp	11.5	11.5	.8	36.9q	4.13	2.1	2.1	65.2	25	19	03-87	1.60	4.0	7	38	56	05-18-87	10.0	1.35	13.5	2.28	30.8	39	1.7	362	8,971	6,968	+15	0.1	12
Crompt & Knwl	-10.1	-10.1	-13.0	1.4q	.19	34.5	34.5	-84.4	-29	-5	03-87	.68	2.8	5	700	72	06-01-87	.7	1.43	1.0	2.00	2.0	28	2.3	155	6,508	1,896	+0	0.5	12
Dexter Cp	14.2	14.2	5.8	34.9q	1.40	15.2	15.2	17.6	4	8	03-87	.60	2.4	6	41	41	06-09-87	5.2	1.19	6.2	2.18	13.5	44	2.1	619	24,893	15,052	-10	0.1	12
Diam Crystal	7.8	1.4	.8	1.3f	.51	NE	292.3	292.3	-34	-1	03-87	.80	2.1	7	157	55	05-11-87	1.1	1.09	1.2	1.33	1.6	1	3.5	98	2,567	281	0	0.0	03
Ferro Corp	17.4	17.4	13.6	26.3q	3.84	44.1	44.1	140.0	2	8	03-87	1.32	2.5	0	34	50	05-11-87	3.5	1.69	5.9	2.00	11.8	30	2.1	365	6,821	4,179	+5	0.1	12
Fuller H B Co	13.9	14.6	16.2	21.4s	2.25	30.4	29.1	30.1	12	13	05-87	.42	1.0	8	18	21	04-24-87	3.8	1.92	7.3	2.16	15.8	27	1.9	382	9,383	4,491	0	0.0	11
Grt Lks Chem	62.7	62.7	23.5	33.4q	2.22	122.9	122.9	29.8	11	11	03-87	.60	1.0	12	29	24	06-25-87	9.7	.70	6.8	2.26	15.4	75	2.4	871	14,977	10,054	0	0.2	12
Kinark Cp	12.7	12.7	11.5	-.8q	-.23	NE	NE	NE	NC	-5	03-87	.00	.0	0	0	0	00-00-00	-2.8	.75	-2.1	2.43	-5.1	78	1.0	14	3,482	321	0	0.8	12
Lawter Int	5.5	5.5	7.1	13.6q	.78	23.5	23.5	NE	NC	7	03-87	.56	3.5	5	76	97	05-11-87	13.0	1.12	14.6	1.68	24.6	9	3.8	280	17,513	5,826	0	3.8	12
LeaRonal Inc	25.9	21.6	21.9	7.5f	1.01	160.0	57.8	57.8	-3	7	02-87	.48	2.6	9	42	35	05-27-87	5.9	1.86	11.0	1.29	14.2	6	6.0	138	7,443	2,884	0	0.0	02
Loctite Cp	34.3	25.2	24.5	29.2n	3.22	81.1	39.5	47.7	15	13	03-87	1.00	1.6	9	31	31	06-01-87	9.3	1.29	12.0	1.58	19.0	9	2.3	561	9,080	3,797	0	0.1	06
Lubrizol Corp	-.8	-.8	5.1	76.1q	1.91	-8.5	-8.5	10.4	2	5	03-87	1.20	3.1	-2	44	67	05-04-87	7.8	1.12	8.7	1.53	13.3	9	2.8	1,553	39,691	26,081	0	2.0	12
MacDermid Inc	6.6	12.5	12.7	5.4f	1.49	60.0	43.3	43.3	9	10	03-87	.52	1.7	4	35	34	06-08-87	5.6	1.57	8.8	1.80	15.8	24	2.0	113	3,630	2,098	0	0.0	03
Morton Thiokol	.3	-2.0	.5	131.8n	2.77	.0	-1.4	119.8	20	12	03-87	.76	1.7	7	25	28	05-19-87	6.9	1.35	9.3	1.72	16.0	4	1.7	2,101	47,224	28,442	0	0.5	06
Nalco Chem	7.3	7.3	3.4	66.4q	1.69	17.9	17.9	-6.6	0	5	03-87	1.20	3.4	3	74	68	05-14-87	8.9	1.27	11.3	1.44	16.3	7	1.8	1,404	39,271	30,339	-1	0.0	12
NCH Corp	18.0	13.9	13.8	19.6f	2.12	31.6	19.8	19.8	10	9	04-87	.72	2.1	0	34	44	05-26-87	4.6	1.57	7.2	1.79	12.9	10	2.6	315	9,262	3,018	-1	0.6	04
Nuclear Metals	-9.9	7.7	16.2	2.6s	.95	-90.9	-24.2	30.1	-6	6	03-87	.00	.0	0	0	0	11-18-80	6.0	.60	3.6	1.72	6.2	27	3.5	43	2,701	1,000	0	0.0	09
Oakite Products	-2.5	-2.5	-2.4	2.7q	1.65	10.4	10.4	-22.2	-4	1	03-87	1.52	5.0	1	95	77	05-14-87	3.4	2.03	6.9	1.48	10.2	7	2.8	50	1,629	435	+1	1.7	12
Petrolite Corp	-8.0	-11.9	-14.0	14.0s	1.22	-28.0	-29.0	-30.3	-10	1	04-87	1.12	3.1	7	74	53	04-06-87	5.3	1.15	6.1	1.39	8.5	3	3.1	412	11,451	3,037	0	0.0	10
Prods Research	5.8	6.0	7.9	7.7s	.82	11.1	11.4	15.5	16	9	03-87	.32	1.8	7	27	38	05-18-87	8.1	1.49	12.1	1.27	15.4	4	4.1	167	9,459	3,883	-38	0.5	09
Quaker Chemical	9.0	9.0	3.9	8.8q	1.32	18.2	18.2	15.8	1	8	03-87	.50	2.5	11	33	31	04-10-87	6.7	1.33	8.9	1.48	13.2	13	3.6	132	6,613	2,183	+0	0.0	12
Sigma-Aldrich	19.8	19.8	18.8	35.6q	1.45	21.2	21.2	21.8	18	18	03-87	.28	.6	19	17	19	05-26-87	13.4	1.08	14.5	1.58	22.9	10	2.6	1,094	24,578	10,310	-99	0.0	12
Univar Cp	106.1	106.1	55.4	3.1q	.36	357.1	357.1	-76.0	-32	3	05-87	.20	.9	-8	318	42	05-11-87	.4	4.25	1.7	4.06	6.9	132	1.4	120	5,603	934	+3	0.9	02
Vista Chem	1.4	4.4	7.0	40.6s	1.95	39.5	25.6	NC	NC	55	03-87	.00	.0	0	0	0	00-00-00	7.2	1.17	8.4	6.50	54.6	356	1.8	537	15,971	2,942	0	0.2	09
WD Forty Co	1.1	5.3	10.9	11.1s	1.48	-25.0	-8.6	8.8	6	4	02-87	1.32	3.9	11	69	66	04-06-87	15.6	1.85	28.8	1.19	34.2	0	6.1	257	7,504	2,055	0	0.0	08

Company	Revenue: Pct. Change Last Qtr	Revenue: Pct. Change FY to Date	Revenue: Pct. Change Last 12 Mos	Revenue: Last 12 Mos	Earnings Per Share: Last 12 Mos	Earnings Per Share: Pct. Change Last Qtr	Earnings Per Share: Pct. Change FY to Date	Earnings Per Share: Pct. Change Last 12 Mos	Earnings: 5-Year Growth Rate	Earnings: Par Growth Rate	Earnings: Date of Report	Dividends: Current Rate Amt	Dividends: Current Rate Yield	Dividends: 5-Year Growth Rate	Dividends: Payout Last FY	Dividends: Payout Last 5 Yrs.	Dividends: Last X-Dvd Date	Ratio Analysis: Profit Margin	Ratio Analysis: Asset Turnover	Ratio Analysis: Return on Total Assets	Ratio Analysis: Leverage Ratio	Ratio Analysis: Return on Equity	Ratio Analysis: Debt to Equity	Ratio Analysis: Current Ratio	Shareholdings: Market Value	Shareholdings: Latest Shares Outstndng.	Shareholdings: Held by Banks-Funds	Shareholdings: Insider Net Trading	Shareholdings: Short Interest Ratio	Shareholdings: Fiscal Year Ends
-	%	%	%	$Mil	$	%	%	%	%	%	-	$	%	%	%	%	-	r/r x	r/a =	r/a x	a/e =	r/e	%	-	$Mil	000	000	000	Days	Mo
Tires and Inner Tubes																														
Ind. Group	6.5	8.8	.8	749.4	3.74	4404.7	1593.4	137.2	9	9	- - -	1.11	1.9	1	61	45	- - - -	4.3	1.19	5.1	2.59	13.2	61	1.5	9,418	161,085	94,968	-1681	1.0	- -
Alliance Tire	58.3	38.8	66.6	3.6s	.41	NE	NE	NE	NC	31	06-86	.00	.0	0	0	0	06-30-83	5.1	1.06	5.4	5.70	30.8	55	1.1	11	6,509	45	0	0.1	12
Bandag Inc	14.1	14.1	12.3	53.5q	3.16	62.0	62.0	22.5	15	22	03-87	.70	1.1	22	45	30	06-15-87	14.0	1.29	18.0	1.55	27.9	5	3.1	1,079	16,865	7,226	-1694	0.3	12
Cooper Tire	20.3	20.3	14.2	26.0q	2.57	85.3	85.3	42.8	1	11	03-87	.44	1.3	10	18	17	03-03-87	4.3	1.65	7.1	1.87	13.3	39	3.1	353	10,136	5,497	+1	0.1	12
Danaher	177.8	177.8	91.1	10.7q	1.02	154.5	154.5	82.1	NC	16	03-87	.00	.0	0	0	0	00-00-00	1.9	.74	1.4	11.71	16.4	610	1.5	241	10,196	1,392	0	1.5	12
Firestone Tire	17.1	10.8	1.5	59.0s	1.56	138.7	150.7	NE	NC	2	04-87	1.00	2.4	8	163	63	06-26-87	1.6	1.44	2.3	2.22	5.1	24	1.5	1,604	38,541	20,804	+13	2.5	10
GenCorp	5.8	5.8	4.1	128.3q	5.75	-8.3	-8.3	90.4	12	9	02-87	1.50	1.5	2	26	44	04-28-87	4.1	1.49	6.1	2.00	12.2	19	1.7	2,301	22,339	12,469	0	0.4	11
Goodyear Tire ◦	-2.8	-2.8	-4.8	468.3q	5.70	NE	NE	129.8	-8	11	03-87	1.60	2.4	4	138	49	05-12-87	5.2	1.04	5.4	2.89	15.6	83	1.4	3,828	56,499	47,535	0	1.8	12
Rubber and Plastic Products																														
Ind. Group	17.5	17.8	14.3	213.9	.86	- 22.6	22.3	24.9	17	10	- - -	.29	1.0	1	28	27	- - - -	4.7	1.45	6.8	2.15	14.6	43	2.2	7,039	247,740	59,453	+1152	4.1	- -
Alpine Grp	120.8	71.9	58.0	1.3n	.28	NE	-11.1	16.7	NC	23	01-87	.00	.0	0	0	0	00-00-00	2.7	2.22	6.0	3.80	22.8	144	2.4	67	3,447	49	-3	0.9	04
Am Biltrite	37.7	37.7	21.4	3.4q	1.52	47.4	47.4	44.8	NC	11	03-87	.15	.9	-15	10	19	06-22-87	2.9	1.69	4.9	2.49	12.2	69	2.5	36	2,185	433	0	5.6	12
Bamberger Poly	2.4	11.5	11.1	1.6f	1.07	4.8	15.1	NC	NC	49	12-86	.00	.0	0	0	0	00-00-00	1.6	2.88	4.6	10.54	48.5	318	1.6	20	2,000	0	0	0.0	12
Carlisle Corp	7.7	7.7	.4	19.0q	2.13	-6.0	-6.0	-7.8	-7	5	03-87	1.10	3.0	6	50	36	05-12-87	4.0	1.48	5.9	1.78	10.5	20	2.2	338	9,107	3,091	-16	1.0	12
Chariot Grp	48.4	48.4	3.5	1.1q	.40	50.0	50.0	-20.0	NC	9	03-87	.16	2.6b	0	32	9	06-08-87	3.8	1.39	5.3	2.77	14.7	68	1.6	16	2,572	272	0	0.0	12
Chelsea Indus	-14.0	-13.2	-6.6	5.3s	2.08	-90.7	-72.9	-21.2	8	6	03-87	.72	3.1	4	26	29	05-22-87	3.2	1.63	5.2	1.79	9.3	34	3.3	50	2,128	797	0	2.0	09
Day Intl ♦ ■	3.5	.6	.6	4.3f	.54	-100.0	-73.5	-73.5	7	0	10-86	.50	1.4	-13	54	24	07-27-87	.5	2.20	1.1	2.00	2.2	19	1.9	366	10,500	4,357	+10	0.3	10
Filtertek Inc	10.0	10.0	3.5	6.9q	.96	9.5	9.5	5.5	20	13	03-87	.44	2.8	0	46	42	07-27-87	23.8	.85	20.3	1.22	24.7	7	3.6	99	6,413	711	0	0.0	12
Fluorocarbon Co	8.3	8.3	2.0	4.4q	1.03	50.0	50.0	-19.5	16	8	04-87	.28	1.8	13	30	22	07-09-87	4.4	1.23	5.4	2.00	10.8	63	3.6	67	4,310	1,672	0	0.0	01
Himont	NA	NA	.0	NA	NA	NA	NA	NA	NA	NC	00-00	.17	.4	NA	NA	NA	05-04-87	NA	NC	NA	NC	NA	NA	NA	2,225	50,000	0	+180	NA	NA
Kleer-Vu Ind	-9.7	-9.7	-61.2	-1.0q	-.11	NE	NE	-100.0	NC	-11	03-87	.03	1.8b	0	NE	52	12-16-85	-8.3	.57	-4.7	1.87	-8.8	35	1.0	12	7,135	472	-15	0.1	12
Mark IV Ind	16.0	16.0	110.4	11.5q	1.35	60.0	60.0	68.8	NC	29	05-87	.00	.0	0	0	0	02-02-87	3.8	.97	3.7	7.70	28.5	516	3.6	136	8,509	748	+1039	30.2	02
Martin Process	-13.2	-13.2	-13.4	2.8q	.48	16.7	16.7	54.8	NC	7	03-87	.12	.6	0	20	NE	06-01-87	6.2	1.02	6.3	1.46	9.2	17	3.2	98	4,964	364	0	51.4	12
O'Sullivan	11.7	11.7	12.5	8.7q	.86	-12.5	-12.5	-23.9	13	10	03-87	.32	1.8	25	36	26	06-08-87	5.1	1.94	9.9	1.54	15.2	0	1.7	179	10,087	794	0	0.3	12
Pantasote Inc	50.7	50.7	.8	-1.2q	-.31	172.7	172.7	NE	NC	-6	03-87	.00	.0	0	0	0	11-02-81	-1.0	1.40	-1.4	4.43	-6.2	89	1.6	38	3,919	297	0	0.0	12
Plymth Rub A	-6.9	-6.9	-2.0	-2.9q	-2.54	NE	NE	NE	NC	-60	02-87	.00	.0	0	0	0	00-00-00	-6.0	1.88	-11.3	5.35	-60.4	38	1.1	2	815	0	0	0.0	11
Porex Tech	125.4	88.2	83.5	37.4n	3.30	-4.5	444.6	358.3	45	32	03-87	.00	.0	0	0	0	00-00-00	15.2	.61	9.3	3.44	32.0	131	3.3	385	11,067	2,837	0	0.0	06
Rubbermaid	28.4	28.4	18.6	75.0q	1.02	27.3	27.3	22.9	18	14	03-87	.36	1.2	13	27	30	08-10-87	8.8	1.47	12.9	1.62	20.9	10	2.1	2,161	72,350	33,450	+0	1.3	12
Schulman, A Inc	14.1	13.2	14.0	17.0s	1.91	64.1	26.7	30.8	31	13	02-87	.40	1.3	12	16	17	04-21-87	4.1	2.37	9.7	1.74	16.9	10	2.5	281	8,928	3,930	-55	0.0	08
Sealed Air	8.6	8.6	11.6	16.3q	2.25	19.2	19.2	11.9	20	11	03-87	.52	1.1	11	22	24	06-01-87	7.7	1.26	9.7	1.53	14.8	13	2.6	335	7,235	4,137	+13	0.1	12
Sun Coast Plastics	26.1	33.9	37.5	.1n	.01	-100.0	-50.0	-50.0	NC	2	03-87	.00	.0	0	0	0	00-00-00	.9	.78	.7	3.00	2.1	142	1.7	36	14,423	126	0	0.0	06
Velcro Industries	11.7	18.8	61.2	4.9s	1.63	-48.0	-27.7	NC	NC	5	03-87	.92	3.9	0	48	40	05-26-87	6.2	.74	4.6	2.37	10.9	12	.8	71	3,010	488	0	0.0	09
Voplex Corp	6.5	6.5	31.6	-2.0q	-.78	8.7	8.7	-100.0	NC	-16	03-87	.40	4.8	10	NE	72	04-27-87	-2.5	2.12	-5.3	1.98	-10.5	25	1.9	22	2,636	428	-2	0.0	12

Recent Performance and Forecast: Electronic Computing Equipment (SIC 3573)

(in millions of dollars except as noted)

					Percent Change				
					Compound Annual		Annual		
	1984	1985[1]	1986[2]	1987[3]	1972-84	1979-84	1984-85	1985-86	1986-87
Industry Data									
Value of shipments[4]	53,524	51,383	49,225	50,505	19.3	20.0	−4.0	−4.2	2.6
Total employment (000)	374	340	316	316	8.2	6.4	−9.0	−7.1	0.0
Production workers (000)	158	130	114	114	7.7	5.3	−17.6	−12.3	0.0
Average hourly earnings ($)	9.77	10.00	10.30	—	7.3	9.0	2.3	3.0	—
Product Data									
Value of shipments[5]	49,275	47,304	45,317	46,495	19.0	19.3	−4.0	−4.2	2.6
Trade Data									
Value of imports (ITA)[6]	7,834	8,285	10,439	13,571	—	51.4	5.8	26.0	30.0
Value of exports (ITA)[7]	13,511	13,964	13,266	13,929	21.2	19.7	3.4	−5.0	5.0
Export/shipments ratio	0.270	0.237	0.293	0.300	1.8	0.0	−12.4	23.8	2.4

[1]Estimated except for exports and imports.
[2]Estimated.
[3]Forecast.
[4]Value of all products and services sold by the Electronic Computing Equipment industry.
[5]Value of products classified in the Electronic Computing Equipment industry produced by all industries.
[6]Import data, developed by the chapter author, are on a C.I.F. valuation basis.
[7]Export data are developed by the chapter author.

SOURCE: U.S. Department of Commerce: Bureau of the Census, Bureau of Economic Analysis, International Trade Administration (ITA). Estimates and forecasts by ITA.

Source: *U.S. Industrial Outlook 1987*, U.S. Department of Commerce.

Company	Revenue: Pct. Change: Last Qtr	Revenue: Pct. Change: FY to Date	Revenue: Pct. Change: Last 12 Mos	Earnings: Last 12 Mos	Earnings: Per Share: Last 12 Mos	Earnings: Per Share: Pct. Change: Last Qtr	Earnings: Per Share: Pct. Change: FY to Date	Earnings: Per Share: Pct. Change: Last 12 Mos	Earnings: 5-Year Growth Rate	Earnings: Par Growth Rate	Earnings: Date of Report	Dividends: Current Rate: Amt	Dividends: Current Rate: Yield	Dividends: 5-Year Growth Rate	Dividends: Payout: Last FY	Dividends: Payout: Last 5 Yrs.	Dividends: Last X-Dvd Date	Ratio Analysis: Profit Margin	Ratio Analysis: Asset Turnover	Ratio Analysis: Return on Total Assets	Ratio Analysis: Leverage Ratio	Ratio Analysis: Return on Equity	Ratio Analysis: Debt to Equity	Ratio Analysis: Current Ratio	Shareholdings: Market Value	Shareholdings: Latest Shares Out-stndng	Shareholdings: Held by Banks-Funds	Shareholdings: Insider Net Trading	Shareholdings: Short Interest Ratio	Shareholdings: Fiscal Year Ends
-	%	%	%	$Mil	$	%	%	%	%	%	-	$	%	%	%	%	-	π/r x	r/a =	π/a x	a/e =	π/e	%	-	$Mil	000	000	000	Days	Mo
Computers,Subsystems and Peripherals																														
Ind. Group	15.0	19.0	8.8	7,235.0	2.09	7.9	12.5	- 6.4	- 1	6	- - -	.94	1.6	1	15	6	- - - -	5.9	1.02	6.0	1.82	10.9	20	2.2	194,361	3,405,270	G	-3326	1.1	- -
Amdahl Corp	59.1	59.1	22.5	62.1q	1.27	920.0	920.0	170.2	20	10	03-87	.20	.6	0	25	31	05-05-87	5.7	1.04	5.9	2.10	12.4	27	2.1	1,690	48,102	19,134	-238	0.5	12
Andersn Jacob	3.9	.0	.0	-7.8f	-2.88	NE	NE	NE	NC	-94	03-87	.00	.0	0	0	0	11-25-83	-20.0	1.47	-29.4	3.20	-94.0	72	2.2	5	2,722	139	0	1.4	03
Apollo Cptr	50.5	50.5	46.2	15.2q	.43	800.0	800.0	NE	NC	8	03-87	.00	.0	0	0	0	03-01-84	3.5	1.17	4.1	1.95	8.0	62	4.4	701	34,635	18,943	+2	0.0	12
Apple Cptr	40.7	31.3	27.1	157.6s	1.21	4.2	1.4	63.5	19	22	03-87	.06	.1	0	0	0	06-16-87	7.2	1.89	13.6	1.67	22.7	0	3.2	5,073	125,256	77,368	-18	0.0	09
Appld Magnet	72.8	51.7	32.5	7.1s	1.05	285.7	169.2	262.1	-18	7	03-87	.00	.0	0	0	0	02-14-84	4.5	1.27	5.7	1.25	7.1	1	2.6	191	6,337	2,637	+10	0.1	09
AST Research	33.2	7.9	4.5	14.3n	1.23	-47.3	-55.8	-53.1	NC	17	03-87	.00	.0	0	0	0	00-00-00	7.8	1.68	13.1	1.26	16.5	0	4.9	161	11,323	2,511	0	0.0	06
Atari Cp	23.3	23.3	57.8	30.3q	.59	60.0	60.0	NC	NC	29	03-87	.00	.0	0	0	0	06-22-87	11.2	1.46	16.4	1.75	28.7	0	2.2	816	57,788	7,088	0	2.3	12
Audiotronics Cp	-163.6	2.3	-14.2	-1.1n	-.88	NE	NE	NE	NC	-50	03-87	.00	.0	0	0	NE	07-10-84	-18.3	1.25	-22.9	2.18	-50.0	68	3.1	3	1,189	33	0	0.0	06
Barry Wright ◇	6.1	6.1	.5	7.4q	.89	25.0	25.0	-28.2	-10	3	03-87	.60	3.2	12	74	40	07-16-87	3.7	1.51	5.6	1.46	8.2	2	2.4	153	8,159	3,160	-1	0.5	12
C 3 Inc	166.1	23.5	8.4	1.8n	.19	NE	15.8	NE	-35	2	12-86	.00	.0	0	0	0	07-14-81	2.3	.91	2.1	1.14	2.4	0	6.6	105	9,701	2,078	0	0.8	03
C COR Electronics	17.2	24.9	8.3	1.1n	.36	NE	NE	NE	NC	6	03-87	.00	.0	0	0	0	00-00-00	4.2	1.19	5.0	1.22	6.1	3	5.9	19	2,033	718	0	0.0	06
Centronics Cp	-22.3	-20.7	-13.6	1.1n	.09	-80.0	NE	NE	NC	2	09-86	.00	.0	0	0	0	12-22-80	.6	1.33	.8	2.50	2.0	83	3.0	95	24,597	2,467	0	0.0	12
Cipher Data	14.4	21.0	26.3	7.1n	.49	-25.0	-4.2	28.9	29	5	03-87	.00	.0	0	0	0	05-25-83	3.8	1.16	4.4	1.23	5.4	0	5.0	162	14,366	9,861	-5	0.0	06
Comdisco Inc	21.7	14.0	26.3	75.5s	1.84	75.0	-7.2	4.0	24	19	03-87	.20	.7	21	8	10	05-18-87	7.8	.56	4.4	4.89	21.5	123	NA	1,209	39,313	9,666	+16	4.3	09
Compaq Cptr	46.5	46.5	25.5	54.8q	1.78	86.7	86.7	61.8	NC	30	03-87	.00	.0	0	0	0	00-00-00	7.9	1.84	14.5	2.06	29.9	40	2.2	1,564	33,370	13,578	-26	0.6	12
CompuScan	3.3	-21.3	-29.4	-4.1n	-.72	NE	NE	NE	NC	-42	02-87	.00	.0	0	0	0	00-00-00	-34.2	.87	-29.7	1.42	-42.3	12	3.1	6	5,635	1,091	0	0.0	05
Comp Automation	11.1	6.9	40.0	1.2n	.56	-75.3	NE	NE	NC	21	03-87	.00	.0	0	0	0	00-00-00	5.7	1.46	8.3	2.49	20.7	28	1.6	29	2,059	111	0	0.0	06
Comp Consoles	67.9	67.9	34.5	3.1q	.27	NE	NE	NE	NC	15	03-87	.00	.0	0	0	0	07-01-83	2.2	.73	1.6	9.50	15.2	622	1.6	117	12,135	2,752	0	3.0	12
Comp Memories	-97.3	-95.4	-94.0	-5.1n	-.45	NE	NE	NE	NC	-17	12-86	.00	.0	0	0	0	06-01-83	-56.7	.24	-13.4	1.27	-17.0	0	4.7	37	11,109	657	0	0.0	03
Comp Prods	-6.4	-6.4	15.7	-6.1q	-.31	NE	NE	NE	NC	-13	03-87	.00	.0	0	0	0	04-01-85	-5.5	.93	-5.1	2.49	-12.7	112	3.1	73	19,800	9,530	0	0.0	12
Computervision □	23.8	23.8	16.5	7.0q	.24	NE	NE	NE	NC	4	03-87	.00	.0	0	0	0	06-22-81	1.3	1.23	1.6	2.38	3.8	77	2.4	433	28,885	15,239	0	6.4	12
Control Data	3.2	3.2	-5.9	-237.8q	-5.77	NE	NE	NE	NC	-24	03-87	.00	.0	-34	NE	NE	09-09-85	-7.1	1.30	-9.2	2.64	-24.3	50	NA	1,173	40,991	26,652	-21	4.1	12
Convergent Inc	-17.8	-17.8	-26.0	-45.9q	-1.02	-100.0	-100.0	-100.0	NC	-21	03-87	.00	.0	0	0	0	00-00-00	-15.8	.98	-15.5	1.35	-20.9	9	3.7	320	46,618	15,130	-500	0.0	12
Corvus Systs	-25.5	-4.2	-4.6	-11.9n	-.40	NE	NE	NE	NC	-75	02-87	.00	.0	0	0	0	00-00-00	-29.0	1.04	-30.1	2.49	-74.8	25	1.6	22	29,646	3,205	0	0.0	05
Cray Research	50.8	50.8	65.5	151.1q	4.78	79.0	79.0	94.3	47	34	03-87	.00	.0	0	0	0	08-19-85	22.6	.96	21.6	1.58	34.2	28	2.7	3,067	30,179	22,272	+15	1.7	12
CSP Inc	-32.4	-38.9	-33.3	.4n	.14	-84.6	-82.1	-81.8	-16	2	05-87	.00	.0	0	0	0	00-00-00	4.0	.53	2.1	1.10	2.3	0	17.2	15	2,826	801	0	0.0	08
Data General ■	-1.2	2.6	7.1	-18.7s	-.70	-100.0	-100.0	NE	NC	-3	03-87	.00	.0	0	0	0	11-21-83	-1.5	1.00	-1.5	1.80	-2.7	35	2.6	822	26,619	16,779	+4	1.7	09
Data Switch Cp	158.2	158.2	62.8	.9q	.16	100.0	100.0	NE	NC	2	03-87	.00	.0	0	0	0	06-15-83	1.6	.44	.7	3.29	2.3	123	1.9	65	9,884	2,416	+24	0.0	12
Datapoint Cp ◆	-4.5	-4.9	-13.0	-67.7n	-4.40	-5.0	NE	NE	NC	-29	04-87	.00	.0	0	0	0	02-09-81	-21.6	.75	-16.1	1.80	-29.0	42	2.6	65	9,932	5,558	-1	1.3	07
Dataproducts	-6.5	-1.2	-5.3	12.7n	.61	100.0	NE	NE	NC	4	12-86	.16	1.4	2	NE	33	06-01-87	3.6	1.06	3.8	1.55	5.9	12	2.9	236	20,984	10,669	0	0.1	03
Dataram Cp	-2.7	-12.6	-16.6	1.0f	.48	-85.7	-76.8	-76.8	NC	8	04-87	.00	.0	0	0	0	05-12-80	6.7	.94	6.3	1.24	7.8	0	6.9	14	1,965	116	0	2.5	04
Datarex Systs	90.0	90.0	81.2	.5q	.40	-12.5	-12.5	NC	NC	10	03-87	.00	.0	0	0	0	00-00-00	1.7	2.53	4.3	2.33	10.0	56	2.3	19	1,590	0	0	0.2	12
Decision Ind	-3.8	-3.8	8.5	4.7q	.50	-100.0	-100.0	NC	21	5	03-87	.00	.0	0	0	0	00-00-00	2.5	1.44	3.6	1.36	4.9	1	3.3	95	9,500	2,657	0	0.5	11
Digital Equip	25.0	24.1	22.4	998.8n	7.50	74.2	89.7	96.3	14	17	03-87	.00	.0	0	0	0	05-12-86	11.2	1.24	13.9	1.25	17.4	6	4.9	21,281	129,864	104,443	-1	1.1	06
Educ Computer	46.2	36.4	34.6	3.4n	.74	69.2	32.6	23.3	25	13	03-87	.16	1.2	0	23	12	06-15-87	9.7	.84	8.1	2.01	16.3	38	4.5	59	4,470	1,553	-1	0.0	06
Electron Assoc	33.9	33.9	.0	.6q	.22	100.0	100.0	83.3	NC	6	03-87	.00	.0	0	0	0	00-00-00	2.0	1.70	3.4	1.71	5.8	6	2.4	13	2,859	324	0	1.1	12
Elron Electronic	-1.7	-4.2	14.0	-.4n	-.04	NE	NE	NE	NC	-1	12-86	.00	.0	0	0	0	01-18-83	-.2	1.00	-.2	2.50	-.5	36	1.6	77	10,739	385	0	0.0	03
ELXSI Ltd	-10.1	-10.1	-37.1	-11.9q	-.15	NE	NE	NE	NC	-66	03-87	.00	.0	0	0	0	00-00-00	-54.1	.41	-22.1	2.99	-66.1	33	1.5	81	78,196	0	0	0.0	12
Emulex Cp	-5.1	-.6	1.9	5.5n	.41	-43.8	-38.5	-14.6	15	9	03-87	.00	.0	0	0	0	02-29-84	5.3	1.30	6.9	1.32	9.1	1	3.7	102	13,319	6,097	0	0.0	06
Encore Cptr	483.3	714.3	900.0	-8.2s	-.37	NE	NE	NE	NC	-93	04-87	.00	.0	0	0	0	00-00-00	-82.0	.72	-59.4	1.57	-93.2	16	3.4	86	21,550	5,182	0	0.0	10

Company	Revenue: Pct. Change: Last Qtr	Revenue: Pct. Change: FY to Date	Revenue: Pct. Change: Last 12 Mos	Earnings: Last 12 Mos	Earnings: Per Share: Last 12 Mos	Earnings: Per Share: Pct. Change: Last Qtr	Earnings: Per Share: Pct. Change: FY to Date	Earnings: Per Share: Pct. Change: Last 12 Mos	Earnings: 5-Year Growth Rate	Earnings: Par Growth Rate	Earnings: Date of Report	Dividends: Current Rate: Amt	Dividends: Current Rate: Yield	Dividends: 5-Year Growth Rate	Dividends: Payout: Last FY	Dividends: Payout: Last 5 Yrs.	Dividends: Last X-Dvd Date	Ratio Analysis: Profit Margin	Ratio Analysis: Asset Turnover	Ratio Analysis: Return on Total Assets	Ratio Analysis: Leverage Ratio	Ratio Analysis: Return on Equity	Ratio Analysis: Debt to Equity	Ratio Analysis: Current Ratio	Shareholdings: Market Value	Shareholdings: Latest Shares Outstndng.	Shareholdings: Held by Banks-Funds	Shareholdings: Insider Net Trading	Shareholdings: Short Interest Ratio	Fiscal Year Ends
-	%	%	%	$Mil	$	%	%	%	%	%	-	$	%	%	%	%	-	ᴨ/r x	r/a =	ᴨ/a x	a/e =	ᴨ/e	%	-	$Mil	000	000	000	Days	Mo
Computers,Subsystems and Peripherals																														
Esprit Syst	-48.1	-21.3	-26.9	-.5n	.00	-100.0	NE	NE	NC	NC	02-87	.00	.0	0	0	0	00-00-00	-2.6	1.62	-4.2	2.83	-11.9	24	1.6	7	7,629	0	0	0.0	05
Fingermatrix	-100.0	-83.3	-100.0	-3.2n	-.59	NE	NE	NE	NC	-63	02-87	.00	.0	0	0	0	00-00-00	NC	NC	NC	NC	-62.7	0	4.5	42	7,640	218	0	0.0	05
Fortune Systs	-31.8	-31.8	-27.0	-3.4q	-.16	-100.0	-100.0	NE	NC	-8	03-87	.00	.0	0	0	0	00-00-00	-9.7	.69	-6.7	1.25	-8.4	1	4.2	50	21,050	2,512	-8	0.0	12
Gandalf Tech	17.4	24.6	24.5	5.7n	.58	60.0	114.3	123.1	-7	10	04-87	.00	NA	0	0	0	00-00-00	4.5	1.56	7.0	1.49	10.4	7	2.4	82	10,050	841	-85	0.0	07
Genisco Tech	-9.8	-4.5	2.5	-.2s	-.07	-100.0	NE	-100.0	NC	-1	03-87	.00	.0	0	0	0	03-10-81	-.5	1.40	-.7	1.86	-1.3	46	3.6	12	2,670	530	0	0.0	09
Gould Inc	-33.4	-33.4	-43.9	-109.6q	-2.43	-56.7	-56.7	NE	NC	-20	03-87	.00	.0	-29	NE	NE	06-09-86	-13.8	.63	-8.7	2.26	-19.7	59	2.4	896	44,537	18,673	+0	0.6	12
Hewlett-Pack	13.4	11.3	12.1	558.0s	2.18	28.6	17.4	16.6	8	12	04-87	.22	.4	17	11	9	06-18-87	7.5	1.19	8.9	1.44	12.8	3	2.5	15,654	256,092	124,789	+3	1.5	10
Honeywell Inc	-1.3	-1.3	-19.3	27.1q	.60	68.4	68.4	-89.3	-37	-3	03-87	2.00	2.4	4	952	42	05-22-87	.5	1.00	.5	2.40	1.2	26	.9	3,628	43,972	29,449	-0	1.7	12
Info International o	23.5	14.8	13.3	2.5f	1.03	-41.2	368.2	368.2	-8	8	04-87	.22	1.6	3	19	23	07-09-87	7.4	1.08	8.0	1.35	10.8	0	3.5	33	2,417	750	+3	0.0	04
Infotron Syst	-13.6	-13.6	6.8	-5.7q	-1.13	-100.0	-100.0	-100.0	NC	-10	03-87	.00	.0	0	0	0	00-00-00	-7.3	.86	-6.2	1.53	-9.5	1	1.7	50	5,128	2,878	0	0.0	12
Intelligent Sys	-368.7	-64.6	.0	.0	.50	-100.0	NC	NC	NC	0	03-87	.00	.0	0	0	0	03-07-83	NC	NC	NC	NC	.0	0	1.9	78	11,286	2,170	0	0.0	12
Intergraph Cp	-12.6	-12.6	4.0	62.4q	1.12	-43.8	-43.8	-13.2	46	13	03-87	.00	.0	0	0	0	06-17-85	10.6	.96	10.2	1.24	12.6	3	4.4	1,259	55,957	27,580	+3	0.0	12
Intermec Cp	78.4	46.2	46.5	3.8f	.65	100.0	132.1	132.1	17	11	03-87	.00	.0	0	0	0	03-09-83	6.0	1.45	8.7	1.31	11.4	0	3.6	84	5,629	2,035	+0	0.0	03
Intl Bus Mach	5.5	5.5	2.7	4557.0q	7.46	-21.2	-21.2	-30.3	5	5	03-87	4.40	2.7	6	56	44	05-07-87	8.8	.90	7.9	1.68	13.3	12	2.2	98,462	605,923	292,155	-2	0.7	12
Iomega Cp	-52.6	-52.6	-14.9	-15.7q	-1.03	-100.0	-100.0	-100.0	NC	-27	03-87	.00	.0	0	0	0	00-00-00	-14.5	1.14	-16.5	1.66	-27.4	13	2.1	57	15,197	2,436	0	0.0	12
ISC Systems	5.8	-1.1	25.9	8.3n	.51	-70.8	-60.9	-40.7	11	9	03-87	.00	.0	0	0	0	06-18-81	5.0	1.08	5.4	1.63	8.8	22	3.2	143	16,087	5,354	0	0.0	06
Kaypro Cp	41.2	70.4	54.5	3.0s	.09	-50.0	NE	NE	NC	12	02-87	.00	.0	0	0	0	00-00-00	2.9	2.28	6.6	1.88	12.4	28	2.5	84	36,140	364	0	0.0	08
Key Tronic •	-4.8	-7.2	-1.8	-2.7n	-.31	-28.6	-100.0	NC	NC	-4	03-87	.00	.0	0	0	0	00-00-00	-2.5	1.24	-3.1	1.32	-4.1	5	3.4	70	8,793	3,099	-40	0.0	06
Lee Data	24.0	23.0	23.6	5.6f	.39	NE	160.0	160.0	-11	6	03-87	.00	.0	0	0	0	00-00-00	4.9	.98	4.8	1.31	6.3	0	4.5	92	14,226	2,858	0	0.0	03
LSI Logic	21.4	21.4	32.4	3.3q	.08	-28.6	-28.6	-72.4	NC	1	03-87	.00	.0	0	0	0	03-17-86	1.6	.44	.7	1.86	1.3	43	8.7	403	39,343	15,963	0	0.0	12
LTX	28.1	22.2	15.6	-9.2n	-.98	NE	NE	NE	NC	-16	04-87	.00	.0	0	0	0	03-22-83	-8.3	.96	-8.0	1.96	-15.7	67	4.5	152	9,351	3,792	+0	0.0	07
Machine Vision	-65.0	-68.5	-66.6	-13.6f	-1.25	NE	NE	NE	NC	0	12-86	.00	.0	0	0	0	00-00-00	NM	NC	NC	NC	NS	-61	.3	9	8,214	535	0	0.0	12
Masstor Sys	91.8	91.8	80.9	1.1q	.07	NE	NE	NE	NC	5	03-87	.00	.0	0	0	0	00-00-00	2.9	1.17	3.4	1.47	5.0	16	3.9	69	16,091	2,628	0	0.0	12
Maxtor Cp	103.4	105.8	105.8	22.4f	1.18	142.9	107.0	107.0	NC	52	03-87	.00	.0	0	0	0	06-13-86	12.8	2.85	36.5	1.42	51.7	8	3.4	348	18,058	10,462	-194	0.0	03
Micom Syst	11.1	3.8	3.6	12.2f	.70	166.7	14.8	14.8	-1	8	03-87	.00	.0	0	0	0	03-14-83	6.2	1.05	6.5	1.18	7.7	4	5.3	221	17,339	8,622	-30	0.0	03
Micropolis Cp	21.9	21.9	72.3	20.7q	1.87	37.5	37.5	152.7	118	19	03-87	.00	.0	0	0	0	00-00-00	9.2	1.70	15.6	1.20	18.7	0	4.9	397	11,231	5,008	-66	0.0	12
Miniscribe Cp	52.4	52.4	58.4	24.1q	.58	14.3	14.3	NE	NC	36	03-87	.00	.0	0	0	0	00-00-00	11.7	1.50	17.6	2.07	36.4	36	2.2	383	23,209	8,478	-57	0.0	12
Mohawk Data	-67.9	-64.2	-64.2	4.8f	.30	-18.2	NE	NE	NC	0	04-87	.00	.0	0	0	0	00-00-00	5.5	1.76	9.7	.00	NS	-34	NA	55	15,104	1,054	0	0.5	04
MSI Data	28.0	13.1	12.6	1.3f	.51	108.3	628.6	628.6	NC	5	03-87	.00	.0	0	0	37	11-16-84	1.8	1.67	3.0	1.60	4.8	10	2.8	46	2,528	641	0	0.0	03
Natl Compt Sys	-.5	-.5	13.4	14.9q	.78	-30.0	-30.0	-16.1	32	10	04-87	.20	1.4	22	18	19	06-08-87	5.7	1.05	6.0	2.13	12.8	66	1.8	264	18,995	8,877	+3	0.0	01
Natl Micronetics o	-2.9	-19.6	-9.7	-5.1n	-.58	NE	NE	NE	NC	-51	03-87	.00	.0	0	0	0	07-01-83	-13.8	1.05	-14.5	3.48	-50.5	50	.9	37	9,338	651	-2	0.0	06
NBI Inc	2.5	1.1	4.0	-8.3n	-.93	NE	NE	-100.0	NC	-8	03-87	.00	.0	0	0	0	03-10-81	-2.9	1.28	-3.7	2.11	-7.8	54	2.5	117	9,728	3,955	0	4.8	06
NCR	16.7	16.7	13.6	347.8q	3.56	27.5	27.5	10.2	12	10	03-87	1.00	1.3	12	27	26	06-08-87	6.9	1.26	8.7	1.67	14.5	5	2.0	7,002	93,984	61,281	+2	1.0	12
Netwk Systems	-15.4	-15.4	11.7	16.0q	.55	-63.6	-63.6	-5.2	31	9	03-87	.00	.0	0	0	0	04-16-85	15.2	.55	8.3	1.13	9.4	2	9.9	286	28,957	17,013	-200	0.0	12
Norsk Data	62.1	39.8	40.0	13.4f	1.74	-36.8	-36.3	-36.3	NC	8	12-86	.15	NA	0	8	5	05-14-86	3.8	.58	2.2	3.82	8.4	86	1.7	621	18,672	8,164	0	0.0	12
Novell Inc	193.8	152.1	146.1	14.8s	.61	111.1	84.2	90.6	NC	0	04-87	.00	.0	0	0	0	04-14-87	11.6	8.23	95.5	.00	NM	18	1.5	444	22,506	6,808	0	0.0	10
Par Tech Cp	-3.2	-3.2	1.4	5.1q	.55	-50.0	-50.0	-33.7	11	11	03-87	.00	.0	0	0	0	00-00-00	7.1	1.24	8.8	1.25	11.0	0	4.4	93	7,725	1,072	0	0.0	12
Priam Cp •	.0	-5.8	-1.6	-43.1n	-1.80	-92.3	-100.0	NE	NC	-55	03-87	.00	.0	0	0	0	00-00-00	-35.0	1.16	-40.5	1.35	-54.8	7	3.2	110	23,852	4,764	-70	0.0	06
Prime Computer	12.7	12.7	11.8	49.5q	1.02	26.3	26.3	-10.5	5	11	03-87	.00	.0	0	0	0	06-13-83	5.6	1.29	7.2	1.57	11.3	3	2.9	1,271	48,172	28,919	-858	2.3	12
Printronix	-11.7	-6.2	-6.0	-4.9f	-1.08	-100.0	NE	NE	NC	-7	03-87	.00	.0	0	0	0	00-00-00	-4.0	1.35	-5.4	1.35	-7.3	0	3.4	55	4,534	1,514	+0	0.0	03

QMS Inc	59.9	59.9	60.7	7.7q	.82	12.5	12.5	30.2	35	17	12-86	.00	.0	0	0	0	09-17-84	9.4	1.01	9.5	1.75	16.6	31	2.9	156	9,429	1,725	0	5.6	09
Quantum Cp	15.6	-.3	.0	8.8f	.95	-54.9	-58.7	-58.7	82	8	03-87	.00	.0	0	0	0	00-00-00	7.3	.96	7.0	1.19	8.3	0	8.2	145	8,962	4,480	+7	0.0	03
Recog Equip	14.4	11.8	27.5	10.6s	1.05	44.4	46.9	144.2	NC	9	04-87	.00	.0	0	0	0	00-00-00	4.2	1.10	4.6	1.98	9.1	48	2.9	195	9,818	4,327	-1	3.9	10
SCI Systs Inc	26.2	12.7	3.6	15.2n	.74	18.8	15.6	7.2	25	13	03-87	.00	.0	0	0	0	06-16-87	3.0	1.87	5.6	2.38	13.3	69	2.9	404	20,716	6,841	0	0.0	06
Seagate Tech	110.3	122.4	117.9	119.0n	2.41	224.0	444.7	517.9	36	57	03-87	.00	.0	0	0	0	06-10-83	14.0	2.79	39.0	1.46	57.1	7	2.7	1,609	47,314	28,999	-565	0.0	06
Sigma Designs	159.5	159.5	169.2	3.4q	.74	73.3	73.3	105.6	NC	35	04-87	.00	.0	0	0	0	03-11-87	9.7	2.21	21.4	1.65	35.4	0	2.5	55	4,250	1,152	0	0.0	01
Storage Technl	11.8	11.8	6.2	23.8q	.69	262.5	262.5	NE	NC	0	03-87	.00	.0	0	0	0	00-00-00	3.3	.82	2.7	.00	NS	-2847	NA	126	34,764	1,442	0	23.4	12
Stratus Cptr	39.0	39.0	46.7	14.1q	.73	18.8	18.8	37.7	NC	19	03-87	.00	.0	0	0	0	00-00-00	10.4	1.27	13.2	1.41	18.6	8	3.2	632	18,582	8,913	-62	0.0	12
System Indus	11.6	17.6	19.3	4.6n	1.01	31.8	78.6	1162.5	NC	18	04-87	.00	.0	0	0	0	06-24-81	3.9	1.85	7.2	2.50	18.0	26	1.6	42	4,267	1,752	+2	0.0	07
System Integ	-15.5	-4.5	9.8	8.3s	.70	-76.2	-41.7	-4.1	34	13	03-87	.00	.0	0	0	0	00-00-00	12.4	.77	9.5	1.39	13.2	0	3.5	106	11,964	2,058	0	0.0	09
Tab Products	8.9	3.4	5.0	6.7n	.99	22.7	24.6	28.6	12	11	02-87	.20	1.1	34	27	15	05-18-87	5.4	1.98	10.7	1.33	14.2	2	3.2	120	6,652	2,040	0	2.1	05
Tandem Cptr	37.5	38.7	35.8	89.2s	.96	64.3	85.7	118.2	16	17	03-87	.00	.0	0	0	0	06-15-87	9.9	1.28	12.7	1.31	16.7	1	3.9	2,835	89,630	67,858	+14	0.5	09
Tandon Cp	38.4	48.1	18.8	-58.9s	-1.17	150.0	140.0	NE	NC	0	03-87	.00	.0	0	0	0	04-13-83	-22.2	1.88	-41.8	.00	NM	12	1.4	276	52,608	5,020	0	0.0	09
TEC Inc	-24.1	-18.8	-26.6	.2n	.20	NE	NE	NE	NC	4	03-87	.00	.0	0	NE	NE	09-08-86	1.8	1.50	2.7	1.56	4.2	15	1.7	4	856	9	0	0.0	06
TeleVideo Sys	.5	3.7	-1.0	-1.9s	-.04	NC	100.0	NE	NC	-2	04-87	.00	.0	0	0	0	00-00-00	-2.0	.65	-1.3	1.23	-1.6	0	4.3	115	41,988	1,610	0	0.0	10
Telex Corp	12.0	18.5	18.6	77.9f	5.28	30.9	14.8	14.8	41	29	03-87	.00	.0	0	0	0	00-00-00	9.3	1.56	14.5	1.99	28.8	38	NA	1,035	14,623	10,124	0	3.2	03
Telxon Cp	117.6	42.0	42.2	12.3f	.91	17.4	46.8	46.8	42	18	03-87	.01	.0	0	1	2	05-13-86	12.2	1.11	13.5	1.31	17.7	1	4.0	323	12,919	7,447	-3	0.0	03
Three Com	79.9	76.1	66.1	10.1n	.71	69.2	69.7	61.4	NC	31	02-87	.00	.0	0	0	0	00-00-00	10.3	2.35	24.2	1.28	30.9	2	4.6	264	13,897	7,135	0	0.0	05
Titan Cp	13.4	13.4	21.3	1.3q	.01	-50.0	-50.0	NE	NC	3	03-87	.00	.0	0	0	0	00-00-00	1.0	1.60	1.6	1.81	2.9	19	3.2	76	12,628	2,417	0	0.5	12
TRW Inc	13.7	13.7	4.4	205.9q	3.42	-20.2	-20.2	2180.0	NC	9	03-87	1.60	3.0	5	42	59	06-02-87	3.3	1.61	5.3	3.25	17.2	66	1.3	3,100	58,914	35,728	-8	1.3	12
Ultimate Cp	16.0	21.2	21.4	13.8f	1.43	-15.1	-15.9	-15.9	38	16	04-87	.00	.0	0	0	0	09-16-83	8.1	.95	7.7	2.01	15.5	6	2.1	262	9,811	3,774	-39	8.7	04
Ungermann Bass	19.5	19.5	34.8	.4q	.02	40.0	40.0	-93.3	NC	1	03-87	.00	.0	0	0	0	00-00-00	.3	1.00	.3	2.00	.6	76	4.1	218	17,239	8,265	-150	0.0	12
Unisys Cp	113.0	113.0	74.0	50.8q	-.27	388.6	388.6	-100.0	NC	24	03-87	2.76	2.2	0	NE	81	06-30-87	.6	.83	.5	4.20	2.1	93	1.4	5,644	45,797	32,241	0	3.2	12
Valid Logic	-23.1	-23.1	5.4	-26.2q	-1.93	-100.0	-100.0	-100.0	NC	-57	03-87	.00	.0	0	0	0	00-00-00	-45.2	.85	-38.3	1.50	-57.3	8	2.7	66	13,543	4,678	-30	0.0	12
Vermont Resch	20.0	27.3	.0	-2.5s	-1.25	NE	NE	NE	NC	-38	03-87	.00	.0	0	0	NE	12-02-82	-50.0	.63	-31.3	1.21	-37.9	0	4.2	14	1,953	153	0	0.0	09
Vermitron Corp ◦	-24.3	-24.3	-33.3	-3.6q	-.60	450.0	450.0	NE	NC	-6	03-87	.00	.0	13	NE	40	09-09-86	-4.2	.74	-3.1	1.97	-6.1	41	2.5	63	6,187	1,080	0	0.0	12
Wang Labs	8.8	4.5	6.5	-101.9n	-.65	-73.3	-100.0	NE	NC	-9	03-87	.16	1.0	19	34	14	06-23-87	-3.7	1.03	-3.8	1.84	-7.0	45	2.2	2,558	161,124	67,816	-17	1.0	06
Wells American ◦	.0	983.3	600.0	-1.0n	-.20	NC	NE	NE	NC	-15	12-86	.00	.0	0	0	0	00-00-00	-14.3	.80	-11.5	1.26	-14.5	4	4.6	14	4,767	284	0	21.5	03
Wespercorp	320.0	-38.0	-58.3	-2.7n	-1.32	-100.0	NE	NE	NC	0	03-87	.00	.0	0	0	NE	01-26-83	-27.0	2.17	-58.7	.00	NS	0	.7	1	2,075	34	0	1.3	06
Wicat Systs	-22.7	-28.9	-28.2	-11.6f	-.55	-100.0	-100.0	-100.0	NC	-26	03-87	.00	.0	0	0	0	00-00-00	-41.4	.47	-19.6	1.33	-26.1	0	3.7	63	21,048	1,696	0	0.0	03
Wyse Technology	87.3	56.3	56.6	18.1f	1.50	36.7	25.0	25.0	NC	25	03-87	.00	.0	0	0	0	00-00-00	7.0	2.40	16.8	1.49	25.1	6	3.6	332	11,870	6,565	-10	0.0	03
Xebec	-5.0	-4.0	-1.7	-2.8s	-.21	NE	NE	NE	NC	-6	03-87	.00	.0	0	0	0	07-11-83	-2.5	1.28	-3.2	1.72	-5.5	12	1.7	12	13,210	408	-130	0.0	09
Zentec	47.8	47.8	76.4	1.6q	.43	-66.7	-66.7	NE	NC	21	03-87	.00	.0	0	0	0	00-00-00	5.3	1.38	7.3	2.85	20.8	0	3.3	16	3,470	431	0	0.0	12
Zycad Cp	117.6	117.6	12.0	-14.9q	-.97	NE	NE	NE	NC	-52	03-87	.00	.0	0	0	0	00-00-00	-53.2	.56	-29.9	1.74	-51.9	25	2.8	59	10,796	914	0	0.0	12

Value of New Construction Put in Place

(in billions of 1982 dollars except as noted)

Type of Construction	1977	1982	1983	1984	1985	1986[1]	1987[2]	Percent Change 1985-86	Percent Change 1986-87
Total New Construction	294.3	244.4	272.0	308.0	324.9	340.6	343.2	4.8	0.8
Residential	149.1	85.4	123.1	146.1	146.3	161.4	167.1	10	4
Single-family	100.2	41.5	70.2	80.6	79.4	89.7	95.1	13	6
Multi-family	16.9	16.2	22.9	27.8	27.5	28.3	26.1	3	−8
Home Improvement	32.0	27.7	30.0	37.6	39.4	43.3	45.9	10	6
Private Nonresidential	87.0	108.1	98.5	109.0	121.6	117.4	112.9	−3	−4
Manufacturing facilities	12.2	17.3	12.4	12.9	14.2	12.8	14.1	−10	10
Office	8.4	23.0	20.0	23.9	28.3	26.3	22.4	−7	−15
Hotels & Motels	1.5	4.1	5.0	6.2	6.6	6.9	6.5	4	−5
Other Commercial	15.1	14.2	14.5	20.4	25.2	25.2	24.7	0	−2
Religious	1.7	1.5	1.7	2.0	2.2	2.3	2.3	4	0
Educational	1.1	1.5	1.5	1.5	1.7	1.9	2.0	10	5
Hospital & Institutional	5.2	5.9	6.3	5.8	5.0	4.9	4.8	−2	−2
Misc. buildings	1.9	1.7	1.8	2.3	2.4	2.3	2.3	−4	0
Telephone & telegraph	6.3	7.1	6.3	6.8	7.0	7.5	7.9	7	5
Railroads	2.0	2.6	3.0	3.4	3.4	3.1	3.2	−8	2
Electric utilities	17.1	18.3	17.4	14.8	15.4	14.2	12.8	−8	−10
Gas utilities	3.8	5.5	3.7	4.2	5.3	5.4	5.5	2	2
Petroleum pipelines	1.8	0.4	0.5	0.3	0.3	0.3	0.3	0	10
Farm structures	7.0	3.7	3.1	2.6	2.1	1.9	1.7	−10	−10
Misc. structures	1.7	1.3	1.5	1.9	2.5	2.5	2.5	0	3
Public Works	58.2	50.9	50.3	52.9	57.0	61.8	63.2	8	2
Housing & redevelopment	1.5	1.7	1.7	1.5	1.4	1.3	1.3	−5	0
Federal industrial	1.3	1.6	1.7	1.7	1.8	1.7	1.6	−5	−6
Educational	8.7	5.9	5.2	5.1	6.0	6.6	6.9	10	5
Hospital	2.8	2.0	2.0	1.9	1.8	1.8	1.8	0	−2
Other public buildings	5.8	5.8	6.1	6.3	7.2	8.1	8.4	12	4
Highways	14.3	13.4	14.4	16.0	17.5	18.9	19.5	8	3
Military facilities	2.2	2.2	2.5	2.7	2.9	3.1	3.0	7	−4
Conservation & development	5.8	5.0	4.8	4.5	4.8	4.4	4.5	−8	2
Sewer systems	8.0	5.5	5.3	6.1	6.9	7.8	8.0	13	3
Water supplies	2.7	2.9	2.1	2.6	2.6	3.1	3.3	20	5
Misc. public structures	5.3	4.9	4.6	4.5	4.1	4.9	4.9	20	3

[1]Estimated.
[2]Forecast.
[3]Value for this category not estimated separately, but included in totals.

SOURCE: U.S. Department of Commerce; Bureau of the Census and International Trade Administration (ITA). Estimates and forecasts by ITA.

Source: *U.S. Industrial Outlook 1987,* U.S. Department of Commerce.

Company	Revenue			Earnings								Dividends						Ratio Analysis							Shareholdings					
	Pct. Change				Per Share							Current Rate			Payout															
	Last Qtr	FY to Date	Last 12 Mos	Last 12 Mos	Last 12 Mos	Pct. Change Last Qtr	Pct. Change FY to Date	Pct. Change Last 12 Mos	5-Year Growth Rate	Par Growth Rate	Date of Report	Amt	Yield	5-Year Growth Rate	Last FY	Last 5 Yrs.	Last X-Dvd Date	Profit Margin	Asset Turnover	Return on Total Assets	Leverage Ratio	Return on Equity	Debt to Equity	Current Ratio	Market Value	Latest Shares Outstndng.	Held by Banks-Funds	Insider Net Trading	Short Interest Ratio	Fiscal Year Ends
-	%	%	%	$Mil	$	%	%	%	%	%	-	$	%	%	%	%	-	π/r	x r/a =	π/a	x a/e =	π/e	%	-	$Mil	000	000	000	Days	Mo
Residential Construction																														
Ind. Group	9.5	40.8	14.9	381.0	1.12	- 26.8	- 2.4	7.6	46	8	- - -	.44	2.8	0	18	22	- - - -	4.0	.73	2.9	4.41	12.8	119	2.8	5,128	323,500	74,578	- 44	4.6	- -
Am Continental	5.0	5.0	21.7	31.1q	1.38	8.0	8.0	-27.4	60	35	03-87	.00	.0	0	5	1	05-11-87	3.6	.19	.7	50.29	35.2	1405	NA	161	18,132	760	0	0.0	12
Anthony Ind	13.1	13.1	6.2	1.9q	.44	.0	.0	-43.6	1	0	03-87	.44	3.1	6	84	38	05-26-87	.8	1.88	1.5	2.87	4.3	66	2.1	62	4,332	1,936	0	45.0	12
Calprop Cp	-20.3	-20.3	100.0	2.5q	.75	-91.7	-91.7	4.2	21	8	03-87	.00	.0	0	0	0	11-17-86	6.9	.86	5.9	1.42	8.4	17	NA	29	3,439	467	0	0.9	12
Calton Inc	-33.3	-33.3	20.0	13.9q	.82	60.0	60.0	-28.1	NC	25	02-87	.00	.0	0	0	0	00-00-00	9.7	.78	7.6	3.34	25.4	157	NA	165	18,298	1,833	0	0.0	11
Centex Cp	-15.2	-8.6	-8.6	44.2f	2.47	-36.1	-5.7	-5.7	NC	11	03-87	.25	.9	0	0	8	06-09-87	3.4	1.29	4.4	2.77	12.2	35	.0	476	17,779	10,176	0	0.3	03
Gen Homes	-48.8	-34.9	.7	3.1s	.21	-100.0	-100.0	-80.2	1	2	03-87	.00	.0	0	0	0	00-00-00	.8	.63	.5	4.00	2.0	96	NA	98	15,009	757	-1	0.2	09
Hovnanian Ent	4.9	24.8	24.7	18.5f	.88	81.8	51.7	51.7	48	27	02-87	.00	.0	0	0	0	04-14-87	6.4	1.03	6.6	4.08	26.9	70	NA	319	21,250	3,492	0	2.9	02
Kauf Broad Ho	71.7	53.3	42.2	31.7s	1.21	71.4	46.4	NC	NC	17	05-87	.20	1.7	0	5	2	05-22-87	5.4	1.33	7.2	2.83	20.4	91	NA	317	27,000	295	0	14.9	11
Key Company	-10.0	-3.3	17.9	.2s	.08	-100.0	-100.0	-73.3	-14	-3	04-87	.20	5.2	13	64	31	06-22-87	.4	2.00	.8	2.38	1.9	0	1.5	4	1,128	51	-1	0.0	10
Lennar Corp	45.7	45.7	7.0	15.1q	1.74	155.0	155.0	58.2	8	9	02-87	.24	.9	0	14	21	08-03-87	6.2	.73	4.5	2.22	10.0	10	NA	230	8,684	2,361	-7	1.2	11
Levitt Cp	58.3	58.3	40.5	2.2q	.65	166.7	166.7	54.8	NC	9	03-87	.00	.0	0	0	0	00-00-00	2.3	.87	2.0	4.45	8.9	254	.0	30	3,390	154	0	0.3	12
Natl Enterpr ◇ ◆	14.6	14.6	26.4	1.8q	.05	NE	NE	-50.0	NC	8	03-87	.00	.0	0	0	0	00-00-00	2.1	1.38	2.8	2.89	8.1	100	2.6	26	7,130	437	0	1.6	12
NVRyan	787.1	787.1	222.0	15.4q	1.53	NE	NE	264.3	NC	33	03-87	.37	3.8	0	0	0	05-01-87	4.1	.68	2.8	15.68	43.9	550	3.2	194	20,200	222	0	0.2	12
Oriole Homes	55.5	55.5	31.5	3.0q	.77	90.9	90.9	-3.8	-1	5	03-87	.25	2.7	-23	22	77	03-16-87	3.0	.73	2.2	3.23	7.1	90	NA	18	1,957	154	-13	24.4	12
Ryland Grp	45.1	45.1	33.7	29.6q	2.29	135.0	135.0	63.6	46	23	03-87	.40	1.8	17	18	25	07-09-87	4.1	1.88	7.7	3.69	28.4	129	3.6	282	12,547	7,417	-20	0.4	12
Std Pacific	17.3	17.3	556.2	27.1q	1.00	-44.0	-44.0	NC	NC	-15	03-87	1.80	14.1	0	22	22	05-13-87	8.6	1.01	8.7	2.20	19.1	72	3.5	335	26,268	7,536	0	0.7	12
Toll Bros	22.0	22.2	193.4	14.3s	.52	71.4	64.3	NC	NC	46	04-87	.00	.0	0	0	0	04-21-87	10.6	1.25	13.2	3.45	45.5	0	1.5	274	29,993	4,290	0	1.4	10
US Home	-2.5	-2.5	-14.5	-76.5q	-1.92	NE	NE	NE	NC	-35	03-87	.00	.0	0	0	NE	08-27-84	-10.0	1.05	-10.5	3.30	-34.6	69	NA	209	39,813	5,776	0	0.4	12
UDC Univ Dev	28.5	28.5	55.0	30.9q	2.76	-25.9	-25.9	29.6	64	7	03-87	2.20	11.1	0	80	60	03-10-87	14.2	1.02	14.5	2.52	36.6	121	NA	210	10,655	2,139	0	0.5	12
Walter, Jim	-2.6	.8	2.0	162.7n	4.37	-54.3	-8.9	-1.6	62	10	05-87	1.40	2.7	4	26	29	06-09-87	6.8	.84	5.7	2.53	14.4	77	NA	1,647	31,750	22,769	-2	1.2	08
Wash Homes	6.0	5.7	16.2	8.3n	1.65	-16.3	.0	16.2	NC	30	04-87	.00	.0	0	0	0	02-17-87	9.7	1.33	12.9	2.33	30.1	57	NA	43	4,746	1,556	0	0.0	07

Company	Revenue: Pct. Change Last Qtr	Revenue: Pct. Change FY to Date	Revenue: Pct. Change Last 12 Mos	Earnings: Last 12 Mos	Earnings Per Share: Last 12 Mos	Per Share Pct. Change: Last Qtr	Per Share Pct. Change: FY to Date	Per Share Pct. Change: Last 12 Mos	5-Year Growth Rate	Par Growth Rate	Date of Report	Dividends Current Rate: Amt	Current Rate: Yield	5-Year Growth Rate	Payout: Last FY	Payout: Last 5 Yrs.	Last X-Dvd Date	Profit Margin	Asset Turnover	Return on Total Assets	Leverage Ratio	Return on Equity	Debt to Equity	Current Ratio	Market Value	Latest Shares Outstndng.	Held by Banks-Funds	Insider Net Trading	Short Interest Ratio	Fiscal Year Ends
-	%	%	%	$Mil	$	%	%	%	%	%	-	$	%	%	%	%	-	π/r x	r/a =	π/a x	a/e =	π/e	%	-	$Mil	000	000	000	Days	Mo
General Contractors																														
Ind. Group	- 23.9	- 17.7	- 5.4	- 17.0	.05	- 100.0	- 100.0	NE	NC	3	- - -	.33	1.6	0	72	59	- - - -	- .1	2.00	- .2	3.00	- .6	42	1.4	3,955	185,782	76,765	- 33	.9	- -
Am Med Bldg	78.7	78.7	73.6	-.8q	-.22	NE	NE	NE	NC	0	03-87	.00	.0	0	0	0	07-20-83	-2.4	3.88	-9.3	.00	NS	-7	1.2	28	7,939	1,008	0	0.2	12
Blount Inc	18.9	18.9	13.3	9.2q	.77	1700.0	1700.0	NE	-19	3	05-87	.45	2.8	16	73	31	06-09-87	.7	1.86	1.3	5.00	6.5	123	1.1	113	7,068	3,218	0	2.7	02
Dravo Corp	12.1	12.1	-14.8	-16.6q	-1.19	NE	NE	-100.0	NC	-11	03-87	.50	2.4	-13	NE	NE	04-28-87	-2.3	1.43	-3.3	2.39	-7.9	22	1.9	297	14,152	7,727	+1	0.3	12
Dyncorp ■	23.3	23.3	19.0	14.0q	1.33	63.6	63.6	232.5	-12	8	03-87	.31	1.7	18	21	23	03-13-87	1.8	2.61	4.7	2.32	10.9	5	1.6	192	10,760	3,185	0	0.6	12
Fluor Corp	-28.4	-23.5	-12.6	-141.3s	-1.37	NE	NE	NE	NC	-15	04-87	.00	.0	-15	NE	NE	12-18-86	-3.5	1.57	-5.5	2.71	-14.9	55	1.4	1,397	79,259	34,805	+1	1.0	10
Foster Wheeler	-4.4	-4.4	-.8	31.1q	.90	40.9	40.9	25.0	-16	4	03-87	.44	2.2	0	54	39	05-11-87	2.5	1.12	2.8	2.57	7.2	45	1.6	699	34,509	17,720	-38	1.7	12
Jacobs Eng	51.6	48.1	22.4	1.3s	.30	266.7	76.9	-18.9	NC	5	03-87	.00	.0	0	0	NE	11-15-83	.5	3.40	1.7	2.82	4.8	3	1.2	43	4,273	428	0	0.0	09
Morrison Knuds	-3.5	-3.5	-2.5	36.9q	3.36	-32.4	-32.4	-13.4	-1	5	03-87	1.48	3.0	6	41	36	05-05-87	1.8	2.11	3.8	2.29	8.7	16	1.6	524	10,660	6,650	+3	1.8	12
Seligman&Assc	-57.1	-79.3	-68.7	1.2n	.66	-47.6	-37.7	-28.3	31	12	04-87	.00	.0	0	0	0	00-00-00	24.0	.30	7.3	1.67	12.2	41	.0	12	1,785	55	0	0.0	07
Stone & Web	14.1	14.1	3.3	36.4q	4.92	134.4	134.4	17.4	-4	8	03-87	1.60	2.3	-1	39	36	06-25-87	13.0	.53	6.9	1.72	11.9	7	1.8	508	7,424	1,192	0	0.4	12
Turner Cp	-96.7	-96.7	-12.8	9.1q	2.17	-58.5	-58.5	-12.1	-1	5	03-87	1.30	5.0	12	54	40	05-18-87	.5	2.00	1.0	12.70	12.7	58	1.0	104	3,986	650	0	1.0	12
Union Valley	28.1	28.1	17.7	2.5q	.70	45.5	45.5	NC	NC	22	03-87	.00	.0	0	0	0	00-00-00	3.4	.88	3.0	7.37	22.1	527	NA	38	3,967	127	0	1.4	12
Other Building - Heavy																														
Ind. Group	- 7.8	2.1	1.4	133.3	.91	- 100.0	161.8	NE	- 22	3	- - -	.51	3.5	1	86	59	- - - -	1.9	1.05	2.0	3.60	7.2	73	1.3	2,089	144,498	34,914	+ 19	2.0	- -
ACMAT Corp ◇	2.3	2.3	-15.0	1.6q	1.13	661.5	661.5	NE	NC	39	03-87	.00	.0	0	0	0	00-00-00	9.4	.91	8.6	4.53	39.0	117	1.4	29	1,030	67	0	0.0	12
Am Ship Bldg	-71.7	-80.5	-77.9	-5.7s	-.95	-100.0	-100.0	-100.0	NC	-18	03-87	.40	6.0	-2	145	206	05-04-87	-16.8	.34	-5.7	2.23	-12.7	40	1.9	40	5,988	1,010	+2	2.2	09
Banister Contl	89.3	89.3	41.1	8.6q	1.71	NE	NE	5600.0	NC	15	03-87	.00	NA	0	0	35	09-17-79	6.0	1.55	9.3	1.58	14.7	2	1.8	50	5,038	376	+15	0.0	12
Bk Bldg Equip	-31.0	-32.5	-33.6	-1.6s	-.94	-100.0	-100.0	-100.0	NC	-22	04-87	.40	5.2	-18	571	NE	05-12-87	-2.1	2.71	-5.7	2.72	-15.5	10	1.4	13	1,650	203	0	0.0	10
Burnup & Sims Inc ◇	5.3	9.0	8.7	2.4n	.10	NE	NE	400.0	NC	3	01-87	.00	.0	0	0	24	08-03-81	1.2	1.17	1.4	2.21	3.1	63	1.8	106	15,961	1,732	0	0.0	04
Fischbach Cp	-5.2	1.3	20.1	-18.5s	-4.71	NE	NE	NE	NC	-14	03-87	.00	.0	0	0	74	08-19-85	-1.4	2.50	-3.5	4.00	-14.0	70	1.8	86	3,911	2,712	0	5.5	09
Goldfield Cp	-87.0	-87.0	-50.0	.0q	.00	NC	NC	NE	NC	NC	03-87	.00	.0	0	0	0	00-00-00	.0	NC	NC	NC	.0	24	3.7	20	26,329	763	0	2.1	12
Kasler Cp	2.9	-2.6	-27.2	-2.1s	-.42	NE	NE	NE	NC	-19	04-87	.00	.0	0	0	2129	06-25-85	-2.0	2.60	-5.2	3.62	-18.8	77	1.2	44	5,026	1,702	0	0.0	10
KDI Cp	8.2	8.2	12.3	7.6q	.80	200.0	200.0	-25.9	8	8	03-87	.30	1.8	0	40	20	05-27-87	2.5	2.00	5.0	2.52	12.6	57	2.0	155	9,437	724	+2	0.0	12
McDermott Intl	-1.6	2.1	.3	175.9n	4.75	-100.0	313.6	NE	-7	9	12-86	1.80	6.0	7	118	69	06-09-87	5.3	.75	4.0	3.65	14.6	76	1.0	1,108	37,077	20,402	0	7.4	03
McDowell Ent	-91.0	-83.5	-73.1	-4.1n	-1.65	NE	NE	NE	NC	-31	09-86	.00	.0	0	0	NE	08-31-81	-22.8	.49	-11.1	2.82	-31.3	5	1.1	11	2,452	158	0	2.9	12
Myers LE Grp	1.4	1.4	-30.0	-8.7q	-3.82	NE	NE	NE	NC	-45	03-87	.00	.0	0	0	NE	03-08-82	-13.8	1.59	-22.0	2.05	-45.1	41	3.3	16	2,261	37	0	0.0	12
Newberry Cp	-23.1	14.7	15.5	-8.6n	-4.71	NC	NE	-100.0	NC	0	12-86	.00	.0	0	0	NE	08-26-85	-9.7	2.37	-23.0	.00	NM	111	1.3	1	1,739	42	0	1.7	03
Std Shares	3.5	8.0	8.0	28.6f	10.90	194.8	47.1	47.1	1	24	02-87	.00	.0	0	37	75	09-27-79	4.6	1.33	6.1	3.98	24.3	25	1.9	270	2,626	876	-0	0.0	02
Tacoma Btbldg	-79.2	-79.2	-9.7	1.0q	.09	-83.3	-83.3	NE	NC	0	03-87	.00	.0	0	0	0	12-07-82	1.0	4.20	4.2	.00	NS	0	1.6	12	11,911	252	0	3.2	12
Todd Shipyards	-41.4	2.9	2.8	-44.1f	-10.90	-100.0	NE	NE	NC	-33	03-87	.00	.0	7	NE	138	01-09-87	-10.4	.86	-8.9	3.75	-33.4	112	1.8	41	4,194	2,178	0	1.8	03
Ultrasystems	-24.4	-24.4	-5.8	1.0q	.12	-52.9	-52.9	-87.6	-7	1	04-87	.08	.7	0	38	14	02-09-87	.7	1.43	1.0	2.30	2.3	69	2.8	89	7,868	1,680	0	7.5	01

Changes in Computer Equipment and Parts Trade by Principal Country

Country	Percent change	
	1984-85	1985-86 (3 mos.)
EXPORTS		
United States	+ 3.4	− 9.8
United Kingdom	+ 28.0	−15.8
Germany	+ 30.9	+ 3.9
France	+125.0	NA
Italy	+ 60.0	NA
Japan	+ 4.8	+ 0.2
IMPORTS		
United States	+ 5.8	+25.6
United Kingdom	+ 10.0	−17.0
Germany	+ 21.2	− 4.7
France	+ 68.0	NA
Italy	+ 46.0	NA
Japan	+ 15.3	−28.8

[1]Change shown is between first quarter 1985 and first quarter 1986.
SOURCE: Compiled by the U.S. Department of Commerce: Office of Computers and Business Equipment, from official trade statistics of each country.
NA = Not available.

Source: *U.S. Industrial Outlook 1987*, U.S. Department of Commerce.

Recent Performance and Forecast: Data Processing Services (SIC 7374)

Item	1984	1985[1]	1986[1]	1987[2]	Percent change: Compound Annual 1972-84	Compound Annual 1979-84	Annual 1984-85	Annual 1985-86	Annual 1986-87
Revenues (billion $)	14.9	17.3	19.5	22.0	15.7	15.7	16.1	12.7	12.8
Employment (000)	249	265	268	273	NA	9.7	6.4	1.1	1.9

[1]Estimated.
[2]Forecast.
NA = Not Available.

SOURCE: ADAPSO; INPUT; U.S. Department of Commerce: International Trade Administration (ITA); Bureau of Labor Statistics. Estimates and forecasts by ITA.

Source: *U.S. Industrial Outlook 1987*, U.S. Department of Commerce.

Company	Revenue: Pct. Change Last Qtr	Revenue: Pct. Change FY to Date	Revenue: Pct. Change Last 12 Mos	Earnings: Last 12 Mos	Earnings: Per Share Last 12 Mos	Earnings: Per Share Pct. Change Last Qtr	Earnings: Per Share Pct. Change FY to Date	Earnings: Per Share Pct. Change Last 12 Mos	Earnings: 5-Year Growth Rate	Earnings: Par Growth Rate	Earnings: Date of Report	Dividends: Current Rate Amt	Dividends: Current Rate Yield	Dividends: 5-Year Growth Rate	Dividends: Payout Last FY	Dividends: Payout Last 5 Yrs.	Dividends: Last X-Dvd Date	Ratio Analysis: Profit Margin	Ratio Analysis: Asset Turnover	Ratio Analysis: Return on Total Assets	Ratio Analysis: Leverage Ratio	Ratio Analysis: Return on Equity	Ratio Analysis: Debt to Equity	Ratio Analysis: Current Ratio	Shareholdings: Market Value	Shareholdings: Latest Shares Outstndng	Shareholdings: Held by Banks-Funds	Shareholdings: Insider Net Trading	Shareholdings: Short Interest Ratio	Shareholdings: Fiscal Year Ends
-	%	%	%	$Mil	$	%	%	%	%	%	-	$	%	%	%	%	-	r/r x	r/a =	r/a x	a/e =	r/e	%	-	$Mil	000	000	000	Days	Mo
Computer Software, Data Processing																														
Ind. Group	22.9	27.4	20.5	467.5	.53	1.7	- 13.9	- 6.2	32	9	- - -	.11	.5	1	10	11	- - - -	5.5	1.18	6.5	1.82	11.8	27	2.4	19,399	885,439	338,458	-1050	.9	- -
AGS Cptr	39.3	39.3	39.8	9.9q	.98	86.7	86.7	44.1	22	19	03-87	.00	.0	0	0	0	06-01-87	2.4	2.25	5.4	3.46	18.7	122	1.7	167	9,976	4,294	-100	15.7	12
Altos Cptr Syst	-234.7	200.8	195.7	12.4n	.89	-69.1	-51.0	-23.9	21	12	03-87	.00	.0	0	0	0	00-00-00	5.9	1.64	9.7	1.25	12.1	4	5.6	165	12,936	3,031	-45	0.0	06
Am Managemnt	28.3	28.3	25.2	5.4q	.53	22.2	22.2	32.5	NC	21	03-87	.00	.0	0	0	0	06-11-87	3.8	2.16	8.2	2.50	20.5	13	1.4	170	9,584	2,692	0	0.0	12
Anacomp Inc	16.3	5.6	-2.6	4.8s	.15	250.0	500.0	NE	NC	62	03-87	.00	.0	0	0	NE	07-14-83	4.3	1.16	5.0	12.46	62.3	788	1.1	286	32,679	5,062	0	8.7	09
Ashton Tate	46.1	46.1	65.4	34.1q	1.38	50.0	50.0	43.8	NC	28	04-87	.00	.0	0	0	0	01-13-87	14.8	1.32	19.5	1.43	27.9	4	2.9	586	23,909	16,264	+4	0.0	01
ASK Cptr Systs	44.3	35.4	34.2	7.5n	.57	18.2	35.5	16.3	17	10	03-87	.00	.0	0	0	0	00-00-00	8.0	.98	7.8	1.32	10.3	1	3.9	160	12,943	8,571	-20	0.0	06
Autodesk Inc	57.3	57.3	68.5	13.1q	.61	50.0	50.0	56.4	NC	62	04-87	.00	.0	0	0	0	03-30-87	22.2	2.39	53.0	1.17	61.8	1	7.4	516	20,436	7,988	0	0.0	01
Autom Data Pr	15.2	16.2	17.0	122.9n	1.66	20.9	20.4	18.6	15	14	03-87	.44	.9	12	23	25	06-15-87	9.1	1.03	9.4	1.97	18.5	47	2.8	3,675	76,973	51,152	-18	0.7	06
BPI Systs Inc	-57.1	-15.6	.0	-1.7n	-.32	-100.0	-100.0	-100.0	NC	-28	12-86	.00	.0	0	0	0	03-02-83	-17.0	.72	-12.3	2.30	-28.3	83	3.2	10	5,648	1,249	0	0.0	03
Chancellor Cptr	.0	-20.0	.0	-1.9f	-.15	NE	NE	NE	NC	0	12-86	.00	.0	0	0	0	00-00-00	NM	NC	NC	NC	NM	50	1.2	6	13,072	0	0	0.0	12
CMX Cp	19.2	12.2	22.2	.5n	.08	300.0	33.3	NE	NC	21	03-87	.00	.0	0	0	0	00-00-00	4.5	1.69	7.6	2.74	20.8	71	2.2	10	5,793	40	0	0.0	06
Comp Assoc	60.1	60.1	52.1	19.5q	.43	25.0	25.0	34.4	36	11	06-86	.00	.0	0	0	0	05-08-87	9.3	.86	8.0	1.39	11.1	3	2.6	1,231	48,996	31,220	0	1.7	03
Comp Factory	84.8	88.0	91.0	5.5s	.84	111.1	123.3	110.0	41	21	03-87	.00	.0	0	0	0	03-04-87	3.7	3.59	13.3	1.59	21.2	0	2.4	176	7,983	2,682	-4	0.0	09
Comp Horizons	21.3	16.3	18.0	2.2f	.83	.0	-3.5	-3.5	34	18	02-87	.00	.0	0	0	0	07-12-83	3.7	3.00	11.1	1.65	18.3	0	2.3	32	2,588	1,028	0	0.0	02
Comp Language	-.3	-.3	-3.1	-.6q	-.03	-13.5	-13.5	-100.0	NC	-7	03-87	.12	1.7	0	600	19	03-11-87	-.6	1.50	-.9	1.44	-1.3	8	2.2	94	13,620	639	0	0.0	12
Comp Sciences	22.7	23.0	23.0	32.2f	2.08	11.5	23.1	23.1	10	15	03-87	.00	.0	0	0	0	00-00-00	3.1	2.23	6.9	2.19	15.1	22	1.5	861	15,277	10,051	+8	1.0	03
Computrac	-13.0	-13.0	25.0	1.8q	.29	-62.5	-62.5	7.4	NC	11	04-87	.07	.8	0	0	0	12-29-87	18.0	.60	10.8	1.40	15.1	11	2.7	49	5,930	2,128	0	0.6	01
Comshare Inc	3.0	-.8	1.4	1.7n	.63	-48.4	34.9	18.9	NC	8	03-87	.00	.0	0	0	0	00-00-00	2.5	1.56	3.9	2.13	8.3	9	1.2	63	2,668	472	0	0.0	06
Continuum Co	26.8	10.4	9.4	3.2f	.75	NE	NE	NE	NC	35	03-87	.00	.0	-14	3	14	03-24-86	5.5	1.33	7.3	4.82	35.2	145	1.3	98	4,322	771	0	0.0	03
Cullinet Softwr ◆	21.4	-5.1	-4.8	-27.6f	-.86	-100.0	-100.0	-100.0	NC	-20	04-87	.00	.0	0	0	0	01-22-85	-15.8	.80	-12.7	1.54	-19.6	0	2.1	375	32,227	6,770	+12	0.5	04
Daisy Syst	5.8	-16.8	-23.6	-8.9s	-.50	NE	-100.0	-100.0	NC	-6	03-87	.00	.0	0	0	0	00-00-00	-9.2	.57	-5.2	1.13	-5.9	0	7.2	141	17,685	8,430	-58	0.0	09
Data I O	3.7	3.7	15.5	4.3q	.43	-16.7	-16.7	13.2	7	6	03-87	.00	.0	0	0	0	08-22-83	6.4	.83	5.3	1.13	6.0	0	5.9	91	10,076	3,445	0	0.0	12
DBA Systs	14.9	10.2	12.6	3.8n	1.13	-10.0	2.5	3.7	12	12	03-87	.00	.0	0	0	0	06-27-83	4.8	.96	4.6	2.61	12.0	123	7.3	52	3,238	957	0	0.0	06
Dicomed Cp	-15.7	-15.7	-9.0	-5.9q	-1.48	NE	NE	NE	NC	-34	03-87	.00	.0	0	0	0	05-31-83	-29.5	.67	-19.9	1.68	-33.5	38	3.4	7	3,953	503	0	0.0	12
DST Syst Inc	63.6	63.6	42.2	15.7q	1.63	131.6	131.6	106.3	14	17	03-87	.20	.5	0	14	9	06-09-87	15.5	.53	8.2	2.30	18.9	53	1.2	388	9,704	488	+4	0.0	12

Dyatron	12.2	12.2	-10.5	1.9q	.53	650.0	650.0	430.0	NC	21	03-87	.00	.0	0	0	0	03-16-81	5.6	2.04	11.4	1.87	21.3	12	1.2	25	4,717	306	0	0.0	12
Epsilon Data Mgmt	-14.6	-4.4	.0	-.9n	-.29	-100.0	NE	-100.0	NC	-7	02-87	.00	.0	0	0	0	00-00-00	-1.7	2.24	-3.8	1.92	-7.3	22	2.0	28	2,750	463	-5	0.0	05
Evans & Suth	16.7	16.7	29.8	12.2q	1.48	100.0	100.0	78.3	0	16	03-87	.00	.0	0	0	0	06-10-81	10.8	.91	9.8	1.62	15.9	7	2.0	263	8,105	4,356	-2	0.0	12
Fidata Cp	-93.2	-93.2	-68.5	-5.0q	-1.10	-100.0	-100.0	-100.0	NC	-10	03-87	.00	.0	0	0	0	08-31-81	-14.7	.50	-7.3	1.34	-9.8	0	NA	31	4,439	767	0	0.0	12
Gen Motors E	NA	NA	.0	NA	NA	NA	NA	NA	NA	NC	00-00	.46	1.2	NA	NA	NA	05-08-87	NA	NC	NA	NC	NA	NA	NA	2,439	63,774	15,949	+8	NA	NA
GTECH Corp	-9.6	59.3	60.0	7.7f	.81	NE	285.7	285.7	17	17	02-87	.00	.0	0	0	0	00-00-00	6.0	.75	4.5	3.71	16.7	157	1.3	209	9,512	2,530	-200	0.0	02
HBO Co	-15.4	-15.4	-21.6	-8.7q	-.37	-84.0	-84.0	-100.0	NC	-14	03-87	.10	.8	-3	NE	19	06-24-87	-5.9	1.14	-6.7	1.64	-11.0	7	2.0	285	23,028	6,033	0	0.0	12
Hogan Systs	86.1	63.3	62.9	9.5f	.37	NE	NE	NE	NC	39	03-87	.00	.0	0	0	0	12-05-83	21.6	1.00	21.5	1.83	39.3	0	1.7	182	13,740	4,696	0	0.0	03
IntelliCorp	1.8	10.6	17.6	1.2n	.20	-75.0	-100.0	11.1	NC	4	03-87	.00	.0	0	0	0	00-00-00	6.0	.55	3.3	1.15	3.8	0	5.3	57	6,970	1,475	-14	0.0	06
ISI Systs	NA	NA	.0	NA	NA	NA	NA	NA	NA	NC	00-00	.20	1.1	NA	NA	NA	07-06-87	NA	NC	NA	NC	NA	NA	NA	83	4,500	0	0	NA	NA
Kalvar Corp	17.0	4.0	5.0	.5f	.07	NC	NE	NE	NC	10	03-87	.00	.0	0	0	0	00-00-00	2.4	2.00	4.8	2.00	9.6	38	1.7	14	5,769	448	0	0.0	03
Kenilworth Systs	-60.0	-7.4	33.3	-1.7n	-.15	-100.0	-33.3	-100.0	NC	-19	09-86	.00	.0	0	0	0	00-00-00	-42.5	.32	-13.7	1.41	-19.3	14	3.4	12	19,823	123	0	0.0	12
Logicon Inc	.4	3.2	3.5	6.1f	1.27	-100.0	-39.5	-39.5	15	9	03-87	.28	1.1	25	20	13	06-11-87	3.0	2.50	7.5	1.55	11.6	0	2.6	119	4,735	2,082	0	9.4	03
Lotus Development	22.4	22.4	19.2	50.6q	1.11	34.8	34.8	37.0	NC	44	03-87	.00	.0	0	0	0	02-24-87	17.0	1.42	24.2	1.83	44.2	26	2.3	1,345	45,990	30,300	-450	0.0	12
MacNeal Sch	25.8	25.8	26.0	7.3q	.60	14.3	14.3	130.8	27	23	04-87	.20	1.1	0	17	20	08-24-87	25.2	1.20	30.2	1.14	34.3	0	6.4	219	12,180	7,038	-56	0.1	01
Mai Basic Four	14.9	10.4	34.0	19.5s	1.29	33.3	21.8	72.0	NC	36	03-87	.00	.0	0	0	0	00-00-00	6.6	1.62	10.7	3.38	36.2	95	2.2	236	14,216	2,470	0	1.4	09
Mgmnt Sci Amer	58.2	58.2	34.3	13.9q	.75	NE	NE	41.5	3	11	03-87	.00	.0	0	0	0	12-20-82	6.6	1.15	7.6	1.41	10.7	0	2.9	209	17,203	9,148	-146	0.0	12
Mentor Graphics	36.1	36.1	31.6	13.3q	.80	108.3	108.3	90.5	NC	9	03-87	.00	.0	0	0	0	00-00-00	7.1	.87	6.2	1.39	8.6	0	3.2	477	16,023	9,187	-175	0.0	12
Micro Pro Intl	-11.5	-15.4	-16.6	-2.1s	-.18	-42.9	-66.7	-100.0	NC	-7	02-87	.00	.0	0	0	0	00-00-00	-6.0	1.00	-6.0	1.18	-7.1	0	6.0	77	12,841	2,160	+1	0.0	08
Natl Data Cp	2.0	2.2	-3.3	8.7n	1.57	19.2	21.9	67.0	9	9	02-87	.44	2.0	17	31	38	05-08-87	6.0	1.20	7.2	1.78	12.8	4	1.4	242	11,273	5,644	0	0.0	05
Pansophic Sys	59.4	40.8	41.9	16.8f	.95	8.3	11.8	11.8	25	16	04-87	.12	.6	0	6	2	06-22-87	14.6	1.10	16.0	1.17	18.7	1	8.1	333	17,066	8,874	+8	0.7	04
Paychex Inc	26.7	27.1	27.0	5.1n	.60	30.0	33.3	39.5	58	27	02-87	.00	.0	0	0	0	06-13-86	8.4	2.29	19.2	1.43	27.4	14	2.8	225	8,590	3,636	+2	0.0	05
Policy Mgmt	29.7	29.7	45.4	14.6q	.90	26.3	26.3	7.1	22	12	03-87	.00	.0	0	0	0	10-03-83	9.1	.89	8.1	1.48	12.0	23	4.1	387	16,288	10,880	-6	0.0	12
SEI Corp	4.2	4.2	10.0	-6.6q	-.57	40.0	40.0	-100.0	NC	-18	03-87	.00	.0	0	0	0	06-23-87	-5.5	1.55	-8.5	2.06	-17.5	41	1.2	198	11,800	4,152	0	0.0	12
Shared Med Systs	10.7	10.7	17.4	33.3q	1.31	10.9	10.9	-24.7	14	9	03-87	.72	2.6	19	48	34	06-24-87	8.7	1.26	11.0	1.72	18.9	8	2.2	703	25,123	13,287	+2	0.0	12
Sftwr Lisco	24.2	33.3	30.0	.2f	.03	25.0	-57.1	-57.1	NC	1	04-87	.00	.0	0	0	0	00-00-00	.8	1.00	.8	1.63	1.3	10	2.2	42	7,182	1,153	+48	0.0	04
Software AG Syst	4.8	1.7	-3.1	4.2n	.72	-88.9	-65.2	-48.9	44	10	02-87	.00	.0	0	0	0	00-00-00	6.9	1.03	7.1	1.41	10.0	1	3.2	75	5,744	1,465	0	0.0	05
Sterling Sftwr	-21.9	-28.9	10.6	7.2s	.82	-29.4	-6.1	30.2	14	10	03-87	.00	.0	0	0	7	06-12-85	3.7	.81	3.0	3.23	9.7	160	2.6	96	9,063	3,544	0	5.5	09
Symbolics	-218.8	141.4	203.8	-19.2n	-.75	-100.0	-100.0	-100.0	NC	-22	03-87	.00	.0	0	0	0	00-00-00	-12.2	1.32	-16.1	1.37	-22.0	3	3.7	109	25,739	7,177	0	0.0	06
Tenera	-490.8	-49.2	.0	.0	.10	NE	47.1	-85.3	NC	0	03-87	.00	.0	0	0	0	00-00-00	NC	NC	NC	NC	.0	0	2.4	55	8,873	927	+118	0.0	12
Total Systs	15.5	15.5	22.5	5.6q	.35	28.6	28.6	16.7	35	23	03-87	.00	.0	0	0	0	05-02-86	14.7	1.39	20.4	1.12	22.8	1	5.7	390	15,916	239	+2	0.0	12
Triad System	3.1	.6	1.7	3.9s	.51	57.1	83.3	537.5	NC	6	03-87	.00	.0	0	0	0	00-00-00	3.4	1.00	3.4	1.74	5.9	2	2.0	90	7,616	4,309	0	0.0	09
UCCEL Cp	13.8	13.8	-25.0	12.8q	.75	257.1	257.1	13.6	35	10	03-87	.00	.0	0	0	0	00-00-00	8.7	.48	4.2	2.36	9.9	57	2.3	693	16,800	3,502	+33	0.5	12
Warner Cptr	42.9	36.2	46.1	1.7s	.29	50.0	41.7	45.0	NC	35	04-87	.00	.0	0	0	0	00-00-00	8.9	2.42	21.5	1.61	34.7	6	1.9	39	5,835	211	0	0.0	10

Recent Performance and Forecast: Drugs (SIC 283)

(in millions of dollars except as noted)

					Percent Change				
					Compound Annual		Annual		
	1984	1985[1]	1986[2]	1987[3]	1972-84	1979-84	1984-85	1985-86	1986-87
Industry Data									
Value of shipments[4]	28,967	31,443	33,426	—	11.3	10.9	8.5	6.3	—
2831 Biological Products	2,669	2,773	2,881	—	18.2	17.4	3.9	3.9	—
2833 Medicinals & Botanicals	3,410	3,435	3,410	—	17.2	7.7	0.7	−0.7	—
2834 Pharmaceutical Preps	22,888	25,235	27,135	—	10.2	10.7	10.3	7.5	—
Value of shipments (1982$)	25,796	26,209	26,681	27,170	4.1	2.7	1.6	1.8	1.8
2831 Biological Products	2,626	2,549	2,591	2,635	11.8	12.9	−2.9	1.6	1.7
2833 Medicinals & Botanicals	3,613	3,758	3,870	3,990	10.4	5.5	4.0	3.0	3.1
2834 Pharmaceutical Preps	19,558	19,902	20,220	20,545	2.7	1.2	1.8	1.6	1.6
Total employment (000)	167	165	165	165	2.1	0.5	−1.1	−0.2	−0.1
2831 Biological Products	26.2	26.0	25.5	25.6	8.3	7.2	−0.8	−1.9	0.4
2833 Medicinals & Botanicals	17.3	16.7	16.8	16.5	6.9	3.5	−3.5	0.6	−1.8
2834 Pharmaceutical Preps	124	123	123	123	0.8	−1.0	−0.9	0.1	0.1
Production workers (000)	81.8	83.9	83.8	83.5	1.7	−0.7	2.6	−0.1	−0.4
2831 Biological Products	12.6	13.2	13.2	13.2	7.5	5.8	4.8	0.0	0.0
2833 Medicinals & Botanicals	9.5	10.2	10.1	9.6	6.2	2.5	7.4	−1.0	−5.0
2834 Pharmaceutical Preps	59.7	60.5	60.5	60.7	0.4	−2.2	1.3	0.0	0.3
Average hourly earnings ($)	10.74	11.36	11.36	—	7.7	8.0	5.8	0.0	—
2831 Biological Products	8.44	9.00	9.60	—	6.7	9.0	6.6	6.7	—
2833 Medicinals & Botanicals	12.50	12.85	13.25	—	7.7	7.8	2.8	3.1	—
2834 Pharmaceutical Preps	10.96	11.45	11.85	—	7.9	8.1	4.5	3.5	—
Product Data									
Value of shipments[5]	26,869	28,961	31,118	—	11.1	11.1	7.8	7.4	—
2831 Biological Products	2,779	2,995	3,245	—	15.5	14.4	7.8	8.3	—
2833 Medicinals & Botanicals	3,398	3,337	3,313	—	12.9	3.2	−1.8	−0.7	—
2834 Pharmaceutical Preps	20,692	22,629	24,560	—	10.4	12.4	9.4	8.5	—

Value of shipments (1982$)	23,861	24,377	24,970	25,560	3.9	2.9	2.2	2.4	2.4
2831 Biological Products	2,734	2,784	2,875	2,950	9.2	10.0	1.8	3.3	2.6
2833 Medicinals & Botanicals	3,630	3,683	3,795	3,910	6.4	1.2	1.5	3.0	3.0
2834 Pharmaceutical Preps	17,497	17,910	18,300	18,700	2.9	2.4	2.4	2.2	2.2
Shipments price index[6] (1982 = 100)	112.8	119.0	124.1	—	6.7	7.9	5.5	4.3	—
2831 Biological Products	102.5	108.8	111.2	—	6.0	4.1	6.2	2.2	—
2833 Medicinals & Botanicals	93.6	90.6	87.3	—	4.5	1.9	−3.2	−3.6	—
2834 Pharmaceutical Preps	118.5	126.8	134.2	—	7.3	9.8	7.0	5.8	—
Trade Data									
Value of imports	1,665	1,896	2,359	3,020	17.3	15.5	13.9	24.4	28.0
2831 Biological Products	76.8	163	169	180	21.7	53.5	111.8	4.1	6.3
2833 Medicinals & Botanicals	1,341	1,517	2,028	2,700	16.1	12.5	13.1	33.7	33.2
2834 Pharmaceutical Preps	247	216	162	140	26.7	34.2	−12.5	−25.1	−13.6
Import/new supply ratio[7]	0.058	0.061	0.070	—	5.3	3.7	5.3	14.7	—
2831 Biological Products	0.027	0.052	0.050	—	5.3	33.7	91.6	−3.7	—
2833 Medicinals & Botanicals	0.283	0.313	0.380	—	2.1	6.8	10.4	21.5	—
2834 Pharmaceutical Preps	0.012	0.009	0.007	—	14.6	19.3	−19.8	−30.8	—
Value of exports	2,637	2,671	2,839	3,085	13.4	10.0	1.3	6.3	8.7
2831 Biological Products	456	516	603	700	18.7	9.1	13.2	16.9	16.0
2833 Medicinals & Botanicals	1,497	1,465	1,625	1,800	13.1	8.4	−2.2	11.0	10.8
2834 Pharmaceutical Preps	684	691	611	585	11.7	15.1	0.9	−11.6	−4.2
Export/shipments ratio	0.098	0.092	0.091	—	2.1	−1.0	−6.0	−1.1	—
2831 Biological Products	0.164	0.172	0.186	—	2.8	−4.6	5.0	7.9	—
2833 Medicinals & Botanicals	0.441	0.439	0.491	—	0.2	5.1	−0.4	11.8	—
2834 Pharmaceutical Preps	0.033	0.031	0.025	—	1.2	2.4	−7.7	−18.5	—

[1]Estimated except for exports and imports.
[2]Estimated.
[3]Forecast.
[4]Value of all products and services sold by the Drugs industry.
[5]Value of products classified in the Drugs industry produced by all industries.
[6]Developed by the Office of Industry Assessment, ITA.
[7]New supply is the sum of product shipments plus imports.

SOURCE: U.S. Department of Commerce: Bureau of the Census, Bureau of Economic Analysis, International Trade Administration (ITA). Estimates and forecasts by ITA.

Source: *U.S. Industrial Outlook 1987*, U.S. Department of Commerce.

Recent Performance and Forecast: Soap, Cleaners, and Toilet Goods (SIC 284)

(in millions of dollars except as noted)

					Percent Change				
					Compound Annual		Annual		
	1984	1985[1]	1986[2]	1987[3]	1972-84	1979-84	1984-85	1985-86	1986-87
Industry Data									
Value of shipments[4]	28,517	29,756	30,998	32,560	9.3	8.0	4.3	4.2	5.0
2841 Soap & Other Detergents	9,468	9,942	10,160	10,570	8.9	6.5	5.0	2.2	4.0
2842 Polishes/Sanitation Gds	4,902	5,100	5,230	5,430	8.4	5.6	4.0	2.5	3.8
2843 Surface Active Agents	2,482	2,574	2,678	2,790	15.0	12.8	3.7	4.0	4.2
2844 Toilet Preparations	11,665	12,140	12,930	13,770	9.2	9.5	4.1	6.5	6.5
Value of shipments (1982$)	26,005	26,392	26,987	27,578	1.5	−0.2	1.5	2.3	2.2
2841 Soap & Other Detergents	9,028	9,240	9,400	9,560	1.2	−0.1	2.3	1.7	1.7
2842 Polishes/Sanitation Gds	4,661	4,735	4,833	4,935	−0.0	−1.5	1.6	2.1	2.1
2843 Surface Active Agents	2,463	2,466	2,524	2,583	8.1	6.9	0.1	2.4	2.3
2844 Toilet Preparations	9,853	9,951	10,230	10,500	1.4	−1.2	1.0	2.8	2.6
Total employment (000)	125	123	123	124	0.9	1.1	−1.1	−0.7	1.3
2841 Soap & Other Detergents	32.8	32.2	32.0	32.4	0.3	−0.2	−1.8	−0.6	1.2
2842 Polishes/Sanitation Gds	21.9	22.4	22.8	23.0	−1.1	−2.2	2.3	1.8	0.9
2843 Surface Active Agents	9.3	9.5	9.7	9.8	2.5	6.5	2.2	2.1	1.0
2844 Toilet Preparations	60.9	59.4	58.1	59.0	2.0	2.4	−2.5	−2.2	1.5
Production workers (000)	73.4	72.0	72.0	73.0	0.3	−0.3	−1.9	0.0	1.4
2841 Soap & Other Detergents	19.2	18.8	18.4	18.7	−0.5	−2.2	−2.1	−2.1	1.6
2842 Polishes/Sanitation Gds	13.8	14.0	14.5	14.6	−0.5	−1.4	1.4	3.6	0.7
2843 Surface Active Agents	4.5	4.6	4.8	4.9	1.4	5.8	2.2	4.3	2.1
2844 Toilet Preparations	35.9	34.6	34.3	34.8	1.0	0.6	−3.6	−0.9	1.5
Average hourly earnings ($)	9.70	10.10	9.98	—	7.6	7.1	4.1	−1.2	—
2841 Soap & Other Detergents	12.11	12.44	12.39	—	7.6	7.2	2.7	−0.4	—
2842 Polishes/Sanitation Gds	8.94	8.87	8.90	—	8.1	8.8	−0.7	0.3	—
2843 Surface Active Agents	11.03	10.94	10.86	—	8.4	8.5	−0.8	−0.7	—
2844 Toilet Preparations	8.38	8.97	8.81	—	7.3	6.5	7.0	−1.8	—
Product Data									
Value of shipments[5]	27,096	28,299	29,511	31,015	9.2	7.9	4.4	4.3	5.1
2841 Soap & Other Detergents	8,265	8,690	8,920	9,275	9.3	6.2	5.1	2.6	4.0
2842 Polishes/Sanitation Gds	4,096	4,283	4,400	4,560	7.5	5.7	4.6	2.7	3.6
2843 Surface Active Agents	2,580	2,666	2,780	2,900	13.2	7.7	3.3	4.3	4.3
2844 Toilet Preparations	12,155	12,660	13,411	14,280	9.2	10.1	4.2	5.9	6.5

Value of shipments (1982$)	24,665	25,014	25,612	26,250	1.4	−0.3	1.4	2.4	2.5
2841 Soap & Other Detergents	7,917	8,114	8,290	8,480	1.6	−0.1	2.5	2.2	2.3
2842 Polishes/Sanitation Gds	3,929	4,014	4,100	4,190	−0.8	−1.3	2.2	2.1	2.2
2843 Surface Active Agents	2,552	2,546	2,612	2,680	6.4	1.8	−0.2	2.6	2.6
2844 Toilet Preparations	10,267	10,340	10,610	10,900	1.4	−0.6	0.7	2.6	2.7
Shipments price index[6] (1982 = 100)	110.7	113.2	115.3	—	7.6	8.4	2.2	1.9	—
2841 Soap & Other Detergents	104.6	107.1	107.6	—	7.6	6.4	2.4	0.5	—
2842 Polishes/Sanitation Gds	104.3	106.7	107.2	—	8.1	7.0	2.3	0.5	—
2843 Surface Active Agents	101.1	104.5	106.4	—	6.4	5.7	3.4	1.8	—
2844 Toilet Preparations	120.1	122.4	126.4	131.0	7.7	11.0	1.9	3.3	3.6
Trade Data									
Value of imports	470	572	706	839	23.8	23.5	21.7	23.4	18.8
2841 Soap & Other Detergents	68.9	80.3	113	120	28.2	38.1	16.5	40.2	6.6
2842 Polishes/Sanitation Gds	23.1	25.3	29.0	34.0	21.6	15.2	9.5	14.6	17.2
2843 Surface Active Agents	95.8	145	181	225	20.1	8.6	51.5	24.9	24.1
2844 Toilet Preparations	282	322	384	460	24.7	30.3	13.9	19.2	19.9
Import/new supply ratio[7]	0.017	—	—	—	13.2	14.3	—	—	—
2841 Soap & Other Detergents	0.006	—	—	—	17.8	30.1	—	—	—
2842 Polishes/Sanitation Gds	0.026	—	—	—	15.0	8.1	—	—	—
2843 Surface Active Agents	0.036	—	—	—	5.9	0.9	—	—	—
2844 Toilet Preparations	0.024	—	—	—	13.8	18.0	—	—	—
Value of exports	715	670	678	731	13.3	2.9	−6.3	1.2	7.8
2841 Soap & Other Detergents	144	132	104	115	9.1	1.1	−8.2	−21.5	10.7
2842 Polishes/Sanitation Gds	85.7	76.3	78.5	81.0	11.4	2.5	−11.0	2.9	3.2
2843 Surface Active Agents	155	149	178	210	14.0	0.4	−3.4	19.0	18.2
2844 Toilet Preparations	331	312	318	325	16.3	5.3	−5.5	1.8	2.2
Export/shipments ratio	0.026	—	—	—	3.7	−4.6	—	—	—
2841 Soap & Other Detergents	0.017	—	—	—	−0.1	−4.8	—	—	—
2842 Polishes/Sanitation Gds	0.021	—	—	—	3.6	−2.9	—	—	—
2843 Surface Active Agents	0.060	—	—	—	0.7	−6.7	—	—	—
2844 Toilet Preparations	0.027	—	—	—	6.6	−4.4	—	—	—

[1]Estimated except for exports and imports.
[2]Estimated.
[3]Forecast.
[4]Value of all products and services sold by the Soap, Cleaners, and Toilet Goods industry.
[5]Value of products classified in the Soap, Cleaners, and Toilet Goods industry produced by all industries.
[6]Developed by the Office of Industry Assessment, ITA.
[7]New supply is the sum of product shipments plus imports.
SOURCE: U.S. Department of Commerce: Bureau of the Census, Bureau of Economic Analysis, International Trade Administration (ITA). Estimates and forecasts by ITA.

Source: *U.S. Industrial Outlook 1987*, U.S. Department of Commerce.

Company	Revenue: Pct. Change Last Qtr	Revenue: Pct. Change FY to Date	Revenue: Pct. Change Last 12 Mos	Earnings: Last 12 Mos	Earnings: Per Share Last 12 Mos	Earnings: Per Share Pct. Change Last Qtr	Earnings: Per Share Pct. Change FY to Date	Earnings: Per Share Pct. Change Last 12 Mos	Earnings: 5-Year Growth Rate	Earnings: Par Growth Rate	Earnings: Date of Report	Dividends: Current Rate Amt	Dividends: Current Rate Yield	Dividends: 5-Year Growth Rate	Dividends: Payout Last FY	Dividends: Payout Last 5 Yrs.	Dividends: Last X-Dvd Date	Ratio Analysis: Profit Margin	Ratio Analysis: Asset Turnover	Ratio Analysis: Return on Total Assets	Ratio Analysis: Leverage Ratio	Ratio Analysis: Return on Equity	Ratio Analysis: Debt to Equity	Ratio Analysis: Current Ratio	Shareholdings: Market Value	Shareholdings: Latest Shares Outstndng.	Shareholdings: Held by Banks-Funds	Shareholdings: Insider Net Trading	Shareholdings: Short Interest Ratio	Shareholdings: Fiscal Year Ends
-	%	%	%	$Mil	$	%	%	%	%	%	-	$	%	%	%	%	-	π/r x	r/a =	π/a x	a/e =	π/e	%	-	$Mil	000	000	000	Days	Mo
Ethical Drugs																														
Ind. Group	12.7	16.7	12.8	5,677.5	2.25	11.2	13.2	13.7	9	10	- - -	1.21	2.0	1	41	44	- - - -	11.9	.95	11.3	1.92	21.7	16	2.0	149,707	2,519,297	G	- 15	4.5	- -
A L Labs	38.2	38.2	35.0	5.5q	.61	.0	.0	.0	101	10	03-87	.12	1.1	0	18	11	06-15-87	4.2	1.10	4.6	2.63	12.1	33	1.3	100	9,128	2,061	0	0.0	12
Abbott Labs	16.0	16.0	13.7	558.6q	2.42	19.2	19.2	19.2	17	18	03-87	1.00	1.6	18	35	35	07-09-87	14.2	1.02	14.5	2.17	31.4	17	1.4	14,274	228,839	108,328	+11	3.6	12
Alco Hlth	41.7	41.9	41.7	16.5s	1.26	24.0	10.2	5.9	NC	13	03-87	.00	.0	0	0	0	00-00-00	1.1	3.91	4.3	2.95	12.7	78	2.2	253	12,884	3,571	+3	0.0	09
Alza Cp A	-22.9	-22.9	-7.6	10.1q	.31	50.0	50.0	47.6	NC	8	03-87	.00	.0	0	0	0	07-09-86	28.1	.26	7.4	1.12	8.3	2	7.3	1,153	30,837	12,139	+13	1.4	12
Am Home Prod	2.0	2.0	4.4	798.4q	5.33	11.5	11.5	10.6	10	13	03-87	3.34	3.9	10	60	60	05-07-87	16.1	1.19	19.1	1.75	33.5	0	2.8	12,794	150,292	81,208	-2	2.1	12
Amgen	128.6	64.5	66.6	1.1f	.08	.0	60.0	60.0	NC	1	03-87	.00	.0	0	0	0	00-00-00	3.1	.39	1.2	1.17	1.4	10	14.9	622	16,262	4,901	-4	0.0	03
Biocraft Labs	88.7	14.9	13.9	6.9f	.51	171.4	2.0	2.0	NC	24	03-87	.00	.0	0	0	0	01-16-86	14.1	1.27	17.9	1.34	24.0	13	3.8	276	13,993	2,275	0	32.5	03
Block Drugs Co	7.3	12.5	12.7	32.6f	2.03	15.6	13.4	13.4	12	12	03-87	.54	1.7	3	25	28	06-02-87	10.6	1.06	11.2	1.46	16.3	16	2.6	492	15,626	2,775	-67	0.0	03
Bolar Pharm	23.5	23.5	38.0	10.3q	1.08	13.8	13.8	31.7	22	19	03-87	.05	.2	8	5	5	02-12-87	17.8	.97	17.3	1.13	19.5	0	4.9	211	8,866	3,239	0	62.6	12
Bristol-Myers	12.8	12.8	9.5	618.8q	2.17	19.6	19.6	9.6	12	8	03-87	1.40	2.8	20	51	45	06-26-87	12.4	1.19	14.8	1.47	21.8	6	2.7	14,207	285,560	154,872	+27	0.7	12
Calif Biotech	46.2	-21.7	.0	.0	-2.06	3100.0	NE	NE	NC	0	03-87	.00	.0	0	0	0	00-00-00	NC	NC	NC	NC	.0	0	8.2	161	11,678	2,378	0	0.0	12
Carter-Wallace	7.6	12.7	12.7	32.3f	4.27	16.0	17.6	17.6	21	11	03-87	.80	.8	12	18	18	04-10-87	7.2	1.21	8.7	1.61	14.0	11	2.4	746	7,573	2,217	-4	0.6	03
Centocor Inc	64.4	64.4	39.1	-38.7q	-4.17	.0	.0	-100.0	NC	-38	03-87	.00	.0	0	0	0	00-00-00	NM	NC	NC	NC	-38.0	6	13.9	378	9,742	3,692	+0	0.0	12
Collaborative Rsh	35.0	16.3	25.0	-1.8s	-.17	NE	NE	NE	NC	-9	02-87	.00	.0	0	0	0	00-00-00	-18.0	.47	-8.4	1.12	-9.4	0	7.2	75	10,579	596	0	0.0	08
Cooper Develop ◇ ■	493.3	495.5	341.6	-3.3s	-.13	NE	NE	NE	NC	-6	04-87	.00	.0	0	0	0	00-00-00	-.9	.56	-.5	11.40	-5.7	537	1.6	37	29,412	1,856	0	0.0	10
Diagnostic Prods	30.3	30.3	29.1	7.0q	1.16	37.5	37.5	41.5	22	19	03-87	.00	.0	0	0	0	09-27-83	22.6	.78	17.7	1.05	18.6	0	17.3	237	5,893	1,077	0	0.0	12
Forest Labs	97.9	68.5	67.5	12.4f	.77	57.1	57.1	57.1	27	16	03-87	.00	.0	0	0	0	05-16-86	18.5	.71	13.1	1.25	16.4	1	4.6	432	15,580	6,591	0	1.5	03
Genentech	33.1	33.1	60.0	-350.8q	-5.07	33.3	33.3	-100.0	NC	0	03-87	.00	.0	0	0	0	03-02-87	NM	NC	NC	NC	NM	3	4.9	3,303	82,563	22,968	+6	0.0	12
ICN Pharm	-10.7	-10.7	35.1	10.3q	.54	16.7	16.7	NE	NC	6	02-87	.00	.0	0	0	0	00-00-00	10.3	.17	1.7	3.35	5.7	166	4.6	190	16,149	5,564	0	6.5	11
Immunex Cp	108.3	108.3	166.6	-.9q	-.10	NE	NE	NE	NC	-3	03-87	.00	.0	0	0	0	00-00-00	-11.3	.11	-1.2	2.67	-3.2	147	23.6	187	7,628	1,704	-25	0.0	12
Integ Genetics	385.7	385.7	83.3	-.8q	-.06	NE	NE	NE	NC	-2	03-87	.00	.0	0	0	0	00-00-00	-7.3	.27	-2.0	1.20	-2.4	8	8.9	115	10,080	1,591	-0	0.0	12
Lilly Eli Co	7.2	7.2	13.1	590.8q	4.17	12.9	12.9	10.0	10	11	03-87	2.00	2.1	8	45	45	05-11-87	15.6	.83	12.9	1.67	21.6	14	1.8	13,054	139,056	95,377	-3	3.0	12
Lyphomed Inc	31.3	31.3	59.7	17.0q	.58	33.3	33.3	70.6	NC	14	03-87	.00	.0	0	0	0	06-23-86	12.2	.90	11.0	1.23	13.5	4	4.5	698	28,764	9,962	-26	0.0	12
Marion Labs	52.5	45.9	44.6	82.8n	.52	77.8	65.4	57.6	48	24	03-87	.20	.6	13	20	28	06-15-87	15.7	1.76	27.6	1.44	39.8	0	1.9	5,386	149,622	62,370	+38	2.0	06
Merck & Co	20.6	20.6	19.5	719.2q	5.19	30.1	30.1	29.8	12	16	03-87	2.20	1.3	7	39	44	06-02-87	16.7	.84	14.1	1.99	28.0	7	1.8	23,256	136,401	86,174	+0	0.5	12
Mylan Labs	18.7	17.7	17.2	23.3f	.65	38.5	14.0	14.0	54	29	03-87	.10	.7	0	11	11	06-24-87	24.5	1.18	29.0	1.18	34.3	7	8.9	537	36,115	2,738	-67	35.1	03
Newport Pharm	-44.7	-6.6	-20.0	-1.2n	-.14	-100.0	NE	NE	NC	-7	01-87	.00	.0	0	0	0	00-00-00	-15.0	.36	-5.4	1.31	-7.1	1	4.2	66	10,419	585	+20	0.0	04
NMS	40.0	15.4	.0	-1.9n	-.34	NE	NE	NE	NC	-31	02-87	.00	.0	0	0	0	12-15-80	-95.0	.27	-25.3	1.23	-31.1	0	5.9	21	5,918	291	0	0.0	05
Novo Industri	52.2	52.2	37.5	78.9q	3.10	29.1	29.1	20.2	4	13	03-87	.31	.8	18	12	28	04-21-86	11.8	.81	9.6	1.50	14.4	15	2.7	1,007	25,487	9,006	0	6.9	12
Pfizer Inc	8.5	8.5	11.0	683.1q	4.03	13.0	13.0	13.5	16	11	03-87	1.80	2.5	16	42	43	05-14-87	15.0	.88	13.2	1.52	20.0	8	2.0	11,881	165,007	96,350	+8	1.1	12
Ribi Immuno	300.0	300.0	.0	-.3q	-.04	NC	NC	NE	NC	-2	03-87	.00	.0	0	0	0	05-01-85	-30.0	.06	-1.9	1.00	-1.9	0	144.0	87	8,620	1,117	+0	0.0	12
Robins, AH ◆	13.3	11.9	11.8	81.8f	3.38	56.5	33.6	33.6	NC	0	12-86	.00	.0	0	0	NE	11-19-84	10.4	.94	9.8	.00	NM	0	3.6	673	24,161	5,738	0	0.7	12
Rorer Group	17.2	17.2	96.8	10.6q	.46	-94.0	-94.0	-93.5	8	-4	03-87	1.16	2.6	4	20	40	05-04-87	1.2	.83	1.0	2.70	2.7	114	1.7	959	21,799	7,771	-24	1.6	12
Scher Plough	12.0	12.0	14.2	278.9q	2.31	23.7	23.7	16.1	5	11	03-87	1.00	2.1	1	41	46	06-02-87	11.3	.82	9.3	2.05	19.1	20	1.5	5,699	117,200	71,810	+13	0.6	12
Smith Labs	-31.4	-35.2	-50.0	4.6s	.34	NE	NE	NE	NC	10	04-87	.00	.0	0	0	0	00-00-00	65.7	.13	8.4	1.21	10.2	11	8.9	36	13,207	1,141	0	0.0	10

Company																														
Smithkline Beck	16.3	16.3	16.0	551.1q	3.78	51.3	51.3	17.8	6	24	03-87	1.66	2.8	7	44	44	06-15-87	14.2	.92	13.1	3.24	42.5	6	1.4	7,588	127,000	100,360	-25	1.2	12
Squibb Corp	-15.8	-15.8	-21.0	292.5q	2.73	32.0	32.0	23.5	29	3	03-87	2.40	2.8	10	38	40	05-11-87	17.2	.70	12.1	1.78	21.5	12	2.0	9,300	107,200	73,406	+46	0.9	12
Syntex Corp	12.8	10.8	4.6	222.6n	1.95	26.8	34.5	-27.5	18	15	04-87	1.00	2.3	25	37	29	06-15-87	21.0	.84	17.7	1.72	30.5	19	2.0	5,231	121,646	56,944	-0	0.8	07
TechAmerica	-15.7	-15.7	-5.7	-2.5q	-.30	NE	NE	NE	NC	-18	03-87	.00	.0	0	0	0	00-00-00	-7.6	1.24	-9.4	1.93	-18.1	42	2.3	31	8,379	484	0	0.0	12
Unimed Inc	16.7	54.5	50.0	-255.0s	-.26	NE	NE	NE	NC	15	03-87	.00	.0	0	0	0	03-02-81	NM	NC	NC	NC	15.1	23	5.3	27	3,227	99	0	0.0	09
Upjohn Co	10.6	10.6	16.7	270.5q	1.15	-58.8	-58.8	-.9	9	9	03-87	.60	1.3	8	37	43	06-29-87	11.5	.89	10.2	1.80	18.4	29	2.1	8,467	187,114	131,192	+30	0.7	12
Ventrex Labs	-56.5	-47.3	-42.8	-2.6s	-.25	NC	NC	NE	NC	-14	03-87	.00	.0	0	0	0	00-00-00	-21.7	.53	-11.6	1.24	-14.4	6	3.5	31	10,726	2,342	0	0.0	09
Warner-Lambrt	10.1	10.1	.8	317.8q	4.33	17.2	17.2	NE	NC	20	03-87	1.80	2.5	3	38	99	05-04-87	10.0	1.26	12.6	2.78	35.0	38	1.6	5,210	72,117	44,352	+12	0.6	12
Zenith Labs	-25.1	-25.1	-43.2	-9.0q	-.42	-100.0	-100.0	-100.0	NC	-31	03-87	.05	.5	0	NE	5	06-19-86	-19.6	.61	-12.0	2.33	-27.9	24	1.3	220	20,948	2,582	+6	31.8	12

Cosmetics and Grooming Aids

Company																														
Ind. Group	18.1	18.4	34.6	273.2	.82	2.1	1.7	-30.6	-8	0	---	.81	2.5	0	91	73	----	2.8	1.04	2.9	3.62	10.5	156	2.5	9,809	309,576	131,897	-9	2.2	--
Alberto-Culver	15.7	15.0	16.5	11.0s	.79	31.6	29.7	113.5	NC	7	03-87	.24	1.0	6	29	53	04-28-87	2.4	2.00	4.8	1.98	9.5	20	1.9	337	13,895	1,650	+10	15.7	09
Alfin Frag	-69.8	-27.2	-6.6	-3.7n	-.54	-100.0	-100.0	-100.0	NC	-16	04-87	.00	.0	0	0	0	02-20-86	-13.2	.92	-12.1	1.30	-15.7	4	4.4	27	6,675	342	0	0.9	07
Avon Products	13.6	13.6	23.1	161.7q	2.29	28.6	28.6	16.2	-8	3	03-87	2.00	5.9	-7	90	92	05-14-87	5.5	1.27	7.0	3.39	23.7	104	1.6	2,371	70,241	42,523	+9	3.5	12
Del Labs	4.0	4.0	3.8	3.2q	2.11	5.8	5.8	-16.3	10	8	03-87	.40	1.4	8	19	18	05-11-87	3.0	1.33	4.0	2.50	10.0	89	2.7	41	1,383	170	0	0.1	12
Gillette Co	16.3	16.3	17.0	25.8q	.24	29.7	29.7	-82.2	-27	-12	03-87	.76	2.0	6	523	61	05-26-87	.9	1.11	1.0	5.60	5.6	199	1.7	4,381	114,908	61,044	-23	1.4	12
Helene Curtis	17.3	10.9	10.8	10.3f	2.80	-12.7	-7.0	-7.0	19	12	02-87	.30	.9	0	5	1	07-27-87	2.6	2.00	5.2	2.56	13.3	37	1.6	128	3,907	1,043	0	0.6	02
Johnson Prdts	.0	-10.1	-3.0	.5n	.13	NE	NE	NE	NC	5	05-87	.00	.0	0	0	0	04-30-80	1.6	1.31	2.1	2.14	4.5	34	1.7	13	3,987	239	0	0.0	08
Lamaur Inc	1.3	1.3	3.2	5.2q	.84	5.6	5.6	58.5	7	10	03-87	.30	2.4	37	29	27	06-16-87	4.1	2.63	10.8	1.44	15.5	2	3.0	76	6,017	1,615	0	0.3	12
Lee Pharm	-14.9	5.0	128.0	6.0s	1.45	-71.4	9.1	400.0	NC	53	03-87	.00	.0	0	0	0	10-27-86	10.5	2.39	25.1	2.10	52.6	0	1.7	20	3,957	400	0	8.5	09
MEM Co	-29.8	-29.8	-11.6	2.7q	1.02	NE	NE	10.9	0	3	03-87	.60	3.6	3	53	50	06-24-87	4.0	1.28	5.1	1.31	6.7	0	3.1	45	2,650	743	0	0.0	12
Minnetonka	75.8	75.8	47.5	10.2q	.70	340.0	340.0	141.4	NC	26	03-87	.00	.0	0	0	0	05-27-87	5.6	2.59	14.5	1.79	25.9	4	2.0	287	17,018	5,962	0	0.0	12
Noxell Cp	15.1	15.1	17.6	39.2q	1.95	17.9	17.9	16.1	17	15	03-87	.64	1.1	17	33	31	06-11-87	8.5	1.88	16.0	1.38	22.0	0	3.0	1,178	20,058	6,342	0	0.0	12
Redken Labs	30.1	17.8	13.5	3.7n	1.21	650.0	103.7	-10.4	-14	6	04-87	.20	.9	11	62	21	06-29-87	3.2	1.38	4.4	1.55	6.8	16	2.7	67	2,991	284	0	0.0	07
Revlon Grp	33.2	33.2	238.5	-2.6q	-.62	NE	NE	NC	NC	0	03-87	.00	.0	0	0	NE	00-00-00	-.1	1.00	-.1	3.00	-.3	276	7.9	838	41,889	9,540	-5	0.3	12

Proprietary Drugs

Company																														
Ind. Group	14.9	15.6	12.4	274.0	1.39	9.2	41.1	75.6	6	8	---	.63	2.2	1	38	41	----	7.1	.97	6.9	2.20	15.2	25	1.9	5,710	197,471	51,797	+650	2.6	--
Erbamont	5.9	5.9	13.0	70.4q	1.59	-45.7	-45.7	8.9	13	10	03-87	.52	1.8	0	23	16	05-11-87	7.7	.56	4.3	3.33	14.3	28	1.5	1,300	44,261	2,458	0	0.0	12
GNC Inc	4.0	4.0	-2.2	6.6q	.20	.0	.0	NE	NC	1	04-87	.16	2.7	49	80	43	05-26-87	1.9	2.11	4.0	1.73	6.9	19	1.7	194	33,015	1,712	-2	0.9	01
IGI Inc	-9.3	-9.3	5.8	.5q	.08	200.0	200.0	NE	NC	6	03-87	.00	.0	0	0	0	00-00-00	2.8	1.00	2.8	2.14	6.0	64	2.3	28	7,457	212	0	0.0	12
Iroquois Brands	21.5	21.5	-28.9	3.0q	3.22	-25.7	-25.7	820.0	NC	35	03-87	.00	.0	0	0	0	12-04-81	3.9	1.13	4.4	8.02	35.3	342	1.8	23	711	253	0	9.0	12
Par Pharm	161.4	154.3	133.3	7.8s	.72	166.7	158.8	118.2	61	25	03-87	.00	.0	0	0	0	03-12-87	12.4	1.18	14.6	1.69	24.7	33	3.3	278	10,785	693	0	15.7	09
Pharmacontrol	62.5	50.0	33.3	-2.3s	-.54	NE	NE	NE	NC	-30	12-86	.00	.0	0	0	0	00-00-00	-57.5	.42	-24.2	1.24	-29.9	0	2.2	22	4,377	256	0	0.0	06
Scherer RP Co	31.4	22.8	22.5	7.5f	.80	NE	NE	NE	NC	6	03-87	.32	1.8	2	40	223	06-12-87	3.3	1.27	4.2	2.31	9.7	55	1.9	171	9,424	1,751	-25	0.0	03
Sterling Drug	17.1	17.1	15.7	177.4q	3.02	18.3	18.3	58.9	4	9	03-87	1.52	2.6	5	44	50	05-01-87	8.6	1.20	10.3	1.77	18.2	21	2.3	3,380	58,913	39,490	-1	3.0	12
Thompson Med	16.0	16.0	-4.5	7.9q	.90	17.1	17.1	-21.7	-4	6	02-87	.40	2.1	0	48	22	03-24-87	6.3	1.51	9.5	1.21	11.5	0	6.1	165	8,824	1,425	0	0.2	11
Viratek Inc	-94.1	-94.1	60.0	-.9q	-.13	-100.0	-100.0	NE	NC	-7	02-87	.00	.0	0	0	0	08-19-86	-11.3	.50	-5.6	1.25	-7.0	0	3.5	100	7,962	550	+678	0.0	11
VLI Corp	23.8	23.8	12.5	-3.9q	-.34	NE	NE	NE	NC	-17	03-87	.00	.0	0	0	0	00-00-00	-21.7	.73	-15.9	1.06	-16.8	0	12.1	50	11,742	2,997	0	0.0	12

Recent Performance and Forecast: Electronic Components and Accessories (SIC 367)

(in millions of dollars except as noted)

					Percent Change				
					Compound Annual		Annual		
	1984	1985[1]	1986[2]	1987[3]	1972-84	1979-84	1984-85	1985-86	1986-87
Industry Data									
Value of shipments[4]	47,983	39,263	39,728	42,961	15.2	16.1	−18.2	1.2	8.1
Value of shipments (1982$)	48,299	46,205	49,565	57,776	12.1	15.9	−4.3	7.3	16.6
Total employment (000)	582	580	543	550	4.7	4.5	−0.4	−6.3	1.2
Production workers (000)	375	353	314	322	4.0	2.9	−5.8	−11.1	2.7
Average hourly earnings ($)	8.17	8.33	8.65	—	7.6	8.3	2.0	3.8	—
Product Data									
Value of shipments[5]	45,489	36,812	37,188	40,135	14.9	16.0	−19.1	1.0	7.9
Value of shipments (1982$)	45,774	44,070	47,569	55,009	11.3	15.5	−3.7	7.9	15.6
Shipments price index[6] (1982=100)	100.7	92.8	91.6	91.8	−5.7	−3.0	−7.9	−1.2	0.2
Trade Data									
Value of imports (ITA)[7]	10,351	8,545	8,231	9,840	28.3	23.8	−17.4	−3.7	19.5
Value of exports (ITA)[8]	7,252	6,188	6,157	7,394	18.4	13.2	−14.7	−0.5	20.1

[1]Estimated except for exports and imports.

[2]Estimated.

[3]Forecast.

[4]Value of all products and services sold by the Electronic Components and Accessories industry.

[5]Value of products classified in the Electronic Components and Accessories industry produced by all industries.

[6]Developed by the Office of Microelectronics and Instrumentation, ITA.

[7]Import data are developed by the chapter author.

[8]Export data are developed by the chapter author.

SOURCE: U.S. Department of Commerce: Bureau of the Census, Bureau of Economic Analysis, International Trade Administration (ITA). Estimates and forecasts by ITA.

Source: *U.S. Industrial Outlook 1987*, U.S. Department of Commerce.

Recent Performance and Forecast: Radio and TV Communication Equipment (SIC 3662)

(in millions of dollars except as noted)

					Percent Change				
					Compound Annual		Annual		
	1984	1985[1]	1986[2]	1987[3]	1972-84	1979-84	1984-85	1985-86	1986-87
Industry Data									
Value of shipments[4]	40,919	46,158	51,700	57,700	13.3	15.8	12.8	12.0	11.6
Value of shipments (1982$)	37,393	40,561	43,800	46,900	7.7	8.8	8.5	8.0	7.1
Total employment (000)	505	551	591	620	3.9	5.5	9.0	7.3	4.9
Production workers (000)	242	259	265	280	3.4	4.0	7.0	2.2	5.7
Average hourly earnings ($)	10.69	11.29	11.32	—	7.5	8.6	5.6	0.3	—
Product Data									
Value of shipments[5]	39,924	45,036	50,400	56,200	13.9	16.5	12.8	11.9	11.5
Value of shipments (1982$)	36,483	39,575	42,700	45,700	8.2	9.4	8.5	7.9	7.0
Shipments price index[6] (1982 = 100)	109.4	113.8	118.0	123.0	5.2	6.4	4.0	3.7	4.2
Trade Data									
Value of imports (ITA)[7]	2,881	3,707	3,990	4,300	22.4	25.1	28.7	7.6	7.8
Import/new supply ratio[8]	0.067	0.076	0.073	0.071	7.1	6.9	13.0	−3.5	−3.1
Value of exports (ITA)[9]	2,768	2,897	3,090	3,300	13.4	9.2	4.7	6.7	6.8
Export/shipments ratio	0.069	0.064	0.061	0.059	−0.4	−6.3	−7.2	−4.7	−4.2

[1]Estimated except for exports and imports.
[2]Estimated.
[3]Forecast.
[4]Value of all products and services sold by the Radio and TV Communication Equipment industry.
[5]Value of products classified in the Radio and TV Communication Equipment industry produced by all industries.
[6]Developed by the Office of Industry Assessment, ITA.
[7]Import data are developed by the chapter author.
[8]New supply is the sum of product shipments plus imports.
[9]Export data are developed by the chapter author.
SOURCE: U.S. Department of Commerce: Bureau of the Census, Bureau of Economic Analysis, International Trade Administration (ITA). Estimates and forecasts by ITA.

Source: *U.S. Industrial Outlook 1987,* U.S. Department of Commerce.

Company	Revenue Pct. Change Last Qtr	Revenue Pct. Change FY to Date	Revenue Pct. Change Last 12 Mos	Earnings Last 12 Mos	Earnings Per Share Last 12 Mos	Per Share Pct. Change Last Qtr	Per Share Pct. Change FY to Date	Per Share Pct. Change Last 12 Mos	5-Year Growth Rate	Par Growth Rate	Date of Report	Dividends Current Rate Amt	Current Rate Yield	5-Year Growth Rate	Payout Last FY	Payout Last 5 Yrs.	Last X-Dvd Date	Profit Margin	Asset Turnover	Return on Total Assets	Leverage Ratio	Return on Equity	Debt to Equity	Current Ratio	Market Value	Latest Shares Outstndng.	Held by Banks-Funds	Insider Net Trading	Short Interest Ratio	Fiscal Year Ends
-	%	%	%	$Mil	$	%	%	%	%	%	-	$	%	%	%	%	-	π/r x	r/a =	π/a x	a/e =	π/e	%	-	$Mil	000	000	000	Days	Mo
Electronic Devices																														
Ind. Group	- 15.6	- 12.7	- 7.1	441.2	.55	NE	NE	444.2	- 11	3	- - -	.25	1.1	0	33	24	- - - -	2.7	1.15	3.1	1.84	5.7	16	2.3	17,251	753,004	264,073	- 118	2.2	- -
Anaren Micrwve	-14.3	-10.8	-6.2	2.2n	.54	-45.0	-42.6	-26.0	21	9	03-87	.00	.0	0	0	0	03-30-81	7.3	.90	6.6	1.33	8.8	16	6.9	31	4,209	1,174	0	0.0	06
Anthem Elects	59.5	42.9	43.2	2.7f	.38	-16.7	-13.6	-13.6	11	7	03-87	.00	.0	13	5	6	03-10-86	1.8	3.22	5.8	1.12	6.5	0	9.5	116	7,210	4,247	-19	1.0	03
Avnet Inc	4.8	7.5	7.9	17.5n	.49	-39.1	-29.0	-41.7	-20	0	03-87	.50	1.5	1	75	33	06-01-87	1.2	1.58	1.9	1.42	2.7	17	5.2	1,169	35,547	24,174	+29	2.9	06
AVX Corp	29.0	29.0	18.7	2.7q	.23	NE	NE	NE	NC	2	03-87	.00	.0	0	0	62	08-06-85	1.3	.86	1.1	1.64	1.8	33	4.0	232	12,995	6,616	0	0.4	12
Burr-Brown	27.2	27.2	23.7	2.8q	.30	-81.8	-81.8	-33.3	7	5	03-87	.00	.0	0	0	0	12-15-86	2.3	1.09	2.5	1.92	4.8	48	2.7	92	9,415	2,589	0	0.0	12
Cetec Corp	10.4	10.4	-3.0	.4q	.23	11.1	11.1	NE	NC	0	03-87	.20	3.1	9	91	61	05-04-87	1.3	1.54	2.0	1.70	3.4	27	2.8	12	1,953	187	0	0.2	12
Comdial Cp	1.7	1.7	-9.1	-3.1q	-.18	NE	NE	NE	NC	-19	03-87	.00	.0	0	0	0	00-00-00	-3.9	1.23	-4.8	4.04	-19.4	4	.9	49	17,975	454	0	0.0	12
E Systems	27.1	27.1	24.7	63.9q	2.06	12.8	12.8	41.1	14	13	03-87	.50	1.5	16	25	26	06-08-87	5.3	1.92	10.2	1.66	16.9	18	3.4	991	30,366	11,972	+36	3.3	12
EDO Cp	6.2	-2.6	-2.5	6.3f	.84	-23.1	-16.8	-16.8	NC	7	12-86	.28	1.8	25	33	26	06-03-87	5.6	.64	3.6	2.81	10.1	62	2.4	110	7,173	2,574	0	5.0	12
Equatorial Commun	-36.7	-36.7	-33.3	-71.0q	-4.81	NE	NE	NE	NC	0	03-87	.00	.0	0	0	0	00-00-00	NM	NC	NC	NC	NM	25	1.7	48	14,822	3,950	+1	0.0	12
GenRad	3.7	3.7	-.4	-22.8q	-1.39	NE	NE	NE	NC	-22	03-87	.00	.0	0	0	NE	09-25-85	-11.1	.92	-10.2	2.12	-21.6	56	2.7	206	16,307	6,924	0	5.7	12
Jetronic Ind	2.0	2.0	7.4	1.2q	.46	35.7	35.7	-30.3	NC	10	04-87	.00	.0	0	0	0	08-11-86	2.1	1.33	2.8	3.46	9.7	62	1.6	13	2,457	149	0	0.0	01
KLA Instruments	10.0	11.0	17.1	9.9n	.55	-7.1	-2.4	.0	41	13	03-87	.00	.0	0	0	0	12-17-84	11.1	.91	10.1	1.30	13.1	0	3.6	352	17,192	7,199	-50	0.0	06
Knogo Cp	39.8	36.1	36.1	8.5f	1.25	-15.4	5.0	5.0	NC	11	02-87	.00	.0	0	0	0	09-22-80	17.3	.52	9.0	1.17	10.5	6	NA	167	6,707	2,565	0	8.2	02
Mitel Cp ◇	-1.3	9.7	.0	.0	-.57	NE	NE	NE	NC	0	03-87	.00	NA	0	0	0	00-00-00	NC	NC	NC	NC	.0	76	5.9	365	78,951	6,592	-225	8.8	03
Northn Telecom	-99.9	-99.9	-37.5	263.2q	1.27	21.1	21.1	-14.8	20	11	03-87	.24	NA	6	16	17	06-04-87	7.7	.86	6.6	2.11	13.9	5	2.2	4,989	234,796	32,528	-4	1.7	12
Pac Scientific	48.2	48.2	16.2	3.0q	.55	14.3	14.3	-43.9	-19	1	03-87	.40	2.2	7	77	30	06-15-87	3.0	.97	2.9	1.76	5.1	47	6.6	99	5,500	2,715	-1	1.9	12
Paradyne Cp	-15.3	-15.3	.4	-42.0q	-1.84	-100.0	-100.0	NE	NC	-29	03-87	.00	.0	0	0	0	03-22-83	-16.7	.87	-14.6	1.97	-28.8	64	3.7	154	22,790	14,829	0	0.8	12
Plantronics	20.8	17.2	20.6	7.8n	1.24	25.0	-7.3	NC	2	11	03-87	.16	.7	0	12	17	04-30-87	7.0	1.10	7.7	1.69	13.0	18	2.5	139	6,229	4,159	-58	1.1	06
Regency Electro	-9.3	-23.9	-23.4	-1.3n	-.12	NE	NE	NE	NC	-8	03-87	.20	3.2	-9	NE	66	05-05-87	-1.7	1.00	-1.7	1.82	-3.1	40	4.1	67	10,732	2,496	+1	0.0	06
Sci-Atlanta	7.3	5.6	7.7	-2.2n	-.09	1150.0	83.3	-100.0	NC	-3	03-87	.12	.6	7	NE	40	07-30-87	-.5	1.40	-.7	1.71	-1.2	3	2.3	448	23,254	7,552	+10	0.7	06
Semtech Cp	12.9	12.9	-7.6	.3q	.14	NC	NC	NE	NC	5	04-87	.00	.0	0	0	0	03-14-83	2.5	1.20	3.0	1.77	5.3	44	4.4	9	2,450	916	0	1.2	01
Servo Cp Am	-15.2	-3.3	5.8	1.0s	1.41	-35.1	-14.1	4.4	19	15	04-87	.00	.0	0	0	0	00-00-00	5.6	1.79	10.0	1.45	14.5	4	3.3	10	686	7	0	0.6	10
Solitron Device	-.8	-1.4	.0	3.3f	.67	226.7	.0	.0	NC	11	02-87	.00	.0	0	0	0	00-00-00	6.6	.88	5.8	1.88	10.9	48	2.6	38	4,322	698	0	0.1	02
Sooner Defense	85.7	90.5	110.0	1.5n	.30	-80.0	-20.0	400.0	NC	22	03-87	.00	.0	0	0	0	00-00-00	7.1	.93	6.6	3.39	22.4	113	.8	27	5,364	597	0	0.0	06
Sun Electric	21.8	21.7	13.2	3.6s	.52	400.0	NE	NE	NC	5	04-87	.00	.0	0	0	NE	02-22-82	1.8	1.33	2.4	2.08	5.0	51	2.6	97	7,030	3,905	-5	23.9	10
Tektronix Inc	8.0	3.1	.0	58.2n	1.51	23.1	65.8	-.7	-8	4	02-87	.60	1.5	2	51	26	07-27-87	4.2	1.17	4.9	1.43	7.0	1	2.3	1,493	38,536	32,706	+2	0.7	05
TeleConcepts	-3.7	-3.7	-20.0	-.6q	-.20	NE	NE	NE	NC	-10	03-87	.00	.0	0	0	0	02-15-83	-5.0	1.04	-5.2	1.96	-10.2	66	5.3	26	3,289	176	0	1.4	12
TeleSciences	-93.4	-93.4	-50.0	-13.1q	-3.91	NE	NE	NE	NC	0	03-87	.00	.0	0	0	0	10-30-79	-65.5	.80	-52.4	.00	NM	0	1.4	8	3,338	1,046	0	0.0	12
Tex Inst	11.1	11.1	6.6	127.6q	1.48	NE	NE	NE	NC	4	03-87	.72	1.2	0	176	107	06-24-87	2.5	1.52	3.8	1.95	7.4	11	1.6	4,675	76,799	57,598	-12	2.8	12
Torotel Inc	-4.0	-2.7	.0	.0	-2.16	NE	NE	-100.0	NC	0	01-87	.00	.0	0	0	0	04-24-85	NC	NC	NC	NC	.0	5	.6	8	2,516	137	0	2.0	04
Varian Assoc	5.0	1.7	-4.7	-4.8s	-.23	NC	587.5	-100.0	NC	-3	03-87	.26	.8	-4	NE	16	04-13-87	-.5	1.20	-.6	2.00	-1.2	12	1.7	685	21,564	13,505	+4	0.9	09
Varo Inc	74.9	26.4	26.6	3.5f	.81	116.0	NE	NE	NC	4	04-87	.40	2.4	0	49	63	03-02-87	3.7	1.27	4.7	1.51	7.1	5	3.2	74	4,341	1,060	+31	0.1	04
Vishay Inter	.0	-.2	.0	7.9n	1.46	8.1	12.6	14.1	24	13	03-87	.00	.0	0	0	0	03-20-87	13.4	.63	8.5	1.58	13.4	29	3.9	166	7,038	1,383	+142	0.0	06
Wavetek □	7.4	6.5	5.5	3.1s	.33	14.3	-6.7	NE	NC	5	03-87	.00	.0	0	0	0	03-25-83	4.1	.95	3.9	1.23	4.8	4	5.5	85	9,151	4,694	0	0.0	09

Company	Revenue: Pct. Change Last Qtr	Revenue: Pct. Change FY to Date	Revenue: Pct. Change Last 12 Mos	Earnings: Last 12 Mos	Earnings Per Share: Last 12 Mos	Per Share Pct. Change: Last Qtr	Per Share Pct. Change: FY to Date	Per Share Pct. Change: Last 12 Mos	5-Year Growth Rate	Par Growth Rate	Date of Report	Dividends: Current Rate Amt	Current Rate Yield	5-Year Growth Rate	Payout Last FY	Payout Last 5 Yrs.	Last X-Dvd Date	Profit Margin	Asset Turnover	Return on Total Assets	Leverage Ratio	Return on Equity	Debt to Equity	Current Ratio	Market Value	Latest Shares Outstndng.	Held by Banks-Funds	Insider Net Trading	Short Interest Ratio	Fiscal Year Ends
-	%	%	%	$Mil	$	%	%	%	%	%	-	$	%	%	%	%	-	π/r x	r/a =	π/a x	a/e =	π/e	%	-	$Mil	000	000	000	Days	Mo
Electronic Systems																														
Ind. Group	48.2	56.7	52.0	311.2	.74	27.4	27.0	24.1	- 2	5	- - -	.16	.3	0	24	15	- - - -	1.5	1.13	1.7	3.88	6.6	59	1.2	26,041	541,694	65,242	- 96	2.5	- -
Adams Rus I	15.1	12.3	-47.7	.4s	.05	-91.9	-91.9	-96.8	-23	0	03-87	.16	.4	10	22	10	05-02-86	.9	.78	.7	.00	NS	-260	.2	247	6,670	2,950	+2	0.9	09
AEL Inds	5.4	5.4	7.8	3.5q	.80	150.0	150.0	14.3	NC	6	05-87	.00	.0	0	0	0	08-09-85	3.2	1.22	3.9	1.62	6.3	14	2.0	62	4,431	1,652	0	0.0	02
ArgoSysts Inc	35.0	23.5	24.0	8.4n	1.27	NE	106.5	69.3	20	17	03-87	.00	.0	0	0	0	05-13-83	9.0	1.28	11.5	1.50	17.3	0	2.6	254	6,891	2,873	0	0.0	06
Cohu Inc	-5.4	-5.4	-6.6	.6q	.37	72.7	72.7	-24.5	-5	2	03-87	.20	2.7	6	69	31	05-28-87	2.1	1.62	3.4	1.24	4.2	0	4.3	13	1,821	191	0	0.0	12
Cubic Corp	4.1	6.4	.8	4.2s	.54	440.0	200.0	-50.9	-31	1	03-87	.39	1.9	9	279	23	03-13-87	1.2	1.58	1.9	2.05	3.9	45	2.7	158	7,780	2,050	0	4.0	09
DSC Commun □	1.2	1.2	7.0	11.4q	.28	20.0	20.0	NE	NC	6	03-87	.00	.0	0	0	0	05-24-83	3.7	.76	2.8	2.04	5.7	66	3.8	311	40,816	15,539	0	0.0	12
EECO Inc	13.2	13.2	14.2	1.3q	.33	-100.0	-100.0	-45.0	NC	2	03-87	.24	1.5	6	38	71	05-12-87	2.0	1.25	2.5	2.20	5.5	50	1.9	63	3,923	451	-4	0.0	12
EG & G Inc	4.6	4.6	-.9	44.5q	1.62	-6.3	-6.3	-22.1	7	12	03-87	.56	1.6	15	32	24	07-20-87	3.8	2.63	10.0	1.88	18.8	9	1.6	946	27,431	14,501	+19	2.7	12
Gen Datacomm	22.2	24.7	14.3	5.0s	.34	266.7	61.5	.0	NC	6	03-87	.00	.0	0	0	0	05-25-84	2.5	1.08	2.7	2.19	5.9	37	3.6	147	15,116	3,178	+16	0.3	09
NEC Cp	72.1	72.1	76.8	43.8s	.46	-66.7	-66.7	-25.8	0	1	09-86	.21	.3	0	9	7	03-21-86	.3	1.00	.3	5.33	1.6	84	1.1	20,488	279,705	295	0	0.0	03
Plessey Co Ltd	-.3	3.8	6.7	177.8n	2.41	21.6	32.0	38.5	5	22	12-86	.07	.2	-3	38	31	09-05-86	8.0	1.16	9.3	2.46	22.9	5	1.8	2,728	73,730	122	0	2.0	03
Porta Syst	19.4	19.4	4.8	2.6q	.47	8.3	8.3	-13.0	9	11	03-87	.00	.0	0	0	0	07-01-83	6.0	.88	5.3	2.04	10.8	83	7.4	48	5,451	914	0	1.4	12
Ramtek Corp	-5.3	2.0	-11.4	-6.2n	-.14	NE	NE	NE	NC	-41	03-87	.00	.0	0	0	0	00-00-00	-20.0	.94	-18.8	2.20	-41.3	17	1.5	20	3,901	518	0	0.0	06
Sensormatic Elec	12.1	11.1	13.1	11.4n	.41	NE	NE	NE	NC	5	02-87	.05	.4	11	NE	11	05-22-87	11.1	.41	4.6	1.33	6.1	12	NA	331	28,160	11,850	+11	0.0	05
Silicon Gen	-2.0	21.5	2.7	.7n	.07	NE	NE	NE	NC	2	03-87	.00	.0	0	0	0	06-15-83	1.8	.56	1.0	2.00	2.0	29	1.2	51	12,096	3,446	-6	0.0	06
Technol for Comm	18.5	7.6	16.2	3.5s	1.11	65.0	40.5	32.1	-6	18	03-87	.00	.0	0	0	0	00-00-00	8.1	1.02	8.3	2.11	17.5	6	1.1	57	2,919	470	-134	0.0	09
Trans-Lux Cp ◇	-29.4	-29.4	-40.0	-2.6q	-1.49	NE	NE	-100.0	NC	-10	03-87	.08	.6b	0	NE	15	07-02-87	-14.4	.35	-5.1	1.92	-9.8	71	5.1	20	1,581	180	0	37.9	12
Univ Sec Inst	16.7	41.9	38.8	1.1f	.29	750.0	222.2	222.2	NC	13	03-87	.00	.0	0	0	0	07-10-81	4.4	1.82	8.0	1.56	12.5	13	2.9	16	3,893	791	0	0.0	03
Vicon Ind	18.5	14.3	16.1	-.4s	-.16	-62.5	-100.0	NE	NC	-3	03-87	.00	.0	0	0	0	07-05-83	-1.1	1.09	-1.2	2.42	-2.9	99	4.5	13	2,349	698	0	0.3	09
VMX Inc	51.4	.0	-9.0	.2n	-.30	NE	NE	NE	NC	1	03-87	.00	.0	0	0	0	00-00-00	.7	.71	.5	1.20	.6	0	9.1	68	13,030	2,573	0	0.0	06
Radio - TV Manufacture																														
Ind. Group	38.2	406.5	25.4	529.0	.96	36.0	35.9	29.6	7	5	- - -	.25	.7	0	27	26	- - - -	2.5	1.24	3.1	2.10	6.5	21	1.7	20,217	588,364	108,594	- 464	2.0	- -
Andrea Radio	-30.8	-30.8	.0	.3q	.51	-8.7	-8.7	18.6	-12	-4	03-87	.72	6.5	2	102	89	05-26-87	7.5	1.03	7.7	1.12	8.6	0	8.5	6	508	3	0	0.0	12
Armatron Intl	-19.0	-43.1	-59.0	-3.7s	-1.42	NE	NE	NE	NC	-73	03-87	.00	.0	0	0	0	00-00-00	-20.6	.57	-11.7	6.20	-72.5	12	1.1	7	2,541	207	0	0.2	09
Compact Video	1881.0	543.4	550.0	-3.7f	-.67	-100.0	-100.0	-100.0	NC	-13	12-86	.00	.0	0	0	0	00-00-00	-2.4	.58	-1.4	9.29	-13.0	561	2.0	25	6,571	262	+11	0.0	12
Craig Corp	3361.9	1316.1	6354.5	1.6n	.85	410.0	85.0	54.5	NC	10	03-87	.00	.0	0	0	0	12-21-79	.2	47.00	9.4	1.10	10.3	0	7.6	31	1,895	238	+5	0.0	06
Digitech	.0	15.6	-50.0	.6s	.02	-40.0	-33.3	NE	NC	9	04-87	.00	.0	0	0	0	00-00-00	10.0	.37	3.7	2.54	9.4	6	1.9	48	12,477	929	0	0.0	10
Emerson Radio	25.8	43.1	43.1	26.6f	.72	-61.5	94.6	94.6	106	43	03-87	.00	.0	0	0	0	10-17-86	3.3	4.48	14.8	2.93	43.3	79	2.7	241	35,662	11,342	-449	1.8	03
Esquire Radio	443.8	443.8	360.0	.3q	.60	900.0	900.0	NE	NC	0	03-87	.72	1.9	0	171	33	03-21-86	1.3	.85	1.1	1.36	1.5	0	4.3	18	483	102	0	0.1	12
Microdyne	-15.4	-30.1	-27.5	-6.5s	-1.42	NE	NE	-100.0	NC	-25	04-87	.06	1.5	0	NE	NE	05-11-87	-31.0	.68	-21.2	1.12	-23.8	4	9.5	18	4,445	631	0	0.0	10
Motorola Inc	15.5	15.5	11.6	205.0q	1.60	18.9	18.9	154.0	-7	4	03-87	.64	1.2	5	42	32	06-15-87	3.4	1.29	4.4	1.68	7.4	12	1.6	6,939	128,200	76,522	-31	1.3	12
Pioneer Elec	35.9	27.0	40.8	40.0s	.57	287.5	111.8	1040.0	NC	3	03-87	.10	.2	-14	26	156	09-23-86	1.6	1.38	2.2	1.77	3.9	4	1.8	5,637	137,498	458	0	2.0	09
Sony Corp	15.3	15.3	19.3	272.8q	1.18	15.2	15.2	-25.3	8	6	01-87	.23	.8	8	19	16	10-24-86	3.2	.97	3.1	2.35	7.3	24	1.6	6,617	231,148	5,226	0	12.1	10
Wells Gard El	59.5	59.5	21.0	.3q	.07	NE	NE	NE	NC	2	03-87	.00	.0	0	0	99	08-26-83	1.3	1.46	1.9	1.26	2.4	0	4.9	28	3,591	305	+1	5.5	12
Zenith Eltrns	36.4	36.4	27.0	-4.6q	-.20	NE	NE	NE	NC	-1	03-87	.00	.0	0	0	5	06-07-82	-.2	2.00	-.4	2.75	-1.1	63	2.0	601	23,345	12,369	0	3.0	12

Recent Performance and Forecast: Measuring and Controlling Instruments (SIC 3822,3823,3824,3829)

(in millions of dollars except as noted)

					Percent Change				
					Compound Annual		Annual		
	1984	1985[1]	1986[2]	1987[3]	1972-84	1979-84	1984-85	1985-86	1986-87
Industry Data									
Value of shipments[4]	9,367	10,200	10,708	—	11.6	8.2	8.9	5.0	—
3822 Environmental Controls	1,966	2,007	2,331	—	8.6	7.6	2.1	16.1	—
3823 Control Instruments	4,308	4,625	4,811	—	13.9	9.9	7.4	4.0	—
3824 Fluid Meters & Devices	811	774	794	—	9.1	−0.8	−4.6	2.6	—
3829 Instruments, nec	2,283	2,794	2,772	—	12.1	9.9	22.4	−0.8	—
Value of shipments (1982$)	8,231	8,684	8,875	9,100	4.3	0.3	5.5	2.2	2.5
3822 Environmental Controls	1,814	1,796	2,024	—	2.5	1.4	−1.0	12.7	—
3823 Control Instruments	3,563	3,703	3,698	—	4.8	−0.2	3.9	−0.1	—
3824 Fluid Meters & Devices	748	691	703	—	3.0	−6.4	−7.6	1.7	—
3829 Instruments, nec	2,106	2,494	2,450	—	5.9	3.6	18.4	−1.8	—
Total employment (000)	131	133	130	—	2.3	−1.1	1.3	−2.1	—
Production workers (000)	75.8	77.8	76.5	—	1.8	−1.9	2.6	−1.7	—
Average hourly earnings ($)	9.34	9.60	9.84	—	7.6	8.3	2.8	2.5	—
Product Data									
Value of shipments[5]	9,055	9,822	10,335	—	11.8	8.1	8.5	5.2	—
3822 Environmental Controls	2,030	2,073	2,407	—	9.8	8.7	2.1	16.1	—
3823 Control Instruments	4,115	4,418	4,595	—	14.7	9.2	7.4	4.0	—
3824 Fluid Meters & Devices	860	821	843	—	8.4	0.7	−4.6	2.7	—
3829 Instruments, nec	2,051	2,510	2,490	—	11.0	9.6	22.4	−0.8	—

Value of shipments (1982$)	7,961	8,360	8,570	8,791	4.5	0.3	5.0	2.5	2.6
3822 Environmental Controls	1,872	1,849	2,090	—	3.7	2.5	−1.2	13.0	—
3823 Control Instruments	3,403	3,537	3,532	—	5.5	−0.9	3.9	−0.1	—
3824 Fluid Meters & Devices	794	734	747	—	2.3	−5.0	−7.5	1.8	—
3829 Instruments, nec	1,892	2,240	2,201	—	4.8	3.3	18.4	−1.7	—
Shipments price index[6]									
(1982 = 100)	114.3	118.1	121.5	—	7.2	8.0	3.3	2.9	—
3822 Environmental Controls	108.4	112.1	115.1	—	5.9	6.0	3.4	2.7	—
3823 Control Instruments	120.9	124.9	130.1	—	8.7	10.2	3.3	4.2	—
3824 Fluid Meters & Devices	108.4	10.7	10.7	—	5.9	6.0	−90.1	0.0	—
3829 Instruments, nec	108.4	112.0	113.2	—	5.9	6.0	3.3	1.1	—
Trade Data									
Value of imports (ITA)[7]	481	606	715	—	15.7	15.5	26.0	18.0	—
Import/new supply ratio[8]	0.050	0.058	0.065	—	3.3	6.5	15.2	11.3	—
Value of exports (ITA)[9]	1,526	1,562	1,528	—	10.7	5.6	2.4	−2.2	—
Export/shipments ratio	0.169	0.159	0.148	—	−1.0	−2.4	−5.6	−7.0	—

[1]Estimated except for exports and imports.
[2]Estimated.
[3]Forecast.
[4]Value of all products and services sold by the Measuring and Controlling Instruments industry.
[5]Value of products classified in the Measuring and Controlling Instruments industry produced by all industries.
[6]Developed by the Office of Industry Assessment, ITA.
[7]Import data are developed by the chapter author.
[8]New supply is the sum of product shipments plus imports.
[9]Export data are developed by the chapter author.
SOURCE: U.S. Department of Commerce: Bureau of the Census, Bureau of Economic Analysis, International Trade Administration (ITA). Estimates and forecasts by ITA.

Source: *U.S. Industrial Outlook 1987*, U.S. Department of Commerce.

Company	Revenue: Pct. Change Last Qtr	Revenue: Pct. Change FY to Date	Revenue: Pct. Change Last 12 Mos	Earnings: Last 12 Mos	Earnings Per Share: Last 12 Mos	Per Share Pct. Change: Last Qtr	Per Share Pct. Change: FY to Date	Per Share Pct. Change: Last 12 Mos	5-Year Growth Rate	Par Growth Rate	Date of Report	Dividends Current Rate: Amt	Current Rate: Yield	5-Year Growth Rate	Payout: Last FY	Payout: Last 5 Yrs.	Last X-Dvd Date	Profit Margin	Asset Turnover	Return on Total Assets	Leverage Ratio	Return on Equity	Debt to Equity	Current Ratio	Market Value	Latest Shares Outstndng.	Held by Banks-Funds	Insider Net Trading	Short Interest Ratio	Fiscal Year Ends
-	%	%	%	$Mil	$	%	%	%	%	%	-	$	%	%	%	%	-	π/r x	r/a =	π/a x	a/e =	π/e	%	-	$Mil	000	000	000	Days	Mo
Electronic Controls and Instruments																														
Ind. Group	- 1.1	- 1.2	5.4	130.4	.54	2.5	- 38.3	- 8.1	- 8	2	- - -	.38	1.6	1	36	29	- - - -	2.2	1.27	2.8	1.82	5.1	24	2.2	5,103	216,246	85,434	+ 143	1.0	- -
Adams Rsl E	11.6	18.0	132.0	5.4s	.83	-65.6	-37.1	NC	NC	6	03-87	.00	.0	0	0	0	00-00-00	4.4	1.09	4.8	1.23	5.9	6	4.9	99	6,376	2,609	0	0.0	09
Ametek Inc	1.8	1.8	8.9	37.2q	1.69	7.1	7.1	5.6	7	7	03-87	1.00	3.1	13	60	50	06-10-87	6.5	1.12	7.3	2.21	16.1	66	3.6	707	21,849	7,962	+7	0.2	12
Bowmar Instr	.0	.4	12.2	.1s	-.01	-100.0	-100.0	-100.0	NC	1	03-87	.00	.0	0	0	0	00-00-00	.2	1.50	.3	3.33	1.0	113	2.3	14	5,986	315	+5	0.4	09
CompuDyne	-96.7	-70.6	.0	.0	2.45	324.0	-98.2	NE	NC	0	03-87	.00	.0	0	0	0	00-00-00	NC	NC	NC	NC	.0	119	2.8	21	1,026	142	0	1.3	09
Daniel Inds	-3.3	-3.3	-9.7	-3.6q	-.36	NE	NE	NE	NC	-6	12-86	.18	1.7	5	NE	57	06-08-87	-3.0	.90	-2.7	1.52	-4.1	15	2.8	110	10,160	1,930	0	0.4	09
Diagnostic Ret	14.2	48.1	47.2	3.4f	.61	116.7	306.7	306.7	-10	14	03-87	.00	.0	0	0	0	07-18-83	6.4	.86	5.5	2.53	13.9	105	4.1	39	3,602	487	0	0.0	03
Dranetz Tech	7.8	7.8	-4.0	2.2q	.46	.0	.0	-34.3	3	5	03-87	.24	2.5	57	43	17	06-22-87	9.2	.98	9.0	1.11	10.0	0	9.9	45	4,749	885	-20	0.0	12
Dynascan Cp	54.2	54.2	26.3	6.3q	.87	20.0	20.0	200.0	NC	17	03-87	.00	.0	0	0	0	06-22-87	3.9	1.49	5.8	2.90	16.8	59	2.2	83	6,820	993	+7	0.0	12
EIP Microwave	-11.1	5.1	5.0	.2s	.11	-66.7	-33.3	.0	-23	0	03-87	.12	1.2	21	86	19	04-29-87	1.0	1.70	1.7	1.88	3.2	24	2.4	22	2,184	354	0	0.0	09
Energy Conv Dev	-48.2	-44.7	-40.9	-27.4n	-5.38	NE	NE	NE	NC	0	03-87	.00	.0	0	0	0	00-00-00	NM	NC	NC	NC	NM	140	2.1	156	5,171	852	0	0.0	06
Fischer & Port	-1.2	-1.2	.5	.8q	.10	-100.0	-100.0	-90.5	19	1	03-87	.00	.0	0	0	0	03-03-87	.5	1.20	.6	2.00	1.2	11	2.6	56	4,044	1,821	0	1.3	12
Fluke, John	-.8	-.9	-1.8	11.0s	1.26	-5.9	-13.9	-18.7	10	9	03-87	.00	.0	0	0	0	02-19-87	5.3	1.17	6.2	1.44	8.9	13	4.4	222	7,643	3,720	+1	0.6	09
Frequency Elec	28.8	25.0	26.6	6.3n	1.35	29.6	31.6	35.0	11	15	01-87	.00	.0	0	0	0	05-27-86	16.6	.67	11.1	1.37	15.2	15	6.5	115	4,584	1,756	0	0.1	04
Imo Delaval	-4.3	-6.8	-7.0	-11.0f	-1.52	-100.0	-100.0	NC	NC	-8	12-86	.56	2.0	0	0	0	06-26-87	-3.1	1.13	-3.5	1.60	-5.6	18	3.3	204	7,270	188	+18	0.2	12
Instron Corp	2.3	2.3	7.3	4.4q	.70	-33.3	-33.3	7.7	72	13	03-87	.12	.8	10	15	24	06-11-87	5.0	1.46	7.3	2.14	15.6	23	1.9	86	6,019	1,497	0	1.0	12
Johnson Contr	-3.7	-9.6	4.4	87.4s	2.13	40.0	-21.7	-7.4	5	5	03-87	1.06	2.9	9	42	38	06-08-87	3.5	1.49	5.2	2.02	10.5	16	1.2	1,370	37,804	19,380	+0	1.0	09
Kollmorgen Cp	-14.9	-14.9	-3.7	-19.5q	-1.92	NE	NE	NE	NC	-29	03-87	.32	2.0	0	NE	356	05-18-87	-6.4	1.53	-9.8	2.51	-24.6	72	2.1	173	10,624	3,354	+1	0.3	12
Mangood Corp	13.0	13.0	16.1	-4.7q	-3.74	NE	NE	NE	NC	0	03-87	.00	.0	0	0	0	02-07-84	-6.5	1.55	-10.1	.00	NS	-724	2.1	16	1,894	33	0	12.2	12
Measurex Corp	21.5	18.0	15.4	23.5s	1.23	14.8	20.4	17.1	NC	12	05-87	.24	.9	0	15	16	06-25-87	11.2	.93	10.4	1.49	15.5	4	3.5	505	18,516	11,806	-15	0.1	11
MTS Systems Cp	15.7	1.2	10.0	6.0s	1.38	-13.6	-39.6	16.0	24	10	03-87	.24	1.0	3	11	19	04-02-87	5.5	1.13	6.2	1.98	12.3	20	2.0	99	4,291	1,318	+3	0.0	09
Nicolet Instr	8.7	6.7	7.0	14.8f	2.25	NE	411.4	411.4	19	23	03-87	.00	.0	-8	5	11	10-31-87	12.1	1.21	14.7	1.54	22.7	13	2.6	128	6,489	3,817	0	0.4	03
Nuclear Data	-.8	-15.3	-15.0	-10.2f	-5.54	NE	NE	NE	NC	-64	02-87	.00	.0	0	0	0	04-13-81	-22.7	1.20	-27.3	2.35	-64.2	71	2.3	7	1,848	142	0	0.0	02
Tenney Engr	-11.1	-11.1	-8.6	.3q	.08	-66.7	-66.7	-71.4	-10	4	03-87	.00	.0	0	0	2	05-25-84	1.4	1.21	1.7	2.06	3.5	44	2.6	12	3,538	555	0	0.8	12
Teradyne Inc	4.9	4.9	-.9	-3.8q	-.16	NC	NC	-100.0	NC	-1	03-87	.00	.0	0	0	0	08-01-83	-1.2	.92	-1.1	1.27	-1.4	5	3.8	611	23,284	16,113	+5	0.9	12
Veeco Instrs	16.7	16.8	19.2	1.3s	.10	17.6	22.2	-83.9	-40	-4	03-87	.40	2.1	18	1000	34	05-05-87	.7	1.14	.8	1.75	1.4	16	3.1	204	10,475	3,405	+130	2.6	09

Energy: Coal, Oil, and Gas

CONSUMPTION BY FUEL TYPE AND SECTOR 1973–1986 [Quadrillon (10^{15}) BTU]

Residential and Commercial*				Transportation*			
Total	Coal	Natural Gas[1]	Petroleum	Total	Coal	Natural Gas[4]	Petroleum
1973	0.254	7.626	4.391	1973	0.003	0.743	17.821
1974	0.257	7.518	3.996	1974	0.002	0.685	17.396
1975	0.209	7.581	3.805	1975	0.001	0.595	17.610
1976	0.203	7.866	4.181	1976	([2])	0.559	18.499
1977	0.205	7.461	4.206	1977	([2])	0.543	19.230
1978	0.214	7.624	4.070	1978	([3])	0.539	20.019
1979	0.187	7.891	3.448	1979	([3])	0.612	19.817
1980	0.145	7.539	3.035	1980	([3])	0.650	19.009
1981	0.168	7.242	2.634	1981	([3])	0.058	18.800
1982	0.188	7.433	2.449	1982	([3])	0.612	18.417
1983	0.196	7.025	2.499	1983	([3])	0.505	18.591
1984	0.212	7.292	2.582	1984	([3])	0.545	19.295
1985	0.179	7.085	R2.573	1985	([3])	0.520	19.558
1986	0.184	6.968	2.573	1986		0.495	20.158

* Geographic coverage: the 50 United States and District of Columbia.

The Residential and Commercial Sector consists of housing units, non-manufacturing business establishments (e.g., wholesale and retail businesses), health and educational institutions, and government office buildings.

R = Revised data.

˙Totals may not equal sum of components due to independent rounding.

The Transportation Sector consists of both private and public passenger and freight transportation, as well as government transportation, including military operations.

[1] Includes supplemental gaseous fuels.

[2] Less than 0.5 trillion BTU.

[3] Negligible quantities are included in the industrial sector.

[4] Pipeline fuel only, including supplemental gaseous fuels.

Industrial*				Electric Utilities*			
Total	Coal	Natural Gas[1]	Petroleum	Total	Coal	Natural Gas[1]	Petroleum[2]
1973	4.057	10.388	9.113	1973	8.658	3.748	3.515
1974	3.870	10.003	8.698	1974	8.534	3.519	3.365
1975	3.667	8.532	8.151	1975	8.786	3.240	3.166
1976	3.661	8.761	9.018	1976	9.720	3.152	3.477
1977	3.454	8.636	9.786	1977	10.262	3.284	4.901
1978	3.314	8.539	9.890	1978	10.238	3.297	3.987
1979	3.593	8.549	10.576	1979	11.260	3.613	3.283
1980	3.155	8.394	9.524	1980	12.123	3.810	2.634
1981	3.157	8.257	8.295	1981	12.583	3.768	2.202
1982	2.552	7.116	7.798	1982	12.582	3.342	1.568
1983	2.490	6.821	7.421	1983	13.213	2.998	1.544
1984	2.842	7.448	7.889	1984	14.020	3.220	1.286
1985	2.777	R7.087	R7.702	1985	14.542	3.130	1.090
1986	2.675	6.364	7.705	1986	14.463	2.699	1.452

* Geographic coverage: the 50 United States and District of Columbia.

The Industrial Sector is made up of construction, manufacturing, agriculture, and mining establishments.

R = Revised data.

˙Totals may not equal sum of components due to independent rounding.

[1] Includes supplemental gaseous fuels.

[2] Includes petroleum products reported as "oil consumed at steam units" through 1979 and "heavy oil" from 1980 forward, which are assumed to be residual fuel oil; petroleum products reported as "oil consumed by gas turbine and internal combustion units" through 1979 and "light oil" from 1980 forward, which are assumed to be distillate fuel oil and kerosene; and petroleum coke.

Source: *Monthly Energy Review,* U.S. Department of Energy, Energy Information Administration, March 1987.

PETROLEUM—CRUDE OIL[1] SUPPLY AND DISPOSITION*

		Supply				
		Field Production		Imports		
		Total Domestic	Alaskan	Total	SPR[2]	Other
		Thousand barrels per day				
1973	AVERAGE	9,208	198	3,244		3,244
1974	AVERAGE	8,774	193	3,477		3,477
1975	AVERAGE	8,375	191	4,105		4,105
1976	AVERAGE	8,132	173	5,287		5,287
1977	AVERAGE	8,245	464	6,615	21	6,594
1978	AVERAGE	8,707	1,229	6,356	162	6,195
1979	AVERAGE	8,552	1,401	6,519	67	6,452
1980	AVERAGE	8,597	1,617	5,263	44	5,219
1981	AVERAGE	8,572	1,609	4,396	256	4,141
1982	AVERAGE	8,649	1,696	3,488	165	3,323
1983	AVERAGE	8,688	1,714	3,329	234	3,096
1984	AVERAGE	8,879	1,722	3,426	197	3,229
1985	AVERAGE	8,971	1,825	3,201	118	3,083
1986	AVERAGE	8,668	1,865	4,111	48	4,063

* Geographic coverage: the 50 United States and the District of Columbia.

' Totals may not equal sum of components due to independent rounding.

[1] Includes lease condensate.

[2] Strategic Petroleum Reserve.

Source: *Monthly Energy Review,* U.S. Department of Energy, Energy Information Administration, March 1987.

Company	Revenue: Pct. Change: Last Qtr	Revenue: Pct. Change: FY to Date	Revenue: Pct. Change: Last 12 Mos	Earnings: Last 12 Mos	Earnings: Per Share: Last 12 Mos	Earnings: Per Share: Pct. Change: Last Qtr	Earnings: Per Share: Pct. Change: FY to Date	Earnings: Per Share: Pct. Change: Last 12 Mos	Earnings: 5-Year Growth Rate	Earnings: Par Growth Rate	Earnings: Date of Report	Dividends: Current Rate: Amt	Dividends: Current Rate: Yield	Dividends: 5-Year Growth Rate	Dividends: Payout: Last FY	Dividends: Payout: Last 5 Yrs.	Dividends: Last X-Dvd Date	Ratio Analysis: Profit Margin	Ratio Analysis: Asset Turnover	Ratio Analysis: Return on Total Assets	Ratio Analysis: Leverage Ratio	Ratio Analysis: Return on Equity	Ratio Analysis: Debt to Equity	Ratio Analysis: Current Ratio	Shareholdings: Market Value	Shareholdings: Latest Shares Outstndng.	Shareholdings: Held by Banks-Funds	Shareholdings: Insider Net Trading	Shareholdings: Short Interest Ratio	Shareholdings: Fiscal Year Ends
-	%	%	%	$Mil	$	%	%	%	%	%	-	$	%	%	%	%	-	π/r	x r/a	= π/a	x a/e	= π/e	%	-	$Mil	000	000	000	Days	Mo
Oil, Natural Gas Producers																														
Ind. Group	1.4	2.5	- 7.1	- 2,043.7	- 1.48	NE	NE	- 100.0	NC	- 28	- - -	.74	5.2	0	349	105	- - - -	- 6.0	.68	- 4.1	4.51	-18.5	206	1.1	24,578	1,722,546	230,823	- 135	2.4	- -
Allegheny & Wstrn	-2.1	-4.7	-6.2	18.3n	2.29	13.3	8.7	10.1	NC	23	03-87	.30	1.1	0	10	6	05-11-87	8.1	1.14	9.2	2.93	27.0	72	1.5	227	7,998	1,762	+35	0.0	06
Asamera Inc	-61.9	-61.9	-43.2	-2.3q	-.22	NE	NE	-100.0	NC	-4	03-87	.20	2.1	10	NE	NE	03-26-87	-1.1	.82	-.9	2.44	-2.2	26	1.3	319	33,116	5,684	+3	0.1	12
Barnwell Indus	3.4	-14.1	-28.5	.9s	.67	457.1	366.7	NE	NC	0	03-87	.00	.0	-9	43	NE	03-10-86	9.0	.48	4.3	.00	NS	-182	1.6	18	1,400	43	0	8.1	09
Baruch-Foster	-18.5	-18.5	-46.6	-3.9q	-1.43	NE	NE	-100.0	NC	-30	03-87	.00	.0	0	0	0	07-08-85	-48.8	.35	-17.3	1.72	-29.8	58	2.3	20	2,718	373	0	0.0	12
Basic Res Intl	125.0	125.0	8.3	.3q	.01	NE	NE	NE	NC	0	03-87	.00	.0	0	0	0	00-00-00	2.3	.13	.3	1.00	.3	0	4.9	51	101,777	40,962	0	0.0	12
Cdn Occid Pet	2.1	2.1	-14.0	44.9q	1.35	37.5	37.5	-48.7	5	4	03-87	.64	NA	15	52	22	06-01-87	8.7	.38	3.3	2.03	6.7	23	1.3	991	33,316	598	-3	1.6	12
Coastal Corp	.9	.9	-12.9	167.7q	3.04	NE	NE	473.6	NC	18	03-87	.40	1.2	10	32	15	05-22-87	2.5	.88	2.2	9.68	21.3	481	1.0	1,526	43,923	17,594	-2	3.8	12
Consol O & G	-33.3	-33.3	-39.2	-21.3q	-3.48	NE	NE	NE	NC	0	02-87	.00	.0	0	0	0	05-28-80	NM	NC	NC	NC	NS	-499	NA	17	5,748	844	-1	12.1	11
Damson Oil	-66.7	-66.7	-58.1	-82.3q	-9.63	NE	NE	NE	NC	0	12-86	.00	.0	0	0	0	00-00-00	NM	NC	NC	NC	NM	987	1.0	10	33,112	696	0	6.9	09
Devon Resourc	-23.1	-23.1	-33.3	-1.3q	-.22	NC	NC	-100.0	NC	-17	03-87	.60	11.4	0	NE	2000	05-11-87	-16.3	.21	-3.5	1.31	-4.6	28	3.0	31	5,998	0	0	0.0	12
Dome Petrol	-16.4	-16.4	-35.2	-2050.0q	-6.48	NE	NE	NE	NC	0	03-87	.00	NA	0	0	0	06-03-81	NM	NC	NC	NC	NS	-240	1.2	298	340,452	18,294	0	0.1	12
Ensource Inc	-31.5	-31.5	-35.2	3.4q	1.00	NE	NE	NE	NC	14	03-87	.00	.0	0	0	0	05-15-86	10.3	.29	3.0	4.63	13.9	169	.3	31	3,356	279	+1	0.0	12
Equity Oil	-32.5	-32.5	-47.3	-.9q	-.08	-66.7	-66.7	-100.0	NC	-2	03-87	.00	.0	0	0	54	11-10-86	-9.0	.18	-1.6	1.44	-2.3	0	4.2	75	12,265	3,876	0	0.0	12
Forest Oil	-9.2	-9.2	-31.1	-3.7q	-1.17	NE	NE	-100.0	NC	-6	03-87	.25	1.8b	-12	NE	102	04-30-87	-4.4	.18	-.8	5.88	-4.7	301	.8	98	6,972	1,216	0	0.0	12
Free Mc Egy	-23.3	-23.3	-21.0	12.3q	.56	NE	NE	NC	NC	-6	03-87	2.20	14.5	0	NE	NE	04-24-87	9.4	.16	1.5	1.40	2.1	26	.7	808	53,424	769	0	0.2	12
Gulf Appld Tech	-24.5	-24.5	46.6	2.0q	.71	NE	NE	NE	NC	7	03-87	.00	.0	0	0	NE	06-29-84	9.1	.58	5.3	1.25	6.6	1	3.1	33	3,267	236	0	0.0	12
Hamilton Oil	5.7	5.7	-18.7	12.1q	.39	10.5	10.5	-66.4	-11	4	03-87	.03	.1	0	23	11	09-09-87	4.5	.31	1.4	2.93	4.1	103	1.2	533	25,386	4,124	+7	0.0	12
Howell Corp	43.1	43.1	2.9	-19.8q	-4.12	400.0	400.0	-100.0	NC	-40	03-87	.32	2.7	2	NE	NE	05-27-87	-19.0	.66	-12.5	2.94	-36.8	80	1.0	58	4,794	369	0	0.0	12
MAPCO	-13.7	-13.7	-18.9	78.2q	3.63	-4.7	-4.7	.6	7	12	03-87	1.00	1.8	-13	27	36	05-19-87	5.2	1.08	5.6	2.86	16.0	80	1.6	1,167	21,323	15,591	0	0.5	12
May Petrol	-46.4	-46.4	-34.6	-17.6q	-1.40	NE	NE	NE	NC	-32	03-87	.00	.0	0	0	0	10-22-80	NM	NC	NC	NC	-32.1	29	1.3	29	12,609	771	0	0.0	12
Maynard Oil	-40.8	-40.8	-57.6	-2.4q	-.39	NE	NE	-100.0	NC	-8	03-87	.00	.0	0	0	0	00-00-00	-21.8	.28	-6.0	1.38	-8.3	20	4.0	32	6,139	649	0	0.0	12
MCO Holding	-11.9	-11.9	34.6	-23.0q	-4.12	NE	NE	-100.0	NC	-37	03-87	.00	.0	0	0	0	00-00-00	-21.9	.20	-4.4	8.34	-36.7	200	.8	85	5,600	809	0	16.9	12
Mitchell Energy	-15.6	-15.6	-31.2	5.5q	.12	-66.7	-66.7	-86.4	-37	-1	04-87	.24	1.7	0	133	23	06-08-87	1.0	.30	.3	3.33	1.0	160	1.0	680	47,333	9,056	+5	1.1	01
N Cdn Oils	-32.6	-32.6	-34.0	16.8q	.05	-59.5	-59.5	-93.9	-29	12	03-87	.00	NA	0	0	0	08-23-85	17.0	.12	2.1	5.90	12.4	242	6.6	237	18,434	350	0	1.0	12
Numac O & G	-35.4	-35.4	-53.0	4.9q	.21	-16.7	-16.7	-73.1	-2	3	03-87	.00	NA	0	0	2	12-12-83	15.8	.13	2.0	1.70	3.4	28	1.7	193	22,750	2,736	0	1.9	12
Occid Petrol	14.5	14.5	9.6	174.9q	.58	-17.4	-17.4	-77.3	-18	-14	03-87	2.50	6.6	0	379	162	06-04-87	1.1	.91	1.0	4.10	4.1	175	1.1	7,458	198,213	68,799	+60	2.7	12
Pauley Petro	-23.4	-24.5	-26.4	5.0s	1.73	NE	2.0	-2.8	NC	18	02-87	.00	.0	0	0	0	00-00-00	3.5	2.20	7.7	2.34	18.0	46	1.2	38	2,902	214	0	2.3	08
Plains Petrol	-8.7	-24.3	-27.7	3.6f	.40	116.7	-18.4	-18.4	NC	16	12-86	.12	.4	0	0	0	06-08-87	27.7	.39	10.9	2.10	22.9	41	1.8	291	9,050	4,624	0	1.7	12
Prairie Oil Roy	-18.0	-18.0	-42.1	2.1q	.28	4.8	4.8	-66.3	-8	4	03-87	.00	NA	0	0	0	01-10-85	19.1	.13	2.5	1.60	4.0	0	4.2	51	7,846	466	0	0.0	12
Ranger Oil	-27.2	-27.2	-43.4	7.5q	.08	28.6	28.6	NE	NC	5	03-87	.00	.0	0	0	0	11-25-80	10.3	.17	1.8	2.50	4.5	22	2.7	430	74,722	7,117	-4	2.5	12
Santa Fe Engy	-22.7	-22.7	158.9	-122.1q	-4.49	NE	NE	NC	NC	-68	03-87	2.88	13.9	0	0	0	06-24-87	NM	NC	NC	NC	-41.3	0	.3	519	25,000	73	0	0.0	12
Saxon Oil Dev	-22.2	-22.2	-40.0	-3.4q	-.52	NC	NC	NE	NC	-15	03-87	.00	.0	0	NE	NE	00-00-00	-28.3	.43	-12.1	1.26	-15.2	18	1.1	24	24,253	10	-236	0.1	12
Sceptre Rscs	-30.3	-30.3	-22.5	4.9q	.05	-28.6	-28.6	-84.8	NC	56	03-87	.00	.0	0	0	0	00-00-00	7.9	.25	2.0	27.85	55.7	1395	1.1	95	25,776	292	+1	0.0	12
Scurry Rainbow	-35.3	-35.3	-32.9	14.9q	1.10	-41.5	-41.5	-50.5	13	4	12-86	.50	NA	0	38	6	06-02-87	22.9	.21	4.8	1.67	8.0	2	3.7	224	13,462	228	0	10.1	09
Summit En ◆	-11.1	-36.8	-40.0	-1.2n	-.54	NE	NE	NE	NC	-26	04-87	.00	.0	0	0	NE	03-11-82	-40.0	.28	-11.0	2.32	-25.5	0	.5	5	2,874	134	0	16.1	07
Sun Engy Prt	-23.5	-23.5	170.9	-47.0q	-.16	-70.4	-70.4	NC	NC	-14	03-87	1.20	6.4	0	5867	5867	05-04-87	-3.4	.32	-1.1	1.55	-1.7	39	.7	5,651	303,400	503	0	0.1	12
Tesoro Petrol	-7.0	-26.2	-32.7	-67.5s	-5.25	NE	NE	NE	NC	-34	03-87	.00	.0	0	NE	NE	08-05-86	-5.4	2.20	-11.9	2.89	-34.4	73	1.4	182	13,729	4,854	0	6.9	09
Tex Pacific	-6.3	-6.3	-50.0	3.1q	.82	.0	.0	-52.0	-10	9	03-87	.40	1.2	10	49	23	02-26-87	51.7	.26	13.2	1.33	17.6	0	NA	130	3,792	510	0	2.1	12
Tosco Corp	23.7	23.7	-37.0	55.6q	2.06	NE	NE	NE	NC	0	03-87	.00	.0	0	0	NE	07-06-82	6.7	1.69	11.3	.00	NS	-394	1.7	83	28,779	2,011	0	8.0	12
Total Petro NA	-14.4	-14.4	-32.8	21.3q	.78	-100.0	-100.0	-73.0	NC	5	03-87	.40	2.1	-7	24	46	05-22-87	1.4	1.64	2.3	4.09	9.4	132	1.3	503	26,108	6,021	-1	4.2	12

Continued

Company	Revenue: Pct. Change Last Qtr	Revenue: Pct. Change FY to Date	Revenue: Pct. Change Last 12 Mos	Earnings: Last 12 Mos	Earnings Per Share: Last 12 Mos	Per Share Pct. Change: Last Qtr	Per Share Pct. Change: FY to Date	Per Share Pct. Change: Last 12 Mos	5-Year Growth Rate	Par Growth Rate	Date of Report	Dividends Current Rate: Amt	Current Rate: Yield	5-Year Growth Rate	Payout: Last FY	Payout: Last 5 Yrs.	Last X-Dvd Date	Profit Margin	Asset Turnover	Return on Total Assets	Leverage Ratio	Return on Equity	Debt to Equity	Current Ratio	Market Value	Latest Shares Outstndng.	Held by Banks-Funds	Insider Net Trading	Short Interest Ratio	Fiscal Year Ends
-	%	%	%	$Mil	$	%	%	%	%	%	-	$	%	%	%	%	-	π/r	x r/a =	π/a	x a/e =	π/e	%	-	$Mil	000	000	000	Days	Mo
Oil, Natural Gas Producers																														
Transco Expl	13.0	13.0	-18.7	-182.2q	-2.60	NE	NE	NE	NC	-39	03-87	1.50	10.8	0	NE	NE	03-26-84	-68.0	.22	-15.1	1.65	-24.9	17	.4	976	70,310	1,321	-0	0.7	12
Unimar Co	.0	.0	0	-24.6f	-2.33	NC	NC	NC	NC	-18	12-86	1.34	13.7	0	NE	NE	05-11-87	-14.1	.25	-3.5	3.20	-11.2	136	.7	103	10,536	2,424	0	0.3	12
Walker Energy	-54.7	-54.7	-38.0	-26.5q	-3.11	NE	NE	NE	NC	-56	03-87	.00	0	0	NE	NE	00-00-00	NM	NC	NC	NC	-55.9	16	.6	20	8,502	25	0	0.1	12
Wichita Indus	-92.3	-92.3	-113.3	-1.1q	-.39	NE	NE	NE	NC	0	03-87	.00	0	0	0	0	11-02-81	55.0	-.80	-44.0	.00	NM	60	.7	3	2,870	159	0	0.0	12
Wilshire Oil	-17.4	-17.4	-45.4	-.6q	-.08	NE	NE	NE	NC	-12	03-87	.10	1.7b	0	0	357	01-06-86	-10.0	.11	-1.1	5.00	-5.5	245	1.9	48	8,143	644	0	0.0	12
Wiser Oil	-28.9	-28.9	-44.4	.8q	.10	-34.8	-34.8	-87.7	-33	-3	03-87	.40	2.0	-10	250	82	05-14-87	3.2	.22	.7	1.29	.9	1	6.4	179	9,069	2,713	+0	0.0	12
Oil Refining and Marketing																														
Ind. Group	- 25.4	- 27.0	- 29.2	39,964.4	3.03	- 19.9	- 21.0	- 17.6	- 6	5	- - -	2.34	3.6	1	46	32	- - - -	10.3	.75	7.7	2.83	21.8	44	1.3	323,896	5,010,083	G	+1304	2.4	- -
Adam Rsc En	-26.2	-26.2	-49.5	1.1q	.11	0	0	-26.7	NC	0	03-87	.00	0	0	0	0	00-00-00	1.9	3.74	7.1	.00	NS	-29	.6	14	6,958	394	-36	0.5	12
Adobe Rscs	-25.2	-25.2	7.9	-42.8q	-2.76	NE	NE	NE	NC	-36	03-87	.00	0	0	0	0	00-00-00	-45.1	.21	-9.4	3.78	-35.5	87	2.1	203	22,196	2,113	-0	20.3	12
Argas Inc	71.6	57.4	57.3	2.6f	.60	-20.8	-21.1	NC	NC	24	03-87	.00	0	0	0	0	00-00-00	2.4	2.46	5.9	4.08	24.1	183	2.0	53	3,871	0	0	0.0	03
Amerada Hess	-13.9	-13.9	-45.3	217.7q	2.58	NE	NE	NE	NC	10	03-87	.15	.4	-14	NE	1114	06-18-87	5.6	.79	4.4	2.41	10.6	66	1.3	3,188	83,063	39,175	0	2.5	12
Am Petrofina	7.0	7.0	-14.8	34.9q	2.78	NE	NE	NE	NC	5	03-87	.00	0	0	0	104	08-28-85	1.7	1.18	2.0	2.65	5.3	69	1.1	698	11,982	160	+0	0.0	12
Amoco Cp	-14.9	-14.9	-19.1	676.0q	2.65	-20.3	-20.3	-61.8	-11	-1	03-87	3.30	3.8	5	113	50	05-07-87	3.5	.83	2.9	2.07	6.0	29	.9	22,313	255,004	101,541	0	2.2	12
Ashland Oil	-11.0	-18.0	-17.5	149.0s	4.47	-97.3	-66.1	-23.1	NC	9	03-87	1.80	2.8	-9	28	91	05-26-87	2.4	1.63	3.9	3.92	15.3	82	1.3	2,062	32,541	11,884	+2	1.1	09
Atlantic Rchfld	-10.1	-10.1	-30.7	566.0q	3.11	-17.1	-17.1	NE	NC	-3	03-87	4.00	4.2	14	118	90	05-11-87	4.0	.65	2.6	4.15	10.8	133	1.3	16,908	177,510	95,044	+6	1.1	12
Brit Petrol	-9.0	-9.0	-31.4	1644.9q	2.39	-39.4	-39.4	-44.5	-2	0	03-87	2.48	3.3	5	92	57	09-08-86	4.2	.93	3.9	2.85	11.1	39	1.5	34,349	457,993	20,428	0	5.5	12
Buckeye Prtnr	9.1	9.1	310.8	27.5q	2.28	12.7	12.7	NC	NC	11	03-87	.00	0	0	0	0	00-00-00	18.1	.27	4.8	2.35	11.3	125	1.8	262	12,121	0	0	0.0	12
Charter Co	-7.4	-7.4	-24.6	50.6q	1.68	NE	NE	NE	NC	0	03-87	.00	0	0	0	NE	00-00-00	4.5	3.60	16.2	.00	NM	353	1.9	237	47,416	324	+22	4.6	12
Chevron Cp	-18.7	-18.7	-39.6	536.0q	1.57	-47.3	-47.3	-65.8	-16	-2	03-87	2.40	3.9	1	115	61	05-05-87	2.3	.65	1.5	2.33	3.5	50	1.4	21,211	342,109	137,677	-13	2.5	12
Crown Ctrl Pet	-20.3	-20.3	-32.4	-17.7q	-3.22	NE	NE	NE	NC	-11	03-87	.00	0	0	0	NE	04-03-84	-1.8	2.28	-4.1	2.56	-10.5	37	1.4	103	6,251	521	0	0.0	12
Diam Sham Off	.0	.0	0	-54.6f	-1.14	NC	NC	NC	NC	-43	12-86	2.80	15.4	0	NE	NE	05-04-87	-54.1	.22	-12.1	1.02	-12.3	0	7.0	816	45,000	177	+3	0.0	12
Exxon	-10.9	-10.9	- 20.7	4720.0q	6.57	-36.2	-36.2	-7.5	7	7	03-87	3.60	3.9	4	49	53	05-07-87	7.0	.97	6.8	2.16	14.7	13	1.1	66,954	718,000	247,921	+4	1.4	12
Getty Petro	20.4	20.4	-23.3	8.8q	.79	-88.2	-88.2	-55.9	NC	10	04-87	.16	7b	3	9	22	06-30-87	.9	3.78	3.4	3.68	12.5	139	1.3	255	11,075	1,798	0	13.5	01
Gulf Canada	-6.1	-6.1	37.9	466.0q	2.25	254.5	254.5	92.3	14	18	03-87	.52	NA	4	26	36	02-23-87	11.9	.59	7.0	3.26	22.8	124	1.2	4,306	195,710	3,320	0	0.4	12
Holly Corp	19.2	-27.7	-29.6	7.5n	1.67	-69.1	-92.5	-53.0	24	35	04-87	.00	0	0	2	8	09-24-85	2.7	2.33	6.3	5.56	35.0	117	1.4	62	4,127	2,236	+0	0.3	07
Imperial Oil	-12.1	-12.1	-20.7	501.0q	3.06	62.7	62.7	-23.5	8	5	03-87	1.60	NA	1	61	50	05-26-87	7.7	.75	5.8	1.69	9.8	20	2.7	8,979	163,635	4,712	0	1.5	12
Kerr-McGee	-23.9	-23.9	-27.4	-293.9q	-6.04	-6.7	-6.7	-100.0	NC	-26	03-87	1.10	3.0	2	NE	136	06-01-87	-12.4	.77	-9.5	2.32	-22.0	51	1.3	1,777	48,358	27,291	+11	4.4	12
Maxus Engy	-79.2	-79.2	-50.1	236.0q	-1.60	NE	NE	NE	NC	21	03-87	.40	2.9	-13	NE	NE	02-03-87	12.2	.55	6.7	2.54	17.0	82	1.2	1,241	91,103	54,860	0	1.2	12
Mobil Corp	-9.7	-9.7	-13.8	1217.0q	2.99	-42.6	-42.6	4.9	-7	2	03-87	2.20	4.3	2	64	67	04-28-87	2.5	1.24	3.1	2.58	8.0	54	1.0	20,794	408,732	174,883	-1	1.9	12
Murphy Oil	-93.4	-93.4	-49.8	-203.2q	-5.88	-37.5	-37.5	-100.0	NC	-31	03-87	1.00	2.7	4	NE	78	05-11-87	-20.2	.51	-10.3	2.54	-26.2	30	1.4	1,230	33,591	14,612	+3	4.6	12
Pac Resources	-5.5	-5.5	-34.5	27.7q	1.41	-9.1	-9.1	62.1	NC	16	03-87	.05	.3	0	0	19	05-26-87	3.5	1.66	5.8	2.93	17.0	59	2.3	267	17,105	2,978	+1387	1.9	12
Pennzoil Co	-13.0	-13.0	-20.9	96.7q	1.97	NE	NE	286.3	-18	-2	03-87	2.20	2.9	0	172	89	05-22-87	5.6	.52	2.9	4.79	13.9	217	3.0	3,119	41,451	17,471	-20	1.0	12
Petro Heat Pwr	10.6	10.6	-11.4	8.2q	.81	-59.6	-59.6	NC	NC	79	03-87	.68	4.8	0	36	6	06-09-87	2.8	2.32	6.5	6.65	43.2	321	1.2	53	3,745	0	0	0.0	12
Phillips Petrol	-18.4	-18.4	-37.7	106.0q	.38	-100.0	-100.0	-76.1	-13	-4	03-87	.60	3.6	2	77	55	05-04-87	1.2	.75	.9	6.78	6.1	334	1.3	3,789	227,883	95,963	-23	1.9	12
Quaker St Oil	-4.4	-4.4	-9.2	45.4q	1.78	-52.3	-52.3	-11.4	6	6	03-87	.85	3.8	1	42	47	05-11-87	5.1	1.33	6.8	1.71	11.6	16	1.9	583	26,335	9,478	+0	0.2	12
Royal Dutch	-99.8	-99.8	-32.1	26751.1q	10.16	18.3	18.3	29.4	1	0	03-87	6.03	4.6	12	54	39	05-19-87	68.3	.85	58.3	.00	NM	17	1.4	35,381	268,037	63,421	0	2.6	12
Salomon Inc	-6.9	-6.9	-71.7	475.0q	3.15	-23.4	-23.4	-23.2	9	11	03-87	.64	1.9	9	18	17	06-16-87	7.1	.08	.6	23.00	13.8	140	.0	4,931	150,000	76,508	0	0.4	12
Shell Transport	-99.7	-99.7	-32.1	1136.4q	5.00	11.3	11.3	-11.3	1	3	03-87	3.02	3.3	7	61	39	09-26-86	4.3	.86	3.7	2.08	7.7	17	1.4	25,273	276,209	14,493	0	1.4	12
Std Oil Ohio	-14.4	-14.4	-25.6	-364.0q	-1.55	-21.3	-21.3	-100.0	NC	-15	03-87	2.80	3.7	4	NE	67	05-04-87	-3.8	.61	-2.3	2.26	-5.2	47	1.4	17,662	234,713	59,266	-35	0.1	12
Sun Co Inc	-28.1	-28.1	-37.1	277.0q	2.55	-73.9	-73.9	-48.4	-7	-1	03-87	3.00	4.6	4	85	54	05-05-87	3.3	.73	2.4	2.17	5.2	29	1.4	7,069	107,712	48,698	+0	3.2	12
Texaco Canada	-21.8	-21.8	-35.0	273.0q	2.25	-12.9	-12.9	-14.4	1	5	03-87	1.20	NA	8	51	42	05-05-87	10.8	.69	7.4	1.53	11.3	4	2.4	3,366	120,768	1,294	-1	1.1	12
vjTexaco	-8.7	-8.7	-29.9	515.0q	2.13	-64.2	-64.2	-59.0	-16	4	03-87	.00	.0	1	100	79	02-04-87	1.7	.88	1.5	2.47	3.7	55	1.3	9,780	241,474	93,553	-7	0.3	12

Recent Performance and Forecast: Health and Medical Services (SIC 80)

(in billions of dollars except as noted)

Item	1984	1985	1986[1]	1987[2]	Percent Change: Compound Annual 1972-84	Compound Annual 1979-84	Annual 1984-85	Annual 1985-86	Annual 1986-87
TOTAL EXPENDITURES	390.2	425.0	465.4	511.9	12.6	12.6	8.9	9.6	10.0
Health services and supplies	374.5	409.5	450.5	496.6	12.9	12.8	9.3	10.0	10.1
Personal health care	341.5	371.4	407.2	447.7	12.8	12.5	8.8	9.6	10.0
Hospital care	155.3	166.7	180.9	197.2	13.2	12.3	7.3	8.5	9.0
Physicians' services	75.4	82.8	91.5	101.1	13.1	13.4	9.8	10.5	10.5
Dentists' services	24.6	27.1	29.8	32.8	13.1	13.1	10.2	10.0	10.2
Other professional services	11.0	12.6	14.4	16.5	16.3	18.5	14.5	14.3	14.5
Drugs and medical sundries[3]	26.5	28.5	30.7	33.1	9.1	9.0	7.6	7.7	7.8
Eyeglasses and appliances	7.0	7.5	8.0	8.6	9.7	8.3	7.1	6.7	7.5
Nursing home care	32.0	35.2	39.2	43.7	14.2	13.5	10.0	11.5	11.5
Other health services	9.5	11.0	12.7	14.7	11.4	13.2	15.8	15.8	15.8
Program administration and net cost of insurance	22.6	26.2	30.3	35.0	13.8	21.3	15.9	15.6	15.5
Government public health activities	10.9	11.9	13.0	14.2	37.7	10.9	9.2	9.2	9.2
Research and construction of medical facilities	15.6	15.4	15.6	15.9	7.4	8.2	9.9	1.3	1.9
Research[4]	6.8	7.4	7.5	7.9	9.1	7.7	8.8	1.4	5.3
Construction	8.9	8.1	8.1	8.2	6.5	9.3	−0.1	0.0	1.2

[1]Estimated by U.S. Department of Commerce, International Trade Administration, (ITA).
[2]Forecast by U.S. Department of Commerce, ITA.
[3]Includes only expenditures for prescription drugs, over-the-counter drugs, and medical sundries dispensed through retail channels. Spending for drugs dispensed in hospitals and by physicians is reported within those cost categories.
[4]Research expenditures of drug companies and other manufacturers and providers of medical equipment and supplies are included in the expenditure class in which the product falls.

SOURCE: Bureau of Data Management and Strategy, Health Care Financing Administration and the U.S. Department of Commerce.

Source: *U.S. Industrial Outlook 1987*, U.S. Department of Commerce.

Recent Performance and Forecast: X-ray and Electromedical Apparatus (SIC 3693)

(in millions of dollars except as noted)

					Percent Change				
					Compound Annual		Annual		
	1984	1985[1]	1986[2]	1987[3]	1972-84	1979-84	1984-85	1985-86	1986-87
Industry Data									
Value of shipments[4]	5,175	5,061	5,324	5,979	22.7	17.1	−2.2	5.2	12.3
Value of shipments (1982$)	4,882	4,797	5,027	5,577	13.3	9.0	−1.7	4.8	10.9
Total employment (000)	46.4	45.6	44.4	45.3	11.9	5.4	−1.7	−2.6	2.0
Production workers (000)	21.7	21.1	20.0	20.0	10.0	2.9	−2.8	−5.2	0.0
Average hourly earnings ($)	8.75	—	—	—	6.9	6.3	—	—	—
Product Data									
Value of shipments[5]	4,782	4,677	4,920	5,525	23.4	15.9	−2.2	5.2	12.3
Value of shipments (1982$)	4,511	4,433	4,646	5,154	13.9	7.9	−1.7	4.8	10.9
Shipments price index[6] (1982=100)	106.0	105.5	105.9	107.2	8.3	7.5	−0.5	0.4	1.2
Trade Data									
Value of imports (ITA)[7]	840	1,053	1,254	1,369	23.6	25.1	25.4	19.1	9.2
Import/new supply ratio[8]	0.149	0.184	0.203	0.199	0.1	6.8	23.0	10.5	−2.2
Value of exports (ITA)[9]	1,099	1,161	1,268	1,449	24.2	8.9	5.6	9.2	14.3
Export/shipments ratio	0.230	0.248	0.258	0.262	0.7	−6.1	8.0	3.8	1.8

[1]Estimated except for exports and imports.
[2]Estimated.
[3]Forecast.
[4]Value of all products and services sold by the X-ray and Electromedical Apparatus industry.
[5]Value of products classified in the X-ray and Electromedical Apparatus industry produced by all industries.
[6]Developed by the Office of Industry Assessment, ITA.
[7]Import data are developed by the chapter author.
[8]New supply is the sum of product shipments plus imports.
[9]Export data are developed by the chapter author.
SOURCE: U.S. Department of Commerce: Bureau of the Census, Bureau of Economic Analysis, International Trade Administration (ITA). Estimates and forecasts by ITA.

Source: *U.S. Industrial Outlook 1987*, U.S. Department of Commerce.

Recent Performance and Forecast: Surgical and Medical Instruments (SIC 3841)

(in millions of dollars except as noted)

					Percent Change				
					Compound Annual		Annual		
	1984	1985[1]	1986[2]	1987[3]	1972-84	1979-84	1984-85	1985-86	1986-87
Industry Data									
Value of shipments[4]	4,630	4,855	5,137	5,471	14.0	15.5	4.9	5.8	6.5
Value of shipments (1982$)	4,323	4,516	4,761	5,019	6.3	8.3	4.5	5.4	5.4
Total employment (000)	61.3	61.3	63.9	66.4	4.9	4.2	0.0	4.2	4.0
Production workers (000)	39.7	38.6	41.0	43.4	4.2	3.4	−2.7	6.2	5.8
Average hourly earnings ($)	7.78	—	—	—	7.3	7.5	—	—	—
Product Data									
Value of shipments[5]	4,600	4,823	5,103	5,435	13.7	13.6	4.9	5.8	6.5
Value of shipments (1982$)	4,295	4,487	4,729	4,986	6.1	6.5	4.5	5.4	5.4
Shipments price index[6] (1982 = 100)	107.1	107.5	107.9	109.0	7.2	6.6	0.4	0.4	1.0
Trade Data									
Value of imports (ITA)[7]	337	399	508	572	22.0	16.6	18.3	27.3	12.6
Import/new supply ratio[8]	0.068	0.076	0.091	0.095	6.9	2.4	11.8	18.5	5.2
Value of exports (ITA)[9]	618	644	716	778	13.1	8.6	4.1	11.2	8.7
Export/shipments ratio	0.134	0.134	0.140	0.143	−0.5	−4.4	−0.7	5.1	2.0

[1]Estimated except for exports and imports.
[2]Estimated.
[3]Forecast.
[4]Value of all products and services sold by the Surgical and Medical Instruments industry.
[5]Value of products classified in the Surgical and Medical Instruments industry produced by all industries.
[6]Developed by the Office of Industry Assessment, ITA.
[7]Import data are developed by the chapter author.
[8]New supply is the sum of product shipments plus imports.
[9]Export data are developed by the chapter author.
SOURCE: U.S. Department of Commerce: Bureau of the Census, Bureau of Economic Analysis, International Trade Administration (ITA). Estimates and forecasts by ITA.

Source: *U.S. Industrial Outlook 1987,* U.S. Department of Commerce.

Recent Performance and Forecast: Dental Equipment and Supplies (SIC 3843)

(in millions of dollars except as noted)

					Percent Change				
					Compound Annual		Annual		
	1984	1985[1]	1986[2]	1987[3]	1972-84	1979-84	1984-85	1985-86	1986-87
Industry Data									
Value of shipments[4]	1,213	1,258	1,351	1,409	9.5	2.4	3.7	7.4	4.3
Value of shipments (1982$)	1,131	1,166	1,229	1,258	2.3	−4.1	3.1	5.4	2.3
Total employment (000)	14.4	14.6	15.3	16.2	1.3	−2.3	1.4	4.8	5.9
Production workers (000)	9.3	9.3	9.8	10.4	0.8	−2.8	0.0	5.4	6.1
Average hourly earnings ($)	7.96	—	—	—	7.1	7.3	—	—	—
Product Data									
Value of shipments[5]	1,023	1,060	1,139	1,188	9.3	1.9	3.6	7.5	4.3
Value of shipments (1982$)	953	957	1,026	1,061	2.2	−4.6	0.4	7.2	3.4
Shipments price index[6] (1982 = 100)	107.3	107.9	109.9	112.0	7.0	6.8	0.6	1.9	1.9
Trade Data									
Value of imports (ITA)[7]	66.3	75.0	89.0	96.0	14.8	9.8	13.1	18.7	7.9
Import/new supply ratio[8]	0.061	0.066	0.072	0.075	4.8	7.4	8.6	9.7	3.2
Value of exports (ITA)[9]	137	132	155	173	12.3	6.3	−3.9	17.4	11.6
Export/shipments ratio	0.134	0.125	0.136	0.146	2.7	4.3	−7.3	9.3	7.0

[1]Estimated except for exports and imports.
[2]Estimated.
[3]Forecast.
[4]Value of all products and services sold by the Dental Equipment and Supplies industry.
[5]Value of products classified in the Dental Equipment and Supplies industry produced by all industries.
[6]Developed by the Office of Industry Assessment, ITA.
[7]Import data are developed by the chapter author.
[8]New supply is the sum of product shipments plus imports.
[9]Export data are developed by the chapter author.

SOURCE: U.S. Department of Commerce: Bureau of the Census, Bureau of Economic Analysis, International Trade Administration (ITA). Estimates and forecasts by ITA.

Source: *U.S. Industrial Outlook 1987,* U.S. Department of Commerce.

Hospital and Laboratory Instruments

Company	Revenue: Pct. Change: Last Qtr	Revenue: Pct. Change: FY to Date	Revenue: Pct. Change: Last 12 Mos	Earnings: Last 12 Mos	Earnings: Per Share: Last 12 Mos	Earnings: Per Share: Pct. Change: Last Qtr	Earnings: Per Share: Pct. Change: FY to Date	Earnings: Per Share: Pct. Change: Last 12 Mos	Earnings: 5-Year Growth Rate	Earnings: Par Growth Rate	Earnings: Date of Report	Dividends: Current Rate: Amt	Dividends: Current Rate: Yield	Dividends: 5-Year Growth Rate	Dividends: Payout: Last FY	Dividends: Payout: Last 5 Yrs.	Dividends: Last X-Dvd Date	Ratio Analysis: Pro-fit Mar-gin	Ratio Analysis: Asset Turn-over	Ratio Analysis: Return on Total Assets	Ratio Analysis: Lever-age Ratio	Ratio Analysis: Return on Equity	Ratio Analysis: Debt to Eq-uity	Ratio Analysis: Curr-ent Ratio	Shareholdings: Mar-ket Value	Shareholdings: Latest Shares Out-stndng.	Shareholdings: Held by Banks-Funds	Shareholdings: Insider Net Trad-ing	Shareholdings: Short Int-erest Ratio	Shareholdings: Fiscal Year Ends
-	%	%	%	$Mil	$	%	%	%	%	%	-	$	%	%	%	%	-	π/r x	r/a =	π/a x	a/e =	π/e	%	-	$Mil	000	000	000	Days	Mo
Ind. Group	6.7	10.8	8.7	- 40.0	- .13	NE	- 73.1	NE	NC	- 4	- - -	.06	.4	1	11	10	- - - -	- 1.4	1.00	- 1.4	2.00	- 2.8	27	2.1	4,976	328,175	88,547	+ 947	1.2	- -
ADAC Labs •	43.1	25.9	15.2	-6.6s	-.24	NE	NE	NE	NC	0	03-87	.00	.0	0	0	0	11-22-82	-12.5	1.59	-19.9	.00	NS	-54	1.3	49	21,561	1,325	0	0.0	09
Biogen NV	42.9	42.9	-46.6	-27.5q	-1.34	NE	NE	NE	NC	-31	03-87	.00	.0	0	0	0	00-00-00	NM	NC	NC	NC	-30.8	5	10.2	232	22,102	6,586	0	0.0	12
Biomet	31.7	26.8	27.2	8.1f	.69	42.9	35.3	35.3	76	30	05-87	.00	.0	0	0	0	05-01-86	14.5	1.67	24.2	1.24	29.9	1	5.3	318	12,102	4,510	-73	0.0	05
Cobe Labs	7.9	7.9	12.0	9.4q	1.40	-5.9	-5.9	8.5	8	11	03-87	.00	.0	0	0	0	01-23-86	5.3	1.51	8.0	1.43	11.4	18	4.4	142	6,544	2,073	-27	0.0	12
Coherent Inc	16.6	8.3	3.5	-3.7s	-.46	-100.0	-100.0	-100.0	NC	-5	03-87	.00	.0	0	0	0	10-01-84	-2.6	1.00	-2.6	1.73	-4.5	5	2.2	101	7,990	2,793	0	0.0	09
Cordis Cp ■	-155.8	-44.8	-33.3	-7.6n	-.58	NE	NE	-100.0	NC	-7	03-87	.00	.0	0	0	0	07-21-83	-6.0	.58	-3.5	2.03	-7.1	54	3.1	203	13,285	6,574	0	0.0	06
Damon Corp	16.4	16.6	15.9	-1.6s	-.25	25.0	NE	NE	NC	-5	02-87	.20	1.0	0	NE	NE	04-28-87	-1.0	1.20	-1.2	2.33	-2.8	51	3.2	127	6,217	2,368	-0	0.6	08
Datascope Cp	33.7	32.2	32.2	4.4n	1.52	81.8	77.3	133.8	20	18	03-87	.00	.0	0	0	0	09-23-86	5.4	1.44	7.8	2.31	18.0	47	2.4	137	3,740	1,611	+20	0.0	06
Diasonics Inc	20.2	20.2	34.5	-17.4q	-.30	.0	.0	-100.0	NC	-25	03-87	.00	.0	0	0	0	00-00-00	-7.7	1.10	-8.5	2.98	-25.3	41	1.5	230	60,259	13,740	+747	0.0	12
Dynatech Cp	25.9	18.7	18.6	23.2f	2.10	-12.2	7.7	7.7	24	24	03-87	.00	.0	0	0	0	03-02-84	7.6	1.97	15.0	1.62	24.3	18	3.0	334	10,953	4,916	0	0.0	03
Electro Biology	.0	.0	5.7	2.1q	.38	-44.4	-44.4	-45.7	2	8	03-87	.00	.0	0	0	0	04-04-83	5.7	1.11	6.3	1.22	7.7	1	4.4	27	5,888	1,345	0	0.0	12
Elscint Ltd •	40.0	-16.0	-16.2	-115.8f	-6.99	NE	NE	NE	NC	0	03-86	.00	.0	0	0	0	00-00-00	-93.4	.58	-53.8	.00	NS	-55	.6	37	16,593	158	0	1.5	03
Fonar Cp	.0	15.6	36.6	1.3n	.08	-25.0	.0	NE	NC	0	03-87	.00	.0	0	0	0	00-00-00	3.2	1.88	6.0	.00	NM	4100	.9	65	16,804	764	0	0.0	06
Gelman Sci	9.6	5.8	8.3	1.2n	.46	42.9	NE	NE	NC	7	04-87	.00	.0	0	0	0	12-31-80	2.3	1.30	3.0	2.30	6.9	76	2.8	35	2,415	457	+1	0.0	07
Healthdyne	-43.2	-43.2	-27.5	-21.0q	-1.45	NC	NC	-100.0	NC	-27	03-87	.00	.0	0	0	0	05-26-83	-24.1	.85	-20.4	1.30	-26.5	5	5.0	81	14,548	2,171	-29	0.0	12
Imatron	93.8	93.8	66.6	-9.3q	-.43	NE	NE	NE	NC	-53	03-87	.00	.0	0	0	0	00-00-00	NM	NC	NC	NC	-52.5	0	4.4	58	23,651	745	0	0.0	12
Intermedics Inc	18.0	-.1	-7.2	1.0s	.06	-58.8	-41.1	NE	NC	1	04-87	.00	.0	0	0	0	08-29-80	.6	1.00	.6	2.00	1.2	13	1.5	255	10,286	3,429	0	2.9	10
Laser Indus	31.3	26.5	28.0	4.3f	.97	73.7	26.0	26.0	33	19	03-87	.00	.0	0	0	0	00-00-00	13.4	.82	11.0	1.75	19.3	4	2.0	64	4,436	320	0	27.6	03
Medtronic Inc	29.5	24.6	24.5	73.8f	5.25	28.8	43.8	43.8	8	17	04-87	1.04	1.1	7	17	21	07-06-87	14.7	.95	14.0	1.51	21.2	4	2.7	1,309	14,004	9,378	0	0.9	04
Micron Prods	.0	3.8	33.3	.5n	.26	-55.6	-44.8	NC	NC	36	03-87	.00	.0	0	0	0	00-00-00	12.5	1.54	19.2	1.86	35.7	21	NA	11	1,915	0	0	0.0	06
Mtn Med Equip	-23.2	-23.6	-25.0	-1.0f	-.31	-100.0	-100.0	-100.0	NC	-10	03-87	.00	.0	0	0	0	02-28-83	-3.7	.70	-2.6	3.85	-10.0	125	1.8	11	3,069	513	0	0.2	03
Newport Cp	-.9	7.4	7.5	5.2n	.55	-33.3	-24.5	-23.6	7	7	04-87	.06	.5	27	9	8	05-20-87	12.1	.64	7.7	1.05	8.1	0	17.5	110	9,391	4,508	0	0.0	07
St Jude Med	17.3	17.3	61.5	13.4q	1.32	40.0	40.0	325.8	NC	27	03-87	.00	.0	0	0	0	10-01-86	21.3	.73	15.6	1.72	26.9	52	8.5	232	9,572	4,298	-7	0.0	12
Stryker Cp	21.2	21.2	19.6	10.8q	.71	21.1	21.1	20.3	19	18	03-87	.00	.0	0	0	0	06-12-87	8.4	1.50	12.6	1.44	18.1	7	3.1	380	15,064	9,150	-3	0.0	12
Survival Tech	10.5	-28.0	-29.4	-3.0n	-1.07	354.5	-100.0	-100.0	NC	-53	04-87	.00	.0	0	0	0	00-00-00	-12.5	1.26	-15.8	3.33	-52.6	86	1.3	44	2,720	53	0	0.0	07
US Surgical	18.1	18.1	13.1	16.3q	1.29	25.0	25.0	63.3	NC	10	03-87	.40	1.3	0	33	28	05-29-87	7.6	1.00	7.6	1.87	14.2	64	2.9	383	12,070	4,721	+319	0.0	12
USR Ind	.0	.0	.0	-.5q	-.50	NE	NE	NE	NC	-12	03-87	.00	.0	0	0	0	00-00-00	-50.0	.20	-10.2	1.17	-11.9	0	.7	2	996	41	0	0.0	12

Company	Revenue: Pct. Change Last Qtr	Revenue: Pct. Change FY to Date	Revenue: Pct. Change Last 12 Mos	Earnings: Last 12 Mos	Earnings: Per Share Last 12 Mos	Earnings: Per Share Pct. Change Last Qtr	Earnings: Per Share Pct. Change FY to Date	Earnings: Per Share Pct. Change Last 12 Mos	Earnings: 5-Year Growth Rate	Earnings: Par Growth Rate	Earnings: Date of Report	Dividends: Current Rate Amt	Dividends: Current Rate Yield	Dividends: 5-Year Growth Rate	Dividends: Payout Last FY	Dividends: Payout Last 5 Yrs.	Dividends: Last X-Dvd Date	Ratio Analysis: Profit Margin	Ratio Analysis: Asset Turnover	Ratio Analysis: Return on Total Assets	Ratio Analysis: Leverage Ratio	Ratio Analysis: Return on Equity	Ratio Analysis: Debt to Equity	Ratio Analysis: Current Ratio	Shareholdings: Market Value	Shareholdings: Latest Shares Outstndng.	Shareholdings: Held by Banks-Funds	Shareholdings: Insider Net Trading	Shareholdings: Short Interest Ratio	Shareholdings: Fiscal Year Ends
-	%	%	%	$Mil	$	%	%	%	%	%	-	$	%	%	%	%	-	π/r x	r/a =	π/a x	a/e =	π/e	%	-	$Mil	000	000	000	Days	Mo
Hospital and Laboratory Supplies																														
Ind. Group	12.1	13.0	26.6	1,668.9	1.67	NE	3306.0	75.5	2	12	- - -	.68	1.7	1	52	38	- - - -	8.5	.98	8.3	2.35	19.5	43	1.6	31,611	787,983	347,768	-1067	2.1	- -
Acme United	-7.1	-7.1	-2.7	-.6q	-.18	-100.0	-100.0	-100.0	NC	-3	03-87	.00	.0	4	NE	58	02-09-87	-1.7	1.18	-2.0	1.55	-3.1	34	6.9	21	3,220	1,304	0	0.0	12
Bard C R	17.7	17.7	18.2	54.1q	1.83	27.5	27.5	25.3	16	16	03-87	.40	.9	12	20	19	04-21-87	9.5	1.35	12.8	1.59	20.3	14	2.3	1,313	29,174	19,076	-4	1.6	12
Bausch Lomb	24.9	24.9	20.0	76.5q	2.53	14.6	14.6	11.5	8	10	03-87	.86	2.0	7	32	40	05-26-87	10.4	.83	8.6	1.81	15.6	42	3.1	1,275	29,992	16,906	0	2.2	12
Baxter Travenol	2.9	2.9	72.5	517.0q	.87	53.3	53.3	20.8	-11	10	03-87	.44	1.8	17	49	33	06-09-87	9.3	.78	7.3	2.85	20.8	63	1.2	5,248	215,303	97,510	-501	1.0	12
Becton, Dick	22.2	25.5	22.9	126.9s	3.00	11.1	33.3	27.1	13	12	03-87	.74	1.2	5	25	33	06-03-87	8.7	.86	7.5	2.11	15.8	49	1.8	2,612	40,980	25,375	-7	0.7	09
Collagen Cp ◇	-19.1	5.8	10.0	1.8n	.23	-33.3	5.9	53.3	NC	6	03-87	.00	.0	0	0	0	07-28-86	8.2	.68	5.6	1.09	6.1	1	7.8	74	7,210	2,117	0	0.0	06
Concept Inc	22.2	25.9	28.5	3.1n	.51	50.0	54.2	168.4	30	14	05-87	.00	.0	0	0	0	02-17-87	8.6	1.26	10.8	1.29	13.9	7	5.3	100	5,796	1,300	+50	0.0	08
Cooper Cos	15.3	13.2	28.3	45.4s	1.96	NE	NE	176.1	NC	16	04-87	.40	2.7	0	NE	36	06-16-87	9.4	.56	5.3	3.87	20.5	164	1.4	336	22,582	6,609	0	3.2	10
Delmed Inc ◇ ◆	-1.4	-1.4	-35.7	-3.5q	-.03	NE	NE	NE	NC	0	03-87	.00	.0	0	0	0	00-00-00	-13.0	.45	-5.8	.00	NS	-166	.5	44	41,725	6,168	0	2.3	12
Durr Fillauer	7.4	7.4	10.6	6.6q	.83	5.3	5.3	3.8	10	9	03-87	.17	1.4	14	20	18	05-18-87	1.3	3.38	4.4	2.59	11.4	69	2.5	94	7,860	2,966	-94	0.0	12
Everest & Jen	1.5	1.5	8.2	2.9q	.23	-100.0	-100.0	-58.9	NC	2	03-87	.10	.6	3	7	33	04-15-87	1.5	1.13	1.7	2.18	3.7	52	2.5	38	2,356	98	+2	1.5	12
Hlth-Chem	40.3	40.3	10.3	1.7q	.24	NE	NE	NE	NC	7	03-87	.00	.0	0	0	0	10-16-80	5.3	.47	2.5	2.68	6.7	81	4.1	75	7,413	938	0	1.8	12
Hillenbrand Ind	8.6	8.6	20.4	51.5q	1.33	10.7	10.7	35.7	10	13	02-87	.35	1.2	21	42	31	04-20-87	7.9	1.11	8.8	2.01	17.7	45	2.5	1,121	38,838	13,596	-59	0.2	11
Intl Hydron	25.2	25.2	26.7	4.2q	.38	266.7	266.7	NC	NC	10	03-87	.00	.0	0	0	0	00-00-00	5.9	.68	4.0	2.45	9.8	94	4.1	89	11,124	390	0	18.6	12
IPCO Corp ◆	2.0	-3.0	-1.8	-.4n	-.04	-50.0	-100.0	-100.0	NC	-6	03-87	.36	2.3	23	33	29	07-02-87	-.2	1.50	-.3	2.00	-.6	53	2.5	82	5,233	1,313	0	0.3	06
Johnsn & John	13.7	13.7	10.1	701.5q	3.96	NE	NE	137.1	-1	14	03-87	1.68	1.8	10	75	44	05-22-87	9.7	1.23	11.9	2.08	24.8	9	1.4	15,881	172,850	111,468	-4	0.6	12
Lumex	6.8	6.8	19.0	5.3q	1.32	-20.0	-20.0	55.3	15	14	03-87	.08	.5	13	6	9	07-14-87	7.1	1.31	9.3	1.56	14.5	27	4.1	61	4,044	1,704	-87	0.1	12
Medex Inc	17.6	17.5	15.7	2.0n	.54	15.4	17.6	17.4	11	13	03-87	.06	.6	20	10	10	09-15-86	9.1	1.20	10.9	1.31	14.3	11	5.9	36	3,744	492	0	0.0	06
Mediq Inc	45.7	53.1	39.7	10.0s	.23	-50.0	-47.2	-73.6	0	7	03-87	.12	1.7	0	38	16	06-09-87	4.3	.98	4.2	3.62	15.2	179	4.0	101	14,681	1,643	0	14.3	09
Mentor Minn	18.4	13.8	13.7	4.2f	.37	12.5	27.6	27.6	49	8	03-87	.16	1.2	0	0	0	04-03-87	12.7	.89	11.3	1.18	13.3	2	4.7	156	11,434	2,834	-63	0.0	03
Natl Patent	105.4	105.4	76.8	-21.9q	-1.78	-100.0	-100.0	NE	NC	-43	03-87	.10	.7	0	NE	NE	03-26-87	-9.2	.58	-5.3	7.68	-40.7	439	2.5	170	11,136	1,840	0	1.4	12
Nova Pharm	200.0	227.3	300.0	-10.3n	-.35	NE	NE	NE	NC	0	09-86	.00	.0	0	0	0	00-00-00	NM	NC	NC	NC	NM	25	1.5	275	20,404	894	-295	0.0	12
Puritan Bennett	21.6	21.6	23.6	11.9q	1.08	69.2	69.2	125.0	NC	19	03-87	.10	.4	0	10	49	06-01-87	7.6	1.61	12.2	1.67	20.4	12	2.4	292	10,934	7,978	+4	0.0	12
Sci Leasing	11.9	10.9	6.8	.4n	.12	-70.0	-68.3	-90.3	-16	1	03-87	.00	.0	0	0	0	00-00-00	.9	.22	.2	4.00	.8	228	NA	39	3,055	830	0	0.5	06
Tambrands Inc	5.3	5.3	12.3	70.7q	3.18	7.9	7.9	10.8	11	12	03-87	1.80	3.0	6	55	60	05-22-87	14.3	1.36	19.4	1.40	27.2	0	2.8	1,315	22,199	13,897	+1	0.1	12
Thermedics	128.6	128.6	216.6	-.3q	-.02	NE	NE	NE	NC	-1	03-87	.00	.0	0	0	0	11-03-86	-1.6	.38	-.6	2.00	-1.2	100	10.0	218	15,197	597	-10	0.0	12
Utd Industrial	13.9	13.9	5.6	-9.2q	-.69	.0	.0	-100.0	NC	-19	03-87	.64	3.9b	24	NE	47	07-29-87	-3.3	1.30	-4.3	2.30	-9.9	15	1.1	217	13,327	3,123	0	6.8	12
West Co	16.4	16.4	25.7	17.4q	1.09	12.0	12.0	17.2	5	9	03-87	.28	1.4	10	24	23	07-15-87	7.1	1.03	7.3	1.71	12.5	21	1.8	327	16,172	4,802	0	0.3	12

Company	Revenue Pct. Change Last Qtr	Revenue Pct. Change FY to Date	Revenue Pct. Change Last 12 Mos	Earnings Last 12 Mos	Earnings Per Share Last 12 Mos	Earnings Per Share Pct. Change Last Qtr	Earnings Per Share Pct. Change FY to Date	Earnings Per Share Pct. Change Last 12 Mos	Earnings 5-Year Growth Rate	Earnings Par Growth Rate	Earnings Date of Report	Dividends Current Rate Amt	Dividends Current Rate Yield	Dividends 5-Year Growth Rate	Dividends Payout Last FY	Dividends Payout Last 5 Yrs.	Dividends Last X-Dvd Date	Ratio Analysis Profit Margin	Ratio Analysis Asset Turnover	Ratio Analysis Return on Total Assets	Ratio Analysis Leverage Ratio	Ratio Analysis Return on Equity	Ratio Analysis Debt to Equity	Ratio Analysis Current Ratio	Shareholdings Market Value	Shareholdings Latest Shares Outstndng	Shareholdings Held by Banks-Funds	Shareholdings Insider Net Trading	Shareholdings Short Interest Ratio	Shareholdings Fiscal Year Ends
-	%	%	%	$Mil	$	%	%	%	%	%	-	$	%	%	%	%	-	π/r	x r/a	= π/a	x a/e	= π/e	%	-	$Mil	000	000	000	Days	Mo
Hospitals and Laboratories																														
Ind. Group	13.8	20.5	15.5	298.8	.47	- 11.5	3.3	- 64.5	- 18	0	- - -	.46	1.9	2	45	24	- - - -	1.5	.93	1.4	3.36	4.7	152	1.3	14,161	588,391	258,663	- 53	.9	- -
Am Hlthcare	35.0	35.0	10.4	-57.8q	-4.79	.0	.0	-100.0	NC	0	03-87	.00	.0	0	0	0	00-00-00	-14.4	.78	-11.2	.00	NM	406	.3	26	12,062	723	0	0.8	12
Am Med Intl	164.3	40.9	25.6	22.9n	.26	44.0	NE	NE	NC	-5	05-87	.72	3.8	-7	NE	38	04-09-87	.7	.86	.6	4.33	2.6	234	1.1	1,662	86,876	27,903	-7	1.5	08
Cetus Corp ♦	54.5	22.6	21.0	-31.4n	-1.20	-100.0	-100.0	-100.0	NC	-16	03-87	.00	.0	0	0	0	00-00-00	-68.3	.23	-15.4	1.04	-16.0	1	31.2	765	26,257	7,684	-3	0.0	06
Charter Med	26.8	25.5	25.8	49.6s	1.60	21.1	18.2	19.4	24	19	03-87	.24	.8	0	13	10	06-10-87	5.5	.98	5.4	4.07	22.0	212	1.5	647	21,130	11,820	-35	1.3	09
Chemex Pharma	.0	100.0	.0	-4.0s	-.47	NE	NE	NE	NC	0	09-86	.00	.0	0	0	0	00-00-00	NC	NC	NC	NC	NM	0	2.0	71	9,801	1,112	0	0.0	03
Commun Psych	10.1	10.1	10.7	53.2q	1.77	14.0	14.0	12.7	25	14	02-87	.48	1.2	22	18	18	06-04-87	22.4	.72	16.1	1.22	19.6	5	3.1	1,246	30,287	18,268	+113	3.7	11
Comprhen Care	-1.7	5.5	6.0	9.7n	.70	-22.7	-20.7	-39.1	6	4	02-87	.36	2.5	33	37	27	04-27-87	5.0	.88	4.4	1.66	7.3	42	3.7	155	10,595	5,475	0	0.0	05
DDI Pharm	.0	.0	50.0	-.4q	-.08	.0	.0	NE	NC	-14	03-87	.00	.0	0	0	0	00-00-00	-13.3	.91	-12.1	1.18	-14.3	0	4.8	29	4,983	116	0	0.0	12
Enzo Biochem	60.0	113.6	140.0	1.1n	.07	-75.0	-50.0	-50.0	NC	5	04-87	.00	.0	0	0	0	06-30-86	9.2	.16	1.5	3.00	4.5	196	28.2	100	10,794	1,238	+108	0.0	07
Hlth Mgmt	123.8	109.4	212.5	2.9s	.59	8.3	8.3	NC	NC	12	03-87	.00	.0	0	0	0	00-00-00	3.9	.97	3.8	3.11	11.8	159	1.4	33	4,232	960	0	0.0	09
Hlthcare Intl	28.5	25.1	23.2	6.2n	.64	21.4	27.3	18.5	NC	15	03-87	.00	.0	0	0	0	00-00-00	2.7	.78	2.1	7.29	15.3	391	1.3	35	3,965	1,449	0	0.2	06
Hlthcare Svc Am	52.4	52.4	52.3	-17.9q	-2.24	-100.0	-100.0	-100.0	NC	-68	03-87	.00	.0	0	0	0	00-00-00	-18.6	.53	-9.9	6.85	-67.8	4	.2	44	7,987	1,276	0	0.0	12
Hosp Cp Am	-13.9	-13.9	-11.2	160.6q	1.96	-10.9	-10.9	-36.4	4	5	03-87	.72	1.6	22	31	18	06-26-87	3.4	.71	2.4	3.33	8.0	152	1.8	3,795	81,843	51,809	-2	0.4	12
Humana Inc	13.0	14.3	45.3	27.4n	.30	.0	-15.9	-86.2	-21	-5	05-87	.80	3.1	25	132	37	06-25-87	.7	1.29	.9	3.44	3.1	136	1.3	2,509	97,441	50,940	-4	2.8	08
Imreg Inc	-33.3	-25.0	.0	-2.1f	-.20	NE	NE	NE	NC	-27	12-86	.00	.0	0	0	0	00-00-00	NM	NC	NC	NC	-26.9	0	17.5	52	6,333	676	+1	0.0	12
Integ Generics	-65.7	-65.7	-25.0	.1q	.02	-100.0	-100.0	-77.8	NC	1	12-86	.00	.0	0	0	0	00-00-00	1.1	1.09	1.2	1.17	1.4	0	8.9	36	7,155	0	0	2.4	09
Intl Clin Lab	26.2	21.2	20.3	4.2n	.54	21.7	.0	14.9	-5	5	05-87	.00	.0	0	0	0	01-03-83	2.2	1.14	2.5	2.08	5.2	64	2.0	138	7,561	2,737	0	0.0	08
Maxicare Hlth	157.6	157.6	99.8	-17.8q	-.53	-100.0	-100.0	-100.0	NC	-8	03-87	.00	.0	0	0	0	07-09-85	-1.5	1.00	-1.5	5.20	-7.8	227	.8	476	33,416	24,164	0	0.0	12
Medicore Inc	26.5	26.5	60.0	.3q	.05	20.0	20.0	-76.2	NC	3	03-87	.00	.0	0	0	0	10-24-85	1.9	.84	1.6	2.00	3.2	28	2.4	17	4,846	162	0	0.0	12
Natl Med Ent	-48.3	-4.4	.8	80.8n	1.04	-11.8	-10.4	-47.2	0	3	02-87	.60	2.2	19	45	28	05-18-87	2.3	1.09	2.5	3.20	8.0	136	1.4	2,046	74,726	39,672	-224	6.4	05
Summit Hlth	299.7	69.5	93.3	3.5n	.11	-33.3	-31.3	-82.3	-4	0	03-87	.12	2.3	0	38	10	06-16-87	.6	1.67	1.0	4.20	4.2	163	1.1	164	31,250	4,915	0	0.0	06
Univ Health ♦	20.0	20.0	16.8	7.7q	.51	-32.4	-32.4	-58.5	3	6	03-87	.00	.0	0	0	0	07-05-83	1.1	1.18	1.3	4.31	5.6	229	1.4	117	14,851	5,564	0	0.0	12

Recent Performance and Forecast: Household Appliances (SIC 363)

(in millions of dollars except as noted)

	1984	1985[1]	1986[2]	1987[3]	Percent Change: Compound Annual 1972-84	1979-84	Annual 1984-85	1985-86	1986-87
Industry Data									
Value of shipments[4]	16,249	15,998	16,036	—	7.3	5.0	−1.5	0.2	—
3631 Household Cooking Equip	3,579	3,273	3,079	—	11.8	8.7	−8.5	−5.9	—
3632 Household Refrigerators	3,088	3,112	3,187	—	5.0	2.8	0.8	2.4	—
3633 Household Laundry Equip	2,716	2,874	2,986	—	6.0	4.2	5.8	3.9	—
3634 Elect Housewares & Fans	3,239	3,010	2,879	—	6.0	2.5	−7.1	−4.4	—
3635 Household Vacuums	1,307	1,430	1,555	—	8.9	10.4	9.4	8.7	—
3636 Sewing Machines	170	161	154	—	0.5	−15.7	−5.2	−4.3	—
3639 Home Appliances, nec	2,151	2,138	2,196	—	10.0	8.6	−0.6	2.7	—
Value of shipments (1982$)	15,304	14,992	15,170	15,422	1.5	−0.5	−2.0	1.2	1.7
3631 Household Cooking Equip	3,256	2,930	2,910	2,925	5.2	2.8	−10.0	−0.7	0.5
3632 Household Refrigerators	2,905	2,908	3,027	3,135	−1.1	−3.2	0.1	4.1	3.6
3633 Household Laundry Equip	2,617	2,750	2,833	2,930	0.0	−1.1	5.1	3.0	3.4
3634 Elect Housewares & Fans	3,081	2,905	2,755	2,675	1.1	−2.5	−5.7	−5.2	−2.9
3635 Household Vacuums	1,268	1,350	1,448	1,505	4.6	6.5	6.5	7.3	3.9
3636 Sewing Machines	164	155	147	142	−6.4	−20.2	−5.8	−5.2	−3.4
3639 Home Appliances, nec	2,013	1,994	2,050	2,110	3.9	2.6	−0.9	2.8	2.9
Total employment (000)	132	122	120	—	−1.7	−3.9	−7.8	−1.5	—
Production workers (000)	105	96.2	94.6	—	−1.8	−3.6	−8.8	−1.7	—
Average hourly earnings ($)	9.38	9.65	10.02	—	7.7	7.4	2.9	3.8	—

Product Data									
Value of shipments[5]	15,359	15,109	15,129	—	7.3	5.0	−1.6	0.1	—
3631 Household Cooking Equip	3,404	3,114	2,917	—	10.5	9.0	−8.5	−6.3	—
3632 Household Refrigerators	2,990	3,012	3,085	—	6.4	5.3	0.7	2.4	—
3633 Household Laundry Equip	2,459	2,602	2,703	—	5.5	5.5	5.8	3.9	—
3634 Elect Housewares & Fans	2,998	2,786	2,665	—	6.3	1.9	−7.1	−4.3	—
3635 Household Vacuums	1,173	1,283	1,396	—	8.5	6.4	9.4	8.8	—
3636 Sewing Machines	178	169	163	—	1.3	−11.2	−5.2	−3.6	—
3639 Home Appliances, nec	2,157	2,143	2,200	—	8.4	4.8	−0.6	2.7	—
Value of shipments (1982$)	14,460	14,156	14,311	14,545	1.5	−0.5	−2.1	1.1	1.6
3631 Household Cooking Equip	3,098	2,788	2,757	2,770	4.0	3.0	−10.0	−1.1	0.5
3632 Household Refrigerators	2,813	2,815	2,930	3,035	0.2	−0.9	0.1	4.1	3.6
3633 Household Laundry Equip	2,370	2,490	2,565	2,650	−0.4	0.2	5.1	3.0	3.3
3634 Elect Housewares & Fans	2,852	2,689	2,550	2,475	1.3	−3.0	−5.7	−5.2	−2.9
3635 Household Vacuums	1,138	1,212	1,300	1,350	4.2	2.6	6.5	7.3	3.8
3636 Sewing Machines	173	163	155	150	−5.7	−15.9	−5.6	−4.9	−3.2
3639 Home Appliances, nec	2,018	1,999	2,054	2,115	2.3	−1.0	−1.0	2.8	3.0
Shipments price index[6] (1982=100)	106.1	106.6	105.8	—	5.6	5.4	0.5	−0.8	—
Trade Data									
Value of imports	2,068	2,387	2,530	—	13.8	16.7	15.4	6.0	—
Import/new supply ratio[7]	0.128	—	—	—	4.8	9.8	—	—	—
Value of exports	1,067	945	855	—	11.0	−1.4	−11.5	−9.5	—
Export/shipments ratio	0.060	—	—	—	3.2	−6.2	—	—	—

[1]Estimated except for exports and imports.
[2]Estimated.
[3]Forecast.
[4]Value of all products and services sold by the Household Appliances industry.
[5]Value of products classified in the Household Appliances industry produced by all industries.
[6]Developed by the Office of Industry Assessment, ITA.
[7]New supply is the sum of product shipments plus imports.

SOURCE: U.S. Department of Commerce: Bureau of the Census, Bureau of Economic Analysis, International Trade Administration (ITA). Estimates and forecasts by ITA.

Source: *U.S. Industrial Outlook 1987*, U.S. Department of Commerce.

Recent Performance and Forecast: Household Furniture (SIC 251)

(in millions of dollars except as noted)

					Percent Change				
					Compound Annual		Annual		
	1984	1985[1]	1986[2]	1987[3]	1972-84	1979-84	1984-85	1985-86	1986-87
Industry Data									
Value of shipments[4]	15,545	16,350	17,078	—	6.4	4.5	5.2	4.5	—
2511 Wood Furniture, House	6,613	6,954	7,270	—	7.2	6.0	5.2	4.5	—
2512 Upholstered Furn, House	4,363	4,660	4,824	—	6.3	3.7	6.8	3.5	—
2514 Metal Furniture, House	1,796	1,841	1,915	—	6.0	3.6	2.5	4.0	—
2515 Mattresses & Bedsprings	1,956	2,039	2,163	—	5.4	2.1	4.2	6.1	—
Value of shipments (1982$)	14,673	14,975	15,407	15,768	0.1	−0.9	2.1	2.9	2.3
2511 Wood Furniture, House	6,041	6,160	6,345	6,504	0.1	−0.7	2.0	3.0	2.5
2512 Upholstered Furn, House	4,181	4,305	4,412	4,500	0.8	−1.2	3.0	2.5	2.0
2514 Metal Furniture, House	1,790	1,816	1,879	1,936	0.3	1.3	1.5	3.5	3.0
2515 Mattresses & Bedsprings	1,895	1,914	1,972	2,011	−0.2	−2.9	1.0	3.0	2.0
Total employment (000)	279	278	279	—	−1.1	−2.4	−0.2	0.1	—
Production workers (000)	237	237	237	—	−1.1	−2.4	−0.0	0.0	—
Average hourly earnings ($)	6.16	6.41	6.71	—	6.6	6.3	4.0	4.7	—

Product Data									
Value of shipments[5]	14,964	15,734	16,433	—	6.4	4.6	5.1	4.4	—
2511 Wood Furniture, House	6,166	6,484	6,779	—	7.1	5.4	5.2	4.5	—
2512 Upholstered Furn, House	4,104	4,383	4,538	—	6.2	4.8	6.8	3.5	—
2514 Metal Furniture, House	1,796	1,841	1,915	—	6.3	4.6	2.5	4.0	—
2515 Mattresses & Bedsprings	2,069	2,157	2,288	—	5.6	1.7	4.2	6.1	—
Value of shipments (1982$)	14,139	14,429	14,846	15,194	0.1	−0.8	2.1	2.9	2.3
2511 Wood Furniture, House	5,633	5,744	5,916	6,064	−0.0	−1.3	2.0	3.0	2.5
2512 Upholstered Furn, House	3,935	4,053	4,154	4,237	0.8	−0.1	3.0	2.5	2.0
2514 Metal Furniture, House	1,790	1,816	1,879	1,936	0.6	2.4	1.5	3.5	3.0
2515 Mattresses & Bedsprings	2,004	2,025	2,086	2,128	−0.0	−3.4	1.0	3.0	2.0
Shipments price index[6] (1982 = 100)	105.8	109.0	110.7	—	6.2	5.4	3.0	1.5	—
2511 Wood Furniture, House	109.5	112.9	114.6	—	7.1	6.8	3.1	1.5	—
2512 Upholstered Furn, House	104.3	108.2	109.2	—	5.4	4.9	3.7	0.9	—
2514 Metal Furniture, House	100.4	101.4	101.9	—	5.7	2.2	1.0	0.5	—
2515 Mattresses & Bedsprings	103.3	106.5	109.7	—	5.6	5.2	3.1	3.0	—
Trade Data									
Value of imports (ITA)[7]	2,010	2,646	3,042	—	21.0	24.1	31.6	15.0	—
Import/new supply ratio[8]	0.118	0.144	0.156	—	12.7	16.9	22.0	8.3	—
Value of exports (ITA)[9]	208	165	153	—	16.9	4.9	−20.7	−7.3	—
Export/shipments ratio	0.014	0.011	0.009	—	9.0	0.0	−21.4	−18.2	—

[1]Estimated except for exports and imports.
[2]Estimated.
[3]Forecast.
[4]Value of all products and services sold by the Household Furniture industry.
[5]Value of products classified in the Household Furniture industry produced by all industries.
[6]Developed by the Office of Industry Assessment, ITA.
[7]Import data, developed by the chapter author, includes an indeterminate amount of office furniture.
[8]New supply is the sum of product shipments plus imports.
[9]Export data are developed by the chapter author.
SOURCE: U.S. Department of Commerce: Bureau of the Census, Bureau of Economic Analysis, International Trade Administration (ITA). Estimates and forecasts by ITA.

Source: *U.S. Industrial Outlook 1987*, U.S. Department of Commerce.

Company	Revenue: Pct. Change Last Qtr	Revenue: Pct. Change FY to Date	Revenue: Pct. Change Last 12 Mos	Earnings: Last 12 Mos	Earnings: Per Share Last 12 Mos	Earnings: Per Share Pct. Change Last Qtr	Earnings: Per Share Pct. Change FY to Date	Earnings: Per Share Pct. Change Last 12 Mos	Earnings: 5-Year Growth Rate	Earnings: Par Growth Rate	Earnings: Date of Report	Dividends: Current Rate Amt	Dividends: Current Rate Yield	Dividends: 5-Year Growth Rate	Dividends: Payout Last FY	Dividends: Payout Last 5 Yrs.	Dividends: Last X-Dvd Date	Ratio Analysis: Profit Margin	Ratio Analysis: Asset Turnover	Ratio Analysis: Return on Total Assets	Ratio Analysis: Leverage Ratio	Ratio Analysis: Return on Equity	Ratio Analysis: Debt to Equity	Ratio Analysis: Current Ratio	Shareholdings: Market Value	Shareholdings: Latest Shares Outstndng.	Shareholdings: Held by Banks-Funds	Shareholdings: Insider Net Trading	Shareholdings: Short Interest Ratio	Shareholdings: Fiscal Year Ends
-	%	%	%	$Mil	$	%	%	%	%	%	-	$	%	%	%	%	-	s/r	x r/a =	s/a	x a/e =	s/e	%	-	$Mil	000	000	000	Days	Mo
Furniture, Home Furnishings																														
Ind. Group	24.1	27.5	19.8	129.2	1.31	4.8	.1	.2	12	9	- - -	.43	1.7	1	30	29	- - - -	4.6	1.85	8.5	1.58	13.4	23	3.5	2,525	97,641	29,659	- 49	1.9	- -
Bassett Furniture	4.3	3.2	3.1	19.5f	2.32	-32.7	-22.9	-22.9	-2	4	11-86	1.05	2.6	9	52	43	05-12-87	4.6	1.52	7.0	1.11	7.8	0	6.9	340	8,393	2,484	+0	0.0	11
Berkline Corp	-5.4	-.2	.0	1.0n	.70	-92.6	-51.7	22.8	45	1	03-87	.50	4.0	0	43	78	06-24-87	1.2	2.25	2.7	1.63	4.4	9	2.5	19	1,520	247	0	0.0	06
Bush Industries	NA	NA	.0	NA	NA	NA	NA	NA	NA	NC	00-00	.00	.0	NA	NA	NA	02-06-87	NA	NC	NA	NC	NA	NA	NA	87	2,999	360	0	NA	NA
Dresher Inc	9.3	15.2	21.6	2.7n	.61	14.3	17.9	19.6	53	19	03-87	.16	1.4	0	17	9	05-05-87	6.0	2.83	17.0	1.54	26.2	0	2.3	46	4,169	1,218	0	0.0	06
Flexsteel Ind	16.4	16.1	15.6	6.4n	1.35	46.2	33.3	32.4	2	8	03-87	.48	2.9	12	43	34	05-20-87	4.1	2.10	8.6	1.38	11.9	16	5.5	79	4,806	1,288	-1	0.0	06
LaZ Boy Chair	16.1	22.9	22.8	24.7f	5.36	14.3	6.8	6.8	23	12	04-87	1.60	1.9	17	29	26	05-13-87	5.9	1.80	10.6	1.58	16.8	17	3.1	387	4,603	738	-1	0.0	04
Ladd Furniture	46.4	46.4	30.5	24.3q	1.26	38.5	38.5	26.0	80	25	03-87	.19	.9	0	16	13	04-27-87	7.4	1.89	14.0	2.08	29.1	60	3.2	394	19,203	8,346	0	0.0	12
Leggett Platt	18.5	18.5	22.4	36.5q	2.16	19.6	19.6	16.8	18	15	03-87	.56	1.6	14	19	20	05-22-87	6.0	1.73	10.4	1.91	19.9	48	2.8	568	16,458	5,788	+2	2.6	12
Ohio Mattress	74.7	74.7	27.9	11.6q	.72	.0	.0	24.1	11	4	02-87	.40	1.8	17	56	54	04-10-87	3.3	2.09	6.9	1.38	9.5	12	3.1	365	16,231	6,146	0	1.4	11
Rowe Furniture	5.9	5.9	1.2	2.3q	1.02	20.0	20.0	-30.6	NC	8	02-87	.26	1.7	32	27	16	06-19-87	2.8	1.86	5.2	2.15	11.2	51	2.2	31	2,038	398	0	0.0	11
Shelby Wms	21.8	21.8	13.2	9.4q	.90	.0	.0	5.9	21	13	03-87	.24	1.4	0	20	12	04-27-87	6.9	1.42	9.8	1.82	17.8	40	3.4	184	10,392	2,335	-50	20.5	12
Sierra Hlth	49.1	49.1	86.7	-8.9q	-1.58	-12.5	-12.5	-100.0	NC	-77	03-87	.00	.0	0	0	0	00-00-00	-7.0	3.07	-21.5	3.57	-76.7	37	NA	22	5,629	291	0	0.1	12
Triangle Home	6.7	6.7	.0	-.3q	-.17	NE	NE	NE	NC	-5	03-87	.00	.0	0	0	0	00-00-00	-1.1	2.91	-3.2	1.41	-4.5	10	3.8	4	1,200	20	0	0.0	12
Appliances																														
Ind. Group	27.2	45.6	33.1	363.9	2.21	14.0	44.9	6.3	5	8	- - -	1.11	3.1	1	45	46	- - - -	4.9	1.88	9.2	1.70	15.6	16	2.2	5,525	154,692	89,246	+ 11	.8	- -
Dynamics Amer	-20.3	-20.3	-8.9	-1.8q	-.45	-100.0	-100.0	-100.0	NC	-3	03-87	.20	.9	5	182	11	02-09-87	-1.4	.86	-1.2	1.67	-2.0	25	2.4	90	4,146	1,453	0	0.5	12
Hlth-Mor	-10.8	-10.8	-11.1	1.6q	.93	-45.8	-45.8	-26.8	0	2	03-87	.68	4.5	12	64	46	03-20-87	6.7	.86	5.7	1.19	6.8	6	5.5	27	1,771	427	0	1.2	12
Maytag Cp	144.5	144.5	185.8	135.4q	2.89	16.7	16.7	2.5	17	9	03-87	1.78	3.3	11	62	65	05-26-87	6.7	2.30	15.4	1.60	24.6	8	2.5	2,250	42,151	19,749	+8	2.3	12
Mor-Flo Inds	5.9	5.9	-3.8	.7q	.29	-10.7	-10.7	-77.3	-15	2	03-87	.01	.1	0	3	1	12-02-86	.4	1.25	.5	3.60	1.8	87	2.0	29	2,506	286	0	0.0	12
Natl Presto	.6	.6	12.3	16.9q	2.28	2.4	2.4	2.2	-11	5	03-87	1.20	3.7	8	48	38	06-01-87	15.5	.52	8.1	1.21	9.8	4	6.7	241	7,371	3,079	0	1.3	12
Preway Inc	-20.3	-12.8	-12.4	-12.3f	-1.82	NE	NE	NE	NC	0	12-86	.00	.0	0	0	NE	08-29-84	-10.9	1.49	-16.2	.00	NM	639	1.7	5	9,901	1,793	0	0.0	12
Rangaire	6.2	4.5	6.4	.8n	.19	-25.0	-50.0	-68.9	3	3	04-87	.00	.0	3	40	50	02-06-87	1.0	1.50	1.5	1.67	2.5	24	2.3	23	3,855	910	-8	0.0	07
Roper Corp	13.8	11.0	1.4	23.5n	2.39	47.9	117.0	326.8	NC	27	04-87	.48	1.9	0	0	29	08-17-87	3.8	2.53	9.6	3.46	33.2	80	1.5	220	8,898	4,915	0	0.9	07
Whirlpool Cp	10.4	10.4	15.3	199.1q	2.69	-1.5	-1.5	2.3	8	9	03-87	1.10	3.1	6	38	40	05-18-87	4.9	1.84	9.0	1.64	14.8	13	2.0	2,640	74,093	56,634	+11	0.8	12

Recent Performance And Forecast: Life Insurance (SIC 6311)

(in billions of dollars except as noted)

					Percent Change				
					Compound Annual		Annual		
	1984	1985	1986[1]	1987[2]	1972-84	1979-84	1984-85	1985-86	1986-87
Premium receipts	134.8	155.9	171.5	190.7	9.7	9.7	15.7	10.0	11.2
New life insurance purchases[3]	1,114.8	1,200.0	1,318.8	1,463.9	15.0	17.7	7.6	9.9	11.0
Life insurance in force[3]	5,550.0	6,053.1	6,602.0	6,940.0	10.8	11.5	9.1	9.1	5.1
Total benefits paid	60.4	66.5	73.0	80.0	10.3	9.7	10.1	9.8	9.6
Life insurance assets	723.0	825.9	945.0	1,040.0	9.6	10.8	14.2	14.4	10.0
Total employment (000)[4]	536.7	552.6	554.0	554.0	.2	.6	3.0	.3	0

[1]Estimated.
[2]Forecast.
[3]Excludes foreign business.
[4]Home office personnel only.

SOURCE: American Council of Life Insurance, estimates and forcasts by U.S. Department of Commerce, International Trade Administration.

Source: *U.S. Industrial Outlook 1987*, U.S. Department of Commerce.

Recent Performance and Forecast: Property/Casualty Insurance (SIC 6331)

(in billions of dollars except as noted)

					Percent Change				
					Compound Annual		Annual		
Industry data	1984	1985	1986[1]	1987[2]	1972-84	1979-84	1984-85	1985-86	1986-87
Net premiums written	118.6	144.3	188.0	214.0	9.6	5.7	21.7	25.0	14.0
Underwriting gain (loss)	(19.4)	(22.5)	(13.0)	(12.0)	N/A	N/A	N/A	N/A	N/A
Net investment income	20.7	24.8	25.0	26.0	21.0	15.7	19.8	0.8	4.0
Operating earnings after taxes	.8	2.0	12.0	14.0	N/A	N/A	150.0	500.0	16.7

[1]Estimated.
[2]Forecast.
N/A - not applicable.

SOURCE: Insurance Information Institute; estimates and forecasts by U.S. Department of Commerce, International Trade Administration.

Source: *U.S. Industrial Outlook 1987*, U.S. Department of Commerce.

Company	Revenue: Pct. Change Last Qtr	Revenue: Pct. Change FY to Date	Revenue: Pct. Change Last 12 Mos	Earnings: Last 12 Mos	Earnings: Per Share Last 12 Mos	Earnings: Per Share Pct. Change Last Qtr	Earnings: Per Share Pct. Change FY to Date	Earnings: Per Share Pct. Change Last 12 Mos	Earnings: 5-Year Growth Rate	Earnings: Par Growth Rate	Earnings: Date of Report	Dividends: Current Rate Amt	Dividends: Current Rate Yield	Dividends: 5-Year Growth Rate	Dividends: Payout Last FY	Dividends: Payout Last 5 Yrs.	Dividends: Last X-Dvd Date	Ratio Analysis: Pro-fit Mar-gin	Ratio Analysis: Asset Turn-over	Ratio Analysis: Return on Total Assets	Ratio Analysis: Lever-age Ratio	Ratio Analysis: Return on Equity	Ratio Analysis: Debt to Eq-uity	Ratio Analysis: Curr-ent Ratio	Shareholdings: Mar-ket Value	Shareholdings: Latest Shares Out-stndng.	Shareholdings: Held by Banks-Funds	Shareholdings: Insider Net Trad-ing	Shareholdings: Short Int-erest Ratio	Shareholdings: Fiscal Year Ends
-	%	%	%	$Mil	$	%	%	%	%	%	-	$	%	%	%	%	-	π/r x	r/a =	π/a x	a/e =	π/e	%	-	$Mil	000	000	000	Days	Mo
Life, Accid., Health Ins.																														
Ind. Group	16.8	20.0	13.3	3,747.4	2.74	13.5	8.9	120.5	7	7	- - -	1.04	3.5	1	35	43	- - - -	4.0	.33	1.3	8.62	11.2	15	2.4	38,935	1,317,217	577,732	+ 132	1.8	- -
Academy Ins Grp	-3.3	-3.3	-7.9	-9.6q	-.28	NE	NE	NE	NC	-13	03-87	.00	.0	0	0	NE	06-24-85	-8.3	.34	-2.8	4.71	-13.2	8	NA	176	68,502	2,755	0	0.0	12
Aetna Life Cas .... □	5.0	5.0	7.9	755.7q	6.53	28.9	28.9	43.8	4	8	03-87	2.76	4.6	3	43	72	07-10-87	3.6	.31	1.1	12.45	13.7	8	NA	6,725	113,033	73,274	-2	0.6	12
Alleghany Cp	.0	.0	.0	.0	NC	NC	NC	NC	NC	NC	00-00	.00	.0	0	0	0	03-24-87	NC	NC	NC	NC	NC	NC	NC	719	6,422	2,808	+0	0.0	NA
Am Bankers Insur ... □	12.1	12.1	21.7	19.2q	1.51	83.3	83.3	19.8	3	8	03-87	.50	3.7	4	38	39	06-01-87	3.0	.53	1.6	7.56	12.1	96	NA	171	12,787	6,728	0	0.0	12
Am Family Cp .... □	46.4	46.4	48.1	81.4q	1.02	19.0	19.0	36.0	34	14	03-87	.22	1.7	13	21	27	05-11-87	5.3	.47	2.5	7.28	18.2	5	NA	1,045	80,396	23,662	+112	0.9	12
Am Heritage Lf .... □	-6.4	-6.4	-.5	9.2q	1.98	10.4	10.4	9.4	7	5	03-87	.96	3.0	12	40	37	07-07-87	4.8	.48	2.3	4.22	9.7	2	NA	150	4,680	436	0	7.8	12
Am Income Life ...... □	1.3	1.3	.8	17.9q	1.34	-8.8	-8.8	.8	1	8	03-87	.40	3.4	0	29	16	06-11-87	14.7	.28	4.1	2.61	10.7	0	NA	160	13,470	4,817	0	0.0	12
Am Integrity .... ◇	34.7	34.7	61.7	4.2q	.62	-45.0	-45.0	-56.0	45	10	03-87	.00	.0	0	0	0	00-00-00	5.5	.75	4.1	2.37	9.7	0	NA	45	6,719	731	-27	0.0	12
Am Natl Ins .... □	5.6	4.8	4.7	86.4f	2.99	-11.3	-4.5	-4.5	6	3	12-86	1.32	3.8	12	41	34	06-10-87	10.4	.21	2.2	2.82	6.2	0	NA	1,011	28,888	4,917	0	0.0	12
Aon Cp .... □	54.6	54.6	43.9	188.8q	2.83	12.1	12.1	13.7	10	10	03-87	1.20	4.7	6	40	45	05-27-87	9.4	.34	3.2	5.16	16.5	23	NA	1,718	66,700	31,520	0	0.0	12
Bus Mens Assur ..... □	8.2	8.2	3.4	-25.5q	2.66	NE	NE	60.2	3	-5	03-87	1.10	2.9	6	43	35	05-19-87	-6.0	.40	-2.4	3.83	-9.2	8	NA	399	10,471	3,799	0	0.0	12
Cap Holding .... □	59.9	59.9	17.1	159.2q	3.01	14.8	14.8	13.6	10	9	03-87	.88	2.9	5	28	31	08-26-87	6.1	.33	2.0	6.50	13.0	16	NA	1,563	50,820	30,731	-7	0.5	12
CIGNA Cp .... □	5.3	5.3	5.7	590.1q	6.96	73.8	73.8	NE	NC	8	03-87	2.80	4.4	8	41	219	06-08-87	3.4	.35	1.2	10.67	12.8	11	NA	4,980	78,584	57,370	-5	1.7	12
Conseco .... □	796.5	796.5	535.0	7.1q	1.61	222.2	222.2	187.5	NC	26	03-87	.00	.0	0	0	0	00-00-00	5.6	.18	1.0	25.60	25.6	498	NA	67	4,696	1,387	0	28.1	12
Durham Cp .... □	11.5	11.5	11.8	14.6q	1.77	-52.4	-52.4	-28.6	10	3	03-87	.92	2.8	11	46	35	05-20-87	5.5	.40	2.2	2.95	6.5	0	NA	190	5,689	2,931	0	0.0	12
Equitable of Iowa ... □	20.1	20.1	1.8	23.0q	2.50	-29.4	-29.4	62.3	10	6	03-87	.92	3.9	0	33	51	05-08-87	5.1	.27	1.4	6.36	8.9	19	NA	213	9,066	3,523	0	0.0	12
Fst Executive	26.7	26.7	34.0	152.4q	1.60	20.0	20.0	24.0	26	11	03-87	.00	.0	0	0	0	09-29-86	4.0	.28	1.1	10.09	11.1	0	NA	1,247	72,809	33,530	0	0.0	12
Home Beneficial	-1.3	-1.3	1.0	43.3q	3.60	3.7	3.7	.8	10	8	03-87	1.04	2.9	10	27	24	05-14-87	23.2	.19	4.3	2.65	11.4	0	NA	406	11,432	1,581	0	0.0	12
Home Group .... □	15.6	15.6	8.5	48.2q	.48	15.8	15.8	-11.1	NC	3	03-87	.20	1.0	0	0	0	06-08-87	2.1	.38	.8	7.38	5.9	43	NA	770	39,002	17,140	+0	0.1	12
ICH Corp	69.2	69.2	19.2	98.8q	1.79	-63.6	-63.6	-23.2	39	17	03-87	.00	.0	0	0	2	05-20-86	5.4	.22	1.2	13.92	16.7	246	NA	706	52,266	11,698	0	0.9	12

Indep Ins Grp □	4.6	4.6	2.0	28.6q	3.27	-45.7	-45.7	-25.0	5	5	03-87	1.52	4.9	6	37	31	05-05-87	6.5	.37	2.4	4.04	9.7	13	NA	228	7,305	1,153	0	0.0	12
Jefferson Pilot	1.7	1.7	3.2	112.9q	2.78	-13.0	-13.0	-6.1	10	5	03-87	1.20	3.8	10	38	36	05-11-87	10.7	.28	3.0	2.97	8.9	0	NA	1,286	40,191	19,264	+1	0.9	12
Kansas City Life □	8.4	8.4	5.9	20.2q	2.62	3.6	3.6	-26.6	-1	4	03-87	.96	3.4	5	37	32	05-05-87	7.5	.19	1.4	5.00	7.0	4	NA	219	7,696	2,371	0	0.0	12
Kauf Broad Inc	53.7	53.7	29.7	48.4q	2.44	141.2	141.2	78.1	NC	21	02-87	.33	1.5	17	15	26	04-28-87	3.9	.56	2.2	11.05	24.3	131	NA	400	17,664	6,495	+50	2.8	11
Laurentain Cap ◇	113.2	113.2	167.3	.7q	.05	NE	NE	-76.2	NC	1	03-87	.00	.0	0	0	0	00-00-00	.5	.20	.1	7.00	.7	5	NA	113	16,125	335	+1	0.0	12
Lawrence Ins	NA	NA	.0	NA	NA	NA	NA	NA	NA	NC	00-00	.00	.0	NA	NA	NA	00-00-00	NA	NC	NA	NC	NA	NA	NA	82	6,655	0	0	NA	NA
Lib Cp	3.3	7.4	7.6	28.2f	2.84	-18.1	18.8	18.8	10	7	12-86	.72	1.8	4	25	34	06-09-87	7.4	.28	2.1	4.67	9.8	4	NA	383	9,715	3,408	0	0.5	12
Linc Natl Cp □	34.4	34.4	27.5	221.5q	4.74	16.5	16.5	10.2	9	6	03-87	2.16	4.2	7	44	45	07-06-87	3.4	.41	1.4	7.93	11.1	10	NA	2,269	44,267	23,928	0	1.3	12
Manhattan Natl	-51.5	-51.5	-29.9	-1.2q	-.23	-100.0	-100.0	NE	NC	-1	03-87	.00	.0	0	NE	59	04-29-86	-.6	.17	-.1	14.00	-1.4	0	NA	42	5,202	880	0	0.0	12
Midland Co	5.3	5.3	7.9	9.0q	2.63	200.0	200.0	192.2	8	13	03-87	.24	1.0	2	9	16	05-08-87	7.4	.64	4.7	3.00	14.1	25	NA	81	3,424	342	0	0.3	12
Monarch Cap	192.9	192.9	92.4	41.9q	5.29	24.0	24.0	-1.7	15	13	03-87	.00	.0	0	0	25	05-24-85	2.2	.50	1.1	12.00	13.2	0	NA	469	6,898	3,821	0	0.1	12
NWn Natl Life	-2.7	-2.7	-2.6	39.2q	3.51	24.0	24.0	53.9	19	8	03-87	.96	3.5	4	26	32	04-20-87	2.3	.30	.7	15.00	10.5	38	NA	306	11,180	7,021	0	0.0	12
Old Rep Intl	6.4	28.1	28.1	47.2f	2.39	NE	-13.7	-13.7	-5	8	12-86	.80	2.6	1	32	22	06-01-87	4.1	.51	2.1	5.90	12.4	30	NA	433	14,128	7,764	0	0.0	12
Orion Cap Cp	-13.8	-13.8	-15.9	-54.9q	-9.97	NE	NE	NE	NC	-58	03-87	.76	3.4	9	NE	NE	06-09-87	-12.0	.53	-6.4	8.36	-53.5	89	NA	146	6,487	3,114	0	10.5	12
PHLCorp Inc	42.9	42.9	340.9	7.9q	4.34	-87.8	-87.8	NC	NC	0	03-87	.00	.0	0	0	0	00-00-00	2.7	.67	1.8	.00	NS	-131	NA	81	13,510	348	+1	1.7	12
Protective Life	4.8	4.8	5.0	17.9q	1.23	-78.0	-78.0	-32.8	-1	3	03-87	.70	5.0	8	45	32	05-11-87	5.8	.29	1.7	4.53	7.7	0	NA	201	14,480	7,049	0	0.0	12
Provident Lf Acc	21.2	21.2	18.1	67.5q	1.81	-53.1	-53.1	-36.9	4	4	03-87	.84	4.1	10	38	29	05-22-87	3.2	.28	.9	7.44	6.7	0	NA	757	37,378	18,667	0	0.0	12
Southland Fincl	-3.1	-3.1	-46.7	-17.2q	-1.02	NE	NE	NE	NC	-9	03-87	.00	.0	0	NE	NE	11-03-86	-29.7	.05	-1.5	6.27	-9.4	0	NA	122	16,772	4,586	0	0.0	12
Torchmark Cp	3.0	3.0	9.4	206.4q	2.80	13.1	13.1	53.0	25	13	03-87	1.20	4.2	16	29	29	04-06-87	13.2	.38	5.0	4.52	22.6	17	NA	1,851	65,241	25,074	0	0.6	12
TPA of Amer	-914.3	26.2	.0	.0	-.07	NE	NE	NC	NC	0	03-87	.00	.0	0	0	0	00-00-00	NC	NC	NC	NC	.0	396	1.5	52	16,697	330	0	17.9	12
Travelers Cp □	16.0	9.9	9.8	443.6f	4.45	20.5	11.3	11.3	1	5	12-86	2.28	5.1	8	49	47	04-24-87	2.8	.36	1.0	9.80	9.8	1	NA	4,467	99,274	69,837	+7	0.5	12
US Hlthcare	18.1	18.1	33.6	76.0q	1.49	5.9	5.9	156.9	158	36	03-87	.16	1.1	0	8	7	06-11-87	13.9	1.96	27.2	1.47	40.1	0	2.5	713	49,615	30,893	0	0.0	12
USLICO Cp □	1.4	1.4	42.2	25.3q	2.26	45.7	45.7	15.9	4	6	03-87	.88	3.6	4	39	27	05-06-87	4.6	.30	1.4	7.21	10.1	24	NA	272	11,221	2,081	0	1.3	12
USLIFE Cp	5.1	5.1	13.0	73.8q	3.38	-39.0	-39.0	-20.8	-1	5	03-87	1.20	3.2	8	29	25	05-04-87	6.2	.32	2.0	4.10	8.2	28	.0	731	19,625	10,517	0	1.0	12
Wash Natl Cp	48.4	48.4	-2.9	22.5q	1.94	-27.0	-27.0	-12.6	-1	2	03-87	1.08	3.9	0	51	46	06-09-87	3.3	.30	1.0	5.20	5.2	1	NA	306	11,165	6,029	0	0.0	12
Westbridge Cap □	-14.4	-15.7	-15.7	-12.2f	-2.91	-100.0	-100.0	-100.0	NC	-43	12-86	.00	.0	0	0	0	08-24-83	-16.3	.60	-9.8	4.34	-42.5	80	.0	11	4,148	318	0	1.0	12
Williams A L	41.9	41.9	48.3	29.8q	1.22	54.2	54.2	50.6	NC	25	03-87	.00	.0	0	0	0	09-16-83	13.5	.67	9.1	2.78	25.3	34	NA	454	24,722	6,769	0	0.0	12

Recent Performance and Forecast: Sawmills and Planing Mills - General (SIC 2421)

(in millions of dollars except as noted)

					Percent Change				
					Compound Annual		Annual		
	1984	1985[1]	1986[2]	1987[3]	1972-84	1979-84	1984-85	1985-86	1986-87
Industry Data									
Value of shipments[4]	13,118	12,984	13,802	14,768	6.0	−1.3	−1.0	6.3	7.0
Value of shipments (1982$)	11,525	11,500	11,837	12,276	−0.5	−1.0	−0.2	2.9	3.7
Total employment (000)	143	138	143	156	−1.3	−5.1	−3.3	3.7	9.1
Production workers (000)	125	121	138	139	−1.5	−5.2	−3.8	14.3	0.9
Average hourly earnings ($)	8.08	8.13	8.28	—	7.1	5.9	0.6	1.8	—
Product Data									
Value of shipments[5]	13,122	12,823	13,631	14,585	6.7	−0.4	−2.3	6.3	7.0
Value of shipments (1982$)	11,514	11,337	11,670	12,465	0.2	−0.1	−1.5	2.9	6.8
Shipments price index[6] (1982 = 100)	114.1	113.2	116.8	117.0	6.6	−0.2	−0.8	3.2	0.2
Quantity shipped (Million Board Feet)	36,765	37,200	—	—	−0.2	−0.7	1.2	—	—
Trade Data									
Value of imports	2,866	3,073	3,334	—	7.9	−0.3	7.2	8.5	—
Import/new supply ratio[7]	0.179	0.193	0.197	—	0.9	0.0	7.8	1.7	—
Value of exports	983	916	1,063	1,167	10.1	−3.7	−6.8	16.0	9.8
Export/shipments ratio	0.075	0.071	0.078	0.080	3.2	−3.4	−4.6	9.1	2.6

[1]Estimated except for exports and imports.
[2]Estimated.
[3]Forecast.
[4]Value of all products and services sold by the Sawmills and Planing Mills - General industry.
[5]Value of products classified in the Sawmills and Planing Mills - General industry produced by all industries.
[6]Developed by the Office of Industry Assessment, ITA.
[7]New supply is the sum of product shipments plus imports.

SOURCE: U.S. Department of Commerce: Bureau of the Census, Bureau of Economic Analysis, International Trade Administration (ITA). Estimates and forecasts by ITA.

Source: *U.S. Industrial Outlook 1987*, U.S. Department of Commerce.

Company	Revenue			Earnings								Dividends						Ratio Analysis							Shareholdings					
	Pct. Change				Per Share							Current Rate			Payout															
					Last 12 Mos	Pct. Change			5-Year Growth Rate	Par Growth Rate	Date of Report			5-Year Growth Rate			Last X-Dvd Date	Pro-fit Mar-gin	Asset Turn-over	Return on Total Assets	Lever-age Ratio	Return on Equity	Debt to Eq-uity	Curr-ent Ratio	Mar-ket Value	Latest Shares Out-stndng.	Held by Banks-Funds	Insider Net Trad-ing	Short Int-erest Ratio	Fiscal Year Ends
	Last Qtr	FY to Date	Last 12 Mos	Last 12 Mos		Last Qtr	FY to Date	Last 12 Mos				Amt	Yield		Last FY	Last 5 Yrs.														
-	%	%	%	$Mil	$	%	%	%	%	%	-	$	%	%	%	%	-	π/r x	r/a =	π/a x	a/e =	π/e	%	-	$Mil	000	000	000	Days	Mo
Lumber and Wood Products																														
Ind. Group	12.8	13.6	5.2	1,461.9	2.60	117.5	120.4	82.6	43	6	---	1.20	2.9	0	51	73	----	5.5	.98	5.4	2.06	11.1	54	1.6	22,599	554,606	262,725	+ 104	.4	--
Bohemia Inc	19.2	11.8	12.0	8.8f	1.93	247.1	2044.4	2044.4	NC	10	04-87	.00	.0	0	0	NE	11-28-86	3.9	1.03	4.0	2.45	9.8	47	1.8	91	4,584	1,845	0	0.0	04
Boise Cascade	.4	.4	1.4	116.7q	3.80	57.8	57.8	20.3	26	4	03-87	1.90	2.6	0	57	85	06-09-87	3.1	1.06	3.3	2.39	7.9	78	1.6	2,120	29,143	18,842	+5	0.5	12
Champ Intl	-2.2	-2.2	-16.8	234.3q	2.47	195.0	195.0	81.6	NC	7	03-87	.64	1.8	-19	25	57	06-11-87	5.4	.72	3.9	2.31	9.0	81	1.1	3,424	94,132	57,863	0	0.5	12
Etz Lavud Ltd	-40.0	-40.4	.0	1.0s	.57	-13.6	-72.7	23.9	-31	6	09-86	.11	1.1	3	12	13	09-17-85	2.6	1.08	2.8	2.79	7.8	26	1.1	18	1,724	7	0	0.0	03
Georgia-Pacifc	15.6	15.6	10.8	346.0q	3.15	184.0	184.0	131.6	25	10	03-87	1.00	2.3	-6	32	60	05-11-87	4.6	1.48	6.8	2.07	14.1	41	1.7	4,710	107,348	70,868	+106	0.8	12
IP Timberlands	-7.0	-7.0	7.5	93.4q	2.27	-3.4	-3.4	-4.2	NC	-2	03-87	2.72	10.4	0	117	96	06-24-87	54.9	.19	10.6	1.09	11.6	0	3.5	1,190	45,332	332	0	0.0	12
La Pacific	31.1	31.1	22.3	79.8q	2.16	975.0	975.0	222.4	NC	5	03-87	.80	2.6b	3	45	94	05-12-87	5.0	.84	4.2	2.02	8.5	61	1.5	1,182	37,975	13,427	+19	1.0	12
Ply-Gem	39.5	39.5	39.7	9.4q	.95	11.5	11.5	31.9	29	10	03-87	.12	.7	6	13	16	05-18-87	3.8	1.45	5.5	2.18	12.0	67	2.9	131	8,025	2,204	+5	0.3	12
Pope & Talbot	35.4	35.4	6.3	23.0q	1.92	NE	NE	500.0	NC	16	03-87	.44	2.0	39	30	65	06-01-87	6.8	1.63	11.1	1.82	20.2	34	2.0	263	12,020	3,618	-4	0.6	12
Potlatch Cp	6.6	6.6	4.5	74.1q	2.64	31.3	31.3	112.9	27	10	03-87	.84	2.6	2	32	59	05-04-87	7.5	.81	6.1	2.31	14.1	66	1.9	866	26,546	9,278	-9	1.2	12
Rayonier Timb	30.9	30.9	337.5	47.9q	2.35	17.9	17.9	NC	NC	-2	03-87	2.60	12.8	0	119	119	02-23-87	68.4	.28	19.2	1.12	21.5	4	.9	408	20,000	1,456	0	0.0	12
Trus Joist Cp	46.6	46.6	43.3	8.9q	1.24	43.8	43.8	90.8	7	13	03-87	.32	1.6	10	20	22	06-22-87	4.6	1.85	8.5	2.13	18.1	53	2.4	141	6,978	2,668	0	0.0	12
Weyerhaeuser	23.8	23.8	13.8	328.6q	2.35	141.9	141.9	69.1	8	5	03-87	1.30	2.6	0	68	93	04-27-87	5.5	.91	5.0	2.02	10.1	45	1.6	6,803	135,393	68,045	-16	0.9	12
Willamette Inc	18.7	18.7	10.1	90.0q	3.54	200.0	200.0	67.8	48	12	03-87	1.08	2.2	3	35	52	05-18-87	7.2	1.14	8.2	2.10	17.2	60	1.6	1,251	25,406	12,272	0	0.0	12

Recent Performance and Forecast: Metal-Cutting Machine Tools (SIC 3541)

(in millions of dollars except as noted)

					Percent Change				
					Compound Annual		Annual		
	1984	1985[1]	1986[2]	1987[3]	1972-84	1979-84	1984-85	1985-86	1986-87
Industry Data									
Value of shipments[4]	3,212	3,480	3,480	3,130	7.0	−6.1	8.4	0.0	−10.1
Value of shipments (1982$)	3,077	3,222	3,135	2,722	−2.6	−12.3	4.7	−2.7	−13.2
Total employment (000)	42.4	—	—	—	−1.8	−9.3	—	—	—
Production workers (000)	24.7	—	—	—	−2.5	−11.6	—	—	—
Average hourly earnings ($)	11.65	—	—	—	7.7	7.3	—	—	—
Product Data									
Value of shipments[5]	2,815	3,000	3,000	2,700	6.9	−7.4	6.6	0.0	−10.0
Value of shipments (1982$)	2,696	2,778	2,703	2,348	−2.8	−13.5	3.0	−2.7	−13.1
Shipments price index[6] (1982 = 100)	103.9	—	—	—	9.2	6.8	—	—	—
Trade Data									
Value of imports	1,322	1,690	2,000	1,800	23.5	6.1	27.9	18.3	−10.0
Import/new supply ratio[7]	0.319	0.360	0.400	0.400	12.6	10.7	12.8	11.0	0.0
Value of exports	455	500	510	520	7.6	−3.7	9.9	2.0	2.0
Export/shipments ratio	0.162	0.167	0.170	0.193	0.6	3.9	3.1	2.0	13.3

[1]Estimated except for exports and imports.
[2]Estimated.
[3]Forecast.
[4]Value of all products and services sold by the Metal-Cutting Machine Tools industry.
[5]Value of products classified in the Metal-Cutting Machine Tools industry produced by all industries.
[6]Developed by the Office of Industry Assessment, ITA.
[7]New supply is the sum of product shipments plus imports.

SOURCE: U.S. Department of Commerce: Bureau of the Census, Bureau of Econom Analysis, International Trade Administration (ITA). Estimates and forecasts by ITA.

Source: *U.S. Industrial Outlook 1987,* U.S. Department of Commerce.

Recent Performance and Forecast: Metal-Forming Machine Tools (SIC 3542)

(in millions of dollars except as noted)

					Percent Change				
					Compound Annual		Annual		
	1984	1985[1]	1986[2]	1987[3]	1972-84	1979-84	1984-85	1985-86	1986-87
Industry Data									
Value of shipments[4]	1,309	1,440	1,296	1,248	5.4	−4.7	10.0	−10.0	−3.7
Value of shipments (1982$)	1,263	1,358	1,200	1,124	−4.7	−11.1	7.6	−11.7	−6.3
Total employment (000)	16.1	—	—	—	−3.3	−9.8	—	—	—
Production workers (000)	10.5	—	—	—	−3.7	−10.9	—	—	—
Average hourly earnings ($)	11.72	—	—	—	7.9	7.6	—	—	—
Product Data									
Value of shipments[5]	1,363	1,500	1,350	1,300	6.1	−3.6	10.1	−10.0	−3.7
Value of shipments (1982$)	1,315	1,415	1,250	1,171	−4.1	−10.0	7.6	−11.7	−6.3
Shipments price index[6] (1982 = 100)	103.2	—	—	—	10.4	7.0	—	—	—
Trade Data									
Value of imports	341	427	510	490	20.9	7.6	25.4	19.3	−3.9
Import/new supply ratio[7]	0.138	0.222	0.274	0.274	10.9	8.2	61.0	23.7	−0.2
Value of exports	289	278	320	325	7.3	−3.4	−3.9	15.3	1.6
Export/shipments ratio	0.212	0.185	0.237	0.250	1.2	0.2	−12.7	28.1	5.5

[1]Estimated except for exports and imports.
[2]Estimated.
[3]Forecast.
[4]Value of all products and services sold by the Metal-Forming Machine Tools industry.
[5]Value of products classified in the Metal-Forming Machine Tools industry produced by all industries.
[6]Developed by the Office of Industry Assessment, ITA.
[7]New supply is the sum of product shipments plus imports.
SOURCE: U.S. Department of Commerce: Bureau of the Census, Bureau of Economic Analysis, International Trade Administration (ITA). Estimates and forecasts by ITA.

Source: *U.S. Industrial Outlook 1987*, U.S. Department of Commerce.

Company	Revenue			Earnings								Dividends						Ratio Analysis							Shareholdings					
	Pct. Change				Per Share							Current Rate			Payout															
	Last Qtr	FY to Date	Last 12 Mos	Last 12 Mos	Last 12 Mos	Pct. Change Last Qtr	Pct. Change FY to Date	Pct. Change Last 12 Mos	5-Year Growth Rate	Par Growth Rate	Date of Report	Amt	Yield	5-Year Growth Rate	Last FY	Last 5 Yrs.	Last X-Dvd Date	Profit Margin	Asset Turnover	Return on Total Assets	Leverage Ratio	Return on Equity	Debt to Equity	Current Ratio	Market Value	Latest Shares Outstndng.	Held by Banks-Funds	Insider Net Trading	Short Interest Ratio	Fiscal Year Ends
-	%	%	%	$Mil	$	%	%	%	%	%	-	$	%	%	%	%	-	π/r x	r/a =	π/a x	a/e =	π/e	%	-	$Mil	000	000	000	Days	Mo
Machine Tools and Accessories																														
Ind. Group	7.1	11.3	5.9	- 17.0	- .32	403.2	746.6	- 100.0	NC	- 2	- - -	.55	2.1	0	182	96	- - - -	- .3	1.00	- .3	2.33	- .7	30	1.9	3,660	138,060	54,513	- 10	.9	- -
Acme-Clevelnd	2.8	.9	-6.5	3.7s	.53	NE	NE	NE	NC	1	03-87	.40	3.1	-27	NE	NE	04-23-87	2.0	.95	1.9	2.26	4.3	36	1.7	80	6,279	2,676	0	0.4	09
Brenco Inc	31.3	31.3	17.3	.5q	.05	.0	.0	NE	NC	-2	03-87	.12	2.5	-25	240	NE	06-15-87	1.9	.63	1.2	1.08	1.3	0	10.2	46	9,728	3,722	0	0.0	12
Brown & Shrpe	19.0	19.0	11.6	-1.4q	-.42	-77.8	-77.8	-100.0	NC	-3	03-87	.40	2.0	-28	NE	NE	05-11-87	-1.0	.90	-.9	1.78	-1.6	24	3.4	70	3,535	1,635	+2	2.9	12
Cinn Milacron ■	4.4	4.4	14.0	22.9q	.95	-15.8	-15.8	955.6	NC	2	03-87	.72	2.3	0	73	154	05-18-87	2.7	1.19	3.2	2.53	8.1	59	2.0	746	23,598	10,341	-6	1.3	12
Conchemco Inc	5.1	1.7	5.0	1.0s	1.80	29.0	23.1	9.1	NC	6	04-87	.50	1.9	0	26	50	06-10-87	4.8	1.25	6.0	1.38	8.3	4	4.9	15	571	126	0	0.0	10
Cross Trecker	10.0	3.8	-.9	-7.7s	-.61	NE	-100.0	-100.0	NC	-4	03-87	.00	.0	2	4000	85	08-18-86	-1.8	1.06	-1.9	1.95	-3.7	7	1.9	244	12,411	7,169	0	0.0	09
Fedl Mogul	9.6	9.6	6.1	4.3q	.34	-8.6	-8.6	-91.0	-24	-5	03-87	1.60	3.6	5	400	58	05-20-87	.4	1.50	.6	2.17	1.3	50	2.0	574	12,753	6,422	-15	0.1	12
Gleason Cp ♦	-9.2	-9.2	5.5	-1.0q	-.16	-100.0	-100.0	-100.0	NC	-1	03-87	.00	.0	0	0	NE	08-02-82	-.4	1.50	-.6	1.83	-1.1	28	2.0	97	5,608	1,858	0	2.3	12
Hein-Werner	8.4	8.4	-6.1	1.2q	.98	45.0	45.0	4.3	NC	7	03-87	.25	2.0	0	28	16	12-19-86	2.6	1.62	4.2	2.36	9.9	56	2.6	15	1,161	35	+10	0.0	12
Kennametal	.3	-2.2	-.8	6.5n	.65	.0	105.4	-34.3	NC	-2	03-87	1.00	3.2	0	1433	99	05-04-87	1.9	1.16	2.2	1.91	4.2	45	2.8	314	10,164	5,524	-5	0.2	06
Mestek Inc	705.1	435.2	443.7	5.2f	.61	433.3	662.5	662.5	NC	29	12-86	.00	.0	0	0	0	00-00-00	6.0	1.38	8.3	3.51	29.1	45	1.6	60	8,292	141	0	0.0	12
Monarch Mach	12.6	12.6	-12.0	1.0q	.28	-66.7	-66.7	-58.2	-31	-3	03-87	.80	4.0	0	267	109	05-12-87	1.5	.80	1.2	1.25	1.5	0	3.7	73	3,674	1,239	0	2.3	12
Newcor	-12.5	-3.4	48.5	.1s	.02	183.3	NE	NE	NC	-9	04-87	.32	3.2	8	NE	97	07-09-87	.1	2.00	.2	3.00	.6	94	1.7	28	2,816	422	+1	0.0	10
Ransburg Corp	5.6	6.2	7.6	-6.7s	-.82	-100.0	-100.0	-100.0	NC	-11	05-87	.40	2.6	1	NE	679	06-19-87	-3.0	1.00	-3.0	2.57	-7.7	9	1.3	124	8,052	3,830	-0	0.5	11
Regal-Beloit	12.4	12.4	32.7	5.9q	1.07	17.4	17.4	42.7	19	9	03-87	.44	2.5	8	39	51	06-24-87	7.3	1.42	10.4	1.50	15.6	12	3.0	102	5,886	1,174	+0	0.2	12
Spectra-Phys	10.9	4.3	4.3	.8s	.11	.0	.0	-65.6	NC	1	03-87	.00	.0	0	0	0	00-00-00	.4	1.00	.4	1.50	.6	24	3.8	275	7,571	2,005	+3	0.4	09
Timken Co	.3	.3	-2.7	-55.6q	-6.60	NE	NE	NE	NC	-8	03-87	1.00	1.6	-19	NE	NE	05-14-87	-5.3	.75	-4.0	1.73	-6.9	20	1.3	778	12,598	6,034	0	4.7	12
Wedco Tech	164.3	15.2	13.3	2.3f	.69	NE	NE	NE	NC	54	03-87	.00	.0	0	0	NE	02-08-85	13.5	.81	11.0	4.86	53.5	181	1.4	18	3,363	160	0	0.0	03

Recent Performance and Forecast: Steel Mill Products (SIC 3312,3315,3316,3317)

(in millions of dollars except as noted)

					Percent Change				
					Compound Annual		Annual		
	1984	1985[1]	1986[2]	1987[3]	1972-84	1979-84	1984-85	1985-86	1986-87
Industry Data									
Value of shipments[4]	50,539	49,982	45,983	45,062	5.0	−5.2	−1.1	−8.0	−2.0
Value of shipments (1982$)	48,233	48,526	45,527	43,750	−3.6	−9.9	0.6	−6.2	−3.9
Total employment (000)	318	290	273	258	−4.4	−9.9	−8.6	−6.0	−5.5
Production workers (000)	244	221	210	199	−4.8	−10.6	−9.2	−5.1	−5.2
Average hourly earnings ($)	14.10	14.52	—	—	8.0	4.0	3.0	—	—
Product Data									
Value of shipments[5]	48,010	47,233	43,453	42,583	5.5	−4.5	−1.6	−8.0	−2.0
Value of shipments (1982$)	45,684	45,857	42,601	41,343	−3.2	−9.4	0.4	−7.1	−3.0
Shipments price index[6] (1982 = 100)	104.2	102.3	100.3	102.3	8.9	5.3	−1.8	−2.0	2.0
Trade Data									
Value of imports	10,102	9,462	8,210	8,114	11.5	7.7	−6.3	−13.2	−1.2
Import/new supply ratio[7]	0.175	0.168	0.160	0.162	5.0	11.0	−4.0	−4.8	0.7
Value of exports	880	818	785	808	2.9	−13.7	−7.0	−4.0	2.9
Export/shipments ratio	0.019	0.018	0.018	0.019	−2.5	−9.5	−5.5	4.3	5.0

[1]Estimated except for exports and imports.
[2]Estimated.
[3]Forecast.
[4]Value of all products and services sold by the Steel Mill Products industry.
[5]Value of products classified in the Steel Mill Products industry produced by all industries.
[6]Developed by the Office of Industry Assessment, ITA.
[7]New supply is the sum of product shipments plus imports.

SOURCE: U.S. Department of Commerce: Bureau of the Census, Bureau of Economic Analysis, International Trade Administration (ITA). Estimates and forecasts by ITA.

Source: *U.S. Industrial Outlook 1987,* U.S. Department of Commerce.

Recent Performance and Forecast: Aluminum, Copper and Zinc (SIC 3331,3333,3334)

(in millions of dollars except as noted)

					Percent Change				
					Compound Annual		Annual		
	1984	1985[1]	1986[2]	1987[3]	1972-84	1979-84	1984-85	1985-86	1986-87
Industry Data									
Value of shipments[4]	9,121	7,674	7,192	7,566	5.0	−5.3	−15.9	−6.3	5.2
3331 Primary Copper	2,753	2,400	2,200	2,270	−0.1	−13.4	−12.8	−8.3	3.2
3333 Primary Zinc	356	320	260	280	−0.5	−9.1	−10.2	−18.8	7.7
3334 Primary Aluminum	6,011	4,954	4,732	5,016	9.8	0.9	−17.6	−4.5	6.0
Value of shipments (1982$)	9,101	7,588	7,059	7,306	−1.6	−6.0	−16.6	−7.0	3.5
3331 Primary Copper	2,967	2,581	2,391	2,441	−2.2	−7.8	−13.0	−7.3	2.1
3333 Primary Zinc	331	308	254	272	−7.3	−11.4	−7.1	−17.6	7.2
3334 Primary Aluminum	5,802	4,700	4,414	4,593	−0.7	−4.6	−19.0	−6.1	4.1
Total employment (000)	32.3	27.7	24.7	26.2	−3.4	−7.8	−14.2	−10.8	6.1
3331 Primary Copper	8.0	6.0	4.8	6.5	−6.2	−7.6	−25.0	−20.0	35.4
3333 Primary Zinc	1.8	1.4	1.4	1.4	−9.9	−18.8	−22.2	0.0	0.0
3334 Primary Aluminum	22.5	20.3	18.5	18.3	−1.1	−6.5	−9.8	−8.9	−1.1
Production workers (000)	23.7	20.7	18.4	19.5	−4.2	−9.5	−12.7	−11.1	6.0
3331 Primary Copper	4.6	4.0	3.2	4.4	−9.1	−14.0	−13.0	−20.0	37.5
3333 Primary Zinc	1.3	1.0	1.0	1.0	−10.9	−20.1	−23.1	0.0	0.0
3334 Primary Aluminum	17.8	15.7	14.2	14.1	−1.0	−6.7	−11.8	−9.6	−0.7
Average hourly earnings ($)	15.64	—	—	—	9.7	7.3	—	—	—
3331 Primary Copper	14.34	14.35	12.90	—	9.5	7.5	0.1	−10.1	—
3333 Primary Zinc	12.29	12.30	12.30	—	9.1	6.2	0.1	0.0	—
3334 Primary Aluminum	16.20	16.50	—	—	9.2	6.8	1.8	—	—
Product Data									
Value of shipments[5]	12,505	9,737	9,677	9,716	6.8	−0.4	−22.1	−0.6	0.4
3331 Primary Copper	3,880	3,100	2,860	2,960	2.5	−2.6	−20.1	−7.7	3.5
3333 Primary Zinc	667	514	420	448	3.2	0.2	−22.9	−18.3	6.7
3334 Primary Aluminum	7,958	6,123	6,397	6,308	10.8	0.8	−23.1	4.5	−1.4

Value of shipments (1982$)	12,082	9,303	9,087	8,964	−0.2	−1.8	−23.0	−2.3	−1.4
3331 Primary Copper	4,134	3,316	3,075	3,159	−0.1	3.0	−19.8	−7.2	2.7
3333 Primary Zinc	604	482	400	423	−4.3	−3.2	−20.2	−17.0	5.9
3334 Primary Aluminum	7,344	5,506	5,612	5,382	0.3	−3.9	−25.0	1.9	−4.1
Shipments price index[6] (1982 = 100)	104.1	105.7	107.4	109.7	6.8	0.5	1.6	1.5	2.2
3331 Primary Copper	94.0	93.5	93.0	93.7	2.5	−5.5	−0.5	−0.5	0.8
3333 Primary Zinc	110.9	106.7	105.0	105.8	7.9	3.9	−3.7	−1.6	0.8
3334 Primary Aluminum	109.8	113.3	116.5	120.0	10.4	4.5	3.2	2.8	3.0
Trade Data									
Value of imports	2,651	2,066	3,127	2,580	11.3	12.4	−22.0	51.3	−17.5
3331 Primary Copper	710	528	700	590	9.2	10.2	−25.6	32.6	−15.7
3333 Primary Zinc	649	521	550	540	11.2	10.3	−19.7	5.6	−1.8
3334 Primary Aluminum	1,293	1,018	1,877	1,450	12.8	14.9	−21.3	84.5	−22.7
Import/new supply ratio[7]	0.175	0.175	0.244	0.210	3.6	11.0	0.1	39.5	−14.1
3331 Primary Copper	0.155	0.146	0.197	0.166	5.8	11.5	−5.9	35.1	−15.5
3333 Primary Zinc	0.493	0.503	0.567	0.547	4.7	5.6	2.1	12.7	−3.6
3334 Primary Aluminum	0.140	0.142	0.227	0.187	1.6	12.4	2.0	59.2	−17.6
Value of exports	556	540	320	349	7.1	5.7	−2.9	−40.8	9.1
3331 Primary Copper	158	95.6	60.0	70.0	−1.5	0.2	−39.5	−37.2	16.7
3333 Primary Zinc	1.7	2.9	4.0	4.0	−1.7	11.2	70.6	37.9	0.0
3334 Primary Aluminum	397	442	256	275	18.5	8.5	11.3	−42.0	7.4
Export/shipments ratio	0.045	0.055	0.033	0.036	0.3	6.1	24.6	−40.4	8.6
3331 Primary Copper	0.041	0.031	0.021	0.024	−3.9	2.9	−24.3	−32.0	12.7
3333 Primary Zinc	0.003	0.006	0.010	0.009	−4.8	10.9	121.3	68.8	−6.3
3334 Primary Aluminum	0.050	0.072	0.040	0.044	6.9	7.6	44.6	−44.5	8.9

[1]Estimated except for exports and imports.
[2]Estimated.
[3]Forecast.
[4]Value of all products and services sold by the Aluminum, Copper and Zinc industry.
[5]Value of products classified in the Aluminum, Copper and Zinc industry produced by all industries.
[6]Developed by the Office of Industry Assessment, ITA.
[7]New supply is the sum of product shipments plus imports.
SOURCE: U.S. Department of Commerce: Bureau of the Census, Bureau of Economic Analysis, International Trade Administration (ITA). Estimates and forecasts by ITA.

Source: *U.S. Industrial Outlook 1987*, U.S. Department of Commerce.

Company	Revenue			Earnings								Dividends						Ratio Analysis							Shareholdings					
	Pct. Change				Per Share							Current Rate			Payout															
					Last 12 Mos	Pct. Change			5-Year Growth Rate	Par Growth Rate	Date of Report			5-Year Growth Rate			Last X-Dvd Date	Profit Margin	Asset Turnover	Return on Total Assets	Leverage Ratio	Return on Equity	Debt to Equity	Current Ratio	Market Value	Latest Shares Outstndng.	Held by Banks-Funds	Insider Net Trading	Short Interest Ratio	Fiscal Year Ends
	Last Qtr	FY to Date	Last 12 Mos	Last 12 Mos		Last Qtr	FY to Date	Last 12 Mos				Amt	Yield		Last FY	Last 5 Yrs.														
-	%	%	%	$Mil	$	%	%	%	%	%	-	$	%	%	%	%	-	π/r	x r/a =	π/a	x a/e =	π/e	%	-	$Mil	000	000	000	Days	Mo
Copper Mining and Refining																														
Ind. Group	7.9	19.5	- 15.9	106.4	.29	NE	NE	NE	NC	2	- - -	.15	.7	- 1	30	65	- - - -	4.3	.40	1.7	2.00	3.4	46	1.4	4,869	241,743	51,301	- 12	2.0	- -
ASARCO Inc ◇	-6.1	-6.1	-13.2	17.0q	-.22	NE	NE	NE	NC	3	03-87	.00	.0	0	0	NE	08-03-84	1.6	.56	.9	2.89	2.6	71	1.6	801	32,368	9,634	0	7.1	12
Atlas Consol B	41.8	41.8	-1.6	-42.7q	-.52	NE	NE	NE	NC	0	03-87	.00	.0	0	0	0	04-06-81	-35.3	.32	-11.4	.00	NM	1065	.3	115	83,611	564	0	0.7	12
Campbell Rsc	-442.9	-72.1	.0	.0	.03	NE	NE	NE	NC	0	03-87	.00	NA	0	0	0	05-21-84	NC	NC	NC	NC	.0	17	1.2	77	34,238	1,072	0	0.8	12
Newmont Mng	-40.9	-40.9	-57.6	84.5q	1.39	207.7	207.7	NE	NC	3	03-87	.60	1.3	-14	45	93	06-11-87	28.1	.15	4.3	1.35	5.8	12	2.0	2,867	60,834	23,922	-11	0.6	12
O'Okiep Copp	1625.0	44.0	47.3	3.3f	.94	-68.9	NE	NE	NC	8	12-85	.00	.0	0	0	NE	02-06-81	11.8	.50	5.9	1.36	8.0	32	3.4	41	3,525	0	0	1.5	12
Phelps Dodge	61.5	61.5	10.5	44.3q	1.15	42.9	42.9	134.7	NC	5	03-87	.00	.0	0	0	NE	05-17-82	4.5	.49	2.2	2.45	5.4	74	1.7	968	27,167	16,109	-1	1.0	12
Aluminum Refining																														
Ind. Group	6.3	6.5	4.6	704.5	2.09	162.6	160.0	NE	NC	5	- - -	.67	1.9	- 1	30	86	- - - -	4.2	.81	3.4	2.26	7.7	56	1.9	11,970	334,584	167,748	+ 224	1.1	- -
Alcan Alum	6.4	6.4	4.6	261.0q	1.71	200.0	200.0	NE	NC	5	03-87	.60	2.0	-12	37	247	06-02-87	4.3	.86	3.7	2.27	8.4	44	2.5	4,784	157,483	66,774	-1	0.9	12
Alum Co Am	7.2	7.2	-5.4	312.1q	3.63	5500.0	5500.0	NE	NC	6	03-87	1.20	2.2	-8	39	82	04-27-87	6.6	.70	4.6	1.85	8.5	36	1.6	4,657	87,255	62,891	+222	0.6	12
Dw Industries	-21.9	-11.1	-5.1	-.7s	-.11	-77.8	-76.5	-100.0	NC	-2	04-87	.00	.0	0	0	0	00-00-00	-.4	2.00	-.8	2.38	-1.9	67	1.9	28	5,247	741	0	2.3	10
Kaisertech Ltd	2.9	2.9	28.3	-69.2q	-1.70	-100.0	-100.0	NE	NC	-6	03-87	.00	.0	0	0	NE	02-04-85	-3.1	.71	-2.2	2.86	-6.3	107	1.7	805	44,710	21,888	0	1.8	12
Reynolds Metal	8.8	8.8	7.9	203.4q	8.70	102.0	102.0	NE	NC	15	03-87	1.20	1.6	-19	9	NE	06-02-87	5.5	1.00	5.5	3.11	17.1	100	1.7	1,667	22,001	15,159	+4	1.0	12
Toth Alum	.0	.0	.0	-2.1q	-.11	NC	NC	NE	NC	-24	11-86	.00	.0	0	0	0	00-00-00	NC	NC	NC	NC	-24.4	1	.1	30	17,888	295	0	0.0	08
Lead, Nck, Tn, Zn Mining & Refining																														
Ind. Group	.1	- .3	- 4.0	.4	- .14	NE	NE	NE	NC	0	- - -	.12	.8	0	464	114	- - - -	.0	NC	.0	NC	.0	92	1.9	2,759	185,669	44,710	+ 10	2.5	- -
Cominco Ltd	-13.4	-13.4	-8.5	-15.5q	-.47	NE	NE	NE	NC	-3	03-87	.00	NA	0	0	NE	12-02-85	-1.2	.75	-.9	3.67	-3.3	101	1.5	797	65,038	1,218	0	2.2	12
Gulf Res & Ch	115.0	115.0	29.3	21.9q	2.80	NE	NE	-49.6	-4	15	03-87	.00	.0	0	0	0	00-00-00	15.5	.40	6.2	2.37	14.7	68	2.7	147	9,278	1,631	0	2.2	12
Inco Ltd	.0	.0	-2.4	-4.9q	-.21	NC	NC	-100.0	NC	-1	03-87	.20	1.2	0	NE	NE	04-28-87	-.3	.67	-.2	2.50	-.5	94	1.9	1,784	104,175	41,285	+10	0.9	12
Utd Park City	.0	.0	.0	-3.1q	-.57	NE	NE	NE	NC	-25	03-87	.00	.0	0	0	0	00-00-00	NM	NC	NC	NC	-24.6	0	.4	7	5,401	514	0	3.6	12
Zemex Cp	8.0	8.0	2.8	2.0q	1.62	166.7	166.7	68.8	NC	6	03-87	.40	3.1	-15	25	NE	06-04-87	5.6	1.04	5.8	1.33	7.7	0	3.1	23	1,777	62	0	3.4	12

Recent Performance and Forecast: Motor Vehicles and Car Bodies (SIC 3711)

(in millions of dollars except as noted)

					Percent Change				
					Compound Annual		Annual		
	1984	1985[1]	1986[2]	1987[3]	1972-84	1979-84	1984-85	1985-86	1986-87
Industry Data									
Value of shipments[4]	118,066	121,689	111,345	106,112	8.8	6.8	3.1	-8.5	-4.7
Value of shipments (1982$)	112,578	113,199	101,039	93,904	2.6	0.9	0.6	-10.7	-7.1
Total employment (000)	296	298	271	255	-1.1	-3.2	0.5	-9.0	-5.8
Production workers (000)	248	249	222	207	-1.1	-3.2	0.6	-10.8	-7.1
Average hourly earnings ($)	14.46	14.86	15.19	—	7.9	5.6	2.8	2.2	—
Product Data									
Value of shipments[5]	112,358	115,806	105,962	100,982	8.8	7.0	3.1	-8.5	-4.7
Value of shipments (1982$)	107,136	107,726	96,329	89,365	2.5	1.1	0.6	-10.6	-7.2
Shipments price index[6] (1982 = 100)	104.9	—	—	—	6.1	5.8	—	—	—
Trade Data									
Value of imports (ITA)[7]	21,400	26,600	33,450	40,000	16.6	10.9	24.3	25.8	19.6
Import/new supply ratio[8]	0.171	0.206	0.255	—	7.0	4.5	20.3	23.8	—
Value of exports (ITA)[9]	1,700	2,043	2,350	2,700	7.3	-11.7	20.2	15.0	14.9
Export/shipments ratio	0.017	0.020	0.023	—	-0.6	-16.0	22.3	14.3	—

[1]Estimated except for exports and imports.
[2]Estimated.
[3]Forecast.
[4]Value of all products and services sold by the Motor Vehicles and Car Bodies industry.
[5]Value of products classified in the Motor Vehicles and Car Bodies industry produced by all industries.
[6]Developed by the Office of Industry Assessment, ITA.
[7]Import data are developed by the chapter author.
[8]New supply is the sum of product shipments plus imports.
[9]Export data are developed by the chapter author.
SOURCE: U.S. Department of Commerce: Bureau of the Census, Bureau of Economic Analysis, International Trade Administration (ITA). Estimates and forecasts by ITA.

Source: *U.S. Industrial Outlook 1987,* U.S. Department of Commerce.

Recent Performance and Forecast: Motor Vehicle Parts and Stampings (SIC 3465,3592,3647,3691,3694,3714)

(in millions of dollars except as noted)

					Percent Change				
					Compound Annual		Annual		
	1984	1985[1]	1986[2]	1987[3]	1972-84	1979-84	1984-85	1985-86	1986-87
Industry Data									
Value of shipments[4]	80,123	86,138	92,336	99,054	9.2	6.0	7.5	7.2	7.3
3465 Automotive Stampings	14,137	15,853	7,788	19,944	8.5	6.3	12.1	12.2	12.1
3592 Pistons, Rings, Etc.	3,096	3,357	3,633	3,937	12.6	10.2	8.4	8.2	8.4
3647 Vehicle Lighting Equip	1,419	1,496	,586	1,682	9.1	6.0	5.5	6.0	6.1
3691 Storage Batteries	2,916	3,128	3,353	3,594	9.6	2.3	7.3	7.2	7.2
3694 Engine Electrical Equip	5,971	6,771	7,369	8,022	9.4	7.7	13.4	8.8	8.9
3714 Parts & Accessories	52,583	55,533	58,607	61,875	9.2	5.7	5.6	5.5	5.6
Value of shipments (1982$)	78,276	82,065	85,800	89,780	0.3	−1.7	4.8	4.6	4.6
3465 Automotive Stampings	13,548	14,830	16,230	17,760	1.2	2.4	9.5	9.4	9.4
3592 Pistons, Rings, Etc.	2,928	3,100	3,270	3,460	1.7	2.1	5.9	5.5	5.8
3647 Vehicle Lighting Equip	1,363	1,410	,450	1,500	0.8	−3.0	3.5	2.8	3.4
3691 Storage Batteries	3,198	3,345	3,500	3,660	4.4	3.2	4.6	4.6	4.6
3694 Engine Electrical Equip	5,730	6,340	6,730	7,150	1.5	1.0	10.7	6.2	6.2
3714 Parts & Accessories	51,508	53,040	54,620	56,250	−0.3	−3.3	3.0	3.0	3.0
Total employment (000)	619	653	686	721	−0.3	−3.2	5.4	5.1	5.1
Production workers (000)	500	534	567	603	−0.5	−3.4	6.7	6.3	6.3
Average hourly earnings ($)	12.54	—	—	—	7.7	6.5	—	—	—

Product Data									
Value of shipments[5]	82,074	88,044	94,488	101,497	9.2	5.9	7.3	7.3	7.4
3465 Automotive Stampings	14,696	16,773	19,153	21,854	9.1	7.4	14.1	14.2	14.1
3592 Pistons, Rings, Etc.	2,565	2,718	2,889	3,061	10.3	7.6	6.0	6.3	6.0
3647 Vehicle Lighting Equip	935	981	1,039	1,087	8.3	7.3	4.9	5.9	4.6
3691 Storage Batteries	2,794	3,040	3,253	3,483	9.4	2.1	8.8	7.0	7.1
3694 Engine Electrical Equip	5,280	5,869	6,532	7,255	9.5	9.0	11.2	11.3	11.1
3714 Parts & Accessories	55,805	58,663	61,622	64,757	9.2	5.4	5.1	5.0	5.1
Value of shipments (1982$)	80,206	83,840	87,755	91,940	0.3	−1.9	4.5	4.7	4.8
3465 Automotive Stampings	14,090	15,690	17,475	19,460	1.8	3.6	11.4	11.4	11.4
3592 Pistons, Rings, Etc.	2,426	2,510	2,600	2,690	−0.4	−0.3	3.5	3.6	3.5
3647 Vehicle Lighting Equip	898	920	950	970	0.1	−1.7	2.5	3.3	2.1
3691 Storage Batteries	3,064	3,200	3,340	3,490	4.1	3.0	4.4	4.4	4.5
3694 Engine Electrical Equip	5,065	5,490	5,960	6,460	1.7	2.6	8.4	8.6	8.4
3714 Parts & Accessories	54,664	56,030	57,430	58,870	−0.3	−3.6	2.5	2.5	2.5
Shipments price index[6] (1982 = 100)	102.3	104.9	107.5	110.2	8.7	7.5	2.5	2.5	2.5
Trade Data									
Value of imports	12,125	13,729	17,475	22,265	15.9	16.2	13.2	27.3	27.4
Import/new supply ratio[7]	0.113	—	—	—	5.2	8.8	—	—	—
Value of exports	11,149	11,734	13,006	14,442	11.9	9.3	5.2	10.8	11.0
Export/shipments ratio	0.133	—	—	—	2.2	3.0	—	—	—

[1]Estimated except for exports and imports.

[2]Estimated.

[3]Forecast.

[4]Value of all products and services sold by the Motor Vehicle Parts and Stampings industry.

[5]Value of products classified in the Motor Vehicle Parts and Stampings industry produced by all industries.

[6]Developed by the Office of Industry Assessment, ITA.

[7]New supply is the sum of product shipments plus imports.

SOURCE: U.S. Department of Commerce: Bureau of the Census, Bureau of Economic Analysis, International Trade Administration (ITA). Estimates and forecasts by ITA.

Source: *U.S. Industrial Outlook 1987*, U.S. Department of Commerce.

Company	Revenue Pct. Change Last Qtr	Revenue Pct. Change FY to Date	Revenue Pct. Change Last 12 Mos	Earnings Last 12 Mos	Per Share Last 12 Mos	Per Share Pct. Change Last Qtr	Per Share Pct. Change FY to Date	Per Share Pct. Change Last 12 Mos	5-Year Growth Rate	Par Growth Rate	Date of Report	Dividends Current Rate Amt	Current Rate Yield	5-Year Growth Rate	Payout Last FY	Payout Last 5 Yrs.	Last X-Dvd Date	Profit Margin	Asset Turnover	Return on Total Assets	Leverage Ratio	Return on Equity	Debt to Equity	Current Ratio	Market Value	Latest Shares Outstndng.	Held by Banks-Funds	Insider Net Trading	Short Interest Ratio	Fiscal Year Ends
-	%	%	%	$Mil	$	%	%	%	%	%	-	$	%	%	%	%	-	π/r x	r/a =	π/a x	a/e =	π/e	%	-	$Mil	000	000	000	Days	Mo
Auto Manufacture																														
Ind. Group	7.7	10.3	12.1	9,079.2	7.18	25.0	15.2	.6	62	11	- - -	2.37	3.8	3	30	26	- - - -	3.9	1.64	6.4	2.47	15.8	19	1.2	71,130	1,129,859	465,198	+ 39	3.4	- -
Am Motors	20.0	20.0	-9.7	-63.7q	-.78	NE	NE	NE	NC	-17	03-87	.00	.0	0	0	0	03-26-80	-1.7	1.71	-2.9	5.79	-16.8	227	1.0	554	130,402	5,098	0	14.5	12
Chrysler Cp	4.4	4.4	5.6	1316.4q	5.98	-21.0	-21.0	.2	NC	20	03-87	1.00	2.9	0	11	8	06-09-87	5.8	1.57	9.1	2.70	24.6	44	1.0	7,395	216,693	129,142	+0	1.1	12
ESI Ind	83.2	83.2	8.0	1.5q	.31	27.3	27.3	-53.7	NC	11	03-87	.00	.0	0	0	0	11-03-86	2.8	1.04	2.9	3.83	11.1	167	1.8	26	3,789	766	+5	0.1	12
Ford Motor Co	22.7	22.7	21.6	4048.4q	15.14	112.2	112.2	68.4	NC	22	03-87	3.00	3.0	47	18	16	04-27-87	6.1	1.75	10.7	2.54	27.2	14	1.2	24,031	242,742	161,931	+4	1.5	12
Ford of Can	2.0	2.0	5.7	167.8q	20.22	1056.6	1056.6	50.7	NC	11	03-87	6.00	NA	0	0	28	03-09-87	1.2	4.50	5.4	2.89	15.6	10	1.2	1,115	8,291	81	0	0.0	12
Gen Motors	-2.7	-2.7	3.1	2803.4q	7.72	-15.8	-15.8	-36.4	40	3	03-87	5.00	6.1	20	61	40	05-08-87	2.7	1.44	3.9	2.36	9.2	14	1.2	26,389	319,384	123,174	+25	1.7	12
Honda Motor	35.7	46.4	72.2	725.8n	5.94	-37.9	-35.4	-26.2	14	15	11-86	.68	.6	2	5	8	08-25-86	3.5	2.23	7.8	2.21	17.2	28	1.3	10,142	89,948	1,670	0	11.3	02
Mack Trucks	11.0	11.0	-8.0	-18.9q	-.71	NE	NE	NE	NC	-4	03-87	.00	.0	0	0	0	00-00-00	-1.1	1.73	-1.9	2.11	-4.0	23	1.9	570	29,423	12,937	+9	0.0	12
Pullman Co	-13.9	-9.7	11.4	16.7s	.40	.0	.0	-2.4	NC	7	03-87	.12	1.5	0	23	8	06-16-87	3.3	1.33	4.4	2.32	10.2	27	1.3	326	40,714	16,664	0	3.5	09
Subaru of Amer	-.7	7.8	11.6	81.8s	1.69	-55.3	-24.2	-5.6	22	20	04-87	.38	3.2	48	16	14	05-26-87	4.1	4.05	16.6	1.56	25.9	13	4.0	582	48,473	13,735	-5	0.0	10
Auto Parts and Accessories																														
Ind. Group	14.6	17.0	10.1	530.4	1.43	17.3	17.8	- 20.2	49	5	- - -	.70	2.3	0	42	37	- - - -	2.8	1.43	4.0	2.30	9.2	50	2.1	11,935	385,773	152,088	- 149	1.7	- -
Allen Group	-2.9	-2.9	.4	-9.8q	-1.48	-100.0	-100.0	-100.0	NC	-9	03-87	.56	3.6	-5	NE	369	06-01-87	-2.3	1.26	-2.9	2.31	-6.7	44	2.0	135	8,594	4,187	0	1.6	12
Amtek Cp	60.0	42.9	21.1	-34.7s	-3.32	200.0	86.5	-100.0	NC	-22	03-87	.48	2.4	9	NE	33	05-28-87	-3.6	1.86	-6.7	2.84	-19.0	87	1.9	196	9,747	6,560	0	12.5	09
Arvin Indus	76.7	76.7	38.9	42.3q	2.48	3.4	3.4	3.8	30	12	03-87	.68	1.9	3	26	35	06-08-87	3.7	1.43	5.3	3.08	16.3	122	2.1	625	17,616	6,586	-30	0.3	12
Barnes Group •	3.9	3.9	7.7	15.6q	2.43	-25.9	-25.9	52.8	60	6	03-87	1.20	3.4	3	39	48	05-26-87	3.5	1.60	5.6	2.27	12.7	26	1.5	231	6,485	3,480	0	3.8	12
Buell Indus	10.5	3.2	-1.3	3.9s	1.63	-32.4	-30.3	-25.6	25	8	04-87	.32	1.6	10	16	15	04-28-87	5.3	1.40	7.4	1.34	9.9	4	5.4	49	2,412	367	0	0.0	10
Champ Parts •	.0	.0	6.7	-41.5q	.21	-100.0	-100.0	320.0	NC	0	03-87	.00	.0	0	0	12	09-19-86	-37.7	1.41	-53.2	.00	NM	151	2.4	27	2,455	387	0	0.0	12
Champ Spark	15.1	15.1	10.0	-10.3q	-.27	NC	NC	-100.0	NC	-3	03-87	.00	.0	-23	NE	107	05-19-86	-1.1	1.45	-1.6	1.81	-2.9	7	1.8	557	38,396	15,152	-134	0.6	12
Dana Corp	4.3	4.3	-.6	82.6q	1.72	6.2	6.2	-37.0	8	2	03-87	1.36	2.9	4	76	54	05-20-87	2.2	1.50	3.3	2.64	8.7	65	1.8	2,459	52,035	24,728	0	1.1	12
Donaldson	14.1	7.9	7.8	12.3n	2.39	-8.8	-24.3	-20.1	NC	8	04-87	.66	1.8	1	22	43	05-19-87	4.3	1.49	6.4	1.69	10.8	15	2.5	180	5,008	2,763	0	0.4	07
Eaton Corp	15.5	15.5	8.2	147.7q	4.79	32.9	32.9	-26.5	NC	7	03-87	2.00	2.2	-2	37	42	04-28-87	3.7	1.32	4.9	2.41	11.8	50	2.6	2,898	31,332	16,582	-4	0.8	12
Echlin Inc	27.0	20.5	16.7	71.2s	1.19	20.0	20.0	19.0	19	9	02-87	.56	3.2	13	42	39	06-29-87	7.2	1.44	10.4	1.62	16.8	22	2.9	957	54,694	30,947	+2	0.4	08
Excel Ind	39.1	39.1	51.4	4.6q	.86	2.9	2.9	11.7	NC	8	03-87	.36	3.6	0	36	22	06-29-87	2.8	2.04	5.7	2.39	13.6	80	2.8	57	5,799	461	0	0.0	12
Facet Entprs	60.5	30.6	16.6	2.2s	.73	140.0	150.0	NE	NC	5	03-87	.00	.0	0	0	0	12-13-80	1.1	1.73	1.9	2.63	5.0	104	2.7	58	3,076	1,111	-6	2.7	09
Hastings Mfg	5.4	5.4	-1.5	1.9q	4.58	NE	NE	52.2	11	10	03-87	.45	1.1	-3	12	17	05-18-87	3.0	1.63	4.9	2.16	10.6	66	3.3	17	420	50	0	2.6	12
Intermet Cp	.6	.6	8.4	19.7q	.92	7.4	7.4	26.0	NC	21	03-87	.18	1.2	0	18	9	05-08-87	6.7	2.00	13.4	1.99	26.7	40	1.7	282	18,042	1,653	0	0.0	12
Kysor Ind	38.2	38.2	29.7	10.1q	2.99	79.1	-79.1	4.2	NC	11	03-87	1.00	2.6	4	33	31	04-09-87	5.6	1.59	8.9	1.82	16.2	21	2.2	124	3,197	1,083	0	2.1	12
Magna Intl	21.2	18.1	22.1	45.2n	1.78	-20.3	-10.1	-14.0	NC	10	04-87	.48	2.6	0	25	20	08-10-87	3.9	1.28	5.0	2.62	13.1	81	1.3	473	25,387	7,312	+9	0.0	07
Modine Mfg	13.4	11.9	11.8	19.6f	2.61	-39.7	-2.2	-2.2	NC	10	03-87	.88	2.6	0	29	25	05-20-87	5.6	1.48	8.3	1.80	14.9	26	2.1	244	7,277	2,040	+11	0.0	03
Mr Gasket	-322.2	-76.8	.0	.0	-.51	1350.0	-86.0	-100.0	NC	0	03-87	.00	.0	0	0	1	00-00-00	NC	NC	NC	NC	.0	121	4.3	65	10,629	1,842	0	0.0	12
Premier Ind	6.1	4.8	2.9	44.9n	1.52	11.4	11.5	10.1	7	13	02-87	.44	1.1	11	27	26	06-17-87	10.0	1.50	15.0	1.25	18.7	3	6.8	1,162	29,604	5,675	+0	1.5	05
Raytech Cp ○	-2.6	1.0	1.7	4.7f	1.59	NE	NE	NE	NC	30	12-86	.00	.0	0	0	NE	06-22-82	4.1	1.34	5.5	5.51	30.3	115	1.2	30	3,012	510	0	4.4	12
Sealed Power	8.6	8.6	7.5	30.5q	2.48	29.6	29.6	9.7	4	6	03-87	1.10	3.1	10	45	36	05-18-87	4.5	1.31	5.9	1.90	11.2	52	3.2	442	12,274	6,253	-5	2.9	12
Seaport Cp	-23.5	-23.8	-25.0	-3.7f	-1.83	-100.0	NE	NE	NC	0	12-86	.00	.0	0	0	0	00-00-00	-20.6	2.25	-46.3	.00	NM	350	1.0	3	2,072	31	+8	6.5	12
Simpson Indust	-18.7	-14.2	-5.5	4.1n	.66	-56.8	-78.6	-54.2	23	1	03-87	.56	3.6	-2	37	56	05-29-87	2.7	1.41	3.8	2.18	8.3	51	1.7	97	6,321	2,780	0	0.0	06
Smith AO	14.7	14.7	5.2	29.5q	2.83	-23.5	-23.5	-20.7	NC	8	03-87	.80	3.5	27	26	544	04-24-87	3.1	1.39	4.3	2.44	10.5	30	1.4	115	4,981	1,374	-1	2.1	12
Sparton Corp	-3.4	14.5	48.3	13.7s	1.71	47.4	814.3	NE	NC	16	12-86	.52	3.3	15	46	50	06-09-87	5.2	2.44	12.7	1.87	23.7	1	1.6	127	7,914	1,514	0	0.3	06
Std Motor Prd	26.3	26.3	21.6	18.7q	1.41	.0	.0	48.4	1	11	03-87	.32	1.7	12	23	22	05-11-87	6.2	1.21	7.5	1.84	13.8	41	3.9	254	13,201	5,262	0	0.2	12
Wynn's Intl	-12.1	-12.1	12.9	5.4q	1.39	-93.9	-93.9	NE	NC	4	03-87	.60	3.3	1	35	47	06-09-87	1.8	1.61	2.9	2.41	7.0	56	2.3	70	3,793	1,398	0	0.3	12

Recent Performance and Forecast: Selected Retail Establishments (SICs 52-59, 5311, 5823)

Type of Retailer	Sales (bil. $)				Percent Change				
					Compound Annual		Annual		
	1984	1985	1986[1]	1987[2]	1972-84	1979-84	1984-85	1985-86	1986-87
Total retailing	1,293	1,374	1,477	1,588	9.2	7.5	6.3	7.5	7.5
Department stores (SIC 531)	129	135	144	154	8.4	7.7	4.7	6.7	6.9
Eating and drinking places (SIC 581)	125	131	142	153	10.8	8.7	4.8	8.4	7.7
Apparel and accessory stores (SIC 56)	65	70	75	81	8.6	7.9	7.7	7.1	8.0

[1]Estimated.
[2]Forecast.

SOURCE: U.S. Department of Commerce: Bureau of the Census, and International Trade Administration (ITA). Estimates and forecasts by ITA.

Source: *U.S. Industrial Outlook 1987*, U.S. Department of Commerce.

Historical Trends: Selected Retail Establishments (SICs 52-59, 5311, 5823)

Item	1972	1973	1974	1975	1976	1977	1978	1979	1980	1981	1982	1983	1984
Retail Trade (total)													
Sales (bil. $)	449.1	509.5	541.0	588.1	657.4	725.2	806.9	899.4	960.8	1,043.5	1,072.1	1,174.2	1,293.1
Total employment (000)	11,836	12,329	12,554	12,645	13,209	13,795	14,496	14,989	15,035	15,189	15,258	15,281	16,261
Avg. hourly earnings ($)	2.75	2.91	3.14	3.36	3.57	3.85	4.19	4.53	4.88	5.25	5.49	5.73	5.89
Department stores (SIC 531)													
Sales (billions)	49.1	54.7	65.7	61.8	68.2	76.5	84.1	89.2	93.3	103.9	107.2	116.6	129.1
Total employment (000)	1,706	1,768	1,758	1,694	1,731	1,788	1,891	1,878	1,871	1,872	1,885	1,885	1,950
Avg. hourly earnings ($)	2.62	2.91	3.13	3.37	3.55	3.71	4.05	4.38	4.77	5.15	5.59	5.82	5.85
Eating & drinking places (SIC 581)													
Sales (bil. $)	36.2	40.4	44.7	51.1	57.2	63.3	71.8	82.2	90.2	98.3	104.4	114.7	124.5
Total employment (000)	2,860	3,054	3,231	3,380	3,656	3,945	4,260	4,513	4,626	4,750	4,781	4,888	5,212
Avg. hourly earnings ($)	2.97	2.18	2.37	2.55	2.69	2.93	3.21	3.45	3.69	3.95	4.09	4.27	4.32
Apparel & Accessory stores													
Sales (bil. $)	24.1	27.7	28.9	31.3	33.7	35.6	41.0	44.6	48.1	53.0	55.3	60.3	65.1
Total employment (000)	784	795	811	806	842	864	884	949	957	968	970	951	978
Avg. hourly earnings ($)	2.52	2.63	2.83	3.03	3.26	3.45	3.72	4.01	4.30	4.65	4.86	5.01	5.15

SOURCE: U.S. Department of Commerce: Bureau of the Census, and International Trade Administration; U.S. Department of Labor: Bureau of Labor Statistics.

Source: *U.S. Industrial Outlook 1987*, U.S. Department of Commerce.

Recent Performance and Forecast: Food Retailing (SIC 54)

Types of Store	1982	1983	1984	1985	1986[1]	1987[2]	Percent Change 1982-83	1983-84	1984-85	1985-86	1986-87
Sales (bil. $)											
All food/grocery stores	245.3	254.9	270.4	282.2	296.3	313.2	3.9	6.1	4.4	5.0	5.7
Chain stores[3]	135.5	141.3	149.0	156.1	162.3	170.4	4.3	5.4	4.8	4.0	5.0
Grocery stores	230.1	239.1	254.2	266.1	280.1	296.6	3.9	6.3	4.7	5.3	5.9
Chain stores[3]	133.8	139.4	147.0	154.1	160.2	168.4	4.2	5.5	4.8	4.0	5.1
Retail bakers	3.7	3.9	4.1	4.0	4.2	4.4	5.4	5.1	−2.4	5.0	4.8
Other food/grocery stores[4]	11.5	11.9	12.1	12.0	12.0	12.2	3.5	1.7	−0.8	0.0	1.6
Employment and earnings											
Total employment (000)	2,478	2,556	2,637	2,779	2,894	2,995	3.1	3.2	5.4	4.1	3.5
Nonsupervisory employment	2,270	2,294	2,374	2,442	2,668	2,750	1.1	3.5	2.9	9.3	3.1
Average hourly earnings, nonsupervisory employees ($)	7.22	7.51	7.64	7.35	7.15	—	4.0	1.7	−3.8	−2.7	—

[1]Estimate.
[2]Forecast.
[3]Companies with 11 or more retail establishments.
[4]Meat/seafood, produce, confectionery, dairy, and miscellaneous food/grocery retailers.
SOURCE: U.S. Department of Commerce: Bureau of the Census and International Trade Administration (ITA); U.S. Department of Labor: Bureau of Labor Statistics. Estimates and forecasts by ITA.

Source: *U.S. Industrial Outlook 1987,* U.S. Department of Commerce.

Company	Revenue: Pct. Change Last Qtr	Revenue: Pct. Change FY to Date	Revenue: Pct. Change Last 12 Mos	Earnings: Last 12 Mos	Earnings Per Share: Last 12 Mos	Per Share Pct. Change: Last Qtr	Per Share Pct. Change: FY to Date	Per Share Pct. Change: Last 12 Mos	5-Year Growth Rate	Par Growth Rate	Date of Report	Dividends Current Rate: Amt	Current Rate: Yield	5-Year Growth Rate	Payout: Last FY	Payout: Last 5 Yrs.	Last X-Dvd Date	Profit Margin	Asset Turnover	Return on Total Assets	Leverage Ratio	Return on Equity	Debt to Equity	Current Ratio	Market Value	Latest Shares Outstndng.	Held by Banks-Funds	Insider Net Trading	Short Interest Ratio	Fiscal Year Ends
-	%	%	%	$Mil	$	%	%	%	%	%	-	$	%	%	%	%	-	π/r x	r/a =	π/a x	a/e =	π/e	%	-	$Mil	000	000	000	Days	Mo
Food Chain Stores																														
Ind. Group	5.2	4.4	- 3.2	1,374.9	1.86	128.6	52.5	25.4	14	11	- - -	.57	1.8	1	33	33	- - - -	1.6	3.75	6.0	2.67	16.0	57	1.3	23,517	727,930	256,682	- 13	.8	- -
Albertson's Inc	9.3	9.3	7.0	104.2q	3.12	16.0	16.0	13.5	12	12	04-87	.96	1.7	14	27	27	08-03-87	1.9	4.32	8.2	2.13	17.5	31	1.6	1,860	33,370	15,344	+1	0.9	01
Allied Super	7.7	8.9	-.9	1.4n	.08	-90.0	-83.9	-74.2	NC	2	03-87	.00	.0	0	0	0	00-00-00	.3	2.33	.7	2.57	1.8	119	5.2	143	13,949	2,042	-0	0.7	06
Arden Group Inc	-12.5	-12.5	-7.4	5.1q	2.16	79.4	79.4	-10.4	27	13	03-87	.00	.0	0	0	0	00-00-00	1.3	3.15	4.1	3.22	13.2	67	1.4	68	2,296	371	0	0.0	12
Big Bear	2.4	.5	-.3	15.0s	1.92	43.8	35.9	12.9	15	19	02-87	.00	.0	0	0	0	01-26-87	1.7	4.29	7.3	2.62	19.1	39	1.4	200	7,837	3,578	-17	0.0	08
Big V Supmkt	5.9	5.9	5.4	6.2q	1.04	-4.2	-4.2	-4.6	-4	6	03-87	.44	2.2	20	41	37	04-14-87	1.0	4.90	4.9	2.18	10.7	63	1.2	126	6,255	2,120	0	0.0	12
Borman's Inc	13.7	8.7	8.7	6.3f	2.23	11.1	26.0	26.0	NC	15	01-87	.20	1.1	0	7	11	05-12-87	.6	6.00	3.6	4.50	16.2	107	1.1	49	2,808	639	0	1.7	01
Bruno's Inc	9.7	11.3	11.4	30.3n	.77	-9.5	.0	2.7	18	13	03-87	.18	.9	16	21	21	05-07-87	2.7	3.86	10.4	1.64	17.1	8	1.6	760	39,459	9,374	0	0.0	06
Circle K Cp	14.0	8.4	8.4	49.4f	.93	11.8	6.9	6.9	54	17	04-87	.28	1.7	2	30	35	06-08-87	2.2	2.64	5.8	4.29	24.9	193	1.5	825	49,264	27,027	0	2.4	04
Cullum Companies	-6.1	-5.4	-3.8	18.0n	1.65	13.9	.0	.6	7	11	03-87	.50	1.6	9	29	30	06-24-87	1.8	4.17	7.5	2.01	15.1	39	1.5	343	10,938	3,902	0	0.0	06
Delchamps Inc	13.1	12.9	11.2	6.4n	.95	10.5	-25.0	-22.8	-1	6	03-87	.28	1.3	0	24	14	04-30-87	.8	5.00	4.0	2.23	8.9	49	1.9	139	6,394	1,518	0	0.0	06
Farm Fresh	55.8	55.8	88.1	11.3q	.80	.0	.0	12.7	6	10	03-87	.00	.0	0	0	0	07-13-84	1.3	3.00	3.9	2.51	9.8	87	1.7	158	13,412	3,966	0	0.0	12
Fisher Foods	-12.8	-12.8	8.9	-5.2q	-1.44	-100.0	-100.0	-100.0	NC	-11	03-87	.05	.4	0	0	NE	11-24-86	-.9	3.67	-3.3	3.24	-10.7	88	1.3	42	3,528	2,403	+0	1.2	12
Food Lion	35.6	29.0	28.9	61.8f	.39	44.4	30.0	30.0	26	15	12-86	.14	.9	0	10	6	07-14-87	2.6	3.92	10.2	2.28	23.3	35	1.4	1,252	80,768	6,968	0	0.0	12
Foodarama	1.0	.2	2.3	1.7s	1.27	-10.2	2.4	-38.6	29	6	04-87	.00	.0	0	0	0	09-17-79	.4	5.00	2.0	3.15	6.3	50	.8	28	1,342	151	0	0.0	10
Gen Host	-18.1	-18.1	-1.4	1.6q	.06	-100.0	-100.0	-94.9	-13	-2	04-87	.24	1.7	15	72	24	06-09-87	.3	.67	.2	4.00	.8	149	2.2	357	25,535	10,050	0	0.6	01
Giant Food A	10.6	10.6	13.0	48.5q	1.61	13.3	13.3	-16.6	16	10	05-87	.66	2.0	26	37	26	05-04-87	1.9	3.37	6.4	2.53	16.2	67	1.4	1,006	30,015	5,511	0	0.6	02
Grt A & P Tea	48.3	18.4	18.4	69.0f	1.82	52.8	23.0	23.0	NC	7	02-87	.40	1.0	0	0	0	04-09-87	.9	3.67	3.3	2.76	9.1	56	1.1	1,474	38,048	8,981	+2	0.8	02
Hannaford Bros	18.3	18.3	14.0	21.1q	2.30	62.5	62.5	23.7	12	13	03-87	.56	1.1	7	24	28	06-08-87	2.3	3.61	8.3	2.12	17.6	46	1.4	482	9,184	2,956	0	0.3	12
Kroger	-5.2	-5.2	-3.2	53.3q	1.53	8.1	8.1	-26.1	-5	1	03-87	1.05	2.9	5	69	56	04-27-87	.3	4.33	1.3	3.46	4.5	60	1.2	3,220	87,609	34,087	0	1.7	12
Lucky Stores	-24.0	-24.0	-37.3	264.5q	5.56	229.3	229.3	245.3	16	92	04-87	.30	1.0	0	25	48	06-09-87	4.5	3.78	17.0	5.72	97.2	132	.7	1,118	36,800	21,333	+17	0.7	01
Marsh Supermkt	6.4	7.5	7.3	6.7f	1.32	13.0	14.8	14.8	7	10	03-87	.40	2.0	3	28	37	07-13-87	.9	4.56	4.1	3.59	14.7	129	1.5	104	5,096	1,665	+0	0.0	03
Mott's Super	2.7	2.7	-1.0	-2.3q	-.86	NE	NE	NE	NC	-9	03-87	.00	.0	0	0	NE	02-04-86	-.8	5.25	-4.2	2.14	-9.0	5	1.1	40	2,786	427	0	0.0	12
Munford Inc	-7.0	-7.0	-3.8	.9q	.24	NE	NE	-83.0	-24	-2	03-87	.54	2.2	26	129	40	06-22-87	.2	3.00	.6	2.83	1.7	90	1.7	95	3,815	1,131	0	1.1	12
Natl Conv Str	-12.7	-20.3	-20.2	-2.8n	-.13	-100.0	-100.0	-100.0	NC	-12	03-87	.36	3.6	12	240	47	06-22-87	-.4	1.75	-.7	4.43	-3.1	268	1.0	227	22,945	9,016	0	0.6	06
Pueblo Intl	16.4	16.4	15.6	6.3q	1.85	44.4	44.4	24.2	21	11	04-87	.20	.8	8	10	14	04-21-87	.9	4.11	3.7	3.38	12.5	95	1.2	92	3,604	881	-14	4.8	01
Seaway Food Town	-.5	2.3	-.4	2.2s	1.39	112.5	102.4	-6.7	-9	3	03-87	.68	2.6	5	70	46	05-13-87	.5	4.00	2.0	3.35	6.7	103	1.4	33	1,257	166	0	0.0	09
Southland Corp ◇	7.4	7.4	-27.7	313.9q	6.34	NE	NE	155.6	11	17	03-87	1.12	1.7	10	28	26	05-26-87	3.8	2.42	9.2	2.21	20.3	41	.8	3,236	48,297	27,468	0	1.7	12
Stop & Shop	13.7	13.7	6.2	43.0q	3.11	121.4	121.4	57.1	0	6	04-87	1.28	1.9	16	40	25	05-22-87	1.1	3.38	3.7	2.70	10.0	81	1.7	954	13,896	7,919	0	0.2	01
Sunshine-Jr	-5.4	-5.4	-10.3	2.6q	1.52	-72.0	-72.0	.7	9	8	03-87	.48	2.4		28	36	05-20-87	1.6	3.63	5.8	1.95	11.3	38	1.0	34	1,702	497	0	0.0	12
Supermkts Gen	4.8	4.8	6.2	59.0q	1.53	-20.6	-20.6	-14.5	13	10	04-87	.28	.7	14	16	15	04-09-87	1.1	4.55	5.0	2.54	12.7	43	1.2	1,522	38,528	18,156	0	0.1	01
Weis Markets	2.4	2.4	6.2	67.7q	1.47	14.7	14.7	10.5	11	12	03-87	.43	1.3	9	19	23	05-26-87	6.1	2.34	14.3	1.16	16.6	0	5.7	1,497	45,890	20,336	+0	0.5	12
Winn-Dixie A	6.4	7.6	6.8	107.8n	2.62	.0	-10.9	-5.1	2	5	03-87	1.80	3.7	4	61	52	06-04-87	1.2	6.67	8.0	1.91	15.3	14	1.7	2,034	41,304	6,699	-2	3.5	06

Company	Revenue Pct. Change Last Qtr	Revenue Pct. Change FY to Date	Revenue Pct. Change Last 12 Mos	Earnings Last 12 Mos	Per Share Last 12 Mos	Per Share Pct. Change Last Qtr	Per Share Pct. Change FY to Date	Per Share Pct. Change Last 12 Mos	5-Year Growth Rate	Par Growth Rate	Date of Report	Dividends Current Rate Amt	Current Rate Yield	5-Year Growth Rate	Payout Last FY	Payout Last 5 Yrs.	Last X-Dvd Date
-	%	%	%	$Mil	$	%	%	%	%	%	-	$	%	%	%	%	-
Department Stores																	
Ind. Group	15.4	19.6	10.7	3,421.9	3.02	14.8	14.6	5.5	5	7	- - -	1.37	2.7	1	41	40	- - - -
Alexander's Inc	4.0	.9	.3	3.0n	.63	NE	9.8	8.6	NC	4	04-87	.00	.0	0	0	0	08-20-80
Ames Dept St	20.1	20.1	15.9	28.3q	.76	18.8	18.8	-36.1	12	6	04-87	.10	.4	9	14	11	08-17-87
Carson Pirie	11.7	11.7	9.0	21.9q	2.14	NE	NE	39.9	15	6	04-87	.70	1.4	1	36	33	08-24-87
Carter Hawley	-4.3	-4.3	1.4	51.0q	1.02	42.9	42.9	-3.8	NC	-3	04-87	1.22	1.9	0	140	116	05-11-87
Crowley Milner	16.0	16.0	11.4	1.7q	3.49	NE	NE	33.7	12	6	04-87	1.00	2.4	21	29	26	04-09-87
Dayton Hudson	14.1	14.1	7.4	256.6q	2.63	-2.5	-2.5	-11.7	9	8	04-87	.92	1.8	10	32	27	05-14-87
Dillard Dept	12.7	12.7	15.1	77.2q	2.41	15.4	15.4	3.4	27	13	04-87	.12	.3	21	5	5	06-24-87
Fedrtd Dep Str	8.1	8.1	6.2	304.7q	3.16	8.2	8.2	6.0	4	6	04-87	1.48	2.8	7	43	39	05-12-87
Gottschalks	20.7	20.7	13.9	4.3q	.60	60.0	60.0	-7.7	NC	15	04-87	.00	.0	0	0	0	04-13-87
Holmes, D.H.	.5	.5	.3	.2q	.06	NE	NE	-90.9	-44	-1	04-87	.25	1.2b	3	970	56	06-15-87
INTERCO Inc	34.9	34.9	12.5	110.7q	3.29	34.8	34.8	8.9	-1	5	05-87	1.60	3.5	2	50	52	06-12-87
May Dept Strs	94.6	94.6	32.1	404.5q	2.39	-10.9	-10.9	.0	9	8	04-87	1.14	2.4	14	42	36	08-26-87
Mercantile Strs	6.9	6.9	7.5	116.6q	3.18	27.6	27.6	10.4	13	12	04-87	.70	1.5	14	19	19	08-25-87
Nordstrom	22.2	22.2	23.1	78.7q	1.94	48.0	48.0	-27.1	24	14	04-87	.36	.5	27	14	16	05-26-87
Penney, JC	5.9	5.9	6.6	497.0q	3.31	-37.9	-37.9	14.1	3	6	04-87	1.48	2.8	5	35	38	05-01-87
Sears, Roebuck	11.6	11.6	9.7	1443.9q	3.85	44.2	44.2	11.6	10	5	03-87	2.00	4.0	6	49	46	05-29-87
Strawbrid & Cloth	11.7	11.7	8.1	21.6q	2.95	41.4	41.4	-1.0	17	9	04-87	.87	1.9b	22	30	20	04-08-87

Company	Ratio Analysis Profit Margin	Asset Turnover	Return on Total Assets	Leverage Ratio	Return on Equity	Debt to Equity	Current Ratio	Shareholdings Market Value	Latest Shares Outstndng.	Held by Banks-Funds	Insider Net Trading	Short Interest Ratio	Fiscal Year Ends
-	π/r x	r/a =	π/a x	a/e =	π/e	%	-	$Mil	000	000	000	Days	Mo
Department Stores													
Ind. Group	3.1	1.06	3.3	3.61	11.9	64	2.3	54,903	1,099,480	597,535	+ 142	2.6	- -
Alexander's Inc	.6	2.67	1.6	2.44	3.9	83	2.2	218	4,540	1,459	+73	0.2	07
Ames Dept St	1.5	2.53	3.8	1.89	7.2	35	2.5	889	37,418	21,289	0	0.5	01
Carson Pirie	1.5	2.13	3.2	2.97	9.5	72	1.7	496	10,175	4,907	0	3.5	01
Carter Hawley	1.3	1.85	2.4	6.54	15.7	218	1.9	1,464	23,287	5,142	0	7.4	01
Crowley Milner	1.5	2.07	3.1	2.55	7.9	76	1.9	21	509	79	0	8.8	01
Dayton Hudson	2.7	1.81	4.9	2.41	11.8	63	1.8	4,928	97,340	61,953	0	0.4	01
Dillard Dept	4.1	1.56	6.4	2.17	13.9	56	2.2	1,524	32,084	10,690	-0	2.0	01
Fedrtd Dep Str	2.8	1.93	5.4	2.11	11.4	30	1.9	4,875	93,294	65,914	+1	1.6	01
Gottschalks	3.3	1.70	5.6	2.59	14.5	88	2.6	124	7,500	1,598	0	0.6	01
Holmes, D.H.	.1	1.00	.1	3.00	.3	75	1.5	75	3,551	340	-30	0.0	01
INTERCO Inc	3.9	1.64	6.4	1.59	10.2	22	3.4	1,296	28,565	21,731	0	9.2	02
May Dept Strs	3.5	1.86	6.5	2.40	15.6	44	2.2	7,294	153,566	92,297	+12	4.6	01
Mercantile Strs	5.7	1.61	9.2	1.65	15.2	27	4.7	1,778	36,845	13,048	0	1.8	01
Nordstrom	4.6	1.91	8.8	1.98	17.4	31	1.5	2,834	40,480	17,350	-6	0.0	01
Penney, JC	3.3	1.33	4.4	2.61	11.5	61	2.8	7,856	149,640	91,034	-267	2.2	01
Sears, Roebuck	3.2	.69	2.2	5.14	11.3	79	NA	18,908	373,494	186,812	+359	1.2	12
Strawbrid & Cloth	2.9	1.59	4.6	2.80	12.9	104	2.6	324	7,192	1,892	0	0.0	01

Company	Revenue: Pct. Change: Last Qtr	Revenue: Pct. Change: FY to Date	Revenue: Pct. Change: Last 12 Mos	Earnings: Last 12 Mos	Earnings: Per Share: Last 12 Mos	Earnings: Per Share: Pct. Change: Last Qtr	Earnings: Per Share: Pct. Change: FY to Date	Earnings: Per Share: Pct. Change: Last 12 Mos	Earnings: 5-Year Growth Rate	Earnings: Par Growth Rate	Earnings: Date of Report	Dividends: Current Rate: Amt	Dividends: Current Rate: Yield	Dividends: 5-Year Growth Rate	Dividends: Payout: Last FY	Dividends: Payout: Last 5 Yrs.	Dividends: Last X-Dvd Date	Ratio Analysis: Profit Margin	Ratio Analysis: Asset Turnover	Ratio Analysis: Return on Total Assets	Ratio Analysis: Leverage Ratio	Ratio Analysis: Return on Equity	Ratio Analysis: Debt to Equity	Ratio Analysis: Current Ratio	Shareholdings: Market Value	Shareholdings: Latest Shares Outstndng.	Shareholdings: Held by Banks-Funds	Shareholdings: Insider Net Trading	Shareholdings: Short Interest Ratio	Shareholdings: Fiscal Year Ends
-	%	%	%	$Mil	$	%	%	%	%	%	-	$	%	%	%	%	-	s/r x	r/a =	s/a x	a/e =	s/e	%	-	$Mil	000	000	000	Days	Mc
Discount and Variety Stores.																														
Ind. Group	5.6	11.3	14.1	1,702.3	1.44	57.8	53.6	41.1	31	12	---	.36	1.0	1	21	23	----	2.6	2.42	6.3	2.51	15.8	58	1.8	45,139	1,188,624	550,752	-99	2.9	--
Best Products	-11.0	-11.0	-6.4	-20.0q	-.74	NE	NE	NE	NC	-5	04-87	.00	.0	-4	NE	37	05-23-86	-1.0	1.60	-1.6	3.25	-5.2	120	2.0	289	27,154	16,138	+0	0.3	01
COMB Co	12.7	12.7	23.0	-4.4q	-.34	25.0	25.0	-100.0	NC	-3	03-87	.00	.0	0	0	0	06-30-86	-2.8	.79	-2.2	1.55	-3.4	9	2.5	348	17,953	5,252	0	0.0	12
Consol Store	NA	NA	.0	NA	NA	NA	NA	NA	NA	NC	00-00	.00	.0	NA	NA	NA	06-17-86	NA	NC	NA	NC	NA	NA	NA	408	40,800	17,562	0	NA	NA
Cook Utd •	14.8	-6.4	-7.1	-16.5n	-2.38	NE	NE	NC	NC	0	10-86	.00	.0	0	0	NE	00-00-00	-7.1	2.45	-17.4	.00	NS	-48	1.7	4	6,815	59	0	0.0	01
Costco Wholesale	85.3	81.4	84.1	3.4n	.13	-50.0	-25.0	NE	NC	4	05-87	.00	.0	0	0	0	00-00-00	.3	4.00	1.2	3.42	4.1	147	2.4	309	24,206	3,651	0	0.0	08
Dollar General Cp	6.7	6.7	-1.0	4.5q	.24	NE	NE	-69.6	-8	1	03-87	.20	1.7	19	87	22	05-01-87	.8	2.38	1.9	2.16	4.1	48	3.0	226	18,802	3,665	+0	0.0	12
Family Dollar	10.3	12.8	15.8	29.1s	1.01	-9.7	-9.4	-1.0	25	15	02-87	.28	1.6	29	22	18	06-09-87	5.6	2.39	13.4	1.54	20.6	0	2.2	507	28,962	10,943	0	11.5	08
Hecks Inc	-.7	8.2	8.2	-17.8f	-2.01	NE	NE	NE	NC	-20	12-86	.00	.0	-11	NE	NE	08-04-87	-3.1	1.90	-5.9	3.32	-19.6	93	1.7	36	8,876	3,190	0	20.9	12
Home Shop	257.6	295.3	340.7	31.8n	.36	60.0	93.3	140.0	NC	67	05-87	.00	.0	0	0	0	01-20-87	6.7	5.04	33.8	1.98	66.9	18	1.6	1,590	85,925	11,824	0	4.6	08
Jamesway Corp	16.7	16.7	17.4	12.5q	.88	50.0	50.0	35.4	10	12	04-87	.08	.6	17	7	6	06-26-87	2.0	3.00	6.0	2.13	12.8	57	3.0	183	13,840	6,054	-1	1.3	01
K mart Cp	7.3	7.3	6.8	621.9q	3.08	21.3	21.3	135.1	13	10	04-87	1.16	2.7	10	33	38	06-08-87	2.6	2.27	5.9	2.68	15.8	66	1.7	8,445	199,893	155,219	+2	1.3	01
Lionel Cp	28.8	28.8	23.2	14.6q	1.11	NE	NE	-45.3	NC	19	04-87	.00	.0	0	0	0	00-00-00	4.9	1.80	8.8	2.18	19.2	45	2.4	111	13,097	3,555	0	0.2	01
Marcade Grp	77.0	77.0	29.4	.6q	-.03	-60.0	-60.0	NE	NC	0	04-87	.00	.0	0	0	0	00-00-00	.7	3.14	2.2	.00	NS	-3	.6	49	9,266	814	0	0.2	01
Mars Stores	-20.3	-20.3	-6.0	-2.0q	-.87	NE	NE	-100.0	NC	-18	04-87	.00	.0	0	0	0	00-00-00	-1.8	3.39	-6.1	2.98	-18.2	85	1.9	9	2,229	125	+3	0.0	01
Michaels Str	60.8	27.9	.0	.0	.35	NE	33.3	84.2	NC	0	04-87	.00	.0	0	0	0	00-00-00	NC	NC	NC	NC	.0	39	2.5	72	9,250	1,440	+3	19.0	01
Nichols, SE	-2.1	-2.1	.9	1.9q	.43	-87.5	-87.5	-50.6	NC	4	04-87	.00	.0	0	0	0	12-31-80	.6	2.33	1.4	2.57	3.6	95	2.9	33	4,665	1,144	0	4.6	01
Pic 'n Save	16.0	16.0	10.2	40.7q	1.03	12.5	12.5	-1.9	18	27	03-87	.00	.0	0	0	0	06-11-86	13.0	1.66	21.6	1.24	26.7	1	4.1	964	39,563	25,989	0	0.0	12
Price Co	22.1	25.5	29.5	70.2n	1.43	25.0	19.4	17.2	63	23	05-87	.00	.0	0	0	0	02-04-86	2.2	6.45	14.2	1.64	23.3	1	1.4	2,194	48,886	23,930	-20	0.0	08
Rose's Stores	16.2	16.2	17.8	25.2q	1.22	15.6	15.6	6.1	18	12	04-87	.21	1.1	23	17	17	03-10-87	2.0	3.15	6.3	2.21	13.9	44	2.3	385	20,524	1,999	+3	0.0	01
Svc Merchandise	14.8	14.8	.5	-36.0q	-1.08	NE	NE	NE	NC	-14	03-87	.08	1.0	1	NE	13	05-15-87	-1.4	1.71	-2.4	5.38	-12.9	276	2.0	262	33,316	15,079	+2	0.0	12
Three D Dept	NA	NA	-30.5	NA	NA	NA	NA	NA	NA	NC	10-86	.10	3.1	NA	NA	NA	04-20-87	NA	NA	NA	NC	NA	NA	NA	6	1,710	129	0	NA	NA
Three D Depts	-3.9	-27.2	-32.6	.5n	.15	NC	-45.8	-58.3	-20	2	04-87	.06	1.9	-2	19	12	04-20-87	1.4	1.86	2.6	1.31	3.4	0	3.8	7	2,111	260	0	0.0	07
Toys R Us	28.7	28.7	26.4	156.4q	1.20	37.5	37.5	30.4	21	17	04-87	.00	.0	0	0	0	06-30-86	6.1	1.69	10.3	1.69	17.4	9	1.3	4,511	124,431	68,470	-78	4.1	01
Wal-Mart Strs	37.0	37.0	39.5	487.1q	1.72	50.0	50.0	39.8	35	25	04-87	.24	.4	35	10	11	06-14-87	3.8	3.16	12.0	2.40	28.8	56	1.8	19,063	281,900	102,758	-24	1.5	01
Woolworth FW	-99.9	-99.9	-15.4	201.0q	3.48	115.0	115.0	21.7	NC	8	04-87	1.32	2.5	4	34	113	04-27-87	3.9	1.82	7.1	1.92	13.6	24	1.9	3,486	65,457	38,248	+3	2.4	01
Zayre Corp	24.1	24.1	30.5	96.7q	1.63	28.6	28.6	.0	20	11	04-87	.40	1.4	40	19	12	08-07-87	1.7	3.00	5.1	2.90	14.8	74	1.8	1,644	58,993	33,255	+8	2.1	01

Recent Performance and Forecast: Telecommunications Services (SIC 4811 & 4821)

(in millions of dollars except as noted)

Item	1983	1984	1985[1]	1986[1]	1987[2]	Percent Change 1983-84	1984-85	1985-86	1986-87
Operating revenues									
Domestic telephone & telegraph	86,870	95,700	103,000	113,250	120,270	10.2	7.6	10.0	6.2
Int'l. telephone & telegraph	2,500	2,800	3,170	3,620	4,130	12.0	13.2	14.2	14.1
Operating Revenues (1982$)									
Domestic telephone & telegraph	83,288	88,950	93,297	97,029	101,007	6.8	4.9	4.0	4.1
Capital expenditures	21,125	21,400	24,300	24,900	24,500	1.3	13.6	2.5	−1.6
Gross cumulative plant investment[3]	216,925	231,690	244,497	251,000	256,770	6.8	5.5	2.7	2.3
Total employment (000)[4]	984	982	931	884	840	−0.2	−5.2	−5.0	−5.0
Production workers (000)[4]	720	731	694	659	624	1.5	−5.1	−5.0	−5.3
Average hourly earnings ($)	11.90	12.43	12.57	12.96	13.37	4.5	1.1	3.1	3.2
No. of telephones (000)	189,000	198,000	205,000	212,000	220,000	4.8	3.5	3.4	3.8
Industry price index[5] (domestic)	104.3	110.4	116.1	118.0	121.2	5.8	5.2	1.6	2.7

[1]Estimated. Includes independents; Regional Bell Operating Companies, AT&T; Southern New England and Cincinnati telephone companies; Western Union Telegraph; and International Record Carriers (IRCs).

[2]Forecast.

[3]Does not include domestic or international carriers.

[4]Includes both telephone and telegraph workers.

[5]Price indexes for international telecommunications services have declined slightly since 1972.

SOURCE: U.S. Department of Commerce: Bureau of the Census; Bureau of Labor Statistics. Estimates and forecast by International Trade Administration.

Source: *U.S. Industrial Outlook 1987*, U.S. Department of Commerce.

Company	Revenue: Pct. Change Last Qtr	Revenue: Pct. Change FY to Date	Revenue: Pct. Change Last 12 Mos	Earnings: Last 12 Mos	Earnings Per Share: Last 12 Mos	Per Share Pct. Change: Last Qtr	Per Share Pct. Change: FY to Date	Per Share Pct. Change: Last 12 Mos	5-Year Growth Rate	Par Growth Rate	Date of Report	Dividends Current Rate: Amt	Current Rate: Yield	5-Year Growth Rate	Payout: Last FY	Payout: Last 5 Yrs.	Last X-Dvd Date	Profit Margin	Asset Turnover	Return on Total Assets	Leverage Ratio	Return on Equity	Debt to Equity	Current Ratio	Market Value	Latest Shares Outstndng.	Held by Banks-Funds	Insider Net Trading	Short Interest Ratio	Fiscal Year Ends
-	%	%	%	$Mil	$	%	%	%	%	%	-	$	%	%	%	%	-	π/r x	r/a =	π/a x	a/e =	π/e	%	-	$Mil	000	000	000	Days	Mo
Broadcasting																														
Ind. Group	20.4	24.9	36.9	521.1·	.89	150.9	- 73.2	40.6	4	9	- - -	.15	.3	0	11	16	- - - -	4.0	.58	2.3	4.61	10.6	222	1.6	28,311	662,362	197,690	-1312	2.9	- -
Acton Cp .... ○	393.8	393.8	116.6	2.7q	.00	NE	NE	NE	NC	NC	03-87	.00	.0	0	0	0	06-25-87	10.4	.70	7.3	.00	NS	-218	.4	21	1,175	108	0	2.0	12
Am Cablesysts	25.5	19.7	18.6	.1n	.11	-100.0	-100.0	-90.4	NC	0	03-87	.00	.0	0	0	0	00-00-00	.2	.50	.1	4.00	.4	523	11.1	223	9,398	3,720	0	0.0	06
Am Comm & TV	.0	33.3	50.0	-2.2s	-.03	NE	NE	NC	NC	0	03-87	.00	.0	0	0	0	00-00-00	-73.3	.29	-21.0	.00	NM	857	.3	10	76,769	10	0	0.0	09
Cablevi Syst	88.1	88.1	67.9	-10.0q	-.58	NE	NE	NE	NC	0	03-87	.00	.0	0	0	0	00-00-00	-5.6	.30	-1.7	.00	NS	-1104	NA	589	21,019	4,924	0	0.1	12
Cap Cities/ABC	5.1	5.1	145.4	203.8q	12.51	1091.7	1091.7	41.2	13	10	03-87	.20	.1	0	2	2	06-24-87	4.9	.80	3.9	2.69	10.5	93	1.5	6,165	16,117	11,998	-8	19.3	12
CBS Inc	8.8	8.8	.2	414.6q	17.09	124.4	124.4	1439.6	2	42	03-87	3.00	1.7	2	19	41	05-20-87	8.7	1.41	12.3	4.18	51.4	78	1.6	4,128	23,519	15,409	0	2.3	12
Chris-Craft	10.6	10.6	16.2	14.5q	.68	NE	NE	-5.6	NC	26	03-87	.00	.0	0	0	0	03-31-87	6.3	.29	1.8	14.56	26.2	429	1.4	555	20,377	4,194	-15	5.0	12
Comcast Cp	129.4	129.4	41.3	-8.4q	-.23	-100.0	-100.0	-100.0	NC	-7	03-87	.12	.5	28	300	17	05-29-87	-4.9	.16	-.8	5.50	-4.4	368	3.1	898	38,193	13,230	+9	0.0	12
Falcon Cable	9.3	9.3	.0	-4.5q	-.77	200.0	200.0	NC	NC	-25	03-87	.54	2.8	0	0	0	03-25-87	-28.1	.28	-7.9	1.87	-14.8	68	NA	112	5,799	0	0	0.0	12
Finl News Net	115.8	98.7	64.2	2.4s	.19	50.0	240.0	171.4	NC	43	02-87	.00	.0	0	0	0	00-00-00	10.4	2.60	27.0	1.59	42.9	0	1.6	131	11,737	1,044	-0	0.0	08
Galaxy Cblvsn	.0	.0	.0	-2.6f	-1.22	NC	NC	NC	NC	-8	12-86	.00	.0	0	0	0	00-00-00	-28.9	.26	-7.4	1.03	-7.6	0	NA	43	2,150	0	0	0.8	12
Herit Comm	87.0	87.0	40.3	-21.2q	-1.01	-100.0	-100.0	-100.0	NC	-9	03-87	.04	.1	0	NE	8	05-27-86	-9.4	.21	-2.0	4.15	-8.3	262	.7	744	22,389	12,416	+22	4.6	12
Jones Intercable	152.3	95.2	93.7	3.7n	.32	-80.0	-45.7	-22.0	16	6	02-87	.00	.0	0	0	0	04-01-85	11.9	.13	1.5	4.20	6.3	220	NA	179	12,777	1,120	0	0.0	05
Jones Intercbl	NA	NA	.0	NA	NA	NA	NA	NA	NA	NC	00-00	.00	.0	NA	NA	NA	00-00-00	NA	NC	NA	NC	NA	NA	NA	50	3,563	76	0	NA	NA
Lin Broadcasting	5.7	5.7	8.7	69.0q	1.24	112.5	112.5	87.9	22	18	03-87	.00	.0	0	0	0	04-01-87	34.8	.37	12.8	1.40	17.9	13	3.4	2,219	53,315	40,224	-16	0.0	12
Malrite Commun	14.9	14.9	5.7	-9.8q	-.42	NE	NE	-100.0	NC	-22	03-87	.00	.0	0	0	1	00-00-00	-10.7	.33	-3.5	6.20	-21.7	304	1.1	154	13,655	1,104	0	0.0	12
Park Commun	8.8	8.8	16.6	15.0q	1.09	7.1	7.1	3.8	13	11	03-87	.00	.0	0	0	0	09-03-85	10.7	.60	6.4	1.78	11.4	51	2.1	4,416	138,000	1,225	+7	0.0	12
Price Comm	30.9	30.9	88.8	-21.0q	-2.02	NE	NE	NE	NC	0	03-87	.00	.0	0	0	0	01-27-87	-20.6	.22	-4.6	.00	NS	-3021	5.4	95	6,975	4,658	-1302	16.2	12
Scripps Howard ...... ○	12.4	12.4	44.0	27.8q	2.69	NE	NE	-2.2	-9	15	03-87	.80	1.0	0	151	45	05-20-87	12.9	.38	4.9	4.37	21.4	221	1.2	826	10,328	965	0	0.0	12
Taft Brdcast	-10.7	5.7	5.7	-53.1f	-5.70	NE	-100.0	-100.0	NC	-19	03-87	.16	.1	5	NE	58	05-11-87	-10.6	.40	-4.2	4.50	-18.9	175	1.2	1,393	9,166	5,596	0	0.5	03
TCA Cable TV	-16.7	22.5	14.8	5.1s	.51	-7.7	-11.5	-8.9	15	10	04-87	.24	.9	0	28	23	04-03-87	9.4	.60	5.6	3.46	19.4	152	NA	276	10,817	2,483	-30	0.0	10
Tele Commun A	149.8	149.8	46.1	109.8q	1.05	433.3	433.3	707.7	44	15	03-87	.00	.0	0	0	0	07-14-86	12.6	.21	2.7	5.67	15.3	401	NA	3,455	98,022	57,934	+15	0.0	12
Turner Brdcst	59.2	59.2	63.8	-220.1q	-12.47	NE	NE	-100.0	NC	0	03-87	.00	.0	0	0	0	07-13-81	-36.2	.32	-11.6	.00	NS	-653	1.3	490	21,790	1,043	0	19.3	12
Utd Cable TV .... •	10.5	13.0	14.3	-1.5n	-.01	-100.0	-54.2	-100.0	NC	-28	02-87	.08	.2	7	67	NE	06-25-87	-.7	.43	-.3	10.33	-3.1	709	NA	789	24,359	11,386	+9	1.3	05
Utd Television	5.5	5.5	12.5	7.0q	.64	NE	NE	-39.6	NC	14	03-87	.00	.0	0	0	0	00-00-00	7.8	.50	3.9	3.69	14.4	119	1.2	350	10,953	2,823	-2	0.0	12

Company	Revenue Pct. Change Last Qtr	Revenue Pct. Change FY to Date	Revenue Pct. Change Last 12 Mos	Earnings Last 12 Mos	Earnings Per Share Last 12 Mos	Earnings Per Share Pct. Change Last Qtr	Earnings Per Share Pct. Change FY to Date	Earnings Per Share Pct. Change Last 12 Mos	Earnings 5-Year Growth Rate	Earnings Par Growth Rate	Earnings Date of Report	Dividends Current Rate Amt	Dividends Current Rate Yield	Dividends 5-Year Growth Rate	Dividends Payout Last FY	Dividends Payout Last 5 Yrs.	Dividends Last X-Dvd Date	Ratio Analysis Profit Margin	Ratio Analysis Asset Turnover	Ratio Analysis Return on Total Assets	Ratio Analysis Leverage Ratio	Ratio Analysis Return on Equity	Ratio Analysis Debt to Equity	Ratio Analysis Current Ratio	Shareholdings Market Value	Shareholdings Latest Shares Outstndng.	Shareholdings Held by Banks-Funds	Shareholdings Insider Net Trading	Shareholdings Short Interest Ratio	Shareholdings Fiscal Year Ends
-	%	%	%	$Mil	$	%	%	%	%	%	-	$	%	%	%	%	-	r/r x	r/a =	r/a x	a/e =	r/e	%	-	$Mil	000	000	000	Days	Mo
Telephone Utility																														
Ind. Group	13.2	33.7	- 1.0	13,295.2	2.61	9.0	16.2	5.6	39	4	- - -	1.73	4.6	0	69	64	- - - -	8.8	.52	4.6	2.70	12.4	70	1.1	187,663	5,046,376	G	+ 44	1.1	- -
ADC Telecomm	19.4	11.7	12.5	12.0s	1.38	17.6	-1.4	16.0	44	20	04-87	.00	.0	0	0	0	04-28-86	7.9	1.78	14.1	1.41	19.9	6	3.0	196	8,617	3,267	0	0.0	10
ALLTEL Cp	3.8	3.8	3.0	58.4q	1.69	10.3	10.3	-25.2	2	2	03-87	1.36	4.9	4	80	63	06-08-87	8.3	.42	3.5	3.29	11.5	121	1.0	857	31,160	6,591	+1	0.2	12
Am Tel & T	-6.8	-6.8	-5.1	229.2q	.14	-14.9	-14.9	-90.8	NC	-13	03-87	1.20	4.3	0	571	127	06-24-87	.7	.86	.6	2.83	1.7	54	1.4	29,614	1,071,987	200,686	+6	1.0	12
Ameritech Cp	.6	.6	3.0	1142.7q	7.95	4.1	4.1	7.0	NC	6	03-87	5.00	5.7	0	59	54	03-25-87	12.2	.50	6.1	2.46	15.0	59	.8	12,417	142,719	48,312	+0	1.5	12
Bell Atlantic	4.5	4.5	7.5	1184.7q	5.94	6.2	6.2	5.3	NC	5	03-87	3.84	5.6	0	61	57	06-24-87	11.8	.47	5.6	2.54	14.2	60	.8	13,555	198,971	64,991	+1	3.0	12
Bell Canada	9.1	9.1	5.6	1031.5q	3.80	-3.2	-3.2	-7.8	6	5	03-87	2.40	NA	8	62	53	06-09-87	7.3	.59	4.3	2.86	12.3	80	1.3	8,389	265,276	7,839	+1	0.5	12
BellSouth	5.0	5.0	5.9	1621.1q	3.41	3.3	3.3	3.0	NC	5	03-87	2.20	5.4	0	59	55	07-06-87	14.0	.44	6.2	2.32	14.4	56	1.0	19,491	476,838	131,607	+6	3.8	12
Brit Telecom	29.2	21.9	21.8	2112.3f	3.36	50.0	36.0	36.0	NC	22	03-87	.00	.0	0	41	34	00-00-00	13.9	.70	9.7	2.31	22.4	49	1.1	27,900	600,006	3,141	0	2.9	03
CTEC Cp	23.2	23.2	12.3	10.0q	1.82	37.2	37.2	-4.7	12	7	03-87	.92	3.8	10	66	47	05-04-87	7.9	.47	3.7	3.62	13.4	133	1.3	134	5,524	186	0	0.0	12
Centel Cp	10.0	10.0	5.7	109.8q	3.86	-1.8	-1.8	-15.9	1	4	03-87	2.50	3.8	3	63	55	07-01-87	7.9	.48	3.8	3.03	11.5	93	.9	1,896	28,671	14,420	+9	0.3	12
Century Tel	.5	.5	-20.0	17.7q	1.51	5.6	5.6	.7	3	6	03-87	.86	4.5	3	56	58	05-22-87	12.0	.32	3.8	3.63	13.8	151	.9	213	11,146	3,242	-5	0.2	12
Checkpoint Sys	-5.7	-5.7	25.0	5.0q	.51	-100.0	-100.0	-15.0	NC	19	03-87	.00	.0	0	0	0	05-28-86	14.3	.97	13.8	1.37	18.9	12	4.0	117	9,477	3,412	+34	0.0	12
Cinn Bell	3.6	3.6	4.1	59.7q	1.84	13.3	13.3	15.7	12	7	03-87	.96	3.9	6	52	53	05-21-87	12.0	.51	6.1	2.31	14.1	50	1.0	780	31,832	7,358	+6	0.3	12
Contel Cp	3.8	3.8	15.8	238.5q	3.11	10.9	10.9	-4.9	8	6	03-87	2.00	6.3	5	61	63	05-12-87	7.7	.57	4.4	3.61	15.9	128	.9	2,430	76,534	35,845	0	2.3	12
Graphic Scanning	-12.8	-11.6	-26.8	37.4n	.69	NE	NE	NE	NC	0	03-87	.00	.0	0	0	0	11-01-83	34.3	.59	20.4	.00	NM	1883	1.0	348	40,377	7,446	0	0.0	06
GTE Cp	938.1	938.1	-61.0	1166.2q	3.45	-9.3	-9.3	NE	NC	4	03-87	2.44	6.3	9	90	86	05-18-87	24.1	.18	4.3	3.53	15.2	116	.9	12,703	329,958	167,247	+3	1.4	12
Inter Tel	22.5	22.5	-15.5	.5q	.07	200.0	200.0	NE	NC	3	02-87	.00	.0	0	0	0	08-17-81	1.3	1.46	1.9	1.79	3.4	37	3.1	25	8,315	118	0	0.0	11
Intl Mobile Mach	300.0	433.3	.0	-9.6f	-.95	NE	NE	NE	NC	0	12-86	.00	.0	0	0	0	00-00-00	NM	NC	NC	NC	NM	1	5.0	119	11,107	521	-4	0.0	12
Linc Telecom	10.0	10.0	11.6	19.5q	4.53	12.8	12.8	30.5	6	8	03-87	2.32	4.6	5	50	58	06-24-87	12.0	.57	6.8	2.29	15.6	61	.0	207	4,149	1,073	+0	0.0	12
MCI Communicatn .. ○	16.5	16.5	33.5	-431.3q	-1.52	-12.5	-12.5	-100.0	NC	-33	03-87	.00	.0	0	0	0	08-22-83	-11.6	.83	-9.6	3.41	-32.7	129	1.0	2,124	283,200	93,412	0	0.0	12
Millicom Inc	50.0	66.7	.0	1.8n	.22	-100.0	500.0	NE	NC	0	09-86	.00	.0	0	0	0	00-00-00	NM	NC	NC	NC	NM	456	.4	141	8,207	567	0	0.0	12
NYNEX Cp	8.3	8.3	10.4	1218.0q	6.74	98.6	98.6	37.8	NC	6	03-87	3.80	5.4	0	57	53	06-24-87	10.5	.53	5.6	2.45	13.7	62	1.2	14,329	204,340	69,223	0	2.5	12
Pac Telecom	3.3	3.3	4.0	42.5q	1.11	-18.2	-18.2	20.7	-9	2	03-87	.88	5.0	11	70	58	05-11-87	8.6	.41	3.5	2.89	10.1	80	.8	670	38,301	1,591	0	0.0	12
Pac Telesis	1.1	1.1	3.8	1098.8q	2.55	6.3	6.3	8.5	NC	5	03-87	1.64	6.2	0	60	57	03-31-87	12.2	.44	5.4	2.63	14.2	71	.9	11,410	430,550	185,020	0	1.8	12
Philipp LD Tel	11.8	18.1	18.9	82.7n	3.96	157.4	217.3	202.3	19	66	09-86	.23	.8	-17	16	39	03-09-87	29.2	.32	9.2	7.61	70.0	527	1.8	527	17,569	1,443	0	0.6	12
Roch Tele	6.8	6.8	-2.1	38.1q	3.54	-1.2	-1.2	-6.8	2	3	03-87	2.64	6.0	7	72	64	07-09-87	9.3	.58	5.4	2.44	13.2	63	.8	452	10,207	3,218	0	0.5	12
So N Eng Tel	9.7	9.7	11.3	140.7q	4.54	7.4	7.4	15.2	5	5	03-87	2.88	5.4	6	63	67	06-16-87	9.6	.58	5.6	2.48	13.9	64	1.0	1,641	30,603	6,883	+0	0.9	12
Swtn Bell	-2.2	-2.2	-.8	1034.9q	3.46	5.3	5.3	8.5	NC	4	03-87	2.32	6.0	0	61	56	05-26-87	13.2	.39	5.1	2.59	13.2	63	.9	11,669	300,180	120,309	0	2.2	12
Telephone Data	22.1	22.1	29.6	15.2q	1.47	13.6	13.6	75.0	6	10	03-87	.50	1.7	10	29	39	03-10-87	9.4	.37	3.5	4.14	14.5	201	1.0	272	9,434	3,503	-12	1.2	12
TIE Comm	-23.7	-23.7	-11.4	-56.5q	-1.58	NE	NE	NE	NC	-36	03-87	.00	.0	0	0	0	07-19-83	-20.3	.94	-19.0	1.90	-36.1	23	2.4	157	35,918	4,498	0	0.6	12
TPI Enterprises ..... □	-17.4	8.2	19.7	-32.4n	-1.14	-100.0	-100.0	-100.0	NC	-16	09-86	.00	.0	0	0	0	08-01-83	-12.7	.65	-8.2	1.99	-16.3	3	2.6	139	30,066	5,339	0	0.0	12
US West	.5	.5	4.6	948.6q	4.99	13.7	13.7	4.8	NC	4	03-87	3.28	6.2	0	62	55	04-10-87	11.4	.45	5.1	2.55	13.0	67	.9	9,969	189,427	74,628	+2	2.0	12
Utd Telcom	-1.8	-1.8	-22.2	147.5q	1.47	-72.3	-72.3	G	-21	-3	03-87	1.92	7.0	3	106	95	06-04-87	6.2	.37	2.3	3.74	8.6	156	1.1	2,697	98,536	47,007	-3	3.8	12
Univ Commun	12.4	29.5	.0	.0	.72	33.3	10.0	-18.2	NC	0	03-87	.00	.0	0	0	0	01-03-83	NC	NC	NC	NC	.0	55	2.7	73	7,174	367	0	4.1	06

Recent Performance and Forecast: Textile Mill Products (SIC 22)

(in millions of dollars except as noted)

				Percent change			
				Compound Annual		Annual	
	1984	1985[1]	1986[2]	1972-84	1979-84	1984-85	1985-86
Industry Data							
Value of shipments[3]	55,489	53,020	55,141	5.8	4.3	−4.4	4.0
Value of shipments (1982$)	53,188	51,326	52,316	0.5	−0.4	−3.5	1.9
Total employment (000)	711	670	669	−2.4	−3.3	−5.7	−0.2
Production workers (000)	611	575	575	−2.6	−3.5	−5.9	0.0
Average hourly earnings ($)	6.56	6.80	7.01	7.4	6.7	3.7	3.1
Product Data							
Value of shipments[4]	52,258	50,147	51,917	6.0	4.2	−4.0	3.5
Value of shipments (1982$)	50,065	48,498	49,210	0.7	−0.5	−3.1	1.5
Shipments price index[5] (1982=100)	104.8	103.8	105.9	5.1	4.7	−0.9	2.0
Trade Data							
Value of imports	3,539	3,697	4,322	8.4	14.0	4.5	16.9
Value of exports	1,541	1,462	1,751	8.1	−6.3	−5.1	19.8

[1]Estimated except for exports and imports.
[2]Estimated.
[3]Value of all products and services sold by the Textile Mill Products industry.
[4]Value of products classified in the Textile Mill Products industry produced by all industries.
[5]Developed by the Office of Industry Assessment, ITA.

SOURCE: U.S. Department of Commerce: Bureau of the Census, Bureau of Economic Analysis, International Trade Administration (ITA). Estimates and forecasts by ITA.

Source: *U.S. Industrial Outlook 1987*, U.S. Department of Commerce.

Company	Revenue: Pct. Change Last Qtr	Revenue: Pct. Change FY to Date	Revenue: Pct. Change Last 12 Mos	Earnings: Last 12 Mos	Earnings: Per Share Last 12 Mos	Earnings: Per Share Pct. Change Last Qtr	Earnings: Per Share Pct. Change FY to Date	Earnings: Per Share Pct. Change Last 12 Mos	Earnings: 5-Year Growth Rate	Earnings: Par Growth Rate	Earnings: Date of Report	Dividends: Current Rate Amt	Dividends: Current Rate Yield	Dividends: 5-Year Growth Rate	Dividends: Payout Last FY	Dividends: Payout Last 5 Yrs.	Dividends: Last X-Dvd Date	Ratio Analysis: Profit Margin	Ratio Analysis: Asset Turnover	Ratio Analysis: Return on Total Assets	Ratio Analysis: Leverage Ratio	Ratio Analysis: Return on Equity	Ratio Analysis: Debt to Equity	Ratio Analysis: Current Ratio	Shareholdings: Market Value	Shareholdings: Latest Shares Outstndng.	Shareholdings: Held by Banks-Funds	Shareholdings: Insider Net Trading	Shareholdings: Short Interest Ratio	Fiscal Year Ends
-	%	%	%	$Mil	$	%	%	%	%	%	-	$	%	%	%	%	-	π/r	x r/a	= π/a	x a/e	= π/e	%	-	$Mil	000	000	000	Days	Mo
Textile Mills																														
Ind. Group	20.3	22.2	18.6	665.7	1.02	63.6	40.8	54.5	17	8	---	.34	1.7	1	32	40	----	3.6	1.44	5.2	2.17	11.3	48	2.3	12,640	655,877	130,290	- 43	1.2	--
Adams-Millis	62.5	62.5	63.8	6.2q	1.34	37.5	37.5	12.6	32	10	03-87	.24	1.5	17	16	15	05-12-87	3.2	1.47	4.7	2.57	12.1	88	2.6	74	4,620	2,842	+7	1.4	12
Aileen Inc	12.2	13.3	-4.0	-3.7s	-.71	-93.3	NE	-100.0	NC	-13	04-87	.00	.0	0	0	0	00-00-00	-7.7	1.22	-9.4	1.35	-12.7	5	2.5	21	5,103	572	0	0.0	10
Alba-Waldens	23.0	23.0	9.5	1.4q	.75	NE	NE	NE	NC	6	03-87	.00	.0	0	0	28	09-07-84	3.0	1.30	3.9	1.54	6.0	10	2.5	16	1,861	259	0	0.0	12
Belding Hemin	15.9	15.9	11.5	4.0q	1.57	59.1	59.1	.0	13	6	03-87	.40	1.7	2	28	27	05-26-87	3.2	1.41	4.5	1.93	8.7	44	3.4	61	2,532	538	-11	1.9	12
Burlington Inds	15.7	9.8	3.8	57.5s	2.09	1.4	8.0	90.0	-14	1	03-87	1.64	2.1	2	82	83	04-21-87	2.0	1.30	2.6	1.92	5.0	39	2.4	2,088	27,290	15,722	-78	0.0	09
Chatham Mfg	7.0	7.0	5.0	5.9q	3.50	95.6	95.6	75.9	25	8	03-87	.80	2.2	8	26	35	06-04-87	4.7	1.74	8.2	1.27	10.4	8	6.0	61	1,682	626	0	0.0	12
Concord Fab ○	17.4	16.6	16.1	2.4s	1.22	51.2	22.7	159.6	-3	10	02-87	.00	.0	0	0	0	00-00-00	2.0	2.40	4.8	2.08	10.0	10	2.0	23	1,783	165	0	0.0	08
Courtaulds Ltd □ ■	31.3	20.7	20.6	168.5f	.44	85.7	46.7	46.7	NC	17	03-86	.07	.9	7	16	35	11-29-85	5.2	1.58	8.2	2.45	20.1	33	1.7	2,987	379,300	772	0	3.9	03
Crown Crafts	20.0	28.7	28.5	2.8f	3.69	124.5	314.6	314.6	NC	36	03-87	.00	.0	0	0	0	05-08-80	5.2	2.71	14.1	2.55	35.9	78	2.9	43	734	5	0	2.3	03
Damon Creat	-2.0	-2.0	-9.3	-.8q	-.75	NE	NE	NE	NC	-8	03-87	.00	.0	0	0	0	00-00-00	-2.1	1.90	-4.0	1.88	-7.5	14	2.2	6	1,100	0	0	0.0	12
Fab Indus	4.2	4.2	9.0	10.8q	2.97	3.0	3.0	16.9	10	11	02-87	.60	1.7	11	17	16	12-04-86	9.0	1.07	9.6	1.42	13.6	1	4.5	127	3,632	1,227	0	0.0	11
Fieldcrest Mill	45.6	45.6	75.2	26.0q	3.15	NE	NE	266.3	11	8	03-87	.68	2.0	-11	27	58	06-10-87	2.2	1.45	3.2	3.03	9.7	122	3.0	332	9,755	3,211	-1	1.6	12
Guilford Mills	32.0	29.1	23.9	21.9n	2.10	23.3	15.5	25.0	3	9	03-87	.60	1.8	13	28	24	05-01-87	4.4	1.95	8.6	1.52	13.1	6	2.5	342	10,536	5,348	0	0.8	06
Hancock Fab	5.5	5.5	302.7	19.1q	1.49	.0	.0	NC	NC	25	04-87	.00	.0	0	0	0	00-00-00	6.5	1.95	12.7	1.99	25.3	48	3.6	239	12,857	0	0	0.0	01
Ruddick Corp	10.2	10.3	7.0	14.5s	1.52	25.9	23.5	22.6	5	9	03-87	.44	2.3	-6	16	25	06-08-87	1.6	3.44	5.5	2.24	12.3	40	1.6	173	9,130	1,329	0	9.1	09
Russell Cp	11.9	11.9	11.6	43.0q	1.07	-4.0	-4.0	24.4	11	14	03-87	.20	1.2	6	15	19	04-28-87	9.6	1.28	12.3	1.41	17.3	15	5.6	667	39,214	14,178	0	0.4	12
Springs Indus	2.7	2.7	28.7	37.0q	2.07	88.9	88.9	146.4	-9	5	03-87	.84	2.5	0	31	43	06-08-87	2.4	1.54	3.7	2.16	8.0	58	3.3	591	17,708	4,354	0	2.1	12
Stanwood Cp	12.2	12.2	-.8	-.6q	-.34	154.5	154.5	-100.0	NC	-2	03-87	.00	.0	0	0	0	00-00-00	-.5	1.60	-.8	3.00	-2.4	150	5.5	24	1,533	180	0	2.8	12
Stevens JP	-12.6	-8.8	-6.6	56.9s	3.22	16.4	18.6	NE	NC	7	04-87	1.20	2.8	0	40	100	06-29-87	3.6	1.64	5.9	1.92	11.3	25	2.7	735	17,138	8,105	-0	0.3	10
Texfi Ind	125.3	94.1	27.6	2.2s	.38	NE	NE	NE	NC	19	04-87	.00	.0	0	0	0	00-00-00	1.8	2.33	4.2	4.55	19.1	211	1.8	55	5,830	647	+64	0.2	10
Unifi Inc	9.3	20.0	24.6	8.6n	.87	50.0	-23.0	-30.4	-4	10	03-87	.00	.0	0	0	0	02-24-86	3.0	1.97	5.9	1.64	9.7	33	3.2	149	9,547	7,383	-10	0.0	06
Utd Mer Mfrs □	-2.8	-8.3	-7.2	-23.0n	-2.54	NE	NE	NE	NC	-20	03-87	.00	.0	0	0	0	00-00-00	-3.1	1.29	-4.0	4.98	-19.9	283	2.6	106	9,117	5,417	0	0.8	06
Vertipile Inc	1.9	1.9	-6.9	2.6q	1.55	NE	NE	1191.7	NC	21	05-87	.00	.0	0	0	30	10-30-84	2.4	2.38	5.7	3.68	21.0	147	2.1	10	1,686	248	0	1.1	02
V.F. Corp	83.6	83.6	20.8	136.3q	2.12	17.1	17.1	-7.0	16	11	03-87	.72	1.8	20	32	27	06-02-87	7.5	.99	7.4	2.23	16.5	53	2.1	2,753	67,556	48,744	+6	0.7	12
West Point-P	17.2	30.2	47.1	66.2s	4.40	23.0	14.2	6.0	-3	4	02-87	2.39	3.7	6	54	48	05-19-87	3.2	1.44	4.6	2.13	9.8	46	2.3	957	14,633	8,418	-19	0.4	08

Purchasing Power of the Dollar: 1940 to 1985

[1967=$1.00. Producer prices prior to 1961, and consumer prices prior to 1964, exclude Alaska and Hawaii. For 1940 and 1945, producer prices based on all commodities index; subsequent years based on finished goods index. Obtained by dividing the average price index for the 1967 base period (100.0) by the price index for a given period and expressing the result in dollars and cents. Annual figures are based on average of monthly data]

YEAR	ANNUAL AVERAGE AS MEASURED BY—		YEAR	ANNUAL AVERAGE AS MEASURED BY—		YEAR	ANNUAL AVERAGE AS MEASURED BY—	
	Producer prices	Consumer prices		Producer prices	Consumer prices		Producer prices	Consumer prices
1940	$2.469	$2.381	1960	$1.067	$1.127	1973	$.782	$.751
1945	1.832	1.855	1961	1.067	1.116	1974	.678	.677
1948	1.252	1.387	1962	1.064	1.104	1975	.612	.620
1949	1.289	1.401	1963	1.067	1.091	1976	.586	.587
1950	1.266	1.387	1964	1.063	1.076	1977	.550	.551
1951	1.156	1.285	1965	1.045	1.058	1978	.510	.512
1952	1.163	1.258	1966	1.012	1.029	1979	.459	.460
1953	1.175	1.248	1967	1.000	1.000	1980	.405	.405
1954	1.172	1.142	1968	.972	.960	1981	.371	.367
1955	1.170	1.247	1969	.938	.911	1982	.356	.346
1956	1.138	1.229	1970	.907	.860	1983	.351	.335
1957	1.098	1.186	1971	.880	.824	1984	.343	321
1958	1.073	1.155	1972	.853	.799	1985	.340	.310
1959	1.075	1.145						

Source: U.S. Bureau of Labor Statistics. Monthly data in U.S. Bureau of Economic Analysis, *Survey of Current Business.*

Source: *Statistical Abstracts of the United States, 1987,* U.S. Department of Commerce.

Financial Statement Ratios by Industry

Many quantitative indicators are used to assess the financial strength of an enterprise and the success of its operations. The simplest is to assemble related financial items, such as sales and profits, and express the relationship in the form of a ratio. Using these ratios, various aspects of corporate operations may be compared with the performance of other corporations or groups of corporations of similar size or in a similar industry.

The Quarterly Financial Report's (QFR) ratio formatted income statement and selected balance sheet ratios are expressed as a percent of net sales and total assets, respectively. The operating and financial characteristics of the respective industries and asset size groups are thus reduced to a common denominator to facilitate analysis.

The ratio tables include the following additional basic operating ratios:

1. *Annual rate of profit on stockholders' equity at end of the period.* This ratio is obtained by multiplying income for the quarter before or after domestic taxes [including branch income (loss) and equity in the earnings of nonconsolidated subsidiaries net of foreign taxes] by four, to put it on an annual basis, and then dividing by stockholders' equity at the end of the quarter. It measures the rate of return which accrues to stockholders on their investment.
2. *Annual rate of profit on total assets.* This ratio is obtained by multiplying income, as defined in deriving the rate of profit on stockholders' equity, both before and after taxes, by four and then dividing by total assets at the end of the quarter. This ratio measures the productivity of assets in terms of producing income.
3. *Total current assets to total current liabilities.* This ratio is obtained by dividing total current assets by total current liabilities. It measures the ability to discharge current maturing obligations from existing current assets.
4. *Total cash, U.S. government and other securities to current liabilities.* This ratio is obtained by dividing total cash, U.S. government and other securities by total current liabilities. It measures the ability to discharge current liabilities from liquid assets.
5. *Total stockholders' equity to total debt.* This ratio is obtained by dividing total stockholders' equity by the total of short-term loans, current installments on long-term debt, and long-term debt due in more than one year. It indicates the extent of leverage financing used.

Source: *Quarterly Financial Report*, Bureau of the Census. The exhibits in this section are from the same publication.

DESCRIPTION OF THE SAMPLE

The sample on which the QFR estimates for mining, wholesale and retail trade are based is a composite sample selected from two mutually exclusive sampling frames. Prior to the third quarter 1977, the sample drawn for manufacturing estimates was similarly based. The frame from which the major portion of the sample continues to be selected consists of the Internal Revenue Service file of those corporate entities which are required to file Form 1120 or 1120-S and which also have as their principal industrial activity manufacturing, mining, or wholesale or retail trade. The IRS file is sampled once each year. At the time the sample is selected, the file does not contain those corporate entities whose first income tax return has not been processed. In addition, several months elapse between the selection of this sample and its introduction into the QFR program. To keep the mining and wholesale and retail trade QFR sample as up to date as possible, a separate sample is drawn each calendar quarter from a frame comprising applications for a Federal Social Security Employer's Identification Number filed with the Social Security Administration (SSA) during the previous quarter by new corporations. In processing the composite list of sample companies, a screening technique is used to insure that corporations drawn from the SSA frame could not have been drawn from the IRS frame.

Stratification is used in the sample selection process. In sampling from the IRS frame, stratification by industry and size is employed. In sampling from the SSA frame, stratification is by division and size alone. The measures of size used in the IRS frame are total assets and gross receipts while the measure of size used in the SSA frame is number of employees. Beginning with the third quarter 1977, the strata comprised of manufacturing firms with assets of less than $250,000 and the strata which contained corporations in the SSA frame are estimated by multivariate techniques. The sampling fractions applied to the other various industry-size strata vary according to both industry and size. They range from approximately one out of

850 to one out of one. Nearly all corporations whose operations are within the scope of the QFR and which have total assets greater than $50 million are included in the sample. Corporations whose total assets are between $10 million and $50 million and whose receipts exceed the estimated average value for a corporation with $25 million in assets in its industry are also in the sample. Thus, for the most part, corporations with assets over $25 million are permanent sample members with a one out of one sampling fraction.

In those industry-size strata for which the sampling fraction is less than one out of one, a replacement scheme is utilized which provides that one eighth of the sample is replaced each quarter. Corporations removed are those that have been in the reporting group longest (usually eight quarters). Therefore, samples of small corporations for adjacent quarters are seven-eighths identical; for quarters ending nine months apart they are five-eighths identical; etc.

Notice of Change

Beginning in the first quarter 1987, the universe of manufacturing corporations was redefined to exclude corporations with less than $250,000 in assets at the time of sample selection. To provide comparability, manufacturing data for the four quarters of 1986 have been restated to reflect this change.

Industry Contents

Ratios for Firms with Assets $25 Million and Under

TABLE

Ratios for Firms with Assets $25 Million and Over

TABLE 1—INCOME STATEMENT
FOR CORPORATIONS INCLUDED IN ESIC MAJOR GROUPS 20 AND 21

(See NOTE below.)

	Food and Kindred Products[1]				
	1Q 1986	2Q 1986	3Q 1986	4Q 1986	1Q 1987
	(percent of net sales)				
INCOME STATEMENT IN RATIO FORMAT					
Net sales, receipts, and operating revenues	100.0	100.0	100.0	100.0	100.0
Less: Depreciation, depletion, and amortization of property, plant and equipment	2.5	2.2	2.4	2.4	2.6
Less: All other operating costs and expenses	91.5	90.7	90.6	89.9	90.8
Income (or loss) from operations	6.0	7.1	7.0	7.7	6.6
Non-operating income (expense)	-0.2	-0.5	-0.8	0.5	-0.8
Income (or loss) before income taxes	5.7	6.5	6.2	8.1	5.9
Less: Provision for current and deferred domestic income taxes	2.1	2.5	2.3	3.0	2.2
Income (or loss) after income taxes	3.6	4.0	3.9	5.2	3.7
	(percent)				
OPERATING RATIOS (see explanatory notes)					
Annual rate of profit on stockholders' equity at end of period:					
Before income taxes	21.08	25.58	24.59	31.51	21.64
After taxes	13.33	15.89	15.54	20.00	13.62
Annual rate of profit on total assets:					
Before income taxes	8.50	10.37	9.30	11.91	8.18
After taxes	5.38	6.44	5.88	7.56	5.15
BALANCE SHEET RATIOS (based on succeeding table)					
Total current assets to total current liabilities	1.52	1.47	1.45	1.35	1.33
Total cash, U.S. Government and other securities to total current liabilities	0.25	0.22	0.23	0.21	0.21
Total stockholders' equity to total debt	1.18	1.24	1.05	1.07	1.02

NOTE: Beginning in the first quarter 1987, the universe of corporations represented by these estimates was redefined to exclude corporations with less than $250,000 in assets at the time of sample selection.

[1]In the first quarter 1987, a number of corporations were reclassified by industry. Also, estimates for corporations with less than $250,000 in assets were discontinued. To provide comparability, the four quarters of 1986 have been restated to reflect these changes.

[2]The 1986 data are restated to exclude estimates for corporations with less than $250,000 in assets at the time of sample selection.

[3]Tobacco industry data have been collapsed into food industry data. Major merger and acquisition activity in recent years resulted in the reclassification of a significant portion of gross receipts and assets from tobacco to food. The remainder, comprised of data from highly specialized tobacco manufacturers, is too small to be considered publishable as a separate industry.

TABLE 2—BALANCE SHEET
FOR CORPORATIONS INCLUDED IN ESIC MAJOR GROUPS 20 AND 21

(See NOTE below.)

	Food and Kindred Products[1]				
	1Q 1986	2Q 1986	3Q 1986	4Q 1986	1Q 1987
	(percent of total assets)				
SELECTED BALANCE SHEET RATIOS					
Total cash, U.S. Government and other securities	6.2	5.7	5.8	5.6	5.6
Trade accounts and trade notes receivable	12.3	13.1	12.6	11.7	11.1
Inventories	17.0	16.2	15.2	15.4	14.9
Total current assets	38.4	37.3	36.4	35.5	35.3
Net property, plant and equipment	35.0	35.5	34.6	34.3	34.1
Short-term debt including installments on long-term debt	7.7	7.2	7.6	7.6	9.4
Total current liabilities	25.2	25.3	25.2	26.4	26.5
Long-term debt	26.6	25.4	28.6	27.6	27.6
Total liabilities	59.7	59.4	62.2	62.2	62.2
Stockholders' equity	40.3	40.6	37.8	37.8	37.8

NOTE: Beginning in the first quarter 1987, the universe of corporations represented by these estimates was redefined to exclude corporations with less than $250,000 in assets at the time of sample selection.

[1]In the first quarter 1987, a number of corporations were reclassified by industry. Also, estimates for corporations with less than $250,000 in assets were discontinued. To provide comparability, the four quarters of 1986 have been restated to reflect these changes.

[2]The 1986 data are restated to exclude estimates for corporations with less than $250,000 in assets at the time of sample selection.

[3]Tobacco industry data have been collapsed into food industry data. Major merger and acquisition activity in recent years resulted in the reclassification of a significant portion of gross receipts and assets from tobacco to food. The remainder, comprised of data from highly specialized tobacco manufacturers, is too small to be considered publishable as a separate industry.

Food and Kindred Products [2] Assets Under $25 Million					Tobacco Manufactures [3]					Tobacco Manufactures [3] Assets Under $25 Million				
1Q 1986	2Q 1986	3Q 1986	4Q 1986	1Q 1987	1Q 1986	2Q 1986	3Q 1986	4Q 1986	1Q 1987	1Q 1986	2Q 1986	3Q 1986	4Q 1986	1Q 1987
(percent of net sales)					(percent of net sales)					(percent of net sales)				
100.0	100.0	100.0	100.0	100.0										
1.9	1.8	1.9	1.9	2.2										
95.1	96.1	95.1	95.2	95.0										
3.0	2.0	2.9	3.0	2.8										
-0.5	-0.3	0.4	-0.2	-0.3										
2.5	1.7	3.3	2.8	2.5										
1.0	0.6	1.0	1.0	1.1										
1.5	1.1	2.3	1.8	1.5										
(percent)					(percent)					(percent)				
19.48	13.87	24.11	18.98	16.50										
11.54	9.01	16.49	12.22	9.54										
7.80	5.60	10.59	8.90	7.31										
4.62	3.63	7.24	5.73	4.22										
1.73	1.69	1.73	1.83	1.94										
0.26	0.25	0.30	0.29	0.31										
1.08	1.11	1.29	1.57	1.36										

Food and Kindred Products [2] Assets Under $25 Million					Tobacco Manufactures [3]					Tobacco Manufactures [3] Assets Under $25 Million				
1Q 1986	2Q 1986	3Q 1986	4Q 1986	1Q 1987	1Q 1986	2Q 1986	3Q 1986	4Q 1986	1Q 1987	1Q 1986	2Q 1986	3Q 1986	4Q 1986	1Q 1987
(percent of total assets)					(percent of total assets)					(percent of total assets)				
8.8	8.6	10.4	9.5	9.2										
23.5	22.9	21.8	22.4	21.6										
22.8	23.2	23.5	24.5	22.1										
57.9	58.0	59.5	60.1	57.3										
34.5	33.8	34.5	33.6	35.9										
12.8	13.3	14.4	11.4	9.7										
33.6	34.4	34.4	32.8	29.6										
24.3	23.1	19.5	18.6	22.9										
60.0	59.6	56.1	53.1	55.7										
40.0	40.4	43.9	46.9	44.3										

TABLE 3—INCOME STATEMENT
FOR CORPORATIONS INCLUDED IN ESIC MAJOR GROUPS 22 AND 26

(See NOTE below.)

	Textile Mill Products[1]				
	1Q[2] 1986	2Q[2] 1986	3Q 1986	4Q 1986	1Q 1987
	(percent of net sales)				
INCOME STATEMENT IN RATIO FORMAT					
Net sales, receipts, and operating revenues	100.0	100.0	100.0	100.0	100.0
Less: Depreciation, depletion, and amortization of property, plant and equipment	3.3	3.2	3.2	2.9	3.2
Less: All other operating costs and expenses	90.7	89.2	88.6	88.6	89.5
Income (or loss) from operations	6.1	7.6	8.2	8.5	7.4
Non-operating income (expense)	-1.2	-1.3	-1.3	-0.9	-1.5
Income (or loss) before income taxes	4.9	6.3	6.8	7.7	5.8
Less: Provision for current and deferred domestic income taxes	2.0	2.6	3.1	3.2	2.5
Income (or loss) after income taxes	2.9	3.7	3.7	4.4	3.4
	(percent)				
OPERATING RATIOS (see explanatory notes)					
Annual rate of profit on stockholders' equity at end of period:					
Before income taxes	17.05	22.13	24.10	27.43	20.76
After taxes	10.23	13.11	13.03	15.86	12.01
Annual rate of profit on total assets:					
Before income taxes	7.91	10.34	11.23	12.90	9.29
After taxes	4.74	6.13	6.07	7.46	5.38
BALANCE SHEET RATIOS (based on succeeding table)					
Total current assets to total current liabilities	2.36	2.38	2.42	2.47	2.42
Total cash, U.S. Government and other securities to total current liabilities	0.28	0.24	0.25	0.29	0.25
Total stockholders' equity to total debt	1.51	1.56	1.53	1.56	1.41

NOTE: Beginning in the first quarter 1987, the universe of corporations represented by these estimates was redefined to exclude corporations with less than $250,000 in assets at the time of sample selection.

[1]The 1986 data are restated to exclude estimates for corporations with less than $250,000 in assets at the time of sample selection.

[2]Revised.

TABLE 4—BALANCE SHEET
FOR CORPORATIONS INCLUDED IN ESIC MAJOR GROUPS 22 AND 26

(See NOTE below.)

	Textile Mill Products[1]				
	1Q[2] 1986	2Q[2] 1986	3Q 1986	4Q 1986	1Q 1987
	(percent of total assets)				
SELECTED BALANCE SHEET RATIOS					
Total cash, U.S. Government and other securities	6.9	5.8	5.9	6.5	5.8
Trade accounts and trade notes receivable	23.4	23.6	23.9	23.2	23.0
Inventories	24.9	25.7	24.2	23.4	24.6
Total current assets	57.4	57.2	56.5	56.1	55.9
Net property, plant and equipment	32.5	32.1	32.6	32.4	32.4
Short-term debt including installments on long-term debt	7.2	7.0	6.7	6.6	6.7
Total current liabilities	24.3	24.0	23.3	22.7	23.1
Long-term debt	23.6	23.0	23.8	23.6	25.1
Total liabilities	53.6	53.3	53.4	53.0	55.2
Stockholders' equity	46.4	46.7	46.6	47.0	44.8

NOTE: Beginning in the first quarter 1987, the universe of corporations represented by these estimates was redefined to exclude corporations with less than $250,000 in assets at the time of sample selection.

[1]The 1986 data are restated to exclude estimates for corporations with less than $250,000 in assets at the time of sample selection.

[2]Revised.

Textile Mill Products[1] Assets Under $25 Million					Paper and Allied Products[1]					Paper and Allied Products[1] Assets Under $25 Million				
1Q 1986	2Q 1986	3Q 1986	4Q 1986	1Q 1987	1Q 1986	2Q[2] 1986	3Q 1986	4Q 1986	1Q 1987	1Q 1986	2Q 1986	3Q 1986	4Q 1986	1Q 1987
(percent of net sales)					(percent of net sales)					(percent of net sales)				
100.0	100.0	100.0	100.0	100.0	100.0	100.0	100.0	100.0	100.0	100.0	100.0	100.0	100.0	100.0
2.7	2.7	2.5	2.2	2.3	4.7	4.6	4.5	4.4	4.8	2.4	2.4	2.6	2.4	3.0
92.0	89.4	90.2	91.6	91.8	88.8	87.2	87.4	86.1	85.9	91.7	91.7	93.2	92.3	91.3
5.3	7.9	7.4	6.2	5.9	6.5	8.3	8.1	9.4	9.3	5.9	5.9	4.2	5.3	5.7
-0.5	-0.4	0.1	0.8	-0.5	-1.2	-0.5	-1.2	-1.3	-1.0	-0.8	-0.8	-0.8	-0.3	-0.3
4.9	7.6	7.4	7.0	5.4	5.3	7.8	6.9	8.2	8.3	5.1	5.2	3.4	5.0	5.4
1.4	2.7	3.0	2.7	2.1	2.0	2.8	2.5	3.4	3.3	2.2	1.8	1.7	1.4	1.7
3.4	4.8	4.4	4.2	3.3	3.3	5.0	4.3	4.8	5.0	2.9	3.3	1.7	3.5	3.7
(percent)					(percent)					(percent)				
21.18	31.76	30.35	29.12	24.47	12.50	18.85	16.73	20.83	20.64	25.97	27.89	17.14	27.93	31.93
14.88	20.35	18.10	17.65	14.75	7.78	12.07	10.56	12.25	12.35	14.56	18.09	8.48	20.02	21.99
10.56	16.44	15.83	15.10	11.47	5.87	8.79	7.58	9.42	9.36	11.64	12.53	7.92	12.20	12.49
7.42	10.54	9.44	9.16	6.91	3.65	5.63	4.79	5.54	5.61	6.53	8.12	3.92	8.74	8.60
2.14	2.23	2.32	2.24	2.04	1.68	1.68	1.72	1.66	1.67	2.12	1.85	1.95	1.85	1.71
0.30	0.31	0.33	0.31	0.24	0.19	0.21	0.21	0.19	0.20	0.40	0.32	0.33	0.28	0.26
1.74	2.02	1.95	2.02	1.55	1.60	1.58	1.46	1.45	1.47	1.42	1.46	1.58	1.47	1.19

Textile Mill Products[1] Assets Under $25 Million					Paper and Allied Products[1]					Paper and Allied Products[1] Assets Under $25 Million				
1Q 1986	2Q 1986	3Q 1986	4Q 1986	1Q 1987	1Q 1986	2Q[2] 1986	3Q 1986	4Q 1986	1Q 1987	1Q 1986	2Q 1986	3Q 1986	4Q 1986	1Q 1987
(percent of total assets)					(percent of total assets)					(percent of total assets)				
9.4	9.5	9.3	9.3	7.7	3.3	3.6	3.6	3.3	3.5	11.7	11.2	10.6	9.8	9.7
28.7	30.2	28.9	30.4	29.7	11.3	11.6	11.8	11.3	11.5	25.2	26.8	26.2	25.8	25.4
25.7	26.6	24.1	25.4	26.9	11.5	11.4	11.2	11.6	12.0	21.1	23.0	21.8	25.2	25.8
66.3	68.3	65.5	66.8	65.8	28.6	29.0	29.6	28.7	29.6	61.7	64.3	62.4	64.0	64.4
30.6	28.9	31.4	28.5	29.3	62.1	61.7	60.5	61.3	60.2	32.2	30.5	30.8	30.2	30.3
11.2	10.0	8.8	9.0	11.1	3.4	3.7	3.5	3.8	4.2	8.1	12.1	9.6	9.8	10.9
31.0	30.6	28.2	29.8	32.3	17.0	17.3	17.1	17.2	17.8	29.1	34.8	32.0	34.5	37.5
17.5	15.6	18.0	16.6	19.2	25.9	25.9	27.7	27.4	26.8	23.5	18.8	19.6	19.9	21.9
50.1	48.2	47.8	48.1	53.1	53.1	53.4	54.7	54.8	54.6	55.2	55.1	53.8	56.3	60.9
49.9	51.8	52.2	51.9	46.9	46.9	46.6	45.3	45.2	45.4	44.8	44.9	46.2	43.7	39.1

TABLE 5—INCOME STATEMENT
FOR CORPORATIONS INCLUDED IN ESIC MAJOR GROUPS 27 AND 28

(See NOTE below.)

	Printing and Publishing[1]				
	1Q 1986	2Q 1986	3Q 1986	4Q 1986	1Q 1987
	(percent of net sales)				
INCOME STATEMENT IN RATIO FORMAT					
Net sales, receipts, and operating revenues	100.0	100.0	100.0	100.0	100.0
Less: Depreciation, depletion, and amortization of property, plant and equipment	3.8	3.7	3.7	3.4	3.7
Less: All other operating costs and expenses	87.4	85.5	85.2	86.3	87.3
Income (or loss) from operations	8.8	10.8	11.2	10.3	9.0
Non-operating income (expense)	1.5	0.4	1.6	1.5	-1.0
Income (or loss) before income taxes	10.3	11.3	12.7	11.8	8.0
Less: Provision for current and deferred domestic income taxes	4.2	5.0	5.4	4.5	3.4
Income (or loss) after income taxes	6.1	6.3	7.3	7.2	4.6
	(percent)				
OPERATING RATIOS (see explanatory notes)					
Annual rate of profit on stockholders' equity at end of period:					
Before income taxes	27.59	30.97	34.96	33.64	21.53
After taxes	16.25	17.19	20.18	20.68	12.45
Annual rate of profit on total assets:					
Before income taxes	12.65	14.08	15.88	14.65	9.41
After taxes	7.45	7.82	9.16	9.01	5.44
BALANCE SHEET RATIOS (based on succeeding table)					
Total current assets to total current liabilities	1.83	1.79	1.85	1.67	1.68
Total cash, U.S. Government and other securities to total current liabilities	0.41	0.39	0.41	0.31	0.32
Total stockholders' equity to total debt	1.69	1.61	1.62	1.50	1.51

NOTE: Beginning in the first quarter 1987, the universe of corporations represented by these estimates was redefined to exclude corporations with less than $250,000 in assets at the time of sample selection.

[1]In the first quarter 1987, a number of corporations were reclassified by industry. Also, estimates for corporations with less than $250,000 in assets were discontinued. To provide comparability, the four quarters of 1986 have been restated to reflect these changes.

[2]The 1986 data are restated to exclude estimates for corporations with less than $250,000 in assets at the time of sample selection.

[3]Revised.

TABLE 6—BALANCE SHEET
FOR CORPORATIONS INCLUDED IN ESIC MAJOR GROUPS 27 AND 28

(See NOTE below.)

	Printing and Publishing[1]				
	1Q 1986	2Q 1986	3Q 1986	4Q 1986	1Q 198
	(percent of total assets)				
SELECTED BALANCE SHEET RATIOS					
Total cash, U.S. Government and other securities	8.8	8.6	8.9	7.2	7.
Trade accounts and trade notes receivable	17.8	17.6	18.4	18.8	18.
Inventories	8.3	8.7	8.7	8.0	8.
Total current assets	39.5	39.4	40.3	38.6	37.
Net property, plant and equipment	31.6	31.3	30.7	29.9	30.
Short-term debt including installments on long-term debt	4.0	4.7	4.3	4.7	4.
Total current liabilities	21.5	22.0	21.8	23.1	22
Long-term debt	23.2	23.5	23.6	24.4	24
Total liabilities	54.2	54.5	54.6	56.4	56
Stockholders' equity	45.8	45.5	45.4	43.6	43

NOTE: Beginning in the first quarter 1987, the universe of corporations represented by these estimates was redefined to exclude corporations with less than $250,000 in assets at the time of sample selection.

[1]In the first quarter 1987, a number of corporations were reclassified by industry. Also, estimates for corporations with less than $250,000 in assets were discontinued. To provide comparability, the four quarters of 1986 have been restated to reflect these changes.

[2]The 1986 data are restated to exclude estimates for corporations with less than $250,000 in assets at the time of sample selection.

[3]Revised.

Printing and Publishing[2] Assets Under $25 Million					Chemicals and Allied Products[1]					Chemicals and Allied Products[2] Assets Under $25 Million				
1Q 1986	2Q 1986	3Q 1986	4Q 1986	1Q 1987	1Q[3] 1986	2Q[3] 1986	3Q 1986	4Q 1986	1Q 1987	1Q 1986	2Q 1986	3Q 1986	4Q 1986	1Q 1987
(percent of net sales)					(percent of net sales)					(percent of net sales)				
100.0	100.0	100.0	100.0	100.0	100.0	100.0	100.0	100.0	100.0	100.0	100.0	100.0	100.0	100.0
3.6	3.6	3.5	3.2	3.3	5.0	4.5	4.7	5.3	4.4	2.1	2.1	2.2	2.1	2.1
90.5	91.3	90.2	91.1	91.1	87.5	87.3	86.2	89.4	86.1	96.6	91.1	92.0	93.5	93.5
5.9	5.1	6.4	5.7	5.5	7.5	8.[illegible]	9[illegible].	5.3	9.5	1.3	6.9	5.8	4.4	4.4
-0.7	-0.8	-0.7	-0.7	-1.0	2.0	2.4	2.8	1.7	3.0	-0.2	-0.5	-0.3	0.2	-1.2
5.3	4.4	5.7	5.0	4.5	9.4	10.6	11.9	7.0	12.5	1.1	6.4	5.5	4.6	3.1
1.9	2.0	2.3	1.9	1.7	3.3	3.5	4.3	2.7	4.3	1.4	2.2	2.1	2.1	1.3
3.3	2.4	3.4	3.0	2.9	6.1	7.0	7.5	4.3	8.2	-0.3	4.2	3.5	2.5	1.9
(percent)					(percent)					(percent)				
23.49	19.66	25.63	25.32	22.69	19.66	22.46	24.04	13.83	25.25	4.39	29.57	24.61	21.89	14.23
14.91	10.93	15.33	15.41	14.33	12.74	14.94	15.28	8.49	16.62	-1.30	19.57	15.42	12.04	8.47
10.14	8.30	10.87	10.05	8.71	9.07	10.56	11.26	6.42	11.71	2.07	14.07	11.22	9.59	6.01
6.43	4.61	6.50	6.12	5.50	5.88	7.02	7.16	3.94	7.71	-0.61	9.31	7.03	5.27	3.58
1.93	1.79	1.90	1.79	1.75	1.50	1.57	1.52	1.49	1.52	2.03	2.07	1.96	1.82	1.79
0.39	0.35	0.42	0.38	0.36	0.20	0.22	0.20	0.22	0.19	0.32	0.34	0.38	0.32	0.27
1.35	1.29	1.34	1.21	1.16	1.62	1.7[illegible]	1.73	1.73	1.71	1.67	1.69	1.62	1.53	1.44

Printing and Publishing[2] Assets Under $25 Million					Chemicals and Allied Products[1]					Chemicals and Allied Products[2] Assets Under $25 Million				
1Q 1986	2Q 1986	3Q 1986	4Q 1986	1Q 1987	1Q[3] 1986	2Q[3] 1986	3Q 1986	4Q 1986	1Q 1987	1Q 1986	2Q 1986	3Q 1986	4Q 1986	1Q 1987
(percent of total assets)					(percent of total assets)					(percent of total assets)				
11.3	10.5	12.4	12.2	11.7	4.7	5.0	4.7	5.1	4.4	10.6	11.2	13.5	11.7	10.0
26.8	25.6	26.7	28.5	27.9	13.8	13.6	13.6	12.7	13.7	26.2	30.4	27.3	26.4	27.5
12.3	12.4	13.0	12.7	13.6	13.5	13.1	12.9	12.9	12.8	25.9	22.7	24.7	25.0	26.9
55.3	53.5	56.3	57.5	56.5	35.7	35.7	35.1	34.8	34.7	66.2	68.6	68.9	67.3	67.4
37.4	36.1	35.5	35.2	36.5	36.8	36.5	36.3	35.7	34.7	24.7	25.7	25.2	26.3	26.2
8.6	8.9	8.5	9.3	8.7	6.3	5.0	5.3	5.3	5.3	9.8	10.6	9.9	11.0	11.5
28.7	29.8	29.6	32.2	32.3	23.8	22.7	23.1	23.4	22.9	32.6	33.2	35.1	37.0	37.6
23.5	23.9	23.2	23.6	24.6	22.1	22.3	21.9	21.6	21.7	18.4	17.7	18.1	17.6	17.9
56.9	57.8	57.6	60.3	61.6	53.9	53.0	53.2	53.6	53.6	52.9	52.4	54.4	56.2	[illegible]7.8
43.1	42.2	42.4	39.7	38.4	46.1	47.0	46.8	46.4	46.4	47.1	47.6	45.6	43.8	2.2

TABLE 7—INCOME STATEMENT
FOR CORPORATIONS INCLUDED IN ESIC MAJOR GROUPS 28.1 AND 28.3

(See NOTE below.)

	Industrial Chemicals and Synthetics[1,2]				
	1Q 1986	2Q 1986	3Q 1986	4Q 1986	1Q 1987
	(percent of net sales)				
INCOME STATEMENT IN RATIO FORMAT					
Net sales, receipts, and operating revenues	100.0	100.0	100.0	100.0	100.0
Less: Depreciation, depletion, and amortization of property, plant and equipment	7.1	6.1	6.9	7.4	6.2
Less: All other operating costs and expenses	85.3	83.6	85.2	88.5	84.4
Income (or loss) from operations	7.6	10.3	8.0	4.1	9.4
Non-operating income (expense)	2.5	3.3	0.9	1.4	1.4
Income (or loss) before income taxes	10.1	13.6	8.8	5.4	10.8
Less: Provision for current and deferred domestic income taxes	3.5	4.9	3.0	2.6	3.7
Income (or loss) after income taxes	6.6	8.7	5.8	2.8	7.1
	(percent)				
OPERATING RATIOS (see explanatory notes)					
Annual rate of profit on stockholders' equity at end of period:					
Before income taxes	21.44	29.37	18.00	10.30	21.72
After taxes	13.99	18.75	11.91	5.28	14.34
Annual rate of profit on total assets:					
Before income taxes	9.22	13.02	7.86	4.71	9.59
After taxes	6.02	8.31	5.20	2.41	6.33
BALANCE SHEET RATIOS (based on succeeding table)					
Total current assets to total current liabilities	1.35	1.50	1.42	1.47	1.46
Total cash, U.S. Government and other securities to total current liabilities	0.10	0.15	0.13	0.17	0.10
Total stockholders' equity to total debt	1.41	1.56	1.51	1.67	1.47

NOTE: Beginning in the first quarter 1987, the universe of corporations represented by these estimates was redefined to exclude corporations with less than $250,000 in assets at the time of sample selection.

[1]Included in Chemicals and Allied Products.

[2]The 1986 data are restated to exclude estimates for corporations with less than $250,000 in assets at the time of sample selection.

TABLE 8—BALANCE SHEET
FOR CORPORATIONS INCLUDED IN ESIC MAJOR GROUPS 28.1 AND 28.3

(See NOTE below.)

	Industrial Chemicals and Synthetics[1,2]				
	1Q 1986	2Q 1986	3Q 1986	4Q 1986	1Q 198
	(percent of total assets)				
SELECTED BALANCE SHEET RATIOS					
Total cash, U.S. Government and other securities	2.4	3.3	3.0	3.8	2.
Trade accounts and trade notes receivable	14.4	13.8	13.3	12.9	14.
Inventories	12.3	12.3	12.0	12.3	12.
Total current assets	32.2	32.7	31.6	32.4	31.
Net property, plant and equipment	43.5	43.1	43.2	42.6	41.
Short-term debt including installments on long-term debt	6.3	4.0	4.3	4.5	4.
Total current liabilities	23.9	21.8	22.2	22.0	21.
Long-term debt	24.2	24.4	24.5	22.9	24.
Total liabilities	57.0	55.7	56.3	54.3	55.
Stockholders' equity	43.0	44.3	43.7	45.7	44.

. NOTE: Beginning in the first quarter 1987, the universe of corporations represented by these estimates was redefined to exclude corporations with less than $250,000 in assets at the time of sample selection.

[1]Included in Chemicals and Allied Products.

[2]The 1986 data are restated to exclude estimates for corporations with less than $250,000 in assets at the time of sample selection.

[3]Revised.

Industrial Chemicals and Synthetics[1,2] Assets Under $25 Million					Drugs[1,2]					Drugs[1,2] Assets Under $25 Million				
1Q 1986	2Q 1986	3Q 1986	4Q 1986	1Q 1987	1Q 1986	2Q 1986	3Q 1986	4Q 1986	1Q 1987	1Q 1986	2Q 1986	3Q 1986	4Q 1986	1Q 1987
(percent of net sales)					(percent of net sales)					(percent of net sales)				
100.0	100.0	100.0	100.0	100.0	100.0	100.0	100.0	100.0	100.0	100.0	100.0	100.0	100.0	100.0
1.9	2.5	3.0	2.4	2.4	3.5	3.7	3.4	3.6	3.1	3.3	2.9	2.6	2.6	3.1
94.5	89.1	88.7	96.0	93.6	85.7	87.4	84.3	88.1	83.7	90.4	91.1	89.2	90.7	94.6
3.6	8.4	8.3	1.6	3.9	10.8	8.9	12.2	8.3	13.2	6.4	6.0	8.2	6.7	2.3
0.0	-1.4	-1.1	-0.7	-2.7	7.6	8.4	12.8	14.0	7.8	-6.5	-1.5	0.9	-0.9	-1.1
3.5	7.0	7.2	0.9	1.2	18.4	17.3	25.0	22.3	20.9	-0.1	4.5	9.1	5.8	1.2
0.4	1.7	1.7	-0.4	1.0	5.7	4.3	9.2	5.5	6.3	2.9	2.0	2.5	1.4	3.7
3.2	5.3	5.5	1.3	0.1	12.7	13.0	15.8	16.7	14.6	-3.1	2.4	6.6	4.4	-2.5
(percent)					(percent)					(percent)				
12.24	29.00	30.74	4.27	8.84	28.92	26.33	38.36	37.25	34.80	-0.53	15.82	34.41	28.26	3.50
11.00	22.08	23.64	6.28	1.09	19.92	19.74	24.22	27.98	24.36	-11.26	8.57	24.97	21.36	-7.26
7.30	14.55	12.59	1.85	2.14	15.46	14.16	20.62	18.27	17.67	-0.23	6.23	15.98	10.63	1.75
6.56	11.08	9.69	2.72	0.26	10.65	10.61	13.02	13.73	12.37	-4.83	3.38	11.59	8.03	-3.63
2.56	2.48	2.05	2.28	1.73	1.54	1.56	1.42	1.39	1.49	1.71	1.77	1.89	1.67	1.91
0.38	0.36	0.46	0.52	0.28	0.27	0.28	0.24	0.27	0.28	0.24	0.46	0.38	0.25	0.62
3.14	1.62	1.11	1.22	0.46	2.54	2.51	2.72	2.21	2.38	1.26	1.10	1.60	1.00	2.09

Industrial Chemicals and Synthetics[1,2] Assets Under $25 Million					Drugs[1,2]					Drugs[1,2] Assets Under $25 Million				
1Q 1986	2Q 1986	3Q 1986	4Q 1986	1Q 1987	1Q[3] 1986	2Q[3] 1986	3Q 1986	4Q 1986	1Q 1987	1Q 1986	2Q 1986	3Q 1986	4Q 1986	1Q 1987
(percent of total assets)					(percent of total assets)					(percent of total assets)				
10.4	9.6	13.7	15.3	9.6	6.4	6.5	5.9	6.7	6.5	8.1	15.5	12.9	9.6	19.7
29.2	27.3	23.6	22.5	22.4	12.4	12.1	12.7	11.8	12.1	22.0	21.6	24.1	21.4	17.7
25.6	22.7	21.7	21.9	24.0	12.2	12.3	11.9	11.9	11.5	21.6	19.6	20.5	24.5	19.8
70.5	65.9	61.9	66.3	58.6	36.2	36.0	35.4	34.8	35.0	57.7	59.7	63.5	63.9	60.3
25.8	31.4	30.6	28.1	31.5	28.6	28.0	27.8	27.6	27.6	33.6	31.9	34.2	32.6	33.7
6.9	8.8	9.5	9.7	13.1	5.2	5.3	5.9	5.0	4.7	12.1	11.8	9.6	14.2	6.2
27.5	26.6	30.1	29.1	33.9	23.5	23.1	25.0	25.1	23.5	33.7	33.8	33.5	38.3	31.5
12.2	22.1	27.3	25.9	39.1	15.7	16.0	13.9	17.2	16.6	21.8	24.0	19.3	23.2	17.7
40.4	49.8	59.0	56.7	75.8	46.5	46.2	46.3	51.0	49.2	57.1	60.6	53.6	62.4	50.0
59.6	50.2	41.0	43.3	24.2	53.5	53.8	53.7	49.0	50.8	42.9	39.4	46.4	37.6	50.0

TABLE 9—INCOME STATEMENT
FOR CORPORATIONS INCLUDED IN ESIC MAJOR GROUPS 29 AND 30

(See NOTE below.)

	Petroleum and Coal Products[1,3]				
	1Q 1986	2Q 1986	3Q 1986	4Q 1986	1Q 1987
	(percent of net sales)				
INCOME STATEMENT IN RATIO FORMAT					
Net sales, receipts, and operating revenues	100.0	100.0	100.0	100.0	100.0
Less: Depreciation, depletion, and amortization of property, plant and equipment	8.3	9.9	10.6	10.3	9.2
Less: All other operating costs and expenses	86.4	85.4	86.7	90.5	87.2
Income (or loss) from operations	5.3	4.7	2.8	-0.8	3.6
Non-operating income (expense)	0.7	2.2	-1.6	3.3	2.6
Income (or loss) before income taxes	6.0	6.9	1.1	2.5	6.2
Less: Provision for current and deferred domestic income taxes	1.8	-0.5	0.4	-0.4	1.1
Income (or loss) after income taxes	4.1	7.4	0.7	2.9	5.2
	(percent)				
OPERATING RATIOS (see explanatory notes)					
Annual rate of profit on stockholders' equity at end of period:					
Before income taxes	10.94	10.81	1.64	3.72	9.50
After taxes	7.58	11.54	1.04	4.33	7.89
Annual rate of profit on total assets:					
Before income taxes	4.51	4.61	0.69	1.58	4.11
After taxes	3.13	4.92	0.44	1.84	3.41
BALANCE SHEET RATIOS (based on succeeding table)					
Total current assets to total current liabilities	0.99	1.05	1.12	1.08	1.13
Total cash, U.S. Government and other securities to total current liabilities	0.20	0.23	0.29	0.28	0.29
Total stockholders' equity to total debt	1.50	1.54	1.55	1.57	1.66

NOTE: Beginning in the first quarter 1987, the universe of corporations represented by these estimates was redefined to exclude corporations with less than $250,000 in assets at the time of sample selection.

[1]In the first quarter 1987, a number of corporations were reclassified by industry. To provide comparability, the four quarters of 1986 have been restated to reflect these reclassifications.

[2]The 1986 data are restated to exclude estimates for corporations with less than $250,000 in assets at the time of sample selection.

[3]The 1986 data are revised and also exclude estimates for corporations with less than $250,000 in assets at the time of sample selection.

TABLE 10—BALANCE SHEET
FOR CORPORATIONS INCLUDED IN ESIC MAJOR GROUPS 29 AND 30

(See NOTE below.)

	Petroleum and Coal Products[1,3]				
	1Q 1986	2Q 1986	3Q 1986	4Q 1986	1Q 1987
	(percent of total assets)				
SELECTED BALANCE SHEET RATIOS					
Total cash, U.S. Government and other securities	3.6	3.8	4.7	5.0	4.9
Trade accounts and trade notes receivable	6.5	6.2	6.0	6.1	6.6
Inventories	5.8	5.6	5.5	5.4	5.2
Total current assets	17.9	17.4	18.2	19.3	19.0
Net property, plant and equipment	58.4	58.4	57.6	57.2	56.9
Short-term debt including installments on long-term debt	4.9	4.4	4.1	5.1	4.0
Total current liabilities	18.0	16.6	16.3	17.9	16.8
Long-term debt	22.6	23.2	23.0	22.0	22.0
Total liabilities	58.8	57.4	58.0	57.5	56.7
Stockholders' equity	41.2	42.6	42.0	42.5	43.3

NOTE: Beginning in the first quarter 1987, the universe of corporations represented by these estimates was redefined to exclude corporations with less than $250,000 in assets at the time of sample selection.

[1]In the first quarter 1987, a number of corporations were reclassified by industry. To provide comparability, the four quarters of 1986 have been restated to reflect these reclassifications.

[2]The 1986 data are restated to exclude estimates for corporations with less than $250,000 in assets at the time of sample selection.

[3]The 1986 data are revised and also exclude estimates for corporations with less than $250,000 in assets at the time of sample selection.

Petroleum and Coal Products[2] Assets Under $25 Million					Rubber and Misc. Plastics Products[1,3]					Rubber and Misc. Plastics Products[3] Assets Under $25 Million				
1Q 1986	2Q 1986	3Q 1986	4Q 1986	1Q 1987	1Q 1986	2Q 1986	3Q 1986	4Q 1986	1Q 1987	1Q 1986	2Q 1986	3Q 1986	4Q 1986	1Q 1987
(percent of net sales)					(percent of net sales)					(percent of net sales)				
100.0	100.0	100.0	100.0	100.0	100.0	100.0	100.0	100.0	100.0	100.0	100.0	100.0	100.0	100.0
3.8	2.9	2.0	2.4	2.7	3.4	3.2	3.3	3.6	3.5	3.0	3.0	3.1	3.6	3.2
101.6	89.8	91.2	90.6	101.7	92.2	90.0	89.6	90.6	89.8	93.1	90.3	88.9	90.3	90.9
-5.4	7.3	6.9	7.0	-4.3	4.5	6.8	7.2	5.8	6.7	4.0	6.7	8.0	6.1	5.9
-0.2	0.0	-0.3	-1.3	0.2	-0.8	-0.7	1.5	-1.9	1.0	-0.4	-0.5	0.7	-0.1	-0.4
-5.6	7.4	6.6	5.7	-4.2	3.7	6.1	8.7	3.9	7.8	3.5	6.2	8.7	6.0	5.5
-0.4	1.8	2.1	1.6	0.4	1.2	2.3	3.2	2.0	2.2	1.3	2.1	2.4	2.3	1.8
-5.2	5.6	4.5	4.1	-4.6	2.4	3.8	5.5	1.9	5.6	2.2	4.1	6.3	3.8	3.7
(percent)					(percent)					(percent)				
-25.34	42.05	56.89	37.05	-17.81	12.70	21.82	29.66	13.84	28.29	17.82	30.88	42.37	29.89	24.88
-23.36	31.66	38.96	26.62	-19.57	8.46	13.62	18.65	6.71	20.34	11.17	20.32	30.67	18.71	16.85
-9.40	16.68	18.74	15.07	-7.93	5.39	9.49	13.19	5.88	11.00	7.16	13.21	18.50	13.14	11.12
-8.66	12.56	12.83	10.83	-8.71	3.59	5.92	8.29	2.85	7.91	4.49	8.70	13.39	8.23	7.53
1.94	1.75	1.66	2.13	2.09	1.62	1.64	1.63	1.62	1.60	1.59	1.66	1.73	1.76	1.86
0.58	0.31	0.29	0.57	0.76	0.17	0.18	0.19	0.20	0.18	0.19	0.22	0.25	0.26	0.27
1.00	1.23	0.94	1.50	1.94	1.49	1.54	1.62	1.45	1.15	1.27	1.39	1.57	1.53	1.48

Petrolum and Coal Products[2] Assets Under $25 Million					Rubber and Misc. Plastics Products[1,3]					Rubber and Misc. Plastics Products[3] Assets Under $25 Million				
1Q 1986	2Q 1986	3Q 1986	4Q 1986	1Q 1987	1Q 1986	2Q 1986	3Q 1986	4Q 1986	1Q 1987	1Q 1986	2Q 1986	3Q 1986	4Q 1986	1Q 1987
(percent of total assets)					(percent of total assets)					(percent of total assets)				
16.8	10.4	10.7	15.4	20.8	5.1	5.3	5.5	6.1	5.5	6.9	7.8	9.1	8.8	9.1
19.0	31.1	34.3	24.1	20.0	21.2	21.1	21.2	21.0	21.5	25.8	25.9	27.0	27.9	27.4
17.1	16.5	15.1	12.7	13.3	19.6	19.6	18.7	17.7	18.2	22.3	22.3	21.8	20.4	21.8
55.8	59.9	62.0	57.2	57.2	48.7	48.7	48.2	48.3	48.4	58.5	59.6	61.8	60.9	61.9
37.8	34.4	34.9	36.2	34.2	37.6	37.9	36.2	37.1	36.5	34.2	35.2	33.3	35.1	33.8
8.2	10.3	9.4	6.4	6.4	7.2	7.6	7.7	8.2	8.7	10.4	11.4	10.4	11.2	10.6
28.8	34.1	37.3	26.9	27.3	30.1	29.7	29.5	29.8	30.3	36.8	35.9	35.8	34.5	33.3
28.8	21.9	25.6	20.7	16.5	21.2	20.7	19.8	21.1	25.0	21.1	19.4	17.4	17.5	19.6
62.9	60.3	67.1	59.3	55.5	57.6	56.5	55.5	57.5	61.1	59.8	57.2	56.3	56.0	55.3
37.1	39.7	32.9	40.7	44.5	42.4	43.5	44.5	42.5	38.9	40.2	42.8	43.7	44.0	44.7

TABLE 11—INCOME STATEMENT
FOR CORPORATIONS INCLUDED IN ESIC MAJOR GROUPS 32 AND 33
(See NOTE below.)

	Stone, Clay and Glass Products [2]				
	1Q 1986	2Q 1986	3Q 1986	4Q 1986	1Q 1987
	(percent of net sales)				
INCOME STATEMENT IN RATIO FORMAT					
Net sales, receipts, and operating revenues	100.0	100.0	100.0	100.0	100.0
Less: Depreciation, depletion, and amortization of property, plant and equipment	4.9	4.2	4.3	4.5	4.9
Less: All other operating costs and expenses	90.1	85.8	85.2	87.6	90.1
Income (or loss) from operations	5.0	10.1	10.5	7.9	4.9
Non-operating income (expense)	-1.1	-2.5	-3.1	0.0	3.1
Income (or loss) before income taxes	3.9	7.5	7.4	7.9	8.1
Less: Provision for current and deferred domestic income taxes	2.2	2.6	2.8	3.5	2.7
Income (or loss) after income taxes	1.7	4.9	4.6	4.4	5.4
	(percent)				
OPERATING RATIOS (see explanatory notes)					
Annual rate of profit on stockholders' equity at end of period:					
Before income taxes	8.46	20.27	19.96	22.82	20.25
After taxes	3.64	13.33	12.50	12.70	13.52
Annual rate of profit on total assets:					
Before income taxes	4.11	9.30	9.36	9.43	8.72
After taxes	1.77	6.12	5.86	5.25	5.82
BALANCE SHEET RATIOS (based on succeeding table)					
Total current assets to total current liabilities	1.83	1.82	1.85	1.69	1.80
al cash, U.S. Government and other securities to total current liabilities	0.28	0.25	0.28	0.32	0.32
;kholders' equity to total debt	1.73	1.46	1.60	1.21	1.31

NOTE: Beginning in the first quarter 1987, the universe of corporations represented by these estimates was redefined to exclude corporations with less than $250,000 in assets at the time of sample selection. See text, page XIII.

[1]In the first quarter 1987, a number of corporations were reclassified by industry. Also, estimates for corporations with less than $250,000 in assets were discontinued. To provide comparability, the four quarters of 1986 have been restated to reflect these changes.

[2]The 1986 data are restated to exclude estimates for corporations with less than $250,000 in assets at the time of sample selection.

[3]Revised.

TABLE 12—BALANCE SHEET
FOR CORPORATIONS INCLUDED IN ESIC MAJOR GROUPS 32 AND 33
(See NOTE below.)

	Stone, Clay and Glass Products [2]				
	1Q 1986	2Q 1986	3Q 1986	4Q 1986	1Q 198
	(percent of total assets)				
SELECTED BALANCE SHEET RATIOS					
Total cash, U.S. Government and other securities	5.8	5.3	6.1	7.5	6.
Trade accounts and trade notes receivable	15.9	16.9	17.8	16.8	15.
Inventories	13.6	13.4	12.6	12.0	12.
Total current assets	38.7	38.5	39.7	39.4	38.
Net property, plant and equipment	46.3	44.9	43.7	43.8	44.
Short-term debt including installments on long-term debt	6.2	6.7	5.9	7.5	5.
Total current liabilities	21.1	21.2	21.4	23.3	21.
Long-term debt	21.8	24.8	23.4	26.7	26.
Total liabilities	51.4	54.1	53.1	58.7	56.
Stockholders' equity	48.6	45.9	46.9	41.3	43.

NOTE: Beginning in the first quarter 1987, the universe of corporations represented by these estimates was redefined to exclude corporations with less than $250,000 in assets at the time of sample selection.

[1]In the first quarter 1987, a number of corporations were reclassified by industry. Also, estimates for corporations with less than $250,000 in assets were discontinued. To provide comparability, the four quarters of 1986 have been restated to reflect these changes.

[2]The 1986 data are restated to exclude estimates for corporations with less than $250,000 in assets at the time of sample selection.

Stone, Clay and Glass Products[2] Assets Under $25 Million					Primary Metal Industries[1]					Primary Metal Industries[2] Assets Under $25 Million				
1Q 1986	2Q 1986	3Q 1986	4Q 1986	1Q 1987	1Q 1986	2Q 1986	3Q 1986	4Q 1986	1Q 1987	1Q 1986	2Q 1986	3Q 1986	4Q 1986	1Q 1987
(percent of net sales)					(percent of net sales)					(percent of net sales)				
100.0	100.0	100.0	100.0	100.0	100.0	100.0	100.0	100.0	100.0	100.0	100.0	100.0	100.0	100.0
4.2	3.1	3.5	3.8	4.1	4.0	4.0	4.1	4.0	4.0	3.0	3.1	3.5	3.1	3.1
94.4	88.4	86.4	91.7	97.2	94.1	92.7	93.3	92.9	91.4	93.4	91.3	91.0	94.8	92.5
1.4	8.6	10.1	4.5	-1.2	1.9	3.3	2.6	3.2	4.6	3.6	5.6	5.5	2.2	4.4
0.5	-0.5	-0.6	-0.2	0.0	-2.0	-2.9	-11.3	-3.8	-0.4	-0.8	0.2	-0.9	-0.5	-0.3
1.8	8.0	9.5	4.3	-1.3	-0.2	0.4	-8.7	-0.6	4.2	2.8	5.9	4.6	1.7	4.1
1.8	2.8	3.7	2.3	1.1	0.7	1.0	0.8	0.8	1.3	1.4	1.8	1.6	0.9	1.8
0.1	5.3	5.9	2.0	-2.4	-0.9	-0.6	-9.5	-1.4	2.9	1.4	4.0	3.1	0.7	2.3
(percent)					(percent)					(percent)				
5.26	37.37	38.71	18.35	-4.52	-0.49	1.13	-28.07	-2.01	14.47	11.89	23.95	16.95	7.23	18.17
0.17	24.57	23.88	8.61	-8.53	-2.68	-2.03	-30.69	-4.65	10.02	6.04	16.56	11.23	3.19	10.05
2.78	16.88	20.25	8.64	-2.30	-0.18	0.41	-9.51	-0.68	4.85	5.40	11.33	8.22	3.26	7.98
0.09	11.10	12.49	4.05	-4.34	-0.97	-0.74	-10.40	-1.57	3.36	2.74	7.84	5.44	1.44	4.41
2.05	1.94	2.01	2.00	1.94	1.58	1.63	1.60	1.58	1.61	1.82	1.79	1.89	1.87	1.78
0.46	0.38	0.38	0.39	0.39	0.16	0.20	0.20	0.23	0.22	0.28	0.27	0.30	0.26	0.26
2.06	1.34	1.94	1.69	1.97	1.08	1.11	1.04	1.06	1.07	1.50	1.73	1.65	1.43	1.42

Stone, Clay and Glass Products[2] Assets Under $25 Million					Primary Metal Industries[1]					Primary Metal Industries[2] Assets Under $25 Million				
1Q 1986	2Q 1986	3Q 1986	4Q 1986	1Q 1987	1Q 1986	2Q 1986	3Q 1986	4Q 1986	1Q 1987	1Q 1986	2Q 1986	3Q 1986	4Q 1986	1Q 1987
(percent of total assets)					(percent of total assets)					(percent of total assets)				
13.3	12.0	11.1	11.8	11.6	4.0	4.9	5.1	6.0	5.8	8.9	8.6	9.3	8.1	8.8
24.5	27.1	28.8	31.2	28.0	16.1	16.2	16.2	15.3	16.6	26.2	26.9	25.2	25.5	26.4
17.8	18.6	15.7	14.4	15.1	17.8	17.5	17.3	17.2	17.4	19.7	18.8	20.1	22.5	23.2
58.8	60.7	59.1	60.5	58.4	39.5	40.4	40.5	40.4	41.8	57.1	57.5	57.5	59.2	60.8
36.0	34.9	34.0	33.8	35.4	45.4	44.9	44.5	45.6	43.6	36.1	35.0	33.9	34.1	32.3
9.1	11.3	9.8	6.5	8.6	6.1	5.6	6.0	6.7	6.0	9.4	9.6	11.5	11.5	13.1
28.7	31.3	29.4	30.2	30.1	25.0	24.8	25.2	25.6	26.0	31.3	32.0	30.5	31.6	34.1
16.6	22.3	17.0	21.4	17.3	27.5	27.0	26.4	25.2	25.2	20.8	17.8	18.0	19.9	17.9
47.2	54.8	47.7	52.9	49.1	63.7	63.7	66.1	66.2	66.5	54.6	52.7	51.5	54.8	56.1
52.8	45.2	52.3	47.1	50.9	36.3	36.3	33.9	33.8	33.5	45.4	47.3	48.5	45.2	43.9

TABLE 13—INCOME STATEMENT
FOR CORPORATIONS INCLUDED IN ESIC MAJOR GROUPS 33.1-2 AND 33.5-6

(See NOTE below.)

	Iron and Steel[1 2]				
	1Q 1986	2Q 1986	3Q 1986	4Q 1986	1Q 1987
	(percent of net sales)				
INCOME STATEMENT IN RATIO FORMAT					
Net sales, receipts, and operating revenues	100.0	100.0	100.0	100.0	100.0
Less: Depreciation, depletion, and amortization of property, plant and equipment	4.0	4.1	4.0	3.8	3.9
Less: All other operating costs and expenses	95.9	93.3	93.6	91.7	91.4
Income (or loss) from operations	0.1	2.6	2.4	4.5	4.7
Non-operating income (expense)	-2.5	-5.0	-20.2	-7.7	-0.8
Income (or loss) before income taxes	-2.4	-2.4	-17.9	-3.2	3.8
Less: Provision for current and deferred domestic income taxes	0.5	0.9	0.9	0.8	0.9
Income (or loss) after income taxes	-2.9	-3.3	-18.8	-4.0	2.9
	(percent)				
OPERATING RATIOS (see explanatory notes)					
Annual rate of profit on stockholders' equity at end of period:					
Before income taxes	-10.38	-11.13	-103.65	-20.10	24.04
After taxes	-12.54	-15.48	-108.85	-25.21	18.50
Annual rate of profit on total assets:					
Before income taxes	-2.84	-2.93	-21.51	-3.98	4.80
After taxes	-3.43	-4.08	-22.59	-5.00	3.70
BALANCE SHEET RATIOS (based on succeeding table)					
Total current assets to total current liabilities	1.42	1.46	1.43	1.45	1.47
Total cash, U.S. Government and other securities to total current liabilities	0.13	0.18	0.19	0.22	0.23
Total stockholders' equity to total debt	0.75	0.74	0.59	0.57	0.60

NOTE: Beginning in the first quarter 1987, the universe of corporations represented by these estimates was redefined to exclude corporations with less than $250,000 in assets at the time of sample selection.

[1]Included in Primary Metal Industries.

[2]In the first quarter 1987, a number of corporations were reclassified by industry. Also, estimates for corporations with less than $250,000 in assets were discontinued. To provide comparability, the four quarters of 1986 have been restated to reflect these changes.

[3]The 1986 data are restated to exclude estimates for corporations with less than $250,000 in assets at the time of sample selection.

TABLE 14—BALANCE SHEET
FOR CORPORATIONS INCLUDED IN ESIC MAJOR GROUPS 33.1-2 AND 33.5-6

(See NOTE below.)

	Iron and Steel[1 2]				
	1Q 1986	2Q 1986	3Q 1986	4Q 1986	1Q 1987
	(percent of total assets)				
SELECTED BALANCE SHEET RATIOS					
Total cash, U.S. Government and other securities	3.9	5.3	5.8	6.9	7.1
Trade accounts and trade notes receivable	17.3	17.5	18.0	17.2	18.2
Inventories	19.4	19.5	19.2	19.3	19.1
Total current assets	41.9	43.7	44.6	45.1	46.1
Net property, plant and equipment	48.4	47.4	46.8	46.3	45.3
Short-term debt including installments on long-term debt	6.6	6.3	6.6	7.3	6.1
Total current liabilities	29.6	29.8	31.1	31.2	31.4
Long-term debt	29.9	29.4	28.8	27.5	27.5
Total liabilities	72.7	73.7	79.2	80.2	80.0
Stockholders' equity	27.3	26.3	20.8	19.8	20.0

NOTE: Beginning in the first quarter 1987, the universe of corporations represented by these estimates was redefined to exclude corporations with less than $250,000 in assets at the time of sample selection.

[1]Included in Primary Metal Industries.

[2]In the first quarter 1987, a number of corporations were reclassified by industry. Also, estimates for corporations with less than $250,000 in assets were discontinued. To provide comparability, the four quarters of 1986 have been restated to reflect these changes.

[3]The 1986 data are restated to exclude estimates for corporations with less than $250,000 in assets at the time of sample selection.

Iron and Steel[13] Assets Under $25 Million					Nonferrous Metals[12]					Nonferrous Metals[13] Assets Under $25 Million				
1Q 1986	2Q 1986	3Q 1986	4Q 1986	1Q 1987	1Q 1986	2Q 1986	3Q 1986	4Q 1986	1Q 1987	1Q 1986	2Q 1986	3Q 1986	4Q 1986	1Q 1987
(percent of net sales)					(percent of net sales)					(percent of net sales)				
100.0	100.0	100.0	100.0	100.0	100.0	100.0	100.0	100.0	100.0	100.0	100.0	100.0	100.0	100.0
4.1	3.9	4.0	3.3	3.1	4.0	3.9	4.2	4.1	4.2	2.4	2.6	3.2	3.0	3.1
92.8	90.1	89.7	93.4	91.6	91.9	92.0	93.0	94.4	91.3	93.7	91.9	91.8	95.4	93.0
3.2	6.0	6.4	3.4	5.3	4.1	4.1	2.8	1.5	4.5	3.9	5.5	5.0	1.6	3.9
-0.8	-0.4	-0.7	-0.5	0.1	-1.5	-0.5	-0.4	1.2	0.2	-0.8	0.5	-1.1	-0.4	-0.5
2.4	5.6	5.7	2.9	5.4	2.6	3.7	2.4	2.7	4.8	3.1	6.0	3.9	1.1	3.5
1.7	2.3	2.1	1.0	2.2	1.0	1.1	0.7	0.7	1.8	1.2	1.5	1.2	0.9	1.7
0.7	3.3	3.5	1.8	3.2	1.6	2.6	1.7	1.9	2.9	1.9	4.4	2.8	0.2	1.8
(percent)					(percent)					(percent)				
7.96	18.90	18.77	10.83	19.65	5.78	8.29	5.14	5.71	10.32	15.34	27.71	15.52	5.12	17.08
2.25	11.18	11.69	6.93	11.72	3.59	5.82	3.65	4.12	6.33	9.37	20.58	10.86	1.00	8.82
3.88	9.64	9.76	5.02	9.42	2.65	3.86	2.41	2.75	4.90	6.57	12.45	7.14	2.28	7.06
1.10	5.70	6.08	3.21	5.62	1.64	2.71	1.71	1.99	3.01	4.02	9.24	5.00	0.44	3.64
1.87	1.83	2.12	2.05	1.88	1.83	1.89	1.87	1.80	1.83	1.80	1.77	1.75	1.79	1.73
0.35	0.32	0.40	0.29	0.28	0.20	0.23	0.23	0.26	0.22	0.24	0.24	0.25	0.24	0.25
1.55	2.02	1.84	1.38	1.51	1.51	1.57	1.59	1.67	1.65	1.46	1.56	1.52	1.46	1.35

Iron and Steel[13] Assets Under $25 Million					Nonferrous Metals[12]					Nonferrous Metals[13] Assets Under $25 Million				
1Q 1986	2Q 1986	3Q 1986	4Q 1986	1Q 1987	1Q 1986	2Q 1986	3Q 1986	4Q 1986	1Q 1987	1Q 1986	2Q 1986	3Q 1986	4Q 1986	1Q 1987
(percent of total assets)					(percent of total assets)					(percent of total assets)				
9.6	9.5	10.7	8.2	9.0	4.0	4.5	4.4	5.0	4.4	8.3	8.1	8.3	8.1	8.7
22.5	25.2	23.2	24.0	25.1	14.7	14.8	14.4	13.3	14.9	29.1	28.0	26.5	26.4	27.3
16.8	16.5	20.4	21.7	25.0	16.2	15.5	15.3	15.0	15.7	21.9	20.3	19.9	23.0	22.0
50.6	54.0	57.3	57.5	61.1	37.0	37.1	36.4	35.6	37.3	62.2	59.7	57.7	60.1	60.7
42.9	40.7	37.3	39.1	33.7	42.2	42.4	42.3	44.8	41.9	30.9	31.2	31.6	31.3	31.5
9.2	7.6	10.6	10.2	14.2	5.4	5.1	5.4	6.0	5.9	9.7	11.0	12.1	12.2	12.5
27.1	29.5	27.0	28.0	32.5	20.2	19.6	19.4	19.7	20.4	34.6	33.7	33.0	33.7	35.1
22.3	17.7	17.8	23.2	17.5	24.9	24.6	24.1	22.9	22.9	19.7	17.9	18.1	18.2	18.0
51.3	49.0	48.0	53.7	52.1	54.3	53.4	53.1	51.8	52.5	57.1	55.1	54.0	55.5	58.7
48.7	51.0	52.0	46.3	47.9	45.7	46.6	46.9	48.2	47.5	42.9	44.9	46.0	44.5	41.3

TABLE 15—INCOME STATEMENT
FOR CORPORATIONS INCLUDED IN ESIC MAJOR GROUPS 34 AND 35

(See NOTE below.)

	Fabricated Metal Products[1]				
	1Q 1986	2Q 1986	3Q 1986	4Q 1986	1Q 1987
	(percent of net sales)				
INCOME STATEMENT IN RATIO FORMAT					
Net sales, receipts, and operating revenues	100.0	100.0	100.0	100.0	100.0
Less: Depreciation, depletion, and amortization of property, plant and equipment	3.3	3.0	3.1	3.2	3.2
Less: All other operating costs and expenses	91.4	90.7	90.8	92.1	90.5
Income (or loss) from operations	5.3	6.3	6.1	4.8	6.3
Non-operating income (expense)	-0.2	-0.2	-1.4	-0.9	-2.7
Income (or loss) before income taxes	5.1	6.1	4.7	3.9	3.6
Less: Provision for current and deferred domestic income taxes	2.1	2.4	2.3	1.8	1.9
Income (or loss) after income taxes	3.0	3.6	2.4	2.1	1.7
	(percent)				
OPERATING RATIOS (see explanatory notes)					
Annual rate of profit on stockholders' equity at end of period:					
Before income taxes	15.39	19.69	14.44	12.17	11.91
After taxes	9.06	11.78	7.50	6.54	5.67
Annual rate of profit on total assets:					
Before income taxes	7.06	8.99	6.62	5.43	5.15
After taxes	4.16	5.38	3.44	2.92	2.45
BALANCE SHEET RATIOS (based on succeeding table)					
Total current assets to total current liabilities	2.02	1.98	2.02	1.97	1.93
Total cash, U.S. Government and other securities to total current liabilities	0.34	0.30	0.34	0.33	0.32
Total stockholders' equity to total debt	1.64	1.68	1.64	1.56	1.46

NOTE: Beginning in the first quarter 1987, the universe of corporations represented by these estimates was redefined to exclude corporations with less than $250,000 in assets at the time of sample selection.

[1]In the first quarter 1987, a number of corporations were reclassified by industry. Also, estimates for corporations with less than $250,000 in assets were discontinued. To provide comparability, the four quarters of 1986 have been restated to reflect these changes.

[2]The 1986 data are restated to exclude estimates for corporations with less than $250,000 in assets at the time of sample selection.

TABLE 16—BALANCE SHEET
FOR CORPORATIONS INCLUDED IN ESIC MAJOR GROUPS 34 AND 35

(See NOTE below.)

	Fabricated Metal Products[1]				
	1Q 1986	2Q 1986	3Q 1986	4Q 1986	1Q 1987
	(percent of total assets)				
SELECTED BALANCE SHEET RATIOS					
Total cash, U.S. Government and other securities	9.0	8.4	9.0	8.8	8.8
Trade accounts and trade notes receivable	21.7	22.3	21.9	20.7	21.4
Inventories	20.1	20.7	19.9	20.4	20.8
Total current assets	53.7	54.2	53.5	52.6	53.7
Net property, plant and equipment	29.8	29.8	29.3	30.0	29.9
Short-term debt including installments on long-term debt	6.1	6.2	6.2	6.1	6.9
Total current liabilities	26.6	27.4	26.5	26.8	27.8
Long-term debt	21.8	21.0	21.8	22.5	22.5
Total liabilities	54.1	54.3	54.1	55.4	56.8
Stockholders' equity	45.9	45.7	45.9	44.6	43.2

NOTE: Beginning in the first quarter 1987, the universe of corporations represented by these estimates was redefined to exclude corporations with less than $250,000 in assets at the time of sample selection.

[1]In the first quarter 1987, a number of corporations were reclassified by industry. Also, estimates for corporations with less than $250,000 in assets were discontinued. To provide comparability, the four quarters of 1986 have been restated to reflect these changes.

[2]The 1986 data are restated to exclude estimates for corporations with less than $250,000 in assets at the time of sample selection.

Fabricated Metal Products[2] Assets Under $25 Million					Machinery, Except Electrical[1]					Machinery, Except Electrical[2] Assets Under $25 Million				
1Q 1986	2Q 1986	3Q 1986	4Q 1986	1Q 1987	1Q 1986	2Q 1986	3Q 1986	4Q 1986	1Q 1987	1Q 1986	2Q 1986	3Q 1986	4Q 1986	1Q 1987
(percent of net sales)					(percent of net sales)					(percent of net sales)				
100.0	100.0	100.0	100.0	100.0	100.0	100.0	100.0	100.0	100.0	100.0	100.0	100.0	100.0	100.0
3.1	3.0	3.1	3.1	3.1	4.7	4.4	4.5	4.4	4.6	3.4	3.2	3.4	3.8	3.5
91.9	92.0	92.2	92.6	91.7	91.1	90.3	91.3	93.0	91.1	92.4	90.9	93.5	95.8	94.0
5.0	5.0	4.8	4.3	5.2	4.2	5.3	4.3	2.6	4.3	4.2	5.9	3.1	0.4	2.5
-1.4	-0.7	-0.2	-0.8	-1.3	0.4	0.5	0.8	1.7	-0.7	-0.7	-0.5	-0.3	-0.3	-0.8
3.6	4.3	4.6	3.5	3.9	4.6	5.8	5.0	4.3	3.6	3.5	5.4	2.8	0.1	1.7
1.7	1.7	2.0	1.7	1.8	1.8	1.6	1.8	1.6	2.1	2.0	2.2	1.7	1.3	1.5
1.9	2.6	2.6	1.8	2.1	2.8	4.2	3.3	2.7	1.5	1.5	3.2	1.1	-1.2	0.2
(percent)					(percent)					(percent)				
13.40	16.89	16.67	13.71	15.20	8.27	10.99	8.90	8.05	6.50	12.54	18.90	9.10	0.46	5.65
7.17	10.39	9.32	7.12	8.05	5.02	7.99	5.77	5.06	2.76	5.37	11.16	3.62	-3.99	0.55
6.63	8.27	8.31	6.51	7.18	4.43	5.87	4.81	4.22	3.35	5.60	8.77	4.44	0.21	2.60
3.55	5.08	4.64	3.38	3.80	2.69	4.26	3.12	2.65	1.42	2.40	5.18	1.76	-1.83	0.25
2.13	2.09	2.18	1.99	2.03	2.00	1.92	1.94	1.82	1.81	2.03	2.06	2.15	2.06	2.08
0.41	0.37	0.43	0.38	0.40	0.33	0.32	0.32	0.29	0.29	0.33	0.39	0.42	0.35	0.36
1.76	1.76	1.81	1.71	1.67	2.58	2.51	2.52	2.32	2.29	1.48	1.59	1.74	-1.51	1.49

Fabricated Metal Products[2] Assets Under $25 Million					Machinery, Except Electrical[1]					Machinery, Except Electrical[2] Assets Under $25 Million				
1Q 1986	2Q 1986	3Q 1986	4Q 1986	1Q 1987	1Q 1986	2Q 1986	3Q 1986	4Q 1986	1Q 1987	1Q 1986	2Q 1986	3Q 1986	4Q 1986	1Q 1987
(percent of total assets)					(percent of total assets)					(percent of total assets)				
12.2	11.7	12.6	12.0	12.8	8.0	7.9	7.8	7.5	7.4	11.4	12.9	13.4	11.7	12.0
26.5	27.2	26.3	25.0	25.5	18.4	18.1	17.6	17.6	18.0	24.8	24.0	23.6	24.2	24.3
22.1	23.3	22.4	23.6	23.2	19.9	19.2	18.5	18.1	18.0	29.3	28.6	27.8	28.0	29.0
64.0	65.4	64.7	63.6	64.5	49.2	48.2	47.1	46.6	46.6	69.1	69.2	68.4	68.5	69.4
30.0	29.5	29.1	30.6	29.7	25.8	25.2	24.9	24.9	24.9	25.5	25.2	25.5	24.7	24.8
9.7	9.7	9.3	9.7	9.8	4.6	5.1	4.9	5.9	5.3	12.6	12.1	10.9	12.2	12.7
30.1	31.2	29.7	32.0	31.8	24.6	25.1	24.2	25.6	25.7	34.1	33.5	31.8	33.2	33.4
18.3	18.0	18.3	18.1	18.6	16.2	16.3	16.6	16.7	17.1	17.6	17.2	17.1	18.1	18.2
50.5	51.1	50.2	52.5	52.8	46.4	46.6	46.0	47.6	48.5	55.4	53.6	51.2	54.2	53.9
49.5	48.9	49.8	47.5	47.2	53.6	53.4	54.0	52.4	51.5	44.6	46.4	48.8	45.8	46.1

TABLE 17—INCOME STATEMENT
FOR CORPORATIONS INCLUDED IN ESIC MAJOR GROUPS 36 AND 37

(See NOTE below.)

	Electrical and Electronic Equipment[1]				
	1Q[3] 1986	2Q[3] 1986	3Q 1986	4Q 1986	1Q 198
	(percent of net sales)				
INCOME STATEMENT IN RATIO FORMAT					
Net sales, receipts, and operating revenues	100.0	100.0	100.0	100.0	100.
Less: Depreciation, depletion, and amortization of property, plant and equipment	4.1	3.9	4.0	3.9	4.
Less: All other operating costs and expenses	90.5	90.7	90.8	92.2	90.
Income (or loss) from operations	5.4	5.4	5.2	3.9	5.
Non-operating income (expense)	0.6	0.9	0.0	0.8	1.
Income (or loss) before income taxes	5.9	6.3	5.2	4.8	6.
Less: Provision for current and deferred domestic income taxes	2.2	1.5	2.0	0.8	2.
Income (or loss) after income taxes	3.7	4.8	3.2	4.0	4.
	(percent)				
OPERATING RATIOS (see explanatory notes)					
Annual rate of profit on stockholders' equity at end of period:					
Before income taxes	13.09	14.85	11.51	11.04	14.6
After taxes	8.19	11.31	7.10	9.12	9.0
Annual rate of profit on total assets:					
Before income taxes	6.50	7.34	5.68	5.50	7.1
After taxes	4.07	5.59	3.50	4.54	4.4
BALANCE SHEET RATIOS (based on succeeding table)					
Total current assets to total current liabilities	1.67	1.65	1.65	1.73	1.6
Total cash, U.S. Government and other securities to total current liabilities	0.17	0.19	0.19	0.24	0.2
Total stockholders' equity to total debt	2.71	2.39	2.37	2.59	2.4

NOTE: Beginning in the first quarter 1987, the universe of corporations represented by these estimates was redefined to exclude corporations with less than $250,000 in assets at the time of sample selection.

[1]In the first quarter 1987, a number of corporations were reclassified by industry. Also, estimates for corporations with less than $250,000 in assets were discontinued. To provide comparability, the four quarters of 1986 have been restated to reflect these changes.

[2]The 1986 data are restated to exclude estimates for corporations with less than $250,000 in assets at the time of sample selection.

[3]Revised.

TABLE 18—BALANCE SHEET
FOR CORPORATIONS INCLUDED IN ESIC MAJOR GROUPS 36 AND 37

(See NOTE below.)

	Electrical and Electronic Equipment[1]				
	1Q[3] 1986	2Q[3] 1986	3Q 1986	4Q 1986	19
	(percent of total assets)				
SELECTED BALANCE SHEET RATIOS					
Total cash, U.S. Government and other securities	5.5	5.6	5.9	7.0	
Trade accounts and trade notes receivable	19.0	17.8	19.0	19.2	1
Inventories	22.5	22.7	21.8	20.5	2
Total current assets	52.2	49.8	50.4	50.6	5
Net property, plant and equipment	26.5	25.4	25.5	24.6	2
Short-term debt including installments on long-term debt	5.5	6.1	6.4	4.5	
Total current liabilities	31.3	30.2	30.6	29.2	3
Long-term debt	12.8	14.6	14.4	14.8	1
Total liabilities	50.3	50.6	50.7	50.2	5
Stockholders' equity	49.7	49.4	49.3	49.8	4

NOTE: Beginning in the first quarter 1987, the universe of corporations represented by these estimates was redefined to exclude corporations with less than $250,000 in assets at the time of sample selection.

[1]In the first quarter 1987, a number of corporations were reclassified by industry. Also, estimates for corporations with less than $250,000 in assets were discontinued. To provide comparability, the four quarters of 1986 have been restated to reflect these changes.

[2]The 1986 data are restated to exclude estimates for corporations with less than $250,000 in assets at the time of sample selection.

[3]Revised.

Electrical and Electronic Equipment [2] Assets Under $25 Million					Transportation Equipment [1]					Transportation Equipment [2] Assets Under $25 Million				
1Q[3] 1986	2Q[3] 1986	3Q 1986	4Q 1986	1Q 1987	1Q 1986	2Q[3] 1986	3Q[3] 1986	4Q 1986	1Q 1987	1Q 1986	2Q 1986	3Q 1986	4Q 1986	1Q 1987
(percent of net sales)					(percent of net sales)					(percent of net sales)				
100.0	100.0	100.0	100.0	100.0	100.0	100.0	100.0	100.0	100.0	100.0	100.0	100.0	100.0	100.0
2.7	2.7	3.0	3.0	2.9	3.6	3.7	3.8	3.6	4.0	2.9	2.4	2.7	2.5	2.5
92.1	90.2	94.0	95.5	93.1	91.3	90.9	92.8	92.7	90.5	93.6	89.6	93.0	93.6	91.1
5.3	7.1	3.0	1.5	4.0	5.2	5.4	3.3	3.7	5.5	3.5	7.9	4.3	3.9	6.4
-0.6	-1.0	-1.4	-1.3	-1.0	1.5	1.8	0.8	-0.9	1.7	-1.8	-1.4	-0.9	-0.4	-0.5
4.7	6.1	1.7	0.2	3.0	6.7	7.2	4.1	2.8	7.1	1.7	6.6	3.4	3.5	6.0
2.2	2.3	2.1	1.6	2.2	2.2	2.4	1.1	0.7	2.4	1.4	2.3	1.4	1.3	2.0
2.4	3.8	-0.4	-1.4	0.8	4.5	4.8	3.1	2.1	4.7	0.4	4.3	2.0	2.3	3.9
(percent)					(percent)					(percent)				
15.88	20.98	5.76	0.60	10.84	23.43	25.49	13.00	9.94	23.91	9.37	37.00	14.31	16.88	29.36
8.31	12.94	-1.49	-4.78	2.84	15.65	17.02	9.60	7.47	15.87	1.96	24.11	8.44	10.87	19.46
7.76	10.69	2.77	0.29	4.92	8.99	9.90	4.94	3.75	8.94	3.01	13.13	6.62	6.95	12.09
4.06	6.59	-0.72	-2.30	1.29	6.00	6.61	3.65	2.82	5.93	0.63	8.56	3.91	4.47	8.01
2.09	2.20	2.13	2.12	1.92	1.18	1.20	1.24	1.24	1.25	1.61	1.82	2.13	2.02	1.81
0.40	0.36	0.38	0.42	0.35	0.19	0.20	0.20	0.20	0.19	0.20	0.28	0.42	0.31	0.24
1.85	1.90	1.72	1.83	1.75	2.89	3.01	2.55	2.33	2.24	0.72	0.87	1.60	1.17	1.18

Electrical and Electronic Equipment [2] Assets Under $25 Million					Transportation Equipment [1]					Transportation Equipment [2] Assets Under $25 Million				
1Q[3] 1986	2Q[3] 1986	3Q 1986	4Q 1986	1Q 1987	1Q 1986	2Q[3] 1986	3Q[3] 1986	4Q 1986	1Q 1987	1Q 1986	2Q 1986	3Q 1986	4Q 1986	1Q 1987
(percent of total assets)					(percent of total assets)					(percent of total assets)				
13.5	11.7	12.5	13.8	12.7	8.0	8.3	7.9	7.9	7.5	7.8	10.5	13.3	10.1	8.7
25.2	26.7	25.1	24.9	24.6	13.9	14.8	15.5	14.2	16.7	23.0	22.6	22.4	23.1	23.3
28.2	29.1	29.2	27.9	30.3	25.7	24.5	24.0	23.6	23.0	30.1	30.9	28.5	29.5	29.7
70.6	71.5	70.1	69.7	70.7	50.8	50.6	50.5	50.0	50.6	64.1	66.8	67.0	65.8	64.8
21.7	21.3	22.9	23.0	21.5	27.0	27.1	27.0	28.0	26.8	30.5	29.2	29.0	29.4	30.6
10.3	11.6	10.6	9.5	10.5	3.1	2.5	1.8	2.5	2.6	19.2	13.9	7.9	10.0	12.7
33.8	32.5	32.8	32.8	36.8	42.9	42.2	40.7	40.2	40.3	39.8	36.8	31.4	32.5	35.7
16.2	15.3	17.4	16.9	15.5	10.1	10.4	13.1	13.6	14.1	25.4	26.8	21.1	25.1	22.2
51.2	49.1	51.8	51.9	54.6	61.6	61.2	62.0	62.3	62.6	67.9	64.5	53.7	58.8	58.8
48.8	50.9	48.2	48.1	45.4	38.4	38.8	38.0	37.7	37.4	32.1	35.5	46.3	41.2	41.2

TABLE 19—INCOME STATEMENT
FOR CORPORATIONS INCLUDED IN ESIC MAJOR GROUPS 37.1 AND 37.7

(See NOTE below.)

	Motor Vehicles and Equipment[1,2]				
	1Q 1986	2Q[3] 1986	3Q[3] 1986	4Q 1986	1Q 1987
	(percent of net sales)				
INCOME STATEMENT IN RATIO FORMAT					
Net sales, receipts, and operating revenues	100.0	100.0	100.0	100.0	100.0
Less: Depreciation, depletion, and amortization of property, plant and equipment	3.9	4.2	4.4	4.0	4.5
Less: All other operating costs and expenses	91.2	90.7	93.9	91.8	90.1
Income (or loss) from operations	4.9	5.1	1.6	4.2	5.4
Non-operating income (expense)	2.3	2.7	1.8	-0.4	2.7
Income (or loss) before income taxes	7.2	7.8	3.4	3.8	8.1
Less: Provision for current and deferred domestic income taxes	2.2	2.3	0.6	0.3	2.5
Income (or loss) after income taxes	5.0	5.5	2.9	3.5	5.6
	(percent)				
OPERATING RATIOS (see explanatory notes)					
Annual rate of profit on stockholders' equity at end of period:					
Before income taxes	25.44	28.01	10.17	12.97	26.90
After taxes	17.55	19.75	8.52	11.93	18.48
Annual rate of profit on total assets:					
Before income taxes	11.59	12.88	4.56	5.76	11.82
After taxes	8.00	9.08	3.83	5.30	8.12
BALANCE SHEET RATIOS (based on succeeding table)					
Total current assets to total current liabilities	1.16	1.19	1.32	1.32	1.39
Total cash, U.S. Government and other securities to total current liabilities	0.29	0.29	0.29	0.29	0.27
Total stockholders' equity to total debt	3.61	3.67	2.97	2.60	2.45

NOTE: Beginning in the first quarter 1987, the universe of corporations represented by these estimates was redefined to exclude corporations with less than $250,000 in assets at the time of sample selection.

[1]Included in Transportation Equipment.

[2]The 1986 data are restated to exclude estimates for corporations with less than $250,000 in assets at the time of sample selection.

[3]Revised.

TABLE 20—BALANCE SHEET
FOR CORPORATIONS INCLUDED IN ESIC MAJOR GROUPS 37.1 AND 37.7

(See NOTE below.)

	Motor Vehicles and Equipment[1,2]				
	1Q 1986	2Q[3] 1986	3Q[3] 1986	4Q 1986	1Q 198
	(percent of total assets)				
SELECTED BALANCE SHEET RATIOS					
Total cash, U.S. Government and other securities	9.8	9.5	9.0	8.8	8.
Trade accounts and trade notes receivable	13.1	13.8	15.8	12.9	17.
Inventories	12.6	11.5	11.3	11.7	10.
Total current assets	39.8	39.4	40.5	39.7	41.
Net property, plant and equipment	31.8	32.2	31.9	33.2	31.
Short-term debt including installments on long-term debt	3.3	2.5	1.2	2.6	2.
Total current liabilities	34.3	33.2	30.6	30.1	30.
Long-term debt	9.3	10.1	14.0	14.6	15.
Total liabilities	54.4	54.0	55.1	55.6	56.
Stockholders' equity	45.6	46.0	44.9	44.4	43.

NOTE: Beginning in the first quarter 1987, the universe of corporations represented by these estimates was redefined to exclude corporations with less than $250,000 in assets at the time of sample selection.

[1]Included in Transportation Equipment.

[2]The 1986 data are restated to exclude estimates for corporations with less than $250,000 in assets at the time of sample selection.

[3]Revised.

Motor Vehicles and Equipment[1,2] Assets Under $25 Million					Aircraft, Guided Missiles and Parts[1,2]					Aircraft, Guided Missiles and Parts[1,2] Assets Under $25 Million				
1Q 1986	2Q 1986	3Q 1986	4Q 1986	1Q 1987	1Q 1986	2Q 1986	3Q 1986	4Q 1986	1Q 1987	1Q 1986	2Q 1986	3Q 1986	4Q 1986	1Q 1987
(percent of net sales)					(percent of net sales)					(percent of net sales)				
100.0	100.0	100.0	100.0	100.0	100.0	100.0	100.0	100.0	100.0	100.0	100.0	100.0	100.0	100.0
2.9	2.3	2.3	2.4	2.2	3.0	3.0	3.0	3.2	3.2	4.0	3.6	4.5	4.1	3.8
93.9	90.5	92.8	94.7	91.3	91.1	91.2	91.2	93.9	91.1	88.8	85.2	85.1	86.2	85.4
3.2	7.3	5.0	3.0	6.5	5.9	5.8	5.8	2.9	5.7	7.2	11.2	10.4	9.7	10.9
-2.0	-0.5	-0.4	0.2	-0.8	0.5	0.8	-0.4	-1.8	0.3	-0.9	-0.6	-0.4	1.9	-1.2
1.2	6.8	4.6	3.2	5.7	6.4	6.6	5.4	1.1	6.0	6.3	10.6	10.1	11.6	9.7
1.1	2.0	1.4	0.9	1.6	2.3	2.5	1.9	1.4	2.2	3.1	3.4	3.6	3.5	2.4
0.2	4.7	3.1	2.3	4.1	4.1	4.1	3.6	-0.2	3.8	3.2	7.2	6.4	8.1	7.2
(percent)					(percent)					(percent)				
6.95	49.01	20.11	15.69	30.76	20.70	22.05	17.96	4.05	19.97	19.56	31.74	28.41	31.42	32.39
0.93	34.21	13.81	11.21	22.07	13.11	13.57	11.77	-0.91	12.57	9.90	21.43	18.15	21.99	24.29
2.11	15.09	10.23	6.87	13.24	6.79	7.35	5.83	1.30	6.25	9.70	16.43	15.08	16.21	16.70
0.28	10.53	7.02	4.91	9.50	4.30	4.52	3.82	-0.29	3.94	4.90	11.09	9.63	11.34	12.52
1.57	1.74	2.39	1.99	1.89	1.20	1.20	1.19	1.18	1.16	2.32	2.52	2.52	2.17	2.13
0.21	0.23	0.41	0.25	0.22	0.11	0.13	0.12	0.13	0.13	0.33	0.56	0.72	0.49	0.47
0.64	0.62	1.85	1.26	1.24	2.97	3.17	2.64	2.53	2.41	1.65	1.82	2.13	2.15	2.22

Motor Vehicles and Equipment[1,2] Assets Under $25 Million					Aircraft, Guided Missiles and Parts[1,2]					Aircraft, Guided Missiles and Parts[1,2] Assets Under $25 Million				
1Q 1986	2Q 1986	3Q 1986	4Q 1986	1Q 1987	1Q 1986	2Q 1986	3Q 1986	4Q 1986	1Q 1987	1Q 1986	2Q 1986	3Q 1986	4Q 1986	1Q 1987
(percent of total assets)					(percent of total assets)					(percent of total assets)				
8.6	8.8	12.2	8.3	7.6	6.0	6.7	6.5	6.7	6.8	9.3	14.3	18.5	14.8	14.8
22.5	24.0	25.6	23.1	23.0	12.9	12.9	12.3	12.8	12.6	22.2	20.5	19.5	18.8	22.8
29.6	31.7	31.4	31.3	32.9	42.2	41.6	41.2	40.1	40.8	30.7	27.9	25.4	29.4	27.2
64.0	67.8	72.0	65.3	65.8	62.8	62.7	61.6	61.1	61.4	64.7	64.6	64.8	65.3	67.2
28.9	27.7	25.3	30.0	30.0	20.8	20.6	20.8	21.6	20.9	32.3	32.6	31.3	30.7	30.6
22.2	19.7	9.1	12.0	13.0	2.4	2.0	2.3	2.0	2.5	9.8	7.5	5.8	7.2	7.8
40.9	39.0	30.1	32.8	34.8	52.5	52.1	51.9	51.7	52.8	27.9	25.7	25.7	30.1	31.5
25.0	29.5	18.3	22.7	21.8	8.6	8.4	10.1	10.7	10.5	20.2	20.9	19.2	16.8	15.4
69.6	69.2	49.1	56.2	57.0	67.2	66.7	67.5	67.9	68.7	50.4	48.2	46.9	48.4	48.5
30.4	30.8	50.9	43.8	43.0	32.8	33.3	32.5	32.1	31.3	49.6	51.8	53.1	51.6	51.5

TABLE 21—INCOME STATEMENT
FOR CORPORATIONS INCLUDED IN ESIC MAJOR GROUP 38 AND OTHER DURABLE MANUFACTURING INDUSTRIES

(See NOTE below.)

	Instruments and Related Products[2]				
	1Q 1986	2Q 1986	3Q 1986	4Q 1986	1Q 1987
	(percent of net sales)				
INCOME STATEMENT IN RATIO FORMAT					
Net sales, receipts, and operating revenues	100.0	100.0	100.0	100.0	100.0
Less: Depreciation, depletion, and amortization of property, plant and equipment	5.6	5.4	5.3	5.7	5.3
Less: All other operating costs and expenses	91.1	90.5	87.9	90.9	89.0
Income (or loss) from operations	3.3	4.2	6.8	3.4	5.7
Non-operating income (expense)	-3.7	2.3	2.3	-5.1	3.9
Income (or loss) before income taxes	-0.4	6.4	9.0	-1.7	9.6
Less: Provision for current and deferred domestic income taxes	0.4	1.8	2.9	1.2	3.3
Income (or loss) after income taxes	-0.8	4.6	6.1	-2.9	6.3
	(percent)				
OPERATING RATIOS (see explanatory notes)					
Annual rate of profit on stockholders' equity at end of period:					
Before income taxes	-0.68	11.08	16.16	-3.15	16.94
After taxes	-1.30	7.95	10.95	-5.36	11.11
Annual rate of profit on total assets:					
Before income taxes	-0.39	6.38	9.21	-1.76	9.37
After taxes	-0.75	4.57	6.24	-3.00	6.14
BALANCE SHEET RATIOS (based on succeeding table)					
Total current assets to total current liabilities	1.89	1.91	1.94	1.80	1.71
Total cash, U.S. Government and other securities to total current liabilities	0.24	0.26	0.23	0.23	0.19
Total stockholders' equity to total debt	3.16	3.03	2.92	2.93	2.70

NOTE: Beginning in the first quarter 1987, the universe of corporations represented by these estimates was redefined to exclude corporations with less than $250,000 in assets at the time of sample selection.

[1]In the first quarter 1987, a number of corporations were reclassified by industry. Also, estimates for corporations with less than $250,000 in assets were discontinued. To provide comparability, the four quarters of 1986 have been restated to reflect these changes.

[2]The 1986 data are restated to exclude estimates for corporations with less than $250,000 in assets at the time of sample selection.

TABLE 22—BALANCE SHEET
FOR CORPORATIONS INCLUDED IN ESIC MAJOR GROUP 38 AND OTHER DURABLE MANUFACTURING INDUSTRIES

(See NOTE below.)

	Instruments and Related Products[2]				
	1Q[3] 1986	2Q[3] 1986	3Q 1986	4Q 1986	1Q 1987
	(percent of total assets)				
SELECTED BALANCE SHEET RATIOS					
Total cash, U.S. Government and other securities	5.8	6.2	5.3	5.6	5.0
Trade accounts and trade notes receivable	17.1	16.8	17.1	16.8	16.7
Inventories	18.8	18.5	18.1	17.3	17.7
Total current assets	46.8	46.2	45.4	44.9	44.3
Net property, plant and equipment	30.5	30.5	30.2	30.2	28.5
Short-term debt including installments on long-term debt	5.9	6.8	6.0	6.4	7.6
Total current liabilities	24.7	24.2	23.4	24.9	25.9
Long-term debt	12.3	12.2	13.5	12.7	12.8
Total liabilities	42.4	42.4	43.0	44.1	44.7
Stockholders' equity	57.6	57.6	57.0	55.9	55.3

NOTE: Beginning in the first quarter 1987, the universe of corporations represented by these estimates was redefined to exclude corporations with less than $250,000 in assets at the time of sample selection.

[1]In the first quarter 1987, a number of corporations were reclassified by industry. Also, estimates for corporations with less than $250,000 in assets were discontinued. To provide comparability, the four quarters of 1986 have been restated to reflect these changes.

[2]The 1986 data are restated to exclude estimates for corporations with less than $250,000 in assets at the time of sample selection.

[3]Revised.

Instruments and Related Products[2] Assets Under $25 Million					Other Durable Mfg. Industries[1]					Other Durable Mfg. Industries[2] Assets Under $25 Million				
1Q 1986	2Q 1986	3Q 1986	4Q 1986	1Q 1987	1Q 1986	2Q 1986	3Q 1986	4Q 1986	1Q 1987	1Q 1986	2Q 1986	3Q 1986	4Q 1986	1Q 1987
(percent of net sales)					(percent of net sales)					(percent of net sales)				
100.0	100.0	100.0	100.0	100.0	100.0	100.0	100.0	100.0	100.0	100.0	100.0	100.0	100.0	100.0
2.8	2.8	2.6	2.8	3.1	3.1	2.9	3.0	3.0	3.2	2.5	2.1	2.3	2.2	2.5
92.5	88.7	87.2	92.6	92.1	92.5	90.2	90.5	90.5	91.1	94.4	93.1	93.2	92.8	94.2
4.7	8.5	10.3	4.6	4.7	4.4	6.9	6.5	6.5	5.7	3.2	4.8	4.4	4.9	3.2
-1.3	-0.7	-0.8	-0.1	-0.8	-0.6	-0.5	-0.5	-0.6	-0.4	-0.6	-0.3	-0.5	-0.6	0.1
3.4	7.8	9.4	4.5	3.9	3.8	6.4	6.0	6.0	5.3	2.6	4.5	4.0	4.3	3.3
1.6	2.5	2.9	1.9	2.8	1.8	2.7	2.4	2.4	2.4	1.3	1.8	1.3	1.7	1.8
1.9	5.3	6.5	2.6	1.2	2.0	3.7	3.6	3.5	2.9	1.3	2.7	2.6	2.6	1.5
(percent)					(percent)					(percent)				
10.80	21.15	29.42	14.01	11.85	11.79	21.81	20.45	20.30	16.99	11.53	21.11	18.23	19.77	13.94
5.88	14.47	20.37	8.08	3.57	6.28	12.68	12.30	12.02	9.27	5.69	12.48	12.09	12.06	6.46
5.13	11.99	15.30	7.34	6.17	5.71	10.74	9.86	9.85	8.11	5.41	10.27	8.58	9.75	6.71
2.79	8.20	10.59	4.23	1.86	3.04	6.24	5.93	5.83	4.43	2.67	6.07	5.69	5.95	3.11
2.38	3.13	2.77	2.82	2.59	2.12	2.12	2.06	1.99	2.01	1.98	2.06	1.97	1.98	1.98
0.41	0.65	0.52	0.55	0.48	0.28	0.25	0.27	0.28	0.25	0.24	0.24	0.26	0.30	0.26
1.68	2.31	1.93	1.92	1.91	1.71	1.78	1.74	1.74	1.64	1.48	1.60	1.54	1.75	1.63

Instruments and Related Products[2] Assets Under $25 Million					Other Durable Mfg. Industries[1]					Other Durable Mfg. Industries[1] Assets Under $25 Million				
1Q 1986	2Q 1986	3Q 1986	4Q 1986	1Q 1987	1Q 1986	2Q 1986	3Q 1986	4Q 1986	1Q 1987	1Q 1986	2Q 1986	3Q 1986	4Q 1986	1Q 1987
(percent of total assets)					(percent of total assets)					(percent of total assets)				
12.7	15.0	13.6	13.7	14.0	7.0	6.4	6.8	7.4	6.4	8.1	8.1	9.0	10.1	8.8
26.2	24.3	25.8	24.7	28.2	19.8	20.8	20.1	18.3	19.6	25.6	27.2	24.9	23.3	25.3
31.2	28.8	28.8	29.2	30.7	21.9	21.1	21.3	21.2	20.9	28.9	28.1	29.7	29.7	28.7
73.4	72.0	72.8	70.9	75.9	53.5	53.4	53.1	52.0	52.2	66.5	67.8	67.4	67.2	67.4
22.4	24.5	22.8	23.7	18.4	37.0	36.6	36.9	37.1	37.4	27.4	26.2	26.7	26.6	26.4
8.2	6.0	6.8	6.7	9.9	8.5	8.2	8.2	8.7	9.0	13.9	13.3	13.7	13.0	13.1
30.8	23.0	26.3	25.1	29.3	25.2	25.2	25.8	26.1	25.9	33.6	33.0	34.2	33.9	34.1
20.1	18.5	20.1	20.5	17.4	19.9	19.5	19.5	19.1	20.2	17.7	17.1	16.8	15.2	16.4
52.5	43.3	48.0	47.6	47.9	51.6	50.8	51.8	51.5	52.2	53.1	51.3	52.9	50.7	51.9
47.5	56.7	52.0	52.4	52.1	48.4	49.2	48.2	48.5	47.8	46.9	48.7	47.1	49.3	48.1

TABLE 23—INCOME STATEMENT
FOR CORPORATIONS INCLUDED IN ESIC MAJOR GROUP 20, ASSETS $25 MILLION AND OVER

	Food and Kindred Products[1]				
	1Q 1986	2Q 1986	3Q 1986	4Q 1986	1Q 1987
INCOME STATEMENT IN RATIO FORMAT	(percent of net sales)				
Net sales, receipts, and operating revenues	100.0	100.0	100.0	100.0	100.0
Less: Depreciation, depletion, and amortization of property, plant and equipment	2.7	2.3	2.5	2.5	2.6
Less: All other operating costs and expenses	90.7	89.5	89.6	88.8	89.9
Income (or loss) from operations	6.7	8.2	7.9	8.7	7.4
Non-operating income (expense)	-1.3	-1.6	-2.0	-0.6	-1.9
Income (or loss) before income taxes	5.3	6.7	5.9	8.1	5.5
Net income (or loss) of foreign branches and equity in earnings (losses) of non-consolidated subsidiaries (net of foreign taxes)	1.2	0.9	0.9	1.2	1.1
Less: Provision for current and deferred domestic income taxes	2.3	2.9	2.5	3.4	2.5
Income (or loss) after income taxes	4.1	4.7	4.2	5.9	4.2
OPERATING RATIOS (see explanatory notes)	(percent)				
Annual rate of profit on stockholders' equity at end of period:					
Before income taxes	21.24	26.73	24.65	32.93	22.20
After taxes	13.51	16.56	15.44	20.88	14.07
Annual rate of profit on total assets:					
Before income taxes	8.57	10.84	9.18	12.17	8.26
After taxes	5.45	6.72	5.75	7.72	5.23

[1]In the first quarter 1987, a number of corporations were reclassified by industry. To provide comparability, the four quarters of 1986 have been restated to reflect these reclassifications.

TABLE 24—INCOME STATEMENT
FOR CORPORATIONS INCLUDED IN ESIC MAJOR GROUP 22, ASSETS $25 MILLION AND OVER

	Textile Mill Products				
	1Q[1] 1986	2Q[1] 1986	3Q 1986	4Q 1986	1Q 1987
INCOME STATEMENT IN RATIO FORMAT	(percent of net sales)				
Net sales, receipts, and operating revenues	100.0	100.0	100.0	100.0	100.0
Less: Depreciation, depletion, and amortization of property, plant and equipment	3.5	3.4	3.5	3.1	3.6
Less: All other operating costs and expenses	90.0	89.1	88.0	87.5	88.4
Income (or loss) from operations	6.4	7.5	8.5	9.4	8.0
Non-operating income (expense)	-1.6	-1.9	-2.1	-1.6	-2.1
Income (or loss) before income taxes	4.8	5.6	6.4	7.8	6.0
Net income (or loss) of foreign branches and equity in earnings (losses) of non-consolidated subsidiaries (net of foreign taxes)	0.2	0.1	0.2	0.1	0.1
Less: Provision for current and deferred domestic income taxes	2.2	2.4	3.2	3.4	2.6
Income (or loss) after income taxes	2.7	3.2	3.4	4.5	3.4
OPERATING RATIOS (see explanatory notes)	(percent)				
Annual rate of profit on stockholders' equity at end of period:					
Before income taxes	15.58	18.68	22.07	26.93	19.53
After taxes	8.57	10.51	11.39	15.32	11.11
Annual rate of profit on total assets:					
Before income taxes	7.05	8.43	9.94	12.32	8.62
After taxes	3.88	4.75	5.13	7.01	4.91

[1]Revised.

TABLE 25—INCOME STATEMENT FOR CORPORATIONS INCLUDED IN ESIC MAJOR GROUP 26, ASSETS $25 MILLION AND OVER

	Paper and Allied Products				
	1Q 1986	2Q[1] 1986	3Q 1986	4Q 1986	1Q 1987
INCOME STATEMENT IN RATIO FORMAT	(percent of net sales)				
Net sales, receipts, and operating revenues	100.0	100.0	100.0	100.0	100.0
Less: Depreciation, depletion, and amortization of property, plant and equipment	5.1	5.0	4.9	4.9	5.1
Less: All other operating costs and expenses	88.3	86.3	86.2	84.8	84.8
Income (or loss) from operations	6.7	8.7	9.0	10.3	10.0
Non-operating income (expense)	-1.6	-1.0	-1.7	-1.6	-1.7
Income (or loss) before income taxes	5.0	7.7	7.2	8.7	8.4
Net income (or loss) of foreign branches and equity in earnings (losses) of non-consolidated subsidiaries (net of foreign taxes)	0.4	0.6	0.4	0.2	0.5
Less: Provision for current and deferred domestic income taxes	1.9	2.9	2.7	3.7	3.7
Income (or loss) after income taxes	3.4	5.3	4.9	5.1	5.3
OPERATING RATIOS (see explanatory notes)	(percent)				
Annual rate of profit on stockholders' equity at end of period:					
Before income taxes	11.48	18.17	16.69	20.22	19.79
After taxes	7.27	11.62	10.75	11.58	11.63
Annual rate of profit on total assets:					
Before income taxes	5.41	8.50	7.55	9.17	9.09
After taxes	3.43	5.44	4.87	5.25	5.34

[1]Revised.

TABLE 26—INCOME STATEMENT FOR CORPORATIONS INCLUDED IN ESIC MAJOR GROUP 27, ASSETS $25 MILLION AND OVER

	Printing and Publishing [1]				
	1Q 1986	2Q 1986	3Q 1986	4Q 1986	1Q 1987
INCOME STATEMENT IN RATIO FORMAT	(percent of net sales)				
Net sales, receipts, and operating revenues	100.0	100.0	100.0	100.0	100.0
Less: Depreciation, depletion, and amortization of property, plant and equipment	3.9	3.8	3.7	3.5	4.0
Less: All other operating costs and expenses	85.8	82.3	82.6	83.8	85.3
Income (or loss) from operations	10.3	14.0	13.6	12.7	10.8
Non-operating income (expense)	2.0	-0.1	1.2	1.8	-1.6
Income (or loss) before income taxes	12.3	13.9	14.8	14.4	9.2
Net income (or loss) of foreign branches and equity in earnings (losses) of non-consolidated subsidiaries (net of foreign taxes)	0.6	1.2	1.6	0.9	0.7
Less: Provision for current and deferred domestic income taxes	5.4	6.7	7.0	5.8	4.3
Income (or loss) after income taxes	7.5	8.4	9.4	9.4	5.6
OPERATING RATIOS (see explanatory notes)	(percent)				
Annual rate of profit on stockholders' equity at end of period:					
Before income taxes	28.65	34.11	37.40	35.60	21.27
After taxes	16.60	18.93	21.45	21.93	12.02
Annual rate of profit on total assets:					
Before income taxes	13.35	15.85	17.31	15.88	9.60
After taxes	7.73	8.80	9.92	9.78	5.42

[1]In the first quarter 1987, a number of corporations were reclassified by industry. To provide comparability, the four quarters of 1986 have been restated to reflect these reclassifications.

TABLE 27—INCOME STATEMENT
FOR CORPORATIONS INCLUDED IN ESIC MAJOR GROUP 28, ASSETS $25 MILLION AND OVER

	Chemicals and Allied Products[1]				
	1Q[2] 1986	2Q[2] 1986	3Q 1986	4Q 1986	1Q 1987
INCOME STATEMENT IN RATIO FORMAT	(percent of net sales)				
Net sales, receipts, and operating revenues	100.0	100.0	100.0	100.0	100.0
Less: Depreciation, depletion, and amortization of property, plant and equipment	5.3	4.7	5.0	5.6	4.6
Less: All other operating costs and expenses	86.8	87.0	85.7	89.0	85.4
Income (or loss) from operations	8.0	8.3	9.4	5.4	10.0
Non-operating income (expense)	-0.7	-0.6	0.4	-0.6	0.3
Income (or loss) before income taxes	7.3	7.8	9.8	4.8	10.3
Net income (or loss) of foreign branches and equity in earnings (losses) of non-consolidated subsidiaries (net of foreign taxes)	2.9	3.2	2.6	2.4	3.1
Less: Provision for current and deferred domestic income taxes	3.4	3.6	4.6	2.8	4.5
Income (or loss) after income taxes	6.6	7.3	7.9	4.5	8.8
OPERATING RATIOS (see explanatory notes)	(percent)				
Annual rate of profit on stockholders' equity at end of period:					
Before income taxes	20.29	22.18	24.02	13.52	25.66
After taxes	13.32	14.75	15.28	8.35	16.92
Annual rate of profit on total assets:					
Before income taxes	9.35	10.43	11.26	6.29	11.95
After taxes	6.14	6.93	7.16	3.89	7.88

[1]In the first quarter 1987, a number of corporations were reclassified by industry. To provide comparability, the four quarters of 1986 have been restated to reflect these reclassifications.

[2]Revised.

TABLE 28—INCOME STATEMENT
FOR CORPORATIONS INCLUDED IN ESIC MAJOR GROUP 28.1, ASSETS $25 MILLION AND OVER

	Industrial Chemicals and Synthetics				
	1Q 1986	2Q 1986	3Q 1986	4Q 1986	1Q 1987
INCOME STATEMENT IN RATIO FORMAT	(percent of net sales)				
Net sales, receipts, and operating revenues	100.0	100.0	100.0	100.0	100.0
Less: Depreciation, depletion, and amortization of property, plant and equipment	7.3	6.3	7.1	7.7	6.3
Less: All other operating costs and expenses	84.8	83.3	85.0	88.1	84.1
Income (or loss) from operations	7.8	10.4	7.9	4.2	9.6
Non-operating income (expense)	0.6	1.5	-0.4	-0.4	-0.8
Income (or loss) before income taxes	8.4	12.0	7.6	3.9	8.8
Net income (or loss) of foreign branches and equity in earnings (losses) of non-consolidated subsidiaries (net of foreign taxes)	2.1	1.9	1.3	1.8	2.3
Less: Provision for current and deferred domestic income taxes	3.7	5.1	3.1	2.8	3.8
Income (or loss) after income taxes	6.8	8.9	5.9	2.9	7.4
OPERATING RATIOS (see explanatory notes)	(percent)				
Annual rate of profit on stockholders' equity at end of period:					
Before income taxes	21.72	29.38	17.73	10.43	21.83
After taxes	14.08	18.67	11.66	5.26	14.45
Annual rate of profit on total assets:					
Before income taxes	9.26	12.99	7.75	4.77	9.71
After taxes	6.01	8.25	5.10	2.41	6.42

TABLE 29—INCOME STATEMENT
FOR CORPORATIONS INCLUDED IN ESIC MAJOR GROUP 28.3, ASSETS $25 MILLION AND OVER

	Drugs				
	1Q 1986	2Q 1986	3Q 1986	4Q 1986	1Q 1987
INCOME STATEMENT IN RATIO FORMAT	(percent of net sales)				
Net sales, receipts, and operating revenues	100.0	100.0	100.0	100.0	100.0
Less: Depreciation, depletion, and amortization of property, plant and equipment	3.5	3.7	3.5	3.6	3.1
Less: All other operating costs and expenses	85.5	87.3	84.2	88.0	83.3
Income (or loss) from operations	10.9	9.0	12.3	8.4	13.5
Non-operating income (expense)	0.8	0.1	6.0	8.0	1.5
Income (or loss) before income taxes	11.7	9.1	18.3	16.4	15.1
Net income (or loss) of foreign branches and equity in earnings (losses) of non-consolidated subsidiaries (net of foreign taxes)	7.2	8.7	7.2	6.4	6.5
Less: Provision for current and deferred domestic income taxes	5.8	4.4	9.4	5.6	6.3
Income (or loss) after income taxes	13.1	13.3	16.1	17.1	15.2
OPERATING RATIOS (see explanatory notes)	(percent)				
Annual rate of profit on stockholders' equity at end of period:					
Before income taxes	29.27	26.45	38.41	37.34	35.43
After taxes	20.29	19.87	24.21	28.05	24.99
Annual rate of profit on total assets:					
Before income taxes	15.70	14.28	20.68	18.37	18.00
After taxes	10.88	10.73	13.04	13.80	12.69

TABLE 30—INCOME STATEMENT
FOR CORPORATIONS INCLUDED IN ESIC MAJOR GROUP 29, ASSETS $25 MILLION AND OVER

	Petroleum and Coal Products[1]				
	1Q[2] 1986	2Q[2] 1986	3Q 1986	4Q 1986	1Q 1987
INCOME STATEMENT IN RATIO FORMAT	(percent of net sales)				
Net sales, receipts, and operating revenues	100.0	100.0	100.0	100.0	100.0
Less: Depreciation, depletion, and amortization of property, plant and equipment	8.3	10.0	10.7	10.4	9.2
Less: All other operating costs and expenses	86.3	85.4	86.6	90.5	87.1
Income (or loss) from operations	5.3	4.6	2.7	-0.9	3.7
Non-operating income (expense)	-1.4	0.0	-2.8	2.6	0.6
Income (or loss) before income taxes	3.9	4.7	0.0	1.8	4.3
Net income (or loss) of foreign branches and equity in earnings (losses) of non-consolidated subsidiaries (net of foreign taxes)	2.2	2.2	1.1	0.7	2.0
Less: Provision for current and deferred domestic income taxes	1.8	-0.5	0.4	-0.4	1.0
Income (or loss) after income taxes	4.2	7.4	0.7	2.9	5.3
OPERATING RATIOS (see explanatory notes)	(percent)				
Annual rate of profit on stockholders' equity at end of period:					
Before income taxes	11.06	10.69	1.50	3.63	9.59
After taxes	7.68	11.47	0.95	4.27	7.98
Annual rate of profit on total assets:					
Before income taxes	4.56	4.56	0.63	1.54	4.15
After taxes	3.17	4.89	0.40	1.81	3.45

[1]In the first quarter 1987, a number of corporations were reclassified by industry. To provide comparability, the four quarters of 1986 have been restated to reflect these reclassifications.

[2]Revised.

TABLE 31—INCOME STATEMENT
FOR CORPORATIONS INCLUDED IN ESIC MAJOR GROUP 30, ASSETS $25 MILLION AND OVER

	Rubber and Misc. Plastics Products[1]				
	1Q 1986	2Q 1986	3Q 1986	4Q 1986	1Q 1987
INCOME STATEMENT IN RATIO FORMAT	(percent of net sales)				
Net sales, receipts, and operating revenues	100.0	100.0	100.0	100.0	100.0
Less: Depreciation, depletion, and amortization of property, plant and equipment	3.7	3.4	3.4	3.7	3.8
Less: All other operating costs and expenses	91.4	89.8	90.1	90.7	88.9
Income (or loss) from operations	4.9	6.8	6.5	5.6	7.3
Non-operating income (expense)	-1.8	-1.5	1.9	-3.3	0.6
Income (or loss) before income taxes	3.1	5.3	8.3	2.2	7.9
Net income (or loss) of foreign branches and equity in earnings (losses) of non-consolidated subsidiaries (net of foreign taxes)	0.7	0.6	0.4	0.0	1.5
Less: Provision for current and deferred domestic income taxes	1.1	2.5	3.9	1.8	2.5
Income (or loss) after income taxes	2.6	3.5	4.8	0.4	7.0
OPERATING RATIOS (see explanatory notes)	(percent)				
Annual rate of profit on stockholders' equity at end of period:					
Before income taxes	10.39	17.42	23.77	6.50	30.07
After taxes	7.24	10.36	13.08	1.21	22.17
Annual rate of profit on total assets:					
Before income taxes	4.52	7.64	10.66	2.72	10.95
After taxes	3.15	4.54	5.86	0.51	8.07

[1]In the first quarter 1987, a number of corporations were reclassified by industry. To provide comparability, the four quarters of 1986 have been restated to reflect these reclassifications.

TABLE 32—INCOME STATEMENT
FOR CORPORATIONS INCLUDED IN ESIC MAJOR GROUP 32, ASSETS $25 MILLION AND OVER

	Stone, Clay and Glass Products				
	1Q 1986	2Q 1986	3Q 1986	4Q 1986	1Q 1987
INCOME STATEMENT IN RATIO FORMAT	(percent of net sales)				
Net sales, receipts, and operating revenues	100.0	100.0	100.0	100.0	100.0
Less: Depreciation, depletion, and amortization of property, plant and equipment	5.1	4.5	4.6	4.8	5.2
Less: All other operating costs and expenses	88.9	85.0	84.7	85.8	87.5
Income (or loss) from operations	6.0	10.5	10.7	9.4	7.3
Non-operating income (expense)	-1.8	-4.0	-4.9	-0.2	3.5
Income (or loss) before income taxes	4.2	6.6	5.7	9.2	10.7
Net income (or loss) of foreign branches and equity in earnings (losses) of non-consolidated subsidiaries (net of foreign taxes)	0.3	0.8	0.8	0.2	0.8
Less: Provision for current and deferred domestic income taxes	2.4	2.5	2.4	4.0	3.3
Income (or loss) after income taxes	2.1	4.8	4.1	5.4	8.3
OPERATING RATIOS (see explanatory notes)	(percent)				
Annual rate of profit on stockholders' equity at end of period:					
Before income taxes	9.07	17.63	15.75	23.98	26.04
After taxes	4.29	11.59	9.95	13.77	18.67
Annual rate of profit on total assets:					
Before income taxes	4.34	8.11	7.22	9.61	10.83
After taxes	2.06	5.33	4.56	5.52	7.76

TABLE 33—INCOME STATEMENT
FOR CORPORATIONS INCLUDED IN ESIC MAJOR GROUP 33, ASSETS $25 MILLION AND OVER

	Primary Metal Industries[1]				
	1Q 1986	2Q 1986	3Q 1986	4Q 1986	1Q 1987
INCOME STATEMENT IN RATIO FORMAT	(percent of net sales)				
Net sales, receipts, and operating revenues	100.0	100.0	100.0	100.0	100.0
Less: Depreciation, depletion, and amortization of property, plant and equipment	4.2	4.2	4.2	4.1	4.2
Less: All other operating costs and expenses	94.2	93.0	93.7	92.6	91.2
Income (or loss) from operations	1.5	2.8	2.1	3.3	4.6
Non-operating income (expense)	-2.1	-3.7	-13.9	-4.2	-1.1
Income (or loss) before income taxes	-0.5	-0.8	-11.8	-0.9	3.6
Net income (or loss) of foreign branches and equity in earnings (losses) of non-consolidated subsidiaries (net of foreign taxes)	-0.2	0.2	0.8	-0.1	0.6
Less: Provision for current and deferred domestic income taxes	0.6	0.8	0.7	0.7	1.2
Income (or loss) after income taxes	-1.3	-1.5	-11.7	-1.7	3.0
OPERATING RATIOS (see explanatory notes)	(percent)				
Annual rate of profit on stockholders' equity at end of period:					
Before income taxes	-2.09	-1.99	-34.83	-3.17	14.01
After taxes	-3.80	-4.57	-36.99	-5.64	10.02
Annual rate of profit on total assets:					
Before income taxes	-0.74	-0.70	-11.29	-1.04	4.56
After taxes	-1.34	-1.61	-11.99	-1.84	3.26

[1]In the first quarter 1987, a number of corporations were reclassified by industry. To provide comparability, the four quarters of 1986 have been restated to reflect these reclassifications.

TABLE 34—INCOME STATEMENT
FOR CORPORATIONS INCLUDED IN ESIC MAJOR GROUPS 33.1-2, ASSETS $25 MILLION AND OVER

	Iron and Steel[1]				
	1Q 1986	2Q 1986	3Q 1986	4Q 1986	1Q 1987
INCOME STATEMENT IN RATIO FORMAT	(percent of net sales)				
Net sales, receipts, and operating revenues	100.0	100.0	100.0	100.0	100.0
Less: Depreciation, depletion, and amortization of property, plant and equipment	4.0	4.1	4.1	3.9	4.0
Less: All other operating costs and expenses	96.3	93.7	94.1	91.5	91.4
Income (or loss) from operations	-0.3	2.2	1.9	4.6	4.6
Non-operating income (expense)	-2.8	-5.8	-22.7	-8.5	-1.1
Income (or loss) before income taxes	-3.1	-3.6	-20.9	-4.0	3.5
Net income (or loss) of foreign branches and equity in earnings (losses) of non-consolidated subsidiaries (net of foreign taxes)	0.1	0.3	0.2	0.2	0.2
Less: Provision for current and deferred domestic income taxes	0.4	0.8	0.8	0.8	0.7
Income (or loss) after income taxes	-3.4	-4.1	-21.5	-4.6	2.9
OPERATING RATIOS (see explanatory notes)	(percent)				
Annual rate of profit on stockholders' equity at end of period:					
Before income taxes	-13.29	-15.98	-132.04	-25.06	24.85
After taxes	-14.89	-19.79	-136.81	-30.37	19.75
Annual rate of profit on total assets:					
Before income taxes	-3.40	-3.91	-24.05	-4.55	4.48
After taxes	-3.81	-4.83	-24.92	-5.51	3.56

[1]In the first quarter 1987, a number of corporations were reclassified by industry. To provide comparability, the four quarters of 1986 have been restated to reflect these reclassifications.

TABLE 35—INCOME STATEMENT
FOR CORPORATIONS INCLUDED IN ESIC MAJOR GROUPS 33.5-6, ASSETS $25 MILLION AND OVER

	Nonferrous Metals[1]				
	1Q 1986	2Q 1986	3Q 1986	4Q 1986	1Q 1987
INCOME STATEMENT IN RATIO FORMAT	(percent of net sales)				
Net sales, receipts, and operating revenues	100.0	100.0	100.0	100.0	100.0
Less: Depreciation, depletion, and amortization of property, plant and equipment	4.5	4.2	4.5	4.4	4.5
Less: All other operating costs and expenses	91.4	92.0	93.2	94.1	90.8
Income (or loss) from operations	4.1	3.8	2.3	1.5	4.7
Non-operating income (expense)	-1.1	-0.7	-1.8	2.2	-1.0
Income (or loss) before income taxes	3.0	3.0	0.5	3.7	3.7
Net income (or loss) of foreign branches and equity in earnings (losses) of non-consolidated subsidiaries (net of foreign taxes)	-0.5	0.0	1.6	-0.6	1.4
Less: Provision for current and deferred domestic income taxes	0.9	1.0	0.5	0.7	1.8
Income (or loss) after income taxes	1.5	2.0	1.5	2.4	3.2
OPERATING RATIOS (see explanatory notes)	(percent)				
Annual rate of profit on stockholders' equity at end of period:					
Before income taxes	4.73	5.92	3.92	5.78	9.63
After taxes	2.95	4.02	2.81	4.47	6.08
Annual rate of profit on total assets:					
Before income taxes	2.18	2.77	1.84	2.81	4.64
After taxes	1.36	1.88	1.32	2.18	2.93

[1]In the first quarter 1987, a number of corporations were reclassified by industry. To provide comparability, the four quarters of 1986 have been restated to reflect these reclassifications.

TABLE 36—INCOME STATEMENT
FOR CORPORATIONS INCLUDED IN ESIC MAJOR GROUP 34, ASSETS $25 MILLION AND OVER

	Fabricated Metal Products[1]				
	1Q 1986	2Q 1986	3Q 1986	4Q 1986	1Q 1987
INCOME STATEMENT IN RATIO FORMAT	(percent of net sales)				
Net sales, receipts, and operating revenues	100.0	100.0	100.0	100.0	100.0
Less: Depreciation, depletion, and amortization of property, plant and equipment	3.5	3.1	3.1	3.2	3.2
Less: All other operating costs and expenses	90.9	89.6	89.7	91.5	89.4
Income (or loss) from operations	5.6	7.4	7.2	5.2	7.3
Non-operating income (expense)	-0.8	-0.9	-3.0	-2.5	-4.5
Income (or loss) before income taxes	4.8	6.5	4.2	2.6	2.8
Net income (or loss) of foreign branches and equity in earnings (losses) of non-consolidated subsidiaries (net of foreign taxes)	1.8	1.2	0.6	1.6	0.6
Less: Provision for current and deferred domestic income taxes	2.5	3.1	2.5	1.9	1.9
Income (or loss) after income taxes	4.1	4.5	2.3	2.3	1.4
OPERATING RATIOS (see explanatory notes)	(percent)				
Annual rate of profit on stockholders' equity at end of period:					
Before income taxes	16.69	21.44	13.04	11.21	9.84
After taxes	10.31	12.66	6.36	6.18	4.17
Annual rate of profit on total assets:					
Before income taxes	7.32	9.39	5.70	4.82	4.04
After taxes	4.52	5.55	2.78	2.66	1.71

[1]In the first quarter 1987, a number of corporations were reclassified by industry. To provide comparability, the four quarters of 1986 have been restated to reflect these reclassifications.

TABLE 37—INCOME STATEMENT FOR CORPORATIONS INCLUDED IN ESIC MAJOR GROUP 35, ASSETS $25 MILLION AND OVER

	Machinery, Except Electrical[1]				
	1Q 1986	2Q 1986	3Q 1986	4Q 1986	1Q 1987
INCOME STATEMENT IN RATIO FORMAT	(percent of net sales)				
Net sales, receipts, and operating revenues	100.0	100.0	100.0	100.0	100.0
Less: Depreciation, depletion, and amortization of property, plant and equipment	5.1	4.7	4.8	4.5	4.9
Less: All other operating costs and expenses	90.7	90.2	90.7	92.3	90.4
Income (or loss) from operations	4.2	5.1	4.6	3.2	4.7
Non-operating income (expense)	-1.9	-1.8	-1.9	-2.0	-2.9
Income (or loss) before income taxes	2.3	3.4	2.7	1.2	1.8
Net income (or loss) of foreign branches and equity in earnings (losses) of non-consolidated subsidiaries (net of foreign taxes)	2.7	2.5	2.9	4.2	2.3
Less: Provision for current and deferred domestic income taxes	1.7	1.5	1.8	1.7	2.2
Income (or loss) after income taxes	3.2	4.5	3.8	3.7	1.9
OPERATING RATIOS (see explanatory notes)	(percent)				
Annual rate of profit on stockholders' equity at end of period:					
Before income taxes	7.75	9.98	8.88	9.01	6.60
After taxes	4.98	7.59	6.05	6.20	3.04
Annual rate of profit on total assets:					
Before income taxes	4.26	5.43	4.86	4.80	3.45
After taxes	2.79	4.13	3.31	3.31	1.59

[1]In the first quarter 1987, a number of corporations were reclassified by industry. To provide comparability, the four quarters of 1986 have been restated to eflect these reclassifications.

TABLE 38—INCOME STATEMENT FOR CORPORATIONS INCLUDED IN ESIC MAJOR GROUP 36, ASSETS $25 MILLION AND OVER

	Electrical and Electronic Equipment[1]				
	1Q[2] 1986	2Q[2] 1986	3Q 1986	4Q 1986	1Q 1987
INCOME STATEMENT IN RATIO FORMAT	(percent of net sales)				
Net sales, receipts, and operating revenues	100.0	100.0	100.0	100.0	100.0
Less: Depreciation, depletion, and amortization of property, plant and equipment	4.3	4.1	4.1	4.0	4.1
Less: All other operating costs and expenses	90.3	90.8	90.3	91.7	89.8
Income (or loss) from operations	5.4	5.1	5.5	4.3	6.1
Non-operating income (expense)	-0.7	-0.2	-1.1	0.3	-0.1
Income (or loss) before income taxes	4.7	4.9	4.5	4.6	5.9
Net income (or loss) of foreign branches and equity in earnings (losses) of non-consolidated subsidiaries (net of foreign taxes)	1.4	1.4	1.3	0.8	1.5
Less: Provision for current and deferred domestic income taxes	2.2	1.4	2.0	0.7	2.7
Income (or loss) after income taxes	3.9	5.0	3.8	4.8	4.8
OPERATING RATIOS (see explanatory notes)	(percent)				
Annual rate of profit on stockholders' equity at end of period:					
Before income taxes	12.83	14.21	12.06	12.06	15.00
After taxes	8.17	11.14	7.93	10.48	9.64
Annual rate of profit on total assets:					
Before income taxes	6.39	7.00	5.96	6.03	7.37
After taxes	4.07	5.49	3.92	5.24	4.73

[1]In the first quarter 1987, a number of corporations were reclassified by industry. To provide comparability, the four quarters of 1986 have been restated to eflect these reclassifications.

[2]Revised.

TABLE 39—INCOME STATEMENT
FOR CORPORATIONS INCLUDED IN ESIC MAJOR GROUP 37, ASSETS $25 MILLION AND OVER

	Transportation Equipment[1]				
	1Q 1986	2Q[2] 1986	3Q[2] 1986	4Q 1986	1Q 1987
INCOME STATEMENT IN RATIO FORMAT	(percent of net sales)				
Net sales, receipts, and operating revenues	100.0	100.0	100.0	100.0	100.0
Less: Depreciation, depletion, and amortization of property, plant and equipment	3.6	3.8	3.9	3.7	4.1
Less: All other operating costs and expenses	91.2	90.9	92.8	92.7	90.5
Income (or loss) from operations	5.2	5.3	3.3	3.7	5.4
Non-operating income (expense)	-0.1	0.0	-0.4	-2.2	-0.6
Income (or loss) before income taxes	5.1	5.2	2.9	1.4	4.7
Net income (or loss) of foreign branches and equity in earnings (losses) of non-consolidated subsidiaries (net of foreign taxes)	1.8	2.0	1.3	1.3	2.4
Less: Provision for current and deferred domestic income taxes	2.3	2.3	1.1	0.6	2.4
Income (or loss) after income taxes	4.6	4.8	3.1	2.1	4.8
OPERATING RATIOS (see explanatory notes)	(percent)				
Annual rate of profit on stockholders' equity at end of period:					
Before income taxes	23.77	25.19	12.96	9.73	23.75
After taxes	15.98	16.84	9.64	7.37	15.77
Annual rate of profit on total assets:					
Before income taxes	9.16	9.81	4.90	3.66	8.85
After taxes	6.16	6.55	3.64	2.77	5.88

[1]In the first quarter 1987, a number of corporations were reclassified by industry. To provide comparability, the four quarters of 1986 have been restated to reflect these reclassifications.
[2]Revised.

TABLE 40—INCOME STATEMENT
FOR CORPORATIONS INCLUDED IN ESIC MAJOR GROUP 37.1, ASSETS $25 MILLION AND OVER

	Motor Vehicles and Equipment				
	1Q 1986	2Q[1] 1986	3Q[1] 1986	4Q 1986	1Q 1987
INCOME STATEMENT IN RATIO FORMAT	(percent of net sales)				
Net sales, receipts, and operating revenues	100.0	100.0	100.0	100.0	100.0
Less: Depreciation, depletion, and amortization of property, plant and equipment	3.9	4.2	4.5	4.0	4.6
Less: All other operating costs and expenses	91.1	90.7	94.0	91.7	90.0
Income (or loss) from operations	5.0	5.0	1.5	4.2	5.4
Non-operating income (expense)	0.1	0.2	-0.2	-2.1	-0.7
Income (or loss) before income taxes	5.1	5.2	1.3	2.1	4.7
Net income (or loss) of foreign branches and equity in earnings (losses) of non-consolidated subsidiaries (net of foreign taxes)	2.3	2.7	2.1	1.7	3.6
Less: Provision for current and deferred domestic income taxes	2.2	2.4	0.5	0.3	2.6
Income (or loss) after income taxes	5.1	5.6	2.9	3.6	5.6
OPERATING RATIOS (see explanatory notes)	(percent)				
Annual rate of profit on stockholders' equity at end of period:					
Before income taxes	25.84	27.64	9.92	12.90	26.81
After taxes	17.90	19.49	8.40	11.95	18.40
Annual rate of profit on total assets:					
Before income taxes	11.90	12.82	4.44	5.73	11.79
After taxes	8.25	9.04	3.76	5.31	8.09

[1]Revised.

TABLE 41—INCOME STATEMENT
FOR CORPORATIONS INCLUDED IN ESIC MAJOR GROUP 37.7, ASSETS $25 MILLION AND OVER

	Aircraft, Guided Missiles and Parts				
	1Q 1986	2Q 1986	3Q 1986	4Q 1986	1Q 1987
INCOME STATEMENT IN RATIO FORMAT	(percent of net sales)				
Net sales, receipts, and operating revenues	100.0	100.0	100.0	100.0	100.0
Less: Depreciation, depletion, and amortization of property, plant and equipment	3.0	3.0	3.0	3.2	3.2
Less: All other operating costs and expenses	91.2	91.4	91.3	94.1	91.2
Income (or loss) from operations	5.8	5.7	5.7	2.8	5.6
Non-operating income (expense)	-0.4	0.1	-0.6	-2.7	-0.2
Income (or loss) before income taxes	5.5	5.7	5.2	0.0	5.3
Net income (or loss) of foreign branches and equity in earnings (losses) of non-consolidated subsidiaries (net of foreign taxes)	0.9	0.8	0.2	0.9	0.6
Less: Provision for current and deferred domestic income taxes	2.4	2.5	1.8	1.4	2.2
Income (or loss) after income taxes	4.1	4.0	3.5	-0.4	3.7
OPERATING RATIOS (see explanatory notes)	(percent)				
Annual rate of profit on stockholders' equity at end of period:					
Before income taxes	20.72	21.84	17.75	3.41	19.72
After taxes	13.17	13.40	11.63	-1.45	12.34
Annual rate of profit on total assets:					
Before income taxes	6.76	7.23	5.72	1.09	6.13
After taxes	4.29	4.43	3.75	-0.46	3.83

TABLE 42—INCOME STATEMENT
FOR CORPORATIONS INCLUDED IN ESIC MAJOR GROUP 38, ASSETS $25 MILLION AND OVER

	Instruments and Related Products				
	1Q[1] 1986	2Q[1] 1986	3Q 1986	4Q 1986	1Q 1987
INCOME STATEMENT IN RATIO FORMAT	(percent of net sales)				
Net sales, receipts, and operating revenues	100.0	100.0	100.0	100.0	100.0
Less: Depreciation, depletion, and amortization of property, plant and equipment	6.1	5.9	5.9	6.3	5.7
Less: All other operating costs and expenses	90.8	90.8	88.1	90.6	88.4
Income (or loss) from operations	3.1	3.3	6.1	3.1	5.9
Non-operating income (expense)	-7.0	-0.4	-0.2	-9.4	2.0
Income (or loss) before income taxes	-3.9	2.9	5.9	-6.3	7.8
Net income (or loss) of foreign branches and equity in earnings (losses) of non-consolidated subsidiaries (net of foreign taxes)	2.8	3.3	3.1	3.3	2.9
Less: Provision for current and deferred domestic income taxes	0.2	1.7	2.9	1.1	3.4
Income (or loss) after income taxes	-1.3	4.5	6.0	-4.1	7.3
OPERATING RATIOS (see explanatory notes)	(percent)				
Annual rate of profit on stockholders' equity at end of period:					
Before income taxes	-1.75	9.95	14.74	-5.18	17.48
After taxes	-1.97	7.21	9.94	-6.95	11.90
Annual rate of profit on total assets:					
Before income taxes	-1.03	5.74	8.48	-2.92	9.73
After taxes	-1.16	4.16	5.72	-3.92	6.63

[1]Revised.

TABLE 43—INCOME STATEMENT
FOR CORPORATIONS INCLUDED IN MINING, ALL WHOLESALE TRADE AND ESIC MAJOR GROUPS 50, 51, ASSETS $25 MILLION AND OVER[1]

	All Mining[3]				
	1Q 1986	2Q 1986	3Q 1986	4Q 1986	1Q 1987
	(percent of net sales)				
INCOME STATEMENT IN RATIO FORMAT					
Net sales, receipts, and operating revenues	100.0	100.0	100.0	100.0	100.0
Less: Depreciation, depletion, and amortization of property, plant and equipment	15.5	15.9	15.9	17.6	15.6
Less: All other operating costs and expenses	90.7	95.4	93.5	93.2	83.8
Income (or loss) from operations	-6.2	-11.3	-9.4	-10.8	0.6
Non-operating income (expense)	-7.4	-9.1	-4.2	-4.8	-3.7
Income (or loss) before income taxes	-13.6	-20.4	-13.6	-15.6	-3.1
Less: Provision for current and deferred domestic income taxes	-2.4	-1.0	-0.7	-1.4	1.2
Income (or loss) after income taxes	-11.2	-19.4	-12.9	-14.2	-4.3
	(percent)				
OPERATING RATIOS (see explanatory notes)					
Annual rate of profit on stockholders' equity at end of period:					
Before income taxes	-16.11	-22.81	-15.46	-18.41	-3.64
After taxes	-13.29	-21.67	-14.68	-16.76	-5.04
Annual rate of profit on total assets:					
Before income taxes	-6.36	-8.81	-5.76	-6.72	-1.31
After taxes	-5.25	-8.37	-5.47	-6.12	-1.82
BALANCE SHEET RATIOS (based on succeeding table)					
Total current assets to total current liabilities	1.32	1.23	1.22	1.39	1.37
Total cash, U.S. Government and other securities to total current liabilities	0.41	0.39	0.38	0.44	0.48
Total stockholders' equity to total debt	1.11	1.05	1.00	0.98	0.97

[1]This asset size cutoff can lead to inconsistencies when comparing data on a quarter-to-quarter basis. Corporations that have exceeded the asset cutoff limit for the first time in the current quarter are not represented in previous quarter's data, and those falling below the cutoff are no longer represented.
[2]In the first quarter 1987, a number of corporations were reclassified by industry. To provide comparability, the four quarters of 1986 have been restated to reflect these reclassifications.
[3]1986 data are revised.

TABLE 44—BALANCE SHEET
FOR CORPORATIONS INCLUDED IN MINING, ALL WHOLESALE TRADE AND ESIC MAJOR GROUPS 50, 51, ASSETS $25 MILLION AND OVER[1]

	All Mining[3]				
	1Q 1986	2Q 1986	3Q 1986	4Q 1986	1Q 1987
	(percent of total assets)				
SELECTED BALANCE SHEET RATIOS					
Total cash, U.S. Government and other securities	6.4	6.5	6.3	6.6	7.3
Trade accounts and trade notes receivable	7.9	7.3	7.5	7.7	7.9
Inventories	4.0	4.0	4.0	3.7	3.7
Total current assets	20.5	20.1	20.2	20.9	20.9
Net property, plant and equipment	62.0	61.5	60.9	59.4	60.9
Short-term debt including installments on long-term debt	4.0	5.6	5.1	3.6	4.1
Total current liabilities	15.5	16.4	16.6	15.0	15.3
Long-term debt	31.5	31.2	32.1	33.7	33.1
Total liabilities	60.5	61.4	62.8	63.5	64.0
Stockholders' equity	39.5	38.6	37.2	36.5	36.0

[1]This asset size cutoff can lead to inconsistencies when comparing data on a quarter-to-quarter basis. Corporations that have exceeded the asset cutoff limit for the first time in the current quarter are not represented in previous quarter's data, and those falling below the cutoff are no longer represented.
[2]In the first quarter 1987, a number of corporations were reclassified by industry. To provide comparability, the four quarters of 1986 have been restated to reflect these reclassifications.
[3]1986 data are revised.

All Wholesale Trade[2]					Wholesale Trade, Durable Goods[2]					Wholesale Trade, Nondurable Goods[2]				
1Q 1986	2Q 1986	3Q 1986	4Q 1986	1Q 1987	1Q 1986	2Q 1986	3Q 1986	4Q 1986	1Q 1987	1Q 1986	2Q 1986	3Q 1986	4Q 1986	1Q 1987
(percent of net sales)					(percent of net sales)					(percent of net sales)				
100.0	100.0	100.0	100.0	100.0	100.0	100.0	100.0	100.0	100.0	100.0	100.0	100.0	100.0	100.0
1.1	1.1	1.1	1.1	1.1	1.2	1.1	1.1	1.1	1.2	1.0	1.1	1.1	1.0	1.0
97.3	96.4	96.9	96.9	97.0	96.1	95.8	96.3	96.8	96.7	98.0	96.9	97.4	97.0	97.2
1.6	2.5	2.0	2.0	2.0	2.7	3.1	2.6	2.1	2.2	1.0	2.0	1.6	2.0	1.8
-0.2	-0.1	-0.2	0.3	0.0	0.0	-0.2	-0.5	0.7	-0.1	-0.3	-0.1	0.0	0.0	0.0
1.4	2.4	1.8	2.4	1.9	2.7	3.0	2.1	2.8	2.1	0.7	1.9	1.6	2.0	1.8
0.7	1.0	0.9	1.1	0.7	1.2	1.4	1.2	1.3	0.9	0.4	0.6	0.6	0.9	0.6
0.7	1.4	0.9	1.3	1.2	1.5	1.5	0.9	1.5	1.2	0.3	1.3	1.0	1.1	1.2
(percent)					(percent)					(percent)				
11.87	17.95	13.50	18.53	14.30	17.14	19.64	13.69	19.20	12.71	6.58	16.28	13.30	17.80	16.03
5.94	10.69	7.00	10.08	8.95	9.33	10.04	6.12	10.08	7.11	2.53	11.33	7.92	10.08	10.96
4.02	6.18	4.56	6.23	4.92	6.24	6.99	4.85	6.80	4.60	2.08	5.42	4.29	5.67	5.25
2.01	3.68	2.36	3.39	3.08	3.40	3.57	2.17	3.57	2.57	0.80	3.77	2.55	3.21	3.59
1.41	1.41	1.39	1.36	1.40	1.58	1.54	1.52	1.48	1.52	1.26	1.28	1.25	1.24	1.27
0.18	0.21	0.21	0.21	0.19	0.23	0.24	0.21	0.22	0.20	0.14	0.19	0.21	0.19	0.17
0.95	1.00	0.97	1.00	1.02	1.11	1.10	1.08	1.09	1.14	0.83	0.91	0.88	0.92	0.91

All Wholesale Trade[2]					Wholoksale Trade, Durable Goods[2]					Wholesale Trade, Nondurable Goods[2]				
1Q 1986	2Q 1986	3Q 1986	4Q 1986	1Q 1987	1Q 1986	2Q 1986	3Q 1986	4Q 1986	1Q 1987	1Q 1986	2Q 1986	3Q 1986	4Q 1986	1Q 1987
(percent of total assets)					(percent of total assets)					(percent of total assets)				
7.9	9.2	9.3	9.5	8.3	10.2	10.8	9.6	10.7	9.5	6.0	7.8	8.9	8.3	7.1
24.6	24.0	24.0	24.3	24.9	26.3	25.8	25.9	25.3	25.8	23.1	22.3	22.1	23.3	24.1
24.9	24.3	24.8	24.7	24.6	29.2	30.0	30.6	28.7	29.5	21.1	19.1	19.2	20.8	19.8
61.0	61.2	61.8	63.0	62.6	69.9	70.9	70.5	70.7	70.7	53.2	52.2	53.4	55.7	54.7
22.7	22.9	22.1	20.9	21.2	18.2	17.8	17.9	17.5	17.4	26.7	27.7	26.0	24.2	24.9
16.9	16.4	17.2	17.5	17.3	17.2	17.6	18.3	19.0	18.2	16.3	15.4	16.1	15.8	16.4
43.2	43.4	44.4	46.3	44.7	44.3	46.1	46.3	47.8	46.5	42.2	40.8	42.5	44.9	43.0
18.7	18.0	17.5	16.2	16.7	15.5	14.6	14.4	13.5	13.6	21.7	21.1	20.5	18.9	19.7
66.2	65.6	66.2	66.4	65.6	63.6	64.4	64.6	64.6	63.8	68.4	66.7	67.8	68.1	67.3
33.8	34.4	33.8	33.6	34.4	36.4	35.6	35.4	35.4	36.2	31.6	33.3	32.2	31.9	32.7

General Business and Economic Indicators

SELECTED BUSINESS STATISTICS

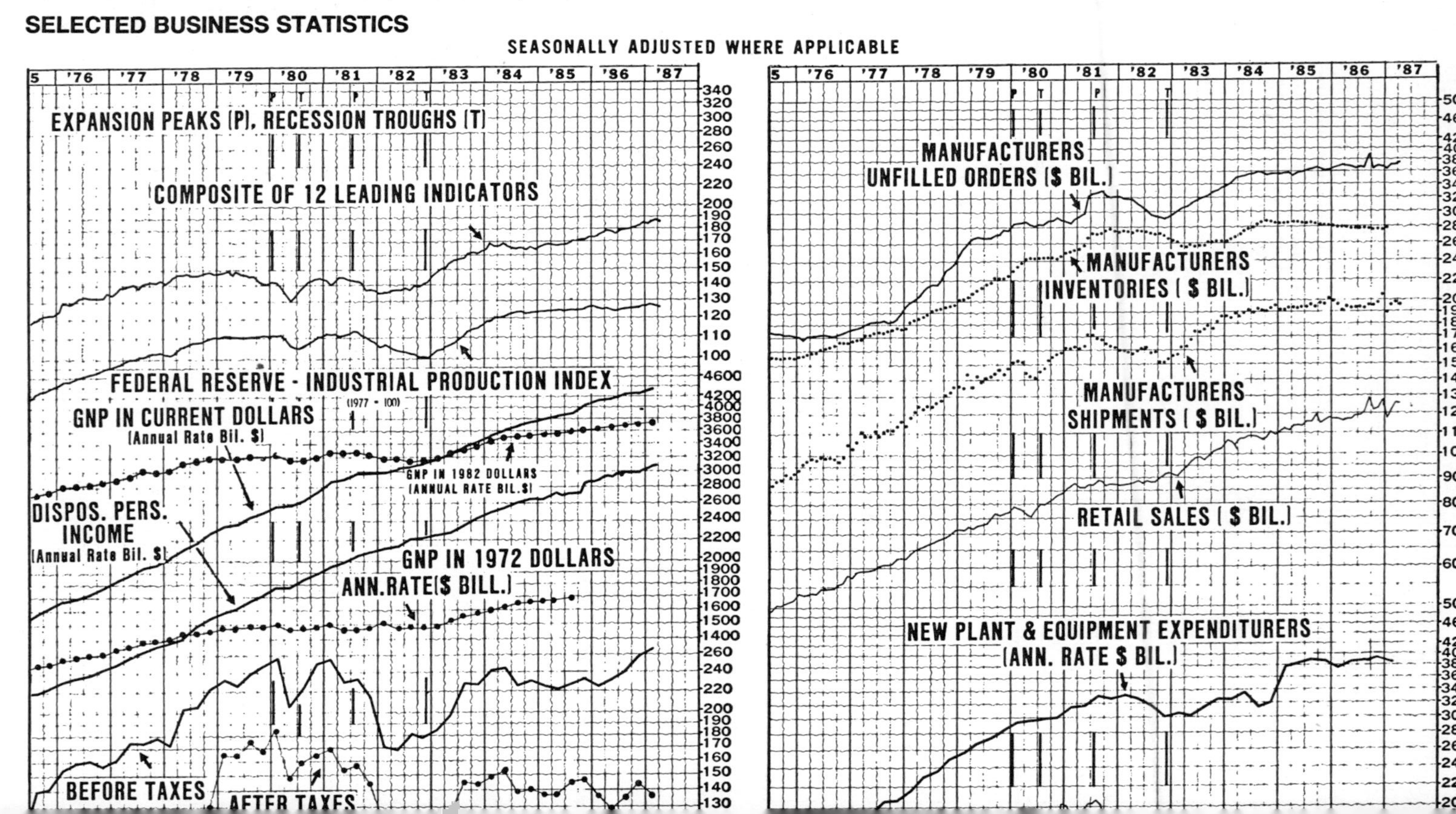

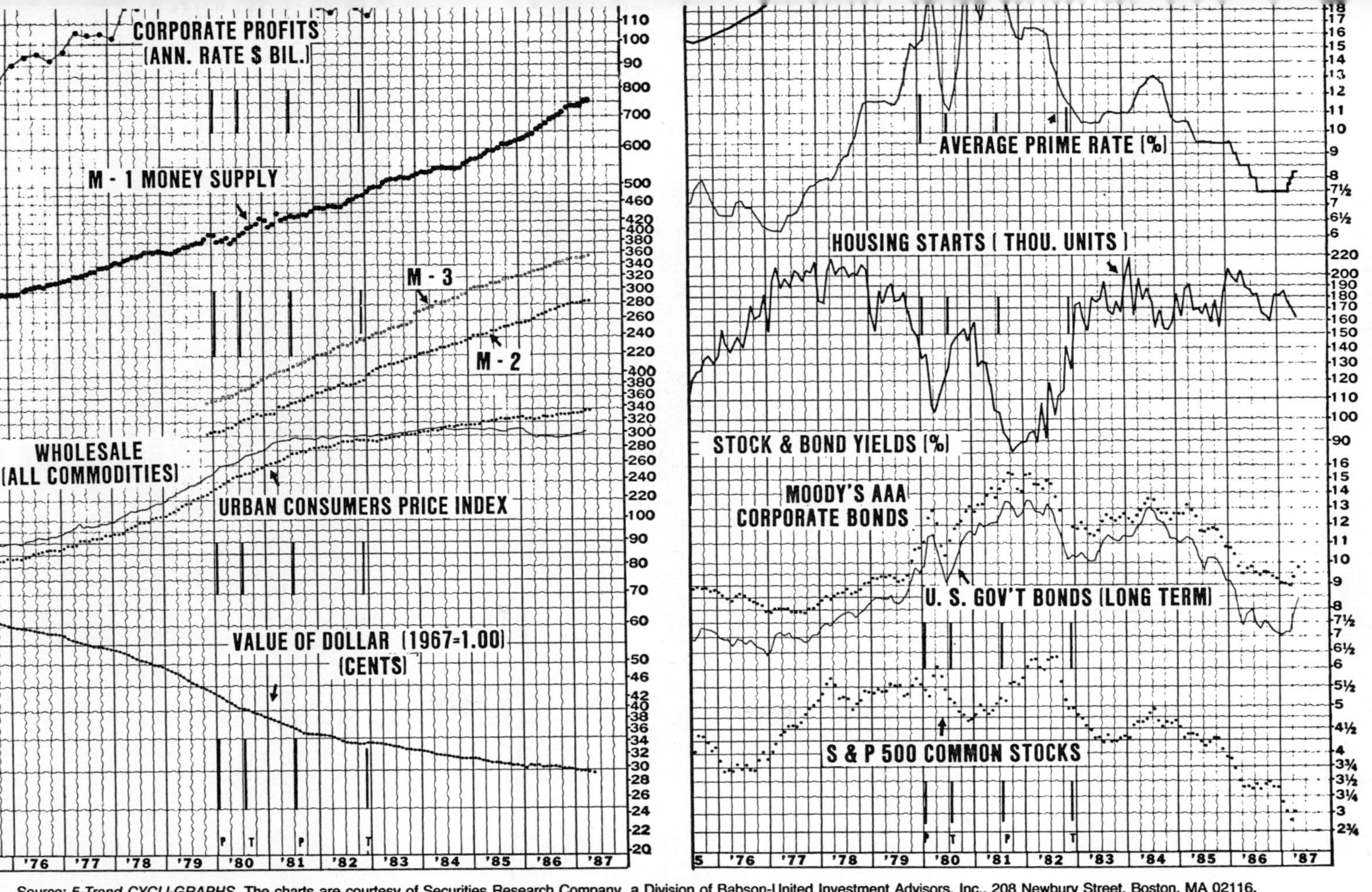

Source: *5-Trend CYCLI-GRAPHS.* The charts are courtesy of Securities Research Company, a Division of Babson-United Investment Advisors, Inc., 208 Newbury Street, Boston, MA 02116, July quarterly edition, 1987.

COMPOSITE INDEXES AND THEIR COMPONENTS

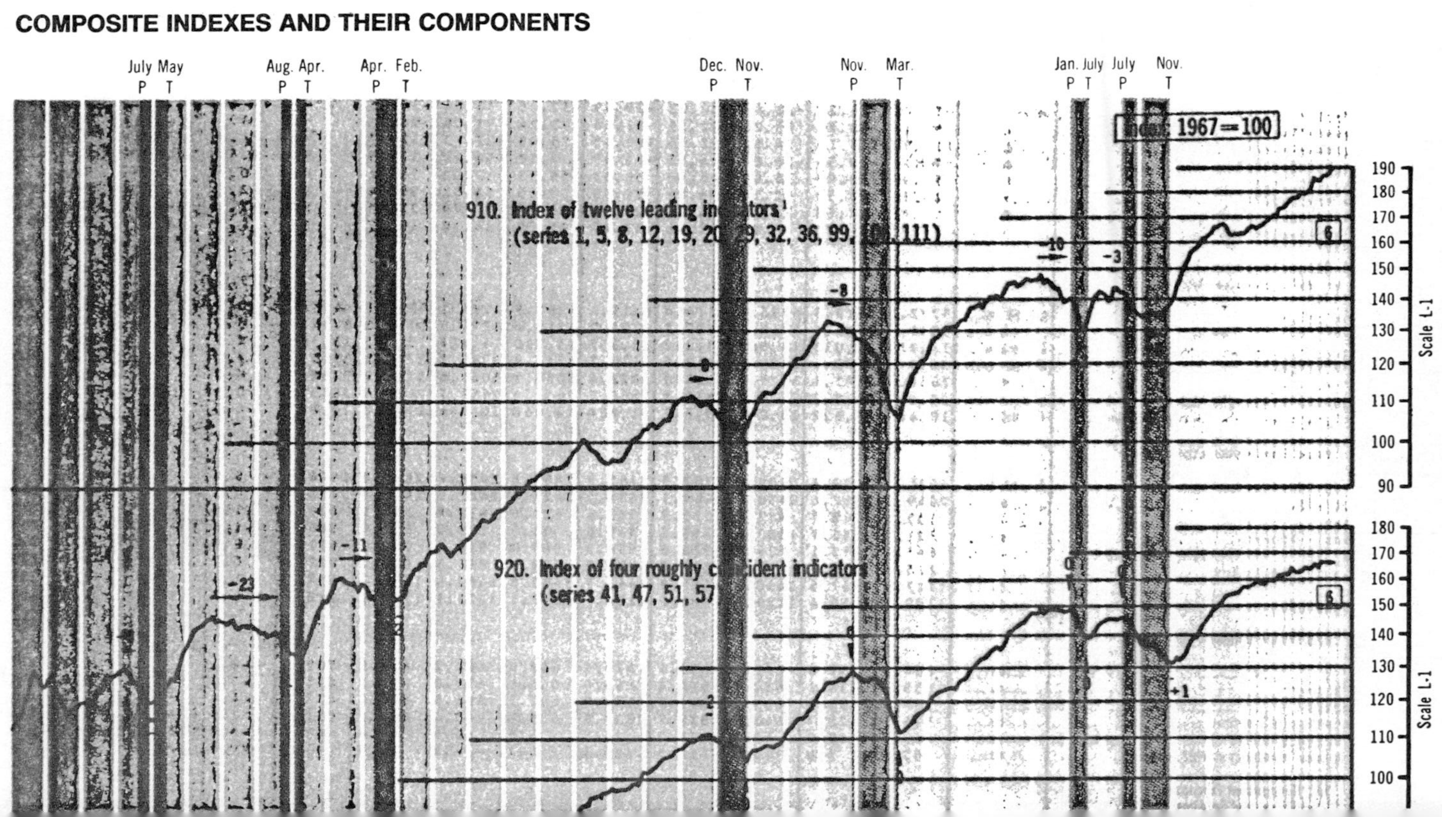

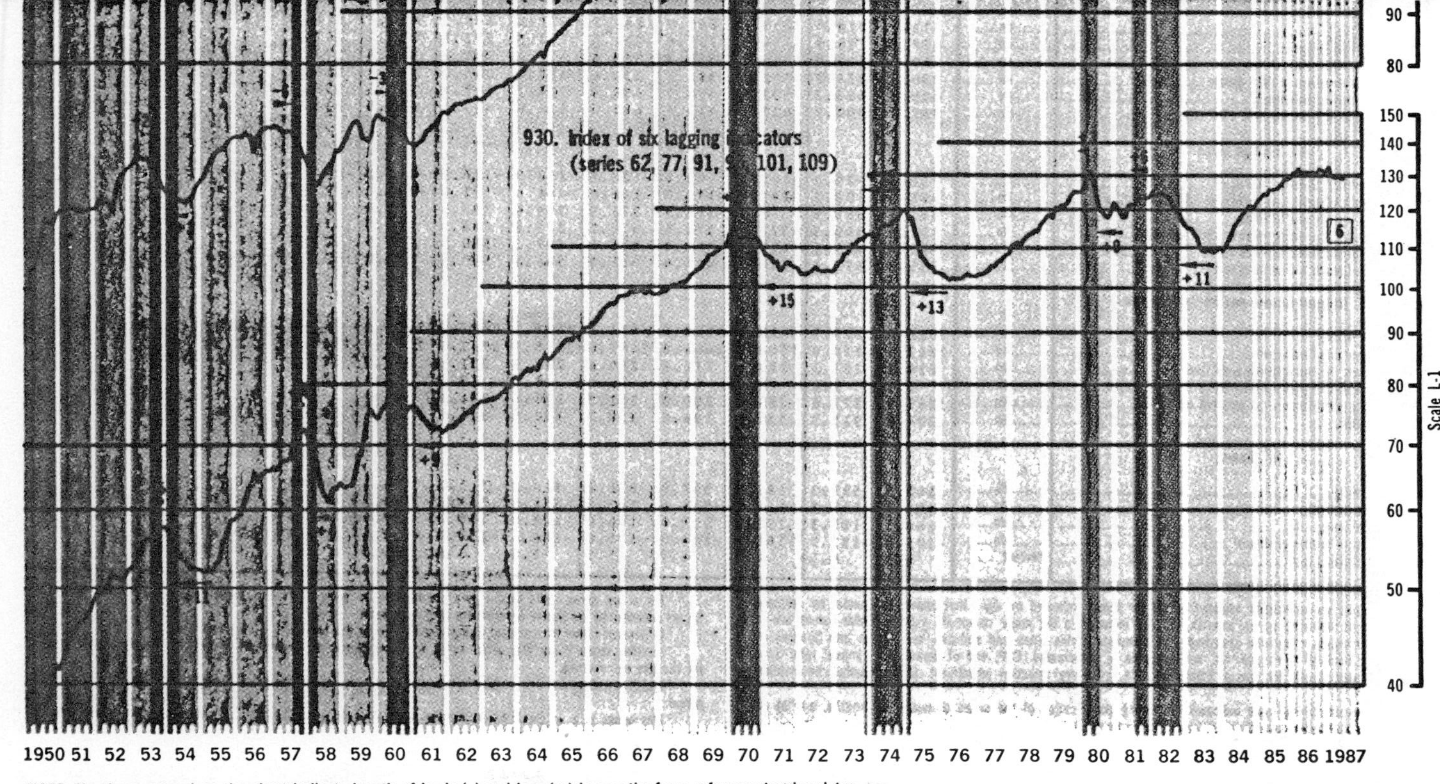

NOTE: Numbers entered on the chart indicate length of leads (–) and lags (+) in months from reference turning dates.
[1] Beginning with data for January 1984, series 12 has been suspended from this index.

Source: *Business Conditions Digest,* U.S. Department of Commerce, Bureau of Economic Analysis, July 1987.

Composition of Leading, Coincident, and Lagging Indicators

I. THE TWELVE LEADING INDICATORS

1. Average weekly hours paid to production or non-supervisory workers in manufacturing.
5. Average weekly claims for Unemployment Insurance (inversely related).
8. New orders for consumer goods and materials in 1982 dollars.
12. Monthly estimate of net formation of new businesses incorporated.
19. Index of 500 common stock prices.
20. Contracts and orders for new plant and equipment in 1982 dollars.
29. Index of new private housing starts.
32. Percentage of purchasing agents in greater Chicago area who experience slower deliveries in current month.
36. Change in manufacturing and trade inventories on hand and on order in 1982 dollars.
99. Change in index of 28 sensitive materials prices.
106. Money supply (M2 in 1982 dollars).
111. Change in business and consumer credit (consumer installment credit, business and real estate loans, etc.).

II. THE FOUR COINCIDENT INDICATORS

41. Employees on non-agricultural payrolls.
47. Index of industrial production, including all stages in manufacturing, mining, gas and electrical utilities.
51. Personal income less transfer payments in 1982 dollars.
57. Monthly volume of sales in manufacturing, wholesale, and retail in 1982 dollars.

III. THE SIX LAGGING INDICATORS

62. Index of labor costs per unit of manufacturing output.
77. Ratio of manufacturing and trade inventories to sales in 1982 dollars.
91. Average duration of unemployment in weeks (inversely related).
95. Ratio of consumer installment credit to personal income.
101. Commercial and industrial loans outstanding in 1982 dollars.
109. Average prime rate charged by banks.

NATIONAL INCOME

[Billions of dollars; quarterly data at seasonally adjusted annual rates]

Period	National income	Compensation of employees[1]	Proprietors' income with inventory valuation and capital consumption adjustments		Rental income of persons with capital consumption adjustment	Corporate profits with inventory valuation and capital consumption adjustments					Net interest
						Total	Profits with inventory valuation adjustment and without capital consumption adjustment			Capital consumption adjustment	
			Farm	Nonfarm			Total	Profits before tax	Inventory valuation adjustment		
1982	2,518.4	1,907.0	24.6	150.9	13.6	150.0	159.2	169.6	−10.4	−9.2	272.3
1983	2,719.5	2,020.7	12.4	178.4	13.2	213.7	196.7	207.6	−10.9	17.0	281.0
1984 r	3,028.6	2,213.9	30.5	204.0	8.5	266.9	234.2	240.0	−5.8	32.7	304.8
1985 r	3,229.9	2,370.8	29.7	227.6	9.0	277.6	224.1	224.8	−.7	53.5	315.3
1986 r	3,422.0	2,504.9	37.2	252.6	16.7	284.4	238.4	231.9	6.5	46.0	326.1
1982: IV	2,548.2	1,931.1	28.5	159.8	15.8	146.1	150.7	164.1	−13.4	−4.5	266.9
1983: IV	2,851.5	2,092.7	19.3	188.6	12.4	248.5	223.4	231.5	−8.1	25.1	290.2
1984: I r	2,962.1	2,152.9	44.3	197.1	12.3	262.7	238.2	253.7	−15.5	24.5	292.8
II r	3,009.0	2,195.2	26.1	202.0	9.3	275.5	246.5	251.4	−5.0	29.0	301.0
III r	3,047.3	2,234.9	23.3	207.5	6.9	262.6	227.4	228.5	−1.1	35.2	312.2
IV r	3,096.1	2,272.7	28.1	209.7	5.6	266.9	224.6	226.1	−1.6	42.3	313.1
1985: I r	3,156.5	2,314.9	31.7	220.4	7.3	265.6	216.1	217.6	−1.5	49.5	316.5
II r	3,204.4	2,351.5	32.2	224.2	9.1	274.2	219.8	218.0	1.8	54.4	313.2
III r	3,254.4	2,386.3	22.9	229.5	9.3	292.8	236.8	230.2	6.5	56.0	313.7
IV r	3,304.4	2,430.5	31.7	236.3	10.1	277.8	223.7	233.5	−9.8	54.2	317.9
1986: I r	3,364.2	2,464.8	28.0	242.8	14.0	288.0	236.7	218.9	17.8	51.3	326.6
II r	3,414.1	2,487.6	48.1	250.1	17.4	282.3	235.6	224.4	11.3	46.7	328.7
III r	3,438.7	2,515.1	36.3	256.2	17.2	286.4	242.4	236.3	6.0	44.0	327.5
IV r	3,471.0	2,552.0	36.6	261.2	18.4	281.1	239.0	247.9	−8.9	42.1	321.7
1987: I r	3,548.3	2,589.9	51.3	269.7	20.0	294.0	245.7	257.0	−11.3	48.2	323.6
II p	....	2,623.4	51.5	276.1	21.8	....	....	....	−18.5	48.8	332.4

[1] Includes employer contributions for social insurance.

Source: Department of Commerce, Bureau of Economic Analysis.

NOTE.—Series revised beginning 1984. See *Survey of Current Business*, July 1987.

Source: *Economic Indicators*, Council of Economic Advisers.

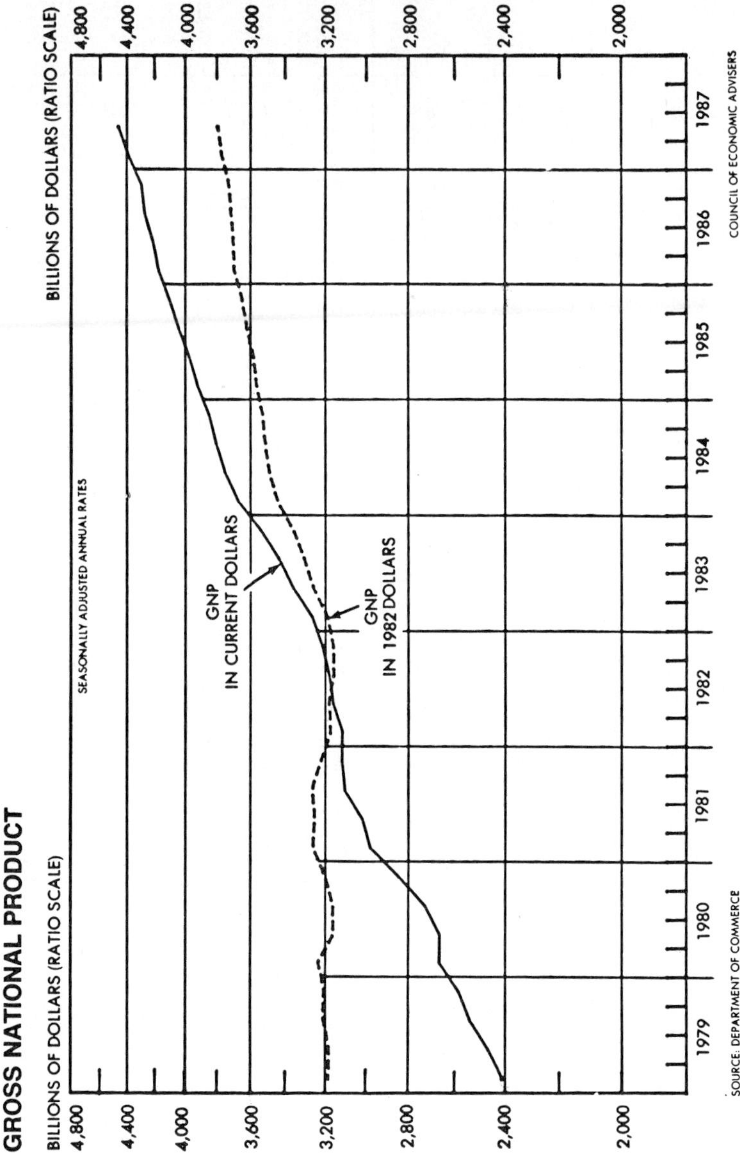
GROSS NATIONAL PRODUCT
BILLIONS OF DOLLARS (RATIO SCALE)
BILLIONS OF DOLLARS (RATIO SCALE)
SEASONALLY ADJUSTED ANNUAL RATES
4,800
4,400
4,000
3,600
3,200
2,800
2,400
2,000
GNP IN CURRENT DOLLARS
GNP IN 1982 DOLLARS
1979
1980
1981
1982
1983
1984
1985
1986
1987
SOURCE: DEPARTMENT OF COMMERCE
COUNCIL OF ECONOMIC ADVISERS

[Billions of current dollars; quarterly data at seasonally adjusted annual rates]

Period	Gross national product	Personal consumption expenditures	Gross private domestic investment	Exports and imports of goods and services			Government purchases of goods and services					Final sales
				Net exports	Exports	Imports	Total	Federal: Total	Federal: National defense	Federal: Nondefense	State and local	
1979	2,508.2	1,566.8	454.8	18.8	291.2	272.5	467.8	178.0	121.9	56.1	289.9	2,495.2
1980	2,732.0	1,732.6	437.0	32.1	351.0	318.9	530.3	208.1	142.7	65.4	322.2	2,740.3
1981	3,052.6	1,915.1	515.5	33.9	382.8	348.9	588.1	242.2	167.5	74.8	345.9	3,028.6
1982	3,166.0	2,050.7	447.3	26.3	361.9	335.6	641.7	272.7	193.8	78.9	369.0	3,190.5
1983	3,405.7	2,234.5	502.3	−6.1	352.5	358.7	675.0	283.5	214.4	69.1	391.5	3,412.8
1984 r	3,772.2	2,430.5	664.8	−58.9	383.5	442.4	735.9	310.5	234.3	76.2	425.3	3,704.5
1985 r	4,010.3	2,629.4	641.6	−79.2	369.9	449.2	818.6	353.9	259.3	94.6	464.7	4,000.3
1986 r	4,235.0	2,799.8	671.0	−105.5	376.2	481.7	869.7	366.2	277.8	88.4	503.5	4,219.3
1982: IV	3,212.5	2,117.0	409.6	14.1	335.9	321.9	671.8	293.2	205.4	87.7	378.7	3,272.4
1983: IV	3,545.8	2,315.8	579.8	−25.8	364.7	390.5	676.1	276.1	221.5	54.6	400.0	3,514.8
1984: I r	3,674.9	2,361.1	663.0	−45.7	374.3	420.0	696.5	284.0	226.9	57.1	412.5	3,580.8
II r	3,754.2	2,417.0	664.2	−62.8	383.2	446.1	735.8	315.0	233.0	81.9	420.8	3,687.4
III r	3,807.9	2,450.3	670.3	−59.3	390.8	450.1	746.6	317.0	233.1	83.9	429.6	3,742.9
IV r	3,851.8	2,493.4	661.8	−67.9	385.7	453.6	764.5	326.0	244.1	81.9	438.5	3,806.8
1985: I r	3,921.1	2,549.9	638.6	−51.5	376.3	427.7	784.1	336.3	250.2	86.1	447.8	3,899.8
II r	3,973.6	2,602.0	648.4	−77.3	370.6	447.8	800.5	339.4	253.7	85.7	461.1	3,955.1
III r	4,042.0	2,665.4	628.6	−84.7	364.2	448.9	832.8	361.9	265.1	96.8	470.9	4,044.4
IV r	4,104.4	2,700.1	650.8	−103.5	368.7	472.2	857.0	378.0	268.2	109.8	479.0	4,101.9
1986: I r	4,174.4	2,737.9	683.4	−93.8	373.5	467.3	846.9	356.7	266.6	90.1	490.2	4,136.1
II r	4,211.6	2,765.8	679.4	−100.8	371.3	472.1	867.2	368.4	278.2	90.2	498.8	4,184.0
III r	4,265.9	2,837.1	660.8	−110.5	376.6	487.1	878.5	371.2	287.6	83.6	507.3	4,262.4
IV r	4,288.1	2,858.6	660.2	−116.9	383.3	500.2	886.3	368.6	279.0	89.6	517.7	4,294.6
1987: I r	4,377.7	2,893.8	699.9	−112.2	397.3	509.5	896.2	366.9	287.5	79.4	529.3	4,326.0
II p	4,448.8	2,944.0	702.3	−108.6	413.3	521.9	911.2	371.8	292.7	79.1	539.4	4,405.3

NOTE.—Series revised beginning 1984. See *Survey of Current Business*, July 1987.

Source: Department of Commerce, Bureau of Economic Analysis.

Source: *Economic Indicators*, Council of Economic Advisers.

GROSS NATIONAL PRODUCT IN 1982 DOLLARS

[Billions of 1982 dollars; quarterly data at seasonally adjusted annual rates]

Period	Gross national product	Personal consumption expenditures	Gross private domestic investment			Exports and imports of goods and services			Government purchases of goods and services					Final sales
			Nonresidential fixed	Residential fixed	Change in business inventories	Net exports	Exports	Imports	Total	Federal			State and local	
										Total	National defense	Non-defense		
1979	3,192.4	2,004.4	389.4	170.8	15.0	3.6	356.8	353.2	609.1	236.2	164.3	71.9	373.0	3,177.4
1980	3,187.1	2,000.4	379.2	137.0	−6.9	57.0	388.9	332.0	620.5	246.9	171.2	75.7	373.6	3,194.0
1981	3,248.8	2,024.2	395.2	126.5	23.9	49.4	392.7	343.4	629.7	259.6	180.3	79.3	370.1	3,225.0
1982	3,166.0	2,050.7	366.7	105.1	−24.5	26.3	361.9	335.6	641.7	272.7	193.8	78.9	369.0	3,190.5
1983	3,279.1	2,146.0	361.2	149.3	−6.4	−19.9	348.1	368.1	649.0	275.1	206.9	68.2	373.9	3,285.5
1984 r	3,501.4	2,249.3	425.2	170.9	62.3	−84.0	371.8	455.8	677.7	290.8	218.5	72.3	387.0	3,439.1
1985 r	3,607.5	2,352.6	454.1	174.6	7.4	−108.2	365.3	473.6	726.9	324.2	236.7	87.5	402.7	3,600.1
1986 r	3,713.3	2,450.5	443.8	196.4	13.8	−145.8	377.4	523.2	754.5	332.5	250.7	81.8	422.1	3,699.5
1982: IV	3,159.3	2,078.7	352.3	115.8	−59.3	11.7	336.0	324.3	660.1	289.5	201.4	88.2	370.6	3,218.6
1983: IV	3,365.1	2,191.9	390.4	159.9	27.0	−46.2	355.5	401.6	642.2	266.0	211.6	54.4	376.2	3,338.1
1984: I r	3,451.7	2,212.1	401.3	170.5	83.4	−68.6	362.7	431.3	653.0	271.5	214.1	57.4	381.6	3,368.3
II r	3,498.0	2,246.7	422.0	173.1	63.2	−87.3	369.1	456.5	680.2	295.6	217.8	77.8	384.7	3,434.8
III r	3,520.6	2,257.3	433.0	170.3	60.9	−85.5	378.7	464.1	684.5	295.5	217.0	78.6	388.9	3,459.6
IV r	3,535.2	2,281.1	444.4	169.6	41.7	−94.8	376.6	471.4	693.2	300.5	225.3	75.2	392.7	3,493.5
1985: I r	3,568.7	2,314.1	440.0	172.6	19.5	−81.0	369.7	450.7	703.4	308.4	229.8	78.6	395.0	3,549.2
II r	3,587.1	2,337.0	457.2	171.2	17.3	−107.7	364.7	472.4	712.1	310.7	232.8	77.8	401.4	3,569.9
III r	3,623.0	2,376.1	454.1	174.9	−5.7	−114.9	360.5	475.4	738.6	332.5	243.3	89.3	406.1	3,628.7
IV r	3,650.9	2,383.2	465.2	179.7	−1.6	−129.3	366.5	495.8	753.7	345.3	241.1	104.2	408.4	3,652.5
1986: I r	3,698.8	2,409.7	453.2	185.9	35.3	−123.0	371.5	494.4	737.6	322.1	240.0	82.0	415.5	3,663.4
II r	3,704.7	2,434.3	441.0	196.5	28.1	−146.8	370.2	517.0	751.6	330.6	250.1	80.4	421.0	3,676.7
III r	3,718.0	2,477.5	437.7	201.1	6.1	−161.6	379.6	541.2	757.2	332.6	259.8	72.8	424.6	3,711.9
IV r	3,731.5	2,480.5	443.2	202.2	−14.4	−151.8	388.3	540.1	771.8	344.6	252.7	91.9	427.1	3,745.8
1987: I r	3,772.2	2,475.9	426.0	198.2	47.6	−135.2	397.8	533.0	759.6	327.3	257.4	69.9	432.3	3,724.5
II p	3,796.4	2,488.7	434.2	198.0	41.2	−127.8	410.7	538.5	762.2	326.3	262.4	63.9	435.9	3,755.3

NOTE.—Series revised beginning 1984. See *Survey of Current Business*, July 1987.

Source: Department of Commerce, Bureau of Economic Analysis.

Source: *Economic Indicators*, Council of Economic Advisers.

SELECTED COMPONENTS OF GNP

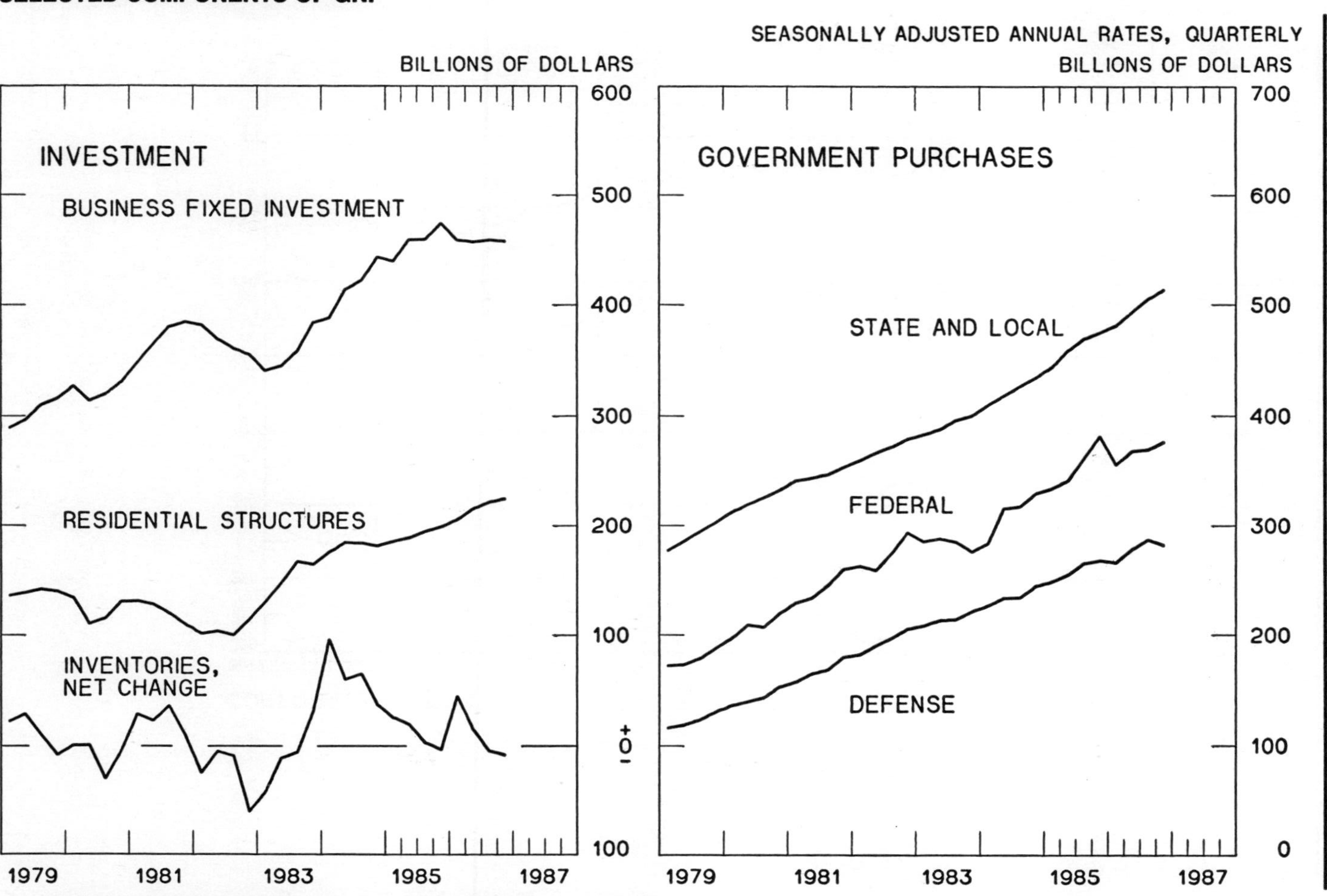

Source: *Federal Reserve Chart Book*, Board of Governors of the Federal Reserve System.

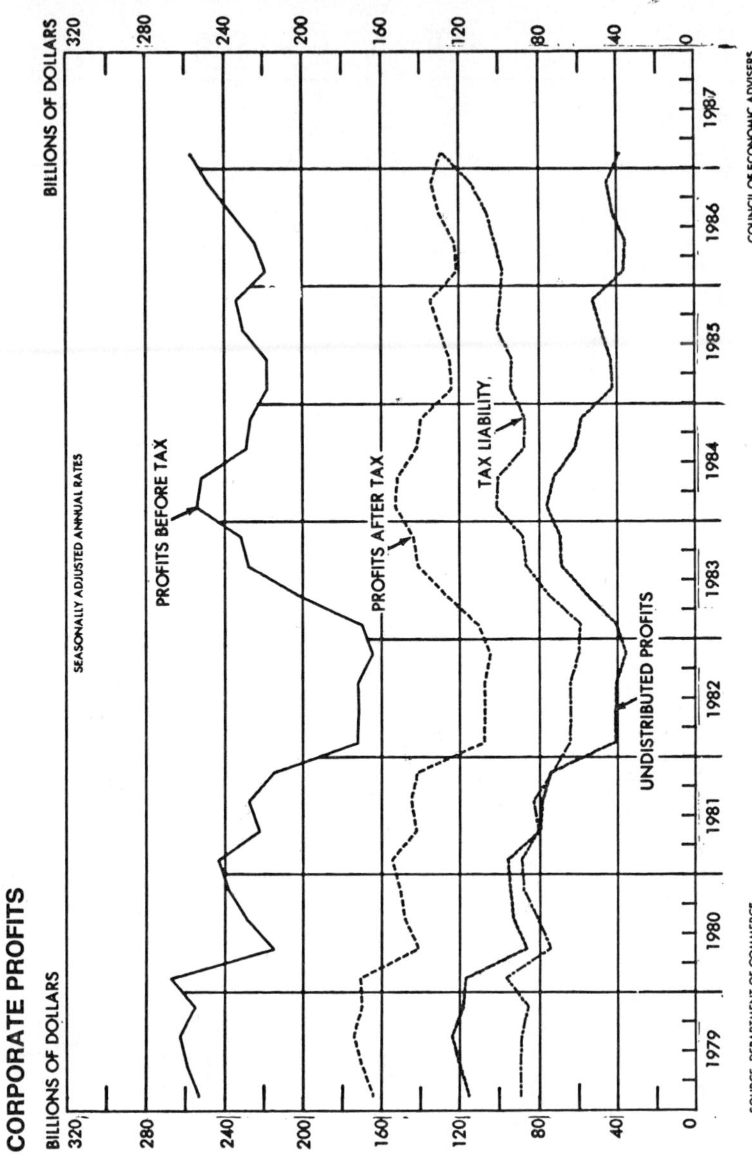
CORPORATE PROFITS
BILLIONS OF DOLLARS
BILLIONS OF DOLLARS
SEASONALLY ADJUSTED ANNUAL RATES
PROFITS BEFORE TAX
PROFITS AFTER TAX
TAX LIABILITY
UNDISTRIBUTED PROFITS
320
280
240
200
160
120
80
40
0
1979
1980
1981
1982
1983
1984
1985
1986
1987
SOURCE: DEPARTMENT OF COMMERCE
COUNCIL OF ECONOMIC ADVISERS

[Billions of dollars; quarterly data at seasonally adjusted annual rates]

Period	Profits (before tax) with inventory valuation adjustment [1]						Profits before tax	Tax liability	Profits after tax			Inventory valuation adjustment
	Total [2]	Domestic industries							Total	Dividends	Undistributed profits	
		Total	Financial	Nonfinancial								
				Total [3]	Manufacturing	Wholesale and retail trade						
1980	194.0	159.6	21.0	138.6	77.1	21.6	237.1	84.8	152.3	54.7	97.6	−43.1
1981	202.3	173.8	16.5	157.3	88.5	32.5	226.5	81.1	145.4	63.6	81.8	−24.2
1982	159.2	131.2	11.8	119.4	58.0	34.6	169.6	63.1	106.5	66.9	39.6	−10.4
1983	196.7	166.6	18.1	148.5	70.1	38.9	207.6	77.2	130.4	71.5	58.9	−10.9
1984 r	234.2	203.3	13.0	190.3	88.8	51.2	240.0	93.9	146.1	79.0	67.0	−5.8
1985 r	224.1	193.6	18.4	175.2	72.2	51.4	224.8	96.7	128.1	81.3	46.8	−.7
1986 r	238.4	207.2	26.1	181.1	69.4	52.1	231.9	105.0	126.8	86.8	40.0	6.5
1982: IV	150.7	121.6	18.7	102.9	46.8	33.6	164.1	59.8	104.3	68.5	35.8	−13.4
1983: IV	223.4	190.7	15.5	175.2	88.6	43.1	231.5	88.1	143.4	73.9	69.5	−8.1
1984: I r	238.2	207.8	14.5	193.3	95.0	48.0	253.7	101.2	152.5	76.6	76.0	−15.5
II r	246.5	216.6	13.1	203.5	97.0	52.7	251.4	100.3	151.2	78.9	72.3	−5.0
III r	227.4	194.8	10.8	184.0	83.3	52.2	228.5	87.2	141.4	79.8	61.5	−1.1
IV r	224.6	193.9	13.6	180.3	79.8	51.8	226.1	87.0	139.2	80.8	58.4	−1.6
1985: I r	216.1	187.1	15.3	171.8	67.8	52.0	217.6	94.0	123.6	81.2	42.4	−1.5
II r	219.8	189.2	19.1	170.1	68.4	52.8	218.0	93.2	124.8	81.3	43.5	1.8
III r	236.8	208.3	18.4	189.9	80.1	55.7	230.2	100.5	129.7	81.2	48.5	6.5
IV r	223.7	189.7	20.8	168.9	72.4	45.0	233.5	99.1	134.4	81.7	52.7	−9.8
1986: I r	236.7	202.3	26.2	176.2	61.9	55.3	218.9	98.1	120.9	84.3	36.6	17.8
II r	235.6	207.0	26.9	180.0	72.5	48.2	224.4	102.1	122.3	86.6	35.7	11.3
III r	242.4	210.2	25.2	185.1	68.0	54.6	236.3	106.1	130.2	87.7	42.5	6.0
IV r	239.0	209.3	26.1	183.2	75.4	49.7	247.9	113.9	134.0	88.6	45.4	−8.9
1987: I r	245.7	213.1	27.6	185.5	75.4	56.2	257.0	128.0	129.0	90.3	38.7	−11.3
II p										92.3		−18.5

[1] See p. 183 for profits with inventory valuation and capital consumption adjustments.
[2] Includes rest of the world, not shown separately.
[3] Includes industries not shown separately.

Source: *Economic Indicators*, Council of Economic Advisers.

NOTE.—Corporate profits and related measures for 1986 reflect retroactive provisions of the Tax Reform Act of 1986.

Series revised beginnig 1984. See *Survey of Current Business*, July 1987.

Source: Department of Commerce, Bureau of Economic Analysis.

Price Data

Definitions are applicable to the exhibits on pages 191 and 196.

Price data are gathered by the Bureau of Labor Statistics from retail and primary markets in the United States. Price indexes are given in relation to a base period (1967 = 100, unless otherwise noted).

DEFINITIONS

The **Consumer Price Index** (CPI) is a measure of the average change in the prices paid by urban consumers for a fixed market basket of goods and services. The CPI is calculated monthly for two population groups, one consisting only of urban households whose primary source of income is derived from the employment of wage earners and clerical workers, and the other consisting of all urban households. The wage earner index (CPI–W) is a continuation of the historic index that was introduced well over a half-century ago for use in wage negotiations. As new uses were developed for the CPI in recent years, the need for a broader and more representative index became apparent. The all urban consumer index (CPI–U) introduced in 1978 is representative of the 1982–84 buying habits of about 80 percent of the noninstitutional population of the United States at that time, compared with 32 percent represented in the CPI–W. In addition to wage earners and clerical workers, the CPI–U covers professional, managerial, and technical workers, the self-employed, short-term workers, the unemployed, retirees, and others not in the labor force.

The CPI is based on prices of food, clothing, shelter, fuel, drugs, transportation fares, doctor's and dentist's fees, and other goods and services that people buy for day-to-day living. The quantity and quality of these items are kept essentially unchanged between major revisions so that only price changes will be measured. All taxes directly associated with the purchase and use of items are included in the index.

Data are collected from more than 21,000 retail establishments and 60,000 tenants in 91 urban areas across the country are used to develop the "U.S. city average."

NOTES ON THE DATA

In January 1983, the Bureau changed the way in which homeownership costs are measured for the CPI–U. A rental equivalence method replaced the asset-price approach to homeownership costs for that series. In January 1985, the same change was made in the CPI–W. The central purpose of the change was to separate shelter costs from the investment component of homeownership so that the index would reflect only the cost of shelter services provided by owner-occupied homes. An updated CP-U and CPI-W were introduced with release of the January 1987 data.

Additional Sources of Information

For a discussion of the general method for computing the CPI, see *BLS Handbook of Methods, Volume II, The Consumer Price Index*, Bulletin 2134–2 (Bureau of Labor Statistics, 1984). The recent change in the measurement of homeownership costs is discussed in Robert Gillingham and Walter Lane, "Changing the treatment of shelter costs for homeowners in the CPI," *Monthly Labor Review*, June 1982, pp. 9–14. An overview of the recently introduced revised CPI, reflecting 1982–84 expenditure patterns, is contained in *The Consumer Price Index: 1987 Revision*, Report 736 (Bureau of Labor Statistics, 1987).

Additional detailed CPI data and regular analyses of consumer price changes are provided in the *CPI Detailed Report*, a monthly publication of the Bureau. Historical data for the overall CPI and for selected groupings may be found in the *Handbook of Labor Statistics*, Bulletin 2217 (Bureau of Labor Statistics, 1985).

Source: *Monthly Labor Review*, U.S. Department of Labor, Bureau of Labor Statistics, July 1987.

CONSUMER PRICE INDEX FOR ALL URBAN CONSUMERS: U.S. CITY AVERAGE

(1967 = 100, unless otherwise indicated)

Series	Annual average		1986								1987				
	1985	1986	May	June	July	Aug.	Sept.	Oct.	Nov.	Dec.	Jan.	Feb.	Mar.	Apr.	May
CONSUMER PRICE INDEX FOR ALL URBAN CONSUMERS:															
All items	322.2	328.4	326.3	327.9	328.0	328.6	330.2	330.5	330.8	331.1	333.1	334.4	335.9	337.7	338.7
All items (1957-59 = 100)	374.7	381.9	379.5	381.4	381.4	382.1	384.1	384.4	384.7	385.1	387.4	388.9	390.7	392.7	393.9
Food and beverages	302.0	311.8	309.4	309.5	312.2	314.6	315.1	315.6	316.4	317.0	320.5	321.6	321.6	322.5	324.0
Food	309.8	319.7	317.0	317.1	320.1	322.7	323.2	323.7	324.6	325.2	328.9	330.1	330.0	331.0	332.5
Food at home	296.8	305.3	302.1	301.6	305.5	308.9	309.0	309.5	309.9	310.2	315.2	316.6	315.8	316.9	318.8
Cereals and bakery products	317.0	325.8	323.8	326.1	326.3	328.2	328.5	328.4	328.5	329.5	331.5	332.7	333.2	335.6	336.5
Meats, poultry, fish, and eggs	263.4	275.1	263.4	265.1	274.9	283.0	284.7	284.9	286.3	287.3	289.2	286.4	286.5	285.9	288.5
Dairy products	258.0	258.4	257.1	257.2	258.4	258.3	258.5	260.0	261.2	262.2	263.3	264.7	263.7	263.2	264.3
Fruits and vegetables	325.7	328.7	336.5	327.8	330.3	332.1	329.1	328.6	327.8	328.5	344.3	355.2	352.5	360.6	365.7
Other foods at home	361.1	373.6	374.6	374.1	373.7	374.0	373.7	374.4	373.9	372.2	378.7	380.0	378.6	377.6	377.5
Sugar and sweets	398.8	411.1	411.2	411.5	412.4	413.1	413.7	413.4	412.4	411.8	415.8	415.8	417.2	417.4	417.7
Fats and oils	294.4	287.8	287.2	287.0	287.3	287.8	285.6	284.6	285.4	286.0	293.2	290.3	294.6	291.8	293.3
Nonalcoholic beverages	451.7	478.2	481.9	480.0	478.3	476.9	475.7	477.5	476.9	470.2	482.6	481.9	475.4	469.8	467.9
Other prepared foods	294.2	301.9	301.4	301.7	301.8	303.2	303.8	304.7	303.9	305.2	308.4	312.1	311.3	313.2	313.5
Food away from home	346.6	360.1	358.8	360.2	360.8	361.8	363.3	364.0	365.8	367.1	368.6	369.6	370.9	371.5	372.3
Alcoholic beverages	229.5	239.7	239.4	240.1	240.4	240.1	240.4	240.6	240.5	240.8	242.5	243.2	243.6	244.3	245.0
Housing	349.9	360.2	358.5	361.2	361.5	362.4	363.7	363.0	361.7	362.1	363.9	365.1	366.4	367.7	368.9
Shelter	382.0	402.9	400.9	401.6	403.5	405.2	407.6	409.5	410.2	410.4	412.3	414.0	415.9	418.0	419.2
Renters' costs (12/82 = 100)	115.4	121.9	121.1	121.6	122.5	122.9	123.6	124.0	124.3	124.2	125.3	125.8	126.4	127.1	127.3
Rent, residential	264.6	280.0	278.4	279.4	281.2	281.7	283.2	284.6	285.6	286.0	287.1	288.0	288.3	288.8	289.4
Other renters' costs	398.4	416.2	411.3	415.2	420.1	425.7	429.1	427.3	425.5	418.2	428.3	430.8	438.7	446.1	446.1
Homeowners' costs (12/82 = 100)	113.1	119.4	118.9	119.0	119.4	119.9	120.7	121.3	121.5	121.6	122.0	122.5	123.0	123.6	124.0
Owners' equivalent rent (12/82 = 100)	113.2	119.4	118.9	119.0	119.4	119.9	120.7	121.3	121.5	121.6	122.0	122.5	123.0	123.6	124.1
Household insurance (12/82 = 100)	112.4	119.2	118.8	118.9	119.9	119.9	120.2	120.6	121.1	121.6	121.8	122.0	122.2	122.4	123.0
Maintenance and repairs	368.9	373.8	367.1	366.6	369.2	376.4	376.2	379.0	377.1	380.0	382.1	381.9	383.4	382.4	381.9
Maintenance and repair services	421.1	430.9	425.5	427.4	430.1	434.2	437.0	437.5	433.7	433.1	437.7	436.1	439.4	437.1	435.3
Maintenance and repair commodities	269.6	269.7	262.9	260.7	262.7	271.3	268.7	273.0	272.9	278.3	277.7	278.8	278.5	278.7	279.6
Fuel and other utilities	393.6	384.7	382.5	393.8	389.4	389.5	388.3	379.1	371.1	371.0	373.7	374.8	374.9	374.2	377.5
Fuels	488.1	463.1	460.6	477.0	469.2	469.0	467.2	450.3	437.8	438.1	443.7	445.1	444.6	442.0	448.7
Fuel oil, coal, and bottled gas	619.5	501.5	496.8	486.6	459.4	447.3	453.5	451.9	452.0	460.6	487.9	503.2	500.6	500.5	497.7
Gas (piped) and electricity	452.7	446.7	444.6	466.0	462.3	464.5	461.1	441.4	426.7	425.3	428.8	428.9	428.7	425.9	433.3
Other utilities and public services	240.7	253.1	251.5	255.2	255.6	255.9	255.6	257.1	255.4	254.9	254.9	255.6	256.2	257.0	257.2
Household furnishings and operations	247.2	250.4	249.9	250.2	250.5	250.5	251.5	251.6	251.2	252.4	253.1	253.5	254.3	255.2	254.9
Housefurnishings	200.1	201.1	200.8	200.8	201.2	200.9	202.2	202.2	201.4	202.5	203.0	203.2	203.8	204.7	203.7
Housekeeping supplies	313.6	319.5	318.3	319.6	319.5	319.8	320.1	319.8	320.4	322.9	324.6	325.3	327.7	328.2	330.1
Housekeeping services	338.9	346.6	345.8	346.1	346.6	347.4	347.8	348.5	348.5	349.3	349.8	350.6	351.0	352.2	353.1

See footnotes at end of table.

Continued

CONSUMER PRICE INDEX FOR ALL URBAN CONSUMERS: U.S. CITY AVERAGE *(continued)*

(1967 = 100, unless otherwise indicated)

Series	Annual average		1986								1987				
	1985	1986	May	June	July	Aug.	Sept.	Oct.	Nov.	Dec.	Jan.	Feb.	Mar.	Apr.	May
Apparel and upkeep	206.0	207.8	206.4	204.5	203.2	207.0	212.1	213.2	213.1	210.9	207.1	208.4	215.2	218.7	218.0
Apparel commodities	191.6	192.0	190.7	188.4	187.0	191.2	196.6	197.6	197.4	194.9	190.9	192.1	199.1	202.6	201.8
Men's and boys' apparel	197.9	200.0	200.2	198.1	195.8	197.8	203.2	204.3	205.3	202.3	199.2	199.9	203.5	205.6	207.1
Women's and girls' apparel	169.5	168.0	164.9	161.3	159.8	167.2	175.7	176.4	175.0	171.7	166.6	167.8	177.0	182.2	179.6
Infants' and toddlers' apparel	299.7	312.7	318.5	319.7	307.5	310.6	309.7	312.0	307.0	312.7	301.8	304.5	319.6	319.1	316.4
Footwear	212.1	211.2	211.5	210.0	209.1	209.6	212.0	215.1	215.1	214.0	209.9	211.0	216.5	219.2	220.8
Other apparel commodities	215.5	217.9	215.4	215.8	218.1	221.6	221.1	219.8	221.1	220.0	223.2	226.0	227.4	227.0	226.7
Apparel services	320.9	334.6	333.6	334.3	334.6	334.7	336.7	338.3	339.0	339.5	342.5	343.2	344.7	344.7	346.8
Transportation	319.9	307.5	305.7	308.6	304.7	301.3	302.2	302.6	304.3	304.8	308.5	310.0	310.6	313.3	314.6
Private transportation	314.2	299.5	297.8	300.8	296.5	292.8	293.7	294.1	295.8	295.9	299.8	301.3	301.9	304.8	306.3
New vehicles	214.9	224.1	222.8	224.0	224.5	224.5	224.2	226.7	230.2	231.7	232.3	229.9	229.2	229.9	230.6
New cars	215.2	224.4	223.0	224.2	224.7	224.7	224.5	227.1	230.7	232.2	233.0	230.2	229.4	230.4	231.3
Used cars	379.7	363.2	363.6	362.5	360.3	358.0	359.5	360.6	361.0	356.6	354.6	356.9	363.0	371.6	378.6
Motor fuel	373.8	292.1	289.3	299.4	280.2	265.9	271.1	263.2	260.9	261.9	275.8	288.1	290.0	297.2	299.7
Gasoline	373.3	291.4	288.7	299.1	279.8	265.3	270.6	262.6	260.2	261.2	275.1	287.5	289.4	296.7	299.3
Maintenance and repair	351.4	363.1	361.3	362.1	363.4	364.3	365.0	365.7	368.4	370.7	371.3	373.0	373.0	376.1	376.1
Other private transportation	287.6	303.9	301.3	303.0	304.5	304.5	302.3	307.6	311.6	312.0	314.9	314.0	314.4	315.1	315.9
Other private transportation commodities	202.6	201.6	202.4	201.5	201.6	201.8	200.3	198.9	200.0	200.4	202.2	201.8	202.3	200.8	202.3
Other private transportation services	312.8	333.9	330.4	332.8	334.6	334.6	332.3	339.3	344.1	344.5	347.7	346.7	347.0	348.6	349.1
Public transportation	402.8	426.4	423.7	425.4	428.0	428.0	428.5	428.7	431.7	437.5	438.9	439.8	441.4	440.8	439.6
Medical care	403.1	433.5	429.7	432.0	434.8	437.5	439.7	442.3	444.6	446.8	449.6	452.4	455.0	457.3	458.9
Medical care commodities	256.7	273.6	272.3	273.3	275.4	276.0	276.7	277.5	278.2	280.8	282.4	283.9	286.3	287.5	289.6
Medical care services	435.1	468.6	464.2	466.8	469.8	473.0	475.7	478.8	481.5	483.4	486.5	489.6	492.1	494.7	496.0
Professional services	367.3	390.9	388.3	390.3	391.7	393.3	396.1	398.0	399.8	401.0	403.7	406.8	409.6	412.5	413.9
Hospital and related services	224.0	237.4	234.4	235.0	237.4	239.5	240.1	242.3	243.8	245.0	246.7	248.1	249.0	250.1	251.0
Entertainment	265.0	274.1	272.9	273.9	274.4	274.7	275.3	276.5	277.4	277.4	278.3	278.7	279.8	281.3	282.0
Entertainment commodities	260.6	265.9	265.3	266.1	265.8	266.1	265.9	266.7	267.6	267.4	268.1	268.1	269.9	270.8	271.7
Entertainment services	271.8	286.3	284.2	285.5	287.0	287.3	289.2	290.8	291.8	292.2	293.3	294.1	294.5	296.6	297.2
Other goods and services	326.6	346.4	342.1	342.6	344.9	346.4	353.3	354.6	354.9	355.2	358.1	359.7	360.3	361.1	362.0
Tobacco products	328.5	351.0	346.5	347.1	354.3	356.2	356.8	357.2	357.3	357.6	364.9	368.3	369.6	370.4	370.9
Personal care	281.9	291.3	290.9	291.0	291.1	292.3	292.0	293.1	293.4	293.6	295.7	296.4	296.4	297.3	299.0
Toilet goods and personal care appliances	278.5	287.9	287.9	287.0	287.1	289.1	288.2	289.9	289.6	289.6	291.3	292.1	292.0	292.9	294.2
Personal care services	286.0	295.4	294.7	295.7	295.8	296.2	296.5	297.1	297.9	298.2	300.8	301.3	301.5	302.3	304.6
Personal and educational expenses	397.1	428.8	419.5	420.4	421.2	422.9	445.2	447.6	448.2	448.8	450.6	452.0	452.8	453.8	454.4
School books and supplies	350.8	380.3	374.5	375.7	375.9	376.9	389.4	392.3	392.5	392.6	400.7	403.4	403.9	404.4	404.9
Personal and educational services	407.7	440.1	430.2	431.0	431.9	433.7	457.8	460.2	460.8	461.6	462.8	464.2	465.0	466.0	466.8

All items	322.2	328.4	326.3	327.9	328.0	328.6	330.2	330.5	330.8	331.1	333.1	334.4	335.9	337.7	338.7
Commodities	286.7	283.9	282.1	282.8	281.9	281.9	283.5	283.6	284.0	284.2	286.3	287.7	289.5	291.4	292.3
Food and beverages	302.0	311.8	309.4	309.5	312.2	314.6	315.1	315.6	316.4	317.0	320.5	321.6	321.6	322.5	324.0
Commodities less food and beverages	274.6	264.7	263.4	264.3	261.4	260.1	262.3	262.1	262.4	262.4	263.7	265.2	267.9	270.4	270.9
Nondurables less food and beverages	282.1	265.2	263.3	264.7	259.8	258.1	261.5	260.4	260.0	260.0	261.8	265.4	269.7	273.2	273.5
Apparel commodities	191.6	192.0	190.7	188.4	187.0	191.2	196.6	197.6	197.4	194.9	190.9	192.1	199.1	202.6	201.8
Nondurables less food, beverages, and apparel	333.3	307.3	305.2	308.4	301.7	296.9	299.5	297.2	296.7	298.0	304.8	310.3	311.9	315.0	316.4
Durables	270.7	270.2	269.6	269.9	269.6	269.0	269.3	270.5	271.8	271.7	272.4	271.2	271.7	273.0	273.6
Services	381.5	400.5	397.9	401.0	402.3	403.7	405.5	406.1	406.1	406.6	408.6	409.9	411.2	412.8	414.2
Rent of shelter (12/82=100)	113.9	120.2	119.7	119.9	120.5	120.9	121.7	122.2	122.4	122.5	123.1	123.6	124.1	124.8	125.1
Household services less rent of' shelter (12/82=100)	111.2	112.8	112.3	115.2	114.9	115.3	114.9	112.9	111.0	110.8	111.3	111.5	111.5	111.4	112.3
Transportation services	337.0	356.3	353.4	355.3	357.1	357.3	356.2	360.5	364.4	366.2	368.5	368.5	369.0	370.5	370.5
Medical care services	435.1	468.6	464.2	466.8	469.8	473.0	475.7	478.8	481.5	483.4	486.5	489.6	492.1	494.7	496.0
Other services	314.1	331.8	328.2	329.2	330.1	330.8	337.9	339.5	340.3	340.8	342.2	343.1	343.7	345.0	345.9
Special indexes:															
All items less food	323.3	328.6	326.7	328.6	328.0	328.1	330.0	330.2	330.4	330.6	332.2	333.6	335.4	337.3	338.3
All items less shelter	303.9	306.7	304.7	306.5	306.1	306.4	307.9	307.8	308.0	308.3	310.3	311.5	312.9	314.6	315.6
All items less homeowners' costs (12/82=100)	109.7	111.2	110.4	111.1	111.0	111.2	111.7	111.7	111.8	111.9	112.7	113.1	113.6	114.2	114.6
All items less medical care	317.7	322.6	320.6	322.2	322.1	322.6	324.2	324.4	324.5	324.8	326.7	328.0	329.4	331.1	332.2
Commodities less food	272.5	263.4	262.1	263.0	260.2	259.0	261.1	260.9	261.2	261.2	262.5	264.0	266.5	268.9	269.4
Nondurables less food	277.2	262.2	260.5	261.8	257.3	255.6	258.9	257.8	257.4	257.5	259.2	262.6	266.4	269.6	270.0
Nondurables less food and apparel	319.2	297.1	295.2	298.1	292.2	287.9	290.2	288.1	287.7	288.9	294.9	299.6	301.0	303.7	305.0
Nondurables	293.2	289.6	287.4	288.2	287.1	287.4	289.4	289.0	289.2	289.5	292.1	294.6	296.8	299.1	300.0
Services less rent of' shelter (12/82=100)	113.5	118.7	117.8	119.2	119.5	119.8	120.2	120.1	120.0	120.2	120.8	121.1	121.3	121.6	122.1
Services less medical care	373.3	390.6	388.3	391.3	392.5	393.6	395.4	395.7	395.4	395.8	397.6	398.8	400.0	401.5	402.9
Energy	426.5	370.3	367.6	380.6	366.5	358.6	360.6	348.6	341.7	342.4	352.2	359.2	360.0	362.4	366.9
All items less energy	314.8	327.0	325.0	325.5	326.9	328.3	330.0	331.4	332.3	332.6	334.0	334.9	336.5	338.2	339.0
All items less food and energy	314.4	327.1	325.3	325.9	326.9	327.9	329.9	331.6	332.5	332.8	333.6	334.5	336.4	338.3	338.9
Commodities less food and energy	259.7	263.2	262.2	262.0	262.0	262.9	264.5	265.5	266.1	265.8	265.5	265.7	268.4	270.3	270.7
Energy commodities	409.9	322.4	319.3	327.1	306.6	292.4	297.7	290.6	288.5	290.5	306.1	319.2	320.9	328.0	330.2
Services less energy	375.9	397.1	394.5	395.9	397.7	399.0	401.4	403.7	405.0	405.7	407.5	408.9	410.4	412.3	413.2
Purchasing power of the consumer dollar:															
1967=$1.00	31.0	30.5	30.6	30.5	30.5	30.4	30.3	30.3	30.2	30.2	30.0	29.9	29.8	29.6	29.5
1957-59=$1.00	26.7	26.2	26.4	26.2	26.2	26.2	26.0	26.0	26.0	26.0	25.8	25.7	25.6	25.5	25.4

Source: *Monthly Labor Review*, U.S. Department of Labor, Bureau of Labor Statistics, July, 1987.

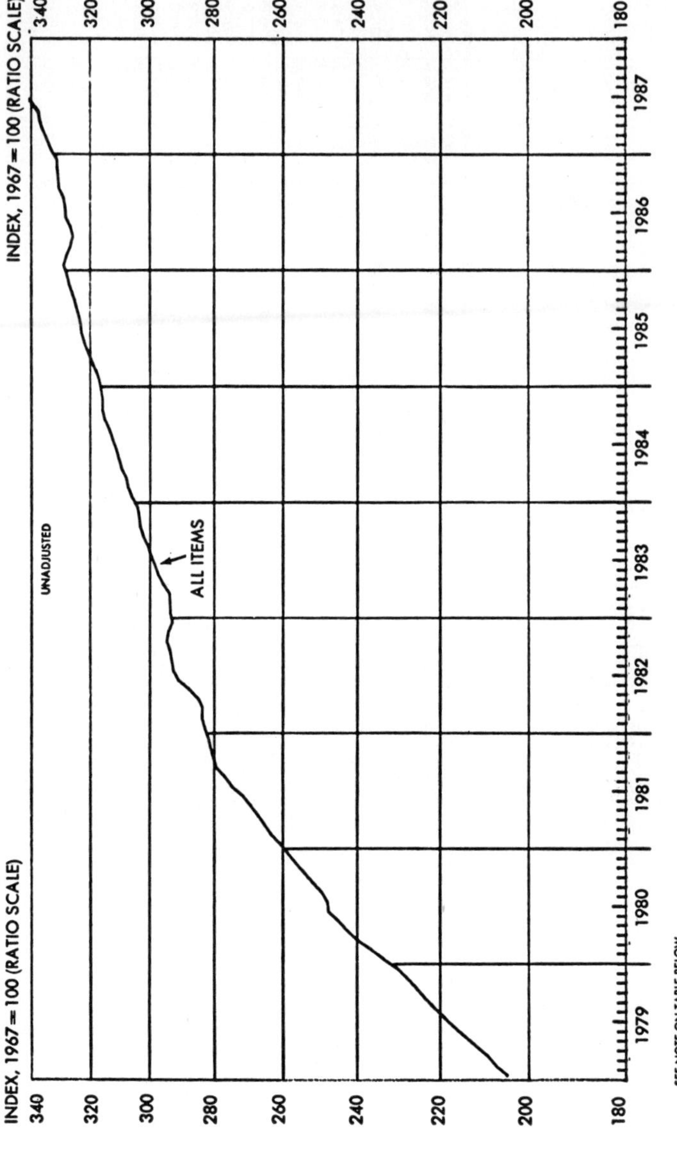
CONSUMER PRICES–ALL URBAN CONSUMERS
INDEX, 1967=100 (RATIO SCALE)
INDEX, 1967=100 (RATIO SCALE)
340
320
300
280
260
240
220
200
180
UNADJUSTED
ALL ITEMS
1979
1980
1981
1982
1983
1984
1985
1986
1987
SEE NOTE ON TABLE BELOW
SOURCE: DEPARTMENT OF LABOR
COUNCIL OF ECONOMIC ADVISERS

[1967=100, except as noted; monthly data seasonally adjusted, except as noted by NSA]

Period	All items [1] NSA	Food	Housing: Total [1]	Housing: Shelter: Total	Housing: Shelter: Renters' costs (Dec. 1982=100)	Housing: Shelter: Home-owners' costs (Dec. 1982=100)	Housing: Shelter: Mainte-nance and repairs NSA	Housing: Fuel and other utilities	Appar-el and upkeep	Transportation: Total [1]	Transportation: New cars	Transportation: Motor fuel	Medical care	Ener-gy [2]	All items less food, energy, and shelter
Rel. imp. [3]	*100.0*	*16.2*	*42.9*	*27.8*	*8.0*	*19.6*	*0.2*	*7.9*	*6.3*	*17.2*	*4.6*	*2.9*	*5.4*	*7.4*	*48.6*
1979	217.4	234.5	227.6	239.7	....	....	256.4	239.3	166.6	212.0	166.0	265.6	239.7	275.9	191.5
1980	246.8	254.6	263.3	281.7	....	....	285.7	278.6	178.4	249.7	179.3	369.1	265.9	361.1	208.3
1981	272.4	274.6	293.5	314.7	....	....	314.4	319.2	186.9	280.0	190.2	410.9	294.5	410.0	228.1
1982	289.1	285.7	314.7	337.0	....	....	334.1	350.8	191.8	291.5	197.6	389.4	328.7	416.1	245.6
1983	298.4	291.7	323.1	344.8	103.0	102.5	346.3	370.3	196.5	298.4	202.6	376.4	357.3	419.3	258.4
1984	311.1	302.9	336.5	361.7	108.6	107.3	359.2	387.3	200.2	311.7	208.5	370.7	379.5	423.6	271.2
1985	322.2	309.8	349.9	382.0	115.4	113.1	368.9	393.6	206.0	319.9	215.2	373.8	403.1	426.5	281.6
1986	328.4	319.7	360.2	402.9	121.9	119.4	373.8	384.7	207.8	307.5	224.4	292.1	433.5	370.3	291.2
1986: June	327.9	317.4	360.1	401.6	121.7	119.1	366.6	388.1	206.3	308.1	224.2	297.2	432.7	375.2	290.6
July	328.0	320.2	360.1	403.0	122.3	119.4	369.2	383.4	207.1	304.2	225.2	276.5	435.3	360.0	291.7
Aug	328.6	322.7	361.0	404.6	122.6	119.9	376.4	382.9	208.0	301.3	225.9	263.2	437.8	352.2	292.4
Sept	330.2	323.9	361.8	406.7	123.1	120.6	376.2	380.6	208.9	302.2	226.4	269.0	440.6	353.7	292.8
Oct	330.5	325.2	361.9	408.3	123.6	121.1	379.0	376.7	209.0	302.5	228.0	263.4	443.0	347.1	293.9
Nov	330.8	326.5	362.0	409.3	124.1	121.3	377.1	374.9	209.6	303.6	229.7	261.7	445.3	345.3	294.8
Dec	331.1	327.2	362.7	410.3	124.5	121.5	380.0	374.3	209.5	303.6	230.9	260.9	448.2	344.6	295.5
1987: Jan	333.1	328.6	364.4	412.2	125.4	122.0	382.1	375.9	210.4	308.3	231.8	278.0	450.2	354.9	297.0
Feb	334.4	329.6	365.8	414.3	126.0	122.6	381.9	377.1	211.8	309.8	229.3	289.5	451.7	361.5	297.4
Mar	335.9	329.2	367.2	416.5	126.7	123.2	383.4	377.6	215.4	311.8	229.4	296.2	453.7	365.2	298.8
Apr	337.7	330.2	368.2	418.0	127.0	123.7	382.4	378.1	218.6	313.4	230.4	298.4	456.5	366.2	300.5
May	338.7	332.0	368.9	419.2	127.2	124.2	381.9	378.1	219.1	314.4	231.1	299.7	459.1	366.8	301.4
June	340.1	334.4	370.1	420.1	127.7	124.3	385.0	381.0	217.3	316.0	232.0	303.6	462.1	372.2	301.9

[1] Includes items not shown separately.
[2] Fuel oil, coal, and bottled gas; gas (piped) and electricity; and motor fuel. Motor oil, coolant, etc. also included through 1982.
[3] Relative importance, December 1986.

NOTE.—Data beginning 1983 incorporate a rental equivalence measure for homeownership costs and therefore are not strictly comparable with figures for earlier periods.
Data beginning 1987 calculated on a revised basis.

Source: Department of Labor, Bureau of Labor Statistics.

Source: *Economic Indicators*, Council of Economic Advisers.

CONSUMER PRICE INDEX—U.S. CITY AVERAGE AND AVAILABLE LOCAL AREA DATA: ALL ITEMS

(1967 = 100, unless otherwise indicated)

Area[1]	Pricing schedule[2]	Other index base	All Urban Consumers							Urban Wage Earners						
			1986		1987					1986		1987				
			May	June	Jan.	Feb.	Mar.	Apr.	May	May	June	Jan.	Feb.	Mar.	Apr.	May
U.S. city average	M	-	326.3	327.9	333.1	334.4	335.9	337.7	338.7	321.4	323.0	327.7	329.0	330.5	332.3	333.4
Region and area size[3]																
Northeast urban	M	12/77	-	174.2	178.4	179.0	179.9	181.0	181.7	-	171.6	175.5	176.0	177.0	178.2	178.9
Size A - More than 1,200,000	M	12/77	-	171.8	176.1	176.8	177.5	178.8	179.5	-	167.7	171.6	172.3	173.0	174.4	175.2
Size B - 500,000 to 1,200,000	M	12/77	-	175.2	179.3	179.1	180.7	182.3	182.8	-	172.2	176.2	176.2	177.7	179.3	179.7
Size C - 50,000 to 500,000	M	12/77	-	183.4	187.1	187.4	188.8	188.9	189.0	-	187.8	191.4	191.7	193.1	193.1	193.5
North Central urban	M	12/77	-	176.1	178.3	178.5	179.5	180.4	180.8	-	172.2	174.3	174.4	175.3	176.2	176.7
Size A - More than 1,200,000	M	12/77	-	180.3	182.1	182.5	183.2	184.0	184.5	-	174.7	176.3	176.6	177.3	178.3	178.8
Size B - 360,000 to 1,200,000	M	12/77	-	174.1	177.2	177.2	177.8	179.5	179.5	-	169.7	172.7	172.6	173.1	174.6	174.8
Size C - 50,000 to 360,000	M	12/77	-	170.7	173.9	173.6	175.3	176.1	176.9	-	167.2	170.3	169.9	171.5	172.2	173.0
Size D - Nonmetropolitan (less than 50,0000	M	12/77	-	171.3	172.5	172.9	174.0	174.6	174.9	-	172.6	173.7	174.1	175.1	175.7	176.2
South urban	M	12/77	-	176.3	178.7	179.5	180.2	180.9	181.4	-	175.2	177.5	178.3	179.0	179.7	180.3
Size A - More than 1,200,000	M	12/77	-	176.8	178.6	179.4	180.4	181.5	182.0	-	176.1	177.8	178.7	179.6	180.7	181.4

Size B - 450,000 to 1,200,000	M	12/77	-	178.5	180.8	181.7	182.3	183.0	183.2	-	174.6	176.5	177.4	178.1	178.7	179.1
Size C - 50,000 to 450,000	M	12/77	-	174.5	177.5	178.5	178.8	179.2	179.8	-	175.2	177.9	179.0	179.3	179.8	180.4
Size D - Nonmetropolitan (less than 50,000)	M	12/77	-	173.9	177.4	177.3	177.8	178.0	178.9	-	174.6	177.9	177.9	178.4	178.6	179.5
West urban	M	12/77	-	178.7	180.6	182.0	182.7	183.8	184.4	-	176.3	177.9	179.3	180.1	181.1	181.7
Size A - More than 1,250,000	M	12/77	-	181.8	183.6	185.3	186.1	187.2	188.1	-	177.1	178.4	180.2	181.0	182.1	182.9
Size B - 330,000 to 1,250,000	M	12/77	-	178.3	179.9	180.6	181.4	182.7	183.2	-	178.7	180.0	180.8	181.5	182.8	183.5
Size C - 50,000 to 330,000	M	12/77	-	171.6	173.8	174.8	175.2	175.8	175.2	-	169.9	171.9	172.7	173.3	173.8	173.2
Size classes:																
A	M	12/77	-	-	100.6	101.1	101.6	102.2	102.5	321.4	323.0	327.7	329.0	330.5	332.3	333.4
B	M	12/77	-	177.0	179.6	180.1	181.0	182.1	182.4	-	174.1	176.5	177.0	177.8	178.9	179.3
C	M	12/77	-	174.7	177.7	178.2	179.1	179.6	180.0	-	174.6	177.5	178.0	178.9	179.4	179.8
D	M	12/77	-	173.4	176.1	176.4	176.9	177.4	178.2	-	174.2	176.7	177.1	177.6	178.1	178.9
Selected local areas																
Chicago, IL-Northwestern IN	M	-	324.2	330.4	334.3	334.2	335.5	337.1	338.4	309.6	315.6	319.1	319.0	320.1	321.6	322.7
Los Angeles-Long Beach, Anaheim, CA	M	-	329.4	331.3	335.1	338.8	341.4	342.8	345.1	322.7	324.5	327.4	331.2	333.4	334.8	337.1
New York, NY-Northeastern NJ	M	-	320.6	322.8	331.6	333.2	334.7	337.0	339.0	312.3	314.4	322.3	324.0	325.7	328.2	330.2
Philadelphia, PA-NJ	M	-	318.9	321.7	327.7	329.0	329.4	333.8	336.2	320.8	323.5	329.1	329.9	330.4	334.9	337.5
San Francisco-Oakland, CA	M	-	-	344.0	345.8	348.8	349.6	353.0	353.5	-	338.1	339.0	342.2	343.4	346.9	347.0

(continued)

CONSUMER PRICE INDEX—U.S. CITY AVERAGE AND AVAILABLE LOCAL AREA DATA: ALL ITEMS *(concluded)*

(1967=100, unless otherwise indicated)

Area[1]	Pricing schedule[2]	Other index base	All Urban Consumers							Urban Wage Earners						
			1986		1987					1986		1987				
			May	June	Jan.	Feb.	Mar.	Apr.	May	May	June	Jan.	Feb.	Mar.	Apr.	May
Baltimore, MD	1	-	329.1	-	334.1	-	335.9	-	340.1	326.8	-	331.1	-	333.2	-	337.4
Boston, MA	1	-	322.6	-	333.2	-	336.8	-	335.1	319.3	-	330.9	-	334.7	-	332.9
Cleveland, OH	1	-	-	350.6	352.9	-	356.8	-	357.5	-	328.2	330.1	-	333.3	-	334.2
Miami, FL	1	11/77	173.0	-	177.2	-	178.4	-	179.1	173.4	-	177.6	-	178.6	-	179.2
St. Louis, MO-IL	1	-	318.6	-	326.7	-	328.8	-	330.5	314.2	-	321.9	-	324.3	-	326.3
Washington, DC-MD-VA	1	-	329.6	-	335.7	-	338.0	-	340.5	330.2	-	337.7	-	340.1	-	343.2
Dallas-Ft. Worth, TX	2	-	-	344.7	-	347.8	-	351.8	-	-	337.4	-	341.1	-	344.4	-
Detroit, MI	2	-	321.7	321.0	-	327.6	-	330.5	-	311.0	310.2	-	316.5	-	319.9	-
Houston, TX	2	-	-	333.3	-	334.9	-	341.1	-	-	330.9	-	333.0	-	338.5	-
Pittsburgh, PA	2	-	-	328.6	-	335.2	-	338.2	-	-	308.3	-	314.2	-	316.6	-

[1] Area is the Consolidated Metropolitan Statistical Area (CMSA), exclusive of farms and military. Area definitions are those established by the Office of Management and Budget in 1983, except for Boston-Lawrence-Salem, MA-NH Area (excludes Monroe County); and Milwaukee, WI Area (includes only the Milwaukee MSA). Definitions do not include revisions made since 1983.

[2] Foods, fuels, and several other items priced every month in all areas; most other goods and services priced as indicated:.

M - Every month.

1 - January, March, May, July, September, and November.

2 - February, April, June, August, October, and December.

[3] Regions are defined as the four Census regions.

- Data not available.

NOTE: Local area CPI indexes are byproducts of the national CPI program. Because each local index is a small subset of the national index, it has a smaller sample size and is, therefore, subject to substantially more sampling and other measurement error than the national index. As a result, local area indexes show greater volatility than the national index, although their long-term trends are quite similar. Therefore, the Bureau of Labor Statistics strongly urges users to consider adopting the national average CPI for use in escalator clauses.

Source: *Monthly Labor Review,* U.S. Department of Labor, Bureau of Labor Statistics.

Federal Budget: Procedure and Timetable

Congressional Budget Timetable

CONGRESSIONAL BUDGET ACT OF 1974: THE NEW BUDGET PROCESS IN TEN STEPS

1. To give Congress an earlier and better start in reviewing and reshaping the budget, the Executive Branch must submit a "current services budget" by November 10th for the new fiscal year that starts the following October 1st. The current services budget should project the spending required to maintain ongoing programs throughout the following fiscal year at existing commitment levels, or at commitment levels specified by existing legislation based on current economic assumptions. The Joint Economic Committee should review and assess the current services budget and report to Congress by December 31st.

2. The President will continue to submit his new budget to Congress in late January or early February. In addition to the traditional budget totals and breakdowns, the budget document must include a list of existing "tax expenditures"—i.e., estimates of revenues lost to the Treasury through preferential tax treatment—as well as any proposed changes in tax expenditures. The budget must also contain estimates of expenditures for programs for which funds are appropriated one year in advance and five-year budget projections of all federal spending under existing programs.

3. Reports of all standing committees to the House and Senate Budget Committees of the spending plans of those committees on all matters under their jurisdiction, including spending under new legislation, are required by March 15th for the upcoming fiscal year.

4. An annual report of the Congressional Budget Office to the Budget Committees on alternative budget levels and national budget priorities is required on or before April 1st.

5. By April 15th, the Budget Committees must report concurrent resolutions to the House and Senate floors, and Congress will have to clear the initial budget resolution by May 15th. This initial budget resolution sets target totals for appropriations, outlays, taxes, the budget surplus or deficit, and the federal debt. Within these overall targets, the resolution will break down appropriations and outlays by the functional categories used in the President's budget document, as well as by classifications used by the appropriations subcommittees for the 13 appropriations bills. The resolution will include any recommended changes in tax revenues and in the level of the federal debt ceiling.

6. Committees report bills or resolutions authorizing new budget authority by May 15th.

7. The basic appropriations process proceeds within the Appropriations Committees, but is subject to targets of the budget resolution.

8. Scorekeeping reports will be issued periodically by the Congressional Budget Office on the status of budget authority, revenue, outlays and debt legislation, comparing the amounts and changes in such legislation with the First Congressional Budget Resolution.

9. Subject to prior authorization, all appropriations bills have to be cleared by the middle of September—no later than the seventh day after Labor Day. By September 15th, after finishing action on all appropriations and other spending bills, Congress must adopt a second, and final, budget resolution that may either affirm or revise the budget targets set by the initial resolution. This resolution must provide for a final budget reconciliation by changing either one or more of the following: (1) appropriations (both for the upcoming fiscal year or carried over from previous fiscal years) and/or entitlements; (2) revenues; and (3) the public debt. The final resolution will direct the committees that have jurisdiction over these matters to report the necessary legislative changes. The Budget Committees will then combine these changes and report them to the floor in the form of a reconciliation bill.

If Congress has withheld all appropriations and entitlement bills from the President until passage of the final reconciliation bill, then this bill becomes the final budget legislation, subject to Presidential signature (or veto). If, on the other hand, each individual appropriations bill has been signed by the President upon passage by the Congress, the final reconciliation bill—upon signature by the President—supersedes all the previously passed individual bills.

10. The new fiscal year begins on October 1st.

FEDERAL BUDGET: PROCEDURE AND TIMETABLE

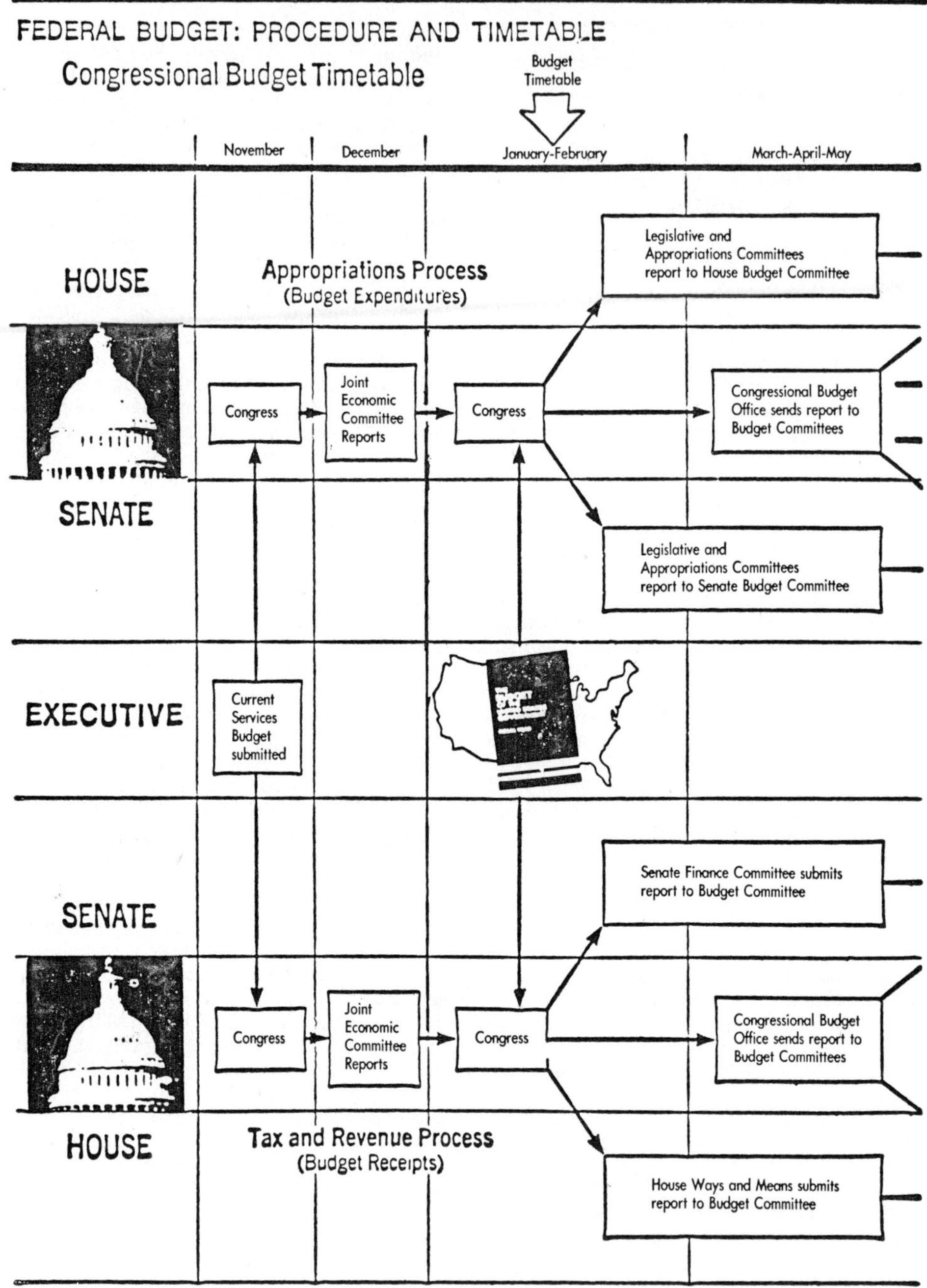

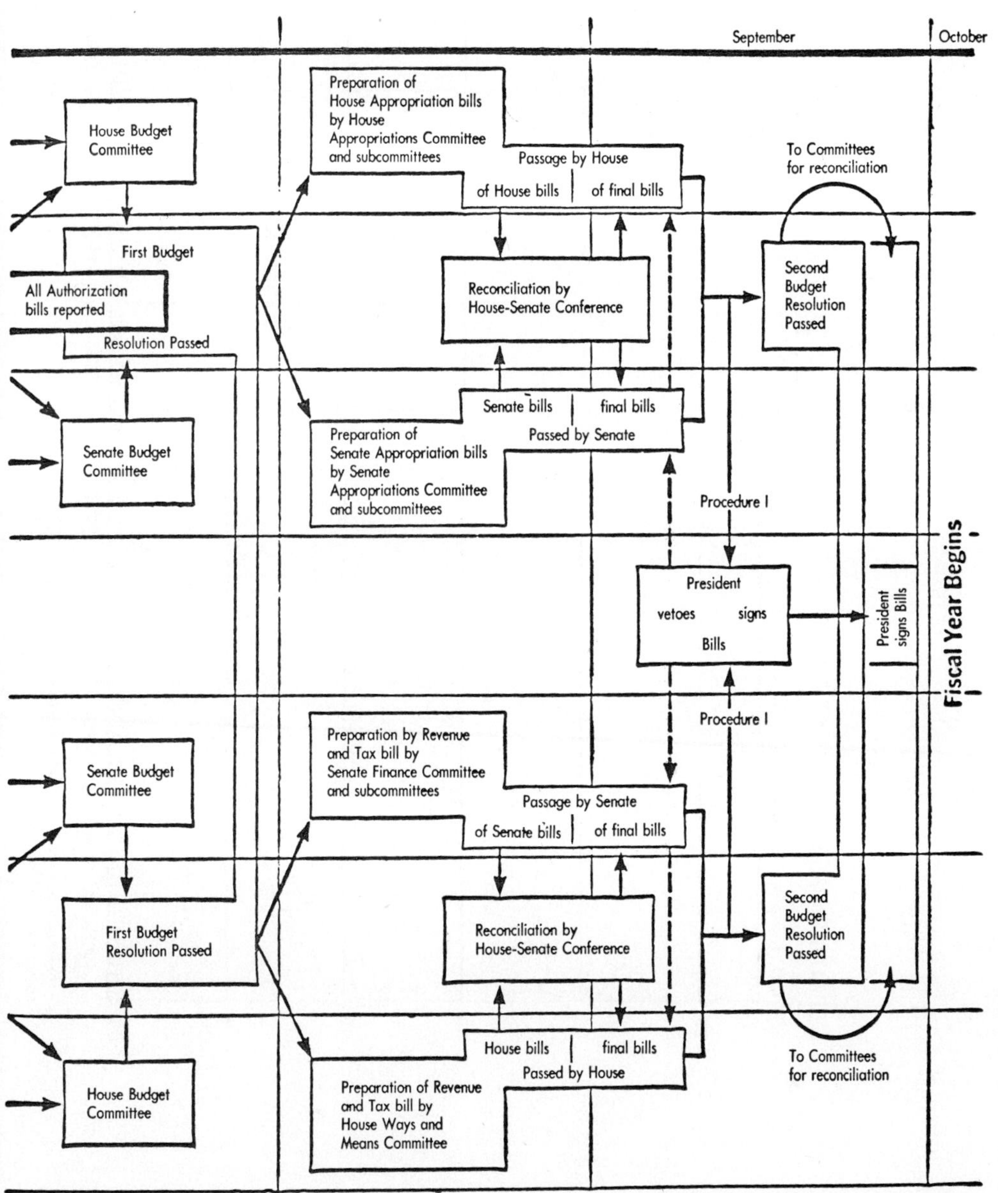

Source: The Conference Board, "The Federal Budget: Its Impact on the Economy," Michael E. Levy, assisted by Delos R. Smith.

SELECTED UNEMPLOYMENT RATES

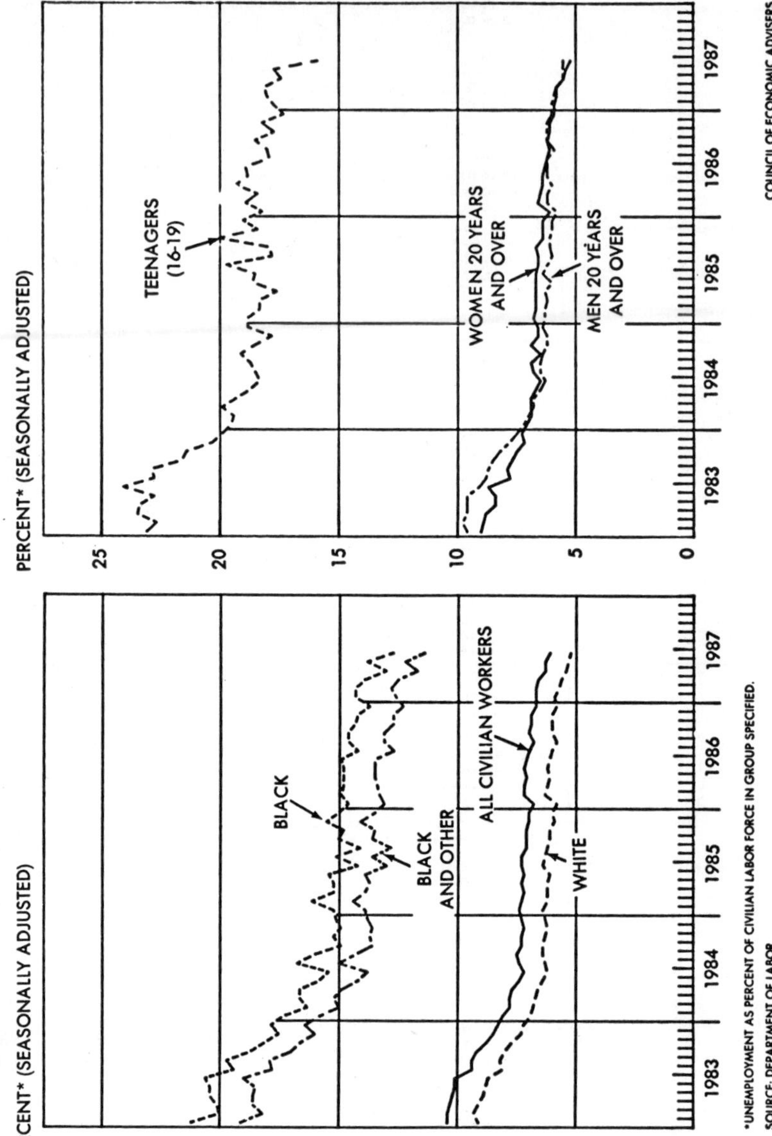

[Monthly data seasonally adjusted]

Period	Unemployment rate, all workers [1]	Unemployment rate (percent of civilian labor force in group)												Labor force time lost (percent) [2]
		All civilian workers	By sex and age			By race			By selected groups					
			Men 20 years and over	Women 20 years and over	Both sexes 16–19 years	White	Black and other	Black	Experienced wage and salary workers	Married men, spouse present	Women who maintain families	Full-time workers	Part-time workers	
1979	5.8	5.8	4.2	5.7	16.1	5.1	11.3	12.3	5.5	2.8	8.3	5.3	8.8	6.3
1980	7.0	7.1	5.9	6.4	17.8	6.3	13.1	14.3	6.9	4.2	9.2	6.9	8.8	7.9
1981	7.5	7.6	6.3	6.8	19.6	6.7	14.2	15.6	7.3	4.3	10.4	7.3	9.4	8.5
1982	9.5	9.7	8.8	8.3	23.2	8.6	17.3	18.9	9.3	6.5	11.7	9.6	10.5	11.0
1983	9.5	9.6	8.9	8.1	22.4	8.4	17.8	19.5	9.2	6.5	12.2	9.5	10.4	10.9
1984	7.4	7.5	6.6	6.8	18.9	6.5	14.4	15.9	7.1	4.6	10.3	7.2	9.3	8.6
1985	7.1	7.2	6.2	6.6	18.6	6.2	13.7	15.1	6.8	4.3	10.4	6.8	9.3	8.1
1986	6.9	7.0	6.1	6.2	18.3	6.0	13.1	14.5	6.6	4.4	9.8	6.6	9.1	7.9
1986: June	7.0	7.1	6.2	6.3	18.9	6.1	13.5	14.9	6.6	4.5	10.0	6.7	9.1	8.1
July	6.9	7.0	6.2	6.2	17.9	6.0	12.7	14.2	6.6	4.4	9.5	6.6	9.2	7.8
Aug	6.7	6.8	5.9	6.1	18.0	5.8	13.1	14.6	6.5	4.2	10.1	6.4	9.3	7.7
Sept	6.9	7.0	6.2	6.2	18.5	6.0	13.1	14.6	6.5	4.3	9.8	6.6	9.3	7.9
Oct	6.8	6.9	6.2	6.1	17.7	6.0	12.7	14.3	6.6	4.6	8.9	6.6	9.2	7.8
Nov	6.8	6.9	6.2	6.1	18.2	6.0	12.7	14.2	6.5	4.5	9.7	6.6	9.1	7.7
Dec	6.6	6.7	6.0	5.9	17.3	5.8	12.3	13.7	6.3	4.3	9.8	6.3	8.8	7.6
1987: Jan	6.6	6.7	6.0	5.9	17.7	5.9	12.6	14.3	6.3	4.2	9.8	6.4	9.0	7.6
Feb	6.6	6.7	5.9	5.8	18.0	5.7	12.8	14.3	6.2	4.2	9.5	6.3	8.7	7.6
Mar	6.5	6.6	5.8	5.8	18.1	5.6	12.5	13.9	6.1	4.1	9.7	6.2	9.2	7.4
Apr	6.2	6.3	5.5	5.5	17.4	5.4	11.7	13.0	5.9	4.1	9.3	5.9	8.6	7.3
May	6.2	6.3	5.5	5.4	17.7	5.3	12.2	13.8	5.9	3.9	9.6	5.9	8.7	7.2
June	6.0	6.1	5.5	5.2	15.9	5.2	11.4	12.7	5.8	4.0	9.7	5.9	6.9	7.1

[1] Unemployed as percent of total labor force including resident Armed Forces.
[2] Aggregate hours lost by the unemployed and persons on part time for economic reasons as percent of potentially available labor force hours.

Source: Department of Labor, Bureau of Labor Statistics.

Source: *Economic Indicators*, Council of Economic Advisers.

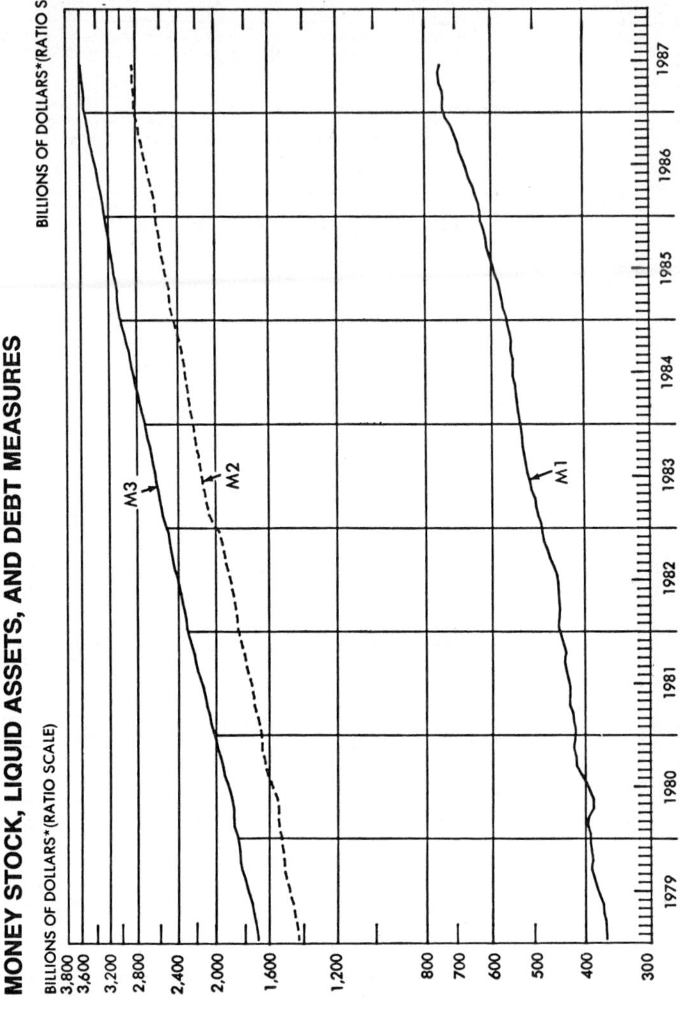

* AVERAGES OF DAILY FIGURES; SEASONALLY ADJUSTED
SOURCE: BOARD OF GOVERNORS OF THE FEDERAL RESERVE SYSTEM

COUNCIL OF ECONOMIC ADVISERS

[Averages of daily figures, except as noted; billions of dollars, seasonally adjusted]

Period	M1	M2	M3	L	Debt	Percent change from year or 6 months earlier [2]			
	Sum of currency, demand deposits, travelers' checks, and other checkable deposits (OCDs)	M1 plus overnight RPs and Eurodollars, MMMF balances (general purpose and broker/dealer), MMDAs, and savings and small time deposits	M2 plus large time deposits, term RPs, term Eurodollars, and institution-only MMMF balances	M3 plus other liquid assets	Debt of domestic nonfinancial sectors (monthly average) [1]	M1	M2	M3	Debt
1980: Dec	416.6	1,633.1	1,990.9	2,327.6	3,895.1	6.5	8.9	10.2	9.7
1981: Dec	443.2	1,795.5	2,236.4	2,598.9	4,275.5	6.4	9.9	12.3	9.8
1982: Dec	481.3	1,953.8	2,443.1	2,853.0	4,658.0	8.6	8.8	9.2	8.9
1983: Dec	526.9	2,184.6	2,692.8	3,154.6	5,206.3	9.5	11.8	10.2	11.8
1984: Dec	557.5	2,369.1	2,985.7	3,529.3	5,946.0	5.8	8.4	10.9	14.2
1985: Dec	627.0	2,569.6	3,205.6	3,838.6	6,774.9	12.5	8.5	7.4	13.9
1986: Dec r	730.5	2,800.1	3,489.1	4,141.1	7,630.4	16.5	9.0	8.8	12.6
1986: June	667.5	2,667.5	3,338.1	3,972.4	r 7,168.3	13.3	7.8	8.4	r 12.0
July	676.6	2,693.8	3,368.3	3,998.8	r 7,234.4	15.7	9.5	9.0	r 10.7
Aug	687.0	2,718.4	3,396.8	4,027.7	r 7,318.7	18.1	10.8	9.7	r 11.9
Sept	693.1	2,736.3	3,422.0	4,057.0	r 7,400.8	17.1	10.9	9.9	12.9
Oct	701.4	2,760.7	3,442.2	4,082.7	r 7,457.2	17.1	10.7	9.3	r 12.7
Nov r	712.4	2,775.4	3,460.1	4,108.5	7,530.5	16.7	9.9	9.0	12.6
Dec r	730.5	2,800.1	3,489.1	4,141.1	7,630.4	19.8	10.2	9.3	13.3
1987: Jan r	737.7	2,822.2	3,514.7	4,174.1	7,695.3	18.9	9.8	8.9	13.1
Feb r	737.4	2,821.5	3,518.4	4,182.6	7,728.6	15.2	7.7	7.3	11.5
Mar r	739.5	2,824.7	3,523.1	4,172.4	7,781.7	13.8	6.6	6.0	10.6
Apr r	750.3	2,839.1	3,540.0	4,187.0	7,844.6	14.4	5.8	5.8	10.7
May r	753.1	2,840.1	3,554.2	4,219.1	7,911.3	11.8	4.7	5.5	10.4
June p	746.7	2,843.2	3,570.1	....	....	4.5	3.1	4.7	....

[1] Consists of outstanding credit market debt of the U.S. Government, State and local governments, and private nonfinancial sectors; data from flow of funds accounts.

[2] Annual changes are from December to December and monthly changes are from 6 months earlier at a seasonally adjusted annual rate.

Source: Board of Governors of the Federal Reserve System.

Source: *Economic Indicators*, Council of Economic Advisers.

Bank Failures and Corporate Bankruptcies

NUMBER AND DEPOSITS OF BANKS CLOSED BECAUSE OF FINANCIAL DIFFICULTIES, 1934–1986

Year	Number					Deposits (in thousands of dollars)					Assets[4]
			Insured					Insured			
	Total	Non-Insured[1]	Total	Without disbursements by FDIC[2]	With disbursements by FDIC[3]	Total	Non-Insured[1]	Total	Without disbursements by FDIC[2]	With disbursements by FDIC[3]	(in Thousands Dollars)
Total	**1,149**	**136**	**1,013**	**8**	**1,005**	**42,998,525**	**143,501**	**42,855,024**	**41,147**	**42,813,877**	**51,999,628**
1934	61	52	9	...	9	37,333	35,365	1,968	...	1,968	2,661
1935	32	6	26	1	25	13,988	583	13,405	85	13,320	17,242
1936	72	3	69	...	69	28,100	592	27,508	...	27,508	31,941
1937	84	7	77	2	75	34,205	528	33,677	328	33,349	40,370
1938	81	7	74	...	74	60,722	1,038	59,684	...	59,684	69,513
1939	72	12	60	...	60	160,211	2,439	157,722	...	157,772	181,514
1940	48	5	43	...	43	142,788	358	142,430	...	142,430	161,898
1941	17	2	15	...	15	29,796	79	29,717	...	29,717	34,804
1942	23	3	20	...	20	19,540	355	19,185	...	19,185	22,254
1943	5	...	5	...	5	12,525	...	12,525	...	12,525	14,058
1944	2	...	2	...	2	1,915	...	1,915	...	1,915	2,098
1945	1	...	1	...	1	5,695	...	5,695	...	5,695	6,392
1946	2	1	1	...	1	494	147	347	...	347	351
1947	6	1	5	...	5	7,207	167	7,040	...	7,040	6,798
1948	3	...	3	...	3	10,674	...	10,674	...	10,674	10,360
1949	9	4	5	1	4	9,217	2,552	6,665	1,190	5,475	4,886
1950	5	1	4	...	4	5,555	42	5,513	...	5,513	4,005
1951	5	3	2	...	2	6,464	3,056	3,408	...	3,408	3,050
1952	4	1	3	...	3	3,313	143	3,170	...	3,170	2,388
1953	5	1	4	2	2	45,101	390	44,711	26,449	18,262	18,811
1954	4	2	2	...	2	2,948	1,950	998	...	998	1,138
1955	5	...	5	...	5	11,953	...	11,953	...	11,953	11,985
1956	3	1	2	...	2	11,690	360	11,330	...	11,330	12,914
1957	3	1	2	1	1	12,502	1,255	11,247	10,084	1,163	1,253
1958	9	5	4	...	4	10,413	2,173	8,240	...	8,240	8,905
1959	3	...	3	...	3	2,593	...	2,593	...	2,593	2,858
1960	2	1	1	...	1	7,965	1,035	6,930	...	6,930	7,506

1961	9	4	5	...	5	10,611	1,675	8,936	...	8,936	9,820
1962	3	2	1	1	...	4,231	1,220	3,011	3,011	...	...[5]
1963	2	...	2	...	2	23,444	...	23,444	...	23,444	26,179
1964	8	1	7	...	7	23,867	429	23,438	...	23,438	25,849
1965	9	4	5	...	5	45,256	1,395	43,861	...	43,861	58,750
1966	8	1	7	...	7	106,171	2,648	103,523	...	103,523	120,647
1967	4	...	4	...	4	10,878	...	10,878	...	10,878	11,993
1968	3	...	3	...	3	22,524	...	22,524	...	22,524	25,154
1969	9	...	9	...	9	40,134	...	40,134	...	40,134	43,572
1970	8	1	7	...	7	55,229	423	54,806	...	54,806	62,147
1971	6	...	6	...	6	132,058	...	132,058	...	132,058	196,520
1972	3	2	1	...	1	99,784	79,304	20,480	...	20,480	22,054
1973	6	...	6	...	6	971,296	...	971,296	...	971,296	1,309,675
1974	4	...	4	...	4	1,575,832	...	1,575,832	...	1,575,832	3,822,596
1975	14	1	13	...	13	340,574	1,000	339,574	...	339,574	419,950
1976	17	1	16	...	16	865,659	800	864,859	...	864,859	1,039,293
1977	6	...	6	...	6	205,208	...	205,208	...	205,208	232,612
1978	7	...	7	...	7	854,154	...	854,154	...	854,154	994,035
1979	10	...	10	...	10	110,696	...	110,696	...	110,696	132,988
1980	10	...	10	...	10	216,300	...	216,300	...	216,300	236,164
1981	10	...	10	...	10	3,826,022	...	3,826,022	...	3,826,022	4,859,060
1982	42	...	42	...	42	9,908,379	...	9,908,379	...	9,908,379	11,632,415
1983	48	...	48	...	48	5,441,608	...	5,441,608	...	5,441,608	7,026,923
1984	79	...	79	...	79	2,883,162	...	2,883,162	...	2,883,162	3,276,411
1985[6]	120	...	120	...	120	8,059,441	...	8,059,441	...	8,059,441	8,741,268
1986[7]	138	...	138	...	138	6,471,100	...	6,471,100	...	6,471,100	6,991,600

[1]For information regarding each of these banks, see table 22 in the 1963 *Annual Report* (1963 and prior years), and explanatory notes to tables regarding banks closed because of financial difficulties in subsequent annual reports. One noninsured bank placed in receivership in 1934, with no deposits at time of closing, is omitted (see table 22 note 9). Deposits are unavailable for seven banks.

[2]For information regarding these cases, see table 23 of the *Annual Report* for 1963.

[3]For information regarding each bank, see the *Annual Report* for 1958, pp. 48-83 and pp. 98-127, and tables regarding deposit insurance disbursements in subsequent annual reports. Deposits are adjusted as of December 31, 1982.

[4]Insured banks only.

[5]Not available.

[6]Includes data for one bank granted financial assistance although no disbursement was required until January, 1986.

[7]Excludes data for banks granted financial assistance under Section 13(c)(1) of the Federal Deposit Insurance Act to prevent failure. Data for these banks are included in table 123.

Source: Federal Deposit Insurance Corporation *1986 Annual Report*

Corporate Reorganizations

REORGANIZATION PROCEEDINGS UNDER CHAPTER 11 OF THE BANKRUPTCY CODE IN WHICH COMMISSION ENTERED APPEARANCE

Debtor	District	Fiscal Year Filed	Fiscal Year Closed
A.H. Robins Co., Inc.	E.D. VA	1985	
AIA Industries, Inc.	E.D. PA	1984	
AIC Photo[4]	E.D. NY	1985	1986
Air Florida System, Inc.	S.D. FL	1984	
Air One, Inc.	E.D. MO	1985	
Airlift International, Inc.	S.D. FL	1981	
Altec Corp.	C.D. CA	1985	
Amarex, Inc.	W.D. OK	1983	
American Monitor Corp.	S.D. IN	1986	
Amfesco Ind., Inc.	E.D. NY	1986	
Amfood Ind.	N.D. IL	1986	
Anglo Energy, Ltd.[2]	S.D. NY	1984	1986
ATI, Inc.	D. NJ	1985	
Avanti Corp.[1,4]	N.D. IN	1986	1986
Baldwin United Corp.[2]	S.D. OH	1984	1986
Bear Lake West, Inc.[1]	D. ID	1982	1986
Beehive International[2]	D. UT	1985	1986
Beker Industries Corp.	S.D. NY	1986	
Berry Industries Corp.	C.D. CA	1985	
Bevill, Bressler & Schulman[1]	D. NJ	1985	
The Bishop's Glen Fndn., Inc.[1]	N.D. FL	1985	
Branch Industries, Inc.	S.D. NY	1985	
Buttes Gas & Oil Co.	S.D. TX	1986	
Capitol Air, Inc.	S.D. NY	1985	
Chalet Gourmet Corp.	C.D. CA	1985	
Charter Co.	M.D. FL	1984	
Chem-Technics, Inc.[3]	N.D. GA	1986	1986
Citel, Inc.	N.D. CA	1985	
Citywide Securities Corp.[1]	S.D. NY	1985	
CLC of America	E.D. MO	1986	
CoElco Ltd.	C.D. CA	1986	
Colonial X-Ray Corp.	S.D. FL	1986	
Columbia Data Products, Inc.	D. MD	1985	
Commodore Corporation	N.D. IN	1985	
Commonwealth Oil Refining Co., Inc.	W.D. TX	1984	
Computer Devices, Inc.[3]	D. MA	1984	1986
Computer Depot, Inc.	D. MN	1986	
Computer Usage Co.[2]	N.D. CA	1985	1986
Conesco Ind., Ltd.	D. NJ	1986	
Consolidated Packaging Corp.[2]	D. CO	1984	1986
Continental Airlines Corp.[2]	S.D. TX	1984	1986
Continental Steel Corp.[3]	S.D. IN	1986	
Cook United, Inc.	N.D. OH	1985	
Crompton Co., Inc.	S.D. NY	1985	
Dakota Minerals, Inc.	D. WY	1986	
The Diet Institute, Inc.[3]	D. NJ	1985	1986
D'Lites of America, Inc.	N.D. GA	1986	
Dreco Energy Service, Ltd.[2]	S.D. TX	1982	1986
DRW Realty Services, Inc.[1,2]	N.D. TX	1986	1986
Eastmet Corp.	D. MD	1986	
Emons Industries, Inc.	S.D. N.Y.	1984	
Empire Oil & Gas Co.[3]	D. CO	1982	1986
Energy Exchange Corp.	W.D. OK	1985	
Energy Management Corp.	D. CO	1986	
Enertec Corp.	N.D. TX	1986	
Enterprise Technologies, Inc.	S.D. TX	1984	

REORGANIZATION PROCEEDINGS UNDER CHAPTER 11 *(continued)*

Debtor	District	Fiscal Year Filed	Fiscal Year Closed
Equestrian Ctrs. of America, Inc.	C.D. CA	1985	
Evans Products Co.	S.D. FL	1985	
Fidelity American Financial Corp.[1]	E.D. PA	1981	
Financial & Bus. Serv., Inc.[1]	W.D. NC	1986	
Flanigan Enterprises	S.D. FL	1986	
General Exploration Co.	N.D. OH	1986	
General Resources Corp.	N.D. GA	1980	
GIC Government Securities, Inc.[1, 3]	M.D. FL	1986	
Global Marine, Inc.	S.D. TX	1986	
Haven Properties, Inc.[1]	D. OR	1981	1986
Homecrafters Warehouse, Inc.	N.D. AL	1986	
ICX, Inc.	D. CO	1984	
International Institute of Applied Tech., Inc.	D. DC	1983	
International Waste Water[1]	M.D. PA	1985	
K-Tel International, Inc.[2]	D. MN	1985	1986
Kelly-Johnston Enterprises, Inc.[2]	W.D. OK	1985	1986
Koss Corp.[2]	D. WI	1985	1986
LTV Corporation	S.D. NY	1986	
Magic Circle Energy Corp.	W.D. OK	1985	
Manoa Finance Co., Inc.[1]	D. HA	1983	
Mansfield Tire & Rubber Co.[2]	N.D. OH	1980	1986
Manville Corp.	S.D. NY	1982	
Marion Corp.[2]	S.D. AL	1983	1986
Microcomputer Memories, Inc.	C.D. CA	1986	
Mid-America Petroleum, Inc.	N.D. TX	1986	
Midland Capital Corp.	S.D. NY	1986	
Midwestern Companies, Inc.[3]	W.D. MO	1984	1986
Mobile Home Industries, Inc.[2]	N.D. FL	1985	1986
National Bus. Communications Corp.	S.D. FL	1986	
ND Resource, Inc.	D. AZ	1985	
New Brothers, Inc.	S.D. GA	1985	
Nicklos Oil & Gas Co.	S.D. TX	1986	
North Atlantic Airlines, Inc.[1, 3]	D. VT	1984	1986
Nucorp Energy, Inc.	S.D. CA	1982	
Oxoco, Inc.	S.D. TX	1986	
Pacific Express Holding, Inc.	E.D. CA	1984	
Paiute Oil & Mining Corp.	D. UT	1985	
Penn Pacific Corp.	C.D. CA	1986	
Peoples Restaurants, Inc.[2]	M.D. FL	1985	1986
Petromac Energy, Inc.[4]	S.D. TX	1986	1986
Pettibone Corp.	N.D. IL	1986	
Provincetown-Boston Airline[2]	M.D. FL	1985	1986
Psych Systems	D. MD	1986	
Roblin Industries, Inc.	W.D. NY	1985	
Ronco Teleproducts, Inc.	N.D. IL	1984	
Rusco Industries, Inc.	S.D. GA	1986	
Salant Corp.	S.D. NY	1985	
Satelco, Inc.[2]	N.D. TX	1985	1986
Seatrain Lines, Inc.	S.D. NY	1981	
Selectors, Inc.	E.D. WA	1986	
Seneca Oil Co.[2]	W.D. OK	1985	1986
Servamatic Systems, Inc.	N.D. CA	1986	
SPW Corporation	N.D. TX	1985	
Standard Metals Corp.	D. CO	1984	
State Capital Corp.	M.D. FL	1985	
Steiger Tractor, Inc.	D. ND	1986	

REORGANIZATION PROCEEDINGS UNDER CHAPTER 11 *(concluded)*

Debtor	District	Fiscal Year Filed	Fiscal Year Closed
Storage Technology, Inc.	D. CO	1985	
Swanton Corp.	S.D. NY	1985	
Sykes Datatronics, Inc.	W.D. NY	1986	
Taco Eds, Inc.[1]	N.D. OH	1984	
Tacoma Boatbuilding Co.	S.D. NY	1986	
Technical Equities Corp.	N.D. CA	1986	
Texscan Corp.	D. AZ	1986	
Tidwell Industries, Inc.	N.D. AL	1986	
Towle Manufacturing Co.	S.D. NY	1986	
Towner Petro.[2]	W.D. OK	1985	1986
Trans Western Exploration	N.D. OK	1985	
Transcontinental Energy Corp.[2]	N.D. TX	1985	1986
Unimet Corp.	N.D. OH	1986	
The Veta Grande Cos., Inc.	C.D. CA	1986	
Victoria Station	N.D. CA	1986	
Videostation, Inc.	C.D. CA	1985	
W & J Sloane Corp.	S.D. NY	1986	
Wheatland Investment Co.[1]	E.D. WA	1985	
Wheeling-Pittsburgh Steel Corp.	W.D. PA	1985	
Windsor Ind., Inc.	N.D. IL	1986	
Wright Air Lines, Inc.[3]	N.D. OH	1985	1986
Xenerex Corp.	W.D. OK	1986	
Total Cases Opened (FY 1986)		52	
Total Cases Closed (FY 1986)			33

[1]Debtor's securities not registered under Section 12(g) of the Exchange Act.
[2]Plan of reorganization confirmed.
[3]Debtor liquidated under Chapter 7.
[4]Chapter 11 case dismissed.

Source: U.S. Securities and Exchange Commission *Fifty Second Annual Report 1986.*

Government Budget, Receipts, and Deficits: Historical Data

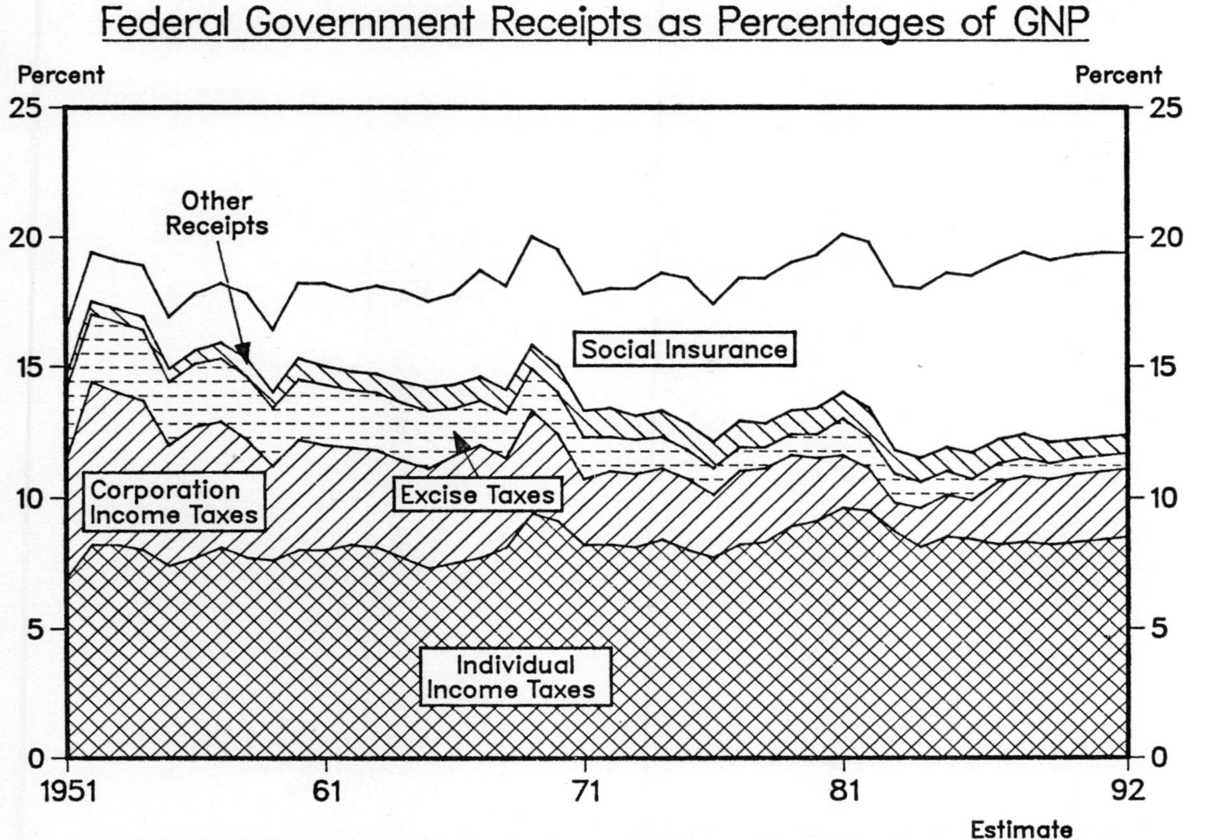

Source: *Historical Tables*, Budget of the United States Government, Fiscal 1988, Executive Office of the President, Office of Management and Budget.

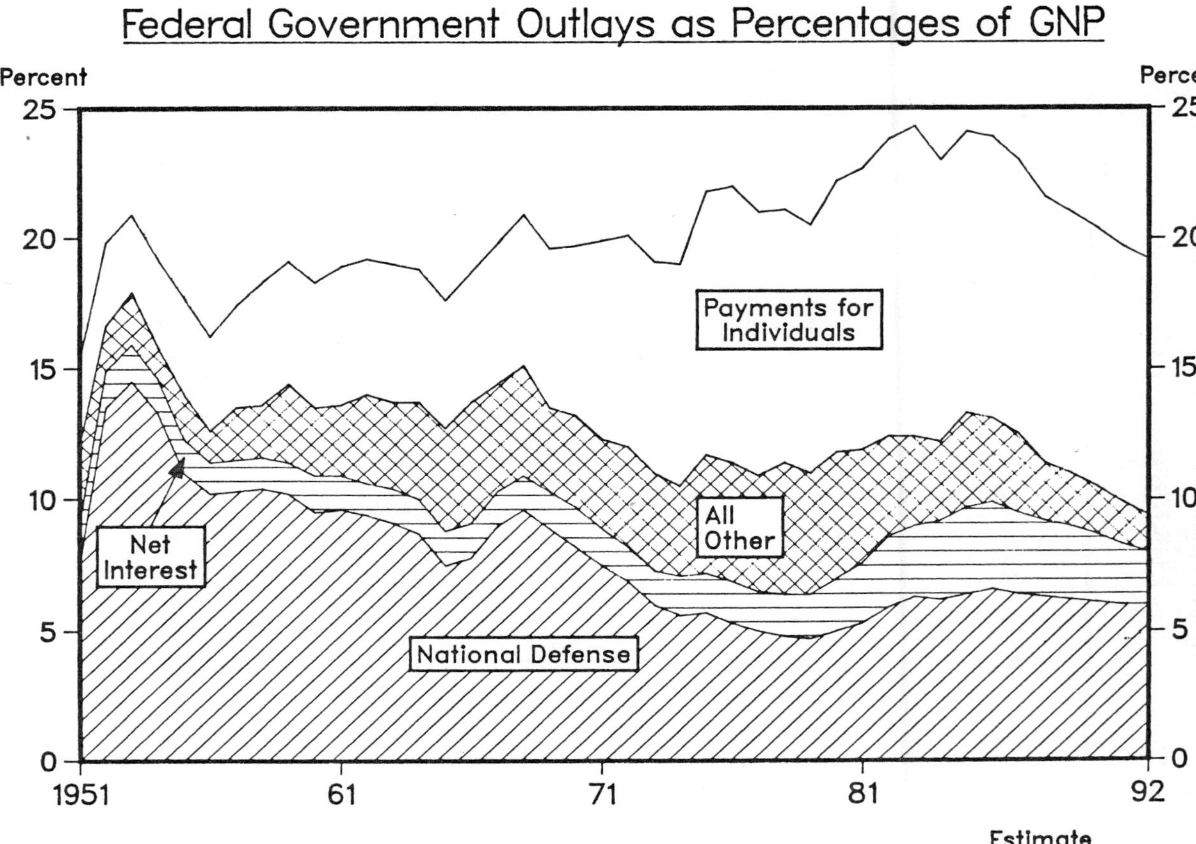

Source: *Historical Tables*, Budget of the United States Government, Fiscal 1988, Executive Office of the President, Office of Management and Budget.

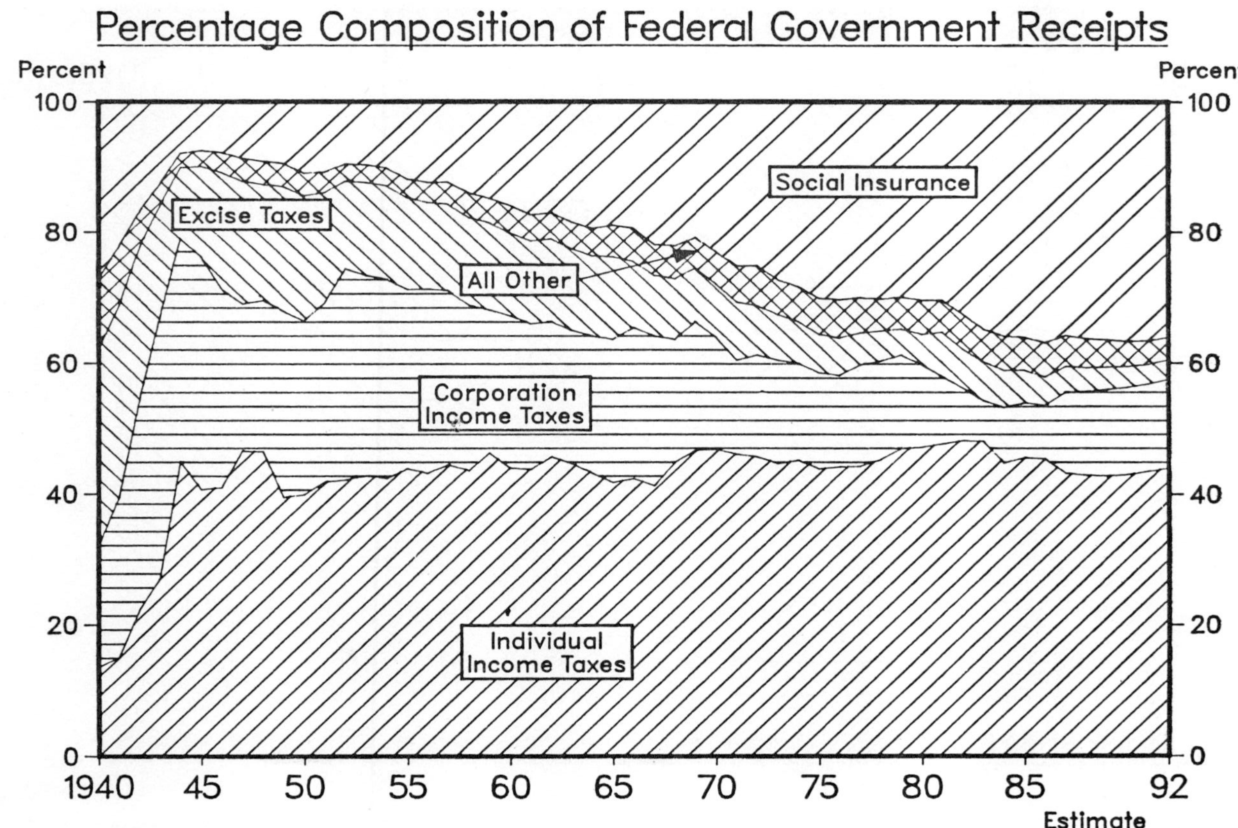

Source: *Historical Tables*, Budget of the United States Government, Fiscal 1988, Executive Office of the President, Office of Management and Budget.

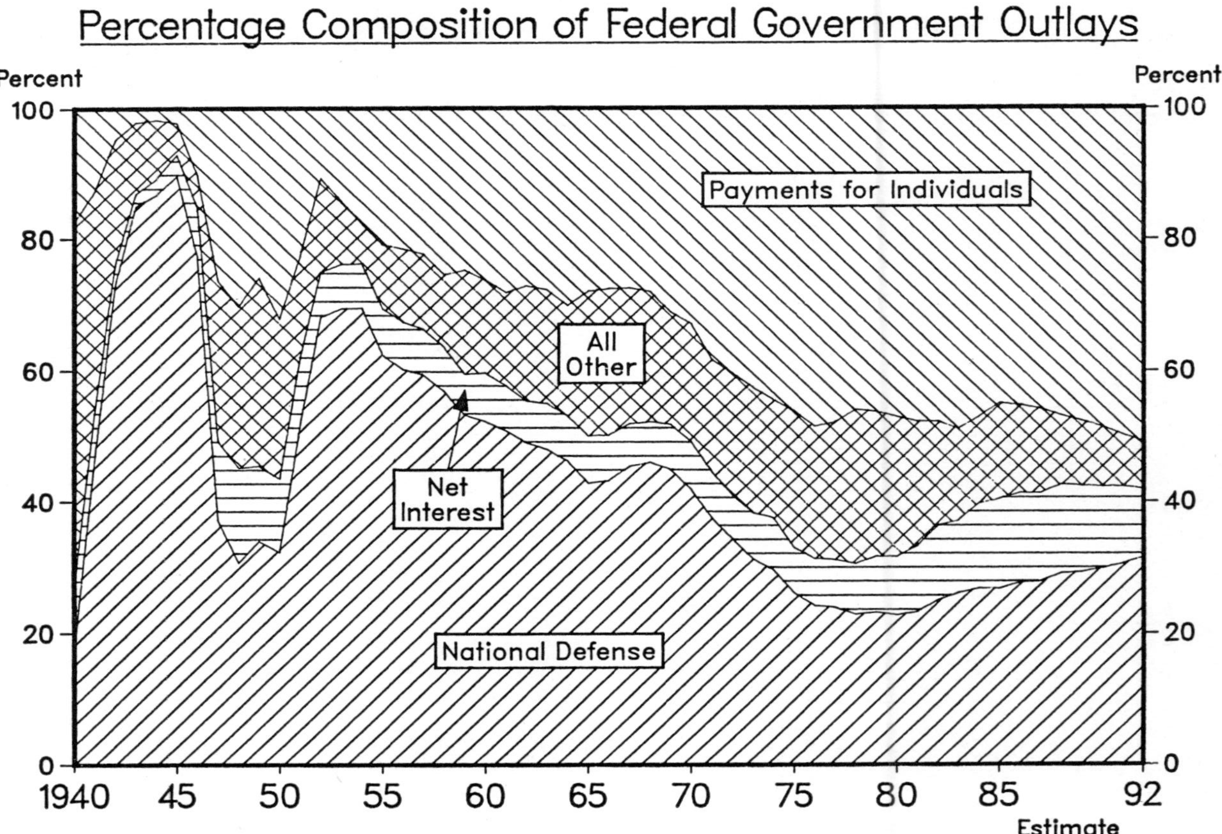

Source: *Historical Tables,* Budget of the United States Government, Fiscal 1988, Executive Office of the President, Office of Management and Budget.

TOTAL GOVERNMENT EXPENDITURES AS PERCENTAGES OF GNP: 1947-1986
(percent)

	Federal outlays			Addendum:	State and Local Government	
	On-budget	Off-Budget	Total Federal	Federal Grants-in-Aid, NIPA Basis	Expenditures From Own Sources Net of Nontax Receipts (NIPA Basis)	Total Government Expenditures
1947	15.3%	0.1%	15.4%	(0.7)%	4.6%	20.1%
1948	11.9	0.1	12.0	(0.7)	5.3	17.3
1949	14.6	0.2	14.7	(0.8)	5.8	20.6
1950	15.8	0.2	16.0	(0.9)	6.7	22.7
1951	14.0	0.4	14.4	(0.8)	6.1	20.5
1952	19.3	0.5	19.8	(0.7)	6.0	25.8
1953	20.2	0.6	20.8	(0.8)	5.9	26.8
1954	18.4	0.8	19.2	(0.8)	6.4	25.6
1955	16.7	1.0	17.7	(0.8)	6.9	24.6
1956	15.7	1.2	16.9	(0.8)	6.9	23.8
1957	16.0	1.4	17.4	(0.8)	7.1	24.5
1958	16.6	1.7	18.3	(1.0)	7.6	25.9
1959	17.3	1.9	19.1	(1.3)	7.7	26.8
1960	16.1	2.1	18.2	(1.4)	7.6	25.8
1961	16.6	2.3	18.9	(1.3)	8.1	27.0
1962	16.7	2.4	19.2	(1.4)	8.1	27.2
1963	16.4	2.5	18.9	(1.4)	8.2	27.1
1964	16.3	2.5	18.8	(1.6)	8.2	27.1
1965	15.1	2.5	17.6	(1.6)	8.3	25.9
1966	15.5	2.7	18.2	(1.7)	8.4	26.6
1967	17.2	2.6	19.8	(1.9)	8.6	28.4
1968	18.3	2.6	21.0	(2.1)	8.9	29.9
1969	17.0	2.7	19.8	(2.1)	9.2	29.0
1970	17.0	2.8	19.8	(2.3)	9.4	29.2
1971	16.8	3.1	19.9	(2.5)	10.0	29.9
1972	16.8	3.2	20.0	(2.8)	9.8	29.8
1973	15.6	3.6	19.2	(3.2)	9.3	28.4
1974	15.3	3.7	19.0	(2.9)	9.5	28.5
1975	17.9	4.0	21.8	(3.2)	10.0	31.8
1976	17.8	4.1	21.9	(3.4)	9.9	31.8
TQ	17.1	4.3	21.4	(3.4)	9.9	31.3
1977	17.0	4.2	21.2	(3.4)	9.1	30.3
1978	17.0	4.1	21.1	(3.4)	8.8	29.9
1979	16.5	4.1	20.6	(3.2)	8.5	29.1
1980	17.8	4.3	22.1	(3.2)	8.6	30.7
1981	18.2	4.5	22.7	(3.0)	8.3	31.0
1982	18.9	4.8	23.8	(2.7)	8.6	32.4
1983	19.9	4.4	24.3	(2.6)	8.6	33.0
1984	18.6	4.5	23.1	(2.5)	8.3	31.4
1985	19.5	4.5	24.0	(2.5)	8.5	32.5
1986	19.4	4.4	23.8	(2.6)	8.6	32.3

* 0.05 percent or less.

See page 219 for explanatory notes

TOTAL GOVERNMENT EXPENDITURES BY MAJOR CATEGORY OF EXPENDITURE AS PERCENTAGES OF GNP: 1947-1988
(in billions of dollars)

	Defense and International	Net Interest	Social Security and Medicare	Other Federal Payments for Individuals	Other Federal	State and Local From Own Sources (Except Net Interest)	Total Government
1947	8.3%	1.9%	0.2%	3.9%	1.2%	4.6%	20.1%
1948	5.5	1.8	0.2	3.4	1.1	5.3	17.3
1949	7.3	1.7	0.2	3.6	1.9	5.8	20.6
1950	6.9	1.8	0.3	4.8	2.1	6.7	22.7
1951	8.6	1.5	0.5	2.8	1.0	6.1	20.5
1952	14.2	1.4	0.6	2.6	1.0	6.0	25.8
1953	15.0	1.4	0.7	2.3	1.4	5.9	26.8
1954	13.8	1.3	0.9	2.5	0.7	6.4	25.6
1955	11.6	1.3	1.1	2.6	1.1	6.9	24.6
1956	10.7	1.2	1.3	2.4	1.3	6.8	23.8
1957	11.0	1.2	1.5	2.4	1.2	7.1	24.5
1958	11.1	1.3	1.8	2.9	1.2	7.6	25.9
1959	10.8	1.2	2.0	2.8	2.3	7.7	26.8
1960	10.1	1.4	2.3	2.5	1.9	7.5	25.8
1961	10.2	1.3	2.4	3.0	2.0	8.1	27.0
1962	10.4	1.3	2.6	2.7	2.3	8.1	27.2
1963	10.0	1.3	2.7	2.6	2.3	8.1	27.1
1964	9.5	1.3	2.6	2.5	2.9	8.2	27.1
1965	8.3	1.2	2.6	2.4	3.0	8.3	25.9
1966	8.6	1.2	2.8	2.3	3.2	8.4	26.6
1967	9.7	1.2	3.1	2.4	3.4	8.7	28.4
1968	10.3	1.2	3.4	2.5	3.5	9.1	29.9
1969	9.4	1.3	3.5	2.6	2.9	9.4	29.0
1970	8.7	1.3	3.7	2.9	3.1	9.6	29.2
1971	7.9	1.3	4.0	3.6	3.0	10.1	29.9
1972	7.3	1.2	4.1	3.9	3.3	9.9	29.8
1973	6.3	1.2	4.5	3.7	3.4	9.4	28.4
1974	6.0	1.3	4.6	3.8	3.0	9.8	28.5
1975	6.1	1.2	5.1	5.0	4.1	10.2	31.8
1976	5.7	1.3	5.3	5.3	4.1	10.1	31.8
TQ	5.5	1.4	5.4	4.8	4.2	10.1	31.3
1977	5.4	1.4	5.4	4.8	4.1	9.3	30.3
1978	5.2	1.4	5.4	4.3	4.6	9.0	29.9
1979	5.1	1.3	5.3	4.2	4.3	8.9	29.1
1980	5.5	1.4	5.6	4.7	4.3	9.2	30.7
1981	5.7	1.6	6.0	4.8	3.9	9.0	31.0
1982	6.3	2.0	6.5	4.9	3.4	9.4	32.4
1983	6.7	1.9	6.7	5.2	3.1	9.4	33.0
1984	6.6	2.3	6.4	4.4	2.7	9.1	31.4
1985	6.8	2.6	6.5	4.3	3.1	9.2	32.5
1986	6.9	2.6	6.5	4.2	2.9	9.2	32.3

See page 219 for explanatory notes.

TOTAL GOVERNMENT EXPENDITURES BY MAJOR CATEGORY OF EXPENDITURE: 1947-1986
(in billions of dollars)

	Defense and International	Net Interest	Social Security and Medicare	Federal Payments for Individuals	Other Federal	State and Local From Own Sources (Except Net Interest)	Total Government
1947	18.6	4.3	0.5	8.6	2.6	10.2	44.9
1948	13.7	4.4	0.6	8.5	2.7	13.1	43.0
1949	19.2	4.6	0.7	9.5	5.0	15.3	54.3
1950	18.4	4.9	0.8	12.9	5.6	17.8	60.5
1951	27.2	4.7	1.6	8.8	3.3	19.1	64.7
1952	48.8	4.7	2.1	8.9	3.3	20.6	88.4
1953	54.9	5.2	2.7	8.3	5.0	21.7	97.8
1954	50.9	4.8	3.4	9.3	2.5	23.6	94.5
1955	45.0	4.9	4.4	10.0	4.3	26.5	95.1
1956	44.9	5.2	5.5	9.8	5.3	28.6	99.4
1957	48.6	5.4	6.7	10.5	5.5	31.4	108.0
1958	50.2	5.7	8.2	12.9	5.5	34.3	116.8
1959	52.2	5.9	9.7	13.2	11.2	36.9	129.2
1960	51.1	7.1	11.6	12.8	9.8	38.2	130.5
1961	52.8	6.8	12.5	15.3	10.4	42.0	139.9
1962	58.0	7.0	14.4	14.9	12.7	45.0	151.9
1963	58.7	7.9	15.8	15.5	13.6	47.9	159.3
1964	59.7	8.2	16.6	16.0	18.1	51.8	170.4
1965	55.9	8.4	17.5	16.0	20.3	55.9	173.9
1966	63.7	9.0	20.8	16.8	23.9	62.2	196.3
1967	77.0	9.5	24.5	18.7	27.0	69.3	226.0
1968	87.2	10.1	28.5	21.3	30.0	76.9	254.1
1969	87.1	11.7	33.0	24.1	26.7	86.9	269.5
1970	86.0	12.8	36.5	28.3	30.5	94.8	288.9
1971	83.0	13.2	42.5	37.8	32.0	106.9	315.5
1972	84.0	14.2	47.6	45.2	38.5	113.9	343.2
1973	80.8	15.3	57.1	47.3	43.1	120.8	364.5
1974	85.1	17.9	65.5	54.4	42.9	138.2	403.9
1975	93.6	18.9	77.5	75.8	62.1	155.9	483.9
1976	96.1	22.8	89.7	90.5	68.8	172.4	540.3
TQ	24.7	6.1	24.0	21.3	18.9	45.4	140.6
1977	103.6	26.2	104.4	91.8	79.5	180.3	585.8
1978	112.0	29.5	116.6	94.2	100.4	196.4	649.2
1979	123.8	32.0	130.6	102.1	104.4	218.6	711.4
1980	146.7	36.9	150.6	126.5	114.6	244.9	820.2
1981	170.6	49.0	178.7	144.3	115.9	268.7	927.2
1982	197.6	61.9	202.5	153.6	107.0	294.0	1,016.6
1983	221.8	63.7	223.3	171.3	103.3	312.4	1,095.8
1984	243.3	84.2	235.8	162.8	98.9	333.9	1,158.8
1985	268.9	102.0	254.4	169.5	124.0	361.2	1,280.1
1986	287.5	109.9	268.9	176.3	121.1	382.1	1,345.8

See page 219 for explanatory notes.

TOTAL GOVERNMENT SURPLUSES OR DEFICITS (-) IN ABSOLUTE AMOUNTS AND AS PERCENTAGES OF GNP: 1947-1986

(dollar amounts in billions)

	Federal Government					As Percentages of GNP		
	On-Budget	Off-Budget	Total Federal	State and Local (NIPA Basis)	Total Government	Total Federal	State and Local	Total Government
1947	2.9	1.2	4.0	1.6	5.6	1.8%	0.7%	2.5%
1948	10.5	1.2	11.8	0.6	12.4	4.8	0.2	5.0
1949	-.7	1.3	0.6	-.2	0.4	0.2	-.1	0.2
1950	-4.7	1.6	-3.1	-1.3	-4.4	-1.2	-.5	-1.7
1951	4.3	1.8	6.1	-.5	5.6	1.9	-.2	1.8
1952	-3.4	1.9	-1.5	-.4	-2.0	-.4	-.1	-.6
1953	-8.3	1.8	-6.5	0.3	-6.2	-1.8	0.1	-1.7
1954	-2.8	1.7	-1.2	-.3	-1.4	-.3	-.1	-.4
1955	-4.1	1.1	-3.0	-1.6	-4.6	-.8	-.4	-1.2
1956	2.5	1.5	3.9	-.8	3.2	0.9	-.2	0.8
1957	2.6	0.8	3.4	-.9	2.5	0.8	-.2	0.6
1958	-3.3	0.5	-2.8	-2.0	-4.8	-.6	-.4	-1.1
1959	-12.1	-.7	-12.8	-1.8	-14.6	-2.7	-.4	-3.0
1960	0.5	-.2	0.3	0.4	0.7	0.1	0.1	0.1
1961	-3.8	0.4	-3.3	-.3	-3.7	-.6	-.1	-.7
1962	-5.9	-1.3	-7.1	*	-7.1	-1.3	*	-1.3
1963	-4.0	-.8	-4.8	0.3	-4.4	-.8	0.1	-.8
1964	-6.5	0.6	-5.9	0.6	-5.3	-.9	0.1	-.8
1965	-1.6	0.2	-1.4	0.8	-.7	-.2	0.1	-.1
1966	-3.1	-.6	-3.7	0.6	-3.1	-.5	0.1	-.4
1967	-12.6	4.0	-8.6	-1.5	-10.1	-1.1	-.2	-1.3
1968	-27.7	2.6	-25.2	0.4	-24.7	-3.0	0.1	-2.9
1969	-.5	3.7	3.2	-.4	2.9	0.3	-*	0.3
1970	-8.7	5.9	-2.8	3.7	0.8	-.3	0.4	0.1
1971	-26.1	3.0	-23.0	-.5	-23.5	-2.2	-*	-2.2
1972	-26.4	3.1	-23.4	8.2	-15.2	-2.0	0.7	-1.3
1973	-15.4	0.5	-14.9	14.9	-*	-1.2	1.2	-*
1974	-8.0	1.8	-6.1	10.6	4.5	-.4	0.8	0.3
1975	-55.3	2.0	-53.2	5.9	-47.4	-3.5	0.4	-3.1
1976	-70.5	-3.2	-73.7	6.8	-66.9	-4.3	0.4	-3.9
TQ	-13.3	-1.4	-14.7	-1.4	-16.2	-3.3	-.3	-3.6
1977	-49.7	-3.9	-53.6	24.4	-29.3	-2.8	1.3	-1.5
1978	-54.9	-4.3	-59.2	31.4	-27.8	-2.7	1.4	-1.3
1979	-38.2	-2.0	-40.2	26.5	-13.7	-1.6	1.1	-.6
1980	-72.7	-1.1	-73.8	25.7	-48.1	-2.8	1.0	-1.8
1981	-73.9	-5.0	-78.9	32.5	-46.5	-2.6	1.1	-1.6
1982	-120.0	-7.9	-127.9	34.8	-93.1	-4.1	1.1	-3.0
1983	-208.0	0.2	-207.8	43.7	-164.1	-6.3	1.3	-4.9
1984	-185.6	0.3	-185.3	63.9	-121.4	-5.0	1.7	-3.3
1985	-221.6	9.4	-212.3	60.9	-151.3	-5.4	1.5	-3.8
1986	-237.5	16.7	-220.7	63.8	-156.9	-5.3	1.5	-3.8

* If dollars, $50 million or less. If percent, 0.05 percent or less.

See page 219 for explanatory notes.

NOTES TO HISTORICAL TABLES AND CHARTS

Because of the numerous changes in the way budget data have been presented over time, there are inevitable difficulties in trying to produce comparable data to cover so many years. The general rule underlying all of these tables is to provide data in as meaningful and comparable a fashion as is possible. The data are always presented on a basis consistent with current budget concepts. Insofar as is possible such changes are made for all years. For example, one major function in the 1986 Budget was entitled "Social Security and Medicare," with separate subfunctions for Social Security and for Medicare. In the 1987 Budget, Social Security and Medicare are shown as separate major functions and the data were reconstructed to show these as separate functions from the origin of the programs.

NOTE ON THE FISCAL YEAR

The Federal fiscal year begins on October 1 and ends on the subsequent September 30. It is designated by the year in which it ends; for example, fiscal year 1985 began October 1, 1984 and ended on September 30, 1985. Prior to fiscal year 1977 the Federal fiscal years began on July 1 and ended on June 30. In calendar year 1976 the July–September period was a separate accounting period (known as the transition quarter or TQ) to bridge the period required to shift to the new fiscal years.

BUDGET SUMMARY

(In billions of dollars)

	1985	1986	1987	1988	1989	1990	1991
Receipts	734.1	777.1	850.4	933.2	996.1	1,058.1	1,124.0
Outlays	946.3	979.9	994.0	1,026.8	1,063.6	1,093.8	1,122.7
Surplus or deficit (−)	−212.3	−202.8	−143.6	−93.6	−67.5	−35.8	1.3
Gramm-Rudman-Hollings deficit targets	....	−171.9	−144.0	−108.0	−72.0	−36.0	0.0
Difference	....	30.9	−0.4	−14.4	−4.5	−0.2	−1.3

Note.—Totals include social security, which is off-budget.

Source: *The United States Budget in Brief,* Fiscal Year 1987, Executive Office of the President, Office of Management and Budget.

Note: The Balanced Budget and Emergency Deficit Control Act is commonly referred to as Gramm-Rudman-Hollings for its principal architects. The proposed budget has as its major objective, a balanced budget by 1991 to meet the deficit reduction targets set out in the Act.

Federal Deficit Projections Under Current Policy and Gramm-Rudman-Hollings

Fiscal Years 1986-1991
($bils)

	1986	1987	1988	1989	1990	1991
(A) Current Services Budget as of August 30, 1985 ..	242.6	253.1	255.9	243.8	237.9	
(B) Mid-Session Review of Fiscal '86 Budget	177.8	139.3	99.8	53.6	17.7	
(C) "Realistic" Current Policy Budget, January 1, 1986 (average of A + B)...............	210	196	178	149	128	100
(D) G-R-H Deficit Targets ..	172	144	108	72	36	0
(E) Potential Mandated Budget Cuts[1]..........	12[2]	52	70	77	92	100

[1]For fiscal 1987-1990, the deficit targets must be missed by more than $10 billion for sequestration to be ordered.
[2]Limited by formula to $11.7 billion in fiscal 1986 only.
Sources: Office of Management and Budget, Tax Foundation computations.

Source: Tax Foundation, Incorporated, One Thomas Circle, NW, Washington, DC 20005.

FEDERAL FISCAL AND FINANCING OPERATIONS
Millions of dollars

Type of account or operation	Fiscal year 1984	Fiscal year 1985	Fiscal year 1986	Calendar year					
				1986		1987			
				Nov.	Dec.	Jan.	Feb.	Mar.	Apr.
U.S. budget[1]									
1 Receipts, total	666,457	734,057	769,091	52,967	78,035	81,771	55,463	56,515	122,897
2 On-budget	500,382	547,886	568,862	38,158	60,694	62,981	37,919	38,469	99,083
3 Off-budget	166,075	186,171	200,228	14,809	17,341	18,790	17,544	18,046	23,814
4 Outlays, total	851,781	946,316	989,815	79,973	89,158	83,942	83,828	84,527	84,240
5 On-budget	685,968	769,509	806,318	63,639	74,669	68,176	67,138	67,872	69,215
6 Off-budget	165,813	176,807	183,498	16,334	14,489	15,766	16,690	16,655	15,025
7 Surplus, or deficit (−), total	−185,324	−212,260	−220,725	−27,006	−11,123	−2,170	−28,366	−28,012	38,657
8 On-budget	−185,586	−221,623	−237,455	−25,481	−13,976	−5,195	−29,219	−29,403	29,867
9 Off-budget	262	9,363	16,371	−1,524	2,853	3,024	854	1,391	8,790
Source of financing (total)									
10 Borrowing from the public	170,817	197,269	236,284	40,352	22,824	4,353	15,248	7,884	9,075
11 Cash and monetary assets (decrease, or increase (−))[2]	6,631	13,367	−14,324	−2,721	−14,751	−9,564	16,574	15,621	−47,189
12 Other[3]	7,875	1,630	−1,235	−10,625	4,004	7,381	−3,456	4,506	−543
Memo									
13 Treasury operating balance (level, end of period)	30,426	17,060	31,384	17,007	30,946	41,307	24,816	8,969	55,744
14 Federal Reserve Banks	8,514	4,174	7,514	2,529	7,588	15,746	3,482	3,576	29,688
15 Tax and loan accounts	21,913	12,886	23,870	14,478	23,357	25,561	21,334	5,394	26,056

1. In accordance with the Balanced Budget and Emergency Deficit Control Act of 1985, all former off-budget entries are now presented on-budget. The Federal Financing Bank (FFB) activities are now shown as separate accounts under the agencies that use the FFB to finance their programs. The act has also moved two social security trust funds (Federal old-age survivors insurance and Federal disability insurance trust funds) off-budget.

2. Includes U.S. Treasury operating cash accounts; SDRs; reserve position on the U.S. quota in the IMF; loans to International Monetary Fund; and other cash and monetary assets.

3. Includes accrued interest payable to the public; allocations of special drawing rights; deposit funds; miscellaneous liability (including checks outstanding) and asset accounts; seigniorage; increment on gold; net gain/loss for U.S. currency valuation adjustment; net gain/loss for IMF valuation adjustment; and profit on the sale of gold.

Sources. "Monthly Treasury Statement of Receipts and Outlays of the U.S. Government" and the *Budget of the U.S. Government.*

Source: *Federal Reserve Bulletin*, Board of Governors of the Federal Reserve System.

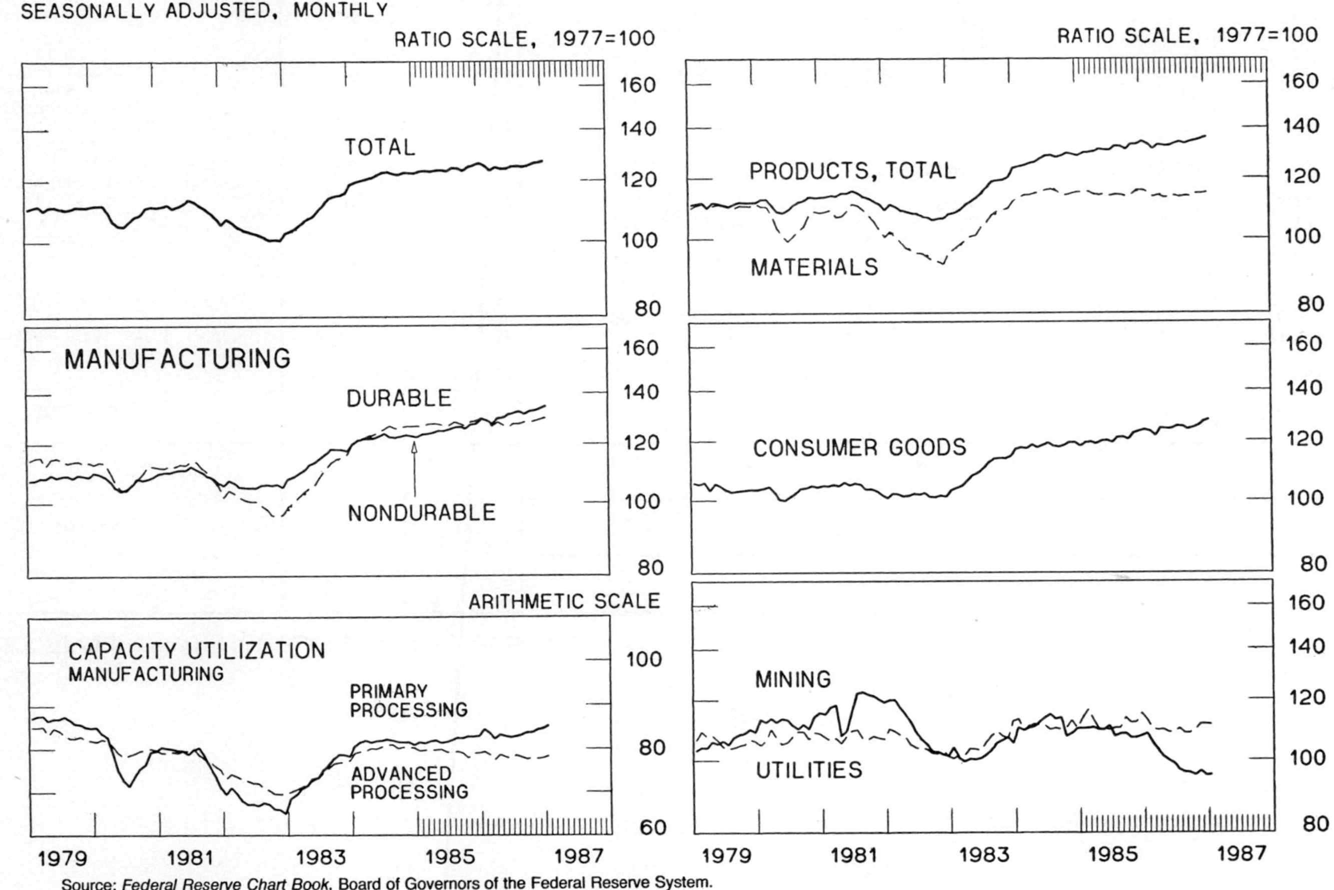

Source: *Federal Reserve Chart Book*, Board of Governors of the Federal Reserve System.

U.S. BUDGET RECEIPTS AND OUTLAYS (millions of dollars)

Source or type	Fiscal year 1985	Fiscal year 1986	Calendar year						
			1985		1986		1987		
			H1	H2	H1	H2	Feb.	Mar.	Apr.
RECEIPTS									
1 **All sources**	**734,057**	**769,091**	**380,618**	**364,790**	**394,345**	**387,524**	**55,463**	**56,515**	**122,897**
2 Individual income taxes, net	334,531	348,959	166,783	169,987	169,444	183,156	22,805	14,240	71,850
3 Withheld	298,941	314,838	149,288	155,725	153,919	164,071	25,486	27,608	26,943
4 Presidential Election Campaign Fund	35	36	29	6	31	4	2	10	7
5 Nonwithheld	101,328	105,994	76,155	22,295	78,981	27,733	1,320	4,106	62,939
6 Refunds	65,743	71,873	58,684	8,038	63,488	8,652	4,003	17,482	18,039
Corporation income taxes									
7 Gross receipts	77,413	80,442	42,193	36,528	41,946	42,108	2,369	15,948	13,290
8 Refunds	16,082	17,298	8,370	7,751	9,557	8,230	1,433	2,834	2,101
9 Social insurance taxes and contributions, net	265,163	283,901	144,598	128,017	156,714	134,006	25,590	23,689	33,646
10 Employment taxes and contributions[1]	234,646	255,062	126,038	116,276	139,706	122,246	22,594	23,128	30,457
11 Self-employment taxes and contributions[2]	10,468	11,840	9,482	985	10,581	1,338	809	669	7,403
12 Unemployment insurance	25,758	24,098	16,213	9,281	14,674	9,328	2,633	186	2,827
13 Other net receipts[3]	4,759	4,742	2,350	2,458	2,333	2,429	364	375	361
14 Excise taxes	35,992	32,919	17,259	18,470	15,944	15,947	2,291	2,511	2,471
15 Customs deposits	12,079	13,323	5,807	6,354	6,369	7,282	1,052	1,220	1,165
16 Estate and gift taxes	6,422	6,958	3,204	3,323	3,487	3,649	553	570	810
17 Miscellaneous receipts[4]	18,539	19,887	9,144	9,861	10,002	9,605	2,235	1,171	1,767

Outlays									
18 All types	**946,223**	**989,789**	**463,842**	**487,188**	**486,037**	**504,785**	**83,828**	**84,527**	**84,240**
19 National defense	252,748	273,369	124,186	134,675	135,367	138,544	23,475	24,742	24,407
20 International affairs	16,176	14,471	6,675	8,367	5,384	8,876	1,319	681	163
21 General science, space, and technology	8,627	9,017	4,230	4,727	12,519	4,594	791	703	653
22 Energy	5,685	4,792	680	3,305	2,484	2,735	189	441	361
23 Natural resources and environment	13,357	13,508	5,892	7,553	6,245	7,141	871	1,092	1,052
24 Agriculture	25,565	31,169	11,705	15,412	14,482	16,160	2,293	2,453	2,641
25 Commerce and housing credit	4,229	4,258	−260	644	860	3,647	−334	1,677	1,129
26 Transportation	25,838	28,058	11,440	15,360	12,658	14,745	1,697	1,982	1,936
27 Community and regional development	7,680	7,510	3,408	3,901	3,169	3,494	380	490	592
28 Education, training, employment, social services	29,342	29,662	14,149	14,481	14,712	15,268	2,669	2,440	2,317
29 Health	33,542	35,936	16,945	17,237	17,872	19,814	3,166	3,263	3,672
30 Social security and medicare	254,446	190,850	128,351	129,037	135,214	138,296	23,081	23,407	23,615
31 Income security	128,200	120,686	65,246	59,457	60,786	59,628	10,551	10,910	11,282
32 Veterans benefits and services	26,352	26,614	11,956	14,527	12,193	14,497	2,053	1,137	2,360
33 Administration of justice	6,277	6,555	3,016	3,212	3,352	3,360	619	570	619
34 General government	5,228	6,796	2,857	3,634	3,566	2,786	631	439	196
35 General-purpose fiscal assistance	6,353	6,430	2,659	3,391	2,179	2,767	120	61	179
36 Net interest[5]	129,436	135,284	65,143	67,448	68,054	65,816	12,967	10,971	11,295
37 Undistributed offsetting receipts[6]	−32,759	−33,244	−14,436	−17,953	−17,193	−17,426	−2,708	−2,932	−4,230

1. Old-age, disability, and hospital insurance, and railroad retirement accounts.
2. Old-age, disability, and hospital insurance.
3. Federal employee retirement contributions and civil service retirement and disability fund.
4. Deposits of earnings by Federal Reserve Banks and other miscellaneous receipts.
5. Net interest function includes interest received by trust funds.
6. Consists of rents and royalties on the outer continental shelf and U.S. government contributions for employee retirement.

SOURCE. "Monthly Treasury Statement of Receipts and Outlays of the U.S. Government," and the *Budget of the U.S. Government, Fiscal Year 1988*.

Source: *Federal Reserve Bulletin*, Board of Governors of the Federal Reserve System.

Largest Companies

The 100 Largest U.S. Industrial Corporations (ranked by sales)

Rank '86	Rank '85	Company	Sales ($000)	Sales % Change	Net Income ($000)	Net Income Rank	Net Income % Change	Assets ($000)	Assets Rank	Stockholders' Equity ($000)	Stockholders' Equity Rank
1	1	General Motors (Detroit)	102,813,700	6.7	2,944,700	4	(26.4)	72,593,000	1	30,678,000	3
2	2	Exxon (New York)	69,888,000	(19.4)	5,360,000	1	10.1	69,484,000	2	32,012,000	2
3	4	Ford Motor (Dearborn, Mich.)	62,715,800	18.8	3,285,100	3	30.6	37,933,000	6	14,859,500	7
4	5	International Business Machines (Armonk, N.Y.)	51,250,000	2.4	4,789,000	2	(26.9)	57,814,000	3	34,374,000	1
5	3	Mobil (New York)	44,866,000*	(19.8)	1,407,000	8	35.3	39,412,000	4	15,239,000	5
6	10	General Electric (Fairfield, Conn.)	35,211,000	24.5	2,492,000	5	6.7	34,591,000	8	15,109,000	6
7	8	American Tel. & Tel. (New York)	34,087,000	(2.4)	139,000	115	(91.1)	38,883,000	5	13,550,000	10
8	6	Texaco (White Plains, N.Y.)	31,613,000	(31.7)	725,000	17	(41.2)	34,940,000	7	13,739,000	9
9	9	E. I. du Pont de Nemours (Wilmington, Del.)	27,148,000	(7.9)	1,538,000	6	37.6	26,733,000	10	13,374,000	11
10	7	Chevron (San Francisco)	24,351,000	(41.7)	715,000	18	(53.8)	34,583,000	9	15,493,000	4
11	13	Chrysler (Highland Park, Mich.)	22,513,500	5.9	1,403,600	9	(14.2)	14,463,200	20	5,344,800	20
12	27	Philip Morris (New York)[1]	20,681,000*	70.2	1,478,000	7	17.8	17,642,000	16	5,655,000	18
13	11	Amoco (Chicago)	18,281,000	(32.8)	747,000	15	(61.8)	23,706,000	12	11,324,000	12
14	23	RJR Nabisco (Winston-Salem, N.C.)[2]	16,998,000*	25.6	1,064,000	10	6.3	17,019,000	18	5,312,000	21
15	14	Shell Oil (Houston)[3]	16,833,000*	(17.1)	883,000	12	(46.5)	26,214,000	11	14,312,000	8
16	21	Boeing (Seattle)	16,341,000	19.8	665,000	22	17.5	11,068,000	29	4,826,000	25
17	16	United Technologies (Hartford)	15,669,157	(0.5)	72,727	187	(76.7)	11,091,787	28	3,803,063	32
18	22	Procter & Gamble (Cincinnati)[4,5]	15,439,000	13.9	709,000	19	11.7	13,055,000	21	5,954,000	16
19	19	Occidental Petroleum (Los Angeles)	15,344,100	5.6	181,000	96	(74.0)	17,466,777	17	4,308,300	30
20	12	Atlantic Richfield (Los Angeles)	14,585,802	(34.8)	615,116	25	—	21,603,543	14	5,258,730	23
21	18	Tenneco (Houston)	14,558,000	(5.5)	(39,000)‡	439	—	18,021,000	15	4,412,000	28
22	15	USX (Pittsburgh)[6]	14,000,000*	(24.0)	(1,833,000)‡	476	—	21,823,000	13	5,634,000	19
23	29	McDonnell Douglas (St. Louis)	12,660,600	10.3	277,500	61	(19.7)	7,910,700	38	2,844,800	46
24	30	Rockwell International (Pittsburgh)[7]	12,295,700	8.5	611,200	26	2.7	7,703,400	41	3,162,100	42
25	37	Allied-Signal (Morristown, N.J.)	11,794,000	29.4	605,000	27	—	11,268,000	27	3,686,000	35
26	33	Eastman Kodak (Rochester, N.Y.)	11,550,000	8.6	374,000	50	12.7	12,902,000	23	6,388,000	15
27	28	Dow Chemical (Midland, Mich.)	11,113,000	(3.7)	732,000	16	162.1	12,242,000	25	5,168,000	24
28	32	Westinghouse Electric (Pittsburgh)	10,731,000	0.3	670,800	21	10.8	8,481,800	34	3,009,600	44
29	35	Goodyear Tire & Rubber (Akron, Ohio)	10,327,700¶	4.4	124,100	128	(69.9)	8,609,500	33	3,002,600	45
30	36	Lockheed (Calabasas, Calif.)[8]	10,273,000	7.7	408,000	44	1.8	5,943,000	51	1,866,000	68
31	17	Phillips Petroleum (Bartlesville, Okla.)	9,786,000	(37.6)	228,000	72	(45.5)	12,399,000	24	1,724,000	73
32	40	Xerox (Stamford, Conn.)[9]	9,377,000	4.8	465,000	37	(2.2)	10,608,000	30	4,687,000	26
33	20	Sun (Radnor, Pa.)	9,376,000*	(31.9)	385,000	48	(26.9)	11,684,000	26	5,287,000	22
34	41	PepsiCo (Purchase, N.Y.)[10]	9,290,800	9.6	457,500	38	(15.9)	8,024,700	37	2,059,400	62
35	24	Standard Oil (Cleveland)	9,219,000*	(29.1)	(345,000)	472	—	15,955,000	19	7,020,000	14
36	42	General Dynamics (St. Louis)	9,211,400	9.5	(52,500)	443	—	4,552,500	71	1,264,400	107
37	34	Kraft (Glenview, Ill.)[11]	8,742,200	(12.1)	413,200	41	(11.4)	4,749,300	64	1,798,000	70
38	44	Coca-Cola (Atlanta)	8,668,556	6.5	934,347	11	29.4	8,373,438	35	3,514,979	37
39	47	Minnesota Mining & Manufacturing (St. Paul)	8,602,000	9.6	779,000	13	17.3	7,348,000	43	4,463,000	27
40	45	Sara Lee (Chicago)[5]	7,937,722	(2.2)	223,455	75	8.3	3,503,106	94	1,154,678	114
41	25	ITT (New York)	7,895,540*	(37.9)	439,720	35	68.2	12,920,407	22	7,145,738	13
42	39	Union Carbide (Danbury, Conn.)	7,828,000¶	(13.1)	496,000‡	34	—	7,571,000	42	1,005,000	130
43	51	Anheuser-Busch (St. Louis)	7,677,200*	9.7	518,000	32	16.8	5,833,800	53	2,313,700	58
44	55	Digital Equipment (Maynard, Mass.)[8]	7,590,357	13.5	617,420	24	38.2	7,173,326	44	5,727,827	17

The definitions and concepts underlying the figures in this directory are explained on page 229.

Market Value	Net Income as Percent of: Sales		Assets		Stock-holders' Equity		Earnings per Share				Total Return to Investors: 1986		1976–86 Growth Rate		Industry Code
									Growth Rate 1976–86						
($000)	%	Rank	%	Rank	%	Rank	'86/$	% Change	%	Rank	%	Rank	%	Rank	
24,767,590	2.9	300	4.1	282	9.6	282	8.21	(33.14)	(2.03)	296	0.22	317	5.68	356	40
59,246,393	7.7	79	7.7	138	16.7	125	7.42	14.86	9.66	144	34.76	112	18.76	152	29
20,782,850	5.2	174	8.7	103	22.1	52	12.32	35.58	12.73	99	51.42	50	16.15	197	40
88,784,982	9.3	49	8.3	114	13.9	178	7.81	(26.80)	6.96	184	(20.41)	399	10.52	301	44
18,495,123	3.1	282	3.6	302	9.2	287	3.45	35.29	4.27	219	41.73	84	16.95	180	29
47,925,962	7.1	97	7.2	151	16.5	130	5.46	6.43	10.24	133	21.93	186	16.96	179	36
25,057,693	0.4	393	0.4	397	0.4§	396	0.05	(96.35)	(38.10)	345	5.18	292	3.94	365	36
8,388,752	2.3	325	2.1	351	5.3	348	3.01	(41.10)	(0.61)	283	31.20	128	11.28	288	29
25,800,000	5.7	150	5.8	216	11.5	243	6.35	37.74	7.43	174	28.41	140	12.76	256	28
18,003,486	2.9	294	2.1	353	4.6	355	2.09	(53.76)	(2.12)	299	25.56	166	14.88	218	29
8,215,443	6.2	128	9.7	73	26.3	30	9.47	0.96	7.30	177	22.49	183	13.12	250	40
20,217,891	7.2	94	8.4	112	26.1	31	6.20	18.43	18.69	32	68.56	20	21.21	110	21
19,593,089	4.1	239	3.2	322	6.6	333	2.91	(60.78)	(0.45)	281	11.23	257	14.17	227	29
14,616,808	6.3	125	6.3	188	18.1§	103	3.83	6.39	9.86	141	62.19	27	20.72	118	21
—	5.3	172	3.4	309	6.2	341	N.A.	—	—		—		—		29
8,105,092	4.1	241	6.0	197	13.8	180	4.28	14.13	19.54	20	(0.04)	319	27.32	45	41
6,881,161	0.5	391	0.7	385	1.9	383	0.27	(87.26)	(20.03)	334	8.21	268	13.89	232	41
15,585,683	4.6	208	5.4	232	11.9	226	4.20	10.53	5.62	197	13.57	240	9.56	314	28
5,106,599	1.2	369	1.0	378	3.4§	366	0.72	(84.11)	(12.61)	322	(2.96)	338	9.75	313	20
12,913,882	4.2	231	2.9	333	11.7	235	3.38	—	2.98	232	1.09	312	13.33	245	29
7,222,275	—		—		—		(0.72)‡	—	—		4.00	295	7.76	336	29
6,481,938	—		—		—		(7.46)‡	—	—		(14.62)	383	(2.40)	397	29
3,164,305	2.2	333	3.5	304	9.8	280	6.86	(20.23)	9.18	153	(1.63)	331	14.54	223	41
7,716,746	5.0	184	7.9	131	19.3	82	4.12	3.00	16.37	52	30.40	131	24.95	69	41
8,259,927	5.1	178	5.4	234	15.6§	148	3.26	—	1.58	258	(1.30)	328	10.42	303	41
16,963,225	3.2	276	2.9	330	5.9	344	1.66	13.70	(4.70)	308	42.06	82	6.71	347	38
15,539,715	6.6	114	6.0	200	14.2	172	3.82	1,132.26	1.47	261	47.95	56	8.52	327	28
9,268,949	6.3	127	7.9	132	22.3	46	4.42	25.57	13.28	89	28.39	141	26.08	57	36
3,023,203	1.2	367	1.4	367	4.1	360	1.16	(69.79)	(3.69)	305	40.29	87	12.97	253	30
3,362,269	4.0	244	6.9	165	21.9	54	6.18	1.31	19.58	19	3.97	297	32.76	12	41
3,225,199	2.3	322	1.8	358	11.8§	228	0.89	(38.19)	(0.09)	276	3.42	301	7.06	343	29
7,104,100	5.0	185	4.4	267	9.9	274	4.28	(3.60)	(0.52)	282	5.73	291	5.94	353	38
6,333,732	4.1	236	3.3	313	7.3	321	3.54	(25.00)	(0.35)	279	11.06	258	14.46	224	29
9,111,158	4.9	188	5.7	219	22.2	48	1.75	(9.95)	10.97	123	9.62	261	15.65	205	49
14,229,454	—		—		—		(1.47)	—	—		5.11	293	14.82	220	29
3,305,353	—		—		—		(1.23)	—	—		(0.14	320	22.27	96	41
8,405,038	4.7	196	8.7	101	23.0	41	2.93	(9.01)	6.10	190	39.39	95	20.82	117	20
18,143,643	10.8	28	11.2	46	26.6	27	2.42	31.76	11.80	110	39.50	94	16.91	181	49
14,197,598	9.1	52	10.6	55	17.5	112	6.80	17.85	8.75	156	34.38	114	12.28	262	38
4,606,621	2.8	302	6.4	185	19.4	80	4.04	11.91	10.45	131	36.76	105	24.32	76	20
8,992,942	6.3	126	3.8	294	6.9	327	3.23	70.90	(2.12)	298	43.55	75	11.76	274	36
3,687,198	6.3	121	6.6	176	49.4	3	4.78§	—	7.21	179	42.54	78	11.38	285	28
10,556,975	6.8	111	8.9	93	21.2§	60	1.69	10.01	23.48	10	25.85	164	24.85	71	49
21,056,835	8.1	72	8.6	105	10.8	259	4.81	29.65	17.13	42	(20.94)	402	6.88	345	44

The 100 Largest U.S. Industrial Corporations (ranked by sales)

Rank			Sales		Net Income			Assets		Stockholders' Equity	
'86	'85	Company	($000)	% Change	($000)	Rank	% Change	($000)	Rank	($000)	Rank
45	31	Unocal (Los Angeles)	7,482,000*	(30.3)	176,000	102	(45.9)	10,133,000	31	1,681,000	77
46	72	Unisys (Detroit)[12]	7,432,400	47.5	(43,400)	442	—	9,408,800	32	3,828,300	31
47	52	Caterpillar (Peoria, Ill.)[13]	7,321,000	8.2	76,000	178	(61.6)	6,288,000	48	3,149,000	43
48	60	Raytheon (Lexington, Mass.)	7,307,952	14.0	393,205	46	4.6	3,555,899	91	1,954,578	66
49	43	LTV (Dallas)	7,271,400	(11.3)	(3,251,600)	477	—	5,498,700	56	(2,558,900)	488
50	54	Georgia-Pacific (Atlanta)	7,223,000	7.6	296,000	59	58.3	5,114,000	60	2,452,000	54
51	58	Hewlett-Packard (Palo Alto, Calif.)[14]	7,102,000	9.2	516,000	33	5.5	6,287,000	49	4,374,000	29
52	56	Honeywell (Minneapolis)	7,086,700¶	7.0	(398,100)	473	—	5,139,000	59	2,221,200	59
53	59	Johnson & Johnson (New Brunswick, N.J.)	7,002,900	9.1	329,500	53	(46.3)	5,876,700	52	2,824,200	48
54	46	Ashland Oil (Russell, Ky.)[7]	6,991,262	(11.4)	208,571	81	42.2	3,804,749	83	971,044	140
55	53	Monsanto (St. Louis)	6,879,000	2.0	433,000	39	—	8,269,000	36	3,781,000	33
56	49	W. R. Grace (New York)	6,808,300¶	(6.2)	472,300	36	221.5	4,097,200	78	1,308,600	102
57	50	Coastal (Houston)	6,668,200	(8.1)	71,600	190	(49.7)	7,777,300	40	788,900	173
58	57	TRW (Cleveland)	6,450,143	(2.5)	217,710	79	—	3,909,300	81	1,197,943	110
59	65	ConAgra (Omaha)[15]	5,911,046	7.5	105,285	139	14.8	1,819,696	180	510,549	237
60	66	Motorola (Schaumburg, Ill.)	5,888,000	8.2	194,000	89	169.4	4,682,000	66	2,754,000	49
61	80	Pillsbury (Minneapolis)[15]	5,847,900	25.2	208,100	82	8.5	3,658,800	88	1,314,200	101
62	68	Weyerhaeuser (Tacoma, Wash.)	5,652,029	8.6	276,685	62	38.3	6,557,652	47	3,253,165	41
63	160	Baxter Travenol Laboratories (Deerfield, Ill.)	5,634,000	139.2	422,000‡	40	208.0	7,068,000	45	3,370,000	40
64	71	Northrop (Los Angeles)	5,608,400	10.9	41,200	260	(80.8)	2,698,800	122	898,700	154
65	61	Ralston Purina (St. Louis)[7]	5,514,600	(6.0)	388,700	47	51.6	4,209,900	75	998,900	132
66	83	International Paper (New York)[16]	5,501,000	22.2	305,00	57	129.3	7,848,000	39	3,664,000	36
67	76	Archer Daniels Midland (Decatur, Ill.)[5]	5,335,975	12.6	230,386	71	40.6	3,315,436	100	2,075,887	61
68	78	American Brands (New York)	5,261,179*	12.1	365,304	51	(13.2)	5,362,791	57	2,578,466	52
69	74	Textron (Providence)[17]	5,226,300	4.7	239,200	69	(5.0)	5,557,100	55	1,847,200	69
70	77	Borden (New York)	5,002,097	6.1	223,312	76	15.2	3,582,189	90	1,438,743	89
71	73	Colgate-Palmolive (New York)	4,984,576	(0.7)	177,465	100	62.2	2,845,935	115	979,916	137
72	75	Texas Instruments (Dallas)	4,974,000	1.0	29,100‡	302	—	3,336,700	99	1,727,100	72
73	81	Emerson Electric (St. Louis)[7]	4,952,900	6.5	408,900	42	1.9	3,769,000	84	2,374,000	57
74	79	American Home Products (New York)	4,926,512	5.2	778,824	14	8.6	4,175,123	77	2,380,846	56
75	89	NCR (Dayton, Ohio)	4,881,641	13.1	336,524	52	6.8	4,014,991	79	2,396,332	55
76	84	Bristol-Myers (New York)	4,835,866	8.8	589,519	28	10.9	4,183,000	76	2,835,572	47
77	85	Martin Marietta (Bethesda, Md.)	4,752,537	7.8	202,344	86	(18.9)	2,470,745	135	843,376	158
78	88	PPG Industries (Pittsburgh)	4,687,100	7.9	316,400	55	4.5	4,641,400	68	1,977,800	65
79	69	Aluminum Co. of America (Pittsburgh)	4,667,200	(9.6)	254,100	66	—	6,766,700	46	3,721,600	34
80	64	General Mills (Minneapolis)[18]	4,586,600	(18.9)	183,500	94	—	2,086,200	156	682,500	195
81	90	CPC International (Englewood Cliffs, N.J.)	4,548,800	8.1	219,200	78	54.4	3,650,600	89	956,100	141
82	86	North American Philips (New York)	4,531,640	3.1	68,520	199	(16.0)	2,885,846	112	1,096,229	122
83	82	Litton Industries (Beverly Hills, Calif.)[18]	4,521,005	(1.5)	71,137	192	(76.3)	4,569,321	70	1,019,896	128
84	99	Pfizer (New York)	4,476,000	11.2	660,000	23	13.9	5,163,700	58	3,415,200	38
85	67	IC Industries (Chicago)	4,439,400	(16.1)	(136,700)	459	—	4,712,900	65	1,528,400	83
86	62	Champion International (Stamford, Conn.)	4,387,623	(24.0)	220,832	87	23.1	6,025,690	50	2,592,395	51
87	100	Campbell Soup (Camden, N.J.)[18]	4,378,714	9.8	223,225	77	12.8	2,762,785	117	1,538,880	82
88	97	H. J. Heinz (Pittsburgh)[19]	4,366,177	7.9	301,734	58	13.4	2,837,364	116	1,360,007	94
89	70	Bethlehem Steel (Bethlehem, Pa.)	4,332,900	(15.3)	(152,700)	460	—	4,660,900	67	849,000	157
90	94	Kimberly-Clark (Dallas)	4,303,100	5.7	269,400	64	0.9	3,676,000	86	1,919,900	67
91	110	Merck (Rahway, N.J.)	4,128,900	16.4	675,700	20	25.2	5,105,200	61	2,569,100	53
92	48	Amerada Hess (New York)	4,014,671	(47.5)	(219,443)	465	—	4,914,054	63	2,050,482	63
93	112	Whirlpool (Benton Harbor, Mich.)	4,008,702	15.4	199,649	88	9.5	2,202,356	149	1,349,791	98
94	109	American Cyanamid (Wayne, N.J.)	3,815,900	4.1	202,500	85	56.9	3,667,000	87	1,720,600	74
95	107	Eaton (Cleveland)	3,811,600	3.7	137,600	118	(40.4)	3,025,100	106	1,255,600	108
96	116	Abbott Laboratories (North Chicago, Ill.)	3,807,634	13.3	540,460	30	16.1	3,865,609	82	1,778,921	71

Market Value	Net Income as Percent of Sales		Assets		Stockholders' Equity		Earnings per Share		Growth Rate 1976–86		Total Return to Investors 1986		1976–86 Growth Rate		Industry Code
($000)	%	Rank	%	Rank	%	Rank	'86/$	% Change	%	Rank	%	Rank	%	Rank	
3,852,685	2.4	320	1.7	361	10.5	264	1.51	(36.02)	(2.04)	297	4.00	296	9.96	311	29
4,586,950	—		—		—		(1.63)	—	—		31.05	129	2.90	373	44
4,620,400	1.0	372	1.2	373	2.4	379	0.77	(61.88)	(16.09)	328	(3.36)	341	(0.36)	391	45
5,750,305	5.4	167	11.1	48	20.1	70	5.10	10.87	13.84	81	28.95	138	19.66	136	36
201,297	—		—		—		(35.41)	—	—		(75.93)	443	(18.25)	414	33
5,256,375	4.1	238	5.8	213	11.8§	232	2.69	64.02	2.53	242	43.07	76	3.85	367	26
14,688,000	7.3	91	8.2	118	11.8	230	2.02	5.76	17.43	37	14.64	229	15.05	217	44
3,160,237	—		—		—		(8.83)	—	—		(18.03)	392	13.14	249	36
15,530,400	4.7	202	5.6	223	11.7	236	1.85	(44.94)	4.63	213	27.44	145	12.54	258	42
2,154,430	3.0	290	5.5	230	20.0§	72	6.15	49.27	6.25	189	54.76	41	15.98	201	29
6,198,567	6.3	122	5.2	239	11.5	246	5.55	—	1.00	265	66.42	24	11.42	283	28
2,547,825	6.9	102	11.5	36	36.1	10	11.25	298.94	12.23	105	6.63	278	11.86	272	28
1,342,945	1.1	371	0.9	380	4.9§	353	084	(76.73)	(7.67)	312	(9.44)	368	19.74	134	29
2,942,005	3.4	268	5.6	226	18.2	100	7.25	—	6.00	193	(0.90)	326	13.41	242	36
2,219,809	1.8	350	5.8	214	20.6	65	3.05	15.09	9.68	143	36.89	103	41.18	4	20
6,380,885	3.3	273	4.1	278	7.0	322	1.53	150.82	4.31	217	(6.80)	359	8.74	325	36
3,695,825	3.6	261	5.7	220	15.8	141	4.77	7.92	13.33	88	13.06	243	17.27	173	20
7,019,751	4.9	191	4.2	275	8.5§	295	1.91	44.70	(1.93)	295	27.22	146	1.73	380	26
5,489,620	7.5	82	6.0	203	12.5	207	170‡	100.00	13.90	80	25.03	171	8.17	330	42
2,177,523	0.7	383	1.5	364	4.6	356	0.89	(80.78)	(0.75)	284	(8.59)	364	21.48	108	41
6,077,944	7.1	99	9.2	83	38.9	6	5.06	60.63	15.70	61	53.09	47	19.49	141	20
5,083,418	5.5	156	3.9	291	8.1‡	300	5.79	168.06	0.33	271	53.43	45	5.96	352	26
3,262,232	4.3	221	7.0	161	11.1	251	1.43	32.41	9.21	151	11.96	250	13.40	243	20
5,396,533	6.9	101	6.8	170	13.7‡	185	3.18	(13.35	10.85	125	35.28	111	22.35	95	21
2,629,176	4.6	210	4.3	269	13.0	204	5.79	(14.22)	6.01	192	32.77	122	15.05	216	41
4,199,247	4.5	216	6.2	191	15.5	150	3.00	20.00	9.47	145	38.92	99	21.59	107	20
3,310,804	3.6	260	6.2	190	18.1	102	2.52	81.29	2.60	239	29.30	137	10.09	308	43
4,194,148	0.6	387	0.9	381	1.7	385	0.71‡	—	(16.38)	329	13.91	236	3.35	372	36
7,573,481	8.3	70	10.9	50	17.2	117	5.62	3.50	10.61	129	6.42	282	13.51	241	36
13,484,357	15.8	5	18.7	4	32.7	15	5.18	10.21	11.46	115	27.00	149	14.78	221	42
5,951,531	6.9	105	8.4	111	14.0	173	3.42	8.57	13.82	82	11.74	253	19.93	130	44
14,194,929	12.2	23	14.1	12	20.8	64	4.13	6.99	12.92	97	28.35	142	28.29	34	42
2,660,881	4.3	227	8.2	120	24.0	36	3.67	(15.83)	14.07	75	11.38	255	22.90	86	41
5,197,866	6.8	110	6.8	169	16.0	139	2.66	17.18	8.17	164	46.97	58	20.18	126	32
3,808,440	5.4	162	3.8	297	6.8	329	2.96	—	3.69	227	(9.22)	367	6.16	350	33
4,735,244	4.0	242	8.8	97	26.9	25	4.11	—	7.26	178	45.55	67	15.55	208	20
3,970,397	4.8	193	6.0	198	22.9	43	2.30	57.53	5.97	194	60.79	29	18.89	150	20
1,182,303	1.5	360	2.4	342	6.3	340	2.36	(16.31)	0.02	275	13.79	239	13.26	246	36
2,127,019	1.6	359	1.6	363	7.0	325	2.52	(65.34)	16.69	48	(11.64)	375	21.16	114	36
12,134,086	14.8	9	12.8	19	19.3	83	3.90	13.37	13.09	94	23.72	176	19.19	144	42
3,332,450	—		—		—		(1.24)	—	—		23.93	174	22.16	97	20
3,552,622	4.6	209	3.3	311	7.8	309	2.08	30.82	(3.72)	306	26.17	159	5.38	360	26
4,261,359	5.1	179	8.1	124	14.5	163	3.45	12.75	8.44	159	18.18	201	16.59	187	20
6,207,445	6.9	104	10.6	53	22.2	49	2.20	13.99	15.18	64	28.18	143	27.06	47	20
377,581	—		—		—		(3.37)	—	—		(60.00)	439	(13.26)	411	33
5,192,893	6.3	124	7.3	147	14.0	174	5.87	0.51	8.46	158	22.89	179	19.94	129	26
20,869,353	16.4	3	13.2	18	26.3	29	4.85	27.97	11.12	121	84.74	12	17.26	174	42
2,461,465	—		—		—		(2.60)	—	—		(11.96)	377	8.62	326	29
2,826,700	5.0	183	9.1	88	14.8	159	2.70	8.43	9.85	142	41.32	85	15.19	213	36
4,437,936	5.3	170	5.5	227	11.8	233	4.36	62.69	4.36	216	38.93	98	16.26	193	28
2,389,389	3.6	258	4.6	266	11.0	252	4.29	(38.80)	2.10	253	17.55	205	14.56	222	36
14,086,904	14.2	12	140.0	13	30.4	18	2.32	19.59	19.00	26	35.99	108	25.18	65	42

The 100 Largest U.S. Industrial Corporations (ranked by sales) *(concluded)*

Rank '86	Rank '85	Company	Sales ($000)	Sales % Change	Net Income ($000)	Net Income Rank	Net Income % Change	Assets ($000)	Assets Rank	Stockholders' Equity ($000)	Stockholders' Equity Rank
97	162	Hanson Industries North America (Iselin, N.J.)[7,20]	3,768,541¶	64.6	103,062	143	(7.1)	3,228,043	101	1,694,688	76
98	114	Time Inc. (New York)	3,762,087	10.5	376,388	49	88.4	4,299,994	73	1,301,657	103
99	121	SmithKline Beckman (Philadelphia)	3,745,400	15.0	521,100	31	1.3	4,222,000	74	1,296,000	105
100	105	Boise Cascade (Boise, Idaho)	3,739,970	0.1	101,540	144	(2.6)	3,533,647	92	1,575,063	81

¶ Includes sales from discontinued operations of at least 10%; see explanations of sales on page 229.
N.A. Not available.
* Does not include excise taxes; see the explanation of "sales" on page 229.
** Reflects an extraordinary credit of at least 10%; see the explanation of "net income" and "earnings per share" on page 229.
‡ Reflects an extraordinary charge of at least 10%; see the explanation of "net income" and "earnings per share" on page 229.
§ Dividends paid by company on its mandatory redeemable preferred stock were subtracted from net income in calculating this figure.
[1] Figures include General Foods (1985 rank: 38) acquired November 1, 1985.
[2] Name changed from R. J. Reynolds Industries April 25, 1986.
[3] Wholly owned by Royal Dutch/Shell Group (1985 International 500 rank: 1).
[4] Figures include Richardson-Vicks (1985 rank: 271) acquired November 13, 1985.
[5] Figures are for fiscal year ended June 30, 1986.
[6] Name changed from U.S. Steel July 8, 1986. Figures include Texas Oil & Gas acquired February 11, 1986.

Market Value	Net Income as Percent of: Sales		Assets		Stockholders' Equity		Earnings per Share				Total Return to Investors: 1986		1976–86 Growth Rate		Industry Code
									Growth Rate 1976–86						
($000)	%	Rank	%	Rank	%	Rank	'86/$	% Change	%	Rank	%	Rank	%	Rank	
—	2.7	306	3.2	321	6.1	342	N.A.	—	—		—		—		20
5,317,997	10.0	34	8.8	98	28.9	22	5.95	88.89	13.96	78	14.19	232	19.60	138	27
7,130,545	13.9	16	12.3	26	40.2	5	6.78	3.35	18.81	29	30.07	132	21.16	115	42
2,258,576	2.7	307	2.9	331	6.5	337	3.32	(3.77)	(0.30)	278	31.76	127	10.93	293	26

[7] Figures are for fiscal year ended September 30, 1986.
[8] Figures include Sanders Associates (1985 rank: 341) acquired August 13, 1986.
[9] Financial subsidiaries would add 25% or more to sales if consolidated.
[10] Figures include MEI (1985 rank: 358) acquired May 30, 1986.
[11] Spun off Premark International October 31, 1986. Name changed from Dart & Kraft November 21, 1986.
[12] Company was formed by the merger of Sperry (1985 rank: 65) and Burroughs (1985 rank: 72) September 16, 1986.
[13] Name changed from Caterpillar Tractor May 22, 1986.
[14] Figures are for fiscal year ended October 31, 1986.
[15] Figures are for fiscal year ended May 31, 1986.
[16] Figures include Hammermill Paper (1985 rank: 199) acquired September 7, 1986.
[17] Figures include Ex-Cell-O (1985 rank: 287) acquired September 17, 1986.
[18] Figures are for fiscal year ended July 31, 1986.
[19] Figures are for fiscal year ended April 30, 1986.
[20] Figures include SCM (1985 rank: 172) acquired March 31, 1986.

Source: *FORTUNE*

NOTES TO THE FORTUNE DIRECTORY

Sales All companies on the list must have derived more than 50% of their sales from manufacturing and/or mining. Sales include rental and other revenues but exclude dividends, interest, and other non-operating revenues. Sales of subsidiaries are included if they are consolidated. Sales from discontinued operations are included when these figures are published. When the sales are at least 10% higher for this reason, there is a symbol (¶) next to the sales figure. All figures are for the year ending December 31, 1986, unless otherwise noted. Sales figures do not include excise taxes collected by the manufacturer, and so the figures for some corporations—most of which sell gasoline, liquor, or tobacco—may be lower than those published by the corporations themselves. If they are at least 5% lower for this reason, there is an asterisk (*) next to the sales figures.

Assets are those shown at the company's fiscal year-end.

Net Income is shown after taxes and after extraordinary credits or charges if any are shown on the income statement. A double asterisk (**) signifies an extraordinary credit reflecting at least 10 percent of the net income shown, a double dagger (‡) an extraordinary charge of at least 10 percent. Cooperatives provide only "net margin" figures, which are not comparable with the net income figures in these listings, and therefore N.A. is shown in that column. Figures in parentheses indicate a loss.

Stockholders' Equity is the sum of capital stock, surplus, and retained earnings at the company's year-end. Redeemable preferred stock is excluded when its redemption is either mandatory or outside the control of the company, except in the case of cooperatives. For purposes of calculating "net income as percent of stockholders' equity," any dividends paid on redeemable preferred stock, if that stock's redemption is either mandatory or outside the control of the company, have been subtracted from the net income figure.

Market Value The figure shown represents the most recent number of common shares outstanding multiplied by the price per common share as of March 13, 1987.

Earnings per Share For all companies, the figures shown are the primary earnings per share that appear on the company's income statement. These figures are based on a weighted average of the number of common shares and common-stock equivalents outstanding during the year. Per-share earnings for 1985 and 1976 are adjusted for stock splits and stock dividends. They are not restated for mergers, acquisitions, or accounting changes made after 1976. A double asterisk (**) signifies an extraordinary credit reflecting at least 10 percent of the net income shown, a double dagger (‡) an extraordinary charge of at least 10 percent. Results are listed as not available (N.A.) where the companies are cooperatives, joint ventures, or wholly owned subsidiaries of other companies, or if the figures were not published in 1976. The growth rate is the average annual growth, compounded. No growth rate is given if the company had a loss in either 1976 or 1986.

Total Return to Investors includes both price appreciation and dividend yield, to an investor in the company's stock. The figures shown assume sales at the end of 1986 of stock owned at the end of 1976 and 1985. It has been assumed that any proceeds from cash dividends, the sale of rights and warrant offerings, and stock received in spin-offs were reinvested at the end of the year in which they were paid. Returns are adjusted for stock splits, stock dividends, recapitalizations, and corporate reorganizations as they occur; however, no effort has been made to reflect the cost of brokerage commissions or of taxes. Results are listed as not available (N.A.) if shares are not publicly traded or traded on only a limited basis. If companies have more than one class of shares outstanding, only the more widely held and actively traded has been considered.

Total-return percentages shown are the returns received by the hypothetical investor described above. The ten-year figures are annual averages, compounded.

Industry Code numbers used in the directory indicate which industry represents the greatest volume of industrial sales for each company. The numbers refer to the industry groups below, which are based on categories established by the U.S. Office of Management and Budget and issued by the Federal Statistical Policy and Standards Office. The median figures in the tables refer only to results of companies among the 500; no attempt has been made to calculate medians in groups with fewer than four companies.

Code No.	Industry
10	Mining, crude-oil production
20	Food
21	Tobacco
22	Textiles
23	Apparel
25	Furniture
26	Forest products
27	Publishing, printing
28	Chemicals
29	Petroleum refining
30	Rubber products
31	Leather
32	Building materials
33	Metals
34	Metal products
36	Electronics
37	Transportation equipment
38	Scientific and photographic equipment
40	Motor vehicles and parts
41	Aerospace
42	Pharmaceuticals
43	Soaps, cosmetics
44	Computers (includes office equipment)
45	Industrial and farm equipment
46	Jewelry, silverware
47	Toys, sporting goods
49	Beverages

The 100 Largest International Industrial Corporations (ranked by sales)

Rank 1986	Rank 1985	Company	Country	Sales $ Thousands	Net Income $ Thousands	Net Income Rank	Assets $ Thousands	Assets Rank	Stockholders' Equity $ Thousands	Stockholders' Equity Rank	Employees	Employees Rank	Industry Code
1	1	Royal Dutch/Shell Group	Neth./Britain	64,843,217	3,725,779	1	76,462,902	1	37,071,395	1	138,000	26	29
2	2	British Petroleum	Britain	39,855,564	731,954	16	42,065,937	3	14,783,490	5	126,700	34	29
3	5	IRI[1]	Italy	31,561,709	197,118	74	74,682,599	2	17,699,776	2	471,366	2	33
4	3	Toyota Motor[2]	Japan	31,553,827	1,717,733	3	26,545,201	10	17,443,803	3	82,620	52	40
5	16	Daimler-Benz	W. Germany	30,168,550	831,600	13	24,440,195	12	5,674,005	22	319,965	5	40
6	7	Matsushita Electric Industrial[3]	Japan	26,459,539	946,571	12	26,867,705	9	13,341,684	8	135,881	28	36
7	6	Unilever	Neth./Britain	25,141,672	973,983	11	20,448,122	18	5,626,087	23	302,000	6	20
8	15	Volkswagen	W. Germany	24,317,154	286,133	53	21,193,030	16	5,316,053	25	281,718	7	40
9	8	Hitachi[4]	Japan	22,668,085	679,609	18	29,077,686	6	9,812,247	9	164,117	16	36
10	4	ENI[1]	Italy	22,549,921	342,275	45	32,474,458	4	6,845,417	18	129,903	32	29
11	13	Philips' Gloeilampenfabrieken	Netherlands	22,471,263	414,418	34	23,304,948	14	7,299,425	15	344,200	4	36
12	17	Nestlé	Switzerland	21,153,285[5]	994,566[5]	10	15,548,327[5]	25	7,253,408[5]	16	162,078[5]	18	20
13	14	Siemens[6]	W. Germany	20,307,037	629,353	22	28,774,413	8	7,087,383	17	363,000	3	36
14	12	Nissan Motor[4]	Japan	20,141,237	158,477	99	20,203,958	19	7,702,066	13	106,282	40	40
15	22	Fiat	Italy	19,669,581	1,449,556	4	28,879,014	7	7,482,450	14	230,293	8	40
16	19	Bayer	W. Germany	18,768,914[5]	619,752[5]	24	16,630,387[5]	23	5,860,878[5]	21	170,000[5]	13	28
17	20	BASF	W. Germany	18,640,985[5]	416,418[5]	32	14,991,368[5]	27	6,088,424[5]	20	131,468[5]	31	28
18	30	Renault[1]	France	17,661,021[5]	(844,233)[5]	496	16,057,237[5]	24	(1,465,893)[5]	499	182,448[5]	11	40
19	21	Hoechst	W. Germany	17,509,344[5]	568,152[5]	27	14,297,531[5]	30	4,563,816[5]	29	181,176[5]	12	28
20	10	Elf Aquitaine[1]	France	17,287,058[5]	617,833[5]	25	24,301,866[5]	13	7,950,917[5]	12	71,350	63	29
21	23	Samsung	South Korea	16,522,664	182,175	82	10,900,652	44	1,273,522	142	147,154	23	36
22	24	Mitsubishi Heavy Industries[4]	Japan	15,932,973	299,241	50	20,874,679	17	2,659,893	57	88,600	47	40
23	38	Peugeot	France	15,152,869	518,350	29	11,304,375	42	1,652,031	103	165,042	14	40
24	31	Toshiba[4]	Japan	15,036,390	268,916	58	17,835,923	22	3,190,073	47	120,000	36	36
25	27	Imperial Chemical Industries	Britain	14,867,911	817,031	14	12,876,995	35	5,433,362	24	121,800	35	28
26	18	Petrobrás (Petróleo Brasileiro)[1]	Brazil	14,701,534	2,073,456	2	15,524,884	26	8,287,636	11	64,319	76	29
27	28	Kuwait Petroleum[1,2]	Kuwait	13,911,716	184,562	79	18,872,720	21	13,729,409	6	15,402	289	29
28	11	Total Cie Française des Pétroles[1]	France	13,821,041[5]	(68,006)[5]	475	12,137,212[5]	40	3,630,861[5]	41	40,253[5]	119	29
29	37	Thyssen[6]	W. Germany	13,818,174	150,463	105	8,645,627	57	1,598,438	106	127,683	33	33
30	32	Nippon Oil[4]	Japan	13,690,884	56,371	225	8,424,521	60	1,947,320	85	10,599	368	29
31	26	General Motors of Canada	Canada	13,335,100[7]	301,085	48	3,410,112	168	1,761,133	97	45,994	100	40
32	36	BAT Industries	Britain	13,210,379	1,273,219	7	13,883,612	31	6,179,060	19	162,580	17	21
33	33	Nippon Steel[4]	Japan	13,034,715	184,174	80	21,373,266	15	3,856,188	34	70,492	65	33
34	41	Honda Motor[8]	Japan	12,481,447	643,578	20	9,279,147	55	4,217,546	31	53,730	87	40
35	42	Volvo	Sweden	11,795,263	414,637	33	10,707,907	46	2,980,567	51	73,147	60	40
36	48	CGE (Cie Générale d'Électricité)[1]	France	11,681,337	167,417	92	26,401,505	11	1,321,515	135	149,010	20	36
37	43	Lucky-Goldstar	South Korea	11,433,748	131,934	114	7,247,470	73	1,333,168	134	64,750	74	36

The definitions and concepts underlying the figures in this directory are explained on page 234.

(continued)

The 100 Largest International Industrial Corporations *(concluded)*

Rank				Sales	Net Income		Assets		Stockholders' Equity		Employees		Industry
1986	1985	Company	Country	$ Thousands	$ Thousands	Rank	$ Thousands	Rank	$ Thousands	Rank		Rank	Code
38	54	Saint-Gobain[1]	France	11,222,417[5]	182,030[5]	83	12,223,177[5]	39	1,994,189[5]	80	147,579[5]	22	32
39	49	Daewoo	South Korea	11,204,191	53,580	233	13,067,635	33	1,180,498	147	91,944	46	45
40	9	Pemex (Petróleos Mexicanos)[1]	Mexico	11,032,902[9]	3,596[9]	417	30,915,214[9]	5	13,616,567[9]	7	155,907[9]	19	29
41	40	Canadian Pacific	Canada	10,807,709	(57,764)	467	12,815,862	37	4,186,770	32	93,800	44	33
42	47	NEC[4]	Japan	10,562,396	122,989	133	14,561,695	28	2,804,279	53	95,796	43	36
43	45	Ford Motor of Canada	Canada	10,308,776[7]	72,717	197	2,255,633	260	777,247	209	27,512	172	40
44	46	Idemitsu Kosan[4]	Japan	10,255,663[9]	3,343[9]	418	8,568,750[9]	59	225,918[9]	425	5,858[9]	443	29
45	58	Robert Bosch	W. Germany	10,003,662	176,770	86	8,320,861	61	2,257,226	71	148,888	21	40
46	62	Mazda Motor[10]	Japan	9,678,888	83,567	174	6,249,896	88	1,913,953	88	30,603	155	40
47	53	Ruhrkohle	W. Germany	9,637,210	25,331	339	9,317,942	54	576,350	261	132,570	29	10
48	52	Mitsubishi Electric[4]	Japan	9,401,584	120,985	135	10,321,047	48	2,609,510	58	71,479	62	36
49	34	Petróleos de Venezuela[1]	Venezuela	9,249,726	1,196,262	8	18,971,739	20	16,596,548	4	44,674	105	29
50	61	Thomson[1]	France	9,045,864	127,350	122	12,591,501	38	882,547	187	105,000	41	36
51	55	Ciba-Geigy	Switzerland	8,869,925	645,439	19	13,815,366	32	8,922,553	10	82,231	54	28
52	56	Montedison	Italy	8,604,813	214,550	69	13,023,898	34	2,414,488	63	66,649	72	28
53	51	Indian Oil[1,4]	India	8,076,784	105,860	148	2,999,301	195	764,138	215	31,998	148	29
54	74	Mannesmann	W. Germany	7,938,097[5]	36,156[5]	291	6,077,782[5]	93	1,590,194[5]	107	108,556[5]	39	45
55	44	Petrofina	Belgium	7,847,250	410,489	35	8,230,042	63	2,462,112	62	22,200	220	29
56	83	Brown Boveri	Switzerland	7,686,342	44,475	260	10,011,152	49	2,602,850	59	97,500	42	36
57	100	Ford-Werke	W. Germany	7,683,589[7]	270,448	57	3,491,391	164	557,733	264	46,311	98	40
58	68	Fujitsu[4]	Japan	7,654,080	173,918	88	10,539,026	47	3,582,990	44	84,277	51	44
59	72	Rhône-Poulenc[1]	France	7,608,344[5]	289,930[5]	51	2,571,742[5]	228	2,116,983[5]	77	84,600[5]	50	28
60	108	Electrolux	Sweden	7,446,908	285,168	54	7,164,367	74	1,469,218	120	141,753	25	36
61	80	Sony[10]	Japan	7,432,628	238,907	65	8,874,816	56	3,711,089	38	48,671	95	36
62	193	British Coal[1,11]	Britain	7,352,956	(68,848)	476	9,446,608	52	(53,046)	495	199,600	10	10
63	101	Norsk Hydro[1]	Norway	7,331,609	(50,544)	463	8,230,373	62	N.A.		43,122	108	28
64	71	Fried. Krupp	W. Germany	7,299,059	36,270	290	5,634,278	102	1,040,549	162	68,043	68	33
65	64	General Electric[4]	Britain	7,233,160	623,624	23	7,590,146	70	3,851,287	35	164,536	15	36
66	57	DSM[1]	Netherlands	7,231,699[5]	168,217[5]	91	4,616,801[5]	130	1,371,231[5]	128	27,315[5]	177	28
67	97	BMW (Bayerische Motoren Werke)	W. Germany	7,166,269	159,677	97	4,709,828	123	1,374,589	125	50,719	89	40
68	29	VÖEST-Alpine	Austria	7,079,471	(3,773)	440	6,775,774	82	359,248	359	65,100	73	33
69	110	Dalgety[2]	Britain	7,072,281	14,836	385	1,748,012	321	453,472	310	20,098	234	20
70	73	Sanyo Electric[12]	Japan	6,916,814	12,246	399	7,068,534	77	2,555,211	60	25,599	193	36
71	96	Adam Opel	W. Germany	6,834,236[7]	(65,189)	472	3,767,282	153	794,276	202	55,438	86	40
72	76	Grand Metropolitan[6]	Britain	6,757,909	384,526	36	6,107,232	92	2,959,429	52	131,493	30	49
73	91	Michelin	France	6,689,030	274,590	55	8,132,416	65	1,500,862	116	119,300	37	30

74	78	Statoil[1]	Norway	6,647,776	154,741	101	6,835,390	81	707,390	223	8,471	393	29
75	107	ASEA	Sweden	6,456,746	247,576	62	7,859,813	69	1,429,907	123	63,124	78	45
76	90	Ford Motor	Britain	6,415,967[7]	115,881	139	5,639,430	101	1,543,282	111	49,000	93	40
77	86	Akzo Group	Netherlands	6,375,425	343,579	44	5,260,345	109	1,984,442	81	68,400	67	28
78	109	Isuzu Motors[10]	Japan	6,325,777	(67,689)	474	4,988,782	114	539,810	271	25,608	191	40
79	60	Showa Shell Sekiyu	Japan	6,168,625[9]	29,181[9]	326	4,318,282[9]	139	308,579[9]	388	2,832[9]	487	29
80	87	Sacilor[1]	France	6,154,075[5]	(1,069,910)[5]	497	7,349,381[5]	72	357,221[5]	362	55,573[5]	85	33
81	70	Nippon Kokan[4]	Japan	6,086,493	30,248	319	14,407,506	29	1,459,623	122	38,106	124	33
82	67	Sunkyong	South Korea	6,005,876	69,507	206	2,883,300	202	534,253	273	19,540	238	29
83	79	Barlow Rand[6]	South Africa	5,944,771	150,697	104	4,559,666	132	885,438	186	143,959	24	20
84	84	Broken Hill Proprietary[13]	Australia	5,937,725	707,301	17	11,829,233	41	4,700,137	28	61,000	80	33
85	95	BTR	Britain	5,895,531	630,889	21	4,745,779	122	1,854,756	92	79,400	55	45
86	128	Nippondenso	Japan	5,879,785	191,426	76	5,437,701	106	2,783,588	54	42,967	109	40
87	81	Alcan Aluminium	Canada	5,756,000	244,000	63	7,118,000	75	3,116,000	49	64,500	75	33
88	65	Veba Oel	W. Germany	5,711,567	107,449	144	2,582,593	226	715,487	222	16,782	273	29
89	98	Kawasaki Steel[4]	Japan	5,585,393[9]	83,095[9]	176	11,011,852[9]	43	1,916,143[9]	87	33,212[9]	136	33
90	88	Kobe Steel[4]	Japan	5,583,004	29,217	325	10,733,074	45	863,176	189	31,486	150	33
91	111	IBM Deutschland	W. Germany	5,537,978[7]	238,437	66	4,274,460	142	1,039,771	163	28,546	165	44
92	89	Sumitomo Metal Industries[4]	Japan	5,459,793	82,869	177	12,821,413	36	1,869,910	90	33,670	133	33
93	106	Sharp[4]	Japan	5,370,672	161,761	95	6,941,143	78	2,136,661	74	28,873	161	36
94	154	Hanson Trust[6]	Britain	5,339,905	535,899	28	9,642,922	51	2,297,518	70	92,000	45	20
95	93	Mitsubishi Chemical Industries[14]	Japan	5,306,188	32,145	308	5,929,631	95	685,585	232	18,400	252	28
96	92	Chrysler Canada	Canada	5,295,095[7]	139,089	111	1,490,514	360	502,896	285	12,093	346	40
97	118	IBM France	France	5,288,329[7]	356,925	41	3,810,726	152	1,576,133	109	22,225	218	44
98	125	Canon	Japan	5,277,304	63,668	214	6,377,157	83	2,125,433	76	35,498	128	44
99	66	Esso (Germany)	W. Germany	5,233,831[7]	141,224	110	2,327,261	249	677,671	235	3,231	484	29
100	130	IBM Japan	Japan	5,213,933[7,9]	379,428[9]	38	3,656,229[9]	158	1,639,255[9]	105	18,822[9]	245	44

The definitions and concepts underlying the figures in this directory are explained on page 234.

• Indicates that a corporation was not among the 500 in 1985.

N.A. Not available.

[1] Company owned by its government.

[2] Figures are for fiscal year ended June 30, 1986.

[3] Figures are for fiscal year ended November 20, 1986.

[4] Figures are for fiscal year ended March 31, 1986.

[5] Figure includes certain subsidiaries owned 50% or less, either fully or on a prorated basis.

[6] Figures are for fiscal year ended September 30, 1986.

[7] Revenues include sales to other affiliates of U.S. parent also on this list.

[8] Figures are for fiscal year ended February 28, 1986.

[9] Figures are for parent company only.

[10] Figures are for fiscal year ended October 31, 1986.

[11] British Coal (62): Name was changed from National Coal Board on March 5, 1987.

[12] Figures are for fiscal year ended November 30, 1986.

[13] Figures are for fiscal year ended May 31, 1986.

[14] Figures are for fiscal year ended January 31, 1986.

NOTES TO THE INTERNATIONAL 100*

Sales All companies on the list must have derived more than 50% of their sales from manufacturing and/or mining. Sales do not include excise taxes or customs duties levied according to either volume or value sales, and so the figures for some companies—most of which sell gasoline, liquor, or tobacco—may be lower than those published by the companies themselves. Unless otherwise noted, figures exclude intracompany transactions and include consolidated subsidiaries more than 50% owned, either fully or on a prorated basis. Figures have been converted to dollars using an exchange rate that consists of the official average rate during each company's fiscal year (ended December 31, 1986, unless otherwise noted).

Assets Totals shown at each company's year-end. Figures have been converted to dollars at the official exchange rate at each company's year-end.

Net Income is shown after taxes, minority interests, and extraordinary items. Figures have been converted to dollars using an exchange rate that consists of the official average rate during each company's fiscal year (ended December 31, 1986, unless otherwise noted).

Stockholders' Equity is shown at each company's year-end. Minority interest is not included. Figures have been converted to dollars at the official exchange rate at each company's year-end.

Employees The figure shown is either a year-end or yearly average number as published.

Industry Code Numbers used in the directory indicate which industry represents the greatest volume of industrial sales for each company. The numbers refer to the industry groups listed on page 230, which are based on categories established by the U.S. Office of Management and Budget and issued by the Federal Statistical Policy and Standards Office. The median figures in the tables refer only to results of companies in the 500. No attempt has been made to calculate medians in groups or countries with fewer than four companies.

* Selected from the Fortune 500.

The 25 Largest Industrial Companies in the World (ranked by sales)

Rank '86	Rank '85	Company	Headquarters	Industry	Sales (000)	Net Income (000)
1	1	General Motors	Detroit	Motor vehicles and parts	102,813,700	2,944,700
2	2	Exxon	New York	Petroleum refining	69,888,000	5,360,000
3	3	Royal Dutch/Shell Group	The Hague/London	Petroleum refining	64,843,217	3,725,779
4	6	Ford Motor	Dearborn, Mich.	Motor vehicles and parts	62,715,800	3,285,100
5	7	International Business Machines	Armonk, N.Y.	Computers	51,250,000	4,789,000
6	4	Mobil	New York	Petroleum refining	44,866,000	1,407,000
7	5	British Petroleum	London	Petroleum refining	39,855,564	731,954
8	12	General Electric	Fairfield, Conn.	Electronics	35,211,000	2,492,000
9	10	American Tel. & Tel.	New York	Electronics	34,087,000	139,000
10	8	Texaco	White Plains, N.Y.	Petroleum refining	31,613,000	725,000
11	16	IRI	Rome	Metals	31,561,709	197,118
12	14	Toyota Motor	Toyota City (Japan)	Motor vehicles and parts	31,553,827	1,717,733
13	31	Daimler-Benz	Stuttgart	Motor vehicles and parts	30,168,550	831,600
14	11	E.I. du Pont de Nemours	Wilmington, Del.	Chemicals	27,148,000	1,538,000
15	20	Matsushita Electric Industrial	Osaka	Electronics	26,459,539	946,571
16	18	Unilever	Rotterdam/London	Food	25,141,672	973,983
17	9	Chevron	San Francisco	Petroleum refining	24,351,000	715,000
18	30	Volkswagen	Wolfsburg (W. Germany)	Motor vehicles and parts	24,317,154	286,133
19	21	Hitachi	Tokyo	Electronics	22,668,085	679,609
20	15	ENI	Rome	Petroleum refining	22,549,921	342,275
21	19	Chrysler	Highland Park, Mich.	Motor vehicles and parts	22,513,500	1,403,600
22	28	Phillips' Gloeilampenfabrieken	Eindhoven (Netherlands)	Electronics	22,471,263	414,418
23	32	Nestlé	Vevey (Switzerland)	Food	21,153,285	994,566
24	●	Philip Morris	New York	Tobacco	20,681,000	1,478,000
25	29	Siemens	Munich	Electronics	20,307,037	629,353

● Not on last year's list.

Source: Reprinted from *FORTUNE*,

The 25 Largest Diversified Service Companies (ranked by sales)

Rank '86	Rank '85	Company	Sales[1] ($000)	Assets ($000)	Assets Rank	Net Income ($000)	Net Income Rank	Stockholders' Equity ($000)	Stockholders' Equity Rank
1	6	Super Valu Stores (Eden Prairie, Minn.)[2]	7,905,016	1,555,451	33	91,247	23	534,830	33
2	5	Fleming Cos. (Oklahoma City)	7,652,624	1,242,289	38	39,315	42	472,732	38
3	7	McKesson (San Francisco)[3]	6,285,000	2,176,000	29	77,900	28	695,800	27
4	8	CBS (New York)	4,900,400	3,370,300	9	375,100	2	806,500	20
5	10	Fluor (Irvine, Calif.)[4]	4,678,661	2,565,393	21	(60,443)	83	950,240	17
6	11	Hospital Corp. of America (Nashville)	4,665,592	6,793,372	1	174,644	12	2,015,383	4
7	13	Alco Standard (Wayne, Pa.)[5]	4,334,022	1,229,711	39	56,963	33	425,590	40
8	15	Electronic Data Systems (Dallas)[6]	4,321,000	2,409,600	22	260,900	7	798,300	21
9	·	American Can (Greenwich, Conn.)[7]	4,292,800¶	5,350,100	2	196,300‡	9	1,354,100	11
10	28	National Intergroup (Pittsburgh)[3]	4,166,294	2,270,904	26	(88,451)	86	763,023	22
11	·	Capital Cities Comm./ABC (New York)[8]	4,124,374	5,191,416	3	447,689**	1	1,948,627	5
12	19	Ryder System (Miami)	3,768,328	4,783,910	4	160,933	13	1,239,231	12
13	14	ARA Holding (Philadelphia)[5]	3,748,749	1,651,231	32	15,502	61	114,384	81
14	9	Halliburton (Dallas)	3,509,439	3,328,028	10	(515,214)	90	2,150,172	3
15	18	Wetterau (Hazelwood, Mo.)[3]	3,482,315	639,564	64	31,825	47	243,127	55
16	21	Sysco (Houston)[9]	3,172,269	781,291	60	58,328	32	397,822	45
17	·	Henley Group (La Jolla, Calif.)[10]	3,172,000	4,698,000	5	(426,000)	89	3,364,000	1
18	20	Dun & Bradstreet (New York)	3,113,506	3,117,664	15	339,990	4	1,448,830	9
19	27	Bergen Brunswig (Orange, Calif.)[11]	3,065,536	785,159	59	20,661	57	176,839	69
20	24	National Medical Enterprises (Los Angeles)[12]	2,962,000	3,296,000	11	85,000‡	26	1,010,000	15
21	32	Warner Communications (New York)	2,848,324	3,223,452	13	185,795	11	1,172,520	13
22	16	ENSERCH (Dallas)	2,722,821	3,233,558	12	26,878	49	973,393	16
23	23	Greyhound (Phoenix)	2,647,428	2,963,731	16	186,158	10	1,054,407	14
24	33	Humana (Louisville, Ky.)[11]	2,600,610	2,916,230	17	54,452	34	896,358	18
25	31	American Medical Int'l (Beverly Hills, Calif.)[11]	2,569,893	3,901,107	8	(97,279)	87	886,748	19

The definitions and concepts underlying the figures in this directory are explained on pages 236–38.
· Not on last year's list.
¶ Includes sales from discontinued operations of at least 10%.
† Average for the year; see the reference to "employees" on page 237.
** Reflects an extraordinary credit of at least 10%; see the explanations of "net income" and "earnings per share" on page 237.
‡ Reflects an extraordinary charge of at least 10%; see the explanations of "net income" and "earnings per share" on page 237.
§ Dividends paid by company on its mandatory redeemable preferred stock were subtracted from net income in calculating this figure.
[1] Net sales include all operating revenues and revenues from discontinued operations when they are published. All figures are for the fiscal year ending December 31, 1986, unless otherwise noted. Sales of subsidiaries are included when they are consolidated. All companies on the list must have derived more than 50% of their revenues from non-manufacturing and/or non-mining businesses. Excluded (but eligible for the lists that follow) are companies deriving more than 50% of their revenues solely from banking, life insurance, finance, retailing, transportation, or utilities.

NOTES TO SERVICE COMPANIES

Assets are those shown at the company's fiscal year-end.

Net income is shown after taxes and after extraordinary credits or charges if any are shown on the income statement. A double asterisk (**) signifies an extraordinary credit reflecting at least 10% of the net income shown, a double dagger (‡) an extraordinary charge of at least 10%. Figures in parentheses indicate a loss.

Stockholders' equity is the sum of capital stock, surplus, and retained earnings at the company's year-end. Redeemable preferred stock is excluded if its redemption is either mandatory or outside the control of the company, except in the case of cooperatives. For purposes of calculating "net income as percent of stockholders' equity," any dividends

Employees		Net Income as Percent of				Earnings per Share					Total Return to Investors			
		Sales		Stock-holders' Equity					Growth Rate 1976–86		1986		1976–86 Average	
Number	Rank	%	Rank	%	Rank	'86($)	'85($)	'76($)	%	Rank	%	Rank	%	Rank
26,575	19	1.2	61	17.1	22	1.23	1.45	0.22	18.51	15	11.42	44	26.38	19
15,880	36	0.5	74	8.3	63	1.80	2.87	1.05	5.54	49	(9.21)	64	20.06	40
17,200	33	1.2	58	11.2	50	3.96	3.60	2.58	4.38	51	26.40	20	22.28	27
18,300	31	7.7	14	44.9§	3	15.42	0.81	5.75	10.37	37	12.09	43	12.78	63
21,391	24	—		—		(0.76)	(8.01)	1.29	—		(23.81)	81	1.90	77
89,000	3	3.7	35	8.7	60	2.08	3.75**	0.54	14.39	28	(13.49)	67	20.83	35
18,700	29	1.3	56	13.2§	41	3.24	2.32	1.55	7.62	46	13.25	42	21.48	31
45,000	10	6.0	22	32.7	7	2.13	1.57	N.A.	—		—		—	
24,300†	20	4.6	30	12.9§	44	3.21‡	2.53	2.55	2.33	55	45.33	11	15.85	53
6,965	59	—		—		(4.50)	(1.44)	4.53	—		(48.22)	85	(6.54)	80
19,960	28	10.9	8	23.0	14	27.55**	10.87	2.30	28.19	4	19.53	30	25.60	20
34,981	15	4.3	33	13.0	43	2.09	1.73	0.49	15.69	22	52.59	6	28.17	16
115,000†	2	0.4	76	13.6	40	N.A.	N.A.	N.A.	—		—		—	
46,909	8	—		—		(4.85)	(3.12)‡	2.61	—		6.67	61	0.80	78
10,200†	52	0.9	65	13.1	42	2.90	2.51	1.54	6.50	47	0.95	51	15.59	55
10,700	51	1.8	48	14.7	33	1.34	1.17	0.26	18.02	16	35.21	14	34.29	12
22,400	23	—		—		(5.33)	N.A.	N.A.	—		—		—	
58,000	6	10.9	7	23.5	13	4.47	3.88	0.90	17.38	17	28.58	18	25.56	21
4,552	71	0.7	71	11.7	48	1.54	1.74	0.16	25.21	7	(31.49)	83	25.40	22
83,000	4	2.9	39	8.4	61	1.08	1.98	0.25	15.96	21	3.03	48	33.91	13
11,660	49	6.5	18	15.9	28	1.26	1.43	0.56	8.48	44	21.94	24	22.09	28
16,300	34	1.0	64	2.4§	75	0.17	(1.12)	1.71	(20.62)	65	(19.96	77	8.88	67
35,922	13	7.2	16	17.7§	20	4.09	2.48	1.76	8.80	42	(0.46)	54	14.74	58
45,300	9	2.1	45	6.1	66	0.56	2.19	0.12	16.37	19	(36.96)	84	35.11	11
47,000	7	—		—		(1.12)	1.94	0.35	—		(21.11)	79	18.74	44

[2] Figures are for fiscal year ended February 28, 1986.
[3] Figures are for fiscal year ended March 31, 1986.
[4] Figures are for fiscal year ended October 31, 1986.
[5] Figures are for fiscal year ended September 30, 1986.
[6] Wholly owned by General Motors (No. 1 on the FORTUNE 500 Industrials).
[7] Company was No. 140 on last year's FORTUNE 500 Industrials.
[8] Company formed January 3, 1986, upon acquisition of American Broadcasting (1985 rank: 17) by Capital Cities Communications (No. 306 on last year's FORTUNE 500 Industrials).
[9] Figures are for fiscal year ended June 30, 1986.
[10] Company comprises 35 businesses spun off from Allied-Signal (No. 25 on the FORTUNE 500 Industrials) May 27, 1986.
[11] Figures are for fiscal year ended August 31, 1986.
[12] Figures are for fiscal year ended May 31, 1986.

Source: Reprinted from *FORTUNE*, "© 1987 Time Inc. All rights reserved."

paid on redeemable preferred stock, if that stock's redemption is either mandatory or outside the control of the company, have been subtracted from the net income figure.

Employees The figure shown is a year-end total except when it is followed by a dagger (†), in which case it is an average for the year.

Earnings per Share For all companies the figures shown are the primary earnings per share that appear on the company's income statement. These figures are based on a weighted average of the number of common shares and common stock equivalents outstanding during the year. Per-share earnings for 1985 and 1986 are adjusted for stock splits and stock dividends. They are not restated for mergers, acquisitions, or accounting changes made after 1976. A double asterisk (**) signifies an extraordinary credit reflecting at least 10% of the net income shown, a double dagger (‡) an extraordinary charge of at least 10%. Figures in parentheses indicate a loss. Results are listed as not available (N.A.)

The 25 Largest Life Insurance Companies (ranked by assets)

Rank 1986	Rank 1985	Company	Assets[1] ($000)	Premium and Annuity Income[2] ($000)	Rank	Net Investment Income ($000)	Rank
1	1	Prudential of America (Newark)*	103,317,115	17,380,277	1	6,221,946	2
2	2	Metropolitan Life (New York)*	81,581,350	12,148,965	2	6,705,678	1
3	3	Equitable Life Assurance (New York)*	48,577,698	5,500,913	4	2,733,134	5
4	4	Aetna Life (Hartford)[7]	42,957,155	10,506,887	3	3,130,175	3
5	5	New York Life*	29,793,627	3,477,186	7	2,412,632	6
6	8	Teachers Insurance & Annuity (New York)	27,887,103	2,654,607	13	2,778,127	4
7	6	John Hancock Mutual Life (Boston)*	27,213,497	4,173,912	5	1,406,348	10
8	7	Travelers (Hartford)[8]	27,210,137	4,023,926	6	2,371,822	7
9	9	Connecticut General Life (Bloomfield)[9]	24,806,504	2,869,639	11	1,544,123	8
10	10	Northwestern Mutual Life (Milwaukee)*	20,187,343	2,934,270	9	1,439,008	9
11	11	Massachusetts Mutual Life (Springfield)*	18,027,848	2,487,919	14	1,338,391	12
12	12	Principal Mutual Life (Des Moines)*[10]	16,993,647	3,112,712	8	1,391,709	11
13	13	New England Mutual Life (Boston)*	12,827,256	2,769,876	12	1,019,988	13
14	14	Mutual of New York*	11,248,982	2,197,790	15	723,087	16
15	19	Executive Life (Los Angeles)	9,870,910	1,615,782	21	800,593	15
16	15	Mutual Benefit Life (Newark)*	9,837,863	1,634,881	19	891,052	14
17	16	Connecticut Mutual Life (Hartford)*	8,934,017	1,763,712	17	645,224	18
18	17	State Farm Life (Bloomington, Ill.)	7,485,062	1,224,966	29	657,372	17
19	18	IDS LIfe (Minneapolis)[11]	7,301,941	1,213,298	31	580,540	19
20	21	Variable Annuity Life (Houston)	6,614,424	1,004,512	36	562,186	20
21	20	Nationwide Life (Columbus, Ohio)	6,444,987	1,013,129	35	386,565	24
22	26	Aetna Life & Annuity (Hartford)[7]	5,610,053	986,995	37	312,460	30
23	24	Continental Assurance (Chicago)[12]	5,601,469	1,488,613	25	178,575	49
24	25	Pacific Mutual Life (Newport Beach, Calif.)*	5,515,535	1,457,421	26	438,057	22
25	30	New York Life & Annuity (Wilmington, Del.)	5,481,656	1,489,552	24	483,440	21

Data for all companies are on the statutory accounting basis required by state insurance regulatory authorities.
* Indicates a mutual company.
[1] As of December 31, 1986.
[2] Includes premium income from life, accident, and health policies, annuities, and from contributions to deposit administration funds.
[3] After dividends to policyholders and federal income taxes, excluding capital gains and losses. Figures in parentheses indicate a loss.
[4] Face value of all life policies, including variable life insurance, as of December 31, 1986.
[5] Change between December 31, 1985, and December 31, 1986.

if the companies are cooperatives, joint ventures, or wholly owned subsidiaries of other companies, or if the figures were not published in 1976. The growth rate is the average annual growth, compounded. No growth rate is given if the company had a loss in either 1976 or 1986.

Total Return to Investors Total return to investors includes both price appreciation and dividend yield to an investor in the company's stock. The figures shown assume sales at the end of 1986 of stock owned at the end of 1976 and 1985. It has been assumed that any proceeds from cash dividends, the sale of rights and warrant offerings, and stock received in spinoffs were reinvested when they were paid. Returns are adjusted for stock splits, stock dividends, recapitalizations, and corporate reorganizations as they occur; however, no effort has been made to reflect the cost of brokerage commissions or of taxes. Results are listed as not available (N.A.) if shares are not publicly traded or are traded on only a limited basis. If companies have more than one class of shares outstanding, only the more widely held and actively traded has been considered.

Total return percentages shown are the returns received by the hypothetical investor described above. The ten-year figures are annual averages, compounded. If corporations were substantially reorganized—e.g., because of mergers—the predecessor companies used in calculating total return are the same as those cited in the footnotes to the earnings-per-share figures.

Net Gain from Operations[3]			Life Insurance in Force[4]		Increase in Life Insurance in Force[5]				Employees[6]	
	Rank									
($000)	Mutual	Stock	($000)	Rank	($000)	Rank	Percent	Rank	Number	Rank
307,946	2		602,393,802	1	41,427,635	1	7.4	30	62,399	1
236,179	3		519,414,564	2	36,614,861	2	7.6	29	35,900	2
332,215	1		291,198,418	3	3,375,770	26	1.2	40	25,000	4
223,676		3	213,119,304	4	5,238,534	22	2.5	39	25,719	3
121,740	5		186,796,438	5	7,912,400	13	4.4	37	18,294	8
182,154		5	17,265,985	41	1,993,630	31	13.1	18	2,780	38
203,433	4		166,532,325	6	7,559,115	15	4.8	36	18,306	7
238,744		2	151,256,243	9	7,111,499	17	4.9	35	N.A.	
359,364		1	120,849,091	11	6,907,952	18	6.1	34	12,537	10
16,873	12		137,078,662	10	16,036,149	5	13.3	17	7,895	17
56,458	7		76,601,093	14	7,965,531	12	11.6	22	8,515	16
64,568	6		72,195,424	15	6,414,580	19	9.8	24	9,723	12
6,515	15		59,358,851	20	7,172,977	16	13.8	16	9,010	14
(53,512)	24		57,472,692	22	6,054,684	20	11.8	21	9,188	13
4,969		21	45,453,517	27	10,482,307	10	30.0	4	800	43
47,024	8		55,626,916	24	4,866	43	9.6	25	4,128	27
39,664	9		47,738,871	25	2,870,590	27	6.4	32	21,680	5
105,411		7	105,964,178	12	13,157,411	6	14.2	14	18,364	6
39,181		14	18,578,247	40	1,973,686	32	11.9	20	6,165	21
13,522		19	3,242	49	(422)	45	—		1,220	42
46,520		13	18,924,656	39	2,114,162	30	12.6	19	7,377	19
(16,932)		24	22,267,006	37	4,036,719	24	22.1	7	12,477	11
81,745		9	69,090	48	8,877	42	—		N.A.	
7,686	14		30,696,149	30	3,743	44	13.9	15	2,830	37
21,665		18	39,135,289	28	9,620,881	11	32.6	2	18,294	9

[6] Includes home office, field force, and full-time agents.
[7] Wholly owned by Aetna Life & Casualty (No. 4 on Diversified Financial list).
[8] Wholly owned by Travelers Corp. (No. 8 on Diversified Financial list).
[9] Wholly owned by CIGNA (No. 6 on Diversified Financial list).
[10] Name changed from Bankers Life July 1, 1986.
[11] Wholly owned by American Express (No. 2 on Diversified Financial list).
[12] Wholly owned by Loews (No. 13 on Diversified Financial list).

Source: Reprinted from *FORTUNE*,

The 25 Largest Commercial Banking Companies (ranked by assets)

Rank '86	Rank '85	Company	Assets[1] ($000)	Deposits ($000)	Deposits Rank	Loans[2] ($000)	Loans Rank	Net Income ($000)	Net Income Rank
1	1	Citicorp (New York)	196,124,000	114,689,000	1	129,206,000	1	1,058,000	1
2	2	BankAmerica Corp. (San Francisco)	104,189,000	82,205,000	2	71,783,000	2	(518,000)	100
3	3	Chase Manhattan Corp. (New York)	94,765,815	66,002,844	3	65,154,782	3	585,363	3
4	5	J. P. Morgan & Co. (New York)	76,039,000	42,960,000	5	33,783,000	9	872,500	2
5	4	Manufacturers Hanover Corp. (New York)	74,397,389	45,544,277	4	55,264,518	4	377,189	7
6	7	Security Pacific Corp. (Los Angeles)	62,606,000	38,408,000	8	43,586,000	5	385,900	6
7	6	Chemical New York Corp.	60,564,123	39,054,910	7	38,756,475	6	402,431	5
8	8	Bankers Trust New York Corp.	56,419,945	29,535,520	10	28,610,057	10	427,912	4
9	9	First Interstate Bancorp (Los Angeles)	55,421,736	39,457,006	6	33,987,675	8	337,934	8
10	13	Wells Fargo & Co. (San Francisco)	44,577,100	32,992,800	9	36,037,100	7	273,500	11
11	10	First Chicago Corp.	39,147,996	27,024,943	11	24,825,398	11	276,202	9
12	11	Mellon Bank Corp. (Pittsburgh)	34,499,370	21,647,152	13	23,034,755	13	183,253	18
13	14	Bank of Boston Corp.	34,045,409	21,724,988	12	23,624,992	12	232,764	14
14	12	Continental Illinois Corp. (Chicago)	32,809,000	18,032,000	16	20,207,000	14	165,200	20
15	15	First Bank System (Minneapolis)	28,012,000	16,261,000	22	14,640,000	19	202,900	15
16	23	NCNB Corp. (Charlotte, N.C.)	27,472,434	18,519,315	15	15,528,982	18	198,765	16
17	32	First Union Corp. (Charlotte, N.C.)	26,820,240	17,003,549	21	13,799,947	22	274,437	10
18	24	SunTrust Banks (Atlanta)	26,165,455	21,284,007	14	16,642,080	16	245,118	12
19	16	Marine Midland Banks (Buffalo and New York)[4]	24,789,596	17,418,418	20	18,420,839	15	144,944	27
20	20	Irving Bank Corp. (New York)	24,232,521	15,327,955	24	13,793,148	23	128,107	30
21	28	Bank of New England Corp. (Boston)	22,472,935	17,676,987	18	15,965,000	17	171,803	19
22	26	PNC Financial Corp. (Pittsburgh)	22,198,930	14,315,971	28	12,397,404	29	237,382	13
23	18	MCorp (Dallas)	21,887,000	17,492,000	19	14,560,000	20	(82,000)	96
24	21	Norwest Corp. (Minneapolis)	21,539,400	14,099,800	30	13,033,900	26	121,700	32
25	31	NBD Bancorp (Detroit)	21,176,031	15,011,323	26	11,151,316	32	145,805	26

† Average for the year; see the reference to "employees" on page 237.

** Reflects an extraordinary credit of at least 10%; see the explanations of "net income" and "earnings per share" on page 237.

§ Dividends paid on mandatory redeemable preferred stock were subtracted from net income.

[1] As of December 31, 1986. All companies on the list must have more than 80% of their assets in chartered commercial banking institutions.

[2] Net of unearned discount and loan loss reserve. Figure includes lease financing.

Stockholders' Equity		Employees		Net Income as Percent of Equity		Earnings per Share					Total Return to Investors			
									Growth Rate: 1976–86		1986		1976–86 Average	
($000)	Rank	Number	Rank	%	Rank	'86($)	'85($)	'76($)	%	Rank	%	Rank	%	Rank
9,060,000	1	88,500	1	11.6§	63	7.14	7.12	3.21	8.32	66	12.29	38	10.89	79
4,038,000	4	73,465	2	—		(3.74)	(2.68)	2.41	—		(6.40)	82	(1.80)	88
4,280,310	3	47,480	3	13.6§	40	6.63	6.39	1.81	13.83	29	4.75	60	16.55	64
5,130,000	2	14,518	16	17.0	6	4.74	3.90	1.26	14.17	27	32.73	7	17.15	60
3,766,354	5	30,316	6	10.0	77	7.99	8.38	4.82	5.18	76	2.62	66	9.41	80
2,875,000	7	35,095	5	13.1§	47	4.86	4.35	1.24	14.61	25	13.14	35	20.36	44
3,119,854	6	20,993	8	12.9	49	7.57	7.33	2.84	10.28	55	(1.78)	75	16.60	63
2,721,300	9	11,069	22	15.7	15	6.01	5.39	1.16	17.83	12	27.43	12	24.39	14
2,759,749	8	35,410†	4	12.3	56	7.19	6.84	2.45	11.35	45	2.87	65	16.15	66
2,342,700	11	21,500	7	11.7	62	5.03	4.15	1.58	12.28	40	65.04	2	20.60	43
2,347,377	10	13,884	17	11.8	61	4.70	2.84	2.67	5.82	75	1.38	67	8.55	81
1,818,982	13	19,800	10	9.5§	81	6.20	7.13	3.27	6.61	71	11.31	40	13.06	76
1,769,309	14	20,000	9	13.2	46	3.69	5.64	0.80	16.55	14	33.50	6	22.43	27
2,048,000	12	9,477	29	8.1	85	0.60	0.53**	3.64	(16.50)	87	(45.37)	88	(11.21)	92
1,417,000	17	9,970†	26	14.3	29	3.42	2.84	1.06	12.37	39	23.93	15	14.50	72
1,308,864	20	12,107	20	15.2§	22	2.53	2.30	0.60	15.48	21	(1.92)	76	18.79	52
1,602,479	15	19,266	12	17.1	3	2.53	2.16	0.61	15.25	22	15.10	29	27.34	4
1,507,858	16	19,711	11	16.3	12	1.86	1.67	0.31[3]	19.48	9	7.46	54	20.79	42
1,368,730	19	12,031†	21	10.6	74	7.19	6.06	1.04	21.33	5	25.28	14	22.64	26
1,052,347	31	10,200	25	12.2	58	6.83	6.14	2.43	10.86	51	8.31	51	20.28	45
1,152,163	26	14,827	15	14.9	25	3.52	3.11	0.80[5]	15.97	19	14.97	31	25.16	10
1,389,970	18	9,328†	30	17.1	5	4.44	3.88	1.24[6]	13.63	30	21.84	19	20.98	39
1,146,000	27	8,472	35	—		(2.21)	3.02	1.50	—		(46.96)	89	2.81	87
1,303,500	21	15,526	14	9.3	82	3.64	3.20	2.61	3.36	79	22.17	18	8.43	82
1,158,007	25	11,038	23	12.6	52	3.87	3.20	1.43	10.44	53	13.13	36	21.34	36

[3] Figure is for Sun Banks.
[4] Company is 52% owned by Hongkong & Shanghai Banking Corp. (No. 27 among last year's Largest International Banks).
[5] Figure is for CBT.
[6] Figure is for Pittsburgh National.

Source: Reprinted from *FORTUNE*,

The 50 Largest International Banks*

The top 50 bank holding companies in the world are listed according to the size of their assets. Also shown are each bank's total deposits and its respective ranking (in parentheses) as well as the total capital and pretax earnings, along with its ranking (again in parentheses) in those categories. For any bank to be ranked in deposits, capital or earnings, the bank must first be among the top 50 in assets. Those cases where bank figures were not available or could not be confirmed for accuracy are indicated by dashes.**

Rank 1985	Rank 1986	Name of Bank	Assets (US$ millions) 1986	Assets (US$ millions) 1985	Deposits (US$ millions) 1986	Capital (US$ millions) 1986	Pretax Earnings (US$ millions) 1986
2	1	Dai-Ichi Kangyo Bank[1,2] Japan	$239,653	$157,614	$182,587(1)	$4,803(14)	$ 986(9)
3	2	Fuji Bank[1,2,3] Japan	212,506	142,088	166,598(2)	5,035(11)	1,089(7)
4	3	Sumitomo Bank[1,2] Japan	205,188	135,349	164,558(3)	6,046(4)	1,242(5)
5	4	Mitsubishi Bank[1] Japan	203,869	132,901	158,720(4)	4,984(12)	971(10)
6	5	Sanwa Bank[1,2] Japan	191,421	122,973	151,918(5)	4,143(16)	947(11)
1	6	Citicorp United States	191,355	167,201	114,689(10)	9,060(1)	1,700(1)
11	7	Norinchukin Bank[1,3,4] Japan	161,619	106,724	145,531(6)	758(156)	—
13	8	Industrial Bank of Japan[1] Japan	160,886	102,662	137,466(7)	3,296(26)	883(12)
7	9	Credit Agricole France	155,128	120,545	107,330(15)	6,756(3)	531(30)
8	10	Banque Nationale de Paris France	142,533	118,857	120,853(8)	4,492(15)	775(16)
17	11	Tokai Bank[1,2] Japan	137,831	90,397	113,295(12)	2,782(35)	525(31)
10	12	Credit Lyonnais France	132,692	109,445	114,311(11)	2,598(41)	631(23)
15	13	Deutsche Bank West Germany	131,861	93,855	120,490(9)	5,176(9)	1,387(3)
18	14	Mitsui Bank[1,3,4] Japan	131,445	88,476	104,384(16)	2,764(36)	630(24)
22	15	Mitsubishi Trust & Banking Corp.[1,3,4] Japan	126,796	80,546	110,563(13)	2,809(34)	716(19)
23	16	Sumitomo Trust & Banking Co.[1] Japan	124,591	79,175	110,170(14)	2,857(33)	730(18)

12	17	National Westminster Bank United Kingdom	123,054	103,697	102,408(17)	6,839(2)	1,493(2)
16	18	Barclays United Kingdom	116,596	92,981	94,921(21)	5,493(5)	1,321(4)
14	19	Societe Generale France	116,554	94,259	98,290(20)	3,383(25)	626(25)
26	20	Taiyo Kobe Bank[1,3,4] Japan	115,988	74,477	91,268(23)	2,004(59)	341(60)
28	21	Mitsui Trust & Banking Co.[1,3] Japan	115,531	72,901	98,949(18)	2,455(44)	507(35)
24	22	Long-Term Credit Bank of Japan[1,3,4] Japan	115,006	78,859	98,676(19)	2,423(45)	517(33)
20	23	Bank of Tokyo[1] Japan	111,489	83,433	86,890(25)	3,678(22)	616(27)
33	24	Daiwa Bank[1,3,4] Japan	102,370	66,826	88,323(24)	1,522(73)	332(62)
9	25	BankAmerica Corp. United States	102,204	114,751	82,205(27)	4,038(18)	−350(183)
25	26	Dresdner Bank West Germany	101,226	74,890	94,803(22)	3,433(24)	550(29)
35	27	Yasuda Trust & Banking Co.[1,3,4] Japan	100,883	62,660	85,927(26)	1,891(61)	392(47)
34	28	Union Bank of Switzerland Switzerland	93,756	66,045	81,104(29)	5,353(7)	666(20)
29	29	Compagnie Financiere de Paribas France	93,675	71,584	60,611(42)	4,010(19)	782(15)
19	30	Chase Manhattan Corp. United States	92,147	84,865	66,003(36)	4,882(13)	844(13)
30	31	Hongkong & Shanghai Banking Corp. Hongkong	90,735	68,833	81,805(28)	1,211(99)	—
37	32	Swiss Bank Corp.[3] Switzerland	84,921	60,589	74,019(30)	5,221(8)	578(28)
51	33	Toyo Trust & Banking Co.[1,3,4] Japan	81,518	47,942	71,537(32)	1,404(80)	342(59)
21	34	Midland Bank United Kingdom	78,519	82,941	65,600(37)	2,984(31)	640(22)
48	35	Nippon Credit Bank[1,3,4] Japan	77,906	49,832	68,822(34)	1,506(77)	274(76)
40	36	Westdeutsche Landesbank West Germany	76,274	56,514	70,875(33)	2,147(52)	163(116)
43	37	Commerzbank West Germany	75,460	54,000	72,334(31)	2,509(42)	374(51)
31	38	J. P. Morgan United States	74,643	67,611	42,960(62)	5,130(10)	1,166(6)
41	39	Banca Nazionale del Lavoro[3,4] Italy	73,058	56,129	61,226(40)	2,487(43)	374(51)
27	40	Manufacturers Honover Corp. United States	72,918	74,359	45,544(57)	3,766(20)	443(41)

The 50 Largest International Banks *(concluded)*

Rank 1985	Rank 1986	Name of Bank	Assets (US$ millions) 1986	Assets (US$ millions) 1985	Deposits (US$ millions) 1986	Capital (US$ millions) 1986	Pretax Earnings (US$ millions) 1986
44	41	Bayerische Vereinsbank West Germany	72,154	52,679	67,774(35)	1,763(65)	330(63)
52	42	Kyowa Bank[1,3,4] Japan	71,313	47,071	57,005(46)	1,328(87)	310(69)
57	43	Shoko Chukin Bank[1] Japan	71,214	45,202	64,279(38)	1,626(69)	—
36	44	Lloyds Bank United Kingdom	70,633	62,566	62,950(39)	4,068(17)	1,033(8)
32	45	Royal Bank of Canada[5] Canada	67,407	67,227	60,657(41)	3,283(27)	480(39)
38	46	Banco do Brasil Brazil	67,382	58,241	26,603(88)	5,477(6)	318(67)
47	47	Algemene Bank Nederland Netherlands	66,944	50,277	55,053(48)	2,347(46)	358(56)
60	48	Credit Suisse[3,4] Switzerland	63,919	41,990	56,829(47)	3,760(21)	469(40)
54	49	Rabobank Nederland Netherlands	63,761	46,541	60,236(43)	3,547(23)	416(45)
53	50	Amsterdam-Rotterdam Bank Netherlands	62,986	46,796	58,374(45)	2,134(53)	269(79)

* In order to compile the global banking rankings, *Institutional Investor* first asked more than 500 of the world's leading bank holding companies to report their assets, deposits, capital and pretax earnings in local currencies as of year-end 1985 and 1986. For the sake of comparability, we then converted the local currencies into U.S. dollars at year-end rates for banks on calendar years. For those not on calendar years, the conversion rates used are those prevailing at the end of each bank's fiscal year. The conversion figures were provided by the money desk of a major U.S. bank.

It should be noted that the banks were asked to report consolidated figures for all other banks in which they have an interest of 50 percent or more. Those that chose not to provide consolidated figures are noted. The banks were also asked if their figures included recent mergers and acquisitions; those that said they did not are also noted. Figures reflect consolidated bank holding company interests only; industrial and other nonbank holdings are not included.

Banks were asked to report their figures published in these tables using the following definitions:

Total assets exclude contra accounts where contra accounts are defined as acceptances, bonds or other securities held for customers; letters of credit; guarantees; and similar instruments.

Total deposits do not include treasury operations.

Capital includes funds supplied by shareholders, such as permanent preferred stock, share capital, retained earnings or undistributed profits and contingent type reserves. It excludes reserves for possible loan losses, subordinated debt and redeemable preferred stock.

Pretax earnings include earnings before taxes and extraordinary items.

** The table reproduced here includes only the top 50 of the top 200 banks in assets listed in the *Institutional Investor.*

[1] As of September 30, 1986, 1985.

[2] Earnings not consolidated.

[3] Figures do not include all subsidiaries owned 50 percent or more.

[4] Not adjusted for all mergers and acquisitions.

[5] As of October 31, 1986, 1985.

Source: *Institutional Investor*, July 1987.

The 100 Largest Brokerage Houses*

Rank 1986	Rank 1987	Name of Firm	Total Capital ($ millions)	Equity Capital ($ millions)	Subordinated Debt ($ millions)	"Excess" Net Capital ($ millions)
1	1	Salomon Brothers	$3,209.2	$2,090.4	$ 1,118.8	$ 537.1
2	2	Shearson Lehman Brothers	3,122.0	1,495.0	1,627.0	342.0
3	3	Merrill Lynch, Pierce, Fenner & Smith	2,864.8	2,014.8	850.0	828.9
5	4	Goldman, Sachs & Co.	1,951.0*	1,529.0	422.0	1,127.7
7	5	Drexel Burnham Lambert	1,870.5	1,289.2	581.3	737.0
6	6	First Boston	1,363.8	958.8	405.0	410.2
4	7	Prudential-Bache Securities	1,288.7	1,031.3	257.4	119.0
8	8	Dean Witter Reynolds	1,213.6	683.2	530.4	256.8
9	9	Bear, Stearns & Co.	1,057.2	709.7	347.5	195.4
10	10	E.F. Hutton & Co.	986.4	601.8	384.6	150.2
13	11	Morgan Stanley & Co.	901.2	576.2	325.0	237.1
12	12	Donaldson, Lufkin & Jenrette	766.1	246.0	520.1	47.4
11	13	Paine Webber	635.1	414.1	221.0	54.8
15	14	Kidder, Peabody & Co.	595.5	358.4	237.1	138.5
14	15	Stephens	418.8	418.8		92.5
17	16	Smith Barney, Harris Upham & Co.	407.9	283.4	124.5	120.1
16	17	Shelby Cullom Davis & Co.	366.6	366.6		271.8
18	18	Allen & Co.	359.5	359.5		
19	19	Thomson McKinnon Securities	298.0	208.0	90.0	22.0
23	20	L.F. Rothschild, Unterberg, Towbin	289.3	201.1	88.2	116.8
22	21	Van Kampen Merritt	236.5	236.5		43.0
20	22	Spear, Leeds & Kellogg	234.0	147.0	87.0	72.1
21	23	A.G. Edwards & Sons	231.0	231.0		72.4
25	24	Oppenheimer & Co.	211.0	134.2	76.8	47.8
32	25	Dillon, Read & Co.	190.9	164.6	26.3	20.9
24	26	John Nuveen & Co.	185.6	185.6		93.2
27	27	UBS Securities	170.3	70.3	100.0	45.8
37	28	Allen & Co. Inc.	150.8	87.3	63.5	66.2
26	29	Neuberger & Berman	144.1	144.1		62.9
33	30	Nomura Securities International	128.0	128.0		57.0
30	31	Charles Schwab & Co.	126.0	75.8	50.2	25.1
29	32	Cowen & Co.	118.1	109.7	8.4	52.0
43	33	Daiwa Securities America	116.6	116.6		8.1
28	34	Jefferies & Co.	112.3	82.3	30.0	65.0
46	35	Nikko Securities Co. International	108.3	58.3	50.0	54.1
36	36	Wertheim Schroder & Co.	107.4	101.8	5.6	34.3
45	37	Alex. Brown & Sons	107.2	97.2	10.0	49.3
67	38	Deutsche Bank Capital Corp.	102.2	52.2	50.0	18.2
34	39	Prescott, Ball & Turben	99.5	89.5	10.0	12.6
35	40	M.A. Schapiro & Co.	99.2	99.2		90.0
56	41	Gruntal & Co. (Consolidated)	92.8	47.2	45.6	44.8
41	42	Brown Brothers Harriman & Co.	82.7	82.7		
61	43	Edward D. Jones	82.5	50.5	32.0	43.8
39	44	Glickenhaus & Co.	81.3	81.3		20.0
47	45	Fidelity Brokerage Services	80.2	80.2		17.9
44	46	Gruss Partners	80.2	80.2		50.4
38	47	Janney Montgomery Scott	77.1	77.1		20.6
31	48	Advest	74.4	74.4		16.6
52	49	Mabon, Nugent and Co.	71.2	71.2		15.2
58	50	Interstate Securities Corp.	70.9	48.4	22.5	33.6
42	51	Lazard Freres & Co.	70.0	70.0		29.2
49	52	Quick & Reilly Group	67.2	66.6	0.6	16.1
48	53	Bateman Eichler, Hill Richards	64.8	46.9	17.9	10.0
55	54	S.D. Securities	64.6	64.6		48.4
50	55	Legg Mason	63.6	61.7	1.9	22.0
64	56	Keefe, Bruyette & Woods	63.2	50.7	12.5	46.0
88	57	Yamaichi International (America)	62.7†	62.7		23.3
59	58	Blunt Ellis & Loewi	61.3	40.8	20.5	14.0‡
60	59	J.C. Bradford & Co.	61.1	61.1		26.2
77	60	McDonald & Co. Securities	59.6	59.6		20.1

The 100 Largest Brokerage Houses *(concluded)*

Rank 1986	Rank 1987	Name of Firm	Total Capital ($ millions)	Equity Capital ($ millions)	Subordinated Debt ($ millions)	Excess Net Capital ($ millions)
70	61	Ryan, Beck Co.	59.0	59.0		37.1
54	62	Piper, Jaffray & Hopwood	56.5	55.2	1.3	18.3
51	63	Kaufmann, Alsberg & Co.	53.0	53.0		26.3
53	64	Ziegler Co.	52.8	52.8		24.3
73	65	Tucker, Anthony & R.L. Day	51.3	48.3	3.0	14.2
57	66	Moseley Securities Corp.	49.7	32.3	17.4	11.4
69	67	Arnhold and S. Bleichroeder	48.3	45.3	3.0	9.2
63	68	Dain Bosworth	47.8	47.8		7.0
71	69	William Blair & Co.	45.0	45.0		16.8
84	70	Furman Seiz Mager Dietz & Birney	44.8	34.8	10.0	22.1
65	71	Ohio Co.	43.8	43.8		6.3
83	72	Montgomery Securities	42.1	37.1	5.0	22.7
62	73	McMahan & Co.	41.7	25.7	16.0	9.3
75	74	Robert W. Baird & Co.	38.7	38.7		20.1
74	75	Easton & Co.	38.5	36.2	2.3	25.1
66	76	Boettcher & Co.	37.1	37.1		6.7
81	77	Morgan Keegan & Co.	36.6	36.6		12.8
76	78	Eppler, Guerin & Turner	36.5	36.5		29.4
68	79	Carl Marks & Co.	35.7	32.7	3.0	13.3
85	80	Bernard L. Madoff	35.0	35.0		20.9
80	81	Rothschild Inc.	34.1	20.1	14.0	15.6
82	82	Crowell, Weedon & Co.	33.2	32.1	1.1	8.0
87	83	MKI Securities Corp.	32.3	18.9	13.4	13.0
93	84	Raymond, James & Associates	31.9	31.9		15.0
72	85	Hambrecht & Quist	31.7†	31.7		16.2
91	86	Herzog, Heine, Geduld	30.9	22.6	8.3	9.9
86	87	Rauscher Pierce Refsnes	30.8	25.6	5.2	4.8
—	88	Johnson, Lane, Space, Smith & Co.	27.2	23.6	3.6	9.1
79	89	Clayton Brown & Associates	27.0	27.0		0.5
78	90	Wedbush Securities	27.0	26.3	0.7	8.8
90	91	Wheat, First Securities	26.9	24.4	2.5	6.8
95	92	Franklin Distributors	26.5	26.5		20.3
94	93	Ernst & Co.	25.0	23.0	2.0	5.7
89	94	Sanford C. Bernstein & Co.	24.5	20.1	4.4	10.4
100	95	Stifel, Nicolaus & Co.	23.3	23.3		1.8
96	96	J.J.B. Hilliard, W.L. Lyons	23.1	21.2	1.9	7.1
92	97	Butcher & Singer	22.4	17.5	4.9	0.6
—	98	Howard, Weil, Labouisse, Friedrichs	22.1	22.1		8.2
—	99	Chicago Corp.	22.0	15.6	6.4	6.8
—	100	Josephthal & Co.	21.9	16.5	5.4	4.7

* Based on broker-dealer capital. • As of 11/28/86

† As of 9/30/86

‡ Based on 6% of funds required to be segregated pursuant to the Commodity Exchange Act

Source: Ranking America's Biggest Brokers, *Institutional Investor,* April 1987.

America's Most and Least Admired Corporations*

AT THE TOP AND BOTTOM OF THE 300 COMPANIES

RANK	COMPANY	SCORE	RANK	COMPANY	SCORE
1	**Merck** Pharmaceuticals	8.38	300	**LTV** Metals	3.11
2	**Liz Claiborne** Apparel	8.02	299	**BankAmerica** Commercial banking	3.28
3	**Boeing** Aerospace	7.99	298	**American Motors** Motor vehicles and parts	3.45
4	**J.P. Morgan** Commercial banking	7.95	297	**Financial Corp. of Amer.** Savings institutions	3.46
5	**Rubbermaid** Rubber and plastic products	7.94	296	**Manville** Glass, building materials	3.64
6	**Shell Oil** Petroleum refining	7.91[1]	295	**Bethlehem Steel** Metals	3.69
7	**IBM** Office equipment, computers	7.91[1]	294	**Pan Am** Transportation	3.73
8	**Johnson & Johnson** Pharmaceuticals	7.86	293	**Union Carbide** Chemicals	4.16
9	**Dow Jones** Publishing, printing	7.84[2]	292	**Manhattan Industries** Apparel	4.30
10	**Herman Miller** Furniture	7.84[2]	291	**Trans World Airlines** Transportation	4.31

The most admired
Merck dethrones IBM, No. 1 since the survey began and the only other company in the top ten every year. Liz Claiborne and Herman Miller make their debut.

The least admired
LTV and Manville are both in Chapter 11 and back at the bottom of the list. The least admired company of 1985, Financial Corp. of America, moves up a little.

[1] Shell Oil scores higher than IBM in five of eight attributes.
[2] Dow Jones scores higher than Herman Miller in six of eight attributes.

Source: "America's Most Admired Corporations" by Edward C. Baig, *Fortune,* "© 1987 Time Inc. All rights reserved."

* To compile the rankings of 300 companies in 33 industry groups, FORTUNE late last year polled more than 8,200 senior executives, outside directors, and financial analysts. About half responded—a good return. One who declined was Lee Iacocca. "I am afraid my bias might skew the results of your study," wrote the Chrysler Chairman. (Even without his vote, however, Chrysler finished a strong second behind Ford in the motor vehicles group.) Respondents were asked to rate the companies in their own industry on eight key measures of reputation, using a scale of 0 (poor) to 10 (excellent). The eight attributes are: quality of management; quality of products or services; innovativeness; long-term investment value; financial soundness; ability to attract, develop, and keep talented people; community and environmental responsibility; and use of corporate assets.

America's Top 100 Growth Companies (above $25 million sales)

Rank	Company	Stk. Exch.	5-Year EPS Growth Rate %	Latest 12-Month EPS	Year-to-Date Price Chg. %
1	Digital Commun.	M	146	1.66	-34.5
2	Rhodes	M	128	1.61	51.9
3	Cannon Group	N	127	3.29	19.1
4	Environdyne Industries	M	123	0.80	124.6
5	Fleetwood Enterprises	N	123	1.69	-5.6
6	United Presidential	M	106	1.35	46.3
7	A.L. Labs	A	104	0.92	46.9
8	National Health	M	102	1.31	4.1
9	Dual Lite	M	100*	0.73	42.1
10	VMX	M	99*	-0.14	-22.0
11	Intertrans	M	97	0.67	50.0
12	Brunswick	N	95	2.37	63.9
13	Virginia Beach Fed. S&L	M	95	0.92	21.7
14	CasaBlanca Industries	A	93*	-0.21	161.9
15	Price	M	93	1.20	40.7
16	Clothes Time	M	92	0.73	93.8
17	RB&W	A	92*	0.84	14.1
18	Royal Int'l Optical	N	92	0.85	-45.3
19	Centuri	M	91*	0.06	43.5
20	Empire of Carolina	A	89*	1.36	63.6
21	Maxco	O	88*	0.61	9.1
22	King World Productions	M	86	1.60	34.1
23	Leucadia National	N	86	2.73	7.5
24	American Integrity	M	85	1.41	-4.4
25	Biomet	M	85	0.47	53.1
26	Atlantic Southeast Air	M	84	0.94	23.3
27	Fedders	N	84*	0.45	117.1
28	Genentech	M	84	0.20	148.7
29	Cipher Data Products	M	83	0.38	-3.6
30	American Continental	M	81	2.86	8.3
31	Kuhlman	N	81	1.06	5.6
32	Siliconix	M	81	0.71	12.1
33	Syntrex	M	81*	0.12	5.6
34	General Shale Products	M	80	2.50	19.0
35	Stratus Computer	M	80	0.53	-7.4
36	Tyson Foods	M	80	0.96	105.5
37	Mylan Labs	N	79	0.86	33.3
38	Zenith Labs	N	79	1.52	31.3
39	Waxman Industries	M	78	0.81	13.3
40	InteCom	M	77*	-0.41	7.5
41	Lam Research	M	77*	0.42	-9.9
42	Winn Enterprises	A	77*	-0.43	-15.6
43	Seton	A	76	0.90	37.8
44	Slattery Group	N	76*	-0.02	-18.6
45	Western S&L	N	75*	2.63	112.0
46	Equatorial Commun.	M	74*	0.15	0.0
47	Fortune Fin'l	M	74*	4.69	42.7
48	Hofmann Industries	A	74*	-0.21	-10.0
49	Transcon	N	74*	0.35	28.6
50	United Fin'l Grp. Del.	M	74*	-0.72	-34.6
51	Fuqua Industries	N	71	4.01	31.0
52	Home Depot	N	71	0.46	67.0

America's Top 100 Growth Companies (above $25 million sales) *(concluded)*

Rank	Company	Stk. Exch.	5-Year EPS Growth Rate %	Latest 12-Month EPS	Year to Date Price Chg. %
53	Hunt (J.B.) Transport	M	71	1.53	81.8
54	Safeguard Scientific	N	71*	0.75	12.5
55	Casey's General Stores	M	70	0.99	43.8
56	NWA	N	70	2.39	8.7
57	Toro	N	70*	1.92	35.7
58	Douglas & Lomason	M	68	3.51	35.3
59	Total Petroleum	A	68*	2.89	21.6
60	Levitt	A	67*	0.42	54.3
61	Triangle	A	67*	0.76	18.2
62	Ultimate	A	66	1.70	25.3
63	Etz Lavud	A	65	0.74	42.7
64	Pauley Petroleum	A	65*	1.78	36.8
65	Circuit City Stores	N	64	1.98	83.9
66	Green Tree Acceptance	N	64	5.14	63.8
67	Mentor Minn.	M	64	0.57	-14.3
68	Pasquale Food Cl. B	M	64	0.46	41.7
69	Republic Gypsum	N	64	0.90	21.2
70	Valid Logic Systems	M	64*	0.01	-32.4
71	Redlaw Industries	A	63*	0.27	16.7
72	Southmark	N	63	2.04	18.1
73	Alza Cl. A	A	62*	0.42	55.3
74	Chrysler	N	62*	8.95	13.8
75	Gibraltar Fin'l	N	62*	2.13	8.2
76	KLM Royal Dutch Air	N	62	3.13	2.7
77	Uniforce Temp.	M	62	0.74	55.1
78	American Software	M	61	0.84	4.0
79	Arundel	A	61*	1.53	12.3
80	Kellwood	N	60	3.03	47.7
81	Sandgate	A	60	3.04	12.0
82	Newbery	A	59*	0.37	41.4
83	Sceptre Resources	A	59*	0.33	-36.0
84	Amcast Industrial	M	58*	-1.22	-9.1
85	National-Standard	N	58*	0.49	2.8
86	Federal Screw Works	M	57*	1.44	44.2
87	Turner Broadcasting	A	57*	0.50	83.2
88	APL	N	56*	2.53	3.5
89	First Southern S&L	M	56*	1.84	20.5
90	United First Fed. S&L	M	55*	2.65	80.0
91	Limited (The)	N	54	1.28	55.6
92	Computer Horizons	M	53	0.86	25.8
93	Decision Industries	N	53	0.64	5.7
94	Hines, Edward Lumber	O	53*	1.46	-82.2
95	Kit Manufacturing	A	53*	0.81	87.2
96	Minstar	M	53*	0.96	45.6
97	Nu-Med	M	53*	0.54	-1.6
98	American Biltrite	A	52*	1.05	29.1
99	Bally's Park Place	N	52	1.00	35.8
100	Comair	M	52	0.47	-5.7

* Other than a quarterly multiple because of fiscal-year change. A—American Stock Exchange. M—Nasdaq National Market Over the Counter. N—New York Stock Exchange. O—Nasdaq Over the Counter.

Source: Reprinted by permission *Financial World*, 1987.

Largest Certified Public Accounting (CPA) Firms*

Alexander Grant & Company
605 Third Avenue
New York, NY 10016
212-599-0100

Arthur Andersen & Company[1]
69 West Washington Street
Chicago, IL 60602
312-346-6262

Arthur Young & Company[1]
277 Park Avenue
New York, NY 10017
212-922-2000

Cherry, Bekaert & Holland
1 NCNB Plaza
Charlotte, NC 28280
704-377-3741

Clifton, Gunderson & Co.
808 Commercial National Bank Building
Peoria, IL 61602
309-671-4511

Coopers & Lybrand[1]
1251 Avenue of the Americas
New York, NY 10020
212-536-2000

Deloitte Haskins & Sells[1]
1114 Avenue of the Americas
New York, NY 10036
219-790-0500

Fox and Company
1660 Lincoln Street
Denver, CO 80264
303-861-5555

Ernst & Whinney[1]
2000 National City Center
Cleveland, OH 44114
216-861-5000

Kenneth Leventhal & Company
2049 Century Park East
Los Angeles, CA 90067
213-277-0880

Laventhol & Horwath
1845 Walnut Street
Philadelphia, PA 19103
215-299-1700

McGladrey Hendrickson & Pullen
640 Capital Square
4th & Locust
Des Moines, IA 50309
515-284-8660

Moss Adams & Co.
2830 Bank of California Center
Seattle, WA 98164
206-223-1820

Oppenheim, Appel, Dixon & Co.
One New York Plaza
New York, NY 10004
212-422-1000

Pannell, Kerr, Forster & Co.
420 Lexington Avenue
New York, NY 10017
212-867-8000

Peat, Marwick, Main & Co.[1]
345 Park Avenue
New York, NY 10022
212-758-9700

Price Waterhouse & Co.[1]
1251 Avenue of the Americas
New York, NY 10020
212-489-8900

Seidman & Seidman
110 Union Bank Building
Grand Rapids, MI 49503
616-744-2111

Touche Ross & Company[1]
1633 Broadway
New York, NY 10019
212-489-1600

* Firms with the largest number of American Institute of Certified Public Accountants (AICPA) members.

[1] One of the "Big 8" accounting firms.

Source: American Institute of Certified Public Accountants.

Capital Sources for Startup Companies and Small Businesses

Sources of Venture Capital

INTRODUCTION

What Is An SBIC?

Although individual investors have been providing venture capital for new and small business in the United States for many years, no institutional sources of such financing existed until 1958 when Congress passed the Small Business Investment Act.

Small business investment companies (SBICs) and minority enterprise small business investment companies (MESBICs) are financial institutions created to make equity capital and long-term credit (with maturities of at least 5 years) available to small, independent businesses. SBICs are licensed by the Federal Government's Small Business Administration, but they are privately-organized and privately-managed firms which set their own policies and make their own investment decisions. In return for pledging to finance only small businesses, SBICs may qualify for long-term loans from SBA. Although all SBICs will consider applications for funds from socially and economically disadvantaged entrepreneurs. MESBICs normally make all their investments in this area.

What Have SBICs Done?

To date, SBICs have disbursed over $6-billion by making over 70,000 loans and investments. The concerns they have financed have far out-performed all national averages as measured by increases in assets, sales, profits, and new employment.

Need Money? Which SBIC Should You See?

This Directory of members of the National Association of Small Business Investment Companies (NASBIC) lists over 400 SBICs and MESBICs. They represent approximately 90% of the industry's resources and are located in all parts of the country.

In using this Directory, you should consider the following factors:

A. *Geography:* Generally speaking, SBICs are more likely to make loans and investments near their offices, even though many of them operate regionally or even nationally. Therefore, it would probably be wise to contact first those SBICs closest to your business.
B. *Investment Policy:* Even though most SBICs have both equity investments and straight loans in their portfolios, each of them has a policy on which type of financing it prefers. This Directory utilizes a code symbol which indicates that policy; you should match your requirements with that information.
C. *Industry Preferences:* Here again, SBICs differ widely. Because of the expertise of its officers and directors, an SBIC often specializes in making loans and investments in certain industries. This Directory indicates such specialization.
D. *Size of Financing:* Because they differ in size and investment policies, SBICs establish different dollar limits on the financings they make. This Directory has a symbol showing the preferred maximum size of loan or investment for each SBIC.

It should be emphasized that the information given in the Directory should be considered only as a general guide. Every SBIC departs from its usual policies in special cases. Furthermore, SBICs often work together in making loans or investments in greater amounts than any of them could make separately. No SBIC should be ruled out as a possible source of financing, since this Directory is designed to give you an idea about which ones are *most likely* to be interested in your application.

Is Your Firm Eligible for SBIC Financing?

Probably so, since the overwhelming majority of all business firms qualify as small. As a general rule, companies are eligible if they have net worth under $6-million and average after-tax earnings of less than $2-million during the past two years. *In addition,* your firm may qualify as small either under

---

Source: *Venture Capital, Where to Find It*, published by the National Association of Small Business Investment Companies, 618 Washington Building, Washington, D.C. 20005. Copies available at $1.00 each.

an employment standard or amount of annual sales. Both these standards vary from industry to industry.

A phone call or a note to any NASBIC member—or to our Washington office—will clear up the eligibility question quickly.

How Do You Present Your Case To An SBIC?

There is nothing mysterious about asking an SBIC for money. You should prepare a report on your operations, financial condition, and requirements. Specifically, the report should include detailed information on key personnel, products, proposed new product lines, patent positions, market data and competitive position, distribution and sales methods, and other pertinent materials.

How Long Will It Take?

There are no hard and fast rules about the length of time it will take an SBIC to investigate and close a transaction. Ordinarily, an initial response, either positive or negative, is made quickly. On the other hand, the thorough study an SBIC must make before it can make a final decision could take several weeks.

Naturally, a well-documented presentation on your part will reduce the amount of time the SBIC will require.

How Are SBIC Financings Structured?

Every single SBIC financing is tailored individually to meet your needs and to make the best use of the SBIC's funds. You and the SBIC will negotiate the terms. The SBIC might buy shares of your stock or it might make a straight loan.

Usually, SBICs are interested in generating capital gains, so they will purchase stock in your company or advance funds through a note, or debenture, with conversion privileges or rights to buy stock at a predetermined later date.

How Can SBIC Money Provide Additional Credit Lines?

If the SBIC money is provided to you in a subordinated position, it will often do double or triple duty. Industry averages show that for every SBIC dollar placed with a small business concern, two additional senior dollars become available from commercial banks or other sources.

Are There Unique Advantages To SBIC Financing?

Yes, indeed! Before it receives its license, an SBIC must prove that its management and directors are experienced individuals with a broad range of business and professional talents.

This expertise will be applied to assist your business, supplementing the skills of your own management team. Here again, the actual pattern of management and financial counseling will be cut to fit each specific situation.

SBICs can make only long-term loans or equity investments; therefore, their interests and yours will coincide—both of you will want your firm to grow and prosper.

Will I Be Treated Fairly?

As mentioned above, SBICs are licensed by the Federal Government only after their officers and directors have been carefully screened. Furthermore, all the SBICs listed in this Directory are NASBIC members and all have voluntarily subscribed to the Association's Code of Ethics and Trade Practice Rules.

The Code provides, in part, that "the constant goal of each SBIC shall be to improve the welfare of the small business concerns which it serves. Each SBIC shall promote and maintain ethical standards of conduct and deal fairly and honestly with all small business concerns seeking its assistance."

What Is NASBIC?

It is the national trade association which represents the overwhelming majority of all active SBICs and MESBICs. It was formed in 1958, soon after the passage of the Small Business Investment Act, and has worked on behalf of small business generally and the SBIC industry in particular for 28 years.

In addition to providing educational and informational services for its members. NASBIC presses for a rational legal and regulatory framework for the industry. It also cooperates closely with other independent business associations in advancing the interests of small business on the Federal level.

Need More Information?

Contact any SBIC in this Directory. Write the National Association of Small Business Investment Companies (NASBIC), 1156 15 Street, N.W., Suite 1101, Washington, D.C. 20005.

EXPLANATION OF CODES

Preferred Limit for Loans or Investments

A—up to $100,000
B—up to $250,000
C—up to $500,000
D—up to $1-million
E—Above $1-million

Investment Policy

* —Will consider either loans or investments
** —Prefers to make long-term loans
***—Prefers financings with the right to acquire stock interest.

Industry Preferences

1. Communications
2. Construction & Real Estate Development
3. Natural Resources
4. Hotels, Motels & Restaurants
5. Manufacturing & Processing
6. Medical & Health Services
7. Recreation & Amusements
8. Research & Technology
9. Retailing, Wholesaling & Distribution
10. Service Trades
11. Transportation
12. Diversified

MESBIC—a specialized SBIC which invests in socially or economically disadvantaged small businesses.

Non-SBIC Members

This Directory also lists a number of Associate Members of NASBIC. Some of these firms are non-SBIC venture capitalists who also invest in small businesses. Others are firms which provide professional services to SBICs and to small business concerns.

ALABAMA
First SBIC of Alabama
Mr. David C. DeLaney, Pres.
16 Midtown Park East
Mobile, AL 36606
(205) 476-0700
C ** 12

Hickory Venture Capital Corp.
J. Thomas Noojin, Pres/Chmn.
Jeffrey C. Atkinson, VP
699 Gallatin St., Ste. A-2
Huntsville, AL 35801
(205) 539-1931
E *** 12

Remington Fund, Inc., (The)
Ms. Lana Sellers, Pres.
P.O. Box 10686
Birmingham, AL 35202
(205) 326-3509

Tuskegee Capital Corp.
Mr. A.G. Bartholomew
VP/Gen. Mgr.
4453 Richardson Rd.
Montgomery, AL 36108
(205) 281-8059
MESBIC A ** 12

ALASKA
Alaska Business Investment Corp.
Mr. James L. Cloud, VP
PO Box 600
Anchorage, AK 99510
(907) 278-2071
B * 12

Calista Business Investment Corp.
Mr. Nelson N. Angapak, Pres.
Mr. Matthew Nicolai, VP/Gen. Mgr.
516 Denali St.
Anchorage, AK 99501
(907) 277-0425
MESBIC B * 12

ARIZONA
FBS Venture Capital Co.
Mr. William McKee
Pres.
Mr. Stephen W. Buchanan
Inv. Ofcr.
6900 E. Camelback Rd., Ste. 452
Scottsdale, AZ 85251
(602) 941-2160
C *** 1,5,6,8

Branch Office
Norwest Growth Fund, Inc.
Mr. Robert F. Zicarelli, Chmn.
Mr. Stephen J. Schewe, Assoc.
8777 East Via de Ventura, Ste 335
Scottsdale, AZ 85258
(602) 483-8940
E *** 1,6,8,12
(Main Office in MN)

Rocky Mountain Equity Corp.
Mr. Anthony J. Nicoli, Pres.
4530 N. Central Ave., Ste. 3
Phoenix, AZ 85012
(602) 274-7558
A ** 4,7,8,10

Sun Belt Capital Corp.
Mr. Bruce Vinci, Pres.
Mr. Joseph Henske, VP
Mr. Craig C. Lindsay, Mgr.
320 N. Central Ave., Ste. 700
Phoenix, AZ 85004
(602) 253-7600
A *** 2,4,8

VNB Capital Corp.
Mr. James G. Gardner, Pres.
Mr. John Holliman, VP/Gen Mgr.
15 E. Monroe, Suite 1200
Phoenix, AZ 85004
(602) 261-1577
D *** 1,5,6,8,11,12

ARKANSAS
Capital Management Services, Inc.
Mr. David L. Hale, Pres.
1910 N. Grant, Ste. 200
Little Rock, AR 72207
(501) 664-8613
MESBIC A * 12

First SBIC of Arkansas, Inc.
Mr. Fred C. Burns, Pres.
Worthen Bank Bldg.
200 W. Capitol Ave., Ste. 700
Little Rock, AR 72201
(501) 378-1876
A *** 12

Independence Financial Services, Inc.
Mr. John Freeman, Pres.
PO Box 3878
Batesville, AR 72503
(501) 793-4533
B * 6,9,12

Kar-Mal Venture Capital, Inc.
Ms. Amelia S. Karam, Pres.
2821 Kavanaugh Blvd.
Little Rock, AR 72205
(501) 661-0010
MESBIC B *** 9

Power Ventures, Inc.
Mr. Dorsey D. Glover, Pres.
Hwy. 270 N./PO Box 518
Malvern, AR 72104
(501) 332-3695
MESBIC A * 12

Worthern Finance & Inv. Inc.
Mr. Ricor de Silveira, Pres.
PO Box 1681
Little Rock, AR 72203
(501) 378-1082
MESBIC C ** 4,5,6,9,10,11

CALIFORNIA
Branch Office
Atalanta Investment Co., Inc.
Mr. Alan W. Livingston, Pres.
141 El Camino Dr.
Los Angeles, CA 90212
(213) 273-1730
D *** 1,2,5,6,7,8
(Main Office in NY)

Bancorp Venture Capital, Inc.
Mr. Paul R. Blair, Pres.
Mr. Ron Miracle
2082 Michelson Dr., Suite 302
Irvine, CA 92715
(714) 752-7220
E *** 12

BankAmerica Ventures, Inc.
Mr. Robert W. Gibson, Pres.
Mr. Patrick J. Topolski, VP
555 California St., #3908
42nd Floor
San Francisco, CA 94104
(415) 622-2230
D * 12

Bay Venture Group
Mr. William R. Chandler
Gen. Ptnr.
One Embarcadero Ctr., Ste. 3303
San Francisco, CA 94111
(415) 989-7680
B *** 1,5,6,8

Brentwood Associates
Mrs. Leslie R. Shaw
VP Fin. & Admin.
11661 San Vicente Blvd., Ste. 707
Los Angeles, CA 90049
(213) 826-6581
E *** 1,12

Business Equity & Dev. Corp.
Mr. Ricardo J. Olivarez, Pres.
1411 W. Olympic Blvd., Ste. 200
Los Angeles, CA 90015
(213) 385-0351
MESBIC B * 1,5,12

CFB Venture Capital Corp.
Mr. Richard J. Roncaglia, VP
530 B St., 2nd Fl.
San Diego, CA 92101
(619) 230-3304
B *** 1,5,6,8

CIN Investment Co.
Mr. Robert C. Weeks, Pres.
545 Middlefield Rd., #160
Menlo Park, CA 94025
(415) 328-4401
D *** 1,8

California Capital Investors, Ltd
Mr. Arthur Bernstein, Gen. Ptnr.
Ms. Lynda Gibson, Off. Admin.
11812 San Vicente Blvd.
Los Angeles, CA 90049
(213) 820-7222
C *** 1,5,6,10,11,12

California Partners
Mr. Tim Draper, VP/CFO
3000 Sand Hill Rd.
Bldg. 4, Ste. 210
Menlo Park, CA 94025
(415) 854-7472
C *** 1,5,6,8

Camden Investments, Inc.
Mr. Edward G. Victor, Pres.
Mr. Craig M. Cogut, Counsel
Ms. Carolyn Zwirn, Asst. Sec.
9560 Wilshire Blvd., #310
Beverly Hills, CA 90212
(213) 859-9738
C *** 12

Charterway Investment Corp.
Mr. Harold Chuang, Pres.
222 S. Hill St., Ste. 800
Los Angeles, CA 90012
(213) 687-8534
MESBIC B *** 2,4,5,7,9

Branch Office
Citicorp Venture Capital, Ltd.
Mr. J. Matthew Mackowski, VP
One Sansome St., Ste. 2410
San Francisco, CA 94104
(415) 627-6472
E *** 1,5,6,8,11
(Main Office in NY)

Branch Office
Citicorp Venture Capital, Ltd.
Mr. David A. Wegmann, VP
2200 Geng Rd., Ste. 203
Palo Alto, CA 94303
(415) 424-8000
E *** 1,5,6,8,11
(Main Office in NY)

Cogeneration Capital Fund
Mr. Howard Cann, Mng. Gen. Ptnr.
Jonathan S. Saiger, Gen. Ptnr.
300 Tamal Plaza, Ste. 190
Corte Madera, CA 94925
(415) 924-3525
D * 8

Continental Investors, Inc.
Mr. Lac Thantrong, Pres.
8781 Seaspray Dr.
Huntington Beach, CA 92646
(714) 964-5207
MESBIC B ** 4,6,9,10,12

Crocker Ventures, Inc.
Mr. Ray McDonough
One Montgomery St.
San Francisco, CA 94104
(415) 983-3636
A * 12

Crosspoint Investment Corp.
Mr. Max S. Simpson, Pres.
1951 Landings Dr.
Mountain View, CA 94043
(415) 964-3545
B *** 1,5,8

Dime Investment Corp.
Mr. Chun Y. Lee, Pres.
2772 W. 8th St.
Los Angeles, CA 90005
(213) 739-1847
MESBIC A * 5,8,9,12

Enterprise Venture Cap. Corp.
Mr. Ernest de la Ossa, Pres.
Mr. Douglas S. Milroy, Op. Mgr.
1922 The Alameda, Ste. 306
San Jose, CA 95126
(408) 249-3507
B * 1,5,8

First American Cap. Funding, Inc.
Dr. Luu Trankiem, Pres.
9872 Chapman Ave., #216
Garden Grove, CA 92641
(714) 638-7171
MESBIC B * 12

First SBIC of California
Mr. Timothy Hay, Pres.
Mr. John Geer, Mng. Ptnr.
Mr. Brian Jones, Mng. Ptnr.
Mr. James McGoodwin, Mng. Ptnr.
Mr. Everett Cox, Mng. Ptnr.
Mr. Dmitry Bosky, Mng. Ptnr.
650 Town Center Drive, 17th Fl.
Costa Mesa, CA 92626
(714) 556-1964
E *** 12

Branch Office
First SBIC of California
Mr. John D. Padgett, Mng. Ptnr.
Mr. Tony Stevens, Mng. Ptnr.
155 N. Lake Ave., Suite 1010
Pasadena, CA 91109
(818) 304-3451
E *** 12

Branch Office
First SBIC of California
Mr. James B. McElwee, Mng. Ptnr.
5 Palo Alto Square, Suite 938
Palo Alto, CA 94304
(415) 424-8011
E *** 12

Hamco Capital Corp.
Mr. William R. Hambrecht, Pres.
Ms. Colleen E. Curry, VP/Sec.
One Post St., 4th Fl.
San Francisco, CA 94104
(415) 393-9813
C * 1,5,6,8

Branch Office
(Bohlen Capital Corp.)
Harvest Ventures, Inc.
Mr. Harvey J. Wertheim, Pres.
Bldg. SW3, 10080 N. Wolfe Rd.
Suite 365
Cupertino, CA 95014
D * 1,3,5,6,8
(Main Office in NY)

InterVen Partners
Mr. David B. Jones, Pres.
Mr. Jonathan E. Funk, VP
Mr. Kenneth M. Deemer, VP
Mr. Keith R. Larson, VP
445 S. Figueroa, Ste. 2940
Los Angeles, CA 90071
(213) 622-1922
E *** 1,6,8,12

Ivanhoe Venture Capital, Ltd.
Mr. Alan Toffler, Mng. Gen. Ptnr.
Mr. P. F. Wulff, Gen. Ptnr.
Mr. William Wright, Gen. Ptnr.
737 Pearl St., Ste. 201
La Jolla, CA 92037
(619) 454-8882
B *** 1,5,6,12

JeanJoo Finance, Inc.
Mr. Frank R. Remski, Gen. Mngr.
Mr. Chul-Ho Kim, Attorney
700 So. Flower St., Suite 3305
Los Angeles, CA 90017
(213) 627-6660
MESBIC B * 12

Lasung Investment & Finance Co.
Mr. Jung Su Lee, Pres.
3600 Wilshire Blvd., Ste. 1410
Los Angeles, CA 90010
(213) 384-7548
MESBIC B ** 9,12

Latigo Capital Partners
Mr. Donald A. Peterson
Gen. Ptnr.
23410 Civic Ctr. Way, Ste. E-2
Malibu, CA 90265
(213) 456-7024
C * 1,4,5,6,7,8,9

Los Angeles Capital Corp.
Mr. Kuytae Hwang, Pres.
606 N. Larchmont Blvd., Ste. 309
Los Angeles, CA 90004
(213) 460-4646
MESBIC B * 2,4,5,12

Branch Office
MBW Management, Inc.
Doan Resources
Mr. James R. Weersing, Mng. Dir.
350 Second St., Suite 7
Los Altos, CA 94022
(415) 941-2392
D *** 1,5,6,8
(Main Office in MI)

MCA New Ventures, Inc.
Mr. W. Roderick Hamilton, Pres.
100 Universal City Plaza
Universal City, CA 91608
(818) 777-2937
MESBIC B *** 1,5,7

Merrill, Pickard, Anderson
& Eyre I
Mr. Steven L. Merrill, Mng. Ptnr.
Two Palo Alto Sq., Ste. 425
Palo Alto, CA 94306
(415) 856-8880
E *** 1,6,8

Myriad Capital, Inc.
Mr. Chuang-I Lin, Pres.
2225 W. Commonwealth Ave., #111
Alhambra, CA 91801
(818) 289-5689
MESBIC B * 1,2,5,8,9,10,11

Branch Office
Nelson Capital Corp.
Mr. Norman Tulchin, Chmn.
10000 Santa Monica Blvd.
Los Angeles, CA 90067
(213) 556-1944
E * 12
(Main Office in NY)

New Kukje Investment Co.
Mr. C.K. Noh, Pres.
958 S. Vermont Ave., #C
Los Angeles, CA 90006
(213) 389-8679
MESBIC B * 12

New West Ventures
Mr. Tim Haidinger, Pres.
4350 Executive Dr., #206
San Diego, CA 92121
(619) 457-0722
E *** 1,4,5,6,9,10,11

Branch Office
New West Ventures
4600 Campus Dr., #103
Newport Beach, CA 92660
E *** 1,5,6,9,10,11,12

Branch Office
Orange Nassau Capital Corp.
Mr. John W. Blackburn, VP
Westerly Place
1500 Quail St., Ste. 540
Newport Beach, CA 92660
(714) 752-7811
C ** 12
(Main Office in MA)

Opportunity Capital Corp.
Mr. J. Peter Thompson, Pres.
50 California St., Ste. 2505
San Francisco, CA 94111
(415) 421-5935
MESBIC B *** 1,5,11,12

PBC Venture Capital, Inc.
Mr. Henry Wheeler
Pres./Gen. Mgr.
PO Box 6008
Bakersfield, CA 93386
(805) 395-3206
A *** 2,5,6,8,9,12

PCF Venture Capital Corp.
Mr. Eduardo B. Cu-Unjieg, Pres.
Ms. Gina M. Guerrero, Inv. Off.
675 Mariner's Island Blvd., #103
San Mateo, CA 94404
(415) 574-4747
B * 12

San Joaquin Capital Corp.
Mr. Chester W. Troudy, Pres.
1675 Chester Ave., Ste. 330
PO Box 2538
Bakersfield, CA 93303
(805) 323-7581
D *** 2,5,7,12

San Jose SBIC, Inc.
Mr. Robert T. Murphy, Pres.
100 Park Ctr. Pl., Ste. 427
San Jose, CA 95113
(408) 293-8052
C * 1,6,12

Seaport Ventures, Inc.
Mr. Michael Stolper, Pres.
Ms. Carole Rhoades, VP
525 B St., Ste. 630
San Diego, CA 92101
(619) 232-4069
B *** 12

Union Venture Corp.
Mr. Brent T. Rider, Pres.
Mr. Christopher L. Rafferty, VP
Mr. Jeffrey Watts, Sr., Inv. Off.
Mr. Thomas H. Peterson, Inv. Off.
225 S. Lake Ave., #601
Pasadena, CA 91101
(818) 304-1989
D *** 1,5,6,8

Branch Office
Union Venture Corp.
Mr. John W. Ulrich, VP
Mr. Lee R. McCracker, Inv. Ofcr.
18300 Von Karman
Irvine, CA 92713
(714) 553-7130
D *** 1,5,6,8

Unity Capital Corp.
Mr. Frank W. Owen, Pres.
4343 Morena Blvd., #3-A
San Diego, CA 92117
(619) 275-6030
MESBIC A ** 5,12

VK Capital Co.
Mr. Franklin Van Kasper
Gen. Ptnr.
50 California St., #2350
San Francisco, CA 94111
(415) 391-5600
A * 12

Westamco Investment Co.
Mr. Leonard G. Muskin, Pres.
Mr. Scott T. Van Every, VP
8929 Wilshire Blvd., Ste. 400
Beverly Hills, CA 90211
(213) 652-8288
C * 12

Wilshire Capital Inc.
Mr. Kyn Han Lee, Pres.
3932 Wilshire Blvd., Ste. 305
Los Angeles, CA 90010
(213) 388-1314
MESBIC A ** 12

Branch Office
Wood River Capital Corp.
Mr. Peter C. Wendell, VP
3000 Sand Hill Rd., Ste. 280
Menlo Park, CA 94025
(415) 854-1000
D *** 1,5,6,10,12
(Main Office in NY)

Branch Office
Worthen Finance & Inv. Inc.
Mr. Ellis Chane, Mgr.
3660 Wilshire Blvd.
Los Angeles, CA 90010
(213) 480-1908
MESBIC D ** 12
(Main Office in AR)

Yosemite Capital Investment
Mr. J. Horace Hampton, Pres.
448 Fresno St.
Fresno, CA 93706
(209) 485-2431
MESBIC A *** 12

COLORADO

Colorado Growth Capital, Inc.
Mr. Nicholas Davis, Chmn./Pres.
Ms. Debra Chauez, Inv. Analyst
1600 Broadway, Ste. 2125
Denver, CO 80202
(303) 831-0205
B * 5,12

Enterprise Fin. Cap. Dev. Corp.
Mr. Robert N. Hampton, Pres.
PO Box 5840
Snowmass Village, CO 81615
(303) 923-4144
E * 12

Branch Office
FBS Venture Capital Company
Mr. Brian P. Johnson, VP
3000 Pearl St., #206
Boulder, CO 80301
(303) 442-6885
C *** 1,5,6,8
(Main Office in AZ)

InterMountain Ventures, Ltd.
Mr. Norman M. Dean, VP
Mr. E. E. Kuhns, Chmn.
1100 10th St., P.O. Box 1406
Greeley, Colorado 80632
(303) 356-3229
B *** 12

Mile Hi SBIC
Mr. E. Preston Sumner, Inv. Adv.
2505 W. 16th Ave.
Denver, CO 80204
(303) 629-5339
MESBIC A *** 1,5,6,8,12

UBD Capital Inc.
Mr. Richard B. Wigton, Pres.
1700 Broadway
Denver, CO 80274
(303) 863-6329
B * 12

CONNECTICUT

Asset Capital & Management Corp.
Mr. Ralph Smith, Pres.
608 Ferry Blvd.
Stratford, CT 06497
(203) 375-0299
A ** 2

Capital Impact
Mr. Kevin S. Tierney, Pres.
Ms. Joann M. Haines, VP
Ms. Francis P. Murray, Inv. Ofcr.
Mr. John Cuticelli, Jr., Sr. VP
961 Main St.
Bridgeport, CT 06601
(203) 384-5670
C * 2,5,9,10,11,12

Capital Resource Co. of CT L.P.
Mr. I. M. Fierberg, Gen. Ptnr.
Ms. Janice Romanowski, Gen. Ptnr.
699 Bloomfield Ave.
Bloomfield, CT 06002
(203) 243-1114
B ** 12

First Connecticut SBIC (The)
Mr. David Engelson, Pres.
177 State St.
Bridgeport, CT 06604
(203) 366-4726
D * 12

Marcon Capital Corp.
Mr. Martin Cohen, Chmn.
49 Riverside Ave.
Westport, CT 06880
(203) 226-6893
C *** 1,2,9,10,12

Northeastern Capital Corp.
Mr. Louis Mingione
Pres./Exec. Dir.
61 High St.
East Haven, CT 06512
(203) 469-7901
A * 12

Regional Financial Enterprises
Mr. Robert M. Williams
Gen. Ptnr.
Mr. George E. Thomassy III
Gen. Ptnr.
Mr. Howard C. Landis
Gen. Ptnr.
36 Grove St.
New Canaan, CT 06840
(203) 966-2800
E *** 1,5,6,8,9,12

SBIC of Connecticut
Mr. Kenneth F. Zarrilli, Pres.
Mr. Emanuel Zimmer, Treas.
1115 Main St., #610
Bridgeport, CT 06604
(203) 367-3282
A * 2,9,12

DISTRICT OF COLUMBIA

Allied Capital Corp.
Mr. George C. Williams, Chmn.
Mr. David Gladstone, Pres.
1625 I St., NW, Ste. 603
Washington, DC 20006
(202) 331-1112
E *** 1,5,6,9,10,12

American Security Capital Corp.
Mr. Brian K. Mercer, VP
730 15th St., NW
Washington, DC 20013
(202) 624-4843
C *** 12

Broadcast Capital, Inc.
Mr. John Oxendine, Pres.
1771 N St., N.W., #404
Washington, D.C. 20036
(202) 429-5393
MESBIC A *** 1

Branch Office
Continental Investors, Inc.
Mr. Lac Thantrong, Pres.
2020 K St., NW, Ste. 350
Washington, DC 20006
(202) 466-3709
MESBIC B * 4,6,9,10,12
(Main Office in CA)

D.C. Bancorp Venture Capital Co.
Mr. Allan A. Weissburg, Pres.
1801 K St., NW
Washington, DC 20006
(202) 955-6970
C *** 5,6,9,10,12

Fulcrum Venture Capital Corp.
Mr. Divakar Kamath, Pres.
Ms. Renate K. Todd, VP
2021 K St., NW, Ste. 701
Washington, DC 20006
(202) 833-9590
MESBIC C *** 1,2,5,6,11,12

Syncom Capital Corp.
Mr. Herbert P. Wilkins, Pres.
1030 15th St., NW, Ste. 203
Washington, DC 20005
(202) 293-9428
MESBIC C **** 1

Washington Finance & Inv. Corp.
Mr. Chang H. Lie, Pres.
2600 Virginia Ave., NW, #515
Washington, DC 20037
(202) 338-2900
MESBIC A *** 2,4,10,12

Branch Office
Worthen Finance & Inv. Inc.
Mr. Vernon Weaver, Mgr.
2121 K St., NW, Ste. 830
Washington, DC 20037
(202) 659-9427
MESBIC C ** 4,5,6,9,10,11
(Main Office in AR)

FLORIDA

Caribank Capital Corp.
Mr. Michael E. Chaney, Pres.
Mr. Harold F. Messner, VP
Ms. Elaine E. Healy, Invst. Ofcr.
255 E. Dania Beach Blvd.
Dania, FL 33004
(305) 925-2211
B *** 1,3,6,7,8,11

FAIC Capital Corp.
Mr. Joseph N. Hardin, Jr., Pres.
2701 S. Bayshore Dr., Ste. 402
Coconut Grove, FL 33133
(305) 854-6840
B *** 12

First Tampa Capital Corp.
Mr. Thomas L. du Pont
Pres.
Mr. Larry S. Hyman
Fin. & Inv. Mgr.
501 E. Kennedy Blvd., Ste. 806
Tampa, FL 33602
(813) 221-2171
C * 12

Ideal Financial Corp.
Mr. Ectore Reynaldo, Gen. Mgr.
780 NW 42nd Ave., Ste. 304
Miami, FL 33126
(305) 442-4653
MESBIC A ** 12

J & D Capital Corp.
Mr. Jack Carmel, Pres.
12747 Biscayne Blvd.
North Miami, FL 33160
(305) 893 0303
D * 2,5,9,12

Market Capital Corp.
Mr. Ernest E. Eads, Pres.
Mr. Jay A. Musleh, VP
Mr. Billy M. Shaw, Sec/Tres.
PO Box 22667
Tampa, FL 33630
(813) 247-1357
B ** 9

Small Business Assistance Corp.
Mr. Charles S. Smith, Pres.
Mr. H. N. Tillman,.Secretary
2612 W. 15th St.
Panama City, FL 32401
(904) 785-9577
B * 4

Southeast Venture Capital Ltd. I
Mr. Clement L. Hofmann, Pres.
One Southeast Financial Ctr.
Miami, FL 33131
(305) 375-6470
D *** 1,5,6,8,12

Universal Financial Services, Inc
Mr. Norman Zipkin, Pres.
3550 Biscayne Blvd., Ste. 702
Miami, FL 33137
(305) 538-5464
MESBIC B ** 12

Venture Opportunities Corp.
Mr. A. Fred March, Pres.
444 Brickell Ave., Ste. 650
Miami, FL 33131
(305) 358-0359
MESBIC A *** 1,5,6,9,11,12

Verde Capital Corp.
Mr. Jose Dearing, Pres.
255 Alhambra Circle, #720
Coral Gables, FL 33134
(305) 444-8938
MESBIC B * 12

GEORGIA

Mighty Capital Corp.
Mr. Gary E. Korynoski
VP/Gen. Mgr.
50 Technology Park
Atlanta, Ste. 100
Norcross, GA 30092
(404) 448-2232
A * 12

North Riverside Capital Corp.
Mr. Thomas R. Barry, Pres.
Ms. Elizabeth G. Anderson, VP
5775-D Peachtree Dunwoody Rd.
Suite #650
Atlanta, GA 30342
(404) 252-1076
D *** 12

HAWAII

Bancorp Hawaii SBIC, Inc.
Mr. Thomas T. Triggs, VP/Mgr.
P.O. Box 2900
Honolulu, HI 96846
(808) 521-6411
A *** 12

Pacific Venture Capital, Ltd.
Mr. Dexter J. Taniguchi, Pres.
1405 N. King St., Ste. 302
Honolulu, HI 96817
(808) 847-6502
MESBIC A * 12

IDAHO

First Idaho Venture Capital Corp.
Mr. Ron J. Twilegar, Pres.
Mr. Dennis J. Clark, VP
P.O. Box 1739
Boise, ID 83701
(208) 345-3460
B *** 6,12

ILLINOIS

Abbott Capital Corp.
Mr. Richard E. Lassar, Pres.
9933 Lawler Ave., Ste. 125
Skokie, IL 60077
(312) 982-0404
A *** 1,6,10

Alpha Capital Venture Partners
Mr. Andrew H. Kalnow, Mng. Ptnr.
Mr. Daniel O'Connell, Gen. Ptnr.
3 First National Pl., Ste. 1400
Chicago, IL 60602
(312) 372-1556
C * 12

Amoco Venture Capital Co.
Mr. Gordon E. Stone, Pres.
200 E. Randolph Dr.
Chicago, IL 60601
(312) 856-6523
MESBIC C *** 3,8

Business Ventures, Inc.
Mr. Milton Lefton, Pres.
20 N. Wacker Dr., Ste. 550
Chicago, IL 60606
(312) 346-1580
B *** 12

Chicago Community Ventures Inc.
Ms. Phyllis E. George, Pres.
104 S. Michigan, #215
Chicago, IL 60603
(312) 726-6084
MESBIC B *** 4,5,12

Combined Fund, Inc. (The)
Mr. E. Patric Jones, Pres.
Ms. Carolyn Sauage, Analyst
1525 E. 53rd St., #908
Chicago, IL 60615
(312) 363-0300
C * 1,12

Continental IL Venture Corp.
Mr. John L. Hines, Pres.
231 S. LaSalle St.
Chicago, IL 60697
(312) 828-8021
E *** 1,5,6,8,9,10

First Capital Corp. of Chicago
Mr. John A. Canning, Jr., Pres.
Three First National Pl.
Ste. 1330
Chicago, IL 60670-0501
(312) 732-5400
E *** 1,5,6,9

Frontenac Capital Corp.
Mr. David A.R. Dullum, Pres.
208 S. LaSalle St., #1900
Chicago, IL 60604
(312) 368-0044
E *** 12

Mesirow Venture Capital
Mr. James C. Tyree
Managing Director
Mr. William P. Sutter, Jr.
Vice President
350 N. Clark
Chicago, IL 60610
(312) 670-6000
E *** 1,2,3,4,5,6,7,8,9,10,11,12

Branch Office
Nelson Capital Corp.
Mr. Irwin B. Nelson, Pres.
2340 Des Plaines Ave.
Des Plaines, IL 60018
(312) 296-2280
E * 12
(Main Office in NY)

Northern Capital Corp.
Mr. Robert L. Underwood, Pres.
50 S. LaSalle St.
Chicago, IL 60675
(312) 444-5399
D *** 12

Tower Ventures, Inc.
Mr. Robert T. Smith, Pres.
Sears Tower, BSC 43-50
Chicago, IL 60684
(312) 875-0571
MESBIC B *** 12

Walnut Capital Corp.
Mr. Burton W. Kanter, Chmn.
Mr. David L. Bogetz, VP
Three First National Plaza
Chicago, IL 60602
(312) 269-1732
C * 1,5,6,8

INDIANA

Circle Ventures, Inc.
Mr. Samuel Sutphin II, VP
20 N. Meridian St., 3rd Flr.
Indianapolis, IN 46240
(317) 636-7242
A *** 12

Equity Resource Co., Inc.
Mr. Michael J. Hammes, VP/Sec.
202 S. Michigan St.
South Bend, IN 46601
(219) 237-5255
B *** 5,12

1st Source Capital Corp.
Mr. Christopher Murphy, III
Pres.
Mr. Eugene L. Cavanaugh, Jr.
VP
100 N. Michigan
South Bend, IN 46601
(219) 236-2180
B *** 1,3,5,6,7,8,9,11

White River Capital Corp.
Mr. David J. Blair, Pres.
Mr. Thomas D. Washburn, Vice-Chmn
500 Washington St., PO Box 929
Columbus, IN 47202
(812) 376-1759
B *** 1,5,9,10,12

IOWA

MorAmerica Capital Corp.
Mr. Donald E. Flynn, Exec. VP
Mr. David R. Schroder, VP
300 American Bldg.
Cedar Rapids, IA 52401
(319) 363-8249
D *** 12

KANSAS
Kansas Venture Capital, Inc.
Mr. Larry High, VP
One Townsite Plaza
1030 First Nat'l Bank Towers
Topeka, KS 66603
(913) 233-1368
A * 5

KENTUCKY
Equal Opportunity Finance, Inc.
Mr. Frank Justice, Pres.
Mr. David Sattich, Mgr.
Mr. Donald L. Davis, Asst. Mgr.
420 Hurstbourne Ln., Ste. 201
Louisville, KY 40222
(502) 423-1943
MESBIC B * 12

Financial Opportunities, Inc.
Mr. Gary F. Duerr, Gen. Mgr.
833 Starks Bldg.
Louisville, KY 40202
(502) 584-8259
A * 9

Mountain Ventures, Inc.
Mr. L. Raymond Moncrief, Pres.
911 N. Main St.
PO Box 628
London, KY 40741
(606) 864-5175
C * 1,5,6,10

LOUISIANA
Commercial Capital, Inc.
Mr. Milton Coxe, Acting Pres.
Mr. Michael D. Whitney, Treas.
Mr. Lou Braddock, Sec.
PO Box 1776
Covington, LA 70434-1776
(504) 345-8820
A * 12

Dixie Business Inv. Co., Inc.
Mr. L. Wayne Baker, Pres.
Ms. Evelyn S. Bolding, Asst. Mgr.
PO Box 588
Lake Providence, LA 71254
(318) 559-1558
A ** 9,10,12

First Southern Capital Corp.
Mr. Charest Thibaut, Chmn./CEO
Ms. Carol S. Perrin, Inv. Ofcr.
PO Box 14418
Baton Rouge, LA 70898
(504) 769-3004
D *** 12

Louisiana Equity Capital Corp.
Mr. Melvin L. Rambin, Pres.
Mr. Jack McDonald, Inv. Ofcr.
Mr. Tom J. Adomek, Inv. Analyst
Louisiana Nat'l Bank-PO Box 1511
Baton Rouge, LA 70821
(504) 389-4421
C *** 1,5,6,12

Walnut Street Capital Co.
Mr. William D. Humphries
Mng. Gen. Ptnr.
231 Carondelet St., #702
New Orleans, LA 70130
(504) 525-2112
B *** 12

MAINE
Maine Capital Corp.
Mr. David M. Coit, Pres.
70 Center St.
Portland, ME 04101
(207) 772-1001
A *** 12

MARYLAND
First Maryland Capital, Inc.
Mr. Joseph Kenary, Pres.
107 W. Jefferson St.
Rockville, MD 20850
(301) 251-6630
A *** 12

Greater Washington Investors, Inc
Mr. Don A. Christensen, Pres.
Mr. Martin S. Pinson, Sr. VP
Mr. Jeffrey T. Griffin, VP
Mr. Cyril W. Draffin, Jr., VP
5454 Wisconsin Ave., Ste. 1315
Chevy Chase, MD 20815
(301) 656-0626
D *** 8,12

Suburban Capital Corp.
Mr. Henry P. Linsert, Jr., Pres.
Mr. Steve Dubin, VP
6610 Rockledge Dr.
Bethesda, MD 20817
(301) 493-7025
D *** 5,6,8,12

MASSACHUSETTS
Atlantic Energy Capital Corp.
Mr. Joost E. Tjaden, Pres.
260 Franklin St., Ste. 1501
Boston, MA 02110
(617) 451-6220
C * 1,3,5,6,8,9,10,11,12

BancBoston Ventures, Inc.
Mr. Paul F. Hogan, Pres.
Mr. Jeffrey W. Wilson, VP/Treas.
Ms. Diana H. Frazier, VP
100 Federal St.
Boston, MA 02110
(617) 434-5700
E * 1,5,6,8

Branch Office
Boston Hambro Capital Co.
Mr. Robert Sherman, VP
One Boston Pl., Ste. 723
Boston, MA 02106
(617) 722-7055
C *** 1,5,6
(Main Office in NY)

Branch Office
Churchill International
Mr. Roy G. Helsing, VP
Ms. Julie Dunbar, Mgr.
9 Riverside Rd.
Weston, MA 02193
(617) 893-6555
D *** 1,8
(Main Office in CA)

Branch Office
First SBIC of California
Mr. Michael Cronin, Mng. Ptnr.
50 Milk St., 15th Fl.
Boston, MA 02109
(617) 542-7601
E *** 12
(Main Office in CA)

Branch Office
Fleet Venture Resources, Inc.
Mr. James A. Saalfield, VP
60 State St.
Boston, MA 02100
(617) 367-6700
E *** 1,5,6,8,9,10,11,12

Branch Office
Narragansett Capital Corp.
265 Franklin St., 11th Floor
Boston, MA 02110
(Main Office RI)

New England Capital Corp.
Mr. Z. David Patterson, Exec. VP
Mr. Thomas C. Tremblay, VP
Mr. Stuart D. Pompian, VP
One Washington Mall, 7th Flr.
Boston, MA 02108
(617) 722-6400
D *** 1,5,6,8,12

New England MESBIC, Inc.
Dr. Etang Chen, Pres.
50 Kearney Rd., Ste. 3
Needham, MA 02194
(617) 449-2066
MESBIC A * 1,4,5,6,8,9,12

Orange Nassau Capital Corp.
Mr. Joost E. Tjaden, Pres.
260 Franklin St., Ste. 1501
Boston, MA 02110
(617) 451-6220
C * 1,6,9,10,11,12

TA Associates
Advent III Capital Co.
Advent IV Capital Co.
Advent V Capital Co.
Advent Atlantic Capital Co.
Advent Industrial Capital Co.
Chestnut Capital Corp.
Chestnut Capital Int'l II
Devonshire Capital Corp.
Mr. David D. Croll, Mng. Ptnr.
Mr. Richard Churchill, Gen. Ptnr.
Mr. Stephen Gormley, Gen. Ptnr.
Mr. William Collatos, Gen. Ptnr.
Mr. James F. Wade, Assoc.
45 Milk St.
Boston, MA 02109
(617) 338-0800
E *** 1

Branch Office
Transportation Capital Corp.
Mr. Jon Hirch, Asst. VP
566 Commonwealth Ave., Ste. 810
Boston, MA 02215
(617) 262-9701
B ** 11
(Main Office in NY)

UST Capital Corp.
Mr. Arthur F.F. Snyder, Chmn.
Mr. C. Walter Dick, VP
30 Court St.
Boston, MA 02108
(617) 726-7138
B * 1,5,6,8,9,12

Vadus Capital Corp.
Mr. Joost E. Tjaden, Pres.
260 Franklin St., Ste. 1501
Boston, MA 02110
(617) 451-6220
C * 1,6,9,10,11,12

Worcester Capital Corp.
Mr. Kenneth Kidd, VP/Mgr.
446 Main St.
Worcester, MA 01608
(617) 793-4508
A *** 1,6,8

MICHIGAN
Comerica Capital Corp.
Mr. John D. Berkaw, Pres.
30150 Telegraph Rd., Ste. 245
Birmingham, MI 48010
(313) 258-5800
D * 1,5,6,8,12

Doan Resources L.P.
Mr. Ian R.N. Bund, Gen. Ptnr.
2000 Hogback Rd., Suite 2
Ann Arbor, MI 48105
(313) 971-3100
D *** 1,5,6,8

Metro-Detroit Investment Co.
Mr. William J. Fowler, Pres.
Mr. George Caracostas, VP
30777 Northwestern Hwy., Ste. 300
Farmington Hills, MI 48018
(313) 851-6300
MESBIC B * 5,6,9

Michigan Cap. & Service, Inc.
Ms. Mary L. Campbell, VP
500 First Nat'l Bldg.
201 S. Main St.
Ann Arbor, MI 48104
(313) 663-0702
D *** 1,5,6,12

Michigan Tech Capital Corp.
Mr. Edward J. Koepel, Pres.
Technology Park, 1700 Duncan Ave.
PO Box 529
Hubbell, MI 49934
(906) 487-2643
B *** 3,5,8

Motor Enterprises, Inc.
Mr. James Kobus, Mgr.
3044 W. Grand Blvd., Rm. 13-152
Detroit, MI 48202
(313) 556-4273
MESBIC A ** 5

Mutual Investment Co., Inc.
Mr. Timothy J. Taylor, Treas.
21415 Civic Center Dr., Ste. 217
Southfield, MI 48076
(313) 559-5210
MESBIC B ** 9

Branch Office
Regional Financial Enterprises
Mr. Barry P. Walsh, Sr. Assoc.
Mr. James A. Parsons, Ptnr.
315 E. Eisenhower Pkwy., Ste.300
Ann Arbor, MI 48104
(313) 769-0941
E *** 1,5,6,8,9,12
(Main Office in CT)

MINNESOTA
Control Data Capital Corp.
Mr. Doug C. Curtis, Jr., Pres.
Mr. D. R. Pickerell, Sec.
3601 W. 77th St.
Minneapolis, MN 55435
(612) 921-4118
D * 1,5,6,8,

Control Data Community Ventures Fund, Inc.
Mr. Thomas F. Hunt, Jr., Pres.
3601 W. 77th St.
Minneapolis, MN 55435
(612) 921-4352
MESBIC C * 1,5,6,8,12

DGC Capital Co.
Mr. Jerry H. Udesen, Chmn.
603 Alworth Bldg.
Duluth, MN 55802
(218) 722-0058
A * 3,5,6,7,9,10

Branch Office
FBS Venture Capital Company
Mr. W. Ray Allen, Exec. VP
Mr. John H. Bullion, VP
7515 Wayzata Blvd., Ste. 110
Minneapolis, MN 55426
(612) 544-2754
C *** 1,5,6,8
(Main Office in AZ)

Northland Capital Corp.
Mr. George G. Barnum, Jr.
Pres.
Ms. Elizabeth Barnum
Asst. Sec./Treas.
613 Missabe Bldg., 277 W. 1st St.
Duluth, MN 55802
(218) 722-0545
B *** 12

North Star Ventures, Inc.
Mr. Terrence W. Glarner, Pres.
100 S. Fifth St., #2200
Minneapolis, MN 55402
(612) 333-1133
D *** 1,5,6,8,12

North Star Ventures II
Mr. Terrence W. Glarner, Pres.
100 S. Fifth St., #2200
Minneapolis, MN 55402
(612) 333-1133
D *** 1,5,6,8,12

Northwest Venture Partners
Mr. Robert F. Zicarelli, Chmn.
222 S. Ninth St., #2800
Minneapolis, MN 55402
(612) 372-8770
E *** 12

Norwest Growth Fund, Inc.
Mr. Daniel J. Haggerty, Pres.
Mr. Douglas E. Johnson, VP
Mr. Leonard J. Brandt, VP
Mr. Timothy A. Stepanek, VP
222 S. Ninth St., #2800
Minneapolis, MN 55402
(612) 372-8770
E *** 1,5,6,8,12

Retailers Growth Fund, Inc.
Mr. Cornell L. Moore, Pres.
Mr. Rick Olson, Treas.
2318 Park Ave.
Minneapolis, MN 55404
(612) 872-4929
A ** 4,9,11

Shared Ventures, Inc.
Mr. Howard Weiner, Pres.
6550 York Ave. S., Ste. 419
Minneapolis, MN 55435
(612) 925-3411
B *** 1,4,5,6,9,11

Threshold Ventures, Inc.
Mr. John L. Shannon, VP
430 Oak Grove St., Ste. 303
Minneapolis, MN 55403
(612) 874-7199
B *** 1,5,6,9,12

MISSISSIPPI
Columbia Ventures, Inc.
Mr. Maurice Reed, Chmn.
Mr. Richard P. Whitney, Pres.
P.O. Box 1066
Jackson, MS 39215
(Fully Invested)

Invesat Capital Corp.
Mr. John Bise, Pres.
PO Box 3288
Jackson, MS 39207
(601) 969-3242
D * 12

Vicksburg SBIC
Mr. David L. May, Pres.
PO Box 852
Vicksburg, MS 39180
(601) 636-4762
A * 12

MISSOURI
Bankers Capital Corp.
Mr. Raymond E. Glasnapp, Pres.
Mr. Lee Glasnapp, VP
3100 Gillham Rd.
Kansas City, MO 64109
(816) 531-1600
A * 12

Capital For Business, Inc.
Mr. James B. Hebenstreit, Pres.
Mr. William O. Cannon, VP
Mr. Bart Bergman, VP
11 S. Meramec, #800
St. Louis, MO 63105
(314) 854-7427
C *** 1,5,6,8,9,10,12

Branch Office
Capital For Business, Inc.
Mr. Bart Bergman, VP
720 Main St., Suite 700
Kansas City, MO 64105
(816) 234-2357
C *** 1,5,6,8,9,10,12

Intercapco, Inc.
Mr. Thomas E. Phelps, Pres.
Mr. Mark J. Lincoln, VP
7800 Bonhomme Ave.
Clayton, MO 63105
(314) 863-0600
C *** 12

Intercapco West, Inc.
Mr. Thomas E. Phelps, Chmn.
Mr. Mark J. Lincoln, Pres.
7800 Bonhomme Ave.
Clayton, MO 63105
(314) 863-0600
C *** 12

Branch Office
MorAmerica Capital Corp.
Mr. Kevin F. Mullane, VP
Ste. 2724 - Commerce Tower Bldg.
911 Main St.
Kansas City, MO 64105
(816) 842-0114
D *** 12
(Main Office in Iowa)

United Missouri Capital Corp.
Mr. Joseph Kessinger
Exec. VP/Mgr.
928 Grand Ave., 1st Flr.
Kansas City, MO 64106
(816) 556-7115
B * 5,6,8,10

NEW HAMPSHIRE
Granite State Capital, Inc.
Mr. Albert Hall, III, Mng. Dir.
10 Fort Eddy Rd.
Concord, NH 03301
(603) 228-9090
A * 1,5,6,10,12

Lotus Capital Corp.
Mr. Richard J. Ash, Pres.
875 Elm St.
Manchester, NH 03101
(603) 668-8617
B *** 1,6,8,12

NEW JERSEY
Capital Circulation Corp.
Ms. Judy M. Kao, Dir/Sec.
208 Main St.
Ft. Lee, NJ 07024
(201) 947-8637
MESBIC B * 12

ESLO Capital Corp.
Mr. Leo Katz, Pres.
2401 Morris Ave., Ste. 220EW
Union, NJ 07083
(201) 687-4920
B * 12

First Princeton Capital Corp.
Mr. S. Lawrence Goldstein, Pres.
227 Hamburg Tpke.
Pompton Lakes, NJ 07442
(201) 831-0330
B *** 12

Monmouth Capital Corp.
Mr. Eugene W. Landy, Pres.
Mr. Ralph B. Patterson, Exec VP
PO Box 335 - 125 Wyckoff Rd.
Eatontown, NJ 07724
(201) 542-4927
C * 4,5,7,12

Branch Office
MBW Management, Inc.
Doan Resources
Philip E. McCarthy, Mng. Dir.
365 South St., 2nd Floor
Morristown, NJ 07960
(201) 285-5533
D *** 1,5,6,8
(Main Office in MI)

Rutgers Minority Investment Co.
Mr. Oscar Figueroa, Pres.
180 University Ave., 3rd Fl.
Newark, NJ 07102
(201) 648-5627
MESBIC B *** 12

Tappan Zee Capital Corp.
Mr. Jack Birnberg, Chmn.
201 Lower Notch Rd.
Little Falls, NJ 07424
(201) 256-8280
D * 12

Unicorn Ventures, Ltd.
Mr. Frank P. Diassi, Gen. Ptnr.
Mr. Arthur B. Baer, Gen. Ptnr.
6 Commerce Dr.
Cranford, NJ 07016
(201) 276-7880
D *** 12

Unicorn Ventures II, L.P.
Mr. Frank P. Diassi, Gen. Ptnr.
Mr. Arthur B. Baer, Gen. Ptnr.
6 Commerce Dr.
Cranford, NJ 07016
(201) 276-7880
D *** 12

NEW MEXICO

Albuquerque SBIC
Mr. Albert T. Ussery, Pres.
PO Box 487
Albuquerque, NM 87103
(505) 247-0145
A *** 12

Associated SW Investors, Inc.
Mr. John R. Rice, Pres.
2400 Louisiana, N.E., #4
Albuquerque, NM 87110
(505) 881-0066
MESBIC B * 1,5,6,8

Equity Capital Corp.
Mr. Jerry A. Henson, Pres.
231 Washington Ave., Ste. 2
Santa Fe, NM 87501
(505) 988-4273
B *** 5,9,12

Fluid Capital Corp.
Mr. George T. Slaughter, Pres.
8421 B Montgomery Blvd., NE
Albuquerque, NM 87111
(505) 292-4747
C *** 1,2,4,5,6,12

Southwest Capital Inv. Inc.
Mr. Martin J. Roe, Pres.
3500-E Commanche Rd., NE
Albuquerque, NM 87107
(505) 884-7161
C * 12

NEW YORK

American Commercial Capital Corp.
Mr. Gerald J. Grossman, Pres.
310 Madison Ave., Ste. 1304
New York, NY 10017
(212) 986-3305
B * 2,4,5,11,12

AMEV Capital Corp.
Mr. Martin S. Orland, Pres.
One World Trade Ctr., Ste. 5001
New York, NY 10048
(201) 775-9100
D *** 1,4,5,6,9,10,11,12

Atalanta Investment Co., Inc.
Mr. L. Mark Newman, Chmn.
450 Park Ave., Ste. 2102
New York, NY 10022
(212) 832-1104
D *** 1,2,5,6,7,8

Atlantic Capital Corp.
Mr. Harald Paumgarten, Pres.
40 Wall St.
New York, NY 10005
(212) 612-0616
E *** 12

Boston Hambro Capital Co.
Mr. Edwin A. Goodman, Pres.
17 E. 71st St.
New York, NY 10021
(212) 288-7778
C *** 1,5,6

BT Capital Corp.
Mr. James G. Hellmuth, Chmn.
Mr. Noel Urben, Pres.
Mr. Keith Fox, VP
Ms. Martha Cassidy, Asst. VP
280 Park Ave.
New York, NY 10017
(212) 850-1916
E *** 5,10

The Central New York SBIC, Inc.
Mr. Albert Wertheimer, Pres.
351 S. Warren St., Ste. 600
Syracuse, NY 13202
(315) 478-5026
A *** 1,7

Chase Manhattan Capital Corp.
Mr. Gustav H. Koven, Pres.
1 Chase Manhattan Plaza
23rd. Fl.
New York, NY 10081
(212) 552-6275
E *** 1,3,5,6,7,8,10,11,12

Chemical Venuture Capital Corp.
Mr. Steven J. Gilbert, Pres./CEO
Mr. Jeffrey C. Walker, VP
Mr. Michael J. Feldman, VP
277 Park Ave., 10th Fl.
New York, NY 10172
(212) 310-4949
E *** 1,4,5,6,7,8,9,10,11,12

Citicorp Venture Capital Ltd.
Mr. Peter G. Gerry, Pres.
Ms. Diane Rivas, Asst Mgr.
153 East 53rd St., 28th Fl.
New York, NY 10043
(212) 559-1127
E *** 12

Clinton Capital Corp.
Mr. Mark Scharfman, Pres.
Mr. Alan Leavitt, VP
419 Park Ave. S.
New York, NY 10016
(212) 696-4334
E ** 12

CMNY Capital Co., Inc.
Mr. Robert Davidoff, VP
77 Water St.
New York, NY 10005
(212) 437-7078
C *** 1,5,9,10,12

College Venture Equity Corp.
Mr. Francis M. Williams, Pres.
Mr. Joseph M. Williams, VP
256 Third St., PO Box 135
Niagara Falls, NY 14303
(813) 248-3878
A ** 2,5,6,11,12

Croyden Capital Corp.
Mr. Victor L. Hecht, Pres.
45 Rockefeller Pl., Ste. 2165
New York, NY 10111
(212) 974-0184
B *** 12

Edwards Capital Co.
Mr. Edward Teitlebaum, Mng. Ptnr.
215 Lexington Ave., #805
New York, NY 10016
(212) 686-2568
A ** 11

Elk Associates Funding Corp.
Mr. Gary C. Granoff, Pres.
600 Third Ave., #3810
New York, NY 10016
(212) 972-8550
MESBIC B ** 11, 12

Equico Capital Corp.
Mr. Duane E. Hill, Pres.
1290 Ave. of the Amer., Ste. 3400
New York, NY 10019
(212) 397-8660
MESBIC C *** 12

Everlast Capital Corp.
Mr. Frank J. Segreto, VP/CEO
350 Fifth Ave., Ste. 2805
New York, NY 10118
(212) 695-3910
MESBIC B * 2,9,10

Fairfield Equity Corp.
Mr. Matthew A. Berdon, Pres.
Mr. Samuel L. Highleyman, VP
200 E. 42nd St.
New York, NY 10017-5893
(212) 867-0150
B * 1,5,7,9

Ferranti High Technology, Inc.
Mr. Sanford R. Simon, Pres.
Mr. Michael R. Simon, VP
Mr. Keith C. Laugworthy, VP Sec.
515 Madison Ave., #1225
New York, NY 10022
(212) 688-9828
D * 1,5,8,12

Fifty-Third Street Ventures, L.P.
Ms. Patricia Cloherty, Gen. Ptnr.
Mr. Daniel Tessler, Gen. Ptnr.
420 Madison Ave., #1101
New York, NY 10017
(212) 752-8010
D *** 1,5,6,8

J.H. Foster & Co., Ltd.
Mr. John H. Foster, Ptnr.
Mr. Michael J. Connelly, Exec. VP
437 Madison Ave.
New York, NY 10024
(212) 753-4810
E *** 6,10,11,12

Franklin Corp. (The)
Mr. Allen Farkas, Pres.
1185 Ave. of the Americas
27th Flr.
New York, NY 10036
(212) 719-4844
E *** 5,6,8,9,11

Fundex Capital Corp.
Mr. Howard Sommer, Pres.
Mr. Martin Albert, VP
525 Northern Blvd.
Great Neck, NY 11021
(516) 466-8550
D * 12

GHW Capital Corp.
Mr. Jack Graff, Pres.
489 Fifth Ave., 2nd Fl.
New York, NY 10017
(212) 687-1708
B * 12

The Hanover Capital Corp.
Mr. John A. Selzer, VP
Mr. Stephen E. Levenson, VP
150 E. 58th St., Ste. 2710
New York, NY 10155
(212) 980-9670
B * 12

Harvest Ventures
  Asea-Harvest Partners I
  Bohlen Capital Corp.
  European Dev. Cap. Ltd.
Ptnrshp.
  Noro Capital Ltd.
  767 Ltd. Ptnrshp.
  WFG-Harvest Ptnrs., Ltd.
Mr. Harvey Wertheim, Gen. Ptnr.
767 Third Ave.
New York, NY 10017
(212) 838-7776
D * 1,3,5,6,8

Ibero-American Investors Corp.
Mr. Emilio L. Serrano, Pres./CEO
Chamber of Commerce Bldg.
55 St. Paul St.
Rochester, NY 14604
(716) 262-3440
MESBIC B * 5,9,12

Intergroup Venture Capital Corp.
Mr. Ben Hauben, Pres.
230 Park Ave., Ste. 206
New York, NY 10169
(212) 661-5428
A * 12

Irving Capital Corp.
Mr. J. Andrew McWethy, Exec. VP
Mr. Barry Solomon, VP
Mr. Steve Tuttle, VP
1290 Ave. of Americas, 3rd Fl.
New York, NY 10104
(212) 408-4800
E *** 12

Key Venture Capital Corp.
Mr. John M. Lang, Pres.
Mr. Mark R. Hursty, Exec. VP/Mng.
Mr. Richard C. VanAuken, Asst. VP
60 State St.
Albany, NY 12207
(518) 447-3227
B *** 12

Kwiat Capital Corp.
Mr. Sheldon Kwiat, Pres.
Mr. Lowell Kwiat, VP/Sec. •
576 Fifth Ave.
New York, NY 10036
(212) 391-2461
A ** 1,5,6,7,8,12

M & T Capital Corp.
Mr. Joseph V. Parlato, Pres.
Ms. Norma E. Gracia, Treas.
One M & T Pl., 5th Fl.
Buffalo, NY 14240
(716) 842-5881
D * 1,5,6,8,9,11,12

Medallion Funding Corp.
Mr. Alvin Murstein, Pres.
205 E. 42nd St., Ste. 2020
New York, NY 10017
(212) 682-3300
MESBIC B ** 11

Minority Equity Capital Co., Inc.
Mr. Donald Greene
Pres.
Mr. Clarence Arrington
Inv. Ofcr.
275 Madison Ave., Ste. 1901
New York, NY 10016
(212) 686-9710
MESBIC C *** 1,5,6,9,11,12

Multi-Purpose Capital Corp.
Mr. Eli B. Fine, Pres.
31 S. Broadway
Yonkers, NY 10701
(914) 963-2733
A *** 12

NatWest USA Capital Corp.
Mr. Orville G. Aarons, Sr. VP
175 Water St.
New York, NY 10038
(212) 602-1200
D * 1,3,5,6,11

Nelson Capital Corp.
Mr. Irwin B. Nelson, Pres.
591 Stewart Ave.
Garden City, NY 11530
(516) 222-2555
E * 12

Norstar Bancorp
Mr. Raymond A. Lancaster, Pres.
Mr. Joseph L. Reinhart, Analyst
Mr. Stephen Puricelli, Analyst
1450 Western Ave.
Albany, NY 12203
(518) 447-4492
D * 12

North American Funding Corp.
Mr. Franklin Wong, VP/Gen. Mgr.
177 Canal St.
New York, NY 10013
(212) 226-0080
MESBIC B * 12

North Street Capital Corp.
Mr. Ralph L. McNeal, Sr., Pres.
250 North St., RA-6S
White Plains, NY 10625
(914) 335-7901
MESBIC B *** 12

NYBDC Capital Corp.
Mr. Marshall R. Lustig, Pres.
41 State St.
Albany, NY 12207
(518) 463-2268
A * 12

Pan Pac Capital Corp.
Dr. Ing-Ping J. Lee, Pres.
19 Rector St., 35th Fl.
New York, NY 10006
(212) 344-6680
MESBIC A ** 12

Questech Capital Corp.
Dr. Earl W. Brian, Chmn.
Mr. John E. Koonce, Pres.
Ms. Barbara J. Hann, VP
600 Madison Ave.
New York, NY 10022
(212) 758-8522
D * 1,5,6,8

R & R Financial Corp.
Mr. Martin Eisenstadt, VP
1451 Broadway
New York, NY 10036
(212) 790-1400
A ** 12

Rand SBIC, Inc.
Mr. Donald A. Ross, Pres.
Mr. Thomas J. Bernard, VP
Mr. Keith B. Wiley, VP
1300 Rand Bldg.
Buffalo, NY 14203
(716) 853-0802
C *** 1,5,6,7,8,9,10,12

Peter J. Schmitt Co., Inc.
Mr. Mark A. Flint, Mgr.
PO Box 2
Buffalo, NY 14240
(716) 821-1400
A *** 9

Small Bus. Electronics Inv. Co.
Mr. Stanley Meisels, Pres.
1220 Peninsula Blvd.
Hewlett, NY 11557
(516) 374-0743
A * 12

Southern Tier Capital Corp.
Mr. Milton Brizel, Pres.
Mr. Harold Gold, Sec.
55 S. Main St.
Liberty, NY 12754
(914) 292-3030
A * 12

Branch Office
Tappan Zee Capital Corp.
120 N. Main St.
New City, NY 10956
(914) 634-8890
D * 12
(Main Office in NJ)

TLC Funding Corp.
Mr. Philip G. Kass, Pres.
141 S. Central Ave.
Hartsdale, NY 10530
(914) 683-1144
B ** 4,9,12

Transportation Capital Corp.
Mr. Melvin L. Hirsch, Pres.
Mr. Robert Silver, VP
Mr. Jon Hirsch, Asst. VP
Ms. Margaret Shiroky, Asst. Sec.
60 E. 42nd St., Ste. 3126
New York, NY 10165
(212) 697-4885
MESBIC B ** 11

Transworld Ventures, Ltd.
Mr. Jack H. Berger, Pres.
331 W. End Ave., Ste. 1A
New York, NY 10023
(212) 496-1010
A *** 5,10,12

Triad Capital Corp. of NY
Mr. L. Jim Barrera, Pres.
960 Southern Blvd.
Bronx, NY 10459
(212) 589-6541
MESBIC A * 1,3,6,8,9,10

Vega Capital Corp.
Mr. Victor Harz, Pres.
Mr. Ronald A. Linden, VP
720 White Plains Rd.
Scarsdale, NY 10583
(914) 472-8550
D * 12

Venture SBIC, Inc.
Mr. Arnold Feldman, Pres.
249-12 Jericho Tpke.
Floral Park, NY 11001
(516) 352-0068
A ** 2,9,12

Branch Office
Walnut Capital Corp.
Mr. Julius Goldfinger, Pres.
110 E. 59th St., 37th Floor
New York, NY 10016
(212) 750-1000
C * 1,5,6,8
(Main Office in IL)

Winfield Capital Corp.
Mr. Stanley Pechman, Pres.
237 Mamaroneck Ave.
White Plains, NY 10605
(914) 949-2600
D * 12

Wood River Capital Corp.
Ms. Elizabeth W. Smith, Pres.
645 Madison Ave.
New York, NY 10022
(212) 750-9420
D *** 1,5,6,10,12

Branch Office
Worthen Finance & Inv. Inc.
Mr. Guy Meeker, Mgr.
535 Madison Ave., 17th Fl.
New York, NY 10022
(212) 750-9100
MESBIC D ** 12
(Main Office in AR)

NORTH CAROLINA

Branch Office
Carolina Venture Capital Corp.
Mr. Thomas H. Harvey, III, Pres.
P.O. Box 646
Chapel Hill, NC 27514
B *** 1,2,4,7,11,12
(Main Office in SC)

Delta Capital, Inc.
Mr. Alex B. Wilkins, Jr., Pres.
Mr. Martha C. Kirker, Sec.
227 N. Tryon St., Ste 201
Charlotte, NC 28202
(704) 372-1410
B * 2,4,5,8,9,10

Falcon Capital Corp.
Dr. P.S. Prasad, Pres.
400 W. Fifth St.
Greenville, NC 27834
(919) 752-5918
A *** 2,4,6,9,10

Heritage Capital Corp.
Mr. Herman B. McManaway, Pres.
Mr. William R. Starnes, VP
Mr. G. Kinsey Roper, VP
2290 First Union Plaza
Charlotte, NC 28282
(704) 334-2867
C *** 12

Kitty Hawk Capital, Ltd.
Mr. Walter H. Wilkinson Jr.
Gen. Ptnr.
One Tryon Ctr., Ste. 2030
Charlotte, NC 28284
(704) 333-3777
C *** 1,5,6,8,12

NCNB SBIC Corp.
Mr. Troy McCrory, Pres.
One NCNB Plaza, T05-2
Charlotte, NC 28255
(704) 374-5000
C * 12

NCNB Venture Corp.
Mr. Mike Elliott, Pres.
One NCNB Plaza, T39
Charlotte, NC 28255
(704) 374-0435
D *** 1,5,6,8,12

OHIO
A.T. Capital Corp.
Mr. Shailesh J. Mehta, Pres.
Mr. Robert C. Salipante, VP
900 Euclid Ave., T-18
Cleveland, OH 44101
(216) 687-4970
C * 1,6,8

Capital Funds Corp.
Mr. Carl G. Nelson, VP/Mgr.
Mr. David B. Chilcote, Asst. VP
127 Public Sq.
Cleveland, OH 44114
(216) 622-8628
C * 1,5,6,9,12

Clarion Capital Corp.
Mr. Morton Cohen
Chmn/Pres.
Mr. Michael Boeckman
VP/Chief Fin. Ofcr.
Mr. Roger W. Eaglen
VP
3555 Curtis Blvd.
Eastlake, OH 44114
(216) 953-0555
C *** 1,3,5,6,8,10,12

First Ohio Capital Corp.
Mr. Michael J. Aust, VP
606 Madison Ave.
Toledo, OH 43604
(419) 259-7146
B *** 12

Gries Investment Co.
Mr. Robert D. Gries, Pres.
Mr. Richard Brezic, VP
720 Statler Office Tower
Cleveland, OH 44115
(216) 861-1146
B *** 12

National City Capital Corp.
Mr. Michael Sherwin, Pres.
623 Euclid Ave.
Cleveland, OH 44114
(216) 575-2491
C *** 12

Branch Office
River Capital Corp.
Mr. Peter D. Van Oosterhout,
Pres.
796 Huntington Bldg.
Cleveland, OH 44115
(216) 781-3655
D *** 12
(Main Office in RI)

SeaGate SBIC
Mr. Donald E. Breese, Sr. VP
245 Summit St., #1403
Toledo, OH 43603
(419) 259-8588
A *** 5,6,12

OKLAHOMA
Alliance Business Investment Co.
Mr. Barry M. Davis, Pres.
Mr. Mark R. Blankenship, VP
One Williams Ctr., Ste. 2000
Tulsa, OK 74172
(918) 584-3581
C *** 1,3,5,6,7,9,11,12

First OK Investment Capital Corp.
Mr. David H. Pendley, Pres.
Mr. Arthur J. Miller, VP
120 N. Robinson, Ste. 880C
Oklahoma City, OK 73102
(405) 272-4693
D *** 1,5,6,9,10,11,12

Southwest Venture Capital, Inc.
Mr. Donald J. Rubottom, Pres.
2700 E. 51st St., Ste. 340
Tulsa, OK 74105
(918) 742-3177
A *** 5,6,9,10

Western Venture Capital Corp.
Mr. William B. Baker, Pres./CEO
4900 S. Lewis
Tulsa, OK 74105
(918) 749-7981
D ** 12

OREGON
Branch Office
InterVen Partners
Mr. Wayne B. Kingsley, Chmn.
Mr. Keith L. Larson, VP
227 SW Pine St., Ste. 200
Portland, OR 97204
(503) 223-4334
E *** 1,6,8,12
(Main Office in CA)

Northern Pacific Capital Corp.
Mr. John J. Tennant, Jr., Pres.
Mr. Joseph P. Tennant, Sec.
1201 SW 12th Ave.
Portland, OR 97205
(503) 241-1255
B *** 5,9,11

Branch Office
Norwest Growth Fund, Inc.
Mr. Anthony Miadich, VP
Mr. Dale J. Vogel, VP
1300 SW Fifth Ave., Ste. 3018
Portland, OR 97201
(503) 223-6622
E *** 1,6,8,12
(Main Office in MN)

Trendwest Capital Corp.
Mr. Mark E. Nicol, Pres.
PO Box 5106
Klamath Falls, OR 97601
(503) 882-8059
B *** 12

PENNSYLVANIA
Alliance Enterprise Corp.
(The Sun Company)
Mr. Terrence Hicks, VP
1801 Market St., 3rd Fl.
Philadelphia, PA 19103
(215) 977-3925
MESBIC B * 1,5

Enterprise Vent. Cap. Corp of PA
Mr. Donald W. Cowie, VP
227 Franklin St., #215
Johnstown, PA 15901
(814) 535-7597
A * 12

Branch Office
First SBIC of California
Mr. Daniel A. Dye, Mng. Ptnr.
PO Box 512
Washington, PA 15301
(412) 223-0707
E *** 12
(Main Office in CA)

First Valley Capital Corp.
Mr. Matthew W. Thomas, Pres.
One Center Sq., Ste. 201
Allentown, PA 18101
(215) 776-6760
B * 12

Gtr. Phil. Ven. Cap. Corp., Inc.
Mr. Martin M. Newman, Gen. Mgr.
225 S. 15th St., Ste. 920
Philadelphia, PA 19102
(215) 732-1666
MESBIC B *** 4,5,6

Meridian Capital Corp.
Mr. Knute C. Albrecht, Pres/CEO
Mr. Jay M. Ackerman, VP
Blue Bell West, Ste. 122
Blue Bell, PA 19422
(215) 278-8907
B *** 12

PNC Capital Corp.
Mr. David M. Hillman, Exec. VP
Mr. Jeffrey H. Schutz, VP
Mr. Peter Del Presto, Inv.
Analyst
5th Ave. & Wood St., 19th Fl.
Pittsburgh, PA 15222
(412) 355-2245
C *** 1,5,6,8,9,10

PUERTO RICO
First Puerto Rico Capital, Inc.
Mr. Eliseo E. Font, Pres.
PO Box 816
Mayaguez, PR 00709
(809) 832-9171
MESBIC A * 12

North America Investment Corp.
Mr. S. Ruiz-Betancourt, Pres.
Banco Popular Ctr., Ste. 1710
Hato Rey, PR 00919
(809) 754-6177
MESBIC B ** 5,6,9,12

RHODE ISLAND
Domestic Capital Corp.
Mr. Nathaniel B. Baker, Pres.
815 Reservoir Ave.
Cranston, RI 02910
(401) 946-3310
B * 4,5,11,12

Fleet Venture Resources, Inc.
Mr. Robert M. Van Degna, Pres.
111 Westminster St.
Providence, RI 02920
(401) 278-6770
E *** 1,5,6,8,9,10,11,12

Narragansett Capital Corp.
Mr. Arthur D. Little, Chmn.
Mr. Gregory P. Barber, VP
Mr. Roger A. Vandenberg, VP
40 Westminster St.
Providence, RI 02903
(401) 751-1000
E * 1,5,7,8,9,12

Old Stone Capital Corp.
Mr. Arthur Barton, VP
One Old Stone Sq., 11th Fl.
Providence, RI 02901
(401) 278-2559
D *** 1

River Capital Corp.
Mr. Peter D. Van Oosterhout
Pres.
Mr. Robert A. Comey, VP
Mr. Peter C. Canepa, VP
One Hospital Trust Plaza
Providence, RI 02903
(401) 278-8819
D *** 12

SOUTH CAROLINA
Carolina Venture Capital Corp.
Mr. Thomas H. Harvey III, Pres.
14 Archer Rd.
Hilton Head Island, SC 29928
(803) 842-3101
B *** 1,2,4,7,11,12

Reedy River Ventures
Mr. John M. Sterling, Gen. Ptnr.
Mr. Tee C. Hooper, Gen. Ptnr.
PO Box 17526
Greenville, SC 29606
(803) 297-9198
B *** 1,5,9,12

TENNESSEE

Chickasaw Capital Corp.
Mr. Thomas L. Moore, Pres.
P.O. Box 387
Memphis, TN 38147
(901) 523-6470
MESBIC D *** 2,5,6,9,10,12

Financial Resources, Inc.
Mr. Milton C. Picard, Chmn.
2800 Sterick Bldg.
Memphis, TN 38103
(901) 527-9411
B *** 1,5,6,8,10,12

Leader Capital Corp.
Mr. Edward Pruitt, Pres.
P.O. Box 708, 158 Madison Ave.
Memphis, TN 38101-0708
(901) 578-2405

Suwannee Capital Corp.
Mr. Peter R. Pettit, Pres.
Mr. Melvin Hill, VP
3030 Poplar Ave.
Memphis, TN 38111
(901) 345-4200
C ** 9

Tennessee Equity Capital Corp.
Mr. Walter S. Cohen, Pres./CEO
1102 Stonewall Jackson
Nashville, TN 37220
(615) 373-4502
MESBIC C *** 1,2,4,5,7,9,10,12

Valley Capital Corp.
Mr. Lamar J. Partridge
Pres.
Ms. Faye Munger
Exec. Sec./Admin. Assist.
100 W. Martin L. King Blvd., #806
Chattanooga, TN 37402
(615) 265-1557
MESBIC B *** 1,5,6,9,11,12

West Tennessee Venture Cap. Corp.
Mr. Osbie Howard, VP
Mr. Bennie L. Marshall, Mgr.
PO Box 300, 152 Beale St.
Memphis, TN 38101
(901) 527-6091
MESBIC B * 1,5,6,7,10,11,12

TEXAS

Branch Office
Alliance Business Investment Co.
3990 One Shell Pl.
Houston, TX 77002
(713) 224-8224
C *** 1,3,5,6,8,11,12
(Main Office in OK)

Allied Bancshares Capital Corp.
Mr. Philip A. Tuttle, Pres.
Ms. Mary Bass, Inv. Ofcr.
P.O. Box 3326
Houston, TX 77253
(713) 226-1625
D *** 1,6,8,9,11,12

Americap Corp.
Mr. James L. Hurn, Pres.
Mr. Ben Andrews, VP
One Shell Plaza, 3rd Floor
910 Louisiana
Houston, TX 77002
(713) 221-4909
C *** 1,5,6,8,12

Brittany Capital Co.
Mr. Steven S. Peden, Gen. Ptnr.
2424 LTV Tower, 1525 Elm St.
Dallas, TX 75201
(214) 954-1515
B *** 12

Business Cap. Corp. of Arlington
Mr. Keith Martin, Pres.
1112 Copeland Rd., Ste. 420
Arlington, TX 76011-4994
(817) 261-4936
A *** 12

Capital Marketing Corp.
Mr. John King Myrick, Pres.
Mr. Morris Whetstone, Gen. Mgr.
PO Box 1000
Keller, TX 76248
(817) 656-7380
E ** 2,9

Capital Southwest Venture Corp.
Mr. William R. Thomas, Pres.
Mr. J. Bruce Duty, VP
Mr. Patrick Hamner, Inv. Assoc.
12900 Preston Rd., Ste. 700
Dallas, TX 75230
(214) 233-8242
D *** 1,3,5,6,8,9,11,12

Central Texas SBIC
Mr. David G. Horner, Pres.
Mr. Ross Miller, Sec.
Mr. David Senior, Dir.
514 Austin Ave., P.O. Box 2600
Waco, TX 76702-2600
(817) 753-6461
A ** 5,9,12

Charter Venture Group, Inc.
Mr. Jerry Finger, Pres.
2600 Citadel Plaza Dr., 6th Fl.
Houston, TX 77008
(713) 863-0704
B *** 12

Branch Office
Citicorp Venture Capital, Ltd.
Mr. Thomas F. McWilliams, VP
Diamond Shamrock Twr., #2920-LB87
717 Harwood
Dallas, TX 75221
(214) 880-9670
E *** 12
(Main Office in NY)

Energy Capital Corp.
Mr. Herbert F. Poyner, Jr., Pres.
953 Esperson Bldg.
Houston, TX 77002
(713) 236-0006
D *** 3

Enterprise Capital Corp.
Mr. Fred S. Zeidman
Pres.
Mr. Fiore Jalarieo, Jr.
CFO/Treas.
Ms. Eta G. Paransky
Consultant/ Inv. Advisor
3501 Allen Pkwy.
Houston, TX 77019
(713) 521-4401
D *** 1,5,6,7,8,12

FCA Investment Co.
Mr. R. S. Baker, Jr., Chmn.
Ms. Peggy Kliesing, Asst. Treas.
3000 Post Oak Blvd., #1790
Houston, TX 77056
(713) 965-0077
D *** 5,6,8,9,12

The Grocers SBI Corp.
Mr. Milton Levit, Pres.
3131 E. Holcombe Blvd., #101
Houston, TX 77021
(713) 747-7913
B ** 9

Branch Office
Hickory Venture Capital Corp.
3811 Turtle Creek Blvd.
#1000, LB33
Dallas, TX 75219
(214) 522-1892
E *** 12
(Main Office in AL)

InterFirst Venture Corp.
Mr. J.A. O'Donnell, Pres.
901 Main St., 10th Floor
Dallas, TX 75283
(214) 977-3164
E *** 12

Livingston Capital Ltd.
Mr. J. Livingston Kosberg, Ptnr.
Mr. Mark J. Brookner, Gen. Ptnr.
Ms. Glory S. Green, Sec.
PO Box 2507
Houston, TX 77252
(713) 872-3213
B *** 12

Lone Star Capital, Ltd.
Mr. Stuart Schube, Pres.
Mr. Martin D. O'Malley, Assoc.
2401 Fountainview, Ste. 950
Houston, TX 77057
(713) 266-6616
E * 1,5,6,9,12

Mapleleaf Capital Corp.
Mr. Edward M. Fink, Pres.
55 Waugh Dr., #710
Houston, TX 77007
(713) 880-4494
E *** 12

MESBIC Financial Corp. of Dallas
Mr. Thomas Gerron, VP/Controller
Mr. Don Lawhorne, Pres.
Mr. Norman Campbell, VP
12655 North Central Expwy., #814
Dallas, TX 75243
(214) 637-1597
MESBIC C *** 12

MESBIC Financial Corp. of Houston
Mr. Richard Rothfeld, Pres.
1801 Main St., Ste. 320
Houston, TX 77002
(713) 228-8321
MESBIC B * 5,8,9,10,12

Mid-State Capital Corp.
Mr. Smith E. Thomasson, Pres.
PO Box 7554
Waco, TX 76714
(817) 776-9500
B *** 12

MVenture Corp.
Mr. Joseph B. Longino, Jr., Pres.
Mr. J. Wayne Gaylord, Exec. VP
PO Box 662090
Dallas, TX 75266-2090
(214) 741-1469
D *** 1,5,6,10,11,12

Omega Capital Corp.
Mr. Ted E. Moor, Jr., Pres.
755 S. 11th St., #250
Beaumont, TX 77701
(409) 832-0221
A *** 5,12

Branch Office
Orange Nassau Capital Corp.
Mr. Richard D. Tadler, VP
One Galleria Tower
13355 Noel Rd., Ste. 635
Dallas, TX 75240
(214) 385-9685
C ** 12
(Main Office in MA)

Red River Ventures, Inc.
Mr. D.W. Morton, Pres.
777 E. 15th St.
Plano, TX 75074
(214) 422-4999
B * 12

Republic Venture Group, Inc.
Mr. Robert H. Wellborn, Pres.
Mr. William W. Richey, VP/Treas.
Mr. Bart A. McLean, Inv. Ofcr.
Ms. Sherry Richardson
Inv. Ofcr.
PO Box 225961
Dallas, TX 75265
(214) 922-5078
D *** 1,3,5,6,12

Retzloff Capital Corp.
Mr. James K. Hines, Pres.
Mr. Steve Retzloff, Exec. VP
Ms. Diane S. Langdon, Sec.
P.O. Box 41250
Houston, TX 77240
(713) 466-4633
C *** 5,6,9,12

San Antonio Venture Group, Inc.
Mr. Tom Woodley, Inv. Advisor
Mr. Mike Parish, Inv. Advisor
2300 W. Commerce
San Antonio, TX 78207
(512) 223-3633
B *** 4,5,6,9,10

SBI Capital Corp.
Mr. William E. Wright, Pres.
PO Box 771668
Houston, TX 77215-1668
(713) 975-1188
C *** 1,5,6,8

Southern Orient Capital Corp.
Dr. Cheng Ming Lee, Chmn.
2419 Fannin, Ste. 200
Houston, TX 77002
(713) 225-3369
MESBIC A * 4,9,10,12

Southwestern Ven. Cap. of TX,Inc.
Mr. James A. Bettersworth, Pres.
PO Box 1719
Seguin, TX 78155
(512) 379-0380
B * 12

Branch Office
Southwestern Ven. Cap. of TX,Inc.
N. Frost Ctr., Ste. 700
1250 NE Loop 410
San Antonio, TX 78209
B * 12

Sunwestern Capital Corp.
Mr. Thomas W. Wright, Pres.
Mr. James F. Leary, Exec. VP
12221 Merit Dr., #1680
Dallas, TX 75251
(214) 239-5650
C *** 1,3,5,6,8,12

Texas Capital Corp.
Mr. David Franklin, VP
Mr. Tom Beecroft, Asst. VP
1341 W. Mockingbird, #1250E
Dallas, TX 75247
(214) 638-0638
C *** 12

United Mercantile Capital Corp.
Mr. L. Joe Justice, Chmn.
PO Box 66
El Paso, TX 79940
(915) 533-6375
A *** 5,11

United Oriental Cap. Co.
Mr. Don J. Wang, Pres.
908 Town & Country Blvd., #310
Houston, TX 77024
(713) 461-3909
MESBIC B * 12

Wesbanc Ventures, Ltd.
Mr. Stuart Schube, Gen. Ptnr.
2401 Fountainview, #950
Houston, TX 77057
(713) 977-7421
E * 1,5,6,9,12

VIRGINIA

East West United Investment Co.
Mr. Doug Bui, Pres.
6723 Whittier Ave., Ste. 206B
McLean, VA 22101
(703) 821-6616
MESBIC A ** 4,9,12

Hillcrest Group
James River Capital Associates
UV Capital Corp.
Mr. A. Hugh Ewing, III
Gen. Ptnr.
Mr. James B. Farinholt, Jr.
Gen. Ptnr.
Mr. John P. Funkhouser
Gen. Ptnr.
9 S. 12th St., P.O. Box 1776
Richmond, VA 23219
(804) 643-7358
C *** 12

Metropolitan Capital Corp.
Mr. S. W. Austin, VP
2550 Huntington Ave.
Alexandria, VA 22303
(703) 960-4698
B *** 5,8

Branch Office
River Capital Corp.
1033 N. Fairfax St.
Alexandria, VA 22314
(703) 739-2100
D *** 12
(Main Office in RI)

Sovran Funding Corp.
Mr. David A. King, Jr., Pres.
Sovran Ctr., 6th Fl.
One Commercial Pl.
Norfolk, VA 23510
(804) 441-4041
C *** 12

WASHINGTON

Peoples Capital Corp.
Mr. R. W. Maider, Pres.
2411 Fourth Ave., Ste. 400
Seattle, WA 98121
(206) 344-8105
B * 1,6,9

Seafirst Capital Corp.
Mr. R. Bruce Harrod, Pres.
Columbia Seafirst Center
14th Floor
P.O. Box C-34103
Seattle, WA 98124-1103
(206) 442-3501
C * 2

WISCONSIN

Bando-McGlocklin Inv. Co., Inc.
Mr. George Schonath, CEO
Mr. Sal Bando, Pres.
Mr. Jon McGlocklin, Exec. VP
13555 Bishops Ct., Ste. 205
Brookfield, WI 53005
(414) 784-9010
C ** 5,6,9,10,11

Capital Investments, Inc.
Mr. Robert L. Banner, VP
744 N. 4th St.
Milwaukee, WI 53203
(414) 273-6560
C * 1,5,9,12

M & I Ventures Corp.
Mr. Daniel P. Howell, VP
770 N. Water St.
Milwaukee, WI 53202
(414) 765-7910
C *** 5,6,8,12

Madison Capital Corp.
Mr. Roger H. Ganser, Pres.
102 State St.
Madison, WI 53703
(608) 256-8185
B * 6,8,12

Marine Venture Capital, Inc.
Mr. H. Wayne Foreman, Pres.
Mr. Reed R. Prior, VP
111 E. Wisconsin Ave.
Milwaukee, WI 53202
(414) 765-2274
C *** 12

Branch Office
MorAmerica Capital Corp.
Mr. Steven J. Massey, VP
600 E. Mason St.
Milwaukee, WI 53202
(414) 276-3839
D *** 12
(Main Office in Iowa)

SC Opportunities, Inc.
Mr. Robert L. Ableman, VP/Sec.
Mr. Richard E. Becker, Asst. Sec.
1112 7th Ave.
Monroe, WI 53566
(608) 328-8540
MESBIC A *** 9

Super Market Investors, Inc.
Mr. John W. Andorfer, Pres.
Mr. David Maass, VP
PO Box 473
Milwaukee, WI 53201
(414) 547-7999
A ** 9

Twin Ports Capital Co.
Mr. Paul Leonidas, Pres.
R. F. Joki, Sec./Treas.
1230 Poplar Ave.
PO Box 849
Superior, WI 54880
(715) 392-5525
A * 12

Wisconsin Community Capital Inc.
Mr. Louis Fortis, Pres.
Ms. Nancy Bornstein, VP
14 W. Mifflin St., #314
Madison, WI 53703
(608) 256-3441
A * 3,5,10

Wisconsin MESBIC, Inc. (The)
Mr. Charles A. McKinney, Chmn.
Mr. William P. Beckett, Pres.
622 N. Water St., Ste. 500
Milwaukee, WI 53202
(414) 278-0377
MESBIC B *** 12

WYOMING

Capital Corp. of Wyoming, Inc.
Mr. Larry J. McDonald, Pres.
Mr. Scott Weaver, VP
Ms. Luella Brown, VP
Ms. Jean Hughley, Asst. VP
PO Box 3599
Casper, WY 82602
(307) 234-5438
B * 3,5,9,10,11,12

NON-SBIC MEMBERS

Mr. Robert B. Leisy
Consultant
14408 E. Whittier Blvd., B-5
P.O. Box 4405
Whittier, CA 90605
(213) 698-4862

Accel Partners
Mr. James R. Swartz, Mng. Ptnr.
Mr. Dixon R. Doll, Mg. Ptnr.
Mr. Arthur Patterson, Mng. Ptnr.
One Palmer Sq.
Princeton, NJ 08542
(609) 683-4500
E * 1,5,6,8,9,10,12

Alimansky Venture Group, Inc.
Mr. Burt Alimansky, Mng. Dir.
790 Madison Ave., Ste. 705
New York, NY 10021
(212) 472-0502
E *** 1,3,5,6,7,8,9,10,11,12

R.W. Allsop & Associates
Mr. Robert W. Allsop, Gen. Ptnr.
Mr. Gregory B. Bultman, Gen Ptnr.
Mr. Robert L. Kuk, Gen. Ptnr.
Mr. Larry C. Maddox, Gen. Ptnr.
Mr. Paul D. Rhines, Gen. Ptnr.
2750 First Ave., NE, Ste. 210
Cedar Rapids, IA 52402
(319) 363-8971
D *** 1,5,6,9,12

Allstate Insurance Co. -
Venture Capital Division
Mr. Leonard A. Batterson
Sr. Inv. Mgr.
Allstate Plaza E-2
Northbrook, IL 60062
(312) 291-5681
E *** 1,4,5,6,8,10,11,12

Arete Ventures, Inc.
Mr. Robert W. Shaw, Jr., Pres.
5995 Barfield Rd., #220
Atlanta, GA 30328
(404) 257-9548

Arthur Andersen & Co.
Mr. John Cherin, Mng. Ptnr.
8251 Greensboro Dr., #400
McLean, VA 22102
(703) 734-7300

Arthur Andersen & Co.
Mr. Brian P. Murphy, Ptnr.
111 SW Columbia, #1400
Portland, OR 97201
(503) 220-6068

Arthur Anderson & Co.
Mr. Robert W. Philip, Ptnr.
P.O. Box 650026
Dallas, TX 75265
(214) 741-8300

Arthur Andersen & Co.
Mr. Richard J. Strotman, Ptnr.
33 W. Monroe St.
Chicago, IL 60603
(312) 580-0033

Atlantic Venture Partners
Mr. Robert H. Pratt, Gen. Ptnr.
PO Box 1493
Richmond, VA 23212
(804) 644-5496
D *** 12

The Babcock Group
Mr. Warner King Babock, Pres.
Mr. Piers Curry, Baystreet Ptnrs.
P.O.Box 1022
49 Locust Ave.
New Cannan, CT 06840
(203) 972-3579

Bain Capital
Mr. Geoffrey S. Rehnert
Sr. Associate
Two Copley Pl.
Boston, MA 02116
(617) 572-3000
C *** 12

Baker & Kirk, P.C.
Mr. Michael A. Baker, Pres.
1020 Holcombe, Suite 1444
Houston, TX 77030
(713) 790-9316

Battery Ventures
Mr. Richard D. Frisbie
Gen. Ptnr.
Mr. Robert G. Barrett
Gen. Ptnr.
Mr. Oliver D. Curme
Assoc.
Mr. Sheryl E. Cuker
Research Assoc.
60 Batterymarch St., #1400
Boston, MA 02110
(617) 542-0100
D *** 1

Beacon Partners
Mr. Leonard Vignola, Jr.
Mng. Ptnr.
71 Strawberry Hill Ave., #614
Stamford, CT 06902
(203) 348-8858
D *** 1,4,5,6,7,9,11

Berry Cash Southwest Ptnrshp.
Mr. Harvey B Cash, Gen. Ptnr.
Mr. Glenn A. Norem, Gen. Ptnr.
Ms. Nancy J. Schuele, Assoc.
1 Galleria Tower, Ste. 1375
13355 Noel Rd.
Dallas, TX 75240
(214) 392-7279
D *** 1,8

William Blair Venture Partners
Mr. Samuel B. Guren, Gen. Ptnr.
135 S. LaSalle St., 29th Floor
Chicago, IL 60603
(312) 236-1600
E *** 12

Brownstein, Zeidman & Schomer
Mr. Thomas C. Evans, Ptnr.
1401 New York Ave., N.W., #900
Washington, DC 20036
(202) 879-5760

Burton & Co., Inc.
Mr. Reginald C. Burton, Pres.
P.O. Box 7319
Philadelphia, PA 19101-7319
(312) 263-6663

Camperdown Ventures
Mr. S. Cary Beckwith, III
Gen Ptnr.
115 E. Camperdown Way
Greenville, SC 29601
(803) 233-7770

Capital Services & Resources, Inc
Mr. Charles Y. Bancroft, Treas.
5159 Wheelis Dr., Ste. 104
Memphis, TN 38117
(901) 761-2156
E * 1,4,5,6,8,9

Cardinal Development Cap. Fund I
Mr. Richard F. Bannon, Ptnr.
155 E. Broad St.
Columbus, OH 43215
(614) 464-5550
E *** 1,5,6,8,9,10,11,12

Centennial Fund, The
Mr. G. Jackson Tankersley
Gen. Ptnr.
Mr. Steven C. Halstedt
Gen. Ptnr.
Mr. Charles T. Closson
Gen. Ptnr.
Mr. Mark Dubovoy
VP/Gen. Ptnr.
1999 Broadway, Suite 2100
P.O. Box 13977
Denver, CO 80202
(303) 298-9066
D *** 1,6,8

Cherry Tree Ventures
Mr. Gordon Stofer, Gen. Ptnr.
Mr. Tony Christianson, Gen. Ptnr.
Mr. Thomas Jackson, Inv. Ofcr.
Mr. John Bergstrom, Inv. Analyst
640 Northland Executive Ctr.
3600 W. 80th St.
Minneapolis, MN 55431
(612) 893-9012
D *** 1,5,6,10

Mr. Roger B. Collins
R & C Investments
PO Box 52586
Tulsa, OK 74152
(918) 744-5604
B * 1,3,4,5,9,10,11,12

Columbine Venture Mgmt., Inc.
Mr. Mark Kimmel, Pres.
5613 DTC Pkwy., #510
Englewood, CO 80111
(303) 694-3222

CooleyGodwardCastroHuddles&Tatum
Mr. James C. Gaither, Gen. Ptnr.
One Maritime Plaza, 20th Floor
San Francisco, CA 94111
(415) 981-5252

Coopers & Lybrand
Mr. Robert H. Stavers
One Almaden Blvd., #500
San Jose, CA 95113
(408) 295-1020
1,2,3,5,6,8,9

Corp. For Innovation Development
Mr. Marion C. Dietrich, Pres/CEO
Mr. Donald K. Taylor, VP
Mr. M. Archie Leslie, VP
One N. Capitol Ave., Ste. 520
Indianapolis, IN 46204
(317) 635-7325
C *** 1,5,6,8,9

Criterion Venture Partners
Mr. David Wicks, Jr., Sr. Ptnr.
Mr. M. Scott Albert, Ptnr.
Mr. C. W. Brown, Assoc.
333 Clay St., Ste. 4300
Houston, TX 77002
(713) 751-2400
D *** 1,6,8,9,10,11,12

Dana Venture Capital Corp.
Mr. Gene C. Swartz, Pres.
P.O. Box 1000
Toledo, OH 43697
(419) 535-4780
E * 12

Deloitte Haskins & Sells
Mr. Sanford Antignas
Sr. Consultant
1114 Ave. of Americas
New York, NY 10036
(212) 790-0539

DeSoto Capital Corp.
Mr. William Rudner, Chmn.
Mr. Rudolph H. Holmes, III, Pres.
Mr. James A. Baker, Exec. VP
60 N. Third St.
Memphis, TN 38103
(901) 523-6894
A *** 5,12

Development Corp. of Montana
Mr. Richard L. Bourke, Pres.
350 N. Last Chance Gulch
PO Box 916
Helena, MT 59624
(406) 442-3850
B *** 12

Development Finance Corp.
of New Zealand
Mr. Chris C. Ellison, Mgr.
Mr. Andrew Stedman
Technology & Invest. Consultant
100 Spear St., Ste. 1430
San Francisco, CA 94105
(415) 777-2847

DnC Capital Corp.
Mr. Jack A. Prizzi, VP
600 Fifth Ave.
New York, NY 10020
(212) 765-4800
C *** 1,5,6,8,12

Early Stages Co. (The)
Mr. Frank W. Kuehn, Ptnr.
Mr. William Lanphear, IV, Ptnr
Mr. Micheline L. Chau, Assoc.
244 California St., Ste. 300
San Francisco, CA 94111
(415) 986-5700
C *** 6,7,9,10

El Dorado Ventures
Mr. Brent Rider, Ptnr.
Mr. Gary Kalbach, Ptnr.
Mr. Greg S. Anderson, Gen. Mgr.
2 N. Lake Ave., Ste. 480
Pasadena, CA 91101
(818) 793-1936
D * 12

Elf Technologies, Inc.
Mr. John H. Mahar, Exec. VP
Ms. Christine Civiale, Asst. VP
High Ridge Park, P.O. Box 10037
Stamford, CT 06904
(203) 358-5120
E *** 3,5,8

Ernst & Whinney
Mr. Larry Gray, Ptnr.
5941 Variel
Woodland Hills, CA 91367
(818) 888-0707

Fine & Ambrogne
Mr. Arnold M. Zaff, Ptnr.
Exchange Place
Boston, MA 02109
(617) 367-0100

First Chicago Investment Advisors
Mr. Patrick A. McGivney, VP
Mr. T. Bondurant French, VP
Mr. Michael I Gallie, VP
Mr. David S. Timson, VP
Three First National Plaza
Ste. 0140, 9th Fl.
Chicago, IL 60670
(312) 732-4919
D *** 1,5,6,8,9

Fostin Capital Corp.
Mr. William F. Woods, Pres.
Mr. Thomas M. Levine, Exec. VP
P.O. Box 67
Pittsburgh, PA 15230
(412) 928-8900
C *** 1,6,8

Gatti Tomerlin & Martin Corp.
Mr. John Gatti, Chmn.
Mr. Monte Tomerlin, Pres.
Mr. Harlon Martin, Jr., Exec. VP
405 N. St. Mary's, Suite 222
San Antonio, TX 78205
(512) 229-9028
E *** 1,3,5,6,9,10,12

General Electric Ven. Cap. Corp.
Mr. Harry T. Rein
Pres.
Mr. Stephen L. Waechter
VP/Treas.
3135 Easton Tnpk.
Fairfield, CT 06431
(203) 373-3356
D *** 1,5,6,8,10,12

Golder, Thoma & Cressey
Mr. Stanley C. Golder, Gen. Ptnr.
Mr. Carl D. Thoma, Gen. Ptnr.
Mr. Bryan C. Cressey, Gen. Ptnr.
Mr. Bruce V. Rauner, Gen. Ptnr.
120 S. LaSalle St., Ste. 630
Chicago, IL 60603
(312) 853-3322
E *** 1,4,5,6,8,10,11

Grayrock Capital, Ltd.
Mr. W. J. Gluck, Pres.
2 International Blvd.
Rexdale, Ont. M9W 1A2, Canada
(416) 675-4808
D *** 1,6,7,9,10

Great American Investment Corp.
Mr. James A. Arias, Pres.
Mr. Tim Scanlon, VP
4209 San Mateo NE
Albuquerque, NM 87110
(505) 883-6273
C *** 12

HLPM, Inc.
Mr. Robert W. Fletcher, Pres.
Mr. Albert L. Earley, VP
545 S. Third St.
Louisville, KY 40202
(502) 588-8459

Heizer Corp.
Mr. E.F. Heizer, Jr., Chmn./Pres.
261 S. Bluffs Edge Dr.
Lake Forest, IL 60045
(312) 641-2200

Heller Financial Inc.
Mr. Robert Spitalnic, Sr. VP
101 Park Ave.
New York, NY 10178
(212) 880-7062
E *** 5,9,10,12

Helms, Mulliss & Johnston
B. Bernard Burns, Jr., Esq.
227 N. Tryon St., PO Box 31247
Charlotte, NC 28231
(704) 372-9510

Houston Venture Partners
Mr. Howard Hill, Jr., Gen. Ptnr.
Mr. Thomas Fatjo, Jr., Gen. Ptnr.
Mr. Roger Ramsey, Gen. Ptnr.
Mr. Kent Smith, Gen. Ptnr.
401 S. Louisiana
Houston, TX 77002
(713) 222-8600
E * 12

Hunton & Williams
C. Porter Vaughan, III, Esq.
P.O. Box 1535
Richmond, VA 23212
(804) 788-8200

Hutton Venture Investment Ptnrs.
Mr. James E. McGrath, Pres.
1 Battery Park Plaza, #1801
New York, NY 10004
(212) 742-6486
D *** 1,5,6,8

IEG Venture Mgmt., Inc.
Mr. Francis I. Blair
Pres.
Mrs. Marian M. Zamlynski
Op. Mgr./VP
401 N. Michigan Ave., #2020
Chicago, IL 60611
(312) 644-0890
C *** 1,3,6,8

Indiana Capital Corp.
Mr. Samuel Rea, Pres.
5612 Jefferson Blvd., W.
Ft. Wayne, IN 46804
(219) 432-8622

Inst. of Private Enterprise
Dr. Rollie Tillman, Dir.
312 Carroll Hall, #012-A
Chapel Hill, NC 27514
(919) 962-8201

Interstate Capital Corp.
Mr. William C. McConnell Jr.
Pres.
701 E. Camino Real, #9A
Boca Raton, FL 33432
(305) 395-8466
B *** 3,5,6,8

Investors in Industry
(See 3i under T)

Japan Associate Finance Co., Ltd.
Mr. Teiji Imahara, Chmn.
Toshiba Bldg., 10th Fl.
1-1-1 Shibaura Minato-KU
Tokyo, Japan
(03) 456-5101
E *** 1,5,9,10

Jenkens, Huchison & Gilchrist
Mr. John R. Holzgraefe, Ptnr.
Mr. Mark Wigder, Ptnr.
Mr. W. Alan Kailer, Ptnr.
1455 Ross Ave., 29th Flr.
Dallas, TX 75202
(214) 855-4500

Kirkland & Ellis
Mr. Edward T. Swan
200 E. Randolph Dr.
Chicago, IL 60601
(312) 861-2465

Kleinwort, Benson (NA) Corp.
Mr. Alan L. J. Bowen, Sr., VP
Mr. Christopher Wright, VP
Ms. Michele Hurtubise
Office Mgr.
333 S. Grand, #2900
Los Angeles, CA 90071
(213) 680-2297
E * 3,5,6,9,11,12

Knight & Irish Associates, Inc.
Dr. Joan S. Irish, Pres.
Ms. Faith I. Bliga, VP
420 Lexington Ave., Ste. 2358
New York, NY 10170
(212) 490-0135

Lord, Bissell & Brook
Mr. John K. O'Connor, Ptnr.
115 S. LaSalle St., #3500
Chicago, IL 60603
(312) 443-0615

Lubrizol Enterprises, Inc.
Mr. Donald L. Murfin, Pres.
Mr. Bruce H. Grasser, VP
Mr. James R. Glynn, VP-Fin./Tres.
Mr. David R. Anderson, VP
29400 Lakeland Blvd.
Wickliffe, OH 44092
(216) 943-4200
E *** 8

MRI Ventures
Mr. Charles Moll, VP
Ms. Carol Radosevich, Ven. Mgr.
1650 University Blvd., NE, #500
Albuquerque, NM 87102
(505) 768-6200
D *** 1,5,6,8,12

Madison Venture Capital Corp.
Mr. Norman C. Schultz, Pres.
26515 Carmel Rancho Blvd., #201
Carmel, CA 93923
(408) 625-9650

Manuf. Hanover Vent. Cap. Corp.
Mr. Thomas J. Sandleitner, Pres.
Mr. Edward L. Koch, III, VP
140 E. 45th St., 30th Fl.
New York, NY 10017
(212) 350-6701
E *** 1,4,5,6,7,9,10,11,12

Mayer, Brown, & Platt
Herbert B. Max, Esq.
520 Madison Ave.
New York, NY 10022
(212) 437-7132

Med-Wick Associates, Inc.
Mr. A.A.T. Wickersham, Chmn/Pres.
1902 Fleet National Bank Bldg.
Providence, RI 02903
(401) 751-5270

Menlo Ventures
Mr. Ken E. Joy, Gen. Ptnr.
3000 Sand Hill Rd.
Menlo Park, CA 94025
(415) 854-8540
E *** 12

Michigan Inv. Div., Treas. Dept.
Mr. Michael J. Finn, Admin.
P.O. Box 15128
Lansing, MI 48901
(517) 373-4330
D * 12

Miller Venture Partners
Mr. William I. Miller
Gen. Ptnr.
Mr. Ira G. Peppercorn
Sr. Inv. Mgr.
P.O. Box 808
Columbus, IN 47202
(812) 376-3331
B *** 3,5,6,8,11

Moore BersonLifflander&Mewhinney
Mr. Joel L. Berson
595 Madison Ave.
New York, NY 10022

Morgan Holland Ventures Corp.
Mr. James F. Morgan, Mng. Ptnr.
Mr. Daniel J. Holland, Mng. Ptnr.
Mr. John A. Delahanty, Gen. Ptnr.
Mr. Robert Rosbe, Jr., Gen. Ptnr.
Mr. Edwin M. Kania, Jr., Assoc.
1 Liberty Sq.
Boston, MA 02109
(617) 423-1765
E *** 1,5,6,8

Morgenthaler Ventures
Mr. David T. Morgenthaler
Mng. Ptnr.
Mr. Robert D. Pavey
Gen. Ptnr.
Mr. Paul S. Brentlinger
Gen. Ptnr.
Mr. Robert C. Bellas, Jr.
Gen. Ptnr.
700 National City Bank Bldg.
Cleveland, OH 44114
(216) 621-3070
E *** 1,5,6,8,10

Morrison & Foerster
Tino Kamarck, Esq.
Marco Adelfrio, Esq.
2000 Pennsylvania Ave., NW
Washington, DC 20006
(202) 887-1500

NEPA Venture Fund, L.P.
Mr. Frederick J. Beste, III
Pres.
Ben Franklin Adv. Tech. Ctr.
Lehigh Univ.
Bethlehem, PA 18015
(215) 865-6550
E *** 12

New Enterprise Associates
Mr. Charles Newhall III,
Gen. Ptnr.
300 Cathedral St., Ste. 110
Baltimore, MD 21201
(301) 244-0115
E * 1,6

Nippon Investment & Finance Co.
Ltd.
Mr. Yasutoshi Sasada, Pres.
Mr. Motoki Sugiyama, Gen. Mgr.
39F, Nishi-Shinjuku 1-25-1,
Shinjuku-ku
Tokyo 163 JAPAN
(03) 349-0961
E *** 12

NBM Participatie Beheer B.V.
Mr. Michiel A. de Haan, Gen. Mgr.
Postbus 1800
1000 BV AMSTERDAM
The Netherlands, NL
(020) 543-3346
E * 1,5,6,8,10,11

Noro-Moseley Partners
Mr. Charles Moseley, Gen. Ptnr.
100 Galleria Pkwy., #1240
Atlanta, GA 30339
(404) 955-0020

North American Capital Corp.
Mr. Stanley P. Roth, Chmn.
510 Broad Hollow Rd., #205
Melville, NY 11747
(516) 752-9696
E * 12

North American Cap. Group, Ltd.
Mr. Gregory I. Kravitt, Pres.
Ms. Mindy Warshawsky, Assoc.
7250 N. Cicero
Lincolnwood, IL 60646
(312) 982-1010
D *** 2,4,5,6,9,10

Olwine, Connelly, Chase, et al
Mr. Roger Mulvihill
299 Park Ave.
New York, NY 10017
(212) 207-1831

Onondaga Vent. Capital Fund, Inc.
Mr. Irving W. Schwartz, Exec. VP
327 State Tower Bldg.
Syracuse, NY 13202
(315) 478-0157
B *** 12

Oxford Partners
Mr. Kenneth Rind, Gen. Ptnr.
1266 Main St.
Stamford, CT 06902
(203) 964-0592
E *** 1,6,8

Ozanam Capital Co.-I, LP
Ms. Janis L. Mullin, Gen. Ptnr.
Mr. Adam Robins, Gen. Ptnr.
Mr. Robert Berliner, Gen. Ptnr.
4711 Golf Rd., #706
Skokie, IL 60076
(312) 674-2297
B *** 5,9

Pathfinder Venture Cap. Fund
Mr. A.J. Greenshields, Gen. Ptnr.
7300 Metro Blvd., Ste. 585
Minneapolis, MN 55435
(612) 835-1121
D *** 1,5,6,8

Peat, Marwick, Mitchell & Co.
Mr. Terence D. Dibble, Ptnr.
725 South Figueroa St.
Los Angeles, CA 90017
(213) 972-4000

Peat, Marwick, Mitchell & Co.
Mr. Ronald R. Booth, Ptnr.
1700 IDS Center
Minneapolis, MN 55402
(612) 341-2222

Peat, Marwick, Mitchell & Co.
Mr. Michael E. Lavin, Ptnr.
303 E. Wacker Dr.
Chicago, IL 60601
(312) 938-5043

Peat, Marwick, Mitchell & Co.
Mr. Edgar R. Wood, Jr., Ptnr.
1800 First Union Pl.
Charlotte, NC 28282
(704) 335-5300

Pepper, Hamilton & Scheetz
Mr. Michael B. Staebler, Ptnr.
Mr. Hugh D. Camitta, Esq.
100 Renaissance Ctr., Ste. 3600
Detroit, MI 48243
(313) 259-7110

Peregrine Associates
Mr. Gene I. Miller, Ptnr.
Mr. Frank LaHaye, Ptnr.
606 Wilshire Blvd., Ste. 602
Santa Monica, CA 90401
(213) 458-1441
E *** 1,5,6,8,9,10,12

Pioneer Capital Corp.
Mr. Christopher W. Lynch, Ptnr.
Mr. Frank M. Polestra, Ptnr.
60 State St.
Boston, MA 02109
(617) 742-7825
D * 12

Piper, Jaffray & Hopwood, Inc.
Mr. Frank Bennett,
Mr. R. Hunt Greene, 1st VP
Piper Jaffray Tower
222 So. 9th St.
P.O Box 28
Minneapolis, MN 55402
(612) 342-6000
D *** 1,5,6,8,9,10

<u>Branch Office</u>
Piper, Jaffray & Hopwood
Mr. Gary L. Takacs, VP
1600 IBM Building
Seattle, WA 98101
D *** 1,5,6,8,9,10

Primus Capital Fund
Mr. Loyal Wilson, Mng. Ptnr.
Mr. David A. DeVore, Ptnr.
Mr. William C. Mulligan, Ptnr.
One Cleveland Ctr., #2140
Cleveland, OH 44114
(216) 621-2185
E *** 1,5,6,8,9,12

RBK Management Co.
Mr. Robert B. Kaplan, Pres.
140 S. Dearborn St., #420
Chicago, IL 60603
(312) 263-6058

Reprise Capital Corp.
Mr. Stanley Tulchin, Chmn.
Mr. Irwin B. Nelson, Pres.
591 Stewart Ave.
Garden City, NY 11530
(516) 222-1028
E *** 12

Riordan & McKinzie
Michael P. Ridley, Esq.
300 South Grand Ave., Ste. 2900
Los Angeles, CA 90017
(213) 629-4824

Rothschild Ventures, Inc.
Mr. Jess L. Belser, Pres.
One Rockefeller Pl.
New York, NY 10020
(212) 757-6000
E *** 1,5,6,8,12

Rust Capital Ltd.
Mr. Jeffery C. Garvey, Pres.
Mr. Kenneth P. DeAngelis, Exec VP
Mr. Joseph C. Aragona, VP
Mr. William P. Wood, VP
114 W. 7th St., 1300 Norwood Twr.
Austin, TX 78701
(512) 479-0055
D **** 1,4,5,6,12

Salomon Brothers, Inc.
Mr. Melvin W. Ellis, VP
One New York Plaza
New York, NY 10004
(212) 747-6293
E * 1,6,8

Santa Fe Private Equity Fund
Mr. A. David Silver, Gen. Ptnr.
Ms. Kay Tsunemori, Assoc.
Mr. Kyle A. Legkoff, Assoc.
Ms. Angela H. Peck, Assoc.
524 Camino Del Monte Sol
Santa Fe, NM 87501
(505) 983-1769
D *** 6

SB Capital Corp., Ltd.
Mr. Mitch Kostuch, Exec. VP
Mr. Peter Standeven, VP
Mr. David McCart, Inv. Ofcr.
85 Bloor St. E., #506
Toronto, Ontario M4W 1A9
(416) 967-5439
D *** 1,5,6,8,12

Scientific Advances, Inc.
Mr. Charles G. James, Pres.
Mr. Paul F. Purcell, VP
Mr. Thomas W. Harvey, VP
Mr. Daniel J. Shea, VP
601 W. Fifth Ave.
Columbus, OH 43201
(614) 294-5541
D *** 8

Security Pacific Bus. Credit, Inc.
Mr. Nicholas Battaglino, VP
Mr. David J. Freidman, VP
228 E. 45th St.
New York, NY 10017
(212) 309-9302
E ** 5,9,12

South Atlantic Venture Fund
Mr. Donald Burton, Gen. Ptnr.
Mr. Richard Brandewie, Gen. Ptnr.
Ms. Sandra Barber, Admin. Ptnr.
220 East Madison, Suite 530
Tampa, FL 33602-4825
(813) 229-7400
D *** 1,5,6,8,10,12

Spensley, Horn, Jubas & Lubitz
Mr. Bruce W. McRoy, Esq., Ptnr.
1880 Century Park E., #500
Los Angeles, CA 90067
(213) 553-5050

Stephenson Merchant Banking
Mr. A. Emmet Stephenson, Jr.
Sr. Ptnr.
Mr. Thomas Kent Mitchell
Dirctor
100 Garfield St.
Denver, CO 80206
(303) 355-6000
E *** 1,5,6,9,10,11,12

S.W.S. Ltd.
Mr. Steven B. Schaffel, Pres.
Mr. Ira B. Raymond, Exec. VP
Mr. Wendell H. Jones, VP
122 E. 42nd St.
New York, NY 10168
(212) 682-9550
E ** 4,11,12

3i Capital Corp.
Mr. David R. Shaw, Pres.
Ms. Dorothy Langer
99 High St., Ste. 1530
Boston, MA 02110
(617) 542-8560

Taylor International
Mr. Don Snow
1801 Quincy St., N.W.
Washington, D.C. 20011
(202) 955-1330

Taylor & Turner
Mr. Marshall Turner, Gen. Ptnr.
Mr. William Taylor, Gen. Ptnr.
220 Montgomery St., Penthouse 10
San Francisco, CA 94104
(415) 398-6821
D * 1,5,6,8

Tektronix Development Co.
Mr. M. H. Chaffin, Jr.
VP/Gen. Mgr.
P.O. Box 4600-M/S 94-383
Beaverton, OR 97075
(503) 629-1121

Texas Infinity Corp.
Mr. C. Charles Bahr, CEO
P.O. Box 2678
Richardson, TX 75083
(214) 231-7070

Tulsa Industrial Authority
Mr. Rick L. Weddle, Gen. Mgr.
616 S. Boston
Tulsa, OK 74119
(918) 585-1201
E *** 5,6

UNC Ventures
Mr. Edward Dugger, III, Pres.
Mr. James W. Norton, Jr., VP
195 State St., #700
Boston, MA 02109
(617) 723-8300
D *** 1,5,6,8,11

Venad Management, Inc.
Ms. Joy London, Ptnr.
375 Park Ave., #3303
New York, NY 10152
(212) 759-2800

Venco SBIC
Bill McAleir, Chmn.
Phil Bardos, Pres.
One Financial Square
Oxnard, CA 93030
(805) 656-4621
B * 5,6,12

The Venture Capital Fund
of New England
Mr. Richard Farrell, Gen. Ptnr.
100 Franklin St.
Boston, MA 02110
(617) 451-2575
C *** 1,5,8

Venture Economics, Inc.
Mr. Stanley Pratt, Chmn.
Ms. Jane K. Morris, VP
16 Laurel Ave., P.O. Box 348
Wellesley Hills, MA 02181
(617) 431-8100

Venture Founders Corp.
Mr. Alexander Dingee, Jr., Pres
Mr. Grogory Hulecki, Inv. Mgr.
Mr. Ross Yeiter, Treas.
One Cranberry Hill
Lexington, MA 02173
(617) 863-0900
D *** 1,5,6,8

Whitehead Associates, Inc.
Mr. Joseph A. Orlando, Pres.
Mr. William E. Engbers, VP
15 Valley Dr.
Greenwich, CT 06830
(203) 629-4633
D *** 1,5,6,8,10,12

William Blair Venture Partners
Mr. Samuel B. Guren
Gen. Ptnr.
Mr. Scott F. Meadow
Gen. Ptnr.
Mr. James Crawford, III
Gen. Ptnr.
Mr. Gregg S. Newmark
Assoc.
135 S. LaSalle St., 29th Fl.
Chicago, IL 60603
(312) 236-1600
E *** 12

Arthur Young
Entrepreneurial Services
Mr. Jerome S. Engel, Ptnr.
Mr. Marc Berger, Ptnr.
1 Sansome St., Suite 3300
San Francisco, CA 94104
(415) 393-2733

Arthur Young & Co.
Mr. Robert J. Brennan, Dir.
1111 Summer St.
Stamford, CT 06905
(203) 356-1800

Arthur Young & Co.
Mr. John J. Huntz, Jr., Ptnr.
235 Peachtree St., NE
2100 Gas Light Tower
Atlanta, GA 30043
(404) 581-1130

Arthur Young & Co.
Mr. Al Boos, Ptnr.
6501 Americas Parkway NE, Ste 400
Albuquerque, NM 87110
(505) 881-6363

Arthur Young & Co.
Mr. Dennis Serlen, Gen. Ptnr.
277 Park Ave.
New York, NY 10172
(212) 407-1611

Arthur Young & Co,
Mr. Paul E. Gricus
1100 Fleet Center
Providence, RI 02903
(401) 274-1800

Arthur Young & Co.
Mr. Edward B. Beanland, Ptnr.
2121 San Jacinto, Ste. 700
Dallas, TX 75201
(214) 969-8666

Small Business Administration (SBA) Field Offices

Alabama
2121 8th Avenue North
Birmingham, Alabama 35203
205/254-1344

Alaska
Federal Building
701 C Street, Box 67
Anchorage, Alaska 99513
907/271-4022

Arizona
2005 North Central Avenue
Phoenix, Arizona 85004
602/241-2200

301 West Congress Street
Federal Bldg., Box 33
Tucson, Arizona 85701
602/792-6715

Arkansas
320 W. Capitol Avenue
Little Rock, Arkansas 72201
501/378-5871

California
2202 Monterey Street
Fresno, California 93721
209/487-5189

660 J Street
Sacramento, California
95814
916/551-1445

880 Front Street
San Diego, California 92188
619/293-5440

*450 Golden Gate Avenue
P.O. Box 36044
San Francisco, California
94102
415/556-7487

211 Main Street
San Francisco, California
94105
415/974-0642

350 South Figueroa Street
Los Angeles, California 90071
213/688-2956

Fidelity Federal Bldg.
2700 North Main Street
Santa Ana, California 92701
714/836-2494

Colorado
*Executive Tower Building
1405 Curtis Street
Denver, Colorado 80202
303/844-5441

721 19th Street
Denver, Colorado 80202
303/844-2607

Connecticut
One Hartford Square W.
Hartford, Connecticut 06106
203/772-3600

Delaware
844 King Street
Wilmington, Delaware 19801
302/573-6294

District of Columbia
1111 18th St., N.W.
Washington, D.C. 20036
202/634-4950

Florida
400 West Bay Street
Jacksonville, Florida 32202
904/791-3782

2222 Ponce De Leon Blvd.
Coral Gables, Florida 33134
305/350-5521

700 Twiggs Street
Tampa, Florida 33602
813/228-2594

3500 45th Street
West Palm Beach, Florida
33407
305/689-2223

Georgia
*1375 Peachtree Street, N.E.
Atlanta, Georgia 30367
404/881-4999

1720 Peachtree Road, N.W.
Atlanta, Georgia 30309
404/881-4749

Source: Small Business Administration.

* Regional Office

52 North Main Street
Statesboro, Georgia 30458
912/489-8719

Guam
Pacific News Bldg.
238 O'Hara Street
Agana, Guam 96910
671/472-7277

Hawaii
300 Ala Moana
P.O. Box 2213
Honolulu, Hawaii 96850
808/546-8950

Idaho
1020 Main Street
Boise, Idaho 83702
208/334-1096

Illinois
*230 South Dearborn Street
Chicago, Illinois 60604
312/353-0359

219 South Dearborn Street
Chicago, Illinois 60604
312/353-4528

Washington Building
Four North Old State
Capitol Plaza
Springfield, Illinois 62701
217/492-4416

Indiana
New Federal Bldg.
575 North Pennsylvania Street
Indianapolis, Indiana 46209
317/269-7272

Iowa
210 Walnut Street
Des Moines, Iowa 50309
515/284-4422

373 Collins Road, N.E.
Cedar Rapids, Iowa 52402
319/399-2571

Kansas
Main Place Bldg.
110 East Waterman Street
Wichita, Kansas 67202
316/269-6271

Kentucky
600 Federal Place
Louisville, Kentucky 40202
502/582-5976

Louisiana
1661 Canal Street
New Orleans, Louisiana
70112
504/589-6685

500 Fannin Street
Federal Bldg. & Courthouse
Shreveport, Louisiana 71101
318/226-5196

Maine
40 Western Avenue
Augusta, Maine 04330
207/622-8378

Maryland
10 N. Calvert Street
Baltimore, Maryland 21204
301/962-4392

Massachusetts
*60 Batterymarch Street
Boston, Massachusetts
02110
617/223-3204

150 Causeway Street
Boston, Massachusetts 02114
617/223-3224

1550 Main Street
Springfield, Massachusetts
01103
413/785-0268

Michigan
477 Michigan Avenue
McNamara Bldg.
Detroit, Michigan 48226
313/226-6075

220 West Washington Street
Marquette, Michigan 49885
906/225-1108

Minnesota
100 North 6th Street
Minneapolis, Minnesota
55403
612/349-3550

Mississippi
One Hancock Plaza
Gulfport, Mississippi 39501
601/863-4449

100 West Capitol Street
New Federal Bldg.
Jackson, Mississippi 39269
601/960-4378

* Regional Office

Missouri
*911 Walnut Street
Kansas City, Missouri 64106
816/374-5288

818 Grande Avenue
Kansas City, Missouri 64106
816/374-3419

815 Olive Street
St. Louis, Missouri 63101
314/425-6600

Federal Court House Bldg.
339 Broadway
Cape Girardeau, Missouri
63701
314/335-6039

309 North Jefferson
Springfield, Missouri 65803
417/864-7670

Montana
2601 First Avenue North
Billings, Montana 59101
406/657-6047

301 South Park Avenue
Helena, Montana 59626
406/449-5381

Nebraska
South 19th Street
Omaha, Nebraska 68102
402/221-4691

Nevada
301 East Stewart Street
Las Vegas, Nevada 89125
702/385-6611

50 South Virginia Street
Reno, Nevada 89505
702/784-5268

New Hampshire
55 Pleasant Street
Concord, New Hampshire
03301
603/224-4041

New Jersey
1800 East Davis Street
Camden, New Jersey 08104
609/757-5183

60 Park Place
Newark, New Jersey 07102
201/645-2434

New Mexico
Patio Plaza Building
5000 Marble Ave., N.E.
Albuquerque, N.M. 87110
505/766-3430

New York
*26 Federal Plaza
New York, New York 10278
212/264-7772

445 Broadway
Albany, New York 12207
518/472-6300

111 West Huron Street
Buffalo, New York 14202
716/846-4301

333 East Water Street
Elmira, New York 14901
607/733-4686

35 Pinelaw Road
Melville, New York 11747
516/454-0750

26 Federal Plaza
New York, New York 10278
212/264-4355

100 State Street
Rochester, New York 14614
716/263-6700

100 South Clinton St.
Federal Bldg.
Syracuse, New York 13260
315/423-5383

North Carolina
230 South Tryon Street
Charlotte, North Carolina
28202
704/371-6563

North Dakota
657 2nd Avenue
Fargo, North Dakota 58102
701/237-5771

Ohio
1240 East 9th St.
AJC Federal Bldg.
Cleveland, Ohio 44199
216/522-4180

85 Marconi Boulevard
Columbus, Ohio 43215
614/469-6860

---

* Regional Office

550 Main Street
Cincinnati, Ohio 45202
513/684-2814

Oklahoma
200 N.W. 5th Street
Oklahoma City, Oklahoma 73102
405/231-4301

Oregon
1220 S.W. Third Avenue
Federal Building
Portland, Oregon 97204
503/423-5221

Pennsylvania
*One Bala Cynwyd Plaza
231 St. Asaphs Road
Bala Cynwyd, Pennsylvania 19004
215/596-5889

100 Chestnut Street
Harrisburg, Pennsylvania 17101
717/782-3840

960 Penn Avenue
Convention Tower
Pittsburgh, Pennsylvania 15222
412/644-2780

Penn Place
20 North Pennsylvania Avenue
Wilkes-Barre, Pennsylvania 18701
717/826-6497

Puerto Rico
Federal Building
Carlos Chardon Avenue
Hato Rey, Puerto Rico 00919
809/753-4002

Rhode Island
380 Westminster Mall
Providence, Rhode Island 02903
401/528-4586

South Carolina
1835 Assembly Street
Columbia, South Carolina 29201
803/765-5376

South Dakota
101 South Main Avenue
Sioux Falls, South Dakota 57102
605/336-2980

Tennessee
404 James Robertson Parkway
Nashville, Tennessee 37219
615/251-5881

Texas
Federal Building
300 East 8th Street
Austin, Texas 78701
512/482-5288

400 Mann Street
Corpus Christi, Texas 78408
512/888-3331

*8625 King George Drive
Bldg. C
Dallas, Texas 75235
214/767-7643

1100 Commerce Street
Dallas, Texas 75242
214/767-0605

10737 Gateway West
El Paso, Texas 79902
915/543-7586

221 West Lancaster Avenue
Ft. Worth Texas 76102
817/334-5463

222 East Van Buren Street
Harlingen, Texas 78550
512/423-8934

2525 Murthworth
Houston, Texas 77054
713/660-4401

1611 10th Street
Lubbock, Texas 79401
806/743-7466

100 South Washington Street
Marshall, Texas 75670
214/935-5257

727 East Durango Street
Federal Bldg.
San Antonio, Texas 78206
512/229-6250

Utah
125 South State Street
Salt Lake City, Utah 84138
801/524-5800

---

* Regional Office

Vermont
87 State Street
Montpelier, Vermont 05602
802/229-0538

Virginia
400 North 8th Street
Richmond, Virginia 23240
804/771-2617

Virgin Islands
Veterans Drive
St. Thomas, Virgin Islands
00801
809/774-8530

P.O. Box 4010
Christiansted, Virgin Islands
00820
809/773-3480

Washington
2615 4th Avenue
Seattle, Washington 98121
206/442-5676

915 Second Avenue
Seattle, Washington 98174
206/442-5534

W. 920 Riverside Avenue
Spokane, Washington 99210
509/456-3783

West Virginia
168 W. Main
Clarksburg, West Virginia
26301
304/623-5631

550 Eagan Street
Charleston, West Virginia
25301
304/347-5220

Wisconsin
500 South Barstow Street
Eau Claire, Wisconsin 54701
715/834-9012

212 East Washington Avenue
Madison, Wisconsin 53703
608/264-5261

310 West Wisconsin Avenue
Milwaukee, Wisconsin 53203
414/291-3941

Wyoming
100 East B Street
Casper, Wyoming 82602
307/261-5761

Returns on Various Types of Investments*

R. S. Salomon, Jr.
Robert D. Arnott
Caroline H. Davenport
Maria A. Fiore

A year ago, we noted a striking pattern of historical asset class returns. During the 1970s, tangible assets dominated asset class comparisons; whereas financial assets have dominated the 1980s. In 1987, however, the consistency in the pattern between financial and tangible assets broke down. Most notably, the results observed for collectibles and tangible assets fell in a very wide range, as did the results for financial assets. Unlike the pattern noted in previous years, no general category of assets clearly dominated other categories. Furthermore, from a foreign investor's perspective, there has been a marked divergence in results relative to returns in U.S. dollar terms. In short, the pattern which developed during the 1980s was not evident during the past year.

As demonstrated in Figure 2, there was remarkable consistency in the pattern of returns during the 1970s: Collectibles and tangible assets soared in response to accelerating inflation, while financial assets lagged. The results for tangible assets ranged broadly, from a high of 34.7% for oil to a low of 10.2% for housing. During this period all collectibles, commodities and tangible assets measurably outpaced the rate of inflation.

By contrast, the acceleration of inflation during the 1970s depressed financial assets, so that none managed to eke out a real return. Stocks, bonds and Treasury bills all lagged the growth in the Consumer Price Index (CPI). The problem for taxable investors was compounded, with after-tax returns falling far short of inflation.

With the deceleration of inflation during the 1980s, financial assets rebounded sharply while tangible and collectible assets faltered (see Figure 1). Indeed, the results for the 1980s demonstrate a marked reversal of the trend in the 1970s. The real rewards provided by financial assets were considerable and fairly consistent. The results for collectible and tangible assets ranged from disappointing to dismal. However, financial assets were even able to achieve positive after-tax real returns for most classes of investors.

Over the past year, returns have generally been good for most classes of assets, but there is no consistent pattern. Collectibles and tangibles range from top-ranked performers such as silver, gold and oil to the worst performers, which include stamps and U.S. farmland. Returns vary from an impressive 39.8% to a grim −7.9%. Financial returns also fall in a wide band, between 20% for stocks and 5% for bonds.

All asset classes except for stamps and farmland provided investors with real returns. The disinflation theory persisted in the past year, permitting continued robust real returns in most asset classes for the U.S. investor. Figure 3 does not include non-U.S. stock and bond investments; but, those assets also reinforce this pattern of strong returns. In essence, it was a good year for the U.S. investor to be fully invested, in virtually any asset class.

The divergence in the returns of stocks compared with bonds appears rooted in earnings power. Financial assets no longer perform as a uniform group and have begun to exhibit fundamental differences in character; consequently, they are beginning to behave more as independent asset classes. Strong corporate profits have been an important foundation for the continued equity bull market.

The pronounced contrast in asset returns over the past year is marked by strong performance from the perspective of the U.S. investor, as opposed to that of the foreign investor.

* Although the information in this report has been obtained from sources which Salomon Brothers Inc. believes to be reliable, we do not guarantee its accuracy and such information may be incomplete or condensed. All opinions and estimates included in this report constitute our judgment as of this date and are subject to change without notice. This report is for information purposes only and is not intended as an offer or solicitation with respect to the purchase or sale of any security.

Editor's Note: Stock returns are for the S&P 500 and include appreciation plus dividends. Bond returns are for Salomon Brothers Index and include appreciation plus interest.

Source: *A Study In Contrasts,* by R. S. Salomon, Jr., Robert D. Arnott, Caroline H. Davenport, and Maria A. Fiore © Salomon Brothers Inc., June 8, 1987.

Figure 1. The 1980s — A Decade for Financial Assets
(Compound Annual Rate of Return, 1980-86)

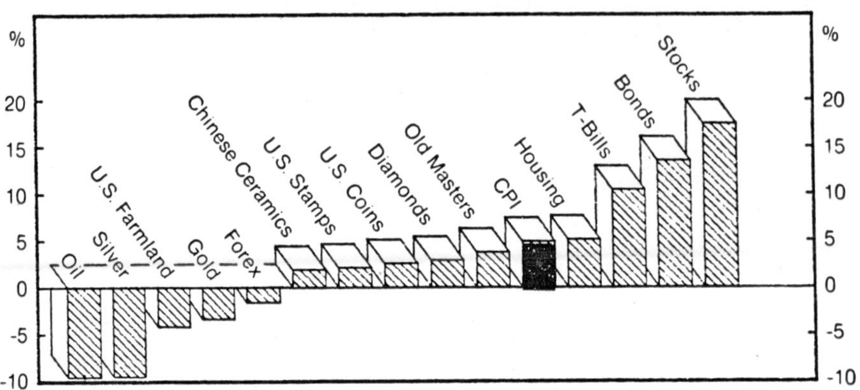

Figure 3 summarizes results denominated in both U.S. dollars and includes returns adjusted for foreign exchange. This measures returns vis-a-vis a basket of currencies, including the German Deutschemark, Japanese yen, Swiss franc, and Dutch guilder. As such, it does not represent an exact measure of returns in yen, pounds or marks; rather, it measures returns from the advantage point of the "average" foreign investor. Results for individual foreign investors will differ somewhat from this perspective, but will generally follow the pattern shown in Figure 3.

Viewed in this manner, only three asset classes exhibited modest positive returns, let alone positive real returns! These were gold, silver and oil, which were all rebounding from a dismal five-year performance. In the five-year period ending June 1, 1986, these three assets were the worst performing asset classes on the entire list. The following are possible future implications:

- Viewed from the perspective of a foreign investor, the U.S. bull market has been a disappointment. As a result, the foreign investor is unlikely to perceive the U.S. bull market as overextended. A foreigner with a strong currency is attracted by the relative value of the U.S. markets.
- Given the global bull market, successes in financial assets might generate renewed interest in tangible assets or collectibles, even in the absence of renewed inflation. As investors' returns lead to increased wealth, diversification and a quest for value may

Figure 2. The 1970s — A Decade for Collectibles and Commodities
(Compound Annual Rate of Return, 1970-80)

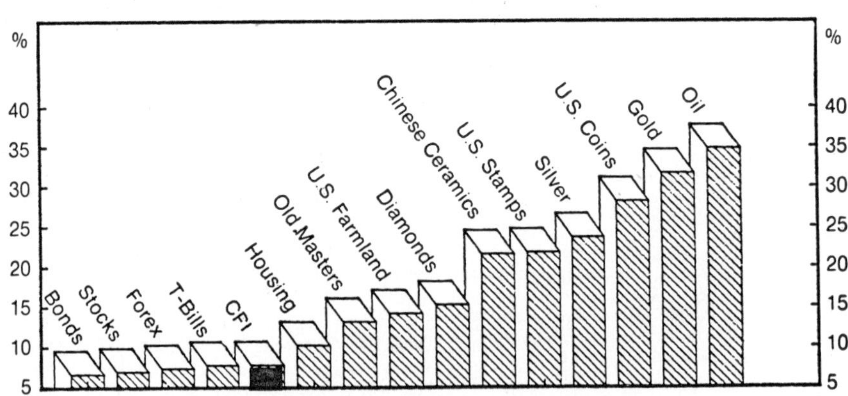

Figure 3. One-Year Ranking, 1987 vs. 1986 for the Period Ended June 1, 1987

	Rank	Return	Returns Denominated in Foreign Exchange
Silver	1	39.8	11.2
Gold	2	29.1	3.3
Oil	3	27.4	1.9
Foreign Exchange	4	25.0	—
Stocks	5	20.6	(3.5)
U.S. Coins	6	10.7	(11.4)
Old Masters	7	8.6	(13.1)
Diamonds	8	7.0	(14.4)
Housing	9	6.8	(14.6)
Chinese Ceramics	10	6.7	(14.6)
Treasury Bills	11	5.7	(15.4)
Bonds	12	5.7	(15.4)
CPI	**13**	**3.8**	**(17.0)**
U.S. Stamps	14	0.5	(19.6)
U.S. Farmland	15	(7.9)	(26.3)

Note: All returns are for the period ended June 1, 1987, based on latest available data.
CPI Consumer Price Index.

lead to investment in collectibles and commodities. We may be seeing the first signs of such a trend in recent art auction behavior, exemplified by the now-famous $40-million Van Gogh painting.

The startling contrasts of the past year represent a departure from the more consistent pattern of prior years. This breakdown, however, has not been sufficient to alter our expectation of continuing domination by financial assets in the 1980s, compared with tangibles in the 1970s. However, these more recent variant return patterns are likely to persist for some time.

Figure 4. Compound Annual Rates of Return

	15 Years	Rank	10 Years	Rank	5 Years	Rank	1 Year	Rank
U.S. Coins	18.8	1	16.3	1	11.4	3	10.7	6
Oil	13.9	2	3.0	13	(11.8)	14	27.4	3
U.S. Stamps	13.6	3	11.8	3	(1.3)	12	0.5	14
Gold	11.9	4	9.2	8	6.8	7	29.1	2
Silver	10.3	5	9.7	6	4.0	9	39.8	1
Treasury Bills	9.2	6	10.2	5	8.5	6	5.7	11
Old Masters[a]	9.2	7	9.7	6	9.5	5	8.6	7
Stocks	8.6	8	13.9	2	24.1	1	20.6	5
Bonds	8.7	9	9.7	7	19.7	2	5.7	12
Chinese Ceramics[a]	8.3	10	11.3	4	3.4	11	6.7	10
Housing	8.2	11	7.4	10	4.8	8	6.8	9
CPI	**6.9**	**12**	**6.5**	**11**	**3.5**	**10**	**3.8**	**13**
U.S. Farmland	6.3	13	1.5	14	(7.8)	13	(7.9)	15
Foreign Exchange	4.6	14	4.1	12	6.8	7	25.0	4
Diamonds[b]	4.1	15	8.9	9	10.2	4	7.0	8

Inflation Scorecard (Number of Assets that Outperformed Inflation)

Tangibles	8 out of 10	8 out of 10	6 out of 10	8 out of 10
• Collectibles	3 out of 4	4 out of 4	2 out of 4	3 out of 4
• Commodities	3 out of 4	3 out of 4	3 out of 4	4 out of 4
• Real Estate	1 out of 2	1 out of 2	1 out of 2	1 out of 2
Financials	3 out of 4	3 out of 4	4 out of 4	4 out of 4

[a] Source: Sotheby's. [b] Source: The Diamond Registry. CPI Consumer Price Index.
Note: All returns are for the period ended June 1, 1987, based on latest available data.

Stock Market: U.S. and Foreign

Stock Exchanges

Common Stocks (shares of ownership in a corporation) are traded on several exchanges. The best known are the New York Stock Exchange and the American Stock Exchange, both located in Manhattan's financial district. Generally, the stocks of the largest companies are traded on the New York Stock Exchange, while somewhat smaller companies are traded on the American Exchange. There are also a number of regional exchanges such as the Midwest Exchange in Chicago and the Pacific Exchange in San Francisco. These exchanges trade stocks of local corporations as well as stocks listed on the New York and American Exchanges.

In addition, there is the Over-The Counter-Market (OTC) which, unlike the exchanges previously mentioned, does not have a specific location but consists of a network of brokers and dealers linked by telephone and private wires. Smaller or relatively new companies are traded on the OTC. Trading information for many (but far from all) stocks on the OTC market is collected and displayed on a computerized system, the National Association of Security Dealers Automatic Quote System (NASDAQ).

Large institutional traders (mutual and pension funds, insurance companies, etc.) often trade blocks of stocks directly with one another. This information is collected and displayed on the Instinet System.

Major Stock Exchanges: U.S. and Canada

UNITED STATES

AMERICAN STOCK EXCHANGE, INC.
86 Trinity Place
New York, New York 10006

BOSTON STOCK EXCHANGE, INC.
53 State Street
Boston, Massachusetts 02109

CHICAGO BOARD OF TRADE
141 West Jackson Boulevard
Chicago, Illinois 60604

THE CINCINNATI STOCK EXCHANGE, INC.
205 Dixie Terminal Building
Cincinnati, Ohio 45202

COMMODITY MERCANTILE EXCHANGE
444 West Jackson Boulevard
Chicago, Illinois 60606

COMMODITY EXCHANGE OF NEW YORK
4 World Trade Center
New York, New York 10048

INTERMOUNTAIN STOCK EXCHANGE, INC.
39 Exchange Place
Salt Lake City, Utah 84111

MIDWEST STOCK EXCHANGE, INC.
120 South LaSalle Street
Chicago, Illinois 60603

NEW YORK FUTURES EXCHANGE
20 Broad Street
New York, New York 10005

NEW YORK STOCK EXCHANGE, INC.
11 Wall Street
New York, New York 10005

PACIFIC STOCK EXCHANGE, INC.
618 South Spring Street
Los Angeles, California 90014

PHILADELPHIA STOCK EXCHANGE, INC.
17th Street & Stock Exchange Place
Philadelphia, Pennsylvania 19103

SPOKANE STOCK EXCHANGE, INC.
225 Peyton Building
Spokane, Washington 99201

CANADA

ALBERTA STOCK EXCHANGE
300–5th Avenue S.W.
Calgary, Alberta T2P 3C4

MONTREAL STOCK EXCHANGE
The Stock Exchange Tower
800 Victoria Square
Montreal, Quebec H4Z 1A9

TORONTO FUTURES EXCHANGE
2 First Canadian Place
Toronto, Ontario M5X 1J2

TORONTO STOCK EXCHANGE
2 First Canadian Place
Toronto, Ontario M5X 1J2

VANCOUVER STOCK EXCHANGE
Stock Exchange Tower
P.O. Box 10333
609 Granville Street
Vancouver, B.C. V7Y 1H1

WINNIPEG STOCK EXCHANGE
303–167 Lombard Avenue
Winnipeg, Manitoba R3B OT6

Investment Returns on Stocks, Bonds, and Bills

Roger G. Ibbotson,* *Laurence B. Siegel,*** *Katse B. Weigel****

Our look at history consists of examining the returns of five capital market sectors. We measure total returns (capital gains plus income) on common stocks, long-term corporate bonds, long-term government bonds, U.S. Treasury bills, and rates of inflation on consumer goods. Comparing the returns from the various sectors gives us insights into the returns available from taking risk and the relationships between capital market returns and inflation.

THE RISKS AND REWARDS

We display graphically the rewards and risks available from the U.S. capital markets over the past 61 years. Exhibit 1 shows the growth of an investment in common stocks, long-term government bonds, and Treasury bills as well as the increase in the inflation index over the 61-year period. Each of the series is initiated at $1 at year-end 1925. The vertical scale is logarithmic so that equal distances represent equal percentage changes anywhere along the axis. The graph vividly portrays that common stocks were the big winner over the entire period. If $1 were invested in stocks at year-end 1925 and all dividends reinvested, the dollar investment would have grown to $330.67 by year-end 1986. This phenomenal growth was not without substantial risk, especially during the earlier portion of the period. In contrast, long-term government bonds (with a constant 20-year maturity) exhibited much less risk, but grew to only $13.72.

A virtually riskless strategy (for those with short-term time horizons) has been to buy U.S. Treasury bills. However, Treasury bills have had a marked tendency to track inflation, with the result that their real (inflation adjusted) return is near zero for the entire 1926–1986 period. Note that the tracking is only prevalent over the latter portion of the period. During periods of deflation (such as the late 1920s and early 1930s) the Treasury bill returns were near zero, but not negative, since no one intentionally buys securities with negative yields. Beginning in the early 1940s, the yields (returns) on Treasury bills were pegged by the government at low rates while high inflation was experienced. The government pegging ended with the U.S. Treasury-Federal Reserve Accord in March 1951.

We summarize the investment returns in Exhibit 2 by presenting the average annual returns over the 1926–1986 period. Common stocks returned a compounded (geometric mean) total return of 10.0 percent per year. The annual compound return from capital appreciation alone was 4.9 percent. After adjusting for inflation, annual compounded total returns were 6.7 percent per year.*

The average total return over any single year (arithmetic mean) for stocks was 12.1 percent, with positive returns recorded in two-thirds of the years (41 out of 61 years). The risk or degree of return fluctuation is measured by standard deviation as 21.2 percent. The frequency distribution (histogram) counts the number of years the returns fell in each 5 percent return increment. Note the wide variations in common stock returns relative to the other capital market sectors. Annual stock returns ranged from 54.0 percent in 1933 to −43.3 percent in 1931.

A simple example illustrates the difference between geometric and arithmetic means. Suppose $1 were invested in a common stock port-folio that experiences successive annual returns of +50 percent and −50 percent. At the end of the first year, the portfolio is worth $1.50. At the end of the second year, the portfolio is worth $0.75. The annual arithmetic mean is 0 percent, whereas the annual geometric mean (compounded return) is −13.4 percent. Naturally, it is the geometric mean that more directly measures the change in wealth over more than one period. On the other hand, the arithmetic mean is a better representation of typical performance over any single annual period.

The other capital market sectors also had returns commensurate with their risks. Long-term corporate bonds outperformed the default-free, long-term government bonds, which in turn outperformed the essentially riskless U.S. Treasury bills. Over the entire period the riskless U.S. Treasury bills had a return almost identical with the inflation rate. Thus, we again note that the real rate of inter-

* Professor, Yale School of Management, New Haven, Connecticut.

** Managing Partner, Ibbotson Associates, Inc., Chicago, Illinois.

*** Research Associate, Ibbotson Associates, Inc.

* Editor's note: While common stock total returns over the current decade have exceeded inflation by a substantial amount, the combined effect of inflation and taxes has made these returns quite meager in real terms. Other asset returns, adjusted for inflation and taxes, have been negative. Thus for common stocks, total returns over 1977–1986 were 13.8 percent as compared with 10.0 percent for long-term corporate bonds and 9.1 percent for U.S. Treasury bills. All figures neglect taxes. The inflation rate over the period was 6.6 percent. After taxes, it is evident that only common stocks earned a positive real return over the period. Assuming a 40 percent tax rate and future 6 percent inflation, and investment must earn 10 percent before taxes to break even.

EXHIBIT 1: WEALTH INDEXES OF INVESTMENTS IN THE U.S. CAPITAL MARKETS, 1926–1986 (assumed initial investment of $1.00 at year-end 1925, includes reinvestment income)

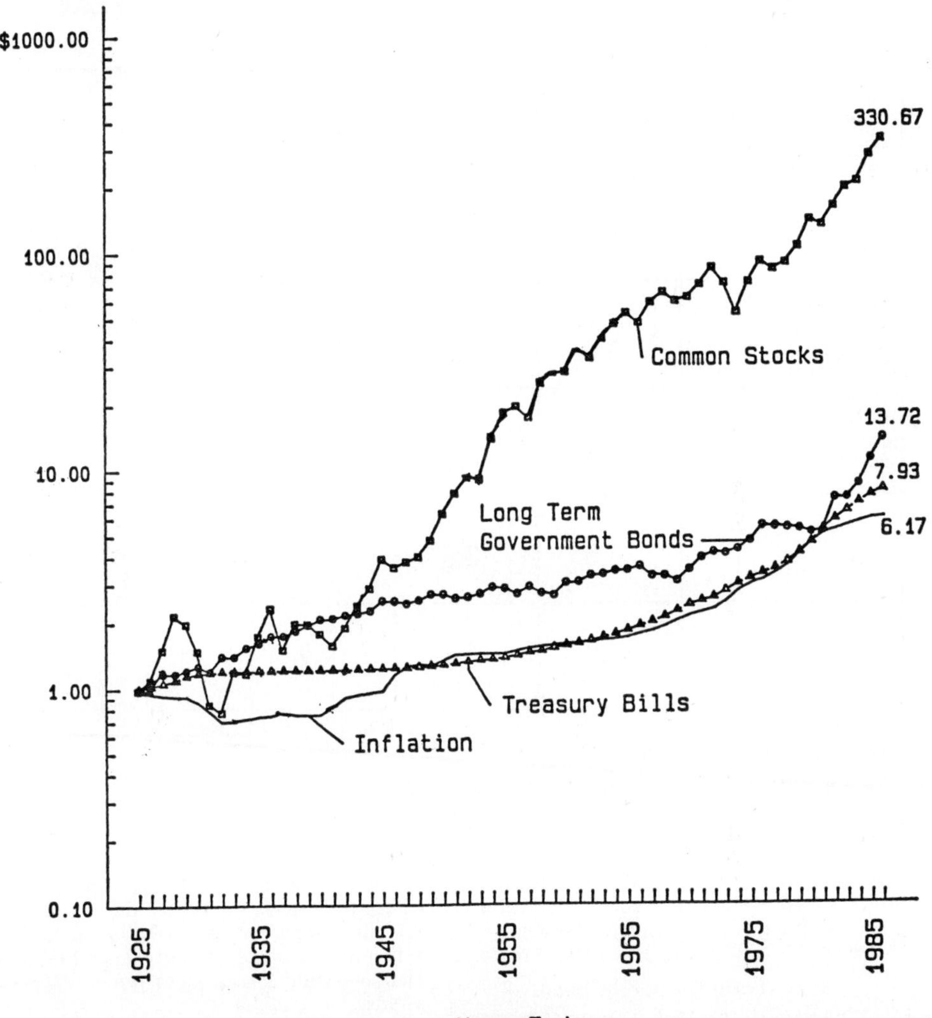

Source: *Stocks, Bonds, Bills, and Inflation: 1987 Yearbook*, published by Ibbotson Associates [8 S. Michigan Avenue, Suite 707, Chicago, IL. 60603, phone 312-263-3434], 1987.

est (the inflation-adjusted riskless rate) has been on average very near 0 percent historically.

MEASUREMENT OF THE FIVE SERIES

The returns were computed by compounding monthly returns, with no adjustments made for transactions costs or taxes. We describe each of the five total return series which are listed annually in Exhibit 3. The index numbers in Exhibit 3 are dollar values of a $1 investment made on December 31, 1925. They can be converted to yearly returns by taking the ratio of a given year-end index value to the previous year-end value, then subtracting one (1). For example, the return for common stocks for 1986 equals (330.668 ÷ 279.115) − 1 = 0.185, or 18.5 percent.

Common Stocks

The total return index is based upon Standard & Poor's (S&P) Composite Index with dividends reinvested monthly. To the extent that the 500 stocks currently included in the

EXHIBIT 2: BASIC SERIES: TOTAL ANNUAL RETURNS, 1926–1986

SERIES	GEOMETRIC MEAN	ARITHMETIC MEAN	STANDARD DEVIATION	DISTRIBUTION
COMMON STOCKS	10.0%	12.1%	21.2%	
SMALL STOCKS	12.5	18.2	36.0	
LONG TERM CORPORATE BONDS	5.0	5.3	8.5	
LONG TERM GOVERNMENT BONDS	4.4	4.7	8.6	
U.S. TREASURY BILLS	3.5	3.5	3.4	
INFLATION	3.0	3.1	4.9	

-90% 0% +90%

Ibbotson Associates • Chicago

Source: *Stocks, Bonds, Bills and Inflation: 1987 Yearbook*, Ibbotson Associates, Inc., Chicago, 1987.

S&P Composite Index (prior to March 1957, there were 90 stocks) are representative of all stocks in the United States, the market value weighting scheme allows the returns of the index to correspond to the aggregate stock market returns in the U.S. economy.

Long-Term Corporate Bonds

We measure the total returns of a corporate bond index with approximately 20 years to maturity. We use Salomon Brothers' High-Grade Long-Term Corporate Bond Index from its beginning in 1969 through 1986. For the period 1946–68 we backdate Salomon Brothers' index using Salomon Brothers' monthly yield data and similar methodology. For the period 1926–45 we compute returns using Standard & Poor's monthly high-grade corporate composite bond yield data, assuming a 4 percent coupon and a 20-year maturity.

Long-Term Government Bonds

To measure the total returns of long-term U.S. government bonds, we use the bond data obtained from the U.S. Government Bond File (constructed by Lawrence Fisher) at the Center for Research in Security Prices (CRSP) at the University of Chicago. We attempt to maintain a 20-year bond portfolio whose returns do not reflect the potential tax benefits, impaired negotiability, or the special redemption or call privileges frequently characterizing government bond prices and yields.

U.S. Treasury Bills

For the U.S. Treasury bill index, we again use the data in the CRSP U.S. Government Bond File. We measure one-month holding period returns for the shortest-term bills not less than one month in maturity. Since U.S. Treasury bills were not initiated until 1929, we use short-term coupon bonds whenever bill quotes are unavailable.

Consumer Price Index

We utilize the Consumer Price Index for All Urban Consumers (CPI-U), not seasonally adjusted, to measure inflation. The CPI-U, and its predecessor, the CPI (which we use prior to January 1978) is constructed by the Bureau of Labor Statistics, U.S. Department of Labor, Washington, D.C.

EXHIBIT 3: BASIC SERIES, INDEXES OF YEAR-END CUMULATIVE WEALTH, 1925–1986 (year-end 1925 = 1.000)

Year	Common Stocks		Long-Term Government Bonds		Long-Term Corporate Bonds	U.S. Treasury Bills	Consumer Price Index
	Total Returns	Capital Appreciation Only	Total Returns	Capital Appreciation Only	Total Returns	Total Returns	Rates of Inflation
1925	1.000	1.000	1.000	1.000	1.000	1.000	1.000
1926	1.116	1.057	1.078	1.039	1.074	1.033	0.985
1927	1.535	1.384	1.174	1.095	1.154	1.065	0.965
1928	2.204	1.908	1.175	1.061	1.186	1.099	0.955
1929	2.018	1.681	1.215	1.059	1.225	1.152	0.957
1930	1.516	1.202	1.272	1.072	1.323	1.179	0.899
1931	0.859	0.636	1.204	0.981	1.299	1.192	0.814
1932	0.789	0.540	1.407	1.108	1.439	1.204	0.730
1933	1.214	0.792	1.406	1.073	1.588	1.207	0.734
1934	1.197	0.745	1.547	1.146	1.808	1.209	0.749
1935	1.767	1.053	1.624	1.170	1.982	1.211	0.771
1936	2.367	1.346	1.746	1.225	2.116	1.213	0.780
1937	1.538	0.827	1.750	1.194	2.174	1.217	0.804
1938	2.016	1.035	1.847	1.228	2.307	1.217	0.782
1939	2.008	0.979	1.957	1.271	2.399	1.217	0.778
1940	1.812	0.829	2.076	1.319	2.480	1.217	0.786
1941	1.602	0.681	2.095	1.305	2.548	1.218	0.862
1942	1.927	0.766	2.162	1.315	2.614	1.221	0.942
1943	2.427	0.915	2.207	1.310	2.688	1.225	0.972
1944	2.906	1.041	2.270	1.314	2.815	1.229	0.993
1945	3.965	1.361	2.513	1.423	2.930	1.233	1.015
1946	3.645	1.199	2.511	1.392	2.980	1.238	1.199
1947	3.853	1.199	2.445	1.327	2.911	1.244	1.307
1948	4.065	1.191	2.528	1.340	3.031	1.254	1.343
1949	4.829	1.313	2.691	1.395	3.132	1.268	1.318
1950	6.360	1.600	2.692	1.366	3.198	1.283	1.395
1951	7.888	1.863	2.586	1.281	3.112	1.302	1.477
1952	9.336	2.082	2.616	1.262	3.221	1.324	1.490
1953	9.244	1.944	2.711	1.270	3.331	1.348	1.499
1954	14.108	2.820	2.906	1.325	3.511	1.360	1.492
1955	18.561	3.564	2.868	1.271	3.527	1.381	1.497
1956	19.778	3.658	2.708	1.164	3.287	1.415	1.540
1957	17.648	3.134	2.910	1.208	3.573	1.459	1.587
1958	25.298	4.327	2.733	1.097	3.494	1.482	1.615
1959	28.322	4.694	2.671	1.029	3.460	1.526	1.639
1960	28.455	4.554	3.039	1.124	3.774	1.566	1.663
1961	36.106	5.607	3.068	1.092	3.956	1.600	1.674
1962	32.955	4.945	3.280	1.122	4.270	1.643	1.695
1963	40.469	5.879	3.319	1.092	4.364	1.695	1.723
1964	47.139	6.642	3.436	1.084	4.572	1.754	1.743
1965	53.008	7.244	3.460	1.047	4.552	1.823	1.777
1966	47.674	6.295	3.586	1.036	4.560	1.910	1.836
1967	59.104	7.560	3.257	0.895	4.335	1.991	1.892
1968	65.642	8.139	3.248	0.846	4.446	2.094	1.981
1969	60.059	7.210	3.083	0.754	4.086	2.232	2.102
1970	62.465	7.222	3.457	0.791	4.837	2.378	2.218
1971	71.406	8.001	3.914	0.843	5.370	2.482	2.292
1972	84.956	9.252	4.136	0.840	5,760	2.577	2.371
1973	72.500	7.645	4.090	0.775	5.825	2.756	2.579
1974	53.311	5.373	4.268	0.748	5.647	2.976	2.894
1975	73.144	7.068	4.661	0.754	6.474	3.149	3.097
1976	90.584	8.422	5.441	0.815	7.681	3.309	3.246
1977	84.076	7.453	5.405	0.750	7.813	3.479	3.466
1978	89.592	7.532	5.342	0.682	7.807	3.728	3.778
1979	106.112	8.459	5.277	0.615	7.481	4.115	4.281
1980	140.513	10.639	5.069	0.530	7.285	4.578	4.812
1981	133.615	9.605	5.162	0.475	7.215	5.251	5.242
1982	162.221	11.023	7.245	0.589	10.374	5.805	5.445
1983	198.744	12.926	7.294	0.530	10.862	6.315	5.652
1984	211.198	13.106	8.420	0.542	12.642	6.937	5.875
1985	279.115	16.558	11.027	0.639	16.549	7.473	6.097
1986	330.668	18.981	13.722	0.735	19.833	7.934	6.166

Source: *Stocks, Bonds, Bills, and Inflation: 1987 Yearbook*, Ibbotson Associates, Inc., Chicago, 1987.

The Constant Dollar Dow

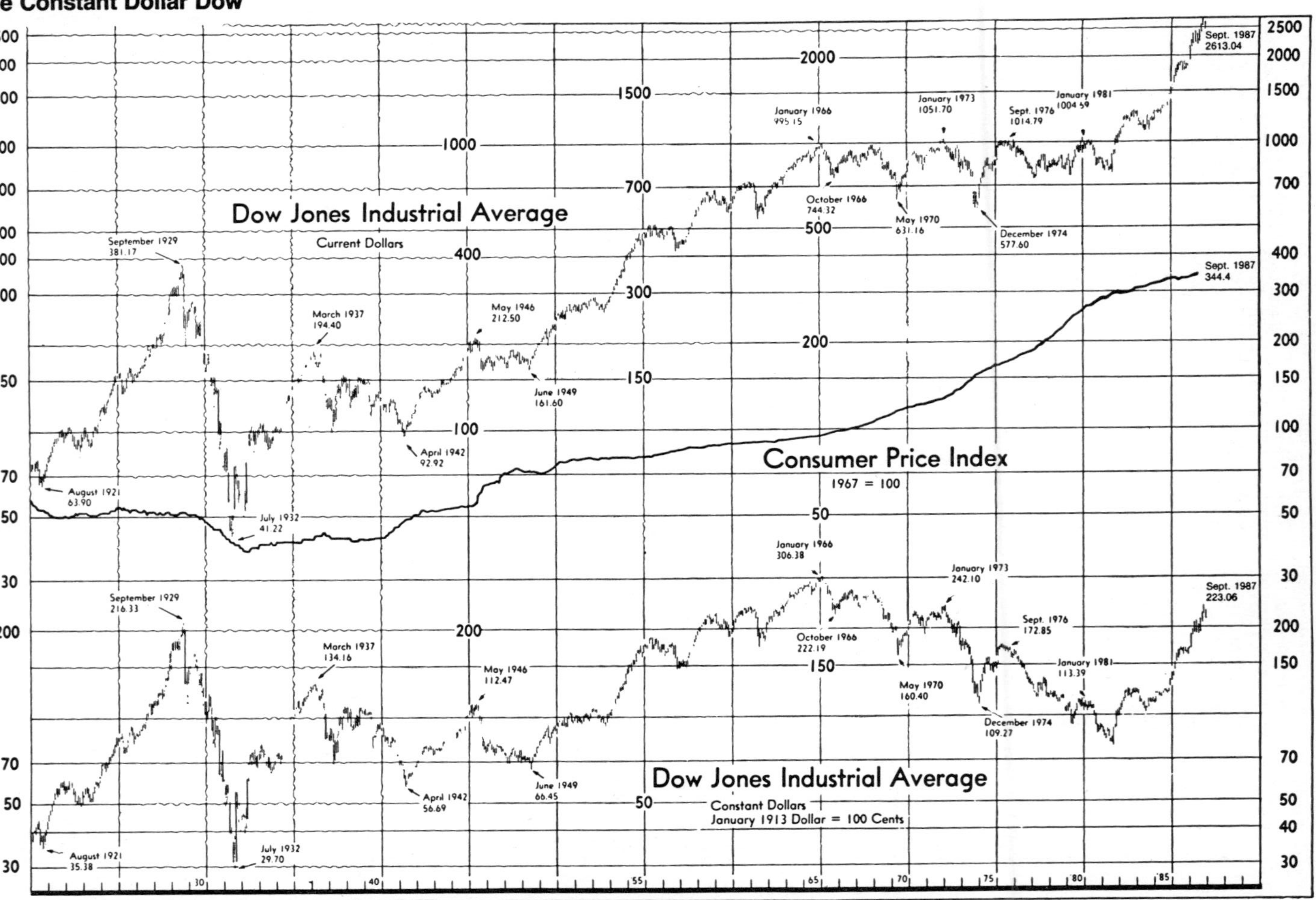

Source: *The Media General Financial Weekly*, Media General Financial Services, 301 East Grace Street, Richmond, VA 23261, October 26, 1987.

Cash Dividends on NYSE Listed Common Stocks

	Common stocks		
	Number of issues listed at year end	Number paying cash dividends during year	Estimated aggregate cash payments (millions)
1929	842	554	$ 2,711
1930	848	576	2,667
1935	776	387	1,336
1940	829	577	2,099
1941	834	627	2,281
1942	834	648	1,997
1943	845	687	2,063
1944	864	717	2,223
1945	881	746	2,275
1946	933	798	2,669
1947	964	851	3,255
1948	986	883	3,806
1949	1,017	887	4,235
1950	1,039	930	5,404
1951	1,054	961	5,467
1952	1,067	975	5,595
1953	1,069	964	5,874
1954	1,076	968	6,439
1955	1,076	982	7,488
1956	1,077	975	8,341
1957	1,098	991	8,807
1958	1,086	961	8,711
1959	1,092	953	9,337
1960	1,126	981	9,872
1961	1,145	981	10,430
1962	1,168	994	11,203
1963	1,194	1,032	12,096
1964	1,227	1,066	13,555
1965	1,254	1,111	15,302
1966	1,267	1,127	16,151
1967	1,255	1,116	16,866
1968	1,253	1,104	18,124
1969	1,290	1,121	19,404
1970	1,330	1,120	19,781
1971	1,399	1,132	20,256
1972	1,478	1,195	21,490
1973	1,536	1,276	23,627
1974	1,543	1,308	25,662
1975	1,531	1,273	26,901
1976	1,550	1,304	30,608
1977	1,549	1,360	36,270
1978	1,552	1,373	41,151
1979	1,536	1,359	46,937
1980	1,540	1,361	53,072
1981	1,534	1,337	60,628
1982	1,499	1,287	62,224
1983	1,518	1,259	67,102
1984	1,511	1,243	68,215
1985	1,503	1,206	74,237
1986	1,536	1,180	76,161

Source: New York Stock Exchange *1987 Fact Book.*

THE MAJOR MARKET AVERAGES

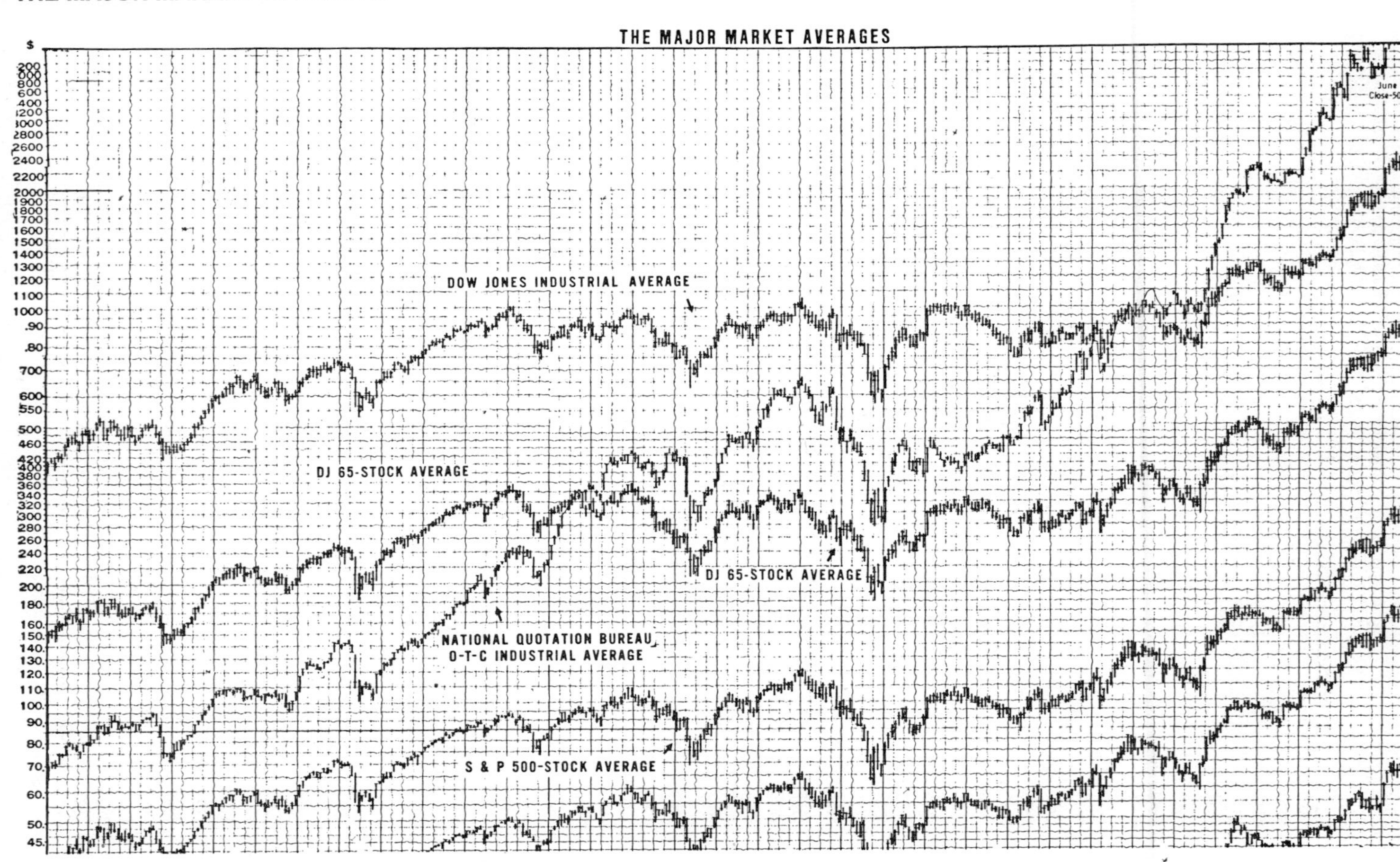

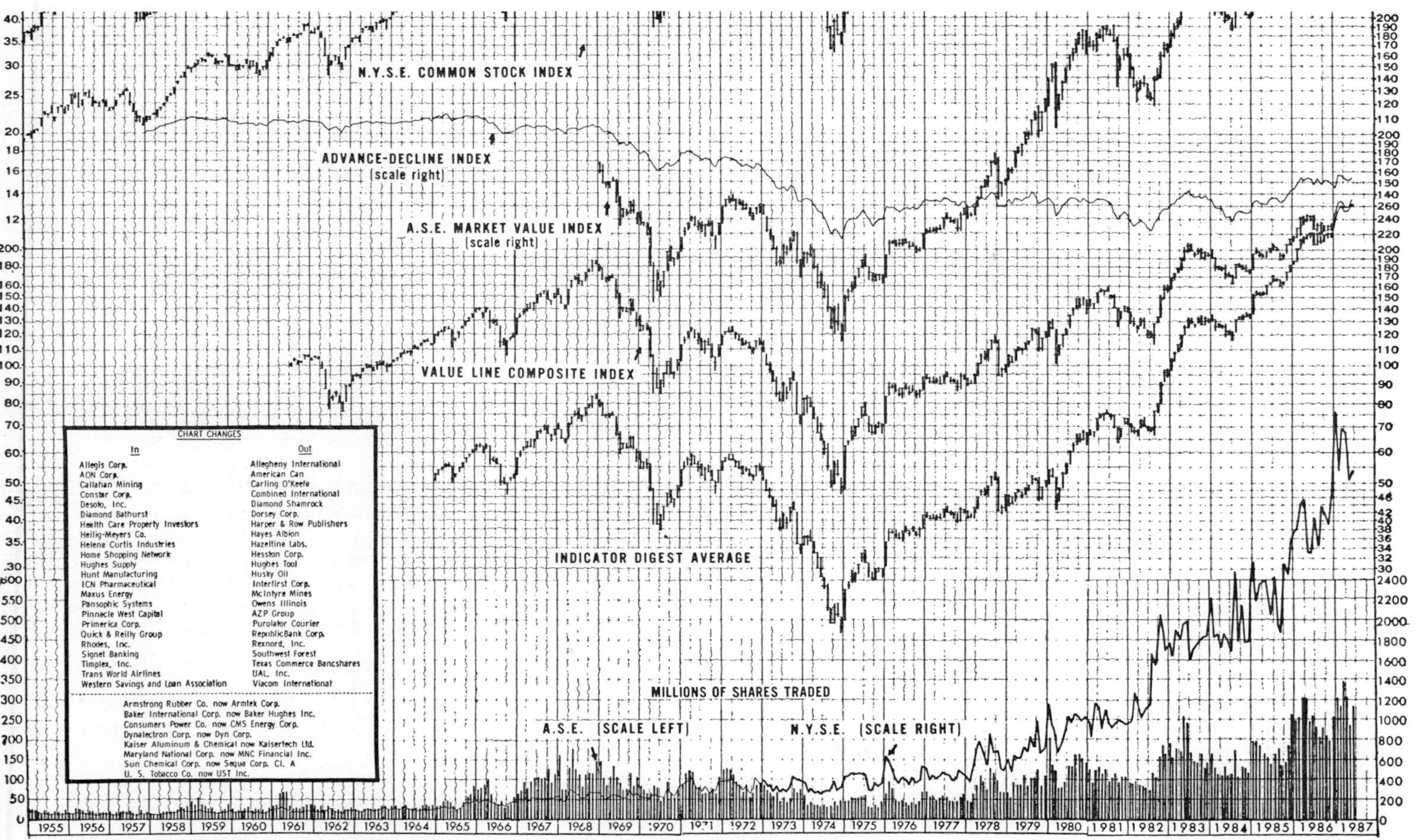

Source: *5-Trend CYCLI-GRAPHS.* The charts are courtesy of Securities Research Company, a Division of Babson-United Investment Advisors, Inc., 208 Newbury Street, Boston, MA 02116, July quarterly edition, 1987.

Quarterly Dow Jones Industrial Stock Average

The table below lists the earnings (losses) of the Dow Jones Industrial Average based on generally accepted accounting principles. The price-earnings ratio for the DJI correctly reflects deficit/negative earnings for the 1982 September and December quarters. The 1985 December quarter and year-end dividend reflects $2.00 GM dividend distribution value of one share of class H common for each 20 shares of common held. The 1984 December quarter and year-end dividend reflects $1.87½ GM dividend distribution value of one share of class E common for each 20 shares of common held. N.A.-Not available. d-Indicates deficit/negative earnings for the quarter.

Year	Quarter Ended	Clos. Avg:	Qtrly Chg.	% Chg.	Qtrly Earns	12-Mth Earns	P/E Ratio	Qtrly Divs	12-Mth Divs	Divs Yield	Payout Ratio
1987	June 30	2418.53	+ 113.84	4.94	N.A.	N.A.	N.A.	18.11	69.36	2.87	N.A.
	Mar. 31	2304.69	+ 408.74	+ 21.56	35.63	126.49	18.2	17.37	68.19	2.96	.5391
1986	Dec. 31	1895.95	+ 128.37	+ 7.26	21.48	115.59	16.4	17.09	67.04	3.54	.5800
	Sept. 30	1767.58	− 125.14	− 6.61	33.01	118.80	14.9	16.79	67.14	3.80	.5652
	June 30	1892.72	+ 74.11	+ 4.08	36.37	103.39	18.3	16.94	65.37	3.45	.6323
	Mar. 31	1818.61	+ 271.94	+ 17.58	24.73	96.43	18.9	16.22	63.38	3.49	.6573
1985	Dec. 31	1546.67	+ 218.04	+ 16.41	24.69	96.11	16.1	17.19	62.03	4.01	.6454
	Sept. 30	1328.63	− 6.83	− 0.51	17.60	90.78	14.6	15.02	61.83	4.65	.6811
	June 28	1335.46	+ 68.68	+ 5.14	29.41	102.26	13.1	14.95	61.53	4.61	.6017
	Mar. 29	1266.78	+ 55.21	+ 4.56	24.41	107.87	11.7	14.87	61.56	4.86	.5707
1984	Dec. 31	1211.57	+ 4.86	+ 0.40	19.36	113.58	10.7	16.99	60.63	5.00	.5338
	Sept. 28	1206.71	+ 74.31	+ 6.56	29.08	108.11	11.2	14.72	58.41	4.84	.5403
	June 29	1132.40	− 32.49	− 2.79	35.02	102.07	11.1	14.98	57.67	5.09	.5650
	Mar. 30	1164.89	− 93.75	− 7.45	30.12	87.38	13.3	13.94	56.39	4.84	.6453
1983	Dec. 30	1258.64	+ 25.51	+ 2.07	13.89	72.45	17.4	14.77	56.33	4.47	.7775
	Sept. 30	1233.13	+ 11.17	+ 0.91	23.04	56.12	22.0	13.98	54.59	4.43	.9727
	June 30	1221.96	+ 91.93	+ 8.13	20.33	11.59	105.4	13.70	54.05	4.42	4.6635
	Mar. 31	1130.03	+ 83.49	+ 7.98	15.19	9.52	118.7	13.88	54.10	4.79	5.6828
1982	Dec. 31	1046.54	+ 150.29	+ 16.77	d2.44	9.15	114.4	13.03	54.14	5.17	5.9169
	Sept. 30	896.25	+ 84.32	+ 10.38	d21.49	35.15	25.5	13.44	55.55	6.20	1.5804
	June 30	811.93	− 10.84	− 1.32	18.26	79.90	10.2	13.75	55.84	6.88	.6989
	Mar. 31	822.77	− 52.23	− 5.97	14.82	97.13	8.5	13.92	56.28	6.84	.5794
1981	Dec. 31	875.00	+ 25.02	+ 2.94	23.56	113.71	7.7	14.44	56.22	6.42	.4944
	Sept. 30	849.98	− 126.90	− 12.99	23.26	123.32	6.9	13.73	56.18	6.61	.4539
	June 30	976.88	− 26.99	− 2.69	35.49	128.91	7.6	14.19	55.98	5.73	.4266
	Mar. 31	1003.87	+ 39.88	+ 4.14	31.40	123.60	8.1	13.86	54.99	5.48	.4449
1980	Dec. 31	963.99	+ 31.57	+ 3.39	33.17	121.86	7.9	14.40	54.36	5.64	.4461
	Sept. 30	932.42	+ 64.50	+ 7.43	28.85	111.58	8.4	13.53	53.83	5.77	.4824
	June 30	867.92	+ 82.17	+ 10.46	30.18	116.40	7.5	13.20	52.81	6.08	.4537
	Mar. 31	785.75	− 52.99	− 6.32	29.66	120.77	6.5	13.23	52.10	6.63	.4314
1979	Dec. 31	838.74	− 39.93	− 4.54	22.89	124.46	6.7	13.87	50.98	6.08	.4096
	Sept. 28	878.67	+ 36.69	+ 4.36	33.67	136.26	6.4	12.51	51.45	5.85	.3776
	June 29	841.98	− 20.20	− 2.34	34.55	128.99	6.5	12.49	50.35	5.98	.3903
	Mar. 30	862.18	+ 57.17	+ 7.10	33.35	124.10	6.9	12.11	49.48	5.74	.3987
1978	Dec. 29	805.01	− 60.81	− 7.02	34.69	112.79	7.1	14.34	48.52	6.03	.4302
	Sept. 29	865.82	+ 46.87	+ 5.72	26.40	101.59	8.5	11.41	47.42	5.48	.4668
	June 30	818.95	+ 61.59	+ 8.13	29.66	91.37	9.0	11.62	46.74	5.71	.5115
	Mar. 31	757.36	− 73.81	− 8.88	22.04	89.23	8.5	11.15	46.53	6.14	.5215
1977	Dec. 30	831.17	− 15.94	− 1.88	23.49	89.10	9.3	13.24	45.84	5.51	.5145
	Sept. 30	847.11	− 69.19	− 7.55	16.18	89.86	9.4	10.73	44.73	5.28	.4978
	June 30	916.30	− 2.83	− 0.31	27.52	97.18	9.4	11.41	43.85	4.79	.4512
	Mar. 31	919.13	− 85.52	− 8.51	21.91	95.51	9.6	10.46	42.63	4.64	.4463
1976	Dec. 31	1004.65	+ 14.46	+ 1.46	24.25	96.72	10.4	12.13	41.40	4.12	.4280
	Sept. 30	990.19	− 12.59	− 1.27	23.50	95.81	10.3	9.85	38.90	3.93	.4060
	June 30	1002.78	+ 3.33	+ 0.33	25.85	90.68	11.1	10.19	38.10	3.80	.4202
	Mar. 31	999.45	+ 147.04	+ 17.25	23.12	81.87	12.2	9.23	36.88	3.69	.4505
1975	Dec. 31	852.41	+ 58.53	+ 7.37	23.34	75.66	11.3	9.63	37.46	4.39	.4951
	Sept. 30	793.88	− 85.11	− 10.72	18.37	75.47	10.5	9.05	38.28	4.82	.5072
	June 30	878.99	+ 110.84	+ 12.61	17.04	83.83	10.5	8.97	38.66	4.40	.4612
	Mar. 31	768.15	+ 151.91	+ 24.65	16.91	93.47	8.2	9.81	38.56	5.02	.4125
1974	Dec. 31	616.24	+ 8.37	+ 1.38	23.15	99.04	6.2	10.45	37.72	6.12	.3809
	Sept. 30	607.87	− 194.54	− 24.24	26.73	99.73	6.1	9.43	37.89	6.23	.3799
	June 28	802.41	− 44.27	− 5.23	26.68	93.26	8.6	8.87	36.82	4.59	.3948
	Mar. 29	846.68	− 4.18	− 0.49	22.48	89.46	9.5	8.97	36.22	4.28	.4049
1973	Dec. 31	850.86	− 96.24	− 11.31	23.84	86.17	9.9	10.62	35.33	4.15	.4100
	Sept. 28	947.10	+ 55.39	+ 6.21	20.26	82.09	11.5	8.36	33.70	3.56	.4105
	June 29	891.71	− 59.30	− 6.23	22.88	77.56	11.5	8.27	33.10	3.71	.4268
	Mar. 30	951.01	− 69.01	− 6.76	19.19	71.98	13.2	8.08	32.70	3.44	.4543
1972	Dec. 29	1020.02	+ 66.75	+ 7.00	19.76	67.11	15.2	8.99	32.27	3.16	.4808
	Sept. 29	953.27	+ 24.24	+ 2.61	15.73	62.15	15.3	7.76	31.13	3.27	.5009
	June 30	929.03	− 11.67	− 1.24	17.30	58.87	15.8	7.87	30.88	3.32	.5245
	Mar. 30	940.70	+ 50.50	+ 5.67	14.32	56.76	16.6	7.65	30.81	3.27	.5428
1971	Dec. 31	890.20	+ 3.01	+ 0.00	14.80	55.09	16.2	7.85	30.86	3.47	.5602
	Sept. 30	887.19	− 3.95	− 0.00	12.45	53.43	16.6	7.51	31.26	3.52	.5851
	June 30	891.14	− 13.23	− 1.46	15.19	53.45	16.7	7.80	31.55	3.54	.5903
	Mar. 31	904.37	+ 65.45	+ 7.80	12.65	52.36	17.3	7.70	32.21	3.56	.6152

Source: Reprinted by courtesy of *Barron's National Business and Financial Weekly*, July 6, 1987.

Stock Market Averages by Industry Group

These definitions apply to the following charts.

Price scale: The price ranges are always read from the scale at the right-hand side of each chart. This scale is equal to 15 times the earnings and dividend scale at the left, so when the price range bars and the earnings line coincide, it shows the price is at 15 times earnings. When the price is above the earnings line, the ratio of price to earnings is greater than 15 times earnings; when below, it is less.

Monthly price ranges represented by the solid vertical bars show the highest and lowest point of each month's transactions. Cross-bars indicate the month's closing price.

Monthly ratio-cator: The plottings for this line are obtained by dividing the closing price of the stock by the closing price of the Dow Jones Industrial Average on the say day. The resulting percentage is multiplied by a factor of 4.5 (450) to bring the line closer to the price bars and is read from the right-hand scale. The plotting indicates whether the stock has kept pace, outperformed, or lagged behind the general market as represented by the DJIA.

Volume: The number of shares traded each month is shown by vertical bars at the bottom of each chart on an arithmetical scale.

Source: 5-*Trend CYCLI-GRAPHS.* The charts are courtesy of Securities Research Company, a Division of Babson-United Investment Advisors, Inc., 208 Newbury Street, Boston, MA 02116, July quarterly edition, 1987.

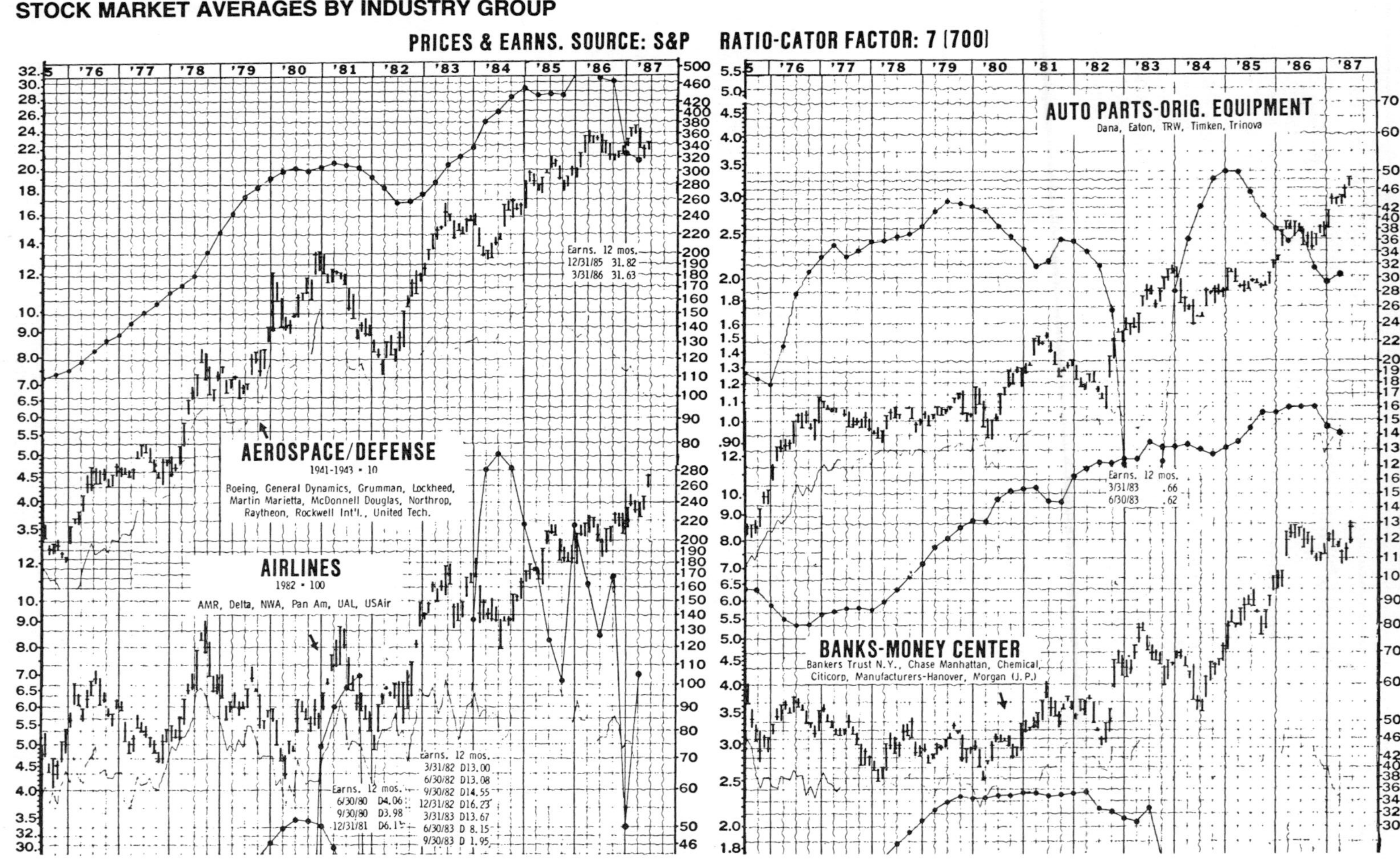
STOCK MARKET AVERAGES BY INDUSTRY GROUP
PRICES & EARNS. SOURCE: S&P
RATIO-CATOR FACTOR: 7 (700)
AEROSPACE/DEFENSE
1941-1943 = 10
Boeing, General Dynamics, Grumman, Lockheed, Martin Marietta, McDonnell Douglas, Northrop, Raytheon, Rockwell Int'l., United Tech.
Earns. 12 mos.
12/31/85 31.82
3/31/86 31.63
AIRLINES
1982 = 100
AMR, Delta, NWA, Pan Am, UAL, USAir
Earns. 12 mos.
6/30/80 D4.06
9/30/80 D3.98
12/31/81 D6.1
Earns. 12 mos.
3/31/82 D13.00
6/30/82 D13.08
9/30/82 D14.55
12/31/82 D16.23
3/31/83 D13.67
6/30/83 D 8.15
9/30/83 D 1.95
AUTO PARTS-ORIG. EQUIPMENT
Dana, Eaton, TRW, Timken, Trinova
Earns. 12 mos.
3/31/83 .66
6/30/83 .62
BANKS-MONEY CENTER
Bankers Trust N.Y., Chase Manhattan, Chemical, Citicorp, Manufacturers-Hanover, Morgan (J.P.)

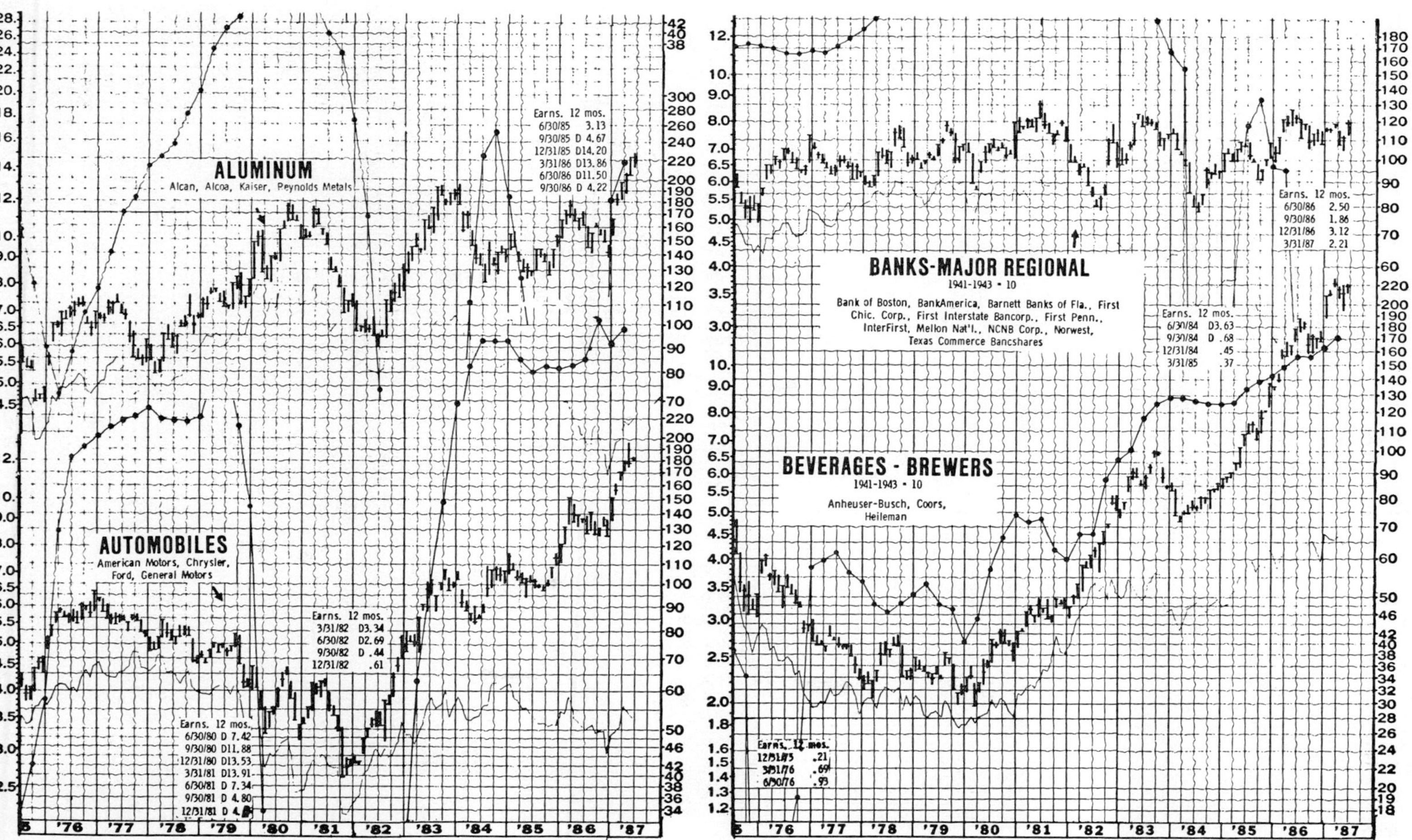
ALUMINUM
Alcan, Alcoa, Kaiser, Reynolds Metals
Earns. 12 mos.
6/30/85 3.13
9/30/85 D 4.67
12/31/85 D14.20
3/31/86 D13.86
6/30/86 D11.50
9/30/86 D 4.22
AUTOMOBILES
American Motors, Chrysler, Ford, General Motors
Earns. 12 mos.
6/30/80 D 7.42
9/30/80 D11.88
12/31/80 D13.53
3/31/81 D13.91
6/30/81 D 7.34
9/30/81 D 4.80
12/31/81 D 4.
Earns. 12 mos.
3/31/82 D3.34
6/30/82 D2.69
9/30/82 D .44
12/31/82 .61
'76 '77 '78 '79 '80 '81 '82 '83 '84 '85 '86 '87
BANKS-MAJOR REGIONAL
1941-1943 = 10
Bank of Boston, BankAmerica, Barnett Banks of Fla., First Chic. Corp., First Interstate Bancorp., First Penn., InterFirst, Mellon Nat'l., NCNB Corp., Norwest, Texas Commerce Bancshares
Earns. 12 mos.
6/30/84 D3.63
9/30/84 D .68
12/31/84 .45
3/31/85 .37
Earns. 12 mos.
6/30/86 2.50
9/30/86 1.86
12/31/86 3.12
3/31/87 2.21
BEVERAGES - BREWERS
1941-1943 = 10
Anheuser-Busch, Coors, Heileman
Earns. 12 mos.
12/31/75 .21
3/31/76 .69
6/30/76 .93
'76 '77 '78 '79 '80 '81 '82 '83 '84 '85 '86 '87

STOCK MARKET AVERAGES BY INDUSTRY GROUP *(continued)*

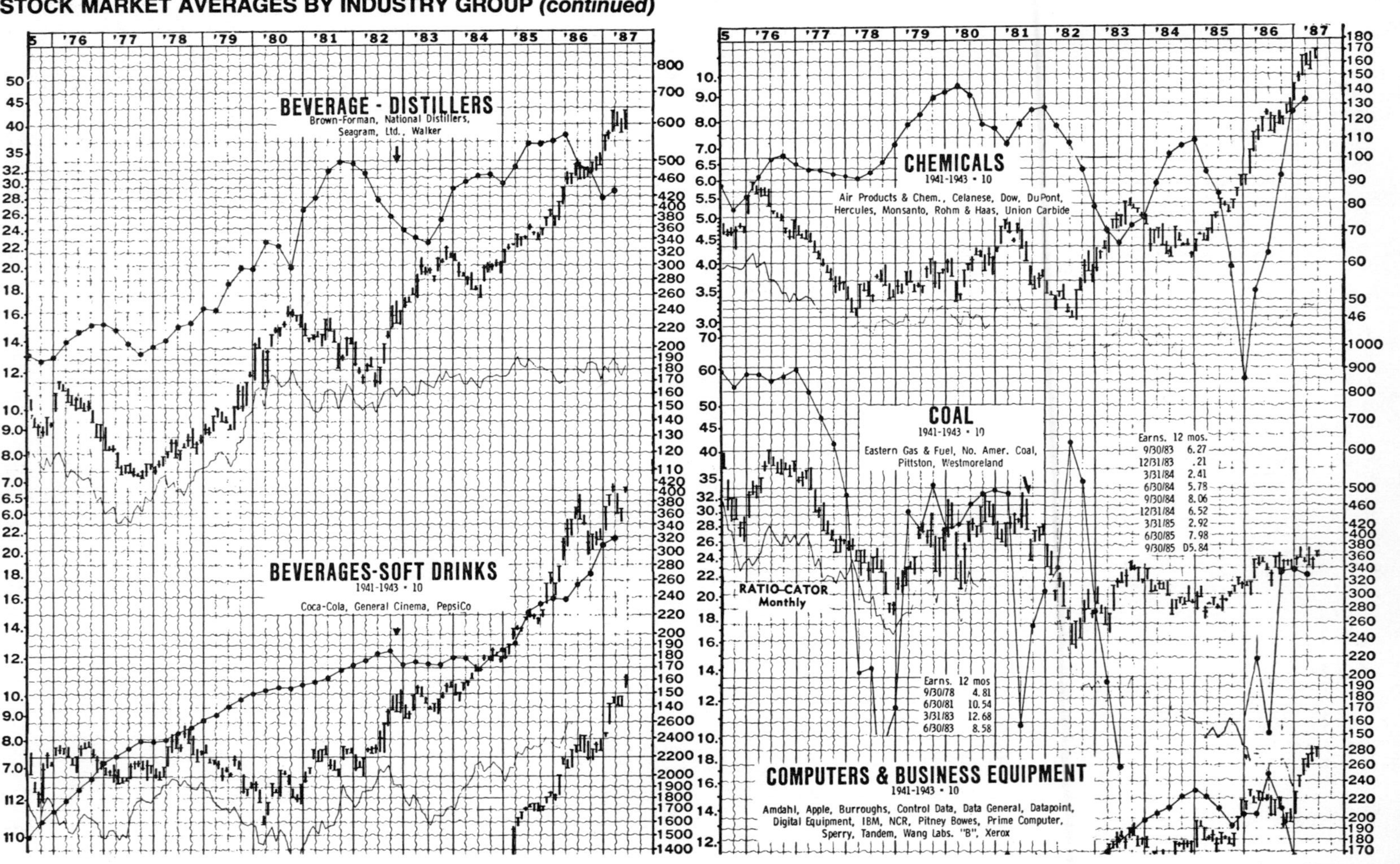

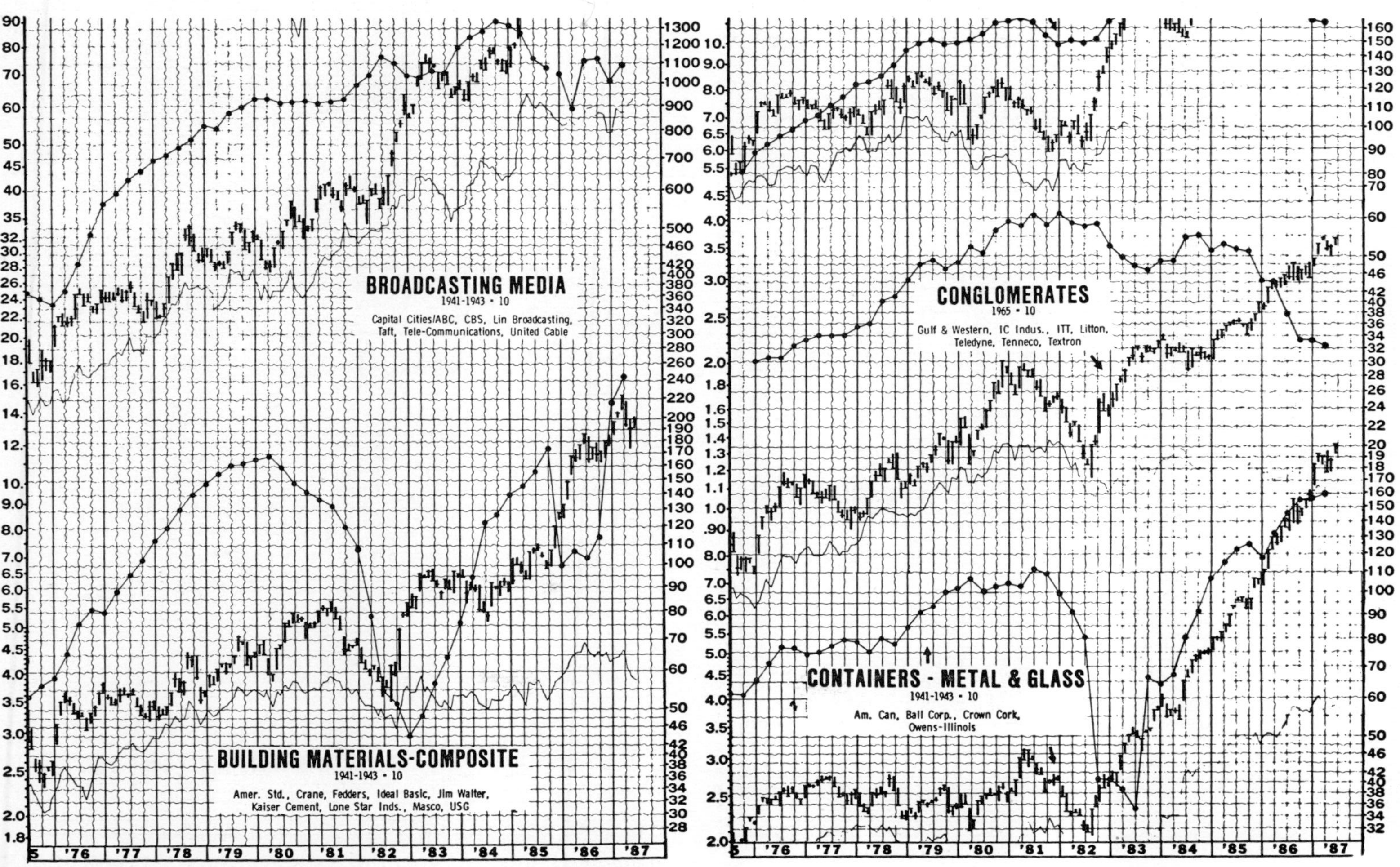
BROADCASTING MEDIA
1941-1943 • 10
Capital Cities/ABC, CBS, Lin Broadcasting,
Taft, Tele-Communications, United Cable
BUILDING MATERIALS-COMPOSITE
1941-1943 • 10
Amer. Std., Crane, Fedders, Ideal Basic, Jim Walter,
Kaiser Cement, Lone Star Inds., Masco, USG
CONGLOMERATES
1965 • 10
Gulf & Western, IC Indus., ITT, Litton,
Teledyne, Tenneco, Textron
CONTAINERS - METAL & GLASS
1941-1943 • 10
Am. Can, Ball Corp., Crown Cork,
Owens-Illinois
'76 '77 '78 '79 '80 '81 '82 '83 '84 '85 '86 '87

STOCK MARKET AVERAGES BY INDUSTRY GROUP (*continued*)

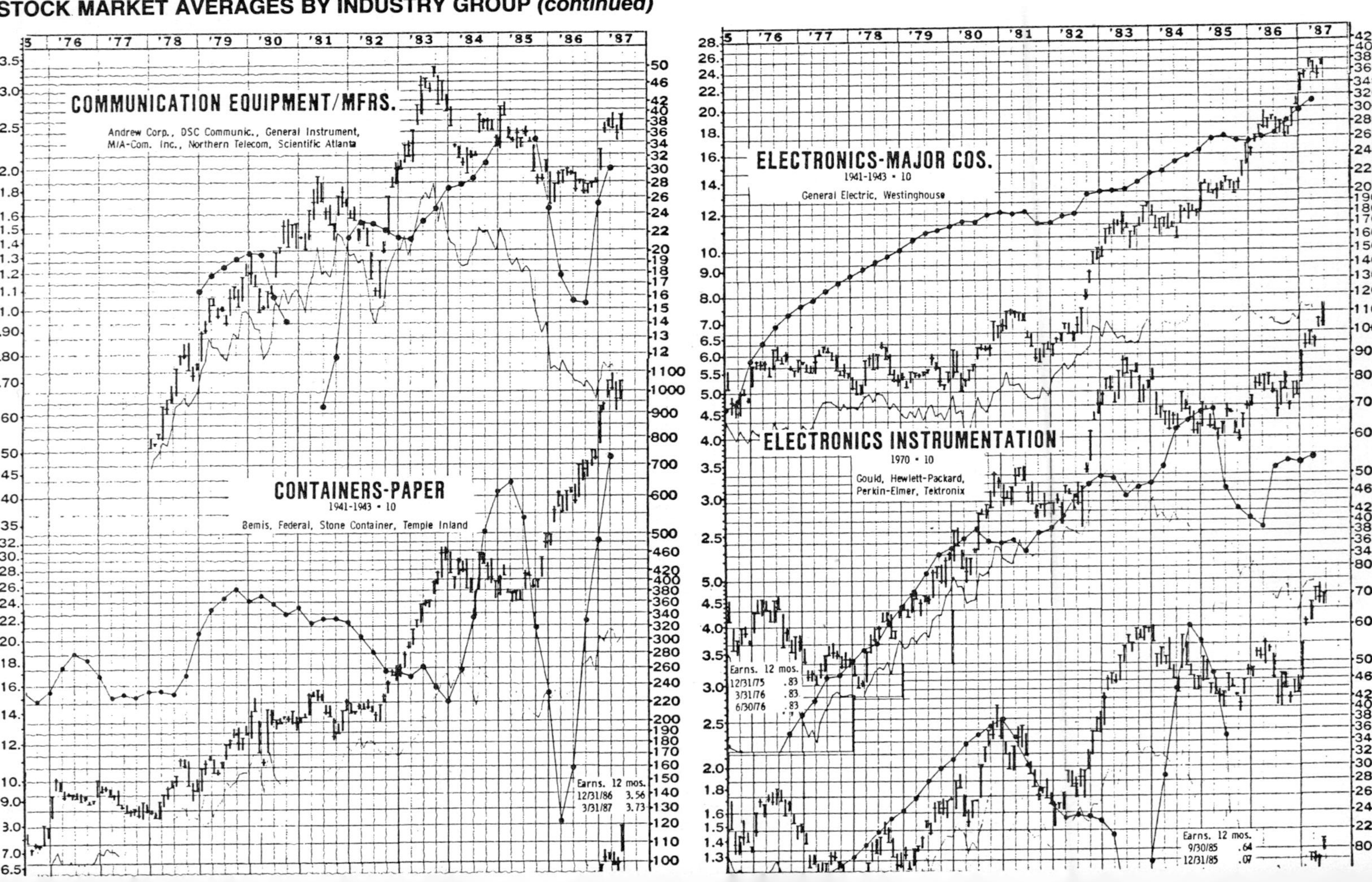

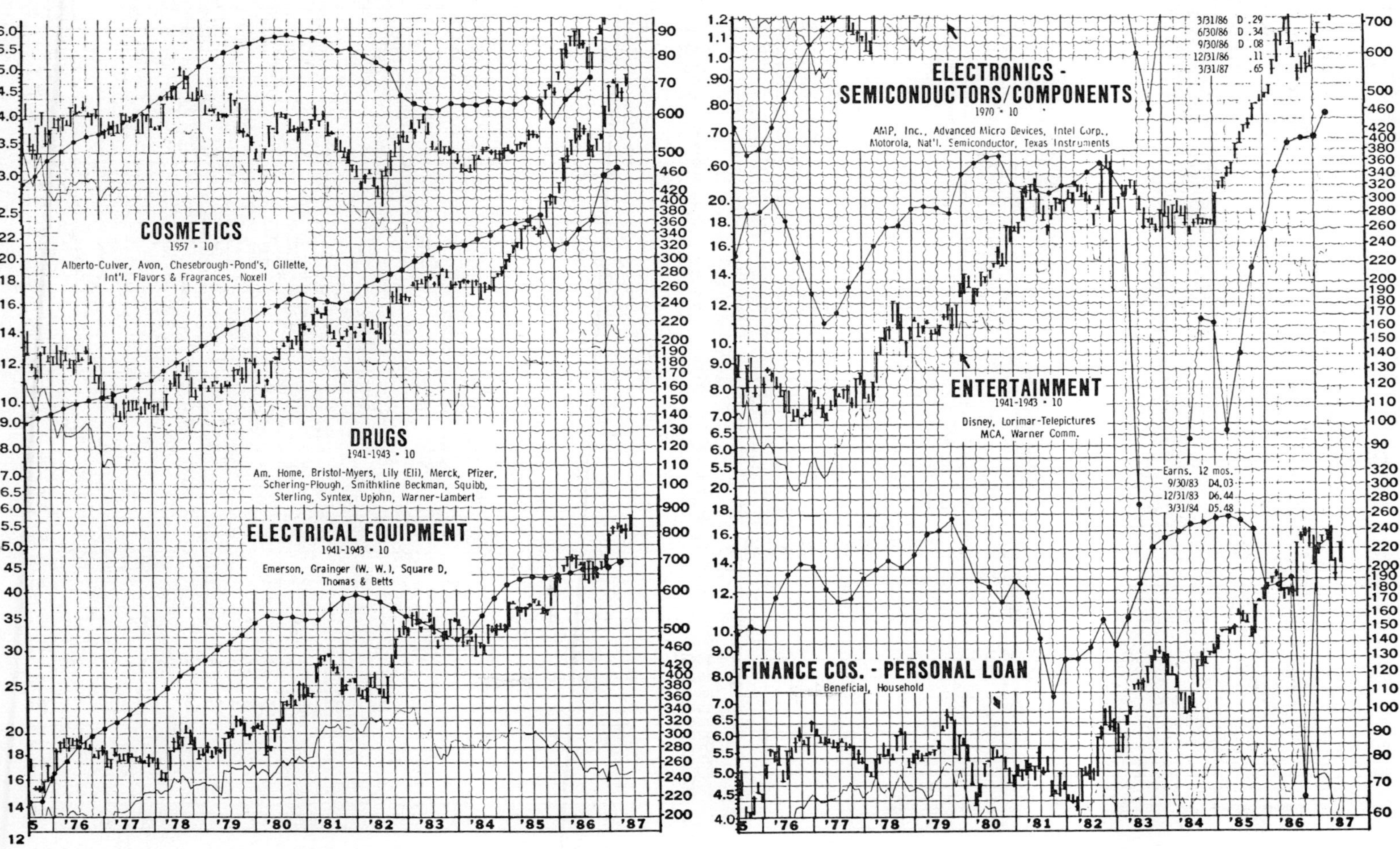

COSMETICS
1957 = 10
Alberto-Culver, Avon, Chesebrough-Pond's, Gillette, Int'l. Flavors & Fragrances, Noxell
DRUGS
1941-1943 = 10
Am. Home, Bristol-Myers, Lily (Eli), Merck, Pfizer, Schering-Plough, Smithkline Beckman, Squibb, Sterling, Syntex, Upjohn, Warner-Lambert
ELECTRICAL EQUIPMENT
1941-1943 = 10
Emerson, Grainger (W. W.), Square D, Thomas & Betts
ELECTRONICS - SEMICONDUCTORS/COMPONENTS
1970 = 10
AMP, Inc., Advanced Micro Devices, Intel Corp., Motorola, Nat'l. Semiconductor, Texas Instruments
3/31/86 D .29
6/30/86 D .34
9/30/86 D .08
12/31/86 .11
3/31/87 .65
ENTERTAINMENT
1941-1943 = 10
Disney, Lorimar-Telepictures MCA, Warner Comm.
Earns. 12 mos.
9/30/83 D4.03
12/31/83 D6.44
3/31/84 D5.48
FINANCE COS. - PERSONAL LOAN
Beneficial, Household
'76 '77 '78 '79 '80 '81 '82 '83 '84 '85 '86 '87

STOCK MARKET AVERAGES BY INDUSTRY GROUP (*continued*)

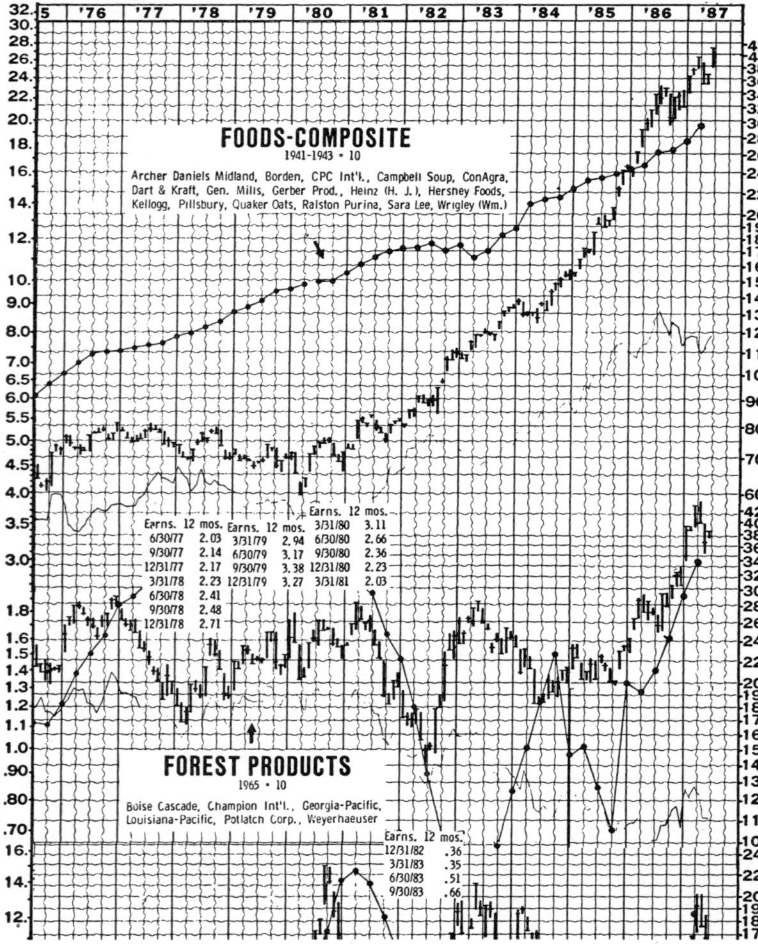

FOODS-COMPOSITE

1941-1943 = 10

Archer Daniels Midland, Borden, CPC Int'l., Campbell Soup, ConAgra, Dart & Kraft, Gen. Mills, Gerber Prod., Heinz (H. J.), Hershey Foods, Kellogg, Pillsbury, Quaker Oats, Ralston Purina, Sara Lee, Wrigley (Wm.)

FOREST PRODUCTS

1965 = 10

Boise Cascade, Champion Int'l., Georgia-Pacific, Louisiana-Pacific, Potlatch Corp., Weyerhaeuser

Earns. 12 mos.	
6/30/77	2.03
9/30/77	2.14
12/31/77	2.17
3/31/78	2.23
6/30/78	2.41
9/30/78	2.48
12/31/78	2.71

Earns. 12 mos.	
3/31/79	2.94
6/30/79	3.17
9/30/79	3.38
12/31/79	3.27

Earns. 12 mos.	
3/31/80	3.11
6/30/80	2.66
9/30/80	2.36
12/31/80	2.23
3/31/81	2.03

Earns. 12 mos.	
12/31/82	.36
3/31/83	.35
6/30/83	.51
9/30/83	.66

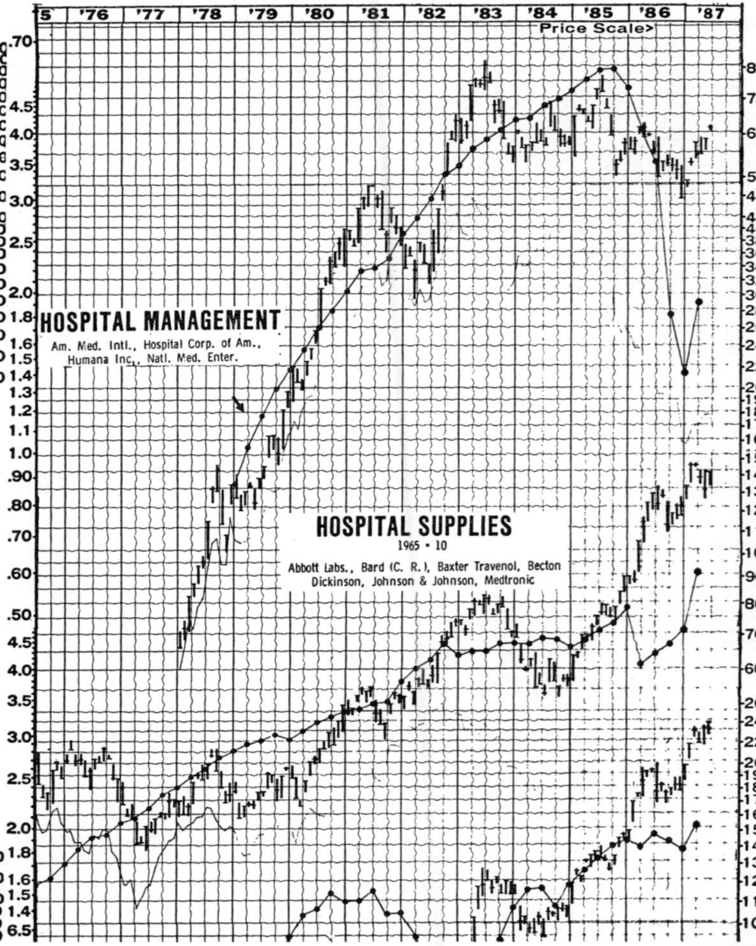

HOSPITAL MANAGEMENT

Am. Med. Intl., Hospital Corp. of Am., Humana Inc., Natl. Med. Enter.

HOSPITAL SUPPLIES

1965 = 10

Abbott Labs., Bard (C. R.), Baxter Travenol, Becton Dickinson, Johnson & Johnson, Medtronic

Price Scale>

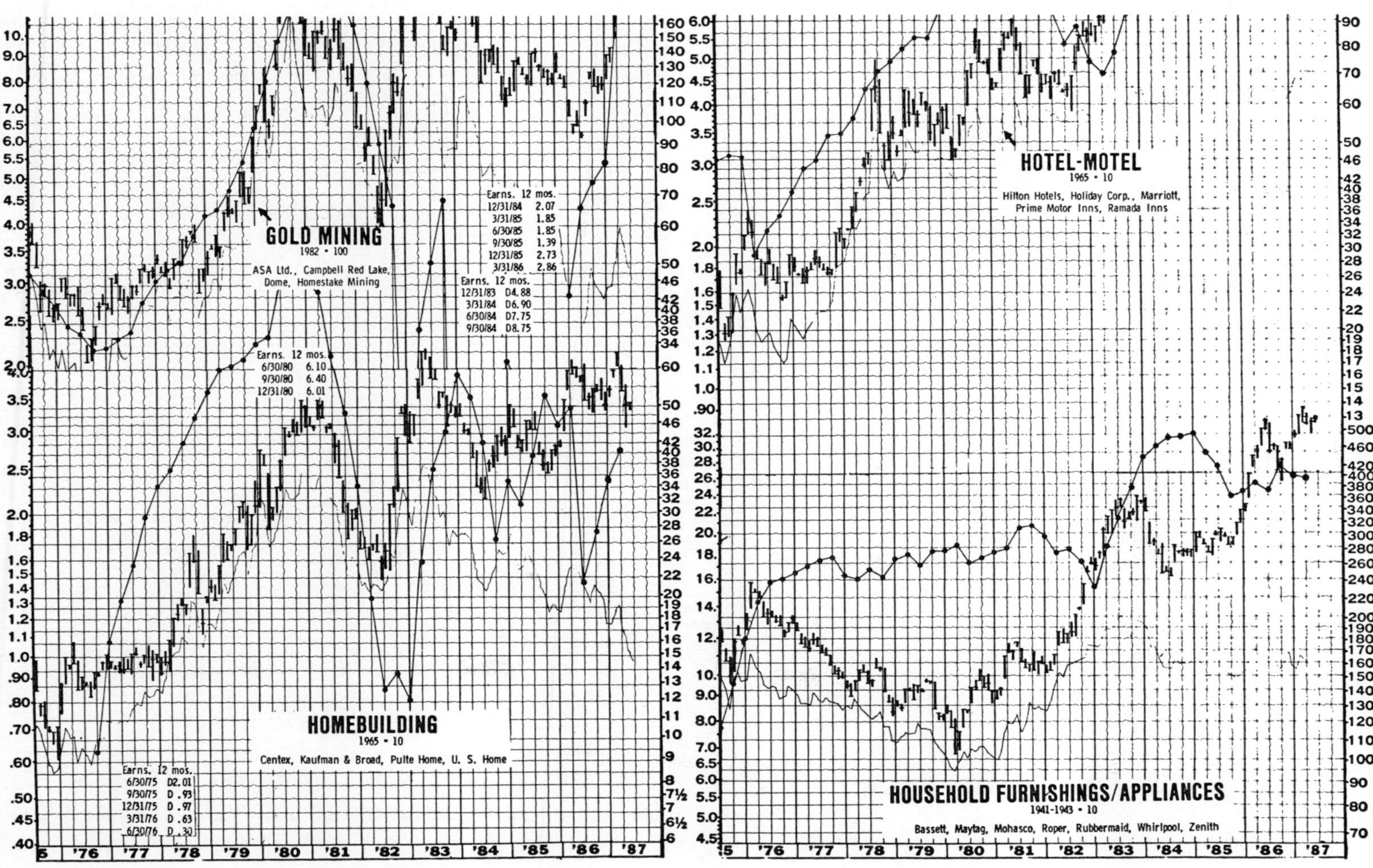
GOLD MINING
1982 = 100
ASA Ltd., Campbell Red Lake, Dome, Homestake Mining
Earns. 12 mos.
12/31/84 2.07
3/31/85 1.85
6/30/85 1.85
9/30/85 1.39
12/31/85 2.73
3/31/86 2.86
Earns. 12 mos.
12/31/83 D4.88
3/31/84 D6.90
6/30/84 D7.75
9/30/84 D8.75
Earns. 12 mos.
6/30/80 6.10
9/30/80 6.40
12/31/80 6.01
HOMEBUILDING
1965 = 10
Centex, Kaufman & Broad, Pulte Home, U. S. Home
Earns. 12 mos.
6/30/75 D2.01
9/30/75 D .93
12/31/75 D .97
3/31/76 D .63
6/30/76 D .30
HOTEL-MOTEL
1965 = 10
Hilton Hotels, Holiday Corp., Marriott, Prime Motor Inns, Ramada Inns
HOUSEHOLD FURNISHINGS/APPLIANCES
1941-1943 = 10
Bassett, Maytag, Mohasco, Roper, Rubbermaid, Whirlpool, Zenith

STOCK MARKET AVERAGES BY INDUSTRY GROUP *(continued)*

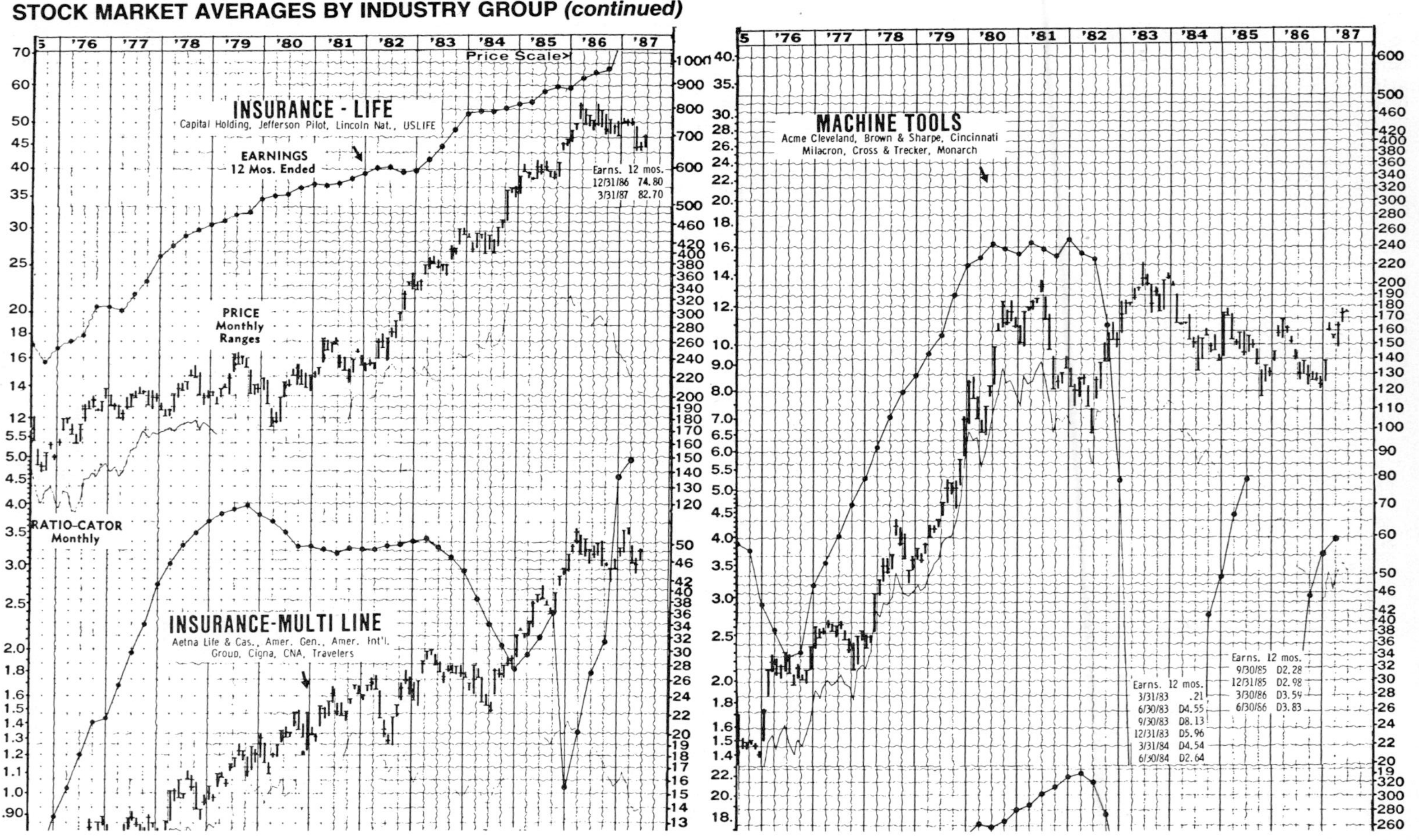

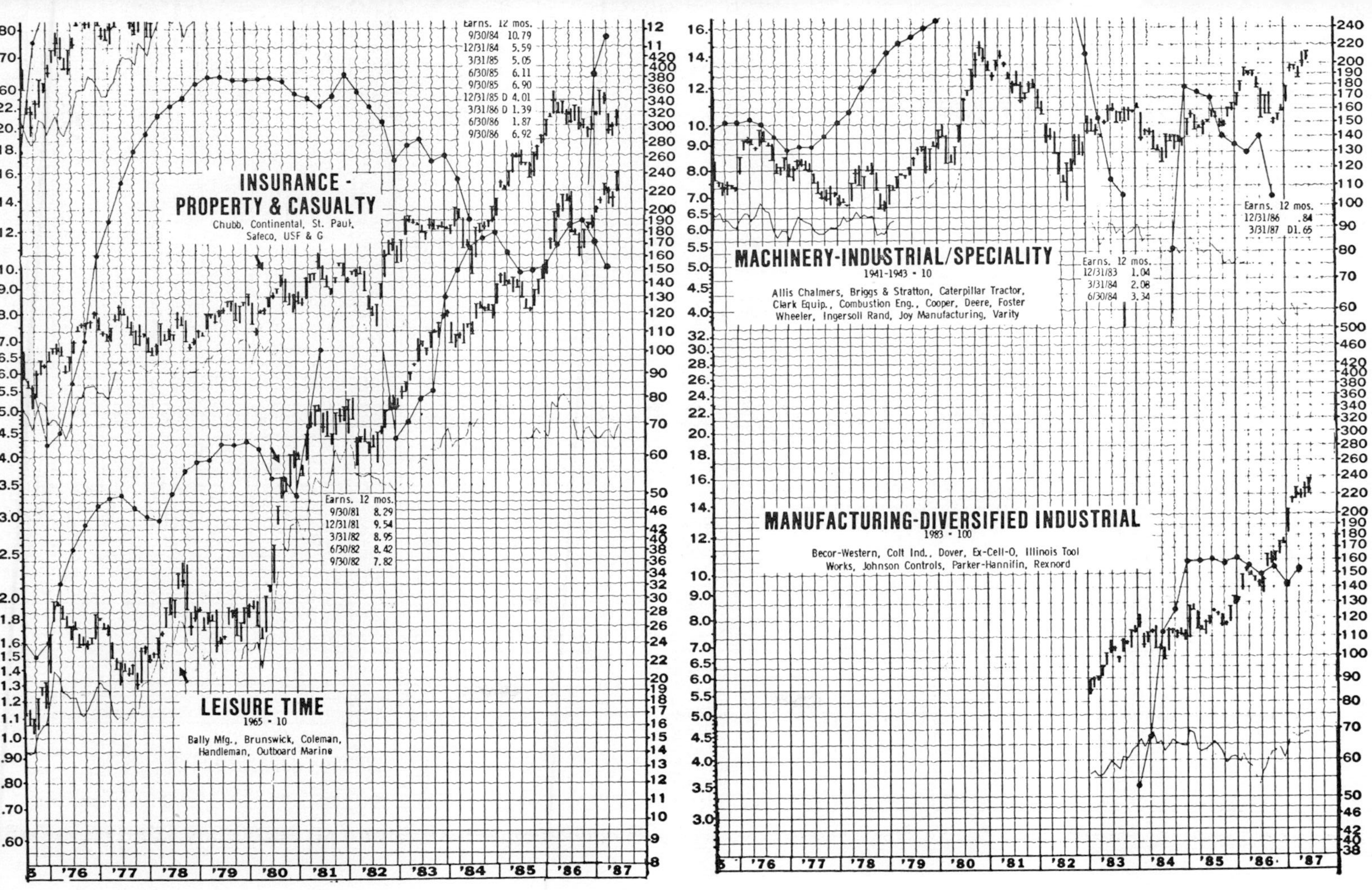

INSURANCE - PROPERTY & CASUALTY
Chubb, Continental, St. Paul, Safeco, USF & G
Earns. 12 mos.
9/30/84 10.79
12/31/84 5.59
3/31/85 5.05
6/30/85 6.11
9/30/85 6.90
12/31/85 D 4.01
3/31/86 D 1.39
6/30/86 1.87
9/30/86 6.92
LEISURE TIME
1965 - 10
Bally Mfg., Brunswick, Coleman, Handleman, Outboard Marine
Earns. 12 mos.
9/30/81 8.29
12/31/81 9.54
3/31/82 8.95
6/30/82 8.42
9/30/82 7.82
MACHINERY-INDUSTRIAL/SPECIALITY
1941-1943 - 10
Allis Chalmers, Briggs & Stratton, Caterpillar Tractor, Clark Equip., Combustion Eng., Cooper, Deere, Foster Wheeler, Ingersoll Rand, Joy Manufacturing, Varity
Earns. 12 mos.
12/31/83 1.04
3/31/84 2.08
6/30/84 3.34
Earns. 12 mos.
12/31/86 .84
3/31/87 D1.65
MANUFACTURING-DIVERSIFIED INDUSTRIAL
1983 - 100
Becor-Western, Colt Ind., Dover, Ex-Cell-O, Illinois Tool Works, Johnson Controls, Parker-Hannifin, Rexnord
'76 '77 '78 '79 '80 '81 '82 '83 '84 '85 '86 '87

STOCK MARKET AVERAGES BY INDUSTRY GROUP *(continued)*

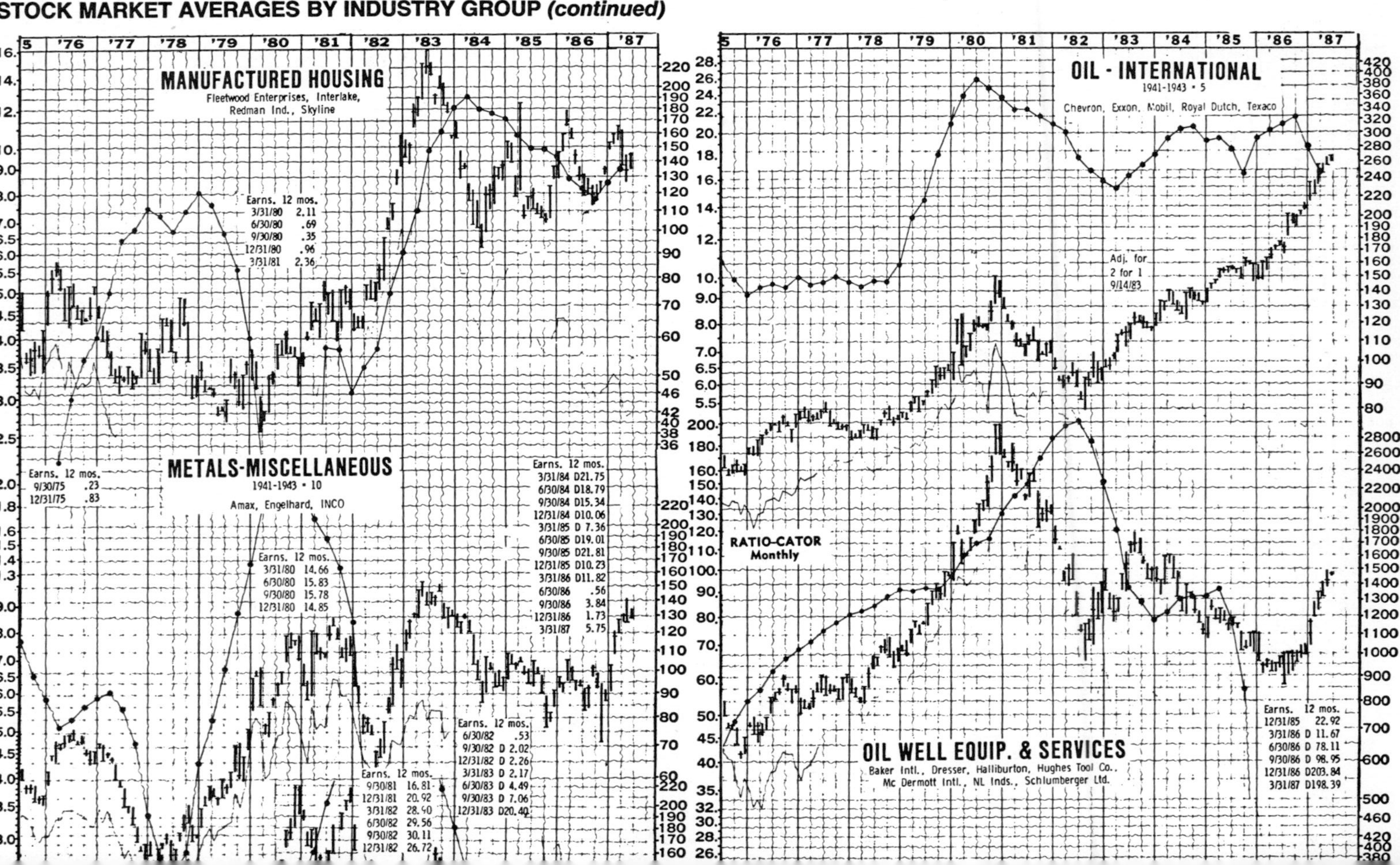

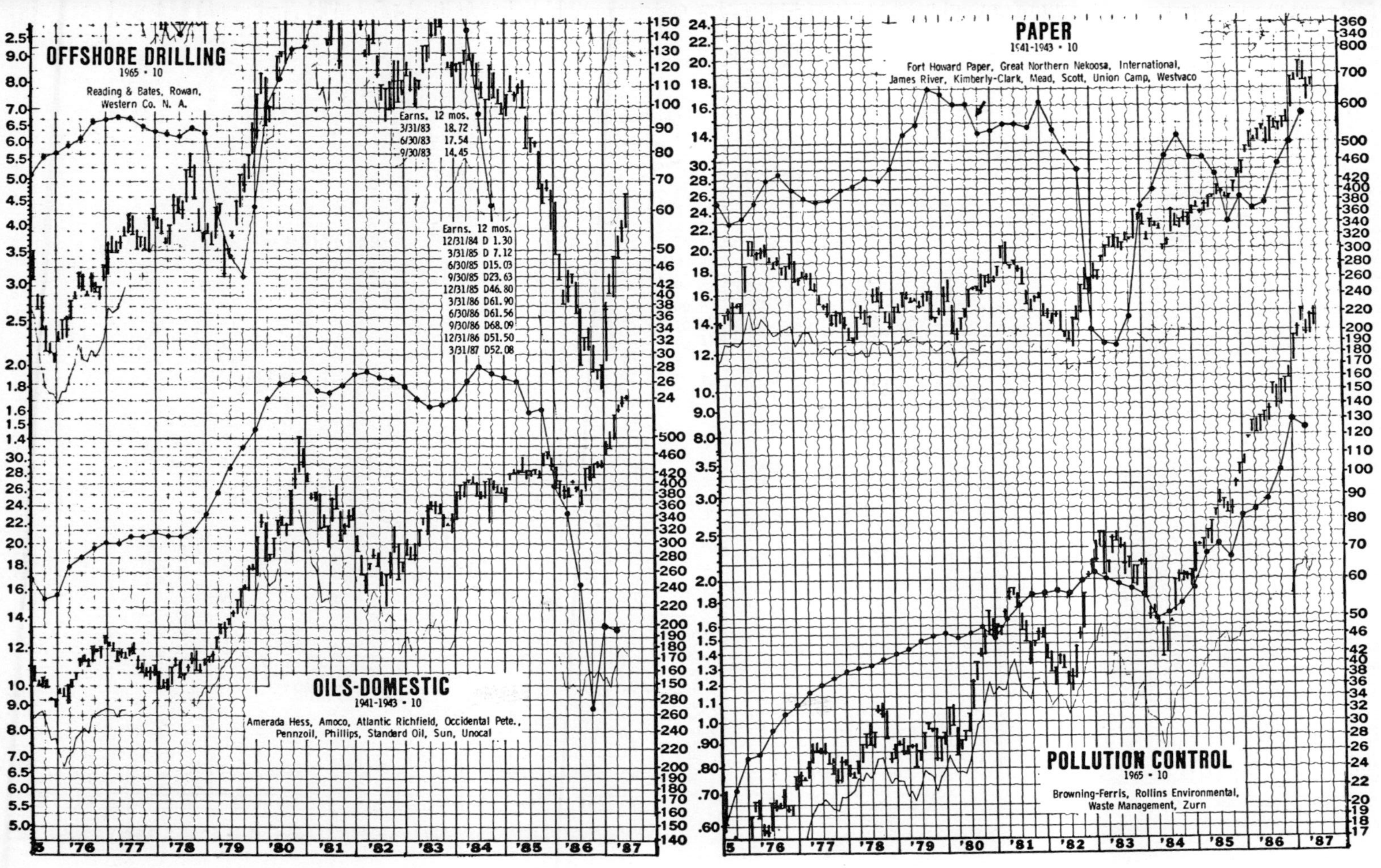
OFFSHORE DRILLING
1965 - 10
Reading & Bates, Rowan, Western Co. N. A.
Earns. 12 mos.
3/31/83 18.72
6/30/83 17.54
9/30/83 14.45
Earns. 12 mos.
12/31/84 D 1.30
3/31/85 D 7.12
6/30/85 D15.03
9/30/85 D23.63
12/31/85 D46.80
3/31/86 D61.90
6/30/86 D61.56
9/30/86 D68.09
12/31/86 D51.50
3/31/87 D52.08
OILS-DOMESTIC
1941-1943 - 10
Amerada Hess, Amoco, Atlantic Richfield, Occidental Pete., Pennzoil, Phillips, Standard Oil, Sun, Unocal
PAPER
1941-1943 - 10
Fort Howard Paper, Great Northern Nekoosa, International, James River, Kimberly-Clark, Mead, Scott, Union Camp, Westvaco
POLLUTION CONTROL
1965 - 10
Browning-Ferris, Rollins Environmental, Waste Management, Zurn
'76 '77 '78 '79 '80 '81 '82 '83 '84 '85 '86 '87

STOCK MARKET AVERAGES BY INDUSTRY GROUP *(continued)*

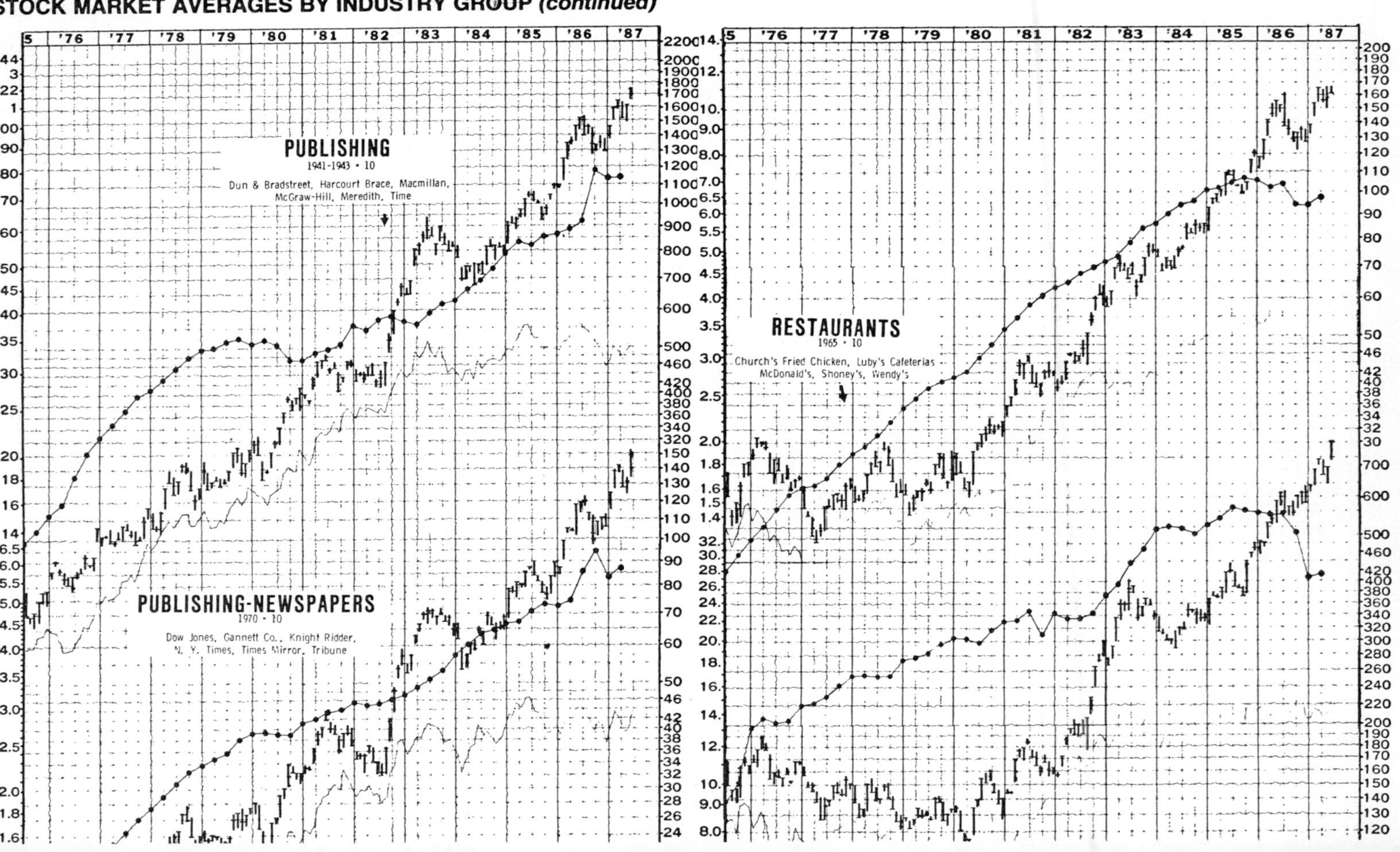

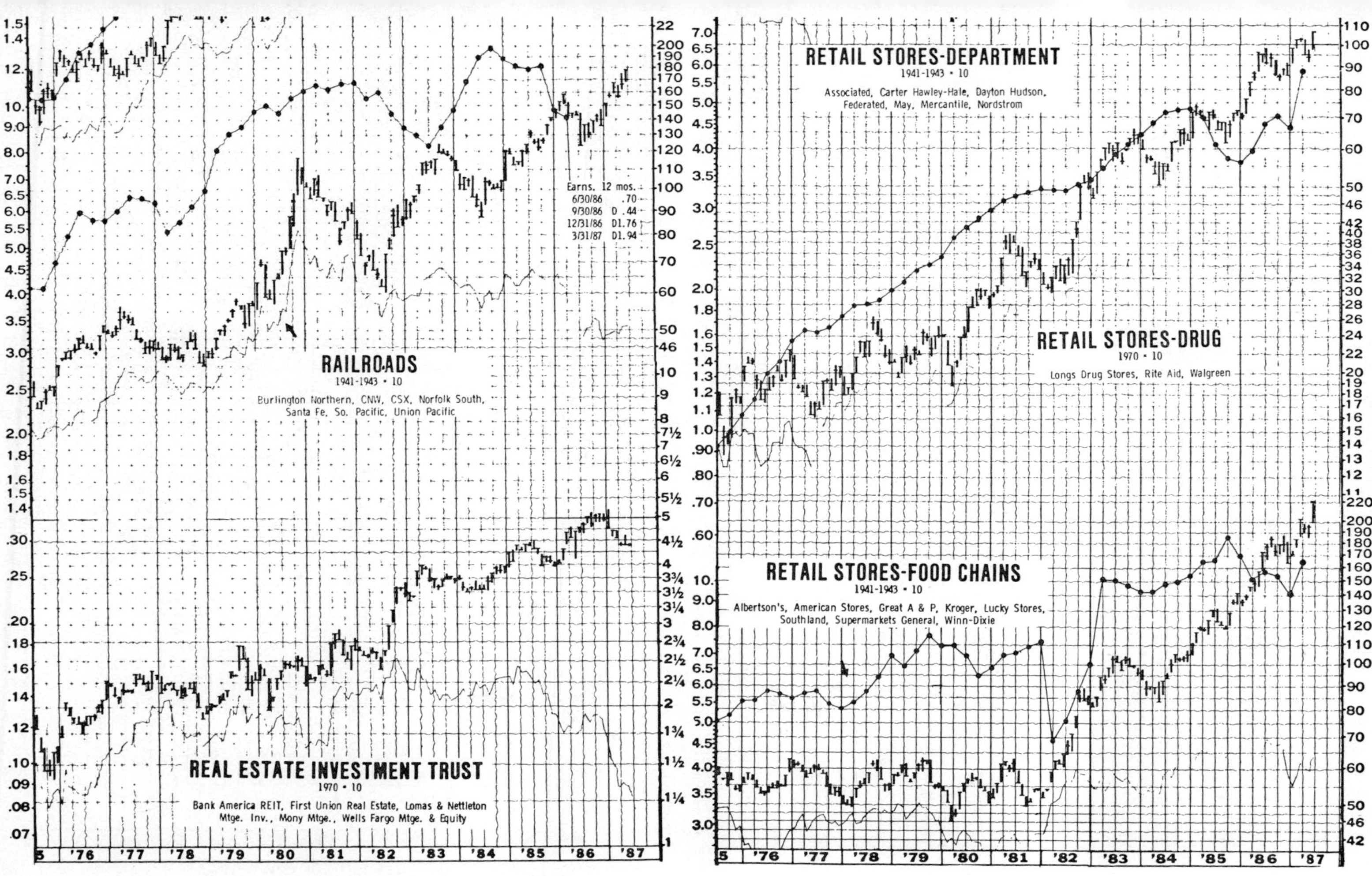
RAILROADS
1941-1943 = 10
Burlington Northern, CNW, CSX, Norfolk South, Santa Fe, So. Pacific, Union Pacific
Earns. 12 mos.
6/30/86 .70
9/30/86 D .44
12/31/86 D1.76
3/31/87 D1.94
REAL ESTATE INVESTMENT TRUST
1970 = 10
Bank America REIT, First Union Real Estate, Lomas & Nettleton Mtge. Inv., Mony Mtge., Wells Fargo Mtge. & Equity
RETAIL STORES-DEPARTMENT
1941-1943 = 10
Associated, Carter Hawley-Hale, Dayton Hudson, Federated, May, Mercantile, Nordstrom
RETAIL STORES-DRUG
1970 = 10
Longs Drug Stores, Rite Aid, Walgreen
RETAIL STORES-FOOD CHAINS
1941-1943 = 10
Albertson's, American Stores, Great A & P, Kroger, Lucky Stores, Southland, Supermarkets General, Winn-Dixie
'76 '77 '78 '79 '80 '81 '82 '83 '84 '85 '86 '87

STOCK MARKET AVERAGES BY INDUSTRY GROUP *(continued)*

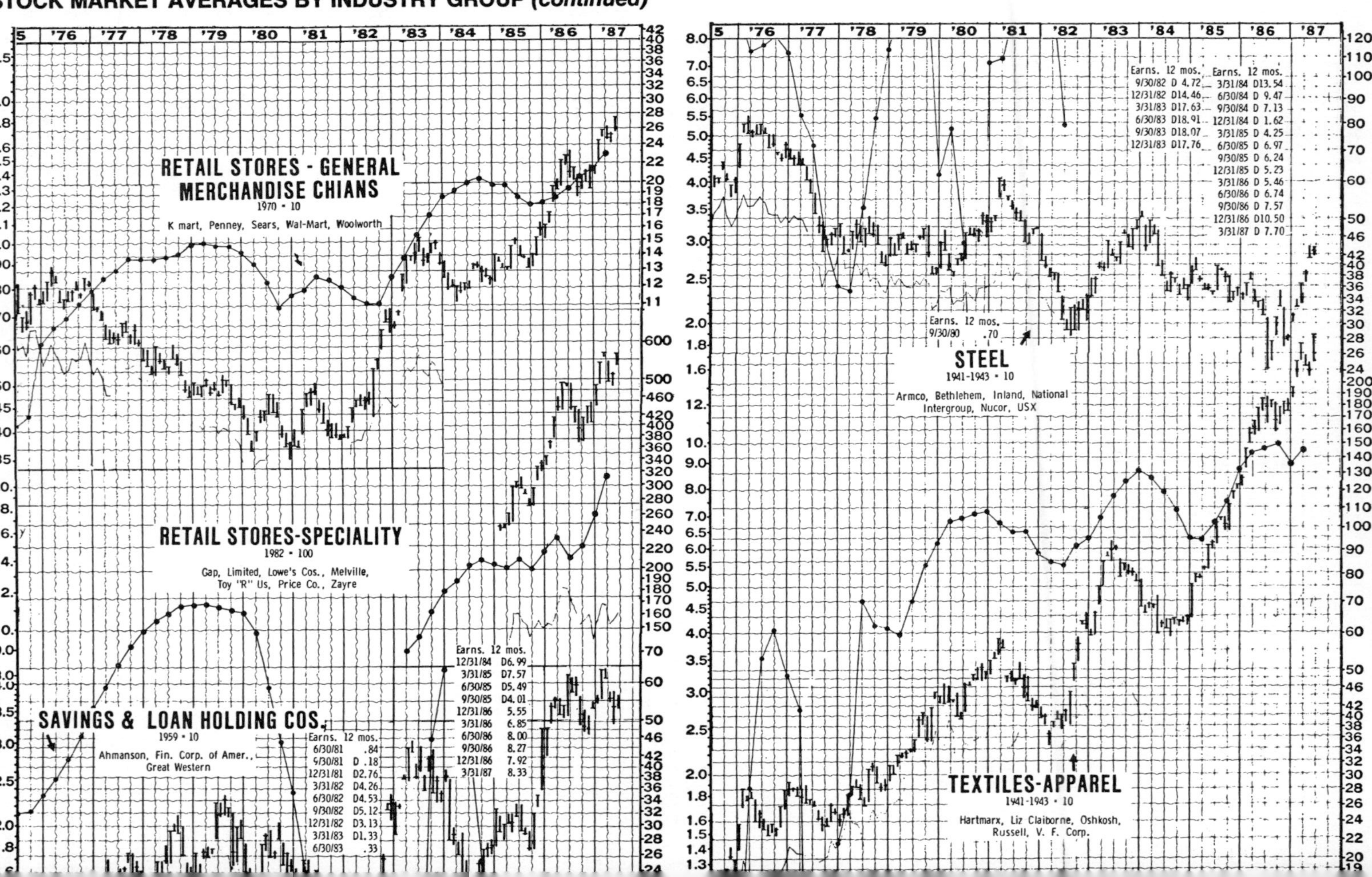

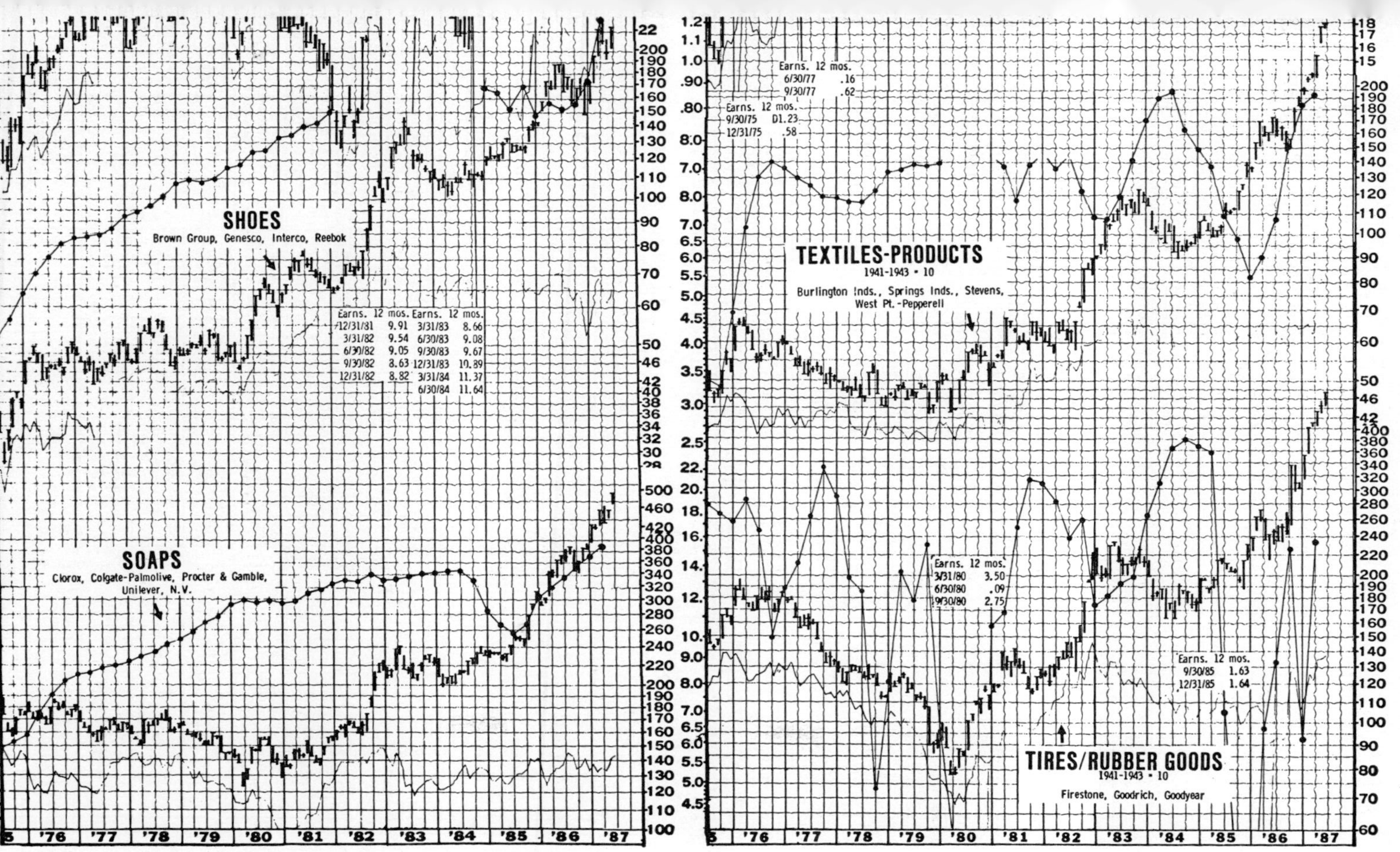

SHOES
Brown Group, Genesco, Interco, Reebok
Earns. 12 mos. Earns. 12 mos.
12/31/81 9.91 3/31/83 8.66
3/31/82 9.54 6/30/83 9.08
6/30/82 9.05 9/30/83 9.67
9/30/82 8.63 12/31/83 10.89
12/31/82 8.82 3/31/84 11.37
6/30/84 11.64
SOAPS
Clorox, Colgate-Palmolive, Procter & Gamble, Unilever, N.V.
TEXTILES-PRODUCTS
1941-1943 = 10
Burlington Inds., Springs Inds., Stevens, West Pt.-Pepperell
Earns. 12 mos.
6/30/77 .16
9/30/77 .62
Earns. 12 mos.
9/30/75 D1.23
12/31/75 .58
TIRES/RUBBER GOODS
1941-1943 = 10
Firestone, Goodrich, Goodyear
Earns. 12 mos.
3/31/80 3.50
6/30/80 .09
9/30/80 2.75
Earns. 12 mos.
9/30/85 1.63
12/31/85 1.64
'76 '77 '78 '79 '80 '81 '82 '83 '84 '85 '86 '87

STOCK MARKET AVERAGES BY INDUSTRY GROUP *(concluded)*

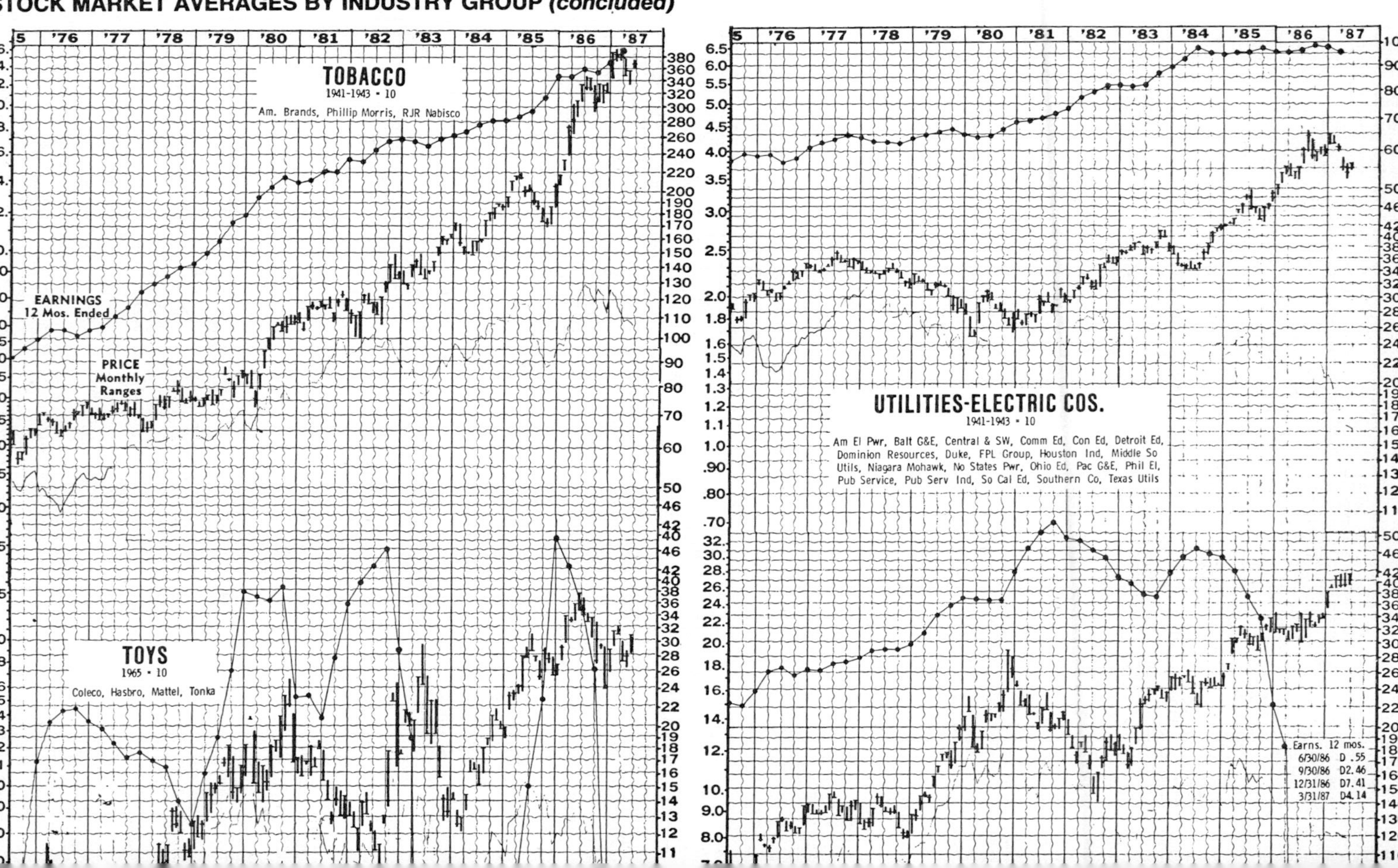

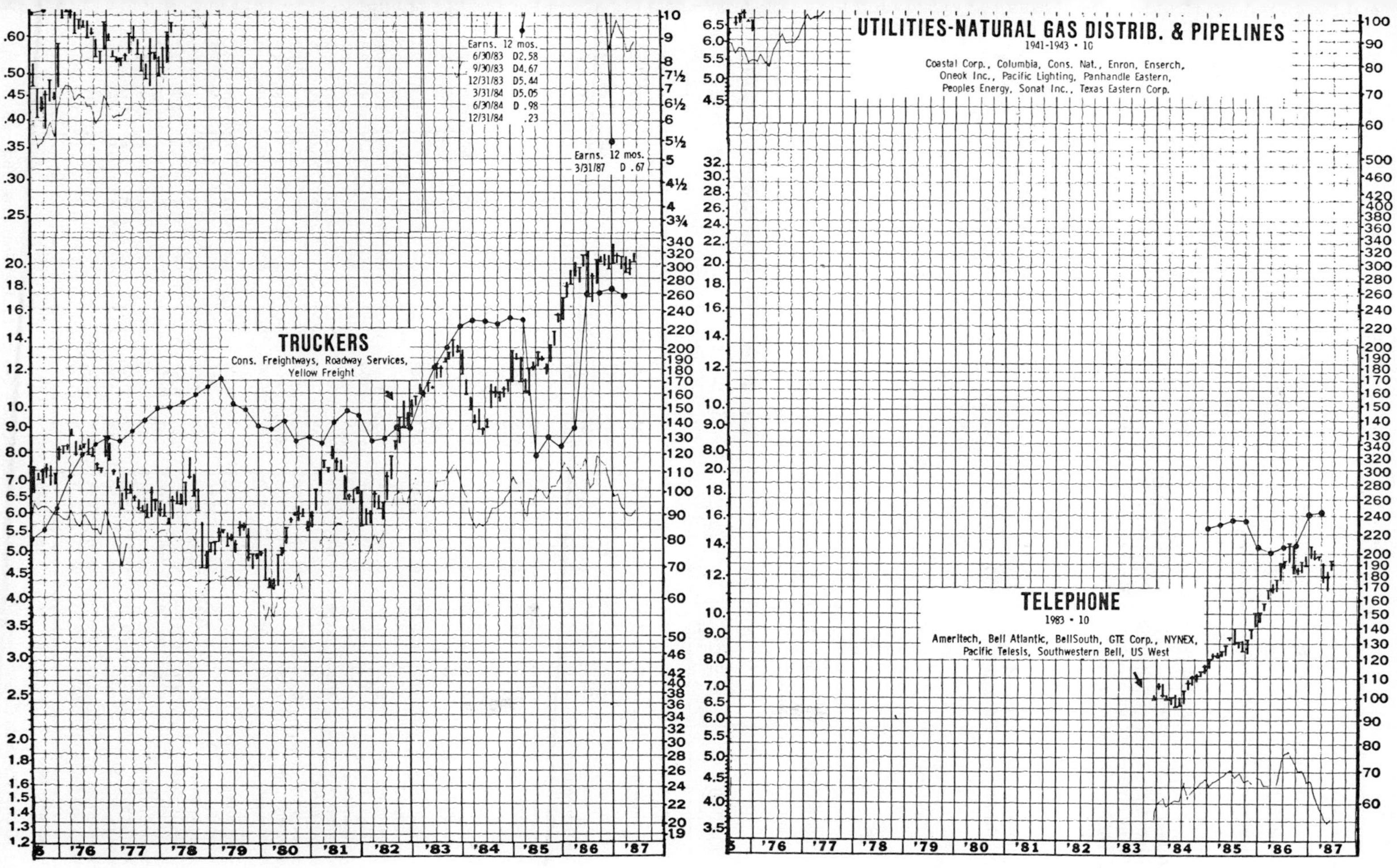

TRUCKERS
Cons. Freightways, Roadway Services, Yellow Freight
Earns. 12 mos.
6/30/83 D2.58
9/30/83 D4.67
12/31/83 D5.44
3/31/84 D5.05
6/30/84 D .98
12/31/84 .23
Earns. 12 mos.
3/31/87 D .67
UTILITIES-NATURAL GAS DISTRIB. & PIPELINES
1941-1943 · 10
Coastal Corp., Columbia, Cons. Nat., Enron, Enserch, Oneok Inc., Pacific Lighting, Panhandle Eastern, Peoples Energy, Sonat Inc., Texas Eastern Corp.
TELEPHONE
1983 · 10
Ameritech, Bell Atlantic, BellSouth, GTE Corp., NYNEX, Pacific Telesis, Southwestern Bell, US West
'76 '77 '78 '79 '80 '81 '82 '83 '84 '85 '86 '87

Components-Dow Jones 65 Stock Averages

INDUSTRIALS

Allied Sig.	Exxon	Philip Morris
Alum Co	Gen Electric	Primerica
Amer Exp	Gen Motors	Proc Gamb
AT&T	Goodyear	Sears
Beth Steel	IBM	Texaco
Boeing	Int'l Paper	Union Carbide
Chevron	McDonald's	United Tech
Coca-Cola	Merck	USX Corp.
Du Pont	Minn M&M	Westinghouse
Eastman	Navistar	Woolworth

TRANSPORTATION

AMR Corp.	Cons Freight	Piedmont
Allegis	Delta Air	Ryder System
Amer Pres	Fed Express	Santa Fe
Burlington	Leaseway	TWA
CSX Corp.	NWA Inc.	Union Pac
Canadian Pac	Norfolk So	USAir
Caro Freight	Pan Am	

UTILITIES

Am El Power	Cons N Gas	Panhandle
Centerior	Detroit Edis	Peoples En
Colum-Gas	Houston Ind	Phila Elec
Comwlth Edis	Niag Mohawk	Pub Serv E
Cons Edison	Pacific G&E	Sou Cal Edis

FINANCIAL DATA ON DOW JONES INDUSTRIALS

	History				Earnings			P/E Ratio			Dvds	
	52-Week		5-Year		Last	%	5-Yr		5-Year Avg		Indic.	
	High	Low	High	Low	12Mos	Ch	Growth	Today	High	Low	Amt	Yield
	$	$	$	$	$	%	%	-	-	-	$	%
Dow Jones Ind	2510.04	1755.20	2510.04	776.92	120.87	9.73	28	20.6	44.8	13.3	67.55	2.7
Allied-Signal	49.25	37.63	NC	NC	3.27	NE	NC	13.9	NC	NC	1.80	4.0
Alum Co Am	60.00	32.63	60.00	21.88	3.63	NE	NC	16.5	18.0	11.6	1.20	2.0
Am Express Co	40.63	26.88	40.63	8.81	1.63	-32.64	8	20.7	15.0	9.2	.76	2.3
Am Tel & T	32.13	22.13	NC	NC	.32	-78.52	NC	95.7	NC	NC	1.20	3.9
Bethlehem Stl	19.38	4.63	29.50	4.63	-1.12	NE	NC	NE	NC	NC	.00	.0
Boeing Co	62.25	42.75	64.88	10.00	4.09	3.54	12	11.6	12.3	7.7	1.40	3.0
Chevron Cp	64.63	34.25	64.63	23.50	1.57	-65.80	-16	38.1	12.1	8.4	2.40	4.0
Coca Cola Co	49.00	32.88	49.00	9.91	2.61	32.49	15	18.0	15.2	10.1	1.12	2.4
Dupont	127.25	73.00	127.25	30.00	6.30	10.53	5	19.9	12.6	8.5	3.20	2.6
Eastman Kodak	92.00	52.38	92.00	40.19	2.23	88.98	-20	39.3	26.7	18.8	2.52	2.9
Exxon	95.50	58.25	95.50	24.88	6.57	-7.46	7	14.1	7.8	5.7	3.60	3.9
Gen Electric	57.25	35.31	57.25	13.75	2.62	-.38	7	21.7	13.6	9.9	1.32	2.3
Gen Motors	92.38	65.88	92.38	34.00	7.72	-36.36	40	11.2	10.2	6.6	5.00	5.8
Goodyear Tire	70.50	30.00	70.50	17.88	5.70	129.84	-8	12.3	16.5	10.3	1.60	2.3
Intl Bus Mach	169.88	115.75	169.88	55.63	7.29	-30.77	3	22.1	15.1	10.6	4.40	2.7
Intl Paper	57.81	30.38	57.81	16.38	3.71	187.60	8	12.4	20.9	15.1	1.25	2.7
McDonald's Cp	57.94	36.94	57.94	11.50	2.55	11.84	13	21.0	15.2	10.0	.50	.9
Merck & Co	185.38	97.00	185.38	32.00	5.69	33.57	14	31.6	18.5	12.4	2.20	1.2
Minn Mng Mfg	73.00	49.56	73.00	24.38	3.54	19.19	4	20.2	15.5	11.6	1.86	2.6
Navistar Intl	8.75	4.13	14.75	2.75	-.22	-100.00	NC	NE	NC	NC	.00	.0
Philip Morris	98.75	63.00	98.75	22.06	8.54	48.78	20	11.2	10.8	7.4	3.00	3.1
Primerica	53.50	35.75	53.50	12.88	3.19	3.57	25	13.1	16.8	11.4	1.60	3.8
Proct & Gambl	99.38	65.88	99.38	38.88	4.56	9.88	-2	20.2	15.0	11.0	2.70	2.9
Sears, Roebuck	56.00	39.00	56.00	15.75	3.85	11.59	10	13.4	12.1	7.9	2.00	3.9
vjTexaco	47.50	27.38	48.38	26.00	2.13	-59.04	-16	22.2	16.5	11.2	.00	.0
Union Carbide	32.50	20.00	33.13	10.91	1.43	NE	NC	19.1	19.1	11.6	1.50	5.5
Utd Technol	55.75	39.25	56.25	15.63	.09	-95.57	-40	NM	51.4	35.8	1.40	2.6
USX Cp	38.75	14.50	38.75	14.50	-5.55	-100.00	NC	NE	10.2	7.2	1.20	3.3
Westinghouse	68.38	50.50	68.38	10.94	4.79	22.82	15	13.6	11.4	7.1	1.72	2.6
Woolworth FW	57.75	37.00	57.75	7.94	3.48	21.68	NC	16.2	11.5	7.1	1.32	2.3
Unweighted Avg	69.10	42.49	71.88	19.91	3.21	1.13	4	21.9	16.1	10.9	1.79	2.7

Source: *The Media General Financial Weekly,* Media General Financial Services, 301 East Grace Street, Richmond, VA 23219, July 27, 1987.

DOW JONES INDUSTRIAL, TRANSPORTATION AND UTILITY AVERAGES

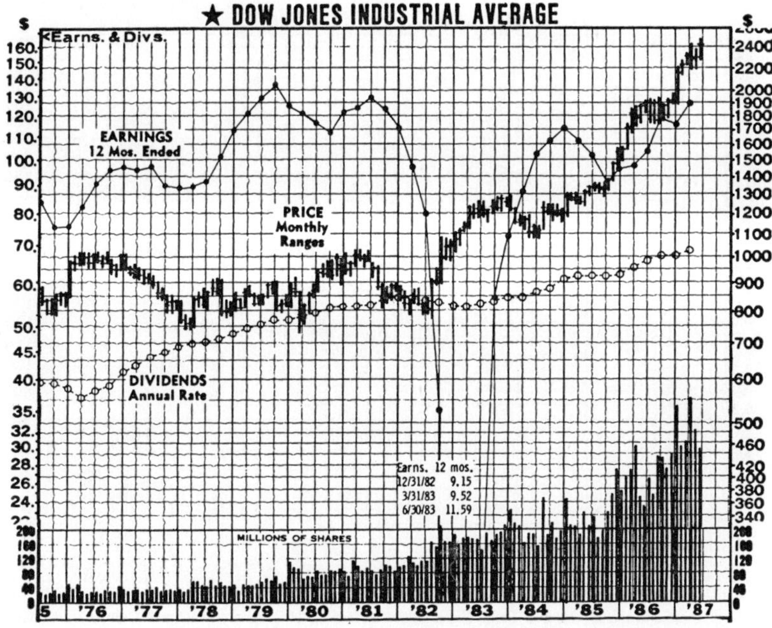

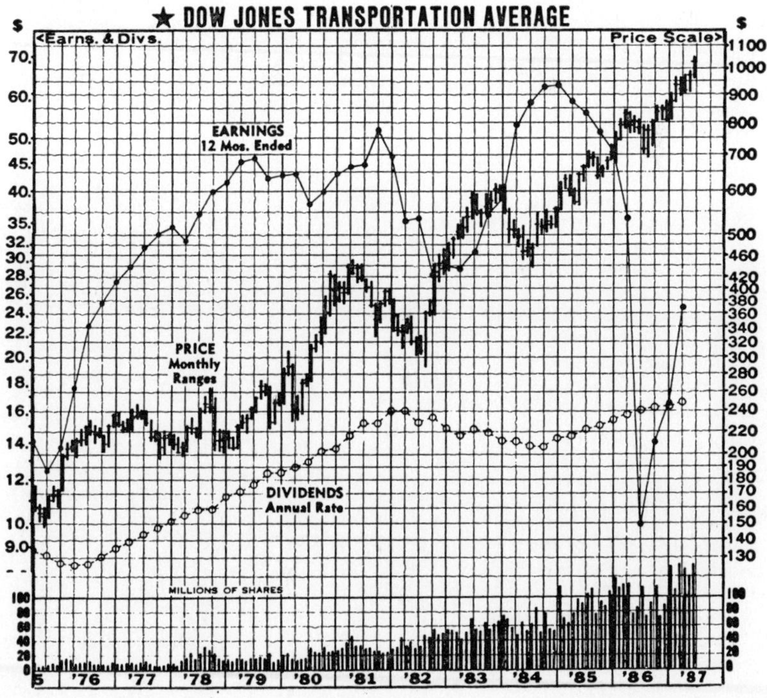

DOW JONES INDUSTRIAL, TRANSPORTATION AND UTILITY AVERAGES *(concluded)*

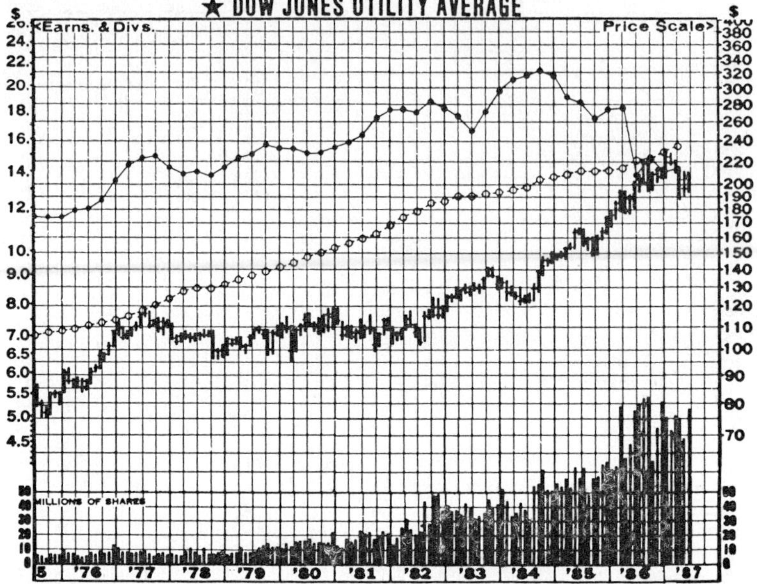

Source: *5-Trend CYCLI-GRAPHS.* The charts are courtesy of Securities Research Company, a Division of Babson-United Investment Advisors, Inc., 208 Newbury Street, Boston, MA 02116, July quarterly edition, 1987.

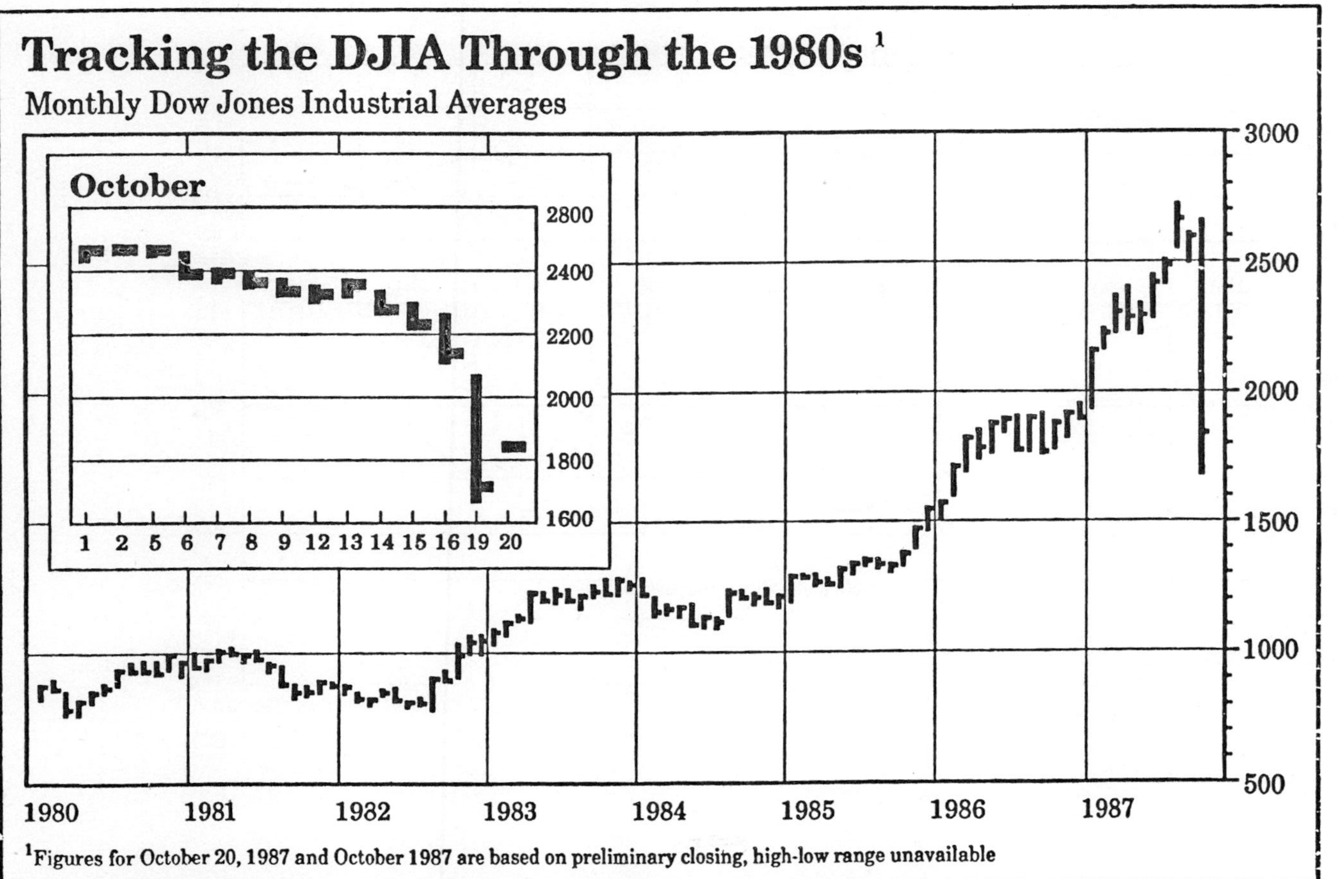

[1]Figures for October 20, 1987 and October 1987 are based on preliminary closing, high-low range unavailable

Source: "Reprinted by permission of *The Wall Street Journal*, © Dow Jones & Company, Inc. 1987. ALL RIGHTS RESERVED."

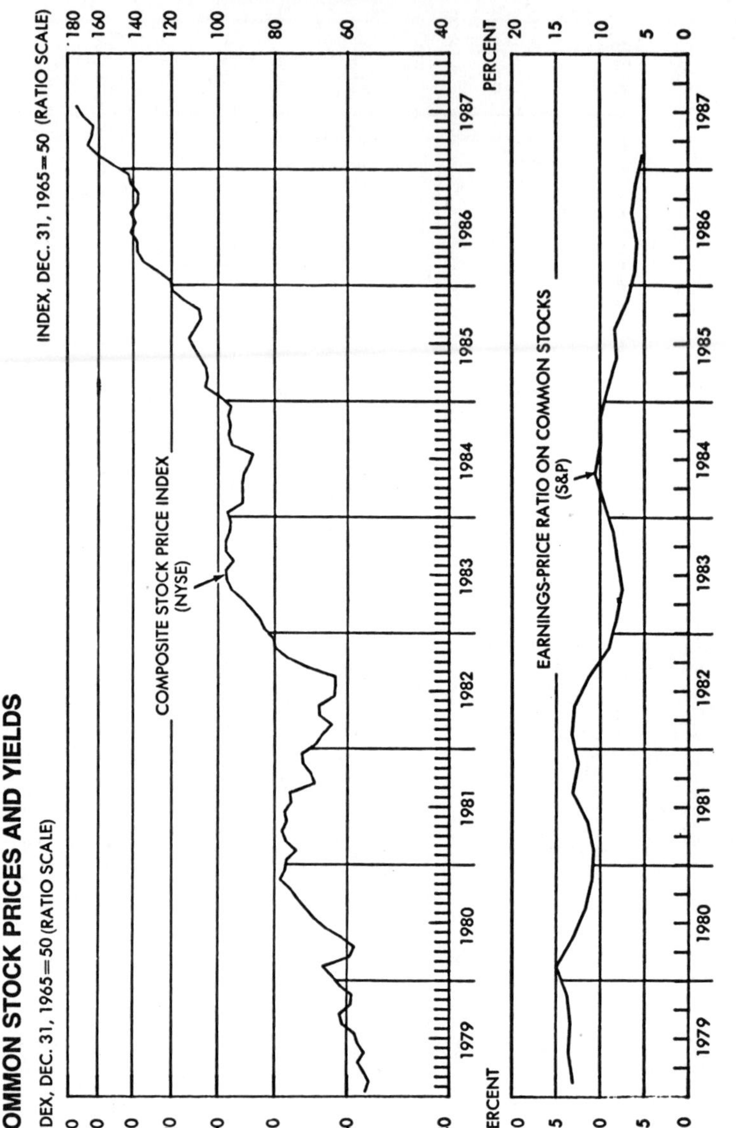
COMMON STOCK PRICES AND YIELDS
INDEX, DEC. 31, 1965=50 (RATIO SCALE)
INDEX, DEC. 31, 1965=50 (RATIO SCALE)
180
160
140
120
100
80
60
40
COMPOSITE STOCK PRICE INDEX
(NYSE)
PERCENT
20
15
10
5
0
EARNINGS-PRICE RATIO ON COMMON STOCKS
(S&P)
1979
1980
1981
1982
1983
1984
1985
1986
1987
SOURCES: NEW YORK STOCK EXCHANGE AND STANDARD & POOR'S CORPORATION
COUNCIL OF ECONOMIC ADVISERS

Period	Common stock prices [1]							Common stock yields (percent) [5]	
	New York Stock Exchange indexes (Dec. 31, 1965=50) [2]					Dow-Jones industrial average [3]	Standard & Poor's composite index (1941–43=10) [4]	Dividend-price ratio	Earnings-price ratio
	Composite	Industrial	Transportation	Utility	Finance				
1981	74.02	85.44	72.61	38.91	73.52	932.92	128.05	5.20	11.96
1982	68.93	78.18	60.41	39.75	71.99	884.36	119.71	5.81	11.60
1983	92.63	107.45	89.36	47.00	95.34	1,190.34	160.41	4.40	8.03
1984	92.46	108.01	85.63	46.44	89.28	1,178.48	160.46	4.64	10.02
1985	108.09	123.79	104.11	56.75	114.21	1,328.23	186.84	4.25	8.12
1986	136.00	155.85	119.87	71.36	147.20	1,792.76	236.34	3.49	r 6.09
1986: July	138.32	158.06	112.03	74.20	150.23	1,809.92	240.18	3.43	
Aug	140.91	160.10	111.24	77.84	152.90	1,843.45	245.00	3.36	
Sept	137.06	156.52	114.06	74.56	145.56	1,813.47	238.27	3.43	6.42
Oct	136.74	156.56	120.04	73.38	143.89	1,817.04	237.36	3.49	
Nov	140.84	162.10	122.27	75.77	142.97	1,883.65	245.09	3.40	
Dec	142.12	163.85	121.26	76.07	144.29	1,924.07	248.61	3.38	r 5.98
1987: Jan	151.17	175.60	126.61	78.54	153.32	2,065.13	264.51	3.17	
Feb	160.23	189.17	135.49	78.19	158.41	2,202.34	280.93	3.02	
Mar	166.43	198.95	138.55	77.15	162.41	2,292.61	292.47	2.93	5.20
Apr	163.88	199.03	137.91	72.74	150.52	2,302.64	289.32	2.99	
May	163.00	198.78	141.30	71.64	145.97	2,291.11	289.12	3.02	
June r	169.58	206.61	150.39	74.25	152.73	2,384.02	301.38	2.92	
July	174.28	214.12	157.48	74.18	152.25	2,481.72	310.09	2.83	
Week ended:									
1987: July 4	171.60	209.35	153.20	75.00	153.15	2,427.98	305.12	2.87	
11	172.92	211.87	154.74	74.49	152.16	2,450.10	307.30	2.84	
18	174.96	215.19	157.40	74.37	151.98	2,485.01	311.20	2.81	
25	173.77	213.88	158.04	73.30	151.21	2,476.62	309.10	2.84	
Aug 1	176.73	217.70	161.21	74.28	153.45	2,538.55	315.07	2.78	

[1] Average of daily closing prices.
[2] Includes all the stocks (more than 1,500) listed on the NYSE.
[3] Includes 30 stocks.
[4] Includes 500 stocks.
[5] Standard & Poor's series. Dividend-price ratios based on Wednesday closing prices. Earnings-price ratios based on prices at end of quarter.

NOTE.—All data relate to stocks listed on the New York Stock Exchange (NYSE).

Sources: New York Stock Exchange, Dow-Jones & Company, Inc., and Standard & Poor's Corporation.

Source: *Economic Indicators*, Council of Economic Indicators.

NEW SECURITY ISSUES OF CORPORATIONS
Millions of dollars

Type of issue or issuer, or use	1984	1985	1986	1986					1987		
				Aug.	Sept.	Oct.	Nov.	Dec.	Jan.	Feb.ʳ	Mar.
1 **All issues**[1]	**132,531**	**155,074**	**294,326**	**24,245**	**16,093**	**28,582**	**28,835**	**25,181**	**23,133ʳ**	**23,986**	**32,799**
2 **Bonds**[2]	**109,903**	**155,074**	**294,326**	**18,481**	**12,830**	**23,476**	**22,236**	**18,933**	**20,218ʳ**	**20,219**	**22,983**
Type of offering											
3 Public	73,579	119,559	232,496	18,481	12,829ʳ	23,476	22,236	18,933	20,218ʳ	20,219	22,983
4 Private placement	36,324	46,195	n.a.	n.a.	n.a.	n.a.	n.a.	n.a.	n.a.	n.a.	n.a.
Industry group											
5 Manufacturing	24,607	52,128	53,358	4,536	2,345	2,055	3,378	3,276	4,165	3,679	6,349
6 Commercial and miscellaneous	13,726	15,140	19,188	1,030	1,387	1,067	1,213	2,067	1,074	1,714	3,723
7 Transportation	4,694	5,743	4,262	550	375	170	0	70	0	100	521
8 Public utility	10,679	12,957	25,585	2,098	1,915	2,537	2,587	2,498	1,491	2,715	694
9 Communication	2,997	10,456	13,430	1,615	417	1,255	1,158	776	65	250	300
10 Real estate and financial	53,199	69,332	116,675	8,652	6,390	16,392	13,901	9,736	13,423ʳ	11,762	11,397
11 **Stocks**[3]	**22,628**	**35,515**	**61,830**	**5,764**	**3,263**	**5,106**	**6,599**	**6,248**	**2,915**	**3,767**	**9,816**
Type											
12 Preferred	4,118	6,505	11,514	1,290	402	817	1,390	1,293	429	905	2,321
13 Common	18,510	29,010	50,316	4,474	2,861	4,289	5,209	4,955	2,486	2,862	7,495
Industry group											
14 Manufacturing	4,054	5,700	14,234	982	250	570	2,565	1,781	365	814	2,134
15 Commercial and miscellaneous	6,277	9,149	9,252	803	1,009	1,271	535	709	148	437	2,264
16 Transportation	589	1,544	2,392	57	28	511	15	183	0	191	299
17 Public utility	1,624	1,966	3,791	208	174	410	218	873	237	509	893
18 Communication	419	978	1,504	379	0	59	104	101	16	9	57
19 Real estate and financial	9,665	16,178	30,657	3,335	1,802	2,285	3,162	2,601	2,149	1,807	4,169

1. Figures, which represent gross proceeds of issues maturing in more than one year, sold for cash in the United States, are principal amount or number of units multiplied by offering price. Excludes offerings of less than $100,000, secondary offerings, undefined or exempted issues as defined in the Securities Act of 1933, employee stock plans, investment companies other than closed-end, intracorporate transactions, and sales to foreigners.

2. Monthly data include only public offerings.

3. Beginning in August 1981, gross stock offerings include new equity volume from swaps of debt for equity.

SOURCES. IDD Information Services, Inc., Securities and Exchange Commission and the Board of Governors of the Federal Reserve System.

Source: *Federal Reserve Bulletin,* Board of Governors of the Federal Reserve System.

How to Understand and Analyze Financial Statements*

Fred B. Renwick†

Analyzing financial statements in corporate annual reports can be easy, fun, and rewarding, if you know what to look for. This short essay explains in a nutshell what to look for and how to analyze financial statements.

Only four statements are important to understand and analyze, namely:

- The *balance sheet*, which states the financial condition of the corporation as of one particular date: the date posted at the top of the statement.
- The *income statement*, which shows the amount of earnings for the year currently ending, and conveys information regarding the efficiency and profitability of the business.
- The *statement of retained earnings*, which gives further information regarding one of the lines on the balance sheet, and also shows the division of net income for the year between dividend payout to stockholders and earnings retained and reinvested in the business.
- The *statement of sources and uses of funds*, which gives further information regarding total current assets and total current liabilities as stated on the balance sheet; and shows the net changes during the year in working capital.

Additionally, corporate annual reports usually contain supplementary information which expands upon items in the four basic statements, and includes: (1) a letter or report of independent accountants and auditors addressed to stockholders and directors of the company certifying and validating the figures in the four statements, (2) notes which report material information regarding line items in each statement, (3) segment information which summarizes selected information by industry and geographic segments, (4) restatement pursuant to Financial Accounting Standards Board (FASB) *Statement of Financial Accounting Standards No. 33* to account for effects of inflation and changing prices on items in the four primary statements, and (5) a long-term (5 or 10-year) summary of selected items from the four primary statements.

The following section explains each statement in detail, Section II explains how to analyze the statements, Section III explains notes and supplementary information.

1. FOUR FINANCIAL STATEMENTS: WHAT TO LOOK FOR

BALANCE SHEETS

Exhibit 1 shows a balance sheet for Universal Manufacturing Corporation (UMC), a hypothetical company which produces and distributes goods and services in the health industry. Universal's single line of business is divided into two industry segments: human and animal health products, and environmental health products and services.

Observe the format of Universal's balance sheet, the *report form*, where total assets, $26 million, are itemized first and total financing (total liabilities and stockholders' equity), $26 million, are itemized below the asset section. Some corporations prefer to use the *account form*, where assets are listed on the left side of the form and liabilities and owners' equity sections are listed to the right of the asset section. UMC is using the *report form*.

The balance sheet shows the ownership of total corporate assets as of the date of the statement. For example, the following calculation implies that if UMC's tangible assets were liquidated as of the date posted at the top of the balance sheet, $17.8 million would be available for distribution among the preferred and common stockholders.

Total assets owned by UMC	$26,000,000
Less: Intangibles	200,000
Total tangible assets owned by UMC	$25,800,000
Amount required to pay total liabilities	8,000,000
Amount remaining for the stockholders	$17,800,000

Further, the above example illustrates a critical point: the difference between *current market value* (the amount UMC's assets would really bring if sold) versus the *accounting book value* (the $17.8 million). Relationships exist between market and book values, but accounting statements (except for FASB *No. 33*) are factual reports of *book*, not *market*, values of corporate assets.

The following paragraphs explain each line entry on balance sheets.

Starting at the top of the balance sheet, after the name of the corporation, title, and date of the statement, total assets are itemized, with current assets (total, $13.6 million) always first.

* See also the definition of financial terms, page 377.

† Fred B. Renwick is Professor of Finance at the Graduate School of Business Administration, New York University, New York, N.Y.

EXHIBIT 1

UNIVERSAL MANUFACTURING CORPORATION
Balance Sheet
December 31, 1983

Assets	1983	1982
Current assets		
Cash	$ 350,000	$ 250,000
Marketable securities at cost (market value: 1983, $2,980,000; 1982, $1,900,000)	2,850,000	1,830,000
Accounts receivable Less: Allowance for bad debt: 1983, $24,000; 1982, $21,000	4,800,000	4,370,000
Inventories	5,600,000	4,950,000
Total current assets	$13,600,000	$11,400,000
Fixed assets (property, plant, and equipment)		
Land	$ 734,000	$ 661,000
Building	5,762,000	5,258,000
Machinery	11,435,000	10,011,000
Office equipment	614,000	561,000
	18,545,000	16,491,000
Less: Accumulated depreciation	6,435,000	5,671,000
Net fixed assets	12,110,000	10,820,000
Prepayments and deferred charges	90,000	61,600
Intangibles (goodwill, patent, trademarks)	200,000	200,000
Total assets	$26,000,000	$22,481,600
Liabilities	**1983**	**1982**
Current liabilities		
Accounts payable	$ 2,910,000	$ 2,300,000
Notes payable	1,420,000	730,000
Accrued expenses payable	430,000	350,000
Federal income taxes payable	1,240,000	1,320,000
Total current liabilities	$ 6,000,000	$ 4,700,000
Long-term liabilities		
First mortgage bonds, 8% interest, due 2003	$ 2,000,000	$ 2,000,000
Total liabilities	$ 8,000,000	$ 6,700,000
Stockholders' Equity		
Capital stock		
Preferred stock, 6% cumulative, $100 par value each; authorized, issued, and outstanding 13,600 shares	1,360,000	1,360,000
Common stock, 30 cents par value each; authorized, issued, and outstanding 760,000 shares	228,000	228,000
Capital surplus	1,112,000	1,112,000
Accumulated retained earnings	15,300,000	13,081,600
Total stockholders' equity	$18,000,000	$15,781,600
Total liabilities and stockholders' equity	$26,000,000	$22,481,600

Current assets consist of:

1. *Cash*, $350,000, which is what you would expect, namely pocket-book currency and coins in the treasurer's office, plus demand deposits at a commercial bank. Cash is synonymous with liquidity,
2. *Marketable securities*, $2.85 million, which usually are cash equivalents or highly liquid securities such as Treasury Bills of the federal government or negotiable certificates of deposit (CDs), or demand notes issued by large corporations,
3. *Accounts receivable*, $4.8 million, which consist of payments due from customers who purchased UMC's goods and services on credit and have not paid yet but are scheduled to pay within the next few months. Since a small fraction of customers might never pay (because of death, financial disaster, flood, or other catastrophe), an allowance is made, $24,000, pursuant to good accounting practices for bad debts,
4. *Inventories*, $5.6 million, which consist of (*a*) finished goods in stock and ready for sale or shipment, (*b*) work and merchandise in process, and (*c*) supplies and raw materials inventories; and are priced on the balance sheet at the lower of cost or market on either a first-in-first-out (Fifo) or last-in-first-out (Lifo) basis. Pricing policy is usually stated in a note.

Total current assets, $13.6 million, are the sum of the four aforecited figures and usually are earmarked for use within the coming 12 months. In other words, *current* means within the next 12 months.

Fixed assets (property, plant and equipment) are the permanent tangible capital owned by the business, and are listed *at cost* (original purchase price) next on the balance sheet; and consists of:

1. *Land,* $734,000, or ground upon which buildings or other assets such as forests, air or water rights, and the like are built,
2. *Building,* $5.762 million, which are structures such as offices, warehouses, and the like where business is conducted,
3. *Machinery,* $11.435 million, which are mechanical apparatuses for increasing productivity and economic efficiency,
4. *Office equipment,* $614,000, which is what you would expect, namely desks, typewriters, copiers, and the like.

Accumulated depreciation, $6.435 million, is the total depreciation (deterioration of property, plant, and equipment due to physical wear and tear) accumulated to date for accounting purposes against UMC's assets. It is important to know about three concepts of depreciation, namely: (1) depreciation calculated for tax purposes which is figured pursuant to the Tax Code to benefit from allowable accelerated rates of depreciation, (2) accounting depreciation, which can be either straight-line or accelerated and is usually explained in a note, (3) economic depreciation, which comes from technological obsolescence and deterioration in ability to continue generating future income at current rates due to changes in demand and markets for the goods and services produced by UMC. The balance sheet states only number two, accounting depreciation.

Net fixed assets, $12,110,000, are the sum of the four above figures, minus accounting depreciation; and are used by the business to generate future (beyond the coming 12 months) income.

Prepayments and deferred charges, $90,000, state total amounts paid in advance for assets not yet obtained (such as paid-up premiums on a fire insurance policy covering the next five years, or rental paid on computers for the next three years); and for benefits to be received in future years for expenditures already made (such as for research and development, moving the business to a new location, or expenses incurred in bringing a new product to market).

Intangibles, $200,000, are assets such as goodwill, trademarks, franchises, patents, copyrights, and the like which have no physical existence; yet are valuable in producing business income.

Total assets, $26 million, are current, plus fixed, plus prepayments and deferred charges, plus intangibles; and state the size of the business and are the total property owned by the business.

Look next at the lower part of the balance sheet, which concerns the financing of the business. Financing must come from either borrowing (liabilities) or ownership equity.

Underneath the asset section of the balance sheet (or on the right side if the company uses the account form), total current liabilities, $6 million, always are itemized next, then long-term liabilities, $2 million, then finally stockholders' equity of $18 million.

Total current liabilities consist of bills due and payable by UMC within the next 12 months, all of which fall into one of four categories:

1. *Accounts payable,* $2.91 million, which are bills currently owed and due to creditors,
2. *Notes payable,* $1.42 million, which are current obligations owed to a bank or other short-term lender,
3. *Accrued expenses payable,* $430,000, include wages due employees, fees to attorneys, current pension or retirement obligations, and the like.
4. *Federal income taxes payable,* $1.24 million, is the current tax payable to the Internal Revenue Service, and is sufficiently important to merit a line of its own on the corporate balance sheet.

Long-term liabilities, $2 million for UMC, can include straight debt (like UMC's which pays 8 percent interest and matures in 2003), convertible bonds (bonds which pay interest like straight bonds but are convertible upon demand of the bond owner into a stated number of shares of common stock), or "other" long-term debt (like pollution control and industrial revenue bonds or sinking-fund debentures). UMC has only straight debt outstanding.

Total liabilities, $8 million, are the sum of current and long-term liabilities and constitute the total financing obtained from borrowings.

Stockholders' equity, $18 million consists of:

1. *Capital stock,* $1.588 million, which includes both preferred stock and common stock but no convertible preferred stock and no warrants or rights to purchase either bonds or common stock,
2. *Capital surplus,* $1.112 million, which is the amount paid in by shareholders over the par or legal value of 30 cents for each common share,
3. *Accumulated retained earnings,* $15.3 million, which are earnings not paid out in dividends but have been retained and reinvested in the business. Further information regarding accumulated retained earnings since inception of the business is set forth below in the *statement of retained earnings.*

Capital stock represents proprietary interest in the company, is represented by stock certificates authorized and issued by the company, and can belong to either of several classes, including:

1. *Preferred stock*, which has preference or takes priority over other shares regarding dividend payout (6 percent in UMC's case), and which can be cumulative, which means that if the company fails to pay dividends for whatever reason for any year, then the 6 percent of $100 or $6 per preferred share accumulates on the books and must be paid before common stockholders can receive future dividends. Total preferred stock authorized and issued by UMC is $100 per share times 13,600 shares or $1.36 million.
2. *Common stock*, which represents the remaining ownership of the company and is entitled to receive a dividend along with fluctuations in value of the stock. Par value is the legal stated value of each common share; so the par value (30 cents per share times 760,000 shares or $228,000) plus the additional amount or capital surplus ($1.112 million) together state the amount UMC received upon issuing 760,000 shares, namely $1.34 million divided by 760,000 or $1.76 per share.

The bottom line, *total liabilities and stockholders equity*, states the financing of the corporation, and shows where UMC obtained the $26 million to buy the total assets itemized at the top of the balance sheet.

We turn next to income statements.

INCOME STATEMENTS

Exhibit 2 shows UMC's income statement, where the important items to look for, after the name of the company, the title, and date of the statement at the heading, are:

1. *Net sales*, which is where most of the business revenue comes from for most businesses, except rental and leasing companies, $23,850,000.
2. *Net Operating Income* (NOI) or profit before interest and taxes, which states profit from business operations, without regard to financing, $5,878,000.
3. *Total Income* before interest and taxes, which states the return on total capital available to the business during the year, $6,220,000.
4. *Less:* provision for federal income tax, $2,240,000.
5. *Total Income*, after tax but before interest deduction, which states the after-tax profitability of the corporation and is widely used in computing cost of capital for a business enterprise, $3,980,000.

EXHIBIT 2

UNIVERSAL MANUFACTURING CORPORATION
Consolidated Income Statement
December 31, 1983 and 1982

	1983	1982
Net sales	$23,850,000	$19,810,000
Cost of sales and operating expenses		
Cost of goods sold	8,940,000	7,209,000
Depreciation	800,000	750,000
Selling and administrating expenses	8,232,000	6,814,000
Operating profit	$ 5,878,000	$ 5,037,000
Other income		
Dividends and interest	342,000	183,000
Total Income	$ 6,220,000	$ 5,220,000
Less: Interest on bonds	160,000	160,000
Income before provision for federal income tax	$ 6,060,000	$ 5,060,000
Provision for federal income tax	2,240,000	1,980,000
Net profit for year	$ 3,820,000	$ 3,080,000
Common shares outstanding	760,000	760,000
Net earnings per share	$ 4.92	$ 3.95

Statement of Accumulated Retained Earnings

	1983	1982
Balance January 1	$13,081,600	$11,413,200
Net profit for year	3,820,000	3,080,000
Total	$16,901,600	$14,493,200
Less: Dividends paid on		
Preferred stock	81,600	81,600
Common stock	1,520,000	1,330,000
Balance December 31	$15,300,000	$13,081,600

6. *Net income* (NI) or profit for the year, which states earnings after taxes and after all fixed charges. The net profit for the year is available for (a) dividend payout to preferred stockholders, (b) dividend payout to common stockholders, and (c) retention and reinvestment in the business, $3,820,000.
7. *Net earnings per share* (EPS), which equals total earnings available for distribution to common stockholders ($3.82 million minus 6% dividend owed on 13,600 shares of $100 par value preferred stock, or $3,738,400), divided by 760,000 common shares outstanding, $4.92.

$$\$3{,}820{,}000 - 0.06(13{,}600)(\$100) = \$3{,}738{,}400$$

$$\$3{,}738{,}400/760{,}000 = \$4.92 \text{ per share}$$

Cost of sales and operating expenses falls into one of three categories:

1. *Cost of goods sold,* which states the amount of labor, material, and other expenses in producing the items sold, $8,940,000.
2. *Depreciation expense,* which states the amount of capital (producer's durables) consumed in producing the goods and services sold and which must be replaced or restored to its original capacity, $800,000.
3. *Selling and administrating expenses,* which includes office expenses, executives salaries, salespersons salaries, advertising and promotion expenses and the like, $8,232,000.

Operating profit, also called net operating income, $5.878 million, is the income from business operations, and is an important indicator of how efficiently the fixed assets were employed during the year.

Other income, $342,000, is from UMC's marketable securities of $1.83 million at cost as of one year ago.

Total income, $6.22 million, is the sum of operating profit from the business and income from other sources.

Interest on bonds, $160,000, (8 percent of 2 million) is itemized next on the income statement, followed by:

Income after interest, before tax	$6,060,000
Provision for federal income tax	2,240,000
Net profit for the year	3,820,000
Net earnings per share	$4.92

We turn next to statements of accumulated retained earnings.

STATEMENTS OF ACCUMULATED RETAINED EARNINGS

The bottom part of Exhibit 2 contains the accumulated retained earnings statement for UMC, and shows at the beginning of the balance, since the starting date of the business to January 1 of the current year, $13,081,600—to which is added the net profit for the year, $3,820,000, to get total accumulated retained earnings of $16,901,600.

Dividends paid to stockholders are itemized next:

Preferred stock dividend: 6 percent of $1,360,000	$ 81,600
Common stock dividend: $2.00 per share declared times 760,000 shares	1,520,000
Total dividends paid	$1,601,600

Balance, December 31 (15.3 million) equals the difference between the total available ($16,901,600) and total dividends paid. Retained earnings are an important source of finance of corporate capital assets.

We turn next to statements of sources and uses of funds.

STATEMENT OF SOURCE AND APPLICATION OF FUNDS

Exhibit 3 is a statement of source and application or use of funds for UMC. Ordinarily, *funds* imply cash; but in a broader sense, *funds* include cash equivalents and substitutes for cash, such as short-term credit, notes, and account payable and accrued liabilities to meet the short-term financing needs of the business. So *funds* in the broader sense imply net *working capital,* which is the difference between current assets and current liabilities.

Sources of funds in general include transactions which increase the amount of working capital, such as:

1. Net profit from operations.
2. Sale or consumption of noncurrent assets.
3. Long-term borrowing.
4. Issuing additional shares of capital stock.
5. Annual depreciation.

Uses of funds in general include transactions which decrease working capital, such as:

1. Declaring cash dividends.
2. Repaying long-term debt.
3. Buying noncurrent assets.
4. Repurchasing outstanding capital stock.

In the case of UMC and Exhibit 3, funds were provided by net income, $3.82 million, and current depreciation expense, $800,000. Some analysts worry that depreciation is not cash, depreciation is a bookkeeping entry. But the capital was consumed in the process of producing the goods and services sold; so the business pays the cash to itself to ultimately replace the consumed capital. Depreciation expense is a source of funds.

Total funds provided for UMC are $4,620,000.

EXHIBIT 3

UNIVERSAL MANUFACTURING CORPORATION
Statement of Source and Application of Funds
December 31, 1983

	1983	
Funds were provided by		
Net income	$3,820,000	
Depreciation	800,000	
Total		$4,620,000
Funds were used for		
Dividends on preferred stock	$ 81,600	
Dividends on common stock	1,520,000	
Plant and equipment	1,720,300	
Sundry assets	398,100	
Total		$3,720,000
Increase in Working Capital		$ 900,000
Analysis of changes in working capital—1983		
Changes in current assets		
Cash	$ 100,000	
Marketable securities	1,020,000	
Accounts receivable	430,000	
Inventories	650,000	
Total		$2,200,000
Changes in current liabilities		
Accounts payable	$ 610,000	
Notes payable	690,000	
Accrued expenses payable	80,000	
Federal income tax payable	(80,000)	
Total		$1,300,000

Uses of funds are itemized next, where all uses fall into one of four categories:

Dividends on preferred stock	$ 81,600
Dividends on common stock	1,520,000
Plant and equipment	1,720,300
Sundry assets	398,100
Total uses or application of funds	$3,720,000

Increase in working capital, $900,000, is the difference between the total funds provided, $4.62 million, and the total funds used, $3.72 million.

An *analysis of changes in working capital* for the year is included in the statement of source and application of funds, and gives further information regarding the $900,000 increase in working capital, which is explained by analyzing changes in current assets together with changes in current liabilities.

Changes in current assets total $2.2 million, itemized as follows:

1. *Cash* increased from $250,000 to $350,000, giving a net change of $100,000,
2. *Marketable securities* increased from $1.83 million to $2.85 million, giving a net change of $1.02 million,
3. *Accounts receivable* increased from $4.37 million to $4.8 million, giving a net change of $430,000,
4. *Inventories* increased from $4.95 million to $5.6 million, giving a net change of $650,000.

Changes in current liabilities total $1.3 million, itemized as follows:

1. *Accounts payable* increased from $2.3 million to $2.91 million, giving a net change of $610,000,
2. *Notes payable* increased from $730,000 to $1.42 million, giving a net change of $690,000,
3. *Accrued expenses payable* increased from $350,000 to $430,000, giving a net change of $80,000,
4. *Federal income taxes payable* decreased from $1.32 million to $1.24 million, giving a net change of ($80,000).

The difference between the changes in current assets ($2.2 million) and changes in current liabilities ($1.3 million) equals the $900,000 increase in working capital.

We turn next to understanding more regarding how to analyze financial statements.

II. ANALYZING FINANCIAL STATEMENTS

The analysis of all four statements consists primarily of calculating ratios; but other methods including the time trend of the ratio, information theory, and flow-of-funds analysis are sometimes used. We shall limit our analysis to using ratios.[1]

In general, financial analysts, investors, creditors, and others look for two kinds of information regarding business enterprises:

1. *Risk*, including financial, business, market, and country or political risks,
2. *Return*, including productivity, efficiency, and profitability of corporate capital investments.

A third factor, *growth rate*, is important too, primarily because high steady growth is usually worth more than low or no growth.

BALANCE SHEET RATIOS

Balance sheet ratios belong to one of the three following categories:

1. *Liquidity and turnover ratios*, which indicate the ability of the corporation to pay current liabilities,
2. *Capitalization*, also called *leverage*, or *debt ratios*, which is the amount of borrowing relative to other factors such as total capitalization, total assets, or total equity,
3. *Net asset ratios*, which indicate the amount of assets backing each class of outstanding securities.

Liquidity ratios are calculated to judge whether the corporation owns sufficient cash and cash-equivalents or substitutes to comfortably pay short-term obligations, and include:

1. *Current liquidity*, the ability to pay current liabilities from current assets:

Current ratio:

$$\frac{\text{Current assets}}{\text{Current liabilities}} = \frac{\$13{,}600{,}000}{\$\ 6{,}000{,}000} = 2.3 \text{ to } 1$$

In total dollar amounts, the numerator in the current ratio, minus the denominator, states *net working capital*, where

Total current assets	$13,600,000
Less: Total current liabilities	6,000,000
Working capital	$ 7,600,000

2. *Quick asset* (sometimes called *acid test*) *ratio:*

$$\frac{\text{Quick assets}}{\text{Current liabilities}} = \frac{\$8{,}000{,}000}{\$6{,}000{,}000} = 1.33$$

Where quick assets are total current assets minus inventories, because inventories usually are less liquid than either cash, marketable securities, or accounts receivable:

Total current assets	$13,600,000	
Less: Inventories	5,600,000	
Quick assets		$8,000,000
Less: Total current liabilities		6,000,000
Net quick assets		$2,000,000

3. The *cash plus marketable securities ratio* indicates the firm's ability to pay current liabilities without relying on either inventories or accounts receivable:

$$\frac{\text{Cash plus marketable securities}}{\text{Total current liabilities}} = \frac{\$3{,}200{,}000}{\$6{,}000{,}000} = 0.53$$

Liquidity and turnover of inventories ratios indicate how close inventories approximate true liquidity through total sales, and are the three following figures:

1. *Inventory as a percent of total current assets:*

$$\frac{\text{Inventory}}{\text{Total current assets}} = \frac{\$5{,}600{,}000}{\$13{,}600{,}000} = 41.18 \text{ percent}$$

2. *Cost of goods sold*, including depreciation and capital consumption, *to average inventory ratio:*

$$\frac{\text{Cost of goods sold plus depreciation}}{\text{Inventory}} = \frac{\$9{,}740{,}000}{\$5{,}600{,}000} = 1.74$$

3. *Inventory turnover ratio:*

$$\frac{\text{Net sales}}{\text{Inventory}} = \frac{\$23{,}850{,}000}{\$5{,}600{,}000} = 4.26 \text{ times}$$

Liquidity of receivables ratios indicate how close accounts receivable approximate true liquidity through total sales, and are the two following figures:

1. Average collection period ratio, which indicates the number of day's sales in accounts receivables:

$$\frac{\text{Receivables} \times \text{Days in year}}{\text{Annual sales}} = \frac{\$4{,}800{,}000 \times 360}{\$23{,}850{,}000} = 72.45$$

2. Accounts receivable turnover ratio:

$$\frac{\text{Annual sales}}{\text{Accounts receivable}} = \frac{\$23{,}850{,}000}{\$4{,}800{,}000} = 4.97$$

Liquidity and turnover of tangible and fixed asset ratios indicate relationships between total sales and total assets, and are given by the following two figures:

1. Fixed asset turnover ratio:

$$\frac{\text{Sales}}{\text{Net fixed assets}} = \frac{\$23{,}850{,}000}{\$12{,}110{,}000} = 1.97$$

2. Total asset turnover ratio:

[1] Comparison of these ratios with those typical of the industry is very helpful. Typical values are given on page 142. More detailed tabulations are provided by Dun & Bradstreet and Robert Morris Associates.

$$\frac{\text{Net sales}}{\text{Average total tangible assets}} = \frac{\$23{,}850{,}000}{\$25{,}800{,}000} = 0.9244$$

Capitalization ratios include:

1. Debt ratio:

$$\frac{\text{Total liabilities}}{\text{Total assets}} = \frac{\$8{,}000{,}000}{\$26{,}000{,}000} = 30.77 \text{ percent}$$

2. Current liabilities as a percent of total liabilities:

$$\frac{\text{Current liabilities}}{\text{Total liabilities}} = \frac{\$6{,}000{,}000}{\$8{,}000{,}000} = 75 \text{ percent}$$

3. Debt-to-net-worth ratio:

$$\frac{\text{Total liabilities}}{\text{Net Worth}} = \frac{\$8{,}000{,}000}{\$18{,}000{,}000} = 0.4444$$

4. Long-term debt capitalization ratio:

$$\frac{\text{Long-term debt}}{\text{Total capitalization}} = \frac{\$2{,}000{,}000}{\$19{,}800{,}000} = 10.10 \text{ percent}$$

5. Preferred stock ratio:

$$\frac{\text{Preferred stock}}{\text{Total capitalization}} = \frac{\$1{,}360{,}000}{\$19{,}800{,}000} = 6.87 \text{ percent}$$

6. Common stock ratio:

$$\frac{\text{Common stock plus accumulated earnings}}{\text{Total capitalization}} = \frac{\$16{,}440{,}000}{\$19{,}800{,}000} = 83.03 \text{ percent}$$

7. Summary:

Total assets	$26,000,000	
Less: Intangibles	$ 200,000	
Less: Total current liabilities	$ 6,000,000	
Total capitalization	$19,800,000	100.00%
Bonds (long-term debt)	2,000,000	10.10
Preferred stock	1,360,000	6.87
Common stock (including capital surplus and retained earnings)	16,440,000	83.03

8. Long-term debt as a percent of total liabilities:

$$\frac{\text{Long-term debt}}{\text{Total liabilities}} = \frac{\$2{,}000{,}000}{\$8{,}000{,}000} = 25.00 \text{ percent}$$

Net asset value ratios include:

1. Net asset value per $1,000 bond; $9,900 per bond.

$$\frac{\text{Net tangible assets available to meet bondholders' claims}}{\text{Number of \$1,000 bonds outstanding}} = \frac{\$19{,}800{,}000}{2{,}000{,}000}$$

where the numerator is calculated as follows:

Total assets	$26,000,000
Less: Intangibles	200,000
Total tangible assets	$25,800,000
Less: Current liabilities	6,000,000
Net tangible assets available to meet bondholders' claims	$19,800,000

2. Net asset value per share of preferred stock: $1,308.82

$$\frac{\text{Net assets backing the preferred stock}}{\text{Number of shares of preferred stock outstanding}} = \frac{\$17{,}800{,}000}{13{,}600}$$

where the numerator is calculated as follows:

Total assets	$26,000,000
Less: Intangibles	200,000
Total tangible assets	$25,800,000
Less: Current liabilities	6,000,000
Less: Long-term liabilities	2,000,000
Net assets backing the preferred stock	$17,800,000

3. Net book value per share of common stock: $21.63

$$\frac{\text{Net assets available for the common stock}}{\text{Total number of shares outstanding}} = \frac{\$16{,}440{,}000}{760{,}000} = \$21.63$$

where the numerator is calculated as follows:

Total assets	$26,000,000
Less: Intangibles	200,000
Total tangible assets	$25,800,000
Less: Current liabilities	6,000,000
Less: Long-term liabilities	2,000,000
Less preferred stock	1,360,000
Net assets available for the common stock	$16,440,000

Finally, estimate the youngest average plant age by dividing the current (1983) depreciation expense accrual ($800,000 from the Statement of Source and Application of Funds) into accumulated depreciation ($6,435,000 from the Balance Sheet) to get 8.04 years. Because some plants and pieces of equipment may have been fully written off over time, we can say that UMC's Fixed Assets, on average, are over 8 years old.

INCOME STATEMENT RATIOS

Income statement ratios belong to one of the two following categories:

1. *Coverage*, which analyzes financial risk by relating the financial charges of a corporation to its ability to service them.
2. *Productivity* or *capital efficiency ratios*, which relate income to total sales and to investment.

Coverage ratios include:

1. Interest coverage ratio: 38.875

$$\frac{\text{Net operating income before interest and taxes}}{\text{Interest charges on bonds}} = \frac{\$6{,}220{,}000}{\$160{,}000} = 38.875$$

2. Cash flow coverage ratio, which indicates the firm's ability to service debt, which is related to both interest and principal payments and is not met out of earnings per se, but out of cash: 19.5 times.

$$\frac{\text{Annual cash flow before interest and taxes}}{\text{Interest on bonds plus principal repayments}/(1-T)} = \frac{\$7{,}020{,}000}{\$\ 360{,}000} = 19.5$$

where:

Net operating income before interest and taxes	$6,220,000	
Plus annual depreciation expense	800,000	
Annual cash flow before interest and taxes	$7,020,000	
Face value 20-year 8% bonds due 2003	$2,000,000	
Annual Repayment rate after taxes $2,000,000 divided by 20 years	100,000	
Before tax annual bond repayment rate $100,000 divided by 1 minus the effective tax rate, say 50 %		$200,000
Plus: 8% interest on $2,000,000		160,000
Interest plus principal repayments		$360,000

Since interest payments are made before taxes, the adjustment is necessary to convert principal repayments which are made after taxes to before-tax equivalents.

3. Preferred dividend coverage ratio: 46.81

$$\frac{\text{Income available for paying preferred dividends}}{\text{Total dividends to preferred shareholders}} = \frac{\$3{,}820{,}000}{\$81{,}600} = 46.81$$

4. Earnings per common share: $4.92

$$\frac{\text{Earnings available for distribution to common shareholders}}{\text{Total number of common shares outstanding}} = \frac{\$3{,}738{,}400}{760{,}000} = \$4.92$$

where:

Net profit for the year	$3,820,000
Less: Dividend requirements on preferred stock	81,600
Earnings available for common stock	$3,738,400

5. Primary earnings for the year: $4.94

$$\frac{\text{Earnings for the year}}{\text{Common stock plus stock equivalents}} = \frac{\$3{,}820{,}000}{773{,}500} = \$4.94$$

Assuming the 13,600 preferred shares had been convertible and converted, on a share-for-share basis, into common stock.

$$13{,}600 + 760{,}000 = 773{,}600 \text{ common shares after conversion}$$

6. Fully diluted earnings per share: $4.79

$$\frac{\text{Adjusted earnings}}{\text{Adjusted shares outstanding}} = \frac{\$3{,}900{,}000}{813{,}600} = \$4.79$$

where:

Earnings for the year	$3,820,000
Plus: interest on convertible bonds	$ 160,000
Less: income tax applicable to interest deduction	80,000
Adjusted earnings for the year	$3,900,000
Common shares outstanding	760,000
Preferred convertible stock equivalent common shares	13,600
Twenty common shares per $1,000 convertible bond (2,000) outstanding	40,000
Adjusted shares outstanding	813,600

7. Summary:

Earnings per share	$4.92
Primary earnings	4.94
Fully diluted earnings	4.79

8. Price-earnings ratio: Approximately 15 times

$$\frac{\text{Market price of stock}}{\text{Earnings per share}} = \frac{\$72.25}{\$4.92} = 14.69$$

Productivity or capital efficiency ratios include:

1. Operating margin of profit: 24.65%.

$$\frac{\text{Operating profit}}{\text{Sales}} = \frac{\$5{,}878{,}000}{\$23{,}850{,}000} = 24.65\%$$

Previous year:

$$= \frac{\$5{,}037{,}000}{\$19{,}810{,}000} = 25.43\%$$

2. Operating cost ratio: 75.35%.

	Amount	Ratio
Net sales	$23,850,000	100.00%
Operating costs	17,972,000	75.35
Operating profit	$ 5,878,000	24.65%

3. Net profit ratio: 16.02%.

$$\frac{\text{Net profit for the year}}{\text{Net sales}} = \frac{\$3{,}820{,}000}{\$23{,}850{,}000} = 16.02\%$$

Previous year: 15.55%

$$= \frac{\$3,080,000}{\$19,810,000} = 15.55\%$$

RATIOS FROM STATEMENTS OF ACCUMULATED RETAINED EARNINGS

Retained earnings statements ratios belong to one of the two following categories:

1. Dividend payout ratio.
2. Earnings retention ratio.

The dividend payout ratio for UMC is: 40.66%.

$$\frac{\text{Dividends paid to common stockholders}}{\text{Income available for common stockholders}} = \frac{\$1,520,000}{\$3,738,400} = 40.66\%$$

where:

Net profit for the year	$3,820,000
Dividends on preferred stock	81,600
Earnings available for common	$3,738,400

The earnings retention ratio for UMC is: 59.34%.

$$\frac{\text{Earnings retained}}{\text{Earnings available for payout}} = \frac{\$2,218,400}{\$3,738,400} = 59.34\%$$

where:

Net profit for the year	$3,820,000
Less: Dividends paid on preferred stock	$ 81,600
Less: Dividends paid on common stock	1,520,000
Earnings retained	$2,218,400

Summary:

Dividend payout ratio	40.66%
Earnings retention ratio	59.34
Earnings available	100.00%

Dividends per share: $2.00.

$$\frac{\text{Total dividends paid to common shareholders}}{\text{Number of common shares outstanding}} = \frac{\$1,520,000}{760,000} = \$2.00$$

Balance December 31, $15,300,000.

RATIOS FROM STATEMENTS OF SOURCE AND APPLICATION OF FUNDS

Since an analysis was stated directly on the statement of source and use of funds in Exhibit 3, that part of the analysis is completed; however we still need to calculate profitability ratios which belong to one of the two following categories:

1. Return on assets.
2. Return on equity.

Return on assets ratios include:

Return on total assets: 27.67%.

$$\frac{\text{Total income}}{\text{Last year's total assets}} = \frac{\$6,220,000}{\$22,481,600} = 27.67\%$$

After tax return on total assets: 17.70%.

$$\frac{\text{Total income after tax but before interest}}{\text{Last year's total assets}} = \frac{\$3,980,000}{\$22,481,600} = 17.70\%$$

where:

Total income	$6,220,000
Less: Provision for total taxes	2,240,000
After tax total income	$3,980,000

Return on equity ratio: 25.92%.

$$\frac{\text{Income available for distribution to common stockholders}}{\text{Last year's total equity of common stockholders}} = \frac{\$3,738,400}{\$14,421,600} = 25.92\%$$

where:

Last year's total stockholder equity	$15,781,600
Less: Preferred stock value	1,360,000
Last year's common stock equity	$14,421,600

We turn next to further discussion of notes and supplemental information.

III. NOTES AND SUPPLEMENTAL INFORMATION

As explained in the introduction, financial statements in corporate annual reports usually are accompanied by:

- A *report of independent accountants and auditors* certifying the statements conform to generally accepted accounting principles and that generally accepted auditing standards and procedures were used.
- *Notes* which further explain details and disclose relevant information regarding line items on all four statements.
- *Segment information,* which summarizes selected items by business, industry, and geographic segment.
- A *restatement* of almost everything in current (in contrast with the traditional historical original purchase) prices, and to account for the effects of inflation on items reported in the standard statements.
- *Long-term record* summarizing selected items over a five- or ten-year time span.

EXHIBIT 4
SEGMENT REPORTING AND FOREIGN OPERATIONS

	Industry Segments			Georgraphic Segments				
					Foreign			
	Segment No. 1	Segment No. 2	Consolidated	Domestic	OECD	Other	Eliminations	Consolidated
1983								
Sales, unaffiliated customers	$20,044,000	$3,806,000	$23,850,000	$12,647,000	$ 9,029,000	$2,175,000		$23,850,000
Sales, intersegment				2,171,000	346,000	21,000	($2,539,000)	
Total sales	$20,044,000	$3,806,000	$23,850,000	$14,818,000	$ 9,375,000	$2,196,000	($2,539,000)	$23,850,000
Pretax operating income	5,435,000	443,000	5,878,000	3,690,000	1,820,000	211,000	157,000	5,878,000
Identifiable assets at December 31	21,700,000	4,300,000	26,000,000	16,549,000	10,168,000	2,353,000	(3,070,000)	26,000,000
Depreciation expense	666,000	134,000	800,000					
Capital spending	1,884,300	234,100	2,118,400					
1982								
Sales, unaffiliated customers	$16,629,000	$3,181,000	$19,810,000	$10,519,000	$ 7,511,000	$1,780,000		$19,810,000
Sales, intersegment				2,614,000	246,000	14,000	($2,878,000)	
Total sales	$16,629,000	$3,181,000	$19,810,000	$13,133,000	$ 7,757,000	$1,794,000	($2,878,000)	$19,810,000
Pretax operating income	4,627,000	410,000	5,037,000	3,512,000	1,449,000	126,000	(50,000)	5,037,000
Identifiable assets at December 31	19,027,000	3,473,000	22,500,000	14,728,000	8,660,000	2,005,000	(2,893,000)	22,500,000
Depreciation expense	611,000	127,000	738,000					
Capital spending	1,751,000	190,000						
1981								
Sales, unaffiliated customers	$14,461,000	$2,779,000	$17,240,000	$ 9,504,000	$ 6,152,000	$1,584,000		$17,240,000
Sales, intersegment				2,677,000	155,000	3,000	($2,835,000)	
Total sales	$14,461,000	$2,779,000	$17,240,000	$12,181,000	$ 6,307,000	$1,587,000	($2,835,000)	$17,240,000
Pretax operating income	4,163,000	378,000	4,541,000	3,552,000	1,234,000	119,000	(364,000)	4,541,000
Identifiable assets at December 31	16,614,000	3,341,000	19,955,000	13,627,000	7,818,000	1,590,000	(3,179,000)	19,955,000
Depreciation expense	551,000	102,000	653,000					
Capital spending	1,969,000	238,000	2,207,000					

REPORT OF INDEPENDENT ACCOUNTANTS

A typical report of independent accountants is addressed to the stockholders and board of directors of the corporation and will read as follows:

"In our opinion, the accompanying consolidated financial statements, appearing on pages — through —, present fairly the financial position of Universal Manufacturing Corporation and its subsidiary companies at December 31, 1983 and 1982, and the results of their operations and changes in financial position for the years then ended, in conformity with generally accepted accounting principles consistently applied. Also, in our opinion, the five-year comparative consolidated summary of operations presents fairly the financial information included therein. Our examinations of these statements were made in accordance with generally accepted auditing standards and accordingly included such tests of the accounting records and such other auditing procedures as we considered necessary in the circumstances."

The report will be signed with the name and address of the accounting firm and dated.

EXHIBIT 5

UNIVERSAL MANUFACTURING CORPORATION
SCHEDULE OF INCOME FROM CONTINUING OPERATIONS
AND OTHER CHANGES IN SHAREHOLDERS' EQUITY
ADJUSTED FOR EFFECTS OF CHANGING PRICES
For the Year Ended December 31, 1983

			Adjusted for	
		As Reported (historical cost)	**General Inflation (constant 1983 $)**	**Specific (current) Costs**
Income from continuing operations				
Net sales	$23,850,000			
Other income	342,000			
Total revenue from continuing operations		$24,192,000	$24,192,000	$24,192,000
Costs and other deductions				
Depreciation expenses		800,000	1,076,000	1,115,000
Other costs and expenses		17,172,000	17,699,000	17,273,000
Interest expense		160,000	160,000	160,000
Federal and foreign income taxes		2,240,000	2,240,000	2,240,000
Total costs and other deductions		$20,372,000	$21,175,000	$20,788,000
Net income from continuing operations		$ 3,820,000	$ 3,017,000	$ 3,404,000
Purchasing power gain on net monetary liabilities (Net amounts owed)			1,000	1,000
Increase in current cost of inventories and property, plant and equipment during 1983				1,911,000
Less: effect of increase in general price level during 1983				2,788,000
Excess of increase in specific prices over increase in the general price level				($ 877,000)
Net income		$ 3,820,000		
Adjusted net income			$ 3,018,000	
Net change in shareholders' equity from above		$ 3,820,000	$ 3,018,000	$ 2,528,000

Summarized Balance Sheet
Adjusted for Changing Prices
At December 31, 1983

		Adjusted for	
	As reported	**General Inflation (constant 1983 $)**	**Specific (current) Costs**
Assets			
Inventories	$ 5,600,000	$ 6,175,000	$ 5,670,000
Property, plant and equipment	12,110,000	13,354,000	16,327,000
All other assets	8,290,000	9,141,000	7,506,000
Total assets	$26,000,000	$28,670,000	$29,503,000
Total liabilities	8,000,000	7,600,000	7,600,000
Shareholders' equity	$18,000,000	$21,070,000	$21,903,000

EXHIBIT 5 *(concluded)*

Supplementary financial data
Five-Year Comparison of Selected Data
Adjusted for Changing Prices

	Years Ended December 31				
	1979	**1980**	**1981**	**1982**	**1983**
Sales					
As reported	$14,020,000	$15,610,000	$17,240,000	$19,810,000	$23,850,000
1983 constant dollars	19,543,000	20,211,000	20,063,000	20,970,000	23,850,000
Net income					
As reported					$ 3,820,000
1983 constant dollars					3,017,000
Current costs					3,404,000
Earnings per share					
As reported					$4.92
1983 constant dollars					3.86
Current costs					4.37
Common stock dividends declared per share					
As reported	$1.40	$1.43	$1.55	$1.75	$2.00
1983 constant dollars	1.95	1.85	1.80	1.85	2.00
Net assets at year-end					
As reported					$18,000,000
1983 constant dollars					21,070,000
Current costs					21,903,000
Purchasing power gain on net monetary liabilities					1,000
Market price per common share at year-end					
Actual	$69.25	$68.13	$55.50	$67.63	$72.25
1983 constant dollars	90.50	84.95	64.80	72.45	68.50
Average consumer price index*	181.5	195.4	217.4	239.0	253.0

* Hypothetical, for illustrative purposes only.

NOTES TO FINANCIAL STATEMENTS

Notes disclose additional information regarding entries in all four primary statements, and usually are considered an integral part of the statements, included in and covered by the auditor's certification. Some corporations include the next three items to be discussed, segment information, effects of inflation, and long-term comparative summary of operations, in the notes. If included in some place other than the notes, then look for whether the statement was excluded from the auditor's audit.

SEGMENT INFORMATION

Notes disclosing geographic area and industry segment information usually summarize selected items such as net sales, operating income, total assets, depreciation and amortization, and capital expenditures for industry segments (business segments or product groups) and foreign operations.

Exhibit 4 shows the segment information for UMC's two segments.

As you can see from Exhibit 4, industry segment number one, Human and Animal Health Products, accounts for 84 percent ($20,044,000 divided by $23,850,000) of total sales, and 92 percent ($5,435,000 divided by $5,878,000) of UMC's operating income; all supported by 83.46 percent ($21,700,000 divided by $26,000,000) of total assets. Eleven percent ($234,100 divided by $2,118,400) of total capital expenditures were made in industry segment number two, Environmental Health Products and Services for the treatment of water and air pollution.

Exhibit 4 also shows, based on the following ratios, that UMC's business is roughly 60 percent domestic United States; 40 percent nondomestic:

Net Sales:

$$\frac{\text{United States}}{\text{Total company}} = \frac{\$14{,}818{,}000}{\$23{,}850{,}000} = 62.13\%$$

Operating income:

$$\frac{\text{United States}}{\text{Total company}} = \frac{\$3{,}690{,}000}{\$5{,}037{,}000} = 62.78\%$$

Total assets:

$$\frac{\text{United States}}{\text{Total company}} = \frac{\$16{,}549{,}000}{\$26{,}000{,}000} = 63.65\%$$

SUPPLEMENTAL INFORMATION ON INFLATION ACCOUNTING

Pursuant to Financial Accounting Standards Board (FASB) *Statement of Financial Accounting Standards No. 33*, public enterprises that have either (1) inventories and property, plant, and equipment (before deducting accumulated

EXHIBIT 6

TEN-YEAR FINANCIAL SUMMARY
UNIVERSAL MANUFACTURING CORPORATION

	1983	1982	1981	1980	1979	1978	1977	1976	1975	1974
Net sales	$23,850,000	$19,810,000	$17,240,000	$15,610,000	$14,020,000	$12,604,000	$11,040,000	$ 9,426,000	$ 8,324,000	$ 7,611,000
Total income before tax	6,060,000	5,060,000	4,535,000	4,164,000	3,783,000	3,619,000	3,195,000	2,747,000	2,521,000	2,286,000
Net profit for the year	3,820,000	3,080,000	2,775,000	2,555,000	2,288,000	2,105,000	1,827,000	1,512,000	1,314,000	1,179,000
Earnings per share	4.92	3.95	3.56	3.28	2.94	2.71	2.36	1.95	1.70	1.53
Dividends per share	2.00	1.75	1.55	1.43	1.40	1.40	1.24	1.12	1.10	1.03
Net working capital	7,600,000	6,700,000	6,300,000	5,500,000	5,023,000	3,596,000	3,424,000	2,964,000	2,604,000	2,261,000
Total assets	26,000,000	22,481,600	19,934,000	17,594,000	15,390,000	12,433,000	9,890,000	8,348,000	7,365,000	6,643,000
Net plant and equipment	12,110,000	10,820,000	9,918,000	8,747,000	6,743,000	4,740,000	3,635,000	3,150,000	2,830,000	2,479,000
Long term debt	2,000,000	2,000,000	2,000,000	2,000,000	2,000,000	2,000,000	2,000,000	1,000,000	1,000,000	1,000,000
Preferred stock	1,360,000	1,360,000	1,360,000	1,360,000	1,360,000	1,360,000	1,360,000	1,360,000	1,360,000	1,360,000
Common stock and surplus	1,340,000	1,340,000	1,340,000	1,340,000	1,340,000	1,340,000	1,340,000	1,340,000	1,340,000	1,340,000
Book value per share	21.63									

depreciation) amounting to more than $125 million or (2) total assets amounting to more than $1 billion (after deducting accumulated depreciation) are required to report supplementary information in addition to the primary financial statements. FASB *Standards No. 33* are:

> For fiscal years ended on or after December 25, 1979, enterprises are required to report:
>
> *a.* Income from continuing operations adjusted for the effects of general inflation.
> *b.* The purchasing power gain or loss on net monetary items.
>
> For fiscal years ended on or after December 25, 1979, enterprises are also required to report:
>
> *a.* Income from continuing operations on a current cost basis.
> *b.* The current cost amounts of inventory and property, plant, and equipment at the end of the fiscal year.
> *c.* Increases or decreases in current cost amounts of inventory and property, plant, and equipment, net of inflation.
>
> Enterprises are required to present a five-year summary of selected financial data, including information on income, sales and other operating revenues, net assets, dividends per common share, and market price per share. In the computation of net assets, only inventory and property, plant, and equipment need be adjusted for the effects of changing prices.

UMC, because of its "small company" asset size, would be exempt from FASB *No. 33*'s reporting requirement. However, Exhibit 5 restates UMC's statement of income from continuing operations, restated for changing prices, for the year ending December 31, 1983; and UMC's five-year comparison of selected data adjusted for changing prices.

A final note on Notes: Feel free to speak with your friendly auditor, or sleuth on your own, regarding additional information which might remain undisclosed and could pertain to:

a. Liabilities arising out of company pension plans (e.g., ERISA).
b. Contractual obligations (e.g., the capitalized value of lease payments).
c. Legal judgments currently enforceable.
d. Contingent liabilities (e.g., pending lawsuits or possible income tax assessment).

TEN-YEAR FINANCIAL SUMMARY

Long-term performance of UMC is summarized and reported on the ten-year financial summary statement, Exhibit 6.

The long-term view is used for detecting trends and changes in trends in important factors such as net sales, total assets, net operating income, earnings per share, and dividends per share. On balance, the trends for UMC look pretty good: upward.

A Guide to SEC Corporate Filings

A basic purpose of the Federal securities laws is to provide disclosure of material financial and other information on companies seeking to raise capital through the public offering of their securities, as well as companies whose securities are already publicly held. This aims at enabling investors to evaluate the securities of these companies on an informed and realistic basis.

The Securities Act of 1933 is a *disclosure* statute. It generally requires that, before securities may be offered to the public, a registration statement must be filed with the Commission disclosing prescribed categories of information. Before the sale of securities can begin, the registration statement must become "effective," and investors must be furnished a prospectus containing the most significant information in the registration statement.

The Securities Exchange Act of 1934 deals in large part with securities already outstanding and requires the registration of securities listed on a national securities exchange, as well as "Over-the-Counter" securities in which there is a substantial public interest. Issuers of registered securities must file annual and other periodic reports designed to provide a public file of current material information. The Exchange Act also requires disclosure of material information to holders of registered securities in solicitations of proxies for the election of directors or approval of corporate action at a stockholder's meeting, or in attempts to acquire control of a company through a tender offer or other planned stock acquisition. It provides that insiders of companies whose equity securities are registered must report their holdings and transactions in all equity securities of their companies.

Effective December 15, 1980, the Securities and Exchange Commission adopted and proposed major changes in its disclosure systems under the Securities Act of 1933 and the Securities Exchange Act of 1934. These changes were intended to reinforce the concept of an integrated disclosure system.

The changes that were adopted include amendments to Form 10-K, amendments to the Proxy rules, expansion of amendments to Regulation S-K (which governs non-financial statement disclosure rules), uniform financial statement instructions, a general revision of Regulation S-X (which governs the form, content and requirements of financial statements), as well as a new simplified optional form for the registration of securities issued in certain business combinations.

The integrated disclosure system is based on the belief that investors expect to be furnished the same basic information package, both to support current information requirements of an active trading market and to provide information in connection with the sale of newly issued securities under the Securities Act.

The program is intended to:

Improve disclosure to investors and other users of financial information
Achieve a single disclosure system at reduced cost
Reduce current impediments to combining shareholder communications with official SEC filings

Form 10-K Items Reported

Part I (must be filed 90 days after close of fiscal year)

1. **Business.** Identifies principal products and services of the company, principal markets and methods of distribution and, if "material," competitive factors, backlog and expectation of fulfillment, availability of raw materials, importance of patents, licenses, and franchises, estimated cost of research, number of employees, and effects of compliance with ecological laws.

   If there is more than one line of business, for each of the last three fiscal years a statement of total sales and net income for each line which, during either of the last two fiscal years, accounted for 10 percent or more of total sales or pretax income.
2. **Properties.** Location and character of principal plants, mines, and other important properties and if held in fee or leased.
3. **Legal Proceedings.** Brief description of material legal proceedings pending; when civil rights or ecological statutes are involved, proceedings must be disclosed.
4. **Principal Security Holders and Security Holdings of Management.** Identification of owners of 10 percent or more of any class of securities and of securities held by directors and officers according to amount and percent of each class.

Source: A *Guide to SEC Corporate Filings,* Disclosure, Inc., 5161 River Road, Bethesda, MD 20816. Provided by Disclosure. To order copies of any SEC filings, call 800–638–8241.

Form 10-K Part II

5. **Market for the Registrants' Common Stock and Related Security Holder Matters.** Includes principal market in which voting securities are traded with high and low sales prices (in the absence thereof, the range of bid and asked quotations for each quarterly period during the past two years) and the dividends paid during the past two years. In addition to the frequency and amount of dividends paid, this item contains a discussion concerning future dividends.
6. **Selected Financial Data.** These are five-year selected data including net sales and operating revenue; income or loss from continuing operations, both total and per common share; total assets; long-term obligations including redeemable preferred stock; cash dividends declared per common share. Also, additional items that could enhance understanding and trends in financial condition and results of operations. Further, the effects of inflation and changing prices should be reflected in the five-year summary.
7. **Management's Discussion and Analysis of Financial Condition and Results of Operations.** Under broad guidelines, this includes: liquidity, capital resources and results of operations; trends that are favorable or unfavorable as well as significant events or uncertainties; causes of any material changes in the financial statements as a whole; limited data concerning subsidiaries; discussion of effects of inflation and changing prices. Projections or other forward-looking information may or may not be included.
8. **Financial Statements and Supplementary Data.** Two-year audited balance sheets as well as three-year audited statements of income and changes in financial condition.

Form 10-K Part III

9. **Directors and Executive Officers of the Registrant.** Name, office, term of office and specific background data on each.
10. **Remuneration of Directors and Officers.** List of each director and 3 highest paid officers with aggregate annual remuneration exceeding $40,000 and total paid all officers and directors.

Form 10-K Part IV

11. **Exhibits, Financial Statement Schedules and Reports on Form 8-K.** Complete, audited annual financial information and a list of exhibits filed. Also, any unscheduled material events or corporate changes filed in an 8-K during the year.

Form 10-K Schedules

- **I.** Marketable securities. Other security investments
- **II.** Amounts due from directors, officers, and principal holders of equity securities other than affiliates
- **III.** Investments in securities of affiliates
- **IV.** Indebtedness of affiliates (not current)
- **V.** Property, plant and equipment
- **VI.** Reserves for depreciation, depletion, and amortization of property, plant and equipment
- **VII.** Intangible assets
- **VIII.** Reserves for depreciation and amortization of intangible assets
- **IX.** Bonds, mortgages, and similar debt
- **X.** Indebtedness to affiliates (not current)
- **XI.** Guarantees of securities of other issuers
- **XII.** Reserves
- **XIII.** Capital shares
- **XIV.** Warrants or rights
- **XV.** Other securities
- **XVI.** Supplementary profit and loss information
- **XVII.** Income from dividends (equity in net profit and loss of affiliates)

18-K (must be filed 9 months after close of fiscal year)

Annual report for foreign governments and political subdivisions thereof.

20-F (must be filed 6 months after close of fiscal year)

Annual report filed by certain foreign issuers of securities trading in the United States.

Item 1 Business

Item 2 Management Discussion & Analysis of the Statements of Income
Item 3 Property
Item 4 Control of Registrant
Item 5 Directors and Officers of Registrant
Item 6 Remuneration of Directors and Officers
Item 7 Options to Purchase Securities from Registrant or Subsidiaries
Item 8 Pending Legal Proceedings
Item 9 Nature of Trading Market
Item 10 Capital Stock to be Registered
Item 11 Debt Securities to be Registered
Item 12 Other Securities to be Registered
Item 13 Exchange Controls and other Limitations Affecting Security Holders
Item 14 Taxation
Item 15 Changes in Securities and Changes in Security for Registered Securities
Item 16 Defaults upon Senior Securities
Item 17 Interest of Management in Certain Transactions
Item 18 Financial Statements and Exhibits

10-Q (must be filed 45 days after close of fiscal quarter)

This is the quarterly financial report filed by most companies, which, although unaudited, provides a continuing view of a company's financial position during the year. It must be filed within 45 days of the close of a fiscal quarter.

Form 10-Q Items Reported Part I

FINANCIAL STATEMENTS

1. Income Statement
2. Balance Sheet
3. Statement of source and application of funds
4. A narrative analysis of material changes in the amount of revenue and expense items in relation to previous quarters, including the effect of any changes in accounting principals.

Form 10-Q Part II

1. **Legal Proceedings.** Brief description of material legal proceedings pending; when civil rights or ecological statutes are involved, proceedings must be disclosed.
2. **Changes in Securities.** Material changes in the rights of holders of any class of registered security.
3. **Changes in Security for Registered Securities.** Material withdrawal or substitution of assets securing any class of registered securities of the registrant.
4. **Defaults upon Senior Securities.** Material defaults in the payment if principal, interest, sinking fund or purchase fund installment, dividend, or other material default not cured within 30 days.
5. **Increase in Amount Outstanding of Securities or Indebtedness.** Amounts of new issues, continuing issues or reissues of any class of security or indebtedness with a reasonable statement of the purposes for which the proceeds will be used.
6. **Decreases in amount Outstanding of Securities or Indebtedness.** Amounts of decreases, through one or more transactions, in any class of outstanding securities or indebtedness.
7. **Submission of Matters to a Vote of Security Holders.** Information relating to the convening of a meeting of shareholders, whether annual or special, and the matters voted upon, with particular emphasis on the election of directors.
8. **Other Materially Important Events.** Information on any other item of interest to shareholders not already provided for in this form.

8-K (corporate changes 1–6 must be filed 15 days after the event. 7 has no mandatory filing time.)

This is a report of unscheduled material events or corporate changes deemed of importance to the shareholders or to the SEC.

1. Changes in Control of Registrant.
2. Acquisition or Disposition of Assets.
3. Bankruptcy or Receivership.
4. Changes in Registrant's Certifying Accountant.
5. Other Materially Important Events.
6. Resignations of Registrant's Directors.
7. Other Materially Important Events.

10-C (must be filed 10 days after change)

"Over-the-counter" companies use this form to report changes in name and amount of NASDAQ-listed securities. It is similar in purpose to the 8-K.

13-F (must be filed 45 days after close of fiscal quarter)

A quarterly report of equity holdings required of all institutions with equity assets of $100 million or more. This includes banks, insurance companies, investment companies, investment advisors and large internally managed endowments, foundations and pension funds.

Proxy Statement

A proxy statement provides official notification to designated classes of stockholders of matters to be brought to a vote at a shareholders' meeting. Proxy votes may be solicited for changing the company name, transferring large blocks of stock, electing new officers, or many other matters. Disclosures normally made via a proxy statement may in some cases be made using Form 10-K (Part III).

Registration Statements

Registration statements are of two principal types: (1) "offering" registrations filed under the 1933 Securities Act, and (2) "trading" registrations filed under the 1934 Securities Exchange Act.

"Offering" registrations are used to register securities before they may be offered to investors. Part I of the registration, a preliminary prospectus or "red herring," is promotional in tone; it carries all the sales features that will be contained in the final prospectus. Part II of the registration contains detailed information about marketing agreements, expenses of issuance and distribution, relationship of the company with experts named in the registration, sales to special parties, recent sales of unregistered securities, subsidiaries of registrant, franchises and concessions, indemnification of directors and officers, treatment of proceeds from stock being registered, and financial statements and exhibits.

"Offering" registration statements vary in purpose and content according to the type of organization issuing stock:

S-1 Companies reporting under the '34 Act for less than 3 years. Permits no incorporation by reference and requires complete disclosure in the prospectus.

S-2 Companies reporting under the '34 Act for 3 years or more but do not meet the minimum voting stock requirement. Reference of '34 Act reports permits incorporation and presentation of financial information in the prospectus or in an annual report to shareholders delivered with the prospectus.

S-3 Companies reporting under the '34 Act for 3 or more years and having at least $150 million of voting stock held by non-affiliates, or as an alternative test, $100 million of voting stock coupled with an annual trading volume of 3 million shares. Requires minimal disclosure in the prospectus and allows maximum incorporation by reference of '34 Act reports.

S-4 Registration used in certain business combinations or registrations. Replaces S-14, S-15, 7/85.

N-1A Used by open end Management Investment Companies other than separate accounts of insurance companies.

N-2 (Formerly S-4) Used by closed-end investment companies.

N-5 Registration of small business investment companies.

NSAR Replaces form N-1R, N-30A-2, N-30A-3, N-5R, 2-MD.

S-6 Used by unit investment trusts registered under the Investment Act of 1940 on Form N-8B-2.

S-8 Used to register securities to be offered to employees under stock option and various other benefit plans.

S-11 Used by real estate companies, primarily limited partnerships and investment trusts.

S-18 Short form registration up to $7.5 million.

SE Non-electronic exhibits of registrants filing with the EDGAR PILOT PROJECT.

F-1 Registration of securities by foreign private issuers eligible to use form 20-F, for which no other form is prescribed.

F-2 Registration of securities of foreign private issuers meeting certain 34 act filing requirements.

F-3 Registration of securities of foreign issuers offered pursuant to certain types of transactions.

F-6 Registration of depository shares evidenced by American depository receipts.

"Trading" registrations are filed to permit trading among investors on a securities exchange or in the over-the-counter market. Registration statements which serve to register securities for trading fall into three categories:

(1) **Form 10** is used by companies during

Quick Reference Chart to Contents of SEC Filings

REPORT CONTENTS	10-K	19-K 20-F	10-Q	8-K	10-C	6-K	Proxy Statement	Prospectus	Registration Statements '34 Act F-10	8-A 8-B	'33 Act "S" Type	ARS	Listing Application	N-1R	N-1Q
Auditor															
☐ Name	A	A	■				■	A	A		A	A	■	A	
☐ Opinion	A	A	■						A			A		A	
☐ Changes				A			■								
Compensation Plans															
☐ Equity	■		■				F	F	A		F		■	■	
☐ Monetary	■		■					F	A		F		■		
Company Information															
☐ Nature of Business	A	A				F		A	A		A	■	■		
☐ History	F	A						A			A	■	■		
☐ Organization and Change	F	F		A	■	F	■	A		F	A	■			
Debt Structure	A					F	■	A	A		A	A		A	
Depreciation & Other Schedules	A	A				F		A	A		A				
Dilution Factors	A	A		F		F		A	A		A	A			
Directors, Officers, Insiders															
☐ Identification	F	A				F	A	A	A		A	F			
☐ Background	■	A				F	F	A	■		A	■			
☐ Holdings	■	A		■			A	A	A		A				
☐ Compensation	■	A		■			A	A	A		A				
Earnings Per Share	A	A	A			F			A			A		A	
Financial Information															
☐ Annual Audited	A	A							A			A		A	
☐ Interim Audited		A					■	■			■				
☐ Interim Unaudited	■		A	■		F		F			F	F			
Foreign Operations	A						■	A	A		A	■	F		
Labor Contracts		■		■			■		F		F				
Legal Agreements	F	■		■					F		F				
Legal Counsel				■				A			A		■		
Loan Agreements	F		F	■			■		F		F			■	
Plants and Properties	A	F		■				F	A		F	■			
Portfolio Operations															
☐ Content (Listing of Securities)															A
☐ Management														A	
Product-Line Breakout	A							A			A	■			
Securities Structure	A	A			■			A	A		A				
Subsidiaries	A	A					■	A	A		A	■	■		
Underwriting				■				A	A		A				
Unregistered Securities	■			■			■	F			F				
Block Movements	■			F			■		A				■		

Legend **A** *– always included • included - if occured or significant* **F** *– frequently included* ■ *special circumstances only*

TENDER OFFER/ACQUISITION REPORTS	13D	13 G	14D-1	14D-9	13E-3	13E-4
Name of Issuer (Subject Company)	A	A	A	A	A	A
Filing Person (or Company)	A	A	A	A	A	A
Amount of Shares Owned	A	A				
Percent of Class Outstanding	A	A				
Financial Statements of Bidders			F		F	F
Purpose of Tender Offer			A	A	A	A
Source and Amount of Funds	A		A		A	
Identity and Background Information			A	A	A	
Persons Retained, Employed or to be Compensated			A	A	A	A
Exhibits	F		F	F	F	F

the first two years they are subject to the 1934 Act filing requirements. It is a combination registration statement and annual report with information content similar to that of SEC-required annual reports.

(2) **Form 8-A** is used by 1934 Act registrants wishing to register *additional* securities for trading.

(3) **Form 8-B** is used by "successor issuers" (usually companies which have changed their name or state of incorporation) as notification that previously registered securities are to be traded under a new corporate identification.

Prospectus

When the sale of securities as proposed in an "offering" registration statement is approved by the SEC, any changes required by the SEC are incorporated into the prospectus. This document must be made available to investors before the sale of the security is initiated. It also contains the actual offering price, which may have been changed after the registration statement was approved.

Annual Report to Shareholders

The Annual Report is the principal document used by most major companies to communicate directly with shareholders. Since it is not a required, official SEC filing, companies have considerable discretion in determining what types of information this report will contain and how it is to be presented.

Recent changes (effective December 15, 1980) required by the SEC were made to standardize the presentation of disclosure items in annual reports to make them consistent with similar requirements in SEC filings. For example, selected financial data relating to a registrant's financial condition and results of continuing operations will be presented in the Annual Report in the same manner as in the 10-K.

In addition to financial information, the Annual Report to Shareholders often provides non-financial details of the business which are not reported elsewhere. These may include marketing plans and forecasts of future programs and plans.

Form 8 (Amendment)

Form 8 is used to amend or supplement filings previously submitted. 1933 Act registration statements are amended by filing an amended registration statement (pre-effective amendment) or by the prospectus itself, as previously noted.

Listing Application

Like the ARS, a listing application is not an official SEC filing. It is filed by the company with the NYSE, AMEX or other stock exchange to document proposed new listings. Usually a Form 8-A registration is filed with the SEC at about the same time.

N-SAR

This report is the equivalent of the 10-K for registered management-investment firms. In addition to annual financial statements, this report shows diversification of assets, portfolio turnover activity, and capital gains experience.

Tender Offers/Acquisition Reports

13-G (must be filed 45 days after end of each calendar year)

An annual report (short form of 13D) which must be filed by all reporting persons (primarily institutions) meeting the 5% equity ownership rule within 45 days after the end of each calendar year.

1. Name of issuer
2. Name of person filing
3. 13D-1 or 13D-2 applicability
4. Amount of shares beneficially owned:
   - Percent of class outstanding
   - Sole or shared power to vote
   - Sole or shared power to dispose
5. Ownership of 5% or less of a class of stock
6. Ownership of more than 5% on behalf of another person
7. Identification of subsidiary which acquired the security being reported on by the parent holding company (if applicable)
8. Identification and classification of members of the group (if applicable)
9. Notice of dissolution of the group (if applicable)

13-D (must be filed within 10 days of the acquisition date)

Similar information of 5% equity ownership in connection with a tender offer filed within ten days of the acquisition date:

1. Security and issuer
2. Identity and background of person filing the statement

3. Source and amount of funds or other consideration
4. Purpose of the transaction
5. Interest in securities of the issuer
6. Contracts, arrangements or relationships with respect to securities of the issuer
7. Material to be filed as exhibits which may include but are not limited to:
   a. Letter agreements between the parties
   b. Formal offer to purchase

14D-1

Tender offer filing made with the SEC at time offer is made to holders of equity securities of target company, if acceptance of offer would give the offerer over 5% ownership of the subject securities:

1. Security and subject company
2. Identity and background information
3. Past contacts, transactions or negotiations with subject company
4. Source and amount of funds or other consideration
5. Purpose of the tender offer and plans or proposals of the bidder
6. Interest in securities of the subject company
7. Contracts, arrangements or relationships with respect to the subject company's securities
8. Persons retained, employed or to be compensated
9. Financial statements of certain bidders
10. Additional information
11. Material to be filed as exhibits which may include but are not limited to:
    a. The actual offer to purchase
    b. The letter to shareholders
    c. The letter of transmittal with notice of guaranteed delivery
    d. The press release
    e. The summary publication in business newspapers or magazines
    f. The summary advertisement to appear in business newspapers or magazines.

14D-9 (must be filed 10 days after making the tender offer)

A solicitation/recommendation statement that must be submitted to equity holders and filed at the SEC by the management of a firm subject to a tender offer within ten days of the making of the tender offer:

1. Security and subject company
2. Tender offer of the bidder
3. Identify and background
4. The solicitation or recommendation
5. Persons retained, employed or to be compensated
6. Recent transactions and intent with respect to securities
7. Certain negotiations and transactions by the subject company
8. Additional information
9. Material to be filed as exhibits

13E-4

Issuer tender offer statement pursuant to the Securities Exchange Act of 1934:

1. Security and issuer
2. Source and amount of funds
3. Purpose of the tender offer and plans or proposals of the issuer or affiliates
4. Interest in securities of the issuer
5. Contracts, arrangements or relationships with respect to the issuer's securities
6. Person retained, employed or to be compensated
7. Financial information
8. Additional information
9. Material to be filed as exhibits which may include but are not limited to:
   The offer to purchase which is being sent to the shareholders to whom the tender offer is being made.

13E-3

Transaction statement pursuant to the Securities Exchange Act of 1934 with respect to a public company or affiliate going private-

1. Issuer and class of security subject to the transaction
2. Identity and background of the individuals
3. Past contacts, transactions or negotiations
4. Terms of the transaction
5. Plans or proposals of the issuer or affiliate
6. Source and amount of funds or other considerations
7. Purpose, alternatives, reasons and effects
8. Fairness of the transaction
9. Reports, opinions, appraisals and certain negotiations
10. Interest in securities of the issuer
11. Contracts, arrangements or relationships with respect to the issuer's securities
12. Present intention and recommendation of certain persons with regard to the transaction
13. Other provisions of the transaction
14. Financial information
15. Persons and assets employed, retained or utilized
16. Additional information
17. Material to be filed as exhibits

How to Read the New York Stock Exchange and American Stock Exchange Quotations

(1)	(2)	(3)	(4)	(5)	(6)	(7)	(8)	(9)	(10)	(11)
52 Weeks				Yld	P-E	Sales				Net
High	Low	Stock	Div.	%	Ratio	100s	High	Low	Close	Chg.
					A A	A				
14¾	9⅛	AAR	.44	4.3	7	26	10½	10¼	10¼	¼
52¼	32¼	ACF	2.76	6.0	10	51	46	45½	46	
27	12⅞	AMF	1.24	5.1	12	1453	24¼	23¾	24⅛ +	¼
24¾	10⅞	AM Intl				51	13⅞	13¾	13¾	
11⅜	6⅜	APL				51	6⅜ d	6¼	6¼	⅛

Source: Reprinted by permission of *The Wall Street Journal*, Dow Jones & Co., Inc., 1981.

The composite quotations take into account prices paid for a stock on the New York or American Exchanges, plus those prices paid on regional exchanges, Over-the-Counter (OTC) and elsewhere, as shown in the example from the Wall Street Journal. The stock market quotations are explained below:

(1) The highest price per share paid in the past 52 weeks in terms of ⅛ of a dollar, i.e., 10⅛ means $10.125.
(2) The lowest price paid per share in the last 52 weeks.
(3) The name of the company in abbreviated form.
(4) The regular annual dividend paid. Special or extra dividends are specified by letters given in the footnotes in the Explanatory Notes shown below.
(5) The yield, that is, the annual dividend divided by the current price of the stock expressed in percent. For example, a stock that sells for $20.00 per share and pays a dividend of $2.00 per share has a yield of 10 percent (2/20).
(6) The P/E ratio is the current price of the stock divided by the company's last reported annual earnings per share. The P/E ratio is generally high for companies which are thought to have a relatively large and persistent earning's growth rate. The average P/E ratio for the Dow Jones stocks varied from 7.7 to 10.2 during the last five years.
(7) The number of shares sold on the day reported in 100s of shares.
(8) The highest price paid per share on the day reported.
(9) The lowest price paid per share on the day reported.
(10) The last price paid per share on the day reported.
(11) The change in the closing price from the previous day's closing price.

EXPLANATORY NOTES
(For New York and American Exchange listed issues)

Sales figures are unofficial.

The 52-Week High and Low columns show the highest and the lowest price of the stock in consolidated trading during the preceding 52 weeks plus the current week, but not the current trading day.

u—Indicates a new 52-week high. d—Indicates a new 52-week low.

s—Split or stock dividend of 25 percent or more in the past 52 weeks. The high-low range is adjusted from the old stock. Dividend begins with the date of split or stock dividend.

n—New issue in the past 52 weeks. The high-low range begins with the start of trading in the new issue and does not cover the entire 52-week period.

g—Dividend or earnings in Canadian money. Stock trades in U.S. dollars. No yield or PE shown unless stated in U.S. money.

Unless otherwise noted, rates of dividends in the foregoing table are annual disbursements based on the last quarterly or semi-annual declaration. Special or extra dividends or payments not designated as regular are identified in the following footnotes.

a—Also extra or extras. b—Annual rate plus stock dividend. c—Liquidating dividend. e—Declared or paid in preceding 12 months. i—Declared or paid after stock dividend or split up. j—Paid this year, dividend omitted, deferred or no action taken at last dividend meeting, k—Declared or paid this year, an accumulative issue with dividends in arrears. r—Declared or paid in preceding 12 months plus stock dividend. t—Paid in stock in preceding 12 months, estimated cash value on ex-dividend or ex-distribution date.

x—Ex-dividend or ex-rights. v—Ex-dividend and sales in full. z—Sales in full.

wd—When distributed. wi—When issued. ww—With warrants. xw—Without warrants.

vi—In bankruptcy or receivership or being reorganized under the Bankruptcy Act, or securities assumed by such companies.

Source: Reprinted by permission of *The Wall Street Journal*, Dow Jones & Co., Inc., 1981.

How to Read Over-the-Counter NASDAQ Listings

(1) (2) Stock & Div.	(3) Sales 100s	(4) Bid	(5) Asked	(6) Net Chg.
CentVtPS 1.92	8	13⅝	13¾ +	⅛
Centrn CP 2.56	4	23¼	23½	. . .
Centura Enrg	135	10½	10¾ –	½
CenturyBK .48	573	13	13⅛ –	⅛
CenturyOil Gs	49	7⅜	7⅝	. . .
Cetus Corptn	231	17⅛	17⅜ +	⅛
CFS Cont .40	18	13⅝	13⅞ +	⅛
CGA Assc Inc	155	10½	11 –	¼
Chalco Ind Inc	2	6	6½ –	¼

Source: Reprinted by permission of *The Wall Street Journal*, Dow Jones & Co., Inc., 1981.

The over-the-counter quotations are explained below.

(1) The company's name, usually abbreviated.

(2) Annual regular dividend per share, unless accompanied by a notation which is explained in the OTC Explanatory Notes (below).

(3) Number of shares sold that day in hundreds, i.e., 2 means 200 shares.

(4) Bid price per share at closing time, i.e., the price at which broker-dealer will buy the stock from the investor. Prices do not include mark-up or commission.

(5) Ask price per share at closing time, i.e., the price at which the broker-dealer will sell the stock.*

(6) The change in the closing bid price from the previous day.

* Bid and ask prices are usually quoted in ⅛ (12.5 cents) of a dollar, i.e., 12⅛ means $12.125, 12½ means $12.50, etc. Very inexpensive stocks are quoted at 1/16 (6.25 cents) and 1/32 (3.125 cents) of a dollar.

OTC EXPLANATORY NOTES

z—Sales in full.

a—Annual rate plus cash extra. b—Paid so far in 1981, no regular rate. c—Payment of accumulated dividends. d—Paid in 1980. e—Cash plus stock paid in 1980. f—Cash plus stock paid in 1981. g—Annual rate plus stock dividend. h—Paid in 1981, latest dividend omitted. i—Percent paid in stock in 1980. j—Percent in stock paid in 1981, latest dividend omitted. k—Percent in stock paid in 1981. n—Asked price not applicable. p—Granted temporary exception from Nasdaq qualifications. q—In bankruptcy proceedings. ut—Units. wt—Warrants. x—Ex-dividend, ex-rights or ex-distribution. (z) No representative quote.

Source: Reprinted by permission of *The Wall Street Journal*, Dow Jones Co., Inc., 1981.

The Ex-dividend Explained

The ex-dividend status of a stock is indicated by an *x* in the newspaper quotation or *xd* on the ticker tape. This is an abbreviation for *without dividend.*

A stock that is purchased during the ex-dividend period will not pay a previously declared dividend to its new owner. The ex-dividend period spans four business days before the so-called record date—the date a dividend issuing corporation uses to tally its shareowners. An ex-dividend stock buyer is not entitled to a dividend because his name is not recorded with the dividend issuing corporation until after the record date.

The New York Stock Exchange requires that the buyer in every transaction be recorded with the issuing corporation on the fifth business day following a trade. A stock buyer, therefore, must purchase his shares at least five business days before the record date in order for the corporation to record his name in time for him to receive his dividend. A purchase one day later disqualifies a buyer from a dividend because the transfer of ownership cannot be completed by the record date. Therefore, on the fourth business day prior to the record date, a stock is sold ex-dividend.

In our example below, the corporation's Board has decided to pay a 50‰ dividend to shareholders of record on Monday, the 10th. A person buying shares up to the close of business on Monday, the 3rd, would be eligible for the dividend because normal settlement (5 business days) will be made on Monday the 10th. On Tuesday, the 4th, however, the stock would begin selling ex-dividend because a stock purchaser as of that date could not settle till after the record date.

On the ex-dividend date, the Exchange specialist will reduce all open buy orders and open sell stop orders by the amount of the dividend. This is done to more equitably reflect the stock's value since purchasers of stock on or after the ex-dividend date are ineligible for a dividend.

EX-DIVIDEND EXPLANATION

Any Month Date	Calendar Day	Status
3	Monday	With/Dividend
4	Tuesday	Ex-Dividend (Without Dividend)
5	Wednesday	" "
6	Thursday	" "
7	Friday	" "
8	Saturday	Not a trading day
9	Sunday	Not a trading day
10	Monday	Record Date/Business Day
11	Tuesday	Business Day

Source: *Taking The Mystery Out of Ex-Dividend,* The New York Stock Exchange, Inc.

Margin Accounts Explained

Stocks may be purchased by paying the purchase price in full (plus commissions and taxes) or on a margin account. With the margin account, the investors put up part of the purchase price in cash or securities, and the broker lends the remainder. The margin investor must pay the usual commissions as well as interest on the broker's loan. The stocks purchased on margin are held by the broker as collateral on the loan. Dividends are applied to the margin account and help offset the interest payments.

Margin (M) is defined as the market value (V) of the securities less the broker's loan (L), divided by the market value of the securities. The ratio is expressed as a percentage:

$$M = \frac{V - L}{V} \times 100$$

Example: You buy 100 shares of a stock at $20 per share at a total cost (V) of $2,000. You put up $1,200 in cash and borrow (L) $800 from the broker. The margin at the time of purchase is

$$M = \frac{\$2{,}000 - \$800}{\$2{,}000} \times 100 = 60\%$$

The margin at the time of purchase is called *initial margin.* The smallest allowed value of initial margin (set by the Federal Reserve) is currently 50%. Thus, with the above stock, if you buy 100 shares at $20 per share on 50% initial margin, you put up $1,000 (.5 × $2,000), and the broker's loan is $1,000.

After the purchase there is a *maintenance margin* (set by the Exchange) below which the margin is not permitted to decrease. The maintenance margin on the New York Stock Exchange is 25%. Some brokers, however, require a higher maintenance margin of about 30%. Thus, if the 100 shares of stocks discussed above decrease in price from $20 to $13 per share, then the margin is

$$M = \left(\frac{\$1{,}300 - \$1{,}000}{\$1{,}300}\right) \times 100 = 23\%$$

The margin of 23% is now below the maintenance margin of 25% set by the Exchange. The securities are said to be *under margined,* and a call for additional cash (or securities) is issued by the broker in order to bring up the margin to 25%. If the investor does not meet the call for additional cash (margin call) within a specified time, the stocks in the margin account are immediately sold.

MARGIN REQUIREMENTS (percent of market value and effective date)

	Mar. 11, 1968	June 8, 1968	May 6, 1970	Dec. 6, 1971	Nov. 24, 1972	Jan. 3, 1974
Margin stocks	70	80	65	55	65	50
Convertible bonds	50	60	50	50	50	50
Short sales	70	80	65	55	65	50

Note: Regulations G, T, and U of the Federal Reserve Board of Governors, prescribed in accordance with the Securities Exchange Act of 1934, limit the amount of credit to purchase and carry margin stocks that may be extended on securities as collateral by prescribing a maximum loan value, which is a specified percentage of the market value of the collateral at the time the credit is extended. Margin requirements are the difference between the market value (100 percent) and the maximum loan value. The term "margin stocks" is defined in the corresponding regulation.

Source: *Federal Reserve Bulletin.*

Short Selling Explained

Short selling provides an opportunity to profit from a decline in the price of a stock. If you believe that a stock is due for a substantial decline, you arrange to have your broker borrow the stock from another investor who owns the shares. The borrowed stock is then sold. This cash is held as collateral against the borrowed shares. When (and if) the stock price declines, you purchase the stock at the market price and use it to replace the borrowed shares. The broker arranges the return of your cash collateral less the cost of the repurchased stock. Your profit per share is the price received on the sale of the stock less the purchase price.

There are certain cash outlays and costs associated with the short sale. Generally there is no charge for borrowing the stock, although occasionally stock lenders may charge a premium over the market price. You must deposit $2,000 or the required initial margin, whichever is the greater, at the time the stock is borrowed. Thus, if you borrow 100 shares of a stock priced at $50 per share and the margin required is 50%, you must put up $2,500 (.5 × $50 × 100) in cash or securities. The margin deposit is returned when you close out the short sale. You pay commission when the stock is sold and when it is repurchased. In addition, you must pay the stock lender any dividends which are declared during the period you are short the stock. It is well to remember that if cash is used for the deposit, there is a loss of the interest which you would have obtained if the cash had been invested.

The dividend payments and interest loss can be reduced or eliminated if you short stocks which pay little or no dividends and use interest-bearing securities (such as T-bills or negotiable certificates of deposit) as the margin deposit.

An increase in the price of the stock can result in substantial losses since you may be forced to repurchase at a higher price than you sold. If there are many short sellers seeking to purchase the stock in order to close out their position, prices may be driven to very high levels.

The short sale cannot be executed while the stock price is declining on the exchange. According to the rules of the SEC, the stock must undergo an increase in price prior to the execution of a short sale.

How to Read Mutual Fund Quotations

The following is an example of typical fund quotations as reported in the Wall Street Journal. The mutual fund quotations are explained in the adjacent column.

(1)	(2) NAV	(3) Offer Price	(4) NAV Chg.
Able Assoc	24.33	N.L.+	.80
Acorn Fnd	28.28	N.L.+	.03
ADV Fund	15.38	N.L.+	.02
Afuture Fd	15.59	N.L.+	.10
AIM funds			
Conv Yld	15.42	16.49+	.09
Edsn Gld	14.59	15.60+	.09
HiYld Sc	8.98	9.60+	.02
Alpha Fnd	17.82	N.L.+	.01
Am Birthrt	12.29	13.43−	.03
American Funds Group			
Am Bal	8.73	9.54	...
Amcap F	6.21	6.79+	.01
Am Mutl	12.46	13.62−	.01

Source: Reprinted by permission of *The Wall Street Journal*, Dow Jones & Co., Inc., 1981.

(1) Name of fund in abbreviated form.

(2) NAV means "net asset value" per share of the stock. It is the price at which the fund will buy shares from investors.

The NAV is obtained from

$$NAV = \frac{M + C - L}{N}$$

M = market value of all stock in the fund's portfolio at the end of the trading day
C = fund's cash or cash equivalent position
L = fund's liabilities
N = number of shares issued by fund

(3) Offer price is the price per share at which the fund will sell shares to investors. With no load (NL, no sale's charge) funds, the offer price and the NAV are the same. With load funds, a sale's charge (load) is added to the NAV to arrive at the sale's price.

(4) The NAV change is the change in net asset value (at the close of the stock market) from that of the previous day.

Top 50 Performing Mutual Funds for 5 Years

What $10,000 Grew to In 5 Years (1982–1986)**

1	+	Fidelity Magellan Fund	$37,075
2	*	Vanguard Qual. Dividend I	35,720
3	*	Loomis-Sayles Capital Dev.	35,641
4	*	Prudential Bache Utility	34,680
5		Merrill Lynch Pacific	33,020
6	+	Fidelity Select-Fincl Ser.	32,877
7		Putnam Intl. Equities	32,405
8		Phoenix Growth Fund Ser.	32,303
9	+	Fidelity Select-Health Cr.	31,911
10		Eaton Vance Total Return	30,815
11	*	The Fairmont Fund	30,391
12		Fidelity Destiny Plan I	30,306
13	*	T. Rowe Price International Stock	30,154
14		Phoenix Stock Fund Series	30,042
15		United Income	29,906
16		Washington Mutual Inv.	29,845
17		NEL Growth Fund	29,735
18		United Continental Income	29,559
19	*	Templeton Global I	29,458
20	*	Northeast Investors Trust	29,238
21	*	Evergreen Total Return	29,183
22	+	Fidelity Select-Utilities	29,182
23	*	Vanguard Windsor (c)	29,124
24		Alliance International	28,932
25	*	SteinRoe Managed Muni. Bd.	28,829
26	*	Elfun Tax Exempt Income	28,752
27		Guardian Park Avenue	28,744
28	*	Sequoia (c)	28,707
29	*	Ivy Growth Fund	28,352
30		IDS Progressive	28,321
31	*	Lehman Opportunity Fund	28,140
32	+	Fidelity Equity Income.	28,131
33		Phoenix Balanced Fund Ser.	28,126
34		Sentinel Common Stock	28,119
35	*	Manhattan Fund	28,035
36	*	Scudder International	27,990
37		United International Grth.	27,986
38	*	Fidelity Puritan Fund	27,922
39		Sogen International Fund	27,844
40		Investment Company of Am.	27,844
41	*	Loomis-Sayles Mutual	27,740
42	*	American Leaders	27,561
43	*	Bruce Fund	27,557
44	*	Twentieth Century Select	27,554
45		Nationwide Growth Fund	27,505
46		Investors Research	27,473
47		Franklin Utilities	27,435
48	*	SAFECO Income	27,352
49	*	Fidelity Qual. Dividend Fd.	27,324
50		Merrill Lynch Basic Value	27,240

Top 50 Performing Mutual Funds for 10 Years

What $10,000 Grew To In 10 Years (1977–1986)**

1	+	Fidelity Magellan Fund	$167,742
2	*	Twentieth Century Select	104,705
3		A-C Pace	94,326
4	*	Twentieth Century Growth	91,740
5	*	Lindner Fund	89,625
6		International Investors	88,850
7		Weingarten Equity	88,378
8	*	Lehman Capital Fund	88,377
9	*	Evergreen Fund	86,610
10	*	Loomis-Sayles Capital Dev.	84,064
11	*	Nicholas	78,214
12		AMEV Growth Fund	76,057
13		Phoenix Stock Fund Series	74,748
14		NEL Growth Fund	73,629
15	*	Value Line Leveraged Grth.	72,396
16		IDS Growth Fund	71,469
17		Franklin Gold	69,844
18	*	US Gold Shares	68,907
19		New York Venture	68,479
20		Growth Fund of America	68,113
21		Fidelity Destiny Plan I	67,784
22	*	Pennsylvania Mutual	67,005
23		United Vanguard	66,426
24	*	SteinRoe Special	65,580
25		O-T-C Securities	65,563
26	*	Sequoia (c)	65,419
27	*	Vanguard Qual. Dividend I	65,072
28		A-C Venture	64,264
29		Mass. Financial Cap. Devel.	63,958
30	+	Tudor Fund	63,664
31		AMCAP	63,401
32	*	Partners Fund	62,911
33		A-C Comstock	62,677
34		Sigma Venture Shares	62,178
35	*	AMEV Special Fund	61,878
36	*	Mutual Shares Corp	61,476
37	+	Fidelity Equity Income	60,796
38	*	Janus	59,787
39		Oppenheimer Aim	59,711
40		Oppenheimer Time	59,649
41	*	Acorn	59,419
42		Pioneer II	58,948
43		Putnam Intl. Equities	58,845
44		Guardian Park Avenue	58,636
45		Shearson Appreciation	58,599
46		Kemper Summit	58,253
47		IDS New Dimensions	57,377
48		AMEV Capital Fund	57,352
49		Strategic Investments	57,182
50		Investors Research	56,667

* No-Load Fund, + Low-Load Fund, (No Symbol) Load Fund.

** Does not take into account loads or income taxes that would have to be paid. Includes reinvestment of all dividends and capital gains.

(c) Fund Closed.

Source: Reprinted from *Donoghue's Mutual Funds' Almanac*, 18th Annual Edition. With permission of William E. Donoghue. For a free sample of Donoghue's MONEYLETTER, call (800) 445-5900; in Massachusetts call (617) 429-5930.

PERFORMANCE OF MUTUAL FUNDS

BARRON'S / LIPPER GAUGE

FUND NAME	OBJ.	LOAD	TOTAL NET ASTS (MIL) 6/30/87	NAV 6/30/87	PERFORMANCE (RETURN ON INITIAL $10,000 INVESTMENT) 12/31/86–6/30/87	6/30/86–6/30/87	6/30/82–6/30/87	YIELD % 6/30/87	PER SHARE LATEST 12 MONTHS CAP GAINS	INC DIVS	LATEST AVAILABLE PRICE/EARNINGS	ANNUAL % TURNOVER
ABT EMERGING GROWTH	CA	SC	$49.0	$10.67	$12,166.50	$10,389.50	$ ☆	0.0	$ 0.00	$ 0.00	29.9	49
ABT GROWTH & INCOME TR	GI	SC	139.9	14.05	12,516.60	12,787.70	28,291.90	2.7	2.70	0.42	21.3	95
ABT SECURITY INCOME	OI	SC	16.9	11.74	11,231.20	11,680.60	☆	1.2	0.82	0.15	N/A	200
ABT UTILITY INCOME FD	UT	SC	133.4	14.52	10,095.10	10,487.20	19,876.20	6.5	0.27	0.95	10.8	45
ACORN FUND (R)	SG	NO	525.8	44.04	12,053.40	11,662.60	30,720.00	0.5	4.64	0.25	25.8	34
ADAM INVESTORS	CA	NO	11.2	15.55	11,731.60	10,977.10	☆	5.5	1.53	0.94	N/A	153
ADDISON CAPITAL	GI	LO	26.1	16.21	12,327.00	☆	☆	0.0	0.00	0.00	N/A	N/A
ADTEK FUND	CA	NO	40.2	12.18	12,125.00	11,887.20	☆	1.5	1.56	0.20	N/A	232
ADVANTAGE TR US GOVT	FI	LO	21.2	9.80	#9,951.30	☆	☆	0.0	0.00	0.15	N/A	N/A
ADVEST ADVANTAGE GOVT (R)	FI	NO	257.4	9.29	9,720.90	10,226.70	☆	7.1	0.24	0.66	N/A	242
ADVEST ADVANTAGE GRO (R)	G	NO	29.9	12.90	12,252.90	12,015.50	☆	0.3	0.33	0.03	N/A	33
ADVEST ADVANTAGE INC (R)	I	NO	67.2	10.55	10,587.90	11,117.30	☆	6.1	0.43	0.68	N/A	79
ADVEST ADVANTAGE SPEC (R)	CA	NO	4.6	9.85	11,042.60	9,733.20	☆	0.0	0.00	0.00	N/A	28
AETNA INCOME SHARES	FI	NO	241.0	13.14	10,023.80	10,610.40	21,386.60	7.8	0.00	1.01	12.3	31
AFFILIATED FUND	GI	SC	4,004.2	12.58	12,243.70	12,535.00	33,713.60	4.0	1.14	0.53	20.6	54
AFUTURE FUND	G	NO	13.8	11.86	11,374.00	9,008.30	14,223.10	0.0	2.18	0.00	N/A	200
AGE HIGH INCOME	FI	LO	1,789.0	3.59	10,368.70	10,599.50	22,267.40	12.7	0.00	0.45	N/A	22
ALGER FIXED INCOME (R)	FI	NO	2.4	9.39	9,645.30	☆	☆	0.0	0.00	0.47	N/A	N/A
ALGER GROWTH (R)	G	NO	5.8	11.77	12,109.10	☆	☆	0.0	0.00	0.00	N/A	N/A
ALGER HIGH YIELD (R)	FI	NO	4.1	9.55	10,355.80	☆	☆	0.0	0.00	0.64	N/A	N/A
ALGER INCOME & GROWTH (R)	GI	NO	2.3	10.96	11,160.90	☆	☆	0.0	0.00	0.00	N/A	N/A
ALGER SMALL CAPITAL (R)	SG	NO	4.2	12.29	12,657.10	☆	☆	0.0	0.00	0.00	N/A	N/A
ALLEGRO GROWTH	G	NO	3.9	14.51	12,152.40	12,567.40	☆	0.6	0.11	0.09	N/A	5
ALLIANCE BALANCED FUND	B	SC	120.2	16.12	11,099.50	11,071.20	30,051.60	4.5	0.53	0.73	14.9	27
ALLIANCE BOND-HIGH YLD	FI	SC	467.4	9.49	10,375.40	10,375.00	☆	12.8	0.00	1.21	N/A	109
ALLIANCE BOND-US GOVT	FI	SC	495.6	8.90	10,126.60	10,699.20	☆	10.9	0.00	0.96	N/A	193
ALLIANCE CANADIAN FUND	IF	SC	27.3	8.99	12,665.00	12,227.40	25,950.40	1.3	1.20	0.12	20.3	94
ALLIANCE CONVERTIBLE	CV	SC	112.1	10.26	11,093.20	10,936.60	☆	5.2	0.00	0.53	N/A	56
ALLIANCE COUNTERPOINT	GI	SC	53.0	17.19	12,282.40	11,757.40	☆	2.0	0.31	0.34	16.5	17
ALLIANCE DIVIDEND SHARES	GI	SC	404.1	4.13	11,882.40	11,653.10	32,267.20	2.9	0.40	0.12	19.1	11
ALLIANCE FUND	G	SC	948.2	8.64	12,728.40	11,742.70	26,387.20	1.1	2.07	0.11	26.5	46
ALLIANCE GLOBAL	GL	SC	11.8	11.48	11,382.80	11,601.10	☆	0.3	0.56	0.04	N/A	126
ALLIANCE INTERNATIONAL	IF	SC	194.7	23.70	11,248.20	12,305.40	38,587.90	0.1	2.75	0.03	N/A	62
ALLIANCE MONTHLY INCOME	FI	SC	41.3	12.24	10,122.30	10,757.80	23,395.70	9.1	0.00	1.11	N/A	240
ALLIANCE MORTGAGE INC	FI	SC	752.9	9.29	10,082.60	10,809.30	☆	10.9	0.02	1.01	N/A	190
ALLIANCE TECHNOLOGY	TK	SC	200.8	31.86	14,628.90	13,849.90	41,540.80	0.0	1.60	0.00	56.7	141
ALPHA FUND	G	SC	32.8	8.76	12,800.30	11,549.60	31,710.00	0.7	0.72	0.06	22.9	35
AARP CAPITAL GROWTH	G	NO	99.9	25.94	12,241.60	11,640.40	☆	0.7	0.90	0.18	N/A	46
AARP GENERAL BOND	FI	NO	113.7	15.26	9,921.00	10,471.00	☆	8.0	0.23	1.22	N/A	63
AARP GNMA	FI	NO	2,959.9	15.48	9,964.90	10,666.80	☆	8.8	0.01	1.36	N/A	62
AARP GROWTH AND INCOME	GI	NO	320.2	24.44	11,640.80	11,727.30	☆	2.6	0.88	0.64	N/A	37
AMANA MUTUAL-INCOME	EI	NO	3.3	11.06	11,419.50	11,875.20	☆	2.4	0.50	0.27	N/A	N/A
AMCAP FUND	G	SC	1,893.7	11.60	12,620.80	12,476.70	27,786.80	1.5	0.97	0.18	27.1	17
AMERICAN BALANCED FUND	B	SC	201.6	11.92	11,374.10	11,560.10	28,138.40	5.2	0.98	0.64	20.1	59
AMER CAPITAL COMSTOCK	CA	SC	1,166.7	17.74	12,729.60	12,601.30	29,115.70	2.0	1.73	0.37	24.6	68
AMER CAPITAL CORP BOND	FI	SC	231.3	7.16	10,380.10	10,651.50	22,613.50	11.3	0.00	0.81	N/A	30
AMER CAPITAL ENTERPRISE	G	SC	719.2	15.22	12,739.40	11,399.70	26,909.50	1.3	1.82	0.21	24.8	90

AMER CAPITAL FED MORT	FI	SC	86.4	13.17	9,753.20	10,254.60	☆	7.0	0.44	0.93	N/A	N/A
AMER CAPITAL GOVT	FI	SC	8,847.1	10.84	9,830.10	10,324.50	☆	7.3	0.59	0.81	N/A	411
AMER CAPITAL GROWTH	G	NO	34.2	27.18	13,530.40	11,342.30	23,221.70	0.1	3.79	0.03	29.3	139
AMER CAPITAL HARBOR	CV	SC	417.5	14.77	11,426.70	10,942.00	27,620.40	5.5	1.06	0.84	17.2	83
AMER CAPITAL HIGH YIELD	FI	SC	595.9	9.86	10,700.70	10,372.60	22,506.70	13.1	0.01	1.29	N/A	86
AMER CAPITAL LIFE STOCK	G	NO	38.7	11.39	12,315.40	11,455.90	☆	0.9	0.00	0.09	N/A	268
AMER CAPITAL LIFE GOVT	FI	NO	128.9	9.12	9,770.20	10,014.90	☆	8.8	0.33	0.82	N/A	115
AMER CAPITAL OTC	SG	SC	92.8	10.20	12,289.20	9,412.90	☆	0.1	0.90	0.01	33.8	107
AMER CAPITAL PACE	CA	SC	3,000.5	28.94	12,822.30	12,653.40	30,384.68	2.2	0.83	0.65	24.0	33
AMER CAPITAL VENTURE	CA	SC	333.3	18.14	12,467.40	10,849.40	22,069.30	1.2	0.29	0.22	30.9	103
AMERICAN GROWTH	G	SC	77.5	9.20	12,293.00	11,520.60	22,675.80	3.2	1.09	0.29	24.2	166
AMERICAN HERITAGE	CA	NO	0.7	1.65	11,619.70	9,934.10	8,415.30	0.0	0.36	0.00	N/A	N/A
AMERICAN INV GROWTH	G	NO	72.2	7.93	12,294.60	10,646.10	13,737.10	0.0	0.60	0.00	25.8	161
AMERICAN INV INCOME	FI	NO	23.3	8.79	10,608.70	10,786.80	19,687.40	13.0	0.00	1.14	N/A	97
AMERICAN INV OPTION	OG	NO	0.8	11.66	12,296.90	☆	☆	0.0	0.33	0.11	N/A	N/A
AMERICAN LEADERS	GI	LO	181.1	14.33	12,006.20	12,165.10	32,961.40	4.6	0.82	0.68	19.6	31
AMA CLASSIC GROWTH	G	NO	47.5	12.38	12,166.50	11,091.20	25,691.90	1.0	2.15	0.13	20.0	127
AMA GLOBAL GROWTH	GL	NO	136.2	21.59	#10,821.40	☆	☆	0.0	0.00	0.05	N/A	N/A
AMA GROWTH & INCOME	GI	NO	15.8	20.62	#10,351.20	☆	☆	0.0	0.00	0.08	N/A	N/A
AMA INC-CLASSIC INCOME	FI	NO	36.1	9.10	9,949.50	10,383.20	19,886.30	6.5	0.00	0.59	N/A	67
AMA-GLOBAL INCOME	WI	NO	14.9	20.10	#10,050.00	☆	☆	0.0	0.00	0.00	N/A	N/A
AMA-GLOBAL SHT TERM	GL	NO	15.6	10.06	#10,060.00	☆	☆	0.0	0.00	0.00	N/A	N/A
AMERICAN MUTUAL	GI	SC	2,696.1	20.31	11,519.20	11,621.00	30,970.90	3.6	1.22	0.76	19.2	18
AMERICAN NATIONAL BOND	FI	SC	9.7	14.56	9,994.90	10,344.40	19,280.40	8.4	0.00	1.22	N/A	11
AMERICAN NATIONAL GROWTH	G	SC	117.2	6.04	13,211.80	12,416.40	28,014.80	0.9	0.43	0.05	31.3	26
AMERICAN NATIONAL INCOME	EI	SC	81.5	22.73	12,060.20	11,657.00	26,551.30	3.0	2.03	0.68	25.0	17
AMER TELECOMMUN-GROWTH	TK	NO	43.5	87.48	11,996.40	11,323.90	☆	1.8	16.96	1.74	21.9	71
AMER TELECOMMUN-INCOME	S	NO	91.7	99.19	10,418.60	10,434.50	☆	5.4	2.91	5.40	11.1	15
AMERITRUST BALANCED	B	NO	3.5	10.40	#10,400.00	☆	☆	0.0	0.00	0.00	N/A	N/A
AMERITRUST US GOVT	FI	NO	3.0	10.08	#10,080.00	☆	☆	0.0	0.00	0.00	N/A	N/A
AMEV CAPITAL FD	GI	SC	145.4	16.03	12,369.70	11,271.60	31,260.60	0.6	0.90	0.09	27.0	80
AMEV FIDUCIARY FD	CA	LO	36.0	22.87	12,561.90	11,099.30	33,072.90	0.1	0.70	0.02	33.0	82
AMEV GROWTH FD	CA	SC	255.9	20.23	12,990.30	11,594.90	31,742.50	0.2	0.92	0.04	35.1	72
AMEV SPECIAL FD	CA	NO	29.5	27.83	12,764.80	11,490.60	31,967.10	0.0	3.56	0.00	34.5	79
AMEV US GOVT FD	FI	SC	104.1	9.85	10,028.50	10,642.40	19,248.30	9.6	0.07	0.95	N/A	147
ANALYTIC OPTIONED EQU	OI	NO	85.9	14.70	11,221.10	11,436.80	21,494.00	5.5	1.51	0.85	N/A	64
API TRUST (R)	CA	NO	22.0	12.19	11,682.60	11,299.80	☆	0.2	1.53	0.05	N/A	169
ARIEL GROWTH	SG	LO	4.8	18.55	11,944.60	☆	☆	0.0	0.00	0.01	N/A	N/A
ARMSTRONG ASSOCIATES	G	NO	12.3	9.66	12,090.10	11,999.90	20,691.80	1.6	0.51	0.16	N/A	54
ASSOCIATED PLANNERS GOVT	FI	SC	1.2	9.35	9,730.10	☆	☆	0.0	0.03	0.36	N/A	N/A
ASSOCIATED PLANNERS STK	CA	SC	10.3	16.35	13,007.20	11,898.10	☆	0.2	1.16	0.04	N/A	139
ASTROP ESTABLISHED GRO	G	NO	0.6	9.98	#9,980.00	☆	☆	0.0	0.00	0.00	N/A	N/A
ASTROP HIGH YIELD BOND	FI	NO	0.2	9.51	#9,546.30	☆	☆	0.0	0.00	0.03	N/A	N/A
ASTROP NEW SOUTH	S	NO	0.4	9.86	#9,860.00	☆	☆	0.0	0.00	0.00	N/A	N/A
AXE-HOUGHTON FUND B	B	NO	204.5	11.41	11,358.60	$11,527.30	$28,081.40	5.0	2.86	0.64	28.1	239
AXE-HOUGHTON INCOME	FI	NO	53.4	5.40	10,086.40	10,634.90	22,884.90	9.3	0.00	0.50	N/A	90
AXE-HOUGHTON STOCK	G	NO	93.4	10.23	13,469.80	12,222.60	31,174.30	0.0	2.43	0.00	27.1	218
BABSON BOND TRUST	FI	NO	69.5	1.61	9,953.30	10,542.50	20,615.00	9.3	0.00	0.15	N/A	41
BABSON ENTERPRISE	SG	NO	55.8	14.42	11,961.50	11,029.80	☆	0.4	1.26	0.06	22.5	32
DAVID L BABSON GROWTH	G	NO	288.7	16.25	12,689.70	12,610.50	29,725.90	0.9	0.60	0.15	20.4	20
BABSON VALUE	GI	NO	15.0	18.65	12,739.10	12,999.30	☆	3.0	0.13	0.56	N/A	28
BAIRD BLUE CHIP	GI	LO	11.1	12.41	#10,914.70	☆	☆	0.0	0.00	0.00	N/A	N/A
BAIRD CAP DEVELOPMENT	G	LO	21.6	18.06	12,352.90	9,842.00	☆	0.3	0.04	0.05	N/A	42
BANKERS GRANIT FIX INC	FI	NO	2.6	9.90	9,889.20	10,284.90	☆	7.4	0.00	0.73	N/A	N/A
BANKERS GRANIT GOVT	FI	NO	9.3	10.00	9,962.90	10,355.10	☆	7.2	0.00	0.71	N/A	N/A
BANKERS GRANIT GR STK	G	NO	10.9	18.29	12,613.80	12,324.80	☆	0.0	0.00	0.00	N/A	12
BANKERS GRANIT STOCK	GI	NO	3.1	13.67	11,667.10	11,586.70	☆	0.3	0.15	0.04	N/A	N/A
BARTLETT BASIC VALUE	GI	NO	99.5	13.42	11,569.30	11,201.40	☆	3.7	1.04	0.52	N/A	82

PERFORMANCE OF MUTUAL FUNDS *(continued)*

FUND NAME	OBJ.	LOAD	TOTAL NET ASTS (MIL) 6/30/87	NAV 6/30/87	PERFORMANCE (RETURN ON INITIAL $10,000 INVESTMENT) 12/31/86-6/30/87	6/30/86-6/30/87	6/30/82-6/30/87	YIELD % 6/30/87	PER SHARE—LATEST 12 MONTHS CAP GAINS	INC DIVS	LATEST AVAILABLE PRICE/EARNINGS	ANNUAL % TURNOVER
BARTLETT CORPORATE CASH	EI	NO	23.3	1.04	10,161.30	10,464.50	☆	7.6	0.00	0.07	N/A	167
BARTLETT FIXED INCOME	FI	NO	149.2	9.87	10,141.30	10,740.00	☆	8.6	0.00	0.84	N/A	N/A
BASCOM HILL BALANCED (R)	B	NO	3.4	20.61	10,305.00	☆	☆	0.0	0.00	0.00	N/A	N/A
BASCOM HILL INVESTORS	GI	NO	8.7	16.03	11,176.70	11,268.30	27,340.30	6.2	3.13	1.09	N/A	55
BBK DIVERSA	CA	NO	74.2	11.29	11,346.70	☆	☆	0.0	0.00	0.00	N/A	N/A
BBK INTERNATIONAL	IF	NO	109.4	21.05	11,165.70	12,370.20	47,498.40	10.2	6.49	2.49	N/A	N/A
BEACON HILL MUTUAL	G	NO	3.8	29.82	12,489.40	11,219.50	25,552.10	0.0	0.99	0.00	N/A	N/A
BENCH BLUE CHIP	G	LO	14.9	13.99	12,437.50	12,571.10	☆	0.2	0.02	0.03	N/A	N/A
BENCH TOTAL RETURN	GI	LO	3.7	11.39	11,448.60	11,580.10	☆	0.3	0.65	0.04	N/A	N/A
BENHAM GNMA	FI	NO	300.9	9.97	9,953.50	10,697.60	☆	8.9	0.00	0.89	N/A	264
BENHAM TARGET 1990	FI	NO	6.3	78.83	9,963.30	10,538.80	☆	0.0	0.00	0.00	N/A	113
BENHAM TARGET 1995	FI	NO	5.0	51.93	9,558.30	10,144.60	☆	0.0	0.00	0.00	N/A	89
BENHAM TARGET 2000	FI	NO	5.0	33.13	9,348.20	9,946.00	☆	0.0	0.00	0.00	N/A	39
BENHAM TARGET 2005	FI	NO	2.8	21.25	8,951.10	9,520.60	☆	0.0	0.00	0.00	N/A	50
BENHAM TARGET 2010	FI	NO	4.1	15.27	8,651.60	9,209.90	☆	0.0	0.00	0.00	N/A	91
BENHAM TARGET 2015	FI	NO	0.7	11.71	8,223.30	☆	☆	0.0	0.00	0.00	N/A	22
BERWYN FUND (R)	GI	NO	8.7	15.71	13,294.80	13,479.50	☆	0.7	0.58	0.11	N/A	17
BLANCHARD STRATEGIC GRO	CA	NO	186.5	10.21	12,319.10	13,240.80	☆	3.2	0.08	0.33	N/A	N/A
BMI EQUITY FUND	CA	NO	2.4	36.50	12,310.20	11,489.80	☆	0.0	7.73	0.00	N/A	88
BOND FUND OF AMERICA	FI	SC	823.1	13.64	10,090.90	10,568.60	22,638.50	10.3	0.40	1.42	N/A	108
BOND PORT FOR ENDOWMENTS	FI	NO	28.1	887.05	9,829.50	10,490.80	21,426.00	9.0	0.00	80.00	N/A	140
BOSTON CO CAPITAL APPREC	G	NO	567.1	37.11	11,782.30	11,832.90	33,466.20	3.2	2.90	1.23	17.5	37
BOSTON CO GNMA	FI	NO	15.9	12.00	9,895.20	10,566.00	☆	8.4	0.00	1.00	N/A	85
BOSTON CO MANAGED INCO	FI	NO	60.4	11.72	10,422.00	10,849.80	20,251.50	10.0	0.10	1.17	N/A	71
BOSTON CO SPECIAL GROWTH	G	NO	44.7	17.58	12,002.40	10,268.90	29,295.70	1.4	6.05	0.29	23.3	192
BOSTON MUTUAL FUND	G	NO	6.8	11.33	12,241.10	11,667.00	25,771.40	1.5	1.52	0.18	N/A	82
BOWSER GROWTH	G	NO	3.4	2.34	12,857.10	9,551.00	☆	0.0	0.00	0.00	N/A	47
BRANDYWINE FUND	G	NO	99.1	15.49	13,341.90	12,373.70	☆	0.2	0.00	0.02	N/A	N/A
BRUCE FUND	G	NO	6.9	112.40	10,275.20	9,672.70	30,144.80	1.1	0.00	1.29	N/A	N/A
BULL&BEAR CAPITAL GROWTH	G	NO	93.9	12.70	12,246.90	10,573.60	23,688.20	0.0	4.22	0.00	23.7	78
BULL&BEAR EQUITY-INCOME	EI	NO	18.5	12.22	11,221.90	11,269.90	24,589.60	2.7	0.74	0.34	N/A	93
BULL&BEAR HIGH YIELD	FI	NO	206.5	13.04	10,218.00	9,917.90	☆	13.3	0.01	1.73	N/A	77
BULL&BEAR SPECIAL EQU	CA	NO	3.3	20.28	12,049.90	10,590.10	☆	0.0	0.00	0.00	N/A	N/A
BULL&BEAR US GOVT SEC	FI	NO	46.7	14.68	10,206.20	10,875.00	☆	9.7	0.00	1.41	N/A	100
CALDWELL FUND	G	NO	1.3	13.39	10,859.70	11,031.80	☆	0.0	1.50	0.00	N/A	106
CALVERT EQUITY	G	NO	10.6	23.79	11,960.80	11,352.40	☆	9.8	0.00	2.32	N/A	56
CALVERT INCOME	FI	SC	22.7	16.08	9,884.20	10,094.50	☆	8.9	0.21	1.44	N/A	23
CALVERT SOCIAL INV GRO	GI	NO	155.8	26.49	11,410.80	10,867.80	☆	1.9	0.00	0.79	N/A	24
CALVERT US GOVT	FI	SC	2.0	14.46	9,924.50	☆	☆	0.0	0.00	1.24	N/A	N/A
CAPITAL PRES T NOTE TR	FI	NO	37.5	10.38	9,707.40	10,264.40	17,980.40	6.5	0.54	0.68	N/A	294
CAP SUPERVISORS HELIOS	G	NO	36.5	3764.56	12,337.90	10,815.80	☆	0.9	103.71	33.67	N/A	76
CARDINAL FUND	GI	SC	130.5	17.12	11,866.20	11,454.50	34,182.20	2.4	1.08	0.42	17.4	6
CARDINAL GOVT GUARTD	FI	SC	162.7	9.10	10,192.20	10,760.70	☆	10.2	0.00	0.92	N/A	N/A
CARNEGIE CAPPIELLO GROW	G	SC	57.0	15.68	11,227.30	10,744.20	☆	1.0	0.88	0.16	N/A	46
CARNEGIE HI YLD GOVT	FI	SC	47.5	9.74	10,018.40	10,546.80	☆	7.4	0.71	0.73	N/A	167
CARNEGIE TOTAL RETURN	GI	SC	90.0	11.35	10,822.60	11,090.70	☆	3.3	0.22	0.33	N/A	35
CASHMAN FARRELL VALUE	CA	SC	8.0	11.79	12,485.30	12,505.20	☆	2.5	0.50	0.31	N/A	N/A
CENTURY SHARES TRUST	S	NO	144.4	19.45	10,756.70	9,723.90	29,754.50	2.6	0.40	0.51	13.3	6
CHARTER FUND	CA	NO	99.4	7.76	12,736.50	12,071.70	25,379.40	1.6	1.86	0.13	29.3	75
CHEAPSIDE DOLLAR	G	NO	37.5	12.46	12,651.20	11,664.80	23,743.80	2.0	2.53	0.27	25.8	41
CIGNA AGGRESSIVE GROWTH	SG	SC	21.5	13.72	11,346.40	10,186.10	☆	0.1	0.23	0.01	N/A	106
CIGNA GOVT	FI	SC	8.5	10.11	#10,179.70	☆	☆	0.0	0.00	0.07	N/A	N/A
CIGNA GROWTH	G	SC	264.2	16.09	12,635.60	11,919.50	28,797.70	1.5	2.56	0.26	26.3	66
CIGNA HIGH YIELD	FI	SC	268.8	10.41	10,448.80	10,794.70	24,496.30	11.5	0.00	1.20	N/A	86
CIGNA INCOME	FI	SC	258.3	7.77	9,921.00	10,447.30	22,373.10	8.6	0.00	0.67	N/A	85
CIGNA VALUE	GI	SC	62.6	14.43	12,003.50	11,826.10	☆	2.4	1.14	0.35	21.0	134

CLAREMONT—BOND	FI	NO	5.9	10.42	9,905.50	10,364.80	☆	6.5	0.06	0.68	N/A	93
CLAREMONT—COMBINED	GI	NO	15.7	13.81	11,639.80	11,079.50	☆	1.9	0.12	0.27	N/A	111
CLAREMONT—STOCK	G	NO	4.5	12.19	11,116.50	10,575.10	☆	1.5	0.23	0.18	N/A	93
CLIPPER FUND	GI	NO	90.2	44.41	11,181.70	11,342.50	☆	3.3	1.88	1.48	19.2	40
COLONIAL ADV STR GOLD	AU	SC	91.7	27.88	15,555.60	20,115.20	☆	1.8	0.00	0.50	54.6	51
COLONIAL CORP CASH I	EI	LO	385.5	48.71	10,358.60	10,788.90	18,802.70	8.4	0.59	4.10	18.3	255
COLONIAL CORP CASH II	EI	LO	282.9	48.01	10,401.00	10,692.40	☆	6.6	0.29	3.17	15.3	87
COLONIAL DVSD INCOME	OI	SC	1,046.2	8.55	11,933.40	11,789.40	22,421.90	1.3	0.91	0.12	28.6	134
COLONIAL EQUITY INCOME	EI	SC	17.0	16.12	11,228.80	11,367.40	28,968.20	3.1	2.81	0.67	N/A	81
COLONIAL FUND	GI	SC	264.0	19.68	11,363.80	11,588.10	29,415.50	3.9	1.31	0.93	14.8	48
COLONIAL GOVT SEC PLUS	FI	SC	4,112.5	11.78	9,826.00	10,402.30	☆	7.1	0.67	0.86	N/A	201
COLONIAL GOVT MORTGAGE	FI	SC	35.5	13.47	9,778.00	10,211.20	☆	6.9	0.43	0.93	N/A	719
COLONIAL GROWTH SHARES	G	SC	98.3	13.73	12,383.90	12,004.50	28,805.80	0.7	2.37	0.12	20.3	65
COLONIAL HIGH YIELD	FI	SC	477.1	7.66	10,510.90	10,990.20	24,598.50	11.3	0.00	0.86	N/A	52
COLONIAL INCOME FUND	FI	SC	174.8	6.97	10,176.90	10,661.70	21,656.10	11.3	0.00	0.79	N/A	42
COLONIAL INCOME PLUS	OI	SC	203.0	11.27	11,426.00	11,349.60	☆	2.4	1.16	0.28	27.4	189
COLONIAL INTL EQ INDEX	IF	SC	9.0	16.77	12,552.00	☆	☆	0.0	0.00	0.01	N/A	N/A
COLONIAL SMAL STK INDEX	SG	SC	38.2	13.81	12,154.80	☆	☆	0.0	0.00	0.03	N/A	N/A
COLONIAL US EQUITY INDEX	G	SC	35.8	15.21	12,575.00	☆	☆	0.0	0.00	0.05	N/A	N/A
COLUMBIA FIXED INCOME	FI	NO	114.2	12.47	9,908.00	10,646.70	☆	9.1	0.22	1.14	N/A	97
COLUMBIA GROWTH	G	NO	250.4	28.43	12,871.80	11,519.70	31,785.70	0.8	4.56	0.25	28.9	131
COLUMBIA SPECIAL (R)	CA	NO	32.3	36.82	13,652.20	11,357.00	☆	0.0	0.74	0.00	30.4	203
COLUMBIA US GOVT	FI	NO	4.6	8.31	10,075.90	☆	☆	0.0	0.00	0.31	N/A	N/A
COMMON SENSE GOVT	FI	SC	10.8	11.56	#10,023.50	☆	☆	0.0	0.00	0.12	N/A	N/A
COMMON SENSE GROWTH	CA	SC	70.5	11.94	#10,437.10	☆	☆	0.0	0.00	0.00	N/A	N/A
COMMON SENSE GRO & INC	GI	SC	26.0	11.86	#10,367.10	☆	☆	0.0	0.00	0.00	N/A	N/A
COMMONWEALTH A&B	GI	NO	10.6	1.64	11,298.00	11,242.70	24,315.70	5.1	0.16	0.08	N/A	103
COMMONWEALTH C	GI	NO	43.6	2.27	11,172.10	11,122.80	22,878.90	4.6	0.16	0.10	19.7	88
COMPANION FUND	G	NO	90.9	14.12	12,655.10	11,888.10	30,071.00	2.0	2.42	0.30	26.6	70
COMPOSITE BOND & STOCK	B	LO	91.3	10.64	10,913.10	11,056.30	25,009.40	5.1	0.71	0.56	14.1	74
COMPOSITE GROWTH FD	GI	LO	78.7	12.16	11,316.20	11,370.50	27,983.20	3.4	1.67	0.44	15.6	58
COMPOSITE INCOME FUND	FI	LO	119.2	9.26	10,351.20	10,900.30	22,844.70	10.9	0.00	1.00	N/A	1.00
COMPOSITE SEL HI YLD	FI	LO	1.2	11.53	10,076.50	☆	☆	0.0	0.00	0.60	N/A	N/A
COMPOSITE SEL VALUE	SG	LO	8.1	13.05	10,812.30	☆	☆	0.0	0.00	0.10	N/A	N/A
COMPOSITE SEL NORTHWEST	G	LO	5.5	15.56	12,952.00	☆	☆	0.0	0.00	0.08	N/A	N/A
COMPOSITE US GOVT SEC	FI	LO	103.5	1.01	9,937.40	10,500.90	☆	9.3	0.00	0.09	N/A	86
CONCORD FUND	G	NO	1.8	31.61	11,870.10	11,450.40	21,140.70	2.4	0.00	0.76	N/A	N/A
CONCORD INCOME-US GOVT	FI	LO	9.0	6.91	#9,929.90	☆	☆	0.0	0.00	0.23	N/A	N/A
CONSTELLATION GROWTH	CA	SC	149.0	13.99	13,693.20	12,769.50	36,825.50	0.0	3.85	0.00	29.2	107
CONTINENTAL EQUITY + (R)	G	LO	11.8	11.70	12,160.50	12,225.00	☆	5.8	0.00	0.67	N/A	N/A
CONTINENTAL GOVT INC	FI	LO	0.9	9.85	10,255.90	☆	☆	0.0	0.00	0.52	N/A	N/A
CONTINENTAL S&P 100	G	LO	0.8	12.07	12,444.10	☆	☆	0.0	0.00	0.40	N/A	N/A
CONTINENTAL OPT INC + (R)	OI	LO	12.2	10.57	11,648.90	11,622.10	☆	7.4	0.00	0.77	N/A	N/A
CONTINENTAL US GOVT + (R)	FI	LO	35.8	9.40	9,891.90	10,447.00	☆	9.5	0.00	0.89	N/A	N/A
CONVERTIBLE YIELD SEC	CV	SC	26.9	11.55	10,789.00	9,610.10	17,994.20	5.5	0.93	0.66	N/A	192
COPLEY FUND	GI	NO	31.0	11.35	10,299.50	10,538.50	25,055.20	0.0	0.00	0.00	12.3	16
CORPORATE LEADERS TR-B (X)	GI	SC	88.8	15.80	12,470.40	13,078.60	34,694.90	8.6	1.54	1.43	N/A	N/A
CORPORATE PREFERRED FD	FI	LO	22.5	45.75	10,141.70	10,138.30	☆	6.4	0.00	2.92	N/A	30
COUNTRY CAPITAL GROWTH	G	SC	79.2	19.43	12,204.80	11,475.10	27,130.00	3.3	2.84	0.63	25.4	65
COUNTRY CAPITAL INCOME	FI	SC	6.0	10.84	10,028.30	10,226.10	21,185.00	6.7	0.00	0.72	N/A	59
COWEN INCOME & GROWTH (R)	EI	NO	30.1	10.61	10,879.50	☆	☆	0.0	0.00	0.31	N/A	N/A
CREDIT UNION GOVT	FI	NO	10.5	9.41	#9,768.70	☆	☆	0.0	0.00	0.34	N/A	N/A
CRITERION COMMERCE INC	I	SC	85.8	11.38	11,705.20	11,441.90	24,265.50	3.3	0.88	0.38	23.8	150
CRITERION CONVERTIBLE	CV	SC	15.7	10.80	11,458.50	☆	☆	0.0	0.00	0.33	N/A	N/A
CRITERION INV QUAL INT	FI	SC	154.4	9.48	9,926.10	10,361.40	21,474.20	11.1	0.22	1.06	N/A	322
CRITERION GLOBAL GROWTH	GL	SC	10.6	13.88	13,880.00	☆	☆	0.0	0.00	0.00	N/A	N/A
CRITERION LTD TRM INSTL	FI	NO	1.5	9.59	10,058.50	☆	☆	0.0	0.00	0.53	N/A	N/A
CRITERION PILOT FUND	CA	SC	78.4	11.95	12,909.30	12,275.40	27,141.70	0.8	1.16	0.10	23.8	101
CRITERION SUNBELT GRO	G	SC	71.1	22.66	12,295.20	11,920.50	25,965.20	0.1	0.00	0.03	24.3	92
CRITERION TECHNOLOGY	TK	SC	4.3	18.50	15,059.30	15,740.20	☆	0.0	4.83	0.00	N/A	267

PERFORMANCE OF MUTUAL FUNDS *(continued)*

FUND NAME	OBJ.	LOAD	TOTAL NET ASTS (MIL) 6/30/87	NAV 6/30/87	PERFORMANCE (RETURN ON INITIAL $10,000 INVESTMENT) 12/31/86–6/30/87	6/30/86–6/30/87	6/30/82–6/30/87	YIELD % 6/30/87	PER SHARE LATEST 12 MONTHS CAP GAINS	INC DIVS	LATEST AVAILABLE PRICE/EARNINGS	ANNUAL % TURNOVER
CRITERION US GOVT HI YLD	FI	SC	1,902.4	9.16	10,004.30	10,413.20	☆	7.4	0.39	0.69	N/A	999
CRITERION US GOVT INSTL	FI	LO	325.4	9.32	10,035.80	10,491.90	☆	7.4	0.34	0.70	N/A	75
CUMBERLAND GROWTH	CA	NO	2.9	11.46	10,836.20	10,420.70	20,412.00	6.1	0.00	0.70	N/A	194
DEAN WITTER AMER VALUE (R)	G	NO	124.7	14.70	11,807.90	11,240.10	23,697.00	1.5	1.84	0.23	25.1	120
DEAN WITTER CONVERT (R)	CV	NO	1,899.8	12.28	11,562.00	11,036.00	☆	5.1	0.28	0.63	N/A	272
DEAN WITTER DEV GRO (R)	SG	NO	167.7	10.18	11,464.00	10,255.80	☆	0.1	0.00	0.01	28.7	90
DEAN WITTER DIVID GRO (R)	GI	NO	2,048.9	21.11	11,653.60	11,701.80	31,063.00	2.4	0.48	0.52	21.5	12
DEAN WITTER GOVT PLUS (R)	FI	NO	1,748.3	9.69	#9,955.40	☆	☆	0.0	0.08	0.18	N/A	N/A
DEAN WITTER HIGH YIELD	FI	SC	1,962.8	13.97	10,544.90	11,061.40	23,599.40	12.9	0.00	1.80	N/A	95
DEAN WITTER NTRL RES (R)	NR	NO	178.9	10.43	13,301.30	14,484.00	21,086.40	1.3	0.00	0.14	28.6	14
DEAN WITTER OPT INC (R)	OI	NO	545.3	9.80	10,769.30	10,730.00	☆	8.4	0.25	0.83	17.3	212
DEAN WITTER TX-ADVAN	FI	NO	274.8	10.23	10,289.80	10,620.90	☆	7.0	0.00	0.71	N/A	36
DEAN WITTER US GOVT (R)	FI	NO	1,409.5	9.97	10,119.70	10,657.90	☆	9.7	0.00	0.96	N/A	93
DEAN WITTER WORLD WIDE (R)	GL	NO	495.5	17.33	11,681.00	12,263.70	☆	0.6	2.06	0.11	23.9	69
DECATUR I	EI	SC	1,636.0	20.24	12,256.20	12,677.20	32,581.90	3.8	2.00	0.80	17.1	72
DECATUR II	GI	SC	133.9	11.98	11,848.10	☆	☆	0.0	0.00	0.08	N/A	N/A
DELAWARE FUND	GI	SC	433.8	22.31	12,253.20	11,470.90	29,602.90	1.8	4.31	0.45	19.6	104
DELAWARE GNMA SR	FI	SC	87.0	8.87	10,051.60	10,613.80	☆	10.3	0.04	0.91	N/A	321
DELAWARE TREAS RESERVE	FI	NO	163.3	9.87	10,234.80	10,546.90	☆	7.2	0.00	0.71	N/A	39
DELAWARE US GOVT SR	FI	SC	67.8	8.67	9,850.40	10,393.50	☆	10.0	0.08	0.86	N/A	349
DELCAP FUND I	CA	SC	91.2	14.22	13,440.50	15,548.10	☆	0.9	7.42	0.16	N/A	293
DELCHESTER BOND FUND	FI	SC	386.6	8.04	10,580.40	11,093.30	24,659.50	12.2	0.00	0.98	N/A	137
DELTA TREND FUND	CA	SC	79.1	9.12	12,701.90	10,235.70	24,315.40	0.0	0.00	0.00	32.2	113
DIT CAPITAL GROWTH	G	NO	15.3	16.23	12,361.00	11,514.60	☆	0.8	2.03	0.13	N/A	118
DIT CURRENT INCOME	FI	NO	7.0	10.14	10,544.60	10,936.80	☆	11.1	0.22	1.13	N/A	163
DFA FIXED INCOME PORT	FI	NO	374.3	101.28	10,257.50	10,598.60	☆	6.6	0.26	6.71	N/A	138
DFA JAPAN SMALL CO	IF	NO	62.0	20.85	14,349.60	13,280.30	☆	0.0	0.00	0.00	N/A	N/A
DFA SMALL COMPANY (R)	SG	NO	1,086.5	10.43	11,988.50	10,791.10	28,338.10	1.0	0.65	0.10	25.1	14
DFA UNITED KINGDOM SM CO	IF	NO	91.3	29.32	16,908.90	17,599.00	☆	0.0	0.00	0.00	N/A	N/A
DIV/GROWTH DIVIDEND SR	EI	NO	4.8	27.76	11,640.80	11,154.80	19,593.00	1.9	0.94	0.55	N/A	43
DIV/GRO LASER & ADV TECH	TK	NO	0.2	10.22	11,012.90	8,639.10	☆	0.0	0.00	0 00	N/A	70
DODGE & COX BALANCED	B	NO	38.5	37.62	11,781.50	12,085.90	28,851.60	4.0	1.76	1.55	19.8	14
DODGE & COX STOCK	GI	NO	71.1	40.18	12,848.70	13,002.00	36,593.30	2.2	1.30	0.91	22.5	10
DOLPHIN FRIC CONVERTIBLE	CV	LO	9.1	10.49	10,701.50	☆	☆	0.0	0.00	0.31	N/A	N/A
DR EQUITY	G	NO	13.6	11.24	11,732.80	☆	☆	0.0	0.00	0.29	N/A	N/A
DREXEL BURNHAM FUND	GI	LO	230.5	24.43	11,747.80	11,754.50	28,970.50	3.2	2.29	0.82	21.4	114
DREXEL SR-BOND-DEB (R)	FI	NO	24.5	11.00	9,844.40	10,347.30	☆	8.6	0.26	0.96	N/A	93
DREXEL SR-CONVERTIBLE (R)	CV	NO	39.7	10.60	11,349.20	10,505.80	☆	2.9	0.36	0.31	N/A	92
DREXEL SR-EMERGING GRO (R)	SG	NO	34.2	15.65	12,391.10	8,973.60	☆	0.0	0.00	0.00	N/A	75
DREXEL SR-GOVT (R)	FI	NO	471.3	9.80	9,631.90	10,192.80	☆	8.3	0.35	0.82	N/A	169
DREXEL SR-GROWTH (R)	G	NO	42.2	14.38	12,411.70	12,178.20	☆	1.6	0.65	0.24	N/A	40
DREXEL SR-OPTION INC (R)	OI	NO	46.2	10.89	11,302.10	11,304.40	☆	1.2	1.19	0.14	N/A	152
DREYFUS A BONDS PLUS	FI	NO	271.7	13.95	9,861.40	10,448.10	20,193.70	9.0	0.46	1.27	N/A	61
DREYFUS CAPITAL VALUE	CA	LO	29.8	23.56	12,625.90	11,052.10	☆	0.3	0.65	0.06	N/A	141
DREYFUS CONVERTIBLE SEC	CV	NO	264.7	9.36	11,239.00	11,476.30	27,674.60	5.0	0.55	0.49	14.3	62
DREYFUS CORP CASH TR	FI	NO	31.0	12.50	10,241.70	☆	☆	0.0	0.00	0.54	N/A	151
DREYFUS FUND	GI	SC	2,689.6	13.97	11,996.30	11,891.30	26,926.00	3.3	1.57	0.49	29.0	149
DREYFUS GNMA	FI	NO	2,343.0	15.05	10,037.60	10,669.50	☆	9.0	0.02	1.36	N/A	245
DREYFUS GRO OPPORTUNITY	G	NO	552.6	12.12	12,532.50	12,474.80	27,504.70	1.4	2.32	0.18	23.0	73
DREYFUS INDEX	G	NO	22.2	12.97	#10,376.00	☆	☆	0.0	0.00	0.00	N/A	N/A
DREYFUS LEVERAGE FUND	CA	SC	588.4	20.24	12,470.70	12,551.80	31,276.00	2.3	4.73	0.52	30.1	141
DREYFUS NEW LEADERS	SG	NO	117.7	25.20	12,411.60	10,516.00	☆	0.3	0.00	0.07	N/A	195
DREYFUS SHT-INTERM GOVT	FI	NO	1.3	11.47	#9,826.40	☆	☆	0.0	0.00	0.31	N/A	N/A
DREYFUS STRAT AGG INV LP	CA	LO	8.1	22.06	#14,706.70	☆	☆	0.0	0.00	0.00	N/A	N/A
DREYFUS STRATEGIC INCO	FI	LO	35.0	13.28	10,260.00	☆	☆	0.0	0.00	0.83	N/A	N/A
DREYFUS STRATEGIC INVEST	CA	LO	113.8	17.16	13,374.90	☆	☆	0.0	0.00	0.05	N/A	N/A

DREYFUS STRAT WORLD LP	GL	LO	3.2	15.74	#12,107.70	☆	☆	0.0	0.00	0.00	N/A	N/A
DREYFUS THIRD CENTURY	G	NO	175.7	7.94	12,196.60	11,918.30	24,668.70	3.9	0.96	0.31	21.4	63
DREYFUS US GOVT BD LP	FI	NO	2.6	13.33	#9,419.10	☆	☆	0.0	0.00	0.32	N/A	N/A
DREYFUS US GOVT INTER LP	FI	NO	5.6	12.89	#9,805.40	☆	☆	0.0	0.00	0.34	N/A	N/A
EAGLE GROWTH SHARES	G	SC	2.9	7.23	10,585.70	9,426.90	15,027.00	0.1	0.08	0.01	N/A	304
EATON & HOWARD STOCK	GI	SC	87.9	15.00	11,556.30	11,427.80	29,696.80	3.4	1.43	0.53	20.8	42
EATON VANCE GOVT OBLIG	FI	SC	418.4	11.87	10,140.60	10,708.30	☆	9.8	0.20	1.17	N/A	37
EATON VANCE GROWTH	G	SC	100.5	8.79	12,912.40	12,021.00	30,336.10	1.3	0.80	0.11	23.5	68
EATON VANCE HIGH INC (R)	FI	NO	212.5	9.88	10,456.40	☆	☆	0.0	0.05	0.93	N/A	N/A
EATON VANCE HIGH YIELD	FI	SC	36.2	5.29	10,518.40	11,162.10	24,026.20	11.3	0.00	0.60	N/A	131
EATON VANCE INC OF BOSTON	FI	SC	45.3	10.20	10,471.00	11,024.90	23,860.70	10.2	0.00	1.04	11.0	74
EATON VANCE INVESTORS	B	SC	240.2	8.42	11,447.90	11,178.70	25,657.60	4.3	0.68	0.38	24.9	89
EATON VANCE SPL EQUITIES	G	SC	40.7	19.03	11,783.30	9,734.00	20,281.80	0.0	1.85	0.00	27.8	58
EATON VANCE TOTAL RETURN	GI	SC	700.0	10.28	10,369.30	10,785.00	29,953.40	5.2	1.57	0.58	12.9	74
ECLIPSE EQUITY	SG	NO	152.3	10.11	#10,159.90	☆	☆	0.0	0.00	0.05	N/A	N/A
EHRENKRANTZ GROWTH	G	NO	1.7	5.27	#10,540.00	☆	☆	0.0	0.00	0.00	N/A	N/A
EHRENKRANTZ EQUITIES	CA	NO	1.3	5.11	#10,220.00	☆	☆	0.0	0.00	0.00	N/A	N/A
88 FUND	G	SC	0.1	7.53	11,340.40	7,233.40	☆	0.0	0.00	0.00	N/A	N/A
ELFUN TRUSTS	G	NO	589.8	32.30	12,241.50	11,728.90	31,814.30	2.6	2.77	0.89	22.7	N/A
ENDOWMENTS INC	GI	NO	38.1	1941.34	11,394.50	11,606.60	29,707.00	4.1	281.00	80.00	18.6	15
ENERGY FUND	NR	NO	473.4	22.87	12,382.20	12,795.50	25,198.80	3.8	1.66	0.88	25.6	28
EQUITEC SIEBEL AGGRES (R)	CA	NO	44.4	13.99	11,688.60	11,088.90	☆	5.7	0.10	0.81	23.7	63
EQUITEC SIEBEL HI YLD (R)	FI	NO	23.2	9.48	10,295.10	10,627.70	☆	10.5	0.00	0.99	N/A	3
EQUITEC SIEBEL TOTL RETN	GI	NO	140.4	14.66	11,296.40	10,943.20	☆	3.5	0.12	0.51	23.8	69
EQUITEC SIEBEL US GOVT (R)	FI	NO	93.1	9.72	10,223.90	10,674.00	☆	8.8	0.00	0.85	N/A	61
EQUITY STRATEGIES (X)	S	NO	59.9	19.72	11,634.20	☆	☆	0.0	0.00	0.00	N/A	N/A
EUROPEAN FUND	IF	SC	2.4	11.09	#11,090.00	☆	☆	0.0	0.00	0.00	N/A	N/A
EUROPACIFIC GROWTH	IF	SC	245.4	28.67	12,137.30	13,497.90	☆	0.7	1.57	0.22	N/A	34
EVERGREEN FUND	G	NO	779.7	14.60	11,931.80	10,754.60	32,142.70	0.9	1.12	0.13	18.9	48
EVERGREEN TOTAL RETURN	EI	NO	1,729.9	19.42	10,628.90	10,854.00	32,734.50	5.6	1.03	1.13	13.7	65
EXPLORER FUND (X)	TK	NO	288.6	33.00	11,930.60	10,137.50	19,523.20	0.1	3.27	0.02	26.6	15
EXPLORER II	SG	NO	67.5	24.00	12,644.90	10,596.30	☆	0.2	0.47	0.04	27.0	23
FAIRFIELD FUND	SG	SC	52.6	10.14	12,246.40	10,988.80	25,878.30	0.9	2.68	0.09	36.0	196
FAIRMONT FUND	CA	NO	109.7	58.85	11,888.90	11,104.40	37,286.20	0.5	5.56	0.29	N/A	1
FAM VALUE (R)	GI	NO	1.3	11.19	#10,556.60	☆	☆	0.0	0.00	0.00	N/A	N/A
FARM BUREAU GROWTH FUND	GI	NO	56.6	15.66	11,035.90	10,582.70	20,138.70	2.6	1.73	0.40	12.8	30
FEDERATED BOND	FI	NO	12.0	9.32	9,751.20	10,321.20	☆	9.6	0.00	0.89	N/A	25
FEDERATED CORP CASH	FI	NO	103.4	10.71	10,353.00	10,537.00	☆	6.1	0.00	0.65	N/A	68
FEDERATED FLOATING RATE	FI	NO	83.7	9.93	10,367.30	☆	☆	0.0	0.00	0.79	N/A	N/A
FEDERATED GNMA TRUST	FI	NO	2,552.8	10.98	10,066.60	10,746.10	19,417.90	9.8	0.00	1.07	N/A	100
FEDERATED GROWTH TRUST	G	NO	143.5	18.28	12,046.30	11,810.10	☆	1.4	0.90	0.25	17.5	42
FEDERATED HIGH INCOME	FI	LO	377.4	12.10	10,411.00	10,677.20	22,755.70	12.0	0.00	1.45	N/A	27
FEDERATED HI QUAL STK	GI	NO	34.4	13.31	12,014.80	12,119.30	☆	1.2	0.04	0.16	19.8	13
FEDERATED HIGH YIELD TR	FI	NO	271.7	10.72	10,468.20	10,962.50	☆	11.9	0.05	1.27	N/A	31
FEDERATED INCOME TRUST	FI	NO	1,604.6	10.38	10,126.70	10,737.20	18,739.10	9.6	0.00	0.99	N/A	146
FEDERATED INTMDT GOVT	FI	NO	1,856.4	9.80	10,042.90	10,562.60	☆	8.3	0.08	0.81	N/A	49
FEDERATED SH-INTMDT GOVT	FI	NO	3,639.6	10.19	10,174.30	10,574.00	☆	7.8	0.04	0.79	N/A	99
FEDERATED STOCK & BOND	B	NO	102.7	16.10	10,814.50	11,114.00	26,842.40	4.9	0.45	0.80	20.1	40
FEDERATED STOCK TRUST	GI	NO	749.7	25.85	12,143.20	12,184.80	36,766.30	2.4	0.81	0.64	20.2	19
FEDERATED US GOVT	FI	NO	6.5	9.30	9,662.60	10,217.10	☆	8.6	0.00	0.79	N/A	89
FEDERATED UTILITY	UT	NO	6.6	9.27	#9,402.40	☆	☆	0.0	0.00	0.15	N/A	N/A
FENIMORE INTL (R)	IF	NO	95.8	14.44	12,051.00	13,603.60	☆	0.0	0.58	0.00	N/A	47
FIDELITY ADJUSTABLE RATE	FI	NO	261.1	10.68	10,596.50	11,060.50	☆	6.4	0.00	0.68	N/A	113
FIDELITY BALANCED	B	NO	169.8	10.85	10,877.20	☆	☆	0.0	0.00	0.20	20.6	N/A
FIDELITY CAPITAL APREC (R)	CA	NO	1,114.2	13.25	13,903.50	☆	☆	0.0	0.00	0.00	25.3	N/A
FIDELITY CONTRAFUND	G	NO	138.5	14.14	12,939.50	12,646.20	27,074.90	0.9	1.63	0.13	19.7	190
FIDELITY CONVERTIBLE	CV	NO	45.7	10.62	10,721.20	☆	☆	0.0	0.00	0.10	N/A	N/A
FIDELITY DESTINY I	G	SC	1,461.5	15.93	12,815.80	12,242.50	39,585.60	2.0	2.54	0.32	22.0	108
FIDELITY DESTINY II	G	SC	39.2	20.98	13,170.10	12,937.10	☆	0.0	0.29	0.00	26.4	228
FIDELITY EQUITY-INCOME	EI	LO	4,178.8	29.14	11,590.40	11,686.20	32,519.00	5.3	3.12	1.64	19.0	110

PERFORMANCE OF MUTUAL FUNDS *(continued)*

FUND NAME	OBJ.	LOAD	TOTAL NET ASTS (MIL) 6/30/87	NAV 6/30/87	PERFORMANCE (RETURN ON INITIAL $10,000 INVESTMENT) 12/31/86–6/30/87	6/30/86–6/30/87	6/30/82–6/30/87	YIELD % 6/30/87	PER SHARE—LATEST 12 MONTHS CAP GAINS	INC DIVS	LATEST AVAILABLE PRICE/EARNINGS	ANNUAL % TURNOVER
FIDELITY EUROPE	IF	LO	200.6	14.66	13,573.60	☆	☆	0.0	0.00	0.01	N/A	9
FIDELITY FLEXIBLE BOND	FI	NO	373.2	6.90	9,808.20	10,244.60	19,632.00	9.6	0.00	0.66	N/A	243
FIDELITY FREEDOM FUND	CA	NO	1,362.2	17.25	13,921.20	12,465.80	☆	0.7	3.50	0.14	26.8	161
FIDELITY FUND	GI	NO	1,111.2	18.29	12,480.30	11,889.30	31,368.40	3.1	3.47	0.62	24.9	214
FIDELITY GNMA	FI	NO	877.5	10.30	9,925.90	10,659.50	☆	8.5	0.01	0.87	N/A	106
FIDELITY GLOBAL BOND	WI	NO	26.6	10.33	10,585.20	☆	☆	0.0	0.00	0.30	N/A	N/A
FIDELITY GOVT SECURITIES	FI	NO	701.4	9.76	9,893.80	10,405.90	18,789.20	8.6	0.00	0.84	N/A	138
FIDELITY GROWTH & INC	GI	NO	1,495.9	16.66	12,568.90	12,237.30	☆	1.5	0.00	0.25	23.9	69
FIDELITY GROWTH CO FUND	G	LO	178.8	16.63	11,869.40	10,627.00	☆	0.0	3.01	0.00	26.9	120
FIDELITY HIGH INCOME	FI	NO	1,794.1	9.54	10,443.50	10,924.00	26,233.00	11.1	0.26	1.07	2.6	104
FIDELITY INTL GR & INC (R)	IF	LO	52.6	12.25	#10,965.00	☆	☆	0.0	0.00	0.02	N/A	N/A
FIDELITY MAGELLAN FUND	G	LO	842.3	54.84	12,605.80	11,996.70	46,733.50	0.6	8.69	0.37	21.9	96
FIDELITY MORTGAGE	FI	NO	611.9	10.16	10,025.90	10,672.30	☆	9.0	0.03	0.91	N/A	59
FIDELITY OVERSEAS	IF	LO	2,313.4	36.35	13,194.10	14,982.90	☆	0.0	3.31	0.00	N/A	107
FIDELITY OTC	SG	LO	1,199.3	20.79	12,623.00	11,034.30	☆	0.1	1.27	0.02	27.1	132
FIDELITY PACIFIC BASIN	IF	LO	317.4	14.76	13,503.70	☆	☆	0.0	0.00	0.01	N/A	N/A
FIDELITY PURITAN	EI	NO	4,645.2	14.52	11,200.40	11,748.30	31,346.90	6.3	0.76	0.92	19.3	85
FIDELITY QUALIFIED DVD	EI	NO	150.5	14.87	10,259.80	10,641.50	26,035.60	6.4	0.76	0.98	13.4	25
FIDELITY REAL ESTATE	S	LO	103.7	10.34	10,613.60	☆	☆	0.0	0.00	0.21	19.7	N/A
FIDELITY SEL AIR TRANS (R)	S	LO	19.6	12.74	11,884.30	12,576.50	☆	0.0	0.00	0.00	N/A	999
FIDELITY SEL AMER GOLD (R)	AU	LO	245.7	17.05	14,412.50	16,748.50	☆	0.0	0.00	0.00	48.4	52
FIDELITY SEL AUTOMATION (R)	S	LO	1.9	11.92	12,494.80	11,920.00	☆	0.0	0.00	0.00	N/A	N/A
FIDELITY SEL AUTO (R)	S	LO	5.4	12.75	13,239.90	12,750.00	☆	0.0	0.00	0.00	N/A	N/A
FIDELITY SEL BIO TECH (R)	S	LO	68.6	13.74	13,275.40	9,717.10	☆	0.0	0.00	0.00	44.6	937
FIDELITY SEL BROADCAST (R)	S	LO	34.9	13.14	13,435.60	13,140.00	☆	0.0	0.00	0.00	N/A	N/A
FIDELITY SEL BROKERAGE (R)	S	LO	10.5	12.46	10,280.50	9,180.00	☆	0.1	0.02	0.01	N/A	347
FIDELITY SEL CAP GOODS (R)	S	LO	3.2	13.10	12,323.60	☆	☆	0.0	0.00	0.00	N/A	N/A
FIDELITY SEL CHEMICAL (R)	TK	LO	147.0	21.29	13,595.10	13,317.30	☆	0.0	0.06	0.00	22.5	125
FIDELITY SEL COMPUTER (R)	TK	LO	46.8	16.19	13,259.60	12,595.10	☆	0.0	0.04	0.00	33.9	269
FIDELITY SEL DEFENSE (R)	S	LO	4.0	15.68	10,601.80	9,576.80	☆	0.1	0.20	0.02	N/A	280
FIDELITY SEL ELECTRONIC (R)	TK	LO	10.1	10.34	12,222.20	10,237.60	☆	0.0	0.00	0.00	N/A	326
FIDELITY SEL ELEC UTIL (R)	UT	LO	6.7	9.41	9,335.30	9,410.00	☆	0.0	0.00	0.00	N/A	N/A
FIDELITY SEL ENERGY (R)	NR	LO	146.3	14.65	12,706.00	14,073.00	22,347.70	0.0	0.00	0.00	31.3	167
FIDELITY SEL ENRGY SER (R)	NR	LO	189.3	12.85	15,011.70	14,028.40	☆	0.0	0.00	0.00	31.7	54
FIDELITY SEL FINANCIAL (R)	S	LO	60.3	33.43	10,592.50	9,218.40	36,285.30	0.6	0.33	0.20	10.2	136
FIDELITY SEL FOOD (R)	S	LO	18.7	18.41	13,056.70	11,946.80	☆	0.0	0.00	0.00	N/A	576
FIDELITY SEL HEALTH (R)	H	LO	399.6	43.40	13,239.80	11,526.50	40,702.10	0.0	0.36	0.00	38.9	217
FIDELITY SEL HEALTH DL (R)	H	LO	20.4	9.55	11,660.60	9,550.00	☆	0.0	0.00	0.00	N/A	N/A
FIDELITY SEL HOUSING (R)	S	LO	2.7	13.20	12,267.70	☆	☆	0.0	0.00	0.00	N/A	N/A
FIDELITY SEL INDUS MAT (R)	S	LO	39.8	14.93	14,151.70	☆	☆	0.0	0.00	0.00	N/A	N/A
FIDELITY SEL LEISURE (R)	S	LO	162.4	26.96	13,144.80	10,996.60	☆	0.0	0.04	0.01	31.1	148
FIDELITY SEL LIFE INS (R)	S	LO	2.4	9.88	10,102.20	8,415.70	☆	0.0	0.00	0.00	N/A	999
FIDELITY SEL PAPER & FRS	S	LO	56.8	15.61	12,986.70	15,610.00	☆	0.0	0.00	0.00	26.7	N/A
FIDELITY SEL PREC-MTLS (R)	AU	LO	402.2	16.50	14,798.20	19,644.20	30,095.20	0.6	0.00	0.09	26.5	65
FIDELITY SEL PROP&CAS (R)	S	LO	9.2	11.51	10,492.30	9,120.40	☆	0.0	0.00	0.00	N/A	299
FIDELITY SEL REGL BANK (R)	S	LO	4.6	9.59	11,229.50	9,590.00	☆	0.0	0.00	0.00	N/A	N/A
FIDELITY SEL RESTAURANT (R)	S	LO	1.4	10.82	12,089.40	10,820.00	☆	0.0	0.00	0.00	N/A	N/A
FIDELITY SEL RETAIL (R)	S	LO	41.0	14.50	12,958.00	10,837.10	☆	0.0	0.00	0.00	N/A	812
FIDELITY SEL S&L (R)	S	LO	23.8	14.20	11,024.80	9,746.10	☆	0.0	0.00	0.00	6.8	312
FIDELITY SEL SOFTWARE (R)	TK	LO	58.0	16.82	13,296.40	12,413.30	☆	0.0	0.00	0.00	37.5	193
FIDELITY SEL TECH (R)	TK	LO	254.2	25.78	12,718.30	11,420.60	25,838.10	0.0	0.08	0.00	24.0	85
FIDELITY SEL TELECOM (R)	TK	LO	28.1	16.87	12,799.70	12,868.00	☆	0.0	0.00	0.00	N/A	237
FIDELITY SEL TRANS (R)	S	LO	4.5	12.37	11,951.70	☆	☆	0.0	0.00	0.00	N/A	N/A
FIDELITY SEL UTILITIES (R)	UT	LO	103.2	26.81	9,816.90	9,914.30	27,856.90	0.8	0.14	0.21	11.8	96
FIDELITY SHORT-TERM BOND	FI	NO	174.7	9.65	10,103.00	☆	☆	0.0	0.00	0.61	N/A	N/A
FIDELITY SPL SITUATIONS	CA	LO	279.6	18.49	11,406.50	11,377.80	☆	0.5	0.97	0.09	22.4	225
FIDELITY THRIFT TRUST	FI	NO	358.4	10.83	9,965.40	10,445.80	19,696.90	5.4	0.32	0.59	N/A	[illegible]

FIDELITY TREND	G	NO	824.8	47.81	12,219.30	11,335.50	28,594.80	1.2	8.25	0.61	26.1	71
FIDELITY VALUE FUND	CA	NO	126.3	26.32	11,663.50	11,051.10	27,781.20	0.5	2.36	0.15	29.7	281
FTP-EQUITY PRT GROWTH	CA	NO	62.3	13.83	11,801.90	10,546.70	☆	0.1	1.22	0.01	N/A	115
FTP-EQUITY PRT INCOME	EI	NO	652.6	13.81	11,638.50	11,787.30	☆	5.1	1.14	0.74	N/A	107
FTP-FIXED INCOME PORT	FI	NO	453.3	10.49	9,970.90	10,464.80	☆	9.1	0.22	0.96	N/A	59
FIDUCIARY CAPITAL GROWTH	SG	NO	54.4	20.76	11,597.80	9,422.50	25,472.50	4.3	2.83	0.95	19.5	57
FIDUCIARY VALQUEST	GI	NO	1.7	11.47	11,516.10	10,923.90	☆	2.7	0.00	0.30	N/A	11
FINANCIAL DYNAMICS	CA	NO	97.8	8.65	13,596.60	11,897.10	24,313.10	0.2	1.74	0.02	29.4	246
FINANCIAL HIGH YIELD BND	FI	NO	43.1	8.37	10,522.30	10,850.50	☆	11.4	0.17	0.96	N/A	134
FINL INDEPENDENCE GRO	G	SC	28.4	16.50	13,080.00	11,748.90	☆	0.0	0.62	0.00	N/A	85
FINL INDEPENDENCE GOVT	FI	LO	51.6	10.24	9,945.70	10,643.10	☆	8.7	0.08	0.89	N/A	110
FINANCIAL INDUST FUND	GI	NO	449.9	4.87	12,432.90	11,727.90	25,823.30	1.6	1.02	0.08	26.2	227
FINANCIAL INDUST INCOME	EI	NO	451.3	8.85	11,979.30	11,421.50	30,991.50	3.7	1.05	0.36	19.2	160
FINANCIAL PORT-ENERGY	NR	NO	20.2	12.19	14,174.40	15,483.00	☆	1.1	0.16	0.13	N/A	629
FINANCIAL PORT-EUROPEAN	IF	NO	4.2	10.09	11,505.10	12,557.20	☆	0.0	0.00	0.00	N/A	4
FINANCIAL PORT-FINANCIAL	S	NO	1.8	7.79	10,512.80	9,612.70	☆	0.3	0.00	0.02	N/A	76
FINANCIAL PORT-GOLD	AU	NO	43.4	8.07	14,699.50	20,320.90	☆	1.0	0.04	0.08	46.1	232
FINANCIAL PORT-HEALTH	H	NO	18.8	16.57	13,256.00	12,122.20	☆	0.0	1.43	0.00	N/A	479
FINANCIAL PORT-LEISURE	S	NO	7.3	13.06	12,217.00	10,398.30	☆	0.0	2.76	0.00	N/A	458
FINANCIAL PORT-PACIFIC	IF	NO	58.8	17.29	13,624.90	16,983.70	☆	0.2	1.77	0.03	N/A	199
FINANCIAL PORT-TECH	TK	NO	31.8	12.90	13,340.20	14,072.30	☆	0.0	1.08	0.00	N/A	368
FINANCIAL PORT-UTILITIES	UT	NO	17.2	8.86	10,355.70	10,893.50	☆	1.7	0.01	0.15	N/A	69
FINANCIAL SELECT INCOME	FI	NO	21.8	6.72	9,907.00	10,515.40	19,373.80	9.6	0.32	0.66	N/A	153
FINANCIAL US GOVT	FI	NO	6.6	7.41	9,703.30	10,459.90	☆	7.4	0.02	0.55	N/A	61
FFB EQUITY	CA	NO	1.9	12.14	12,757.60	12,179.40	☆	1.7	0.27	0.21	N/A	N/A
FIRST INV ADJ RATE PRF	FI	NO	26.9	0.92	10,544.40	10,658.70	☆	6.4	0.00	0.05	N/A	58
FIRST INV BOND APPREC	FI	SC	221.8	13.10	10,941.80	10,641.50	19,729.70	10.0	0.27	1.32	N/A	143
FIRST INV DISCOVERY	SG	SC	35.2	11.50	12,735.30	10,464.10	18,158.00	0.0	0.00	0.00	33.7	37
FIRST INV FD FOR GROWTH	G	SC	59.7	7.19	12,614.00	10,927.10	16,796.60	0.0	0.00	0.00	20.0	74
FIRST INV FD FOR INCOME	FI	SC	1,772.0	5.82	10,354.90	10,689.70	19,294.00	12.0	0.00	0.70	60.7	168
FIRST INV GOVT	FI	SC	355.0	11.28	9,732.60	10,490.50	☆	9.0	0.27	1.03	N/A	287
FIRST INV HIGH YIELD	FI	SC	147.0	14.55	10,386.10	☆	☆	0.0	0.02	1.10	N/A	11
FIRST INV INTERNATIONAL	GL	SC	69.2	4.62	14,002.40	16,821.20	29,802.80	0.2	0.00	0.00	N/A	94
FIRST INV NTRL RESOURCES	NR	SC	26.2	5.02	13,954.80	15,929.60	11,520.60	0.8	0.00	0.04	N/A	101
FIRST INV VALUE FUND	OG	SC	6.9	12.74	10,331.10	10,438.80	☆	3.5	0.00	0.44	N/A	277
FIRST INV OPTION FD	OI	SC	225.0	5.31	11,976.30	11,891.30	18,049.20	1.6	0.53	0.09	25.4	155
FIRST INV SPECIAL BOND	FI	SC	37.9	14.36	10,715.80	11,101.00	☆	11.1	0.19	1.61	N/A	112
FIRST INV US GOVT PLUS-I	FI	SC	1.9	12.87	9,051.60	9,841.00	☆	9.6	0.62	1.26	N/A	21
FIRST LAKESHORE DVRSFD	I	NO	5.1	11.11	10,682.60	11,311.70	☆	6.0	0.02	0.66	N/A	15
FPA CAPITAL	G	SC	58.8	13.50	12,760.20	12,006.00	24,381.50	2.1	0.76	0.30	20.1	34
FPA NEW INCOME	FI	LO	6.8	9.39	10,310.50	10,847.60	20,729.10	8.9	0.03	0.84	N/A	73
FPA PARAMOUNT (X)	GI	SC	134.7	15.68	13,284.20	13,453.60	33,518.10	2.1	1.28	0.34	32.9	137
FPA PERENNIAL FUND	GI	SC	65.5	19.56	11,271.50	11,337.30	☆	3.1	1.68	0.63	16.3	84
FIRST TRUST US GOVT	FI	SC	313.1	10.27	10,016.20	10,821.00	☆	8.6	0.05	0.88	N/A	263
FIRST UTILITY	UT	NO	5.3	10.35	10,550.50	☆	☆	0.0	0.00	0.00	N/A	N/A
FLAG INTERNATIONAL	IF	LO	36.4	12.94	12,563.10	☆	☆	0.0	0.00	0.00	N/A	N/A
FLAG INV TELEPHONE INC	I	NO	102.7	16.09	10,544.00	10,571.70	☆	5.6	2.23	0.96	N/A	30
FLAGSHIP CORPORATE CASH	FI	NO	237.3	46.51	10,479.20	10,792.10	☆	7.0	0.00	3.24	N/A	183
FLEX FUND-BOND	FI	NO	17.2	20.27	10,069.40	10,561.10	☆	9.0	0.30	1.83	N/A	150
FLEX FUND-INC & GROWTH	EI	NO	5.3	21.62	10,165.70	9,952.00	☆	6.5	0.73	1.43	N/A	219
FLEX FUND-GROWTH	CA	NO	14.0	12.39	11,830.30	10,551.40	☆	0.4	1.14	0.05	N/A	152
FLEX FUND-RETIRMNT GRO	CA	NO	93.1	13.36	12,315.90	10,986.60	☆	0.5	1.26	0.07	20.2	141
FLORIDA INDEX	G	NO	0.1	0.00	N/A	☆	☆	0.0	0.00	0.00	N/A	N/A
FORTRESS CONVERTIBLE	CV	LO	11.0	10.04	#10,555.00	☆	☆	0.0	0.09	0.38	N/A	N/A
44 WALL STREET	CA	NO	19.2	3.81	12,330.10	9,049.90	4,940.00	0.0	0.00	0.00	N/A	104
44 WALL STREET EQUITY	CA	LO	12.1	7.21	12,539.10	11,230.50	16,028.60	0.0	0.00	0.00	N/A	82
FOUNDERS EQUITY INCOME	EI	NO	15.2	16.88	11,333.70	11,829.40	22,513.80	4.5	0.88	0.78	N/A	178
FOUNDERS FRONTIER	CA	NO	4.4	12.51	#12,510.00	☆	☆	0.0	0.00	0.00	N/A	N/A
FOUNDERS GROWTH	G	NO	92.0	10.71	12,903.60	11,838.30	28,609.50	3.4	1.05	0.38	23.0	142
FOUNDERS MUTUAL	GI	NO	227.7	9.49	12,248.70	11,542.40	32,818.50	2.6	3.21	0.28	20.8	42

PERFORMANCE OF MUTUAL FUNDS *(continued)*

FUND NAME	OBJ.	LOAD	TOTAL NET ASTS (MIL) 6/30/87	NAV 6/30/87	PERFORMANCE (RETURN ON INITIAL $10,000 INVESTMENT) 12/31/86–6/30/87	6/30/86–6/30/87	6/30/82–6/30/87	YIELD % 6/30/87	PER SHARE LATEST 12 MONTHS CAP GAINS	INC DIVS	LATEST AVAILABLE PRICE/EARNINGS	ANNUAL % TURNOVER
FOUNDERS SPECIAL	CA	NO	87.2	35.08	12,537.50	11,610.40	27,038.80	0.8	3.46	0.28	28.7	138
FRANKLIN CORP CASH	EI	NO	56.9	9.12	10,694.40	10,746.30	☆	6.4	0.00	0.58	N/A	28
FRANKLIN DYNATECH	TK	LO	45.5	13.05	13,191.20	11,285.60	23,892.50	0.5	0.00	0.06	33.3	15
FRANKLIN EQUITY FUND	G	LO	298.6	7.73	12,455.20	11,942.60	33,404.60	1.0	0.60	0.08	17.2	49
FRANKLIN GOLD FUND	AU	LO	273.9	14.09	15,865.20	21,363.90	30,921.90	2.2	0.00	0.31	33.8	3
FRANKLIN GROWTH	G	LO	86.6	19.70	12,568.90	12,597.50	30,461.80	1.5	0.05	0.30	27.6	1
FRANKLIN INCOME	I	LO	410.6	2.30	10,672.30	11,582.60	25,309.40	8.7	0.02	0.20	10.3	31
FRANKLIN OPTION	OI	LO	41.1	6.32	11,369.00	11,057.10	23,113.40	1.9	0.66	0.12	23.6	105
FRANKLIN US GOVERNMENT	FI	LO	4,273.7	7.15	10,122.40	10,824.80	20,373.60	10.6	0.01	0.76	N/A	36
FRANKLIN UTILITIES	UT	LO	650.7	7.92	10,021.60	10,488.90	25,612.40	7.1	0.01	0.56	10.7	3
FREEDOM FINANCIAL (R)	S	NO	3.2	10.90	10,972.20	☆	☆	0.0	0.12	0.02	N/A	N/A
FREEDOM GLOBAL	GL	NO	64.7	12.77	13,019.10	☆	☆	0.0	0.33	0.11	N/A	N/A
FREEDOM GLOBAL INCOME	WI	NO	24.5	10.66	11,399.40	☆	☆	0.0	0.00	0.44	N/A	N/A
FREEDOM GOLD & GOVT (R)	AU	NO	80.6	15.44	10,228.30	10,968.10	☆	6.1	0.59	0.98	55.9	336
FREEDOM GOVT PLUS (R)	FI	NO	174.6	9.78	9,875.70	10,496.30	☆	8.9	0.00	0.86	N/A	N/A
FREEDOM REGIONAL BANK (R)	S	NO	52.1	12.26	11,746.60	10,489.20	☆	1.4	1.47	0.19	11.1	43
FT INTERNATIONAL	IF	NO	119.3	24.20	11,498.80	13,101.70	☆	0.2	2.35	0.05	N/A	70
FUND FOR US GOVT SEC	FI	NO	1,135.5	8.44	10,236.70	10,784.30	20,759.30	9.1	0.00	0.77	N/A	179
FUND OF AMERICA	GI	SC	193.1	13.90	13,493.80	13,056.80	31,593.60	1.6	1.34	0.23	28.8	45
FUNDAMENTAL INVESTORS	GI	SC	691.3	17.51	12,687.20	12,734.40	36,391.30	2.2	1.52	0.40	27.3	19
FUNDTRUST AGGRESSIVE GR	CA	NO	47.1	15.60	11,780.60	11,330.70	☆	0.1	0.37	0.02	N/A	133
FUNDTRUST GROWTH FUND	G	NO	43.9	15.11	11,608.80	11,644.80	☆	0.9	0.24	0.14	N/A	107
FUNDTRUST GROWTH & INC	GI	NO	87.0	14.23	11,221.00	11,288.30	☆	2.3	0.36	0.33	N/A	87
FUNDTRUST INCOME FUND	I	NO	56.7	10.44	10,248.60	10,481.60	☆	9.1	0.00	0.95	N/A	125
FUND SOURCE EQUITY TR	G	NO	3.5	12.05	11,468.70	10,957.00	☆	1.8	0.00	0.22	N/A	N/A
FUND SOURCE HIGH YLD	FI	LO	4.3	10.05	10,246.90	10,925.10	☆	12.2	0.02	1.22	N/A	N/A
FUND SOURCE INTL EQ	IF	NO	28.2	16.92	11,744.50	13,424.20	☆	0.1	0.67	0.02	N/A	N/A
GABELLI ASSET	G	NO	86.1	13.93	12,836.40	12,928.00	☆	0.6	0.41	0.09	31.3	127
GABELLI GROWTH (R)	CA	NO	2.2	10.84	#10,840.00	☆	☆	0.0	0.00	0.00	N/A	N/A
GAM GLOBAL	GL	NO	26.7	117.22	11,196.90	11,435.00	☆	0.0	0.00	0.00	N/A	N/A
GAM INTERNATIONAL	IF	NO	34.2	203.62	12,709.10	14,345.90	☆	0.6	63.29	1.48	N/A	N/A
GAM PACIFIC BASIN	IF	NO	1.6	102.12	#10,212.00	☆	☆	0.0	0.00	0.00	N/A	N/A
GAM TOKYO	IF	NO	1.8	120.97	#12,097.00	☆	☆	0.0	0.00	0.00	N/A	N/A
GATEWAY GROWTH PLUS	G	NO	3.9	11.88	11,918.30	11,069.40	☆	0.7	0.00	0.08	N/A	96
GATEWAY OPTION INCOME	OI	NO	47.5	15.73	11,076.60	11,338.30	19,523.60	2.5	0.95	0.40	23.9	85
GEICO QUAL DIVIDEND	FI	NO	63.9	25.26	10,443.90	10,743.70	☆	6.3	0.28	1.58	N/A	95
GENERAL AGGRESSIVE GRO	CA	NO	49.2	24.20	12,648.90	10,904.50	☆	0.4	0.40	0.10	N/A	183
GENL ELEC LT INTEREST	FI	NO	754.1	11.21	9,784.60	10,382.30	22,597.10	8.7	0.64	1.00	N/A	N/A
GENL ELEC S&S PROGRAM	G	NO	976.4	41.19	12,157.50	11,866.40	29,288.70	2.8	7.50	1.27	21.5	N/A
GENERAL SECURITIES (R)	CA	NO	17.2	12.02	10,780.80	10,628.10	25,757.70	4.5	2.13	0.59	N/A	1
GIBRALTAR FUND	GI	NO	1.3	15.35	11,412.60	11,058.60	☆	1.1	0.30	0.17	N/A	N/A
GINTEL CAPITAL APPREC	CA	NO	25.0	12.10	11,065.20	11,196.80	☆	1.1	0.91	0.14	17.1	119
GINTEL ERISA	GI	NO	103.3	43.69	11,508.40	11,696.90	27,595.70	0.0	7.65	0.00	12.0	69
GINTEL FUND	G	NO	120.9	67.12	10,979.50	11,145.00	26,298.70	2.0	33.35	1.70	13.6	77
GIT EQUITY INCOME	EI	NO	2.7	13.62	10,849.00	10,791.10	☆	4.6	0.14	0.63	N/A	19
GIT A RATED INCOME	FI	NO	8.0	10.82	9,775.90	10,374.30	☆	8.3	0.00	0.89	N/A	47
GIT MAX INCOME	FI	NO	14.6	9.27	10,285.70	10,323.70	☆	11.1	0.00	1.02	N/A	47
GIT SELECT GROWTH	G	NO	4.5	17.41	11,892.60	11,712.30	☆	1.5	0.08	0.26	N/A	35
GIT SPECIAL GROWTH	SG	NO	19.3	18.24	11,548.80	10,239.30	☆	0.8	0.12	0.13	N/A	35
GOLCONDA INVESTORS LTD	AU	NO	61.9	18.77	14,595.60	18,858.80	21,327.60	0.2	0.00	0.03	35.1	33
GOVAARS GOVT	FI	NO	0.9	9.91	10,115.30	☆	☆	0.0	0.00	0.47	N/A	N/A
GOVAARS MORTGAGE	FI	NO	27.6	10.50	10,574.80	☆	☆	0.0	0.00	0.62	N/A	N/A
GPM FUND	GI	NO	7.1	21.82	11,586.00	11,365.70	30,737.90	3.2	3.03	0.70	N/A	N/A
GOVERNMENT INC SEC (R)	FI	SC	2,551.0	9.45	10,133.30	10,763.10	☆	0.0	0.00	0.88	N/A	N/A
GRADISON OPPORTUNITY GRO	SG	NO	20.4	13.26	11,445.00	9,924.20	☆	0.7	0.45	0.10	N/A	83
GRADISON ESTABLISHED GRO	G	NO	58.2	17.52	12,000.80	12,632.50	☆	1.9	1.17	0.35	17.8	88
GREENFIELD FUND	GI	NO	1.2	13.61	10,315.70	10,422.00	20,495.50	6.5	0.00	1.25	N/A	145

GREENSPRING FUND	G	NO	17.9	13.59	11,373.70	12,010.40	☆	12.6	0.65	1.74	N/A	502
GREENWAY FUND	CA	SC	19.6	12.20	12,383.40	11,603.00	26,274.70	1.0	0.52	0.12	N/A	65
GROWTH FUND OF AMERICA	G	SC	1,139.4	19.77	12,544.40	11,898.90	28,640.30	1.4	0.79	0.28	32.8	24
GROWTH FD OF WASHINGTON	G	SC	57.4	13.00	11,845.50	10,700.90	☆	1.3	0.45	0.17	N/A	32
GROWTH INDUSTRY SHARES	G	NO	81.8	11.04	12,246.20	11,017.90	25,465.30	1.3	1.56	0.15	23.8	26
GT AMERICA GROWTH	GL	SC	1.2	10.41	#10,410.00	☆	☆	0.0	0.00	0.00	N/A	N/A
GT EUROPE GROWTH	IF	SC	17.5	22.51	12,442.30	15,012.00	☆	0.0	1.29	0.00	N/A	102
GT INTERNATIONAL GRO	IF	SC	23.9	21.51	12,121.60	13,794.40	☆	0.0	0.70	0.00	N/A	122
GT JAPAN GROWTH	IF	SC	7.2	23.36	12,538.00	13,910.70	☆	0.0	1.18	0.00	N/A	207
GT PACIFIC GROWTH FD	IF	SC	59.6	25.70	12,071.50	14,253.80	31,302.10	0.0	9.27	0.00	N/A	229
GT WORLDWIDE GROWTH	GL	SC	2.9	10.38	#10,380.00	☆	☆	0.0	0.00	0.00	N/A	N/A
GUARDIAN BOND FUND	FI	NO	108.9	11.47	9,830.00	10,430.10	☆	10.5	0.09	1.21	N/A	55
GUARDIAN MUTUAL	GI	NO	595.6	46.28	12,278.50	11,670.00	31,059.20	3.1	4.50	1.51	19.6	70
GUARDIAN PARK AVENUE	G	SC	178.5	24.69	12,107.30	11,173.00	37,023.80	2.1	1.66	0.54	21.8	48
GUARDIAN STOCK FUND	G	NO	138.4	20.34	12,134.30	11,276.20	☆	1.8	0.26	0.36	22.5	36
GUIDANCE INVESTMENTS	I	SC	1.6	1.42	10,140.30	10,482.10	☆	4.1	0.10	0.06	N/A	80
J HANCOCK BOND	FI	SC	1,150.3	15.11	9,994.80	10,575.10	21,739.00	9.6	0.55	1.48	N/A	163
J HANCOCK GLOBAL	GL	SC	158.1	18.26	12,523.10	12,442.20	☆	0.0	0.26	0.00	30.1	41
J HANCOCK GROWTH	G	SC	118.8	17.36	12,638.60	10,921.30	30,094.90	0.6	1.69	0.10	28.6	62
J HANCOCK HIGH INCOME	FI	SC	34.4	9.76	10,512.30	☆	☆	0.0	0.00	0.88	N/A	N/A
J HANCOCK SPEC EQUITY	SG	SC	16.8	6.95	12,171.60	9,718.00	☆	0.0	0.04	0.00	N/A	64
J HANCOCK US GOVT SEC	FI	SC	214.0	9.18	9,819.90	10,351.80	18,748.50	8.4	0.00	0.77	N/A	6
J HANCOCK US GUAR MORT	FI	SC	440.7	10.16	9,909.90	10,577.60	☆	9.5	0.16	0.96	N/A	160
J HANCOCK VAR SR AGG GRO	CA	NO	5.6	11.94	12,395.30	12,443.00	☆	2.4	0.12	0.28	N/A	N/A
J HANCOCK VAR SR BOND	FI	NO	221.3	9.85	10,350.90	10,883.70	☆	8.6	0.03	0.84	N/A	N/A
J HANCOCK VAR SR STOCK	G	NO	375.6	11.44	12,064.30	12,290.80	☆	2.9	0.43	0.34	N/A	N/A
J HANCOCK VAR SR TOT RTN	B	NO	43.3	11.11	11,277.00	11,764.70	☆	4.4	0.15	0.49	N/A	N/A
HARBOR GROWTH	G	NO	116.0	13.08	12,773.40	☆	☆	0.0	0.00	0.00	N/A	N/A
HARTWELL GROWTH FUND	CA	NO	26.2	16.29	14,031.40	14,173.40	32,368.00	0.0	1.37	0.00	N/A	102
HARTWELL LEVERAGE FUND	CA	NO	46.3	23.21	14,371.50	13,039.30	26,297.40	0.0	0.00	0.00	41.0	123
HEARTLAND VALUE	CA	LO	37.4	16.62	12,223.60	11,268.20	☆	2.6	0.63	0.43	N/A	89
HEARTLAND US GOVT	FI	LO	7.2	9.39	#9,987.60	☆	☆	0.0	0.00	0.14	N/A	N/A
HERITAGE CAPITAL APPREC	CA	LO	53.1	12.77	11,791.30	10,993.40	☆	0.7	0.00	0.09	N/A	21
HIDDEN STRENGTH GOVT	FI	SC	4.0	10.04	#11,048.40	☆	☆	0.0	0.00	0.20	N/A	N/A
HIDDEN STRENGTH GROWTH	G	SC	17.2	10.72	13,418.70	☆	☆	0.0	0.00	0.10	N/A	N/A
HIDDEN STRENGTH QUALITY	FI	SC	5.5	8.80	10,078.00	☆	☆	0.0	0.00	0.54	N/A	N/A
HIDDEN STRENGTH TOTAL RN	B	SC	11.2	7.78	11,815.50	☆	☆	0.0	0.00	0.12	N/A	N/A
HIGH YIELD SECURITIES	FI	SC	86.3	9.65	10,512.00	10,774.60	21,662.30	11.9	0.00	1.14	N/A	84
HOME INV GUAR INCOME (R)	FI	NO	209.3	10.21	9,962.60	10,554.00	☆	8.4	0.00	0.85	N/A	43
HUTTON INV SR-BASIC VAL (R)	G	NO	527.3	14.08	11,826.40	11,485.80	☆	2.0	0.51	0.28	N/A	59
HUTTON INV SR-BOND (R)	FI	NO	485.2	11.03	9,573.10	10,196.20	21,563.40	9.9	1.06	1.15	N/A	211
HUTTON INV SR-GOVT (R)	FI	NO	6,234.4	9.66	9,708.30	10,263.70	☆	10.9	0.08	1.06	N/A	353
HUTTON INV SR-GROWTH (R)	G	NO	1,661.8	15.69	11,981.30	11,436.90	28,681.90	1.3	2.82	0.22	N/A	524
HUTTON INV SR-OPTION	OI	NO	62.1	9.73	12,162.30	11,898.00	☆	2.2	0.67	0.22	N/A	173
HUTTON INV SR-PREC METAL (R)	AU	NO	129.2	18.64	14,712.20	20,968.90	☆	0.9	0.31	0.17	N/A	68
HUTTON MSTR CONVERTIBLE	CV	LO	12.7	9.97	#10,385.40	☆	☆	0.0	0.00	0.00	N/A	N/A
HUTTON SPECIAL EQU (R)	SG	NO	265.7	15.09	11,711.00	10,428.10	☆	0.0	1.13	0.00	N/A	114
IDEX FUND (X)	CA	SC	80.8	14.47	12,933.00	12,647.70	☆	2.1	1.37	0.33	N/A	149
IDEX FUND II (X)	CA	SC	72.4	13.05	12,923.10	12,552.70	☆	0.5	0.00	0.07	N/A	8
IDEX FUND 3	CA	SC	9.9	10.45	#10,450.00	☆	☆	0.0	0.00	0.00	N/A	N/A
IDEX TOTAL INCOME	CA	SC	0.4	10.00	#	☆	☆	0.0	0.00	0.00	N/A	N/A
IDS BOND FUND	FI	LO	1,899.2	5.11	10,068.70	10,604.20	23,866.60	9.0	0.17	0.45	N/A	135
IDS DISCOVERY FUND	SG	SC	258.1	8.76	11,758.40	10,617.90	21,626.40	1.0	0.50	0.08	30.3	63
IDS EQUITY +	GI	SC	462.3	11.96	12,815.40	12,244.50	29,099.20	1.9	1.30	0.24	25.7	72
IDS EXTRA INCOME	FI	SC	1,105.3	5.10	10,398.80	10,793.30	☆	10.5	0.14	0.53	N/A	117
IDS FEDERAL INCOME	FI	SC	181.2	5.03	9,977.90	10,661.00	☆	8.0	0.00	0.40	N/A	108
IDS GROWTH FUND	G	SC	903.5	26.81	13,174.40	11,738.80	30,635.80	0.5	2.68	0.13	32.3	24
IDS INTERNATIONAL	IF	SC	353.6	11.31	12,213.80	14,282.60	☆	0.3	1.51	0.04	N/A	146
IDS LIFE CAPITAL RES	G	NO	436.0	18.49	12,088.90	11,811.50	☆	3.0	1.60	0.55	N/A	115
IDS LIFE EQUITY	G	NO	3.7	12.40	12,870.50	12,101.70	☆	0.7	0.05	0.09	N/A	15

PERFORMANCE OF MUTUAL FUNDS *(continued)*

FUND NAME	OBJ.	LOAD	TOTAL NET ASTS (MIL) 6/30/87	NAV 6/30/87	PERFORMANCE (RETURN ON INITIAL $10,000 INVESTMENT) 12/31/86–6/30/87	6/30/86–6/30/87	6/30/82–6/30/87	YIELD % 6/30/87	PER SHARE LATEST 12 MONTHS CAP GAINS	INC DIVS	LATEST AVAILABLE PRICE/EARNINGS	ANNUAL % TURNOVER
IDS LIFE GOVT	FI	NO	1.5	9.25	9,518.20	9,837.20	☆	6.9	0.00	0.63	N/A	N/A
IDS LIFE INCOME	I	NO	2.8	9.31	9,530.00	9,925.80	☆	7.2	0.00	0.66	N/A	N/A
IDS LIFE MANAGED	B	NO	13.3	11.55	11,518.10	11,409.60	☆	2.6	0.07	0.30	N/A	10
IDS LIFE SPEC INCOME	FI	NO	416.6	11.66	10,135.70	10,803.50	☆	9.4	0.68	1.09	N/A	170
IDS MANAGED RETIREMENT	GI	SC	724.6	8.77	12,857.50	12,444.90	☆	1.6	0.27	0.14	N/A	127
IDS MUTUAL	B	SC	1,536.2	13.74	11,499.60	11,980.70	29,263.20	5.5	1.13	0.75	12.6	91
IDS NEW DIMENSIONS	G	SC	728.8	11.04	12,957.70	11,753.80	33,837.80	1.6	2.18	0.17	32.7	128
IDS PAN PACIFIC GRO (R)	GL	NO	52.6	4.81	#9,620.00	☆	☆	0.0	0.00	0.00	N/A	N/A
IDS PRECIOUS METALS	AU	SC	101.2	8.94	15,738.90	22,153.80	☆	0.4	0.35	0.03	N/A	169
IDS PROGRESSIVE	CA	SC	215.7	8.47	12,679.60	12,251.40	30,398.10	2.9	0.93	0.24	27.5	85
IDS SELECTIVE	FI	SC	1,186.5	8.72	10,020.00	10,647.30	24,109.80	8.8	0.00	0.76	N/A	108
IDS STOCK	GI	SC	1,579.8	23.70	12,514.30	12,073.50	27,491.00	2.3	2.28	0.56	22.3	55
IDS STRATEGY AGGR EQ (R)	CA	NO	323.9	12.12	12,854.30	11,682.40	☆	0.0	0.31	0.00	35.3	67
IDS STRATEGY EQUITY (R)	GI	NO	151.0	8.21	11,809.60	11,768.10	☆	2.6	0.44	0.22	N/A	28
IDS STRATEGY INCOME (R)	FI	NO	149.9	5.87	10,175.70	10,739.50	☆	7.6	0.24	0.45	N/A	87
INCOME FUND OF AMERICA	EI	SC	925.6	12.72	10,922.70	11,202.90	28,386.90	6.8	0.59	0.88	20.3	42
INDUSTRIAL-AMERICAN	G	SC	18.5	11.74	13,748.50	13,161.80	☆	0.3	0.25	0.04	N/A	N/A
INDUSTRIAL-BOND	FI	SC	0.2	9.30	10,085.50	10,292.10	☆	3.4	0.00	0.32	N/A	N/A
INDUSTRIAL-GOVERNMENT	FI	SC	18.2	8.24	9,266.60	9,856.40	☆	10.2	0.00	0.84	N/A	322
INDUSTRIAL-OPTION INC	OI	SC	271.1	9.56	11,643.60	12,247.60	☆	8.2	0.60	0.80	23.7	522
INDUSTRY FUND OF AMERICA	CA	NO	0.6	3.65	11,889.30	10,767.00	10,767.00	0.0	2.06	0.00	N/A	N/A
INSIDER REPORTS	G	LO	3.7	12.76	10,915.30	9,508.20	☆	0.0	0.00	0.00	N/A	33
INTEGRATED CAP APPREC (R)	G	NO	243.2	15.25	12,010.10	11,216.50	☆	1.5	0.79	0.23	N/A	60
INTEGRATED CORP INVESTOR	FI	NO	9.7	23.07	10,427.50	10,536.90	☆	6.7	0.00	1.54	N/A	168
INTEGRATED EQ-AGGR GRO	CA	SC	10.5	12.92	#10,848.00	☆	☆	0.0	0.00	0.00	N/A	N/A
INTEGRATED EQ-GROWTH	G	SC	10.3	13.58	#11,402.20	☆	☆	0.0	0.00	0.00	N/A	N/A
INTEGRATED INC-CONVERT	CV	SC	26.2	12.01	#10,279.30	☆	☆	0.0	0.00	0.22	N/A	N/A
INTEGRATED INC-GOVT PLUS	FI	SC	4.7	11.15	#9,640.60	☆	☆	0.0	0.00	0.33	N/A	N/A
INTEGRATED INC-HI YIELD	FI	SC	11.6	11.24	10,290.60	☆	☆	0.0	0.00	0.96	N/A	N/A
INTEGRATED INCOME PLUS (R)	FI	NO	17.4	9.42	10,387.00	☆	☆	0.0	0.00	0.66	N/A	N/A
INTL FD FOR INSTITUTIONS	IF	NO	29.9	19.00	12,511.80	14,151.00	☆	0.3	3.27	0.06	N/A	77
INTL HERITAGE GOVT (R)	FI	SC	1.3	9.46	#9,835.00	☆	☆	0.0	0.00	0.37	N/A	N/A
INTL HERITAGE GR & INC (R)	GI	SC	0.7	9.89	#10,080.50	☆	☆	0.0	0.00	0.19	N/A	N/A
INTL HERITAGE HI YLD (R)	FI	SC	2.3	9.66	#10,234.30	☆	☆	0.0	0.00	0.58	N/A	N/A
INTL HERITAGE OVSEA GR (R)	IF	SC	0.7	10.76	#10,760.00	☆	☆	0.0	0.00	0.00	N/A	N/A
INTL HERITAGE OVSEA IN (R)	WI	SC	1.8	9.82	#10,081.20	☆	☆	0.0	0.00	0.26	N/A	N/A
INTL CASH-EUROCASH	IF	LO	28.1	13.44	10,664.60	11,259.40	☆	3.8	0.10	0.51	N/A	N/A
INTERNATIONAL INVESTORS	AU	SC	1,132.3	17.01	14,305.60	18,812.30	31,846.10	2.3	0.20	0.40	40.0	3
INTERSTATE CAP GROWTH	CA	LO	16.8	7.52	11,750.00	11,190.50	11,453.10	0.0	0.00	0.00	N/A	430
INVESTMENT CO OF AMERICA	GI	SC	4,578.3	15.69	12,109.60	12,176.90	33,763.00	2.7	1.02	0.44	21.4	11
INVEST PORT-EQUITY (R)	G	NO	294.8	13.55	12,604.70	11,867.40	☆	0.0	0.21	0.00	25.8	145
INVEST PORT-GOVT PLUS (R)	FI	NO	6,246.9	8.06	9,926.80	10,428.60	☆	9.2	0.09	0.74	N/A	313
INVEST PORT-HIGH YLD (R)	FI	NO	316.2	9.90	10,563.10	11,270.60	☆	9.1	0.11	0.90	N/A	137
INVEST PORT-TOTL RTN (R)	B	NO	435.3	10.32	11,934.60	☆	☆	0.0	0.00	0.05	22.4	N/A
INVEST PORT-OP INC (R)	OI	NO	468.1	7.96	11,342.20	11,107.10	☆	10.9	0.18	0.86	27.2	217
INVESTMENT TRUST BOSTON	GI	SC	72.7	12.38	11,841.20	11,215.10	25,589.50	2.4	1.52	0.34	17.6	21
ITB HIGH INCOME PLUS	FI	SC	20.6	13.86	10,370.30	10,613.20	☆	11.1	0.43	1.56	N/A	86
INVESTORS RESEARCH	CA	SC	88.9	6.48	12,582.50	10,449.90	34,170.10	0.4	1.27	0.03	29.9	72
IRI STOCK FUND	G	SC	10.3	9.46	11,648.90	10,909.30	26,844.80	1.4	1.97	0.15	N/A	127
ISI GROWTH FUND	G	SC	13.2	7.90	12,191.40	10,626.00	18,431.90	0.0	0.40	0.00	N/A	103
ISI INCOME FUND	I	SC	4.4	3.20	9,718.90	8,992.90	14,604.30	6.4	0.00	0.20	N/A	59
ISI TRUST FUND	GI	SC	105.3	11.15	11,206.20	11,049.00	18,190.50	5.3	0.47	0.60	28.6	113
IVY GROWTH	G	NO	204.0	14.88	11,773.10	12,146.50	34,119.00	3.6	3.44	0.60	20.9	95
IVY INSTITUTIONAL (X)	G	NO	165.6	144.93	12,219.50	12,406.30	☆	2.7	29.85	4.25	20.9	104
IVY INTERNATIONAL	IF	NO	15.9	16.61	13,638.10	15,167.10	☆	0.0	0.25	0.00	N/A	20
IVY MGD US GOVT	FI	NO	1.9	11.58	#9,882.20	☆	☆	0.0	0.00	0.27	N/A	N/A

JANUS FUND	CA	NO	479.6	13.71	11,602.10	10,779.20	27,277.10	4.5	2.20	0.67	23.7	254
JANUS VALUE	CA	NO	19.4	14.10	11,681.90	10,864.40	☆	5.7	0.82	0.80	N/A	152
JANUS VENTURE	SG	NO	44.1	33.32	12,138.40	11,172.50	☆	4.4	1.04	1.48	28.4	248
JP GROWTH FUND	G	SC	28.2	15.95	11,862.00	11,280.80	26,826.70	2.6	2.13	0.44	20.5	64
JP INCOME FUND	FI	SC	18.4	9.55	10,010.90	10,546.50	22,797.60	9.0	0.00	0.86	N/A	6
KAUFMANN FUND	SG	NO	3.2	1.19	10,531.00	10,258.60	☆	0.0	0.00	0.00	N/A	125
KEMPER GROWTH FUND	G	SC	351.8	12.80	12,824.50	12,747.70	30,481.50	0.7	3.57	0.10	28.0	181
KEMPER HIGH YIELD	FI	SC	444.9	11.66	10,741.60	11,345.60	26,288.00	10.8	0.00	1.26	N/A	95
KEMPER INCOME & CAP PRES	FI	SC	254.1	8.76	10,142.30	10,580.70	22,476.70	10.3	0.00	0.90	N/A	87
KEMPER INTERNATIONAL FD	IF	SC	236.8	22.18	11,680.60	13,581.80	36,519.10	0.9	6.69	0.24	N/A	149
KEMPER OPTION INCOME	OI	SC	581.7	10.67	11,748.00	11,630.80	20,305.20	11.9	0.12	1.28	28.7	181
KEMPER SUMMIT FUND	SG	SC	353.0	6.24	12,211.40	11,710.40	29,774.40	0.0	1.02	0.00	21.8	113
KEMPER TOTAL RETURN	B	SC	1,231.8	18.29	12,182.80	11,928.20	28,447.30	2.9	1.96	0.56	26.8	172
KEMPER US GOVT SEC	FI	LO	4,376.5	9.49	10,092.00	10,668.70	21,308.20	10.6	0.00	1.01	N/A	252
KEYSTONE AMER EQ INC (R)	EI	LO	3.2	10.37	#10,370.00	☆	☆	0.0	0.00	0.00	N/A	N/A
KEYSTONE AMER GOVT (R)	FI	LO	2.5	10.31	#10,380.40	☆	☆	0.0	0.00	0.07	N/A	N/A
KEYSTONE AMER HI YLD (R)	FI	LO	4.9	10.18	#10,270.80	☆	☆	0.0	0.00	0.09	N/A	N/A
KEYSTONE AMER INV GRD (R)	FI	LO	1.1	9.80	#9,870.50	☆	☆	0.0	0.00	0.07	N/A	N/A
KEYSTONE B-1 (R)	FI	NO	523.4	16.37	9,748.90	10,231.80	20,837.00	9.0	0.07	1.47	N/A	97
KEYSTONE B-2 (R)	FI	NO	932.2	18.93	10,195.00	10,478.10	21,463.70	9.8	0.14	1.85	N/A	69
KEYSTONE B-4 (X,R)	FI	NO	1,495.1	7.65	10,411.80	10,442.90	20,752.80	11.8	0.07	0.90	57.6	87
KEYSTONE INTERNATIONAL (R)	IF	NO	161.5	9.05	12,639.70	15,158.40	34,705.80	0.6	1.11	0.06	N/A	97
KEYSTONE K-1 (R)	I	NO	726.9	9.74	11,548.70	11,539.60	26,949.80	5.5	1.49	0.54	19.3	92
KEYSTONE K-2 (R)	G	NO	379.7	9.28	12,146.60	12,176.30	31,560.60	1.3	1.51	0.13	22.6	104
KEYSTONE PREC METALS (R)	AU	NO	206.9	21.6/	15,001.10	20,805.00	26,897.90	1.8	0.00	0.39	57.4	42
KEYSTONE S-1 (R)	GI	NO	218.9	24.82	12,756.50	12,142.90	28,663.80	1.7	4.52	0.42	22.5	106
KEYSTONE S-3 (R)	G	NO	285.6	9.85	12,421.20	11,770.80	28,555.40	1.4	1.93	0.14	25.0	117
KEYSTONE S-4 (R)	G	NO	672.2	6.96	12,959.70	11,549.80	25,096.60	0.0	0.79	0.00	30.2	83
KIDDER PEABODY EQU INC (R)	EI	NO	83.6	19.93	11,538.50	11,530.10	☆	2.4	0.00	0.48	N/A	131
KIDDER PEABODY GOV INC (R)	FI	NO	157.5	14.53	10,003.20	10,698.00	☆	7.7	0.06	1.12	N/A	219
KIDDER PEABODY MKTGUARD	S	LO	64.1	15.02	#10,423.30	☆	☆	0.0	0.00	0.00	N/A	N/A
KIDDER PEABODY SPL GR (R)	G	NO	30.9	16.71	12,004.30	10,407.60	☆	0.2	0.00	0.04	N/A	171
LANDMARK CAPITAL GROWTH	CA	NO	19.3	13.12	13,148.40	☆	☆	0.0	0.00	0.08	N/A	N/A
LANDMARK GROWTH & INCOME	GI	NO	17.5	11.45	11,582.30	☆	☆	0.0	0.00	0.39	N/A	N/A
LANDMARK US GOVT INC	FI	NO	50.7	9.33	10,011.70	☆	☆	0.0	0.00	0.56	N/A	N/A
LAZARD FRERES EQUITY	CA	NO	10.4	10.31	#10,310.00	☆	☆	0.0	0.00	0.00	N/A	N/A
LAZARD SPECIAL EQUITY	CA	NO	75.2	13.52	11,864.40	11,518.70	☆	0.0	0.29	0.00	N/A	N/A
LEGG MASON SPECIAL INV	SG	NO	55.8	12.62	12,007.60	10,679.10	☆	0.2	0.22	0.02	17.1	41
LEGG MASON TOTAL RETURN	G	NO	44.6	10.67	11,624.60	10,841.20	☆	1.4	0.90	0.16	23.1	40
LEGG MASON VALUE TRUST	G	NO	871.1	29.50	11,837.50	11,001.50	37,803.40	1.2	2.77	0.39	18.2	33
LEHMAN CAPITAL FUND	CA	SC	120.2	20.27	12,392.30	11,273.30	32,765.60	0.6	3.06	0.13	32.0	279
LEHMAN INVESTORS	GI	SC	471.6	20.79	12,362.00	11,823.20	30,158.70	2.3	2.91	0.51	22.0	62
LEHMAN OPPORTUNITY	CA	NO	103.7	27.16	12,017.70	11,269.60	37,274.00	2.0	2.78	0.58	24.4	28
LEPERCQ-ISTEL AGGR GRO	CA	NO	0.9	10.94	#10,940.00	☆	☆	0.0	0.00	0.00	N/A	N/A
LEPERCQ-ISTEL FUND	GI	NO	28.1	15.57	11,909.60	11,556.80	21,183.60	3.1	1.09	0.50	16.1	45
LEPERCQ-ISTEL INTL	IF	NO	1.7	11.79	#11,790.00	☆	☆	0.0	0.00	0.00	N/A	N/A
LEVERAGE FUND OF BOSTON	CA	NO	29.1	9.59	13,209.40	11,871.30	24,075.90	0.0	0.85	0.00	25.9	53
LEXINGTON GNMA INCOME	FI	NO	129.2	7.89	10,054.90	10,873.50	18,905.70	8.9	0.03	0.70	N/A	300
LEXINGTON GLOBAL	GL	SC	12.7	10.10	#9,970.40	☆	☆	0.0	0.00	0.00	N/A	N/A
LEXINGTON GOLDFUND	AU	NO	80.1	6.50	14,561.70	18,680.60	31,762.00	0.5	0.00	0.03	42.9	15
LEXINGTON GROWTH	G	NO	42.3	13.27	12,729.30	12,123.20	25,099.70	1.4	1.42	0.20	23.5	54
LEXINGTON RESEARCH	G	NO	145.1	19.62	12,027.20	11,879.00	29,237.90	3.8	2.77	0.80	21.2	82
LIBERTY FUND	FI	NO	10.5	4.65	10,279.50	11,293.80	21,788.10	8.8	0.00	0.41	N/A	256
LIFE OF VIRGINIA-BOND	FI	NO	2.5	10.62	10,660.70	11,147.20	☆	6.9	1.28	0.77	N/A	N/A
LIFE OF VIRGINIA-COM STK	G	NO	2.2	13.58	11,304.30	10,791.30	☆	3.8	1.54	0.54	N/A	N/A
LIFE OF VIRGINIA-TOT RTN	GI	NO	1.6	11.27	10,755.60	10,650.20	☆	5.3	1.11	0.62	N/A	N/A
LINDNER DIVIDEND (X,R)	EI	NO	61.4	23.17	10,314.60	11,161.80	29,655.50	7.2	2.70	1.76	11.7	N/A
LINDNER FUND (X,R)	G	NO	405.8	19.14	11,873.40	12,262.20	28,104.30	7.5	4.08	1.49	17.1	33
LMH FUND	GI	NO	76.7	25.49	10,616.40	10,716.00	☆	4.3	4.41	1.09	14.5	50
LOOMIS-SAYLES CAPITAL (X)	G	NO	290.3	27.83	13,236.90	12,519.00	43,618.60	0.3	3.92	0.10	31.0	208

PERFORMANCE OF MUTUAL FUNDS *(continued)*

FUND NAME	OBJ.	LOAD	TOTAL NET ASTS (MIL) 6/30/87	NAV 6/30/87	PERFORMANCE (RETURN ON INITIAL $10,000 INVESTMENT) 12/31/86–6/30/87	6/30/86–6/30/87	6/30/82–6/30/87	YIELD % 6/30/87	PER SHARE LATEST 12 MONTHS CAP GAINS	INC DIVS	LATEST AVAILABLE PRICE/EARNINGS	ANNUAL % TURNOVER
LOOMIS-SAYLES MUTUAL	B	NO	304.7	27.11	12,263.90	12,084.30	32,489.90	3.0	1.90	0.83	29.9	127
LORD ABBETT BOND-DEB	FI	SC	801.5	10.42	10,691.70	10,708.50	21,819.50	11.1	0.00	1.16	N/A	137
LORD ABBETT DEVEL GROWTH	SG	SC	253.9	9.56	12,132.00	10,681.60	19,570.90	0.0	0.00	0.00	27.7	7
LORD ABBETT FUNDMNTL VAL	GI	SC	22.2	11.31	11,699.20	☆	☆	0.0	0.00	0.09	N/A	N/A
LORD ABBETT US GOVT	FI	SC	659.4	3.06	9,883.50	10,640.70	20,885.10	11.3	0.04	0.34	N/A	370
LORD ABBETT VALUE APPREC	G	SC	290.4	12.00	11,432.00	10,700.70	☆	2.5	2.24	0.33	14.9	21
LOWRY MARKET TIMING	CA	SC	35.5	10.23	12,007.00	10,174.00	☆	3.4	0.00	0.35	N/A	426
LUTHERAN BRO FUND	GI	SC	295.6	19.53	11,733.20	11,915.10	30,957.00	3.0	0.50	0.60	20.4	40
LUTHERAN BRO HI YLD	FI	SC	18.8	10.25	#9,996.10	☆	☆	0.0	0.00	0.18	N/A	N/A
LUTHERAN BRO INCOME	FI	SC	682.7	8.62	10,072.50	10,660.20	20,907.90	9.8	0.00	0.84	N/A	39
MACKAY-SHIELDS CAP APR (R)	CA	NO	32.1	12.20	12,668.70	11,223.60	☆	0.0	0.00	0.00	N/A	10
MACKAY-SHIELDS CONV (R)	CV	NO	35.8	10.11	10,446.00	10,396.30	☆	4.0	0.00	0.40	N/A	19
MACKAY-SHIELDS GLOBAL (R)	GL	NO	12.9	9.99	#9,990.00	☆	☆	0.0	0.00	0.00	N/A	N/A
MACKAY-SHIELDS GOVT (R)	FI	NO	338.3	9.54	10,189.50	10,775.40	☆	9.7	0.00	1.06	N/A	78
MACKAY-SHIELDS HI YLD (R)	FI	NO	75.5	9.49	10,440.10	10,697.10	☆	11.9	0.00	1.21	N/A	45
MACKAY-SHIELDS VALUE (R)	GI	NO	18.4	10.79	11,949.10	10,335.20	☆	0.0	0.00	0.00	N/A	N/A
MANHATTAN FUND	CA	NO	528.0	11.14	12,728.00	12,249.20	38,025.30	0.8	0.79	0.09	25.0	96
HORACE MANN BALANCED	B	NO	17.2	15.89	10,657.30	10,942.10	☆	2.2	0.22	0.35	N/A	45
HORACE MANN GROWTH	G	NO	96.1	26.76	12,569.30	11,991.80	30,697.50	1.7	3.96	0.49	N/A	53
HORACE MANN INCOME	I	NO	2[illegible]	13.61	9,749.30	10,116.40	☆	4.1	0.01	0.56	N/A	8
MARINER EQUITY	CA	NO	8.[illegible]	12.37	12,368.10	12,776.70		1.9	0.11	0.24	N/A	19
MARINER INTERM BOND	FI	NO	12.[illegible]	9.95	10,278.90	10,524.20		5.3	0.09	0.52	N/A	N/A
MASS CAPITAL DEVELOPMENT	G	SC	1,098.5	13.91	12,718.60	[illegible]	2[illegible],592.30	1.1	1.29	0.16	22.6	117
MASS FINL BOND	FI	SC	310.0	13.31	9,769.40	10,339.20	22,285.10	8.9	0.82	1.24	N/A	218
MASS FINL DEVELOPMENT	GI	SC	303.2	13.89	12,851.20	11,806.40	30,462.70	1.5	2.44	0.21	23.6	102
MASS FINL EMERGING GRO	SG	SC	317.6	20.85	12,396.00	10,612.00	32,830.00	0.0	1.64	0.00	28.0	56
MASS FINL HIGH INCOME	FI	SC	1,221.5	6.87	10,560.30	10,835.[illegible]	25,305.30	13.1	0.00	0.90	23.5	49
MASS FINL INTL TR-BOND	WI	SC	148.5	12.03	10,837.60	11,818.90	24,051.40	6.2	1.59	0.82	N/A	371
MASS FINL SPECIAL	CA	SC	153.6	9.99	13,259.10	12,149.00	☆	0.3	1.81	0.03	20.9	156
MASS FINL TOTAL RETURN	B	SC	487.2	11.55	11,609.70	11,690.60	30,638.50	4.9	0.88	0.56	22.1	94
MASS INVESTORS GROWTH	G	SC	1,055.2	11.98	12,802.20	11,866.10	26,820.90	1.5	2.97	0.20	25.7	77
MASS INVESTORS TRUST	GI	SC	1,484.3	15.35	12,862.00	12,502.20	30,499.00	2.4	1.75	0.39	23.5	26
MATHERS FUND	G	NO	160.5	18.80	12,474.40	12,348.60	27,985.50	2.0	4.19	0.42	26.5	174
MAXIM BOND	FI	NO	29.6	1.20	9,946.00	10,435.50	☆	6.7	0.01	0.08	N/A	N/A
MAXIM GROWTH	G	NO	99.9	1.50	12,253.90	12,186.30	☆	2.8	0.04	0.04	N/A	N/A
MBL GROWTH FUND	G	NO	36.6	15.20	11,883.70	11,776.20	☆	2.3	1.47	0.36	N/A	44
MEDICAL RESEARCH INV	H	LO	3.7	14.99	12,944.70	10,834.20	☆	0.0	0.79	0.00	N/A	69
MEDICAL TECHNOLOGY FUND	H	NO	59.1	16.62	12,421.50	10,605.40	24,772.60	1.1	0.00	0.18	40.6	15
MEESCHAERT CAPITAL	G	NO	43.0	30.59	11,824.50	11,024.30	21,656.40	8.5	0.00	2.61	24.1	102
MEESCHAERT INTL (R)	WI	NO	9.3	10.46	#10,460.00	☆	☆	0.0	0.00	0.00	N/A	N/A
MERIDIAN FUND	G	NO	18.7	15.29	11,267.50	9,742.90	☆	0.5	1.16	0.07	N/A	75
MERIT GRO OPPORTUNITIES	G	NO	6.3	14.50	12,169.20	☆	☆	0.0	1.19	0.16	N/A	14
MERIT US GOVT	FI	NO	12.9	12.11	9,976.20	☆	☆	0.0	0.10	0.69	N/A	11
MERRILL LYN BASIC VALUE	GI	SC	1,159.0	20.26	12,095.60	12,236.70	35,639.00	3.2	0.86	0.64	15.7	23
MERRILL LYN CAPITAL	GI	SC	730.8	24.49	11,821.50	11,899.20	30,527.10	1.4	3.88	0.40	17.4	87
MERRILL LYN CORP DIV	EI	LO	232.9	10.90	10,524.50	11,165.60	☆	7.1	0.19	0.77	14.0	131
MERRILL LYN EQUI-BOND (R)	GI	LO	16.6	14.08	10,853.20	10,941.00	22,871.90	4.0	0.74	0.58	N/A	6
MERRILL LYN EUROFUND (R)	IF	NO	488.1	11.07	#11,070.00	☆	☆	0.0	0.00	0.00	N/A	N/A
MERRILL LYN FEDERAL	FI	SC	6,229.5	9.45	9,997.00	10,582.60	☆	8.5	0.36	0.80	N/A	300
MERRILL LYN FD TOMOROW (R)	G	NO	892.7	17.33	11,924.30	10,893.60	☆	0.5	0.73	0.08	20.4	7
MERRILL LYN HIGH INCOME	FI	LO	835.2	8.40	10,647.70	10,963.30	22,749.60	11.4	0.00	0.95	N/A	33
MERRILL LYN HIGH QUALITY	FI	LO	269.3	11.28	9,837.20	10,464.70	20,809.90	8.8	0.00	0.99	N/A	94
MERRILL LYN INST INTER	FI	NO	601.3	9.66	10,037.70	☆	☆	0.0	0.00	0.47	N/A	N/A
MERRILL LYN INTL HLDGS	GL	SC	359.2	14.38	11,857.90	12,698.70	☆	1.3	2.54	0.22	24.0	73
MERRILL LYN INTERMEDIATE	FI	LO	122.0	11.25	9,856.90	10,428.30	19,922.10	8.5	0.00	0.95	N/A	67
MERRILL LYN NATRL RES (R)	NR	NO	954.3	17.66	13,879.40	17,034.00	☆	0.4	0.28	0.07	37.0	49
MERRILL LYN PACIFIC	IF	SC	482.4	41.95	13,623.00	16,205.40	58,596.70	0.4	3.65	0.18	N/A	31

MERRILL LYN PHOENIX	GI	SC	127.1	14.29	11,751.30	11,919.80	☆	3.7	1.01	0.55	12.8	44
MERRILL LYN RET BENFT (R)	GI	NO	3,151.9	12.17	11,208.30	11,374.20	☆	3.1	0.28	0.38	N/A	N/A
MERRILL LYN RET EQTY (R)	CA	NO	658.6	10.09	#	☆	☆	0.0	0.00	0.06	N/A	N/A
MERRILL LYN RET GLOBAL (R)	WI	NO	363.0	10.59	10,763.30	☆	☆	0.0	0.00	0.57	N/A	N/A
MERRILL LYN RET INC (R)	FI	NO	2,161.8	9.56	9,944.00	10,505.10	☆	8.1	0.01	0.77	21.8	194
MERRILL LYN SPEC VALUE	G	SC	141.2	14.64	10,986.70	9,286.70	21,973.00	0.4	0.65	0.05	20.2	40
METLIFE CAPITAL APPREC	CA	SC	23.6	11.86	13,283.50	☆	☆	0.0	0.00	0.02	N/A	N/A
METLIFE EQUITY INCOME	EI	SC	31.2	10.35	11,022.80	☆	☆	0.0	0.00	0.20	N/A	N/A
METLIFE EQU INVESTMENTS	GI	SC	22.1	11.33	12,195.90	☆	☆	0.0	0.00	0.12	N/A	N/A
METLIFE GOVT SECS	FI	LO	25.1	7.04	9,789.70	☆	☆	0.0	0.00	0.49	N/A	N/A
METLIFE GOVT INCOME	FI	NO	2,807.5	11.95	#9,785.80	☆	☆	0.0	0.00	0.28	N/A	N/A
METLIFE HIGH INCOME	FI	SC	28.0	7.48	10,604.30	☆	☆	0.0	0.01	0.67	N/A	N/A
METRO PORTFOLIO INV STK	CA	NO	7.8	15.38	11,704.70	10,800.50	☆	0.1	0.67	0.01	N/A	40
MFS GOVT GUARANTEED SEC	FI	LO	1,124.8	9.74	9,929.70	10,518.90	☆	9.3	0.06	0.91	N/A	128
MFS GOVT SEC HIGH YIELD	FI	NO	896.1	8.96	9,749.40	10,308.70	☆	8.6	0.36	0.79	N/A	296
MFS LIFETIME CAP GRO (R)	CA	NO	62.9	10.48	14,118.30	☆	☆	0.0	0.00	0.01	N/A	N/A
MFS LIFETIME DIV PLUS (R)	GI	NO	87.4	9.83	10,820.40	☆	☆	0.0	0.08	0.25	N/A	N/A
MFS LIFETIME EMER GRO (R)	SG	NO	50.6	7.99	14,553.70	☆	☆	0.0	0.00	0.00	N/A	N/A
MFS LIFETIME GLOBAL EQ (R)	GL	NO	21.6	11.87	14,131.00	☆	☆	0.0	0.00	0.00	N/A	N/A
MFS LIFETIME GOVT INC (R)	FI	NO	962.6	8.78	9,629.60	☆	☆	0.0	0.15	0.19	N/A	N/A
MFS LIFETIME HI INC (R)	FI	NO	73.9	7.48	10,277.50	☆	☆	0.0	0.00	0.19	N/A	N/A
MFS LIFETIME MGD SECTR (R)	S	NO	72.1	9.60	15,015.50	☆	☆	0.0	0.00	0.01	N/A	N/A
MFS-MANAGED SECTOR TR	S	SC	201.6	12.61	13,259.40	11,220.20	☆	0.7	0.00	0.08	24.1	167
MIDAMERICA HIGH GROWTH	CA	SC	13.3	5.60	12,903.20	11,857.30	22,687.40	1.2	0.99	0.07	N/A	180
MIDAMERICA HIGH YIELD FD	FI	SC	10.0	10.45	10,110.30	10,413.50	☆	10.1	0.07	1.06	N/A	30
MIDAMERICA MUTUAL	G	SC	37.1	7.25	12,282.80	12,108.20	26,622.50	2.7	1.38	0.21	20.3	75
MIDAS GOLD SHS & BULLION	AU	SC	17.0	11.46	14,524.70	17,962.40	☆	0.0	0.00	0.00	N/A	8
MIDWEST INCOME TR/INTMDT	FI	NO	59.6	10.33	9,950.50	10,420.50	16,666.20	7.6	0.00	0.78	N/A	33
MAS EQUITY	G	NO	215.4	40.43	11,766.40	11,069.30	☆	2.5	1.61	1.03	N/A	52
MAS FIXED INCOME	FI	NO	207.4	28.67	10,152.10	10,923.30	☆	8.0	1.24	2.35	N/A	169
MAS QUANTITATIVE GROWTH	G	NO	10.5	30.01	12,106.40	☆	☆	0.0	0.00	0.11	N/A	N/A
MAS SMALL CAPITALIZATION	SG	NO	200.5	25.46	11,007.30	☆	☆	0.8	0.00	0.21	N/A	N/A
MAS VALUE	GI	NO	688.8	37.79	11,354.20	11,200.40	☆	3.5	2.34	1.35	N/A	33
MIMLIC INVESTORS I	GI	SC	7.8	12.69	12,677.30	11,748.90	☆	1.7	0.00	0.22	N/A	81
MIMLIC MORTGAGE	FI	SC	13.9	10.04	9,879.30	10,678.20	☆	8.6	0.19	0.87	N/A	86
MONETTA FUND	GI	NO	2.6	11.12	11,591.40	11,268.90	☆	1.8	0.00	0.19	N/A	80
MONEY MARKET/OPTIONS	OG	NO	7.6	21.12	12,440.80	11,744.40	23,235.80	3.4	3.11	0.83	N/A	N/A
MONITREND FUND	CA	LO	29.8	18.64	9,951.90	9,636.80	☆	1.4	0.71	0.26	N/A	166
WL MORGAN GROWTH	TK	NO	736.6	14.88	12,939.10	12,150.00	30,051.70	1.3	1.75	0.20	27.5	31
MORGAN KEEGAN SOUTHERN	G	LO	9.9	12.16	12,184.40	☆	☆	0.0	0.00	0.00	N/A	N/A
MORISON ASSET ALLOCATION	CA	SC	18.0	5.72	11,237.70	☆	☆	0.0	0.00	0.00	N/A	N/A
MUTUAL BEACON FUND (X)	GI	NO	112.8	23.42	12,564.40	12,677.00	25,692.60	1.3	0.94	0.31	25.6	113
MUTUAL BENEFIT FUND	GI	SC	19.0	15.72	11,843.50	11,697.40	34,423.70	1.8	1.32	0.29	21.0	48
MUTUAL OMAHA AMERICA	FI	NO	55.5	10.07	9,842.10	10,324.30	16,348.80	8.5	0.00	0.86	N/A	76
MUTUAL OMAHA GROWTH	G	SC	44.1	8.54	12,045.10	11,230.10	24,727.50	1.1	0.42	0.09	22.4	45
MUTUAL OMAHA INCOME	I	SC	150.1	9.41	10,952.50	10,858.70	20,708.10	8.1	0.27	0.77	19.8	76
MUTUAL QUALIFIED INCOME (X)	GI	NO	759.8	24.27	12,098.70	12,272.00	32,922.60	2.9	1.27	0.73	23.7	124
MUTUAL SHARES (X)	GI	NO	1,904.7	72.22	11,951.00	12,045.40	33,497.90	2.3	4.15	1.70	23.4	122
NAESS & THOMAS SPECIAL	SG	NO	33.2	43.80	12,478.60	10,204.90	20,955.10	0.0	5.67	0.00	34.7	82
NATL AVIATION & TECH	TK	SC	92.3	13.05	12,155.90	12,022.70	24,029.50	6.4	0.15	0.84	36.2	10
NATIONAL BALANCED	B	SC	2.6	14.30	11,126.60	10,934.80	27,687.30	5.7	1.67	0.88	N/A	53
NATIONAL BOND	FI	SC	823.1	2.97	10,128.20	9,953.60	20,490.00	15.6	0.00	0.46	N/A	259
NATIONAL FEDERAL SEC TR	FI	SC	1,239.9	10.06	9,492.30	9,950.30	☆	11.4	0.18	1.15	N/A	235
NATIONAL GROWTH	G	SC	71.2	12.36	11,335.90	10,618.20	19,856.10	1.9	0.00	0.24	23.2	84
NATIONAL INDUSTRIES (R)	GI	NO	32.4	14.33	12,311.00	11,152.20	19,351.20	0.9	1.32	0.13	23.3	74
NATIONAL PREFERRED	FI	SC	6.0	8.42	10,349.30	10,519.80	24,664.00	9.0	0.00	0.76	19.0	52
NATIONAL PREMIUM INC	OI	SC	15.1	12.75	11,523.20	11,179.30	☆	7.9	0.60	1.02	N/A	N/A
NATIONAL REAL ESTATE	S	SC	19.5	10.23	10,844.50	10,351.90	☆	3.5	0.32	0.36	N/A	32
NATIONAL STOCK	GI	SC	228.5	8.51	11,877.10	11,457.20	26,199.80	3.9	3.53	0.44	N/A	83
NATL TELECOM & TECH	TK	SC	58.6	16.87	12,321.80	11,491.20	☆	1.1	0.00	0.18	34.0	6

PERFORMANCE OF MUTUAL FUNDS (continued)

FUND NAME	OBJ.	LOAD	TOTAL NET ASTS (MIL) 6/30/87	NAV 6/30/87	PERFORMANCE (RETURN ON INITIAL $10,000 INVESTMENT) 12/31/86–6/30/87	6/30/86–6/30/87	6/30/82–6/30/87	YIELD % 6/30/87	PER SHARE LATEST 12 MONTHS CAP GAINS	INC DIVS	LATEST AVAILABLE PRICE/EARNINGS	ANNUAL % TURNOVER
NATIONAL TOTAL INCOME	EI	SC	150.1	8.27	10,831.60	10,579.70	28,059.50	5.3	0.15	0.44	16.9	10
NATIONAL TOTAL RETURN	EI	SC	330.7	7.97	10,998.00	10,875.30	28,117.40	4.8	0.00	0.38	18.4	6
NATIONAL VALUE	CA	SC	2.8	13.45	11,980.60	12,206.10	☆	6.0	0.25	0.80	N/A	98
NATIONWIDE BOND	FI	SC	34.5	9.62	9,851.10	10,336.80	19,944.50	9.1	0.04	0.88	N/A	39
NATIONWIDE FUND	GI	SC	466.6	16.49	12,384.90	12,055.20	30,532.70	2.2	0.81	0.37	20.4	17
NATIONWIDE GROWTH	G	SC	235.3	10.44	12,196.30	11,912.50	35,589.10	2.7	1.21	0.30	24.2	64
NAUTILUS FUND	TK	SC	20.8	14.28	11,753.10	10,959.30	16,159.60	0.0	0.00	0.00	N/A	31
NEUBERGER & BERMAN LT BD	FI	NO	108.1	9.89	10,055.60	10,459.50	☆	6.1	0.00	0.60	N/A	41
NEUWIRTH FUND	G	NO	31.4	15.80	12,260.40	10,344.50	27,188.40	0.0	2.55	0.00	24.3	74
NEW ALTERNATIVES FUND	NR	SC	4.1	46.44	11,096.80	11,099.40	☆	0.0	0.00	0.00	N/A	28
"NEW BEGINNING" GROWTH	SG	NO	56.1	33.53	13,216.40	11,746.90	☆	0.1	3.82	0.05	N/A	99
"NEW BEGINNING" INC & GR	GI	NO	10.3	21.33	12,077.50	11,856.20	☆	2.0	0.92	0.42	N/A	72
"NEW BEGINNING" INV RESV	FI	NO	2.4	9.96	10,308.70	10,582.40	☆	5.5	0.00	0.54	N/A	N/A
"NEW BEGINNING" YIELD	FI	NO	9.5	10.69	10,030.60	10,693.40	☆	7.6	0.01	0.80	N/A	200
NEW ECONOMY FUND	G	SC	970.4	23.57	12,143.20	11,679.30	☆	1.6	1.12	0.38	27.2	26
NEW ENG BOND INCOME	FI	SC	58.8	11.18	9,936.50	10,598.30	19,681.00	8.5	0.00	0.95	N/A	352
NEW ENG EQUITY FUND	GI	SC	48.2	11.45	11,643.80	11,258.80	25,822.90	2.5	1.95	0.31	15.4	91
NEW ENG GOVERNMENT SEC	FI	SC	201.7	12.26	9,744.80	10,185.50	☆	7.5	0.45	0.93	N/A	66
NEW ENG GROWTH FUND	G	SC	471.8	11.74	13,409.50	12,554.90	36,303.80	0.4	0.69	0.04	34.0	153
NEW ENG RETIREMENT EQU	GI	SC	152.7	9.14	12,866.70	12,380.20	31,580.70	1.0	1.65	0.09	26.8	164
NEW ENG ZENITH BOND INC	FI	NO	16.5	102.12	9,946.20	10,633.60	☆	9.3	11.10	10.04	N/A	303
NEW ENG ZENITH CAP GRO	CA	NO	15.2	275.56	16,725.40	17,787.40	☆	0.1	122.84	0.44	N/A	527
NEW ENG ZENITH MNGD SRS	GI	NO	5.3	104.09	#10,408.00	☆	☆	0.0	0.00	0.00	N/A	N/A
NEW ENG ZENITH STK INDEX	G	NO	10.6	105.64	#10,615.00	☆	☆	0.0	0.00	0.00	N/A	N/A
NEW PERSPECTIVE FUND	GL	SC	1,118.6	12.46	12,566.50	13,950.30	33,966.70	1.7	1.25	0.22	27.5	17
NEW YORK VENTURE	G	SC	228.8	10.58	11,608.70	11,791.50	36,239.90	0.9	1.68	0.10	21.6	98
NEWPORT FAR EAST (R)	IF	NO	4.1	26.64	13,220.80	16,116.20	☆	0.0	0.00	0.00	N/A	19
NEWPORT GLOBAL GROWTH (R)	GL	NO	1.6	12.13	12,130.00	11,121.30	☆	0.0	0.00	0.00	N/A	10
NEWTON GROWTH FUND	G	NO	48.2	26.05	12,560.30	12,647.30	28,700.80	1.2	4.27	0.35	30.7	136
NEWTON INCOME FUND	FI	NO	13.8	8.17	10,033.90	10,406.90	19,319.00	8.1	0.00	0.66	N/A	56
NICHOLAS FUND (R)	G	NO	1,294.2	36.57	11,548.40	11,195.20	32,767.10	2.9	2.37	1.14	17.9	14
NICHOLAS INCOME	FI	NO	71.5	3.94	10,285.30	10,771.80	21,880.40	9.3	0.00	0.36	7.6	20
NICHOLAS LIMITED EDITION	G	NO	6.6	10.15	#10,150.00	☆	☆	0.0	0.00	0.00	N/A	N/A
NICHOLAS II (R)	SG	NO	407.3	20.45	12,607.90	11,699.80	☆	2.0	0.51	0.42	20.6	15
NODDINGS CALAMOS GROWTH	CV	NO	12.1	11.21	10,468.60	10,756.20	☆	3.4	0.61	0.40	N/A	37
NODDINGS CALAMOS INCOME	CV	NO	26.2	12.06	10,984.80	10,836.40	☆	4.4	0.43	0.54	N/A	26
NOMURA PACIFIC BASIN	IF	NO	102.8	25.41	13,574.10	16,128.80	☆	0.0	3.32	0.00	N/A	3
NORTH STAR APOLLO	CA	NO	25.3	12.92	13,518.70	12,655.10	☆	1.2	0.72	0.16	N/A	85
NORTH STAR BOND FUND	FI	NO	40.9	9.90	9,931.30	10,422.50	21,079.70	8.5	0.05	0.84	N/A	76
NORTH STAR INTERNATIONAL	IF	NO	11.8	10.09	#10,059.80	☆	☆	0.0	0.00	0.00	N/A	N/A
NORTH STAR REGIONAL FUND	G	NO	100.2	20.60	12,066.70	11,266.00	32,264.10	1.7	3.34	0.39	19.9	112
NORTH STAR RESERVE	FI	NO	34.8	10.18	10,267.20	10,549.80	☆	5.3	0.00	0.54	N/A	N/A
NORTH STAR STOCK FUND	CA	NO	91.7	17.88	13,088.90	12,621.20	30,198.40	1.0	1.64	0.19	23.7	50
NORTHEAST INV GROWTH	G	NO	28.9	22.62	12,457.40	11,613.20	30,722.40	0.2	0.35	0.04	N/A	13
NORTHEAST INV TRUST	FI	NO	361.0	13.52	10,405.70	11,071.70	25,160.00	10.8	0.00	1.46	N/A	43
NOVA FUND	TK	SC	33.8	18.44	12,823.40	12,495.60	25,542.80	0.00	2.00	0.00	29.6	99
OBERWEIS EMERGING GRO (R)	SG	LO	20.5	12.84	#11,413.30	☆	☆	0.0	0.00	0.00	N/A	N/A
OHIO NATIONAL-BOND (R)	FI	NO	2.3	10.32	9,986.50	10,505.60	☆	8.6	0.00	0.88	N/A	N/A
OHIO NATIONAL-EQUITY (R)	G	NO	23.6	20.21	12,806.60	12,426.90	☆	2.1	2.31	0.45	N/A	N/A
OHIO NATIONAL-OMNI (R)	G	NO	22.3	13.09	10,951.90	10,797.40	☆	4.0	0.23	0.52	N/A	N/A
OLYMPIC TR-B SERIES	CA	NO	8.5	19.27	12,376.40	10,653.70	☆	0.2	0.00	0.04	N/A	N/A
OLYMPIC TR-EQ INCOME	EI	NO	0.1	0.00	N/A	☆	☆	0.0	0.00	0.00	N/A	N/A
OLYMPIC TR-TOTL RETN	GI	NO	4.0	15.16	10,755.50	10,925.70	☆	4.8	0.25	0.72	N/A	N/A
OMEGA FUND	CA	NO	37.7	16.73	12,946.00	12,310.90	26,510.50	1.3	2.09	0.23	26.7	178
ONE HUNDRED FUND	G	NO	12.2	24.78	12,572.30	11,051.90	23,293.60	0.0	1.16	0.00	N/A	122
ONE HUNDRED & ONE FUND	GI	NO	3.7	17.17	11,656.00	11,022.90	31,489.30	2.9	3.00	0.55	N/A	187
OPPENHEIMER ASSET ALOCTN	B	SC	31.7	10.18	#10,241.40	☆	☆	0.0	0.00	0.00	N/A	N/A

OPPENHEIMER BLUE CHIP	GI	SC	17.4	15.28	10,693.80	☆	☆	0.0	0.00	0.18	N/A	N/A
OPPENHEIMER CHALLENGER	CA	LO	14.4	14.13	12,627.30	10,608.30	☆	0.0	2.08	0.00	N/A	252
OPPENHEIMER DIRECTORS	CA	SC	200.3	25.84	12,065.50	11,149.90	24,245.50	2.1	0.00	0.53	23.1	89
OPPENHEIMER EQUITY	EI	SC	730.1	9.85	11,945.90	12,051.30	34,888.30	4.9	0.61	0.48	21.8	105
OPPENHEIMER FUND	G	SC	273.8	12.16	12,416.60	10,864.30	22,944.80	0.2	1.15	0.02	35.8	44
OPPENHEIMER GNMA	FI	SC	58.1	13.58	10,004.40	☆	☆	0.0	0.00	1.08	N/A	N/A
OPPENHEIMER GLD & SP MIN	AU	SC	76.5	12.10	14,319.50	19,222.70	☆	1.1	0.00	0.13	28.8	53
OPPENHEIMER GLOBAL FUND	GL	SC	517.1	33.55	12,430.50	13,472.40	35,756.00	0.3	3.81	0.11	37.7	25
OPPENHEIMER HIGH YIELD	FI	SC	760.9	17.09	10,877.40	11,061.50	21,116.70	12.6	0.00	2.16	N/A	91
OPPENHEIMER OTC	SG	SC	31.3	19.86	13,186.10	☆	☆	0.0	0.00	0.02	29.7	N/A
OPPENHEIMER PREMIUM INC	OI	SC	365.6	21.39	12,419.10	12,567.40	21,409.40	2.9	1.83	0.65	26.8	267
OPPENHEIMER REGENCY	CA	SC	177.9	15.90	12,210.70	11,407.90	☆	1.5	2.66	0.26	31.5	135
OPPENHEIMER SPECIAL	G	SC	690.5	20.37	10,777.80	10,969.20	22,215.90	3.8	4.20	0.77	24.9	67
OPPENHEIMER TARGET	CA	SC	114.2	23.29	11,526.10	9,699.00	28,170.20	0.5	0.19	0.11	19.7	70
OPPENHEIMER TIME	CA	SC	347.5	20.59	12,702.00	11,639.10	33,275.10	1.1	2.07	0.23	30.8	107
OPPENHEIMER TOTAL RETURN	GI	SC	280.6	8.01	12,202.20	12,143.40	27,151.70	4.4	1.12	0.38	26.6	88
OPPENHEIMER US GOVT TR	FI	SC	216.5	9.77	9,992.60	10,515.80	☆	8.7	0.06	0.85	N/A	367
OVER-THE-COUNTER SEC	SG	SC	304.5	19.28	11,707.50	10,170.70	27,735.10	1.1	1.89	0.22	24.9	N/A
OTC 100 FUND	G	NO	92.2	15.60	12,544.30	11,237.60	☆	0.3	0.00	0.04	26.2	46
PACIFIC HORIZON AGG GRO	CA	LO	241.5	17.37	13,648.20	11,405.60	☆	0.1	0.00	0.01	23.6	250
PACIFIC HORIZON HI YLD	FI	LO	29.9	16.03	10,353.90	10,913.80	☆	11.6	0.00	1.86	N/A	131
PAINEWEBBER AMERICA	GI	SC	103.2	17.03	11,549.50	11,096.70	☆	4.5	1.06	0.76	23.1	83
PAINEWEBBER ASSET ALLO (R)	B	NO	710.0	9.89	10,242.20	☆	☆	0.0	0.00	0.10	18.5	N/A
PAINEWEBBER ATLAS	GL	SC	321.8	20.00	12,547.10	13,453.10	☆	4.7	2.14	0.99	26.9	95
PAINEWEBBER GNMA	FI	LO	2,847.5	9.62	9,897.00	10,606.90	☆	11.1	0.00	1.06	N/A	224
PAINEWEBBER HIGH YIELD	FI	LO	831.9	10.09	10,431.70	10,734.40	☆	13.6	0.04	1.37	N/A	169
PAINEWEBBER INV GRADE	FI	LO	681.4	9.96	9,795.40	10,388.10	☆	11.6	0.02	1.16	N/A	81
PAINEWEBBER MSTR GLOBAL	GL	NO	679.6	10.21	#10,310.30	☆	☆	0.0	0.00	0.10	N/A	N/A
PAINEWEBBER MSTR GRO (R)	G	NO	129.4	11.37	12,018.50	☆	☆	0.0	0.00	0.07	N/A	N/A
PAINEWEBBER MSTR INC (R)	FI	NO	450.1	9.31	9,694.20	10,375.70	☆	9.8	0.00	0.91	N/A	N/A
PAINEWEBBER OLYMPUS	G	SC	127.7	14.22	13,093.90	11,298.90	☆	1.4	0.31	0.19	29.2	72
PARIBAS MCU 450	GI	NO	24.4	11.95	12,435.00	☆	☆	0.0	0.00	0.00	N/A	4
PARIBAS QUANTUS EQ (R)	G	NO	18.3	11.60	11,623.20	11,150.10	☆	0.1	0.00	0.01	N/A	88
PARNASSUS FUND	G	LO	5.8	22.94	13,063.80	12,063.50	☆	0.1	0.67	0.03	N/A	31
PARTNERS FUND	G	NO	757.7	20.83	11,991.90	11,671.40	29,150.20	2.1	2.25	0.44	21.2	181
PASADENA GROWTH (R)	SG	NO	14.2	16.32	11,673.80	10,314.70	☆	0.4	0.00	0.06	N/A	N/A
PATRIOT CORP CASH	FI	LO	37.3	50.00	10,232.80	☆	☆	0.0	0.00	1.58	N/A	N/A
PAX WORLD FUND	B	NO	71.6	13.97	11,473.90	10,847.30	26,307.60	3.1	0.83	0.45	22.8	57
PBHG GROWTH	CA	SC	28.1	13.81	13,367.80	13,067.20	☆	0.4	2.69	0.07	N/A	N/A
PDC&J PERFORMANCE	CA	NO	9.2	14.31	11,354.30	10,491.20	☆	12.2	0.00	1.74	N/A	66
PDC&J PRESERVATION	FI	NO	8.8	10.89	10,068.60	10,491.10	☆	5.6	0.00	0.61	N/A	10
PENN SQUARE MUTUAL	GI	NO	231.4	11.26	12,513.80	12,235.80	30,297.90	3.4	0.68	0.39	22.4	22
PENNSYLVANIA MUTUAL	SG	NO	358.4	7.85	11,601.40	11,036.30	34,118.30	1.7	0.82	0.14	20.7	19
PERMANENT PORTFOLIO	S	NO	87.8	15.04	11,411.20	11,898.70	☆	0.0	0.00	0.00	30.6	31
PHILADELPHIA FUND	GI	SC	113.3	7.94	11,954.60	11,204.70	22,086.60	2.0	2.35	0.18	24.5	147
PHOENIX BALANCED	B	SC	333.9	14.29	11,567.80	11,516.40	31,706.20	3.6	1.59	0.55	21.4	129
PHOENIX CONVERTIBLE	CV	SC	155.6	19.87	11,657.00	11,878.50	29,458.50	4.0	1.72	0.83	23.2	187
PHOENIX GROWTH	G	SC	526.7	19.89	12,128.00	12,036.70	37,696.90	1.6	2.91	0.33	24.2	170
PHOENIX HIGH QUAL BOND	FI	SC	19.2	9.55	9,698.50	10,144.50	☆	7.0	0.17	0.67	N/A	248
PHOENIX HIGH YIELD	FI	SC	154.3	9.40	10,370.20	10,763.50	22,101.80	12.8	0.00	1.20	N/A	91
PHOENIX STOCK	CA	SC	127.3	15.66	12,359.90	11,954.00	37,044.50	1.5	3.51	0.24	22.0	241
PHOENIX TOTAL RETURN	GI	SC	18.2	14.78	11,948.30	11,436.30	24,390.80	2.9	0.00	0.42	N/A	378
PIERPONT CAP APPREC	G	NO	0.0	0.00	N/A	N/A	☆	0.0	0.00	0.00	N/A	48
PIERPONT EQUITY	GI	NO	0.0	0.00	N/A	N/A	☆	0.0	0.00	0.28	N/A	52
PILGRIM ADJUSTABLE RATE	FI	LO	665.5	21.77	10,237.70	10,489.40	☆	7.1	0.00	1.55	N/A	70
PILGRIM CORP CASH	FI	NO	30.8	10.00	10,230.60	10,473.10	☆	4.5	0.00	0.46	N/A	408
PILGRIM GNMA	FI	LO	288.4	14.52	9,920.60	10,531.00	☆	9.8	0.00	1.42	N/A	75
PILGRIM FORGN GOVT	FI	LO	22.1	9.73	#9,730.00	☆	☆	0.0	0.00	0.00	N/A	N/A
PILGRIM FORGN HI INC	FI	LO	17.5	9.77	#9,770.00	☆	☆	0.0	0.00	0.00	N/A	N/A
PILGRIM FORGN INTL BOND	IF	LO	11.3	10.42	#10,420.00	☆	☆	0.0	0.00	0.00	N/A	N/A

PERFORMANCE OF MUTUAL FUNDS *(continued)*

FUND NAME	OBJ.	LOAD	TOTAL NET ASTS (MIL) 6/30/87	NAV 6/30/87	PERFORMANCE (RETURN ON INITIAL $10,000 INVESTMENT) 12/31/86–6/30/87	6/30/86–6/30/87	6/30/82–6/30/87	YIELD % 6/30/87	PER SHARE LATEST 12 MONTHS CAP GAINS	INC DIVS	LATEST AVAILABLE PRICE/ EARNINGS	ANNUAL % TURNOVER
PILGRIM HIGH YIELD	FI	LO	53.3	7.95	10,550.00	10,855.80	21,317.60	12.1	0.00	0.96	N/A	66
PILGRIM MAGNACAP	G	SC	245.7	11.56	11,928.50	11,371.80	32,592.10	2.2	0.23	0.26	16.9	16
PILGRIM PREFERRED	FI	LO	196.9	24.56	10,327.10	10,681.20	☆	11.0	0.00	2.70	N/A	55
PILGRIM RISING PROFIT	CA	SC	11.3	10.29	#10,290.00	☆	☆	0.0	0.00	0.00	N/A	N/A
PINE STREET FUND	GI	NO	70.7	14.57	11,759.50	11,295.70	29,080.50	2.4	1.10	0.36	21.7	90
PINNACLE FUND	CA	NO	3.0	31.65	12,351.40	11,212.90	☆	0.3	1.30	0.09	N/A	57
PIONEER BOND FUND	FI	SC	50.9	9.22	10,009.50	10,472.60	20,166.60	9.2	0.00	0.84	N/A	27
PIONEER FUND	GI	SC	1,575.5	24.06	12,415.50	12,374.10	28,570.30	2.2	3.87	0.58	22.0	18
PIONEER II	GI	SC	4,069.9	22.16	12,348.30	12,317.50	30,775.30	2.2	1.03	0.49	23.1	29
PIONEER THREE	GI	SC	712.7	17.79	11,835.60	11,126.00	☆	2.0	1.17	0.36	19.5	24
PIPER JAFFRAY BALANCED	B	LO	14.6	9.80	#9,886.50	☆	☆	0.0	0.00	0.08	N/A	N/A
PIPER JAFFRAY GOVT INC	FI	LO	82.5	9.65	#9,830.00	☆	☆	0.0	0.00	0.17	N/A	N/A
PIPER JAFFRAY SECTOR	S	LO	35.9	10.02	#10,050.20	☆	☆	0.0	0.00	0.03	N/A	N/A
PIPER JAFFRAY VALUE	G	LO	19.4	10.32	#10,376.80	☆	☆	0.0	0.00	0.05	N/A	N/A
PLYMOUTH AGGRESSIVE INC	FI	LO	7.5	10.09	#10,598.60	☆	☆	0.0	0.00	0.50	N/A	N/A
PLYMOUTH GOVERNMENT	FI	LO	3.9	9.40	#9,742.60	☆	☆	0.0	0.00	0.34	N/A	N/A
PLYMOUTH INC & GROWTH	GI	LO	28.9	10.97	#11,089.60	☆	☆	0.0	0.00	0.12	N/A	N/A
PORT WASHINGTON FUND	CA	NO	0.1	9.71	10,576.10	9,755.60	☆	4.8	0.00	0.47	N/A	N/A
PREMIER GNMA	FI	LO	3.7	14.18	#10,176.50	☆	☆	0.0	0.00	0.57	N/A	N/A
PREMIER INCOME	FI	LO	1.3	11.41	#8,973.20	☆	☆	0.0	0.00	0.25	N/A	N/A
T ROWE PRICE CAP APPREC	CA	NO	81.0	11.65	11,235.30	12,190.30	☆	1.2	0.36	0.14	N/A	375
T ROWE PRICE EQUITY INC	EI	NO	219.8	14.38	11,560.90	12,157.70	☆	4.4	0.49	0.65	N/A	73
T ROWE PRICE GNMA	FI	NO	349.6	9.71	9,926.80	10,649.40	☆	9.0	0.02	0.87	N/A	226
T ROWE PRICE GROWTH & INC	GI	NO	471.8	14.56	11,757.10	11,379.90	☆	5.1	1.13	0.77	16.6	100
T ROWE PRICE GROWTH STK	G	NO	1,560.5	19.78	12,155.20	12,149.50	28,858.40	1.3	3.46	0.29	25.1	60
T ROWE PRICE HIGH YIELD	FI	NO	892.0	10.73	10,576.10	10,840.50	☆	11.8	0.14	1.27	N/A	166
T ROWE PRICE INTL FUND	IF	NO	1,003.8	30.48	12,199.50	14,785.50	42,019.70	0.6	3.13	0.19	N/A	56
T ROWE PRICE INTL BOND	WI	NO	200.8	10.32	10,829.50	☆	☆	0.0	0.00	0.79	N/A	218
T ROWE PRICE NEW AMER GR	G	NO	98.2	14.54	11,338.70	10,183.60	☆	0.4	0.59	0.06	24.7	81
T ROWE PRICE NEW ERA	NR	NO	765.9	21.95	12,954.80	13,213.60	30,092.30	1.6	2.95	0.37	34.5	32
T ROWE PRICE NEW HORIZON	SG	NO	1,216.5	14.51	11,994.00	10,309.10	23,035.90	0.1	2.52	0.02	28.6	35
T ROWE PRICE NEW INCOME	FI	NO	818.2	8.65	9,851.80	10,336.20	18,914.10	8.3	0.00	0.71	N/A	126
T ROWE PRICE SH-TERM BD	FI	NO	218.5	5.07	10,121.20	10,507.70	☆	7.5	0.00	0.37	N/A	7
PRIMARY TREND	GI	NO	31.3	11.62	11,573.70	☆	☆	0.0	0.00	0.00	N/A	N/A
PRIMECAP	G	NO	236.2	52.73	12,386.70	12,851.80	☆	0.6	0.63	0.32	29.2	15
PRINCIPAL EQUITY	G	SC	1.8	7.53	12,391.00	10,873.50	☆	0.5	0.48	0.04	N/A	119
PRINCIPAL PRES DV ACHEVR	G	SC	8.0	10.48	#11,112.10	☆	☆	0.0	0.00	0.13	N/A	N/A
PRINCIPAL PRES GOVT	FI	LO	33.4	9.38	10,016.90	10,338.30	☆	7.6	0.12	0.71	N/A	307
PRINCIPAL PRES S&P 100	GI	LO	17.0	13.04	12,683.80	12,669.00	☆	2.7	0.05	0.35	N/A	13
PRINCIPAL WORLD	GL	SC	15.5	10.03	11,858.20	12,909.20	☆	1.1	0.91	0.11	N/A	166
PRINCOR CAPITAL ACCUM	CA	SC	93.5	21.66	12,690.90	12,095.50	36,958.50	1.4	2.15	0.30	24.2	45
PRINCOR GOVT SEC INCOME	FI	SC	65.9	10.40	9,857.70	10,705.40	☆	8.4	0.28	0.87	N/A	141
PRINCOR GROWTH FUND	G	SC	37.0	23.27	12,673.40	12,100.90	30,098.70	1.1	2.24	0.26	25.5	29
PROVIDENT FD FOR INCOME	EI	SC	116.4	5.23	12,032 20	12,362.20	29,183.10	5.5	0.50	0.30	28.0	53
PRU-BACHE ADJ RATE PRF	FI	NO	214.0	23.14	10,370.70	10,440.60	☆	6.9	0.00	1.60	N/A	225
PRU-BACHE EQUITY (R)	G	NO	557.5	10.99	12,547.50	12,062.90	32,541.40	0.9	0.85	0.09	N/A	123
PRUDENTIAL BACHE EQ IN (R)	EI	LO	86.7	10.40	#10,774.90	☆	☆	0.0	0.00	0.05	N/A	N/A
PRU-BACHE GLOBAL (R)	GL	NO	831.0	12.27	12,728.20	13,356.40	☆	0.1	1.09	0.01	N/A	80
PRU-BACHE GNMA (R)	FI	NO	289.3	15.13	9,954.10	10,662.90	18,203.30	7.6	0.36	1.17	N/A	254
PRU-BACHE GROWTH OPP (R)	G	NO	178.2	13.88	12,175.40	11,196.30	26,233.40	0.0	2.87	0.00	25.9	139
PRU-BACHE GOVT INTMDT	FI	LO	914.2	10.35	9,950.60	10,494.70	☆	8.8	0.06	0.91	N/A	139
PRU-BACHE GOVT PLUS (R)	FI	NO	3,865.1	9.94	9,878.20	10,389.60	☆	6.6	0.35	0.67	N/A	266
PRU-BACHE GOVT PLUS II (R)	FI	LO	231.9	9.33	9,763.80	☆	☆	0.0	0.08	0.41	N/A	N/A
PRU-BACHE HIGH YIELD (R)	FI	NO	2,266.9	10.55	10,490.20	10,908.20	22,969.70	11.3	0.00	1.19	N/A	38
PRU-BACHE INCOMVRTIBLE (R)	S	NO	528.6	11.91	11,318.80	11,410.10	☆	5.3	0.30	0.64	N/A	110
PRU-BACHE OPTION GRO (R)	OG	NO	86.8	9.34	12,007.80	11,990.40	☆	1.8	1.21	0.19	20.7	141
PRU-BACHE RESEARCH (R)	G	NO	477.1	15.03	12,603.30	11,935.20	☆	0.8	0.86	0.12	N/A	216
PRU-BACHE UTILITY (R)	UT	NO	1,682.2	14.34	9,999.40	10,594.80	31,800.40	5.7	0.81	0.84	N/A	49

PUTNAM CAPITAL (X)	SG	NO	13.6	8.92	12,549.90	11,060.90	30,876.00	0.2	0.77	0.02	N/A	99
PUTNAM CONV INC-GRO TR	CV	SC	1,279.5	17.68	11,369.20	11,178.00	26,606.30	5.4	0.27	0.96	16.5	78
PUTNAM CORP CASH ARP	FI	LO	499.0	46.17	10,426.70	10,605.90	☆	7.7	0.00	3.56	N/A	115
PUTNAM CORP CASH DSP	EI	LO	401.5	46.81	10,097.50	10,526.00	☆	10.7	0.09	5.01	N/A	260
PUTNAM ENERGY RESOURCES	NR	SC	116.9	14.64	13,190.50	13,657.30	20,787.70	2.6	0.00	0.38	22.3	216
GEORGE PUTNAM FD BOSTON	B	SC	435.2	14.77	11,616.80	11,761.70	27,328.70	5.1	1.78	0.80	18.1	143
PUTNAM GNMA PLUS	FI	SC	2,273.0	10.46	9,733.10	10,201.90	☆	12.5	0.00	1.30	N/A	N/A
PUTNAM GROWTH & INCOME	GI	SC	1,705.0	14.00	11,965.00	12,244.50	31,004.40	4.3	1.93	0.65	18.5	176
PUTNAM HEALTH SCIENCE	H	SC	316.4	22.57	12,941.50	11,210.90	25,346.00	0.8	2.74	0.20	36.0	31
PUTNAM HIGH INCOME GOVT	FI	SC	1,171.2	11.35	9,727.10	10,298.20	☆	8.5	0.60	0.99	N/A	187
PUTNAM HIGH YIELD (X)	FI	SC	2,332.4	15.45	10,507.50	10,934.90	23,509.90	12.8	0.00	1.97	N/A	77
PUTNAM HIGH YIELD II	FI	SC	299.1	11.55	10,510.40	10,654.20	☆	11.4	0.00	1.32	N/A	101
PUTNAM INCOME	FI	SC	295.8	6.98	9,932.60	10,480.60	21,958.30	11.3	0.00	0.79	N/A	202
PUTNAM INFO SCIENCE	TK	SC	144.8	19.26	13,679.00	13,148.80	☆	0.2	0.00	0.03	31.9	141
PUTNAM INTL EQUITIES	GL	SC	611.5	32.67	12,354.60	13,105.00	45,593.40	0.5	4.17	0.17	23.0	176
PUTNAM INVESTORS	G	SC	1,020.2	10.28	12,503.20	11,702.60	29,806.80	1.6	3.78	0.20	22.6	120
PUTNAM OPTION INCOME (X)	OI	SC	1,244.4	11.64	11,891.70	12,090.60	23,844.00	0.6	1.60	0.08	23.7	205
PUTNAM OPTION INCOME II	OI	SC	1,789.7	11.41	11,352.40	11,304.80	☆	3.1	1.37	0.37	23.0	198
PUTNAM OTC EMERGING GRO	SG	SC	149.7	30.44	12,838.50	11,323.50	☆	0.0	2.29	0.00	N/A	92
PUTNAM US GOVERNMENT	FI	SC	1,245.3	14.24	10,173.10	10,893.30	☆	10.1	0.00	1.44	N/A	116
PUTNAM VISTA BASIC VALUE	CA	SC	265.2	21.82	12,629.90	12,371.20	31,643.10	3.2	2.84	0.70	17.0	276
PUTNAM VOYAGER	CA	SC	574.4	25.05	12,787.10	11,774.60	33,744.10	0.6	2.73	0.15	29.7	76
QUANTUM FUND	CA	SC	0.5	10.51	10,896.10	9,768.30	☆	0.0	1.48	0.00	N/A	N/A
QUASAR ASSOCIATES (X)	G	NO	134.9	68.51	12,051.00	10,154.30	34,479.70	0.0	9.21	0.00	29.9	84
QUEST FOR VALUE FUND	CA	NO	110.3	28.22	11,548.40	11,098.30	33,351.20	0.9	1.68	0.26	21.3	68
RAINBOW FUND	CA	NO	2.4	6.52	12,051.80	11,663.70	22,717.80	0.0	0.00	0.00	N/A	190
REA-GRAHAM FUND	B	SC	49.0	14.33	10,281.00	10,869.80	☆	3.2	0.74	0.48	N/A	208
REICH & TANG EQUITY	G	NO	120.6	17.03	11,978.10	11,377.30	☆	1.8	0.60	0.31	N/A	35
REICH & TANG GNMA INC	FI	NO	6.6	9.67	9,679.20	10,466.70	☆	9.5	0.00	0.92	N/A	N/A
RESERVE EQUITY CONTRARIAN	GI	NO	28.4	19.14	12,488.10	11,914.30	☆	1.3	0.46	0.24	N/A	26
RESERVE EQUITY GROWTH	G	NO	2.2	17.46	12,721.50	12,190.90	☆	0.8	0.61	0.14	N/A	21
RETIREMENT PLAN AM-BOND	FI	NO	72.0	7.49	9,894.50	10,527.70	17,765.60	9.0	0.10	0.68	N/A	33
RETIREMENT PLAN AM-EQU	EI	NO	19.4	24.13	12,631.20	12,216.30	29,290.50	0.2	1.15	0.05	N/A	94
RIGHTIME FUND	S	NO	212.4	34.42	11,515.60	10,500.20	☆	0.0	1.95	0.00	N/A	231
RIGHTIME GOVT	FI	NO	8.4	14.13	9,705.60	☆	☆	0.0	0.00	0.43	N/A	N/A
RNC CONVERTIBLE	CV	SC	32.5	10.74	11,106.00	☆	☆	0.0	0.00	0.28	N/A	14
RNC CORP CASH	FI	NO	7.7	9.06	9,530.70	☆	☆	0.0	0.00	0.62	N/A	N/A
RNC INCOME	I	SC	9.3	9.95	10,466.00	10,598.30	☆	5.9	0.00	0.58	N/A	8
RNC REGENCY FUND	G	SC	18.3	14.53	11,627.70	11,178.90	☆	1.6	0.00	0.23	N/A	10
RNC WESTWIND	B	SC	6.5	10.68	10,818.10	☆	☆	0.0	0.00	0.14	N/A	N/A
ROCHESTER CONVERT GRO	CV	LO	5.7	11.09	11,382.80	11,158.80	☆	2.1	0.00	0.23	N/A	41
ROCHESTER CONVERT INC	CV	LO	9.0	8.50	10,354.50	8,976.70	☆	5.5	0.00	0.47	N/A	78
ROCHESTER GROWTH FUND	G	SC	3.1	10.64	11,679.50	8,457.90	☆	0.0	0.00	0.00	N/A	199
ROCHESTER TAX-MGD	G	SC	24.2	11.51	10,848.30	9,974.00	18,191.90	0.0	0.00	0.00	N/A	66
ROCKWOOD GROWTH	CA	NO	0.3	12.75	12,259.60	12,512.50	☆	0.0	0.74	0.00	N/A	N/A
RODNEY SQUARE GROWTH	GI	NO	34.6	10.38	#10,400.00	☆	☆	0.0	0.00	0.02	N/A	N/A
RODNEY SQUARE TOTL RETN	CA	NO	13.0	10.04	#	☆	☆	0.0	0.00	0.04	N/A	N/A
LF ROTHSCHILD CORP CASH	FI	LO	24.2	24.08	#9,840.00	☆	☆	0.0	0.00	0.52	N/A	N/A
LF ROTHSCHILD INVEST GRD	I	LO	15.7	9.36	#9,566.90	☆	☆	0.0	0.00	0.20	N/A	N/A
LF ROTHSCHILD RISING DVD	GI	LO	28.0	10.04	#10,090.30	☆	☆	0.0	0.00	0.05	N/A	N/A
ROYCE EQUITY INC (R)	EI	NO	6.2	5.42	10,871.60	9,986.50	☆	3.5	0.02	0.19	N/A	83
ROYCE HIGH YIELD (R)	FI	NO	17.7	9.42	10,516.10	10,351.40	☆	11.5	0.00	1.08	N/A	63
ROYCE VALUE (R)	SG	NO	173.0	9.67	11,845.50	10,910.20	☆	0.5	0.72	0.05	22.5	28
RUSHMORE GNMA	FI	NO	10.8	9.45	9,810.90	10,428.90	☆	8.4	0.01	0.79	N/A	44
RUSHMORE OTC	G	NO	3.3	14.07	13,262.20	11,737.30	☆	0.6	0.08	0.07	N/A	5
RUSHMORE STK MKT	G	NO	18.5	14.57	12,799.80	12,526.40	☆	1.9	0.00	0.27	N/A	7
RUSHMORE US GOVT	FI	NO	0.4	9.91	9,850.60	10,195.40	☆	6.3	0.00	0.62	N/A	N/A
SAFECO EQUITY FUND	GI	NO	62.7	11.84	12,529.40	11,583.80	28,927.60	1.9	2.03	0.23	23.4	86
SAFECO GROWTH FUND	G	NO	67.5	17.12	12,306.20	11,132.70	25,669.90	1.3	1.58	0.23	21.1	46
SAFECO INCOME FUND	EI	NO	290.5	16.92	11,332.90	11,465.70	32,457.70	4.5	0.72	0.77	15.5	29

PERFORMANCE OF MUTUAL FUNDS *(continued)*

FUND NAME	OBJ.	LOAD	TOTAL NET ASTS (MIL) 6/30/87	NAV 6/30/87	PERFORMANCE (RETURN ON INITIAL $10,000 INVESTMENT) 12/31/86–6/30/87	6/30/86–6/30/87	6/30/82–6/30/87	YIELD % 6/30/87	PER SHARE LATEST 12 MONTHS CAP GAINS	INC DIVS	LATEST AVAILABLE PRICE/EARNINGS	ANNUAL % TURNOVER
SAFECO US GOVT	FI	NO	21.9	9.47	9,905.90	☆	☆	0.0	0.00	0.81	N/A	N/A
SALEM FUNDS	G	NO	25.9	14.71	12,095.30	11,935.30	☆	1.1	0.36	0.16	N/A	20
SANTA BARBARA FUND	CA	NO	2.4	12.67	11,649.20	13,858.80	☆	0.4	1.23	0.06	N/A	N/A
SBSF FUND	G	NO	99.3	14.23	11,348.60	10,791.60	☆	3.8	1.01	0.56	N/A	65
SCHIELD AGGRESSIVE GRO	CA	LO	7.3	12.17	11,735.80	9,522.70	☆	0.0	0.00	0.00	N/A	26
SCHIELD VALUE PORT	G	LO	6.2	12.55	11,265.70	9,661.30	☆	0.0	0.00	0.00	N/A	18
SCI/TECH HOLDINGS	TK	SC	297.5	12.22	12,025.70	11,888.10	☆	0.5	2.04	0.06	36.4	90
SCUDDER CAPITAL GROWTH	G	NO	545.5	19.08	12,238.60	11,713.60	34,052.20	1.1	2.47	0.23	25.1	56
SCUDDER DEVELOPMENT	SG	NO	386.7	25.37	12,250.10	10,740.90	22,002.70	0.0	1.33	0.00	27.6	29
SCUDDER GLOBAL	GL	NO	101.8	15.42	12,405.50	☆	☆	0.0	0.00	0.00	N/A	N/A
SCUDDER GOVT MORT	FI	NO	262.3	14.79	9,941.70	10,672.40	☆	8.7	0.00	1.29	N/A	124
SCUDDER GROWTH & INCOME	GI	NO	471.6	17.01	11,745.00	11,447.10	26,620.40	3.8	1.12	0.66	15.3	45
SCUDDER INCOME	FI	NO	251.0	12.77	9,931.20	10,562.20	21,687.20	9.0	0.00	1.15	9.6	24
SCUDDER INTERNATIONAL	IF	NO	807.4	41.96	11,827.50	13,969.30	40,610.70	0.9	8.82	0.45	N/A	36
SCUDDER TARGET GENL 1987	FI	NO	3.7	10.59	10,301.80	10,617.40	☆	5.0	0.12	0.53	N/A	7
SCUDDER TARGET GENL 1990	FI	NO	15.4	10.34	10,077.50	10,545.90	☆	5.2	0.28	0.54	N/A	35
SCUDDER TARGET GENL 1994	FI	NO	8.4	11.62	10,067.80	10,750.50	☆	6.3	0.18	0.73	N/A	16
SCUDDER TARGET USGT 1987	FI	NO	1.7	9.28	10,199.10	10,472.70	☆	4.6	0.73	0.44	N/A	162
SCUDDER TARGET USGT 1990	FI	NO	1.6	9.72	9,870.20	10,255.50	☆	4.8	0.53	0.47	N/A	80
SCUDDER ZERO TARGT 1990	FI	NO	1.6	11.03	9,928.20	10,510.10	☆	4.0	0.03	0.44	N/A	23
SCUDDER ZERO TARGT 1995	FI	NO	1.6	11.12	9,619.40	10,195.20	☆	4.2	0.02	0.46	N/A	41
SCUDDER ZERO TARGT 2000	FI	NO	1.7	11.20	9,360.50	9,901.90	☆	4.9	0.11	0.55	N/A	79
SECURITY ACTION FUND	CA	SC	118.0	10.56	11,812.90	10,912.00	☆	2.9	0.57	0.31	25.8	71
SECURITY EQUITY FUND	G	SC	275.7	6.45	12,455.30	11,741.20	29,587.50	2.1	0.32	0.14	22.2	108
SECURITY INC-CORP BOND	FI	SC	46.0	8.06	10,203.10	10,599.20	20,690.20	10.5	0.00	0.84	N/A	77
SECURITY INC-HIGH YIELD	FI	SC	9.6	8.46	10,255.60	☆	☆	0.0	0.00	0.95	N/A	34
SECURITY INC-US GOVT	FI	SC	4.5	5.10	10,124.80	10,606.60	☆	10.5	0.00	0.53	N/A	48
SECURITY INVESTMENT FUND	GI	SC	110.2	10.36	11,885.20	11,594.70	21,232.00	4.9	0.42	0.52	17.4	37
SECURITY OMNI	CA	SC	22.9	3.29	11,305.80	9,453.80	☆	6.1	1.32	0.24	N/A	178
SECURITY ULTRA FUND	CA	SC	100.5	7.95	11,848.00	10,586.50	25,197.60	3.9	1.88	0.35	28.1	179
SELECTED AMERICAN SHARES	GI	NO	301.7	14.51	11,989.00	11,618.70	33,167.20	2.6	1.49	0.40	15.7	40
SELECTED SPECIAL SHARES	G	NO	41.9	22.09	12,703.70	12,079.10	28,831.00	2.1	1.75	0.48	22.0	133
SELIGMAN CAPITAL	CA	SC	234.6	15.86	12,587.00	11,354.10	33,375.10	0.0	2.49	0.00	23.5	32
SELIGMAN COMM & INFORMTN	TK	SC	52.5	15.21	13,353.80	12,278.10	☆	0.0	0.35	0.00	31.4	59
SELIGMAN COMMON STOCK	GI	SC	633.0	15.46	12,037.00	11,701.30	33,597.10	2.9	2.03	0.48	22.3	46
SELIGMAN GROWTH	G	SC	718.3	6.60	12,668.40	11,355.70	28,391.30	1.4	1.14	0.10	22.3	64
SELIGMAN HIGH YIELD	FI	SC	78.2	7.42	10,185.10	10,598.60	☆	11.3	0.14	0.84	N/A	110
SELIGMAN INCOME FUND	I	SC	181.6	13.00	10,063.50	10,402.10	23,141.50	8.0	0.62	1.07	11.2	72
SELIGMAN SECURED MORT	FI	SC	46.7	6.91	9,910.50	10,476.00	☆	8.2	0.20	0.57	N/A	365
SELIGMAN US GOVT	FI	SC	147.8	7.27	9,446.90	9,645.20	☆	7.2	0.41	0.53	N/A	245
SENTINEL BALANCED FUND	B	SC	68.9	13.40	11,180.40	11,367.90	28,901.80	5.6	0.40	0.75	17.2	58
SENTINEL BOND FUND	FI	SC	24.5	6.27	9,963.50	10,598.70	20,421.50	9.2	0.34	0.59	N/A	88
SENTINEL COMMON STOCK	GI	SC	604.6	28.04	12,094.50	11,871.40	33,613.00	3.3	1.08	0.93	17.2	8
SENTINEL GOVT	FI	NO	22.4	9.55	9,928.90	☆	☆	0.0	0.00	0.64	N/A	7
SENTINEL GROWTH FUND	G	SC	65.6	17.72	12,809.40	11,986.80	32,478.60	1.6	2.64	0.31	31.7	102
SENTRY FUND	G	SC	50.0	15.43	12,251.10	11,140.10	26,255.90	1.8	1.21	0.29	19.4	24
SEQUOIA FUND (X)	G	NO	801.2	44.95	11,717.70	11,376.50	32,040.90	3.3	5.09	1.59	21.2	40
SHEARSON AGGRESSIVE GRO	CA	SC	139.2	19.72	13,146.70	12,105.90	☆	0.0	0.84	0.00	48.1	24
SHEARSON APPRECIATION	G	SC	514.8	31.95	12,397.40	12,013.40	32,134.60	1.3	1.10	0.42	22.6	30
SHEARSON FUNDAMENTAL VAL	G	SC	109.1	7.96	12,614.90	12,433.20	27,320.40	3.8	0.73	0.31	19.8	91
SHEARSON GLOBAL	GL	SC	268.7	33.77	11,230.50	11,901.70	☆	0.4	6.03	0.15	17.7	85
SHEARSON HIGH YIELD	FI	SC	562.8	19.06	10,670.80	10,841.60	22,483.20	11.3	0.00	2.15	N/A	46
SHEARSON LEHMAN CONV (R)	CV	NO	227.5	13.84	10,950.60	☆	☆	0.0	0.03	0.54	N/A	N/A
SHEARSON LEHMAN GLOBAL (R)	GL	NO	162.6	16.44	10,744.30	☆	☆	0.0	0.00	0.24	N/A	N/A
SHEARSON LEHMAN HI INC (R)	FI	NO	206.3	14.49	10,740.20	☆	☆	0.0	0.02	0.90	N/A	N/A
SHEARSON LEHMAN INTL (R)	IF	NO	184.8	22.09	11,423.80	12,335.50	☆	0.0	0.64	0.00	N/A	N/A
SHEARSON LEHMAN INTMDT (R)	FI	NO	40.7	11.31	9,918.50	10,358.80	☆	6.1	0.08	0.69	N/A	116

SHEARSON LEHMAN LG GVT (R)	FI	NO	1,718.5	8.63	9,778.10	10,276.10	☆	6.4	0.27	0.56	N/A	293
SHEARSON LEHMAN MORT (R)	FI	NO	57.1	11.34	9,858.90	☆	☆	0.0	0.01	0.55	N/A	N/A
SHEARSON LEHMAN MLT OP (R)	CA	NO	520.2	49.54	#9,908.00	☆	☆	0.0	0.00	0.00	N/A	N/A
SHEARSON LEHMAN OPT (R)	OI	NO	946.4	14.21	10,693.10	10,881.30	☆	1.9	1.41	0.28	16.1	212
SHEARSON LEHMAN PR MET (R)	AU	SC	70.6	22.23	14,605.80	☆	☆	0.0	0.00	0.00	N/A	N/A
SHEARSON LEHMAN SP EQ (R)	CA	NO	33.1	16.88	11,684.90	9,664.60	☆	1.0	0.00	0.16	24.0	N/A
SHEARSON LEHMAN SP GRO (R)	G	NO	179.4	15.53	11,236.00	11,157.00	☆	1.6	0.07	0.25	N/A	N/A
SHEARSON LEHMAN STRGIC (R)	GI	NO	176.1	14.50	#10,372.10	☆	☆	0.0	0.00	0.02	15.0	N/A
SHEARSON MANAGED GOVT	FI	SC	1,402.5	12.69	9,969.50	10,694.60	☆	8.4	0.34	1.08	N/A	136
SHERMAN, DEAN FUND	CA	NO	3.3	8.84	16,870.20	18,728.80	15,529.30	0.0	0.00	0.00	N/A	N/A
SIEBEL CAPITAL PARTNERS	CA	NO	26.6	13.28	11,892.20	11,125.50	☆	9.1	1.64	1.29	N/A	125
SIGMA CAPITAL SHARES	CA	SC	98.5	10.21	11,789.80	10,845.20	32,126.10	1.5	0.47	0.15	21.4	11
SIGMA INCOME SHARES	FI	SC	34.3	8.77	10,078.10	10,720.20	23,094.00	8.2	0.00	0.71	N/A	22
SIGMA INVESTMENT SHARES	GI	SC	100.4	11.55	11,764.70	11,635.30	30,869.90	2.1	0.72	0.24	23.2	17
SIGMA SPECIAL FUND	G	SC	21.1	11.95	13,148.00	12,639.60	31,059.50	1.1	0.73	0.13	N/A	4
SIGMA TRUST SHARES	B	SC	48.8	14.42	10,855.90	11,133.90	26,593.60	4.9	0.61	0.72	18.3	19
SIGMA VENTURE SHARES	SG	SC	75.3	13.10	11,844.50	10,085.50	25,137.00	0.4	0.97	0.04	26.9	7
SIGMA WORLD	IF	SC	10.7	18.85	11,968.30	13,547.30	☆	0.0	0.65	0.00	N/A	39
SIMMS GLOBAL	GL	SC	16.3	10.83	#11,400,00	☆	☆	0.0	0.00	0.00	N/A	N/A
SMITH, BARNEY EQUITY	G	LO	90.3	17.08	12,372.00	11,957.00	29,061.80	2.2	2.35	0.40	25.2	49
SMITH, BARNEY INC & GR	GI	SC	658.7	12.40	11,444.80	12,191.30	29,288.60	5.4	0.46	0.68	16.2	54
SMITH, BARNEY US GOVT	FI	LO	465.2	12.89	10,029.40	10,731.20	☆	10.8	0.33	1.40	N/A	131
SOGEN INTERNATIONAL	G	LO	102.4	21.47	12,123.10	12,475.30	34,054.50	0.0	0.00	0.00	25.7	59
SOUND SHORE	G	NO	31.1	14.24	11,336.10	11,188.70	☆	0.9	0.81	0.13	N/A	82
SOUTHEASTERN GROWTH (R)	G	NO	118.7	14.41	11,518.30	10,406.40	☆	0.0	0.39	0.00	N/A	35
SOVEREIGN INVESTORS	GI	SC	44.6	13.77	11,361.30	10,901.60	28,284.20	3.9	0.86	0.56	17.2	33
STATE BOND COMMON STOCK	G	SC	36.6	8.15	12,911.80	11,917.70	25,220.80	1.2	0.50	0.10	19.6	7
STATE BOND DIVERSIFIED	GI	SC	20.3	8.68	11,860.80	11,758.90	29,906.20	2.8	0.54	0.25	N/A	20
STATE BOND PROGRESS	G	SC	8.9	12.49	12,411.30	10,851.30	23,815.80	0.9	0.35	0.11	N/A	9
STATE FARM BALANCED	B	NO	36.2	19.40	11,424.80	11,374.50	28,606.60	3.7	0.71	0.73	22.0	13
STATE FARM GROWTH	G	NO	170.2	14.40	12,203.80	11,844.10	28,893.30	2.5	0.92	0.37	25.1	14
STATE FARM INTERIM	FI	NO	16.8	10.09	10,103.60	10,565.10	18,772.60	7.9	0.00	0.80	N/A	6
STATE STREET INVESTMENT (R)	GI	LO	648.3	96.53	12,907.60	12,494.10	29,809.10	2.2	7.50	2.25	20.1	10
STEADMAN AMER INDUSTRY	CA	NO	6.9	2.99	12,887.90	9,432.20	11,361.00	0.0	0.00	0.00	N/A	420
STEADMAN ASSOCIATED FUND	EI	NO	20.4	0.90	10,549.40	8,667.90	16,076.90	4.4	0.03	0.04	N/A	375
STEADMAN INVESTMENT	G	NO	8.5	1.85	11,562.50	11,144.60	14,698.50	0.0	0.00	0.00	N/A	129
STEADMAN OCEANOGRAPHIC	G	NO	5.2	6.46	14,419.60	10,487.00	12,125.20	0.0	0.00	0.00	N/A	197
STEINROE CAPITAL OPP	G	NO	345.9	36.12	13,602.40	11,897.30	26,496.40	0.1	1.03	0.05	38.2	116
STEINROE DISCOVERY	SG	NO	65.8	13.24	12,537.90	9,672.80	☆	0.3	0.03	0.04	42.8	157
STEINROE GOVT PLUS	FI	NO	22.8	9.79	9,830.60	10,387.10	☆	7.2	0.00	0.70	N/A	91
STEINROE HIGH YLD BOND	FI	NO	92.2	9.71	10,229.90	10,780.90	☆	10.1	0.00	0.98	N/A	84
STEINROE MANAGED BONDS	FI	NO	188.7	8.77	9,848.50	10,340.90	20,256.70	8.1	0.74	0.73	N/A	334
STEINROE PRIME EQUITIES	CA	NO	13.0	10.18	#10,180.00	☆	☆	0.0	0.00	0.00	N/A	N/A
STEINROE SPECIAL FUND	CA	NO	271.9	19.57	12,229.70	11,646.80	36,394.40	1.6	3.95	0.35	24.3	116
STEINROE STOCK	G	NO	308.0	21.81	13,145.60	12,325.90	27,272.90	1.2	3.30	0.27	27.5	137
STEINROE TOTAL RETURN	B	NO	178.0	26.43	11,137.30	11,113.50	25,338.30	5.7	2.18	1.58	18.2	108
STEINROE UNIVERSE FUND	CA	NO	94.4	21.64	12,379.90	10,749.60	24,553.50	1.0	3.61	0.21	28.6	147
STOCK MARKETAMERICA	GI	LO	17.4	22.97	12,714.60	☆	☆	0.0	0.00	0.11	N/A	N/A
STOVALL/21 CONSISTNT RET	CA	SC	8.6	9.20	#9,819.00	☆	☆	0.0	0.00	0.03	N/A	N/A
STRATEGIC CAPITAL GAINS	EI	SC	3.6	5.65	8,639.10	7,179.20	11,232.60	0.0	0.00	0.00	N/A	30
STRATEGIC INVESTMENTS	AU	SC	108.1	6.01	13,420.60	18,923.70	19,736.00	5.7	0.00	0.34	N/A	21
STRATEGIC SILVER	S	SC	32.6	5.47	13,848.10	14,743.90	☆	0.0	0.00	0.00	N/A	34
STRATTON GROWTH FUND	GI	NO	19.8	22.86	11,418.60	10,558.60	26,190.70	0.0	0.65	0.00	N/A	29
STRATTON MONTHLY DIV	UT	NO	44.4	28.09	10,106.20	10,230.40	25,726.80	8.0	0.83	2.28	11.0	15
STRONG GOVT	FI	NO	6.2	9.10	9,362.50	☆	☆	0.0	0.00	0.49	N/A	N/A
STRONG INCOME	I	NO	178.7	12.22	10,431.90	10,861.80	☆	12.0	0.05	1.46	N/A	N/A
STRONG INVESTMENT	B	LO	341.2	19.84	10,442.70	10,303.30	28,417.90	6.3	2.07	1.30	N/A	80
STRONG OPPORTUNITY	CA	LO	166.8	20.48	12,965.90	11,550.10	☆	0.4	0.15	0.09	N/A	170
STRONG TOTAL RETURN	CA	LO	899.2	22.52	11,832.00	11,409.60	33,688.90	5.0	1.81	1.17	N/A	154
SUMMIT INVESTORS FD	G	SC	111.7	8.45	12,711.40	11,793.40	☆	0.5	0.38	0.04	22.6	118

PERFORMANCE OF MUTUAL FUNDS (continued)

FUND NAME	OBJ.	LOAD	TOTAL NET ASTS (MIL) 6/30/87	NAV 6/30/87	PERFORMANCE (RETURN ON INITIAL $10,000 INVESTMENT) 12/31/86–6/30/87	6/30/86–6/30/87	6/30/82–6/30/87	YIELD % 6/30/87	PER SHARE LATEST 12 MONTHS CAP GAINS	INC DIVS	LATEST AVAILABLE PRICE/EARNINGS	ANNUAL % TURNOVER
SURVEYOR FUND	G	SC	107.0	14.09	12,241.50	10,740.40	24,640.80	0.2	4.48	0.04	31.9	107
TECHNOLOGY FUND	TK	SC	701.6	14.31	12,989.70	12,771.60	28,964.80	1.0	2.72	0.16	28.3	37
TEMPLETON FOREIGN	IF	SC	276.3	20.83	13,517.20	14,459.80	☆	1.7	1.07	0.36	N/A	21
TEMPLETON GLOBAL I (X)	GL	SC	337.0	48.09	11,783.90	11,662.10	36,195.70	2.2	2.20	1.09	19.8	4
TEMPLETON GLOBAL II	GL	SC	587.0	14.69	11,548.70	10,880.40	☆	2.1	0.43	0.32	19.6	12
TEMPLETON GROWTH	GL	SC	1,446.5	15.49	12,035.70	12,584.00	33,072.30	1.2	0.00	0.19	16.7	28
TEMPLETON INCOME	WI	SC	118.6	10.42	10,602.00	☆	☆	0.0	0.04	0.47	N/A	N/A
TEMPLETON/TAFT PHIL (R)	GL	NO	1.9	10.08	#10,080.00	☆	☆	0.0	0.00	0.00	N/A	N/A
TEMPLETON WORLD	GL	SC	4,199.0	17.46	11,845.30	12,042.80	34,217.10	2.4	1.28	0.44	20.5	28
TENNECO-FD OF SOUTHWEST	CA	SC	16.1	10.98	11,768.50	10,096.40	18,017.50	0.0	1.85	0.00	N/A	134
TENNECO-INVESTORS INCOME	FI	SC	24.2	5.29	10,319.80	11,023.20	21,965.20	9.1	0.00	0.48	N/A	187
TENNECO-US TREND FD	G	SC	106.2	13.43	12,627.10	12,046.20	27,550.50	2.1	3.76	0.32	N/A	214
THE BOND ACCUMULATION	FI	SC	16.8	10.68	10,022.40	10,533.30	☆	6.7	0.04	0.72	N/A	35
THE STOCK ACCUMULATION	CA	SC	7.7	13.96	10,927.50	10,806.20	☆	1.7	1.09	0.24	N/A	58
THOMSON MCKINNON GLOBL (R)	GL	NO	105.1	12.27	12,369.00	☆	☆	0.0	0.00	0.00	N/A	N/A
THOMSON MCKINNON GOVT (R)	FI	NO	877.7	9.90	9,857.90	10,453.40	☆	9.5	0.11	0.94	N/A	252
THOMSON MCKINNON GRO (R)	G	NO	419.0	17.06	12,915.00	12,989.70	☆	1.3	1.92	0.24	N/A	169
THOMSON MCKINNON INC (R)	I	NO	425.6	10.11	10,359.50	10,751.30	☆	10.0	0.00	1.01	N/A	59
THOMSON MCKINNON OPPTY (R)	CA	NO	66.0	15.40	12,409.30	10,579.80	☆	0.0	1.27	0.00	N/A	109
THOMPSON UNGER & PLUMB	B	NO	2.9	10.23	#	☆	☆	0.0	0.00	0.00	N/A	N/A
THOROUGHBRED BOND	FI	NO	10.5	9.67	#9,993.60	☆	☆	0.0	0.00	0.32	N/A	N/A
THOROUGHBRED STOCK	GI	NO	7.8	12.33	#12,487.50	☆	☆	0.0	0.00	0.15	N/A	N/A
TOCQUEVILLE FUND	CA	LO	9.7	11.13	#11,030.70	☆	☆	0.0	0.00	0.00	N/A	N/A
TRANSATLANTIC GRO FD	IF	NO	100.9	26.93	12,321.60	14,065.50	35,396.30	0.0	4.93	0.00	N/A	76
TRANSATLANTIC INCOME	IF	NO	6.3	10.57	#10,570.00	☆	☆	0.0	0.00	0.00	N/A	N/A
TREASURY FIRST	FI	NO	2.0	9.87	10,254.20	☆	☆	0.0	0.00	0.43	N/A	N/A
TRINITY TAX-ADVANTAGED	FI	NO	16.8	9.95	#10,113.80	☆	☆	0.0	0.00	0.16	N/A	N/A
TRUSTEES COMMINGLED INTL	IF	NO	814.2	49.69	12,953.50	15,109.60	☆	1.9	6.55	1.03	N/A	24
TRUSTEES COMMINGLED US	GI	NO	179.8	36.16	12,930.40	13,130.90	29,793.90	2.8	6.58	1.11	24.6	19
TUDOR FUND	CA	NO	212.9	25.21	12,979.00	11,859.10	33,311.80	0.0	3.86	0.00	33.6	128
TWENTIETH CENTURY GIFT (R)	G	LO	11.4	8.74	12,948.10	11,324.30	☆	0.0	1.25	0.00	N/A	123
TWENTIETH CENTURY GROWTH	CA	NO	1,416.4	19.27	13,788.70	12,498.30	33,279.90	0.4	5.07	0.08	34.2	105
TWENTIETH CENTURY SELECT	G	NO	2,974.8	39.74	12,722.60	11,786.40	36,608.70	0.9	3.46	0.38	28.3	85
TWENTIETH CENTURY LG BD	FI	NO	5.9	94.07	#9,620.30	☆	☆	0.0	0.00	2.13	N/A	N/A
TWENTIETH CENTRY ULTRA (R)	CA	LO	360.0	12.07	13,541.80	11,936.10	30,068.70	0.1	0.00	0.00	40.1	99
TWENTIETH CENTURY US GOV	FI	NO	336.2	96.53	10,064.30	10,506.70	☆	8.2	1.22	7.93	N/A	464
TWENTIETH CENTURY VISTA (R)	CA	LO	276.3	7.86	13,210.10	11,253.10	☆	0.0	0.65	0.00	45.2	121
UNIFIED GROWTH FUND	G	NO	28.9	24.14	11,415.50	10,667.00	27,009.60	1.3	2.45	0.33	21.9	27
UNIFIED INCOME FUND	I	NO	15.1	12.88	10,532.00	10,561.70	21,467.50	6.8	0.00	0.87	N/A	49
UNIFIED MUTUAL SHARES	GI	NO	23.0	18.99	11,304.10	10,751.30	27,907.70	3.1	0.17	0.59	N/A	41
UNITED ACCUMULATIVE	G	SC	821.7	8.31	12,052.30	11,391.10	32,793.40	2.1	2.07	0.20	26.0	261
UNITED BOND FUND	FI	SC	322.0	6.19	10,047.50	10,578.90	23,519.30	8.6	0.00	0.53	N/A	252
UNITED CONTL INCOME	B	SC	383.9	19.08	11,092.50	10,628.40	33,615.10	3.9	1.87	0.81	23.2	212
UNITED GOLD & GOVT	AU	SC	113.5	9.85	14,504.80	18,284.40	☆	1.3	0.10	0.13	N/A	160
UNITED GOVERNMENT	FI	LO	175.7	4.98	9,530.80	10,136.50	☆	8.7	0.19	0.44	N/A	380
UNITED HIGH INCOME	FI	SC	1,310.4	13.44	10,472.20	10,905.60	23,492.50	12.2	0.34	1.68	N/A	66
UNITED HIGH INCOME II	FI	SC	147.3	4.92	10,479.40	☆	☆	0.0	0.00	0.49	N/A	5
UNITED INCOME	EI	SC	1,060.0	19.57	11,865.80	11,646.80	36,830.40	2.4	1.94	0.50	22.0	30
UNITED INTL GROWTH	IF	SC	291.6	9.08	12,768.20	13,822.60	37,269.30	0.9	1.62	0.08	21.4	168
UNITED MISSOURI BK BOND	FI	NO	31.1	10.98	10,008.10	10,487.70	☆	3.6	0.00	0.40	N/A	23
UNITED MISSOURI QUAL DVD	FI	NO	6.3	10.03	#10,299.50	☆	☆	0.0	0.00	0.26	N/A	N/A
UNITED MISSOURI BK STOCK	GI	NO	39.4	15.26	12,124.30	11,812.30	☆	1.3	0.40	0.20	N/A	38
UNITED NEW CONCEPTS	SG	SC	103.6	6.33	12,057.50	10,760.60	☆	0.4	1.04	0.03	35.4	273
UNITED RETIREMENT SHARES	GI	SC	109.4	6.66	11,178.50	10,645.70	25,012.40	3.3	0.94	0.22	15.9	128
UNITED SCIENCE & ENERGY	TK	SC	242.9	12.72	12,952.60	12,779.80	28,863.50	1.2	1.36	0.16	30.1	92
UNITED VANGUARD FUND	G	SC	650.8	7.58	12,220.00	12,036.00	29,335.80	2.0	0.96	0.16	33.2	126

US BOSTON-BOSTON I (R)	GI	NO	$ 34.8	$ 16.20	$ 12,235.60	$ 12,171.30	$ ☆	0.0	$ 0.00	$ 0.00	N/A	N/A
US BOSTON-INTL (R)	AU	NO	7.8	19.12	13,287.00	16,611.60	☆	0.0	0.00	0.00	N/A	N/A
US GOLD SHARES	AU	NO	407.4	6.32	14,219.90	20,595.50	26,214.20	5.5	0.00	0.35	24.8	14
US GOOD & BAD TIMES	GI	NO	37.1	20.24	12,134.30	11,259.10	23,557.30	1.9	0.00	0.38	17.2	91
US GOVT GUARANTEED SEC	FI	SC	361.8	14.14	9,889.60	10,613.20	☆	9.9	0.02	1.40	N/A	N/A
US GOVT SEC FUND	FI	NO	13.2	9.82	9,935.80	10,667.00	☆	9.5	0.00	0.93	N/A	N/A
US GNMA	FI	NO	6.7	9.44	9,666.50	10,309.10	☆	8.3	0.00	0.78	N/A	N/A
US GROWTH FUND	CA	NO	9.2	10.11	11,462.60	10,310.30	☆	0.7	0.00	0.07	N/A	60
US INCOME FUND	I	NO	3.6	10.50	10,206.50	10,332.20	☆	4.6	0.56	0.50	N/A	179
US LOCAP FUND (R)	SG	NO	4.3	8.39	12,284.00	9,979.10	☆	0.2	0.00	0.02	N/A	70
US NEW PROSPECTOR (R)	AU	NO	126.4	2.05	15,648.90	21,679.20	☆	0.0	0.02	0.00	56.4	31
US PROSPECTOR FUND (X,R)	AU	NO	76.2	1.10	15,493.00	20,754.70	☆	0.0	0.00	0.00	54.6	20
USAA CORNERSTONE	S	NO	478.9	18.59	12,459.80	14,881.40	☆	1.6	0.21	0.30	28.8	70
USAA GOLD	AU	NO	180.2	13.79	14,940.40	22,716.80	☆	0.7	0.00	0.10	54.5	62
USAA GROWTH FUND	G	NO	257.8	18.64	12,628.70	11,285.00	24,237.40	1.0	1.59	0.19	22.7	110
USAA INCOME STOCK	EI	NO	7.4	10.50	#10,500.00	☆	☆	0.0	0.00	0.00	N/A	N/A
USAA INCOME FUND	FI	NO	269.4	11.57	10,089.90	10,789.40	20,567.90	10.7	0.06	1.24	8.5	38
USAA SUNBELT ERA	SG	NO	151.4	21.64	12,655.00	10,571.40	23,973.10	0.3	0.35	0.07	29.1	57
UST MASTER EQUITY	CA	NO	15.4	13.43	12,185.60	11,375.90	☆	1.1	0.74	0.15	N/A	207
UST MASTER INC & GROWTH	GI	NO	5.5	9.02	#11,426.10	☆	☆	0.0	0.07	0.04	N/A	N/A
UST MASTER MGD INC	FI	NO	7.9	8.43	10,197.90	11,054.80	☆	7.7	0.31	0.67	N/A	265
VALLEY FORGE FUND (R)	G	NO	9.3	10.58	10,643.90	10,962.40	19,782.10	6.3	0.06	0.67	N/A	40
VALSEARCH TOTL RETURN	GI	NO	0.2	12.54	12,540.00	☆	☆	0.0	0.00	0.00	N/A	N/A
VALUE LINE AGGRES INC	FI	NO	64.9	9.68	10,606.00	10,642.20	☆	12.8	0.00	1.24	N/A	N/A
VALUE LINE FUND	GI	NO	255.9	17.55	12,156.60	10,961.20	20,525.20	1.3	1.92	0.24	30.3	145
VALUE LINE CENTURION	G	NO	243.9	14.16	12,225.90	10,986.50	☆	0.6	0.89	0.08	28.1	210
VALUE LINE CONVERTIBLE	CV	NO	90.9	12.28	10,899.70	10,455.90	☆	4.5	0.71	0.56	N/A	164
VALUE LINE INCOME	EI	NO	182.0	7.29	11,160.20	10,871.30	21,830.40	6.3	0.53	0.48	26.0	167
VALUE LINE LVGE GROWTH	CA	NO	421.0	27.93	12,415.80	11,542.00	23,833.20	0.5	2.82	0.15	25.4	115
VALUE LINE SPECIAL SIT	G	NO	211.8	17.72	11,978.20	10,192.70	18,242.30	0.3	0.27	0.06	33.2	73
VALUE LINE US GOVT SEC	FI	NO	218.7	12.26	10,065.60	10,678.40	20,813.10	10.2	0.23	1.26	N/A	73
VANCE, SANDERS SPECIAL	G	SC	84.5	12.56	11,837.60	10,145.30	17,023.20	0.4	1.04	0.05	30.6	52
VAN ECK GOLD/RESOURCES	AU	SC	162.7	19.32	16,526.90	22,623.00	☆	0.0	0.00	0.00	65.0	N/A
VAN ECK WORLD INCOME	WI	SC	2.1	9.27	#10,021.60	☆	☆	0.0	0.00	0.00	N/A	N/A
VAN ECK WORLD TRENDS	GL	SC	99.5	15.37	11,634.50	13,116.40	☆	1.5	0.13	0.23	45.5	32
VANGUARD BOND MARKET	FI	NO	26.6	9.42	9,895.40	☆	☆	0.0	0.00	0.42	N/A	N/A
VANGUARD CONVERTIBLE	CV	NO	108.1	10.07	10,685.30	10,605.60	☆	5.4	0.00	0.54	N/A	N/A
VANGUARD FI GNMA PORT	FI	NO	2,307.3	9.55	9,947.80	10,706.90	20,390.10	9.6	0.00	0.91	N/A	28
VANGUARD FI HIGH YIELD	FI	NO	1,206.7	8.94	10,391.20	10,953.90	22,260.70	11.5	0.11	1.03	N/A	67
VANGUARD FI INC SHT TERM	FI	NO	426.3	10.40	10,128.70	10,609.60	☆	7.6	0.18	0.79	N/A	278
VANGUARD FI INV GRADE	FI	NO	612.6	8.13	9,887.70	10,579.80	20,422.30	9.8	0.12	0.80	N/A	47
VANGUARD FI US TREASURY	FI	NO	42.7	9.41	9,585.10	9,973.70	☆	8.2	0.03	0.77	N/A	182
VANGUARD INDEX TRUST	GI	NO	906.3	30.52	12,725.20	12,463.80	33,258.90	2.8	2.02	0.89	21.9	29
VANGUARD QUAL DVD I (X)	EI	NO	192.5	18.69	11,250.10	12,113.70	38,687.70	6.7	3.29	1.36	10.6	70
VANGUARD QUAL DVD II	FI	NO	141.9	8.90	9,711.10	10,742.10	32,758.70	9.0	0.00	0.80	N/A	48
VANGUARD QUAL DVD III	FI	NO	126.4	22.49	10,330.00	10,624.40	☆	6.6	0.00	1.49	N/A	47
VANGUARD QUANTITATIVE	GI	NO	171.7	12.22	12,646.00	☆	☆	0.0	0.00	0.03	18.1	N/A
VANGUARD SPECIAL-ENERGY (R)	NR	NO	59.1	14.82	13,571.60	15,435.50	☆	1.1	0.12	0.17	28.5	34
VANGUARD SPECIAL-GOLD (R)	AU	NO	176.0	13.18	14,762.10	20,875.30	☆	1.5	0.15	0.20	25.5	32
VANGUARD SPECIAL-HEALTH (R)	H	NO	72.7	21.82	12,807.90	12,246.00	☆	1.1	1.18	0.24	24.3	27
VANGUARD SPECIAL-SERV (R)	S	NO	51.3	19.61	12,099.70	10,677.50	☆	1.8	1.89	0.38	19.8	96
VANGUARD SPECIAL-TECH (R)	TK	NO	28.1	13.95	12,036.10	11,396.40	☆	0.3	0.68	0.05	27.3	108
VANGUARD STAR	B	NO	638.2	12.28	11,256.10	11,403.70	☆	4.9	0.53	0.62	N/A	N/A
VANGUARD WORLD-INTL GRO	IF	NO	560.1	13.06	11,598.60	13,382.60	48,452.00	0.5	0.80	0.07	N/A	39
VANGUARD WORLD-US GRO	G	NO	189.6	12.18	11,802.30	10,892.00	29,744.00	2.3	1.94	0.28	25.3	77
VAN KAMPEN MERRITT-GOVT	FI	SC	5,304.6	15.51	9,863.50	10,633.40	☆	11.3	0.00	1.75	N/A	154
VAN KAMPEN MERRITT GR&IN	GI	SC	30.9	16.75	11,964.20	☆	☆	0.0	0.00	0.10	N/A	N/A
VAN KAMPEN MERRITT HI YD	FI	SC	120.2	14.57	10,845.70	☆	☆	0.0	0.00	1.51	N/A	N/A
VARIABLE STOCK FUND	G	NO	9.4	10.43	11,838.80	10,871.50	23,957.60	1.7	1.33	0.19	N/A	61
VENTURE INCOME (+) PLUS	FI	SC	71.8	10.01	10,857.30	10,563.20	22,380.80	14.4	0.00	1.44	7.5	155

PERFORMANCE OF MUTUAL FUNDS *(concluded)*

FUND NAME	OBJ.	LOAD	TOTAL NET ASTS (MIL) 6/30/87	NAV 6/30/87	PERFORMANCE (RETURN ON INITIAL $10,000 INVESTMENT) 12/31/86-6/30/87	6/30/86-6/30/87	6/30/82-6/30/87	YIELD % 6/30/87	PER SHARE LATEST 12 MONTHS CAP GAINS	INC DIVS	LATEST AVAILABLE PRICE/EARNINGS	ANNUAL % TURNOVER
VOLUMETRIC FUND	G	NO	2.8	13.71	12,226.20	11,815.40	☆	0.5	1.54	0.06	N/A	N/A
WADE FUND	G	NO	0.7	45.02	12,381.70	12,453.50	25,742.20	1.1	3.22	0.51	N/A	9
WALL STREET FUND	G	SC	12.7	8.85	12,715.50	11,704.40	27,307.20	0.0	1.80	0.00	N/A	166
WASATCH AGGRES EQU	SG	NO	1.4	12.14	#9,934.50	☆	☆	0.0	0.00	0.00	N/A	N/A
WASATCH GROWTH	G	NO	2.5	11.18	#9,911.30	☆	☆	0.0	0.00	0.00	N/A	N/A
WASATCH INCOME	FI	NO	0.4	10.04	#9,990.00	☆	☆	0.0	0.00	0.00	N/A	N/A
WASHINGTON AREA GRO (R)	G	NO	23.0	21.13	11,452.60	10,898.10	☆	3.4	0.00	0.72	N/A	29
WASHINGTON MUTUAL INV	GI	SC	2,881.6	14.03	12,023.00	12,157.30	35,500.10	3.6	0.65	0.52	17.6	13
WAYNE HUMMER GROWTH FUND	G	NO	20.6	15.84	11,979.20	11,609.40	☆	1.5	0.0	0.24	N/A	27
WEALTH MONITORS	CA	SC	6.4	9.64	12,191.60	☆	☆	0.0	0.46	0.00	N/A	N/A
WEINGARTEN EQUITY	CA	NO	258.1	21.69	13,001.90	11,861.10	39,133.70	0.7	4.74	0.16	25.4	113
WEITZ VALUE (R)	GI	NO	7.9	10.42	10,410.60	10,574.10	☆	2.3	0.11	0.24	N/A	N/A
WELLESLEY INCOME	I	NO	590.8	15.92	10,121.30	10,673.80	26,078.70	8.2	0.47	1.33	10.5	20
WELLINGTON FUND	B	NO	1,540.9	18.07	11,636.30	11,856.80	31,201.70	5.2	0.34	0.94	18.2	25
WESTERGAARD FUND	CA	SC	13.4	10.99	11,483.80	8,866.50	☆	1.7	0.26	0.19	N/A	89
WESTWOOD FUND	CA	LO	29.9	14.14	#11,803.00	☆	☆	0.0	0.00	0.00	N/A	N/A
WINDSOR FUND (X)	GI	NO	5,996.1	16.90	12,344.90	12,559.10	37,949.70	4.7	2.59	0.85	10.8	51
WINDSOR II	GI	NO	1,554.3	14.52	11,890.80	11,874.70	☆	2.9	0.52	0.43	13.4	50
WINTHROP FOCUS FIX INC (R)	FI	NO	4.9	9.49	9,796.50	☆	☆	0.0	0.00	0.33	N/A	N/A
WINTHROP FOCUS GROWTH (R)	G	NO	66.4	11.60	11,848.80	☆	☆	0.0	0.00	0.00	N/A	N/A
WORLD OF TECHNOLOGY	TK	NO	10.0	11.57	11,952.50	11,698.70	☆	0.0	0.00	0.00	N/A	147
WPG FUND	CA	NO	47.7	25.75	12,659.20	11,644.90	28,580.80	0.3	4.13	0.08	33.5	71
WPG GOVT	FI	NO	70.7	9.91	9,992.60	10,539.50	☆	7.1	0.12	0.70	N/A	N/A
WPG GROWTH	SG	NO	153.1	127.11	12,812.20	11,809.90	☆	0.0	0.00	0.00	N/A	N/A
YES FUND	FI	LO	116.1	7.17	9,718.30	10,223.10	☆	10.6	0.00	0.76	N/A	592

How to read the *Barron's*/Lipper gauge. These tables show the return on a $10,000 investment over three periods: first six months, one year and five years.

FUND NAME-Mutual fund name, occasionally shortened, appearing in alphabetical order. The majority of open-end funds registered with the Securities and Exchange Commission are included with the exception of the money market and municipal bond funds.

OBJ.-Investment objective of the fund as determined by both the language in the prospectus and a review of the funds' investment characteristics, such as yield, turnover, etc.

INVESTMENT OBJECTIVE DEFINITIONS:

AU-GOLD ORIENTED FUND-A fund which has at least 65% of its assets in shares of gold mines, gold-oriented mining finance houses, gold coins or bullion.

B-BALANCED FUND-A fund whose primary objective is stability of net asset value, achieved by maintaining a balanced portfolio of both stocks and bonds. Typically, the stock/bond ratio ranges around 60%/40%.

CA-CAPITAL APPRECIATION FUND-Any fund which meets at least two of the following criteria: (1) The investment objective shown in the prospectus is capital appreciation or similar wording. (2) A turnover rate of 100% or more is either expected or realized. (3) The fund is permitted to borrow more than 10% of the value of its portfolio. (4) The prospectus permits short selling, the purchase of options, or investing in common stocks or unregistered securities.

CV-CONVERTIBLE SECURITIES FUND-A fund that invests primarily in convertible bonds and convertible preferred shares.

EI-EQUITY INCOME FUND-A fund which normally has 60% or more of its assets in equities and has an above average yield.

LO-Low-load fund. A fund which charges a load up to 4½%.

NO-No-load fund. A fund which has no sales charge.

TOTAL NET ASSETS-Fund assets minus liabilities, fund expenses, advisory fees and commissions.

NAV (Net Asset Value)-Total net assets divided by the number of shares outstanding.

PERFORMANCE-The theoretical ending value of a $10,000 investment for the period analyzed. For complete comparability and regardless of a fund's stated policy, calculations include all capital gains distributions and income dividends, reinvested on the ex-dividend date at ex-date net asset value. Any fund charges not reflected in net asset value or gross income and any tax consequences incurred by the shareholder aren't taken into consideration.

YIELD-The latest 12 months' worth of income dividends divided by the adjusted ending net asset value. The ending net asset value is adjusted periodically for the impact of capital gains paid during the previous 12 months.

PER SHARE-LATEST 12 MONTHS CAP GAINS-Total amount of capital gains per share paid during the last 12 months.

PER SHARE-LATEST 12 MONTHS INC DIVS-Total amount of income dividends per share paid during the last 12 months.

LATEST AVAILABLE-PRICE/EARNINGS-The weighted, average reported price/earnings per share ratio of the underlying equities in the portfolio, based on latest 12 months earnings reported in the latest issue of the "Lipper-Equity Analysis Report on the Weighted Average Holdings of Large Investment Companies."

LATEST AVAILABLE—ANNUAL TURNOVER-The ratio of the smaller of purchases and sales divided by average total net assets expressed as a percentage. The turnover shown is for the latest reported fiscal year.

FI-FIXED INCOME FUND-A fund which typically has more than 75% of its assets in fixed income issues, such as money market instruments, bonds and preferred stocks.
G-GROWTH FUND-A fund which normally invests in companies whose long-term earnings are expected to grow significantly faster than the earnings of the stocks represented in the major unmanaged stock averages.

GI-GROWTH & INCOME FUND-A fund which combines a growth of earnings objective and an income requirement for level and/or rising dividends.
GL-GLOBAL FUND-A fund which invests at least 25% of its portfolio in securities traded outside of the United States and may own U.S. securities as well.
H-HEALTH FUND-A fund which invests 65% of its equity portfolio in health and medical company shares.
I-INCOME FUND-A fund which normally invests less than 75% in fixed income issues and less than 50% in equities, and whose principal aim is the generation of income.
IF-INTERNATIONAL FUND-A fund which invests more than 50% of its assets in securities whose primary trading markets are outside of the United States.
OG-OPTION GROWTH FUND-A fund which attempts to increase its net asset value by investing at least 5% of its portfolio in options.
OI-OPTION INCOME FUND-A fund which writes covered options on at least 50% of its portfolio.
NR-NATURAL RESOURCE FUND-A fund which typically invests more than 65% of its equity commitment in natural resource stocks.
S-SPECIALTY FUND-A fund which, by prospectus, limits its investments to a well-defined specialty, such as banks and utilities.
SG-SMALL COMPANY GROWTH FUND-A fund whose prospectus language and portfolio practice limits its investment to companies on the basis of the size of the company. (Those funds that use smaller companies some of the time or in conjunction with larger companies will not be considered a Small Company Growth Fund.)
TK-SCIENCE & TECHNOLOGY FUND-A fund which invests 65% of its equity portfolio in science and technology stocks.
UT-UTILITY FUND-A fund which invests 65% of its equity portfolio in utility shares.
WI-WORLD INCOME FUND-A fund that invests primarily in U.S. dollar and non-U.S. dollar debt instruments. The fund also may invest in common and preferred stocks.
LOAD-This tells whether a fund has a sales charge known as a load. Load definitions are:
SC-Sales charge-The fund is a load fund up to a maximum 8½% load.

Source: Publisher; Lipper Analytical Services, Inc. Reprinted by courtesy of *Barron's National Business and Financial Weekly*, August 10, 1987.

☆-Fund not in existence for full time period covered.
#-Fund's first public offering occurred during the present calendar year.
N/A-Not available due either to size or availability of data.
(W)-Fund writes options; (PW)-Purchase/Write options; and (P)-Purchases options; (R)-Fund charges ½ of 1% each on sales and redemption. (X)-Fund closed to new accounts.

AMA MEMBERS RETIREMENT PLAN EQUITY-Available to certain members of the American Medical Association. The first public offering was Dec. 31, 1963. Data is only available from Dec. 31, 1979.
BOND PORTFOLIO FOR ENDOWMENTS, INC. and ENDOWMENTS, INC. FUNDS.-Shares are available only to institutions exempt from federal taxation under Section 501 (c) (1) of the Internal Revenue Code.

EATON VANCE TAX MANAGED-The performance reflects the impact of a reversal of a tax reserve of $2.14 per share on Dec. 31, 1985 when the fund became a regulated investment company under Sub Chapter M of the IRS code.

ELFUN TRUSTS-Available to certain employees of the General Electric Co., regular and senior members of the Elfun Society.
GENERAL ELECTRIC S-5 PROGRAM: GENERAL ELECTRIC LONG TERM INTEREST-Available to General Electric employees.

HARTWELL GROWTH FUND-On Feb. 6, 1984, the net asset value for Hartwell Growth Fund was increased by $0.79 per share to reflect the receipt of payment in settlement of a class action lawsuit against Viatron Computer Systems.
IVY GROWTH-A new investment adviser was appointed to the fund on April 1, 1985.

PRUDENTIAL BACHE UTILITY-For periods which include Aug. 24, 1984, the dividend, and therefore the performance: includes a reversal of a reserve for taxes of $2.95 per share when the company became a regulated investment company under Sub Chapter M under the IRS code. On that date the net asset value was $20.35.

SCUDDER GROWTH & INCOME FUND-On Nov. 13, 1984 this Fund adopted its present name and objective. Prior performance is attributed to Scudder Common Stock Fund which had an objective of long-term capital growth.

SECTOR INVESTMENT FUND-Does not accrue an advisory fee. The shareholders pay to the adviser a quarterly fee of 1.00% per annum on their accounts on the average daily value. The fund is not permitted to purchase unregistered securities options, or borrow money.

Selected Mutual Funds Which Invest Abroad

Foreign investments provide a possible opportunity for increased returns and portfolio diversification. Since most investors lack the time, background and information, the only practical way for them to participate is through the purchase of U.S. based mutual funds which invest abroad. A number of these funds are listed below. In general, these mutual funds are divided into three categories: **global funds** which invest in both U.S. and foreign stocks, **international funds** which invest in foreign stocks, and **regional funds** which invest in the equities of a specific country or region. Here we have combined the first two categories.

Global/International Funds	Telephone in State	Out-of-State
Alliance International	(800) 522-2322 (NY)	(800) 221-5672
Financial Program & World Technology[1]	(303) 779-1233 (CO)	(800) 525-8085
Fidelity Overseas	(617) 523-1919	(800) 544-6666
First Investors International	(201) 855-2500	(800) 423-4026
Kemper International Fund	(312) 332-6472	(800) 537-3863
Keystone International	(617) 338-3395	(800) 225-2618
Merrill/Lynch Sci/Tech	(609) 282-2042	(212) 282-2042
Prudential Bache Global	(212) 214-2271	(212) 214-2271
Putnam International Equities	(617) 292-1000	(800) 225-1581
Scudder International[1]	(800) 225-2470 (MA)	(800) 453-3305
Templeton Foreign/Global/ World Funds	(813) 823-8712	(800) 237-0738
T. Rowe Price International[1]	(301) 542-2308	(800) 638-5660
United International Growth	(800) 892-5811 (MO)	(800) 821-5664
Vanguard-TCF International[1]	(215) 648-6000 (PA)	(800) 662-7447

[1] no-load

Regional Funds	Telephone in State	Out-of-State
Alliance Canadian	(800) 221-5672 (NY)	(800) 221-5672
GT Pacific[1]	(800) 824-8361	(800) 824-1580
Merrill Lynch Pacific	(212) 692-2049	(212) 692-2049
Japan Fund	(Closed end, NYSE)	
Korean Fund	(Closed end, NYSE)	
Mexico Fund	(Closed end, NYSE)	
Taiwan	(Closed end, AMEX)	

[1] no-load

Selected Mutual Funds Investing in Gold and Precious Metals

Fidelity Select Portfolio-Precious Metals
82 Devonshire Street
Boston, MA 02109
Telephone: (800) 544-6666
(617) 523-1919

Financial Programs—Gold
P.O. Box 2040
Denver, CO 80201
Telephone: (800) 525-9831
(303) 779-1233 (CO)

Golconda Investors (Bull and Bear)
11 Hanover Square
New York, NY 10005
Telephone: (800) 431-6060
(212) 847-4200

Lexington Goldfund
P.O. Box 1515
Saddlebrook, NJ 07662
Telephone: (800) 526-0056

Strategic Investments
2030 Royal Lane
Dallas, TX 75229
Telephone: (800) 527-5027
(214) 484-1326

USSA Gold Fund
USSA Building
San Antonio, TX 78288
Telephone: (800) 531-8000
(512) 498-8000

United Services Gold Shares
P.O. Box 29467
San Antonio, TX 78229
Telephone: (800) 531-5777
(512) 696-1234

Vanguard Gold and Precious Metals
P.O. Box 2600
Valley Forge, PA 19496
Telephone: (800) 662-SHIP
(215) 648-6016

Selected No Load/Low Load Mutual Fund Families with Switching Privileges

No load funds do not charge an initial sales fee while low load funds apply an initial sales fee of 1% to 3%. In comparison load funds charge a sales fee of about 8½%. With no load funds all of your investment is put to work immediately. The performance of no load funds is comparable to that of load funds.

The funds listed below permit switching (exchanges) between other members of the fund family (including money market funds) unless otherwise indicated. Thus, investors who expect a marked decline have the option of switching into a money market fund while investors who expect a bull market may choose to switch into a growth oriented fund. Switching may be done by mail or by phone, generally with no additional charge. For income tax purposes any exchange of shares is treated both as a new purchase and a new sale.

Since the performance of funds is quite variable, it is probably best for investors to diversify among three or four fund families.

Investors should study the fund prospectus carefully prior to investing, paying particular attention to average rates of return over the last five and ten year periods, and to risk level (fluctuations in the net asset value). Investors should also familiarize themselves with the switching procedures and restrictions, if any. The information can be obtained by phoning the fund.

Fund objectives vary and it is important to select the fund with objectives similar to yours. A detailed listing of funds by objective, performance record, and much more is given in Donoghues's *Mutual Fund Almanac* (Box 540, Holliston, MA 01746).

We employ the following classifications:

M = Money market fund
B = Bond funds with income as the primary objective
I = Income funds provide income through investments in a mixture of high dividend stocks and bonds with limited capital gains opportunity
GI = Growth income funds invest in common stock and attempt to achieve both capital gains and income through dividend payments and interest. Similar to so called balanced funds. Suited for many conservative investors seeking capital gains.
G = These funds primarily seek capital gains though equity investment in companies with high growth potential. For the more aggressive investor willing to assume greater risks to obtain greater gains.

Jones and Babson
2440 Pershing Road
Kansas City, MO 64108
(800) 821-5591
(816) 471-5200

Babson Growth Fund (G)
Babson Income (B)
Babson MMF Federal Portfolio (M)
Babson MMF Prime Portfolio (M)
Babson Tax Free Income Fund MMP (M)
Babson Tax Free Inc Long Term (I)
Babson Tax Free Inc Short Term (I)
UMB M.M.F. Federal Portfolio (M)
UMB M.M.F. Prime Portfolio (M)

Bull & Bear Management Corporation
11 Hanover Square
New York, NY 10005
(800) 847-4200
(212) 363-1100

Bull & Bear Capital Growth (G)
Bull & Bear Dollar Reserves (M)
Bull & Bear Equity Income (I)
Golconda Investors (Goldfund) (GI)

Columbia Management Company
P.O. Box 1350
Portland, OR 97207
(800) 547-1037
(503) 222-3600

Columbia Daily Income(I)
Columbia Fixed Income Securities (I)
Columbia Growth (G)

Dreyfus Service Corporation
666 Old Country Road
Garden City, NY 11530
(718) 895-1206 (general information)
(800) 242-8671
Dreyfus A Bonds Plus (I)
Dreyfus CA Tax Exempt Bond Fund (B)
[1] **Dreyfus Fund (G)**
Dreyfus Growth Opportunity (G)
[2] **Dreyfus Leverage (G)**
Dreyfus Liquid Assets (M)
Dreyfus Money Market Instruments Government Series (M)
Dreyfus Money Market Instruments MM Series (M)
Dreyfus NY Tax Exempt Bond Fund (B)
Dreyfus Tax Exempt MMF, Inc. (M)
Dreyfus Convertible Securities (I)
Dreyfus Tax Exempt Bond (B)
Dreyfus Third Century (G)
General Government Securities, MMF (M)
General Money Market Fund (M)
General Tax Exempt Money Market (M)
Fidelity Investments Corporation
82 Devonshire Street
Boston, MA 02109
(800) 544-6666
(617) 523-1919
Fidelity Cash Reserves (M)
Contrafund (G)
Financial Reserves Fund (M)
Fidelity Corp. Bond (B)
Fidelity Daily Income (M)
[1] **Fidelity Destiny (G)**
Fidelity Value Fund (G)
[3] **Fidelity Equity Income (I)**
Fidelity Freedom Fund (GI)
Fidelity Fund (GI)
Fidelity Gov't Securities (I)
Fidelity High Income (B)
Fidelity High Yield Muni (I)
Fidelity Limited Term Municipals (B)
Fidelity Mass Tax-Free Money Market Portfolio (M)
[3] **Fidelity Growth Company Fund (G)**
Fidelity MMT/Domestic (M)
Fidelity MMT/Government (M)
Fidelity MMT/U.S. Treasury (M)
Fidelity Muni Bond (B)
Fidelity Thrift Trust (B)
Fidelity Trend (G)
[3] **Fidelity Select-American Gold (G)**
[3] **Fidelity Select-Bio-Technology (G)**
[3] **Fidelity Select-Energy (G)**
[3] **Fidelity Select-Energy Services (G)**
[3] **Fidelity Select-Financial Services (G)**
[3] **Fidelity Select-Health Care (G)**
[3] **Fidelity Select-Precious Metals and Minerals (G)**
[2] **Fidelity Select-Technology (G)**
[2] **Fidelity Select-Utilities (G)**
Fidelity Tax Exempt MM Trust (M)
Fidelity U.S. Gov't Reserves (M)
Freedom Fund (GI)
[3] **Magellan Fund (G)**
[3] **Puritan (I)**
Rodney Square Fund Money Market (M)
Rodney Square Fund U.S. Government (M)

Financial Programs Inc.
P.O. Box 2040
Denver, CO 80201
(800) 525-9831
(303) 779-1233 (Denver)
(800) 332-9145 (Colorado)
Financial Bond Shares/Select Income (I)
Financial Daily Income Shares (M)
Financial Dynamics (G)
Financial Industrial Fund (GI)
Financial Industrial Inc. (I)
Financial Tax Free Income Shares (I)
Financial Tax Free Money Fund (M)

Lehman Management Co.
55 Water Street
New York, NY 10041
(800) 221-5350
(212) 668-4308
Lehman Capital Fund (G)
Lehman Cash Management Reserves (M)
Lehman Management Government Fund (M)
Lehman Tax Free MMF, Inc. (M)
Lehman Investors Fund (GI)
Lehman Opportunity Fund (GI)

Lexington Management Corp.
P.O. Box 1515
Saddle Brook, NJ 07662
(800) 526-0056/7
Lexington GNMA Income (I)
Lexington Goldfund Inc. (G)
Lexington Growth (G)
Lexington Government Secs. MMF (M)
Lexington Money Market Trust (M)
Lexington Research (G)
Lexington Tax Exempt Bond Fund (B)
Lexington Tax Free Money Fund (M)

Neuberger & Berman Management Inc.
342 Madison Avenue
New York, NY 10017
(800) 367-0776
(212) 850-8300
Energy (G)
Guardian Mutual (GI)
Liberty (I)
Manhattan (G)

---
[1] 8.5% sales charge on purchase less than $500.00.
[2] 4.5% front end load.
[3] Low-load fund (2%–3% sales charge).

Neuberger & Berman Government MF (M)
Neuberger & Berman Tax Free Money Fund (M)
Partners Fund (G)

Scudder Fund Distributors, Inc.
175 Federal Street
Boston, MA 02110
(800) 225-2470
(617) 426-8300
Scudder Capital Growth (G)
Scudder Cash Investment Trust (M)
Scudder Common Stock (GI)
Scudder Development (G)
Scudder Gov't Money Fund (M)
Scudder Income (GI)
Scudder International (G)
Scudder Managed Muni Bond (B)
Scudder NY Tax Free Bond (B)
Scudder Tax Free Money Fund (M)

Stein Roe & Farnham
P.O. Box 1131
Chicago, IL 60690
(800) 621-0320
(312) 368-7800
Stein Roe Discovery (G)
Stein Roe Tax Exempt Bond Fund (B)
Stein Roe Universe (G)
Stein Roe Cash Reserves (M)
Stein Roe Gov't Reserves (M)
Stein Roe Tax Exempt MF (M)
Stein Roe Total Return (G)
Stein Roe & Farnham Capital Opportunity (G)
Stein Roe & Farnham Stock (G)
Stein Roe Bond (I)
Stein Roe Special Fund (G)

T. Rowe Price Investor Services, Inc.
100 E. Pratt Street
Baltimore, MD 21202
(800) 638-5660
(301) 547-2008
T. Rowe Price Growth & Income Fund (GI)
T. Rowe Price Growth Stock (G)
T. Rowe Price International Fund (G)
T. Rowe Price New Era (G)
T. Rowe Price New Horizons (G)
T. Rowe Price New Income (I)
T. Rowe Price Tax Free Income (I)
T. Rowe Price Prime Reserve (B)
T. Rowe Price Tax Exempt MF (M)
T. Rowe Price Tax Free Income Fund (I)
T. Rowe Price U.S. Treasury MF (M)

Twentieth Century Investors, Inc.
P.O. Box 200
Kansas City, MO 64112
(800) 345-2021
Twentieth Century Cash Reserves (M)
Twentieth Century Growth (G)
Twentieth Century Select (GI)
Twentieth Century US Government (I)
[4]**Twentieth Century Ultra (G)**
Twentieth Century Vista Investors (G)

Value Line Securities, Inc.
711 Third Avenue
New York, NY 10017
(800) 223-0818
(212) 687-3965
The Value Line Cash Fund, Inc. (M)
Value Line U.S. Government Security Fund (I)
Value Line Fund (G)
Value Line Income (I)
Value Line Leveraged Growth (G)
Value Line Special Situations (G)
Value Line Tax Exempt Fund (I)
Value Line Tax Exempt High Yield Portfolio (B)

Vanguard Group
P.O. Box 2600
Valley Forge, PA 19496
(800) 662-SHIP
Energy (G)
Explorer (G)
Gold & Precious Metals (G)
Health Care (G)
Ivest (G)
Morgan Growth (G)
Qualified Dividend Port II (I)
Qualified Dividend Port I (GI)
Service Economy (G)
Technology (G)
Trustees' Commingled Fund-U.S. Portfolio (GI)
Vanguard Fixed Income GNMA (B)
Vanguard MMT Federal Fund (M)
Vanguard MMT Insured Portfolio (M)
Vanguard MMT Prime (M)
Vanguard Muni. Bond Fund Long Term M.M. (M)
Vanguard Fixed Income High Yield (B)
Vanguard Fixed Income Investment Grade (B)
Vanguard Index Trust (G)
Vanguard Muni High Yield (B)
Vanguard Muni Intermediate Term (B)
Vanguard Muni Long Term (B)
Vanguard Muni Short Term (B)
Wellesley Income (I)
Wellington (GI)
Windsor (G)

[4] .05% adjustment fee.

Foreign Securities Investments

This section provides data on the performance of major foreign securities markets and also listings of foreign stocks traded on the New York and American Exchanges. Over 200 foreign stocks and ADRs are also traded on the Over-The-Counter (OTC) market. A complete listing of foreign OTC stocks is available from the National Association of Securities Dealers, 1735 K Street, Washington, DC 20006.

Foreign securities not traded on the above exchanges may generally be purchased through stock brokers or major foreign banks in the country of interest. Most of these banks, which have U.S. branches in New York and other major cities, provide details concerning opening a foreign brokerage account.

A difficulty associated with foreign stock selection is that of obtaining timely information. The following general information sources may be helpful in this regard.

The Wall Street Journal
The Asian Wall Street Journal
Dow Jones & Company
22 Cortlandt Street
New York, NY 10007

The Asian Wall Street Journal, a weekly, is particularly helpful for the Asian region, including stock market coverage.

Barron's
20 Burnett Road
Chicopee, MA 01021

The weekly *International Trader* section is of special interest.

Capital International Perspectives
3 Place Des Bergues
1201 Geneva, Switzerland

Capital International Perspectives is a leading monthly publication dealing with international investments.

The Financial Times
Bracken House
10 Cannon Street
London EC4P 4BY, England

The Financial Times provides comprehensive coverage of European businesses and securities markets and is published daily.

Moody's Investor Services, International Manual
99 Church Street
New York, NY 10007

The International Manual provides financial information on about 3,000 major foreign corporations.

Worldwide Investment Research, Ltd.
7730 Carondelet
St. Louis, MO 63105

This publication provides annual and other financial reports on thousands of foreign firms and also publishes *Worldwide Investment Notes.*

Disclosure
5161 River Road
Bethesda, MD 20816

This service also provides annual reports and filings on foreign firms.

A listing of mutual funds investing in foreign securities is given on page 364.

RETURN ON WORLD STOCK MARKETS

	Market Value	Return in each Currency %				Currency Valuation %				Return in U.S. Dollar %				β
	Billion Dollar	3m	1y	5yr	σ_{A}	3m	1y	5yr	σ_{B}	3m	1y	5yr	σ_{C}	
New York	2535.8	20.5	22.1	21.1	4.4	0.0	0.0	0.0	0.0	20.5	22.1	21.1	4.4	0.90
Tokyo	2503.8	20.2	47.8	28.5	4.3	5.4	18.3	10.5	3.5	26.7	74.9	42.1	6.3	1.23
London	551.1	20.0	13.5	22.6	4.5	8.2	9.4	-2.1	3.8	29.9	24.1	20.1	6.1	1.06
Toronto	194.5	22.0	22.7	18.8	4.5	5.7	6.9	-1.2	1.3	28.9	31.2	17.4	5.2	0.89
Frankfurt	230.9	-13.0	-14.6	19.9	5.6	6.2	29.6	5.9	3.8	-7.6	10.6	27.0	6.8	0.76
Sydney	92.1	14.7	48.7	29.6	5.1	6.0	-1.5	-7.7	3.8	21.6	46.5	19.7	7.3	0.47
Paris	188.4	15.4	34.2	31.8	5.4	5.7	19.6	0.8	3.8	22.0	60.5	32.8	6.7	1.15
Zurich	136.7	0.0	-0.4	18.1	3.9	6.6	29.4	5.1	4.0	6.6	28.9	24.1	5.3	0.83
Hong Kong	59.4	5.7	66.9	18.4	9.3	-0.2	0.2	-5.6	1.9	5.5	67.2	11.8	10.3	0.16
Milano	142.0	-1.8	-0.4	28.4	8.4	3.8	23.7	0.5	3.4	2.0	23.2	29.1	8.8	1.07
Amsterdam	76.4	-7.4	0.8	28.5	5.1	6.3	29.4	5.6	3.7	-1.6	30.5	35.6	5.9	0.76
Singapore	38.7	18.6	78.2	7.8	6.1	1.7	1.7	0.0	1.5	20.6	81.2	7.7	6.4	0.39
Total	**6749.9**									**21.8**	**44.5**	**29.6**	**3.9**	

Source: *Tokyo Stock Market Quarterly Review,* 1987 Vol. 2. March 31, 1987. A publication of Daiwa Securities Co. Ltd. Available through Daiwa Securities America, Inc. One World Financial Center, New York, NY 10281.

NOTES

Market Value Estimate for the end of March, 1987.

Return in each currency Return derived solely based upon each market's Stock Price Index (dividends are not included) for the periods ending on the last trading date of the latest quarter. Five-years data are shown in the annual compound rate. Stock price indices referred to are; S & P500, Tokyo Stock Price Index, FT industrial, Toronto composite, Commerzbank general index, Sydney Stock Exchange all ordinaries, CAC industrial, Swiss Bank Corporation general, index, Hang Seng Bank index, Banca Commerciale Italiana index, ANP-CBS industrial, and Straits Times industrial.

Currency valuation Rate of change of each currency's value in U.S. dollar terms (NY market) for the corresponding periods. Five-years data are shown in the annual compound rate.

Return in U.S. Dollar Return of each market in U.S. $ terms. Five-years data are shown in the annual compound rate.

PERFORMANCES OF FOREIGN SECURITIES MARKETS

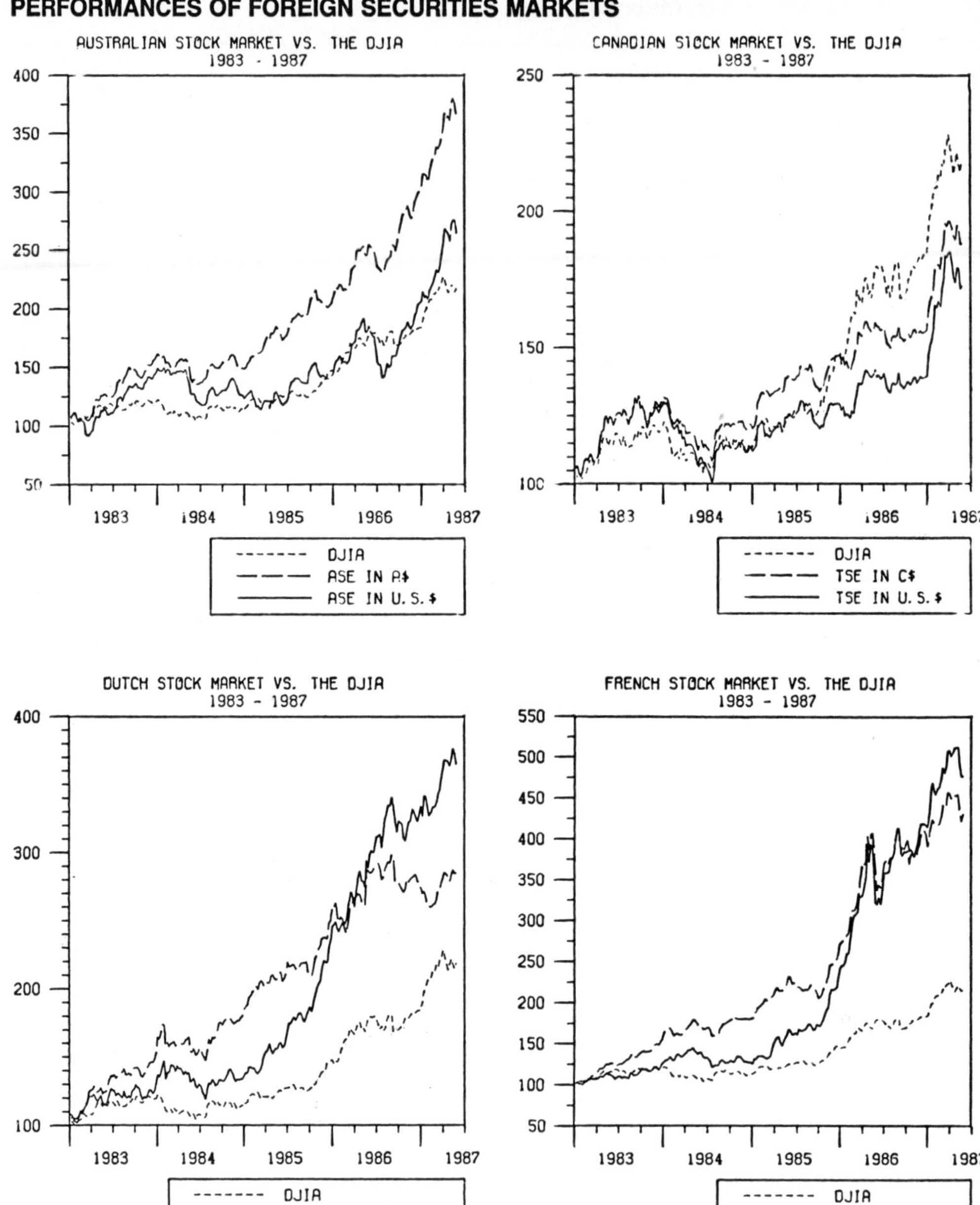

PERFORMANCES OF FOREIGN SECURITIES MARKETS *(continued)*

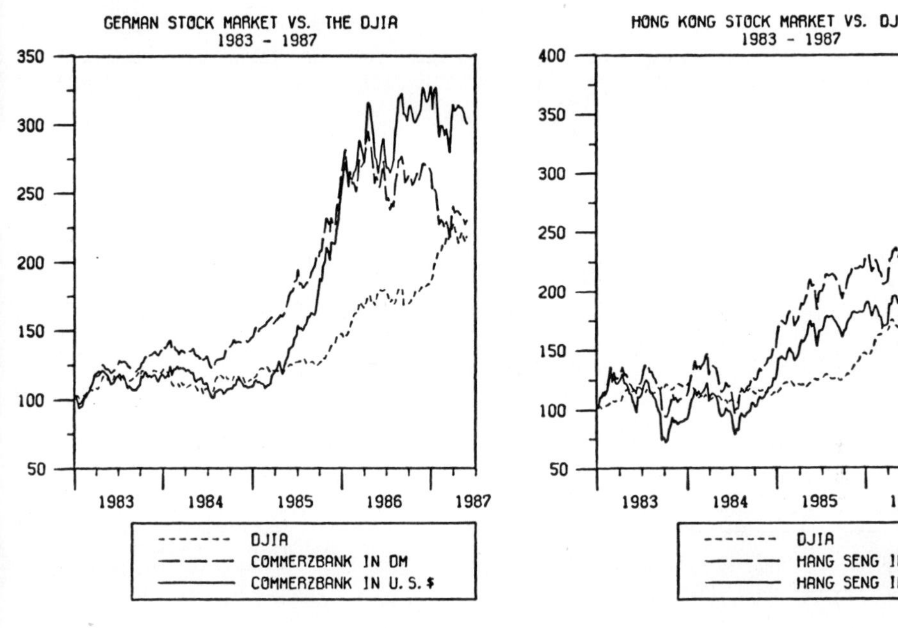

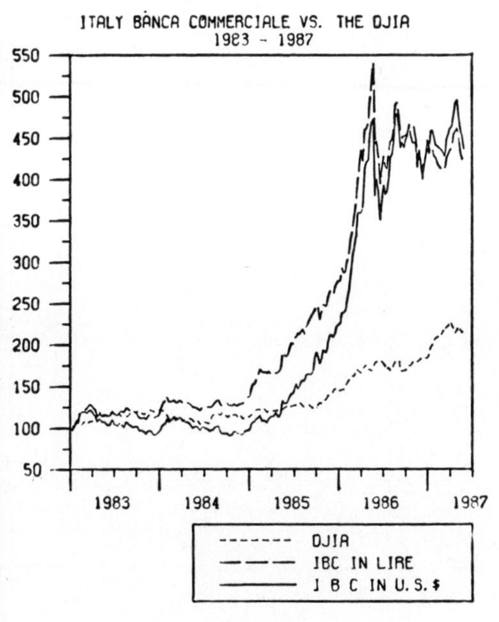

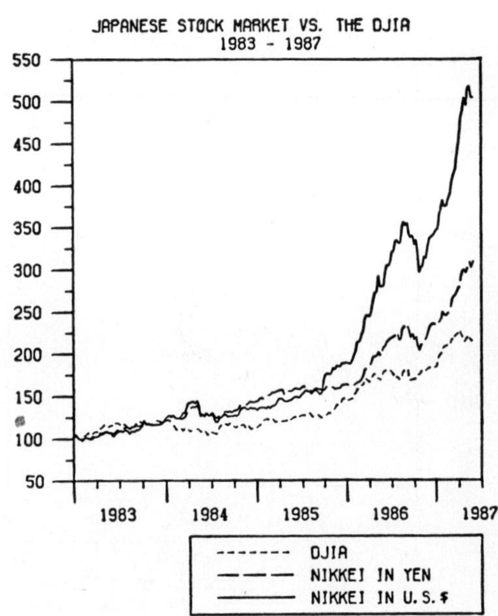

PERFORMANCES OF FOREIGN SECURITIES MARKETS *(concluded)*

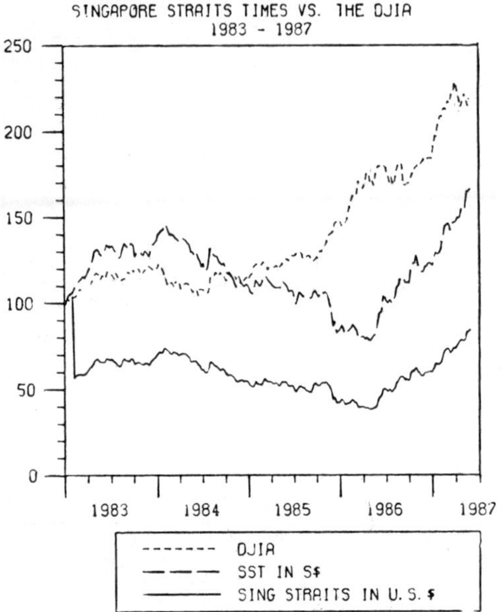

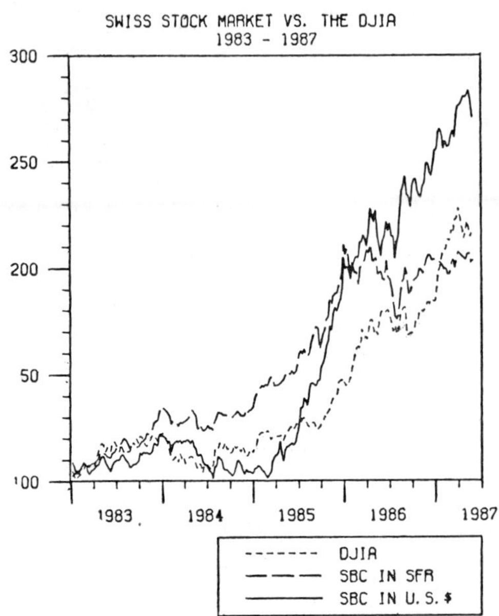

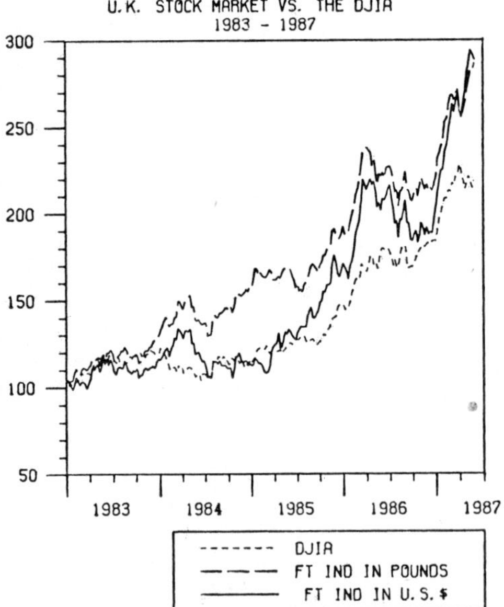

Source: *International Investment Monthly,* Drexel Burnham Lambert Incorporated, International Research Department.

FOREIGN STOCKS LISTED ON THE NEW YORK STOCK EXCHANGE

Listed foreign stocks, December 31, 1986

Country	Company	Industry
Australia	News Corporation Ltd.*	Publishing; broadcasting
Bahamas	Commodore International Ltd.	Integrated microcomputer manufacturer
Bermuda	Sea Containers Ltd. (5 issues)	Cargo container lessor
	Universal Matchbox Group Ltd. Inc.	Designs and manufactures toys
British W.I.	Club Med, Inc.	Hotel, resort operator
Canada	Alcan Aluminium Ltd.	Aluminum producer
	AMCA International Limited	Industrial prods.; construct. services
	Bell Canada Enterprises Inc.	Holding co.-telecommunications services
	Campbell Red Lake Mines Ltd.	Gold mining
	Campbell Resources Inc.	Holding co.-diversified natural resources
	Canadian Pacific Limited	Transportation; telecom.; oil; mining
	Carling O'Keefe Limited	Beer, wine producer
	Dome Mines Limited	Gold mining
	Inco Ltd.	Nickel, copper producer
	Inspiration Resources Corporation	Metals; agricultural chemicals
	LAC Minerals Ltd.	Gold mining
	McIntyre Mines Ltd.	Coal mining
	Mitel Corporation	Telecommunications equip. manufacturer
	Moore Corporation Ltd.	Business forms manufacturer
	Northern Telecom Ltd.	Telecommunications equip. manufacturer
	Northgate Exploration Limited	Holding co.- metal producer
	Ranger Oil Limited	Oil & gas exploration, production
	Seagram Co. Ltd.	Distilled spirits producer
	TransCanada PipeLines Ltd.	Natural gas transmission
	Varity Corporation	Farm equipment producer
	Westcoast Transmission Co., Ltd.	Natural gas distributor
Denmark	Novo Industri A/S*	Industrial enzymes; pharmaceuticals
England	Barclays PLC*	Holding company - bank
	British Gas PLC*	Natural gas distributor
	British Petroleum Company Ltd.*	Holding co. - integrated int'l oil co.
	British Telecommunications PLC*	Telecommunications services & products
	Hanson Trust PLC*	Consumer goods; building products
	Imperial Chemical Industries PLC*	Diversified chemical producer
	National Westminster Bank PLC*	Holding company - bank
	Plessey Company Ltd.*	Telecommunications & electronic equipment
	"Shell" Transport and Trading Co., PLC*	Holding co., - integrated int'l oil co.
	Tricentrol PLC*	Oil & gas production, oil trading
	Unilever PLC*	Holding co. - branded foods
Israel	Elscint Ltd.	Diagnostic medical imaging equipment
Japan	Hitachi, Ltd.*	Electronic eq.; machinery; consumer products
	Honda Motor Co., Ltd.*	Motor vehicle manufacturer
	Kubota, Ltd.*	Agricultural equipment; pipe manufacturer
	Kyocera Corp.*	Ceramic products; electronic equipment
	Matsushita Electric Industrial Co., Ltd.*	Consumer electronic manufacturer
	Pioneer Electronic Corporation*	Consumer electronic manufacturer
	Sony Corporation*	Consumer electronic manufacturer
	TDK Corporation*	Electronic comp.; magnetic tape producer
Netherlands	Ausimont Compo N.V.	Chemicals
	KLM Royal Dutch Airlines	Air transportation
	Royal Dutch Petroleum Co.	Holding co. - integrated int'l oil co.
	Unilever N.V.	Holding co. - branded foods
Netherlands Antilles	Erbamont N.V.	Pharmaceuticals
	Schlumberger Limited	Oilfield services; electronics
Norway	Norsk Hydro a.s.*	Agriculture; oil & gas
Panama	Service Resources Corporation	Financial, corporate printers
	Syntex Corporation	Pharmaceuticals
Philippines	Benguet Corporation	Mining; industrial construction
South Africa	ASA Limited	Closed-end inv. co. - gold mining
Spain	Banco Central, S.A.*	Holding company - bank

*American depository receipts/shares

Source: New York Stock Exchange *1987 Fact Book*.

Securities Markets: Notable Dates

1792 Original brokers' agreement subscribed to by 24 brokers (May 17).

1817 Constitution and the name "New York Stock Exchange Board" adopted (March 8).

1830 Dullest day in history of exchange—31 shares traded (March 16).

1840s Outdoor trading in unlisted securities begins at Wall and Hanover Streets, moves to Wall and Broad, then shifts south along Broad Street.*

1863 Name changed to "New York Stock Exchange" (NYSE) (January 29).

1867 Stock tickers first introduced (November 15).

1868 Membership made salable (October 23).

1869 Gold speculation resulted in "Black Friday" (September 24).

1871 Continuous markets in stocks established.

1873 NYSE closed September 18–29.

Failure of Jay Cooke & Co. and others (September 18).

Trading hours set at 10 A.M. to 3 P.M.; Saturdays, 10 A.M. to noon (December 1).

1878 First telephones introduced in the exchange (November 13).

1881 Annunciator board installed for paging members (January 29).

1885 Unlisted Securities Department established (March 25).

1886 First million-share day—1,200,000 shares traded (December 15).

1908 E. S. Mendels forms New York Curb Agency in first departure from informal trading.*

1910 Unlisted Securities Department abolished (March 31).

1911 Trading rules established with formation of New York Curb Market Association.*

1914 Exchange closed from July 31 through December 11—World War I.

1915 Stock prices quoted in dollars as against percent of par value (October 13).

1919 Separate ticker system installed for bonds (January 2).

1920 Stock Clearing Corporation established (April 26).

1921 New York Curb Market association moves indoors at 86 Trinity Place; name shortened to New York Curb Market and ticker service initiated (June 21).*

1927 Start of ten-share unit of trading for inactive stocks (January 3).

1929 Stock market crash; 16,410,000 shares traded (October 29).

New York Curb Market modifies its name to New York Curb Exchange.*

1930 Faster ticker—500 characters per minute—installed (September 2).

1931 Exchange building expanded; Telephone Quotation Department formed to send stock quotes to member firm offices.*

1933 New York Stock Exchange closed for bank holiday, March 4–14.

1934 Enactment of Securities Exchange Act of 1934 (June 6).

1938 First salaried president elected—Wm. McC. Martin, Jr. (June 30).

1946 Listed stocks outnumber unlisted stocks for first time since the 1934 act imposed restrictions on unlisted trading.*

1952 Trading hours changed: weekdays, 10 A.M. to 3:30 P.M. Closed Saturdays (September 29).*

1953 Name of New York Curb Exchange changed to American Stock Exchange.*

1958 First member corporation—Woodcock, Hess & Co. (June 4).

Mary C. Roebling becomes first woman governor.*

1962 Committee system of administration replaced by expanded paid staff reporting to president. Specialist system strengthened, surveillance of trading increased, listing and delisting standards introduced, and board restructured to give greater representation to commission and out-of-town brokers.*

1964 New member classification—Registered Trader (August 3).

New ticker—900 characters per minute—put into service (December 1).†

Am-Quote computerized telephone-quotation service was completed as first step in major automation program.*

1965 Fully automated quotation service introduced (March 8).

---

* Refers to American Exchange (AMEX) (formerly Curb Exchange).

† Applies to both the New York Stock Exchange and the American Exchange. Other entries refer to the New York Stock Exchange.

Sources: New York Stock Exchange *1985 Fact Book* and American Stock Exchange *Data Book* and *The Wall Street Journal*.

Electronic Systems Center created (October 15).

First women, Phyllis S. Peterson and Julia Montgomery Walsh, elected to regular membership.*

1966 New NYSE Stock Price Index inaugurated (July 14).

AMEX Price Change Index System introduced; computer complex installed for ticker, surveillance, and compared-clearance operations.*

1967 First woman member admitted—Muriel F. Siebert (December 28).

1968 Ticker speed increased to maximum 900 characters per minute; transmission begun to six European countries. Trading floor modernized; line capacity for communications doubled. Visitors gallery expanded.*

1969 Central Certificate Service fully activated (February 26).

1970 Public ownership of member firms approved (March 26).

Securities Investor Protection Corporation Act signed (December 30).

1971 First negotiated commission rates effective (April 5).

First member organization listed—Merrill Lynch (July 27).

AMEX incorporates and marks 50th anniversary of move indoors; Listed Company Advisory Committee formed, composed of nine chief executives of AMEX-listed companies.*

1972 NYSE reorganization, based on Martin Report, approved (January 20).

Board of Directors, with ten public members, replaced Board of Governors (July 13).

Securities Industry Automation Corporation established with AMEX to consolidate facilities of both exchanges (July 17).*

First salaried chairman took office—James J. Needham (August 28).

Board of Governors reorganized to include ten public and ten industry representatives plus full-time salaried chairman as chief executive officer.*

1973 Depository Trust Company succeeded Central Certificate Service (May 11).

Chicago Board of Options Exchange opened with trading in 16 classes of call options (April 26).

AMEX formally adopts affirmative action employment plan; Market Value Index System introduced to replace Price Change Index.*

1974 Trading hours extended to 4 P.M. (October 1).

Consolidated tape begun; 15 stocks reported (October 18).

1975 Fixed commission system abolished (April 30).

Full consolidated tape begun (June 16).

AMEX trades call options.*

Trading begins in call options and odd lots of U.S. government instruments.*

1976 New data line installed, handling 36,000 characters per minute (January 19).

Specialists began handling odd lots in their stocks (May 24).

Varo, Inc.—first stock traded on both NYSE and AMEX (August 23).

Competition between specialists begun (October 11).

1977 Independent audit committee on listed companies' boards required (January 6).

Competitive Trader category for members approved (January 19).

National Securities Clearing Corporation (NSCC) began merging the clearing operations of the Stock Clearing Corporation of NYSE with American Stock Exchange Clearing Corporation and National Clearing Corporation of the NASD (January 20).

Foreign broker/dealers permitted to obtain membership (February 3).

Full Automated Bond System in effect (July 27).

1978 First 60 million share day in history (63,493,000 shares) (April 17).

Intermarket Trading System (ITS) began.

Registered Competitive Market-Maker category for members approved (May 2).

First 65 million share day in history (66,370,000 shares) (August 3).

Trading in Ginnie Maes inaugurated on the AMEX Commodities Exchange (ACE)* (September 12).

AMEX reached an index high of 176.87 (September 13).

1979 Trading began at pilot post on the exchange floor. First stage in a $12-million upgrading of exchange facilities (January 29).

Board of Directors of NYSE approved plan for the creation of the New York Futures Exchange, a wholly owned subsidiary of NYSE. Futures contracts in seven financial instruments will be traded on the NYSE (March 1).

New York Commodities Exchange and NYSE terminated merger talks (March 15).

81,619,000 shares were traded on the NYSE, making it the heaviest trade day in exchange history (October 10).

1980 American Stock Exchange reached an all-time daily stock volume record of 14,980,680 shares sold (January 15).*

NYSE volume of 67,752,000 shares traded was second largest volume on record to date (January 16).

NYSE Futures Exchange opened (August 7).

Option seat on the American Stock Exchange sold at an all-time high of $160,000 (December 24).*

NYSE index reached an all time high of 81.02 (November 28).

1981 First 90 million share day in the history of the Exchange, 92,881,000 (January 7).

The New York Stock Exchange subsidiary, the New York Futures Exchange, started trading futures in Domestic Bank Certificates of Deposit.

1982 A new AMEX subsidiary The American Gold Coin Exchange (AGCE) began trading in the Canadian Maple Leaf (January 21).*

Trading in NYSE Common Stock Index Futures began on the New York Futures Exchange (May 6).*

Trading started through experimental linkage between ITS operated by NYSE and six other exchanges and Computer Assisted Execution Service (CAES) operated by NASD, in 30 stocks exempted from exchange off-board trading rules under SEC Rule 19c-3. (May 17)

Record advance of 38.81 points reached in NYSE trading as measured by Dow Jones Industrial Average (August 17).

First 100 million share day (132,-681,120 shares. (August 18).

Trading in Interest Rate Options on U.S. Treasury Bills & Notes started in May on the AMEX.*

Trading soared to an all time high of 147,081,070 shares on the NYSE (October 7).

All time options high of 340,550 contracts were traded on the AMEX (October 7).*

Dow Jones Industrial Average plunged 36.33 points, the largest one-day loss since the record plunge of 38.33 points on October 28, 1929 (October 25).

1983 Trading in options on NYSE Common Stock Index Futures started on New York Futures Exchange (January 28).

NYSE started trading options on the NYSE Common Stock Index (September 23).

Dow Jones Industrial Average reached an all time high of 1260.77 (September 26).

New shares of common stocks of seven regional telephone companies and shares of the "new" AT&T began trading on a "when issued" basis. Divestiture of AT&T effective January 1, 1984 (November 21).

AMEX stock trading went over the two billion share mark for the first time.

The AMEX list of stock options increased by four index options, two on specific industry groups, one on the AMEX Market Value Index.*

1984 Largest NYSE trading day of 159, 999,031 shares traded (January 5).

CBOT (Chicago Board of Trade) began trading a futures contract on the Major Market Index (July 23).*

Trading began in NYSE Double Index Options (July 23).

NYSE volume soared to a record 236,565,110 shares traded (August 3).

Super DOT 250 (electronic order-routing system) launched on NYSE (November 16).

1985 For the first time the NYSE index went over 100, closing at 101.12 (January 21).

19,091,950 shares were traded on the AMEX, the highest single day volume ever. (February 6).*

Ronald Reagan visited the NYSE, the first President to do so while in office (March 28).

Trading in options on gold bullion started on AMEX (April 26).*

50 billionth share listed in NYSE (May 30).

NYSE began trading options in three over-the-counter stocks (June 3).

NYSE reached an all time index high of 113.49 (July 17).

Amex and Toronto Stock Exchange linked together as part of the first two-way electronic hookup between primary equity markets in different countries (September 24).

Instinet Corporation and the AMEX reached an agreement enabling European institutional investors to have access to the AMEX options market via Reuter's electronic terminals.

The opening trading time on both the NYSE and AMEX went from 10:00 A.M. to 9:30 A.M. (September 30).

The Dow Jones Industrial Average reached an all-time high of 1368.50 (October 16).

Options traded on two listed stocks on the NYSE (October 16).

Tokyo Stock Exchange admitted its first foreign member firms (December 1).

A daily record of 119,969 contracts traded on the AMEX Major Markets Index Option (December 13).*

1986 The Dow Jones Industrial Average for the first time closed above 1600 at 1600.69 (February 6).

The Dow Jones Industrial Average for the first time closed above 1700 at 1713.99. (February 27).

The Dow Jones Industrial Average for the first time closed above 1800 at 1804.24 (March 20).

NYSE began trading the NYSE Beta Index Option (May 22).

NYSE Board of Directors expanded to 24 outside directors: 12 public members and 12 industry members (June 5).

New York Futures Exchange (NYFE) began trading the Commodity Research Bureau (CRB) futures contract (June 5).

The Dow Jones Industrial Average for the first time closed above 1900 at 1903.54 (July 1).

The Directors of the NYSE voted to abandon the one-share-one-vote rule which gives common shareholders equal voting rights (July 3).

The Dow Jones Industrials nose-dived a record 86.61 points on a record volume of 237,600,000 shares traded (September 11).

$600,000.00 (the highest price ever) was paid for membership in the NYSE (December 1).

1987 The Dow Jones industrials passed the 2000 mark, closing at 2000.25 (January 8).

The Dow Jones Industrials closed above 2300 for the first time, up 33.95 points to 2333.52 (March 20).

The Dow Jones Industrials climbed above 2400 for the first time to close at 2405.54 (April 7).

The Chicago Board of Trade and the Chicago Board Options Exchange agreed to permit members of both exchanges to trade financial futures and options contracts side by side (June 25).

For the first time the Dow Jones Industrials closed over 2500 at 2510.04 (July 16).

An advance of 43.83 points pushed the Dow Jones Industrials over 2600 for the first time to close at 2635.84 (Au-

A gain of 15.14 points brought the Dow Jones Industrials above 2700 points for the first time with the market closing at 2700.52 (August 17).

The stock market 'crashed' with the Dow Jones Industrials down 508.00 points or 22% to close at 1738.74 on a record volume of 604.3 shares. Other record declines were: Dow Jones transportations off 164.78; utilities off 29.16; the S & P 500 stock index off 57.86; the AMEX index down 41.05, the NYSE down 30.51, and the NASDAQ composite of over-the-counter stocks off 46.12 (October 19).

A record volume of 608,120,000 shares traded on the NYSE and 43,432,760 on the AMEX (October 20).

The Dow Jones Industrials rocketed 186.84 points, the highest ever, on a volume of 449,350,000 shares (October 21).

Investment and Financial Terms

Abandonment value The amount that can be realized by liquidating a project before its economic life has ended.*

Accelerated depreciation Depreciation methods that write off the cost of an asset at

* Entries from *Managerial Finance*, 6th edition, by J. Fred Weston and Eugene F. Brigham.

† Entries from *The Language of Investing Glossary*.

** Entries from *Tax-Exempt Securities & the Investor*.

†† Entries from the *Glossary*.

¶ Entries from the Federal Reserve *Glossary*.

Sources: From *Managerial Finance*, 6th ed., by J. Fred Weston and Eugene F. Brigham. Copyright © 1978 by The Dryden Press, Copyright © 1962, 1966, 1969, 1972, 1975 by Holt, Rinehart and Winston. Reprinted by permission of Holt, Rinehart and Winston, CBS College Publishing.

The *Language of Investing Glossary* published by the New York Stock Exchange, Inc.

The *Glossary* published by the New York Stock Exchange.

Tax-Exempt Securities & the Investor published by the Securities Industry Association.

The *Glossary* published by the Board of Governors of the Federal Reserve System.

a faster rate than the write-off under the straight-line method. The three principal methods of accelerated depreciation are: (1) sum-of-the-years'-digits, (2) double-declining balance, and (3) units-of-production.*

Accountant's Opinion (See: *Auditor's Report.*)

Accruals Accruals Continuing recurring short-term liabilities. Examples are accrued wages, accrued taxes, and accrued interest.*

Accrued interest Interest accrued on a bond since the last interest payment was made. The buyer of the bond pays the market price plus accrued interest. Exceptions include bonds that are in default and income bonds. (See: *Flat income bond.*)†

Acquisition The acquiring of control of one corporation by another. In "unfriendly" takeover attempts, the potential buying company may offer a price well above current market values, new securities and other inducements to stockholders. The management of the subject company might ask for a better price or try to join up with a third company. (See: *Merger, Proxy.*)††

Ad valorem tax A tax based on the value (or assessed value) of property.**

Aging schedule A report showing how long accounts receivable have been outstanding. It gives the percent of receivables not past due and the percent past due by, for example, one month, two months, or other periods.*

American Depository Receipt (ADR) Issued by American banks, an ADR is a certificate which serves as a proxy for a foreign stock deposited in a foreign bank. For all practical purposes, trading an ADR is equivalent to trading the foreign stock. Hundreds of ADRs are traded on U.S. stock exchange.

Amortization Accounting for expenses or charges as applicable rather than as paid. Includes such practices as depreciation, depletion, write-off of intangibles, prepaid expenses, and deferred charges.†

Amortize To liquidate on an installment basis; an amortized loan is one in which the principal amount of the loan is repaid in installments during the life of the loan.*

Annual report The formal financial statement issued yearly by a corporation. The annual report shows assets, liabilities, earnings—how the company stood at the close of the business year, how it fared profit-wise during the year and other information of interest to shareowners.†

Annuity A series of payments of a fixed amount for a specified number of years.*

Arbitrage A technique employed to take advantage of differences in price. If, for example, ABC stock can be bought in New York for $10 a share and sold in London at $10.50, an arbitrageur may simultaneously purchase ABC stock here and sell the same amount in London, making a profit of 50 cents a share, less expenses. Arbitrage may also involve the purchase of rights to subscribe to a security, or the purchase of a convertible security—and the sale at or about the same time of the security obtainable through exercise of the rights or of the security obtainable through conversion. (See: *Convertible, Rights.*)††

Arrearage Overdue payment; frequently omitted dividend on preferred stock.

Assessed valuation The valuation placed on property for purposes of taxation.**

Assets Everything a corporation owns or due to it: Cash, investments, money due it, materials and inventories, which are called current assets; buildings and machinery, which are known as fixed assets; and patents and good will, called intangible assets. (See: *Liabilities.*)†

Assignment A relatively inexpensive way of liquidating a failing firm that does not involve going through the courts.*

Assignment Notice to an option writer that an option holder has exercised the option and that the writer will now be required to deliver (receive) under the terms of the contract.††

Ask (See: *Bid and asked.*)†

Auction market The system of trading securities through brokers or agents on an exchange such as the New York Stock Exchange. Buyers compete with other buyers while sellers compete with other sellers for the most advantageous price.††

Auditor's report Often called the accountant's opinion, it is the statement of the accounting firm's work and its opinion of the corporation's financial statements, especially if they conform to the normal and generally accepted practices of accountancy.††

Averages Various ways of measuring the trend of securities prices, one of the most popular of which is the Dow-Jones average of 30 industrial stocks listed on the New York Stock Exchange. The prices of the 30 stocks are totaled and then divided by a divisor which is intended to compensate for past stock splits and stock dividends and which is changed from time to time. As a result point changes in the average have only the vaguest relationship to dollar price changes in stocks included in the average. (See: *NYSE composite index.*)††

Balance sheet A condensed financial statement showing the nature and amount of a company's assets, liabilities and capital on a given date. In dollar amounts the balance sheet shows what the company owned, what it owed, and the ownership interest in the company of its stockholders. (See: *Assets, Earnings report.*)†

Balloon payment When a debt is not fully amortized, the final payment is larger than the preceding payments and is called a *balloon* payment.*

Bankers acceptance Bankers acceptances are negotiable time drafts, or bills of exchange, that have been accepted by a bank which, by accepting, assumes the obligation to pay the holder of the draft the face amount of the instrument on the maturity date specified. They are used primarily to finance the export, import, shipment, or storage of goods.¶

Bankruptcy A legal procedure for formally liquidating a business, carried out under the jurisdiction of courts of law.*

Basis book A book of mathematical tables used to convert yields to equivalent dollar prices.**

Basis point One gradation on a 100-point scale representing one percent; used especially in expressing variations in the yields of bonds. Fixed income yields vary often and slightly within one percent and the basis point scale easily expresses these changes in hundredths of one percent. For example, the difference between 12.83% and 12.88% is 5 basis points.††

Basis price The price expressed in yield or percentage of return on the investment.**

Bear market A declining market. (See: *Bull market.*)†

Bearer bond A bond which does not have the owner's name registered on the books of the issuer and which is payable to the holder. (See: *Coupon bond, Registered bond.*)†

Bearer security A security that has no identification as to owner. It is presumed to be owned, therefore, by the bearer or the person who holds it. Bearer securities are freely and easily negotiable since ownership can be quickly transferred from seller to buyer.**

Beta coefficient Measures the extent to which the returns on a given stock move with "the stock market."*

Bid and asked Often referred to as a quotation or quote. The bid is the highest price anyone has declared that he wants to pay for a security at a given time, the asked is the lowest price anyone will take at the same time. (See: *Quote.*)†

Block A large holding or transaction of stock—popularly considered to be 10,000 shares or more.†

Blue chip A company known nationally for the quality and wide acceptance of its products or services, and for its ability to make money and pay dividends.†

Blue-sky laws A popular name for laws various states have enacted to protect the public against securities frauds. The term is believed to have originated when a judge ruled that a particular stock had about the same value as a patch of blue sky.†

Board room A room for registered representatives and customers in a broker's office where opening, high, low, and last prices of leading stocks used to be posted on a board throughout the market day. Today such price displays are normally electronically controlled although most board rooms have replaced the board with the ticker and/or individual quotation machines.†

Bond Basically an IOU or promissory note of a corporation, usually issued in multiples of $1,000 or $5,000, although $100 and $500 denominations are not unknown. A bond is evidence of a debt on which the issuing company usually promises to pay the bondholders a specified amount of interest for a specified length of time, and to repay the loan on the expiration date. In every case a bond represents debt—its holder is a creditor of the corporation and not a part owner as is the shareholder. (See: *Collateral, Convertible, Debenture, General Mortgage Bond, Income Bond.*)††

Bond funds Registered investment companies whose assets are invested in diversified portfolios of bonds.*

Book A notebook the specialist in a stock uses to keep a record of the buy and sell orders at specified prices, in sequence of receipt, which are left with him by other brokers. (See *Specialist.*)†

Book value The accounting value of an asset. The book value of a share of common stock is equal to the net worth (common stock plus retained earnings) of the corporation divided by the number of shares of stock outstanding.*

Break-even analysis An analytical technique for studying the relation between fixed cost, variable cost, and profits. A break-even *chart* graphically depicts the nature of break-even analysis. The break-even *point* represents the volume of sales at which total costs equal total revenues (that is, profits equal zero).*

Broker An agent, who handles the public's orders to buy and sell securities, commodities, or other property. For this service a commission is charged. (See: *Commission broker, dealer.*)†

Brokers' loans Money borrowed by brokers from banks or other brokers for a variety of uses. It may be used by specialists and to help finance inventories of stock they deal in; by brokerage firms to finance the underwriting of new issues of corporate and municipal securities; to help finance a firm's own investments; and to help finance the purchase of securities for customers who prefer to use the broker's credit when they buy securities. (See: *Margin.*)†

Bull market An advancing market. (See: *Bear market.*)†

Business risk The basic risk inherent in a firm's operations. Business risk plus financial risk resulting from the use of debt equals total corporate risk.*

Call (1) An option to buy (or "call") a share of stock at a specified price within a specified period. (2) The process of redeeming a bond or preferred stock issue before its normal maturity. (See: *Options.*)*

Call premium The amount in excess of par value that a company must pay when it calls a security.*

Call price The price that must be paid when a security is called. The call price is equal to the par value plus the call premium.*

Call privilege A provision incorporated into a bond or a share of preferred stock that gives the issuer the right to redeem (call) the security at a specified price.*

Callable A bond issue, all or part of which may be redeemed by the issuing corporation under definite conditions before maturity. The term also applies to preferred shares which may be redeemed by the issuing corporation.†

Capital asset An asset with a life of more than one year that is not bought and sold in the ordinary course of business.*

Capital budgeting The process of planning expenditures on assets whose returns are expected to extend beyond one year.*

Capital gain or capital loss Profit or loss from the sale of a capital asset. A capital gain, under current federal income tax laws, may be either short-term (12 months or less) or long-term (more than 12 months). A short-term capital gain is taxed at the reporting individual's full income tax rate. A long-term capital gain is subject to a lower tax. The capital gains provisions of the tax law are complicated. You should consult your tax advisor for specific information.†

Capital market line A graphical representation of the relationship between risk and the required rate of return on an efficient portfolio.*

Capital markets Financial transactions involving instruments with maturities greater than one year.*

Capital rationing A situation where a constraint is placed on the total size of the capital investment during a particular period.*

Capital stock All shares representing ownership of a business, including preferred and common. (See: *Common stock, Preferred stock.*)†

Capital structure The permanent long-term financing of the firm represented by long-term debt, preferred stock, and net worth (net worth consists of capital, capital surplus, and retained earnings). Capital structure is distinguished from *financial structure,* which includes short-term debt plus all reserve accounts.*

Capitalization Total amount of the various securities issued by a corporation. Capitalization may include bonds, debentures, preferred and common stock, and surplus. Bonds and debentures are usually carried on the books of the issuing company in terms of their par or face value. Preferred and common shares may be carried in terms of par or stated value. Stated value may be an arbitrary figure decided upon by the directors or may represent the amount received by the company from the sale of the securities at the time of issuance. (See: *Par.*)†

Capitalization rate A discount rate used to find the present value of a series of future cash receipts; sometimes called *discount rate.**

Carry-back; carry forward For income tax purposes, losses that can be carried backward or forward to reduce federal income taxes.*

Cash budget A schedule showing cash flows (receipts, disbursements, and net cash) for a firm over a specified period.*

Cash cycle The length of time between the purchase of raw materials and the collection of accounts receivable generated in the sale of the final product.*

Cash flow Reported net income of a corporation *plus* amounts charged off for depreciation, depletion, amortization, extraordinary charges to reserves, which are bookkeeping deductions and not paid out in actual dollars and cents. (See: *Amortization, Depreciation.*)††

Cash sale A transaction on the floor of the Stock Exchange which calls for delivery of the securities the same day. In "regular way" trades, the seller is to deliver on the fifth business day except for bonds, which is the next day. (See: *Regular way delivery.*)†

Certainty equivalents The amount of cash (or rate of return) that someone would require *with certainty* to make him indifferent between this certain sum (or *rate of return*) and a particular uncertain, risky sum (or rate of return).*

Certificate The actual piece of paper which is evidence of ownership of stock in a corporation. Watermarked paper is finely engraved with delicate etchings to discourage forgery.††

Certificate of Deposit (CD) A money market instrument issued by banks. The time CD is characterized by its set date of maturity and interest rate and its wide acceptance among investors, companies and institutions as a highly negotiable short-term investment vehicle.††

CFTC The Commodity Futures Trading Commission, created by Congress in 1974 to regulate exchange trading in futures.††

Characteristic line A linear least-squares regression line that shows the relationship between an individual security's return and returns on "the market." The slope of the characteristic line is the beta coefficient.*

Chattel mortgage A mortgage on personal property (not real estate). A mortgage on equipment would be a chattel mortgage.*

Closed-end investment company (See: *Investment company.*)

Coefficient of variation Standard deviation divided by the mean: CV.*

Collateral Assets that are used to secure a loan.*

Collateral trust bond A bond secured by collateral deposited with a trustee. The collateral is often the stocks or bonds of companies controlled by the issuing company but may be other securities.†

Commercial paper Unsecured, short-term promissory notes of large firms, usually issued in denominations of $1 million or more. The rate of interest on commercial paper is typically somewhat below the prime rate of interest *

Commission The broker's basic fee for purchasing or selling securities or property as an agent.†

Commission broker An agent who executes the public's orders for the purchase or sale of securities or commodities.†

Commitment fee The fee paid to a lender for a formal line of credit.*

Commodities (See: *Futures.*)

Common stock Securities which represent an ownership interest in a corporation. If the company has also issued preferred stock, both common and preferred have ownership rights. Common stockholders assume the greater risk, but generally exercise the greater control and may gain the greater reward in the form of dividends and capital appreciation. The terms of common stock and capital stock are often used interchangeably when the company has no preferred stock.†

Compensating balance A required minimum checking account balance that a firm must maintain with a commercial bank. The required balance is generally equal to 15 to 20 percent of the amount of loans outstanding. Compensating balances can raise the effective rate of interest on bank loans.*

Competitive trader A member of the Exchange who trades in stocks on the Floor for an account in which he has an interest. Also known as a Registered Trader.†

Composite cost of capital A weighted average of the component costs of debt, preferred stock, and common equity. Also called the *weighted-average cost of capital,* but it reflects the cost of each additional dollar raised, not the average cost of all capital the firm has raised throughout its history.*

Composition An informal method of reorganization that voluntarily reduces creditors' claims on the debtor firm.*

Compound interest An interest rate that is applicable when interest in succeeding periods is earned not only on the initial principal but also on the accumulated interest of prior periods. Compound interest is contrasted to *simple interest,* in which returns are not earned on interest received.*

Compounding The arithmetic process of determining the final value of a payment or series of payments when compound interest is applied.*

Conditional sales contract A method of financing new equipment by paying it off in installments over a one-to-five-year period. The seller retains title to the equipment until payment has been completed.*

Conglomerate A corporation that has diversified its operations, usually by acquiring enterprises in widely varied industries.†

Consolidated balance sheet A balance sheet showing the financial condition of a corporation and its subsidiaries. (See: *Balance sheet.*)†

Consolidated tape The ticket tape reporting transactions in NYSE listed securities that take place on the NYSE or any of the participating regional stock exchanges and other markets. Similarly, transactions in AMEX-listed securities, and certain other securities listed on regional stock exchanges, are reported and identified on a separate tape.††

Consolidated tax return An income tax return that combines the income statement of several affiliated firms.*

Continuous compounding (discounting) As opposed to discrete compounding, interest is added continuously rather than at discrete points in time.*

Conversion price The effective price paid for common stock when the stock is obtained by converting either convertible preferred stocks or convertible bonds. For example, if a $1,000 bond is convertible into 20 shares of stock, the conversion price is $50 ($1,000/20).*

Conversion ratio or conversion rate The number of shares of common stock that may be obtained by converting a convertible bond or share of convertible preferred stock.*

Convertibles Securities (generally bonds or preferred stocks) that are exchangeable at the option of the holder for common stock of the issuing firm.*

Correlation coefficient Measures the degree of relationship between two variables.*

Correspondent A securities firm, bank, or other financial organization which regularly performs services for another in a place or market to which the other does not have direct access. Securities firms may have correspondents in foreign countries or on exchanges of which they are not members. Correspondents are frequently linked by private wires. Member organizations of the N.Y.S.E. with offices in New York City may also act as correspondents for out-of-town member organizations which do not maintain New York City offices.†

Cost of capital The discount rate that should be used in the capital budgeting process.*

Coupon bond Bond with interest coupons attached. The coupons are clipped as they come due and are presented by the holder for payment of interest. (See: *Bearer bond, Registered bond.*)†

Coupon rate The stated rate of interest on a bond.*

Covariance The correlation between two variables multiplied by the standard deviation of each variable:

$$\text{Cov} = r_{xy}\sigma_x\sigma_y.*$$

Covenant Detailed clauses contained in loan agreements. Covenants are designed to protect the lender and include such items as limits on total indebtedness, restrictions on dividends, minimum current ratio, and similar provisions.*

Coverage A term usually connected with revenue bonds. It is a ratio of net revenues pledged to principal and interest payments to debt service requirements. It is one of the factors used in evaluating the quality of an issue.**

Covered option An option position that is offset by an equal and opposite position in the underlying security.††

Covering Buying a security previously sold short. (See: *Short sale, Short covering.*)†

Cumulative dividends A protective feature on preferred stock that requires all past preferred dividends to be paid before any common dividends are paid.*

Cumulative preferred A stock having a provision that if one or more dividends are omitted, the omitted dividends must be paid before dividends may be paid on the company's common stock.†

Cumulative voting A method of voting for corporate directors which enables the shareholder to multiply the number of his shares by the number of directorships being voted on and cast the total for one director or a selected group of directors. A 10-share holder normally casts 10 votes for each of, say 12 nominees to the board of directors. He thus has 120 votes. Under the cumulative voting principle he may do that or he may cast 120 (10 × 12) votes for only one nominee, 60 for two, 40 for three, or any other distribution he chooses. Cumulative voting is required under the corporate laws of some states, is permitted in most others.†

Current assets Those assets of a company which are reasonably expected to be realized in cash, or sold, or consumed during the normal operating cycle of the business. These include cash, U.S. government bonds, receivables and money due usually within one year, and inventories.†

Current liabilities Money owed and payable by a company, usually within one year.†

Current return (See: *Yield.*)

Current yield A relation stated as a percent of the annual interest to the actual market price of the bond.**

Cut-off point In the capital budgeting process, the minimum rate of return on acceptable investment opportunities.*

Day order An order to buy or sell which, if not executed expires at the end of the trading day on which it was entered.†

Dealer An individual or firm in the securities business who buys and sells stocks and bonds as a principal rather than as an agent.

The dealer's profit or loss is the difference between the price paid and the price received for the same security. The dealer's confirmation must disclose to the customer that the principal has been acted upon. The same individual or firm may function, at different times, either as broker or dealer. (See: *NASD, Specialist.*)††

Debenture A long-term debt instrument that is not secured by a mortgage on specific property.*

Debit balance In a customer's margin account that portion of purchase price of stock, bonds, or commodities covered by credit extended by the broker to the margin customer.†

Debt limit The statutory or constitutional maximum debt that a municipality can legally incur.**

Debt ratio Total debt divided by total assets.*

Debt service Refers to the payments required for interest and retirement of the principal amount of a debt.**

Default The failure to fulfill a contract. Generally, default refers to the failure to pay interest or principal on debt obligations.*

Degree of leverage The percentage increase in profits resulting from a given percentage increase in sales. The degree of leverage may be calculated for financial leverage, operating leverage, or both combined.*

Denomination The face amount or par value of a security which the issuer promises to pay on the maturity date. Most municipal bonds are issued with a minimum denomination of $5,000, although a few older issues are available in $1,000 denominations.**

Depletion accounting Natural resources, such as metals, oil and gas, and timber, which conceivably can be reduced to zero over the years, present a special problem in capital management. Depletion is an accounting practice consisting of charges against earnings based upon the amount of the asset taken out of the total reserves in the period for which accounting is made. A bookkeeping entry, it does not represent any cash outlay nor are any funds earmarked for the purpose.†

Depository trust company (DTC) A central securities certificate depository through which members effect security deliveries between each other via computerized bookkeeping entries thereby reducing the physical movement of stock certificates.†

Depreciation Normally, charges against earnings to write off the cost, less salvage value, of an asset over its estimated useful life. It is a bookkeeping entry and does not represent any cash outlay nor are any funds earmarked for the purpose.†

Devaluation The process of reducing the value of a country's currency stated in terms of other currencies; for example, the British pound might be devalued from $2.30 for one pound to $2.00 for one pound.*

Director Person elected by shareholders to establish company policies. The directors appoint the president, vice presidents, and all other operating officers. Directors decide, among other matters, if and when dividends shall be paid. (See: *Management, Proxy.*)†

Discount The amount by which a preferred stock or bond may sell below its par value. Also used as a verb to mean "takes into account" as the price of the stock has discounted the expected dividend cut. (See: *Premium.*)†

Discount rate [1]The interest rate used in the discounting process; sometimes called *capitalization rate.**

[2]The interest rate at which eligible depository institutions may borrow funds, usually for short periods, directly from the Federal Reserve Banks. The law requires the board of directors of each Reserve Bank to establish the discount rate every 14 days subject to the approval of the Board of Governors.¶

Discounted cash flow techniques Methods of ranking investment proposals. Included are (1) internal rate of return method, (2) net present value method, and (3) profitability index or benefit/cost ratio.*

Discounting The process of finding the present value of a series of future cash flows. Discounting is the reverse of compounding.*

Discounting of accounts receivable Short-term financing where accounts receivable are used to secure the loan. The lender does not *buy* the accounts receivable but simply uses them as collateral for the loan. Also called *assigning accounts receivable.**

Discretionary account An account in which the customer gives the broker or someone else discretion, which may be complete or within specific limits, either to the purchases, or sale of securities or commodities including selection, timing, amount, and price to be paid or received.†

Diversification Spreading investments among different companies in different fields. Another type of diversification is also offered by the securities of many individual companies because of the wide range of their activities. (See: *Investment trust.*)†

Dividend The payment designed by the board of directors to be distributed pro rata among the shares outstanding. On preferred shares, it is generally a fixed amount. On common shares, the dividend varies with the fortunes of the company and the amount of cash on hand, and may be omitted if business is poor or the directors determine to withhold earnings to invest in plant and equipment. Sometimes a company will pay a dividend out of past earnings even if it is not currently operating at a profit.†

Dividend yield The ratio of the current dividend to the current price of a share of stock.*

Dollar bond A bond that is quoted and traded in dollars rather than in terms of yield.**

Dollar cost averaging A system of buying securities at regular intervals with a fixed dollar amount. Under this system the investor buys by the dollars' worth rather than by the number of shares. If each investment is of the same number of dollars, payments buy more when the price is low and fewer when it rises. Thus temporary downswings in price benefit the investor if he continues periodic purchases in both good times and bad and the price at which the shares are sold is more than their average cost. (See: *Formula investing.*)†

Double-barrelled bond A bond secured by the pledge of two or more sources of repayment, e.g., secured by taxes as well as revenues.**

Double exemption Refers to securities that are exempt from state as well as Federal income taxes.**

Double taxation Short for *double taxation of dividends.* The federal government taxes corporate profits once as corporate income; any part of the remaining profits distributed as dividends to stockholders may be taxed again as income to the recipient stockholder.†

Dow theory A theory of market analysis based upon the performance of the Dow-Jones industrial and transportation stock price averages. The theory says that the market is in a basic upward trend if one of these averages advances above a previous important high, accompanied or followed by a similar advance in the other. When the averages both dip below previous important lows, this is regarded as confirmation of a basic downward trend. The theory does not attempt to predict how long either trend will continue, although it is widely misinterpreted as a method of forecasting future action.†

Down tick (See: *Up tick.*)

Dow theory A theory of market analysis based upon the performance of the Dow Jones industrial and transportation stock price averages. The Theory says that the market is in a basic upward trend if one of these averages advances above a previous important high, accompanied or followed by a similar advance in the other. When the averages both dip below previous important lows, this is regarded as confirmation of a downward trend. The Dow Jones is one type of market index. (See: *NYSE Composite Index.*)††

Earnings report A statement—also called an *income statement*—issued by a company showing its earnings or losses over a given period. The earnings report lists the income earned, expenses, and the net result. (See: *Balance sheet.*)†

EBIT Acronym for *earnings before interest and taxes.**

Economical ordering quantity (EOQ) The optimum (least cost) quantity of merchandise which should be ordered.*

EPS Acronym for *earnings per share.**

Equipment trust certificate A type of security, generally issued by a railroad, to pay for new equipment. Title to the equipment, such as a locomotive, is held by a trustee until the notes are paid off. An equipment trust certificate is usually secured by a first claim on the equipment.†

Equity The net worth of a business, consisting of capital stock, capital (or paid-in) surplus, earned surplus (or retained earnings), and occasionally, certain net worth reserves. *Common equity* is that part of the total net worth belonging to the common stockholders. *Total equity* would include preferred stockholders. The terms *common stock, net worth,* and *common equity* are frequently used interchangeably.†

Exchange acquisition A method of filling an order to buy a large block of stock on the floor of the exchange. Under certain circumstances, a member-broker can facilitate the purpose of a block by soliciting orders to sell. All orders to sell the security are lumped together and crossed with the buy order in the regular action market. The price to the buyer may be on a net basis or on a commission basis.†

Exchange distribution A method of selling large blocks of stock on the floor of the exchange. Under certain circumstances, a member-broker can facilitate the sale of a block of stock by soliciting and getting other member-brokers to solicit orders to buy. Individual buy orders are lumped together and crossed with the sell order in the regular auction market. A special commission is usually paid by the seller; ordinarily the buyer pays no commission.†

Exchange rate The rate at which one currency can be exchanged for another; for example, $2.30 can be exchanged for one British pound.*

Excise tax A tax on the manufacture, sale, or consumption of specified commodities.*

Ex-dividend A synonym for "without dividend." The buyer of a stock selling ex-dividend does not receive the recently declared dividend. Every dividend is payable on a fixed date to all shareholders recorded on the books of the company as of a previous date of record. For example, a dividend may be declared as payable to holders of record on the books of the company on a given Friday. Since five business days are allowed for delivery of stock in a "regular way" transaction on the New York Stock Exchange, the Exchange would declare the stock "ex-dividend" as of the opening of the market on the preceding Monday. That means anyone who bought it on and after Monday would not be entitled to that dividend. When stocks go ex-dividend, the stock tables include the symbol "x" following the name. (See: *Cash sale, Net change, Transfer.*)†

Ex-dividend date The date on which the right to the current dividend no longer accompanies a stock. (For listed stock, the ex-dividend date is four working days prior to the date of record.)*

Exercise Action taken by an option holder that requires the writer to perform the terms of the contract.††

Exercise price The price that must be paid for a share of common stock when it is bought by exercising a warrant.*

Expected return The rate of return a firm expects to realize from an investment. The expected return is the mean value of the probability distribution of possible returns.*

Expiration date The date the option contract expires.††

Ex-rights the date on which stock purchase rights are no longer transferred to the purchaser of the stock.*

Extension An informal method of reorganization in which the creditors voluntarily postpone the date of required payment on past-due obligations.*

External funds Funds acquired through borrowing or by selling new common or preferred stock.

Extra The short form of *extra dividend.* A dividend in the form of stock or cash in addition to the regular or usual dividend the company has been paying.†

Face value The value of a bond that appears on the face of the bond, unless the value is otherwise specified by the issuing company. Face value is ordinarily the amount the issuing company promises to pay at maturity. Face value is not an indication of market value. Sometimes referred to as par value. (See: *Par.*)†

Factoring A method of financing accounts receivable under which a firm sells its accounts receivable (generally without recourse) to a financial institution (the *factor*).*

Federal funds Reserve balances that depository institutions lend each other, usually on an overnight basis. In addition, Federal funds include certain other kinds of borrowings by depository institutions from each other and from federal agencies.¶

Field warehousing A method of financing inventories in which a "warehouse" is established at the place of business of the borrowing firm.*

Financial accounting standards board (FASB) A private (nongovernment) agency which functions as an accounting standards-setting body.*

Financial intermediation Financial transactions which bring savings surplus units together with savings deficit units so that savings can be redistributed into their most productive uses.*

Financial lease A lease that does not provide for maintenance services, is not cancellable, and is fully amortized over the life of the lease.*

Financial leverage The ratio of total debt to total assets. There are other measures of financial leverage, especially ones that relate cash inflows to required cash outflows.*

Financial markets Transactions in which the creation and transfer of financial assets and financial liabilities take place.*

Financial risk That portion of total corporate risk, over and above basic business risk, that results from using debt.*

Fiscal year A corporation's accounting year. Due to the nature of their particular business, some companies do not use the calendar year for their bookkeeping. A typical example is the department store which finds December 31 too early a date to close its books after the Christmas rush. For that reason many stores wind up their accounting year January 31. Their fiscal year, therefore, runs from February 1 of one year through January 31 of the next. The fiscal year of other companies may run from July 1 through the following June 30. Most companies, though, operate on a calendar year basis.†

Fixed charges Costs that do not vary with the level of output, especially fixed financial costs such as interest, lease payments, and sinking fund payments.*

Flat income bond This term means that the price at which a bond is traded includes consideration for all unpaid accruals of interest. Bonds which are in default of interest or principal are traded flat. Income bonds, which pay interest only to the extent earned are usually traded flat. All other bonds are usually dealt in "and interest," which means that the buyer pays to the seller the market price plus interest accrued since the last payment date.†

Float The amount of funds tied up in checks that have been written but are still in process and have not yet been collected.*

Floating exchange rates Exchange rates may be fixed by government policy *(pegged)* or allowed to *float* up or down in accordance with supply and demand. When market forces are allowed to function, exchange rates are said to be floating.*

Floor The huge trading area—about two-thirds the size of a football field—where stocks and bonds are bought and sold on the New York Stock Exchange.†

Floor broker A member of the Stock Exchange who executes orders on the floor of the exchange to buy or sell any listed securities. (See: *Commission broker, Two-dollar broker.*)†

Flotation cost The cost of issuing new stocks or bonds.*

Formula investing An investment technique. One formula calls for the shifting of funds from common shares to preferred shares or bonds as the market, on average, rises above a certain predetermined point—and the return of funds to common share investments as the market average declines. (See: *Dollar cost averaging.*)†

Free and open market A market in which supply and demand are freely expressed in terms of price. Contrasts with a controlled market in which supply, demand, and price may all be regulated.†

Fundamental research Analysis of industries and companies based on factors such as sales, assets, earnings, products or services, markets, and management. As supplied to the economy, fundamental research includes consideration of gross national product, interest rates, unemployment, inventories, savings, and so on. (See: *Technical research.*)†

Funded debt Usually long-term, interest-bearing bonds or debentures of a company. Could include long-term bank loans. Does *not* include short-term loans, preferred, or common stock.†

Funding The process of replacing short-term debt with long-term securities (stocks or bonds).*

General mortgage bond A bond which is secured by a blanket mortgage on the company's property, but which may be outranked by one or more other mortgages.†

General obligation bond A bond secured by the pledge of the issuer's full faith, credit and taxing power.**

General purchasing power reporting A proposal by the FASB that the current values of nonmonetary items in financial statements be adjusted by a general price index.*

Gilt-edged High-grade bond issued by a company which has demonstrated its ability to earn a comfortable profit over a period of years and pay its bondholders their interest without interruption.†

Give up A term with many different meanings. For one, a member of the exchange on the floor may act for a second member by executing an order for him with a third member. The first member tells the third member that he is acting on behalf of the second member and "gives up" the second member's name rather than his own.††

Gold fix The setting of the price of gold by dealers (especially in an twice-daily London meeting at the central bank); the fix is the fundamental worldwide price for setting prices of gold bullion and gold-related contracts and products.††

Good delivery Certain basic qualifications must be met before a security sold on the exchange may be delivered. The security must be in proper form to comply with the contract of sale and to transfer title to the purchaser.†

Good 'til cancelled order (GTC) or open order An order to buy or sell which remains in effect until it is either executed or cancelled.†

Goodwill Intangible assets of a firm established by the excess of the price paid for the going concern over its book value.*

Government bonds Obligations of the U.S. government, regarded as the highest grade issues in existence.†

Growth stock Stock of a company with a record of growth in earnings at a relatively rapid rate.†

Guaranteed bond A bond which has interest or principal, or both, guaranteed by a company other than the issuer. Usually found in the railroad industry when large roads, leasing sections of trackage owned by small railroads, may guarantee the bonds of the smaller road.†

Guaranteed stock Usually preferred stock on which dividends are guaranteed by another company; under much the same circumstances as a bond is guaranteed.†

Hedge (See: *Arbitrage, Options, Short sale.*)

Hedging The purchase or sale of a derivative security (such as options or futures) in order to reduce or neutralize all or some portion of the risk of holding another security.††

Holding company A corporation which owns the securities of another, in most cases with voting control.†

Hurdle rate In capital budgeting, the minimum acceptable rate of return on a project. If the expected rate of return is below the hurdle rate, the project is not accepted. The hurdle rate should be the marginal cost of capital.*

Hypothecation The pledging of securities as collateral—for example, to secure the debit balance in a margin account.†

Improper accumulation Earnings retained by a business for the purpose of enabling stockholders to avoid personal income taxes.*

Inactive stock An issue traded on an exchange or in the over-the-counter market in which there is a relatively low volume of transactions. Volume may be no more than a few hundred shares a week or even less. On the New York Stock Exchange many inactive stocks are traded in 10-share units rather than the customary 100. (See: *Round lot.*)†

In-and-out Purchase and sale of the same security within a short period—a day, a week, even a month. An in-and-out trader is generally more interested in day-to-day price fluctuations than dividends or long-term growth.†

Income bond Generally income bonds promise to repay principal but to pay interest only when earned. In some cases unpaid interest on an income bond may accumulate as a claim against the corporation when the bond becomes due. An income bond may also be issued in lieu of preferred stock.†

Incremental cash flow Net cash flow attributable to an investment project.*

Incremental cost of capital The average cost of the increment of capital raised during a given year.*

Indenture A written agreement under which bonds and debentures are issued, setting forth maturity date, interest rate, and other terms.†

Independent broker Members on the floor of the NYSE who execute orders for other brokers having more business at that time than they can handle themselves, or for firms who do not have their Exchange member on the floor. Formerly known as *two-dollar brokers* from the time when these independent brokers received $2 per hundred shares for executing such orders. Their fees are paid by the commission brokers. (See: *Commission broker.*)†

Index A statistical yardstick expressed in terms of percentages of a base year or years. For instance, the Federal Reserve Board's index of industrial production is based on 1967 as 100. An index is not an average. (See: *Averages, NYSE common stock index.*)†

Industrial revenue bond A security backed by private enterprises that have been financed by a municipal issue.**

Insolvency The inability to meet maturing debt obligations.*

Institutional Investor An organization whose primary purpose is to invest its own assets or those held in trust by it for others. Includes pension funds, investment companies, insurance companies, universities, and banks.†

Interest Payments a borrower pays a lender for the use of his money. A corporation pays interest on its bonds to its bondholders. (See: *Bond, dividend.*)†

Intermarket Trading System (ITS) An electronic communications network now linking the trading floor of seven registered exchanges to foster competition among them in stocks listed on either the NYSE or AMEX and one or more regional exchanges. Through ITS, any broker or market-maker on the floor of any participating market can reach out to other participants for an execution whenever the nationwide quote shows a better price is available.††

Internal financing Funds made available for capital budgeting and working-capital expansion through the normal operations of the firm; internal financing is approximately equal to retained earnings plus depreciation.*

Internal rate of return (IRR) The rate of return on an asset investment. The internal rate of return is calculated by finding the discount rate that equates the present value of future cash flows to the cost of the investment.*

Intrinsic value [1]That value which, in the mind of the analyst, is justified by the facts. It is often used to distinguish between the *true value* of an asset (the intrinsic value) and the asset's current market price.*

[2]The dollar amount of the difference between the exercise price of an option and the current cash value of the underlying security. Intrinsic value and time value are the two components of an option premium, or price.††

Investment The use of money for the purpose of making more money, to gain income or increase capital, or both.††

Investment banker Also known as an *underwriter*. The middleman between the corporation issuing new securities and the public. The usual practice is for one or more investment bankers to buy outright from a corporation a new issue of stocks or bonds. The group forms a syndicate to sell the securities to individuals and institutions. Investment bankers also distribute very large blocks of stocks or bonds—perhaps held by an estate. (See: *Primary Distribution, Syndicate.*)††

Investment company A company or trust which uses its capital to invest in other companies. There are two principal types: the closed-end and the open-end, or mutual fund. Shares in closed-end investment companies, some of which are listed on the New York Stock Exchange, are readily transferable in the open market and are bought and sold like other shares. Capitalization of these companies remains the same unless action is taken to change, which is seldom. Open-end funds sell their own new shares to investors, stand ready to buy back their old shares, and are not listed. Open-end funds are so called because their capitalization is not fixed; they issue more shares as people want them.†

Investment counsel One whose principal business consists of acting as investment adviser and a substantial part of his business consists of rendering investment supervisory services.†

Investment tax credit Business firms can deduct as a credit against their income taxes a specified percentage of the dollar amount of new investments in each of certain categories of assets.*

IRA Individual Retirement Account. A pension plan with major tax advantages. Any worker can begin an IRA and obtain a tax deduction for cash contributions up to $2,000 annually. IRA permits investment through intermediaries like mutual funds, insurance companies and banks or directly in stocks and bonds through stockbrokers. (See: *Keogh Plan.*)††

Issue Any of a company's securities, or the act of distributing such securities.†

Issuer A municipal unit that borrows money through the sale of bonds or notes.**

Keogh Plan Tax advantaged personal retirement program that can be established by a self-employed individual. Currently, annual contributions to a plan can be up to $15,000. Such contributions and reinvestments are not taxed as they accumulate but will be when withdrawn (presumably at retirement when taxable income may be less). (See: *IRA.*)††

Legal list A list of investments selected by various states in which certain institutions and fiduciaries, such as insurance companies and banks, may invest. Legal lists are often restricted to high quality securities meeting certain specifications. (See: *Prudent Man Rule.*)††

Legal opinion An opinion concerning the legality of a bond issue usually written by a recognized law firm specializing in public borrowings.**

Leverage The effect on a company when the company has bonds, preferred stock, or both outstanding. Example: If the earnings of a company with 1,000,000 common shares increases from $1,000,000 to $1,500,000—earnings per share would go from $1 to $1.50, or an increase of 50 percent. But if earnings of a company that had to pay $500,000 in bond interest increased that much—earnings per common share would jump from 50 cents to $1 a share, or 100 percent.††

Leverage factor The ratio of debt to total assets.*

Liabilities All the claims against a corporation. Liabilities include accounts and wages and salaries payable, dividends declared payable, accrued taxes payable, fixed or long-term liabilities such as mortgage bonds, debentures, and bank loans. (See: *Assets, balance sheet.*)†

Lien A lender's claim on assets that are pledged for a loan.*

Limit, limited order, or limited price order An order to buy or sell a stated amount of a security at a specified price, or at a better price, if obtainable after the order is represented in the Trading Crowd.†

Limited tax bond A bond secured by a pledge of a tax or group of taxes limited as to rate or amount.**

Line of credit An arrangement whereby a financial institution (bank or insurance company) commits itself to lend up to a specified maximum amount of funds during a specified period. Sometimes the interest rate on the loan is specified, at other times, it is not. Sometimes a commitment fee is imposed for obtaining the line of credit.*

Liquidation The process of converting securities or other property into cash. The dissolution of a company, with cash remaining after sale of its assets and payment of all indebtedness being distributed to the shareholders.†

Liquidity [1]Refers to a firm's cash position and its ability to meet maturing obligations.*

[2]The ability of the market in a particular

security to absorb a reasonable amount of buying or selling at reasonable price changes. Liquidity is one of the most important characteristics of a good market.†

Listed stock The stock of a company which is traded on a securities exchange. The various stock exchanges have different standards for listing. Some of the guides used by the New York Stock Exchange for an original listing are national interest in the company, a minimum of 1.1-million shares publicly held among not less than 2,000 round-lot stockholders. The publicly held common shares should have a minimum aggregate market value of $18 million. The company should have net income in the latest year of over $2.5-million before federal income tax and $2-million in each of the preceding two years.††

Load The portion of the offering price of shares of open-end investment companies in excess of the value of the underlying assets which cover sales commissions and all other costs of distribution. The load is usually incurred only on purchase, there being, in most cases, no charge when the shares are sold (redeemed).†

Lock-box plan A procedure used to speed up collections and to reduce float.*

Locked in An investor is said to be locked in when he had a profit on a security he owns but does not sell because his profit would immediately become subject to the capital gains tax. (See: *Capital gain.*)†

Long Signifies ownership of securities: "I am long 100 U.S. Steel" means the speaker owns 100 shares. (See: *Short position, short sale.*)†

Management The board of directors, elected by the stockholders, and the officers of the corporation, appointed by the board of directors.†

Manipulation An illegal operation. Buying or selling a security for the purpose of creating a false or misleading appearance of active trading or for the purpose of raising or depressing the price to induce purchase or sale by others.†

Margin The amount paid by the customer when using a broker's credit to buy or sell a security. Under Federal Reserve regulations, the initial margin required since 1945 has ranged from the current rate 50 percent of the purchase price up to 100 percent. (See: *Brokers' loans, Equity, Margin call.*)††

Margin call A demand upon a customer to put up money or securities with the broker. The call is made when a purchase is made; also if a customer's equity in a margin account declines below a minimum standard set by the exchange or by the firm. (See: *Margin.*)†

Margin—profit on sales The *profit margin* is the percentage of profit after tax to sales.*

Marginal cost The cost of an additional unit. The marginal cost of capital is the cost of an additional dollar of new funds.*

Marginal efficiency of capital A schedule showing the internal rate of return on investment opportunities.*

Marginal revenue The additional gross revenue produced by selling one additional unit of output.*

Marketability The measure of the ease with which a security can be sold in the secondary market.**

Market order An order to buy or sell a stated amount of a security at the most advantageous price obtainable after the order is represented in the trading crowd. (See: *Good 'til cancelled order, Limit order, Stop order.*)††

Market price In the case of a security, market price is usually considered the last reported price at which the stock or bond sold.†

Maturity The date on which a loan or a bond or debenture comes due and is to be paid off.†

Member corporation A securities brokerage firm, organized as a corporation, with at least one member of the New York Stock Exchange, who is an officer or an employee of the corporation.††

Member firm A securities brokerage firm organized as a partnership and having at least one general partner who is a member of the New York Stock Exchange, Inc. (See: *Member corporation.*)†

Member organization This term includes New York Stock Exchange Member Firm *and* Member Corporation. (See: *Member corporation, Member firm.*)†

Merger Any combination that forms one company from two or more previously existing companies.*

Money market Financial markets in which funds are borrowed or lent for short periods (i.e., less than one year). (The money market is distinguished from the capital market, which is the market for long-term funds.)*

Mortgage A pledge of designated property as security for a loan.*

Mortgage bond A bond secured by a mortgage on a property. The value of the property may or may not equal the value of the bonds issued against it. (See: *Bond, Debenture.*)††

Municipal bond A bond issued by a state or a political subdivision, such as county, city, town, or village. The term also designates bonds issued by state agencies and authorities. In general, interest paid on municipal bonds is exempt from federal income taxes and state and local income taxes within the state of issue.†

Mutual fund (See: *Investment company.*)

Naked option An option position that is *not* offset by an equal and opposite position in the underlying security.††

NASD The National Association of Securities Dealers, Inc. An association of brokers and dealers in the over-the-counter securities business.††

NASDAQ An automated information network which provides brokers and dealers with price quotations on securities traded over-the-counter. NASDAQ is an acronym for National Association of Securities Dealers Automated Quotations.†

Negotiable Refers to a security, title to which is transferable by delivery. (See: *Good delivery.*)†

Negotiable Order of Withdrawal account An interest earning account on which checks may be drawn. Withdrawals from NOW accounts may be subject to a 14-day or more notice requirement although such is rarely imposed. NOW accounts may be offered by commercial banks, mutual savings banks, and savings and loan associations and may be owned only by individuals and certain nonprofit organizations and governmental units.¶

Net asset value Usually used in connection with investment companies to mean net asset value per share. An investment company computes its assets daily, or even twice daily, by totaling the market value of all securities owned. All liabilities are deducted, and the balance divided by the number of shares outstanding. The resulting figure is the net asset value per share. (See: *Assets, Investment Company.*)††

Net change The change in the price of a security from the closing price on one day and the closing price on the following day on which the stock is traded. The net change is ordinarily the last figure on the stock price list. The mark + 1⅛ means up $1.125 a share from the last sale on the previous day the stock traded.†

Net debt Gross debt less sinking fund accumulations and all self-supporting debt.**

Net present value (NPV) method A method of ranking investment proposals. The NPV is equal to the present value of future returns, discounted at the marginal cost of capital, minus the present value of the cost of the investment.*

Net worth The capital and surplus of a firm—capital stock, capital surplus (paid-in capital), earned surplus (retained earnings), and, occasionally, certain reserves. For some purposes, preferred stock is included; generally, net worth refers only to the common stockholders' position.*

New housing authority bonds A bond issued by a local public housing authority to finance public housing. It is backed by Federal funds and the solemn pledge of the U.S. Government that payment will be made in full.**

New issue A stock or bond sold by a corporation for the first time. Proceeds may be issued to retire outstanding securities of the company, for new plant or equipment, or for additional working capital, or to acquire a public ownership interest in the company for private owners.††

New York Futures Exchange (NYFE) A subsidiary of the New York Stock Exchange devoted to the trading of futures products.††

New York Stock Exchange (NYSE) The largest organized securities market in the United States, founded in 1792. The Exchange itself does not buy, sell, own, or set the prices of securities traded there. The prices are determined by public supply and demand. The Exchange is a not-for-profit corporation of 1,366 individual members, governed by a Board of Directors consisting of 10 public representatives, 10 Exchange members or allied members and a full-time chairman, executive vice chairman and president.††

New issue market Market for new issues of municipal bonds and notes.**

Nominal interest rate The contracted or stated interest rate, undeflated for price-level changes.*

Noncumulative A type of preferred stock on which unpaid dividends do not accrue. Omitted dividends are, as a rule, gone forever. (See: *Cumulative preferred.*)††

Normal probability distribution A symmetrical, bell-shaped probability function.*

Notes Short-term unsecured promises to pay specified amounts of money. For municipal notes maturities generally range from six to twelve months.**

NYSE composite index A composite index covering price movements of all common stocks listed on the "Big Board." It is based on the close of the market December 31, 1965 as 50.00 and is weighted according to the number of shares listed for each issue. The index is computed continuously and printed on the ticker tape each half hour. Point changes in the index are converted to dollars and cents so as to provide a meaningful measure of changes in the average price of listed stocks. The composite index is supplemented by separate indexes for four industry groups: industries, transportation, utilities, and finances. (See: *Averages.*)††

Odd lot An amount of stock less than the established 100-share unit. (See: *Round lot.*)††

Off-board This term may refer to transactions over-the-counter in unlisted securities, or to a transaction involving listed shares that is not executed on a national securities exchange.††

Offer The price at which a person is ready to sell. Opposed to bid, the price at which one is ready to buy. (See: *Bid and asked.*)†

Official statement Document prepared by or for the issuer that gives in detail the security and financial information about the issue.**

Open interest In options and futures trading, the number of outstanding option contracts, at a given point in time, which have not been exercised and have not yet reached expiration.††

Open order (See: *Good 'til cancelled order.*)

Open-end investment company (See: *Investment company.*)

Operating leverage The extent to which fixed costs are used in a firm's operation. Break-even analysis is used to measure the extent to which operating leverage is employed.*

Opportunity cost The rate of return on the best *alternative* investment that is available. It is the highest return that will *not* be earned if the funds are invested in a particular project. For example, the opportunity cost of *not* investing in bond A yielding 8 percent might be 7.99 percent, which could be earned on bond B.*

Option A right to buy (call) or sell (put) a fixed amount of a given stock at a specified price within a limited period of time. The purchaser hopes that the stock's price will go up (a call) or down (a put) by an amount sufficient to provide a profit when the stock is sold. If the stock price holds steady or moves in the opposite direction, the price paid for the option is lost entirely. There are several other types of options available to the public but these are basically combinations of puts and calls. Individuals may write (sell) as well as purchase options. Options are also traded on stock indexes, futures, and debt instruments.††

Orders good until a specified time A market or limited price order which is to be represented in the Trading Crowd until a specified time, after which such order or the portion thereof not executed is to be treated as cancelled.†

Ordinary income Income from the normal operations of a firm. Operating income specifically excludes income from the sale of capital assets.*

Organized security exchanges Formal organizations having tangible, physical locations. Organized exchanges conduct an auction market in designated ("listed") investment securities. For example, the New York Stock Exchange is an organized exchange.*

Overbought An opinion as to price levels. May refer to a security which has had a sharp rise or to the market as a whole after a period of vigorous buying, which it may be argued, has left prices "too high."†

Overdraft system A system where a depositor may write checks in excess of his balance, with his bank automatically extending a loan to cover the shortage.*

Oversold The reverse of overbought. A single security or a market which, it is believed, has declined to an unreasonable level.††

Over-the-counter A market for securities made up of securities dealers who may or may not be members of a securities exchange. The over-the-counter market is conducted over the telephone and deals mainly with stocks of companies without sufficient shares, stockholders, or earnings to warrant listing on an exchange. Over-the-counter dealers may act either as principals or as brokers for customers. The over-the-counter market is the principal market for bonds of all types. (See: *NASD, NASDAQ.*)††

Paper profit (LOSS) An unrealized profit or loss on a security still held. Paper profits and losses become realized profits only when the security is sold. (See: *Profit taking.*)††

Par In the case of a common share, par means a dollar amount assigned to the share by the company's charter. Par value may also be used to compute the dollar amount of the common shares on the balance sheet. Par value has little relationship to the market value of common stock. Many companies issue no-par stock but give a stated per share value on the balance sheet. In the case of preferred stocks, it signifies the dollar value upon which dividends are figured. With bonds, par value is the face amount, usually $1,000.††

Par value The nominal or face value of stock or bond.*

Participating preferred A preferred stock which is entitled to its stated dividend and, also, to additional dividends on a specified basis upon payment of dividends on the common stock.†

Passed dividend Omission of a regular or scheduled dividend.†

Payback period The length of time required for the net revenues of an investment to return the cost of the investment.*

Paying agent Place where principal and interest is payable. Usually a designated bank or the treasurer's office of the issuer.**

Payout ratio The percentage of earnings paid out in the form of dividends.*

Pegging A market stabilization action taken by the manager of an underwriting group during the offering of new securities. He does this by continually placing order to buy at a specified price in the market.*

Penny stocks Low-priced issues often highly speculative, selling at less than $1 a share. Frequently used as a term of disparagement, although a few penny stocks have developed into investment-caliber issues.†

Perpetuity A stream of equal future payments expected to continue forever.*

Pledging of accounts receivable Short-term borrowing from financial institutions where the loan is secured by accounts receivable. The lender may physically take the accounts receivable but typically has recourse to the borrower; also called *discounting of accounts receivable.**

Point In the case of shares of stock, a point means $1. If ABC shares rises 3 points, each share has risen $3. In the case of bonds a point means $10, since a bond is quoted as a percentage of $1,000. A bond which rises 3 points gains 3 percent of $1,000, or $30 in value. An advance from 87 to 90 would mean an advance in dollar value from $870 to $900. In the case of market averages, the word point means merely that and no more. If, for example, the NYSE Composite Index rises from 90.25 to 91.25, it has risen a point. A point in this average, however, is not equivalent to $1. (See: *Indexes.*)††

Pooling of interest An accounting method for combining the financial statements of firms that merge. Under the pooling-of-interest procedure, the assets of the merged firms are simply added to form the balance sheet of the surviving corporation. This method is different from the "purchase" method, where goodwill is put on the balance sheet to reflect a premium (or discount) paid in excess of book value.*

Portfolio Holdings of securities by an individual or institution. A portfolio may contain bonds, preferred stocks, common stocks and other securities.††

Portfolio effect The extent to which the variation in returns on a combination of assets (a "portfolio") is less than the sum of the variations of the individual assets.*

Portfolio theory Deals with the selection of optimal portfolios; that is, portfolios that provide the highest possible return for any specified degree of risk.*

Preemptive right A provision contained in the corporate charter and by laws that gives holders of common stock the right to purchase on a pro rata basis new issues of common stock (or securities convertible into common stock.)*

Preferred stock A class of stock with a claim on the company's earnings before payment may be made on the common stock and usually entitled to priority over common stock if the company liquidates. Usually entitled to dividends at a specified rate—when declared by the board of directors and before payment of a dividend on the common stock—depending upon the terms of the issue. (See: *Cumulative preferred, Participating preferred.*)†

Premium The amount by which a bond or preferred stock, may sell above its par value. For options, the price that the buyer pays the writer for an option contract ("option premium") is synonymous with "the price of an option." (See: *Discount.*)††

Present value (PV) The value today of a future payment, or stream of payments, discounted at the appropriate discount rate.*

Price-earnings ratio A popular way to compare stocks selling at various price levels. The PE ratio is the price of a share of stock divided by earnings per share for a twelve-month period. For example, a stock selling for $50 a share and earning $5 a share is said to be selling at a price-earnings ratio of 10.††

Primary distribution Also called primary offering. The original sale of a company's securities. (See: *Investment banker.*)††

Primary market Market for new issues of securities.

Prime rate The lowest interest rate charged by commercial banks to their most credit-worthy and largest corporate customers; other interest rates, such as personal, automobile, commercial and financing loans are often pegged to the prime.††

Principal The person for whom a broker executes an order, or dealers buying or selling for their own accounts. The term *principal* may also refer to a person's capital or to the face amount of a bond.††

Productivity The amount of physical output for each unit of productive input.¶

Pro forma A projection. A *pro forma* financial statement is one that shows how the actual statement will look if certain specified assumptions are realized. *Pro forma* statements may be either future or past projections. An example of a backward *pro forma* statement occurs when two firms are planning to merge and shows what their consolidated financial statements would have looked like if they had been merged in preceding years.*

Profit center A unit of a large, decentralized firm that has its own investments and for which a rate of return on investment can be calculated.*

Profit margin The ratio of profits after taxes to sales.*

Profitability index (PI) The present value of future returns divided by the present value of the investment outlay.*

Profit-taking Selling stock which has appreciated in value since purchase, in order to realize the profit. The term is often used to explain a downturn in the market following a period of rising prices. (See: *Paper profit.*)††

Progressive tax A tax that requires a higher percentage payment on higher incomes. The personal income tax in the United States, which is at a rate of 14 percent on the lowest increments of income to 70 percent on the highest increments, is progressive.*

Prospectus The official selling circular that must be given to purchasers of new securities registered with the Securities and Exchange Commission. It highlights the much longer Registration Statement filed with the commission.††

Proxy Written authorization given by a shareholder to someone else to represent him and vote his shares at a shareholders' meeting.††

Proxy statement Information given to stockholders in conjunction with the solicitation of proxies.††

Prudent man rule An investment standard. In some states, the law requires that a fiduciary, such as a trustee, may invest the fund's money only in a list of securities designated by the state—the so-called legal list. In other states, the trustee may invest in a security if it is one that would be bought by a prudent man of discretion and intelligence, who is seeking a reasonable income and preservation of capital.††

Public Offering (See: *Primary Distribution.*)

Pure (or primitive) security A security that pays off $1 if one particular state of the world occurs and pays off nothing if any other state of the world occurs.*

Put An option to sell a specific security at a specified price within a designated period.*

Puts and calls (See: *Option.*)

Quote The highest bid to buy and the lowest offer to sell a security in a given market at a given time. If you ask your broker for a "quote" on a stock, he may come back with something like "45¼ to 45½." This means that $45.25 is the highest price any buyer wanted to pay at the time the quote was given on the floor of the exchange and that $45.50 was the lowest price which any seller would take at the same time. (See: *Bid and asked.*)††

Rally A brisk rise following a decline in the general price level of the market, or in an individual stock.†

Rate of return The internal rate of return on an investment.*

Ratings Designations used by investors' services to give relative indications of quality.**

Record date The date on which you must be registered as a shareholder of a company in order to receive a declared dividend or, among other things, to vote on company affairs. (See: *Ex dividend, Transfer.*)††

Recourse arrangement A term used in connection with accounts-receivable financing. If a firm sells its accounts receivable to a financial institution under a recourse agreement, then, if the accounts receivable cannot be collected, the selling firm must repurchase the account from the financial institution.*

Redemption price The price at which a bond may be redeemed before maturity, at the option of the issuing company. Redemption value also applies to the price of the company must pay to call in certain types of preferred stock. (See: *Callable.*)†

Red Herring (See: *Prospectus.*)

Rediscount rate The rate of interest at which a bank may borrow from a Federal Reserve Bank.*

Refinancing Same as refunding. New securities are sold by a company and the money is used to retire existing securities. Object may be to save interest costs, extend the maturity of the loan, or both.*

Refunding Sale of new debt securities to replace an old debt issue.*

Registered bond A bond which is registered on the books of the issuing company in the name of the owner. It can be transferred only when endorsed by the registered owner. (See: *Bearer bond, Coupon bond.*)†

Registered representative The man or woman who serves the investor customers of a broker/dealer. In a New York Stock Exchange Member Organization, a Registered Representative must meet the requirements of the exchange as to background and knowledge of the securities business. Also known as an Account Executive or Customer's broker.††

Registrar Usually a trust company or bank charged with the responsibility of keeping a record of the owners of corporation's securities and preventing the issuance of more than the authorized amount. (See: *Transfer.*)††

Registration Before a public offering may be made of new securities by a company, or of outstanding securities by controlling stockholders—through the mails or in interstate commerce—the securities must be registered under the Securities Act of 1933. A statement is filed with the SEC by the issuer. It must disclose pertinent information relating to the company's operations, securities, management and purpose of the public offering.

Before a security may be admitted to dealings on a national securities exchange, it must be registered under the Securities Exchange Act of 1934. The application for registration must be filed with the exchange and the SEC by the company issuing the securities.††

Regression analysis A statistical procedure for predicting the value of one variable (dependent variable) on the basis of knowledge about one or more other variables (independent variables).*

Regulation T The federal regulation governing the amount of credit which may be advanced by brokers and dealers to customers for the purchase of securities. (See: *Margin.*)†

Regulation U The federal regulation governing the amount of credit which may be advanced by a bank to its customers for the purchase of listed stocks. (See: *Margin.*)†

Reinvestment rate The rate of return at which cash flows from an investment are reinvested. The reinvestment rate may or may not be constant from year to year.*

REIT Real Estate Investment Trust, an organization similar to an investment company in some respects but concentrating its holdings in real estate investments. The yield is generally liberal since REIT's are required to distribute as much as 90 percent of their income. (See: *Investment company.*)†

Reorganization When a financially troubled firm goes through reorganization, its assets are restated to reflect their current market value, and its financial structure is restated to reflect any changes on the asset side of the statement. Under a reorganizations the firm continues in existence; this is contrasted to bankruptcy, where the firm is liquidated and ceases to exist.*

Replacement-cost accounting A requirement under SEC release no. 190 (1976) that large companies disclose the replacement costs of inventory items and depreciable plant.*

Repurchase agreements When the Federal Reserve makes a repurchase agreement with a government securities dealer, it buys a security for immediate delivery with an agreement to sell the security back at the same price by a specific date (usually within 15 days) and receives interest at a specific rate. This arrangement allows the Federal Reserve to inject reserves into the banking system on a temporary basis to meet a temporary need and to withdraw these reserves as soon as that need has passed.¶

Required rate of return The rate of return that stockholders expect to receive on common stock investments.*

Residual value The value of leased property at the end of the lease term.*

Retained earnings That portion of earnings not paid out in dividends. The figure that appears on the balance sheet is the sum of the retained earnings for each year throughout the company's history.*

Return (See: *Yield.*)

Revenue bond A bond payable from revenues derived from tolls, charges, or rents paid by users of the facility constructed from the proceeds of the bond issue.**

Rights When a company wants to raise more funds by issuing additional securities, it may give its stockholders the opportunity, ahead of others, to buy the new securities in proportion to the number of shares each owns. The piece of paper evidencing this privilege is called a right. Because the additional stock is usually offered to stockholders below the current market price, rights ordinarily have a market value of their own and are actively traded. In most cases they must be exercised within a relatively short period. Failure to exercise or sell rights may result in actual loss to the holder. (See: *Warrant.*)†

Rights offering A securities flotation offered to existing stockholders.*

Risk The probability that actual future returns will be below expected returns. It is measured by standard deviation or coefficient of variation of expected returns.*

Risk-adjusted discount rates The discount

rate applicable for a particular risky (uncertain) stream of income: the riskless rate of interest plus a risk premium appropriate to the level of risk attached to the particular income stream.*

Risk premium The difference between the required rate of return on a particular risky asset and the rate of return on a riskless asset with the same expected life.*

Risk-return trade-off function (See *Security market line.*)

Round lot A unit of trading or a multiple thereof. On the NYSE the unit of trading is generally 100 shares in stocks and $1,000 or $5,000 par value in the case of bonds. In some inactive stocks, the unit of trading is ten shares. (See: *Odd Lot.*)††

Sale and leaseback An operation whereby a firm sells land, buildings, or equipment to a financial institution and simultaneously executes an agreement to lease the property back for a specified period under specific terms.*

Salvage value The value of a capital asset at the end of a specified period. It is the current market price of an asset being considered for replacement in a capital budgeting problem.*

Scale order An order to buy (or sell) a security which specifies the total amount to be bought (or sold) and the amount to be bought (or sold) at specified price variations.†

Seat A traditional figure-of-speech for a membership on an exchange.††

SEC The Securities and Exchange Commission, established by Congress to help protect investors. The SEC administers the Securities Act of 1933, the Securities Exchange Act of 1934, the Securities Act Amendments of 1975, the Trust Indenture Act, the Investment Company Act, the Investment Advisers Act, and the Public Utility Holding Company Act.†

Secondary distribution Also known as a secondary offering. The redistribution of a block of stock, sometimes after it has been sold by the issuing company. The sale is handled off the NYSE by a securities firm or group of firms and the shares are usually offered at a fixed price related to the current market price of the stock. Usually the block is a large one, such as might be involved in the settlement of an estate. The security may be listed or unlisted. (See: *Investment banker, Primary distribution.*)††

Secondary market Market for issues previously offered or sold.**

Securities and Exchange Commission (See *SEC.*)

Securities, junior Securities that have lower priority in claims on assets and income than other securities *(senior securities).* For example, preferred stock is junior to debentures, but debentures are junior to mortgage bonds. Common stock is the most junior of all corporate securities.*

Securities, senior Securities having claims on income and assets that rank higher than certain other securities *(junior securities).* For example, mortgage bonds are senior debentures, but debentures are senior to common stock.*

Security market line A graphic representation of the relation between the required return on a security and the product of its risk times a normalized market measure of risk. Risk-return relationships for individual securities or investments.*

Self-supporting debt Debt incurred for a project or enterprise requiring no tax support other than the specific tax or revenue earmarked for that purpose.*

Seller's option A special transaction on the NYSE which gives the seller the right to deliver the stock or bond at any time within a specified period, ranging from not less than 6 business days to not more than 60 days.††

Selling group A group of stock brokerage firms formed for the purpose of distributing a new issue of securities; part of the investment banking process.*

Sensitivity analysis Simulation analysis in which key variables are changed and the resulting change in the rate of return is observed. Typically, the rate of return will be more sensitive to changes in some variables than it will in others.*

Serial bond An issue which matures in part at periodic stated intervals.†

Service lease A lease under which the lessor maintains and services the asset.*

Settlement Conclusion of a securities transaction when a customer pays a broker/dealer for securities purchased or delivers securities sold and receives from the broker the proceeds of a sale. (See: *Regular Way Delivery, Cash Sale.*)††

Short covering Buying stock to return stock previously borrowed to make delivery on a short sale.†

Short position Stocks, options, or futures sold short and not covered as of a particular date. On the NYSE, a tabulation is issued once a month listing all issues on the Exchange in which there was a short position of 5,000 or more shares and issues in which the short position had changed by 2,000 or more shares in the preceding month. Short position also means the total amount of stock an individual has sold short and has not covered, as of a particular date.††

Short sale A transaction by a person who believes a security will decline and sells it, though the person does not own any. For instance: You instruct your broker to sell short 100 shares of XYZ. Your broker borrows the stock so delivery of the 100 shares can be made to the buyer. The money value of the shares borrowed is deposited by your broker with the lender. Sooner or later you must cover your short sale by buying the same amount of stock you borrowed for return to the lender. If you are able to buy XYZ at a lower price than you sold it for, your profit is the difference between the two prices—not counting commissions and taxes. But if you have to pay more for the stock than the price you received, that is the amount of your loss. Stock exchange and federal regulations govern and limit the conditions under which a short sale may be made on a national securities exchange. Sometimes people will sell short a stock they already owns in order to protect a paper profit. This is known as selling short against the box.††

Sinking fund Money regularly set aside by a company to redeem its bonds, debentures or preferred stock from time to time as specified in the indenture or charter.††

SIPC Securities Investor Protection Corporation, which provides funds for use, if necessary, to protect customers' cash and securities which may be on deposit with a SIPC member firm in the event the firm fails and is liquidated under the provisions of the SIPC Act. SIPC is not a government agency. It is a nonprofit membership corporation created, however, by an act of Congress.†

Special bid A method of filling an order to buy a large block of stock on the floor of the New York Stock Exchange. In a special bid, the bidder for the block of stock—a pension fund, for instance, will pay a special commission to the broker who represents him in making the purchase. The seller does not pay a commission. The special bid is made on the floor of the exchange at a fixed price which may not be below the last sale of the security or the current bid in the regular market, whichever is higher. Member firms may sell this stock for customers directly to the buyer's broker during trading hours.†

Special offering Opposite of special bid. A notice is printed on the ticker tape announcing the stock sale at a fixed price usually based on the last transaction in the regular auction market. If there are more buyers than stock, allotments are made. Only the seller pays the commission. (See: *Secondary distribution.*)†

Special tax bond A bond secured by a special tax, such as a gasoline tax.**

Specialist A member of the New York Stock Exchange, Inc., who has two functions: First, to maintain an orderly market in the securities registered to the specialist. In order to maintain an orderly market, the Exchange expects specialists to buy or sell for the own account, to a reasonable degree, when there is a temporary disparity between supply and demand. Second, the specialist acts as a broker's broker. When a commission broker on the Exchange floor receives a limit order, say, to buy at $50 a stock then selling at $60—he cannot wait at the post where the stock is traded to see if the price reaches the specified level. So he leaves the order with the specialist, who will try to execute it in the market if and when the stock declines to the specified price. At all times the specialist must put his customers' interests above his own. There are about 400 specialists on the NYSE. (See: *Limited Order.*)††

Speculation The employment of funds by a speculator. Safety of principal is a secondary factor. (See: *Investment.*)†

Speculator One who is willing to assume a relatively large risk in the hope of gain.††

Spin off The separation of a subsidiary or division of a corporation from its parent by issuing shares in a new corporate entity. Shareowners in the parent receive shares in the new company in proportion to their original holding and the total value remains approximately the same.††

Split The division of the outstanding shares of a corporation into a larger number of shares. A 3-for-1 split by a company with 1 million shares outstanding results in 3 million shares outstanding. Each holder of 100 shares before the 3-for-1 split would have 300 shares, although his proportionate equity in the company would remain the same; 100 parts of 1 million are the equivalent of 300 parts of 3 million. Ordinarily splits must be voted by directors and approved by shareholders. (See: *Stock dividends.*)

Standard deviation A statistical term that measures the variability of a set of observations from the mean of the distribution (σ.)*

State-preference model A framework in which decisions are based on probabilities of payoffs under alternative states of the world.*

Stock ahead Sometimes an investor who has entered an order to buy or sell a stock at a certain price will see transactions at that price reported on the ticker tape while his own order has not been executed. The reason is that other buy and sell orders at the same price came in to the specialist ahead of his and had priority. (See: *Book, Specialist.*)†

Stock dividend A dividend paid in securities rather than cash. The dividend may be additional shares of the issuing company, or shares of another company (usually a subsidiary) held by the company.††

Stock split An accounting action to increase the number of shares outstanding; for example, in a 3-for-1 split, shares outstanding would be tripled and each stockholder would be tripled and each stockholder would receive three new shares for each one formerly held. Stock splits involve no transfer from surplus to the capital account.*

Stockholder of record A stockholder whose name is registered on the books of the issuing corporation.†

Stock Index Futures Futures contracts based on market indexes, e.g., NYSE Composite Index Futures Contracts.††

Stop limit order A stop order which becomes a limit order after the specified stop price has been reached. (See: *Limit order, Stop order.*)†

Stop order An order to buy at a price above or sell at a price below the current market. Stop buy orders are generally used to limit loss or protect unrealized profits on a short sale. Stop sell orders are generally used to protect unrealized profits or limit loss on a holding. A stop order becomes a market order when the stock sells at or beyond the specified price and, thus, may not necessarily be executed at that price.†

Stopped stock A service performed—in most cases by the specialist—for an order given him by a commission broker. Let's say XYZ just sold at $50 a share. Broker A comes along with an order to buy 100 shares at the market. The lowest offer is $50.50. Broker A believes he can do better for his client than $50.50, perhaps might get the stock at $50.25. But he doesn't want to take a chance that he'll miss the market—that is, the next sale might be $50.50 and the following one even higher. So he asks the specialist if he will stop 100 at ½ ($50.50). The specialist agrees. The specialist guarantees Broker A he will get 100 shares at 50½ if the stock sells at that price. In the meantime, if the specialist or broker A succeeds in executing the order at $50.25, the stop is called off. (See: *Specialist.*)†

Street name Securities held in the name of a broker instead of his customer's name are said to be carried in a *street name.* This occurs when the securities have been bought on margin or when the customer wishes the security to be held by the broker.†

Subdivision Any legal and authorized political entity under a state's jurisdiction (county, city, water district, school district, etc.).**

Subjective probability distributions Probability distributions determined through subjective procedures without the use of statistics.*

Subordinated debenture A bond having a claim on assets only after the senior debt has been paid off in the event of liquidation.*

Subscription price The price at which a security may be purchased in a rights offering.*

Switch order or contingent order An order for the purchase (sale) of one stock and the sale (purchase) of another stock at a stipulated price difference.†

Swapping Selling one security and buying a similar one almost at the same time to take a loss, usually for tax purposes.††

Switching Selling one security and buying another.†

Syndicate A group of investment bankers who together underwrite and distribute a new issue of securities or a large block of an outstanding issue.†

Synergy A situation where "the whole is greater than the sum of its parts"; in a synergistic merger, the postmerger earnings exceed the sum of the separate companies' premerger earnings.*

Systematic risk That part of a security's risk that cannot be eliminated by diversification.*

Take-over The acquiring of one corporation by another—usually in a friendly merger but sometimes marked by a "proxy fight." In "unfriendly" take-over attempts, the potential buying company may offer a price well above current market values, new securities, and other inducements to stockholders. The management of the subject company might ask for a better price or fight the take-over or merger with another company. (See: *Proxy.*)†

Tangible assets Physical assets as opposed to intangible assets such as goodwill and the stated value of patents.*

Tax base The total resources available for taxation.**

Tax-exempt bond Another name for a municipal bond. The interest on a municipal bond is presently exempt from Federal income tax.**

Tax shelter A medium or process intended to reduce or eliminate the tax burden of an individual. They range from such conventional ones as tax-exempt municipal securities and interest or dividend exclusion to sophisticated limited partnerships in real estate, cattle raising, equipment leasing, oil drilling, research and development activities and motion picture production.††

Technical research Analysis of the market and stocks based on supply and demand. The technician studies price movements, volume, and trends and patterns which are revealed by charting these factors, and attempts to assess the possible effect of current market action on future supply and demand for securities and individual issues. (See: *Fundamental research.*)†

Tender offer A public offer to buy shares from existing stockholders of one public corporation by another company or other organization under specified terms good for a certain time period. Stockholders are asked to "tender" (surrender) their holdings for stated value, usually at a premium above current market price, subject to the tendering of a minimum and maximum number of shares.††

Term issue An issue that has a single maturity.**

Term loan A loan generally obtained from a bank or an insurance company with a maturity greater than one year. Term loans are generally amortized.*

Thin market A market in which there are comparatively few bids to buy or offers to sell, or both. The phrase may apply to a single security or to the entire stock market. In a thin market, price fluctuations between transactions are usually larger than when the market is liquid. A thin market in a particular stock may reflect lack of interest in that issue or a limited supply of or demand for stock in the market. (See: *Bid and asked, Liquidity, Offer.*)†

Third market Trading of stock exchange listed securities in the over-the-counter market by non-exchange-member brokers.††

Time order An order which becomes a market or limited price order at a specified time.†

Time value The part of an option premium that is in excess of the intrinsic value.††

Tips Supposedly "inside" information on corporation affairs.†

Trader Individuals who buy and sell for their own accounts for short-term profit. Also, an employee of a broker/dealer or financial institution who specializes in handling purchases and sales of securities for the firm and/or its clients. (See: *Investor, Speculator.*)††

Trading floor (See: *Floor.*)

Trading market The secondary market for outstanding securities.**

Trading post One of 23 trading locations on the floor of the New York Stock Exchange at which stocks assigned to that location are bought and sold. About 75 stocks are traded at each post.†

Transfer This term may refer to two different operations. For one, the delivery of a stock certificate from the seller's broker to the buyer's broker and legal change of ownership, normally accomplished within a few days. For another, to record the change of ownership on the books of the corporation by the transfer agent. When the purchaser's name is recorded, dividends, notices of meetings, proxies, financial reports, and all pertinent literature sent by the issuer to its securities holders are mailed direct to the new owner. (See: *Registrar, Street name.*)††

Transfer agent A transfer agent keeps a record of the name of each registered shareowner, his or her address, the number of shares owned, and sees that certificates presented for transfer are properly cancelled and new certificates issued in the name of the new owner. (See: *Registrar.*)††

Treasury bills Short-term U.S. Treasury securities issued in minimum denominations of $10,000 and usually having original maturities of 3, 6, or 12 months. Investors purchase bills at prices lower than the face value of the bills; the return to the investors is the difference between the price paid for the bills and the amount received when the bills are sold or when they mature. Treasury bills are the type of security used most frequently in open market operations.¶

Treasury bonds Long-term U.S. Treasury securities usually having initial maturities of more than 10 years and issued in denominations of $1,000 or more, depending on the specific issue. Bonds pay interest semiannually, with principal payable at maturity.¶

Treasury notes Intermediate-term coupon-bearing U.S. Treasury securities having initial maturities from 1 to 10 years and issued in denominations of $1,000 or more, depending on the maturity of the issue. Notes pay interest semiannually, and the principal is payable at maturity.¶

Treasury stock Stock issued by a company, but later reacquired. It may be held in the company's treasury indefinitely, reissued to the public, or retired. Treasury stock receives no dividends, and has no vote while held by the company.††

Trust receipt An instrument acknowledging that the borrower holds certain goods in trust for the lender. Trust receipt financing is used in connection with the financing of inventories for automobile dealers, construction equipment dealers, appliance dealers, and other dealers in expensive durable goods.*

Trustee The representative of bondholders who acts in their interest and facilitates communication between them and the issuer. Typically these duties are handled by a department of a commercial bank.*

Turnover rate The volume of shares traded in a year as a percentage of total shares listed on an exchange, outstanding for an individual issue, or held in an institutional portfolio.††

Underwriter (See: *Investment banker.*)

Underwriting (1) The entire process of issuing new corporate securities. (2) The insurance function of bearing the risk of adverse price fluctuations during the period in which a new issue of stock or bonds is being distributed.*

Underwriting syndicate A syndicate of investment firms formed to spread the risk associated with the purchase and distribution of a new issue of securities. The larger the issue, the more firms typically are involved in the syndicate.*

Unlimited tax bond A bond secured by pledge of taxes that are not limited by rate or amount.**

Unlisted A security not listed on a stock exchange. (See: *Over-the-counter.*)†

Unsystematic risk That part of a security's risk associated with random events; unsystematic risk can be eliminated by proper diversification.*

Up tick A term used to designate a transaction made at a price higher than the preceding transaction. Also called a *plus-tick.* A *zero-plus* tick is a term used for a transaction at the same price as the preceding trade but higher than the preceding different price.

Conversely, a *down tick,* or *minus* tick, is a term used to designate a transaction made at a price lower than the preceding trade.

A plus sign, or a minus sign, is displayed throughout the day next to the last price of each company's stock traded at each trading post on the floor of the New York Stock Exchange. (See: *Short sale.*)†

Utility theory A body of theory dealing with the relationships among money income, utility (or "happiness"), and the willingness to accept risk.*

Value additivity principle Neither fragmenting cash flows or recombining them will affect the resulting values of the cash flows.*

Variable annuity A life insurance policy where the annuity premium (a set amount of dollars) is immediately turned into units of a portfolio of stocks. Upon retirement, the policyholder is paid according to accumulated units, the dollar value of which varies according to the performance of the stock portfolio. Its objective is to preserve, through stock investment, the purchasing value of the annuity which otherwise is subject to erosion through inflation.††

Volume The number of shares traded in a security or an entire market during a given period. Volume is usually considered on a daily basis and a daily average is computed for longer periods.†

Voting right The common stockholder's right to vote their stock in the affairs of a company. Preferred stock usually has the right to vote when preferred dividends are in default for a specified period. The right to vote may be delegated by the stockholder to another person. (See: *Cumulative voting, Proxy.*)††

Warrant A certificate giving the holder the right to purchase securities at a stipulated price within a specified time limit or perpetually. Sometimes a warrant is offered with securities as an inducement to buy. (See: *Rights.*)††

Weighted cost of capital A weighted average of the component costs of debt, preferred stock, and common equity. Also called the *composite cost of capital.**

When issued A short form of "when, as, and if issued." The term indicates a conditional transaction in a security authorized for issuance but not as yet actually issued. All "when issued" transactions are on an "if" basis, to be settled if and when the actual security is issued and the exchange or National Association of Securities Dealers rules the transactions are to be settled.†

Wire house A member firm of an exchange maintaining a communications network linking either its own branch offices, offices of correspondent firms, or a combination of such offices.†

Working capital Refers to a firm's investment in short-term assets—cash, short-term securities, accounts receivable, and inventories. *Gross working capital* is defined as a firm's total current assets. *Net working capital* is defined as current assets minus current liabilities. If the term *working capital* is used without further qualification, it generally refers to gross working capital.*

Working control Theoretically, ownership of 51 percent of a company's voting stock is necessary to exercise control. In practice—and this is particularly true in the case of a large corporation—effective control sometimes can be exerted through ownership, individually or by a group acting in concert, of less than 50 percent.†

Yield Also known as return. The dividends or interest paid by a company expressed as a percentage of the current price. A stock with a current market value of $3.20 is said to return 8 percent ($3.20 ÷ $40.00). The current yield on a bond is figured the same way.††

Yield to maturity The yield of a bond to maturity takes into account the price discount from or premium over the face amount. It is greater than the current yield when the bond is selling at a discount and less than the current yield when the bond is selling at a premium.†

Zero coupon bonds Bonds which do not convey a coupon (i.e., do not pay interest) but which are offered at a substantial discount from par value and appreciate to their full value (usually $1,000) at maturity. However, under U.S. tax law, the imputed interest is taxed as it accrues. The appeal of Zero coupon bonds is primarily for IRA and other tax sheltered retirement accounts.

Acquisition Takeover Glossary

Asset Play A firm whose underlying assets are worth substantially more (after paying off the firm's liabilities) than the market value of its stock.

Breakup value The sum of the values of the firm's assets if sold off separately.

Crown jewel option The strategem of selling off or spinning off the asset that makes the firm an attractive takeover candidate.

Four-nine position A holding of approximately 4.9% of the outstanding shares of a company. At 5%, the holder must file a form [13d] with the SEC, revealing his position. Thus, a four-nine position is about the largest position that one can quietly hold.

Black knight A potential acquirer that management opposes and would prefer to find an alternative to (i.e. a *white knight*).

Going private The process of buying back the publicly held stock so that what was heretofore a public firm becomes private.

Golden handcuffs Employment agreement that makes the departure of upper level managers very costly to them. For instance, such managers may lose very attractive stock option rights by leaving prior to their normal retirement age.

Golden handshake A provision in a preliminary agreement to be acquired in which the target firm gives the acquiring firm an option to purchase its shares or assets at attractive prices or to receive a substantial bonus if the proposed takeover does not occur.

Golden parachute Extremely generous separation payments for upper level executives that are required to be fulfilled if the firm's control shifts.

Greenmail Incentive payments to dissuade the interest of outsiders who may otherwise seek control of a firm. The payment frequently takes the form of a premium price for the outsiders' shares, coupled with an agreement from them to avoid buying more stock for a set period of time.

The firm bears the cost of the payment. The stock price generally falls after the payment and the removal of the outside threat.

In play The status of being a recognized takeover candidate.

Junk bonds High-risk, high-yield bonds that are often used to finance takeovers.

LBO A leveraged buyout. A purchase of a company financed largely by debt that is backed by the firm's own assets.

Loaded laggard A stock of a company whose assets, particularly its liquid assets, have high values relative to the stock's price.

Lockup agreement An agreement between an acquirer and target that makes the target very unattractive to any other acquirer; similar to a *golden handshake.*

PacMan defense The tactic of seeking to acquire the firm that has targeted your own firm as a takeover prospect.

Poison pill A provision in the corporate bylaws or other governance documents providing for a very disadvantageous result for a potential acquirer should its ownership position be allowed to exceed some preassigned threshold. For example, if anyone acquires more than 20% of Company A's stock, the acquirer might then have to sell $100 worth of its own stock to other shareholders at $50.

Raider A hostile outside party that seeks to take over other companies.

Scorched earth defense A tactic in which the defending company's management engages in practices that reduce their company's value to such a degree that it is no longer attractive to the potential acquirer. This ap-

---

Source: From the *AAII Journal*, American Association of *Individual Investors*, 612 North Michigan Avenue, Chicago, IL 60611. Excerpted from Ben Branch "White Knight Rescues Investors From Terminology."

proach is more often threatened than actually employed.

Shark repellant Anti-takeover provisions such as the poison pill.

Short swing profit A gain made by an insider (including anyone with more than 10% of the stock) who holds stock for less than six months. Such gains must be paid back to the company whose shares were sold.

Standstill agreement A reciprocal understanding between a company's management and an outside party that usually owns a significant minority position. Each party gives up certain rights in exchange for corresponding concessions by the other party. For example, the outside group may agree to limit its stock purchases to keep its ownership percentage below some level (for instance, 20%). In exchange, management may agree to a minority board representation by the outsider.

13d A form that must be filed with the SEC when a single investor or an associated group owns 5% or more of a company's stock. The form reveals the size of the holding and the investor's intentions.

Two-tier offer A takeover device in which a relatively high per share price is paid for controlling interest in a target and a lesser per share price is paid for the remainder.

White knight defense Finding an alternative and presumably more friendly acquirer than the present takeover threat.

White squire defense Finding an important ally to purchase a strong minority position (for example, 25%) of the potential acquisition's stock. Presumably this ally (the "white squire") will oppose and hopefully block the efforts of any hostile firm seeking to acquire the vulnerable firm.

Securities and Exchange Commission

Judiciary Plaza
450 Fifth Street, NW
Washington, DC 20549
Information: 202-272-2650
Freedom of Information Act:
202-272-7450
Filings by Registered Companies:
202-272-2624

FULL AND FAIR DISCLOSURE

The Securities Act of 1933 requires issuers of securities making public offerings of securities in interstate commerce or through the mails, directly or by others on their behalf, to file registration statements containing financial and other pertinent data about the issuer and the securities being offered. A similar requirement applies to such offerings on behalf of a controlling person of the issuer. Unless a registration statement is in effect with respect to such securities, it is unlawful to sell the securities in interstate commerce or through the mails. (There are certain limited exemptions, such as government securities, nonpublic offerings, and intrastate offerings, as well as offerings not exceeding $1,500,000 in amount, which comply with the commission's Regulation A.) The effectiveness of a registration statement may be refused or suspended after a public hearing, if the statement contains material misstatements or omissions, thus barring sale of the securities until it is appropriately amended. Registration of securities does not imply approval of the issue by the commission or that the commission has found the registration disclosures to be accurate. It does not insure investors against loss in their purchase but serves rather to provide information upon which investors may make an informed and realistic evaluation of the worth of the securities.

Persons responsible for filing false information with the commission subject themselves to the risk of fine or imprisonment or both; and persons connected with the public offering may be liable in damages to purchasers of the securities if the disclosures in the registration statement and prospectus are materially defective. Also, the above act contains antifraud provisions which apply generally to the sale of securities, whether or not registered (48 Stat. 74; 15 U.S.C. 77a et seq.).

REGULATION OF SECURITIES MARKETS AND PERSONS CONDUCTING A SECURITIES BUSINESS

The Securities Exchange Act of 1934 assigns to the commission board regulatory responsibilities over the securities markets, the self-regulatory organizations within the securities industry, and persons conducting a business in securities. The commission is directed to facilitate the establishment of a national market system for securities and a national system for the clearance and settlement of securities transactions. Securities exchanges and certain clearing agencies are required to register with the commission, and associations of brokers or dealers are permitted to register with the commission. The securities Exchange Act also provides for the

Source: This material was abstracted from the United States Government Manual.

establishment of the Municipal Securities Rulemaking Board to formulate rules for the municipal securities industry. The commission oversees the self-regulatory activities of the national securities exchanges and associations, registered clearing agencies, and the Municipal Securities Rulemaking Board. In addition, the commission regulates industry professionals, such as securities brokers and dealers, certain municipal securities professionals, and transfer agents.

The Securities Exchange Act authorizes national securities exchanges, national securities associations, clearing agencies, and the Municipal Securities Rulemaking Board to adopt rules that are designed, among other things to promote just and equitable principles of trade and to protect investors. The commission is required to approve or disapprove most proposed rules of these self-regulatory organizations and has the power to abrogate or amend existing rules of the national securities exchanges, national securities associations, and the Municipal Securities Rulemaking Board.

In addition, the commission has broad rulemaking authority over the activities of brokers, dealers, municipal securities dealers, securities information processors, and transfer agents. The commission may regulate such securities trading practices as short sales and stabilizing transactions. It may regulate the trading of options on national securities exchanges and the activities of members of exchanges who trade on the trading floors and may adopt rules governing broker-dealer sales practices in dealing with investors. The commission also is authorized to adopt rules concerning the financial responsibility of brokers and dealers and reports to be made by brokers and dealers. The Securities Exchange Act also empowers the Board of Governors of the Federal Reserve System to prescribe rules relating to the extension of credit by brokers and dealers for securities transactions. Such rules include the establishment of minimum margin requirements with respect to securities registered on national securities exchanges and certain securities traded over-the-counter (48 Stat. 881; U.S.C. 78a et seq.).

The Securities Exchange Act also requires the filing of registration applications and annual and other reports with national securities exchanges and the commission by companies whose securities are listed upon the exchanges, by companies that have assets of $3 million or more and 500 or more shareholders of record, and by companies that distributed securities pursuant to a registration statement declared effective by the commission under the Securities Act of 1933. Such applications and reports must contain financial and other data prescribed by the commission as necessary or appropriate for the protection of investors and to issue fair dealing. In addition, the solicitation of proxies, authorizations, or consents from holders of such registered securities must be made in accordance with rules and regulations prescribed by the commission. These rules provide for disclosures to securities holders of information relevant to the subject matter of the solicitation.

Disclosure of the holdings and transactions by officers, directors, and large (10 percent) holders of equity securities of companies is also required, and any and all persons who acquire more than 5 percent of certain equity securities are required to file detailed information with the commission and any exchange upon which such securities may be traded. Moreover, any person making a tender offer for certain classes of equity securities is required to file reports with the commission, if as a result of the tender offer such person would own more than 5 percent of the outstanding shares of the particular class of equity involved. The commission also is authorized to promulgate rules governing the repurchase by a corporate issuer of its own securities.

REGULATION OF MUTUAL FUNDS AND OTHER INVESTMENT COMPANIES

The Investment Company Act of 1940 provides for the registration with the commission of investment companies and subjects their activities to regulation to protect investors. The regulation covers sales and management fees, composition of boards of directors, and capital structure. Also, various transactions of investment companies, including transactions with affiliated interests, are prohibited unless the commission first determines that such transactions are fair. Under the act, the commission may institute court action to enjoin the consummation of mergers and other plans for reorganization of investment companies if such plans are unfair to security holders. It also may impose sanctions by administrative proceedings against investment company managements for violations of the act and other federal securities laws, and file court actions to enjoin acts and practices of management officials involving breaches of fiduciary duty involving personal misconduct and to disqualify such officials from office (54 Stat. 789; 15 U.S.C. 80a–1—80a–52).

REGULATION OF COMPANIES CONTROLLING ELECTRIC OR GAS UTILITIES

The Public Utility Holding Company Act of 1935 provides for regulation by the commission of the purchase and sale of securities and assets by companies in electric and gas utility holding company systems, their intra-system transactions and service and management arrangements. It limits holding companies to a single coordinated utility system and requires simplification of complex corporate and capital structures and elimination of unfair distribution of voting power among holders of system securities.

The issuance and sale of securities by holding companies and their subsidiaries, unless exempt (subject to conditions and terms which the commission is empowered to impose) as an issue expressly authorized by the state commission in the state in which the issuer is incorporated, must be found by the commission to meet statutory standards, namely: that the new security is reasonably adapted to the security structure and earning power of the issuer; that the proposed financing is necessary and appropriate to the economical and efficient operation of the company's business; that the consideration received, and fees, commissions, and other remuneration paid, are fair; and that the terms and conditions of the sale are not detrimental to investors, consumers, or the public.

The purchase and sale of utility properties and other assets may not be made in contravention of rules, regulations, or orders of the commission regarding the consideration to be received, maintenance of competitive conditions, fees and commissions, accounts, disclosure of interest, and similar matters. In passing upon proposals for reorganization, merger, or consolidation, the commission must be satisfied that the objectives of the act generally are complied with and that the terms of the proposal are fair and equitable to all classes of security holders affected (49 Stat. 803; 15 U.S.C 79–92z–6).

REGULATION OF INVESTMENT COUNSELORS AND ADVISERS

The Investment Advisers Act of 1940 provides that persons who, for compensation, engage in the business of advising others with respect to their security transactions must register with the commission. The act prohibits certain types of fee arrangements, makes unlawful practices of investment advisers involving fraud or deceit, and requires, among other things, disclosure of any adverse interests the advisers may have in transactions executed for clients. The act authorizes the commission to issue rules proscribing acts and practices that may operate as a fraud or deceit upon investors (54 Stat. 847; 15 U.S.C. 80b–1—80b–21).

REHABILITATION OF FAILING CORPORATIONS

Chapter 11, section 1109(a), of the Bankruptcy Code (92 Stat. 2629; 11 U.S.C. 1109) provides for Commission participation as a statutory party in corporate reorganization proceedings administered in Federal courts. The principal functions of the Commission are to protect the interests of public investors involved in such cases through efforts to ensure their adequate representation and to participate on legal and policy issues which are of concern to public investors generally.

INDEPENDENT REPRESENTATION OF THE INTERESTS OF HOLDERS OF DEBT SECURITIES

The interests of purchasers of publicly offered debt securities issued pursuant to trust indentures are safeguarded under the provisions of the Trust Indenture Act of 1939. This act, among other things, requires the exclusion from such indentures of certain types of exculpatory clauses and the inclusion of certain protective provisions. The independence of the indenture trustee, who is a representative of the debt holder, is assured by proscribing certain relationships that might conflict with the proper exercise of his duties (53 Stat. 1149; 15 U.S.C. 77aaa–77bbbb).

ENFORCEMENT ACTIVITIES

The commission's enforcement activities are designed to secure compliance with the federal securities laws administered by the commission and the rules and regulations adopted thereunder. These activities include measures to compel obedience to the disclosure requirements of the registration and other provisions of the acts; to prevent fraud and deception in the purchase and sale of securities; to obtain court orders enjoining acts and practices that operate as a fraud upon investors or otherwise violate the laws; to revoke the registrations of brokers, dealers, and investment advisers who willfully engage in such acts and practices; to suspend or expel from national securities exchanges or the National Association of Securities Dealers, Inc., any member or officer who has violated any provision of the federal securities laws; and to prosecute persons who have engaged in fraudulent activities, or other willful violations of those laws. In addition, attorneys or accountants who violate the securities laws face possible loss of their privilege to practice before the commission. To this end, private investigations are conducted into complaints or other evidences of securities violations. Evidence thus established of law violations in the purchase and sale of securities is used in appropriate administrative proceedings to revoke registration or in actions instituted in federal courts to restrain or enjoin such activities. Where the evidence tends to establish fraud or other willful violation of the securities laws, the facts are referred to the Attorney General for criminal prosecution of the offenders. The commission may assist in such prosecutions.

INVESTOR INFORMATION AND PROTECTION

Complaints and inquiries may be directed to the home office or to any regional office. Registration statements and other public documents filed with the commission are available for public inspection in the public reference room at the home office. Much of the information also is available in its New York, Chicago, and Los Angeles regional offices, and to a lesser extent in the other regional offices of the commission. Reproduction of the public material may be purchased from the commission as prescribed rates.

Small Business Activities Information on security laws which pertain to small businesses in relation to securities offerings may be obtained from the Commission. Phone, 202-272-2644.

Consumer Activities Publications detailing the Commission's activities, which include material of assistance to the potential investor, are available from the Publications Unit. In addition, the Office of Consumer Affairs and Information Services answers questions from investors, assists investors with specific problems regarding their relations with broker-dealers and companies, and advises the Commission and other offices and divisions regarding problems frequently encountered by investors and possible regulatory solutions to such problems. Phone, 202-272-7440.

Reading Rooms The Commission maintains a public reference room (phone, 202-272-7450) and also a library (phone, 202-272-2618) where additional information may be obtained.

Contracts Contact the Office of Administrative Services. Phone, 202-272-7000.

REGIONAL OFFICES (Securities and Exchange Commission)

Region	Address
1. New York, New Jersey	26 Federal Plaza, New York, NY 10078 Phone: 212-264-1636
2. Maine, Vermont, New Hampshire, Massachusetts, Connecticut, Rhode Island	150 Causeway Street, Boston, MA 02114 Phone: 617-223-2721
3. Tennessee, North Carolina, South Carolina, Mississippi, Alabama, Georgia, Florida, Louisiana (southeastern portion only)	1375 Peachtree Street NE, Atlanta, GA 30367 Phone: 404-881-4768
4. Minnesota, Wisconsin, Michigan, Iowa, Missouri, Illinois, Indiana, Ohio, Kentucky	219 S. Dearborn Street, Chicago, IL 60604 Phone: 312-353-7390
5. Kansas, Oklahoma, Texas, Arkansas, Louisiana (except southeastern portion)	411 W. 7th Street, Fort Worth, TX 76102 Phone: 817-334-3821
6. North Dakota, South Dakota, Colorado, Kansas, Utah, Wyoming, New Mexico	410 17th Street, Denver, CO 80202 Phone: 303-837-2071
7. California, Nevada, Arizona, Hawaii, Guam	5757 Wilshire Boulevard, Los Angeles, CA 90036 Phone: 213-468-3167
8. Washington, Oregon, Alaska, Montana, Idaho	915 Second Avenue, Seattle, WA 98174 Phone: 206-442-7990
9. Pennsylvania, West Virginia, Virginia, Maryland, Delaware, Washington, D.C.	600 Arch St., Philadelphia, PA 19106 Phone: 215-597-3100

Source: "Reprinted by permission of *The Wall Street Journal*, © Dow Jones & Company, Inc. 1987. ALL RIGHTS RESERVED."

Hulbert Performance Rating of Investment Advisory Letters

PERFORMANCE RATING

NEWSLETTER (Composition of Portfolio)	1/1 to 6/30/87 Gain	1986 Gain	1985 Gain	1984 Gain	1983 Gain	1982 Gain	1981 Gain	7/1 to 12/31/80 Gain	Risk Rating Note 1	See Note #2
Addison Report										
a. Monitored List of Conservative Stocks (Stocks and, at times, T-Bills)	+12.2%	+20.7%	+15.3%	+4.4%	+28.9%	n/a	n/a	n/a	4.36	29-B
b. Monitored List of Speculative Stocks (Stocks and, at times, T-Bills)	+7.4%	-1.8%	+17.6%	-13.6%	+89.6%	n/a	n/a	n/a	5.44	30-C
Astute Investor (Model Portfolio: Stocks and, at times, T-Bills)	+9.8%	+15.0%	+44.3%	-5.9%	n/a	n/a	n/a	n/a	5.09	26-A
(Astute Investor–Timing Only)	*+16.9%*	*+16.0%*	*+26.2%*	*+0.5%*	*n/a*	*n/a*	*n/a*	*n/a*	*n/a*	*n/a*
BI Research (Portfolio fully invested in stocks rated "Buy")	+28.7%	-10.4%	+65.9%	+14.3%	n/a	n/a	n/a	n/a	13.54	4-C
Bob Brinker's Markettimer (Model Portfolios: Funds and, at times, T-Bills)										
a. Mutual Fund Portfolio I	+20.9%	n/a	n/a	n/a	n/a	n/a	n/a	n/a	n/a	3-A
b. Mutual Fund Portfolio II	+21.2%	n/a	n/a	n/a	n/a	n/a	n/a	n/a	n/a	3-A
c. Mutual Fund Portfolio III	+21.6%	n/a	n/a	n/a	n/a	n/a	n/a	n/a	n/a	2-A
Cabot Market Letter										
a. Model Portfolio: Stocks and, at times, T-Bills	+16.2%	+8.0%	+37.4%	-22.7%	+7.3%	+32.8%	+2.5%	n/a	7.82	7-A
(Cabot Market Letter--Timing Only)	*+22.0%*	*+14.4%*	*+26.3%*	*+0.7%*	*+16.4%*	*+13.9%*	*-3.7%*	*n/a*	*n/a*	*n/a*
b. Mutual Fund Portfolio	+17.0%	n/a	n/a	n/a	n/a	n/a	n/a	n/a	n/a	3-A
The Cafritz Report (Mutual Funds)										
a. Buy-and-Hold Portfolio	+19.6%	n/a	n/a	n/a	n/a	n/a	n/a	n/a	n/a	5-A
b. Switching Portfolio	+17.6%	n/a	n/a	n/a	n/a	n/a	n/a	n/a	n/a	7-A
Calif. Technology Stock Letter (Model Portfolio: Stocks & T-Bills)	+40.2%	+14.1%	-5.9%	-47.9%	+1.7%	n/a	n/a	n/a	7.04	3-A
(Calif. Technology Stock Letter–Timing Only)	*+11.1%*	*+13.5%*	*+25.5%*	*+1.2%*	*+15.4%*	*n/a*	*n/a*	*n/a*	*n/a*	*n/a*
Canadian Business Service *Investment Report*										
a. Very Conservative Stocks (Fully invested)	+34.5%	+7.6%	+20.7%	-4.9%	n/a	n/a	n/a	n/a	5.40	25-C
b. Conservative stocks (fully invested)	+26.2%	+29.6%	+17.2%	+.3%	n/a	n/a	n/a	n/a	4.57	28-C
c. Average risk stocks (fully invested)	+19.2%	+32.2%	+39.7%	-6.4%	n/a	n/a	n/a	n/a	5.81	7-C
d. Higher risk stocks (fully invested)	+33.0%	+15.1%	+21.4%	-10.7%	n/a	n/a	n/a	n/a	3.58	8-C
e. Speculative stocks (fully invested)	+26.4%	-1.3%	+13.8%	-10.8%	n/a	n/a	n/a	n/a	8.27	3-C
The Chartist										
a. Actual Cash Account (Stocks and, at times, T-Bills)	+23.6%	+15.5%	+23.3%	+1.0%	+25.1%	+32.7%	-9.7%	+23.4%	3.05	18-A
(Actual Cash Account--Timing Only)	*+13.0%*	*+10.1%*	*+20.6%*	*+5.0%*	*+16.2%*	*+12.1%*	*n/a*	*n/a*	*n/a*	*n/a*
b. Traders' Stocks (fully invested)	+26.1%	+11.7%	+52.2%	+6.4%	+30.5%	n/a	n/a	n/a	6.82	27-C
Dessauer's Journal (International Portfolio: Stocks, Bonds, Currencies)	+16.8%	+20.2%	+41.8%	-0.0%	+21.0%	+20.1%	n/a	n/a	3.82	61-B

The Dines Letter (Supervised Lists of Stocks, Bonds, Options, T-Bills)										
#1. Good-Grade for Moderate Gains	+18.9%	-7.3%	+12.5%	-41.1%	+43.5%	+15.1%	-20.4%	+10.2%	11.43	7-A
#2. Speculative	-1.0%	+11.2%	+18.1%	+37.0%	+8.6%	+9.1%	+15.5%	+5.8%	10.05	5-A
#3. Growth	+41.8%	+12.9%	+23.3%	+71.9%	+7.0%	+25.1%	+14.2%	+5.8%	9.78	8-A
#4. Short-Term Trading	+31.7%	+59.1%	-2.6%	+27.4%	+90.1%	-4.3%	-13.2%	+19.3%	16.68	4-A
(Short-Term Trading Portfolio--Timing Only)	*+6.8%*	*+19.2%*	*+18.0%*	*+1.9%*	*+15.2%*	*+18.1%*	*+16.5%*	*+11.3%*	*n/a*	*n/a*
Income (Discontinued early 1984)	n/a	n/a	n/a	n/a	+13.2%	+20.1%	+14.2%	+5.8%	n/a	n/a
Gold (Discontinued early 1984)	n/a	n/a	n/a	n/a	+9.1%	-8.4%	-39.4%	+28.9%	n/a	n/a
Donoghue's Moneyletter (Moel Portfolio: Mutual Funds)	+21.7%	n/a	n/a	n/a	n/a	n/a	n/a	n/a	n/a	9-A
(Donoghue's Moneyletter Model Portfolio--Timing Only)	*+22.8%*	*n/a*	*n/a*	*n/a*	*n/a*	*n/a*	*n/a*	*n/a*	*n/a*	*n/a*
Dow Theory Forecasts (Portfolios fully invested in each list's stocks)										
a. Income Stocks (Invested in those "especially recommended")	+3.8%	+32.2%	+35.1%	+12.9%	+20.5%	+20.2%	-8.2%	+14.9%	5.02	13-C
b. Investment Stocks (Invested in those "especially recommended")	+27.8%	+24.1%	+35.3%	+2.3%	+15.6%	+28.4%	-4.2%	+21.8%	6.08	21-C
c. Growth Stocks (Invested in those "especially recommended")	+28.0%	+6.1%	+28.8%	-6.8%	+11.7%	+14.9%	+5.2%	+22.5%	6.54	16-C
d. Speculative Stocks (Invested in those "especially recommended")	+35.4%	+5.9%	+35.3%	-4.7%	+11.7%	+13.4%	-5.9%	+27.5%	6.13	25-C
e. Low-Priced & Spec. Situations (Invested in those "especially recommended")	+20.8%	+5.4%	n/a	n/a	n/a	n/a	n/a	n/a	4.68	23-C
Dow Theory Letters (Recommendations in "Investment Position" Box)	n/a	-1.8%	-5.9%	+1.8%	-6.8%	+19.2%	+10.2%	n/a	3.48	6-D
Dowse Market Letter (Mutual Fund Portfolios)										
a. Equity Portfolio	+27.3%	n/a	n/a	n/a	n/a	n/a	n/a	n/a	n/a	1-A
b. Bond Portfolio	-0.7%	n/a	n/a	n/a	n/a	n/a	n/a	n/a	n/a	0-A
c. Gold Portfolio	+45.6%	n/a	n/a	n/a	n/a	n/a	n/a	n/a	n/a	1-A
Emerging & Special Situations (Fully invested in stocks rated "buy")	+27.0%	-5.5%	+44.2%	-4.6%	+6.6%	n/a	n/a	n/a	7.31	16-C
Fidelity Monitor (Mutual Funds)										
a. Medium Risk Portfolio	+21.5%	n/a	n/a	n/a	n/a	n/a	n/a	n/a	n/a	4-A
b. Fidelity Select Portfolio	+20.9%	n/a	n/a	n/a	n/a	n/a	n/a	n/a	n/a	3-A
Financial World (Fully invested in A+-rated stocks)	+18.2%	+7.0%	+19.3%	n/a	n/a	n/a	n/a	n/a	6.35	39-C
Fund Exchange Report (Mutual Funds)										
a. Balanced Model Portfolio (discontinued 1987)	n/a	+5.2%	+20.2%	n/a	n/a	n/a	n/a	n/a	n/a	n/a
b. Aggressive Balanced Portfolio	+18.5%	n/a	n/a	n/a	n/a	n/a	n/a	n/a	n/a	3-A
c. Conservative Balanced Portfolio	+12.2%	n/a	n/a	n/a	n/a	n/a	n/a	n/a	n/a	3-A
d. Conservative Growth Model Portfolio	+11.9%	-3.0%	+28.6%	n/a	n/a	n/a	n/a	n/a	4.51	0-A
c. Conservative Growth Margined Portfolio	+20.0%	+2.7%	+45.5%	n/a	n/a	n/a	n/a	n/a	8.14	0-A
d. Aggressive Growth Model Portfolio	+20.1%	-1.4%	+29.7%	n/a	n/a	n/a	n/a	n/a	5.45	0-A
e. Aggressive Growth Margined Portfolio	+41.7%	-11.9%	+40.1%	n/a	n/a	n/a	n/a	n/a	10.74	0-A
f. Taxable Bond Model Portfolio	+7.4%	+9.3%	+18.9%	n/a	n/a	n/a	n/a	n/a	1.24	5-A
g. Gold Model Portfolio	+39.7%	+20.6%	-9.9%	n/a	n/a	n/a	n/a	n/a	8.37	0-A
Fundline ("Accumulation Portfolio"--Mutual Funds)	+18.0%	+18.5%	n/a	n/a	n/a	n/a	n/a	n/a	3.53	4-A
(Fundline--Timing Only)	*+19.9%*	*+10.1%*	*n/a*	*n/a*	*n/a*	*n/a*	*n/a*	*n/a*	*n/a*	*n/a*
Garside Forecast (Fully invested in recommended stocks)	-22.6%	+8.9%	+17.8%	+1.6%	n/a	n/a	n/a	n/a	6.74	21-C
Granville Market Letter (*Not* including phone service)										
a. Open Stock Positions (was "Aggressive Traders' Portfolio)	+47.1%	-13.7%	-22.7%	+2.9%	-25.2%	-29.7%	-3.3%	+10.6%	7.02	23-C
b. Option Portfolio (Fully invested when in options))	+56.7%	-89.7%	-97.8%	n/a	n/a	n/a	n/a	n/a	134.78	31-C

PERFORMANCE RATING *(continued)*

NEWSLETTER (Composition of Portfolio)	1/1 to 6/30/87 Gain	1986 Gain	1985 Gain	1984 Gain	1983 Gain	1982 Gain	1981 Gain	7/1 to 12/31/80 Gain	Risk Rating Note 1	See Note #2
Growth Fund Guide										
a. Aggressive Growth Funds (Invested in funds most highly rated)	+4.5%	+10.9%	+33.8%	-18.3%	+22.4%	n/a	n/a	n/a	5.03	7-B
b. Growth Funds (Invested in funds most highly rated)	+5.1%	+15.5%	+31.2%	+0.8%	+24.2%	n/a	n/a	n/a	4.37	8-B
c. Quality Growth Funds (Invested in funds most highly rated)	+6.7%	+13.1%	+26.4%	+5.5%	+22.4%	n/a	n/a	n/a	2.75	1-B
d. Special Situations Funds (Invested in funds most highly rated)	+19.1%	+33.1%	+20.9%	-3.6%	+30.3%	n/a	n/a	n/a	4.29	2-B
Growth Stock Outlook (Supervised Portfolio: Stocks, T-Bills)	+6.4%	+7.4%	+24.7%	+3.5%	+33.1%	+24.0%	+11.8%	+34.0%	2.01	23-A
(Growth Stock Outlook–Timing Only)	*+7.1%*	*+10.0%*	*+19.5%*	*+5.4%*	*+17.6%*	*+18.5%*	*-0.6%*	*+14.9%*	*n/a*	*n/a*
Harry Browne's Special Reports (Variable [Speculative] Portfolio)	+14.0%	+18.1%	+14.8%	+4.1%	+8.1%	+17.2%	-6.9%	n/a	2.65	5-A
Heim Investment Letter (Typically stocks, options, or commodities)										
a. Conservative Portfolio	-3.6%	+13.2%	+4.8%	+1.6%	+2.6%	-8.4%	+10.5%	+2.6%	3.11	0-A
b. Aggressive Portfolio	-10.7%	+19.8%	+4.8%	+1.6%	+2.6%	n/a	n/a	n/a	6.22	0-A
High Technology Growth Stocks										
a. Model Portfolio: Stocks, T-Bills	+41.5%	+8.8%	-4.8%	-36.3%	n/a	n/a	n/a	n/a	8.92	34-A
High Technology Growth Stocks Model Portfolio–Timing Only)	*+22.9%*	*+13.8%*	*+25.5%*	*+1.5%*	*n/a*	*n/a*	*n/a*	*n/a*	*n/a*	*n/a*
b. Timeliness Portfolio (Stocks, T-Bills)	+36.5%	+15.8%	n/a	n/a	n/a	n/a	n/a	n/a	8.99	27-A
High Technology Investments										
a. Long-Term Portfolio I (Stocks and, at times, T-Bills)	+38.5%	+18.8%	+50.0%	-23.3%	+3.5%	n/a	n/a	n/a	10.80	0-A
b. Long-Term Portfolio II (Stocks and, at times, T-Bills)	+46.5%	+23.0%	+103.3%	-2.6%	-19.2%	n/a	n/a	n/a	9.16	0-A
(Long-Term Portfolio II–Timing Only)	*+18.5%*	*+3.9%*	*+15.8%*	*+8.6%*	*+12.0%*	*n/a*	*n/a*	*n/a*	*n/a*	*n/a*
Howard Ruff's *Ruff Times*										
a. "Phantom Investor" (Stocks, commodities, coins, T-Bills)	n/a	n/a	+2.3%	-13.2%	-14.9%	+43.8%	-2.4%	-6.8%	n/a	n/a
b. "Optimum Switch Hitter" (Mutual Funds)	n/a	n/a	+12.6%	n/a	n/a	n/a	n/a	n/a	n/a	n/a
c. Portfolio of investments rated "Buy" (Fully invested)	+25.2%	n/a	n/a	n/a	n/a	n/a	n/a	n/a	n/a	2-C
Holt Advisory (Fully invested in current recommendations)	+19.8%	-9.9%	-17.4%	-0.4%	-8.2%	-11.8%	+7.9%	-6.1%	6.37	11-C
ITA Mutual Fund Advisor (Mutual Funds)										
a. $100,000 Aggressive Model Portfolio	+15.2%	n/a	n/a	n/a	n/a	n/a	n/a	n/a	n/a	6-A
($100,000 Aggressive Model–Timing Only)	*+10.9%*	*n/a*	*n/a*	*n/a*	*n/a*	*n/a*	*n/a*	*n/a*	*n/a*	*n/a*
b. $100,000 Conservative Model Portfolio	+22.3%	n/a	n/a	n/a	n/a	n/a	n/a	n/a	n/a	7-A
Indicator Digest										
a. Growth Portfolio: Stocks, Options, T-Bills	+4.1%	-0.8%	+6.9%	-10.3%	+11.8%	n/a	n/a	n/a	2.98	7-B
(Indicator Digest Growth Portfolio–Timing Only)	*+9.4%*	*+10.2%*	*+18.7%*	*+1.1%*	*+17.0%*	*n/a*	*n/a*	*n/a*	*n/a*	*n/a*
b. Total Return Portfolio (Stocks, Funds, T-Bills)	+7.3%	+15.4%	n/a	n/a	n/a	n/a	n/a	n/a	1.93	11-B
Insider Indicator (Portfolio fully invested in past year's 'buys')	+20.5%	+6.9%	+25.6%	n/a	n/a	n/a	n/a	n/a	4.49	230-C
Insiders (Insiders' Portfolio)	+28.9%	+6.4%	+20.2%	n/a	n/a	n/a	n/a	n/a	4.85	42-C
International Harry Schultz Letter										
a. US Stocks in the "List" (formerly "Investment Table")	+21.8%	+6.8%	+8.7%	+7.4%	+2.1%	-5.5%	-17.5%	+41.2%	3.24	32-B
b. Non-U.S. Stocks in the "List" (Fully invested)	+27.0%	+44.2%	n/a	n/a	n/a	n/a	n/a	n/a	4.06	74-C
c. Portfolio constructed out of gold/silver trading advice (non-margined)	+0.4%	+0.5%	-2.8%	+20.3%	n/a	n/a	n/a	n/a	2.44	0-C

Investech Market Analyst (Model Portfolio: Stocks, Options, T-Bills	+25.1%	+2.2%	+32.7%	-16.7%	n/a	n/a	n/a	n/a	3.92	4-A
(Investech Model Portfolio–Timing Only)	*+11.5%*	*+10.5%*	*+15.8%*	*+1.8%*	*n/a*	*n/a*	*n/a*	*n/a*	*n/a*	*n/a*
Investech Mutual Fund Advisor (Mutual Fund Portfolio)	+27.9%	+35.3%	n/a	n/a	n/a	n/a	n/a	n/a	3.97	2-A
Investment Horizons (Model Stock PortfolIOS: Stocks and, at times, T-Bills)										
a. Aggressive Portfolio	+12.7%	n/a	n/a	n/a	n/a	n/a	n/a	n/a	n/a	44-B
(Aggressive Portfolio–Timing Only)	*+15.2%*	*n/a*	*n/a*	*n/a*	*n/a*	*n/a*	*n/a*	*n/a*	*n/a*	*n/a*
b. Conservative Portfolio	+11.1%	n/a	n/a	n/a	n/a	n/a	n/a	n/a	n/a	44-B
Investment Quality Trends (Fully invested in 'undervalued stocks')	+12.8%	+18.5%	n/a	n/a	n/a	n/a	n/a	n/a	4.90	47-C
Investment Values (Fully invested in stocks rated 'buy')	+6.4%	+11.1%	+18.6%	n/a	n/a	n/a	n/a	n/a	4.59	20-C
Investor's Intelligence (Mutual Fund Portfolio)	+31.8%	n/a	n/a	n/a	n/a	n/a	n/a	n/a	n/a	4-A
(Investor's Intelligence Mutual Fund Portfolio–Timing Only)	*+20.7%*	*n/a*	*n/a*	*n/a*	*n/a*	*n/a*	*n/a*	*n/a*	*n/a*	*n/a*
Kenneth Gerbino Investment Letter (Fully invested in "buys")	+62.2%	+18.7%	+0.4%	n/a	n/a	n/a	,n/a	n/a	11.12	20-C
Kinsman's Low-Risk Growth Letter										
a. Conservative Model Portfolio (Stocks, Bonds, Funds)	+7.4%	+9.7%	+10.3%	+7.3%	+9.0%	+18.2%	+7.2%	+6.0%	1.84	9-A
b. Aggressive Model Portfolio (Stocks, Bonds, Funds)	+10.4%	+3.8%	n/a	n/a	n/a	n/a	n/a	n/a	3.74	7-C
LaLoggia's Special Situations Report										
a. Master List of Takeover Candidates (Fully Invested in "Buys")	+25.7%	+9.9%	+31.3%	-6.3%	n/a	n/a	n/a	n/a	5.06	27-C
b. Breakout Stocks for Traders (Fully Invested in "Buys")	+13.1%	+13.2%	n/a	n/a	n/a	n/a	n/a	n/a	4.35	15-C
Lynn Elgert Report (Model Portfolio: Stocks and, at times, T-Bills)	+6.5%	+2.0%	+41.7%	n/a	n/a	n/a	n/a	n/a	5.44	13-A
(Lynn Elgert Report–Timing Only)	*+12.1%*	*+12.6%*	*+22.5%*	*n/a*	*n/a*	*n/a*	*n/a*	*n/a*	*n/a*	*n/a*
Margo's Market Monitor										
a. Model Portfolio: Stocks and, at times, T-Bills	+19.9%	+24.4%	+22.2%	-5.8%	n/a	n/a	n/a	n/a	5.66	14-A
(Margo's Market Monitor Model Portfolio–Timing Only)	*+19.1%*	*+16.6%*	*+22.9%*	*+4.0%*	*n/a*	*n/a*	*n/a*	*n/a*	*n/a*	*n/a*
b. Model Sector Fund Portfolio (Mutual Funds)	+63.6%	+9.5%	n/a	n/a	n/a	n/a	n/a	n/a	8.77	0-A
Market Logic										
a. Master Portfolio (Stocks and at times T-Bills)	+24.7%	+12.6%	+37.3%	-13.7%	+28.0%	+41.0%	+8.6%	+18.9%	5.77	35-B
(Market Logic–Timing Only)	*+23.4%*	*+14.0%*	*+26.2%*	*+1.3%*	*+17.5%*	*+17.9%*	*+2.2%*	*+12.5%*	*n/a*	*n/a*
b. Actual Options Portfolio (Options, T-Bills)	+2.9%	+7.5%	+22.2%	+5.8%	+13.5%	+25.9%	+14.2%	+5.8%	1.48	0-A
Market Mania ('Under Observation Portfolio: Stocks, Options, T-Bills)	+14.0%	-6.6%	+1.8%	+6.4%	n/a	n/a	n/a	n/a	8.94	46-A
(Market Mania–Timing Only)	*+32.5%*	*+14.0%*	*+24.5%*	*+3.5%*	*n/a*	*n/a*	*n/a*	*n/a*	*n/a*	*n/a*
McKeever Strategy Letter ($50,000 Model Portfolio: Commodities, T-Bills)	+9.9%	+55.2%	+99.3%	-13.3%	n/a	n/a	n/a	n/a	26.90	3-A
Medical Technology Stock Letter (Model Portfolio: Stocks, T-Bills)	+33.9%	+6.3%	+83.3%	n/a	n/a	n/a	n/a	n/a	11.25	12-A
(Medical Technology Stock Letter–Timing Only)	*+23.5%*	*+14.0%*	*+26.2%*	*n/a*	*n/a*	*n/a*	*n/a*	*n/a*	*n/a*	*n/a*
Merrill Lynch Stockfinder Research Service										
a. Stocks Rated "Buy" for Intermediate Term (Fully invested)	+28.1%	+16.1%	n/a	n/a	n/a	n/a	n/a	n/a	5.83	118-C
b. Convertible Preferred and Bond Portfolio (Fully Invested)	+7.0%	+16.2%	n/a	n/a	n/a	n/a	n/a	n/a	3.19	29-C
MJF Growth Stock Advisory (Fully Invested in "Open Recommendations")	+33.6%	+3.7%	n/a	n/a	n/a	n/a	n/a	n/a	7.92	20-C
Mutual Fund Forecaster (Traders' portfolio of mutual funds)	+22.0%	+14.8%	n/a	n/a	n/a	n/a	n/a	n/a	4.59	8-B
Mutual Fund Investing										
a. Portfolio I ("Moderate Risk")	+10.9%	+25.7%	n/a	n/a	n/a	n/a	n/a	n/a	2.03	4-A
(Mutual Fund Investing Port. I–Timing Only)	*+13.6%*	*+12.6%*	*n/a*	*n/a*	*n/a*	*n/a*	*n/a*	*n/a*	*n/a*	*n/a*
b. Portfolio II ("Safe & Secure")	+4.6%	+12.8%	n/a	n/a	n/a	n/a	n/a	n/a	1.53	2-A
Mutual Fund Letter										
a. Highly Aggressive Portfolio	+11.6%	+15.9%	n/a	n/a	n/a	n/a	n/a	n/a	3.05	4-A
b. Moderately Aggressive Portfolio	+11.9%	+17.3%	n/a	n/a	n/a	n/a	n/a	n/a	2.12	3-A
c. Growth & Income Portfolio	+11.4%	+12.4%	n/a	n/a	n/a	n/a	n/a	n/a	2.11	3-A
d. Income Portfolio	+3.8%	+12.6%	n/a	n/a	n/a	n/a	n/a	n/a	1.54	4-A

PERFORMANCE RATING *(continued)*

NEWSLETTER (Composition of Portfolio)	1/1 to 6/30/87 Gain	1986 Gain	1985 Gain	1984 Gain	1983 Gain	1982 Gain	1981 Gain	7/1 to 12/31/80 Gain	Risk Rating Note 1	See Note #2
Mutual Fund Monitor										
a. Investment Portfolio	+12.4%	+7.3%	n/a	n/a	n/a	n/a	n/a	n/a	4.00	4-A
b. IRA/Keogh Portfolio	+9.2%	+13.8%	n/a	n/a	n/a	n/a	n/a	n/a	3.17	3-A
c. International Portfolio	+11.4%	+70.3%	n/a	n/a	n/a	n/a	n/a	n/a	5.21	5-A
d. Traders' Portfolio	+17.0%	+10.3%	n/a	n/a	n/a	n/a	n/a	n/a	4.60	6-A
(Mutual Fund Monitor Traders' Portfolio–Timing Only)	*+23.4%*	*+13.7%*	*n/a*	*n/a*	*n/a*	*n/a*	*n/a*	*n/a*	*n/a*	*n/a*
e. U.S.-based International Portfolio	+21.5%	n/a	n/a	n/a	n/a	n/a	n/a	n/a	n/a	2-A
Mutual Fund Strategist										
a. Diversified Portfolio (was "Buy-and-Hold" Portfolio)	+25.0%	+28.8%	+23.9%	n/a	n/a	n/a	n/a	n/a	3.63	1-A
b. Sector Fund Portfolio (was "Compuvest Timing" Portfolio)	+49.7%	+13.2%	+30.9%	n/a	n/a	n/a	n/a	n/a	5.30	1-A
Mutual Fund Switch Service (Mutual Funds)										
a. Very Aggressive Funds	+23.4%	n/a	n/a	n/a	n/a	n/a	n/a	n/a	n/a	2-B
b. Aggressive Funds	+38.1%	n/a	n/a	n/a	n/a	n/a	n/a	n/a	n/a	2-A
c. Less Aggressive Funds	+27.0%	n/a	n/a	n/a	n/a	n/a	n/a	n/a	n/a	2-A
d. Conservative Funds	+15.8%	n/a	n/a	n/a	n/a	n/a	n/a	n/a	n/a	3-B
e. Bond Funds	+1.2%	n/a	n/a	n/a	n/a	n/a	n/a	n/a	n/a	7-B
f. Gold Funds	+12.6%	n/a	n/a	n/a	n/a	n/a	n/a	n/a	n/a	3-B
New Issues (Fully invested in all open recommendations)	+29.2%	-9.4%	+18.1%	-30.7%	+11.6%	n/a	n/a	n/a	6.97	172-C
New Mutual Fund Advisor (Mutual funds)										
a. Growth Portfolio	+8.5%	n/a	n/a	n/a	n/a	n/a	n/a	n/a	n/a	11-A
(Growth Portfolio–Timing Only)	*+20.5%*	n/a	n/a	n/a	n/a	n/a	n/a	n/a	n/a	n/a
b. Growth and Income Portfolio	+14.1%	n/a	n/a	n/a	n/a	n/a	n/a	n/a	n/a	9-A
c. Income Portfolio	+0.8%	n/a	n/a	n/a	n/a	n/a	n/a	n/a	n/a	10-A
Nicholson Report (Model Portfolio: Stocks and T-Bills)	+16.3%	-4.5%	+21.4%	-7.2%	-11.4%	n/a	n/a	n/a	3.93	41-A
No Load Fund-X ("Follow the Stars Strategy")										
a. Class 1 Funds (Most Speculative Growth Funds)	+25.8%	+14.7%	+22.7%	n/a	n/a	n/a	n/a	n/a	6.47	5-C
b. Class 2 Funds (Speculative Growth Funds)	+8.0%	+26.9%	+25.2%	n/a	n/a	n/a	n/a	n/a	4.27	5-C
c. Class 3 Funds (Higher Quality Growth Funds)	-3.4%	+40.6%	+38.1%	n/a	n/a	n/a	n/a	n/a	4.22	5-C
d. Class 4 Funds (Total Return Funds)	+12.6%	n/a	n/a	n/a	n/a	n/a	n/a	n/a	n/a	5-C
No-Load Fund Investor										
a. Funds for aggressive investors	+26.6%	+16.8%	n/a	n/a	n/a	n/a	n/a	n/a	5.38	4-B
b. Middle of the Road Funds	+15.2%	+18.1%	n/a	n/a	n/a	n/a	n/a	n/a	3.81	5-B
c. Funds for conservative, long-term investors	+16.9%	n/a	n/a	n/a	n/a	n/a	n/a	n/a	n/a	5-B
d. International funds	n/a	+31.5%	n/a	n/a	n/a	n/a	n/a	n/a	n/a	n/a
Nourse Investor Report										
a. Portfolio started 12/7/84 (Stocks, T-Bills)	+11.6%	+12.0%	+22.1%	n/a	n/a	n/a	n/a	n/a	5.30	62-B
(Nourse Investor Report's 12/7/84 Portfolio–Timing Only)	*+14.6%*	*+14.2%*	*+11.9%*	*n/a*	*n/a*	*n/a*	*n/a*	*n/a*	*n/a*	*n/a*
b. Portfolio started 8/30/85 (Stocks, T-Bills)	+13.6%	-6.5%	n/a	n/a	n/a	n/a	n/a	n/a	4.51	62-A
O'Malley's Fidelity Watch (Mutual Funds)										
a. Regular Model Portfolio	+24.7%	n/a	n/a	n/a	n/a	n/a	n/a	n/a	n/a	4-A

(O'Malley's Regular Model–Timing Only)	*+23.4%*	*n/a*	*n/a*	*n/a*	*n/a*	*n/a*	*n/a*	*n/a*	*n/a*	*n/a*
b. Fidelity Select Model Portfolio	+21.5%	n/a	n/a	n/a	n/a	n/a	n/a	n/a	n/a	4-A
Option Advisor										
a. Conservative Portfolio (Options and T-Bills)	-15.1%	+93.4%	+0.6%	+153.3%	-83.5%	n/a	n/a	n/a	12.19	6-A
b. Aggressive Portfolio (Options and T-Bills)	+6.7%	-41.9%	-43.2%	+27.6%	-83.1%	n/a	n/a	n/a	20.48	15-A
OTC Insight (Model Portfolios: Stocks, T-Bills)										
a. $10,000 Conservative	+25.7%	+50.9%	+52.6%	n/a	n/a	n/a	n/a	n/a	5.53	9-A
b. $10,000 Moderately Aggressive	+45.2%	+55.0%	+70.0%	n/a	n/a	n/a	n/a	n/a	9.14	10-A
c. $10,000 Aggressive	+42.4%	+59.9%	+59.4%	n/a	n/a	n/a	n/a	n/a	8.56	8-A
d. $25,000 Conservative	+38.4%	+33.4%	+66.7%	n/a	n/a	n/a	n/a	n/a	6.84	10-A
e. $25,000 Moderately Aggressive	+39.5%	+37.2%	+66.0%	n/a	n/a	n/a	n/a	n/a	8.99	12-A
f. $25,000 Aggressive	+49.7%	+46.8%	+77.8%	n/a	n/a	n/a	n/a	n/a	9.93	10-A
g. $50,000 Conservative	+31.5%	+46.7%	+60.5%	n/a	n/a	n/a	n/a	n/a	5.77	12-A
h. $50,000 Moderately Aggressive	+37.1%	+66.1%	+77.5%	n/a	n/a	n/a	n/a	n/a	7.87	16-A
i. $50,000 Aggressive	+27.1%	+85.7%	+59.0%	n/a	n/a	n/a	n/a	n/a	8.56	14-A
OTC Review and Special Situations (Fully invested in stocks rated "Buy")	+13.3%	n/a	n/a	n/a	n/a	n/a	n/a	n/a	n/a	12-C
Outlook (Standard & Poor's)										
a. Foundation Stocks (Those best situated for purchase)	+21.4%	+13.6%	+19.6%	-14.5%	+12.3%	+19.9%	+8.8%	+18.1%	5.91	3-C
b. Growth Stocks (Those best situated for purchase)	+26.1%	+14.9%	+5.4%	+1.0%	+10.5%	+11.0%	+19.6%	+17.6%	7.08	4-C
c. Speculative Stocks (Those best situated for purchase)	+33.7%	-6.3%	+50.7%	+1.0%	+21.4%	+31.0%	-1.6%	+19.6%	6.79	5-C
d. Income Stocks (Those best situated for purchase)	+7.5%	+28.9%	+29.0%	+12.8%	+28.0%	+10.6%	+10.8%	+17.9%	4.38	3-C
Patient Investor (Fully invested in stocks rated 'Buy')	n/a	+26.4%	+25.1%	n/a	n/a	n/a	n/a	n/a	n/a	n/a
Personal Finance										
a. Income Portfolio (Fully invested in those recommended as "buys")	-1.2%	+22.2%	+63.7%	+5.8%	n/a	n/a	n/a	n/a	5.79	27-B
b. Growth Portfolio (Fully invested in those recommended as "buys")	+26.3%	-0.1%	+34.8%	-26.8%	n/a	n/a	n/a	n/a	4.87	23-B
Peter Dag Investment Letter (Model Portfolio: Mutual Funds)	+2.4%	+13.2%	+14.5%	+5.5%	+6.0%	n/a	n/a	n/a	1.40	6-A
(Peter Dag Investment Letter–Timing Only)	*+18.5%*	*+10.7%*	*+16.2%*	*+7.7%*	*+15.9%*	*n/a*	*n/a*	*n/a*	*n/a*	*n/a*
Plain Talk Investor										
a. Personal Portfolio (Stocks and T-Bills)	+21.9%	+7.1%	+35.5%	n/a	n/a	n/a	n/a	n/a	5.48	21-A
b. High Risk Portfolio	+21.6%	-26.0%	+1.4%	n/a	n/a	n/a	n/a	n/a	7.02	9-A
Professional Investor										
a. NYSE Scan (Fully invested)	+14.6%	+9.2%	+20.4%	-22.1%	+14.1%	+34.5%	-6.1%	+14.4%	4.24	42-C
b. AMEX Scan (Fully invested)	+25.5%	+9.7%	+21.0%	-9.8%	+48.2%	+39.1%	-6.9%	+34.0%	4.29	54-C
c. OTC Scan (Fully invested)	+13.1%	+4.6%	+31.4%	-1.7%	+29.3%	+21.6%	-4.4%	+30.8%	3.78	47-C
d. Investment Grade Scan (Fully invested)	+44.2%	+32.5%	+50.2%	-10.5%	-18.5%	+23.7%	+3.0%	+12.5%	9.55	1-C
Professional Tape Reader										
a. Model Portfolio: Stocks and, at times, T-Bills)	+13.8%	+1.1%	+6.4%	-23.6%	-9.8%	+30.0%	-6.7%	+22.9%	2.94	18-A
(Professional Tape Reader Mode Portfolio–Timing Only)	*+10.4%*	*-2.1%*	*+12.1%*	*-3.1%*	*+8.6%*	*+20.8%*	*+2.4%*	*+13.5%*	*n/a*	*n/a*
b. Mutual Fund Portfolio	+12.1%	+5.9%	n/a	n/a	n/a	n/a	n/a	n/a	1.53	4-A
Professional Timing Service										
a. Open Stock Positions (Fully Invested)	n/a	-13.6%	+27.6%	-19.0%	+22.4%	-2.5%	n/a	n/a	n/a	n/a
b. Gold futures trading (non-margined)	+18.0%	+12.6%	+11.4%	n/a	n/a	n/a	n/a	n/a	2.80	1-C
c. Stock index futures trading (non-margined)	+5.7%	+7.8%	+3.6%	n/a	n/a	n/a	n/a	n/a	1.78	0-C
d. Investors' Model Portfolio (Stocks, T-Bills)	+7.3%	n/a	n/a	n/a	n/a	n/a	n/a	n/a	n/a	5-A
e. Traders' Model Portfolio (Stocks, T-Bills)	+17.5%	n/a	n/a	n/a	n/a	n/a	n/a	n/a	n/a	5-A
f. Mutual Fund Model Portfolio (Mutual Funds)	+4.8%	n/a	n/a	n/a	n/a	n/a	n/a	n/a	n/a	1-A

PERFORMANCE RATING *(concluded)*

NEWSLETTER (Composition of Portfolio)	1/1 to 6/30/87 Gain	1986 Gain	1985 Gain	1984 Gain	1983 Gain	1982 Gain	1981 Gain	7/1 to 12/31/80 Gain	Risk Rating Note 1	See Note #2
Prudent Speculator (Actual TPS Portfolio*: Stocks and at times T-Bills)	+26.6%	+16.9%	+62.2%	-13.1%	+72.9%	+49.0%	+2.9%	+26.5%	11.61	153-A
PSR Prophetwatch										
a. Micro-Cap Model Portfolio	n/a	+6.0%	+17.4%	n/a	n/a	n/a	n/a	n/a	n/a	n/a
b. Mini Cap Model Portfolio	n/a	+11.9%	n/a	n/a	n/a	n/a	n/a	n/a	n/a	n/a
c. $25,000 Model Portfolio	+14.6%	n/a	n/a	n/a	n/a	n/a	n/a	n/a	n/a	7-A
d. $50,000 Model Portfolio	+10.5%	n/a	n/a	n/a	n/a	n/a	n/a	n/a	n/a	5-A
e. $100,000 Model Portfolio	+3.7%	n/a	n/a	n/a	n/a	n/a	n/a	n/a	n/a	5-A
Puetz Investment Report										
a. Aggressive Portfolio (Stocks, Options, T-Bills)	-49.9%	n/a	n/a	n/a	n/a	n/a	n/a	n/a	n/a	8-A
(Puetz Investment Report Aggressive Portfolio—Timing Only)	*-10.2%*	*n/a*	*n/a*	*n/a*	*n/a*	*n/a*	*n/a*	*n/a*	*n/a*	*n/a*
b. Conservative Portfolio (Stocks, Options, T-Bills)	-9.5%	n/a	n/a	n/a	n/a	n/a	n/a	n/a	n/a	4-A
RHM Survey of Warrants, Options & Low-Priced Stocks (Invested in 'Buys')	+40.9%	+16.1%	+6.6%	-42.2%	+8.6%	+23.2%	-50.1%	n/a	7.23	14-C
Sector Funds Newsletter (Model Portfolio of Mutual Funds)	+3.7%	n/a	n/a	n/a	n/a	n/a	n/a	n/a	n/a	3-A
Speculator										
a. Selected Stocks (Fully invested in those best situated for purchase)	+26.6%	+1.2%	+21.9%	-38.6%	+8.8%	+45.3%	-10.8%	n/a	5.62	64-C
b. Trading Portfolio (Stocks and T-Bills)	+31.7%	+20.0%	-3.2%	+5.1%	n/a	n/a	n/a	n/a	6.01	9-A
(Speculator Trading Portfolio—Timing Only)	*+21.4%*	*+15.9%*	*+19.4*	*+0.0%*	*n/a*	*n/a*	*n/a*	*n/a*	*n/a*	*n/a*
Stockmarket Cycles										
a. Model Portfolio (Stocks, T-Bills)	+3.0%	-1.0%	+23.6%	n/a	n/a	n/a	n/a	n/a	5.08	3-A
(Stock Market Cycles Model Portfolio—Timing Only)	*+8.0%*	*+15.0%*	*+25.1%*	*n/a*	*n/a*	*n/a*	*n/a*	*n/a*	*n/a*	*n/a*
b. Mututal Fund Portfolio	+20.7%	+17.0%	+11.4%	n/a	n/a	n/a	n/a	n/a	5.45	1-A
Switch Fund Advisory (Model Portfolio: Mutual Funds)	+11.1%	+16.2%	+20.8%	+1.8%	+16.4%	n/a	n/a	n/a	2.18	9-A
(Switch Fund Advisory Model Portfolio—Timing Only)	*+14.7%*	*+10.9%*	*+18.5%*	*+2.5%*	*+14.6%*	n/a	n/a	n/a	n/a	n/a
Switch Fund Timing (Model Stock Portfolio: Stocks and, at times, T-Bills)	+1.9%	n/a	n/a	n/a	n/a	n/a	n/a	n/a	n/a	9-A
Systems & Forecasts (Stocks, Bonds, Options, Mutual Funds)	+10.1%	+7.0%	+22.0%	+22.2%	-6.9%	n/a	n/a	n/a	3.54	8-B
(Systems & Forecasts--Timing Only)	*+10.7%*	*+9.7%*	*+20.1%*	*+4.1%*	*+8.2%*	*n/a*	*n/a*	*n/a*	*n/a*	*n/a*
Telephone Switch Newsletter										
a. Equity/Cash Switch Plan	+29.4%	+10.7%	+8.5%	-12.1%	+19.0%	+39.2%	+6.0%	+31.7%	5.50	5-A
(Telephone Switch Newsletter—Equity Timing Only)	*+23.4%*	*+8.7%*	*+23.6%*	*+4.7%*	*+17.5%*	*+30.3%*	*+0.7%*	*+19.2%*	*n/a*	*n/a*
b. Gold/Cash Switch Plan	+46.2%	+12.9%	-1.1%	-5.9%	-7.8%	n/a	n/a	n/a	7.30	0-A
c. International Funds/Cash Switch Plan	+22.8%	+54.0%	+37.4%	-1.5%	n/a	n/a	n/a	n/a	4.44	4-A
Tony Henfrey's Gold Letter (Gold Share Portfolio for U.S. $ Investors)	+39.1%	n/a	-28.3%	-28.1%	+6.9%	+93.3%	n/a	n/a	n/a	8-A
United & Babson Reports										
a. Growth Stocks (Fully invested in those best situated for purchase)	+17.4%	+12.2%	+21.6%	-5.5%	+1.7%	+6.7%	-14.1%	+15.8%	5.98	39-C
b. Cyclical Stocks (Fully invested in those best situated for purchase)	+19.3%	-9.1%	+15.2%	-16.9%	+7.0%	+15.6%	-12.9%	+28.2%	5.70	14-C
c. Income Stocks (Fully invested in those best situated for purchase)	-3.7%	+21.7%	+20.3%	+4.2%	+14.7%	+13.8%	-3.8%	+4.6%	4.74	12-C
United Mutual Fund Selector (Invested in those best situated for current purhase)										
a. Aggressive Growth Funds (No-load and low-loads only)	+24.9%	+21.2%	n/a	n/a	n/a	n/a	n/a	n/a	5.57	3-C
b. Growth Funds (No-load and low-loads only)	+19.2%	+13.1%	n/a	n/a	n/a	n/a	n/a	n/a	4.19	2-C
c. Growth & Income Funds (No-load and low-loads only)	+13.7%	+9.8%	n/a	n/a	n/a	n/a	n/a	n/a	3.79	1-C
d. Income Funds (No-load and low-loads only)	+4.1%	+13.1%	n/a	n/a	n/a	n/a	n/a	n/a	1.33	1-C

Value Line Convertibles (Fully Invested in "Recommended Issues")	+13.8%	+33.6%	n/a	n/a	n/a	n/a	n/a	n/a	4.57	12-C
Value Line Inv. Survey (Fully invested in "Group I" Timeliness Stocks)	+25.5%	+14.7%	+35.1%	-8.6%	+34.8%	n/a	n/a	n/a	6.33	100-C
Value Line New Issues Service (Fully invested in stocks rated "Buy")	+29.3%	+13.0%	+47.4%	-29.8%	n/a	n/a	n/a	n/a	10.86	8-C
Value Line OTC Spec'l Sit. Survey (Fully invested in "esp.-recc." stocks	+35.6%	-1.8%	+23.7%	-24.0%	+24.1%	+50.2%	-17.6%	+72.3%	8.28	20-C
Volume Reversal Survey (Model Portfolio: Stocks, Options, Futures, T-Bills)	+10.9%	n/a	n/a	n/a	n/a	n/a	n/a	n/a	n/a	48-A
Wall Street Digest (Fully invested in stocks rated "buy")	+33.2%	+9.0%	+13.1%	n/a	n/a	n/a	n/a	n/a	6.57	24-C
Wall Street Generalist ("Select Trading Portfolio": Stocks, T-Bills)	+36.7%	n/a	n/a	n/a	n/a	n/a	n/a	n/a	n/a	3-A
(Wall Street General Select Trading Portfolio—Timing Only)	*+35.7%*	*n/a*	*n/a*	*n/a*	*n/a*	*n/a*	*n/a*	*n/a*	*n/a*	*n/a*
Weber's Fund Advisor (Real World Portfolio: Mutual Funds)	+35.3%	+14.0%	+22.1%	n/a	n/a	n/a	n/a	n/a	4.94	2-A
Wellington's Worry-Free Investing										
a. Model Mutual Fund Portfolio	+24.5%	+24.6%	+29.5%	n/a	n/a	n/a	n/a	n/a	3.71	6-A
b. Leveraged Mutual Fund Portfolio	+41.0%	+27.6%	n/a	n/a	n/a	n/a	n/a	n/a	7.69	6-A
Your Window Into The Future										
a. Portfolio A: Gold Mutual Funds Portfolio	+20.2%	+38.0%	n/a	n/a	n/a	n/a	n/a	n/a	10.69	0-A
b. Portfolio B: General Mutual Funds Portfolio	+20.2%	n/a	n/a	n/a	n/a	n/a	n/a	n/a	n/a	0-A
c. Portfolio C: Trading Portfolio (Stocks, Options, etc.)	+172.0%	n/a	n/a	n/a	n/a	n/a	n/a	n/a	n/a	0-A
Zweig Forecast (Model Portfolio: Stocks, T-Bills)	+24.2%	+11.0%	+41.8%	+2.7%	+1.5%	+24.6%	+24.0%	+23.2%	4.62	10-A
(Zweig Forecast—Timing Only)	*+13.3%*	*+9.7%*	*+24.3%*	*+0.5%*	*+14.3%*	*+13.5%*	*+4.5%*	*+13.6%*	*n/a*	*n/a*
Zweig Performance Ratings Report (Fully invested in 'buys' and 'shorts')	+8.0%	+28.9%	+29.8%	+5.9%	+17.5%	n/a	n/a	n/a	4.41	46-C
The Riskless rate of return: a T-Bill only portfolio	+2.9%	+6.1%	+7.6%	+9.8%	+9.0%	+10.9%	+14.2%	+5.8%	0.05	
STOCK AVERAGES										
a. DJIA (including dividends, reinvested monthly)	+29.4%	+27.4%	+33.6%	+1.0%	+25.9%	+27.2%	-3.7%	+14.3%	5.11	
b. Standard & Poor's 500 (dividends reinvested monthly)	+27.3%	+18.6%	+31.7%	+6.2%	+22.5%	+21.6%	-4.9%	+21.7%	5.07	
c. Wilshire 5000 Value-Weighted Index (dividends reinvested monthly)	+25.3%	+16.1%	+32.6%	+3.0%	+23.5%	+18.7%	-3.7%	+23.2%	4.93	
d. AMEX Market Value Index (without dividends)	+28.4%	+7.0%	+20.5%	-8.4%	+31.0%	+6.2%	-8.0%	+17.3%	4.89	
e. NASDAQ OTC Composite (without dividends)	+21.7%	+7.4%	+31.4%	-11.2%	+19.9%	+18.7%	-3.2%	+27.2%	5.22	

In general when constructing these model portfolios, the HFD adheres to each newsletter's actual recommendations, resorting to the following procedures only when the newsletter is silent or vague about what to do. If a newsletter says nothing to the contrary, the portfolio the HFD constructs will be fully invested (with no margin) in those recommendations most highly recommended at a given time, with each position carrying equal weight. With each transaction, furthermore, the portfolio is rebalanced to keep this equal weighting. Cash positions earn the T-Bill rate, dividends are credited, and a 2% round-trip commission is deducted (0.05% for commodities). Transactions are made at the closing price on the day the newsletter is received (or at the average of the high and low in trading after hotline recommendations); initial public offerings are purchased at the average of their high and low aftermarket prices (therefore the gains and losses for new issues newsletters *exclude* first day premiums). A more complete description is available upon request.

The Timing Portfolios (those in italics following some letters' listings) were constructed exactly as were their corresponding portfolios, except that the stock portions were replaced by the NYSE Composite Index. For example, if a newsletter recommends that 60% be in stocks and 40% in T-Bills, its corresponding Timing Portfolio will have 60% "invested" in the NYSE Composite and 40% earning the T-Bill rate. You thus can see whether a newsletter's stock picks did better or worse than the market as a whole

(1) The risk ratio is the standard deviation of each newsletter's monthly performance since 1/1/86; the larger the number, the greater the risk.

(2) The figure to the left in this column is the number of securities in the portfolio at the end of the month (cash equivalents don't count). The figure to the right signifies how clear and complete are each newsletter's recommendations, with 'A' the most clear and complete to 'D' the least. An 'A' rating signifies that the letter recommends a model portfolio; a 'B' rating signifies that the letter gives overall portfolio allocations but not advice on what to buy or sell to get in line with that advice; a 'C' rating is for letters with just lists of recommended stocks. A 'D' rating is reserved for those letters for which advice sometimes is missing from issue to issue and for which recommendations sometimes come in the form of categories of investments rather than specific securities.

• *The Prudent Speculator's* actual portfolio utilizes margin. As an on-going portfolio, its margin level need only be kept above the maintenance level of 30%; a new subscriber, however, would be unable to use anything less than 50% margin. The HFD's calculations assume that each year the portfolio starts out with 50% margin.

Source: *Hulbert Financial Digest*, 643 S. Carolina Avenue, S.E., Washington, D.C. 20003. A five month trial to the digest is $37.50.

Bonds and Money Market Instruments

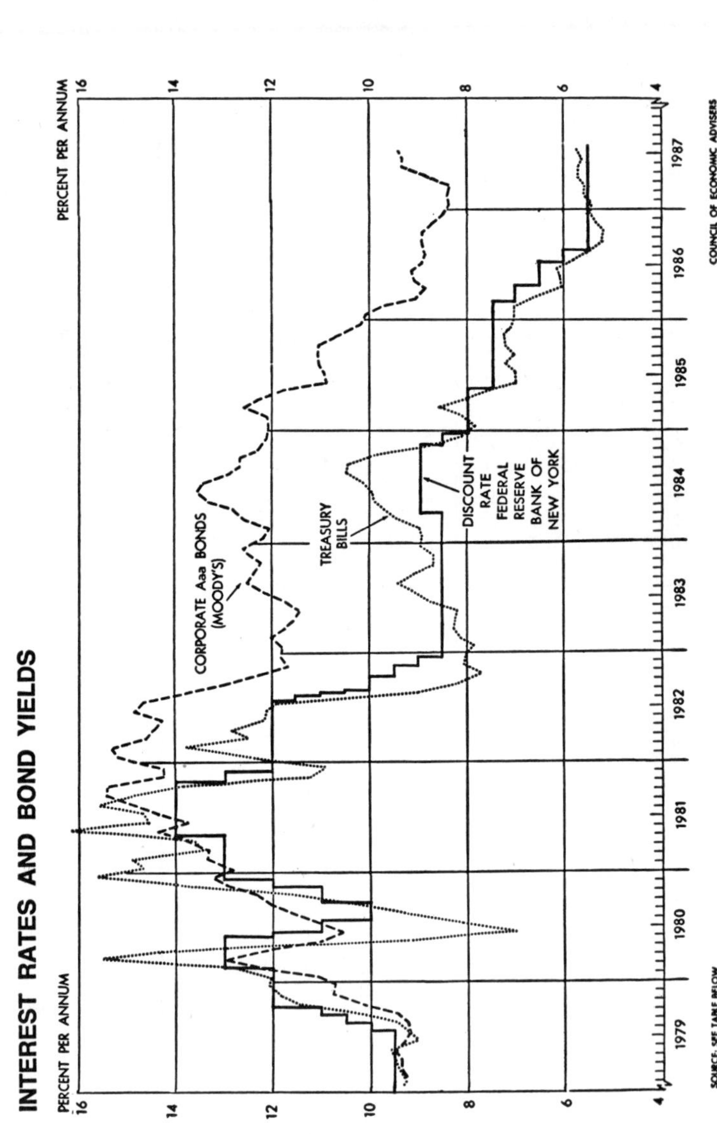

[Percent per annum]

Period	U.S. Treasury security yields			High-grade municipal bonds (Standard & Poor's) [3]	Corporate Aaa bonds (Moody's) [4]	Prime commercial paper, 6 months [1]	Discount rate (N.Y. F.R. Bank) [5]	Prime rate charged by banks [5]	New-home mortgage yields (FHLBB) [6]
	3-month bills (new issues) [1]	Constant maturities [2]							
		3-year	10-year						
1981	14.029	14.44	13.91	11.23	14.17	14.76	13.41	18.87	14.70
1982	10.686	12.92	13.00	11.57	13.79	11.89	11.02	14.86	15.14
1983	8.63	10.45	11.10	9.47	12.04	8.89	8.50	10.79	12.57
1984	9.58	11.89	12.44	10.15	12.71	10.16	8.80	12.04	12.38
1985	7.48	9.64	10.62	9.18	11.37	8.01	7.69	9.93	11.55
1986	5.98	7.06	7.68	7.38	9.02	6.39	6.33	8.33	10.17
1986: July	5.84	6.86	7.30	7.62	8.88	6.24	6.50–6.00	8.50–8.00	10.30
Aug	5.57	6.49	7.17	7.31	8.72	5.83	6.00–5.50	8.00–7.50	10.26
Sept	5.19	6.62	7.45	7.14	8.89	5.61	5.50–5.50	7.50–7.50	10.17
Oct	5.18	6.56	7.43	7.12	8.86	5.61	5.50–5.50	7.50–7.50	10.02
Nov	5.35	6.46	7.25	6.86	8.68	5.69	5.50–5.50	7.50–7.50	9.91
Dec	5.49	6.43	7.11	6.93	8.49	5.88	5.50–5.50	7.50–7.50	9.69
1987: Jan	5.45	6.41	7.08	6.63	8.36	5.76	5.50–5.50	7.50–7.50	9.51
Feb	5.59	6.56	7.25	6.66	8.38	5.99	5.50–5.50	7.50–7.50	9.23
Mar	5.56	6.58	7.25	6.71	8.36	6.10	5.50–5.50	7.50–7.50	9.14
Apr	5.76	7.32	8.02	7.62	8.85	6.50	5.50–5.50	7.75–7.75	9.21
May	5.75	8.02	8.61	8.10	9.33	7.04	5.50–5.50	8.00–8.25	r9.37
June	5.69	7.82	r8.40	7.89	9.32	7.00	5.50–5.50	8.25–8.25	9.50
July	5.78	7.74	8.45	7.83	9.42	6.72	5.50–5.50	8.25–8.25	....
Week ended:									
1987: July 4	5.82	7.72	8.35	7.91	9.33	6.91	5.50–5.50	8.25–8.25	....
11	5.62	7.65	8.32	7.77	9.31	6.75	5.50–5.50	8.25–8.25	....
18	5.55	7.65	8.38	7.80	9.36	6.66	5.50–5.50	8.25–8.25	....
25	....	7.77	8.52	7.80	9.46	6.67	5.50–5.50	8.25–8.25	....
Aug 1	6.14	7.91	8.62	7.87	9.56	6.75	5.50–5.50	8.25–8.25	....

[1] Bank-discount basis.
[2] Yields on the more actively traded issues adjusted to constant maturities by the Treasury Department.
[3] Weekly data are Wednesday figures.
[4] Series excludes public utility issues for January 17, 1984 through October 11, 1984 due to lack of appropriate issues.
[5] Average effective rate for year; opening and closing rate for month and week.
[6] Effective rate (in the primary market) on conventional mortgages, reflecting fees and charges as well as contract rate and assumed, on the average, repayment at end of 10 years.

Sources: Department of the Treasury, Board of Governors of the Federal Reserve System, Federal Home Loan Bank Board, Moody's Investors Service, and Standard & Poor's Corporation.

Source: *Economic Indicators*, Council of Economic Advisers.

SHORT-TERM INTEREST RATES

MONTHLY AVERAGES, EXCEPT FOR DISCOUNT AND PRIME RATES, WHICH ARE EFFECTIVE DATES OF CHANGE

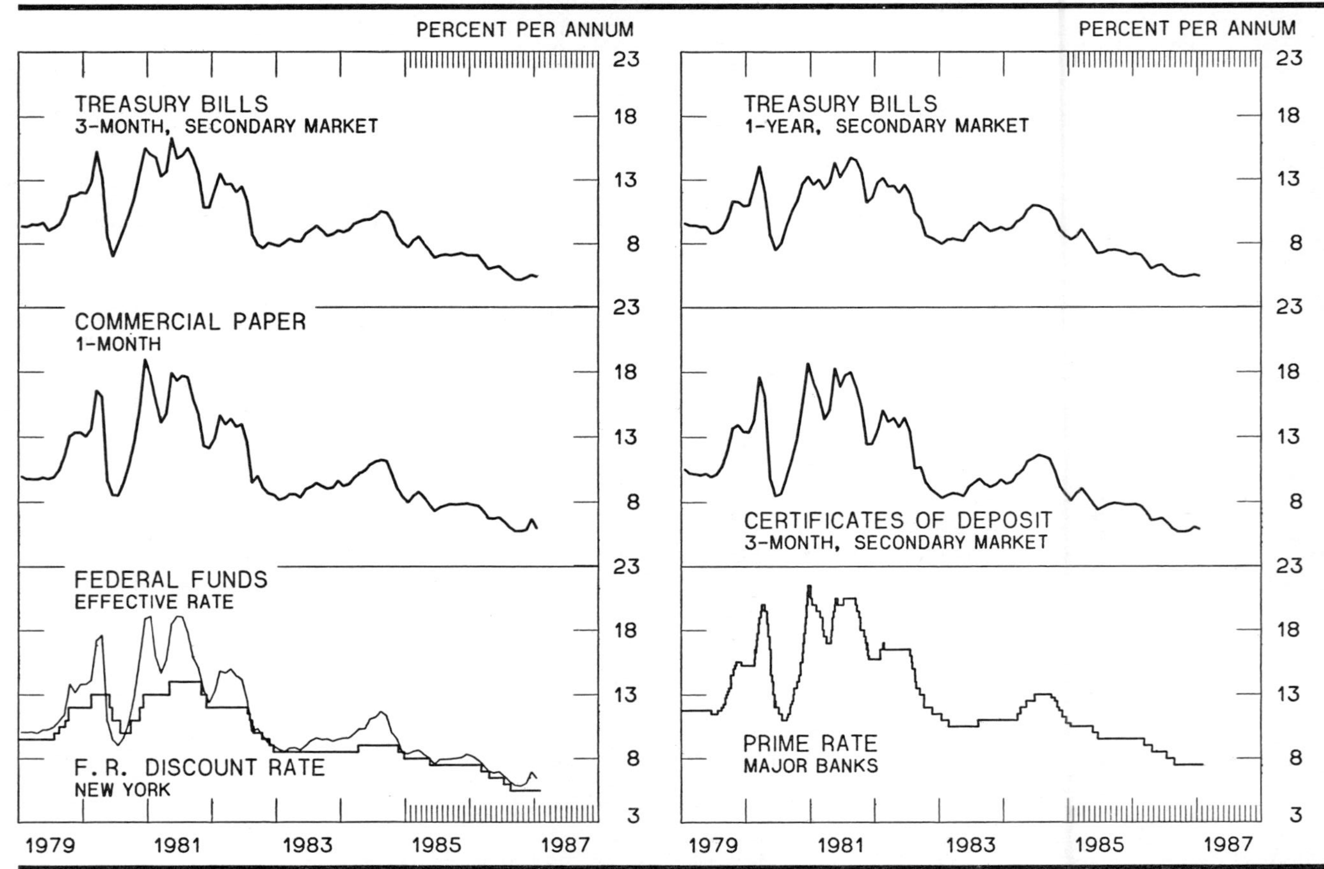

Source: *Federal Reserve Chart Book*, Board of Governors of the Federal Reserve System.

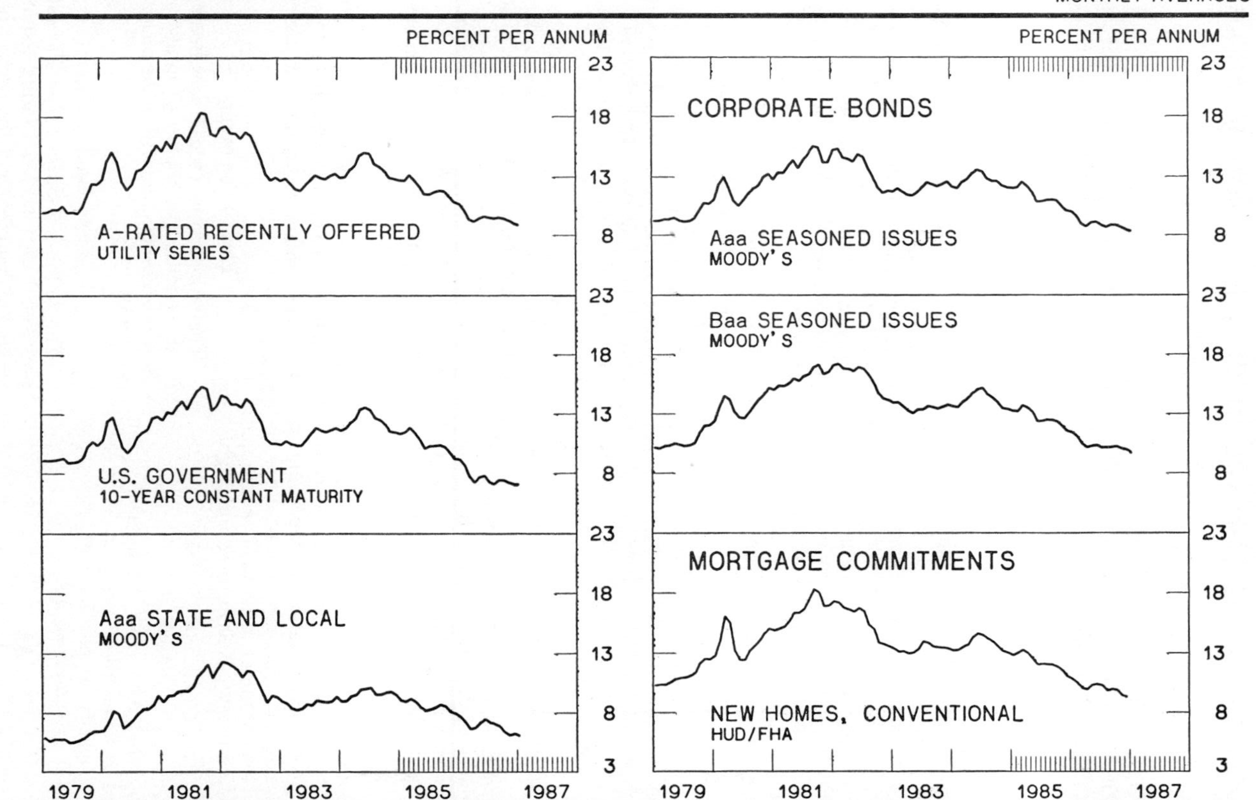

Source: *Federal Reserve Chart Book*, Board of Governors of the Federal Reserve System.

Credit Ratings of Fixed Income and Money Market Securities

KEY TO STANDARD & POOR'S CORPORATE AND MUNICIPAL BOND RATING DEFINITIONS

A Standard & Poor's corporate or municipal debt rating is a current assessment of the creditworthiness of an obligor with respect to a specific debt obligation. This assessment may take into consideration obligors such as guarantors, insurers, or lessees.

The debt rating is not a recommendation to purchase, sell or hold a security, inasmuch as it does not comment as to market price or suitability for a particular investor.

The ratings are based on current information furnished by the issuer or obtained by Standard & Poor's from other sources it considers reliable. Standard & Poor's does not perform an audit in connection with any rating and may, on occasion, rely on unaudited financial information. The ratings may be changed, suspended or withdrawn as a result of changes in, or unavailability of, such information, or for other circumstances.

The ratings are based, in varying degrees, on the following considerations:

I. Likelihood of default—capacity and willingness of the obligor as to the timely payment of interest and repayment of principal in accordance with the terms of the obligation;
II. Nature of and provisions of the obligation;
III. Protection afforded by, and relative position of, the obligation in the event of bankruptcy, reorganization or other arrangement under the laws of bankruptcy and other laws affecting creditor's rights.

AAA

Debt rated **AAA** have the highest rating assigned by Standard & Poor's to a debt obligation. Capacity to pay interest and repay principal is extremely strong.

AA

Debt rated **AA** have a very strong capacity to pay interest and repay principal and differ from the highest rated issues only in a small degree.

A

Debt rated **A** have a strong capacity to pay interest and repay principal although they are somewhat more susceptible to the adverse effects of changes in circumstances and economic conditions than debts in higher rated categories.

BBB

Debt rated **BBB** are regarded as having an adequate capacity to pay interest and repay principal. Whereas they normally exhibit adequate protection parameters, adverse economic conditions or changing circumstances are more likely to lead to a weakened capacity to pay interest and repay principal for debts in this category than for debts in higher rated categories.

BB, B, CCC, CC

Debt rated **BB, B, CCC,** and **CC** are regarded, on balance, as predominantly speculative with respect to capacity to pay interest and repay principal in accordance with the terms of the obligation. **BB** indicates the lowest degree of speculation and **CC** the highest degree of speculation. While such debts will likely have some quality and protective characteristics, these are outweighed by large uncertainties or major risk exposures to adverse conditions.

C

The rating **C** is reserved for income bonds on which no interest is being paid.

D

Debt rated **D** are in default, and payment of interest and/or repayment of principal is in arrears.

Plus (+) or minus (−)

The ratings from **AA** to **B** may be modified by the addition of a plus or minus sign to show relative standing within the major rating categories.

Provisional ratings

The letter *p* indicates that the rating is provisional. A provisional rating assumes the successful completion of the project being financed by the debts being rated and indicates that payment of debt service requirements is largely or entirely dependent upon the successful and timely completion of the project. This rating, however, while addressing credit quality subsequent to completion of the proj-

Source: From Standard & Poor's Debt Rating Division.

* Continuance of the rating is contingent upon S&P's receipt of an executed copy of the escrow agreement or closing documentation confirming investments and the cash flows.

ect, makes no comment on the likelihood of, or the risk of default upon failure of, such completion. The investor should exercise his own judgment with respect to such likelihood and risk.

L*

The letter "L" indicates that the rating pertains to the principal amount of those bonds where the underlying deposit collateral is fully insured by the Federal Savings & Loan Insurance Corp. or the Federal Deposit Insurance Corp.

NR

Indicates that no rating has been requested, that there is insufficient information on which to base a rating or that S&P does not rate a particular type of obligation as a matter of policy.

Debt Obligations

Debt Obligations of issuers outside the United States and its territories are rated on the same basis as domestic corporate and municipal issues. The ratings measure the creditworthiness of the obligor but do not take into account currency exchange and other uncertainties.

Bond Investment Quality Standards

Under present commercial bank regulations issued by the Comptroller of the Currency, bonds rated in the top four categories (**AAA, AA, A, BBB,** commonly known as "Investment Grade" ratings) are generally regarded as eligible for bank investment. In addition, the Legal Investment Laws of various states impose certain rating or other standards for obligations eligible for investment by savings banks, trust companies, insurance companies and fiduciaries generally.

KEY TO STANDARD & POOR'S PREFERRED STOCK RATING DEFINITIONS

A Standard & Poor's preferred stock rating is an assessment of the capacity and willingness of an issuer to pay preferred stock dividends and any applicable sinking fund obligations. A preferred stock rating differs from a bond rating inasmuch as it is assigned to an equity issue, which issue is intrinsically different from, and subordinated to, a debt issue. Therefore, to reflect this difference, the preferred stock rating symbol will normally not be higher than the bond rating symbol assigned to, or that would be assigned to, the senior debt of the same issuer.

The preferred stock ratings are based on the following considerations.

I. Likelihood of payment—capacity and willingness of the issuer to meet the timely payment of preferred stock dividends and any applicable sinking fund requirements in accordance with the terms of the obligation.
II. Nature of, and provisions of, the issue.
III. Relative position of the issue in the event of bankruptcy, reorganization, or other arrangements affecting creditors' rights.

AAA

This is the highest rating that may be assigned by Standard & Poor's to a preferred stock issue and indicates in extremely strong capacity to pay the preferred stock obligations.

AA

A preferred stock issue rated **AA** also qualifies as a high-quality fixed income security. The capacity to pay preferred stock obligations is very strong, although not as overwhelming as for issues rated **AAA.**

A

An issue rated **A** is backed by a sound capacity to pay the preferred stock obligations, although it is somewhat more susceptible to the adverse effects of changes in circumstances and economic conditions.

BBB

An issue rated **BBB** is regarded as backed by an adequate capacity to pay the preferred stock obligations. Whereas it normally exhibits adequate protection parameters, adverse economic conditions or changing circumstances are more likely to lead to a weakened capacity to make payments for a preferred stock in this category than for issues in the **A** category.

BB, B, CCC

Preferred stock rated **BB, B,** and **CCC** are regarded, on balance, as predominately speculative with respect to the issuer's capacity to pay preferred stock obligations. **BB** indicates the lowest degree of speculation and **CCC** the highest degree of speculation. While such issues will likely have some quality and protective characteristics, these are outweighed by large uncertainties or major risk exposures to adverse conditions.

CC

The rating **CC** is reserved for a preferred stock issue in arrears on dividends or sinking fund payments but that is currently paying.

C

A preferred stock rated **C** is a non-paying issue.

D

A preferred stock rated **D** is a non-paying issue with the issuer in default on debt instruments.

NR

NR indicates that no rating has been requested, that there is insufficient information on which to base a rating, or that S&P does not rate a particular type of obligation as a matter or policy.

Plus (+) or Minus (−) To provide more detailed indications of preferred stock quality, the ratings from **AA** to **B** may be modified by the addition of a plus or minus sign to show relative standing within the major rating categories.

The preferred stock rating is not a recommendation to purchase or sell a security, inasmuch as market price is not considered in arriving at the rating. Preferred stock *ratings* are wholly unrelated to Standard & Poor's earnings and dividend *rankings* for common stocks.

MUNICIPAL NOTES

A Standard & Poor's role rating reflects the liquidity concerns and market access risks unique to notes. Notes due in 3 years or less will likely receive a long-term debt rating. The following criteria will be used in making that assessment.

—Amortization schedule (the larger the final maturity relative to other maturities the more likely it will be treated as a note).

—Source of Payment (the more dependent the issue is on the market for its refinancing, the more likely it will be treated as a note).

Note rating symbols are as follows:

SP-1 Very strong or strong capacity to pay principal and interest. Those issues determined to possess overwhelming safety characteristics will be given a plus (+) designation.

SP-2 Satisfactory capacity to pay principal and interest.

SP-3 Speculative capacity to pay principal and interest.

TAX-EXEMPT DEMAND BONDS

Standard & Poor's assigns "dual" ratings to all long-term debt issues that have as part of their provisions a demand or double feature.

The first rating addresses the likelihood of repayment of principal and interest as due, and the second rating addresses only the demand feature. The long-term debt rating symbols are used for bonds to denote the long-term maturity and the commercial paper rating symbols are used to denote the put option (for example, "AAA/A-1+"). For the newer "demand notes," S&P's note rating symbols, combined with the commercial paper symbols, are used (for example, "SP-1+/A-1+").

KEY TO STANDARD & POOR'S COMMERCIAL PAPER RATING DEFINITIONS

A Standard & Poor's Commercial Paper Rating is a current assessment of the likelihood of timely payment of debt having an original maturity of no more than 365 days.

Ratings are graded into four categories, ranging from **A** for the highest quality obligations to **D** for the lowest. The four categories are as follows:

A

Issues assigned this highest rating are regarded as having the greatest capacity for timely payment. Issues in this category are further refined with the designations 1, 2, and 3 to indicate the relative degree of safety.

A-1 This designation indicates that the degree of safety regarding timely payment is very strong.

A-2 Capacity for timely payment on issues with this designation is strong. However, the relative degree of safety is not as overwhelming as for issues designated **A-1.**

A-3 Issues carrying this designation have a satisfactory capacity for timely payment. They are, however, somewhat more vulnerable to the adverse effects of changes in circumstances than obligations carrying the higher designations.

B

Issues rated **B** are regarded as having only an adequate capacity for timely payment. However, such capacity may be damaged by changing conditions for short-term adversities.

C

This rating is assigned to short-term obligations with a doubtful capacity for payment.

D

This rating indicates that the issue is either a default or is expected to be in default upon maturity.

The Commercial paper Rating is not a recommendation to purchase or sell a security. The ratings are based on current information furnished to Standard & Poor's by the issuer or obtained from other sources it considers reliable. The ratings may be changed, suspended, or withdrawn as a result of changes in, or unavailability of, such information.

KEY TO MOODY'S MUNICIPAL RATINGS*

Aaa

Bonds which are rated **Aaa** are judged to be of the best quality. They carry the smallest degree of investment risk and are generally referred to as "gilt edge." Interest payments are protected by a large or by an exceptionally stable margin and principal is secure. While the various protective elements are likely to change, such changes as can be visualized are most unlikely to impair the fundamentally strong position of such issues.

Aa

Bonds which are rated **Aa** are judged to be of high quality by all standards. Together with the **Aaa** group they comprise what are generally known as high grade bonds. They are rated lower than the best bonds because margins of protection may not be as large as in **Aaa** securities or fluctuation of protective elements may be of greater amplitude or there may be other elements present which make the long term risks appear somewhat larger than in **Aaa** securities.

A

Bonds which are rated **A** possess many favorable instrument attributes and are to be considered as upper medium grade obligations. Factors giving security to principal and interest are considered adequate, but elements may be present which suggest a susceptibility to impairment sometime in the future.

Baa

Bonds which are rated **Baa** are considered as medium grade obligations; i.e., they are neither highly protected nor poorly secured. Interest payments and principal security appear adequate for the present but certain protective elements may be lacking or may be characteristically unreliable over any great length of time. Such bonds lack outstanding investment characteristics and in fact have speculative characteristics as well.

Ba

Bonds which are rated **Ba** are judged to have speculative elements; their future cannot be considered as well assured. Often the protection of interest and principal payments may be very moderate, and thereby not well safeguarded during both good and bad times over the future. Uncertainty of position characterizes bonds in this case.

B

Bonds which are rated **B** generally lack characteristics of the desirable investment. Assurance of interest and principal payments or of maintenance of other terms of the contract over any long period of time may be small.

Caa

Bonds which are rated **Caa** are of poor standing. Such issues may be in default or there may be present elements of danger with respect to principal or interest.

Ca

Bonds which are rated **Ca** represent obligations which are speculative in a high degree. Such issues are often in default or have other marked shortcomings.

C

Bonds which are rated **C** are the lowest rated class of bonds, and issues so rated can be regarded as having extremely poor prospects of ever attaining any real investment standing.

Con.(—)

Bonds for which the security depends upon the completion of some act or the fulfillment of some condition are rated conditionally. These are bonds secured by (a) earnings of projects under construction, (b) earnings of projects unseasoned in operation experience, (c) rentals which begin when facilities are completed, or (d) payments to which some other limiting condition attaches. Parenthetical rating denotes probable credit stature upon completion of construction or elimination of basis of condition.

* **Note:** Those bonds in the **Aa, A, Baa, Ba** and **B** groups which Moody's believes possess the strongest investment attributes are designated by the symbols **Aa 1, A 1, Baa 1, Ba 1** and **B 1.**

Source: Moody's Investors Service, Inc.

KEY TO MOODY'S CORPORATE RATINGS*

Aaa

Bonds which are rated **Aaa** are judged to be of the best quality. They carry the smallest degree of investment risk and are generally referred to as "gilt edge." Interest payments

* ***Note:*** Moody's applies numerical modifiers, **1, 2** and **3** in each generic rating classification from **Aa** through **B** in its corporate bond rating system. The modifier **1** indicates that the security ranks in the higher end of its generic rating category; the modifier **2** indicates a mid-range ranking; and the modifier **3** indicates that the issue ranks in the lower end of its generic rating category.

are protected by a large or by an exceptionally stable margin and principal is secure. While the various protective elements are likely to change, such changes as can be visualized are most unlikely to impair the fundamentally strong position of such issues.

Aa

Bonds which are rated **Aa** are judged to be of high quality by all standards. Together with the **Aaa** group they comprise what are generally known as high grade bonds. They are rated lower than the best bonds because margins of protection may not be as large as in **Aaa** securities or fluctuation of protective elements may be of greater amplitude or there may be other elements present which make the long term risks appear somewhat larger than in **Aaa** securities.

A

Bonds which are rated **A** possess many favorable investment attributes and are to be considered as upper medium grade obligations. Factors giving security to principal and interest are considered adequate but elements may be present which suggest a susceptibility to impairment sometime in the future.

Baa

Bonds which are rated **Baa** are considered as medium grade obligations, i.e., they are neither highly protected nor poorly secured. Interest payments and principal security appear adequate for the present but certain protective elements may be lacking or may be characteristically unreliable over any great length of time. Such bonds lack outstanding investment characteristics and in fact have speculative characteristics as well.

Ba

Bonds which are rated **Ba** are judged to have speculative elements; their future cannot be considered as well assured. Often the protection of interest and principal payments may be very moderate and thereby not well safeguarded during both good and bad times over the future. Uncertainty of position characterizes bonds in this class.

B

Bonds which are rated **B** generally lack characteristics of the desirable investment. Assurance of interest and principal payments or of maintenance of other terms of the contract over any long period of time may be small.

Caa

Bonds which are rated **Caa** are of poor standing. Such issues may be in default or there may be present elements of danger with respect to principal or interest.

Ca

Bonds which are rated **Ca** represent obligations which are speculative in a high degree. Such issues are often in default or have other marked shortcomings.

C

Bonds which are rated **C** are the lowest rated class of bonds and issues so rated can be regarded as having extremely poor prospects of ever attaining any real investment standing.

KEY TO MOODY'S COMMERCIAL PAPER RATINGS

The term "Commercial Paper" as used by Moody's means promissory obligations not having an original maturity in excess of nine months. Moody's makes no representation as to whether such Commercial Paper is by any other definition "Commercial Paper" or is exempt from registration under the Securities Act of 1933, as amended.

Moody's Commercial Paper ratings are opinions of the ability of issuers to repay punctually promissory obligations not having an original maturity in excess of nine months. Moody's makes no representation that such obligations are exempt from registration under the Securities Act of 1933, nor does it represent that any specific note is a valid obligation of a rated issuer or issued in conformity with any applicable law. Moody's employs the following three designations, all judged to be investment grade, to indicate the relative repayment capacity of rated issuers:

Issuers rated **Prime-1** (or related supporting institutions) have a superior capacity for repayment of short-term promissory obligations. Prime-1 repayment capacity will normally be evidenced by the following characteristics:

- Leading market positions in well established industries.
- High rates of return on funds employed.
- Conservative capitalization structures with moderate reliance on debt and ample asset protection.
- Broad margins in earnings coverage of fixed financial charges and high internal cash generation.
- Well established access to a range of financial markets and assured sources of alternate liquidity.

Issuers rated **Prime-2** (or related supporting institutions) have a strong capacity for short-term promissory obligations. This will normally be evidenced by many of the characteristics cited above but to a lesser degree. Earnings trends and coverage ratios, while sound, will be more sub-

Source: Moody's Investors Service, Inc.

ject to variation. Capitalization characteristics, while still appropriate, may be more affected by external conditions. Ample alternate liquidity is maintained.

Issuers rated **Prime-3** (or related supporting institutions) have an acceptable capacity for repayment of short-term promissory obligations. The effect of industry characteristics and market composition may be more pronounced. Variability in earnings and profitability may result in changes in the level of debt protection measurements and the requirement for relatively high financial leverage. Adequate liquidity is maintained.

Issuers rated **Not Prime** do not fall within any of the Prime rating categories.

If an issuer represents to Moody's that its Commercial Paper obligations are supported by the credit of another entity or entities, the name or names of such supporting entity or entities are listed within parenthesis beneath the name of the issuer. In assigning ratings to such issuers, Moody's evaluates the financial strength of the indicated affiliated corporations, commercial banks, insurance companies, foreign governments or other entities, but only as one factor in the total rating assessment. Moody's makes no representation and gives no opinion on the legal validity or enforceability of any support arrangement. You are cautioned to review with your counsel any questions regarding particular support arrangements.

KEY TO MOODY'S PREFERRED STOCK RATINGS*

Moody's Rating Policy Review Board Extended its rating services to include quality designations on preferred stocks on October 1, 1973. The decision to rate preferred stocks, which Moody's had done prior to 1935, was prompted by evidence of investor interest. Moody's believes that its rating of preferred stocks is especially appropriate in view of the ever-increasing amount of these securities outstanding, and the fact that continuing inflation and its ramifications have resulted generally in the dilution of some of the protection afforded them as well as other fixed-income securities.

Because of the fundamental differences between preferred stocks and bonds, a variation of our familiar bond rating symbols is being used in the quality ranking of preferred stocks. The symbols, presented below, are designed to avoid comparison with bond quality in absolute terms. It should always be borne in mind that preferred stocks occupy a junior position to bonds within a particular capital structure.

Preferred stock rating symbols and their definitions are as follows:

aaa

An issue which is rated **aaa** is considered to be a top-quality preferred stock. This rating indicates good asset protection and the least risk of dividend impairment within the universe of preferred stocks.

aa

An issue which is rated **aa** is considered a high-grade preferred stock. This rating indicates that there is reasonable assurance that earnings and asset protection will remain relatively well maintained in the foreseeable future.

a

An issue which is rated **a** is considered to be an upper-medium grade preferred stock. While risks are judged to be somewhat greater than in the "aaa" and "aa" classifications, earnings and asset protection are, nevertheless, expected to be maintained at adequate levels.

baa

An issue which is rated **baa** is considered to be medium grade, neither highly protected nor poorly secured. Earnings and asset protection appear adequate at present but may be questionable over any great length of time.

ba

An issue which is rated **ba** is considered to have speculative elements and its future cannot be considered well assured. Earnings and asset protection may be very moderate and not well safeguarded during adverse periods. Uncertainty of position characterized preferred stocks in this class.

b

An issue which is rated **b** generally lacks the characteristics of a desirable investment. Assurance of dividend payments and maintenance of other terms of the issue over any long period of time may be small.

caa

An issue which is rated **caa** is likely to be in arrears on dividend payments. This rating designation does not purport to indicate the future status of payments.

"ca"

An issue which is rated **"ca"** is speculative in a high degree and is likely to be in arrears on dividends with little likelihood of eventual payment.

***Note:** Moody's applies numerical modifiers **1**, **2** and **3** in each rating classification from **1** indicates that the security ranks in the higher end of its generic rating category; the modifier **2** indicates a mid-range ranking; and the modifier **3** indicates that the issue ranks in the lower end of its generic rating category.

Source: Moody's Investors Service, Inc.

"c"

This is the lowest rated class of preferred or preference stock. Issues so rated can be regarded as having extremely poor prospects of ever attaining any real investment standing.

KEY TO SHORT-TERM LOAN RATINGS

MIG 1/VMIG 1

This designation denotes best quality. There is present strong protection by established cash flows, superior liquidity support or demonstrated broadbased access to the market for refinancing.

MIG 2/VMIG 2

This designation denotes high quality. Margins of protection are ample although not so large as in the preceding group.

MIG 3/VMIG 3

This designation denotes favorable quality. All security elements are accounted for but there is lacking the undeniable strength of the preceding grades. Liquidity and cash flow protection may be narrow and market access for refinancing is likely to be less well established.

MIG 4/VMIG 4

This designation denotes adequate quality. Protection commonly regarded as required of an investment security is present and although not distinctly or predominantly speculative, there is specific risk.

Issues or the features associated with **MIG** or **VMIG** ratings are identified by date of issue, date of maturity or maturities or rating expiration date and description to distinguish each rating from other ratings. Each rating designation is unique with no implication as to any other similar issue of the same obligor. **MIG** ratings terminate at the retirement of the obligation while **VMIG** rating expiration will be a function of each issue's specific structural or credit features.

MAJOR MONEY MARKET AND FIXED INCOME SECURITIES

Type	Interest: When Paid	Marketability	Minimum Amount of Issue	Maturity
A. Interest Fully Taxable				
Corporate Bonds and Notes	S[1]	Very good to poor depending on quality	$1,000	1 to 50 years
Corporate Preferred Stock (Pays dividends as a fixed percentage of face value. Dividends not obligatory, but if declared must be paid before that of the common stock. Dividends fully taxable for individuals, but 85% exempt from federal tax for corporations)	Generally quarterly	Good to poor depending on quality	$100 or less	No maturity
Federal Home Loan Mortgage Corporate Bonds	S	Fair	$25,000	Up to 25 years
Federal Home Loan Mortgage Certificates	S	Fair	$100,000	Up to 3 years
Farmers' Home Administration Notes and Certificates	Annual	Fair	$25,000	1 to 25 years
Federal Housing Administration Debentures (Guaranteed by the U.S. Government)	S	Very good	$50	1 to 40 years
Federal National Mortgage Association Bonds	S	Fair	$25,000	2 to 25 years
Government National Mortgage Modified Pass through Certificates (interest plus some repayment of principal, guaranteed by U.S. Government)	Monthly	Good	$25,000	30 years; average life 12 years
Federal Home Loan Bank Bonds and Notes	S	Good	$10,000	1 to 20 years
Export-Import Bank Debentures and Certificates	S	Good	$5,000	3 to 7 years

MAJOR MONEY MARKET AND FIXED INCOME SECURITIES *(continued)*

Type	Interest: When Paid	Marketability	Minimum Amount of Issue	Maturity
International Bank for Reconstruction Development (World Bank), Inter-American Development Bank, Asia Development Bank	S	Fair to poor	$1,000	3 to 25 years
Foreign and Eurodollar Bonds and Notes	May be Annual or S	Poor	$1,000 (amounts vary in foreign currencies)	1 to 30 years
Bankers Acceptances (short-term debt obligations (resulting from international trade and guaranteed by a major bank)	Discounted[2] on a 360-day year basis	Fair	$5,000	1 to 270 days
Commercial Paper (short-term debt issued by a major corporation)	Discounted on a 360-day year basis	No secondary market	$100,000 (occasionally smaller)	1 to 270 days
Negotiable Certificates of Deposit (short-term debt issued by banks and which can be sold on the open market)	Interest paid on maturity; 360-day year basis	Fair	$100,000 (occasionally smaller)	30 days to 1 year
Non-negotiable Certificate of Deposit (savings certificates)	Interest paid on maturity; 360-day year basis	Non-negotiable	$500 $10,000	30 months 6 months
Collateralized Mortgage Obligations (CMO)	S or monthly	Good	$1,000	typically 2 to 20 years
Repurchase Agreements (generally short term loans by large investors, secured by U.S. Government or other high quality issues)[3]	Interest paid on maturity; 360-day year basis	No secondary market	$100,000	1 to 30 days (sometimes more)
Zero Coupon Bonds (Bonds stripped of coupons)	Bonds issued at deep discount. Full yield realized at maturity	Good	$1,000 on maturity	1 to 30 years
B. Interest Exempt from State and Local Income Taxes				
U.S. Treasury Bonds and Notes	S	Very good	$1,000	1 to 20 years
U.S. Treasury Bills	Discounted on a 360-day basis	Very good	$10,000	90 days to 1 year
U.S. Series EE Savings Bonds[4]	Issued at discount, full interest, paid on maturity	No secondary market: available for resale	$50 minimum $15,000 maximum	11 years (can be redeemed before maturity at reduced yields
U.S. Series HH Savings Bonds	S	No secondary market	$500 $15,000 maximum	10 years
Federal Land Bank Bonds	S	Good	$1,000	1 to 10 years
Federal Financing Bank Notes and Bonds	S	Good	$1,000	1 to 20 years
Tennessee Valley Authority Notes and Bonds	S	Fair	$1,000	5 to 25 years
Banks for Cooperatives Bonds	Interest: 360-day year basis	Good	$5,000	180 days
Federal Intermediate Credit Bank Bonds	Interest: 360-day year basis	Good	$5,000.	270 days
Federal Home Loan Bank Notes and Bonds	Discounted: 360-day year basis	Good	$10,000.	30 to 360-day year basis (some more)

MAJOR MONEY MARKET AND FIXED INCOME SECURITIES *(concluded)*

Type	Interest: When Paid	Marketability	Minimum Amount of Issue	Maturity
Farm Credit Bank Notes and Bonds	Interest: 360-day year basis	Good	$50,000.	270 days (some more)
C. Interest Exempt from Federal Income Tax				
State and Local Notes and Bonds (in-State issues, usually exempt from State and local income taxes)	S	Good to fair depending on rating	$5,000.	1 to 50 years
Housing Authority Bonds (in-State issues usually exempt from State and local income taxes)	S	Good to fair	$5,000.	1 to 40 years

[1] S means semiannually.

[2] A discount means interest paid in advance, thus a 10% discounted security maturing at $10,000 would cost $9,000 to purchase.

[3] Recently some banks have issued repurchase agreements for smaller amounts of money, i.e., several thousands of dollars.

[4] Since November 1982, U.S. Savings Bonds pay variable interest equal to 85% of the 5 year Treasury securities' rate adjusted semi-annually and have a minimum guaranteed rate which is adjustable.

U.S. Treasury Bonds, Notes, and Bills: Terms Defined*

U.S. Treasury bonds, notes and bills are interest paying securities representing a debt on the part of the U.S. Government. Treasury bonds have a maturity of over 5 years, while notes mature within 5 to 7 years. Bills are discussed below. Both Treasury bonds and notes are generally issued in minimum denominations of $1,000 and pay interest semiannually. The amount of semiannual interest paid is determined by the coupon rate specified on the bond and is calculated on a 365-day year basis. For a $1,000 face value† bond the interest is given by:

$$\text{semiannual interest} = 1/2\,(\$1{,}000 \times \text{coupon rate})$$

Bonds may be priced higher (at a premium) or lower (at a discount) than the face value (par) depending on current interest rates. The *current yield* is the rate the investor receives based on the prices actually paid for a bond. The price is given by:

$$\text{current yield} = \frac{\$1{,}000 \times \text{coupon rate}}{\text{purchase price}}$$

Thus, a $1,000 face value bond with an 8% coupon rate purchased at $850 has a current yield by:

$$\text{current yield} = \frac{\$1{,}000 \times 8\%}{\$850} = 9.41\%$$

The *yield to maturity* (YTM) is the yield obtained on taking into account the years remaining to maturity, annual interest payments, and the capital gain (or loss) realized at maturity. It is obtained from special tables.

However, the yield to maturity (YTM) may be found approximately from the formula

$$\text{YTM} = \frac{I + A}{B}$$

$$I = \text{annual interest rate}$$

$$A = \frac{\$1{,}000 - M}{N}$$

$$B = \frac{\$1{,}000 + M}{2}$$

where M = current market price of the bond
N = years remaining to maturity

As an example, a bond ($1,000 face value) has a 10% coupon and is currently priced at $1,100 with 10 years remaining to maturity. What is the approximate YTM?

$$I = \$1{,}000 \times .1 = \$100 \text{ interest per year}$$

$$A = \frac{\$1{,}000 - \$1{,}100}{10} = \$-10$$

$$B = \frac{\$1{,}000 + \$1{,}100}{2} = \$1{,}050$$

$$\text{YTM} = \frac{\$100 - \$10}{\$1{,}050} = .0857 = 8.57\%$$

U.S. Treasury bills (T-bills) are U.S. Government debt obligations which mature within one year. They are offered by the Federal Reserve Bank with maturities of 90 days (3 month bills) and 182 days (six month bills). Nine-month bills and one-year bills are also available. Treasury bills are sold in a minimum denomination of $10,000. Interest is paid by the discount method based on a 360-day year. With the discount method, interest is, in effect, paid at the time the bill is purchased. Thus a 91-day $10,000 bill (face value) with an 8% discount interest rate

* The terms *current yield*, *yield to maturity*, etc. defined in this section are generally applicable to all fixed incomes.

† Face value is the amount of the bond or note payable upon maturity.

would provide the buyer with \$202.22 (\$10,000 $\times$ .08 $\times$ $^{91}/_{360}$) interest at the time of purchase. This amount is deducted from the face value of the bill at the time of purchase so the buyer actually pays a net amount of \$9,797.78 (\$10,000 − \$202.22). When the bill matures, the buyer receives \$10,000 on redemption.

Since T-bills pay interest at the time of purchase (discount basis) on a 360-day year basis, while bonds (and notes) pay interest semiannually on a 365-day year basis, the two rates cannot be compared directly. To compare the two rates, the discount rate must be converted to the so-called *bond equivalent yield*, given by

$$\text{bond equivalent yield} = \frac{365 \times \text{discount rate}}{360 - (\text{discount rate} \times \text{days to maturity})}$$

As an example, a newly issued 91-day note with a discount rate of 12% has a

$$\text{bond equivalent yield} = \frac{365 \times (.12)}{360 - (.12 \times 91)} = 12.55\%$$

Interest from U.S. Treasury bonds, notes, and bills are subject to federal income tax, but are exempt from state and local income taxes.

How to Read U.S. Government Bond and Note Quotations

TREASURY BONDS AND NOTES

(1) Rate	(2) Mat.	(3) Date	(4) Bid	(5) Asked	(6) Bid Chg.	(7) Yld.
6¾s,	1981	Jun n . . .	99.3	99.7	+.1	16.51
9⅛s,	1981	Jun n . . .	99.12	99.16	+.2	15.10
9⅜s,	1981	Jul n	98.21	98.25	+.3	16.54
7s,	1981	Aug	97.26	98.10	+.2	15.19
7⅝s,	1981	Aug n . . .	97.30	98.2	+.6	17.66
8⅜s,	1981	Aug n . . .	98.2	98.6	+.2	17.15
9⅝s,	1981	Aug n . . .	98.5	98.9	+.4	16.53
6¾s,	1981	Sep n . . .	96.29	97.1	+.5	16.10
10⅛s,	1981	Sep n . . .	97.28	98	+.4	16.28
12⅝s,	1981	Oct n . . .	98.14	98.18	+.4	16.18
7s,	1981	Nov n . . .	96.4	96.8	+.10	15.86
7¾s,	1981	Nov n . . .	96.18	96.22	+.13	15.55
12⅛s,	1981	Nov n . . .	98.1	98.5	+.3	16.14
7¼s,	1981	Dec n . . .	95.12	95.16	+.10	15.14

Source: Reprinted by permission of *The Wall Street Journal*, Dow Jones & Co., Inc., 1981. All rights reserved.

The above exhibit is an example of U.S. Government bond and note quotations as it appears in *The Wall Street Journal*.

(1) Indicates the coupon rate of interest which is designated by *s*. Rates are quoted to ⅛ of a percent. Thus 8⅜ means 8.375%. The semiannual interest payments are calculated, as described elsewhere, using this rate.

(2) Indicates the year of maturity.

(3) Indicates the month (of the above year) in which the bond or note matures. The letter *n* means the security is a note. Otherwise a bond is implied.

(4) The *bid price* per bond or note (the price at which the bond can be sold to the dealer), expressed as a percentage of the face value (\$1,000) of the bond. Prices are quoted in terms of $^{1}/_{32}$ of a percent. Thus 98.5 means 98$^{5}/_{32}$. To find the dollar value of the price, convert 98$^{5}/_{32}$ to a decimal (98$^{5}/_{32}$ = .98156) and multiply by the face value of the bond to give \$981.56 (.98156 $\times$ \$1,000).

(5) The *ask price* per bond or note (the price at which the dealer will sell the bond). The dollar value is found as indicated above.

(6) The change in the bid price from the closing price of the previous day.

(7) The yield if the bond is held to maturity, based on the ask price.

Some U.S. Treasury bonds can be called back for redemption prior to maturity. These are shown with two dates (under item 2 for example)—*1993–98* indicating that the bonds mature in 1998, but may be called back and redeemed any time after 1993.

Some newspapers (such as *The New York Times*) use a slight modification of the above arrangement, though the various terms have the same meaning as defined above. Thus, a bond maturing in June of 1985 and bearing a 10⅜% coupon is indicated by *May '85 10⅜*.

How to Read U.S. Treasury Bill Quotations

(1) U.S. Treas. Mat. date	(2) Bills Bid	(3) Asked Discount	(4) Yield
-1981-			
6–18	17.62	17.44	17.69
6–25	17.15	17.03	17.33
7– 2	15.39	15.01	15.31
7– 9	15.18	15.04	15.39
7–16	15.02	14.78	15.17
7–23	14.83	14.67	15.10
7–30	14.72	14.42	14.88
8– 6	14.11	13.89	14.36
8–13	13.94	13.72	14.22
8–20	13.94	13.72	14.26
8–27	13.92	13.70	14.28
9– 3	13.97	13.63	14.24
9–10	13.72	13.64	14.29
9–17	13.52	13.34	14.00
9–24	13.63	13.43	14.14
10– 1	13.74	13.54	14.30

Source: Reprinted by permission of *The Wall Street Journal*, Dow Jones & Co., Inc. 1981. All rights reserved.

The above exhibit is an example of Treasury bill quotations as it appears in *The Wall Street Journal*.

(1) The date of maturity, i.e., 6–18 means June 18, 1981.

(2) The bid price at market close quoted as a *discount* rate in percent. This bid price is the price at which the dealer will buy the bill. To convert the discount rate to a dollar price use the formula

$$\text{dollar price} = \$10{,}000 - (\text{discount rate} \times \text{days to maturity} \times .2778)$$

In the above, the discount must be expressed in percent. For example, if the dealer bids 16.18% discount for a bill which will mature in 110 days, the dollar price is given by

$$\text{dollar price} = \$10{,}000 - (16.18 \times 110 \times .2778) = \$9{,}505.57 \text{ per bill}$$

(3) The asked price at market close expressed as a discount rate in percent. The asked price is the price at which the dealer will sell a bill to a buyer. To convert to a dollar price use the above formula.

(4) The bond equivalent yield expressed in percent. This is calculated (as explained elsewhere) from the asked price expressed as a discount rate. This rate is used to compare T-bill yields to that of bonds, notes and certificates of deposit.

Some newspapers (e.g., *The New York Times*) use a somewhat different arrangement, though the meaning of the terms is the same as defined above. Thus, a bill maturing on June 4, 1981, is indicated as such. Also included in some newspapers is the change in bid price expressed as a discount rate.

How to Read Corporate Bond Quotations*

Corporate bonds are debt securities issued by private corporations. They generally have a face value (the amount due on maturity) of $1,000 and a specified interest rate (coupon rate) paid semiannually. Many corporate bonds have a *call* provision which permits the company to recall and redeem the bond after a specified date. Call privileges are usually exercised when interest rates fall sufficiently. Investors, therefore, cannot count on *locking in* high interest rates with corporate bonds. Bond quality designations used by Moody's and Standard & Poor's are given elsewhere in the Almanac (pp. 418–424).

The following is an example of price quotations for bonds traded on The New York Stock Exchange as they appear in *The Wall Street Journal.*

CORPORATION BONDS

VOLUME, $18,990,000

(1) Bonds		(2) Cur YID	(3) Vol	(4) High	(5) Low	(6) Close	(7) Net Chg.
AlaP	9s2000	14.	6	63	62	63	2
AlaP	8½s01	15.	10	57½	57½	57½	. . .
AlaP	8⅞s03	15.	25	60	59½	60	+ ½
AlaP	10⅞05	15.	3	72	72	72	− 2¼
AlaP	10½05	15.	12	70½	70½	70½	− 1
AlaP	12⅝10	16.	7	81¼	81⅛	81⅛	− 1⅝
AlaP	15¼10	16.	111	94⅝	93⅝	94	. . .
AlaP	14¾91	15.	31	97	96½	96½	. . .
AlaP	17⅜11	17.	99	104	103½	103¾	− ¼
Alexn	5½96	cv	34	61¾	61⅝	61¾	+ ¾
Allgl	10¾99	15.	2	70½	70½	70½	. . .
AllstF	8⅛87	11.	2	76⅜	76⅜	76⅜	+ 1⅞
AllstF	9⅝86	12.	10	83⅛	83	83	+ 1⅞

Source: Reprinted by permission of *The Wall Street Journal,* Dow Jones and Company, Inc. 1981.

(1) The name of the issue in abbreviated form, followed by the coupon rate of interest in percent (designated by the letter *s*), and the year in which the bond matures. The coupon rate is stated in terms of ⅛ of a percent; 9⅜ means 9.375%.

(2) This is the current yield which is calculated as stated elsewhere. (See U.S. Treasury Bonds, Notes, and Bills, p. 426.)

(3) This item is the number of bonds sold that day.

(4) This is the highest price quoted for the bond sold on that day, expressed as a percentage of face value ($1,000). To convert to dollars, express the price as a decimal and multiply by the face value of the bond. As an example:

$$58\tfrac{1}{2} = (.5850 \times \$1{,}000.) = \$585$$

(5) This is the lowest price quoted that day. It is converted into dollars as described above.

(6) This is the price at the close of the market that day.

(7) This is the change in the closing price from that of the previous day. To convert to dollars, express as a decimal and multiply by $1,000. Thus, −1⅞ means a decrease per bond of $18.75 (.01875 × $1,000) from that of the previous day.

* Yield terms are the same as those defined in the section on U.S. Treasury Bonds, Notes and Bills, p. 426.

TAX EXEMPT VERSUS TAXABLE YIELDS

tax bracket	To equal a tax-free yield of:											
	5½%	6%	6½%	7%	7½%	8%	8½%	9%	9½%	10%	10½%	11%
	a taxable investment has to earn:											
28%	7.64%	8.33%	9.03%	9.72%	10.42%	11.11%	11.81%	12.50%	13.19%	13.89%	14.58%	15.28%
30	7.86	8.57	9.29	10.00	10.71	11.43	12.14	12.86	13.57	14.29	15.00	15.71
31	7.97	8.70	9.42	10.14	10.87	11.59	12.32	13.04	13.77	14.49	15.22	15.94
32	8.09	8.82	9.56	10.29	11.03	11.76	12.50	13.24	13.97	14.71	15.44	16.18
34	8.33	9.09	9.85	10.61	11.36	12.12	12.88	13.64	14.39	15.15	15.91	16.67
36	8.59	9.38	10.16	10.94	11.72	12.50	13.28	14.06	14.84	15.63	16.41	17.19
37	8.73	9.52	10.32	11.11	11.90	12.70	13.49	14.29	15.08	15.87	16.67	17.47
39	9.02	9.84	10.66	11.48	12.30	13.11	13.93	14.75	15.57	16.39	17.21	18.03
42	9.48	10.34	11.21	12.07	12.93	13.79	14.66	15.52	16.38	17.24	18.10	18.97
43	9.65	10.53	11.40	12.28	13.16	14.04	14.91	15.79	16.67	17.54	18.42	19.30
44	9.82	10.71	11.61	12.50	13.39	14.29	15.18	16.07	16.96	17.86	18.75	19.64
46	10.19	11.11	12.03	12.96	13.89	14.81	15.74	16.67	17.59	18.52	19.44	20.37
49	10.78	11.76	12.75	13.73	14.71	15.69	16.67	17.65	18.63	19.61	20.59	21.57
54	11.96	13.04	14.13	15.22	16.30	17.39	18.48	19.57	20.65	21.74	22.83	23.91
55	12.22	13.33	14.44	15.56	16.67	17.78	18.89	20.00	21.11	22.22	23.33	24.44
59	13.41	14.63	15.85	17.07	18.29	19.51	20.73	21.95	23.17	24.39	25.61	26.83
63	14.86	16.22	17.57	18.92	20.27	21.62	22.97	24.32	25.68	27.03	28.38	29.73
64	15.28	16.67	18.06	19.44	20.83	22.22	23.61	25.00	26.39	27.78	29.17	30.56
68	17.19	18.75	20.31	21.88	23.44	25.00	26.56	28.13	29.69	31.25	32.81	34.38
70	18.33	20.00	21.67	23.33	25.00	26.67	28.33	30.00	31.67	33.33	35.00	36.67

Tax-Exempt Bonds

Tax exempt (municipal) bonds are issued by state and local governments and are free from federal income tax on interest payments. The bonds are often issued in $5,000 denominations and pay interest semiannually. Capital gains are taxable. In addition, holders of out-of-state bonds may be subject to state and local income taxes of the state in which they reside. For example, a New York City resident holding Los Angeles municipal bonds would be subject to New York State and City income taxes on the interest.

The taxable equivalent yield of a tax exempt bond is obtained by means of the expression

$$\text{taxable equivalent yield} = \frac{\text{tax exempt yield}}{1-(F+S+L)}$$

where

F is the federal tax bracket of the investor
S is the state tax bracket of the investor
L is the local tax bracket of the investor

Thus, an investor in the 50% federal bracket, 10% state bracket and 3% local bracket who holds a bond with a current yield of 6% which is exempt from all income taxes would enjoy a taxable equivalent yield (TEY) given by

$$\text{TEY} = \frac{6\%}{1-(.5+.1+.03)} = 16.21\%$$

A taxable yield of 16.21% would be necessary to provide the same yield as the 6% current yield on the tax exempt security.

TYPES OF TAX EXEMPT BONDS AND NOTES

General Obligation bonds, also known as GO's, are backed by a pledge of a city's or state's full faith and credit for the prompt repayment of both principal and interest. Most city, county and school district bonds are secured by a pledge of unlimited property taxes. Since general obligation bonds depend on tax resources, they are normally analyzed in terms of the size of the resources being taxed.

Revenue bonds are payable from the earnings of a revenue-producing enterprise such as a sewer, water, gas or electric system, airport, toll bridge, college dormitory, lease payments from property rented to industrial companies, and other income-producing facilities. Revenue bonds are analyzed in terms of their earnings.

Limited and Special Tax bonds are payable from the pledge of the proceeds derived by the issuer from a specific tax such as a property tax levied at a fixed rate, a special assessment, or a tax on gasoline.

Municipal notes are short term obligations maturing from 30 days to a year and are issued in anticipation of revenues coming from the sales of bonds (BANS), taxes (TANS), or other revenues (RANS).

Project notes, issued by local housing and urban renewal agencies, are backed by a U.S. Government guarantee and are also tax exempt.

How to Understand Tax-Exempt Bond Quotations

Generally the prices of municipal bonds are quoted in terms of the yield to maturity (defined elsewhere) rather than in percentage of face value, as with other bonds. The yield to maturity can be converted to a dollar price if the years remaining to maturity and the rate of interest due are known. Certain tables used for this purpose are given in the *Basis Book* (published by the Financial Publishing Company, 82 Brookline Avenue, Boston, Massachusetts). The books list the dollar price (per $1,000 face value of the bond) corresponding to a given coupon rate, yield, and years to maturity.

Some municipal bonds, however, are quoted directly in terms of percentage of face value. Thus, a bid price (the price at which the dealer will buy the bonds from the investor) of 98⅝ for a $5,000 face value bond can be converted to a dollar price by first converting the bid to a decimal expression (.98625) and then multiplying by the face value of the bond. The result in this case is $4,931.25 (.98625 × $5,000). The same calculation applies to the ask price (the price at which the dealer will sell the bond to the investor).

Prices of tax exempt bonds are not quoted in the daily press. They can be obtained by calling municipal bond dealers. Extensive quotations are given in some relatively expensive publications:

The Blue List
Standard & Poor's
25 Broadway
New York, New York 10004
(212) 208-8471

The Daily Bond Buyer
and
The Weekly Bond Buyer
The Bond Buyer
1 State Street Plaza
New York, New York 10004
(212) 943-8200

Bond Week (Formerly Money Manager)
Institutional Investor
488 Madison Avenue
New York, New York 10022
(212) 303-3300

Government National Mortgage Association (GNMA) Modified Pass Through Certificates

A GNMA Mortgage-Backed Security is a government-guaranteed security which is collateralized by a pool of federally-underwritten residential mortgages. The investor receives a monthly check for a proportionate share of the principal and interest on a pool of mortgages whether or not the payments have actually been collected from the borrowers.

The GNMA Mortgage-Backed Security offers the highest yield of any federally-guaranteed security. In addition, the GNMA security offers a very competitive return in comparison to private corporation debt issues. Moreover, the investor receives a monthly return on the GNMA guaranteed investment, rather than semi-annual payments as on most bonds. This monthly payment represents a cash flow available for reinvestment and has the effect of increasing the yield on GNMAs by 10 to 18 basis points (a basis point is 0.1%) when compared to the yield equivalent received on a bond investment with the same "coupon" rate but paying interest semi-annually.

On single-family securities (the most popular form) the maturity is typically 30 years. However, statistical studies have determined that the average life of a single-family security is approximately 12 years, due to prepayments of principal. Nevertheless, some of the mortgages in any pool are likely to remain outstanding for the full 30-year period.

The minimum size of original individual certificates is $25,000 with increments of $5,000 above that amount.

Due to the uncertainties in the maturity of the above mentioned pass-through certificates, collateralized mortgage obligations (CMOs) have been introduced. CMOs are bonds backed by Ginnie Maes, Freddie Macs, and other mortgage instruments providing investors with a wide choice of maturities ranging from 2 to 20 years. Essentially, the monthly payments from the underlying mortgage instruments are initially allocated to the nearest maturity CMO and subsequently to CMO maturities of successively longer duration. CMO interest payments are made semiannually or monthly.

How to Understand Convertible Securities

The term "Convertible Securities" refers to securities that can be exchanged for another type of security, usually the common stock of the company issuing the convertible.

Source: Reprinted, with permission, from *Understanding Convertible Securities*, © New York Stock Exchange, Inc., 1982. Further reprinting is prohibited without express written approval of New York Stock Exchange, Inc.

The two basic types of convertible securities are debentures (commonly known as bonds) and preferred stock. These securities have intrinsic value. Bonds represent a debt of the issuing company. Preferred stock represents an ownership interest. Intrinsic value may be enhanced by the convertible feature.

There are other certificates or contracts which are sometimes considered to be convertible securities but which have no intrinsic value based on ownership interest or debt. Their value is derived solely from their ability to be converted into another type of security. To do so requires a payment in addition to the surrender of the security. These are rights, warrants and options. To many investors these securities may offer certain advantages. However, our emphasis here will be on convertible securities—bonds and preferred stock—which have broader application as investment vehicles.

CONVERTIBLE BONDS

Convertible debt securities are almost always issued in the form of debentures. That is, there is no specific collateral pledged by the issuing corporation in the indenture which states the terms under which the security is issued. Rather, the promise to pay interest on stated dates and the principal amount at maturity is backed by the full faith and credit of the corporation. However, even the most sophisticated investors and those in the securities industry commonly refer to this type of security as a convertible bond.

Convertible bonds have been extolled as the ultimate investment medium offering the desirable features of other securities without the normal risks. If this were so, it would not be for long. Demand for such a security would be so great that the price would be driven up to the point where the element of risk would be very evident. Convertible bonds like all other securities have both advantages and disadvantages and the informed investor can measure these against his own objectives.

Here are the three most important characteristics:

1. Convertible bonds pay interest—which, as a general rule yields more than the dividends on common stock of comparable quality and less than the interest on straight (non-convertible) bonds of equivalent quality and maturity.

   The issuing company's obligation to pay this interest comes before dividends on preferred and common stock.
2. Convertible bonds offer appreciable possibilities linked to the earnings and growth of the company. As the common stock rises in value to reflect this growth, the price

of the convertible bond should also increase. Conversely, as the common stock declines in value, so should the convertible bond decline.

3. Convertible bonds enjoy some of the stability and relative safety associated with straight bonds and preferred stock. For each outstanding convertible bond, it is possible to estimate an investment value. This is the price below which the convertible bond is not expected to fall, if interest rates remain constant, even if the common stock price falls to such an extent as to render the convertible feature virtually valueless. Investment value is arrived at by estimating a price that would produce a yield comparable to straight bonds of equivalent quality. Investment value, it should be stressed, is only an estimate and subject to change from many influences such as fluctuating interest rates, economic and business conditions, ratings given by investment advisory services and the general well-being of the issuing company.

These characteristics can perhaps best be understood by examining how convertible bonds come into existence and how they behave in various circumstances.

XYZ COMPANY ISSUES CONVERTIBLE BONDS

Let's assume that the XYZ Company wants to raise more capital to expand its business. Interest rates are high and XYZ does not want to pay 12% or more to borrow money in the conventional bond market. XYZ is also reluctant at this time to issue additional common stock as a means of raising additional capital. This could be due to a number of reasons, one of which might be unwillingness to dilute the equity interest of its present stockholders. For example, if there are presently ten million shares outstanding and an additional million are issued, earnings per share will normally be reduced by ten percent at the moment of issue, and the market price of the common stock probably would fall proportionately unless it could support the higher price earnings ratio. (The dilution problem is not quite the same when additional stock is issued to acquire an interest in or control of another company. The acquired company will presumably have its own earnings to contribute to earnings per share.) The XYZ Company is also mindful of the fact that dividends on stock are paid after federal income taxes, whereas interest on debt securities, like bonds, is a deduction before taxes.

Accordingly, the management of the XYZ Company decides to issue convertible bonds. In conjunction with the underwriting firm, the interest is set at 10% and the bonds are priced at par—an even $1,000 per $1,000 face amount bond. Bond prices are commonly stated as a percentage of par which, in this case, would be 100. It is further stipulated that each $1,000 bond can be converted into 25 shares of XYZ common stock. At the time that the bonds are marketed, the common stocks is trading at $32 per share.

DEFINITION OF TERMS

In any discussion of convertible bonds, various terms, related to the above figures, are widely used. Before proceeding, these should be defined.

Market Price Price at which a convertible bond can be bought or sold at a given point in time. Market price is stated as a percentage of par, usually $1,000. 100 means $1,000, 90 means $900, 110 means $1,100, etc.

Conversion Ratio Number of shares of common stock obtainable through conversion of one bond. In the case of XYZ, conversion ratio is 25.

Conversion Price The reciprocal of conversion ratio or the price of the stock when the number of shares obtainable through conversion of one $1,000 bond equals exactly $1,000. Conversion price is $40 when conversion ratio is 25.

Conversion Value Current value of total shares into which a bond can be converted. Conversion value of XYZ $1,000 bond with conversion ratio of 25 shares is $800 when XYZ common stock is trading at $32 per share.

Conversion Premium Percentage difference between conversion value and market value of bond. When conversion value is $800 and market value is $1,000, conversion premium is 25% since difference between conversion and market values ($1,000 − $800 = $200) is 25% of conversion value ($800). This figure represents the judgment of investors, as expressed in the marketplace, with respect to the worth of the three characteristics of convertible securities discussed above. These were yield, appreciation potential and relative safety. With some issues, supply and demand is also a factor in the premium.

Investment Value Estimated price, usually set by investment advisory services, at which bond would be selling if it had no convertible feature. Investment value is arrived at by estimating the price at which the convertible bond would have to sell to provide a percentage yield comparable to percentage yield on a non-convertible bond of equivalent quality and maturity. Investment value, like market price, is normally stated as a percentage of $1,000. For the XYZ Bonds, investment value will be assumed to be 75 providing a current yield of 13.33%.

Premium Over Investment Value Percentage difference between estimated investment value and market price of bond. When market price is 100 and investment value is estimated at 75, the difference is 25 which is 33% of 75. Thus, the premium over investment value is 33%. This figure can be considered a measurement of the worth of the conversion privilege as well as an indication of the proportion of the price that is subject to the risks associated with common stock.

To summarize, the position of XYZ Convertible Bonds, and the related stock at the time the bonds are marketed, is as follows:

Market Price of Bond............100	($1,000)
Yield.............................10%	
Conversion Ratio....................25	
Conversion Price............$40	($\frac{\$1,000}{25}$)
Market Price of Stock...............$32	
Conversion Value............$800	(25 × $32)
Conversion Premium...25%	($\frac{\$1,000 - \$800}{\$800}$)
Investment Value.........75	($750)
Premium Over Investment Value.....33%	($\frac{\$1,000 - \$750}{\$750}$)

Obviously, no owners of the bonds would convert them into the common stock at this time, since they would be exchanging $1,000 for $800. However, it is not necessary to convert a convertible bond into stock in order to enjoy its advantages. Bonds are frequently sold many times before they are finally converted into stock and many investors have actively participated in the convertible bond market without ever exercising the conversion privilege. Let's now explore what could happen to the XYZ Convertible Bonds under various circumstances.

IF THE STOCK GOES UP

If the XYZ Company prospers and is considered to have appreciation potential, the price of the common stock should go up. By the same token, the price of the XYZ Convertible Bond should also rise. Let's assume the stock goes up by 25% to $40 per share. Normally, the bond will also go up but not necessarily at the same rate as the stock. There is a good reason for this. As the bond price increases, it acts more like a stock and less like a bond. Investment value is left further behind. The risk increases. Yield diminishes too. Accordingly, even though the appreciation potential of the stock may not have changed, the other factors (greater risk and lower yield) will tend to hold back the price of the bond. Therefore, a rise in the XYZ stock of 25% from $32 to $40 might be reflected in a rise in the bond of 20% from 100 to 120. The most significant figures are now as follows:

Market Price of Bond............120	($1,200)
Current Yield.........8.33%	($\frac{\$100}{\$1,200}$)
Market Price of Stock...............$40	
Conversion Value..........$1,000	(25 × $40)
Conversion Premium..20%	($\frac{\$1,200 - \$1,000}{\$1,000}$)
Premium Over Investment Value.....60%	($\frac{\$1,200 - \$750}{\$750}$)

Conversion is still unrealistic. But bondholders who bought at the offering may want to take profits by selling their bonds to other investors who believe the stock will continue to go up but are not quite certain enough in their belief to buy the stock itself. Let's assume now that XYZ common stock goes up to $60 per share, an increase of 87½% since the bonds were issued. What is likely to happen to the XYZ bonds? The bond price may now rise to the level where virtually all of the bond-like characteristics are lost and, from the standpoint of risk, the bond is interchangeable with the stock. If we assume this is so, the bond's conversion value should be approximately the same as its market value and conversion premium will disappear. The picture would now look like this:

Market Price of Bond.............150	($1,500)
Current Yield..........6.67%	($100 / $1,500)
Market Price of Stock....................$60	
Conversion Value..........$1,500	(25 × $60)
Conversion Premium....0	(($1,500 - $1,500) / $1,500)
Premium Over Investment Value.......................................100%	

Now the owner of the bond will think very seriously about converting. His decision may depend to some extent on the comparative yields of the bond and the stock. Interest on the bond is $100 per year. If the dividend on the stock is less than $4.00 per share, conversion would result in less income. If, on the other hand, the dividend is $4.20 (a yield of 7%) conversion would result in more current income.

In the meantime, while the stock has been rising from $32 to $60 per share, the company has presumably been using the money received from the sale of the convertible bonds to expand its business and improve its earnings. This should have put it in a better position to absorb the dilution that conversion into common stock entails.

When a convertible bond's conversion value and market price become the same, the stock and the bond should move up and down together within a limited range to maintain this relationship. It is virtually impossible for a convertible bond to sell with a negative conversion premium (below its conversion value) for any length of time. If this should happen, professional traders will quickly move in and employ a device known as arbitrage to make a small but rapid profit. They will buy the bonds and simultaneously sell the stock short. Converting the bonds enables them to replace the stock borrowed for the short sale. If, for example, XYZ convertibles are selling at $1,450 while the conversion value is $1,500, the trader can buy ten bonds for $14,500. By selling short 250 shares, he receives $15,000 for an immediate gross profit of $500. This activity will tend to drive the price of the bond back up to or above conversion value.

IF THE STOCK GOES DOWN

Let us now consider what might happen to the XYZ convertible bonds if the common stock took an opposite course and declined from the price of $32 per share which it was enjoying at the time that the convertible bonds were issued. As the price falls the convertible bond's price will also fall. However, the bond's downside potential is less than that of the stock, since the bond should not decline below its investment value which is the estimated value of the bond when we disregard the conversion feature. We have assumed this to be a price of 75 which is 25% below par. Therefore, while the stock is falling from $32 to an unknown level, the bond should only travel from 100 to 75. This factor serves as a brake on the bond and is the reason why convertible bonds are generally considered to be a more conservative investment than the stock of the same issuing company. In reality, conditions which would cause a stock to decline drastically would probably produce a re-adjustment in the investment value of the convertible bond. Investment value is also subject to adjustment when money rates change.

To see how the convertible bond might be affected by a decline in the common stock of the XYZ Company, let's assume that the market price of the stock sags from its original price of $32 all the way down to $16 per share. It has lost half its value. If we estimated correctly the investment value of the convertible bond, and if other factors are the same, it will be selling in the area of $750. Thus, a drop of 50% in the price of the stock produces a drop of 25% in the price of the bond. The table of values will now be as follows:

Market Price of Bond...............75	($750)
Current Yield...........13.33%	($100 / $750)
Market Price of Stock...................$16	
Conversion Value............$400	(25 × $16)
Conversion Premium...87½%	(($750 - $400) / $400)
Premium Over Investment Value...0	

Thus, we have seen in this example that the price of a convertible bond is controlled primarily by the price of the stock into which it is convertible. However, when the stock goes up, the bond's rise should be held back somewhat as risk increases and yield decreases. Conversely, when the stock goes down, the bond's decline is cushioned as yield increases and investment value is approached. This is an oversimplification which disregards other influences but, hopefully, it provides a basic understanding of how convertible bonds behave. Prices, yields and ratios were chosen in order to illustrate the example and simplify the arithmetic. They are not intended to reflect actual market conditions at any time.

HEDGING

We have seen that convertible bonds offer an investor opportunities to participate in the stock market with somewhat less risk (and less profit potential) than is normally encountered with direct investment in common stocks. This opportunity can be pursued even further by employing hedges. Although extremely complex in practice, the basic principles of hedging are actually quite simple.

Typically, a hedge is established when an investor buys convertible bonds and, at the same time, sells short the stock into which the bond is convertible. If the stock goes up, there should be a profit in the bonds and a loss in the stock. If the stock goes down, there should be a profit in the stock and a loss in the bonds. Obviously, there is no advantage in a hedge unless the profit exceeds the loss and expenses. There is no way to assure a profit but the skillful and judicious use of hedges can greatly reduce the risk of loss and enhance the possibility of profit. An essential feature is the ability to sell stock short without margin when the corresponding convertible security is held.

Convertible hedges are a highly sophisticated investment technique and should not be attempted without a complete understanding of all of their ramifications.

CALLABILITY AND OTHER LIMITATIONS

An important factor to consider with convertible bonds is the call feature. This is the right of the issuing company to redeem the bonds before maturity at a stated price slightly above par. Usually the original purchasers of a bond are given some protection against this privilege of the company through an initial period during which the bond is non-callable. If a bond has been on the market for four years and commands a price of 130, this price may be short lived if the bond can be called at 105 after five years. When a convertible bond issue listed on the New York Stock Exchange is called for redemption some notice is always given in a newspaper of general circulation to permit the holders to exercise their conversion privilege or sell the bond to someone else who may convert it. Holders of record of registered bonds are notified directly. If, for some reason, the bond is not converted before expiration date for conversion, which may be the same or a few days before the redemption date, it is then worth no more nor less than the call price. It is, therefore, most important for holders of convertible bonds to know what the call features are and to be sure that they will receive information about calls when and if they occur. Obviously, the best way to do this is to hold registered bonds.

Most convertible bonds are convertible into stock at a fixed rate during the entire life of the bond. However, this rate may change because of a stock split, stock dividend, merger or other circumstances. The conversion privilege may expire before the bond matures or it may not be effective until some time after the bond is issued. Sometimes the conversion rate declines at regular intervals. A bond that is convertible into 25 shares of common stock when first issued may become convertible into only 20 shares after five years, 15 shares after ten years, etc. Although the typical convertible bond is exchangeable for the common stock of the issuing company, this is also subject to variation. Conversion may be made into a combination of common and preferred stock. Or a bond of one company may be convertible into the stock of a parent company.

All of these possible limitations should be checked by investors when investigating convertible securities. A member firm of the New York Stock Exchange, Inc. can usually supply the essential information.

MARGIN AND COMMISSION

Two other features of convertible bonds have traditionally appealed to investors—margin requirements and commission rates. Although the current margin requirement for the purchase of common stock or convertible bonds is the same—50%, the convertible bond rate has usually been significantly less. In 1973, for instance, an investor with $6,500 available in cash could have bought $10,000 worth of common stock or $13,000 of convertible bonds. (Margin requirements are subject to change by the Federal Reserve Board).

The commission paid to a member firm broker for the purchase or sale of listed stocks is one of the lowest fees paid for the transfer of property of any kind. However, in most cases, the commission paid for the purchase or sale of bonds is even lower on a given dollar investment.

CONVERTIBLE PREFERRED STOCK

Convertible preferred stock possesses many of the basic characteristics of convertible bonds and will normally perform in approximately the same manner when subject to the same conditions and influences. However, there are also basic differences which should be pointed out.

Convertible preferred stock represents an equity interest and is, therefore, junior to all debt securities including convertible bonds and would not—all else being equal—have as high a degree of relative safety as convertible bonds. However, all else is rarely equal and the convertible preferred stock of Company A could have more relative safety than the convertible bonds of Company B. Convertible preferred stocks do not have maturity dates as do bonds but are usually subject to redemption.

Convertible preferreds, like common stock, require 50% margin currently, and are subject to the same commission structure.

FOREIGN SHORT-TERM AND LONG-TERM INTEREST RATES: SELECTED COUNTRIES

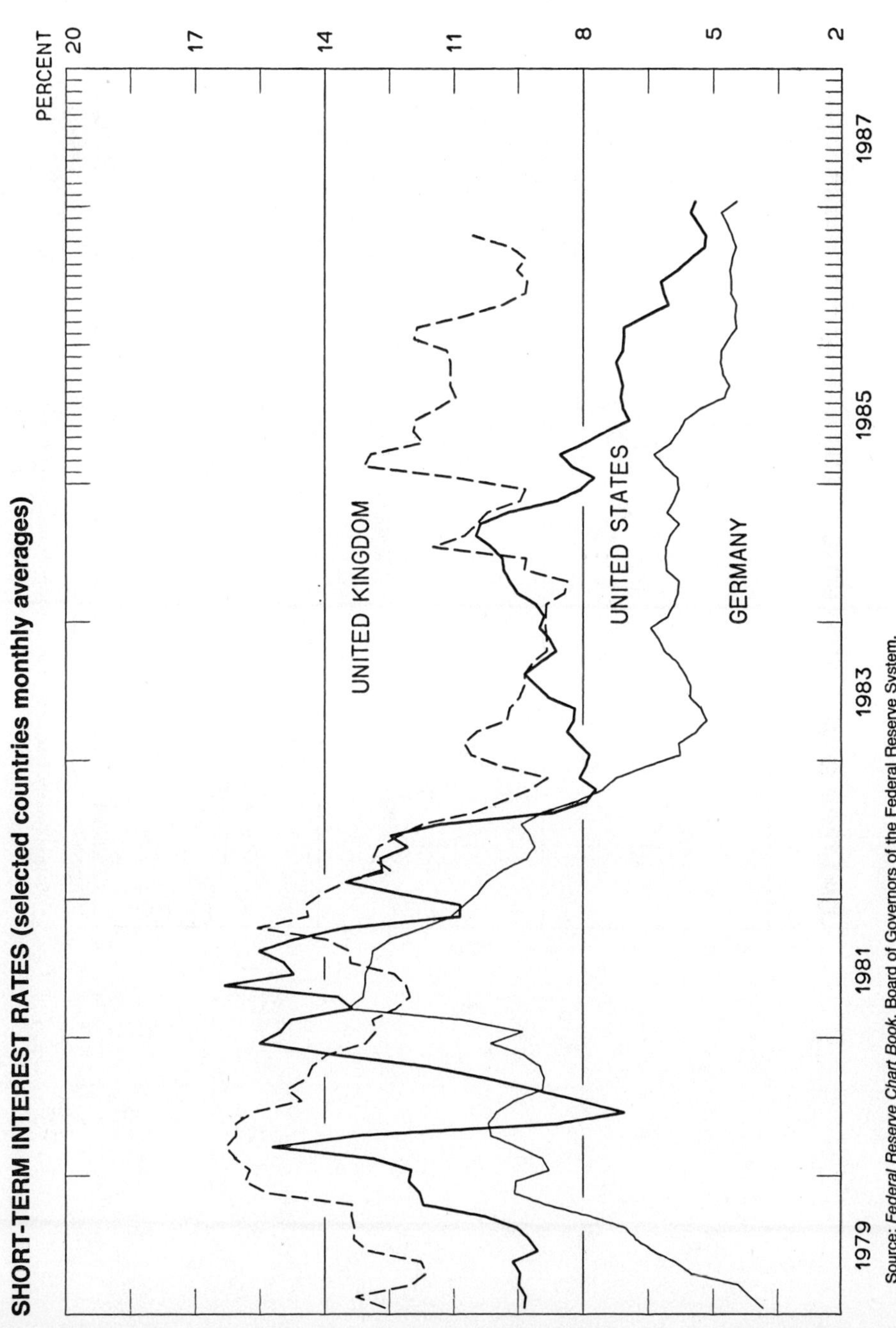

Source: *Federal Reserve Chart Book*, Board of Governors of the Federal Reserve System.

LONG-TERM GOVERNMENT BOND YIELDS (selected countries monthly)

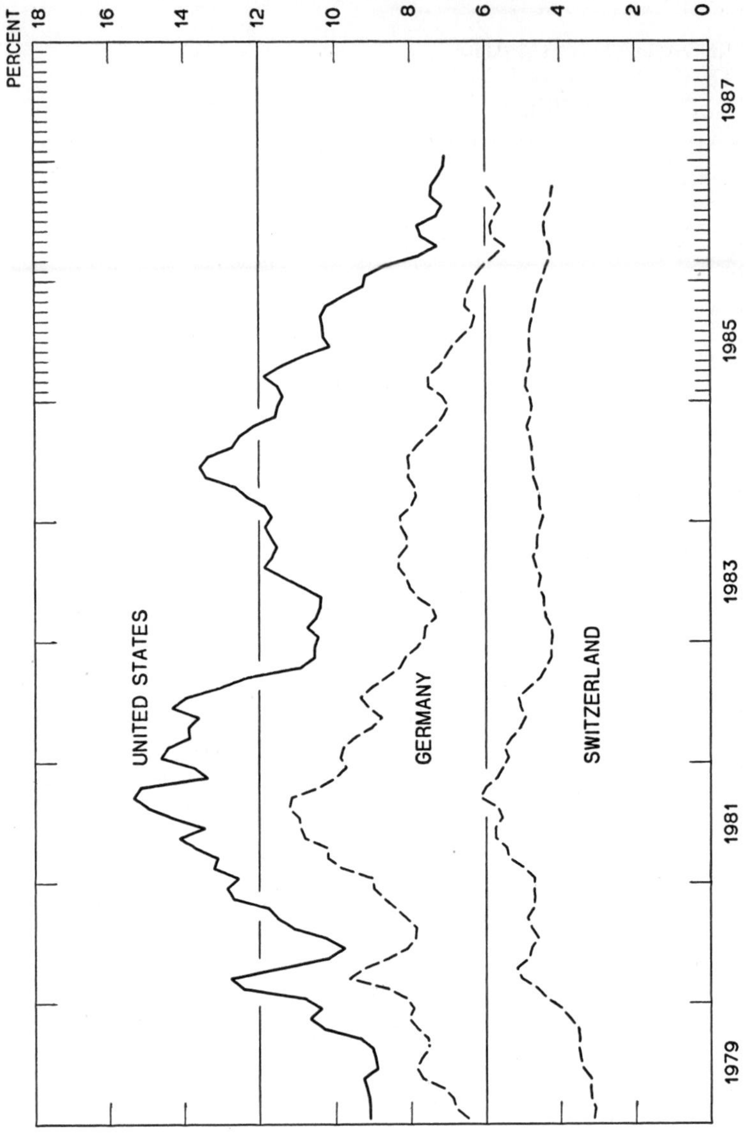

Source: *Federal Reserve Chart Book*, Board of Governors of the Federal Reserve System.

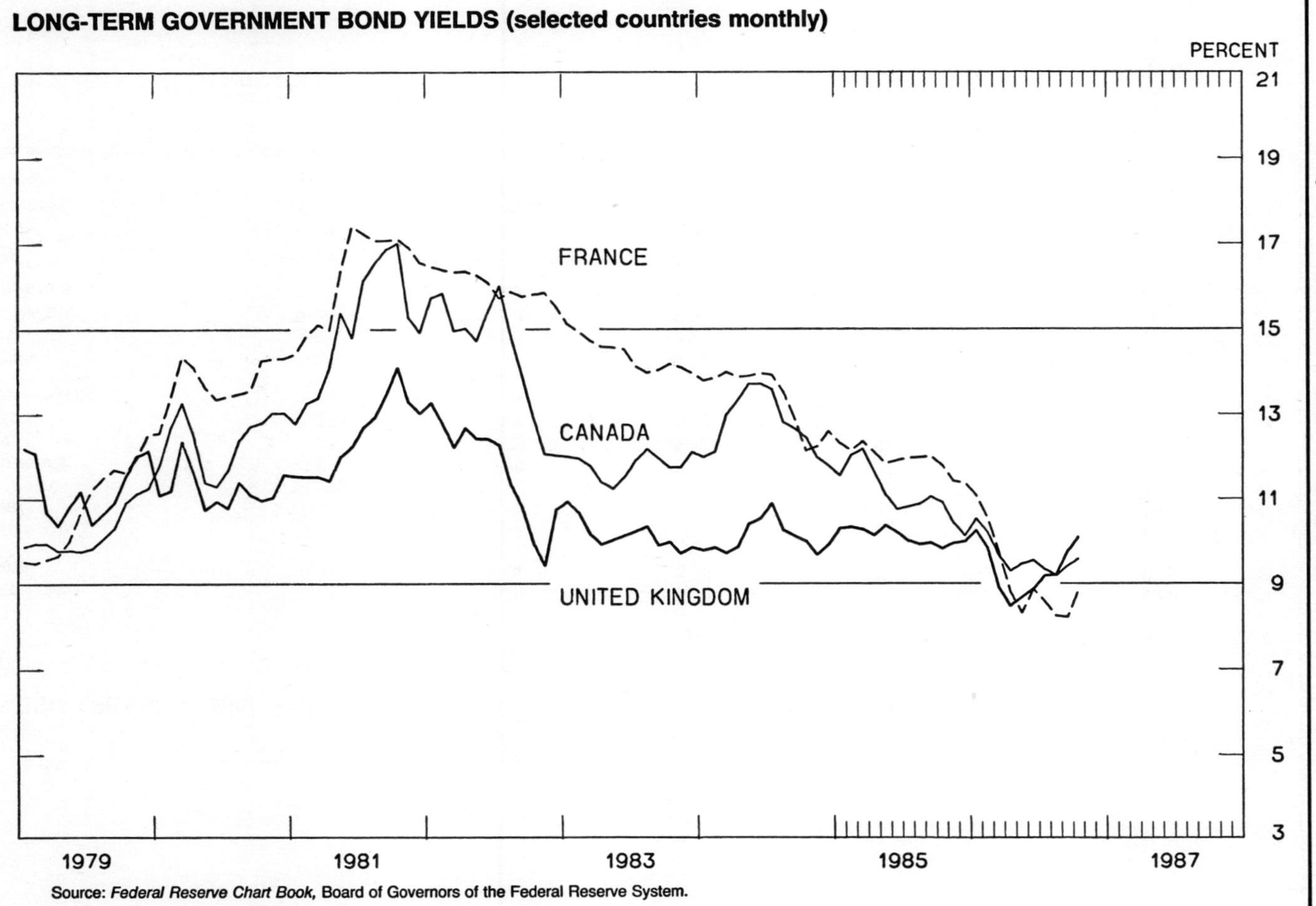

Source: *Federal Reserve Chart Book*, Board of Governors of the Federal Reserve System.

FOREIGN TREASURY BILL RATES (bond-equivalent yields, at or near end of month)

	1983	1984	1985	1986		1987					
	Dec	*Dec*	*Dec*	*Nov*	*Dec*	*Jan*	*Feb*	*Mar*	*Apr*	*May*	*Jun*
United States	9.28	7.99	7.25	5.44	5.73	5.66	5.48	5.76	5.61	5.82	5.90
Canada	9.71	9.84	9.24	8.24	8.22	7.24	7.28	6.80	8.08	8.19	8.29
Belgium	11.00	10.90	9.89	7.45	7.50	7.99	7.86	7.50	7.35	7.15	6.84
Ireland	12.01	15.10	11.15	14.22	13.60	13.91	13.67	13.51	11.29	10.86	n.a.
Italy	16.29	14.19	12.70	10.00	10.00	9.94	9.74	9.66	9.60	9.60	9.60
Netherlands	5.63	5.88	5.69	5.81	6.37	5.94	5.87	5.44	5.31	5.31	4.75
Spain	15.27	12.27	9.52	8.26	8.37	6.94	7.67	n.t.	9.61	10.40	9.59
Sweden	11.75	11.83	12.49	9.05	9.20	10.25	10.80	10.31	9.25	9.16	8.60
United Kingdom	9.04	9.33	11.49	11.01	10.79	10.59	10.46	9.54	9.39	8.68	8.96
Australia	8.54	12.27	19.40	15.49	14.91	16.64	16.32	15.47	14.00	13.10	n.a.
Japan	4.91	4.91	4.91	2.89	2.89	2.89	2.89	2.38	2.38	2.38	2.38
New Zealand	7.80	13.50	17.62	16.44	19.69	22.36	25.38	24.70	25.29	19.48	n.a.
South Africa	18.43	21.94	12.99	8.62	8.84	8.77	8.78	8.26	8.60	8.96	8.64
Brazil	179.15	273.03	379.77	33.00	149.00	276.40	n.t.	n.t.	n.t.	n.a.	n.a.
Mexico	53.78	48.67	72.98	103.77	104.03	104.64	104.83	100.66	99.01	98.60	98.40
Philippines	15.99	47.14	16.45	11.32	n.a.	n.a.	7.71	11.76	11.80	n.a.	n.a.
Singapore	2.59	2.91	2.94	1.93	2.10	2.19	1.67	1.93	2.12	2.61	2.63

Source: *World Financial Markets*, a publication of Morgan Guaranty Trust Company of New York.

FOREIGN MONEY-MARKET RATES (bond-equivalent yields on major short-term (mostly 3–4-month) money-market instruments other than Treasury bills, at or near end of month)

	1983	1984	1985	1986		1987					
	Dec	*Dec*	*Dec*	*Nov*	*Dec*	*Jan*	*Feb*	*Mar*	*Apr*	*May*	*Jun*
United States	9.89	8.34	8.01	5.96	8.04	6.97	6.24	6.70	6.98	7.12	7.10
Canada	9.85	10.00	9.40	8.35	8.35	7.45	7.40	6.90	8.15	8.30	8.45
Belgium	11.15	10.85	9.89	7.50	7.60	7.86	7.81	7.50	7.40	7.25	7.00
France	12.19	10.69	9.12	7.60	8.37	8.50	8.25	7.87	8.00	8.12	8.12
Germany	6.30	5.75	4.80	4.65	4.85	3.90	3.85	3.85	3.80	3.65	3.65
Ireland	12.19	15.13	12.00	14.44	14.06	14.12	14.25	13.37	10.87	11.19	n.a.
Italy	17.88	16.88	15.13	11.12	11.37	11.37	11.12	10.12	10.00	10.50	11.00
Netherlands	6.00	5.75	5.75	5.81	6.19	5.44	5.50	5.55	5.31	5.25	5.25
Portugal	24.11	24.57	20.71	15.93	16.07	14.95	14.94	14.95	14.96	15.03	n.a.
Spain	19.00	12.21	10.51	11.52	11.79	12.35	12.60	14.60	17.09	19.80	18.29
Switzerland	3.88	5.00	4.75	4.00	4.50	3.75	4.00	3.87	3.75	3.87	3.81
United Kingdom	9.31	9.88	12.75	11.44	11.25	11.12	10.19	10.06	9.25	9.00	9.25
Australia	9.05	12.90	19.75	15.90	15.10	16.40	16.60	16.27	14.50	13.80	n.a.
Japan	6.45	6.33	7.03	4.43	4.34	4.22	3.96	3.98	3.89	3.70	3.75
New Zealand	11.75	15.00	20.00	16.50	24.25	23.60	25.15	25.60	25.70	20.35	n.a.
South Africa	19.12	22.78	13.35	8.90	8.55	9.20	9.05	8.40	9.10	9.00	8.80
Chile	20.68	20.68	22.42	20.98	19.56	25.34	25.34	23.87	22.42	28.32	14.03
Hong Kong	14.88	8.25	6.50	4.44	4.62	3.44	4.37	4.87	5.50	6.25	6.87
Indonesia	19.50	19.00	15.00	14.50	19.50	16.50	16.00	17.00	16.50	18.00	27.00
Korea	8.00	8.00	8.00	8.00	8.00	8.00	8.00	8.00	8.00	8.00	8.00
Malaysia	9.80	10.30	8.20	6.70	6.00	5.30	3.30	2.60	2.70	2.80	2.75
Philippines	15.61	33.21	14.61	10.31	8.31	8.34	7.05	8.72	10.05	n.a.	n.a.
Singapore	8.44	7.00	5.88	3.19	3.94	3.34	3.31	3.26	3.73	4.44	4.31
Taiwan	8.07	7.85	4.10	2.86	n.a.	n.a.	n.a.	n.a.	n.a.	n.a.	n.a.
Thailand	16.00	12.00	15.50	7.75	7.75	7.75	7.75	7.75	7.75	7.75	7.75

Source: *World Financial Markets,* a publication of Morgan Guaranty Trust Company of New York.

FOREIGN GOVERNMENT BOND YIELDS (long-term issues, at or near end of month)

	1983	1984	1985	1986		1987					
	Dec	Dec	Dec	Nov	Dec	Jan	Feb	Mar	Apr	May	Jun
United States	12.00	11.61	9.49	7.69	7.79	7.47	7.48	7.81	8.45	8.65	8.50
Canada	12.02	11.66	10.04	9.26	9.23	8.94	9.10	8.98	9.82	9.92	9.78
Austria	8.02	8.04	7.61	7.36	7.33	7.25	7.05	6.93	6.86	6.74	6.61
Belgium	11.89	11.56	9.60	7.41	7.70	7.57	7.57	7.64	7.66	7.76	7.82
Denmark	12.96	14.60	9.67	11.80	11.70	11.33	12.63	12.23	11.96	11.87	12.06
Finland	11.16	10.73	10.58	7.74	7.80	7.78	7.82	7.89	7.77	7.88	7.85
France	13.96	12.70	11.33	9.49	9.89	9.54	9.84	9.42	9.51	9.86	10.40
Germany	8.38	7.17	6.57	6.33	6.25	6.20	6.26	6.12	5.98	5.99	6.31
Ireland	14.25	14.90	11.84	13.49	13.97	12.97	11.16	12.41	n.a.	n.a.	n.a.
Italy	17.69	14.52	13.66	10.33	10.05	9.78	9.84	10.03	10.08	10.20	10.41
Netherlands	8.58	7.72	6.96	6.30	6.40	6.21	6.15	6.22	6.12	6.07	6.26
Norway	12.50	12.00	13.10	n.a.	n.a.	n.a.	n.a.	n.a.	n.a.	n.a.	n.a.
Portugal	22.11	22.23	n.a.	n.a.	n.a.	n.a.	n.a.	n.a.	n.a.	n.a.	n.a.
Spain	17.25	13.93	12.30	10.29	10.36	10.74	10.59	10.95	12.04	13.43	13.20
Sweden	12.30	12.04	12.11	10.35	10.66	11.70	11.23	10.70	11.07	11.77	11.37
Switzerland	4.53	4.60	4.42	4.07	4.05	3.93	4.01	4.04	4.03	4.10	4.08
United Kingdom	9.94	10.25	10.35	10.58	10.17	10.64	9.51	9.15	8.87	8.79	9.15
Australia	13.65	13.50	14.85	13.60	13.40	13.80	14.00	13.45	13.05	12.97	n.a.
Japan	6.94	6.30	5.82	4.73	4.61	4.25	3.96	3.72	3.42	3.38	3.91
New Zealand	10.50	16.90	17.00	16.00	16.00	16.20	16.80	16.30	15.95	15.65	n.a.
South Africa	13.64	16.55	18.09	14.13	15.06	15.33	15.30	14.66	15.30	15.70	15.60
Philippines	14.47	18.54	n.t.	n.t.	n.t.	n.t.	n.t.	n.t.	n.t.	n.a.	n.a.
Venezuela	13.50	14.00	12.00	12.00	12.00	12.00	12.00	12.00	12.00	12.00	12.00

Source: *World Financial Markets*, a publication of Morgan Guaranty Trust Company of New York.

FOREIGN CORPORATE BOND YIELDS (long-term issues, at or near end of month)

	1983	1984	1985	1986		1987					
	Dec	Dec	Dec	Nov	Dec	Jan	Feb	Mar	Apr	May	Jun
United States	12.63	12.25	10.15	8.88	8.88	8.50	8.55	8.65	9.60	9.55	9.55
Canada	12.89	12.42	10.74	10.21	10.18	9.67	9.90	9.79	10.44	10.44	10.46
France	14.35	12.94	11.76	9.77	10.18	9.92	10.06	9.79	9.72	10.05	10.38
Germany	8.30	7.20	6.90	6.60	6.50	6.50	6.40	6.60	6.50	6.40	6.50
Netherlands	8.51	7.51	n.t.	n.t.	n.t.	n.t.	n.t.	n.t.	n.t.	n.t.	n.t.
Norway	13.25	12.75	14.00	n.a.	n.a.	n.a.	n.a.	n.a.	n.a.	n.a.	n.a.
Spain	20.07	18.32	14.92	13 61	13.40	13.72	14.13	14.82	15.52	15.76	16.39
Sweden	12.21	12.33	13.25	11 72	11.99	13.00	12.63	12.15	12.15	12.89	12.47
Switzerland	4.92	5.09	4.93	4.71	4.72	4.62	4.56	4.58	4.57	4.56	4.56
United Kingdom	11.57	11.64	11.47	11.43	11.71	11.30	10.58	10.21	10.09	10.19	10.15
Japan	7.49	7.11	6.79	6.05	5.93	5.46	5.35	5.20	4.99	4.71	n.a.
Korea	14.20	15.00	13.60	12.70	12.80	12.80	12.70	13.00	13.00	12.70	12.70
Venezuela	18.00	18.00	17.00	17.00	17.00	17.00	17.00	17.00	17.00	17.00	17.00

Source: *World Financial Markets*, a publication of Morgan Guaranty Trust Company of New York.

Composition of Dow Jones 20 Bonds Averages

Components—Dow Jones 20 Bond Average

The Dow Jones Bond Averages are a simple arithmetic average compiled daily by using the New York Exchange closing bond prices. A list of the bonds on which these averages are based follows:

10 Public Utilities

Name	Coupon	Age
Alabama Pwr	9¾%	2004
Amer T&T	8.8%	2005
Comwlth Ed	8¾%	2005
Cons Ed	7.9%	2001
Cons Pwr	9¾%	2006
Detroit Edison	9%	1999
Mich Bell	7%	2012
Pac G&E	7¾%	2005
Phil Elec	7⅜%	2001
Pub Svc Ind	9.6%	2005

10 Industrials

Name	Coupon	Age
BankAm	7⅞%	2003
Beth Steel	6⅞%	1999
Eastman	8⅝%	2016
Exxon	6%	1997
Ford Mtr	8⅛%	1990
General Elec	8½%	2004
GM Accept	12%	2005
Pfizer	9⅛%	2000
Socony	4⅛%	1993
Weyerhaeusr	5.20%	1991

Source: Reprinted by courtesy of Barron's *Business and Financial Weekly.*

Components—Barron's Confidence Index

Barron's Confidence Index is the ratio of the average yield to maturity on best grade corporate bonds to the intermediate grade corporate bonds average yield to maturity. The ratio is high when investors are confidently buying bonds below top grade and low when investors take refuge in high grade bond issues. A list of the bonds on which the confidence index is based follows:

Best Grade Bonds

Name	Coupon	Age
AT&T	8¾%	2000
Balt G&E	8⅜%	2006
Exxon	9%	2004
Gen. Elec.	8½%	2004
GMAC	8¼%	2006
IBM	9⅜%	2004
Ill. Bell T	7⅝%	2006
Pfizer	9¼%	2000
Proc. & G.	8¼%	2005
Sears Roe	7⅞%	2007

Intermediate Grade Bonds

Name	Coupon	Age
Ala Power	9¾%	2004
Beneficial	9%	2005
Cater Trac	8%	2001
Comwlth Ed	9⅛%	2008
Crown Zell	9¼%	2005
Firestone	9¼%	2004
GTE	9⅜%	1999
Union Carbide	8½%	2005
USX Corp	7¾%	2001
Woolworth	9%	1999

Source: Reprinted by courtesy of *Barron's National Business and Financial Weekly.*

Monetary Aggregates Defined

Money supply data has been revised and expanded to reflect the Federal Reserve's redefinition of the monetary aggregates. The redefinition was prompted by the emergence in recent years of new monetary assets—for example, negotiable order of withdrawal (NOW) accounts and money-market mutual fund shares—and alterations in the basic character of established monetary assets—for example, the growing similarity of and substitution between the deposits of thrift institutions and those of commercial banks.

M1-A has been discontinued with M1-B now designated as "M-1." M-1 is currency in circulation plus all checking accounts including those which pay interest, such as NOW accounts. M-1 excludes deposits due to foreign commercial banks and official institutions.

M-2 as redefined adds to M1-B overnight repurchase agreements (RPs) issued by commercial banks and certain overnight Eurodollars (those issued by Carribbean branches of member banks) held by U.S. nonbank residents, money-market mutual fund shares, and savings and small-denomination time deposits (those issued in denominations of less than $100,000) at all depository institutions. Depository institutions are commercial banks (including U.S. agencies and branches of foreign banks, Edge Act Corporations, and foreign investment companies), mutual savings banks, savings and loan associations, and credit unions.

M-3 as redefined is equal to new M-2 plus large-denomination time deposits (those issued as in denominations of $100,000 or more) at all depository institutions (including negotiable CDs) plus term RPs issued by commercial banks and savings and loan associations.

L, the very broad measure of liquid assets, equals new M-3 plus other liquid assets consisting of other Eurodollar holdings of U.S. nonbank residents, bankers acceptances, commercial paper, savings bonds, and marketable liquid Treasury obligations.

Federal Reserve Banks

Federal Reserve Bank of	
BOSTON	600 Atlantic Avenue, Boston, Massachusetts 02106—(617) 973-3462
NEW YORK	33 Liberty Street (Federal Reserve P.O. Station). New York, New York 10045—(212) 791-5823 (Telephone 24 hours a day, including Saturday & Sunday)
Buffalo Branch	160 Delaware Avenue (P.O. Box 961), Buffalo, New York 14240—(716) 849-5046
PHILADELPHIA	100 North Sixth Street (P.O. Box 90), Philadelphia, Pennsylvania 19105—(215)574-6580
CLEVELAND	1455 East Sixth Street (P.O. Box 6387), Cleveland, Ohio 44101—(216) 241-2800
Cincinnati Branch	150 East Fourth Street (P.O. Box 999), Cincinnati, Ohio 45201—(513) 721-4787 ext 333
Pittsburgh Branch	717 Grant Street (P.O. Box 867), Pittsburgh, Pennsylvania 15230—(412) 261-7864
RICHMOND	701 East Byrd Street (P.O. Box 27622), Richmond, Virginia 23261— (804) 643-1250
Baltimore Branch	502 South Sharp Street, Baltimore, Maryland 21201 (P.O. Box 1378), Baltimore, Maryland 21203—(301) 576-3300
Charlotte Branch	401 South Tyron Street (P.O. Box 300), Charlotte, North Carolina 28230—(704) 373-0200
ATLANTA	104 Marietta Street, N.W., (P.O. Box 1731) Atlanta, Georgia 30301—(404) 586-8657
Birmingham Branch	1801 Fifth Avenue, North (P.O. Box 10447), Birmingham, Alabama 35202—(205) 252-3141 ext. 215
Jacksonville Branch	515 Julia Street, Jacksonville, Florida 32231—(904) 632-4245
Miami Branch	9100 N.W. Thirty-sixth Street Extension, Miami, Florida 33178 (P.O. Box 520847), Miami, Florida 33153—(305) 591-2065
Nashville Branch	301 Eighth Avenue, North, Nashville, Tennessee 37203—(615) 259-4006
New Orleans Branch	525 St. Charles Avenue (P.O. Box 61630), New Orleans, Louisiana 70161 (540) 586-1505 ext. 230, 240, 242
CHICAGO	230 South LaSalle Street (P.O. Box 834), Chicago, Illinois 60690—(312) 786-1110 (Telephone 24 hours a day, including Saturday & Sunday)
Detroit Branch	160 Fort Street, West (P.O. Box 1059), Detroit, Michigan 48231—(313) 961-6880 ext. 372, 373
ST. LOUIS	411 Locust Street (P.O. Box 442), St. Louis, Missouri 63166—(314) 444-8444
Little Rock Branch	325 West Capitol Avenue (P.O. Box 1261), Little Rock, Arkansas 72203—(501) 372-5451 ext. 270
Louisville Branch	410 South Fifth Street (P.O. Box 32710), Louisville, Kentucky 40232 (502) 587-7351 ext. 237, 301
Memphis Branch	200 North Main Street (P.O. Box 407), Memphis, Tennessee 38101—(800) 238-5293 ext. 225
MINNEAPOLIS	250 Marquette Avenue, Minneapolis, Minnesota 55480—(612) 340-2051
Helena Branch	400 North Park Avenue, Helena, Montana 59601—(406) 442-3860
KANSAS CITY	925 Grand Avenue (Federal Reserve Station), Kansas City, Missouri 64198—(816) 881-2783
Denver Branch	1020 16th Street (P.O. Box 5228, Terminal Annex), Denver, Colorado 80217 (303) 292-4020
Oklahoma City Branch	226 Northwest Third Street (P.O. Box 25129), Oklahoma City, Oklahoma 73125—(405) 235-1721 ext. 182
Omaha Branch	102 South Seventeenth Street, Omaha, Nebraska 68102—(402) 341-3610 ext. 242

DALLAS	400 South Akard Street (Station K), Dallas, Texas 75222—(214) 651-6177
El Paso Branch	301 East Main Street (P.O. Box 100), El Paso, Texas 79999—(915) 544-4730 ext. 57
Houston Branch	1701 San Jacinto Street (P.O. Box 2578), Houston, Texas 77001—(713) 659-4433 ext 19, 74, 75, 76
San Antonio Branch	126 East Nueva Street (P.O. Box 1417), San Antonio, Texas 78295—(512) 224-2141 ext 61, 66
SAN FRANCISCO	101 Market Street (P.O. Box 7702), San Francisco, California 94120—(415) 392-6639
Los Angeles Branch	409 West Olympic Boulevard (P.O. Box 2077, Terminal Annex), Los Angeles, California 90051 (213) 683-8563
Portland Branch	915 S.W. Stark Street (P.O. Box 3436), Portland, Oregon 97208—(503) 228-7584
Salt Lake City Branch	120 South State Street (P.O. Box 30780), Salt Lake City, Utah 84130—(801) 355-3131
Seattle Branch	1015 Second Avenue (P.O. Box 3567), Seattle, Washington 98124—(206) 442-1650
TREASURY	**General information concerning Treasury Securities and requests for forms:** Bureau of the Public Debt, Dept. F Washington, D.C. 20226 Telephone: (202) 287-4113 **Specific questions concerning Bills:** Bureau of the Public Debt, Dept. X Washington, D.C. 20226 Telephone: (202) 287-4113 **Specific questions concerning registered Notes or Bonds:** Bureau of the Public Debt, Dept. A Washington, D.C. 20226 Telephone: (202) 287-4113

Options and Futures

What Are Stock Options?

There are two types of stock options—call and put. A call option is the right to buy a specified number of shares of a stock at a given price before a specific date. A put option is the right to sell a specific number of shares of a stock at a given price before a specific date. Options, unlike a futures contract, are a right *not an obligation* to buy or sell stock. The price at which the stock may be bought or sold is referred to as the exercise (or striking) price. The date at which the option expires is the *expiration* date. The term "in-the-money" option refers to either a call option with an exercise price less than that of the market price of the stock, or a put option with an exercise price above the market price of the stock.

Expiration months are set at intervals of three months for the cycles: the January–April–July–October cycle, February–May–August–November cycle, and the March–June–September–December cycle. Options expire at 11:59 P.M. Eastern Standard Time on the Saturday immediately following the third Friday of the expiration month.

The exercise prices are set at 5 point (dollar) intervals for stocks trading below \$50, 10 point intervals for stocks trading between \$50 to \$200, and 20 point intervals for securities trading above \$200. Initial exercise prices are set above and below the price of the security. Thus, if a security is priced at 32½ on the New York Stock Exchange at the time new options are opened, the opening exercise prices would be set at 30 and 40. If the price of the security is close to a standard exercise price, three prices are set: at the standard price, as well as above and below the latter.

Standard option contracts are written for 100 shares of stock of the underlying security. The price at which the seller (writer) agrees to sell an option to the buyer is called the *premium.* The premium is quoted *per share* of the underlying stock so that the price per contract is 100 times the quote.

After the option is issued, the premium will fluctuate with the price of the stocks. With call options the premium will increase with an increase in the price of stock. With put options the premium will increase when the stock price declines. The reason should be clear from the following examples. Assume that in January a July call option is written at the exercise price of 50 (\$50 per share) on the XYZ Corporation stock. We assume that the stock is selling at \$51. The call option writer (seller) asks and receives a premium of \$2 (\$200 per option contract). After brokerage commission on the sale (say \$25 per contract) the option writer nets a profit of \$175 per contract. The call option buyer pays \$200 for the contract plus the commission or \$225. Assume that the stock increases to 60 per share. The option holder (buyer) can, in principle, purchase the stock at 50 (the Exercise price) and sell it at 60 netting a profit on transaction of \$10 per share (neglecting commissions). Clearly the call option has acquired increased value which will be reflected in the premium (option price). Let us assume that the premium increases from 2 to 10 (\$200 to \$1,000 per contract). If the option holder now sells the option, he will make a profit (after commissions) of \$750 on a \$250 investment (\$200 premium and \$50 commission).

Alternatively, the option holder may elect to exercise the option and acquire the shares at 50 (the exercise price). The option writer must then deliver 100 shares of XYZ Corporation at \$50 per share.

If the stock price drops below the exercise price and remains so until expiration of the option, the call option buyer can lose his entire investment. Sometimes the loss may be reduced if the option is sold before it matures. The holder then is said to have *closed out* his position.

Similar arguments apply to put options. In this case the option holder benefits if the price of the stock decreases below the exercise price. Assume that the above stock drops to 40. The put holder could, in principle, buy the stock at 40 and sell it at 50 (the exercise price) to the put writer. The put holder would make a profit of \$10 per share (neglecting commissions). The put premium would reflect this situation and, as a result, increase.

Instead of selling the option and taking a profit, the put holder may elect to exercise the option and sell 100 shares to the put writer who must purchase these shares at the 50 exercise price.

If the market price of the stock is greater than the exercise price when the put option expires, the holder will lose his investment.

Options are traded on the Chicago Board of Options Exchange, the American Stock Exchange, the Pacific Stock Exchange and the Philadelphia Stock Exchange.

How to Read Option Quotations

(1) Option & NY Close	(2) Strike Price	(3) Calls—Last Aug	Nov	Feb	(4) Puts—Last Aug	Nov	Feb
Slb							
94¾	100	2½	7	9½	5⅞	7¾	a
94¾	110	⅝	3⅜	5½	a	16	a
94¾	120	⅛	1⅛	b	a	a	b
94¾	130	1/16	b	b	a	b	b
Skylin	15	3⅜	4	a	a	⅝	a
17⅝	20	⅝	1 11/16	2¼	a	a	a
Southn	10	a	2⅜	2 7/16	b	b	b

Source: Reprinted by permission of *The Wall Street Journal*

(1) The name of the company in abbreviated form. Below the company name is the New York or American Exchange closing price of the stock in terms of ⅛ of a dollar.
(2) The striking (exercise) price of the option.
(3) The expiration month of the call option, beneath which is the option's premium (price) per share of stock. Contracts are for 100 shares of stock so that, for example, the price of a contract quoted as 2⅛ ($2.125 per share) is $212.50. Options expire on the Saturday following the third Friday of the expiration month. The premium does not include commissions.
(4) The same as item 3, but for a put option. The letter *a* means the option was not traded that day, and *b* means the option is not offered.

Stock Market Futures*

Standard & Poor's 500 Stock Index futures† combine the unique aspects of the futures market with the opportunities of stock ownership and stock options by helping many investors manage their inherent stock market risks, and at the same time allowing others to participate in broad market moves. S&P 500 Index futures can play an important role in an individual's or institution's overall market strategy.

Stock ownership is subject to several risks. Lower earnings reports or changes in industry fundamentals can cause severe declines in individual issues. Or, a promising industry or company might drop because the entire market is heading down. A myriad of decisions go into individual stock selection—but the first question is usually what is the state and direction of the entire market.

The introduction of the Standard & Poor's 500 Stock Index contract allows investors to hedge, and therefore, virtually eliminate their portfolio exposure in a declining market without disturbing their holdings. At the same time, others can purchase or sell the contract according to their expectations of future market activity. This simultaneous ability to hedge the risks of stock ownership and to take advantage of broad market moves creates opportunities for everyone with positions in or opinions about the stock market.

A NEW MARKET FOR TODAY'S INVESTOR

S&P 500 Index futures are traded on the Index and Option Market division of the Chicago Mercantile Exchange. One of the largest commodity exchanges in the world, the CME introduced financial futures trading in 1972 when it formed the International Monetary Market to trade contracts in foreign currencies. Later, the IMM added futures contracts in Gold, 90-Day Treasury Bills, Three-Month Domestic Certificates of Deposit, and Three-Month Eurodollar Time Deposits.

THE S&P 500 INDEX

The Standard & Poor's Stock Price Index has been the standard by which professional portfolio managers and individuals have measured their performance for 65 years. Begun in 1917 as an index based on 200 stocks, the list was expanded to 500 issues in 1957.

Currently, the Index is one of the U.S. Commerce Department's 12 leading economic indicators.

The S&P 500 Index is made up of 400 industrial, 40 public utilities, 20 transportation, and 40 financial companies and represents approximately 80% of the value of all issues traded on the New York Stock Exchange.

The S&P 500 Index is calculated by giving more "weight" to companies with more stock issued and outstanding in the market. Basically, each stock's price is multiplied by its number of shares outstanding. This assures that each

* Although every attempt has been made to ensure the accuracy of the information in this section, the Chicago Mercantile Exchange assumes no responsibility for any errors or omissions. All matters pertaining to rules and specifications herein are made subject to and are superseded by official Exchange rules.

† Editor's Note: Futures based on the Value Line (Kansas City Exchange) and the New York Stock Exchange (New York Futures Exchange) indices are also traded. The principles are the same as with the S&P 500 futures.

Source: *Opportunities in Stock Futures*, Index and Option Market, Chicago Mercantile Exchange, 444 West Jackson Street, Chicago, IL 60606.

stock influences the Index with the same importance that it carries in the actual stock market.

The Index is calculated by multiplying the shares outstanding of each of the 500 stocks by its market price. These amounts are then totaled and compared to a 1941–43 base period.

Calculations are performed continually while the market is open for each of the 500 stocks in the Index. The resulting Index is available minute-by-minute via quote machines throughout the world.

WHAT IS FUTURES TRADING?

The practice of buying or selling goods at prices agreed upon today, but with actual delivery made in the future, dates back to the 12th century. In the United States, organized futures exchanges were active as early as the 1840s. Today, the markets offer futures in grains, meats, lumber, metals, poultry products, currencies and interest-bearing securities.

The ability to contract today at a fixed price for future delivery performs two vital economic functions: risk transfer and price discovery.

For example, suppose a producer of cattle sees that someone is willing to buy his animals for delivery six months hence at a price that insures him an adequate profit. He decides to sell his production, with delivery after the animal matures, at the contracted price. In the process, he has locked in a price that is satisfactory to him and has insulated himself against the risk that the price may fall. In other words, he has transferred the risk of lower prices to someone else. Conversely, the purchaser of his animals has locked in his price and is assured that he will not have to pay a higher price in the future. This transaction could take place directly between the two men, or could be accomplished through futures trading at the CME—without the need for buyer and seller to actually meet. The open public trading system at the CME makes it easy to discover what the market currently considers to be a fair price for future delivery.

If the sale takes place on the Chicago Mercantile Exchange, the Exchange guarantees that both parties adhere to their agreement by placing itself and its resources between them. The Exchange thus becomes the buyer and the seller of the contract. This assures both parties that the contract will be carried out because the Exchange stands behind both parts of the agreement.

When delivery day arrives, the product is delivered to designated delivery points and inspected to make sure it is of the quality stipulated by the contract. The seller receives payment at the agreed price and buyer receives the produce.

Since full payment does not occur until the delivery day, the performance of both parties to the contract requires a good faith deposit or performance bond—known as the margin—when the contract is entered. Margins usually amount to a small percentage of the contract's total face value.

This payment differs from margin for stock purchases in that it is not a partial payment. It serves as a guarantee for both buyer and seller that there are sufficient funds on either side to cover adverse price movements that might otherwise bring the ability to meet contract terms into question.

At the close of business each day, each futures position is revalued at the contract's current closing price. This price is compared to the previous day's close (or if an initial position, the purchase or sale price) and the net gain or loss is calculated. Gains and losses are taken or made from the margin account each day in cash. There are no paper gains or losses in futures trading. If a margin account falls below a specified level, futures traders are required to deposit more money to maintain their positions.

All futures market participants should understand the operation of futures markets and consult with a Registered Commodity Representative before opening a futures trading account.

The S&P 500 Index futures contract is quoted in terms of the actual Index, but carries a face value of 500 times the Index. The contract does not move point-for-point with the actual Index, but it says close enough to act as an effective proxy for the Index, and by extension, for the stock market as a whole.

If, for example, the futures price is quoted at 108.75, then the face value of the contract would be $54,375 (500 × 108.75). Minimum futures price increments, or movements, are .05 of the Index or $25. So if the futures quote is at 108.75, trades can continue to take place at that level, or move to 108.80 or to 108.70, with each .05 move equal to $25.

Trading opens at 9:00 A.M. and closes at 3:15 P.M. (Chicago time) with contracts trading for settlement in March, June, September and December. The final settlement day is the third Thursday of the contract month. At the close of business on that day all open positions have one final mark-to-market calculation—only on this day the expiration of the contract is marked to the actual closing level of the S&P 500 Index itself. Unlike traditional commodities, there is no physical delivery of the underlying commodity or resulting payment for the commodity in S&P 500 futures.

It is this unique cash settlement feature of the S&P 500 futures contract that eliminates the prohibitively expensive costs of delivering 500 individual issues in varying amounts. Since there are little or no delivery costs, investors are assured that there will be no institutional factors to influence the futures contract's price. Thus, the price of the futures contract will reflect the current expectations about the direction of future stock prices. The International Monetary Market division of the CME pioneered this innovative concept in 1981, when its Eurodollar Time Deposit contract became the first cash settlement futures contract ever traded.

The S&P 500 futures contract should be viewed as a complement to equity ownership, not a substitute for it. Among the many benefits of S&P futures is the hedging ability that holders of stock can employ to provide an effective, cost efficient means of protecting security holdings against temporary market declines rather than selling and disturbing stock holdings. In addition, investors find the futures market equally as liquid for both buyers and sellers. Unlike the stock exchanges, short sellers do not require an up-tic before a trade can take place and there are no additional margin requirements.

SITUATIONS & STRATEGIES

Outright positions, either long or short, spreading and hedging are all uses for S&P futures. The contract also offers an unusually large number of hedging strategies when combined with equity portfolios and options. The following examples will show some of these uses in more detail.

LONG POSITION

Situation: An individual sees that interest rates are declining, the economy is firming and believes the entire market is undervalued. He notes that the S&P 500 futures contract for September delivery is at 108.85 and the actual S&P 500 Index is at 108.70.

It is apparent that most futures market participants also believe a move up is imminent. As supply and demand factors are balanced in an open marketplace, the intrinsic value of the September contract is established. The market is willing to pay a slight premium (.15) for the futures contract over the actual Index.

He calls his Registered Commodity Representative, enters an order to buy one September S&P 500 futures contract at the market and makes a good faith deposit to his account to guarantee his ability to meet his contractual commitment. For purposes of the following example, a margin account balance of $5,000 will be used. Margin requirements for actual positions vary. Individuals should contact their Registered Commodity Representatives for current information.

Day	Position	Cost	S&P Future Closing Price	Gain or (Loss) Points X $5 (.01 equals 1 point)		Account Balance	Cumulative Gain or (Loss)
1	Long one contract	108.85	108.90	.05	$ 25	$5,025	$ 25
2	same	108.85	108.60	(.30)	(150)	4,875	(125)
3	same	108.85	108.40	(.20)	(100)	4,775	(225)
4	same	108.85	107.00	(1.40)	(700)	4.075	(925)
5	same	108.85	108.00	1.00	500	4.575	(425)
6	same	108.85	108.70	.70	350	4.925	(75)
7	same	108.85	109.50	.80	400	5.325	325
Sub Total Period one		108 85	109 50	65	$325	$5 325	$325

Period one: Our investor was a little off on his timing and his margin account was debited each day that losses occurred If his margin balance had fallen to the maintenance minimum ($2 000 per contract) in this example he would have been required to make an additional payment to bring his balance back to the initial margin level ($5.000) As it is he ended the period with a credit of $325 in cash

Period two: With minor backing and filling the trend is up and the S&P futures price closes period two at a level of 115 65

	Position	Cost	S&P Future Closing Price	Gain or (Loss) Points X $5 (.01 equals 1 point)		Account Balance	Cumulative Gain or (Loss)
Sub Total Period Two	Long one contract	108.85	115.65	6.80	$3.400	$8.400	$3.400

Observations: During the first two weeks our investor's judgment of the market was correct and the S&P futures price advanced 680 index points or 6 25% This translated into a gain of $3.400 on his initial investment of $5.000. or a gain of 68%

At this point our investor believes that the market is due for a correction and decides to lock in his profit He calls his RCR and instructs him to "cover" his September long position His broker will then enter a sell order After the close of business. the Exchange Clearing House will match the investor's previous long position and his new short position for a net zero position. All margins will be returned with cash credited to the investor's account with his broker the next day Brokerage commissions have not been included in this example. but they are usually extremely reasonable and generally are quoted to include *both* the purchase and sale of the contract

SHORT POSITION

If, instead of a rising market our investor believed that tight money would increase interest rates and the economy was weakening, he might have concluded that the S&P 500 Index futures price of 108.85 was an overvaluation and that the price was vulnerable to a decline.

He decides to call his Registered Commodity Representative and enter a sell order for one September S&P 500 Stock Index future. Selling is just as easy as buying in an open outcry market. All bids to buy and offers to sell must be made publicly in the trading arena and are subject to immediate acceptance by any member. This differs greatly from stock exchanges where specialists or market makers require an up-tic from the previous sale to transact a short sale.

Let's again assume the initial margin required is $5,000. The above table shows the status of the short position over the course of seven trading days.

Day	Position	Cost	S&P Future Closing Price	Gain or (Loss) Points X $5 (.01 equals 1 point)		Account Balance	Cumulative Gain or (Loss)
1	Short one contract	108.85	110.05	(1.20)	$ 600	$4,400	($ 600)
2	same	108.85	112.50	(2.45)	(1,225)	3,175	(1,825)
3	same	108.85	112.00	(.50)	(250)	3,425	(1,575)
4	same	108.85	109.50	(2.50)	(1,250)	4,675	(325)
5	same	108.85	108.75	.75	375	5,050	50
6	same	108.85	107.40	1.35	675	5,725	725
7	same	108.85	107.05	.35	175	5,900	900
Sub Total		108.85	107.05	1.80	$ 900	$5,900	$ 900

In our hypothetical example, the short position eventually worked. If the price had gone to a closing level of 114.85, the investor's account balance would have dropped to the maintenance margin level of $2,000 and he would have been required to add additional funds to bring his balance back to $5,000.

Our investor decides at this point that he wants to cover his short position and lock in his profit. The next morning before the opening of trading, he enters an order to buy one September S&P Index contract to cover his short at the opening.

The opening is down on news that industrial production was weak and his position is covered at 106.55. His gain on his short then amounts to 2.30 at $25 per .05 or $1,150. The money is credited to his account the following day.

REDUCING THE VOLATILITY OF A STOCK PORTFOLIO

One reason for equity ownership is to take advantage of the long-term growth prospects of the company in which stock is purchased. Over time, higher earnings per share might be translated into a higher dividend payout. In the case of a company with a high return on investment and profits that are reinvested in the company's own growth, the expectation is that the growth will be reflected in higher share prices. However carefully constructed and diversified a portfolio may be, it is still subject in varying degrees to the risk that the market will decline. In order to protect principal values in a declining market, investors have traditionally sold stock to raise cash or shifted to more defensive issues with less volatility. These tactics very often are short-run solutions that disturb carefully tailored long-run objectives. S&P 500 Index futures can be used to add protection against a market downturn and allow an investor to maintain his equity holdings based on the prospects of the companies rather than the direction of the market.

SHORT HEDGE AGAINST A DIVERSIFIED PORTFOLIO

Situation: An investor owns a well-diversified portfolio with a current market value of $110,000. The S&P 500 futures contract is at 108.85. The market appears weak and the investor believes that there is substantial downside risk during the next three months. He decides to short S&P 500 futures to protect his portfolio.

Action: The S&P 500 futures contract at 108.85 represents a contract value of $54,425 (500 × 108.85). In order to protect his portfolio, he sells two contracts ($110,000 divided by $54,425 equals 2.02).

This hypothetical example assumed that the volatility of the portfolio very closely matched that of the market as measured by the S&P 500 futures contract prices. In reality, portfolios may be more or less sensitive to market moves. Statistical regression analysis for individual issues and entire portfolios can be calculated to measure past price volatility relative to the market. Expressed as "beta," it is a statistical measure of past movements which may change in the future. However, it is useful when hedging market risk in portfolios that are more volatile than the market.

Day	Position Short 2 Contracts	Closing Price S&P Contract	Gain or (Loss) Contract Points X $5 X 2 Contracts (.01 equals 1 point)		Value of Stock Portfolio	Portfolio Gain or (Loss)
1	108.85	110.05	(1.20)	($1.200)	$111.213	$1.213
18	108.85	109.50	(.65)	(650)	110.657	657
36	108.85	107.40	1.45	1.450	108.535	(1.465)
54	108.85	106.05	2.80	2.800	107.171	(2.829)
72	108.85	103.10	5.75	5.750	104.190	(5.810)
90	108.85	100.65	8.20	8.200	101.714	(8.286)
Position Closed	108.85	100.65	8.20	$8.200	$101.714	($8.286)

Observations: The market dropped and our investor hedged the cash decline in his portfolio with an offsetting gain in his futures position. Of course, if he were wrong about the direction of the market and it went up, he would have had losses in his futures positions but his stocks may have participated in the advance. The investor throughout this period, did not have to disturb his holdings and continued to receive his dividend payments.

Let us assume that the S&P 500 has a beta of 1.00, (that is, a given percentage move in the market gives rise to the same percentage move in the S&P 500) and our hypothetical portfolio has a beta of 1.50. Our portfolio's past market action relative to moves in the market was 50% greater than a given move in the general market. To compensate for this greater volatility, our hedger would require more S&P contracts to offset a greater decline in the value of his portfolio. Known as a hedge ratio, the dollar value of the portfolio is divided by the dollar value of the S&P 500 futures contract, the resulting figure is multiplied by the beta of the portfolio. Using our investor's portfolio and having calculated a beta of 1.5, we arrive at three contracts instead of two when the beta was 1.00:

$$\frac{\$110{,}000}{54{,}425} \times 1.5 = 3.03 \text{ contracts}$$

Thus, our investor would have sold three contracts to offset the portfolio's greater volatility to the market.

The concept of volatility and hedge ratios also may be applied to industry groupings and individual stocks. However, as the number of individual stock holdings that are being hedged decreases, then the greater is the chance that factors affecting that smaller group will make their prices react differently relative to the market than they have in the past.

ADDITIONAL USES OF THE S&P 500 FUTURES CONTRACT

Spreads: The simultaneous purchase and sale of different contract months to take advantage of perceived price discrepancies is called "spreading." The technique is considered by many to be less volatile than an outright long or short position, and as such, spreads generally carry lower margin requirements.

A characteristic of the futures market is that the closest contract date behaves more like the cash market. (In the S&P 500 futures contract, the cash market is the actual S&P 500 Index.) More distant months or back months have a greater component of their price determined by the expectations of what the price will be in the future.

These changing expectations of price levels of the S&P 500 contract into the future creates spreading opportunities. Options strategists will use the S&P 500 futures contract to reduce market risk when writing uncovered puts and calls. Block traders, investment bankers, stock specialists, options principals and anyone with the risk of stock market volatility, now have a vehicle and a well-capitalized liquid market to buy and sell market risk—the Standard & Poor's 500 Stock Index futures contract.

CONTRACT TERMS SUMMARY

Size	500 times the value of the S&P 500 Index
Delivery	Mark-to-market at closing value of the actual S&P 500 Index on Settlement Date
Hours	9:00 am to 3:15 pm Central Time
Months Traded	March, June, September, December
Clearing House Symbol	SP
Ticker Symbol	SP
Prices	Contract quoted in terms of S&P 500 Index
Minimum Fluctuation in Price	.05 ($25)
Limit Move	3.00 ($1,500)
Last Day of Trading	3rd Thursday of Contract Month
Settlement Date	Last Day of Trading

Understanding the Commodities Market

COMMODITY EXCHANGES

A Commodity Exchange is an organized market of buyers and sellers of various types of commodities. It is public to the extent that anyone can trade through member firms. It provides a trading place for commodities, regulates the trading practices of the members, gathers and transmits price information, inspects and governs commodities traded on the Exchange, supervises warehouses that store the commodity, and provides means for settling disputes between members. All transactions must be conducted in a pit on the Exchange floor within certain hours.

FUTURES CONTRACT

A futures contract is a contract between two parties where the buyer agrees to accept delivery at a specified price from the seller of a particular commodity, in a designated month in the future, if it is not liquidated before the contract reaches maturity. A futures contract is not an option; nothing in it is conditional. Each contract calls for a specified amount, and grade of product. For example: *A person buying a February Pork Belly contract at 52.40 in effect is making a legal obligation, now, to accept delivery of 38,000 pounds of frozen Pork Bellies, to be delivered during the month of February, for which the buyer will pay 52.40 per pound.*

The average trader does not take delivery of a futures contract, since he normally will close out his position before the futures contract matures. As a matter of fact, a survey conducted by a leading exchange has estimated that less than 3% of the contracts traded are settled by actual delivery.

Editor's Note: The scope of the commodities market has been broadened in recent years to include contracts on financial (debt) instruments (T-bills, bonds, etc.) and composite stock market indices such as Value Line, S&P 500, and the New York Stock Exchange. With the stock market index futures, settlement is made in cash in amount based on the underlying index. Cash, not the securities, is used to offset the long and short positions. The cash value of the contract is defined as the index quotation × 500.

THE HEDGER AND SPECULATOR

A hedger buys or sells a futures contract in order to reduce the risk of loss through price variation. A short hedger sells a futures contract to protect the possible decline in the actual commodity owned by him. A long hedger purchases a futures contract to protect the possible advance in the value of an actual commodity needed to be purchased in the future.

The speculator is an important factor in the volume of future trading today. He, in effect, voluntarily assumes the risk, which the hedger tries to avoid, with the expectations of making a profit. He is somewhat of an insurance underwriter. The largest number of traders on any commodity exchange is the speculator. In order for the hedger to participate, he must have continuous trading interests and activity in the market. This trading activity stems from the role of the speculator, because he involves himself in buying or selling of futures contracts with the idea of making a profit on the advance or decline of prices. The speculator tries to forecast prices in advance of delivery and is willing to buy or sell on this basis. A speculator involves himself in an inescapable risk.

CAN YOU BE A SPECULATOR?

Now, can you be a speculator? Before considering entering into the futures market as a speculator, there are several facts which you should understand about the market and also about yourself. In order to enter into the futures market, you must understand that you are dealing with a margin account. Margins are as low as 5 to 10% of the total value of the futures contract, so you are obtaining a greater leverage on your capital.

Fluctuations in price are rapid, volatile, and wide. It is possible to make a very large profit in a short period of time, but also, it is possible to take a substantial loss. In fact, surveys taken by the Agricultural Department have shown that up to 75% of the individuals speculating in commodity markets have lost money. This does not mean that some of their trades were not profitable, but after a period of time with a given sum of money they ended up being a loser.

Now taking you as an individual, let us see whether you have the characteristics to become a commodity trader. Number one and the most important is that you do not take money that you have set aside for your future, or money you need daily to support your family or yourself. Number two, and almost equally important, is that you must be willing to assume losses and be willing to assume these losses with such a temperament that it is not going to affect your everyday life. Money used in the futures market should be money that has been set aside for strictly risk purposes, and if this money is not risk capital, your methods of trading could be seriously affected, because you cannot afford to be a loser.

Source: Commodity Educational Services, Division of Commodity Cassettes, Inc., 778 Frontage Road, Northfield, IL 60093.

Another very important factor is that you must not feel that you are going to take a thousand, two thousand, five or ten thousand dollars and place this with a brokerage firm and not follow the daily happenings of the market. Price fluctuations are fast, and as stated before, wide, so you must not only be in contact with your Account Executive daily, but know and study the technical facts that may be affecting the particular market in which you are speculating.

The individual who makes his first trade by buying a contract on Monday and selling this contract on the following Wednesday, making six hundred dollars on a $1,000 investment, in a period of two days, suddenly says to himself, "*Where has this market been all my life? Why am I working? Why not just concentrate on this market, if every two days or so I can make six hundred dollars?*" This is a fallacy, since this is an individual that is going to destroy himself and most likely his family. The next trade he will feel confident that because of his first profitable trade the market will always go his way even though he is now showing a loss in his position. He still feels that the market will turn around in his direction. If you become married to a particular commodity futures contract and constantly feel that the losses you are taking at the present time will reverse into profits, you are really fighting the market and in most cases fighting a losing battle. This could lead to disaster. There is a saying that you let your profits ride, but liquidate your losses fast.

In any way that you are uneasy with a position that you are holding, it is better to liquidate it. If, prior to the time of buying or selling a contract, you are not sure that this is the right step to take, do not take it. To protect yourself against this hazard you should pre-decide on every trade and exactly how much you intend to lose.

Another important point is not to involve yourself in too many markets. It is difficult to know all the technical facts and be able to follow numerous markets. In addition, if you are in a winning position, be conservative as to how you add additional contracts or pyramid your position. Being conservative will sometimes cause you to miss certain moves in certain markets and you may feel this to be wrong, but over a long period of time, this conservatism will be profitable to you.

If at this point you feel that you are ready, both financially and mentally to trade commodities, the next step is to begin the actual mechanics of trading a futures contract.

OPENING AN ACCOUNT

The first important factor is to decide which brokerage firm will afford you the best service. To accomplish this, you should do a little research by checking with the various exchanges about different brokerage firms. You should study their advertising, market letters, and other information. These should all be presented in a business-like manner and have no unwarranted claims, such as a guarantee of profit without indicating the possibility of loss.

The brokerage firm must be able to handle orders on all commodity exchanges. Do not pick just any Account Executive in a firm, but one you feel confident to help you make market decisions. Become acquainted with the Account Executive through phone or personal conversations. His knowledge of the factors entering into the market and the understanding of current market trends are important in your final choice.

After making a decision on the brokerage firm and the Account Executive that would be best for you, contact him and have him send you the literature concerning different contracts, and also, any additional information as to his organization. He will then send you the necessary signature cards required by the firm to open an account, and ask you for a deposit of margin money.

You will be trading in regulated commodities, and margin money will be deposited in a segregated fund at the brokerage firm's bank. A segregated account means that the money will only be used for margin and not for expenses of the brokerage firm.

Now you decide to enter into your first trade. Your Account Executive and you decide to enter into a December Live Cattle contract on the Chicago Mercantile Exchange. Your order will be executed as follows: Your Account Executive will place this order with his order desk who will then transmit the order to the floor of the Chicago Mercantile Exchange. There your order will be executed on the trading floor, in the pit. All technical details connected with the transaction will be handled by the brokerage firm.

Upon filling of your order, the filled order will be transmitted back to your Account Executive, who will then contact you, advising you that you have purchased one December Live Cattle contract at a given price. You will also receive a written confirmation on this transaction. You will now show an open position in December Live Cattle on the books of the brokerage firm.

MECHANICS OF A TRADE

Let us go back one step to explain in detail just how your order to buy one December Cattle was handled on the floor of the exchange. All buying and selling in the pit is done by open out-cry, and every price change is reported on the exchange ticker system. Each firm has brokers in the different pits, a pit meaning a trading area for the purpose of buying and selling contracts.

When your order was received on the exchange floor, it was time stamped and then given to a runner. This is a person who takes the order from the desk on the exchange floor and gives it to one of the brokers in the December Cattle trading pit. He is then responsible to the brokerage firm to fill that order, if possible, at the stated price. After filling the order, he then has the runner return it to the desk where it is time stamped and transmitted back to the order desk at the brokerage house, and the filled order is reported to you.

MARGIN

Futures trading requires the trader to place margin with his brokerage firm. Initial margin is required and this amount varies with each commodity. The minimum margin is established by each commodity exchange. Additional funds are needed when the equity of your account falls below this level. This is known as a maintenance margin call.

All margin calls must be met immediately. Normally you will be given a reasonable amount of time to comply with this request. If you do not comply, the firm has the right to liquidate your trades or a sufficient number of trades to restore your account to margin requirements.

The brokerage firm has the right to raise margin requirements to the customer at any time. This is normally done if the price of the commodity is changing sharply or if it is the brokerage firm's opinion that due to the volatility of the market the margin requirement is not sufficient at that particular time.

Most commodity contracts have a minimum fluctuation and also a maximum fluctuation for any one particular day. For example, if you are trading frozen Pork Bellies on the Chicago Mercantile Exchange the fluctuation is considered in points. A point equals three dollars and eighty cents. This means that if you buy a contract at 52.40 and the next price tick is 52.45, you have made a paper profit of five points or nineteen dollars. The maximum fluctuation on a belly contract is 200 points, so your profit or loss cannot exceed in one day more than 200 points from the previous day's settlement. There are exceptions in some commodity contracts, where the spot month has no limit.

Let us assume that you had originally placed in the hands of your brokerage firm two thousand dollars margin money, and that you and your Account Executive decide to purchase a December Live Cattle contract whose initial margin is $1200 with maintenance of $900.00. After the purchase of the contract your account would show initial margin required $1200 dollars with excess funds of eight hundred dollars. At the end of each day the settlement price of December Cattle would be applied to your purchase price and your account would be adjusted to either an increase due to profit or decrease due to loss in your contract.

Further, assume that in a period of two or three days there is a decline in the price of the December Cattle contract and your account now shows a loss of three hundred dollars. Since maintenance margin is only nine hundred dollars on this contract, you will still show an excess of eight hundred dollars over and above maintenance margin. But, in the next four days suppose there is an additional loss of nine hundred dollars. Your account will now need one hundred dollars to maintain the maintenance margin and four hundred dollars additional in order to bring your account up to initial margin. Your Account Executive, or a man from the margin department of the brokerage firm will then contact you, stating that you must place additional money with the firm in order to maintain the December Cattle contract.

At this point, you must decide whether you should continue with the contract, feeling that it may be profitable in the next few days, and thus sending the brokerage firm the required four hundred dollars to maintain your position, or whether to assume your loss and sell the contract.

Let us assume that you decide to sell your December contract at this point and that the selling price causes a loss of four hundred dollars. Added to this loss would be the commission of forty dollars, so your total loss on the transaction would be four hundred forty dollars. A confirmation and purchase and sales statement will be sent to you, showing the original price paid for the contract, the price for which it was sold, the gross loss of four hundred dollars plus the commission of forty dollars making the total loss four hundred forty dollars, and your new ledger balance on deposit with the firm as fifteen hundred sixty dollars.

As shown in our example, commission was charged only when the contract was closed out. A single commission is charged for each round-turn transaction consisting of the creation and liquidation of a single contract.

CONTROLLED, DISCRETIONARY, AND MANAGED ACCOUNTS

There are two methods of trading your account. The first is the professional approach where you and your Account Executive decide on each trade with no discretion being given directly to your Account Executive. This method was illustrated in the discussion about margins. The second method is called a controlled discretionary or managed account. Under this method, you are giving your Account Executive authorization to trade your account at his discretion at any time and as many times that he considers that a trade should be made. The Chicago Mercantile Exchange, and the Board of Trade have rules governing this type of relationship. The following is an excerpt from the C.M.E. rule regarding controlled, discretionary and managed accounts.

REQUIREMENTS

No clearing member shall accept or carry an account over which any individual or organization, other than the person in whose name the account is carried, exercises trading authority or control, hereinafter referred to as controlled accounts, unless:

> The account is initiated with a minimum of $5000*, and maintained at a minimum equity of $3,750*, regardless of lesser applicable margin requirements. In determining equity the accounts or ledger balances and positions in all commodities traded at the clearing member shall be included. Whenever at the close of any business day the equity, calculated with all open positions figured to the settling price, in any such account is below the required minimum, the clearing member shall immediately notify the customer in person, by telephone or telegraph and by written confirmation of such notice mailed directly to the customer, not later than the close of the following business day. Such notice shall advise the customer that unless additional funds are promptly received to restore the customer's controlled account to no less than $5,000*, the clearing member shall liquidate all of the customer's open futures positions at the Exchange.
>
> In the event the call for additional equity is not met within a reasonable time, the customer's entire open position shall be liquidated. No period of time in excess of five business days shall be considered reasonable unless such longer period is approved in writing by an officer or partner of the clearing member upon good cause shown.

REVIEWING YOUR CONFIRMATIONS AND STATEMENTS

An important factor in trading is that you must be sure that no errors occur in your account. For every trade made you should receive a confirmation, and for every close-out a profit and loss statement known as a Purchase-and-Sale, showing the financial results of each transaction closed out in your account. In addition, a monthly statement showing your ledger balance, your open position, the net profit or loss in all contracts liquidated since the date of your last previous statement, and the net unrealized profit and loss on all open contracts figured to the market should be sent to you.

You should carefully review these statements. Upon receiving a confirmation of a trade you should immediately check its accuracy as far as type of commodity, month, trading price and quantity of contracts. If this does not agree with your original order, it should be immediately reported to the main office of your brokerage firm, and any differences should be explained and adjustments should be made.

If you do not receive a confirmation on a trade after it was orally reported to you by your Account Executive, be sure to contact him and the main office so that if an error was made it can be corrected immediately. You should receive written confirmation when you deposit money with your brokerage firm. If within a few days, you have not received this confirmation, report it immediately to the main office of your brokerage firm.

Never assume that an order has been filled until you receive an oral confirmation from your broker. A ticker or a board that you may be observing can be running several minutes behind and is not the determining factor as to whether your trade was executed or not. Until you receive this oral confirmation, never re-enter an order to buy or sell, against that position.

If you receive a confirmation in the mail showing a trade not belonging to you, immediately notify the main office of your brokerage firm and have them explain why this is on a confirmation with your account number. If it is an error, be sure that it is adjusted immediately and a written confirmation sent to you showing the adjustment of the error. If an error is made and it is profitable to you do not consider this any differently than if it was not profitable. Regardless of whether there is a profit or loss, all errors should be immediately reported to the brokerage firm.

Be sure that when you request funds to be mailed from your account that they are received within a few days from the time of your request. If not, contact the accounting department of the brokerage firm to see what is the cause of the delay.

Never make a check out to an individual. Always make your check out to the brokerage firm.

DAY TRADING

Day trading is where there is a buy and sell made during the trading hours on one particular day. Day trading is not considered to be a sound practice for the new speculator and inexperienced trader. Day trading is something that should be executed only by a sophisticated trader who is in frequent communication with the floor, and even then, on a limited basis.

* Minimums can be changed by each exchange, so consult your Account Executive for current regulations.

ORDERS

In order to trade effectively in the commodity market there are several basic types of orders. The most common order is a market order. A market order is one which you authorize your Account Executive to buy or sell at the existing price. This is definitely not a predetermined price, but is executed at a bid or offer at that particular moment.

Example: Buy 5 Feb Pork Bellies at the market.

LIMITED OR PRICE ORDERS AND "OB" DESIGNATION

This type of order to buy or sell commodities at a fixed or "limited" price and the ordinary "market" order are the most common types of orders.

Example: Buy Three Jan Silver 463.10. This limit order instructs the floor broker to buy three contracts of January Silver futures at 463.10. Even with this simple order, however, one presumption is necessary—that the market price prevailing when the order enters the pit is 463.10 or higher. If the price is below 463.10, the broker could challenge on the basis that the client may have meant *"Buy Three Jan Silver 463.10 stop."* Therefore, while it is always assumed that a "limit: order means 'or better,' " if possible, it saves confusion and challenges if the "OB" designation is added to the limit price. This is particularly true on orders near the market, or on pre-opening orders with the limit price based on the previous close, because no one knows whether the opening will be higher or lower than the close, *i.e., Buy Three Jan Silver 463.10 OB.*

STOP ORDERS *(Orders having the effect of market orders)*

Buy Stop Buy stop orders must be written at a price higher than the price prevailing at the time of entry. If the prevailing price for December Wheat is 456 per bushel, a buy stop order must designate a price above 456.

Example: "Buy 20 Dec Wht 456½ Day Stop." The effect of this order is that if December Wheat touches 456½ the order to buy 20 December Wheat becomes a market order. From that point, 456½ on, all the above discussion regarding market orders applies.

Sell Stop Sell stop orders must be written at a price lower than the price prevailing at the time of entry in the trading pit. If the prevailing price of December Wheat is 456 per bushel, a sell stop order must designate a price below 456.

Example: "Sell 20 Dec Wht 455 Day Stop." If this order enters the trading pit with the above price of 456 prevailing, the order to sell 20 December Wheat becomes a market order. From that point 455 on, all the above discussion regarding market orders applies.

Buy stop orders have several specific uses. If you are short a December Wheat at 456, and wish to limit your loss to ½ cent per bushel, the above buy stop order at 456½ would serve this purpose. However, it is important to realize that such *"stop loss"* orders do not actually limit the loss to exactly ½ cent when *"elected"* or *"touched off"* because they become market orders and must be executed at whatever price the market conditions dictate.

Another use is when you are without a position and believe that, because of chart analysis or for other reasons, a buy of December Wheat at 456½ would signal the beginning of an important uptrend in Wheat prices. Thus, the same order to *"Buy 20 Dec Wheat 456½ Day Stop"* would serve this purpose.

Sell stop orders have the same uses in reverse. That is, if you are long 20 December Wheat at 456 and wish to limit this loss to 1 cent per bushel, the above sell stop order at 455 would serve this purpose, within the limitations of the market order possibilities. Similarly, if you are without a position and believe that a sale of December Wheat at 455 would signal a downtrend in wheat prices, and you wish to be short the market, you could use the order to *"Sell 20 December Wheat 455 Day Stop"* for this purpose.

STOP LIMIT ORDERS *(Variations of stop orders)*

Stop limit orders should be used by you when you wish to give the floor broker a limit beyond which he cannot go in executing the order which results when a stop price is *"elected."*

Example: "Buy 20 Dec Wheat 456½ Day Stop Limit." This instructs the broker that when the price of 456½ is reached and *"elects"* this stop order, instead of making it a market order, it becomes a limited order to be executed at 456½ *(or lower)*, but no higher than 456½. Another possibility:

Example: "Buy One February Pork Belly 58.10 Day Stop Limit 58.25 (or any other price above 58.10)." This instructs the broker that when the price of 58.10 *"elects"* the stop order instead of making it a market order, it becomes a limited order to buy at 58.25 *(or lower)*, but no higher as with any limit order.

Stop limit orders are particularly useful to you when you have no position and wish to enter a market via the stop order, but want to put some reasonable limit as to what you will pay. On the other hand, stop limit orders are not useful to you when you have an open position and wish to prevent a loss beyond a certain point. The reason is that by limiting the broker to a certain price after a *"stop loss"* order is elected, **you also run the risk that the market may exceed the limit too fast for the broker to execute.** This would leave you with your original position because the broker would have to wait for the return to the limit before executing. With a straight stop *(no limit)* order, the broker must execute *"at the market."*

> *Example: "Buy One February Pork Belly 58.10 Day Stop Limit 58.25."* Suppose the market moves to 58.10 but then only 20 February Pork Bellies are offered at that price. Your broker bids for one at 58.10 but another broker in the pit catches the seller's eye first and buys 20 and your broker misses the sale. Your broker then bids 58.20 but the best offer is 58.30. He bids 58.25, but the offer at 58.30 remains unchanged. Then another broker bids for and buys February Pork Bellies at 58.30 and the market moves on up. Your broker is left with no execution to your order unless the market later declines to your limit making a fill possible.

If you did not have a position you might be disappointed, but you would be unhurt financially. However, if you had a position and were trying to limit your loss you would have defeated your purpose with the stop limit order, if you truly wanted *"out"* after the stop was elected.

Stop limit orders on the sell side have exactly the same uses, advantages and disadvantages as discussed above, but in reverse:

> *Example: "Sell 20 December Wheat 455 Day Stop Limit."* This means that when the market declines to 455 per bushel, the broker may sell at 455 *(or higher)*, but no lower.

> *Another Example: "Sell One February Pork Belly 58.25 Stop Limit 58.10."* This instructs the broker to sell a belly after the stop price of 58.25 is reached and *"elects"* the stop order, but no lower than 58.10.

M.I.T. ORDERS *(Market-if-touched)*

By adding MIT *(Market-If-Touched)* to a limit order, the limit order will have the effect of a market order when the limit price is reached or touched. This type of order is useful to you, when you have an open position and if a certain limit price is reached.

> *Example: "Sell One September Sugar 950 MIT."* The floor broker is told that if and when the price of September Sugar rises to 9½¢ per pound, he is to sell one contract at the market. At this price of 9½¢ all prior discussion on market orders applies.

Under certain market conditions, not enough contracts are bid at 9½ cents to fill all offers to sell. Thus, you may see your straight limit price appear on the ticker, but your broker fails to make the sale.

But by adding MIT to the limit price, you will receive an execution, because the order becomes a market order, if the price is touched. However, the price will not necessarily be a good one in your eyes, since it became a market order when touched.

The same reasoning is true on the buy side of MIT orders but in reverse. Assume you are short one contract of September Sugar, with the prevailing price at 9½¢ per pound and you want to cover or liquidate your short at 9¢.

> *Example: "Buy One September Sugar 9¢ MIT."* If and when the price of September sugar declines to 9¢ per pound, the floor broker must buy one contract at the market. Aside from the disadvantages of any market order, the MIT designation on the buy order prevents the disappointment which might arise if a straight limit buy at 9¢ were entered without the MIT added.

SPREAD ORDERS

As explained in the Glossary, a spread is a simultaneous long or short position in the same or related commodity. Thus a spread order would be to buy one month of a certain commodity and sell another month of the same commodity, or buy one month of one commodity and sell the same or another month of a related commodity.

> *Example: "Buy 5 July Beans Market and Sell 5 May Beans Market" or "Buy 10 Kansas City Dec Wheat Market and Sell 10 Chicago May Wheat Market."*

> *Another Example: "Buy 5 May Corn Market and Sell 5 May Wheat Market."*

In the example of the related commodity spread, normally the reason you would use such a spread, is that you expect to make a profit out of an expected tightness in the Corn Market, in the hope the corn contract will gain in value faster than wheat.

There may be a situation where you have a position either long or short in a commodity and want to change to a nearer or more distant option of the same commodity. For example you are long 5,000 bushels of May Soybeans on May 20 and want to avoid a delivery notice by moving your position forward into the July option. The basic spread order would be:

> *"Buy 5 July Beans Market and Sell 5 May Beans Market."*

Sometimes you may prefer not to use market orders, in which case you use the difference spread.

Example: "Buy 5 July Beans and Sell 5 May Beans July 2¢ Over." Even though the prices of the two options are not specified, the broker is allowed to execute at any time he can do so with July selling at 2¢ or less above May. Over or under designations are a necessity for clarity to the floor broker. Omitting either is like omitting the price.

All orders, except market orders, can be cancelled, prior to execution. Naturally, a market order is executed immediately upon reaching the pit, so its cancellation is almost impossible.

There are other variations of orders, but for you the new speculator, the types mentioned are sufficient for your trading.

Options on Stock Market Indices, Bond Futures, and Gold Futures

STOCK MARKET INDEX OPTIONS

Stock market index related options are options whose prices are determined by the value of a stock market average such as the Standard and Poor (S&P) 500 Index or the New York Stock Exchange Composite Index, among others. Two types of such options are currently traded; index options and index futures options. The former are settled in cash while the latter are settled by delivery of the appropriate index futures contract.

Both types of options move in the same way in response to the underlying market index, thereby providing investors the opportunity to speculate on the market averages. The buyer of a call index option is betting that the underlying market index value will increase significantly above the strike price (before the option expires) so as to provide a profit when the option is sold. On the other hand, the buyer of a put option is speculating that the market index value will fall sufficiently below the strike price before the option expires so as to provide a profit when the put option is sold. Options writers (sellers), on the other hand, assume an opposite position.

While index futures (page 448) also permit speculation on the market averages, index option tend to be less risky since option *buyers* are not subject to margin calls and losses are limited to the price (premium) paid for the option. However, index option writers (sellers), in return for the premium received, are subject to margin calls and are exposed to losses of indeterminate magnitude. However, writers of call options on index *futures* can protect themselves by holding the underlying futures contract.

Index Options

A number of index options based on the broad market averages are now traded:

S&P 100 Index [Chicago Board of Options Exchange (CBOE)]
S&P 500 Index (Chicago Board of Options Exchange)
Major Market Index [American Exchange (Amex)]
Institutional Index (American Exchange)
NYSE Options Index (New York Stock Exchange)
Value Line Index (Philadelphia Exchange)
National OTC Index (Philadelphia Exchange)

A brief description of some of the more important indices follows.

The S&P 100 Index is a so-called weighted index obtained by multiplying the current price of each of the 100 stocks by the number of shares outstanding and then adding all of the products to obtain the weighted sum. The weighted sum is then multiplied by a scaling factor to provide an index of a convenient magnitude. The S&P 500 Index is calculated similarly except that all of the S&P 500 stocks are included.

The NYSE Index is based on the weighted sum of all of the stocks traded on the New York Exchange while the AMEX Index is based on the weighted sum of all of the issues traded on the American Exchange. The Institutional Index consists of 75 stocks most widely held by institutional investors.

The Major Market Index differs from the above in that it is just the simple (unweighted) sum of 20 blue chip stocks multiplied by a factor of one tenth. This index behaves very similarly to the Dow Jones Index.

Generally index options expire on the Saturday following the third Friday of the expiration month. Hence the last trading day is on the third Friday of the expiration month. The price of an index option contract is $100 times the premium as quoted in the financial press.

Example: The July 120 (an option with a strike price of 120 expiring in July) Major Market Index call option is quoted (Exhibit 1, see page 460) at 3.00. The cost of an option contract is $300 ($100 × 3).

Option premiums consist of the sum of two components; the intrinsic value and the time value. The intrinsic value of a *call* option is $100 times the difference obtained by subtracting the strike price from the current value of the index. The instrinsic value of a *put* option is $100 times the difference ob-

EXHIBIT 1 INDEX OPTIONS QUOTATIONS

CHICAGO BOARD

CBOE 100 INDEX

Strike	Calls—Last			Puts—Last		
Price	June	Sept	Dec	June	Sept	Dec
145	15¼	....	....	1/16	1	....
150	13¾	....	....	⅛	1¾	....
155	9⅛	10	....	7/16	3⅛	....
160	5⅛	9¼	....	17/16	4⅝	8¼
165	2⅛	6½	8⅝	3⅞	7¼	10½
170	11/16	3¾	6	7⅝	12	13½

Total call volume 20846. Total call open int. 62006.
Total put volume 25167. Total put open int. 103733.
The index closed at 163.55, +1.91.

AMERICAN EXCHANGE

MAJOR MARKET INDEX

Strike	Calls—Last			Puts—Last		
Price	Jul	Oct	Jan	Jul	Oct	Jan
115	5¾	8⅝	10	1⅞	3¾	5½
120	3	5¾	7	4	5⅞	7½
125	1⅛	3¼	....	7⅜	....	....
130	7/16	2¼	3⅝	....	....	

Total call volume 2351. Total call open int. 14572.
Total put volume 5276. Total put open int. 9593.
The index closed at 118.69, +1.00.

Source: Reprinted by permission of *The Wall Street Journal*, Dow Jones & Co., Inc.

tained by subtracting the current value of the index from the strike price. The time value is the money which an option buyer is willing to pay in the expectation that the option will become more valuable (*increase its intrinsic value*) before it expires. Obviously the time value decreases as the time to expiration decreases.

It should be noted that there is a distinction between exercising an index option and selling an index option to close out a position. Exercising an option gives the holder the right to a cash amount equal to the *intrinsic* value of the option. Hence, the time value of the option is lost. When an option is sold to close out a position, the option holder receives a cash amount equal to the *premium* which contains both the intrinsic value and the time value of the option. Thus, in most cases it is more profitable to sell the option. The profit realized (before commissions and taxes) on the *sale* of an option contract is equal to $100 times the difference obtained by subtracting the premium paid when the option was purchased from the premium received when the option was sold.

Example: On May 24 the CBOE 100 Index was 163.55. In anticipation of a market decline, an investor buys a September 165-put option quoted at 7¼ for a total premium of $725 (7.25 × 100) per option. Assume that on August 10 the puts were selling at a total premium of $850 due to a decline in the CBOE 100 Index to 160.10. If the investor sells the put option he will realize a profit, before commissions and taxes, of $125 (850 − 725). If the market moves in a contrary direction he could lose his entire investment.

Index Futures Options

Index futures options (also called futures options) are the right to buy (call) or sell (put) the underlying index futures contracts (see page 448). Futures options are currently traded on the New York Futures Exchange and the Chicago Mercantile Exchange. The dollar value of the underlying contract for the New York Futures Exchange option is equal to the New York Stock Exchange Composite Index multiplied by 500 while that for the Chicago Mercantile Exchange option is equal to the S&P 500 Index multiplied by 500. Quotations for futures options as they appear in *The Wall Street Journal* are shown in Exhibit 2. The total futures option premium per option is equal to the quoted value multiplied by 500. Gains and losses are calculated in the same way as index options.

The expiration day of the S&P 500 futures option is on the third Thursday of the expiration month while that for the NYSE futures option is the business day prior to the last business day of the expiration month.

Example: On May 24, 1983, the New York Composite Index is 94.39. An investor expects the Index to increase during the next six months and buys a September 96 futures call option at a total premium of $1750 (3.50 × 500), as indicated in Exhibit 2. Assume that by August 10 the Index is at 100 and that the September call premium is quoted at 8.00 corresponding to a total premium per option of $4000 (8.00 × 500). By selling the option at the current value the investor can realize a profit of $2250 (4000 − 1750) before commissions and taxes.

Example: Assume that on May 24, 1983 when the S&P 500 Index is at 163.43, an investor expects a market decline within six months. He purchases a September 155 S&P put option at a total premium per option of $1150 (2.30 × 500), as indicated in the quotations shown in Exhibit 2. Assume that the Index declines to 150 on August 10 and that the quoted put premium is 6.50 corresponding to a total premium per option of $3250 (6.50 × 500). By selling the option at the current value the investor can realize a profit of $2100 (3250 − 1150), before commissions and taxes.

While a number of the same basic concepts apply to both index options and future options, there are differences between the two because the futures options have underlying index futures contracts which are traded on the open market. This makes possible a

EXHIBIT 2 FUTURES OPTIONS

CHICAGO MERCANTILE EXCHANGE

S&P 500 STOCK INDEX – Price = $500 times premium.

Strike Price	Calls—Settle Jun	Sep	Dec	Puts—Settle Jun	Sep	Dec
135	....	....	....	.05	....	....
140	23.90	24.25	....	.05	.45	....
145	18.90	20.20	....	.05	.90	....
150	13.95	15.25	....	.10	1.25	....
155	9.20	11.50	....	.30	2.30	4.50
160	4.95	8.60	....	1.05	3.60	....
165	1.90	5.50	8.75	3.00	5.75	7.80
170	.45	3.50	....	6.50	9.50	....
175	.10	1.80	....	11.15	14.00	....

Estimated total vol. 1,440
Calls: Fri. vol. 766; open int. 6,216
Puts: Fri. vol 532; open int. 6,552

N.Y. FUTURES EXCHANGE

NYSE COMPOSITE INDEX – Price = $500 times premium.

Strike Price	Calls—Settle Jun	Sep	Dec	Puts—Settle Jun	Sep	Dec
84	10.90	11.70	....	.05	.40	.75
86	8.90	10.00	11.00	.05	.70	1.50
88	5.95	8.50	9.70	.05	1.00	1.75
90	5.15	7.00	8.30	.25	1.50	2.30
92	3.35	5.50	7.00	.50	2.00	2.95
94	1.95	4.50	6.00	1.15	3.00	3.75
96	.95	3.50	5.00	2.10	3.90	4.95
98	.40	2.75	3.95	3.50	5.25	6.05
100	.15	1.75	3.25	....	6.25	7.00

Estimated total vol. 1,405
Calls: Fri. vol. 844; open int. 4,836
Puts: Fri. vol. 549; open int. 4,801
S&P 500 Index 163.43
New York Composite Index = 94.39
Source: Reprinted by permission of *The Wall Street Journal*, Dow Jones & Co., Inc. All rights reserved.

number of trading strategies with futures options which are not available with index options; for example, simultaneously buying an index futures contract and writing a corresponding call option. Also, for the reason given above, there is a distinction between selling a futures option, the usual procedure, and exercising the option. When a futures option is exercised, the option is exchanged for a position in the index futures market which may result in a loss in the time value of the option.

Investors planning to trade options should read two free booklets available from any of the options exchanges:

Understanding the Risks and Uses of Options

Listed Options On Stock Indices

Subindex Options

Subindex options are based on an index made up of leading publicly traded companies within a specific industry. These options permit speculation on an industry without the necessity of selecting specific stocks within the industry. As with all stock index options they are settled in cash.

Subindex options currently traded are:

American Stock Exchange (AMEX)
  Computer Technology Index Option
  Oil and Gas Index Option
  Transportation Index Option

Pacific Stock Exchange
  Technology Index Option

Philadelphia Stock Exchange
  Gold/Silver Index Option

U.S. TREASURY BOND FUTURES OPTIONS

Options on U.S. Treasury Bonds (T-Bonds), traded on the Chicago Board of Trade, are the right to buy (call) or sell (put) a T-Bond futures contract. The T-Bond futures contract underlying the option is for $100,000 of Treasury Bonds, bearing an 8% or equivalent coupon, which do not mature (and are non-callable) for at least 15 years. When long term interest rates decline, the value of the futures contract and the call option increases while the value of a put option decreases. The reverse is true when long term rates increase.

Premiums for T-bond futures *options* are quoted in 1/64 of 1% (point): Hence each 1/64 of a point is equal to $15.63 ($100,000 × .01 × 1/64) per option. Thus a premium quote of 2–16 means 2 16/64 or (2 × 64 + 16) × $15.63 or $2250.72 per option. It should be noted that prices of T-bond *futures* are quoted in 1/32 (of a point) worth $31.25 per futures contract.

As with options trades in general, the profit (before taxes and commissions) is the premium received (per option) when the option is sold minus the premium paid when the option was purchased.

The last trading day for the options is the first Friday, preceded by at least five business days, in the month *prior* to the month in which the underlying futures contract expires. For example, in 1983 a December option stops trading on November 18, 1983.

GOLD FUTURES OPTIONS

The most widely traded gold futures option is on the New York Comex Exchange. The option is the right to buy (call) or sell (put) a gold futures contract for 100 Troy ounces of pure gold. Both the futures contract and the corresponding call option increase or decrease with the price of gold. Put option premiums move in the opposite direction to the price of gold.

Option premiums are in dollars per ounce

of gold. Thus a quoted premium of 2.50 corresponds to total premium of $2500 (2.50 × 100) per option.

The profit (before commissions and taxes) to an option buyer is simply the premium received when the option is sold less the premium paid when the option was purchased.

The last trading day for gold futures options is the second Friday in the month *prior* to the expiration date of the underlying gold futures contract. Thus in 1983 a December option expires on Friday November 11, 1983. Example: In August an investor buys a December 400 (an option with a strike price of 400 on a December gold futures contract) Comex call option quoted at 25.00. The total price per option is $2500 (25.00 × 100).

On November 5, the price of gold has increased and the investor sells the option at a quoted premium of 50.00 or $5000.00 (50 × 100) per option. His profit is $2500 (5000 − 2500).

The Commodities Glossary

Acreage allotment The portion of a farmer's total acreage that he can harvest and still qualify for government price supports, low interest crop loans and other programs. It currently applies to specialty crops—tobacco, peanuts and extra long staple cotton—for which complex federal marketing orders have been written to control production closely. Before the 1977 farm bill was passed, the same term also applied more loosely to the portion of a farmer's wheat or feed grain acreage for which government payments would be made. A farmer could harvest 100 acres of wheat, for instance, but he'd receive price support payments only for 70 acres if that was his allotment. The allotment in this sense is called "program acreage" in the new farm bill.

Arbitrage The simultaneous buying and selling of futures contracts to profit from what the trader perceives as a discrepancy in prices. Usually this is done in futures in the same commodity traded on different exchanges, such as cocoa in New York and cocoa in London or silver in New York and silver in Chicago. Some arbitrage occurs between cash markets and futures markets.

Asking price The price offered by one wishing to sell a physical commodity or a futures contract. Sometimes a futures market will close with an asking price when no buyers are around.

Backwardation An expression peculiar to New York markets. It means "nearby" contracts are trading at a higher price, or "premium," to the deferreds. See also *Inverted market.*

Basis A couple of meanings: (1) The difference between the price of the physical commodity (the cash price) and the futures price of that commodity. (2) A geographic reference point for a cash price; for example, the price of a beef carcass is quoted "basis Midwest packing plants."

Bear A trader who thinks prices will decline. "Bearish" is often used to describe news or developments that have, or are expected to have, a downward influence on prices. A bear market is one in which the predominant price trend is down. Some think this term originated with an old axiom about "selling the skin before you've caught the bear."

Bid The price offered by one who wishes to purchase a physical commodity or a futures contract. Sometimes a futures market will close with a bid price when no sellers are around.

Broker An agent who buys and sells futures on behalf of a client for a fee. They work for brokerage firms, some of which have extensive research and analysis departments that occasionally issue trading advice. A few firms have so many customers who follow such advisories that recommendations to buy or sell can influence market prices materially.

Bull A trader who thinks prices will go up. "Bullish" describes developments that have, or are expected to have, an upward influence on prices. A bull market is one in which the predominant price trend is up. Some theorize this term originally related to a bull's habit of tossing its head upward.

Butterfly An unusual sort of spread involving three contract months rather than two. Often used to move profits or losses from one year to the next for tax purposes.

Cash The price at which dealings in the physical commodity take place. Used more sweepingly, it can mean simply the physical commodity itself (as in "cash corn" or "cash lumber"), or refer to a market. For example, the cash hog market is a terminal (or, collectively, all terminals) where live hogs are sold by farmers and bought by meat packers.

Chart A graph of futures prices (and sometimes other statistical trading information) plotted in such a way that the charter believes gives insight into future price movements. Several futures markets regularly are influenced by buying or selling based on traders' price-chart indications.

Clearing house The part of all futures exchanges (usually a separate corporation with its

Source: The *Dow Jones Commodities Handbook*, edited by Dan Ruck, Dow Jones Books, Dow Jones Company, Inc. 1979.

own members, fees, etc.) which clears all trades made on the exchange during the day. It matches the buy transactions with the equal number of sell transactions to provide orderly control over who owns what and who owes what to whom. Although futures traders theoretically trade contracts among themselves, the clearing house technically is in the middle of each transaction—being the buyer to every seller and the seller to every buyer. That's how it keeps track of what is going on.

Close The end of the trading session. On some exchanges, the "close" lasts for several minutes to accommodate customers who have entered buy or sell orders to be consummated "at the close." On those exchanges, the closing price may be a range encompassing the highest and lowest prices of trades consummated at the close. Other exchanges officially use settlement prices as the closing prices.

Cold storage Refrigerated warehouses where perishable commodities are stored. In effect. the warehouses are secondary sources of commodities that aren't immediately available from the producers. The Agriculture Department periodically reports the quantities of various commodities stored in warehouses. Futures traders watch these reports to see if the supplies are building or dwindling abnormally fast, which indicates how closely supply and demand are balanced.

Commission The fee charged by a broker for making a trade on behalf of customers.

Contract In the case of futures, an agreement between two parties to make and in turn accept delivery of a specified quantity and quality of a commodity (or whatever is being traded) at a certain place (the delivery point) by a specified time (indicated by the month and year of the contract).

Country Refers to a place relatively close to a farmer where he can sell or deliver his crop or animals. For instance, a country elevator typically is located in a small town and accepts grain from farmers in the immediate vicinity. A country shipping point is a place where farmers in an area combine their marketings for shipment. A country price is the one these elevators, shipping points or whatever pay for the farmers' goods; it's based on the terminal-market prices, less transportation and handling costs.

Covering Buying futures contracts to offset those previously sold. "Short covering" often causes prices to rise even though the overall market trend may be down.

Crop report Estimates issued periodically by the Department of Agriculture on estimated size and condition of major U.S. crops. Similar reports are made on livestock.

Crush The process of reducing the raw, unusable soybean into its two major components, oil and meal. A "crush spread" is a futures spreading position in which a trader attempts to profit from what he believes to be discrepancies in the price relationships between soybeans and the two products. The "crush margin" is the gross profit that a processor makes from selling oil and meal minus the cost of buying the soybeans.

Deferred contracts In futures, those delivery months that are due to expire sometime beyond the next two or three months.

Delivery The tendering of the physical commodity to fulfill a short position in futures. This takes place only during the delivery month and normally takes the form of a warehouse receipt (from an exchange-accredited warehouse, elevator or whatever) that shows where the cash commodity is.

Delivery point The place(s) at which the cash commodity may be delivered to fulfill an expiring futures contract.

Discretionary accounts A futures trading account in which the customer puts up the money but the trading decisions are made at the discretion of the broker or some other person, or maybe a computer. Also known as "managed accounts."

Evening up Liquidating a futures position in advance of a significant crop report or some other scheduled development so as not to be caught on the wrong side of a surprise. In concentrated doses, evening up can cause a bull market to retreat somewhat and a bear market to rebound somewhat.

First notice day The first day of a delivery period when holders of short futures positions can give notice of their intention to deliver the cash commodity to holders of long positions. The number of contracts circulated on first notice day and how they are accepted or not accepted by the longs is often interpreted as an indication of future supply-demand expectations and thus often influence prices of all futures being traded, not just the delivery-month price. This effect also sometimes occurs on subsequent notice days. Rules concerning notices to deliver vary from contract to contract.

F.O.B. Free on Board, meaning that the commodity will be placed aboard the shipping vehicle at no cost to the purchaser, but thereafter the purchaser must bear all shipping costs.

Forward Contract A commercial agreement for the merchandising of commodities in which actual delivery is contemplated but is deferred for purposes of commercial convenience or necessity. Such agreements normally specify the quality and quantity of goods to be delivered at the particular future date. The forward contract may specify the price at which the commodity will be exchanged, or the agreement may stipulate that the price will be determined at some time prior to delivery.

Fundamentalist A trader who bases his buy-sell decisions on supply and demand trends or developments rather than on technical or chart considerations.

Futures Contracts traded on an exchange that call for a cash commodity to be delivered and received at a specified future time, at a specified place and at a specified price. Similar arrangements made directly between buyer and seller are called "forward contracts." They aren't traded on an exchange.

Hedge Using the futures market to reduce the risks of unforeseen price changes that are inherent in buying and selling cash commodities. For example, as an elevator operator buys cash grain from farmer, he can "hedge" his purchases by selling futures contracts; when he sells the cash commodity, he purchases an offsetting number of futures contracts to liquidate his position. If prices rise while he owns the cash grain, he sells the cash grain at a profit and closes out his futures at a loss, which almost always is no greater than his profit in the cash transaction. If prices fall while he owns the cash grain, he sells the cash grain at a loss but recoups all or almost all of the loss by buying back futures contracts at a price correspondingly lower than at which he first sold them. Some users of commodities assure themselves of supplies of their raw materials at a set price by buying futures, which is another form of hedging. When the time comes to acquire inventories, they can either take delivery on their futures contracts or, more likely, simply buy their supplies in the cash market. Futures-contract prices tend to match cash prices at the time the futures expire, so if cash prices have risen the users' higher costs are offset by profits on their futures contracts.

Hedger The Commodity Futures Trading Commission says a hedger in a general sense is someone who uses futures trading as a temporary, risk-reducing substitute for a cash transaction planned later in his main line of business. All other futures traders are classified as speculators. There are more legally specific definitions of hedging and hedgers in such markets as grains, soybeans, potatoes and cotton, where limits are placed on the number of contracts speculators may trade or own. The Commission has broadened these limits to allow hedging in closely related, rather than exactly matching, commodities. A sorghum producer, for instance, can use corn futures as a hedging tool where he couldn't before this rule-broadening. The more general distinction between hedgers and speculators may be important to potential traders. Some may want to use a market like interest rate futures to offset some expected heavy borrowing. The government hasn't set any speculative trading limits in those markets, but lenders or company directors are more apt to back a plan to trade futures for hedging purposes rather than speculation.

Inverted market A futures market where prices for deferred contracts are lower than those for nearby-delivery contracts because of great near-term demand for the cash commodity. Normally, prices of deferred contracts are higher, in part reflecting storage costs.

Last trading day The day when trading in an expiring contract ceases, and traders must either liquidate their positions or prepare to make or accept delivery of the cash commodity. After that, there is no more futures trading for that particular contract month and year.

Life of contract The period of time during which futures trading in a particular contract month and year may take place. This is usually less than a year, but sometimes up to 18 months.

Limit move The maximum that a futures price can rise or fall from the previous session's settlement price. This limit, set by each exchange, varies from commodity to commodity. Some exchanges have variable limits, whereby the limit is expanded automatically if the market moves by the limit for a certain number of consecutive trading sessions. When prices fail to move the expanded limit, or after a specified period of time, the limits revert to normal.

Liquidation Closing out a previous position by taking an opposite position in the same contract. Thus, a previous buyer liquidates by selling, and a previous seller liquidates by buying.

Long A trader who has bought futures, speculating the prices will rise. He is "long" until he liquidates by selling or fulfills his contracts by making delivery.

Margin The amount of "good faith" money that commodity traders must put in order to trade futures. The margins, set by each exchange, usually amount to 5% to 10% of the total value of the commodity contract. The "initial margin" is the amount of money that must be put up to establish a position in a futures market. Exchanges establish this margin, too, but brokerage firms often require even larger amounts to protect their own financial interests. "Maintenance margin" is the money that traders must put up to retain their position in the futures markets.

Margin call A request by a brokerage firm that a customer put up more money. That means the market price has gone against the customer's position and the brokerage firm wants the customer to cover his paper loss, which would become a real loss if the position were liquidated.

Nearby contracts The futures that expire the soonest. Those that expire later are called deferred contracts.

New crop The supply of a commodity that will be available after harvest. The term also is sometimes used in connection with pigs and hogs because the major farrowing periods in the spring and fall are referred to as "crops." There sometimes are substantial price differences between futures contracts related to new-crop supplies and those related to old-crop supplies.

Nominal price An artificial price—usually the midpoint between a bid and an asked price—that gives an indication of the market price level even though no actual transactions may have taken place at that price.

Old crop The supply from previous harvests.

Open The period each session when futures trading commences. Sometimes the open lasts several minutes to accommodate customers who have placed orders to buy or sell contracts "on the open." On these exchanges, opening prices often are reported by the exchange as a range, although these seldom are widely disseminated because of space restrictions in newspapers and periodicals; they are carried on tickers and display panels during that trading day, however.

Open interest Outstanding futures contracts that haven't been liquidated by purchase or sale of offsetting contracts, or by delivery or acceptance of the physical commodity.

Option The right to buy or sell a futures contract over a specified period of time at a set price.

Overbought A term used to express the opinion that prices have risen too high too fast and so will decline as traders liquidate their positions.

Oversold Like "overbought," except the opinion is that prices have fallen too far too fast and so probably will rebound.

Pit The areas on exchange floors where futures trading takes place. Pits usually have three or more levels and can accommodate a large number of traders. On several New York exchanges the trading areas are called rings and consist of open-center, circular tables around which traders sit or stand.

Position A trader's holdings, either long or short. A position limit is the maximum number of contracts a speculator can hold under law; it doesn't apply to bona-fide hedgers, although there really isn't any objective way of telling whether a person in position to hedge actually is hedging or is speculating instead.

Profit taking A trader holding a long position turns paper profits into real ones by selling his contracts. A trader holding a short position takes profits by buying back contracts.

Reaction A decline in prices following a substantial advance.

Recovery An increase in prices following a substantial decline.

Settlement price The single closing price, determined by each exchange's price committee of directors. It is used primarily by the exchange clearing house to determine the need for margin capital to be put up by brokerage-firm members to protect the net position of that firm's total accounts. It's also issued by some exchanges as the official closing price, and it is used to determine the price limits and net price changes on the following trading day. (See also: *Close.*)

Set-aside Acreage withdrawn from crop production for a season and used for soil conservation under a production-control program. Wheat farmers this year must set aside two acres of land for each 10 acres they plant to wheat in order to get any federal price support or disaster aid. The Agriculture Department has also said corn, sorghum and barley producers similarly may be required to set aside some of their acreage if it appears that surpluses will grow too much otherwise.

Short A trader who has sold futures, speculating that prices will decline. He is "short" until he liquidates by buying back contracts or fulfills his contracts by taking delivery.

Short squeeze A situation in which "short" futures traders are unable to buy the cash commodity to deliver against their positions and so are forced to buy offsetting futures at prices much higher than they'd ordinarily be willing to pay.

Speculation Buying or selling in hopes of making a profit. The word connotes a high degree of risk.

Spot The same as cash commodities. Literally, delivery "on the spot" rather than in the future.

Spreads and straddles Terms for the simultaneous buying of futures in one delivery month and selling of futures in another delivery month (or even the simultaneous buying of futures in one commodity and selling of futures in a different but related commodity). One purpose is to profit from perceived discrepancies in price relationships. Another purpose is to transfer current trading profits to some future time to avoid immediate tax liability.

Stop-loss order An open order given to a brokerage firm to liquidate a position when the market reaches a certain price so as to prevent losses from mounting or profits from eroding. Sometimes market price trends are accelerated when concentrations of stop-loss orders are touched off.

Support price A level below which the government tries to keep the agricultural-commodity prices that farmers receive from falling. They're set basically by Congress when farm legislation is passed and adjusted from time to time by the President or Agriculture Secretary. Subsidy payments, commodity purchases, production controls or commodity-secured loans are among the devices used to make up the difference when market prices dip below the support level. Futures and cash prices often tend to remain near the support level when there are large crop surpluses because lower prices keep commodities off the market and higher ones quickly draw willing sellers.

Switch A trading maneuver in which a trader liquidates his position in one futures delivery and takes the position in another delivery month in expectation that prices will change more rapidly in the second contract than in the first. Thus, a trader might switch out of a position in an October silver futures contract into a position in a December silver futures contract. Warning: Some people use the word "switch" when they mean "spread" or "straddle." Feel free to correct them.

Technical factors Futures prices often are affected by influences related to the market itself, rather than to supply-demand fundamentals of the commodity with which the market is concerned. For example, if a market moves up or down the limit several days in succession there frequently is a subsequent "technical reaction" caused in part by the liquidation of contracts held by traders on the wrong side of the price move.

Terminal Refers to an elevator or livestock market at key distribution points to which commodities are sent from a wide area.

Trading range The amount that futures prices can fluctuate during one trading session—essentially, the price "distance" between limit up and limit down. If, for instance, the soybean futures price can advance or fall by a maximum of 20 cents per bushel in one day, the trading range is double that, or 40 cents per bushel. In one market, cocoa, price movements are restricted to a daily range of six cents a pound.

Visible supply The amount of a commodity that can be accounted for and computed accurately, usually because it is being kept in major known storage places.

Warehouse or elevator receipt The negotiable slip of paper that a short can hand over to fulfill an expiring futures contract's delivery requirement. The receipt shows how much of the commodity is in storage.

Dow Jones Futures and Spot Commodity Indexes

The method for arriving at the Dow Jones Futures and Spot Commodity Indexes differs from some others in the order in which the computations are made. Instead of first weighting each price, then adding them up and finally calculating the percentage or index, this method first turns each price into an index or percentage of its base-year price, then weights each individual index, and finally adds them up. Stated mathematically, the more usual method calculates the percentage relation of one average to another, while the Dow Jones Commodity Index method calculates the average of a set of percentage changes. These two methods do not result in exactly the same figures. However, they are equally valid when used consistently, and the indexes they produce are of the same general magnitude.

The Dow Jones Commodity Index method has two advantages. One is that it saves computation, because the factors or multipliers perform two computations at once. They calculate the individual percentages and weight them at one stroke. The other advantage is that if you have yesterday's index, you can apply the multipliers to today's individual price changes. Then all you do is add the resulting figures to yesterday's index, or subtract them from it, depending on whether they're up or down. That gives today's index. No need to recalculate the whole thing each day.

As for the weights, they were obtained by the usual mathematical methods. Basically, the weight of each commodity is the percentage of its commercial production value to the total commercial production value of all commodities in the index, in this case for the years 1927–31. In calculating the weights, consideration also was given to the relation between volume of trading in each commodity and its commercial production.

A further refinement was necessary because price changes of the various commodities are quoted in different units. Grain prices change in eighths of a cent, wool prices change in tenths of a cent, and all the other staples in the Dow Jones index move in hundredths of a cent. This adjustment merely required appropriate treatment in each case of the multiplier, so that it would give the right figure for any price change. In the case of grains it meant an adjustment of 20%, since one-tenth is that much smaller than one-eighth. In other cases a mere adjustment of decimal points was sufficient.

The twelve commodities, with the weight of each and the multiplier applied to the price changes of each, are:

Source: The *Dow Jones Commodities Handbook*, edited by Dan Ruck, Dow Jones Books, Dow Jones & Company, Inc.

	Weight	Multiplier
Wheat	19.5	16
Corn	8	11
Oats	5	13
Rye	4	5
Wool Tops	5.5	4
Cotton	23	10
Cottonseed Oil	4.5	4
Coffee	7	3
Sugar	8.5	27
Cocoa	5	5
Rubber	6	3
Hides	4	3

These are the essentials for calculating the spot index. However, the futures index requires one more set of unusual steps. That's because several times a year an actual quoted "future" disappears. For instance, while early in the year it is possible to buy wheat to be delivered in December, when the month of December actually arrives that "delivery" expires and is no longer quoted.

The result is that futures prices are affected not only by market conditions but also by how close the delivery date looms. Interest charges and other such factors influence them. On July 1, the December delivery is just five months off, but a month later it is only four months away, and a five-month delivery should not, in a precise index, be compared with a four-month delivery.

This problem is overcome by the use of two futures quotations for each commodity. They are combined to produce on each market day the calculated price that would apply to a delivery exactly five months off.

On the first day of July, only the December delivery is used, since it is just five months away and thus no adjustment need be made. On the second day, the two quotations used are those for the same December delivery and the one for May of the following year. The quoted price for December is adjusted by one day's proportion of the difference between it and May's quoted price. Since there are 151 days between December and May (except in leap years) the figure for one day's proportion is 1/151 of the price difference between the two. The resulting fraction is added to December's price, or subtracted from it, depending on whether May is quoted above or below December.

The following day 2/151 of the difference are added or subtracted, the third day 3/151 and so on until December 1, on which day only the May contract's price is used. On December 2, the combination used is May and July, and so on around the year.

To facilitate the work of calculating the futures index every hour of each business day and the spot index once a day, tables have been prepared—resembling somewhat tables of logarithms or bond yields—which give the figures arrived at by multiplying the various quotational units of each commodity by its factor or multiplier. For instance, the tables show the proper multiples for one-eighth, one-quarter, three-eighths, etc., when each is multiplied by each grain's factor or multiplier.

The commodity futures index is published once an hour and as of the close of commodity markets each day on the Dow Jones News Service, where also the spot index is published once daily. Both are published likewise in *The Wall Street Journal.*

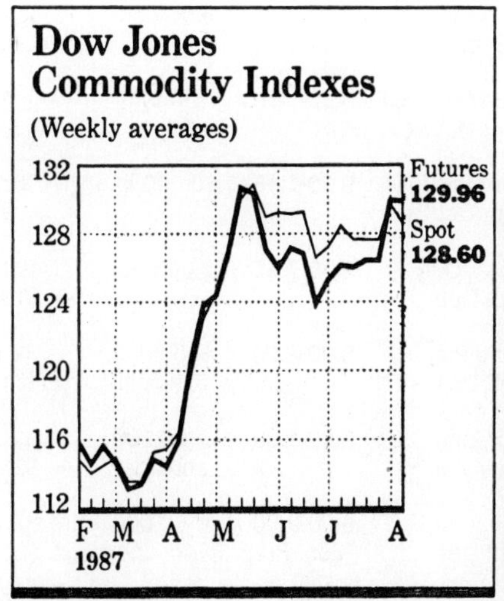

	Close		Net Chg.	Yr. Ago
Dow Jones Futures	128.84	−	.50	115.50
Dow Jones Spot	128.45	−	.72	116.99
Reuter United Kingdom	1661.6	+	14.2	1448.1
C R B Futures*	224.16	−	.31	204.45

*Division of Knight-Ridder.

Source: "Reprinted by permission of The Wall Street Journal

Commodity Trading Facts and Figures

The following provides as complete a list of futures, options on futures and options on actuals contracts as we could put together. It is possible we may have overlooked some contract because of the number of new contracts that have been introduced in the last year, or we may have listed a contract that has become inactive. The list includes some contracts that may be awaiting approval by exchange and/or government officials and are not trading yet.*

Details of all contracts are current, to the best of our knowledge, but any one of the areas listed is subject to change. The daily limit figure given is the normal limit that prices can move up or down from the previous day's close. A number of exchanges have variable limit policies, which can alter these limits in a volatile market. In addition, there are no limits on spot month contracts in many cases. For more information on limit changes, current minimum margin requirements or other contract details, you should check with your broker.

* Only the U.S. and Canadian markets are included in the Dow Jones-Irwin *Business and Investment Almanac.*

U.S. Futures Contracts

Chicago Board of Trade

Commodity	Contract months	Trading hours (local time)	Contract size	Minimum price fluctuation	Daily limit
Corn	Mar/May/July Sept/Dec	9:30-1:15	5,000 bu.	1/4¢/bu. = $12.50	10¢/bu. = $500
Oats	Mar/May/July Sept/Dec	9:30-1:15	5,000 bu.	1/4¢/bu. = $12.50	6¢/bu. = $300
Soybeans	Jan/Mar/May/July Aug/Sept/Nov	9:30-1:15	5,000 bu.	1/4¢/bu. = $12.50	30¢/bu. = $1,500
Soybean Meal	Jan/Mar/May/July Aug/Sept/Oct/Nov	9:30-1:15	100 tons	10¢/ton = $10	$10/ton = $1,000
Soybean Oil	Jan/Mar/May/July Aug/Sept/Oct/Dec	9:30-1:15	60,000 lb.	1/100¢/lb. = $6	1¢/lb. = $600
Wheat (Soft winter)	Mar/May/July Sept/Dec	9:30-1:15	5,000 bu.	1/4¢/bu. = $12.50	20¢/bu. = $1,000
GNMA CDR	Mar/June Sept/Dec	8:00-2:00	$100,000 principal	1/32 pt. = $31.25	63/32 pt. = $2,000
GNMA (Cash-settled)	Mar/June Sept/Dec	8:00-2:00	$100,000 principal	1/32 pt. = $31.25	64/32 pt. = $2,000
U.S. Treasury Bonds	Mar/June Sept/Dec	8:00-2:00 (Mon.-Fri.) (Sun.-Thurs.) 5:00-8:30 p.m.	$100,000 8% coupon	1/32 pt. = $31.25	64/32 pt. = $2,000

Source: Reproduced with permission of *Futures Magazine,* 219 Parkade, Cedar Falls, Iowa 50613.

Commodity	Contract months	Trading hours (local time)	Contract size	Minimum price fluctuation	Daily limit
U.S. Treasury Notes (6½-10 yr.)	Mar/June Sept/Dec	8:00-2:00 (Mon.-Fri.)	$100,000 8% coupon	1/32 pt. = $31.25	64/32 pt. = $2,000
		(Sun.-Thurs.) 5:00-8:30 p.m.			
Municipal Bond Index	Mar/June Sept/Dec	8:00-2:00	$1,000 × Bond Buyer Index	1/32 pt. = $31.25	64/32 pt. = $2,000
Major Market Index-Maxi	March cycle plus next three consecutive months	8:15-3:15	$250 × AMEX Major Market Index	1/20 pt. = $12.50	None
Institutional Index	Next three months plus March cycle	8:15-3:15	$500 × Index	5/100 pt. = $25	None
Gold	Current month and next two months plus Feb/Apr/June	7:20-1:40 (Mon.-Fri.)	100 troy oz.	10¢/oz. = $10	$50/oz. = $5,000
		(Sun.-Thurs.) 5:00-8:30 p.m.			
Gold	Feb/Apr Aug/Oct/Dec	7:20-1:40	1 kilogram = 32.15 oz.	10¢/oz. = $3.22	$50/oz. = $1,607.50
Silver	Current month and next two months plus Feb/Apr/June	7:25-1:25 (Mon.-Fri.)	5,000 troy oz.	1/10¢/oz. = $5	$1/oz. = $5,000
		(Sun.-Thurs.) 5:00-8:30 p.m.			
Silver	Feb/Mar/June Aug/Oct/Dec	7:25-1:25	1,000 troy oz.	1/10¢/oz. = $5	50¢/oz. = $500

*CBOE 250 and 50 stock indexes and Japanese Government Bond futures are pending CFTC approval.

Chicago Mercantile Exchange

Commodity	Contract months	Trading hours (local time)	Contract size	Minimum price fluctuation	Daily limit
Cattle, Feeder	Jan/Mar/Apr/May Aug/Sept/Oct/Nov	9:05-1:00	44,000 lb.	2.5¢/cwt. = $11	1.5¢/lb. = $660
Cattle, Live	Feb/Apr/June Aug/Oct/Dec	9:05-1:00	40,000 lb.	2.5¢/cwt. = $10	1.5¢/lb. = $600
Eggs, Fresh White (Inactive)	All months except August	9:20-1:00	22,500 doz.	5/100¢/doz. = $11.25	2¢/doz. = $450
Hogs, Live	Feb/Apr/June/July Aug/Oct/Dec	9:10-1:00	30,000 lb.	2.5¢/cwt. = $7.50	1.5¢/lb. = $450
Pork Bellies	Feb/Mar/May July/Aug	9:10-1:00	40,000 lb.	2.5¢/cwt. = $9.50	2¢/lb. = $760
Lumber (Random-length)	Jan/Mar/May July/Sept/Nov	9:00-1:05	130,000 bd. ft.	10¢/1,000 bd. ft. = $13	$5/1,000 bd. ft. = $650

Commodity	Contract months	Trading hours (local time)	Contract size	Minimum price fluctuation	Daily limit
Chicago Mercantile Exchange International Monetary Market Division					
Deutsche Mark	Jan/Mar/Apr/June July/Sept/Oct/Dec and spot month	7:20-1:20	125,000 DM	$0.0001/DM = $12.50	None
Canadian Dollar	"	7:20-1:26	100,000 CD	$0.0001/CD = $10	None
French Franc	"	7:20-1:28	250,000 FF	$0.00005/FF = $12.50	None
Swiss Franc	"	7:20-1:16	125,000 SF	$0.0001/SF = $12.50	None
British Pound	"	7:20-1:24	25,000 BP	$0.0005/BP = $12.50	None
Mexican Peso (Inactive)	"	7:20-1:18	1,000,000 MP	$0.00001/MP = $10	None
Japanese Yen	"	7:20-1:22	12,500,000 JY	$0.000001/JY = $12.50	None
Australian Dollar	"	7:20-1:18	100,000 AD	$.0001/AD = $12.50	None
European Currency Unit (ECU)	Mar/June Sept/Dec	7:10-1:30	125,000 ECU	$0.0001/ECU = $12.50	None
Treasury Bills (90-day)	Mar/June Sept/Dec	7:20-2:00	$1,000,000	1 pt. = $25	None
Domestic Certificates of Deposit (3-month)	Mar/June Sept/Dec	7:20-2:00	$1,000,000	1 pt. = $25	None
Eurodollar Time Deposit (3-month)	Mar/June/Sept/Dec and spot month	7:20-2:00	$1,000,000	1 pt. = $25	None
Gold	Aug/Sept/Oct	7:20-1:30	100 oz.	10¢/oz. = $10	None

Commodity	Contract months	Trading hours (local time)	Contract size	Minimum price fluctuation	Daily limit
Chicago Mercantile Exchange Index and Option Market Division					
Standard & Poor's 500 Stock Index	Mar/June Sept/Dec	8:30-3:15	500 × S&P 500 Stock Index	5 pt. = $25	None
Standard & Poor's 100 Stock Index	Next four months and Mar/June Sept/Dec	8:30-3:15	500 × S&P 100 Stock Index	5 pt. = $25	None
Standard & Poor's Over-The-Counter Index (250 stocks)	Mar/June Sept/Dec	8:30-3:15	500 × S&P OTC Index	5 pt. = $25	None

* The Nikkei 225 Stock Average Index is pending CFTC approval.

Chicago Rice and Cotton Exchange

Commodity	Contract months	Trading hours (local time)	Contract size	Minimum price fluctuation	Daily limit
Rough Rice	Jan/Mar/May Sept/Nov	9:15-1:30	2,000 cwt. (200,000 lb.)	0.5¢/cwt. = $10	30¢/cwt. = $600

Coffee, Sugar & Cocoa Exchange Inc.

Commodity	Contract months	Trading hours (local time)	Contract size	Minimum price fluctuation	Daily limit
Cocoa	Mar/May/July Sept/Dec	9:30-2:15	10 metric tons	$1/metric ton = $10	$88/metric ton = $880
Coffee "C"	Mar/May/July Sept/Dec	9:45-2:28 (2:30 closing call)	37,500 lb.	1/100¢/lb. = $3.75	6¢/lb. = $2,250
Sugar No. 11 (World)	Jan/Mar/May July/Oct	10:00-1:43 (1:45 closing call)	112,000 lb.	1/100¢/lb. = $11.20	1/2¢/lb. = $560
Sugar No. 14	Jan/Mar/May July/Sept/Nov	9:45-1:43 (Closing call begins when Sugar No. 11's closing call is completed.)	112,000 lb.	1/100¢/lb. = $11.20	1/2¢/lb. = $560
Sugar (White)	Jan/Mar/May July/Oct	"	50 metric tons	20¢/metric ton = $10	$10/metric ton
Inflation Rate	Jan/Apr July/Oct	9:30-2:30	$1,000,000	.005% = $12.50	100 pt.
Consumer Price Index (CPI-W)	Jan/Apr July/Oct	9:30-2:30	1,000 × CPI-W	0.01 pt. = $10	3.00 pt. = $3,000

Commodity	Contract months	Trading hours (local time)	Contract size	Minimum price fluctuation	Daily limit
Commodity Exchange Inc. (COMEX)					
Aluminum	Current calendar month, next two months and Jan/Mar/May July/Sept/Dec	9:30-2:10	44,000 lb.	5/100¢/lb. = $20	None
Copper	"	9:25-2:00	25,000 lb.	5/100¢/lb. = $12.50	None
Silver	"	8:25-2:25	5,000 troy oz.	10/100¢/oz. = $5	None
Gold (Linked to Sydney Futures Exchange)	Current calendar month, next two months and Feb/Apr/June Aug/Oct/Dec	8:20-2:30	100 troy oz.	10¢/oz. = $10	None
Kansas City Board of Trade					
Wheat (Hard red winter)	Mar/May/July Sept/Dec	9:30-1:15	5,000 bu.	1/4¢/bu. = $12.50	25¢/bu. = $1,250
Value Line Stock Index	Mar/June Sept/Dec	8:30-3:15	500 × the futures price	0.05 = $25	None
Mini Value Line Stock Index	Mar/June Sept/Dec	8:30-3:15	100 × the futures price	0.05 = $5	None
MidAmerica Commodity Exchange					
Cattle, Live	Feb/Apr/June Aug/Oct/Dec	9:05-1:15	20,000 lb.	2.5/100¢/lb. = $5	1.5¢/lb. = $300
Hogs, Live	Feb/Apr/June July/Aug/Oct/Dec	9:10-1:15	15,000 lb.	2.5/100¢/lb. = $3.75	1.5¢/lb. = $225
Corn	Mar/May/July Sept/Dec	9:30-1:30	1,000 bu.	1/8¢/bu. = $1.25	10¢/bu. = $100
Oats	Mar/May/July Sept/Dec	9:30-1:30	1,000 bu.	1/8¢/bu. = $1.25	10¢/bu. = $100
Soybeans	Jan/Mar/May July/Aug/Sept/Nov	9:30-1:30	1,000 bu.	1/8¢/bu. = $1.25	30¢/bu. = $300
Soybean Meal	Jan/Mar/May/July Aug/Sept/Oct/Dec	9:30-1:30	20 tons	10¢/ton = $2	$10/ton = $200
Wheat (Soft winter)	Mar/May/July Sept/Dec	9:30-1:30	1,000 bu.	1/8¢/bu. = $1.25	20¢/bu. = $200

Commodity	Contract months	Trading hours (local time)	Contract size	Minimum price fluctuation	Daily limit
New York Gold	All months	7:20-1:40	33.2 fine troy oz.	10¢/oz. = $3.32	None
New York Silver	All months	7:25-1:40	1,000 troy oz.	10/100¢/oz. = $1	None
Platinum	Current three months and Jan/Apr July/Oct	7:20-1:40	25 fine troy oz.	10¢/oz. = $2.50	$25/oz. = $625
U.S. Treasury Bonds	Mar/June Sept/Dec	7:20-3:15	$50,000 face value	1/32 pt. = $15.62	96/32 pt. = $1,500
U.S. Treasury Bills (90-day)	Mar/June Sept/Dec	7:20-2:15	$500,000 face value	1 pt. = $12.50	None
British Pound	Mar/June Sept/Dec	7:20-1:34	12,500 BP	$0.0005/BP = $6.25	None
Canadian Dollar	Mar/June Sept/Dec	7:20-1:36	50,000 CD	$0.0001/CD = $5	None
Deutsche Mark	Mar/June Sept/Dec	7:20-1:30	62,500 DM	$0.0001/DM = $6.25	None
Japanese Yen	Mar/June Sept/Dec	7:20-1:32	6,250,000 JY	$0.000001/ JY = $6.25	None
Swiss Franc	Mar/June Sept/Dec	7:20-1:26	62,500 SF	$0.0001/SF = $6.25	None

*Australian Dollar futures have been approved by the CFTC but are not yet listed.

Minneapolis Grain Exchange

Commodity	Contract months	Trading hours (local time)	Contract size	Minimum price fluctuation	Daily limit
Wheat (Hard red spring)	Mar/May/July Sept/Dec	9:30-1:15	5,000 bu.	1/8¢/bu. = $6.25	20¢/bu. = $1,000
High Fructose Corn Syrup	Mar/May/July Sept/Dec	9:00-1:25	48,000 lb.	1¢/cwt. = $4.80	$1/cwt. = $480

New York Cotton Exchange

Commodity	Contract months	Trading hours (local time)	Contract size	Minimum price fluctuation	Daily limit
Cotton No. 2	Mar/May/July Oct/Dec	10:30-3:00	50,000 lb. (approx. 100 bales)	1/100¢/lb. = $5	2¢/lb. = $1,000

Citrus Associates of the New York Cotton Exchange Inc.

Commodity	Contract months	Trading hours (local time)	Contract size	Minimum price fluctuation	Daily limit
Orange Juice	Jan/Mar/May July/Sept/Nov	10:15-2:45	15,000 lb.	5/100¢/lb. = $7.50	5¢/lb. = $750

Commodity	Contract months	Trading hours (local time)	Contract size	Minimum price fluctuation	Daily limit
Financial Instrument Exchange (FINEX)					
U.S. Dollar Index	Mar/June Sept/Dec	8:20-2:40	$500 × U.S. Dollar Index	0.01 (1 basis pt.) = $5	None
European Currency Unit (ECU)	Mar/June Sept/Dec	8:20-2:40	100,000 ECU	0.01¢/ECU = $10	None
Five-Year U.S. Treasury Note (FYTR)	Mar/June Sept/Dec	9:00-3:00	U.S. Treasury notes with face values at maturity of $100,000	1/2 of 1/32 pt. = $15.625	None
New York Futures Exchange					
NYSE Composite Stock Index	Mar/June Sept/Dec	9:30-4:15	$500 × NYSE Index	0.05 pt. = $25	None
CRB Futures Price Index	Mar/May/July Sept/Dec	9:00-3:15	$500 × CRB Index	0.05 pt. = $25	None
Russell 2000 Index	Mar/June Sept/Dec	9:30-4:15	$500 × Index	$25	None
Russell 3000 Index	"	"	"	"	"
New York Mercantile Exchange					
Palladium	Mar/June Sept/Dec	8:10-2:20	100 troy oz.	5¢/oz. = $5	$6/oz. = $600
Platinum	Jan/Apr July/Oct	8:20-2:30	50 troy oz.	10¢/oz. = $5	$25/oz. = $1,250
No. 2 Heating Oil (New York)	All months	9:50-3:05	42,000 gal.	1/100¢/gal. = $4.20	2¢/gal. = $840
Unleaded Gasoline	All months	9:50-3:05	42,000 gal.	1/100¢/gal. = $4.20	2¢/gal. = $840
Crude Oil (Light sweet)	All months	9:45-3:10	1,000 barrels (42,000 gal.)	1¢/barrel = $10	$1/barrel = $1,000
Propane	All months	9:40-3:05	42,000 gal.	1/100¢/gal. = $4.20	2¢/gal. = $840
Philadelphia Board of Trade					
National Over-The-Counter Index	Mar/June Sept/Dec plus two near months	9:30-4:15	$500 × index	0.05 pt. = $25	None

Commodity	Contract months	Trading hours (local time)	Contract size	Minimum price fluctuation	Daily limit
British Pound	"	8:00-2:30	25,000 BP	$0.0005/BP = $12.50	None
Canadian Dollar	"	8:00-2:30	100,000 CD	$0.0001/CD = $10	None
***Deutsche Mark**	"	8:00-2:30	125,000 DM	$0.0001/DM = $12.50	None
Swiss Franc	"	8:00-2:30	125,000 SF	$0.0001/SF = $12.50	None
French Franc	"	8:00-2:30	250,000 FF	$0.00005/FF = $12.50	None
***Japanese Yen**	"	8:00-2:30	12,500,000 JY	$0.000001/JY = $12.50	None
European Currency Unit (ECU)	"	8:00-2:30	125,000 ECU	$0.0001/ECU = $12.50	None
***Australian Dollar**	"	8:00-2:30	100,000 AD	$0.0001/AD = $10	None

* Also trade 7:00-11.00 p.m. night session.

Canadian Futures Contracts

Toronto Futures Exchange

Commodity	Contract months	Trading hours (local time)	Contract size	Minimum price fluctuation	Daily limit
Canadian Bonds (15-year)	Mar/June Sept/Dec	9:00-3:15	100,000 CD	1/32 pt. = $31.25	2 pt. = $2,000
Canadian T-Bills (13-week)	Four consecutive near months plus Mar/June/Sept/Dec	9:00-3:15	1,000,000 CD	0.01 pt. = $24	0.60 pt. = $1,440
Toronto Stock Exchange (TSE) 300 Index	Next three months	10:00-4:15	$10 × Index	1 pt. = $10	150 pt. = $1,500
TSE 300 Spot Contract	Daily	9:20-4:10	$10 × Index	1 pt. = $10	None
TSE Oil and Gas Index	Next three months	10:00-4:15	$10 × Index	1 pt. = $10	200 pt. = $2,500
U.S. Dollar	Next three months	8:30-4:00	U.S. $100,000	0.01¢ = $10	1¢ = $1,000
Toronto 35 Index	Three consecutive near months	9:15-4:15	$500 × Index	.02 pt. = $10	9 pt. = $4,500

Commodity	Contract months	Trading hours (local time)	Contract size	Minimum price fluctuation	Daily limit

The Winnipeg Commodity Exchange

Commodity	Contract months	Trading hours (local time)	Contract size	Minimum price fluctuation	Daily limit
Domestic Feed Barley	Mar/May/July Oct/Dec	9:30-1:15	100 metric tons	10¢/ton = $10	$5/ton = $500
Alberta Domestic Feed Barley	Feb/Apr/June Sept/Nov	9:30-1:15	20 metric tons	10¢/ton = $2	$5/ton = $100
Flaxseed	Mar/May/July Oct/Dec	9:30-1:15	100 metric tons	10¢/ton = $10	$10/ton = $1,000
Domestic Feed Oats	Mar/May/July Oct/Dec	9:30-1:15	100 metric tons	10¢/ton = $10	$5/ton = $500
Canola/ Rapeseed	Jan/Mar/June Sept/Nov	9:30-1:15	100 metric tons	10¢/ton = $10	$10/ton = $1,000
Rye	Mar/May/July Oct/Dec	9:30-1:15	100 metric tons	10¢/ton = $10	$5/ton = $500
Domestic Feed Wheat	Mar/May/July Oct/Dec	9:30-1:15	100 metric tons	10¢/ton = $10	$5/ton = $500
Gold	Mar/June Sept/Dec	10:00-1:25	20 oz.	10¢/oz. = $2	$25/oz. = $500
Silver	Jan/Apr July/Oct	10:00-1:25	200 oz.	1¢/oz. = $2	50¢/oz. = $100

Options on Futures

Options on futures have the same contract months, trading hours, limits, etc., as their underlying futures contracts. However, expiration of the options is earlier.

Chicago Board of Trade

Underlying futures contract	Contract size	Strike price increments	Minimum fluctuation	Last trading day
U.S. Treasury Bonds	$100,000	2 pt.	1/64 pt. = $15.62 (1.0 = $1,000)	Noon on Friday at least five business days before first notice day for underlying futures
T-Notes	$100,000	2 pt.	1/64 pt. = $15.625 (1.0 = $1,000)	"

Underlying futures contract	Contract size	Strike price increments	Minimum fluctuation	Last trading day
Municipal Bond Index	$100,000	2 pt.	1/64 pt. = $15.625 (1.0 = $1,000)	8 p.m. on last day of trading
Wheat (Soft winter)	5,000 bu.	10¢	1/8¢/bu. = $6.25	10 a.m. on first Saturday following last day of trading
Soybeans	5,000 bu.	25¢ under $8; 50¢ above $8	1/8¢/bu. = $6.25 (1.0 = $50)	1 p.m. on Friday at least 10 business days prior to first notice day for underlying futures
Soybean Meal	100 tons	5¢/ton = $5	5¢/ton = $5	10 a.m. on first Saturday following last day of trading
Soybean Oil	60,000 lb.	1¢/lb.	.005¢/lb. = $3	"
Corn	5,000 bu.	10¢	1/8¢/bu. = $6.25 (1.0 = $50)	Noon on Friday at least 10 business days before first notice day for underlying futures
Silver	1,000 oz.	25¢ below $8/oz.; 50¢ between $8-$20; $1 above $20	10/100¢/oz. = $1 (1.0 = $10)	Last Friday at least five business days before first notice day for underlying futures

Chicago Mercantile Exchange Index and Option Market

Underlying futures contract	Contract size	Strike price increments	Minimum fluctuation	Last trading day
S&P 500 Stock Index	500 × S&P Index	5 pt.	0.05 pt. = $25 (1.0 = $500)	Third Thursday of contract month
Deutsche Mark	125,000 DM	1¢	0.01¢/DM = $12.50 (1.0 = $1,250)	Second London bank business day before third Wednesday of underlying futures contract month
Eurodollar Time Deposit (Three-month)	$1,000,000	0.50 on IMM Index	0.01 (1 basis pt.) = $25 (1.0 = $2,500)	"
Swiss Franc	125,000 SF	1¢	0.01¢/SF = $12.50 (1.0 = $1,250)	"

Underlying futures contract	Contract size	Strike price increments	Minimum fluctuation	Last trading day
British Pound	25,000 BP	2½¢	0.05¢/BP = $12.50 (1.0 - $250)	"
Cattle, Live	40,000 lb.	2¢	0.025¢/lb. = $10 (1.0 = $400)	Last Friday more than three business days before first business day of delivery month of underlying futures
Cattle, Feeder	44,000 lb.	2¢	2.5¢/cwt. = $11	Last Thursday of contract month
Hogs, Live	30,000 lb.	2¢	0.025¢/lb. = $7.50 (1.0 = $300)	Last Friday more than three business days before first business day of delivery month of underlying futures
Pork Bellies	40,000 lb.	4¢	2.5¢/cwt. = $9.50	Friday at least three business days prior to first business day of contract month
Lumber (Random-length)	130,000 bd. ft.	$10/1,000 bd. ft.	10¢/1,000 bd. ft. = $13	Last Friday prior to delivery month

Coffee, Sugar and Cocoa Exchange

Underlying futures contract	Contract size	Strike price increments	Minimum fluctuation	Last trading day
Cocoa	10 metric tons	$100 if price is below $3,600; $200 if above or equal to $3,600	$1/metric ton $ eq $10	First Friday of month before futures expire
Sugar No. 11	112,000 lb. (50 long tons)	Varies*	1/100¢/lb. = $11.20 (1.0 = $1,120)	Second Friday of month before futures expire
Coffee "C"	37,500 lb.	5¢ if price is below $2; 10¢ if above or equal to $2	1/100¢/lb.	First Friday of month before futures expire

*For first two option months: 1/2¢/lb. if price is between 1¢ and 10¢, 1¢ if between 10¢ and 40¢, 2¢ if greater than or equal to 40¢; For last two option months: 1¢/lb. if price is between 1¢ and 16¢, 2¢ if between 16¢ and 40¢, 4¢ if greater than or equal to 40¢.

Commodity Exchange Inc. (COMEX)

Underlying futures contract	Contract size	Strike price increments	Minimum fluctuation	Last trading day
Copper	25,000 lb.	1¢/lb. below 40¢; 2¢/lb. 40¢-$1 5¢/lb. above $1	5/100¢/lb. = $12.50	Second Friday of month before futures expire

Underlying futures contract	Contract size	Strike price increments	Minimum fluctuation	Last trading day
Gold	100 troy oz.	$10/oz. below $300; $20/oz. $300-$500; $30/oz. $500-$800; $40/oz. above $800	10¢/oz. = $10 (1.0 = $100)	Second Friday of month before futures expire
Silver	5,000 troy oz.	25¢ below $5/oz.; 50¢ between $5-$14.99/oz.; $1 above $15/oz.	1/10¢/oz. = $5 (1.0 = $100)	Second Friday of month prior to futures month

Kansas City Board of Trade

Underlying futures contract	Contract size	Strike price increments	Minimum fluctuation	Last trading day
Wheat (Hard red winter)	5,000 bu.	10¢	1/8¢/bu. = $6.25 (1.0 = $50)	1 p.m. on Friday at least five business days before first notice day for underlying futures

MidAmerica Commodity Exchange

Underlying futures contract	Contract size	Strike price increments	Minimum fluctuation	Last trading day
Gold	33.2 troy oz.	$10-$40/oz. (depends on price level)	10¢.oz. = $3.32 (1 = $33.20)	12 noon Friday at least five business days before first notice day for underlying futures
Wheat (Soft winter)	1,000 bu.	10¢	1/8¢/bu. = $1.25 (1.0 = $10)	1 p.m. on Friday at least five business days before first notice day for underlying futures
Soybeans	1,000 bu.	25¢	1/8¢/bu. = $1.25 (1.0 = $10)	12:15 p.m. on Friday at least five business days before first notice day for underlying futures

Minneapolis Grain Exchange

Underlying futures contract	Contract size	Strike price increments	Minimum fluctuation	Last trading day
Wheat (Spring)	5,000 bu.	10¢	1/8¢/bu. = $6.25 (1.0 = $50)	1 p.m. on Friday at least 10 business days before first notice day for underlying futures

Underlying futures contract	Contract size	Strike price increments	Minimum fluctuation	Last trading day
New York Cotton Exchange				
Cotton No. 2	50,000 lb.	Nearest three delivery months: 1¢ up to 74¢/lb., 2¢ at 75¢/lb. and above.	1/100¢/lb. = $5 (1.0 = $500)	3 p.m. on first Friday in month preceding delivery month
Citrus Associates of the New York Cotton Exchange Inc.				
Orange Juice	15,000 lb.	2.5¢	5/100¢/lb. = $7.50	First Friday of month preceding futures delivery month
Financial Instrument Exchange (FINEX)*				
U.S. Dollar Index	$500 × U.S. Dollar Index	2 pt.	0.01 pt. = $5	Two Fridays before third Wednesday of contract month
New York Futures Exchange				
NYSE Composite Stock Index	500 × NYSE Composite Index	2 pt.	0.05 pt. = $25 (1.0 = $500)	Last trading day of underlying futures
New York Mercantile Exchange				
Crude Oil (Light Sweet)	1,000 barrels (42,000 gal.)	$1/barrel	1¢/barrel = $10	3:10 p.m. on first Friday in month preceding delivery month
Heating Oil	42,000 gal.	2¢/gal.	1/100¢/gal. = $4.20	3:05 p.m. on second Friday in month preceding delivery month
Winnipeg Commodity Exchange				
Gold (Calls only)	20 oz.	$20/oz.	10¢/oz. $2 (1.0 = $20)	Six business days before delivery month

* Division of the New York Cotton Exchange, Inc.

Options on Actuals

This section includes exchange-traded options on physical commodities, such as metals or currencies, or on actual indexes or interest rate instruments. It does not include options on individual stocks or options offered by leverage transactions firms.

Underlying instrument	Contract months	Trading hours (local time)	Contract size	Strike price increments	Minimum price fluctuation
American Stock Exchange (AMEX)					
Major Market Index (XMI) (20 stocks)	Three consecutive near-term expiration months	9:30-4:15	100 × index value	5 pt.	Premium 1/16 up to $3; 1/8 above $3 (1.0 = $100)
Institutional Index (European-style) (75 stocks)	Three consecutive near-term expiration months plus two months from March cycle	9:30-4:10	100 × index value	5 pt.	"
Computer Technology Index	Three consecutive near-term expiration months plus next nearest month in January cycle	9:30-4:10	100 × index value	5 pt.	"
Oil Index	"	9:30-4:10	100 × index value	5 pt.	"
U.S. Treasury Bills (90-day) (European-style)	Mar/June Sept/Dec	9:30-3:00	$1 million principal	1/5 pt. = 0.2%	0.01 pt. = $25 (1.0 = $2,500)
U.S. Treasury Notes (10-year)	Feb/May Aug/Nov	9:30-3:00	$100,000	2 pt.	1/32 pt. = $31.25 (1.0 = $1,000)
Chicago Board Options Exchange (CBOE)					
S&P 100 Stock Index	Four sequential months	8:30-3:15	100 × Index	5 pt.	Premium 1/16 up to $3; 1/8 above $3 (1.0 = $100)
S&P 500 Stock Index	Mar/June Sept/Oct/Dec	8:30-3:15	100 × Index	5 pt.	"
U.S. 30-Year Treasury Bonds (7¼%, 9¼%, 9⅞%)	Mar/June Sept/Dec	8:00-2:00	$100,000	2 pt.	1/32 pt. = $31.25 (1.0 = $1,000)

Underlying instrument	Contract months	Trading hours (local time)	Contract size	Strike price increments	Minimum price fluctuation
U.S. Five-Year Treasury Notes (7½%, 8⅛%, 9⅛%)	"	8:00-2:00	$100,000	1 pt.	"

Coffee, Sugar & Cocoa Exchange Inc.

Underlying instrument	Contract months	Trading hours (local time)	Contract size	Strike price increments	Minimum price fluctuation
Inflation Rate	Jan/Apr July/Oct	9:30-2:30	$1,000,000	1 full percentage point	.005% = $12.50

New York Stock Exchange

Underlying instrument	Contract months	Trading hours (local time)	Contract size	Strike price increments	Minimum price fluctuation
New York Stock Exchange Composite Index	Next three months	9:30-4:15	100 × Index	5 pt.	1/16 pt. (1.0 = $100)
NYSE Beta Index	"	9:30-4:15	100 × Index	5 pt.	1/16 pt. (1.0 = $100)

Pacific Stock Exchange

Underlying instrument	Contract months	Trading hours (local time)	Contract size	Strike price increments	Minimum price fluctuation
PSE Technology Index	Four sequential months	6:30-1:15	100 × Index	5 pt.	1/16 pt. (1.0 = $100)
Financial News Composite Index (FNCI)	Four sequential months	6:30-1:15	100 × Index	5 pt.	None

Philadelphia Board of Trade

Underlying instrument	Contract months	Trading hours (local time)	Contract size	Strike price increments	Minimum price fluctuation
Eurodollar	Mar/June Sept/Dec	8:30-3:00	$1 million	25 pt.	0.01 pt. = $25

Philadelphia Stock Exchange (PHLX)

Underlying instrument	Contract months	Trading hours (local time)	Contract size	Strike price increments	Minimum price fluctuation
Deutsche Mark	Next two months and Mar/June Sept/Dec	8:00-2:30	62,500 DM	$0.01	$0.0001/DM = $6.25 (1.0 = $625)
European Currency Unit (ECU)	"	8:00-2:30	62,500 ECU	$0.02	$0.0001/ECU = $6.25 (1.0 = $625)

Underlying instrument	Contract months	Trading hours (local time)	Contract size	Strike price increments	Minimum price fluctuation
Swiss Franc	"	8:00-2:30	62,500 SF	$0.01	$0.0001/SF = $6.25 (1.0 = $625)
Canadian Dollar	"	8:00-2:30	50,000 CD	$0.01	$0.0001/CD = $5 (1.0 = $500)
British Pound	"	8:00-2:30	12,500 BP	$0.05	$0.0005/BP = $6.25 (1.0 = $125)
[1]**Japanese Yen**	"	8:00-2:30	6,250,000 JY	$0.0001	$0.000001/ JY = $6.25 (1.0 = $625)
French Franc	"	8:00-2:30	125,000 FF	$0.005	$0.00005/FF = $6.25 (1.0 = $1,250)
[1]**Australian Dollar**	"	8:00-2:30	50,000 AD	$.01	$0.0001/AD = $5
Value Line Index	Next three months and March cycle	9:30-4:15	100 × Index	5 pt.	1/16 pt. (1.0 = $100)
Value Line Index (European-style)	Next three months and March cycle plus two near months	9:30-4:15	100 × Index	5 pt.	1/16 pt. (1.0 = $100)
Utility Index	"	9:30-4:10	100 × Index	5 pt.	1/16 pt. (1.0 = $100)
Gold/Silver Stock Index	Next three months and March cycle	9:30-4:10	100 × Index	5 pt.	1/16 pt. (1.0 = $100)
National Over-The-Counter Index	"	9:30-4:15	100 × Index	5 pt.	1/16 pt. (1.0 = $100)

*All currency options now trade European- and American-style.
[1] Also trade a 7:00-11:00 p.m. night session.

The Montreal Exchange

Underlying instrument	Contract months	Trading hours (local time)	Contract size	Strike price increments	Minimum price fluctuation
Canadian Bonds	Next three months plus two on March cycle	9:00-4:00	$25,000 face value	2.5 pt. or 2.0 pt.	$0.01 × 250 per contract
ME T-Bill Index	Next three months plus two on March cycle	8:35-3:00	$250,000 face value	50 basis pt.	1 pt. = $6

Underlying instrument	Contract months	Trading hours (local time)	Contract size	Strike price increments	Minimum price fluctuation
		Toronto Futures Exchange			
Silver	Three consecutive near months plus six and nine months	9:05-4:00	100 oz.	25¢ below $5/oz.; 50¢ from $5-$15/oz.; $1 above $15/oz.	5¢ below $2; 12½¢ above $2
Canadian Bonds (11¾%, 9% maturing Feb. 1, 2003; 8¾% maturing June 1, 1996)	"	9:00-4:00	$25,000 face value at maturity	5¢ below $5; 12½¢ above $5	2.5 pt. for 11¾% and 9% bonds; 2 pt for 8¾% bonds
		Toronto Stock Exchange			
TSE 300 Index	Next three months	9:30-4:10	100 × Index	$5	5¢ below $2; 1/8 above $2
Toronto 35 Index	Three consecutive near months	9:15-4:15	$100 × Index	5 pt. intervals	1¢ under 10¢; 5¢ under $5; 12½¢ for $5 and above

Commodity Futures Trading Commission

Federal laws regulating commodity futures trading are enforced by the Commodity Futures Trading Commission. For information on commodity brokers call (202) 254-8630.

National Office

Commodity Futures Trading Commission
2033 K Street, NW
Washington, DC 20581
Telephone: (202) 254-6387

Regional Offices

Eastern Region
1 World Trade Center
New York, NY 10048
Telephone: (212) 466-2061

Central Region
233 S. Wacker Drive
Chicago, IL 60606
Telephone: (312) 353-5990

Southwestern Region
4901 Main Street
Kansas City, MO 64112
Telephone: (816) 374-2994

510 Grain Exchange Building
Minneapolis, MN 55415
Telephone: (612) 349-3255

Western Region
10850 Wilshire Boulevard
Los Angeles, CA 90024
Telephone: (213) 209-6783

The Commodity Futures Trading Commission (CFTC), the Federal regulatory agency for futures trading, was established by the Commodity Futures Trading Commission Act of 1974 (88 Stat. 1389; 7 U.S.C. 4a), approved October 23, 1974. The Commission began operation in April 1975, and its authority to regulate futures trading was renewed by Congress in 1978 and in 1982.

The CFTC consists of five Commissioners who are appointed by the President with the advice and consent of the Senate. One Commissioner is designated by the President to serve as Chairman. The Commissioners serve staggered 5-year terms, and by law no more than three Commissioners can belong to the same political party.

Source: U.S. Government Manual.

FUNCTIONS AND ACTIVITIES

The Commission consists of five major operating components: the divisions of enforcement, economics and education, trading and markets, and the offices of the executive director and the general counsel.

The Commission regulates trading on the 11 U.S. futures exchanges, which at the end of fiscal 1983 were offering 93 active futures contracts. It also regulates the activities of some 5,025 commodity exchange members, 461 public brokerage houses (futures Commission merchants), about 55,000 Commission-registered futures industry salespeople and associated persons, and 4,100 commodity trading advisers and commodity pool operators. Some off-exchange transactions involving instruments similar in nature to futures contracts also fall under CFTC jurisdiction.

The Commission's regulatory and enforcement efforts are designed to ensure that the futures trading process is fair and that it protects both the rights of customers and the financial integrity of the marketplace. The CFTC approves the rules under which an exchange proposes to operate and monitors exchange enforcement of those rules. It reviews the terms of proposed futures contracts, and registers companies and individuals who handle customer funds or give trading advice. The Commission also protects the public by enforcing rules that require that customer funds be kept in bank accounts separate from accounts maintained by firms for their own use, and that such customer accounts be marked to present market value at the close of trading each day.

Futures contracts for agricultural commodities were traded in the United States for more than 100 years before futures trading was diversified to include trading in contracts for precious metals, raw materials, foreign currencies, commercial interest rates, and U.S. Government and mortgage securities. Contract diversification has grown in exchange trading volume, a growth not limited to the newer commodities.

Futures and Options Exchanges: Addresses

UNITED STATES

American Stock Exchange (AMEX)
86 Trinity Place
New York, NY 10006
(212) 306-1000

AMEX Commodity Corporation (ACC)
86 Trinity Place
New York, NY 10006
(212) 306-1000

Chicago Board of Trade (CBT)
141 West Jackson Boulevard
Chicago, IL 60604
(312) 435-3500

Chicago Board Options Exchange (CBOE)
400 South LaSalle
Chicago, IL 60605
(312) 786-5600

Chicago Mercantile Exchange (CME) and International Monetary Market (IMM)
30 South Wacker Drive
Chicago, IL 60606
(312) 930-8200

Chicago Rice & Cotton Exchange (CRCE)
444 W. Jackson Boulevard
Chicago, IL 60606
(312) 341-3078

Coffee, Sugar & Cocoa Exchange (CSCE)
4 World Trade Center
New York, NY 10048
(212) 938-2800

Commodity Exchange, Inc. (COMEX)
4 World Trade Center
New York, NY 10048
(212) 938-2900

International Monetary Market [IMM] (see Chicago Merchantile Exchange [CME]

Kansas City Board of Trade (KCBT)
4800 Main Street
Kansas City, MO 64112
(816) 753-7500

Midamerica Commodity Exchange (MCE)
444 West Jackson Boulevard
Chicago, IL 60606
(312) 341-3000

Minneapolis Grain Exchange (MGE)
150 Grain Exchange Building
400 S. Fourth Street
Minneapolis, MN 55415
(612) 338-6212

New York Cotton Exchange & Associates (NYCE)
4 World Trade Center
New York, NY 10048
(212) 938-2650

New York Futures Exchange (NYFE)
20 Broad Street
New York, NY 10005
(212) 623-4949
(800) 221-7722

New York Mercantile Exchange (NYME)
4 World Trade Center
New York, NY 10048
(212) 938-2222

New York Stock Exchange
11 Wall St.
New York, NY 10005
(800) 656-8533

Pacific Stock Exchange
301 Pine St.
San Francisco, CA 94104
(415) 393-4000

Philadelphia Board of Trade
1900 Market St.
Philadelphia, PA 19103
(215) 496-5025

Philadelphia Stock Exchange
1900 Market St.
Philadelphia, PA 19103
(215) 496-5000

CANADIAN

Montreal Stock Exchange
800 Victoria Square
Montreal, Quebec, Canada H4Z 1A9
(514) 871-2424

Toronto Futures Exchange
2 First Canadian Place
Exchange Tower
Toronto, Ontario, Canada M5X 1J2
(416) 947-4700

Toronto Stock Exchange
2 First Canadian Place
Exchange Tower
Toronto, Ontario, Canada M5X 1J2
(416) 947-4700

Vancouver Stock Exchange
609 Granville
Vancouver, British Columbia
Canada V7Y 1H1
(604) 689-3334

The Winnipeg Commodity Exchange
500 Commodity Exchange Tower
360 Main Street
Winnipeg, Manitoba
Canada R3C 3Z4
(204) 949-0495

SELECTED FOREIGN EXCHANGES

London Commodity Exchange Co. Ltd.
Cereal House, 58 Mark Lane
London, England EC3R 7NE
01-481-2080

The London International Financial Futures Exchange Ltd. (LIFFE)
Royal Exchange
London, England EC3
01-623-0444

The Hong Kong Futures Exchange Ltd.
Hutchison House, Second Floor
Harcourt Road
Hong Kong
5-251005

European Options Exchange (EOE)
DAM 21
1012 JS Amsterdam
The Netherlands
20-26 27 21

Paris Commodity Exchange
Bourse de Commerce
2, rue de Viarmes B.P. 53/01
75040 Paris, Cedex 01 France
1-508-82-50
(212) 751-9050-New York

The Singapore International Monetary Exchange Ltd.
24 Raffles Place
29-04 Clifford Centre
Singapore 0104

Sydney Futures Exchange Ltd.
13-15 O'Connell St.
Sydney, NSW, Australia 2000
02-233-7633

Futures and Securities Organizations

Futures Industry Association, Inc. (FIA)
1825 I Street, NW
Washington, DC 20006
(202) 466–5460

National Association of Futures Trading Advisors (NAFTA)
111 East Wacker Drive
Chicago, IL 60601
(312) 644–6610

National Association of Securities Dealers (NASD)
1735 K Street, NW
Washington, DC 20006
(202) 728-8000

National Futures Association (NFA)
200 West Madison
Chicago, IL 60606
(312) 781–1300

North American Securities Administrators Association, Inc. (NASAA)
425 13th Street, NW
Washington, DC 20004
(202) 783-2303

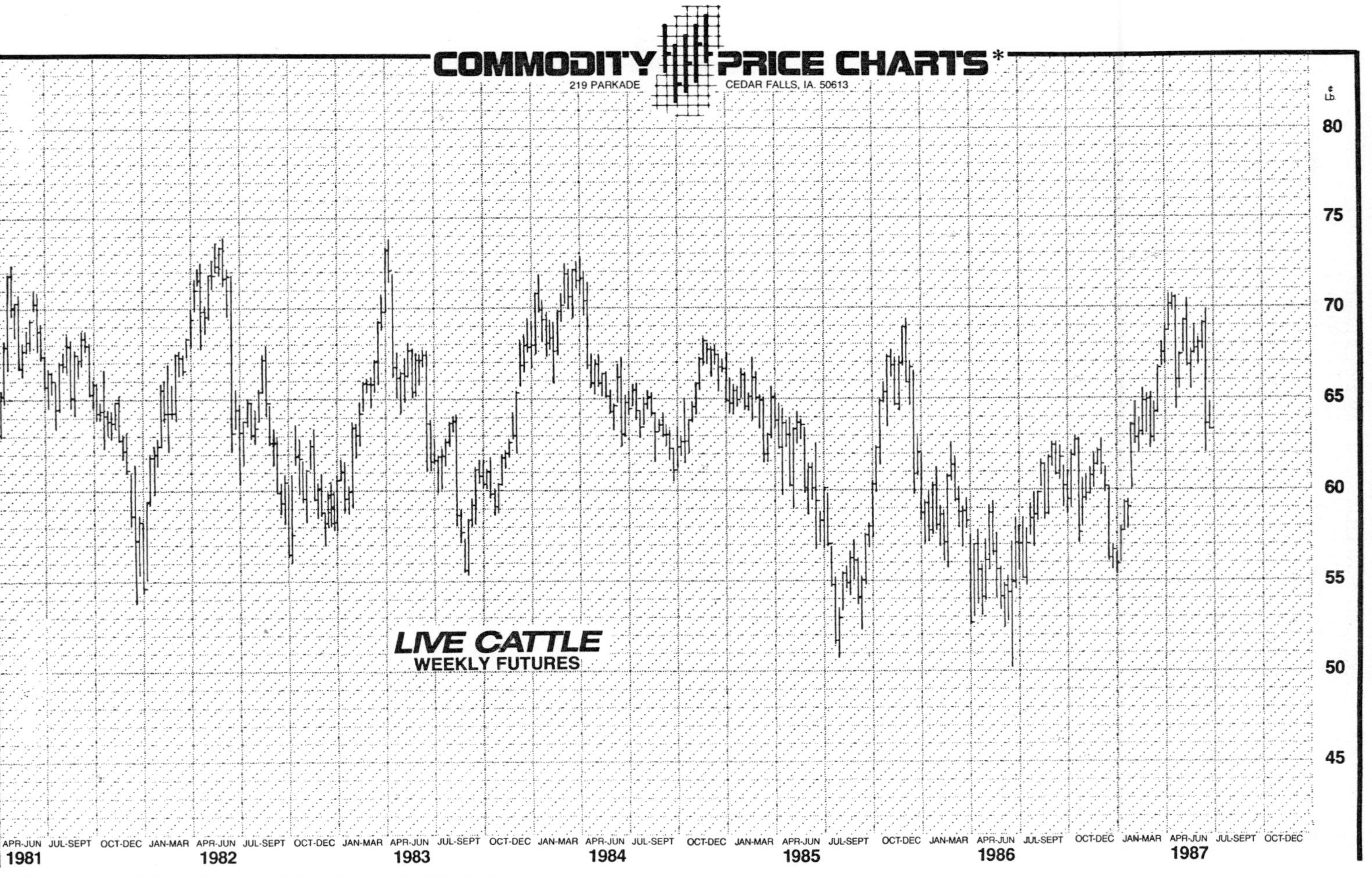

Source: *Commodity Price Charts*, 210 Parkade, Cedar Falls, Iowa 50613.
* See page 534 for data used in plotting.

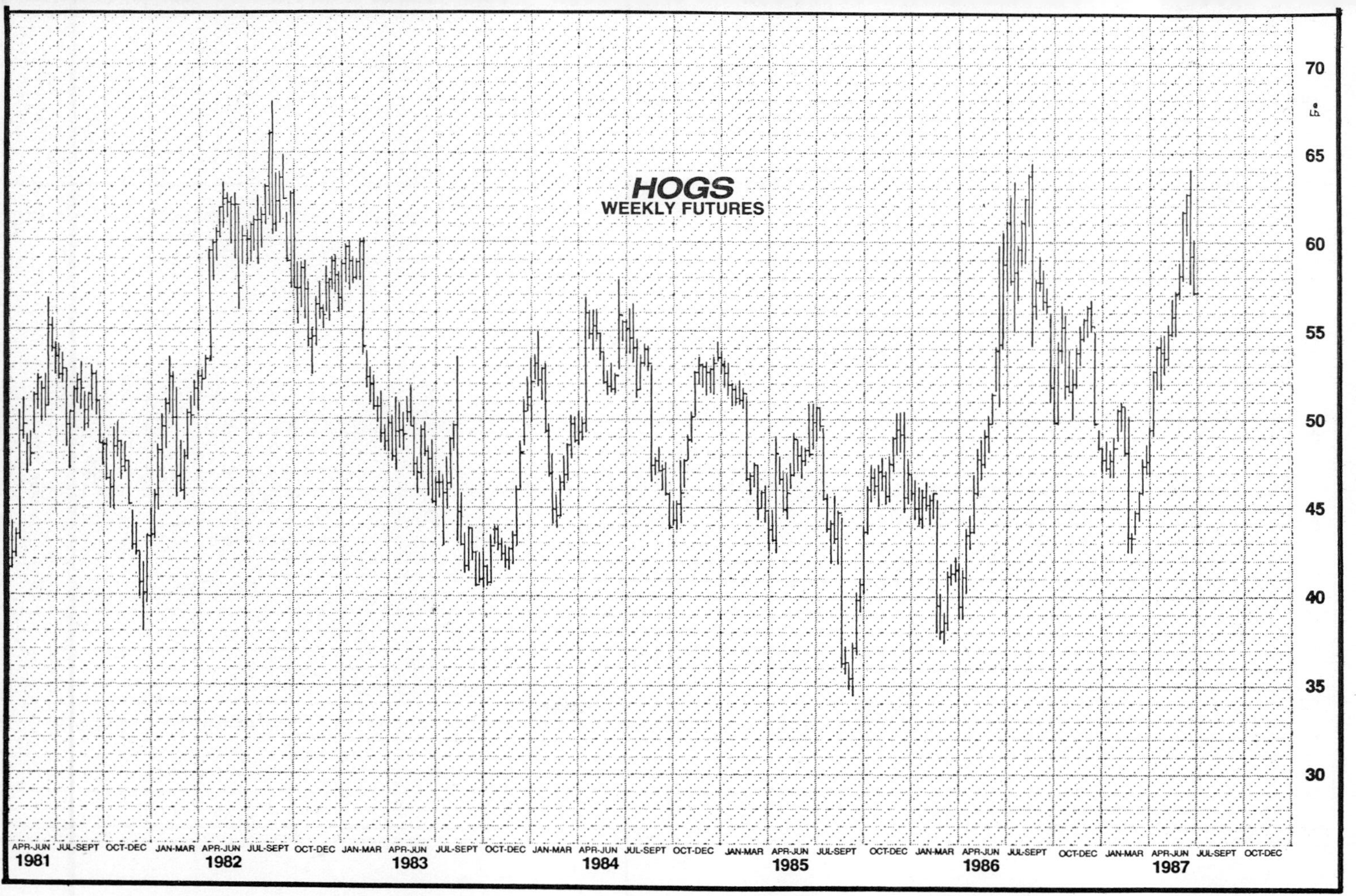
HOGS
WEEKLY FUTURES
70
65
60
55
50
45
40
35
30
APR-JUN JUL-SEPT OCT-DEC
1981
JAN-MAR APR-JUN JUL-SEPT OCT-DEC
1982
JAN-MAR APR-JUN JUL-SEPT OCT-DEC
1983
JAN-MAR APR-JUN JUL-SEPT OCT-DEC
1984
JAN-MAR APR-JUN JUL-SEPT OCT-DEC
1985
JAN-MAR APR-JUN JUL-SEPT OCT-DEC
1986
JAN-MAR APR-JUN JUL-SEPT OCT-DEC
1987

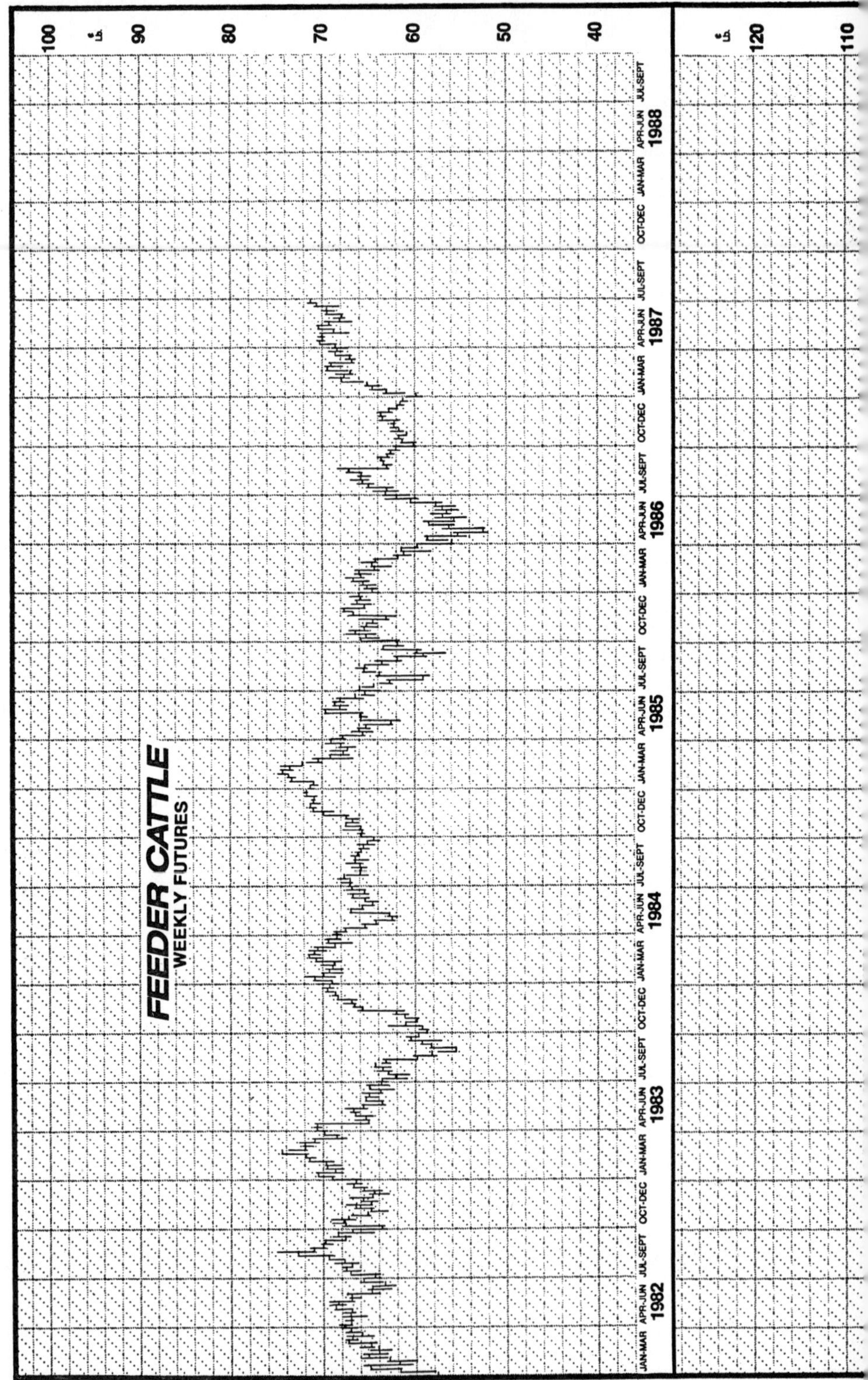
FEEDER CATTLE
WEEKLY FUTURES
¢ Lb.
100
90
80
70
60
50
40
120
110
JAN-MAR APR-JUN JUL-SEPT OCT-DEC
1982
1983
1984
1985
1986
1987
1988

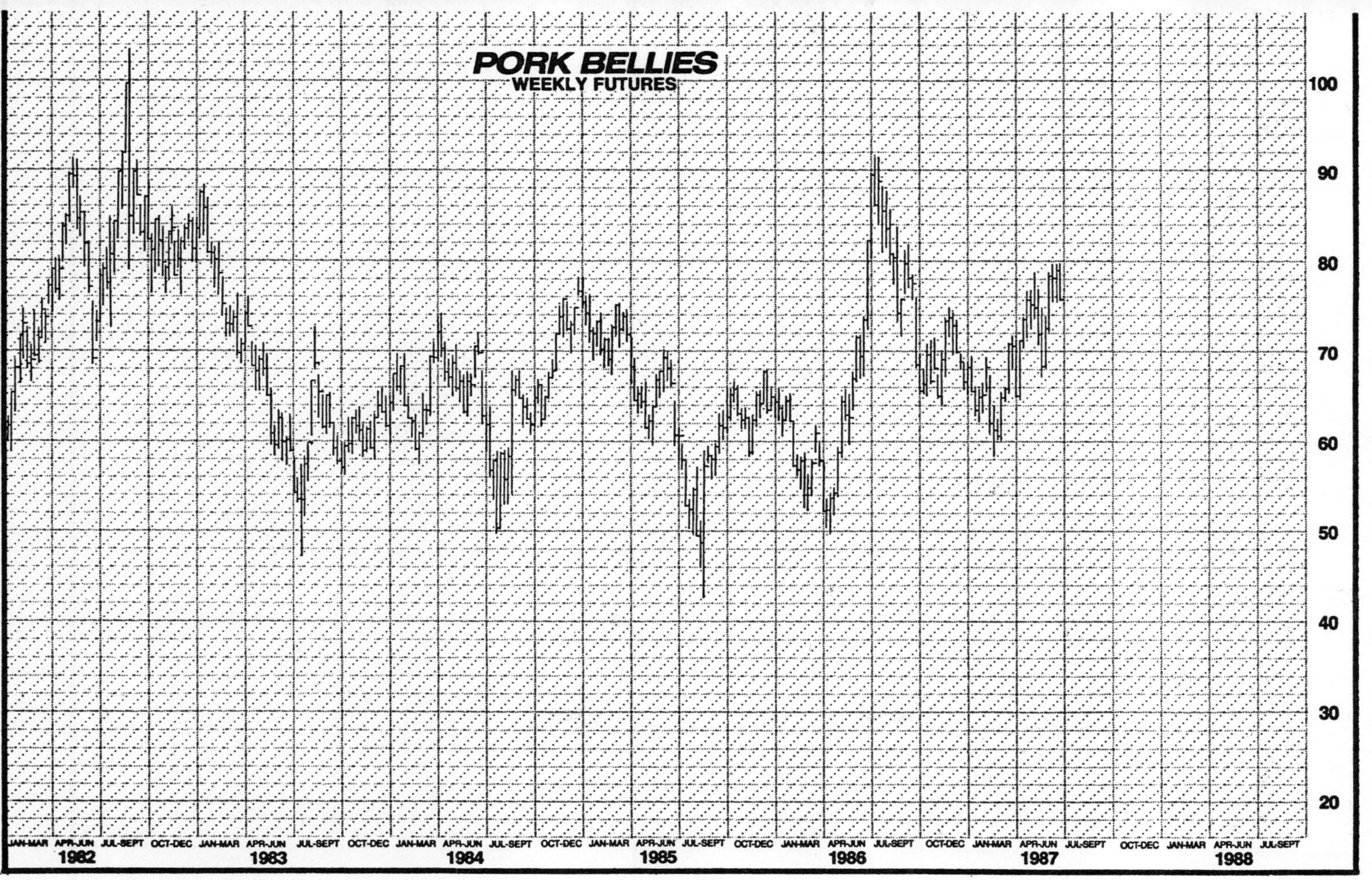
PORK BELLIES
WEEKLY FUTURES
100
90
80
70
60
50
40
30
20
JAN-MAR APR-JUN JUL-SEPT OCT-DEC
1982
JAN-MAR APR-JUN JUL-SEPT OCT-DEC
1983
JAN-MAR APR-JUN JUL-SEPT OCT-DEC
1984
JAN-MAR APR-JUN JUL-SEPT OCT-DEC
1985
JAN-MAR APR-JUN JUL-SEPT OCT-DEC
1986
JAN-MAR APR-JUN JUL-SEPT OCT-DEC
1987
JAN-MAR APR-JUN JUL-SEPT
1988

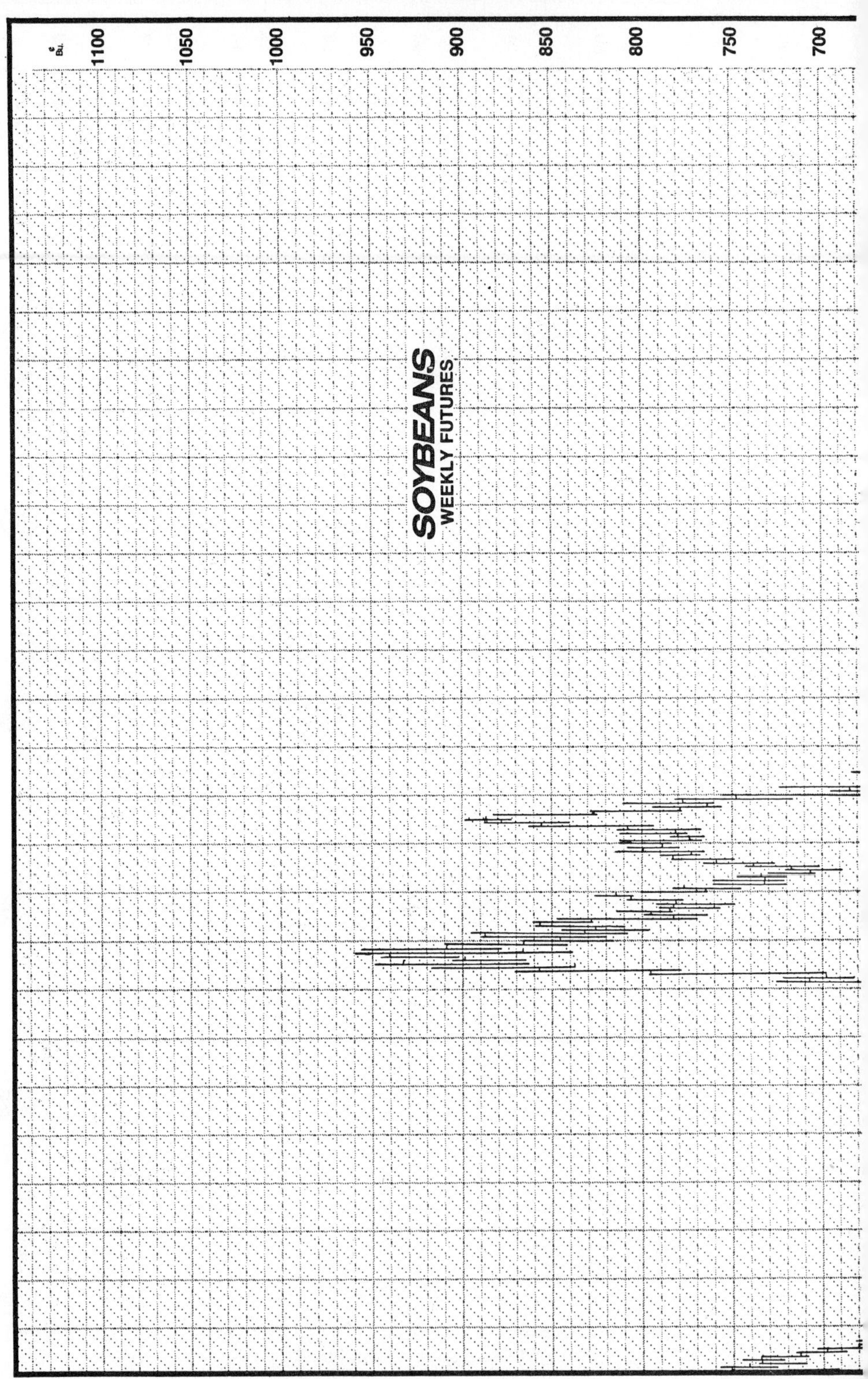

SOYBEANS
WEEKLY FUTURES
¢ Bu.
1100
1050
1000
950
900
850
800
750
700

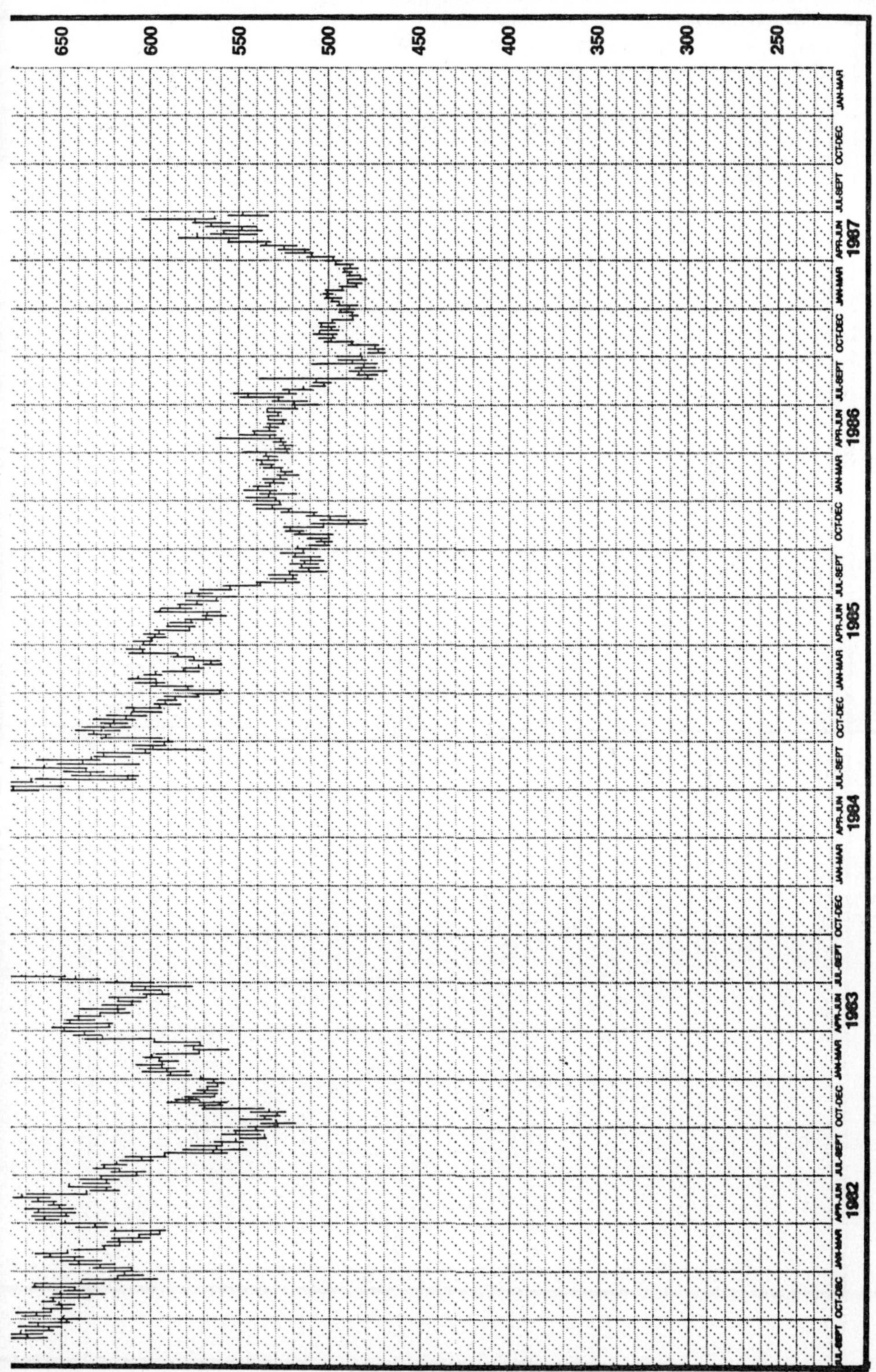
650
600
550
500
450
400
350
300
250
JUL-SEPT
OCT-DEC
JAN-MAR
APR-JUN
1982
1983
1984
1985
1986
1987

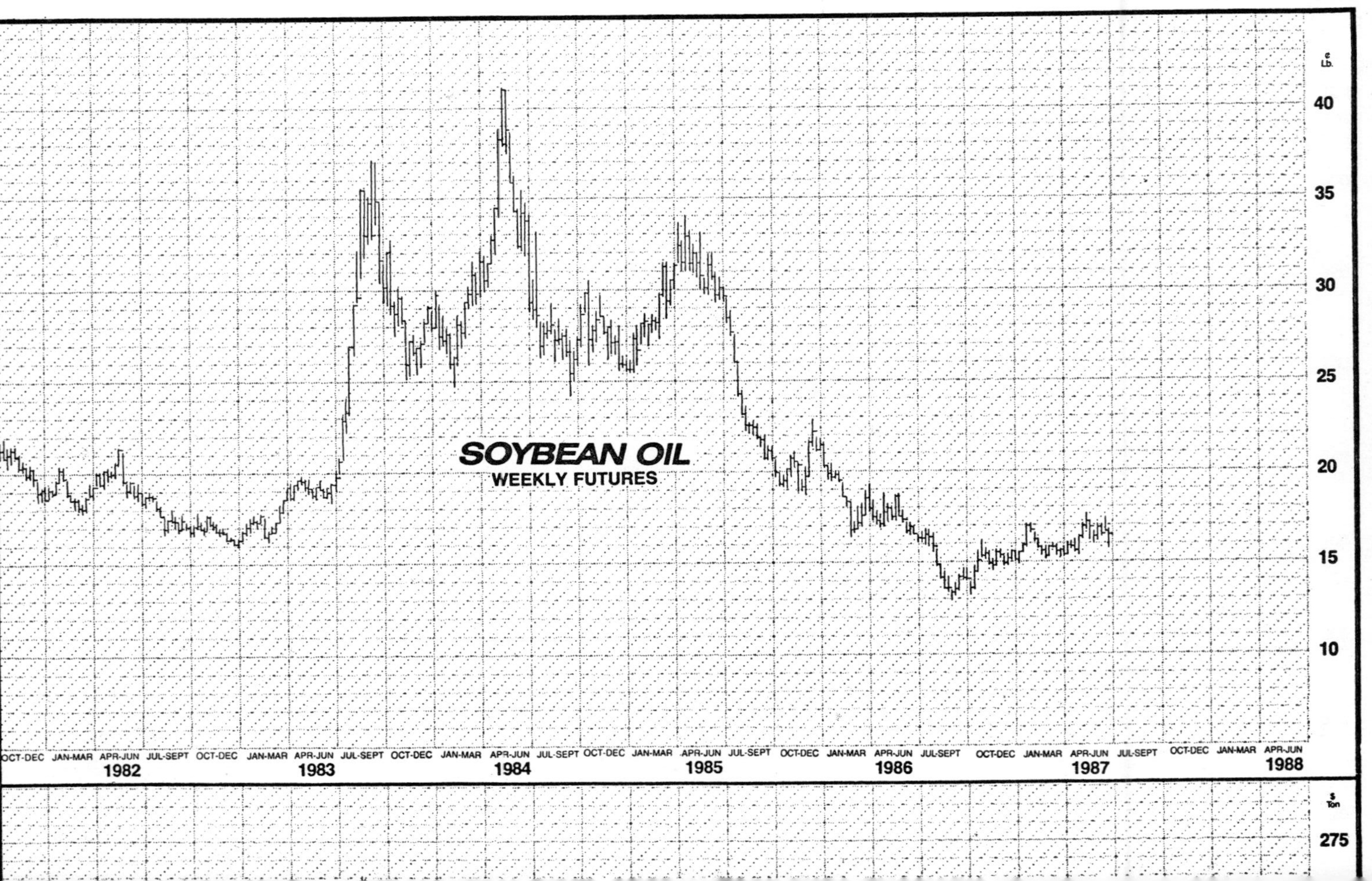
SOYBEAN OIL
WEEKLY FUTURES
¢/Lb.
40
35
30
25
20
15
10
OCT-DEC JAN-MAR APR-JUN JUL-SEPT OCT-DEC JAN-MAR APR-JUN JUL-SEPT OCT-DEC JAN-MAR APR-JUN JUL-SEPT OCT-DEC JAN-MAR APR-JUN JUL-SEPT OCT-DEC JAN-MAR APR-JUN JUL-SEPT OCT-DEC JAN-MAR APR-JUN JUL-SEPT OCT-DEC JAN-MAR APR-JUN
1982
1983
1984
1985
1986
1987
1988
$/Ton
275

SOYBEAN MEAL
WEEKLY FUTURES
250
225
200
175
150
125
100
75
50
OCT-DEC JAN-MAR APR-JUN JUL-SEPT OCT-DEC JAN-MAR APR-JUN JUL-SEPT OCT-DEC JAN-MAR APR-JUN JUL-SEPT OCT-DEC JAN-MAR APR-JUN JUL-SEPT OCT-DEC JAN-MAR APR-JUN JUL-SEPT OCT-DEC JAN-MAR APR-JUN JUL-SEPT OCT-DEC JAN-MAR APR-JUN
1982
1983
1984
1985
1986
1987
1988

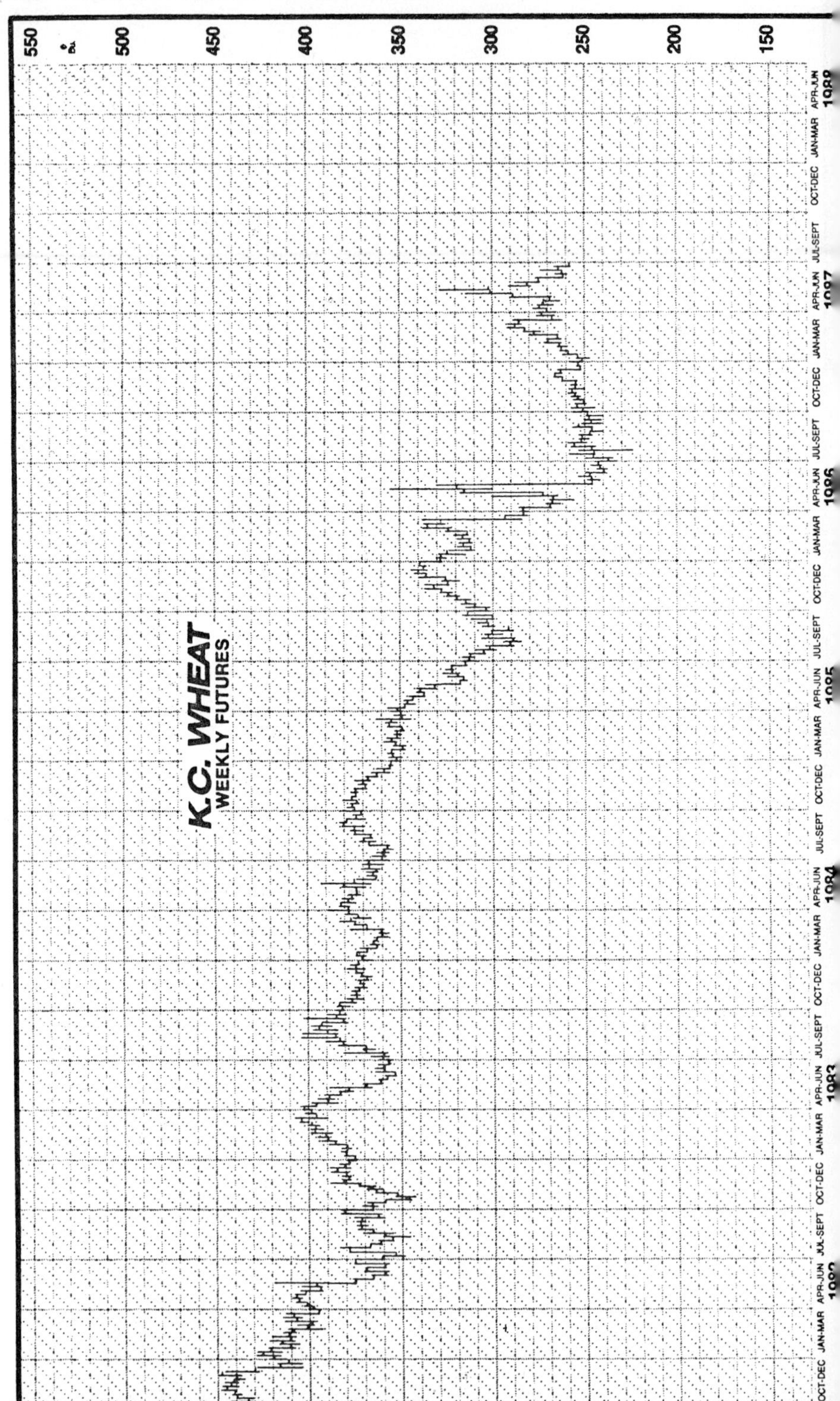
K.C. WHEAT
WEEKLY FUTURES
550
500
450
400
350
300
250
200
150

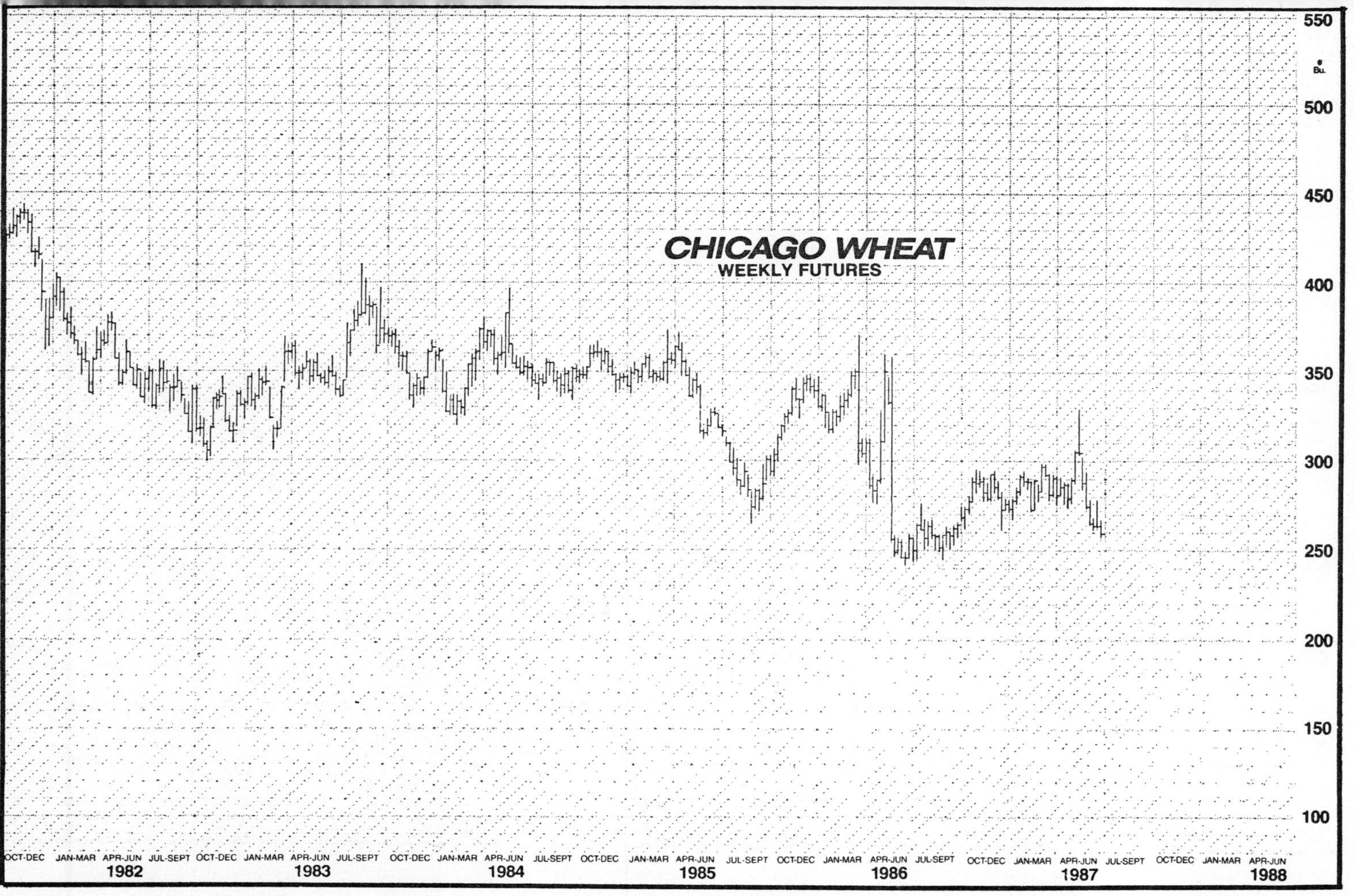
CHICAGO WHEAT
WEEKLY FUTURES
550
¢ Bu.
500
450
400
350
300
250
200
150
100
OCT-DEC JAN-MAR APR-JUN JUL-SEPT OCT-DEC JAN-MAR APR-JUN JUL-SEPT OCT-DEC JAN-MAR APR-JUN JUL-SEPT OCT-DEC JAN-MAR APR-JUN JUL-SEPT OCT-DEC JAN-MAR APR-JUN JUL-SEPT OCT-DEC JAN-MAR APR-JUN JUL-SEPT OCT-DEC JAN-MAR APR-JUN
1982
1983
1984
1985
1986
1987
1988

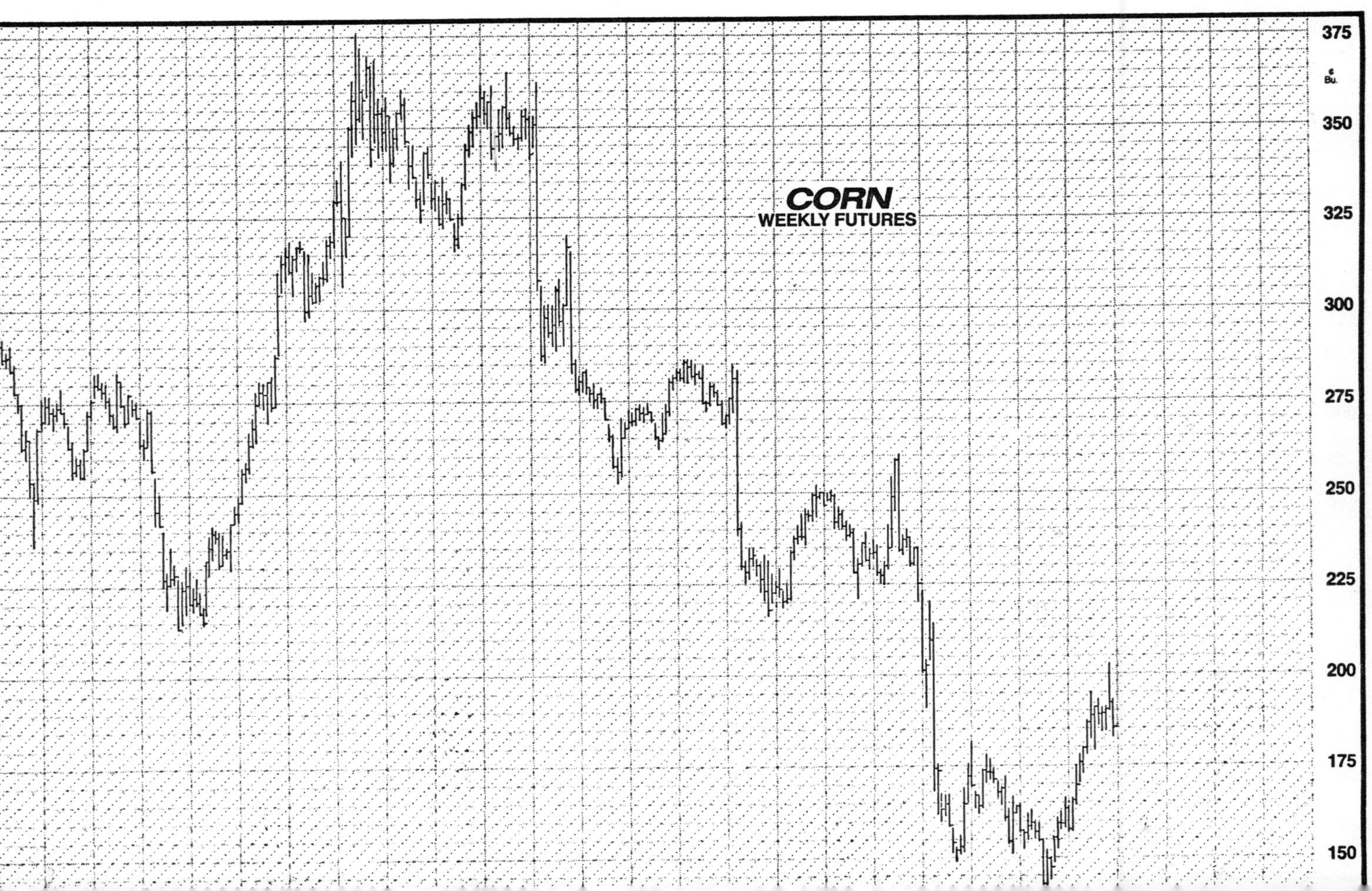
CORN
WEEKLY FUTURES
375
¢ Bu.
350
325
300
275
250
225
200
175
150

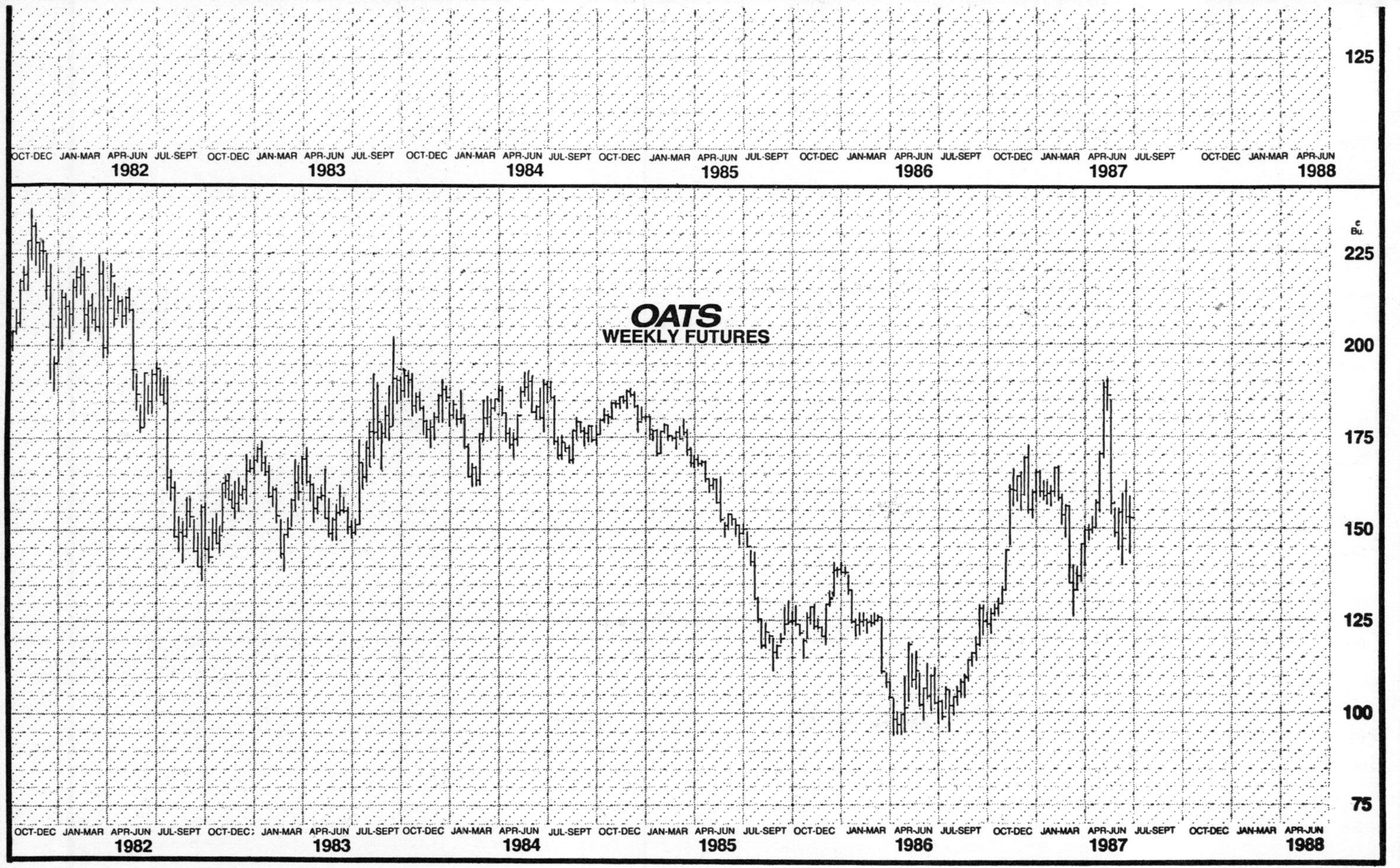
OATS
WEEKLY FUTURES
¢ Bu.
225
200
175
150
125
100
75
OCT-DEC JAN-MAR APR-JUN JUL-SEPT
1982
1983
1984
1985
1986
1987
1988

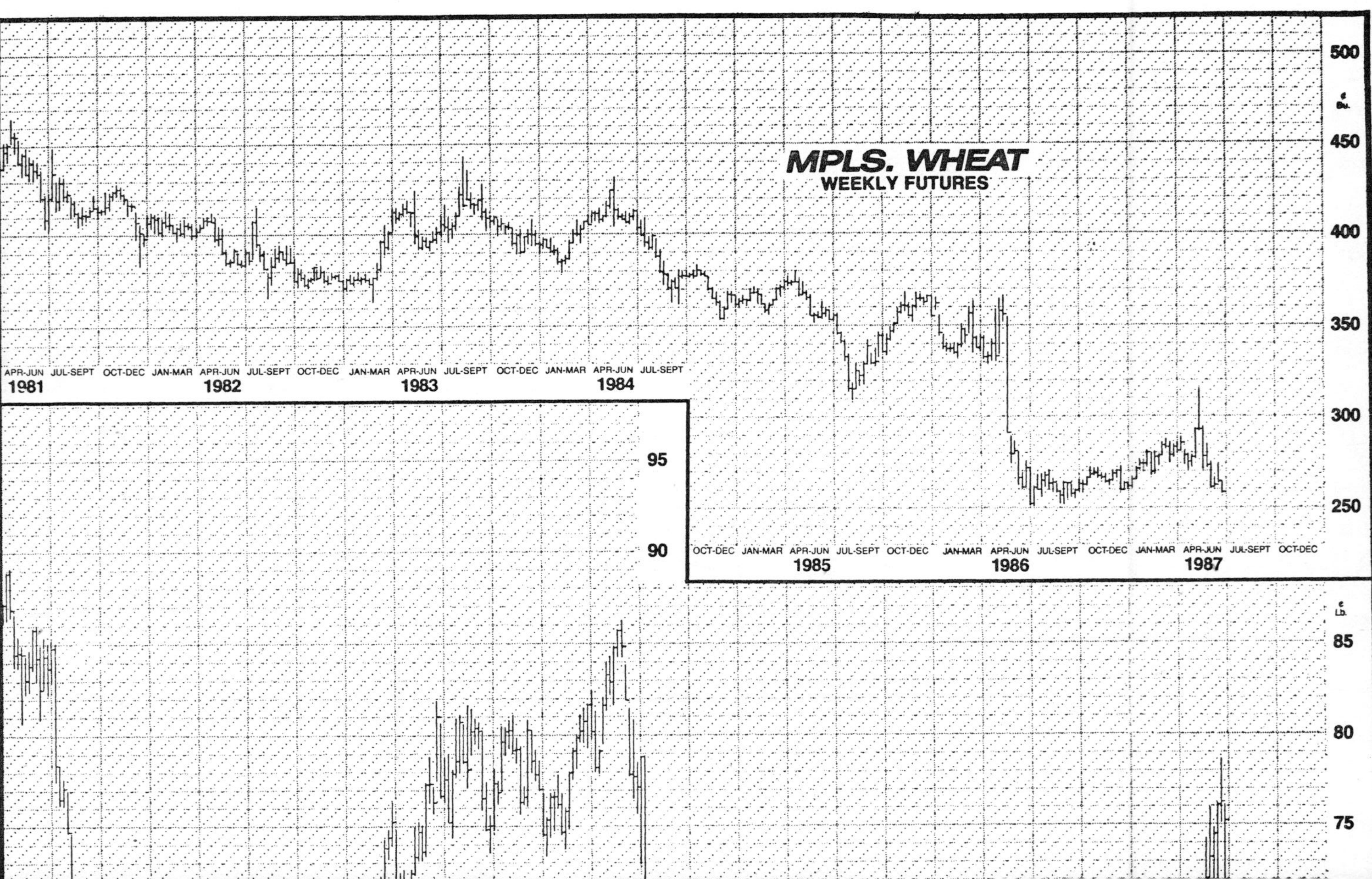
MPLS. WHEAT
WEEKLY FUTURES
¢ Bu.
500
450
400
350
300
250
APR-JUN JUL-SEPT OCT-DEC JAN-MAR APR-JUN JUL-SEPT OCT-DEC JAN-MAR APR-JUN JUL-SEPT OCT-DEC JAN-MAR APR-JUN JUL-SEPT
1981 1982 1983 1984
OCT-DEC JAN-MAR APR-JUN JUL-SEPT OCT-DEC JAN-MAR APR-JUN JUL-SEPT OCT-DEC JAN-MAR APR-JUN JUL-SEPT OCT-DEC
1985 1986 1987
95
90
¢ Lb.
85
80
75

COTTON
WEEKLY FUTURES
70
65
60
55
50
45
40
35
30
APR-JUN JUL-SEPT OCT-DEC JAN-MAR APR-JUN JUL-SEPT OCT-DEC JAN-MAR APR-JUN JUL-SEPT OCT-DEC JAN-MAR APR-JUN JUL-SEPT OCT-DEC JAN-MAR APR-JUN JUL-SEPT OCT-DEC JAN-MAR APR-JUN JUL-SEPT OCT-DEC JAN-MAR APR-JUN JUL-SEPT OCT-DEC
1981
1982
1983
1984
1985
1986
1987

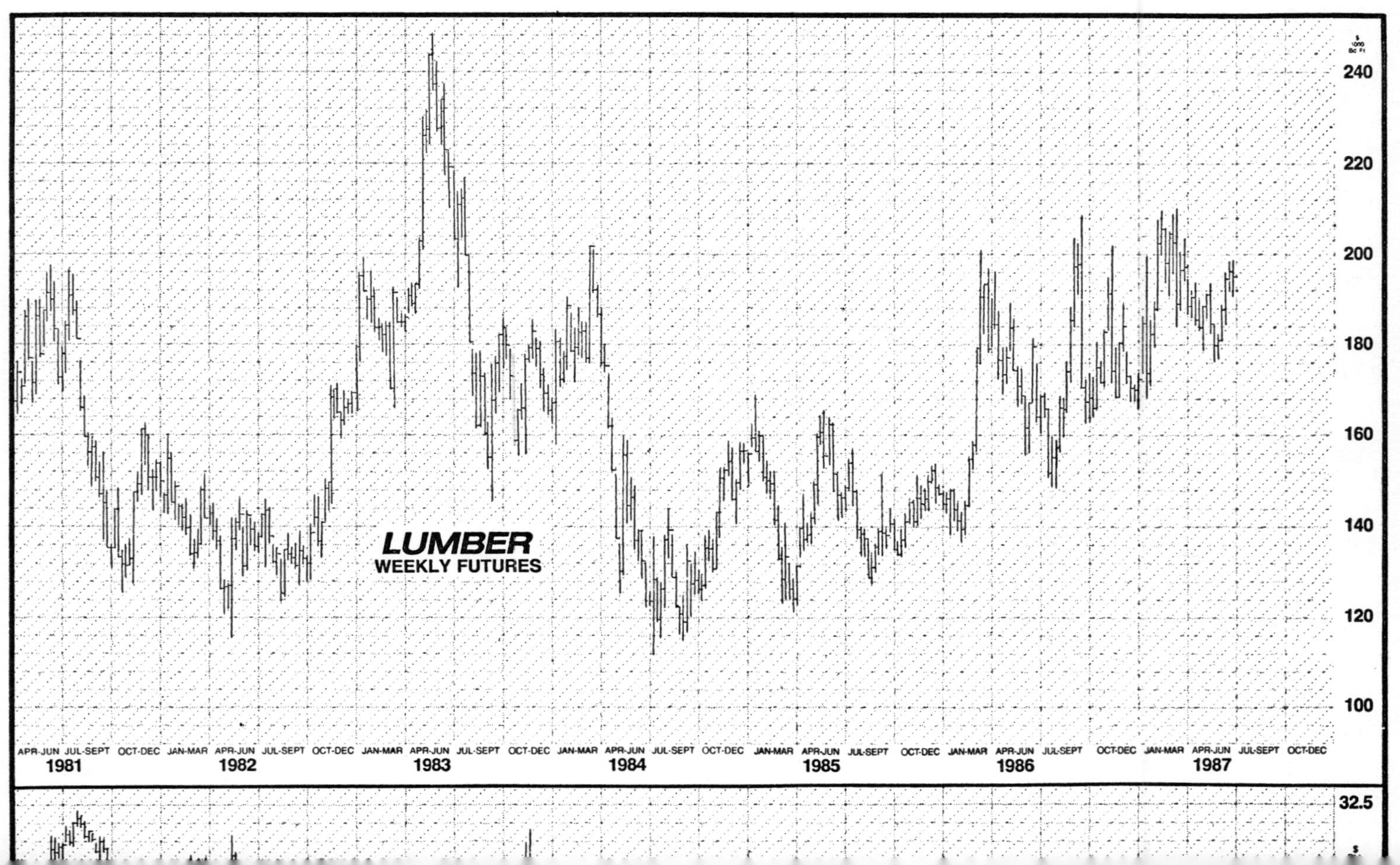
LUMBER
WEEKLY FUTURES
$ 1000 Bd Ft
240
220
200
180
160
140
120
100
APR-JUN JUL-SEPT OCT-DEC JAN-MAR APR-JUN JUL-SEPT OCT-DEC JAN-MAR APR-JUN JUL-SEPT OCT-DEC JAN-MAR APR-JUN JUL-SEPT OCT-DEC JAN-MAR APR-JUN JUL-SEPT OCT-DEC JAN-MAR APR-JUN JUL-SEPT OCT-DEC JAN-MAR APR-JUN JUL-SEPT OCT-DEC
1981 1982 1983 1984 1985 1986 1987
32.5

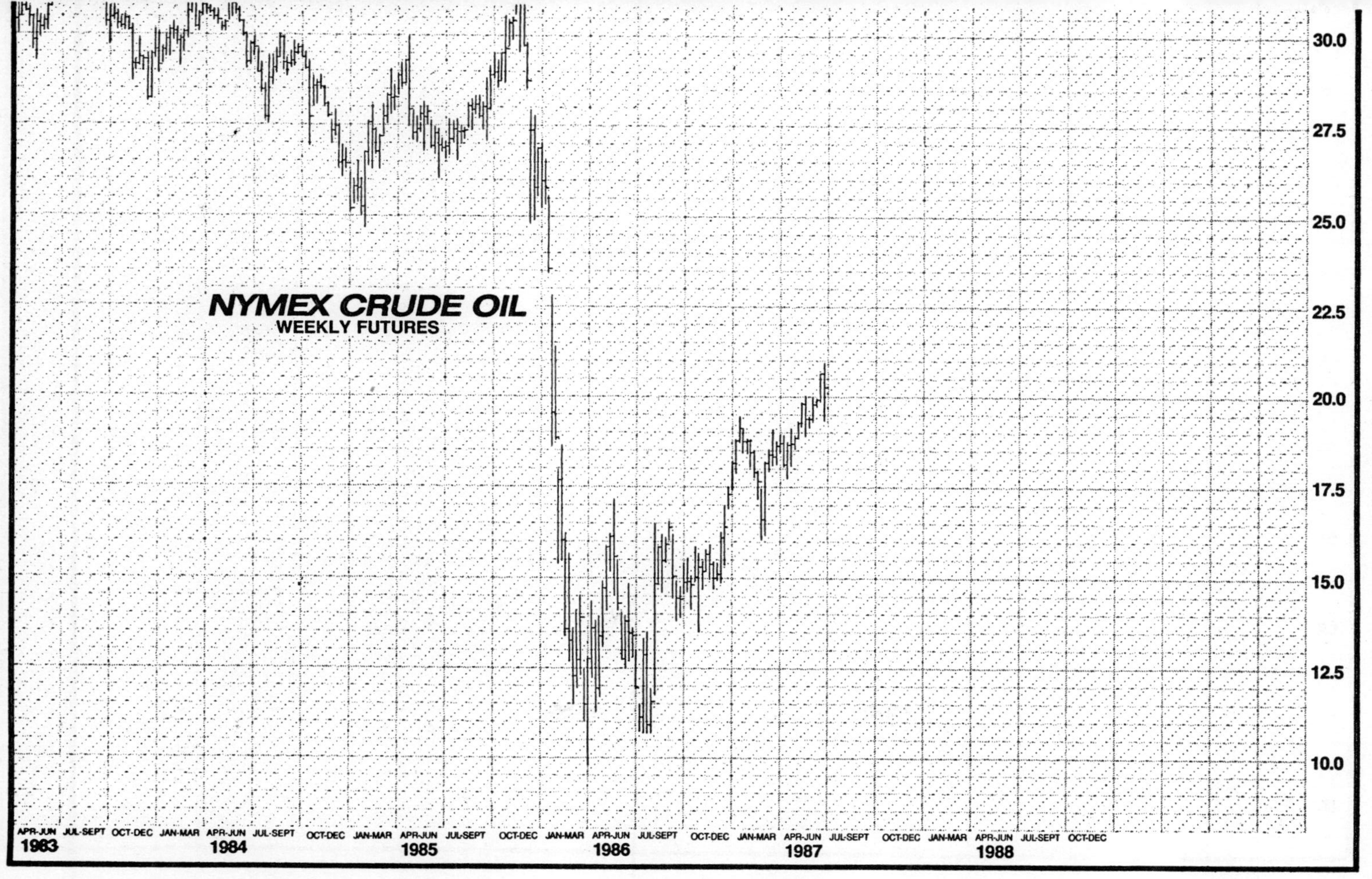
NYMEX CRUDE OIL
WEEKLY FUTURES
30.0
27.5
25.0
22.5
20.0
17.5
15.0
12.5
10.0
APR-JUN JUL-SEPT OCT-DEC
1983
JAN-MAR APR-JUN JUL-SEPT OCT-DEC
1984
JAN-MAR APR-JUN JUL-SEPT OCT-DEC
1985
JAN-MAR APR-JUN JUL-SEPT OCT-DEC
1986
JAN-MAR APR-JUN JUL-SEPT OCT-DEC
1987
JAN-MAR APR-JUN JUL-SEPT OCT-DEC
1988

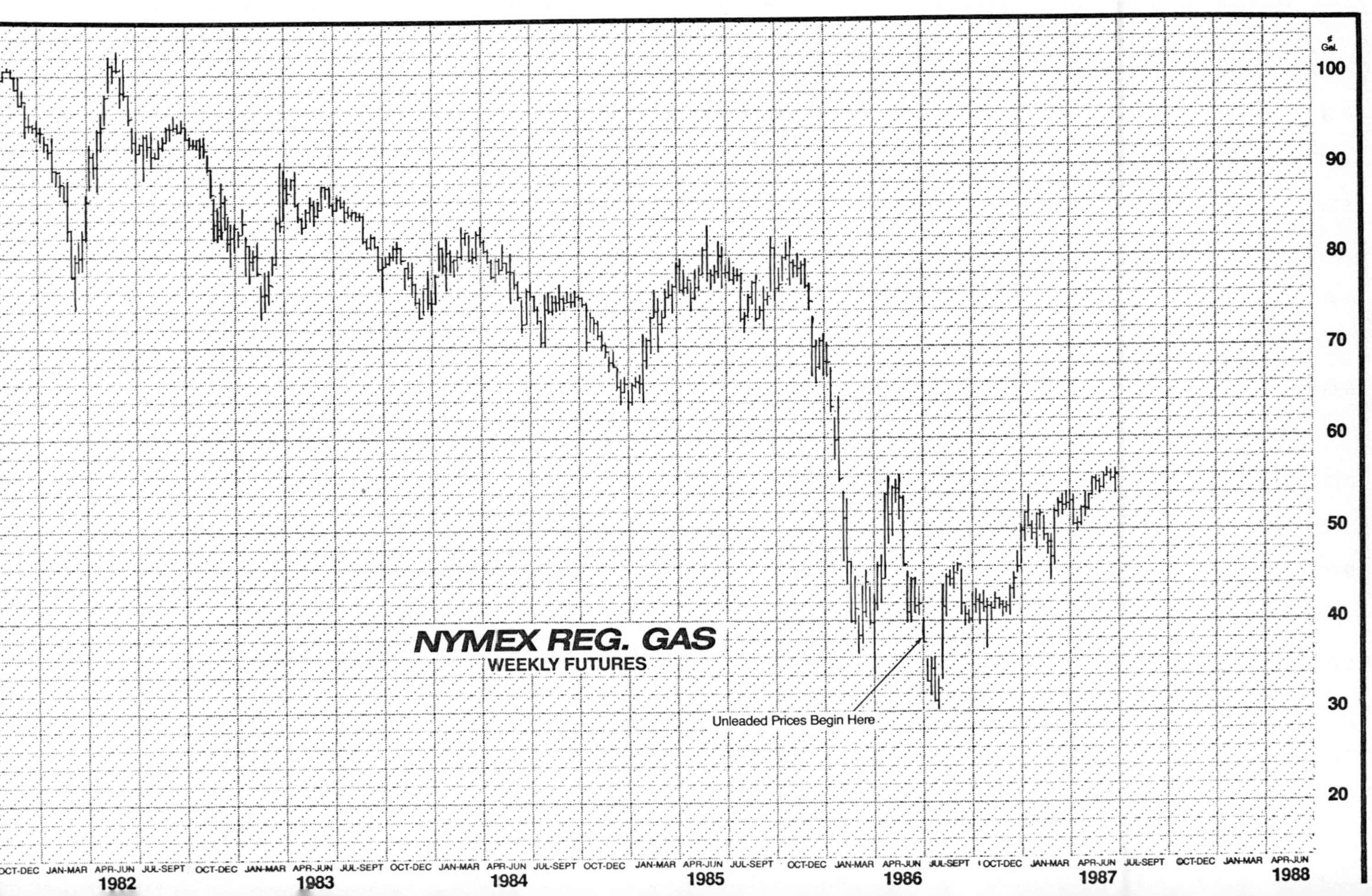

NYMEX REG. GAS
WEEKLY FUTURES
Unleaded Prices Begin Here
¢/Gal.
100
90
80
70
60
50
40
30
20
OCT-DEC
JAN-MAR
APR-JUN
JUL-SEPT
OCT-DEC
1982
1983
1984
1985
1986
1987
1988

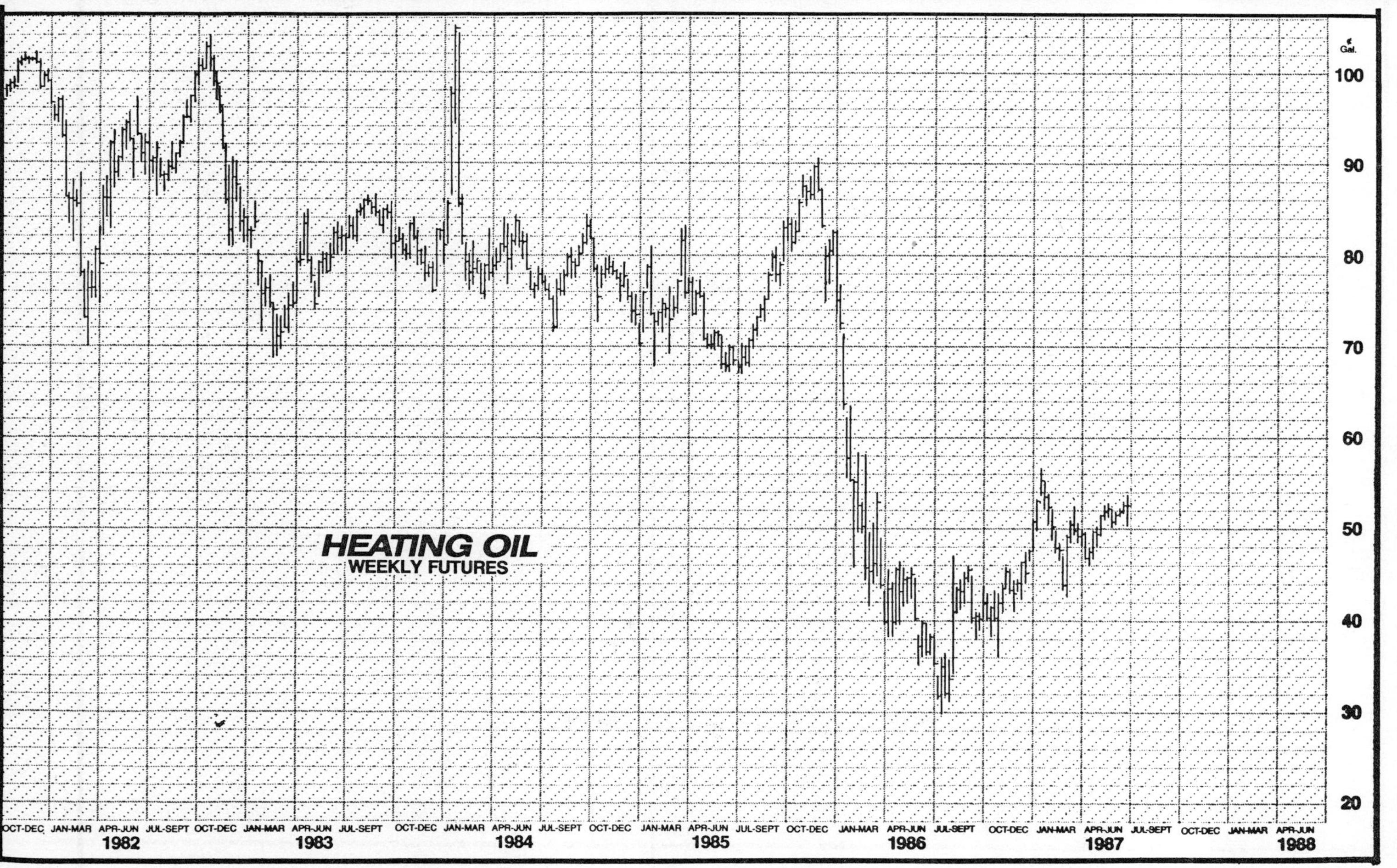
HEATING OIL
WEEKLY FUTURES
¢ Gal.
100
90
80
70
60
50
40
30
20
OCT-DEC JAN-MAR APR-JUN JUL-SEPT OCT-DEC JAN-MAR APR-JUN JUL-SEPT OCT-DEC JAN-MAR APR-JUN JUL-SEPT OCT-DEC JAN-MAR APR-JUN JUL-SEPT OCT-DEC JAN-MAR APR-JUN JUL-SEPT OCT-DEC JAN-MAR APR-JUN JUL-SEPT OCT-DEC JAN-MAR APR-JUN
1982
1983
1984
1985
1986
1987
1988

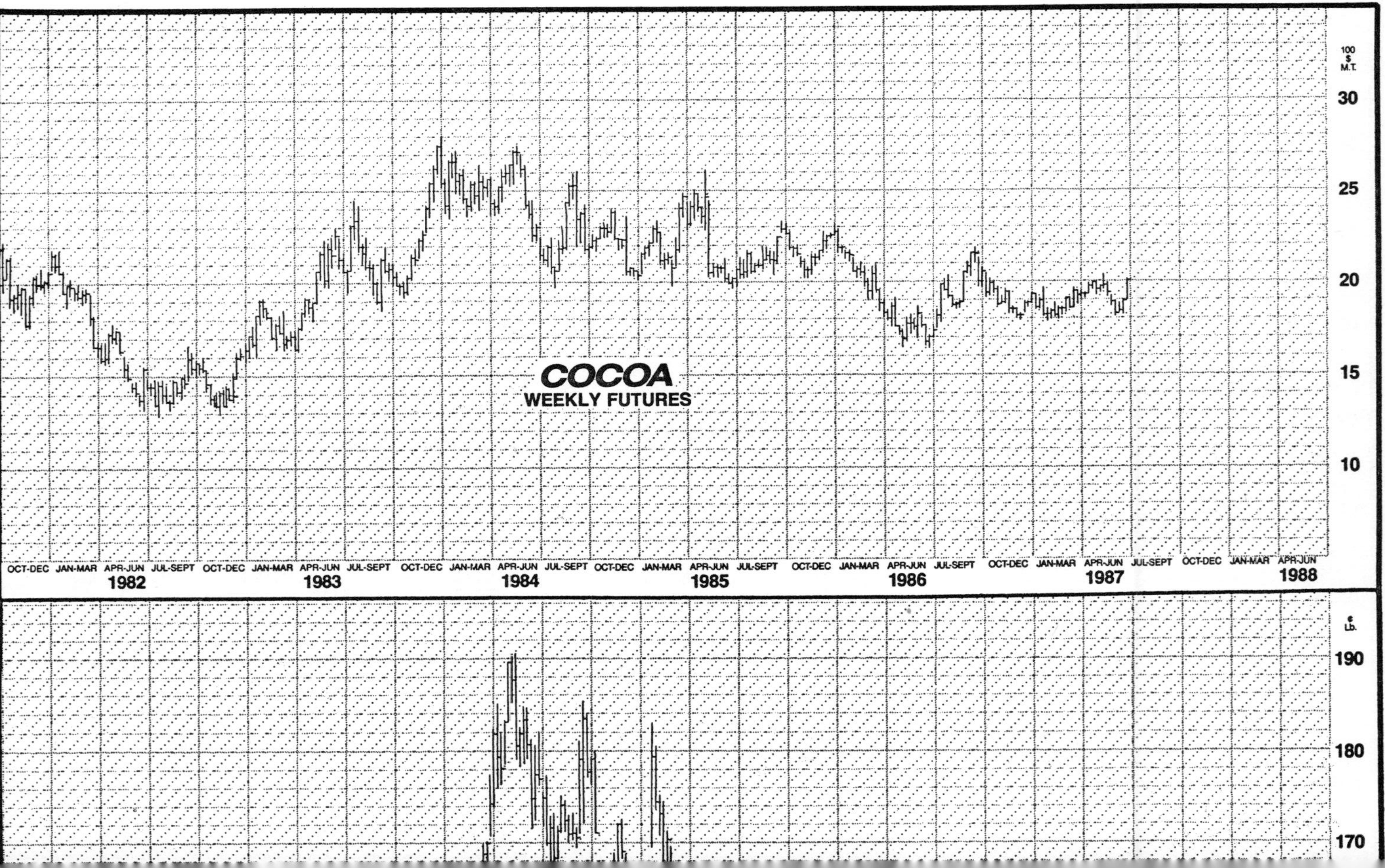
COCOA
WEEKLY FUTURES
100 $ M.T.
30
25
20
15
10
OCT-DEC JAN-MAR APR-JUN JUL-SEPT
1982
OCT-DEC JAN-MAR APR-JUN JUL-SEPT
1983
OCT-DEC JAN-MAR APR-JUN JUL-SEPT
1984
OCT-DEC JAN-MAR APR-JUN JUL-SEPT
1985
OCT-DEC JAN-MAR APR-JUN JUL-SEPT
1986
OCT-DEC JAN-MAR APR-JUN JUL-SEPT
1987
OCT-DEC JAN-MAR APR-JUN
1988
¢ Lb.
190
180
170

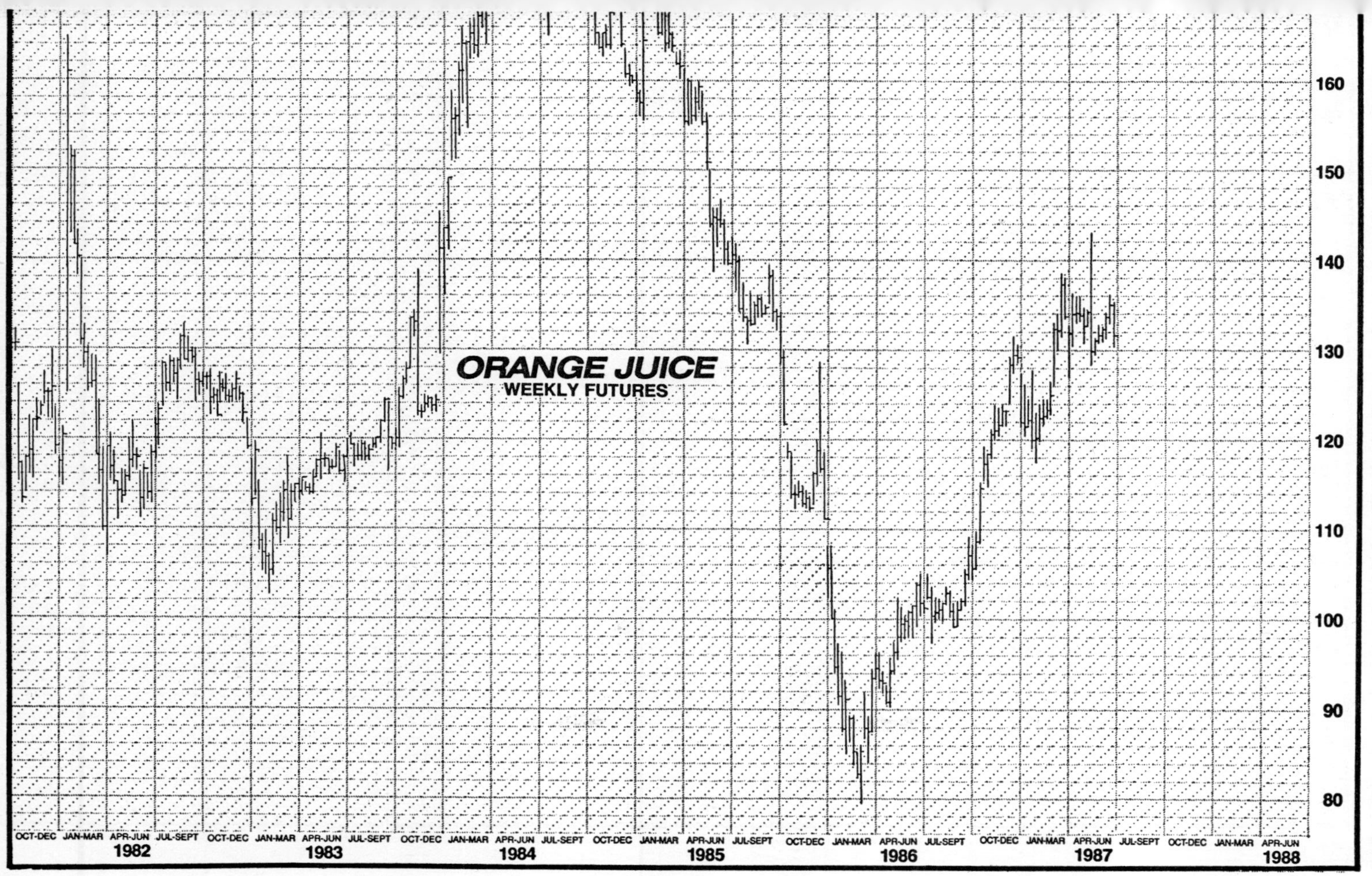
ORANGE JUICE
WEEKLY FUTURES
160
150
140
130
120
110
100
90
80
OCT-DEC
JAN-MAR APR-JUN JUL-SEPT OCT-DEC
1982
JAN-MAR APR-JUN JUL-SEPT OCT-DEC
1983
JAN-MAR APR-JUN JUL-SEPT OCT-DEC
1984
JAN-MAR APR-JUN JUL-SEPT OCT-DEC
1985
JAN-MAR APR-JUN JUL-SEPT OCT-DEC
1986
JAN-MAR APR-JUN JUL-SEPT OCT-DEC
1987
JAN-MAR APR-JUN
1988

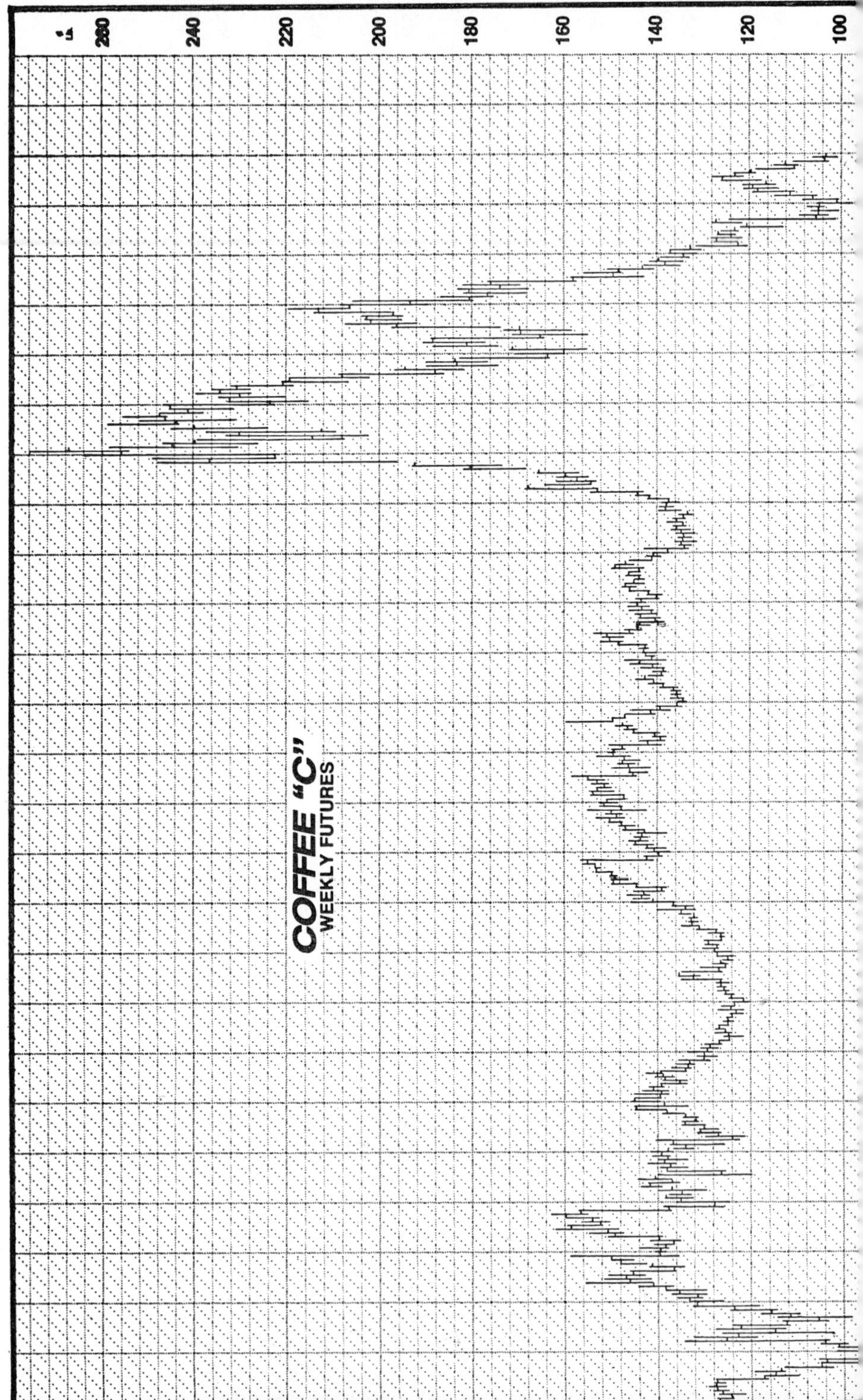
COFFEE "C"
WEEKLY FUTURES
280
240
220
200
180
160
140
120
100

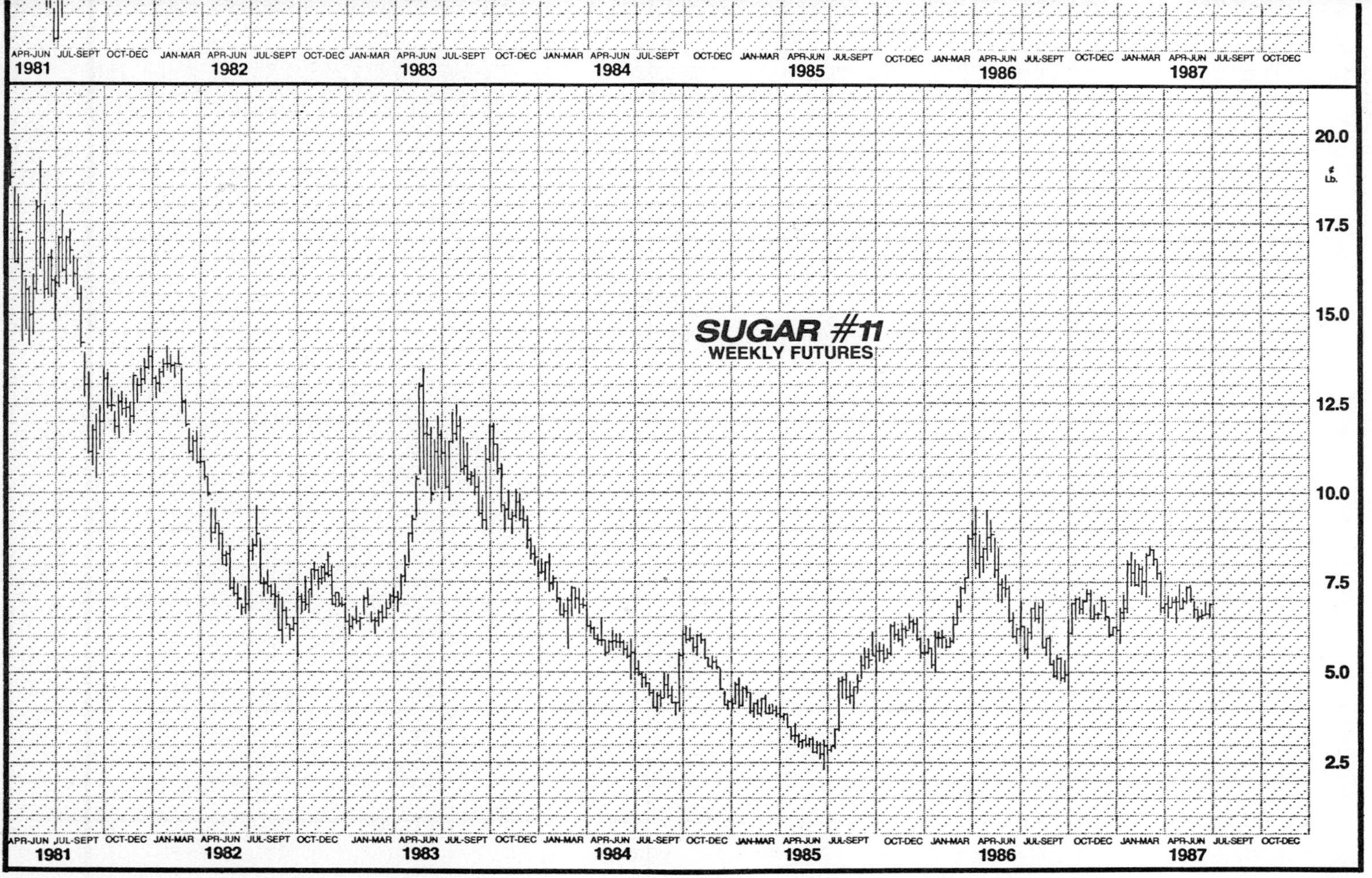
SUGAR #11
WEEKLY FUTURES
¢
Lb.
20.0
17.5
15.0
12.5
10.0
7.5
5.0
2.5
APR-JUN JUL-SEPT OCT-DEC
1981
JAN-MAR APR-JUN JUL-SEPT OCT-DEC
1982
JAN-MAR APR-JUN JUL-SEPT OCT-DEC
1983
JAN-MAR APR-JUN JUL-SEPT OCT-DEC
1984
JAN-MAR APR-JUN JUL-SEPT OCT-DEC
1985
JAN-MAR APR-JUN JUL-SEPT OCT-DEC
1986
JAN-MAR APR-JUN JUL-SEPT OCT-DEC
1987

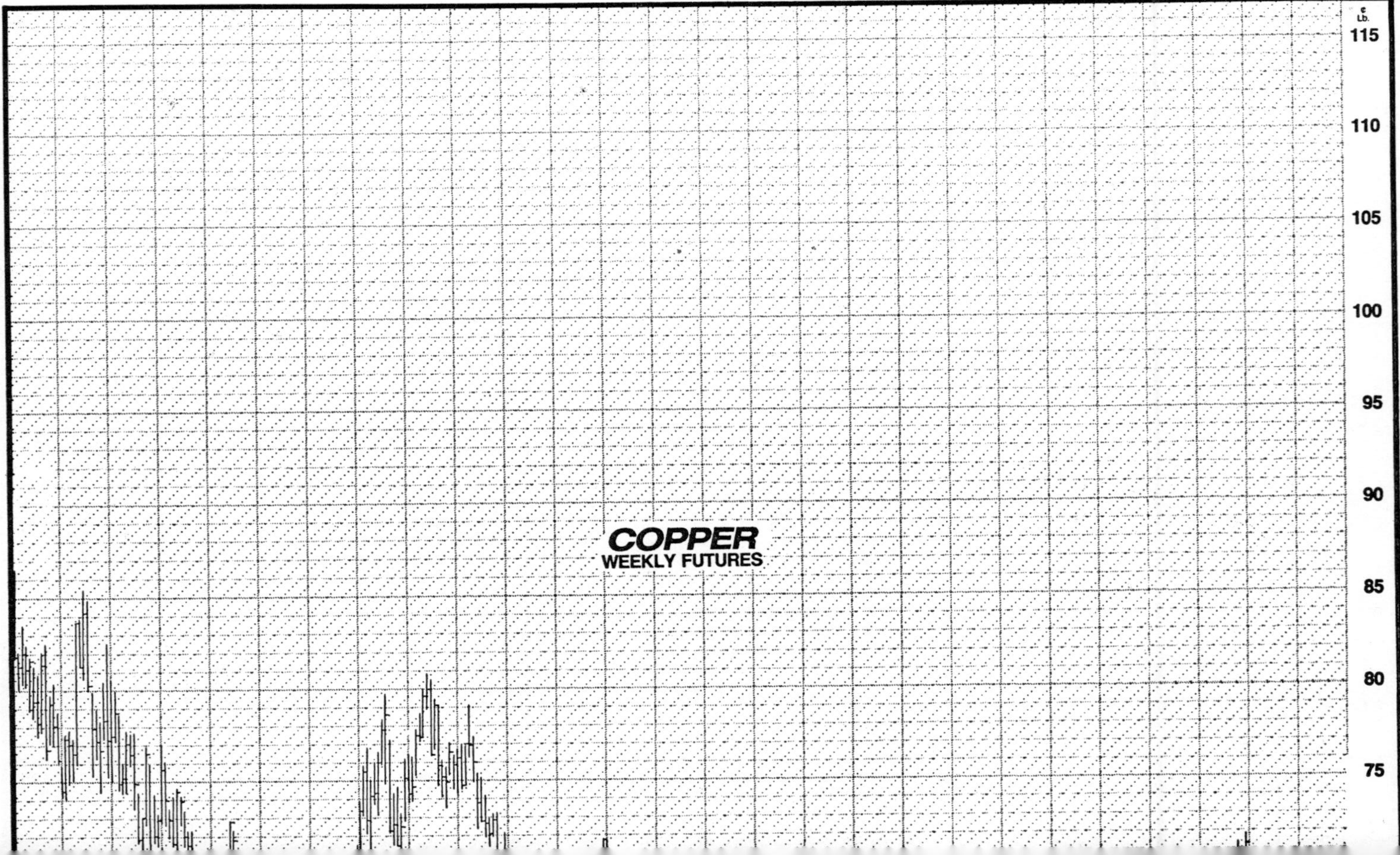

COPPER
WEEKLY FUTURES
¢ Lb.
115
110
105
100
95
90
85
80
75

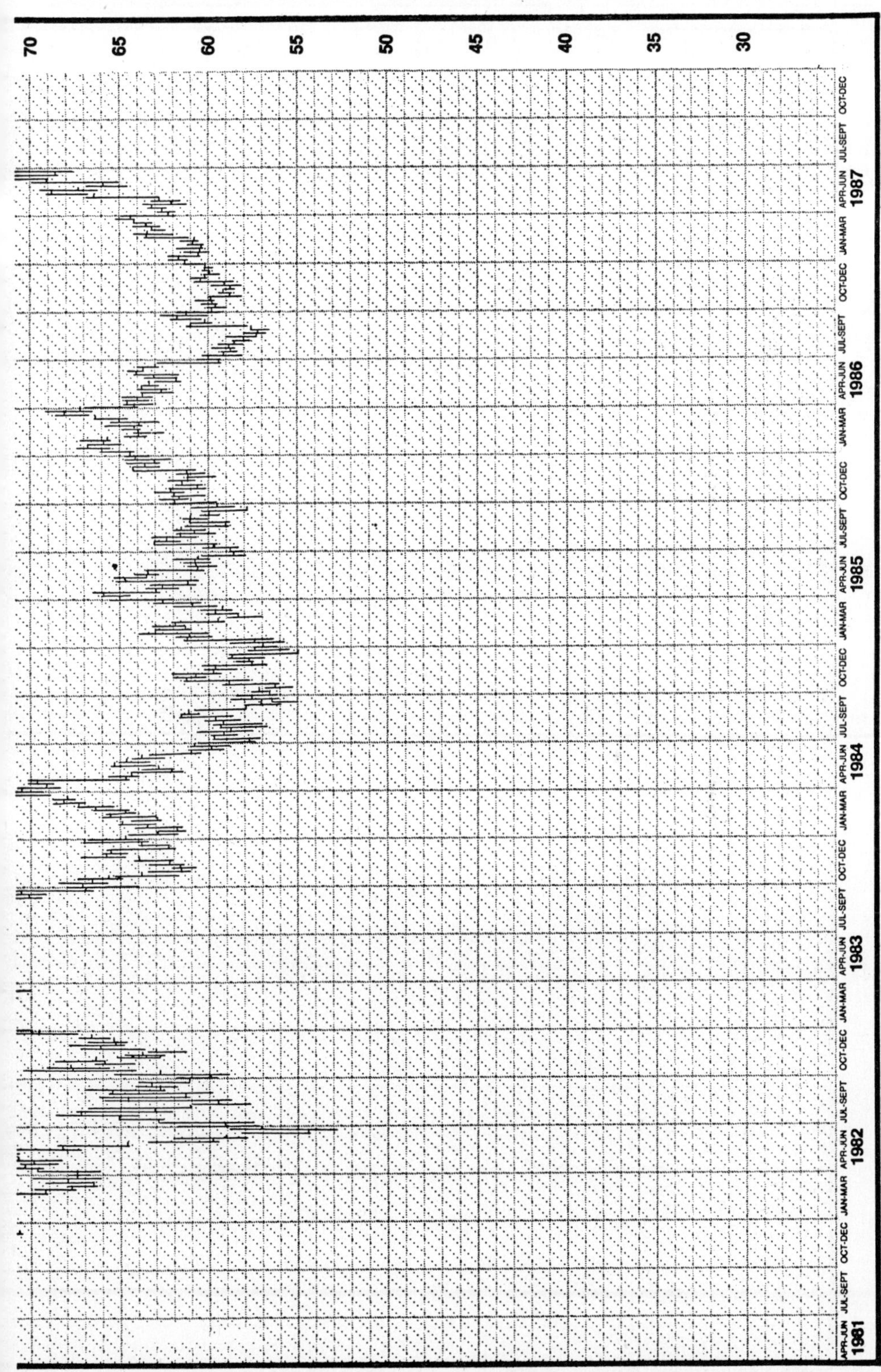
70
65
60
55
50
45
40
35
30
APR-JUN JUL-SEPT OCT-DEC
1981
JAN-MAR APR-JUN JUL-SEPT OCT-DEC
1982
JAN-MAR APR-JUN JUL-SEPT OCT-DEC
1983
JAN-MAR APR-JUN JUL-SEPT OCT-DEC
1984
JAN-MAR APR-JUN JUL-SEPT OCT-DEC
1985
JAN-MAR APR-JUN JUL-SEPT OCT-DEC
1986
JAN-MAR APR-JUN JUL-SEPT OCT-DEC
1987

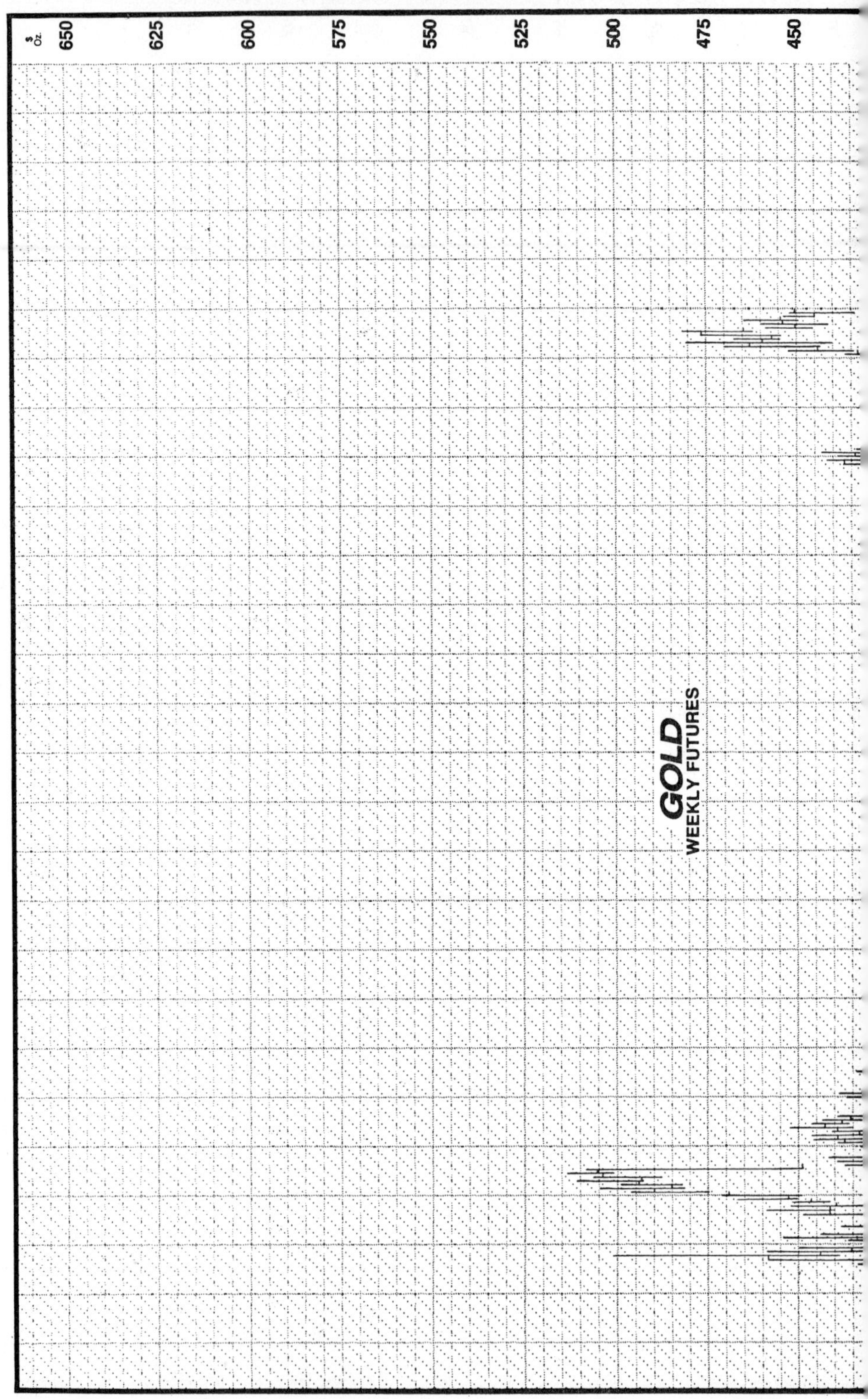
$ Oz.
650
625
600
575
550
525
500
475
450
GOLD
WEEKLY FUTURES

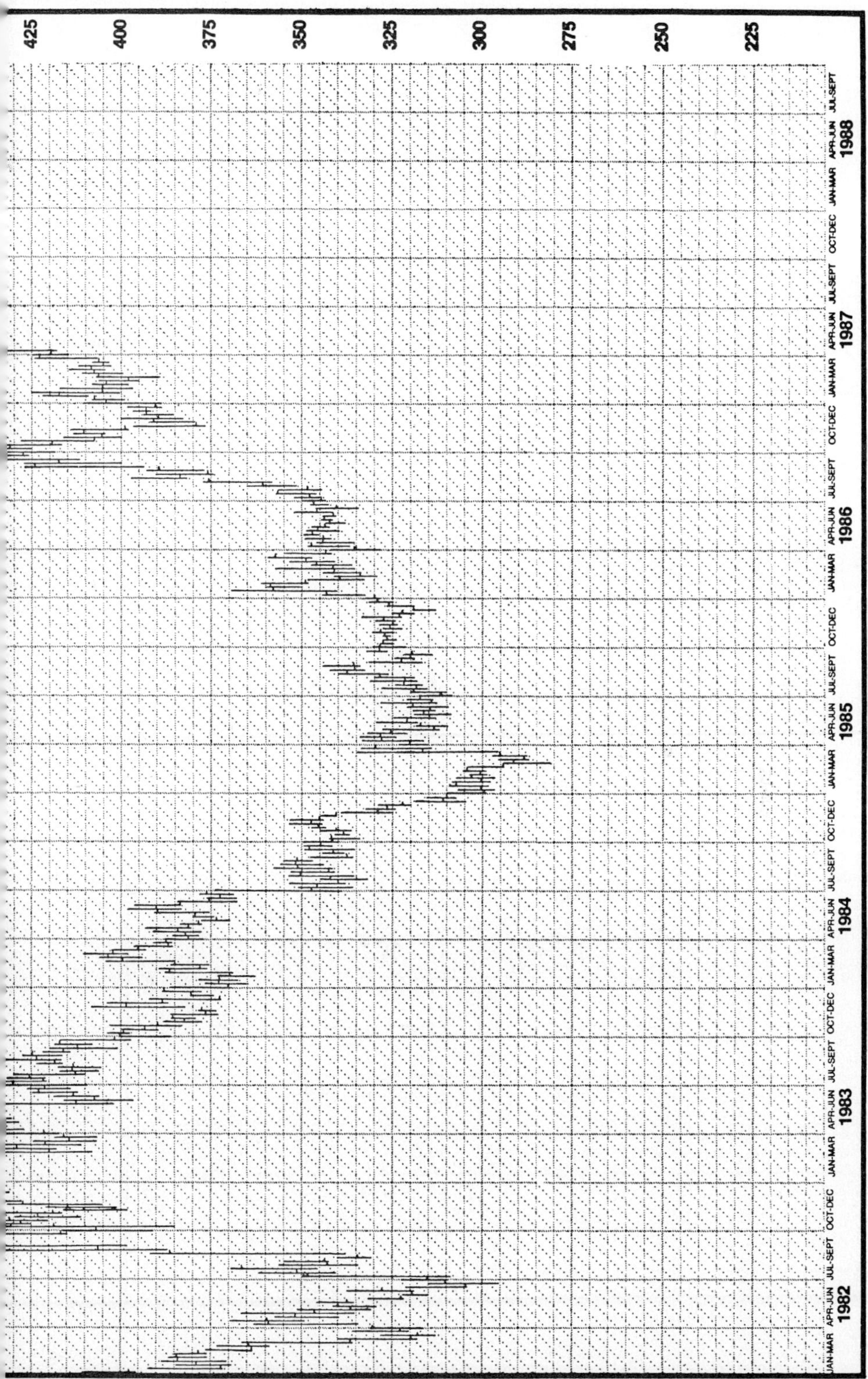
425
400
375
350
325
300
275
250
225
JAN-MAR APR-JUN JUL-SEPT OCT-DEC
1982
1983
1984
1985
1986
1987
1988

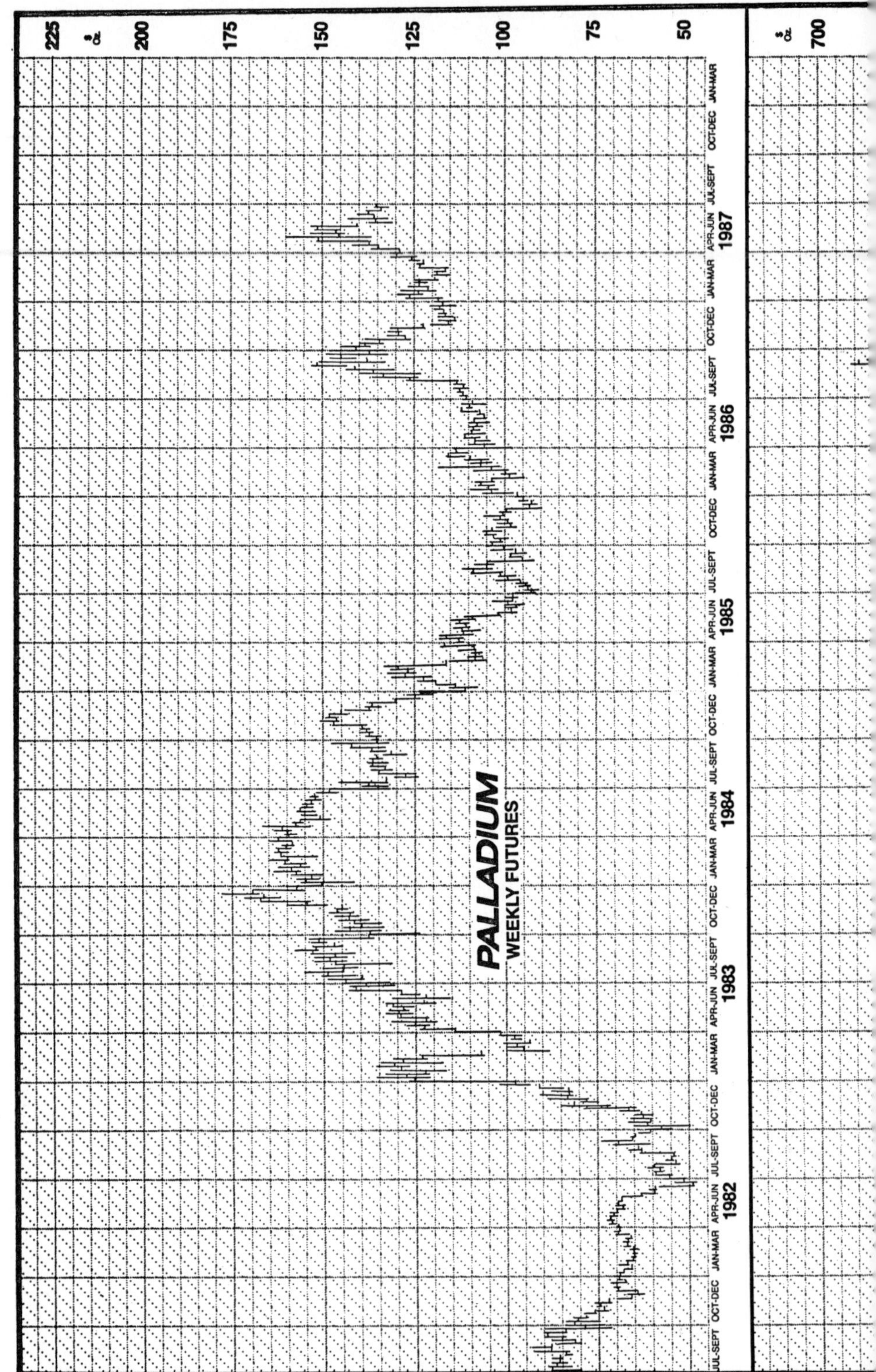
PALLADIUM
WEEKLY FUTURES
$ Oz.
225
200
175
150
125
100
75
50
700
1982
1983
1984
1985
1986
1987
JUL-SEPT
OCT-DEC
JAN-MAR
APR-JUN

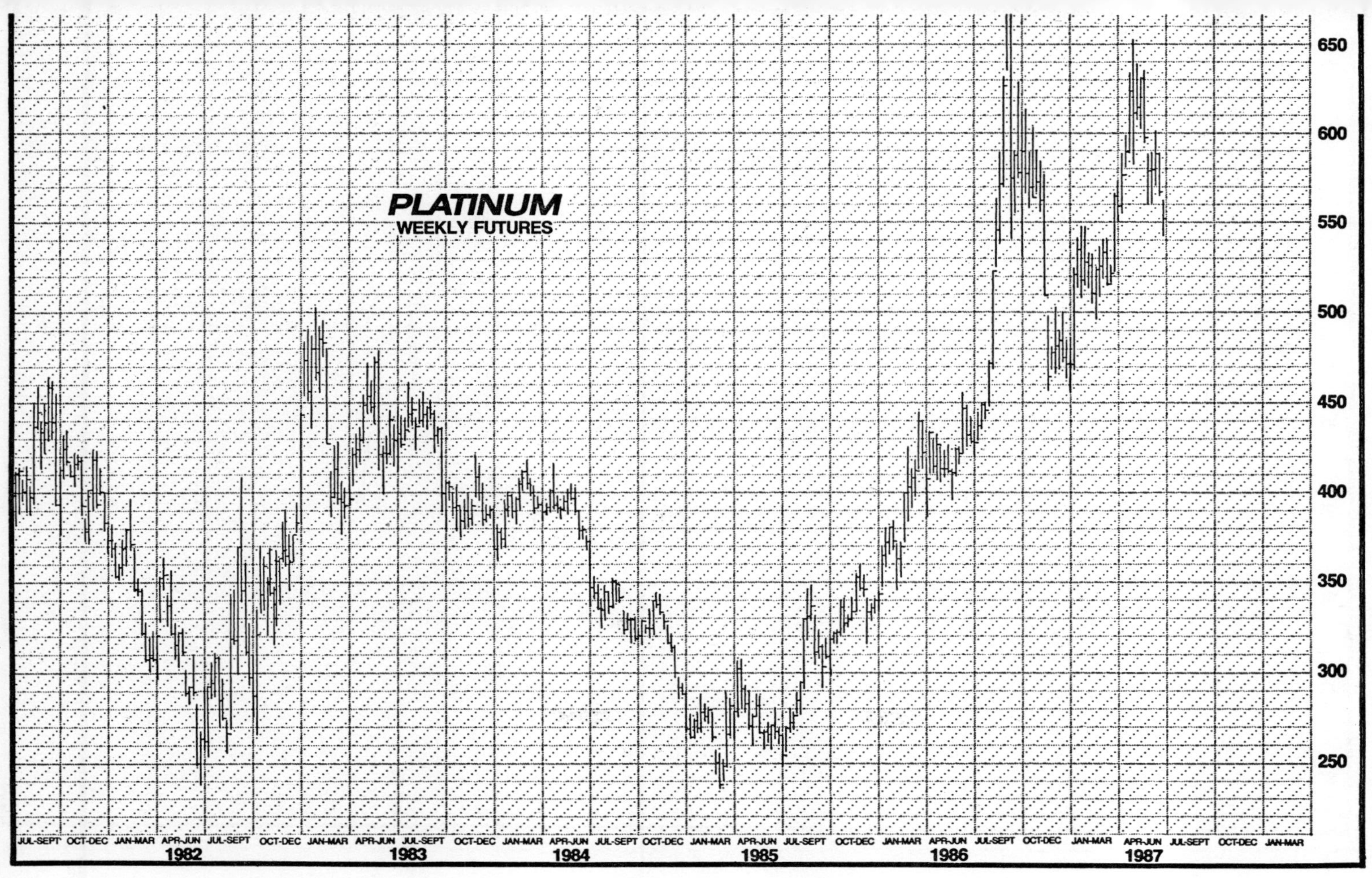
PLATINUM
WEEKLY FUTURES
650
600
550
500
450
400
350
300
250
JUL-SEPT OCT-DEC JAN-MAR APR-JUN JUL-SEPT OCT-DEC JAN-MAR APR-JUN JUL-SEPT OCT-DEC JAN-MAR APR-JUN JUL-SEPT OCT-DEC JAN-MAR APR-JUN JUL-SEPT OCT-DEC JAN-MAR APR-JUN JUL-SEPT OCT-DEC JAN-MAR APR-JUN JUL-SEPT OCT-DEC JAN-MAR
1982
1983
1984
1985
1986
1987

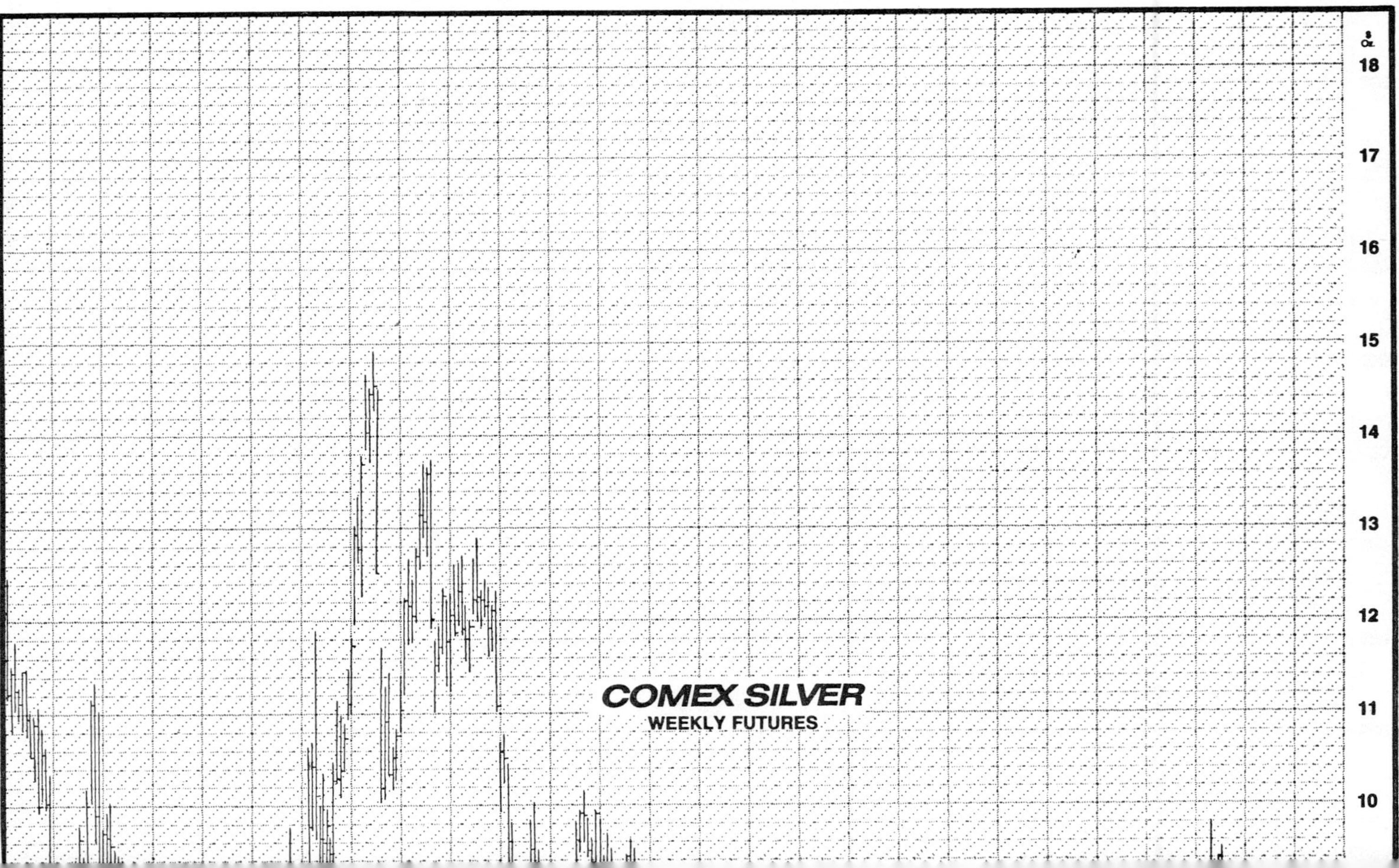
COMEX SILVER
WEEKLY FUTURES
$ Oz.
18
17
16
15
14
13
12
11
10

9
8
7
6
5
4
3
2
1
APR-JUN JUL-SEPT OCT-DEC JAN-MAR APR-JUN JUL-SEPT OCT-DEC JAN-MAR APR-JUN JUL-SEPT OCT-DEC JAN-MAR APR-JUN JUL-SEPT OCT-DEC JAN-MAR APR-JUN JUL-SEPT OCT-DEC JAN-MAR APR-JUN JUL-SEPT OCT-DEC JAN-MAR APR-JUN JUL-SEPT OCT-DEC
1981 1982 1983 1984 1985 1986 1987

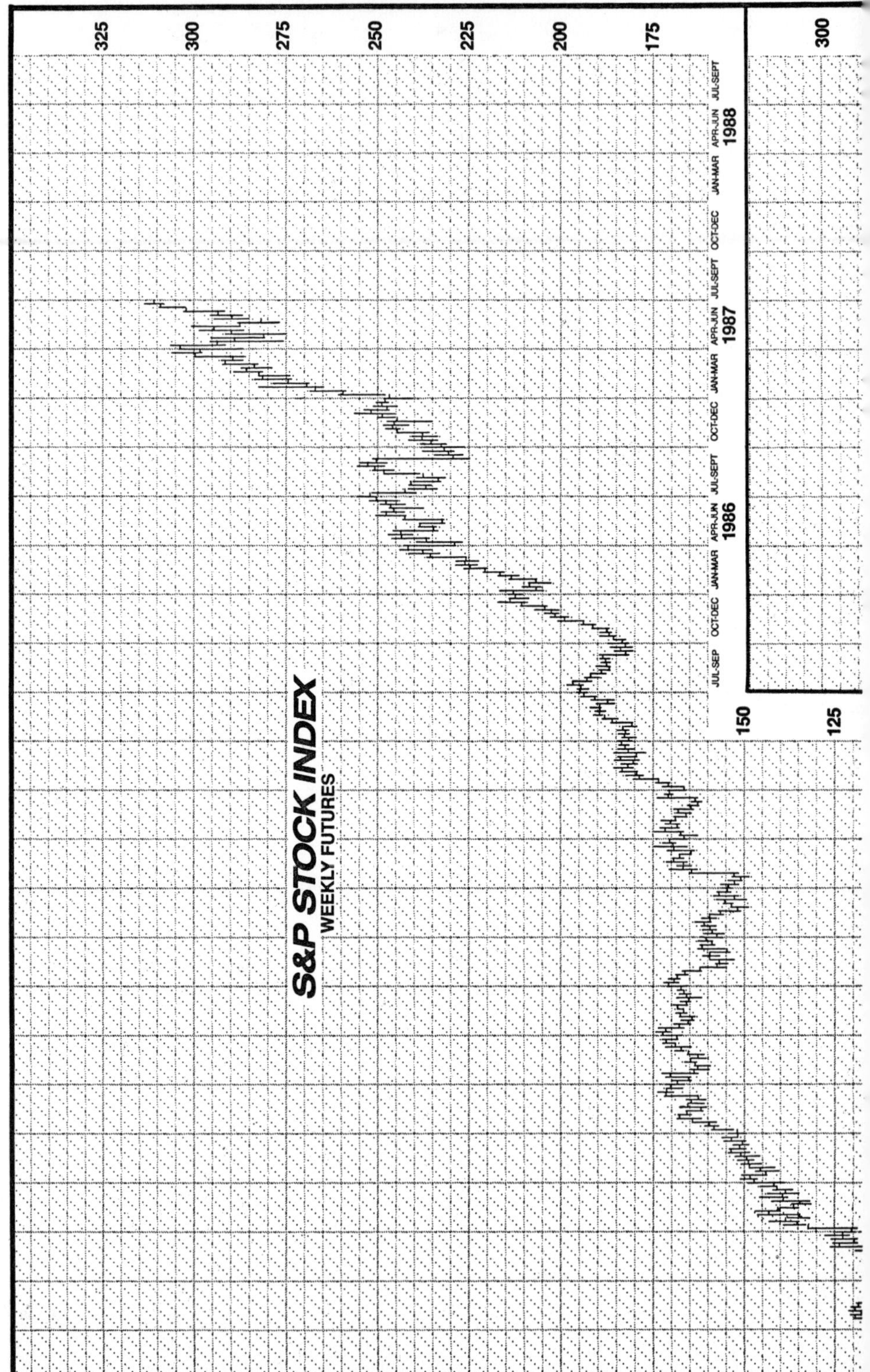
S&P STOCK INDEX
WEEKLY FUTURES
325
300
275
250
225
200
175
150
125
300
JUL-SEP
OCT-DEC
JAN-MAR
APR-JUN
1986
JUL-SEPT
OCT-DEC
JAN-MAR
APR-JUN
1987
JUL-SEPT
OCT-DEC
JAN-MAR
APR-JUN
1988
JUL-SEPT

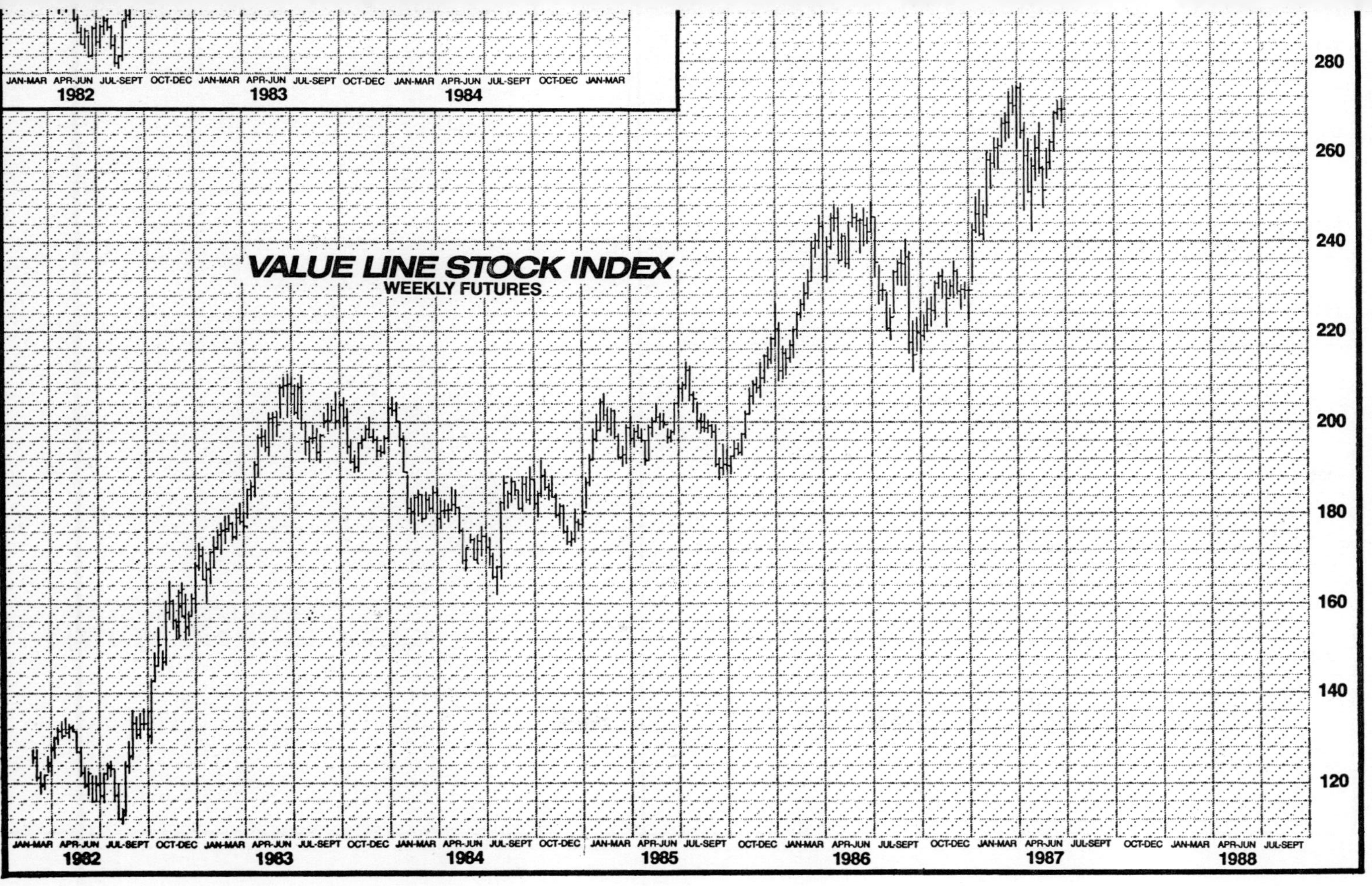
VALUE LINE STOCK INDEX
WEEKLY FUTURES
280
260
240
220
200
180
160
140
120
JAN-MAR APR-JUN JUL-SEPT OCT-DEC JAN-MAR APR-JUN JUL-SEPT OCT-DEC JAN-MAR APR-JUN JUL-SEPT OCT-DEC JAN-MAR
1982 1983 1984
JAN-MAR APR-JUN JUL-SEPT OCT-DEC JAN-MAR APR-JUN JUL-SEPT OCT-DEC JAN-MAR APR-JUN JUL-SEPT OCT-DEC JAN-MAR APR-JUN JUL-SEPT OCT-DEC JAN-MAR APR-JUN JUL-SEPT OCT-DEC JAN-MAR APR-JUN JUL-SEPT OCT-DEC JAN-MAR APR-JUN JUL-SEPT
1982 1983 1984 1985 1986 1987 1988

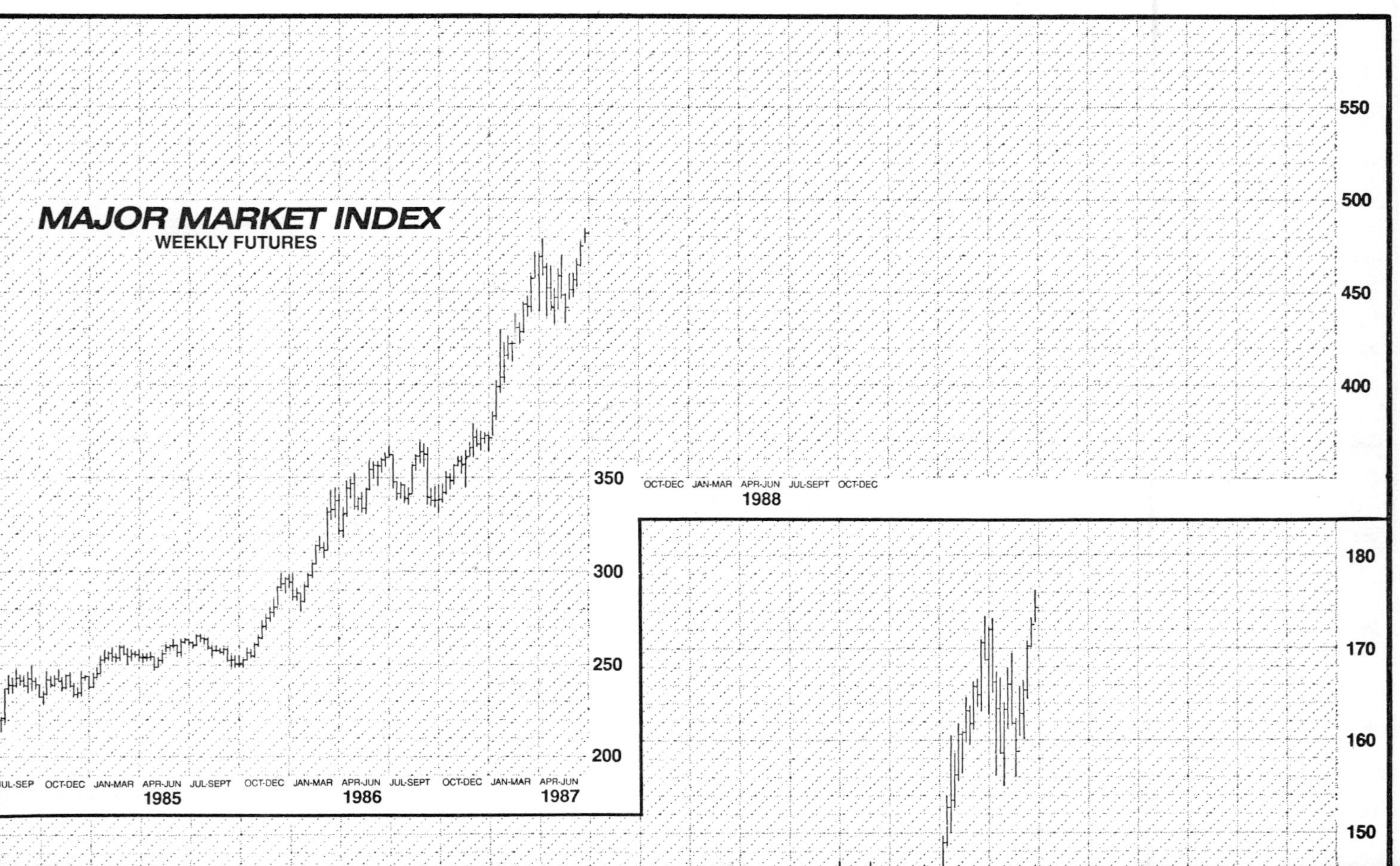
MAJOR MARKET INDEX
WEEKLY FUTURES
550
500
450
400
350
300
250
200
JUL-SEP OCT-DEC JAN-MAR APR-JUN JUL-SEPT OCT-DEC JAN-MAR APR-JUN JUL-SEPT OCT-DEC JAN-MAR APR-JUN
1985
1986
1987
OCT-DEC JAN-MAR APR-JUN JUL-SEPT OCT-DEC
1988
180
170
160
150

NYSE STOCK INDEX
WEEKLY FUTURES
140
130
120
110
100
90
80
70
60
APR-JUN
JUL-SEP
OCT-DEC
1982
JAN-MAR
APR-JUN
JUL-SEPT
OCT-DEC
1983
JAN-MAR
APR-JUN
JUL-SEPT
OCT-DEC
1984
JAN-MAR
APR-JUN
JUL-SEPT
OCT-DEC
1985
JAN-MAR
APR-JUN
JUL-SEPT
OCT-DEC
1986
JAN-MAR
APR-JUN
JUL-SEPT
OCT-DEC
1987
JAN-MAR
APR-JUN
JUL-SEPT
OCT-DEC
1988

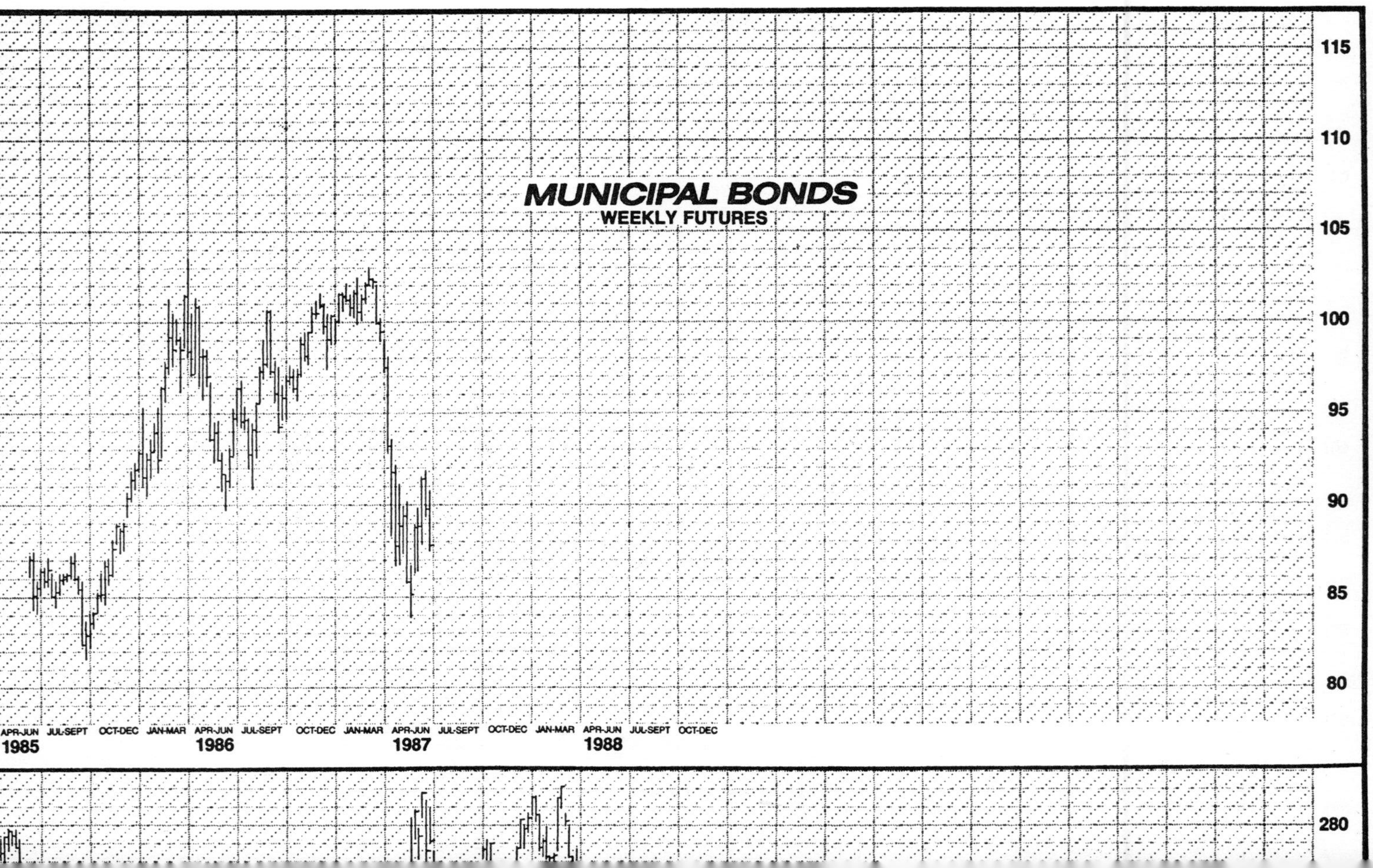
MUNICIPAL BONDS
WEEKLY FUTURES
115
110
105
100
95
90
85
80
280
APR-JUN JUL-SEPT OCT-DEC
1985
JAN-MAR APR-JUN JUL-SEPT OCT-DEC
1986
JAN-MAR APR-JUN JUL-SEPT OCT-DEC
1987
JAN-MAR APR-JUN JUL-SEPT OCT-DEC
1988

CRB FUTURES INDEX
WEEKLY
270
260
250
240
230
220
210
200
190
JUL-SEPT OCT-DEC JAN-MAR APR-JUN JUL-SEPT OCT-DEC JAN-MAR APR-JUN JUL-SEPT OCT-DEC JAN-MAR APR-JUN JUL-SEPT OCT-DEC JAN-MAR APR-JUN JUL-SEPT OCT-DEC JAN-MAR APR-JUN JUL-SEPT OCT-DEC JAN-MAR APR-JUN JUL-SEPT OCT-DEC JAN-MAR
1982
1983
1984
1985
1986
1987

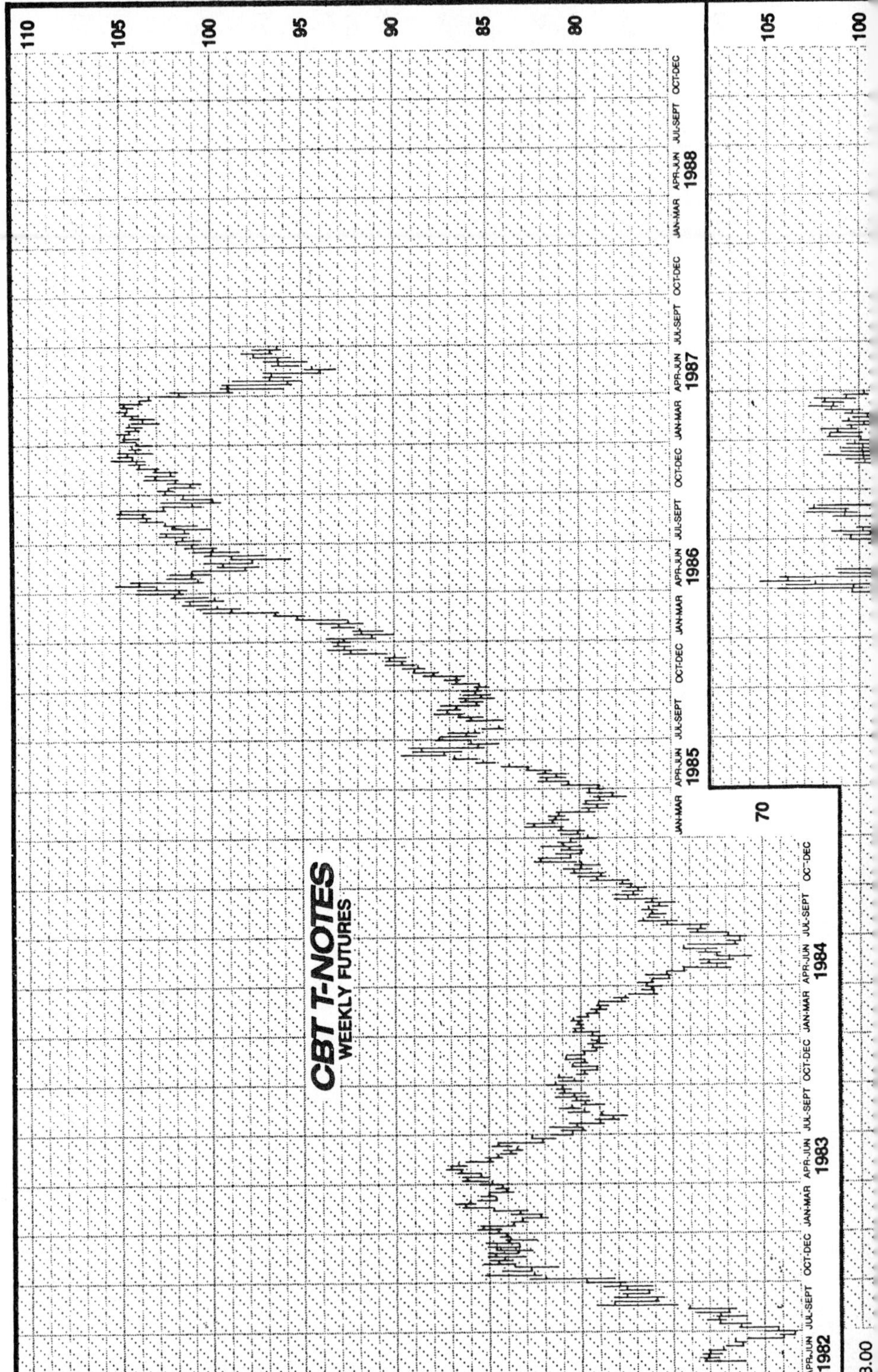
CBT T-NOTES
WEEKLY FUTURES
110
105
100
95
90
85
80
70
APR-JUN JUL-SEPT OCT-DEC JAN-MAR APR-JUN JUL-SEPT OCT-DEC
1982
1983
1984
1985
1986
1987
1988
8.00

T-BONDS
WEEKLY FUTURES
95
90
85
80
75
70
65
60
55
% Yld.
8.56
9.09
9.71
10.39
11.15
11.98
12.93
14.00
JUL-SEPT OCT-DEC JAN-MAR APR-JUN JUL-SEPT OCT-DEC JAN-MAR APR-JUN JUL-SEPT OCT-DEC JAN-MAR APR-JUN JUL-SEPT OCT-DEC JAN-MAR APR-JUN JUL-SEPT OCT-DEC JAN-MAR APR-JUN JUL-SEPT OCT-DEC JAN-MAR APR-JUN JUL-SEPT OCT-DEC
1983
1984
1985
1986
1987
1988

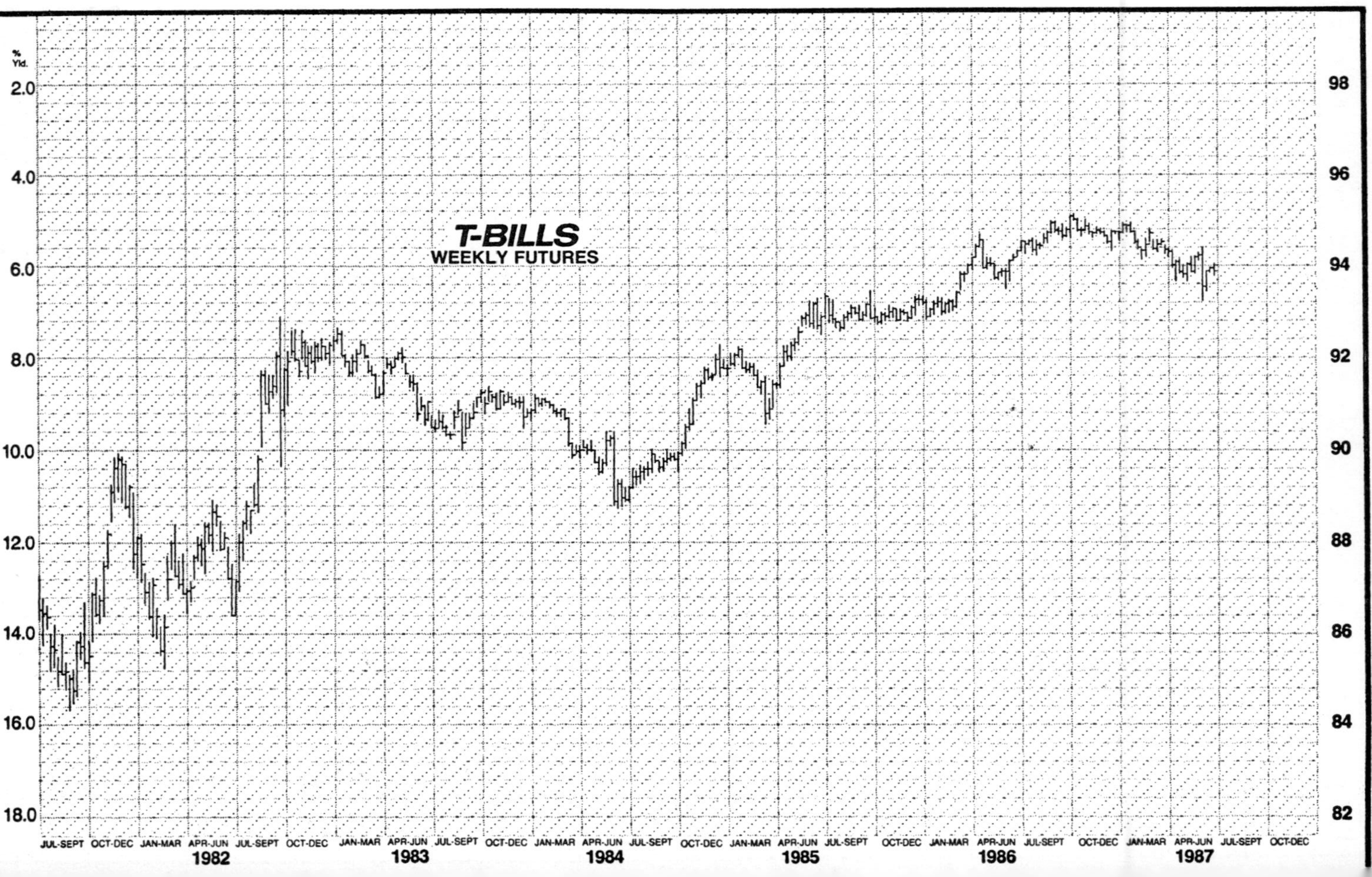
T-BILLS
WEEKLY FUTURES
% Yld.
2.0
4.0
6.0
8.0
10.0
12.0
14.0
16.0
18.0
98
96
94
92
90
88
86
84
82
JUL-SEPT OCT-DEC JAN-MAR APR-JUN JUL-SEPT OCT-DEC JAN-MAR APR-JUN JUL-SEPT OCT-DEC JAN-MAR APR-JUN JUL-SEPT OCT-DEC JAN-MAR APR-JUN JUL-SEPT OCT-DEC JAN-MAR APR-JUN JUL-SEPT OCT-DEC JAN-MAR APR-JUN JUL-SEPT OCT-DEC
1982
1983
1984
1985
1986
1987

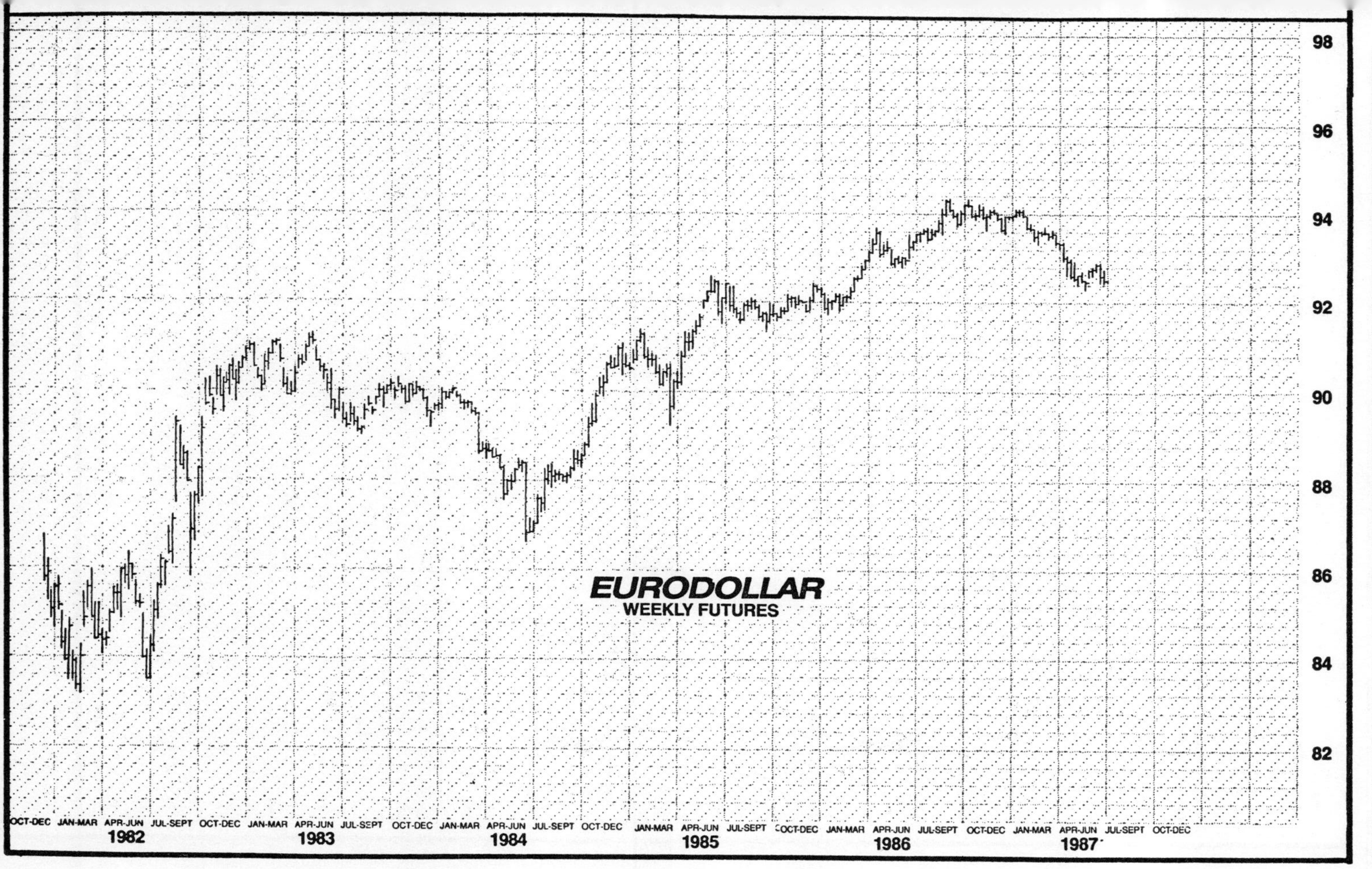
EURODOLLAR
WEEKLY FUTURES
98
96
94
92
90
88
86
84
82
OCT-DEC JAN-MAR APR-JUN JUL-SEPT OCT-DEC JAN-MAR APR-JUN JUL-SEPT OCT-DEC JAN-MAR APR-JUN JUL-SEPT OCT-DEC JAN-MAR APR-JUN JUL-SEPT OCT-DEC JAN-MAR APR-JUN JUL-SEPT OCT-DEC JAN-MAR APR-JUN JUL-SEPT OCT-DEC
1982
1983
1984
1985
1986
1987

U.S. $
2.500
2.400
2.300
2.200
2.100
2.000
1.900
1.800
1.700
BRITISH POUND
WEEKLY FUTURES

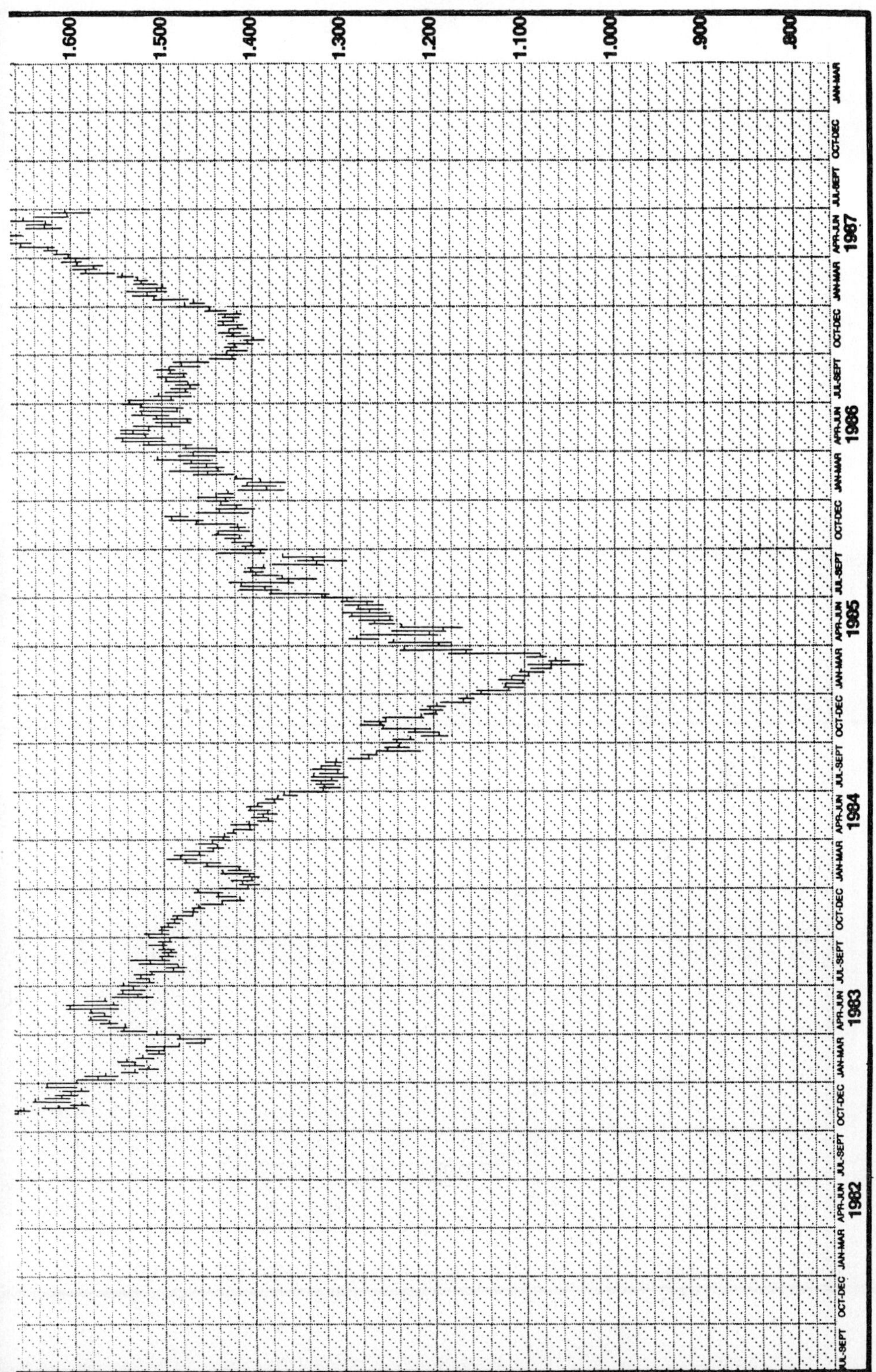
1.600
1.500
1.400
1.300
1.200
1.100
1.000
.900
.800
JUL-SEPT
OCT-DEC
JAN-MAR
APR-JUN
1982
JUL-SEPT
OCT-DEC
JAN-MAR
APR-JUN
1983
JUL-SEPT
OCT-DEC
JAN-MAR
APR-JUN
1984
JUL-SEPT
OCT-DEC
JAN-MAR
APR-JUN
1985
JUL-SEPT
OCT-DEC
JAN-MAR
APR-JUN
1986
JUL-SEPT
OCT-DEC
JAN-MAR
APR-JUN
1987
JUL-SEPT
OCT-DEC
JAN-MAR

CANADIAN DOLLAR
WEEKLY FUTURES
U.S. $
.875
.850
.825
.800
.775
.750
.725
.700
.675
JUL-SEPT
OCT-DEC
JAN-MAR
APR-JUN
1982
1983
1984
1985
1986
1987

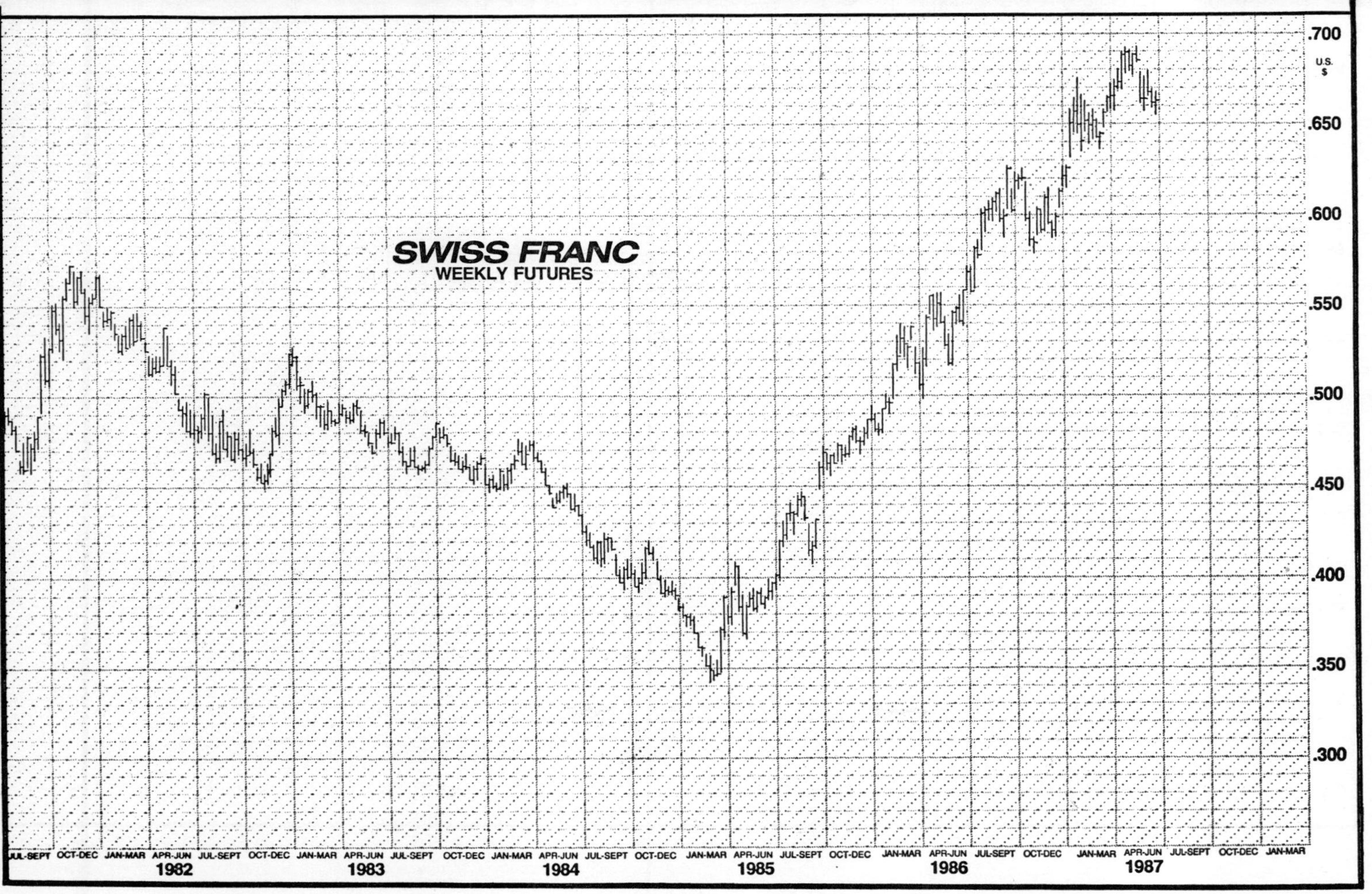
SWISS FRANC
WEEKLY FUTURES
.700
U.S.
$
.650
.600
.550
.500
.450
.400
.350
.300
JUL-SEPT
OCT-DEC
JAN-MAR
APR-JUN
1982
JUL-SEPT
OCT-DEC
JAN-MAR
APR-JUN
1983
JUL-SEPT
OCT-DEC
JAN-MAR
APR-JUN
1984
JUL-SEPT
OCT-DEC
JAN-MAR
APR-JUN
1985
JUL-SEPT
OCT-DEC
JAN-MAR
APR-JUN
1986
JUL-SEPT
OCT-DEC
JAN-MAR
APR-JUN
1987
JUL-SEPT
OCT-DEC
JAN-MAR

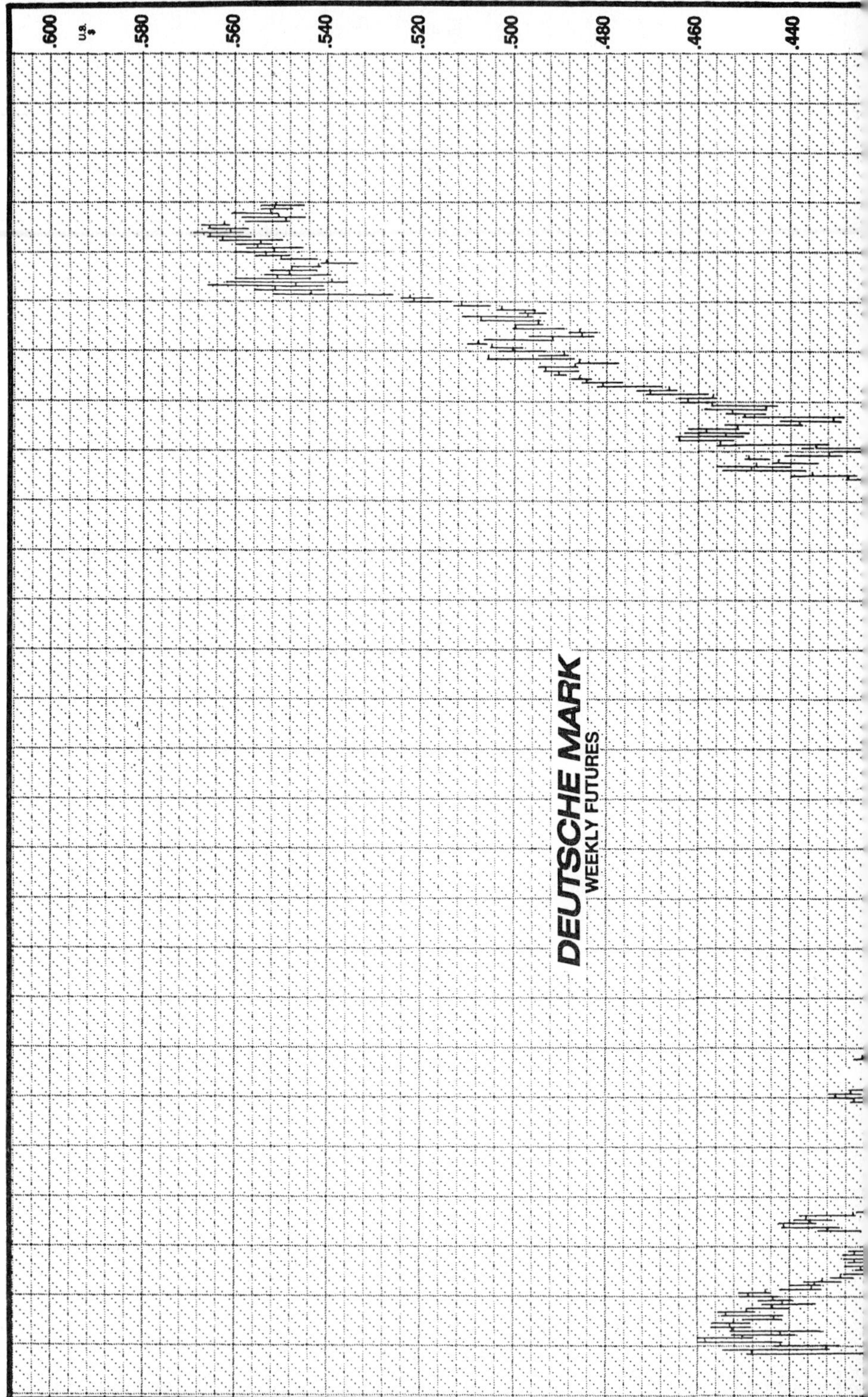

DEUTSCHE MARK
WEEKLY FUTURES
.600
U.S. $
.580
.560
.540
.520
.500
.480
.460
.440

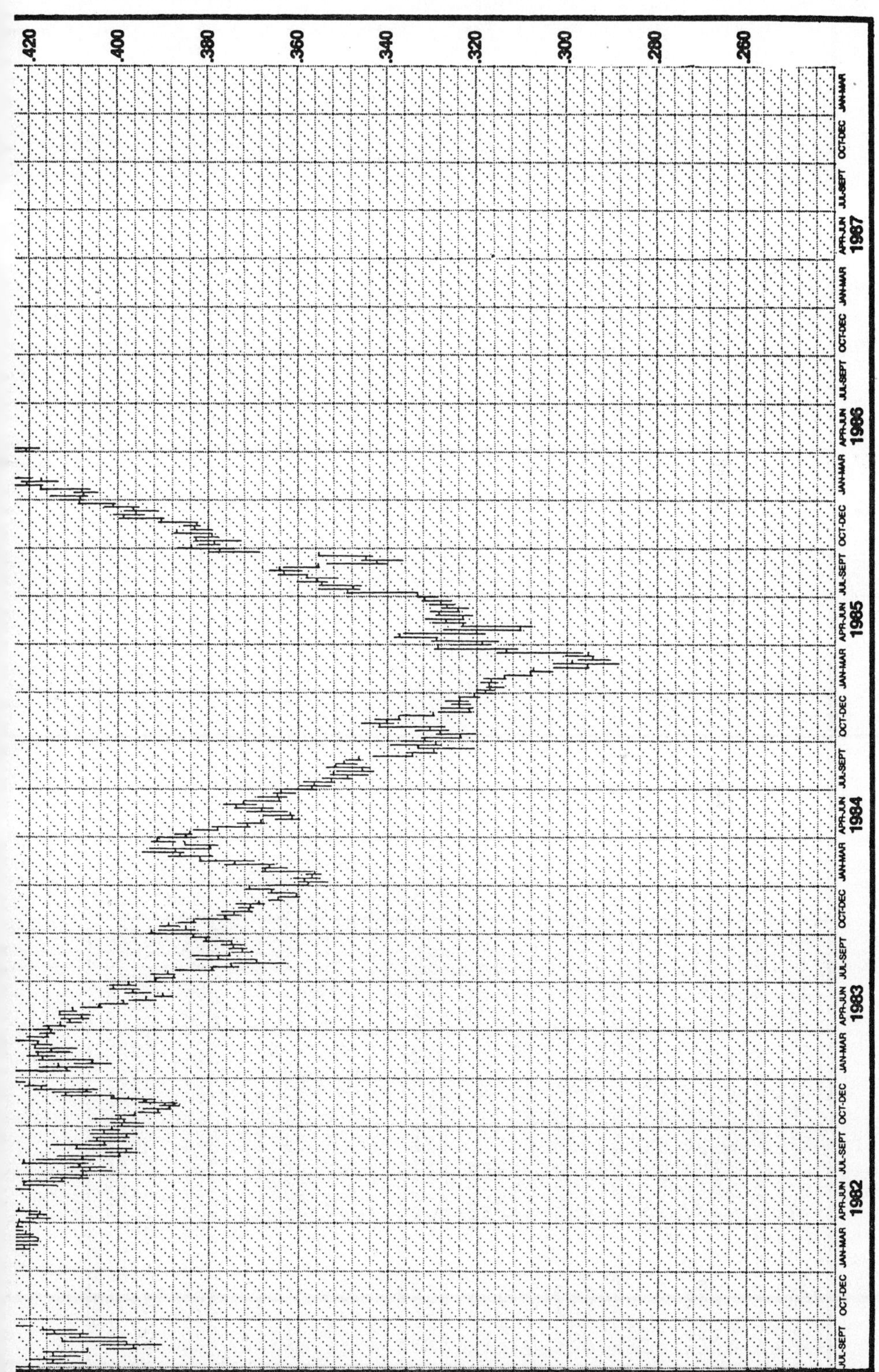
.420
.400
.380
.360
.340
.320
.300
.280
.260
JUL-SEPT
OCT-DEC
JAN-MAR
APR-JUN
1982
JUL-SEPT
OCT-DEC
JAN-MAR
APR-JUN
1983
JUL-SEPT
OCT-DEC
JAN-MAR
APR-JUN
1984
JUL-SEPT
OCT-DEC
JAN-MAR
APR-JUN
1985
JUL-SEPT
OCT-DEC
JAN-MAR
APR-JUN
1986
JUL-SEPT
OCT-DEC
JAN-MAR
APR-JUN
1987
JUL-SEPT
OCT-DEC
JAN-MAR

Weekly High, Low & Close Charts of the Nearest Futures Contract: Long-term charts are plotted for the nearest futures contract on a weekly basis. During the week of change-over, the price action of both the expiring contract and the next one are included in the week's range.

Contract months used for plotting CPC weekly and monthly supplements.

Cattle	Apr., June, Aug., Oct., Dec., Feb.
Hogs	Apr., June, July, Aug., Oct., Dec., Feb.
Feeder Cattle	Jan., March, Apr., May, Aug., Sept., Oct., Nov.
Pork Bellies	Feb., March, May, July, Aug.
Corn	March, May, July, Sept., Dec.
Oats	March, May, July, Sept., Dec.
Soybeans	Jan., March, May, July, Aug., Sept., Nov.
Soybean Meal	Jan., March, May, July, Aug., Sept., Oct., Dec.
Soybean Oil	Jan., March, May, July, Aug., Sept., Oct., Dec.
Chicago Wheat	March, May, July, Sept., Dec.
K.C. Wheat	March, May, July, Sept., Dec.
Mpls. Wheat	March, May, July, Sept., Dec.
Cotton	March, May, July, Oct., Dec.
Lumber	Jan., March, May, July, Sept., Nov.
Crude Oil	All contracts
Reg. Gas	All contracts
Heating Oil	All contracts
Currencies	March, June, Sept., Dec.
Int. Rates	March, June, Sept., Dec.
Stock Indices	March, June, Sept., Dec. (except MMI)
Major Market Index	All contracts
Cocoa	March, May, July, Sept., Dec.
Coffee	March, May, July, Sept., Dec.
Orange Juice	Jan., March, May, July, Sept., Nov.
Sugar	March, May, July, Oct.
Copper	March, May, July, Sept., Dec.
Silver	March, May, July, Sept., Dec.
Gold	Feb., April, June, Aug., Oct., Dec.
Palladium	March, June, Sept., Dec.
Platinum	Jan., Apr., July, Oct.

These weekly charts are plotted through June 26, 1987. Weekly charts are published on a quarterly schedule, and the next mailing is on Oct. 9, 1987. Monthly charts are published semi-annually. The next mailing will be August 14, 1987.

.900
U.S. ¢
.850
.800
.750
.700
.650

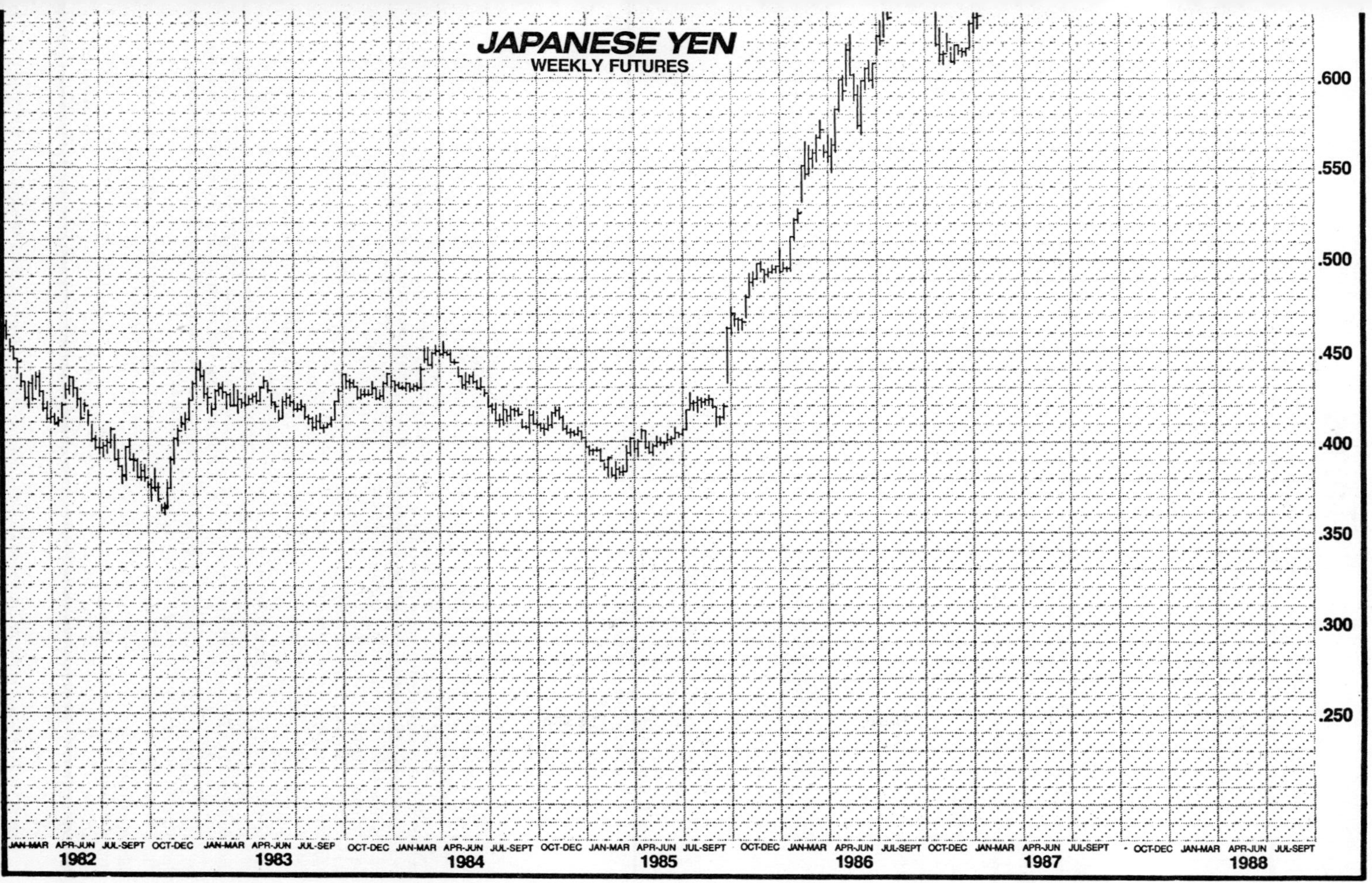
JAPANESE YEN
WEEKLY FUTURES
.600
.550
.500
.450
.400
.350
.300
.250
JAN-MAR APR-JUN JUL-SEPT OCT-DEC
1982
JAN-MAR APR-JUN JUL-SEP OCT-DEC
1983
JAN-MAR APR-JUN JUL-SEPT OCT-DEC
1984
JAN-MAR APR-JUN JUL-SEPT OCT-DEC
1985
JAN-MAR APR-JUN JUL-SEPT OCT-DEC
1986
JAN-MAR APR-JUN JUL-SEPT OCT-DEC
1987
JAN-MAR APR-JUN JUL-SEPT
1988

Taxes

UNDER THE 1986 LAW

Individual Taxation

Basic Rate Structure

The Act replaces the current 14-bracket rate structure, which has rates ranging from 11 to 50 percent, with a five-bracket structure for 1987 and a two-bracket structure for 1988 and later years.

Joint Returns—1987:

Taxable Income	Marginal Tax Rate
0–$ 3,000	11%
$ 3,000– 28,000	15
28,000– 45,000	28
45,000– 90,000	35
90,000 and over	38.5

Joint Returns—1988:

Taxable Income	Marginal Tax Rate
0–$29,750	15%
$29,750 and over	28

Single Returns—1987:

Taxable Income	Marginal Tax Rate
0–$ 1,800	11%
$ 1,800– 16,800	15
16,800– 27,000	28
27,000– 54,000	35
54,000 and over	38.5

Single Returns—1988:

Taxable Income	Marginal Tax Rate
0–$17,850	15%
$17,850 and over	28

For 1988 and later years, the benefit of the 15 percent tax bracket is phased out for higher income individuals and families. The phase out is accomplished by imposing a 5 percent surcharge on taxable income between $71,900 and $149,250 for joint returns and between $43,150 and $89,560 for single individuals. *The surcharge produces the effective marginal tax rate of 33 percent.* For 1987, there is no phase out of the benefits of the lower tax brackets.

For joint returns, the 15 percent tax bracket on the first $29,750 of taxable income saves $3,867.50 in taxes, compared with imposing a 28 percent rate on that income. A 5 percent surcharge on the $77,350 of taxable income between $71,900 and $149,250 will just recapture the $3,867.50. Thus, a taxpayer with $149,250 of taxable income will pay $41,790 in tax, 28 percent of $149,250.

The drop in marginal rates between 1986 and 1987 and between 1987 and 1988 will increase the advantage of deferring income and accelerating deductible expenses. Taxpayers will want to be careful that plans for income deferral do not push the taxpayer into the alternative minimum tax or the limit on investment interest.

Standard Deduction

Under the Act, the zero bracket amount (ZBA) is replaced by a standard deduction. For 1987 and 1988, the standard deduction is as follows:

Filing Status	Standard Deduction 1987	Standard Deduction 1988
Joint returns	$3,760	$5,000
Heads of households	2,540	4,400
Single individuals	2,540	3,000
Married individuals filing separately	1,880	2,500

Note: The elderly and blind may apply the 1988 standard deductions in 1987.

For those age 65 or over or blind, an extra standard deduction of $600 is allowed an individual if married, or $750 if single. The amounts are indexed for inflation beginning in 1989. These deductions replace the extra personal exemptions which are repealed. For those both elderly and blind, two extra standard deductions are allowed.

Personal Exemption

The Act increases the personal exemption for individuals, spouses, and dependents from its 1986 level of $1,080 to $1,900 for 1987, $1,950 for 1988, and $2,000 for 1989. The $2,000 personal exemption will be indexed for inflation beginning in 1990. The personal exemption is phased out for higher income individuals and families by imposing a 5 percent surcharge on taxable income above specified levels. The phase out begins at taxable income of $149,250 for joint returns, $123,790 for heads of household, $89,560 for single individuals, and $113,300 for married individuals filing separately. The phase out range is $10,920 per exemption in 1988 and $11,200 per exemption in 1989. For a four-person family, the phase out in 1988 ends at $192,930 of taxable income. *During the phase out of personal exemptions, the effective marginal tax rate is 33 percent on additional dollars of income. After personal exemptions are phased out, the marginal tax rate falls to 28 percent.*

In addition, an individual who is eligible to be claimed as a dependent on another taxpayer's return is not permitted a personal exemption. To reduce the number of dependents required to file tax returns and pay tax on small amounts of income, dependents may use up to $500 (reduced first by any earned income) of their standard deduction to offset unearned income.

Chart 1 compares the marginal rate schedules for joint returns for 1986, 1987 and 1988.

The personal exemption and the standard deduction together define the minimum income that an individual may receive without owing federal income tax, as shown in Table 1.

PERSONAL INCOME TAXES – MARRIED COUPLES

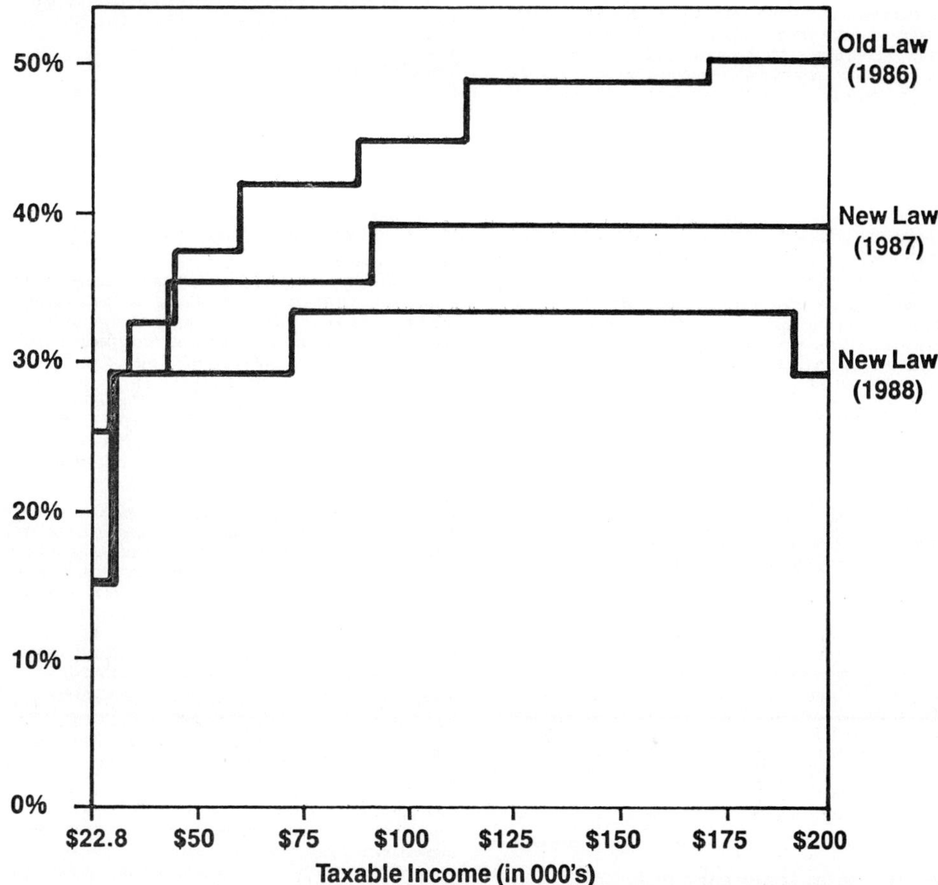

Notes: The rate schedule for 1986 has been adjusted to convert the zero bracket amount into a standard deduction. Also, for 1988, a four-person family is assumed.

Table 1. Income Tax Thresholds in 1987 and 1988

	Prior Law[a]	New Law
1987		
Single, No Dependents	$3,650	$ 4,440
Head of Household, 1 Dependent[b]	4,760	6,340
Married Couple	5,980	7,560
Married Couple, 2 Dependents[b]	8,200	11,360
1988		
Single, No Dependents	$3,700	$ 4,950
Head of Household, 1 Dependent[b]	4,820	8,300
Married Couple	6,060	8,900
Married Couple, 2 Dependents[b]	8,300	12,800

[a]Assumes inflation adjustment of 2.5 percent in 1987 and 4 percent in 1988.
[b]Excludes the effect of the earned income credit.

The dramatic increase in the income tax thresholds will remove 6 million low-income families and individuals from the income tax rolls.

Two-Earner Deduction; Income Averaging

Both the two-earner deduction and income averaging are repealed. *The flatter rate schedule and wider tax brackets reduce the marriage penalty for most two-earner couples and the need for averaging. Because of the phase-outs of the 15 percent tax bracket and personal exemptions, however, some higher-income two-earner families will have a marriage penalty greater than under prior law.*

Individual Capital Gains

The Act repeals the capital gains exclusion for individuals. Capital gains will be taxed at the same rates as other income, but in 1987, the top capital gains rate will be limited to 28 percent by means of an alternative tax computation like the old 25 percent alternative tax repealed in 1978. The Act does not provide for indexing the basis of capital assets.

As full taxation of capital gains does not begin until 1987, taxpayers may want to accelerate into 1986 the realization of long-term gains that otherwise might be realized in 1988 or 1989. But taxpayers probably should not accelerate the realization of gains that otherwise would not be realized for a number of years because the deferral of tax can be more valuable than the lower rate. Also, Congress could once again lower the tax rate on capital gains. If the taxpayer wants to continue to hold an investment, a wash sale to trigger gain in 1986 may still be advisable if the benefit of a lower tax on built-in gain exceeds the income potential for the amount of tax liability triggered in 1986. Brokerage commissions on such wash sales may be lower than on other types of sales.

As with ordinary income, the top marginal rate on capital gains can be as high as 33 percent if the taxpayer is in the 5 percent surcharge range or as high as 49.5 percent if the taxpayer also has real estate losses that are being phased out between $100,000 and $150,000 of income.

The Act does not repeal the concept of capital gains; rather it applies the same rates to capital gains that apply to ordinary income. The present law $3,000 limitation on the deduction of net capital losses is retained, but under the new law, a dollar of capital loss will be able to offset a full dollar of ordinary income up to the $3,000 limit.

The new law applies to gains realized before the effective date but reported on the installment method after the effective date.

Incentive Stock Options
Repeal of the capital gains exclusion will reduce the relative attractiveness of incentive stock options as a compensation technique since gain recognized upon disposition of stock acquired under the options will be taxed at ordinary rates. Nonetheless, the Act limits the granting of ISOs to grants of no more than $100,000 first exercisable in any given year. Restrictions on the order in which ISOs may be exercised are repealed. Given repeal of capital gains, no incentive exists to hold stock after exercise. Taxpayers will want to delay exercise until close to expiration or the time they wish to sell.

Exclusions from Income

The Act modifies a variety of the exclusions from income provided under prior law. Under the Act, unemployment compensation is fully taxed, the $100/$200 dividend exclusion is repealed, awards for artistic, scientific and charitable achievement are taxed unless assigned to a charity, and employee productivity awards are treated as compensation. The exclusion for scholarships is limited to the amount of tuition and course-required fees, books and supplies awarded to degree candidates (effective for taxable years beginning on or after January 1, 1987 for awards granted on or after August 16, 1986). The employee educational assistance exclusion is extended through 1987 and the limit is increased to $5,250. The dependent care assistance exclusion is limited to $5,000 ($2,500 for married filing separately). Finally, the pre-paid legal services exclusion is extended through 1987.

Itemized and Other Deductions

Medical Expenses and Health Insurance
The floor under the medical expense deduction is increased from 5 to 7.5 percent of the taxpayer's adjusted gross income. The Act permits self-employed individuals to deduct 25 percent of the amounts paid for health insurance on behalf of the self-employed individuals (but not in excess of self-employment income) and dependents, if such individuals are not eligible to participate in an employer-subsidized health plan. The provision is effective for taxable years beginning in 1987, 1988, and 1989.

State and Local Taxes
The itemized deduction for state and local sales taxes is repealed. *Taxpayers will want to consider accelerating planned major purchases into 1986 so as to preserve the sales tax deduction.* However, sales taxes (and other nonfederal taxes) which are not allowed as an itemized deduction and which are attributable to the purchase of property are added to the basis of such property. The deduction for state and local income and property taxes is unchanged.

Interest Expense
The Act disallows any deduction for personal interest (such as interest on credit card debt for personal expenses, automobile loans, and tax deficiencies). Mortgage interest on the taxpayer's principal and one other residence is deductible to the extent the mortgage does not exceed the cost of the home plus improvements. Interest on additional mortgage indebtedness (up to fair market value) incurred for qualified educational or medical expenses can also be deducted. In addition, investment interest may be deducted only to the extent of investment income. This latter limitation is discussed below in the section on "Tax Shelters and Real Estate."

These interest limitation rules will place a premium on the characterization of interest expenses. For example, taxpayers in the past may have treated interest used to fund investments or to buy into a business venture as personal interest. Under the new law, care should be taken to create a record establishing the link between a business or investment and related debt. For example, business expenses could be financed through credit card debt while the charges on a separate card used for personal purposes are paid currently.

Taxpayers who have outstanding disputes with the IRS will want to consider their options either to settle the case or to pay tax and sue for a refund before the interest with respect to the disputed liability becomes nondeductible.

Special effective date. — The disallowance of personal interest is phased in over five years starting in 1987. In 1987, 35 percent of previously deductible interest is non-deductible. Interest on mortgage debt incurred prior to August 17, 1986, is not subject to the limitation relating to purchase price plus improvements. The disallowance increases to 60 percent in 1988, 80 percent in 1989, 90 percent in 1990, and 100 percent in later years. *The limitations on mortgage interest to an amount not exceeding the interest on the purchase price and cost of improvements may adversely affect .axpayers who refinanced homes to pull out post-acquisition appreciation after August 16, 1986.*

Charitable Deduction
For taxpayers who itemize, the deduction for charitable contributions is unchanged except the cost of certain charitable travel is no longer deductible. Also, untaxed appreciation on charitable gifts is included in the base of the alternative minimum tax. The charitable deduction for non-itemizers is allowed to expire after 1986, as was scheduled under prior law. *Many charities are concerned that the steep decline in rates and the attendant increase in the tax cost of philanthropy will reduce charitable giving.*

Casualty and Theft Losses
The Act retains the prior law treatment for casualty and theft losses except under the new law taxpayers must file timely insurance claims. *Thus, if a taxpayer fails to pursue a claim for fear of a rate increase, no deduction is allowed.*

Treatment of Losses on Deposits in Insolvent Financial Institution
The Act permits individuals to deduct losses on deposits in qualified bankrupt or insolvent financial institutions as a

casualty loss in the year in which the loss can reasonably be estimated.

Special effective date. – Taxable years beginning after 1982. *Taxpayers who experienced qualified losses in prior years should consider filing amended returns.*

Employee Business Expenses and Miscellaneous Deductions
Under the Act, employee business expenses (other than those that are reimbursed) are permitted only as itemized deductions. Furthermore, the itemized deductions for unreimbursed business expenses and miscellaneous deductions are allowed only to the extent they exceed 2 percent of adjusted gross income.

Some employee business expenses and miscellaneous deductions are deductible as itemized deductions but not subject to the 2 percent floor: (1) moving expenses, (2) certain work expenses incurred by handicapped employees, (3) estate taxes incurred as a result of a decedent's income, (4) amortizable bond premiums, (5) interest expenses of short sales, (6) certain expenses incurred by cooperative housing corporations, (7) amounts included in the prior year's gross income because taxpayer was deemed to have unrestricted rights, (8) certain terminated annuity payments, and (9) gambling losses to the extent of gambling winnings.

Expenses for Travel and Entertainment
Deductions for meal and entertainment expenses are limited to 80 percent of the amount incurred. Those expenses not subject to the 80 percent limit on deductibility include items taxed as compensation to the recipient; expenditures for which the taxpayer receives reimbursement (the 80 percent limit is applied to the party reimbursing the taxpayer); recreational expenses paid on behalf of the employees; items made available to the general public; or banquet expenses in 1987 and 1988 with respect to a legitimate business purpose.

Meals
The Act increased the requirements for the deductibility of business meals to conform with current rules for the deductibility of entertainment expenses. Under these rules, business meals are deductible only if (1) business is discussed before, during, or after the meal (except for an individual eating alone), and (2) the meal has a clear business purpose directly related to the active conduct of the taxpayer's trade or business.

Entertainment
The Act imposes special restrictions on certain entertainment expenses. Specifically, the deduction for ticket cost is limited to 80 percent of face value. However, a premium added to the cost of sports tickets for charitable fundraising events is deductible.

Deductions for the rental or use of a luxury skybox at a sports arena, if used by the taxpayer for more than one event, are also limited to 80 percent of the cost of regular tickets. The disallowance of the skybox deduction is phased in during taxable years beginning in 1987 and 1988 with one-third disallowed in 1987 and two-thirds disallowed in 1988. In addition, deductions for luxury water transportation are limited to twice the highest Federal per diem for U.S. travel, times the number of days in transit.

Travel
The Act eliminates deductions for expenses incurred for (1) travel as a form of education, (2) charitable travel that serves personal, recreational, or vacation purposes, or (3) the expenses of attending a convention or seminar for investment purposes.

Two Percent Floor
Otherwise allowable travel, meals, and entertainment expenses will be aggregated with miscellaneous deductions and subject to the 2 percent of AGI floor. As a result, the taxpayer may not be able to fully utilize the 80 percent deduction for meals and entertainment expenses.

Other Individual Changes
The Act also

- repeals the deduction for certain adoption expenses
- repeals the credit for political contributions
- allows ministers and military personnel a full deduction for mortgage interest and real property taxes
- makes permanent the special filing status rule for spouses of MIAs
- increases the earned income credit
- tightens the hobby loss and home office deduction rules.

Individual Income Tax Effective Dates

Except where otherwise explicitly noted, the changes made to the individual income tax are effective for taxable years beginning after 1986.

Income Shifting and Trusts and Estates

Income Shifting
The Act substantially restricts a parent's ability to lower the effective tax rate on investment income by transferring assets to a child. Specifically, the net unearned income of a child under age 14 is taxed to the child as if it were the parent's income. The tax is calculated by determining what the parent's tax would have been if the child's net unearned income were added to the parent's taxable income. As a result, the child's income may be subject to the 5 percent surcharge effecting a phase out of lower bracket and personal exemption benefits. An exception is provided for the first $500 of taxable, unearned income. A dependent is also allowed to use the greater of $500 of the standard deduction or the amount of allowable deductions which are directly connected with the production of the unearned income to offset unearned income. *Thus, effectively, a child may have up to $1,000 or more if allowable deductions exceed $500 of unearned income before tax is imposed at the parent's rates.* The child's earned income and the first $500 of taxable, unearned income are taxed to the child at the child's marginal tax rate.

Effective date. – Taxable years beginning after date of enactment. No relief is provided for income attributable to assets previously transferred to children.

Trusts
The rate structure for non-grantor trusts is revised to reduce the benefits derived from income-splitting. Specifically, the first $5,000 of taxable income of the trust is taxed at 15 percent. Any excess is taxed at 28 percent. In addition, the benefit of the 15 percent rate is phased out between $13,000 and $26,000 of such income.

Prior law provided a rather complex set of rules requiring the person who created a trust to pay tax on the income of that trust (commonly referred to as the grantor trust rules). The Act amends existing rules to classify as grantor trusts two special trusts which previously escaped these provisions – the Clifford Trust and the Spousal Remainder Trust. A Clifford Trust or Spousal Remainder Trust allowed the shifting of income to the trust or a beneficiary. After the trust terminated, the trust property was returned to the grantor or the grantor's spouse. The Act provides that income from transfers after March 1, 1986, which will revert to either the grantor or his spouse will be taxed at the grantor's tax rates if, as of the inception of the trust, the revisionary interest exceeds 5 percent of the value of such trust. Thus, the Clifford Trust and Spousal Remainder Trust will cease to be viable income shifting techniques.

All trusts, other than tax exempt trusts and wholly charitable trusts, must adopt a calendar year as their taxable year. In addition, trusts are now required to pay estimated taxes in the same manner as individuals.

Estates
Under the Act, the undistributed income of estates is taxed at the same rates as are applicable to trusts. In addition, the Act now requires estates to make estimated income tax payments. However, there is an exception which provides that estates are not required to pay estimated taxes for their first two taxable years. Any amount not paid as estimated taxes may no longer be paid in four quarterly installments, but must be paid in full on the due date of the estate's income tax return.

Effective dates. – The rate changes are effective on July 1, 1987. 1987 returns will use a schedule that blends the old and new rates. The changes in grantor trust rules are generally effective for transfers in trust made after March 1, 1986. The change in taxable year rules is effective beginning after December 31, 1986. Net income distributed to beneficiaries in a short taxable year is included in the beneficiary's income over a four-year period. The requirement that trusts and estates pay estimated taxes is effective after December 31, 1986.

Generation-Skipping Transfer Tax
The Act imposes a simplified, flat rate tax on generation-skipping transfers, including direct generation-skipping transfers. However, a skip to a grandchild whose parent was a direct descendant of the transferor, but is deceased at the time of transfer, is not treated as a generation-skipping transfer. The new rate is equal to the maximum estate and gift tax rate. The present credit and grandchild exclusion are replaced by a $1 million exemption per transferor. Additional exemptions are provided for aggregate transfers of up to $2 million per grandchild for direct skips prior to January 1, 1990. In addition, a credit equal to 5 percent of state taxes on generation-skipping transfers is permitted against the generation-skipping transfer tax.

Effective date. – Testamentary transfers occurring after enactment and inter vivos transfers after September 25, 1985. The present generation-skipping transfer tax is repealed retroactively to June 11, 1976.

Compliance and Tax Administration

Information Reporting
The Act imposes new reporting requirements on real estate transactions, awards of federal contracts, and royalty payments beginning in 1987. For real estate transactions, gross proceeds and other information generally must be reported by the person responsible for closing the transaction, such as the attorney. For federal contracts, the executive agency awarding the contract must report the award.

Individuals filing returns must report the social security number of claimed dependents who are at least 5 years old (beginning in 1987) and the amount of tax-exempt interest received (beginning in 1988).

Penalties Relating to Information Returns. – The maximum penalty for failure to file information returns or supply copies is raised from $50,000 to $100,000 for each category of failure. In addition, the Act imposes a new $5 penalty per return for failure to include correct information on an information return or copy required after 1986. The maximum penalty is $20,000 in any calendar year, except for cases of intentional disregard.

Penalties

Fraud and Negligence. – The Act expands the scope of the negligence penalty by making it applicable to all Internal Revenue taxes and to any failures to properly report an amount shown on an information return. The negligence penalty applies to the entire amount of the underpayment, not just the portion of the underpayment attributable to negligence. The component which bears interest is not changed.

The fraud penalty is increased from 50 to 75 percent and restricted to the amount of underpayment attributable to fraud. The component of the fraud penalty which bears interest is not altered.

Beginning in 1987, various other penalties are increased as follows:

- from 1/2 a percent a month to 1 percent a month per month after notice of levy for failure to pay
- from 10 to 20 percent for substantial understatements
- from $50 to $250 for failure to report tax shelter ID numbers
- to 1 percent of amounts invested for failure to register a shelter.

Interest Rates

For periods after December 31, 1986, the new law provides that the interest rate that Treasury pays to taxpayers on overpayments is the federal short-term rate plus two percentage points. The interest rate that the taxpayers pay to Treasury is the federal short-term rate plus three percentage points.

The special higher interest rate on tax shelter deficiencies (120 percent of the otherwise applicable rate) is extended to tax motivated shams or fraudulent transactions.

Interest is imposed on the accumulated earnings tax from the due date (without regard to extensions) of the income tax return for the year the tax is initially imposed.

Estimated Tax Payments by Individuals
For taxable years beginning after 1986, the individual estimated tax payment requirement is increased from 80 percent to 90 percent of the portion of the current year's tax liability. The alternative test of 100 percent of the preceding year's liability remains unchanged. Under the new law, quarterly estimated payments must be made for the unrelated business income tax and the excise tax on private foundations.

Under the Act, authority is granted to the IRS to suspend various administrative actions and abate interest in specific cases.

Tax Shelters and Real Estate

The new law severely restricts the benefits of tax shelters by imposing new limitations on the utilization of passive losses to shelter non-passive income, by tightening the limitations on the deductibility of investment interest expense, and by cutting back on the deductions and credits that give rise to tax shelters. For taxpayers with significant investments in tax shelters, timely planning for the new system of income taxation will be especially critical.

Passive Loss Limitations

The most significant attempt to eliminate investments in tax shelters is a provision of the Act limiting the ability of individuals to offset losses or credits from "passive" trade or business activities against "active" or "portfolio" income under both the regular tax and the minimum tax. Items of income or loss are assigned to the "passive," "active" or "portfolio" categories by reference to the nature of the activity the taxpayer engaged in to generate the particular item.

Limitation of Passive Losses and Credits
The passive loss limitation does not disallow losses and credits from passive activities but, rather, determines how and when the losses and credits can be claimed by a taxpayer. Losses from a passive activity are deductible only against income from that or another passive activity. Unused or "suspended" losses can be carried forward (but not back) indefinitely and can be used to offset passive income realized by the taxpayer in subsequent years. Taxpayers are allowed to apply prior-year suspended passive losses against current year passive income prior to the application of net operating loss carryovers or other losses from non-passive activities.

The determination of whether a loss is suspended under the passive loss limitation is made after the application of the at-risk rules and most other provisions relating to the measurement of taxable income.

Any interest expense and income attributable to a passive activity will generally be subject to the passive loss limitation and will not be subject to the limitation on investment interest. Interest on debt secured by a taxpayer's principal or second residence will not be subject to the passive loss limitation.

Credits generated by passive activities are generally treated in the same manner as losses and can only be used against the tax attributable to such activities. Credits, like losses, can be carried forward indefinitely. However, once a credit becomes allowable under the passive loss rule it is aggregated with other credits for purposes of determining whether it is subject to other limitations (e.g., the 75 percent tax liability limitation).

A taxable disposition by a taxpayer of the entire interest in a passive activity will trigger the recognition of any suspended losses attributable to that activity. The Act provides an election for property used in the activity if the basis thereof was reduced by a tax credit. Upon final disposition, the taxpayer may elect to increase the basis of the credit property (by an amount not exceeding the original basis reduction) to the extent the credit has yet to be allowed under the passive loss rules. Exchanges of a taxpayer's entire interest in an activity in a nonrecognition transaction will not trigger suspended losses.

The passive loss limitation applies to individuals, estates, trusts, and most personal service corporations. A modified form of the rule also applies to closely held corporations. Although these corporations may offset passive losses and credits against active trade or business income, the losses may not be offset against portfolio income earned by the corporation. If an affiliated group of closely held corporations files a consolidated return, the passive loss rules will be applied on a consolidated basis whereby the passive losses of one group member may be offset against the passive income of another member. The limitation is applied at the shareholder level of S corporations and will focus upon the participation of the shareholders in the business activity of the S corporation.

Definition of Passive Activity
A passive activity generally involves the conduct of a trade or business. If the taxpayer investing in that trade or business does not materially participate in the conduct of the activity, the investment is "passive." Whether an activity constitutes a passive activity must be determined separately for each taxpayer holding an interest in the activity and for each separate activity in which a taxpayer holds an interest.

Generally, rental activities with respect to real or personal property will be treated as passive activities without regard to whether the taxpayer materially participates in the activity. However, activities in which substantial services are provided, such as operating a hotel or other transient lodging facility or daily equipment rentals, do not come within this presumption that an activity is passive. In addition, the activities of a dealer in real estate are not generally treated as a rental activity.

The Act establishes a conclusive presumption that a taxpayer holding a limited partnership interest in an activity does not materially participate in that activity. Thus, income and losses attributable to a limited partnership interest will be classified as passive (with an exception for oil and gas working interests).

The new passive loss provisions should increase the number of real estate syndications structured to produce passive activity income. The real estate in these limited partnerships will be purchased with little or no debt. Taxpayers should determine what their present passive income or loss position will be for 1987 and subsequent years before making any investment decisions as to purchases or sales of limited partnership interests or interests in real estate.

Active Income or Loss
Salaries and income or loss from the conduct of a trade or business in which the taxpayer materially participates are classified as "active" under the Act. The material participation of a taxpayer in an activity is determined separately for each year the taxpayer holds an interest in the trade or business. When determining whether an activity (other than a rental activity) conducted by a closely held consolidated group is active, the material participation test is applied on a group basis and will take into account material participation by shareholders. A taxpayer must be involved in the operations of the activity on a regular, continuous, and substantial basis to be a material participant therein. In determining material participation, the performance of management functions is treated no differently than the rendering of physical labor or other types of services. Providing legal, tax, or accounting services to an activity that does not involve the providing of such services, by itself, generally will not be viewed as a material participation in such activity.

Portfolio Income and Expense
The Act provides that portfolio income is not passive income and thus may not be sheltered by passive losses and credits. Dividends on stock, REIT dividends, interest, royalties, income from annuities, RICs and REMICs (explained below), and gain or loss realized on the sale of properties providing such income are portfolio income or loss. However, income

attributable to the business of a partnership, or an S corporation, or to a lease of property is not treated as portfolio income. Any portfolio income earned by a passive activity must be accounted for separately from the other items of income or expense relating to the activity. Consequently, dividends and interest earned by a limited partnership will be separately stated and represent portfolio income of the partners.

Portfolio income is reduced by the deductible expenses (other than interest) that are clearly and directly allocable to such income. Interest expenses that are properly allocable to portfolio income will also reduce the amount thereof. Such deductions will not be attributed to a passive activity.

The legislative history states that the gain from the disposition of a passive activity is passive activity income. Conference language does not state whether the interest income received on an installment sale of a passive activity will be treated as portfolio income or passive activity income. This determination will be extremely important to holders of installment notes from current or prior years' sales of passive activities, partners in partnerships that hold installment notes, or taxpayers who own real estate directly or indirectly through limited partnerships.

Rental Real Estate Activity

As previously indicated, rental activities are treated as passive without regard to whether the taxpayer materially participates in the activity. However, the Act provides some relief by allowing individuals to offset up to $25,000 of non-passive income with losses from rental real estate activities in which the taxpayer "actively participates." The $25,000 allowance is applied by first netting income and loss from all of the rental real estate activities the taxpayer actively participates in. This relief provision will apply only if the individual does not have adequate net passive income from other sources against which the losses and credits from the rental real estate activity can be fully offset.

The $25,000 allowance is reduced by 50 percent of the amount by which the taxpayer's adjusted gross income for the year (exclusive of passive losses, IRA contributions and taxable social security benefits) exceeds $100,000. Thus, the $25,000 allowance is eliminated for taxpayers with at least $150,000 of adjusted gross income. For a married taxpayer filing separately, the allowance is $12,500 and is reduced by 50 percent of adjusted gross income in excess of $50,000. However, if married individuals live together at any time during the taxable year and file separately, the $25,000 allowance is not available.

A taxpayer will not be considered an active participant in an activity unless the taxpayer and the taxpayer's spouse own at least 10 percent (by value) of all interest in such activity. In addition, the taxpayer must actively participate in the management of the real estate by making management decisions or arranging for others to provide services (such as repairs) in a significant sense. Relevant management decisions would include approving new tenants, determining rental terms, approving capital or repair expenditures, and other similar decisions. The standard of "actively participates" is not as tough to meet as "materially participates." Nevertheless, a limited partner in such an activity will generally not be treated as meeting the active participation standard.

The Act also contains an exception for rehabilitation and low income housing credits regardless of the taxpayer's level of participation in the passive activity. These credits can be offset against the tax on up to $25,000 of non-passive income.

This exception is phased out as a taxpayer's adjusted gross income (exclusive of passive losses, IRA contributions and taxable social security benefits) increases from $200,000 to $250,000. This exception is available only to the extent non-passive income has not been offset with $25,000 of losses from rentals of real estate in which the taxpayer actively participated.

Working Interest in Oil and Gas Property

The passive loss limitation does not apply to a working interest in an oil and gas property.

Effective Date. – The passive loss limitation is effective for tax years beginning after 1986. The rule applies to all losses incurred on or after that date (without regard to when the activity was entered into) and to passive activity credits for property placed in service on or after that date. The Act does, however, contain a specific phase-in rule for passive activities that were entered into prior to the date of enactment of the Act or acquired pursuant to a contract to purchase that was binding on that date. Losses and credits attributable to those activities will be allowed against non-passive income in accordance with the following percentages:

Taxable Years Beginning In:	Percentage Allowed
1987	65%
1988	40
1989	20
1990	10
1991	0

Passive losses that are disallowed during the transitional period must be carried forward to the succeeding year. However, once carried forward, a passive loss is no longer eligible to be deducted under the transitional rule and can be offset only against net passive income during the succeeding years. The phase-in rules do not apply to application of the passive loss limitations for minimum tax purposes.

The Act also contains a specific transitional rule for investments in low-income housing that were made after 1983. Losses from that activity may be exempted from the passive loss limitation for a period up to seven years from the original investment in the low income housing.

Investment Interest Limitations

The Act generally limits the amount of nonbusiness interest a taxpayer can deduct. The disallowance of personal interest deductions and the limitations on mortgage interest deductions are discussed above under individual taxation.

The deduction for investment interest is limited to the amount of net investment income. Any disallowed investment interest expense may be carried forward indefinitely. Investment interest includes all interest (other than consumer interest and mortgage interest on the taxpayer's principal or second home) on debt not incurred in connection with the taxpayer's trade or business.

Net investment income is the excess of investment income over investment expense. The current definition of net investment income is expanded to include gain or loss from the disposition of investment property, and from a limited business interest. Investment expense is determined by using the amount of depreciation and depletion the taxpayer actually utilizes. Interest (and income) from any activity that is subject to the passive loss rules is not treated as investment interest (or investment income). However, to the extent that passive losses are allowed as a deduction under the passive loss phase-in rule, they must be subtracted from net investment income.

Effective Date. – Interest paid or incurred after 1986 regardless of when the debt arose. The new interest expense limitations are phased in over a five-year period. The phase-in generally applies to interest that would not have been disallowed under prior law, whereupon the taxpayer is allowed to deduct a portion of the newly disallowed interest. The percentages for the phase-in period are the same as those used for the phase-in of the passive loss limitation (see previous discussion).

Vacation Homes

Section 280A limits the amount an individual may deduct for expenses attributable to the rental of a vacation home whenever the personal use thereof exceeds the greater of 14 days or 10 percent of the number of days during the year for which the dwelling is rented at a fair rental. Under the limitation, deductions attributable to the rental of a vacation home cannot exceed rental income. Section 280A, however, does not limit deductions for interest or taxes. Disallowed expenses cannot be carried forward for use in future years but are instead lost forever.

The Act provides that rental activities, including the rental of a vacation home, by an individual are subject to the passive loss limitations. It also provides that all qualified interest on first and second residences is fully deductible without limitation. For a vacation home to qualify as a residence, the taxpayer's personal use of the dwelling must be extensive enough to cause the section 280A limitation to apply. Whether a taxpayer should cause a vacation home to be a second residence will require careful analysis.

If the taxpayer is not concerned with the passive loss rules because of high passive income or eligibility for the $25,000 loss exception, vacation home classification will never provide an advantage. If the passive loss rules limit a taxpayer's deductions, deliberately falling into the vacation home rules may be advantageous because all of the interest can be deducted under the second residence mortgage exception as well as those taxes allocable to personal use. However, this advantage must be offset by the permanent loss, rather than suspension, of certain deductible expenses such as those incurred for insurance, utilities, maintenance and repairs.

At-Risk Rules

The Act extends the at-risk rules of prior law to real estate activities but provides exceptions for qualified nonrecourse financing. These rules will be significant, notwithstanding the passive activity loss rules, since the at-risk rules apply first. If the at-risk rules limit a loss, it will not be available even though the taxpayer has excess passive income.

Effective date. – Property placed in service after December 31, 1986, and losses attributable to an interest in a partnership or S corporation or other pass-through entity acquired after that date.

Tax Credit for Rehabilitation Expenditures

The Act reduces the credit for rehabilitating certified historic structures from 25 percent to 20 percent and requires a full basis adjustment for the amount of the credit. For non-historic structures, a single 10 percent credit is provided for rehabilitation of structures originally placed in service before 1936. *Although historic rehabilitations will now be one of the few clear tax shelter opportunities, application of the passive loss limitations and the minimum tax will adversely affect many of these projects.*

Effective dates. – Property placed in service after 1986.

Real Estate Investment Trusts

The Act liberalizes the rules relating to REITs to provide greater flexibility in their use. In general, entities may elect REIT status, even though they failed to qualify in an earlier year, provided they have been treated as a REIT for all taxable years beginning after February 28, 1986, or have no accumulated earnings and profits for pre-REIT years. REITs may now have wholly owned subsidiaries and treat the assets, liabilities, deductions and income of a subsidiary as belonging to the REIT. The definition of "rents from real property and interest" is expanded to allow the REIT to provide services in connection with rentals, and the minimum distribution requirements are liberalized for accrued and unpaid original issue discount. The Act also provides more generous safe harbors under the prohibited transaction rules.

Effective date. – Taxable years beginning after 1986.

Cooperative Housing Corporations

Under the Act, individuals, corporations, trusts, and other taxpayers may be treated as tenant-stockholders in cooperative housing corporations. The Act provides that maintenance and lease expenses are disallowed if payments by tenant stockholders are allocated to amounts properly chargeable to the capital account of the cooperative. Separately allocated amounts of interest and taxes are deductible by the tenant-stockholders when made on a reasonable basis.

Effective date. – Taxable years beginning after 1986.

Multi-Family Residential Rental

The Act replaces prior law incentives for low income housing (preferential depreciation, amortization of rehabilitation expenditures, and special treatment of construction period interest and taxes) with a new tax credit. The Act provides two separate credits that are claimed annually for 10 years. These credits are designed to produce a credit, on a present value basis, of either 70 percent or 30 percent of qualifying expenditures. The 70 percent credit applies to non-subsidized qualifying expenditures for new construction or rehabilitation. The 30 percent credit applies to expenditures for the construction and rehabilitation of low income units financed with tax-exempt bonds and similar federal subsidies or the acquisition and rehabilitation of existing low income housing units.

The new credits are generally effective for property placed in service after December 31, 1986, and before January 1, 1990.

Real Estate Mortgage Investment Conduits

The Act creates a new tax vehicle called a real estate mortgage investment conduit (REMIC) that is intended to facilitate the issuance of mortgage-backed securities. A REMIC is an entity that holds a fixed pool of mortgages and issues multiple classes of interests in itself. A corporation, association, trust or partnership may qualify as a REMIC, if it meets certain requirements and makes a proper election to be treated as such. The assets a REMIC is allowed to hold are generally limited to mortgages secured by real property.

Investments in a REMIC consist of "regular" and "residual" interests. A regular interest entitles the holder to the receipt of a specific sum of money, the timing of which may depend upon prepayment of the mortgages held by the REMIC. A residual interest is any interest other than a regular interest. It involves payments that are contingent upon several factors and more closely resembles an equity interest. A REMIC can only have one class of residual interest and all distributions from that class must be made on a pro rata basis.

Effective date. – Taxable years beginning after December 31, 1986.

Business Income

Corporate Tax Rates

The Act reduces the top corporate tax rate from 46 percent to 34 percent. The graduated rate structure for small companies is also modified so that taxable income of $50,000 and below is taxed at a 15 percent rate and taxable income from $50,000 to $75,000 is taxed at a 25 percent rate. The benefits of the graduated rate structure are phased out as taxable income increases from $100,000 to $335,000 with an effective marginal tax rate of 39 percent in this income range. Corporations with income in excess of $335,000, in effect, will pay a flat tax at a 34-percent rate. The revised corporate rates are fully effective for taxable years beginning on or after July 1, 1987. However, income in taxable years that include July 1, 1987, will be subject to blended rates. A calendar year corporation will have a top rate of 40 percent for 1987, for example. Public utilities must normalize any excess deferred tax reserve resulting from lower corporate tax rates.

Capital Gains

The Act increases the alternative tax on capital gains recognized after 1986 from 28 to 34 percent, which is the same rate that applies to ordinary income after July 1, 1987.

Gain on Disposition

The Act eliminates the recapture of depreciation on the sale of both residential and nonresidential real property. *This will have little significance, as net capital gains will be subject to the 34 percent rate applicable to ordinary income.*

Effective date. – Gains recognized after December 31, 1986.

Investment Tax Credit

The Act repeals the regular investment tax credit (ITC) for property placed in service after December 31, 1985 except for certain transition property (see effective date discussion below). Moreover, for years beginning after December 31, 1986, any ITC allowable either as a credit for transition property or as a carryover credit is reduced by 17 1/2 percent in 1987 and by 35 percent in 1988 and later years. *Taxpayers with an NOL for 1986 may wish to carry the NOL forward rather than back if the result of a carryback would be to create excess credits from prior years which would be cut back when carried forward to subsequent years.*

In addition, the basis of transition property in which an ITC is earned must be adjusted for the entire ITC without regard to the 35 percent reduction in current and carryover credits or any election to claim a reduced credit. The Act continues to apply normalization rules to the unamortized portion of ITCs allowed to public utilities.

Capital Cost Provisions

Capital Cost Recovery Classes

The Act modifies the ACRS system for property placed in service after 1986. Two new ACRS classes are provided and depreciable property is reclassified based generally on the asset depreciation range (ADR) system of pre-1981. The recovery method is double declining balance with switch to straight line for most machinery and equipment.

The new recovery system has eight classes of property as follows:

Recovery Period	Recovery Method	Assets
3-year	Double declining balance	ADR midpoint life of 4 years and less excluding cars and light trucks
5-year	Double declining balance	ADR midpoint life of more than 4 years and less than 10 years plus: cars and light trucks, qualified technological equipment, certain renewable resource property, R&D property
7-year	Double declining balance	ADR midpoint life of 10 years and less than 16 years plus: property without an ADR life
10-year	Double declining balance	ADR midpoint life of 16 years and less than 20 years
15-year	150 percent declining balance	ADR midpoint life of 20 years and less than 25 years plus: sewage plants
20-year	150 percent declining balance	ADR midpoint life of 25 years or more, other than real property with an ADR life of 27.5 or longer
27.5-year	Straight line	Residential rental real estate, elevators, and escalators
31.5-year	Straight line	Other real property

Certain assets are assigned new ADR lives by the Act.

Asset	ADR Life
Semi-conductor manufacturing equipment	5 years
Computer based central office switching equipment	9.5 years
Railroad track	10 years
Single purpose agricultural and horticultural structures	15 years

Asset	ADR Life
Telephone distribution plant and comparable two-way communication equipment	24 years
Municipal waste-water treatment plants	25 years
Sewer pipes	50 years

Generally, the Act permits Treasury to adjust the class lives of assets (other than real estate) based on experience, under factors outlined in the conference agreement. Treasury is prohibited from extending class lives of assets placed in service before 1992. Thereafter, Congress must be notified of any changes.

The Act requires lessees to recover the cost of leasehold improvements over the general recovery periods, without regard to the lease term. For purposes of amortizing leasehold acquisition costs, the lease term includes all renewable options and any reasonably expected renewals.

Conventions. – The Act generally continues the mid-year convention for determining when personal property is placed in service or disposed of and the mid-month convention for real property. In addition, a mid-quarter convention applies if more than 40 percent of all property is placed in service during the last quarter of the taxable year.

Alternative Recovery System

Under the Act, an alternative cost recovery system is prescribed for purposes of applying the minimum tax provisions, computing earnings and profits of a domestic corporation, and computing the depreciation deduction for foreign use and tax-exempt property and property financed through tax-exempt bonds. Satellites launched from the U.S. and used by U.S. persons are not foreign use property. Generally, the applicable depreciation method is straight line, using the asset's ADR midpoint life. However, for purposes of computing the minimum tax, 150 percent declining balance depreciation over ADR midpoint life is used to measure the tax preference on personal property.

For purposes of computing regular depreciation on property otherwise eligible for ACRS, taxpayers may elect either the alternative depreciation system described above or the straight-line method over the ACRS recovery period on a class-by-class, year-by-year basis. The Act grants the President authority to deny a taxpayer the right to use the accelerated depreciation method on property produced abroad. This authority is limited to assets that have not yet been ordered.

Expensing

Taxpayers may elect to expense up to $10,000 of the cost of personal property used in a trade or business provided that the amount expensed does not exceed the income derived from any active trade or business. The $10,000 ceiling is reduced dollar for dollar for taxpayers whose total investment in tangible personal property is greater than $200,000. Furthermore, if the property is converted to non-business use prior to the end of the property's recovery period, the difference between expensing and the allowable ACRS deductions is recaptured.

Effective Dates for Depreciation and ITC

The new depreciation rules are generally effective for assets placed in service after December 31, 1986. A special election is provided to apply the modified depreciation rules to property placed in service after July 31, 1986. In addition, the Act provides anti-churning rules to prevent the use of post-effective-date transactions among related parties to depreciate property placed in service prior to January 1, 1987 under the new depreciation system.

As noted above, the repeal of the *ITC* is generally effective for property placed in service after December 31, 1985.

The Act provides that ACRS will continue to apply and the investment credit will be available for qualifying "transition property." Transition property generally is property which was subject to a binding contract or under construction before 1986 in the case of ITC and before March 1986 in the case of recovery property.

To qualify for transition relief under the Act, transition property must actually be placed in service before specific deadlines which differ for cost recovery and ITC purposes as follows:

ADR Midpoint	Recovery Property	ITC Property
under 5	N/A	July 1, 1986
under 7	N/A	January 1, 1987
under 20	January 1, 1989	January 1, 1989
20 or more	January 1, 1991	January 1, 1991
residential rental	January 1, 1991	N/A
other real property	January 1, 1991	N/A

Limitation on Business Tax Credits

The Act reduces the amount of tax liability (in excess of $25,000) which may be offset by business tax credits from 85 percent to 75 percent. *However, the imposition of a minimum tax, in many instances, will prevent a taxpayer from fully utilizing the available business credit.*

Effective Date. – Taxable years beginning after 1985. *The early effective date of this change will frustrate taxpayers seeking to maximize current use of ITC carryovers before the 35 percent cutback takes effect.*

Treatment of Corporate Distributions

Appreciated Property

The Act generally repeals the limited exceptions to gain recognition on distributions of appreciated property to shareholders in nonliquidating distributions. Thus, the exceptions to gain recognition for certain distributions of appreciated property to 10 percent noncorporate shareholders and distributions in connection with the payment of estate taxes are repealed. The Act also provides that no losses can be recognized on nonliquidating distributions.

Effective date. – Distributions of ordinary income or short-term capital gain property after December 31, 1986 and distributions of other property after December 31, 1988.

Dividends Received Deduction

Under the Act, the 85 percent dividends received deduction is reduced to 80 percent. *Under present law the combination of the 46 percent rate and the 85 percent exclusion produces an effective tax of 6.9 percent on dividends received by corporations. The new rate structure and 80 percent exclusion will yield a 6.8 percent tax.* The 100 percent deduction for qualifying dividends received from affiliates is not affected.

Effective date. – Dividends received after 1986.

Extraordinary Dividends

The Act extends the 1984 Act rules requiring a basis adjustment for the non-taxed portion of extraordinary dividends received by a corporation. The rule now applies to dividends announced or agreed to within two years of acquisition of the stock rather than only those paid within one year of the acquisition. The Act extends the definition of extraordinary dividends to include all non-pro-rata redemptions of stock and distributions in partial liquidation regardless of holding period or size of the distribution. Except as provided in regulations, the extraordinary dividend rules will not apply to distributions between members of an affiliated group filing a consolidated return.

Effective date. – Dividends announced after July 18, 1986, except date of enactment for non-pro-rata redemptions and partial liquidations.

Greenmail Payments

No deduction is allowed for any amount paid or incurred by a corporation in connection with the redemption of its stock.

This rule applies to so-called "greenmail payments." *Any such amounts paid to a selling shareholder in connection with the redemption of stock will not be deductible if paid by the corporation or a related party.*

Effective date. – Payments on or after March 1, 1986.

Liquidating Distributions

The Act generally requires corporate liquidations to be taxed at both the corporate and shareholder levels. A liquidating corporation is required to recognize gain or loss as if its assets were sold at their fair market value. This rule also requires a corporation to recognize full gain on the deemed sale of its assets if an election under section 338 is made to step up the basis of its assets following the purchase of its stock.

The Act prohibits loss recognition on non-pro-rata distributions of property to related persons if the property was acquired as a contribution to capital within five years of the liquidation. Also, a pre-contribution built-in loss may not be recognized on liquidating distribution if the property distributed was acquired as a contribution to capital within two years of the adoption of the plan of liquidation, unless no tax avoidance motive for the contribution can be shown.

The Act furthers the repeal of the "General Utilities Doctrine" begun in the 1982 and 1984 Acts. Basically, the General Utilities Doctrine permitted a corporation non-recognition treatment on distributions to shareholders. As a result of the changes in the Act, the tax cost will rarely make asset acquisitions practical unless the acquisition can qualify under the tax-free reorganization provisions of the Code. Under prior law, the total tax on the liquidation would have been the 20 percent individual tax on the capital gain plus any corporate level recapture tax. Under the Act, the total tax will rise to 52.5 percent – 34 percent at the corporate level plus 18.5 percent (28 percent of 66 percent) at the individual level.

Transition rules preserve corporate level non-recognition treatment for the following transactions involving liquidating distributions:

1. All liquidations completed before January 1, 1987. *This transition rule also includes deemed sales under section 338 even if the election is made in 1987, if the stock purchase occurred prior to January 1, 1987.*
2. Liquidating distributions pursuant to a plan of liquidation adopted before August 1, 1986 if the liquidation is completed prior to January 1, 1988.
3. Liquidating distributions and liquidating sales where there was a binding contract entered into prior to August 1, 1986 to acquire a majority of the liquidating corporation's voting stock or substantially all of its assets, if the liquidation is completed on or before December 31, 1987.
4. Deemed liquidating sales under section 338 relating to stock acquisitions occurring on or after August 1, 1986 and before January 1, 1988 when a binding contract to acquire the stock existed prior to August 1, 1986.
5. Liquidations of closely held companies valued at less than $5 million (with no more than 10 individuals owning more than 50 percent of the stock) completed before January 1, 1989 are provided relief from recognition of gain on long-term capital gain property. There is also partial relief for closely held companies valued between $5 million and $10 million.
6. Liquidations completed before January 1, 1988 in which the company had taken significant action by November 20, 1985 (e.g., the board of directors approved a plan of liquidation or entered into a binding contract to sell substantially all of its assets).

The Act generally retains present law non-recognition treatment for liquidations of a subsidiary corporation into its parent corporation. Gain on distributions of appreciated property to minority shareholders is treated as under the rules for nonliquidating distributions.

The Act provides that if a subchapter S corporation liquidates within 10 years of converting from a subchapter C corporation, it must recognize its aggregate net unrealized gains at the date of the conversion.

Effective date. – Generally, liquidating sales and distributions after July 31, 1986.

Allocation of Purchase Price in Certain Sales of Assets

The Act requires both the buyer and the seller to allocate the purchase price in asset acquisitions using the residual method. Under the residual method, the purchase price is first allocated to the fair market value of tangible and intangible assets and then allocated to the value of goodwill and going concern. In addition, the Act authorizes the Treasury Department to require further information from the parties pertaining to the allocation.

Effective date. – Transactions after May 6, 1986.

Special Limitations on Net Operating Loss (NOL) Carryovers

The NOL carryover limitations adopted in 1976 that would have become effective January 1, 1986 are repealed retroactively. Thus, the NOL rules without the 1976 changes continue to apply for 1986. Starting in 1987, the Act provides that if there is greater than 50 percent ownership change in a loss corporation within a three year period, an annual limit on the use of NOLs will be imposed. The amount of an NOL that may be used to offset earnings is limited to the value of the loss corporation at the date of ownership change multiplied by the highest federal tax-exempt long term bond rate as adjusted for differences between rates on long term taxable and tax exempt obligations in effect during the three-month period ending with the month of ownership change.

The value of a loss corporation is reduced by capital contributions motivated by tax avoidance. Except as specified by regulation, capital contributions made within the two years preceding to the ownership change are presumed to have a tax avoidance motive.

In addition, a loss corporation may not utilize NOL carryovers following taxable purchases and tax-free reorganizations unless it continues substantially the same business for two years after the change in ownership.

Exceptions to the limitations on NOL carryovers are provided for stock acquired by gift, separation, divorce or death. In addition, exceptions are generally provided for acquisitions by ESOPs or ESOP participants if the ESOP owns at least 50 percent of the stock immediately after the transfer.

If the unrealized built-in gains or losses exceed 25 percent of the value of the corporation's assets before the ownership change, then special rules apply. Under these rules, built-in gains recognized within five years of the change may be fully sheltered by carryover NOLs, and built-in losses recognized during this period are treated as pre-change losses. Furthermore, the income against which NOL carryovers can be applied is reduced, if at least one-third of the loss corporation's assets are passive. An exception is provided for both RICs and REITs.

Bankruptcy Proceedings and Stock-for-Debt Exchanges

Special rules apply to NOL carryovers following bankruptcy reorganizations. The Act provides that if the shareholders and creditors of the loss corporation own at least 50 percent of the stock of the loss corporation after bankruptcy proceedings, the change in ownership limitations will not apply. This special rule requires that the debt exchanged for stock be held for an 18-month period prior to filing for bankruptcy or be incurred in the corporation's ordinary course of business. In any event, the NOL carryover must be reduced by 50 percent of the amount by which the discharged debt exceeds the value of the stock received by the former creditors. A modified version of the bankruptcy exception applies to certain ownership changes of thrift institutions.

Effective Date. – Generally, applies to purchases made after December 31, 1986, and reorganizations pursuant to plans adopted after December 31, 1986.

For purposes of determining if a greater than 50 percent ownership change has occurred under the new rules, less than 50 percent changes in ownership occurring after May 5, 1986, and before January 1, 1987, must be aggregated with post-1986 changes.

Research and Development

The tax credit for eligible research and development expenses is extended through December 31, 1988; however, the present 25 percent tax credit is reduced to 20 percent. In addition, the general limitation on business credits is made applicable to the research credit. The Act modifies the definition of qualified research to target research that is aimed at technical discoveries. The augmented charitable deduction for the donation of newly manufactured scientific equipment to a college is extended to comparable donations to certain tax-exempt scientific research organizations.

The Act also reduces the credit for university basic research from 75 percent of corporate expenditures to 20 percent of the excess of (1) all corporate expenditures for university basic research over (2) the sum of a fixed research floor plus any decrease in nonresearch giving.

The credit for orphan drug clinical testing is extended through 1990.

Effective date. – The research credit is extended for taxable years ending after 1985. The other provisions are effective for taxable years beginning after 1985, except that modifications to the university basic research credit are effective beginning after 1986.

Other Business Changes

The Act also:

- permanently extends the elective deduction for removal of architectural barriers
- repeals elective amortization of trademarks and tradenames, and railroad gradings and tunnel bores
- reduces the depreciation limits on luxury cars to $2,560 for the first year, $4,100 for the second year, $2,450 for the third year, and $1,475 for each succeeding taxable year in the recovery period
- generally treats amortized bond premium as interest expense for all tax purposes
- repeals the exclusion for discharge of indebtedness income of solvent taxpayers which was permitted if an appropriate basis adjustment was made
- expands the definition of related party for purposes of the limits on installment sales reporting on sale of depreciable assets between related parties (effective August 14, 1986, except for binding contracts)
- provides a new simplified LIFO inventory method for taxpayers with less than $5 million in annual gross receipts
- limits the deduction for accrued vacation pay to amounts expected to be paid within 8 1/2 months of year-end
- repeals the special deduction for costs of redeeming "qualified" discount coupons
- retroactively excludes from the definitions of personal holding company income and foreign personal holding company income certain computer software royalties
- repeals the statutory finance lease rules
- generally, the Act scales back the targeted job credit and extends it for three years.

Accounting Methods

Long-Term Contracts

Under the Act, all long-term contracts other than those reported on the percentage of completion method, are subject to a modified form of the rules currently governing extended period long-term contracts. Amounts which must be capitalized include certain interest expense incurred, and costs identified by the taxpayer as being attributable to the contract. For example, general and administrative expenses identified pursuant to a cost-plus contract or pursuant to a contract with a federal agency in which costs are certified under federal statute or regulations must be capitalized regardless of whether such costs may be treated as period costs under existing regulations. However, independent research and development costs are generally not capitalized.

The prior-law completed contract method prescribed by regulations is replaced by a new "percentage of completion – capitalized cost method," which applies to any long-term contracts except certain real property construction contracts discussed below. Under this new method, the taxpayer must take into account 40 percent of the items with respect to the contract under the percentage of completion method; the remaining 60 percent of the items will be taken into account under the taxpayer's normal method of accounting.

Current rules are retained for real property construction contracts not requiring more than two years to complete and performed by a taxpayer with average annual gross receipts of $10 million or less.

Effective date. – Contracts entered into on or after March 1, 1986.

Capitalization Rules for Inventory, Construction, and Development Costs

The Act provides uniform capitalization rules for costs incurred in manufacturing property, constructing property (whether for use in a trade or business or sale to others), or purchasing and holding property for resale. The rules are patterned after the rules applicable to the extended period long-term contracts as set forth in final regulations recently issued by the Internal Revenue Service. Included are all "financial conformity" costs, all tax depreciation, current pension and fringe benefit costs, and a portion of general and administrative expenses.

Costs subject to capitalization for wholesalers and retailers include costs incident to purchasing inventories (e.g., wages of employees responsible for purchasing, repackaging and assembly), costs incurred in processing the goods while the taxpayer is in possession, costs of storing goods (only the *offsite* storage costs of retailers), and the portion of general and administrative costs allocable to these functions.

The Treasury Department is directed to provide a simplified method for applying the uniform capitalization rules to wholesalers and retailers.

In the case of property acquired by a taxpayer for resale, the uniform capitalization rules apply only if the taxpayer's average annual gross receipts for the three preceding taxable years were more than $10 million.

The new capitalization rules do not apply to research and experimental expenditures, to property produced under a long-term contract, or to property produced in a farming business.

The new rules require the capitalization of interest on debt incurred or continued to finance the construction or production of real property, long-lived personal property (a 20-year class life or longer) or other tangible property requiring two or more years to produce or construct (one year for property costing more than $1 million).

Effective date. —The new capitalization rules with respect to self-constructed property and noninventory property produced for resale will apply to costs incurred after December 31, 1986, unless incurred with respect to property on which substantial construction occurred before March 1, 1986. The same rule applies for interest. In the case of capitalized costs for inventory, the new rules take effect for taxable years beginning after December 31, 1986, and will be treated as a change in accounting method initiated by the taxpayer. The adjustment necessary to effect the change will be included in income ratably over a period of not more than four years.

The uniform capitalization rules will require taxpayers to identify certain period costs that will continue to be expensed for books but must now be capitalized for tax reporting purposes.

Installment Sales

One of the more important accounting provisions of the Act is the change made to installment sales reporting. Under the provision, the use of the installment method is completely eliminated for sales made pursuant to a revolving credit plan and for sales of certain publicly traded property. This provision is effective for sales of property after December 31, 1986. Taxpayers who will no longer be able to use the installment method for sales made under a revolving credit plan may include the resulting adjustment in income over a period not exceeding four years, taking 15 percent into account in the first year, 25 percent in the second year, and 30 percent in each of the succeeding two taxable years.

The provision effectively denies the use of the installment method for a portion of the sale made by dealers selling under the installment plan (rather than a revolving credit plan) and non-dealers selling business or rental property, the selling price of which exceeds $150,000. This denial is achieved by determining the taxpayer's "allocable installment indebtedness" (AII) for each taxable year and treating such amount as a payment immediately before the close of the taxable year on "applicable installment obligations" (AIO) which arose during the year and are still outstanding as of year end. The AII is determined by dividing (1) the AIO outstanding at year end by (2) the sum of (a) the face amount of all installment obligations and (b) the adjusted basis of all other assets. The result is then multiplied by the average quarterly indebtedness (annual basis for taxpayers who have no AIOs that arose from the sale on the installment method of either personal property by a person who regularly sells property of the same type on the installment method, or real property that was held for sale to customers in the ordinary course of a trade or business). Finally any AII that is attributable to AIOs in prior years is subtracted. In computing the AIO, installment obligations arising from the sale of personal use property by an individual and property used or produced in the trade or business of farming are omitted.

A special election is available for sales of "time shares" or unimproved land by a dealer to an individual. If the election is made, the proportionate disallowance rules will not apply to such installment obligations provided interest is paid on the deferral of the tax liability attributable to the use of the installment method.

An exception is provided for installment sales by a manufacturer to a dealer if (1) the terms are dependent upon when the property is disposed of by the dealer, (2) the manufacturer has the right to repurchase the property from the dealer if it is not disposed of within a specified period, (3) and the amount of these installment obligations exceeds 50 percent of the total sales to dealers giving rise to such obligations.

Generally, the limitation on the use of the installment method based on the proportionate disallowance rule is effective for taxable years ending after December 31, 1986, with respect to sales of property after February 28, 1986. Special transitional rules are provided for, depending on the type of property sold and the activity of the seller.

Limitations on the Use of Cash Method of Accounting

The Act prohibits the use of the cash method of accounting by any C corporation, partnership that has a C corporation as a partner, tax exempt trust with unrelated business income, or tax shelter. An exception from this prohibition is provided for certain entities (other than tax shelters), including farming and timber businesses, entities with average annual gross receipts of $5 million or less (based on the average of the prior three taxable years), and qualified personal service corporations.

A qualified personal service corporation is one that performs substantially all of its activities in certain fields and is substantially employee-owned (i.e., at least 95 percent). The specified fields include: (1) health, (2) law, (3) engineering, (4) architecture, (5) accounting, (6) actuarial science, (7) performing arts, and (8) consulting. Employee ownership includes: (1) present or retired employees who perform or had performed service for such corporation in connection with the qualified services performed by the company, (2) the estate of such present or retired employees, and (3) persons who acquired an ownership interest as a result of the death of a present or retired employee within a two-year period beginning with the death of such employee. Stock held by any plan described in section 401(a) of the Code that is exempt from tax under section 501(a) is treated as held by the employees of the entity. At the election of the common parent of an affiliated group, all members of such affiliated group may be treated as a single entity for the purposes of applying the ownership test if substantially all of the activities of such members involve the performance of services in the same qualified field.

In addition, payments made by a personal service corporation to employee-owners will not be deductible prior to the time that such employee-owners would include the payment in gross income.

Effective date. —The provision is effective for taxable years beginning after December 31, 1986, with any adjustment required to be taken into income over a period not to exceed four years.

Taxable Years of Partnerships, S Corporations, and Personal Service Corporations

The Act significantly changes the current rules regarding the adoption of or change in the taxable year of partnerships, S corporations, and personal service corporations.

A partnership must use the same year end as that of the partners owning the majority interest in the profits and capital. If such a majority does not have the same taxable year, the partnership is then required to adopt the taxable year of all of its principal partners. If neither of these first two situations applies, the partnership must adopt a calendar year.

S corporations and personal service corporations do not have the same flexibility as partnerships do, and must use a calendar year end. However, as under current IRS procedures, a partnership, S corporation, or personal service corporation may adopt or change to a different taxable year than that prescribed above, if it establishes to the satisfaction of the Secretary of the Treasury a business reason for doing so, such as a "natural business year." The Act repeals the present rule that accepts a year end which results in a three months' or less deferral to the partners or shareholders as being an adequate business reason.

Any partnership that received IRS permission under Rev. Proc. 74-33 to use a fiscal year on the basis that it had a natural business year rather than under the automatic rules permitting deferrals of three months or less is allowed to retain such year. The same is true for S corporations that received permission after the effective date of Rev. Proc. 74-33 to use a fiscal year end (other than a year end that resulted in a three month or less deferral).

Effective date. – Taxable years beginning after December 31, 1986. A partner in a partnership or a shareholder in an S corporation that would otherwise be required by this provision to include more than 12 months of income in a single taxable year may include such excess (income minus expenses for the short year required to effect the changes) in income ratably over a period of four taxable years. The rule applies to income from an S corporation only if such corporation was an S corporation for a taxable year beginning in 1986.

Income realized during the adjustment period will be spread over the years 1987 through 1990 in the case of partnerships and subchapter S corporations. By accelerating 1988 income into the adjustment period, taxpayers will be able to defer half of this income to 1989 and 1990, but one-quarter of the income will be accelerated into 1987.

Reserve Method for Bad Debts

The use of the reserve method for deducting bad debts and for losses on debts guaranteed by a dealer is repealed. An exception is provided for thrift institutions and "small" banks. (See below for a discussion of financial institutions changes.) Taxpayers affected by this change will be required to switch to the specific charge-off method allowed under current law. The switch to the specific charge-off method is a change in accounting method whereby the reserve balance is to be restored to income over a four-year period. *Taxpayers will want to carefully evaluate reserve additions for the last year under the reserve method.*

Under the specific charge-off method, a deduction for a partially worthless debt can be taken only in the year the debt is charged off on the books. No such rule applies to wholly worthless debts.

Effective date. – Taxable years beginnning after December 31, 1986.

Utilities Using Accrual Accounting

Under prior law, many utilities did not include services provided to customers after the last meter reading or billing for the year (unbilled revenue) in current income. The Act requires providers of utility services who use the accrual basis of accounting to recognize income attributable to the furnishing or sale of utility services to customers not later than the taxable year in which such services are provided. The adjustment to income resulting from the change in accounting method is recognized ratably over four years.

Effective date. – Taxable years beginning after December 31, 1986.

Contributions in Aid of Construction

Prior tax law permitted regulated public utility providers of electric, gas, water or sewer services to treat contributions in aid of construction (CIAC) as non-taxable contributions to capital. Property purchased with such contributions could not be depreciated for tax purposes.

The Act repeals the special provisions pertaining to contributions in aid of construction, thus taxing CIAC as ordinary income in the year received. Property purchased with these funds may be depreciated for tax purposes under ACRS or any other applicable depreciation method. (No ITC will be available under the new tax bill.)

Effective date. – Contributions received after December 31, 1986.

Financial Accounting Implications

The Act has important implications for financial reporting: When should the effects of the Act be recognized in financial statements? How will deferred taxes be adjusted? How will the 35 percent reduction in carryover investment tax credits be treated?

Timing

The effects of the new legislation *must* be recognized in year end and interim financial statements issued for periods ending on or after the date of enactment, that is, the date the President signs the legislation into law. Year end and interim financial statements for periods ending before the date of enactment, but issued after that date, cannot recognize the effects of the new legislation under the Financial Accounting Standards Board's proposals for implementing the accounting aspects of the Act. These proposals may change before final adoption.

Deferred Taxes

Many companies have set up deferred taxes at a 46 percent rate. Should these deferred taxes be adjusted to reflect the lower corporate tax rate? Under current rules, the reductions in corporate rates are reflected in financial statements only when the timing differences that caused them reverse. However, the Financial Accounting Standards Board (FASB) has proposed to replace the current method of accounting for deferred taxes with the "liability" method. If the FASB adopts this method for deferred taxes (expected in 1987), companies will make a one-time adjustment in their deferred taxes to reflect the reduction in corporate rates. This will boost shareholder equity.

Investment Tax Credit
Companies with ITC carryovers often are able to book them for financial accounting purposes. If the allowable carryovers are reduced by 35 percent, must this change be reflected in financial statements? Current accounting standards do not permit companies to make an adjustment. If the FASB adopts the liability method for deferred taxes, the reduction in the ITC carryover probably would be netted against the deferred tax adjustment.

Minimum Tax

Under prior law, minimum taxes were imposed on individuals and corporations as a back-stop to the regular tax. Congress was concerned that wealthy individuals and profitable corporations should pay at least some tax. Under the Act, the minimum tax is elevated from its back-stop role to a central position in the tax system. Congressional policy is now that all high income individuals and corporations should pay a substantial tax.

Basic Structure

Taxpayers must pay the higher of their regular tax liability or their minimum tax liability. The minimum tax liability is 21 percent (20 percent in the case of corporations) of the taxpayer's alternative minimum taxable income reduced by the allowable exemption amount. The exemption amount is $40,000 for corporations and married taxpayers filing a joint return, and $30,000 for single taxpayers. The exemption amount is reduced 25 cents for each dollar by which AMTI exceeds $150,000 ($112,500 for single taxpayers). For married taxpayers filing a separate return, the exemption amount is $20,000 and phases out above $75,000 of AMTI.

The impact of the minimum tax will be expanded dramatically simply by reason of the narrowing of the gap between the minimum tax rates and the regular tax rates. Under prior law, the individual minimum tax rate was only 40 percent of the top regular individual tax rate; now the individual minimum tax rate (21 percent) is 75 percent of the top regular individual tax rate (28 percent). If an individual is in the midst of the phase out of the exemption amount, an additional dollar of income will be taxed at an effective marginal rate of 26.25 percent under the minimum tax.

The alternative minimum tax may be reduced by foreign tax credits (up to 90 percent of liability). For corporations, ITC on transition property or ITC carried over from prior years may reduce regular tax liability down to 75 percent of minimum tax liability, or if minimum tax exceeds regular tax, these credits may offset up to 25 percent of minimum tax liability. The 35 percent reduction in ITC under the regular tax also applies for minimum tax purposes.

The prohibition on offsetting more than 90 percent of minimum tax liability with foreign tax credits expands the traditional reach of U.S. taxation. A U.S. taxpayer who has only foreign source income taxed at a rate higher than the U.S. rate has, in the past, paid only the foreign tax on that income. Now, the U.S. will impose an effective tax of 2 percent on that income (2.1% in the case of individuals).

Computation of AMTI
The computation of income for minimum tax purposes differs substantially from the computation of income for purposes of the regular tax. The Act prescribes specific adjustments to the regular tax and specific preference amounts that must be taken into account in determining AMTI. These are described below.

Adjustments and Preferences

Adjustments and Preferences for Both Individuals and Corporations
Depreciation. — For minimum tax purposes, depreciation on personal property is computed using the 150 percent declining balance method over an asset's ADR midpoint life for assets (other than transition property) placed in service after 1986. Real estate (other than transition property) placed in service after 1986 is depreciated using the straight line method over 40 years. This adjustment effectively treats accelerated depreciation on real and personal property as a tax preference. Since depreciation is a substantial portion of many taxpayers' tax calculation, this provision will subject many taxpayers to the minimum tax.

For property placed in service before 1987, or under the transition rules of the Act, accelerated depreciation is a preference only to the extent provided under prior law.

When property acquired after 1986 (other than transition property) is disposed of, gain or loss for minimum tax purposes will be computed by reference to basis as adjusted for depreciation allowed under the minimum tax.

Tax-exempt interest. — Generally, tax-exempt interest on private activity bonds issued after August 7, 1986, is included in income for minimum tax purposes.

Untaxed appreciation on charitable contributions. — The charitable deduction for contributions of appreciated property is computed by limiting the value of the contribution to its adjusted basis.

Accounting methods. — The percentage of completion method of accounting must be used with respect to long-term contracts entered into after February 1, 1986 and installment sales treatment is not available for almost all installment sales made after March 1, 1986.

Intangible drilling costs. — Excess IDC deductions (but only to the extent that amount is in excess of 65 percent of net income from oil, gas and geothermal properties) are added to income as a tax preference.

Mining exploration and development costs. — Exploration and development costs incurred after 1986 and expensed for purposes of the regular tax must be amortized over 10 years for purposes of the minimum tax. As with depreciation, separate basis adjustments will be made for regular tax and minimum tax.

Net operating loss. — For minimum tax purposes, a separate net operating loss must be computed in a manner consistent with the adjustments and preferences defined by the minimum tax. Pre-1987 NOLs do not have to be recomputed. NOLs cannot offset more than 90 percent of AMTI.

Preferences from prior law. — The Act continues to treat as preferences: (1) excess amortization on pollution control facilities, (2) percentage depletion in excess of basis, and (3) expensing of mining exploration and development costs.

Adjustments and Preferences for Individuals Only

Passive losses. – No deduction for passive farm losses is allowed, and the limitations on passive activity losses are applied without a phase in. As with the regular tax, disallowed losses may be carried forward. The loss limitations apply to passive activity income or loss as computed for minimum tax purposes. Thus, a taxpayer who has a suspended loss for regular tax purposes may not have any loss for minimum tax purposes.

Interest expense. – The limitations on investment interest and personal interest apply (with necessary conforming modifications) under the minimum tax.

Prior law adjustments and preferences. – The Act continues the prior law minimum tax treatment of (1) circulation expenses, (2) research and experimentation expenditures, (3) itemized deductions, and (4) incentive stock options.

Adjustments and Preferences for Corporations Only

Merchant Marine Capital Construction Funds. – No deduction is allowed for amounts contributed to a capital construction fund of a shipping company and any tax free earnings after 1986 are included in income.

Bad debts. – The excess of bad debt deductions over deductions computed on the basis of actual experience is added to income of thrifts and small banks still permitted to use reserves.

Book income. – The Act requires an increase in AMTI for one-half of any excess of pre-tax book income over AMTI. Book income is the income of a corporation as reported on its financial statements. When more than one statement exists, the following priority is established: (1) SEC statements, (2) audited financials used for credit purposes or other substantial non-tax purposes, (3) regulatory filings, and (4) other non-audited statements used for credit or other substantial non-tax purposes.

The adoption of a book income preference is a novel and controversial approach to the publicity that surrounds the payment of low taxes by profitable companies. The provision necessarily removes from the government any ability to define this element of the tax base because the government, as a practical matter, will not be able to prescribe accounting rules. Given the variety of choices in accounting methods, the provision will treat similarly situated taxpayers differently. For example, taxpayers using full cost accounting and successful efforts accounting in the oil and gas industry will show different annual results for the same activity.

Similarly, a taxpayer facing the minimum tax may establish a larger reserve for a future liability than one facing the regular tax. Book income is computed using special consolidation rules designed to restate book income on a basis comparable to the basis upon which the taxpayer consolidates for income tax purposes.

The book income preference will typically tend to create tax liability in four cases: (1) when a taxpayer has significant exempt income, (2) when a taxpayer books a large liability in one year, but cannot recognize it for tax purposes until a later year, (3) when reserves established for book purposes, but never deducted for tax purposes, are released with resulting book income, and (4) when depreciable lives on major assets are significantly longer for book purposes than for minimum tax purposes.

The Act provides for a switch from the preference based on book income to one based on current earnings and profits after 1989. *The use of earnings and profits would return control of the preference to the government. Thus, reserves would no longer reduce the preference and accounting methods would be those used for tax purposes. The scheduled shift to an earnings and profits preference is likely to be the subject of controversy and legislation in future years.* The transition rules would have to be very complex because of the timing differences between book income and earnings and profits.

Minimum Tax Credit

If, in any post-1986 year, a taxpayer pays minimum tax in excess of its regular tax liability, then the excess (except to the extent attributable to exclusion preferences such as tax exempt interest) may be carried forward as a credit against any subsequent-year regular tax in excess of minimum tax. The amount of this credit is not affected by any investment credit used to reduce the minimum tax liability. The minimum tax credit provides some relief from the minimum tax resulting from timing differences between the regular and minimum taxes. *As there is no carryback for the minimum tax credit, the relief is inadequate when a company books a large liability before it is recognized for tax purposes.*

Estimated Tax Payments

Corporations must now make estimated tax payments with respect to minimum tax liability.

Retirement Savings and Qualified Plans

In General

The Act makes numerous direct changes to the rules governing tax-qualified plans, executive compensation and employee benefit plans. Moreover, other changes to the Internal Revenue Code discussed in this book have an indirect but profound influence on these compensation issues. For example, lower individual tax rates (an indirect change) and the $7,000 cap on 401(k) deferrals (a direct change) may combine to favor cash compensation. With corporate tax rates (34 percent) that exceed individual rates (28 percent or 33 percent), the tax efficiency of current compensation has increased.

Individuals and employers, however, must still provide funds for retirement needs. The changes to IRAs, qualified retirement plans, and employee-benefit plans will restrict the ability of those with higher income to take advantage of these plans. For example, the new 15 percent excise tax on excess retirement income and the new 10 percent excise taxes on excess contributions and early withdrawals may severely limit the attractiveness of these plans (including IRAs) to some people. These new restrictions on qualified plans may mean that, in some circumstances, an individual's retirement needs cannot be satisfied wholly from qualified plans and social security. Here, employers will need to re-evaluate whether and how much of the short-fall should come from non-qualified arrangements and/or from the retiree's personal savings.

Other direct changes, such as the new vesting and integra-

tion rules, may result in a greater proportion of plan costs flowing to lower compensated employees (a clear congressional intention behind the changes). Here, employers will face the issue of cost containment: should costs be increased to continue present levels of benefits, or should the benefit formula be adjusted to contain costs?

Many employers may conclude that the combination of these factors justifies a fresh look at all compensation techniques—tax qualified plans, executive compensation, and employee benefits.

Tax Qualified Plans—Retirement Savings

Individual Retirement Accounts
The Act phases out the deduction for IRA contributions by any moderate and high income taxpayer who is covered by a qualified plan, or whose spouse is covered by a plan. This phase out applies to taxpayers with adjusted gross income between $40,000 and $50,000 on a joint return or $25,000 and $35,000 on a single return. *During this phase out, taxpayers who would otherwise pay at a 15 or 28 percent tax rate will experience effective marginal rates of 18, 21, 33.6, or even 39.2 percent.*

To the extent the IRA deduction is reduced or eliminated by the phase out rule, a taxpayer may elect to make nondeductible IRA contributions. Earnings on the IRA would not be taxed until withdrawn. Total combined contributions to both types of IRAs may not exceed the $2,000 ($2,250 spousal) limitation on IRA contributions. As before, the regular income tax plus a 10 percent excise tax is applied if withdrawals are made before age 59 1/2, death, or disability, unless received in the form of an annuity payable over one's life expectancy. Withdrawals to the extent made from nondeductible contributions are free from income and excise taxes. IRAs may be invested in U.S. gold or silver coins. Rollovers to IRAs are not changed.

Taxpayers subject to the new IRA limits and their employers should carefully review other retirement savings options. Frequently, IRAs have been used where 401(k) plans, Keogh plans, and simplified employee pensions could now be substituted.

Effective date.—These changes are effective in 1987.

Cash or Deferred Arrangements (Section 401(k) Plans)
Beginning in 1987, pre-tax salary deferrals are limited to $7,000 per year. The limit is indexed to inflation. As before, employers may contribute up to the lesser of 25 percent of taxable compensation or $30,000, less the amount of salary deferral. For example, at a salary of $57,000, the employee can defer $7,000 and the employer may contribute $5,500, totaling $12,500 which is 25 percent of $50,000 ($57,000 less the $7,000 salary deferral.)

CHART
401(k) Plan Deferral Test

Non-Highly Compensated Employees' Deferral Percentage				Highly Compensated* Employees' Deferrals
OLD LAW:				
0% to 2%	×	2.5	=	0% to 5%
2% to 6%	+	3%	=	5% to 9%
6% to 10%	×	1.5	=	9% to 15%
NEW LAW:				
0% to 2%	×	2	=	0% to 4%
2% to 8%	+	2%	=	4% to 10%
8% to 12%	×	1.25	=	10% to 15%

*Top 1/3 under old law, and now newly defined by the Act.

The qualification rules, beginning in 1987, will further limit pre-tax deferrals of 401(k) plans (see chart) by members of a newly defined "highly compensated" group of employees. Excess contributions will not be excluded from income and must be returned to employees to avoid a 10 percent excise tax and eventual disqualification of the cash or deferred arrangement.

As before, withdrawals of pre-tax deferrals are prohibited before age 59-1/2, death, disability, severance of employment or hardship. A new exception permits total withdrawals upon plan termination, the sale of a subsidiary or the sale of substantially all of the assets used in a trade or business after 1984.

Beginning in 1989, hardship withdrawals will be limited to the amount of pre-tax deferrals (excluding earnings thereon), and plans cannot require participants to have more than one year of service to enter the plan.

These plans may not now be established by tax-exempt or public-sector employers.

Matching Contributions
New rules apply to all qualified plans in 1987 to limit employer matching and employee after-tax contributions in a manner similar to pre-tax deferrals in a 401(k) plan. *Consequently, highly compensated employees may experience lower employer matches and reduced after-tax contributions.* Excess matching contributions must be distributed to avoid a 10 percent excise tax and eventual plan disqualification.

Simplified Employee Plans (SEPs)
The Act modifies the SEP to permit salary deferrals up to $7,000 under rules similar to 401(k) plans. The new SEP is available to employers with 25 or fewer employees.

Tax Deferred [403(b)] Annuities

In general, the treatment of tax deferred annuity plans offered by charitable organizations or public schools, colleges, and universities will be brought more closely into conformity with qualified plans with respect to coverage, nondiscrimination, minimum distributions, early withdrawals and benefit commencement issues. Effective in 1987, the amount that an employee can defer under all taxed deferred annuities is limited to the greater of $9,500 or the indexed limit on elective deferrals to 401(k) plans. A special catch-up election will be available.

Contribution and Benefit Limits
The Act retains the current limit on annual additions to a defined contribution plan, which is the lesser of 25 percent of compensation or $30,000; and it retains the limit on annual benefits from a defined benefit plan, which is the lesser of 100 percent of compensation or $90,000. The $90,000 limit will be indexed for inflation after 1987; however, the $30,000 annual addition limit will not be indexed until the $90,000 limit reaches $120,000.

Currently, employee after-tax contributions are included in annual additions only to the extent they exceed the lesser of the excess over 6 percent of compensation or one-half of the employee's contribution. For years beginning after 1986, all employee contributions will be treated as annual additions. *Therefore, employees will be precluded from making after-tax contributions if the employer contributes the maximum.*

After 1986, early retirement benefits from defined benefit plans will be limited to the actuarial equivalent of the maximum dollar benefit at normal retirement age (currently age 65). Although former law required actuarial reduction for early retirement benefits, the reduced maximum benefit was $90,000 at age 62 and $75,000 at age 55. The new law produces significantly lower maximum early retirement benefits:

Age	Actuarial Equivalent of $90,000 Limit* Current Law	New Law
65	90,000	90,000
62	90,000	72,000
55	75,000	37,404
50	51,200	25,800

*Assume: 5 percent interest compounded annually and UP-1984 Mortality Table.

An important exception is provided for benefits already accrued. Anyone planning early retirement should examine the consequences of the new actuarial reduction rules.

Sponsors of defined contribution plans may wish to revise their plans to limit employee contributions so that the annual addition limit cannot be exceeded when all employee contributions are treated as annual additions. Sponsors of defined benefit plans in which early retirements are prevalent, particularly among key employees, should consider a redesign of their benefit formula. The early retirement benefits of non-highly-compensated employees may be disproportionately high when compared with similar benefits of highly-compensated employees. The new provisions with regard to includable compensation (discussed elsewhere) may restrict the sponsor's ability to redesign the benefit formula.

Qualification and Nondiscrimination

Definition of Highly Compensated Employee
The Act adopts a uniform definition of "highly compensated employee" to replace the prior law "prohibited group" for purposes of satisfying the nondiscrimination rules for qualified plans (including 401(k) plans) and other employee welfare benefit plans, including group term insurance and insured and self insured health plans. An employee is treated as highly compensated if, at any time during the current or preceding year, the employee (1) was a 5 percent owner, (2) earned more than $75,000 (to be indexed), (3) earned more than $50,000 (to be indexed) and was among the top 20 percent of employees by pay, or (4) was an officer earning more than $45,000 (to be indexed). Individuals coming into the highly compensated group under the second through fourth criteria for the current year must also be among the highest paid 100 employees. The determination of who is highly compensated is to be determined on a controlled group basis.

Effective date. —The definition of highly compensated employee is effective for qualified plans in years beginning after December 31, 1988, and for the special nondiscrimination tests applicable to 401(k) plans in years beginning after December 31, 1986. For employee welfare benefit plans, the rules may apply for post-1987 plan years, depending upon when regulations are issued by Treasury.

Plan Coverage
The Act modifies the coverage rules by requiring all qualified plans to meet one of three coverage tests that are more objective than the prior law. These tests are:

1. Percentage Test. —Seventy percent of all non-highly-compensated employees must be covered; or
2. Ratio Test. —The percentage of non-highly-compensated employees covered by the plan must be at least 70 percent of the percentage of highly compensated employees covered; or
3. Average Benefits Test. —The prior law classification test must be met and the average benefit for non-highly-compensated employees must be at least 70 percent of the average benefit for highly compensated employees (as a percentage of compensation).

The new coverage tests may be met with respect to a separate line of business. A transition rule is provided for certain dispositions or acquisitions.

Minimum Participation
The Act also requires a qualified plan to benefit at least the lesser of 50 employees or 40 percent of all employees. Plans not meeting this test must be merged or terminated by the end of the first plan year in which this rule takes effect. *This rule will require many professional organizations and closely held companies to merge or terminate plans established separately for partners or officers.*

Effective date. —The provisions are effective for plan years beginning after December 31, 1988. A special effective date applies to plans maintained pursuant to a collective bargaining agreement.

Vesting
The Act accelerates the vesting requirements for qualified plans (other than multi-employer plans) to require either 100 percent vesting after 5 years of service, or a graded schedule whereby a participant must be 20 percent vested after 3 years, increasing to 100 percent after 7 years. Under the Act, participants with at least 3 years of service may elect to remain under the plan's current vesting schedule.

Effective date. —The vesting provisions are effective for plan years beginning after December 31, 1988, with respect to all employees who have at least one hour of service in a plan year to which the provisions apply. As a result, benefits earned prior to 1986 under a slower vesting formula will vest in plan years beginning in 1988. A special effective date applies to plans maintained pursuant to a collective bargaining agreement.

Integration with Social Security
The Act significantly changes the social security integration rules and requires a minimum contribution or benefit with respect to earnings below the social security wage base. Conceptually, these rules limit the integrated benefit to no less than one-half of the non-integrated benefit.

Effective date. —The provisions are effective for plan years beginning after December 31, 1988. A special effective date applies to plans maintained pursuant to a collective bargaining agreement.

Distributions and Loans

Lump Sums
After December 31, 1986, 10-year averaging is replaced by a one-time-only 5-year averaging election for lump sum distributions received after the individual attains age 59 1/2. Beginning in 1987, capital gain treatment of the pre-1974 portion of a lump sum distribution is phased out over a six-year period as follows:

Year	Percentage of Pre-1974 Portion Treated as Capital Gain
1987	100%
1988	95%
1989	75%
1990	50%
1991	25%
1992	NONE

Individuals age 50 as of January 1, 1986 may elect 10-year averaging at present rates or 5-year averaging at new rates and to treat the entire pre-1974 amount as capital gain taxed at a rate of 20 percent. One transition election is permitted either before or after attaining age 59-1/2.

Basis Recovery
For distributions with an annuity starting date after July 1, 1986, the special 3-year basis recovery rule is repealed. *This repeal was expected to be the subject of a closely-fought floor fight in the House and may not have survived to final enactment.* For post-1986 distributions received prior to the annuity starting date a pro rata recovery of employee contributions and earnings will apply. Pre-1987 employee contributions are not subject to the pro rata recovery rule.

Minimum Distributions
Beginning January 1, 1989, the benefit commencement date and minimum distribution rules that apply to qualified plans and tax deferred annuities will be conformed to match the rules that currently apply to IRAs. Non-5-percent owners who attain age 70-1/2 by January 1, 1988 can continue to defer distribution to actual retirement. Individuals will be subject to a 50 percent excise tax on the amount which is not distributed.

Early Withdrawals
Subject to numerous exceptions, the 10 percent excise tax that currently applies to premature withdrawals from IRAs will apply to distributions from qualified plans and tax sheltered annuities if made prior to age 59 1/2. The new uniform early withdrawal rules generally are effective for distributions after 1986.

Excess Retirement Distributions
A new 15 percent excise tax will apply to an individual's aggregate distributions in excess of $112,500 received in a year from all qualified plans, tax deferred annuities and IRAs. As the defined benefit limit of $90,000 is indexed upward after 1987, the aggregate annual distribution limit (initially $112,500) will be increased to 125 percent of the indexed annual benefit limit. If an individual elects capital gain or 5-year averaging for a lump sum distribution, the aggregate annual distribution limit will be the lesser of the portion of the distribution to which capital gain or 5-year averaging applies or an amount that is five times the otherwise applicable aggregate annual distribution limit for the year. While the new limitation generally applies to distributions received after 1986, individuals with excess benefits accrued prior to August 1, 1986 will be allowed an election to exempt such pre-August 1, 1986 benefits or to use an alternative limitation.

Plan Loans
The $50,000 limit on plan loans is reduced by the participant's highest outstanding loan balance during the prior 12 months. The exception to the 5-year repayment period is more narrowly limited to loans applied to purchase the participant's principal residence. The interest deduction is denied for loans to key employees and for loans secured by elective deferrals under a qualified cash or deferred arrangement or tax sheltered annuity. The new loan limitations are effective for loan proceeds received after December 31, 1986.

Deductions and Funding

Defined Contribution Plans
Beginning in 1987, excess contributions to qualified plans are subject to a 10 percent excise tax. The Act eliminates the ability to make up for profit sharing and stock bonus contributions of less than 15 percent in a future year by repealing the credit-limit carryforward. Pre-1987 unused credit limits may still be carried forward. Furthermore, for deductions and most other plan purposes, "compensation" is limited to $200,000 per year (indexed for inflation after 1987). The $200,000 includable compensation change is effective after 1988.

The Act modifies the deduction limits for combinations of plans that include a money purchase pension plan (MPPP) for taxable years beginning in 1987. The combined limit for a defined benefit plan and an MPPP (or any other defined contribution plan) is 25 percent of compensation, or the required minimum funding requirement for the defined benefit plan, if greater.

Beginning in 1986, an an employer's contribution to a profit-sharing plan is not limited to current or accumulated profits. This will permit employers to amend plans now to take advantage of this rule change in 1986.

Defined Benefit Plans
After enactment, a new tax penalty is imposed on certain excess deductions due to the overvaluation of pension liabilities if the deductions result in an income tax underpayment.

As to pension plan terminations in 1986 and later, any assets reverting to the employer are subject to a 10 percent excise tax. For plans terminated prior to 1989 an exception is provided for transfers to an ESOP. Tax exempt employers are not subject to this new excise tax.

Employee Stock Ownership Plans

The numerous provisions favoring the use of ESOPs basically are retained and, in a few instances, enhanced by this Act.

The payroll-based tax credit is repealed for compensation paid after December 31, 1986. Distribution of employer securities from a terminated tax credit ESOP is permitted after 1984 without regard to the 84-month rule. ESOPs will be subject to new coverage and nondiscrimination requirements, more rapid vesting schedules, and includable compensation limits described elsewhere.

Beginning in 1987, a new diversification provision requires that older ESOP participants must be allowed annually to direct diversification of a portion of their account balance.

New distribution rules are added that will accelerate distributions from ESOPs. Payments upon the exercise of a put option for stock distributed from an ESOP must be made over five years. The new option payment rules apply to stock acquired after the date of enactment.

Incentives for ESOP financing include (1) a deduction for dividends used to repay the ESOP loan (tax years beginning after enactment), (2) extension of the 50 percent interest income exclusion to loans to the employer if securities are transferred to the ESOP within 30 days (loans after enactment), and (3) an estate tax exclusion for 50 percent of the proceeds from the qualified sale of employer securities to an ESOP (sales after enactment and before January 1, 1992).

International Taxation

The Act radically changes the taxation of U.S. companies doing business abroad, in part by reducing foreign tax credits available to offset their U.S. income tax liabilities. *By reducing the availability of foreign tax credits, the Act is likely to force many U.S. companies into an excess foreign tax credit position. Thus, the Act places a premium on U.S. corporations reducing foreign taxes imposed on their overseas earnings.*

Foreign Tax Credits

Separate Limitation Categories
Under the prior foreign tax credit (FTC) limitation, a taxpayer could generally average high-taxed foreign source income with low-taxed foreign source income, and thus increase the amount of foreign taxes available for credit in a year. To reduce the credit, the Act generally prevents averaging by creating separate categories of low-taxed foreign source income to which the FTC limitation is applied separately. These new categories are:

- income from the active conduct of a banking or financing business and offshore insurance income (referred to as "financial services income");
- shipping income from vessels or aircraft in foreign commerce;
- interest income subjected to a foreign withholding tax of at least five percent (referred to as "high withholding tax interest");
- dividends from non-controlled foreign corporations (non-CFCs) for which an indirect foreign tax credit can be claimed;
- passive income which includes dividends, interest, annuities, net gains from sales of non-inventory assets, certain foreign currency gains, rents and royalties other than those received from unrelated parties in the conduct of an active rental or leasing business, and other items.

Passive income does not include income on which the effective foreign tax rate exceeds 34 percent for corporations and 28 percent for individuals.

Subpart F income realized by a U.S. shareholder of a controlled foreign corporation (CFC) will be allocated to the above categories to the same extent the CFC's income was attributable to those categories. Generally, a similar look-through rule is applied to dividends, interest, rents, and royalties received by a U.S. shareholder from its CFC and similar controlled entities. Passive rents and royalties and all interest received by U.S. shareholders from foreign corporations that are not CFCs is now treated as passive income, whether or not the shareholder owns 10 percent of the CFC's voting stock.

Foreign Loss Recapture Provisions
The allowable foreign tax credit is further reduced by the manner in which losses are allocated to each separate limitation category. Specifically, a foreign-source loss occurring in one category is applied to reduce income in the other categories in proportion to the net foreign-source income in each category. Any remaining unallocated loss reduces U.S. source income. U.S. source losses are allocated on a similar basis to each of the separate foreign limitation categories. Foreign-source income realized in a later year in the separate limitation category producing the original loss is reallocated to the separate categories to which the prior loss was originally allocated.

Foreign Tax Credit for Alternative Minimum Tax Purposes
The Act imposes an alternative minimum tax (AMT) on corporations but limits the allowable foreign tax credit used to offset that tax to no more than 90 percent of the AMT.

Indirect Foreign Tax Credit
In computing the indirect foreign tax credit for actual dividends paid by a foreign corporation as well as for deemed dividends under subpart F, the annual concept of accumulated earnings and profits is repealed for years after 1986. Thus, the indirect foreign tax credit formula is as follows:

$$\text{Foreign income taxes for post-1986 years} \times \frac{\text{Dividends}}{\text{Earnings and profits for post-1986 years}}$$

In the case of actual dividends, earnings and profits are to be computed in this formula using the same rules as earnings and profits for deemed dividends under the subpart F provisions.

Carrybacks and Carryovers of Unused Foreign Tax Credits
Unused foreign tax credits generated on low-taxed foreign source income after the effective date of the Act can be carried back to offset U.S. income tax on high-taxed foreign source income earned in pre-Act years. However, in determining the amount of the carryback allowable, the foreign tax credit limitation for the carryback year is computed for this purpose using the appropriate U.S. tax rates in effect in the year the carryback arises.

By contrast, unused foreign tax credits arising in years prior to the effective date of the Act can be carried over to post-Act years. However, these credits can generally only offset U.S. taxes imposed on the same categories of income on which the carryover taxes were imposed.

Source Rules

The Act also reduces the allowable foreign tax credit by treating many items of income that would be foreign source under prior law as U.S. source in whole or in part.

Sources of Specific Items of Income
Under prior law income from the sale of personal property is generally sourced at the location where title to the property passes. However, the Act eliminates this title test in part by providing that income from sales of personal property (a) is U.S. source if the seller is a U.S. resident, and (b) is foreign source if the seller is a foreign resident, with the following exceptions:

- payments of income from the sale of intangibles that are contingent on productivity, use or disposition are generally sourced where the intangible is used.
- income from the sale of stock of a foreign corporate affiliate conducting an active business is foreign source if sold by a U.S. affiliate corporation in the foreign country where the foreign affiliate derived 50 percent of its gross income for the prior three years.
- income from sales by a U.S. resident of personal property (other than inventory, depreciable property, stock of a foreign affiliate, and intangibles contingent on productivity or use) is foreign source if attributable to a foreign office of the seller, and provided such income is subjected to a foreign income tax of at least 10 percent.
- income from the sale of both inventory property not manufactured by the seller and inventory property manufactured by the seller continues to be sourced under current law rules with exceptions for nonresidents.
- income (other than subpart F income) from the sale of all personal property by a nonresident (NR) will be U.S. source rather than foreign source (except for foreign tax credit

purposes) if the income is attributable to an office maintained by the NR in the U.S. and if the sale did not involve inventory property sold for use outside the United States in which a foreign office of the seller materially participated.

- income from the sale of depreciable property is sourced where the depreciation deductions on that property were sourced, and income in excess of those deductions is sourced where title passes.

For purposes of the Act, the seller is a resident of the country in which his tax home is located, except that a U.S. citizen or resident alien will not be treated as a nonresident of the U.S. on any income from the sale of personal property, unless foreign income tax of at least 10 percent was paid.

The new sourcing rules appear to override income tax treaties to the extent of any inconsistencies and apply to all sales by foreign persons (other than controlled foreign corporations) after March 18, 1986.

Transportation and Other Income From Offshore and Space Activities
The Act treats as U.S. source income 50 percent of all income realized by U.S. or foreign persons from transportation by vessel or aircraft which begins or ends in the U.S. The other 50 percent is foreign source.

The Act modifies prior law by providing that earnings of a nonresident alien or foreign corporation from the operation of a ship or aircraft will only be exempt from U.S. income tax if the foreign country of residence or incorporation (rather than the country where the vessel or aircraft is registered) grants an equivalent exemption to U.S. citizens and corporations. Foreign corporations claiming this exemption are subject to a look-through rule regarding their benefical owners. Income from leasing vessels on a bareboat charter basis is treated as "earnings from the operation of a ship," thus reversing the result in Rev. Rul. 74-170.

The Act also levies a four percent tax on non-effectively connected, U.S. source, gross transportation income earned by foreign persons unless exempted by a treaty or the reciprocal exemption. A special definition of effectively connected income is provided for this purpose.

Income derived from space or ocean activities (including those in Antarctica) will be U.S. source if realized by a U.S. person and foreign source if realized by a foreign person, with exceptions for income from transportation, international communications, and mineral deposits including oil and gas.

Sourcing Rules for 80/20 Companies
Prior law treats all interest and dividend payments as foreign source income when paid by a U.S. corporation (an 80/20 company) that has realized more than 80 percent of its income from foreign sources for the three preceding years. The Act repeals this provision. Thus, the above payments when made to foreign persons are no longer exempt from U.S. withholding tax, except generally for (a) interest payments to unrelated parties from an 80/20 company deriving more than 80 percent of its income from an active business in a foreign country, (b) interest payments on any debt outstanding on December 31, 1985, (c) dividend payments made by an 80/20 company that is a possessions corporation, and (d) interest payments to related parties and dividend payments to the extent attributable to foreign-source gross income of an 80/20 company that derives at least 80 percent of its income from an active business in a foreign country.

Allocation and Apportionment of Expenses
The Act allocates and apportions additional expenses to foreign source taxable income in the foreign tax credit limitation formula. This has the effect of further reducing allowable foreign tax credits in any taxable year.

To reach this result, the Act (a) requires interest and all other expenses (except research and development expenses) incurred by members of a consolidated group to be allocated and apportioned to foreign source taxable income on a consolidated basis instead of a separate company basis, (b) requires interest expense to be allocated and apportioned in the same percentage that the tax basis of the group's foreign assets bears to all assets, thus eliminating the gross income apportionment methods permitted by current law, (c) requires generally that the tax basis of any such asset which is stock of a 10-percent-owned foreign corporation be adjusted for earnings and profits or deficits accumulated during the period the taxpayer held the stock, and (d) requires that tax exempt assets and intragroup debt, equity, interest payments and other expenses be eliminated for allocation and apportionment purposes, subject to certain transition rules.

The Act *does not renew* Congress's moratorium barring the IRS from apportioning U.S. based research and development expenditures to foreign source taxable income under the existing IRS regulations. Instead, the Act says that for taxable years commencing after August 1, 1986 and before August 2, 1987, any part of these expenses (other than for FSC and DISC purposes) incurred to meet legal requirements imposed by a political entity are generally apportioned to income realized in the geographic area governed by that entity. One-half of the remaining expenses are apportioned to U.S. source income, and the other half is apportioned to U.S. or foreign source income in an amount equal to the percentage that sales or gross income from foreign or U.S. sources, respectively, bears to total sales or gross income. Congress will decide later what rules will apply for taxable years beginning after August 1, 1987.

Taxation of U.S. Shareholders of Foreign Corporations

Definition of Controlled Foreign Corporation
The Act treats all foreign corporations as controlled foreign corporations (CFCs) where more than 50 percent of either their voting stock or the value of all their stock is directly or constructively owned by U.S. shareholders, each of whom owns at least 10 percent of the voting stock. If a foreign corporation is a CFC, any tax-haven income earned by it is taxed currently to its U.S. shareholders. Similar ownership rules are adopted for foreign personal holding companies (FPHC). Also, previously exempted corporations organized in U.S. possessions are now treated as CFCs if the above ownership requirements are met.

Subpart F Income Exclusions and Limitations
The prior subjective test for determining whether a CFC was availed of to reduce tax on certain tax-haven income is replaced by an objective test under the Act. This new test requires that the effective rate of foreign tax paid by the CFC on certain tax-haven income (including certain insurance income) must be greater than 90 percent of the U.S. corporate rate. *Thus, if the effective foreign tax rate is greater than 30.6 percent (90% of 34%) on this income, U.S. shareholders of a CFC are not currently taxed on their pro rata share of this income.*

The Act reduces the CFC's income threshold for determining when a U.S. shareholder is currently taxable on the CFC's tax-haven income. Specifically, if the CFC's foreign base company income (i.e., a component of tax-haven income) does not exceed the lesser of 5 percent of the CFC's total gross income or $1 million, then none of the CFC's tax-haven income is taxed currently to the U.S. shareholder. However, if foreign base company income exceeds either 5 percent of the CFC's total gross income or $1 million, the U.S. shareholder is currently taxed on this income.

Under prior law, prior years' deficits in earnings and profits (or current year's deficits from a chain of foreign subsidiaries) reduce the CFC's tax haven income currently taxable to its U.S. shareholders. The Act no longer permits current year's deficits from a chain of foreign subsidiaries to be used for this purpose. In addition, the use of prior years' deficits of a

CFC to reduce its current year tax haven income have been eliminated except for deficits attributable to certain shipping, oil-related, insurance and banking income.

Controlled Partnerships as Related Parties
The Act treats a partnership or trust (which is controlled by a CFC or the CFC's controlling shareholders) as a related person for purposes of the subpart F provisions of the Code. *Thus, tax haven income received by the CFC from a controlled partnership or trust will now be taxable to the U.S. shareholders of the CFC.*

Types of Includable Tax-Haven Income
The Act expands the type of tax haven income earned by a CFC that is currently taxable to its U.S. shareholders. Specifically, under prior law foreign personal holding company (FPHC) income, a type of tax haven income, includes passive income such as dividends, interest, rents, royalties, and annuities. FPHC income is now expanded to include:

- net gains from sales of non-inventory assets which generate passive income or no current income;
- net income from certain non-hedging transactions in commodities but not including income from the active conduct of a commodities business;
- foreign currency net gains from transactions in a nonfunctional currency;
- passive leasing or licensing income;
- income equivalent to interest, such as loan commitment fees;
- interest, rent or royalty payments received by a CFC from a related person (payor) operating in the same foreign country as the CFC that reduces the payor's tax haven income.

In addition, the Act repeals the exceptions from FPHC income for gains from stock or securities, dividends, and interest (except interest in connection with certain export financing) received by a CFC that is a bank or financial institution.

Tax haven insurance income of a CFC is expanded to include income from foreign risks located outside the CFC's country of incorporation. In addition, generally if a foreign insurance company that is not publicly traded (typically a captive) is (1) owned 25 percent or more by U.S. shareholders, whether or not they own 10 percent of the CFC's voting stock, and (2) earns income from insuring risks of its shareholders or related parties, such income will be currently taxable to those shareholders. However, this result can be avoided if the foreign insurance company elects to treat this related person insurance income as effectively connected with the conduct of a U.S. trade or business.

Tax-haven income from shipping operations realized by a CFC is likewise expanded to include any income derived from space and ocean activities (including Antarctica) conducted outside the jurisdiction of any country. Also, the Act repeals the provision that says that tax haven shipping income of a CFC reinvested in certain shipping operations is not currently taxable to the U.S. shareholders.

Taxation of Possession and Other Foreign Income

Possessions Corporations Credit
U.S. companies (possessions corporations) can currently elect to claim a credit equal to the U.S. taxes imposed on certain taxable income derived in most U.S. possessions. This privilege is now extended to such corporations doing business in the Virgin Islands. The Act increases the amount of active business income from a possession that must be earned by these corporations to qualify for the credit from 65 to 75 percent of their gross income. In addition, the Act effectively increases the intercompany price for intangibles that possessions corporations must pay their U.S. affiliates by increasing their cost sharing payment to U.S. affiliates or the amount of allocable product area research expenditures in determining the combined taxable income. *The effect of this change is to reduce the income of possessions corporations eligible for the credit and correspondingly to increase the taxable income of U.S. affiliates.*

Virgin Islands
The Act repeals for open years (i.e., the statute of limitations has not expired) the rules which had permitted U.S. citizens and corporations to qualify as permanent inhabitants of the Virgin Islands (V.I.) and thus to pay income tax on their worldwide income only to the V.I. and not the U.S.

Special Tax Provisions for Americans Working or Living Abroad
The Act reduces the prior exclusion from U.S. income tax for foreign compensation earned by American taxpayers working overseas from $80,000 to $70,000. Additionally, any individual who applies for a U.S. passport (or renewal thereof) is required to file an IRS information return disclosing his taxpayer information number and his foreign residence, if any.

The Act also imposes withholding on all pension payments to U.S. persons living outside the United States.

Transfers of Intangibles to Related Parties Outside the U.S.
Prior law required that a U.S. person who transfers or licenses intangibles to foreign related parties must receive an "arm's-length" payment for their use. The Act now requires that these payments must be commensurate with the income attributable to using the intangible. *Thus, U.S. companies which transfer or license their intangibles offshore after November 16, 1985, may have to adjust annually the payment for any significant changes in the income attributable to the intangible realized by the related party.*

Taxation of Foreign Taxpayers

Branch-Profits Tax and Other Income Subject to U.S. Withholding Taxes
Prior law did not require a foreign corporation (FC) doing business through a branch in the United States to pay U.S. withholding tax when its branch profits are remitted to the home office overseas. The Act now levies a 30 percent withholding tax on an FC's branch profits (earnings and profits effectively connected with the conduct of a U.S. business) whether or not remitted. If effectively connected income is not attributable to a permanent establishment under a treaty, no branch tax will generally be imposed on that income. Also, a tax treaty may reduce the 30 percent tax rate (except in treaty shopping cases) to the treaty branch-profits tax rate, or if none, then the treaty dividend rate. No foreign tax credits can be claimed against the branch-profits tax.

If a treaty bars the U.S. from imposing a branch-profits tax on an FC, none will be imposed except in treaty shopping cases and then only if the treaty prevents U.S. withholding tax from being imposed on dividends paid by the FC.

The Act reduces the threshold for when U.S. withholding tax is imposed on dividends paid by an FC to only those cases in which 25 percent or more of the FC's gross income for the three preceding years was effectively connected with the conduct of its U.S. business. However, if the branch profits tax is payable, no withholding tax will be imposed on dividends paid by the FC.

The Act modifies prior law treatment of U.S. withholding tax on interest paid by a foreign corporation (FC) with a branch in the U.S. Specifically, the Act levies a 30 percent withholding tax (reduced by applicable treaty) on, in effect, the greater of the interest paid or deductible by the branch. If an FC is found to be treaty shopping, the withholding tax rate is not reduced by an applicable treaty unless the recipient of the interest is protected by another treaty.

Withholding on Foreign Investors in Partnerships
The Act levies a 20% withholding tax on that part of any distribution made to a foreign partner by a partnership attributable to income effectively connected (ECI) with the partnership's conduct of a U.S. business. Moreover, the tax will be levied on the entire distribution if ECI is, at least, 80 percent of the partnership's total gross income. This provision is effective for distributions after December 31, 1987, unless regulations are issued before that date.

Income of Foreign Governments
Effective July 1, 1986, the Act taxes a foreign government on any income derived directly or indirectly from engaging in commercial activity in the U.S. (including athletic and cultural group activities). *Additionally, if a controlled entity is itself engaged in commercial activity anywhere in the world, its income is treated like income of a privately owned entity.*

Transfer Prices for Imports
For U.S. income tax purposes the Act requires that transfer prices on import transactions between related persons after March 18, 1986 not exceed those used for U.S. customs purposes.

Dual Resident Companies
The Act denies a U.S. corporation managed and controlled in the U.K. or Australia (a dual resident) the right to deduct any expenses in excess of its income in a U.S. consolidated return with its subsidiaries to the extent those expenses have been deducted by a related foreign corporation for U.K. or Australian tax purposes. However, those excess expenses can be used for U.S. tax purposes by the dual resident in future years when it generates sufficient income to absorb them. In addition, net operating losses incurred by a dual resident prior to the effective date of the Act and deducted by a related foreign corporation can still be deducted in the dual resident's U.S. consolidated return for taxable years after the effective date of the Act.

Foreign Exchange Gains and Losses

The Act adopts uniform rules for the tax treatment of foreign currency.

Functional Currency of an Entity
The Act requires that all income or expenses of a taxpayer must be computed in its "functional currency." In general, a taxpayer's functional currency is the currency in which it keeps its books and records and in which a significant part of its activities are conducted. Thus, the functional currency of most U.S. taxpayers operating in the United States would be the U.S. dollar.

The functional currency of most foreign persons operating in a foreign country would be foreign currency of that country, with exceptions. However, if either the activities of the foreign person are conducted primarily in U.S. dollars, or the foreign person keeps its books and records in U.S. dollars and elects the dollar as its functional currency, then the U.S. dollar is the functional currency.

It is possible for a U.S. taxpayer or a foreign person to have more than one functional currency, provided it has a qualified business unit, the unit maintains separate books and records in a different currency, and other requirements are met. For this purpose, a "qualified business unit" (QBU) is any separate and clearly identified unit of a business conducted by the taxpayer that "is capable of producing income independently." Thus, a QBU includes foreign branches as well as foreign subsidiaries of a U.S. corporation.

Foreign Branch
A foreign branch is required to compute its profit (or loss) in its functional currency and then translate it into U.S. dollars at the weighted average exchange rate for the taxable year. This amount is then included in the taxpayer's income without reduction for remittances from the branch during the year. Only realized exchange gains and losses from foreign currency transactions are reflected in the U.S. taxpayer's income. *Thus, taxpayers are no longer permitted to accelerate the recognition of unrealized foreign exchange gains or losses by use of the net worth method for measuring the U.S. tax results of branch operations.*

Translated branch losses are deductible in computing the taxpayer's taxable income only to the extent of the taxpayer's dollar basis in the branch. That basis initially is equal to the translated value of net assets contributed to the branch and by unremitted branch profits. All contributions to the branch are translated for this purpose at the exchange rate on the date they are made. Similarly, the taxpayer's basis is reduced for branch losses deducted and for remittances to the head office in the U.S.

All branch remittances are treated as paid first out of its post-1986 accumulated earnings. Exchange gains or losses on branch remittances are treated as foreign source income if the remittances are foreign source.

For foreign tax credit purposes foreign income taxes paid by the branch including any refund or credit thereof are translated into U.S. dollars on the date the tax is paid.

Foreign Corporation
In determining the U.S. tax of any shareholder of a foreign corporation (FC), the FC's earnings and profits are computed annually in its functional currency and are *not* translated into U.S. dollars, until distributed to the shareholder. When actual dividend distributions (including deemed dividends under section 1248) are made, both the dividends and the FC's earnings and profits are translated into U.S. dollars at the exchange rate on the date of distribution (or deemed distribution). Thus, no exchange gains and losses are recognized for exchange rate fluctuations between the time the FC's earnings and profits are realized and the time they are distributed.

If an FC's earnings and profits are deemed distributed to U.S. shareholders because of subpart F, an investment in U.S. property, or the foreign personal holding company provisions, they are translated at the weighted average exchange rate for the FC's taxable year.

Although generally no income is realized by U.S. shareholders upon the actual distribution of previously taxed subpart F income (PTI), gain or loss caused by fluctuating exchange rates between the time of the deemed and actual distributions is recognized and treated as foreign source if the PTI was foreign source.

For indirect foreign tax credit purposes, foreign income taxes paid by FCs (including any refund or credit thereof) is translated into U.S. dollars on the date the tax is paid. Thus, the Act repeals the *Bon Ami* rule which had required taxes to be translated at the exchange rate on the date dividends were distributed.

Foreign Currency Transactions
Transactions denominated in nonfunctional currencies generally produce exchange gains and losses. Exchange gains or losses arise when taxpayers

- accrue income or expenses (payables or receivables) in nonfunctional currency,
- borrow or lend in such currency (notes payable or receivables),
- or dispose of non-functional currency, coins, currency-denominated demand or time deposits issued by a bank, or forward contracts, futures contracts or options not marked to market,

when the exchange rate fluctuates between the date these items are booked and their disposition. These exchange gains or losses are classified as ordinary income or losses, and are generally sourced (or the losses are allocated) by the residence of the taxpayer on whose books the underlying assets (or liabilities) are reflected. Treasury is to issue regulations prescribing when the above exchange gains or losses are treated as interest income or expense.

Foreign Exchange Hedging Contracts
The Treasury is to issue special rules for hedging transactions.

Taxpayers Using U.S. Dollar as Functional Currency
The Act generally does not change current law for a taxpayer or qualified business unit using the U.S. dollar as its functional currency.

Revocation of Contiguous Country Corporation Elections To Be Included in U.S. Consolidated Return
The Act requires Treasury to issue regulations allowing a U.S. parent corporation to revoke its election to include wholly-owned contiguous country corporations (Canada or Mexico) in its consolidated U.S. tax return. This is being done because these contiguous corporations can no longer recognize unrealized exchange gains or losses in computing their taxable income for U.S. purposes.

Effective Dates for International Provisions

The effective dates for most provisions affect taxable years beginning after December 31, 1986, or transactions occurring after that date. Where different effective dates are imposed for certain provisions of the Act, an attempt has been made to describe those. Various transitional rules and grandfather rules have been omitted from this explanation.

Rate Structure as of 1987: Summary

For taxable years beginning in 1987, five-bracket rate schedules are provided, as shown in the table below.

For married individuals filing separate returns, the taxable income bracket amounts for 1987 begin at one-half the amounts for joint returns.

Tax rate	Taxable income brackets		
	Married, filing joint returns	Heads of household	Singles
11%	0-$3,000	0-$2,500	0-$1,800
15%	3,000-28,000	2,500-23,000	1,800-16,800
28%	28,000-45,000	23,000-38,000	16,800-27,000
35%	45,000-90,000	38,000-80,000	27,000-54,000
38.5%	Above 90,000	Above 80,000	Above 54,000

Source: Joint Committee on Taxation, *Summary of Conference Agreement on H.R. 3838* (Tax Reform Act of 1986 (JCS-16-86), August 29, 1986.

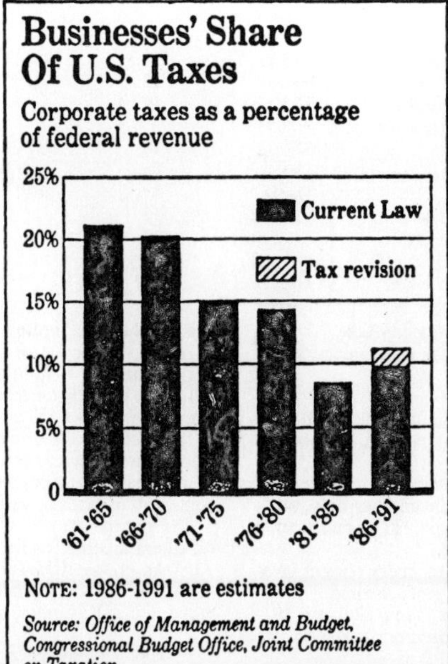

Source: "Reprinted by permission of *The Wall Street Journal*, © Dow Jones & Company, Inc., 1986. ALL RIGHTS RESERVED."

MAJOR TAXES AND RATES USED BY STATES*

State	Income Taxes: Corporation	Income Taxes: Individual	General Sales and Use Tax	Gasoline Tax (per gallon)	Cigarette Tax (per pack of 20)	Property Tax
AL	5%(F)	2 to 5%(F)	4%(a)	11 cents	16.5 cents	X
AZ	2.5 to 10.5(F)	2 to 8(F)	5(a)	16	15	X
AR	1 to 6	1 to 7	4(a)	13.5	21	X
CA	9.6	1 to 11	4.75(a)	9	10	X
CO	5 to 5.5	3 to 8(F)	3(a)	18(b)	20	X
CT	11.5(c)	1 to 12(d)	7.5	17(e)	26	X
GA	6	1 to 6	3(a)	7.5 + 3% of retail	12	X
HI	5.85 to 6.435	2.25 to 11	4	16 to 19	40% wholesale	
ID	8	2 to 8.2	5	14.5	18	X
IL	4	2.5	5(a)	13	20	X
IN	3.4(f)	3.4	5	14	15.5	X
IA	6 to 12(F)	.5 to 13(F)	4(a)	16	26	
KS	4.5(g)	2 to 9(F)	4(a)	11	24	X
KY	3 to 7.25	2 to 6(F,n)	5(a)	15(i)	3.001	X
LA	4 to 8(F)	2 to 6(F)	4(a)	16	16	
ME	3.5 to 8.93	1 to 10	5	14	28	X
MD	7	2 to 5	5	18.5(i)	13	X
MA	8.33(j)	5(k)	5	11	26	X
MI	2.35	4.6	4	15	21	X
MN	9.5	4 to 9(p)	6(a)	17	38	X
MS	3 to 5	3 to 5	6	15(e)	18	X
MO	5(F)	1.5 to 6(F)	4.225(a,b)	11	13	X
NE	4.75 to 6.65	2 to 5.9	4(a)	19	27	X
NJ	9(l)	2 to 3.5	6	8	25	X
NM	4.8 to 7.6	1.8 to 8.5(m)	4.75(a)	14	15	X
NY	10(c)	2 to 8.75(b)	4(a)	8	21	
NC	6	3 to 7	3(a)	15.5	2	X
ND	3 to 10.5(F)	2.67 to 12(F,n,o)	5.5(b)	17	27	X
OH	5.1 to 9.2(c)	.751 to 6.9(b)	5(a)	12	14	X
OK	5	.5 to 6(F,m)	4(a)	16	23	
PA	8.5	2.1	6	12	18	X
RI	8(c)	23.96% of Federal income tax	6	13(i)	25	X
SC	6	2 to 7	5	13	7	X
TN	6	6(d)	5.5(a)	17	13	
UT	5	2.25 to 7.75(F)	5.094(a,b)	19	23	X
VT	6 to 9(b)	25.8% of Federal income tax	4(b)	13	17	X
VA	6	2 to 5.75	3.5(a)	17.5	2.5	X
WV	9.75(b)	3 to 6.5	5	10.5	17	X
WI	7.9	5 to 7.9	5(a)	18	25	X
FL	5.5	These 7 states (FL, NV, SD, TX, WA, WY, AK) have no individual income tax	5(a)	4	24	X
NV	These 5 states (NV, SD, TX, WA, WY) have no corporate income tax		5.75(a)	11.25	15	X
SD			5(a,b)	13	23	
TX			5.25(a,b)	15(b)	20.5	
WA			6.5(a)	18	31	X
WY			3(a)	8	8	X
AK	1 to 9.4		These 5 states (AK, DE, MT, NH, OR) have no general sales tax	8	16	X
DE	8.7	1 to 8.8(F,h)		13	14	
MT	6.75(e,m)	2 to 11(F)		20	16	X
NH	8	5(d)		14	17	X
OR	6.6	5 to 9(F,h)		12	27	X

(X) Indicates state levies a property tax.
(F) Allows Federal income tax as a deduction.

(a) Local taxes are additional.
(b) Future reduction scheduled under current law.
(c) Alternative methods of calculation may be required.
(d) In Connecticut, New Hampshire, and Tennessee, tax applies to income from intangibles only, at various rates according to type. In Connecticut, capital gains are taxed at 7%.
(e) Future increases scheduled under current law.
(f) Tax is 3.4% of adjusted gross income. A supplemental net income tax is imposed at 4.5%.
(g) A 2-1/4% surtax is imposed on taxable income in excess of $25,000.
(h) Deductions limited.
(i) Tax imposed at percent of wholesale value.
(j) Additional 14% surtax is imposed.
(k) Tax of 10% on income derived from intangibles, and 5% on all other income.
(l) Additional tax on net worth is part of the corporate franchise tax.
(m) Qualified taxpayers may elect to pay alternative taxes at varying rates.
(n) Optional tax of 14% of taxpayer's adjusted Federal income tax liability.
(o) Additional 10% surtax is imposed for 1987.
(p) Plus 10% of Federal tax paid under Sec. 1(g) of Internal Revenue Code.

Source: Compiled by Tax Foundation from data reported by Commerce Clearing House.

* As reported through June 2, 1987

Source: Reprinted by permission of Tax Foundation, Incorporated. One Thomas Circle, N.W., Washington, D.C. 20005.

FEDERAL INCOME TAXES PAID BY HIGH- AND LOW-INCOME TAXPAYERS 1979 AND 1985[a]

Adjusted Gross Income Class	Income Level 1979	Income Level 1985	Percent of Tax Paid 1979	Percent of Tax Paid 1985	Average Tax 1979	Average Tax 1985
Highest 5%	$39,900 or more	$63,450 or more	37.6%	38.8%	$17,407	$25,040
Highest 10%	32,710 or more	46,970 or more	49.5	51.8	11,456	16,747
Highest 25%	21,760 or more	30,960 or more	73.1	74.5	6,769	9,623
Highest 50%	11,870 or more	16,483 or more	93.2	93.1	4,315	6,017
Lowest 50%	11,869 or less	16,482 or less	6.8	6.9	313	445
Lowest 25%	5,565 or less	7,673 or less	.5	.7	46	91
Lowest 10%	2,212 or less	3,053 or less	(b)	(b)	9	16

1985 Income and Tax Data

Adjusted Gross Income Class	Total Individual Returns (thousands)	Total Adjusted Gross Income ($billions)	Percentage of Adjusted Gross Income	Average Tax Rate
Highest 5%	5,087	522.6	22.5%	24.4%
Highest 10%	10,174	793.5	34.2	21.5
Highest 25%	25,434	1,368.2	58.9	17.9
Highest 50%	50,869	1,955.4	84.2	15.7
Lowest 50%	50,869	366.5	15.8	6.2
Lowest 25%	25,434	66.1	2.8	3.5
Lowest 10%	10,174	–15.6	—	—

(a) 1985 data are preliminary
(b) Less than .05%

Source: Tax Foundation computations based on *Statistics and Income,* Internal Revenue Service, U.S. Department of the Treasury.

Source: Tax Foundation, One Thomas Circle, N.W., Washington, DC 20005.

HOW FEDERAL, STATE, AND LOCAL GOVERNMENTS SPEND EACH DOLLAR OF PUBLIC FUNDS SELECTED FISCAL YEARS 1960–1985

How Federal, State, and Local Governments Spend Each Dollar of Public Funds Selected Fiscal Years 1960-1985

Function	1960	1970	1980	1985
	Cents per dollar of total spending			
Major social welfare programs, total	20.6	25.8	33.6	31.9
Social Security (OASDHI)	7.1	10.8	15.6	16.0
Social services and income maintenance (a)	8.5	10.7	13.0	11.4
Government employee retirement	1.4	1.9	3.0	3.0
Veterans (not elsewhere classified)	2.5	1.6	1.3	1.1
Railroad retirement	.6	.5	.5	.4
National defense and international relations	32.3	25.3	15.6	18.3
Education	12.8	16.7	15.0	13.0
Interest on general debt	6.2	5.5	7.9	10.9
Environment and housing	5.4	4.4	4.9	5.7
Utilities and liquor stores	3.4	2.8	3.8	3.8
Transportation	7.6	6.2	4.4	3.6
Public safety	1.8	2.0	2.3	3.2
Government administration	1.8	1.9	2.2	2.3
Postal service (Federal)	2.5	2.3	1.9	1.8
Sanitation	1.1	1.0	1.4	1.1
All other	4.5	6.1	7.0	4.4
Exhibit (billions):				
Total spending	$151.3	$333.0	$958.7	$1,581.1

(a) Comprises public welfare, hospitals, health, and unemployment insurance benefits.
Sources: *Facts and Figures on Government Finance*, 1986, Tax Foundation; and other data from U.S. Department of Commerce, Bureau of the Census.

Source: Tax Foundation, One Thomas Circle, N.W., Washington, DC 20005.

Big Deficit Gap Remains

The accompanying table illustrates starkly where the real Federal budget problem lies: spending outstripping tax resources. From a base of a little over $92 billion and 18 percent of gross national product in 1960, total outlays have exploded eleven-fold to over a trillion dollars in fiscal 1987. Spending grew much faster than the overall economy, peaking at 24.4 percent of GNP in fiscal 1983 before dropping back a bit to 23 percent this year.

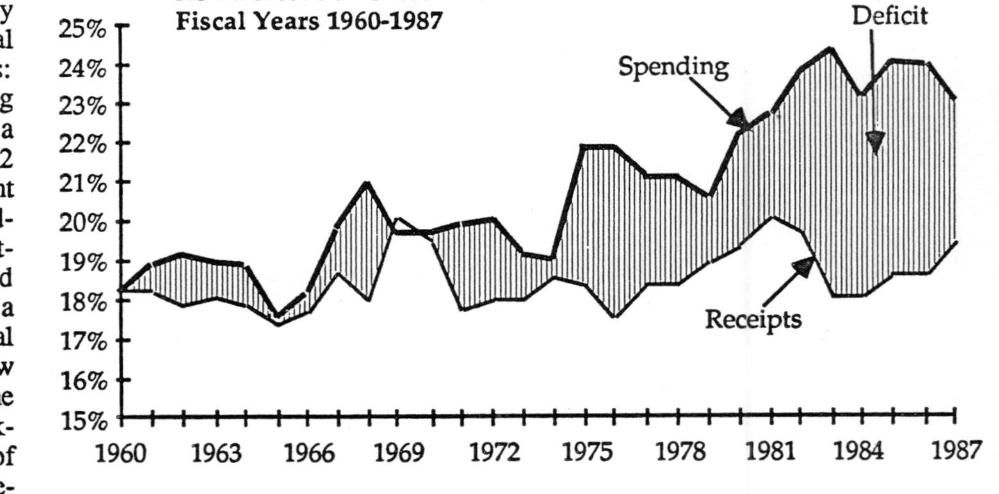

In the meantime, overall tax receipts, starting from the same base of just over 18 percent of GNP in 1960 have kept fairly even pace with the economy. There was a dip in receipts as a percent of GNP after the 1981 tax cuts, but by 1987 taxes were back up over 19 percent of GNP, about one-half percentage point higher than the average over the preceding 27 years.

The difference, of course, is the deficit which reached a post-war high of 6.3 percent of GNP in fiscal 1983 and an historic dollar high of $221 billion in fiscal 1986. Unless stringent fiscal restraint is applied, deficits close to $200 billion will persist into the 1990s.

It is well to remember how we got into this situation. Certainly on the basis of the post-war record, we are not undertaxed but overspent!

Source: *Federal Tax Policy Memo*, September 1987, Tax Foundation, One Thomas Circle, N.W., Washington, DC 20005.

Investing in Gold, Diamonds and Collectibles

Investing in Gold

Gold has been one of the more widely promoted investment vehicles over the last several years. Prices moved from about $140 per ounce in early 1977 to over $800 in early 1980. However, by August 1985 prices declined to $291 an ounce but climbed to over $450.00 by August 1987. Because of such large fluctuations, the metal has stimulated a great deal of speculative interest among many investors.

Investment in gold can be made in a variety of ways:

Gold bullion (bars and wafers) This can be purchased through many stock brokers, bullion currency dealers, and some investment (mutual fund) companies. The purity of gold is indicated by the fineness. Pure gold has a fineness of 1.000 and corresponds to 24 karats.* Each bar is stamped with the fineness as determined by an assay, the refiner's number, a bar identification number and the weight. A bar fineness of .995 or better is acceptable.

Individuals who accept delivery of gold bars and who subsequently wish to resell must have the bar reassayed prior to sale because of the possibility of adulteration with cheaper metals. Because of the latter possibility, individuals should always buy from reputable dealers, and the bar should bear the stamp of well recognized refiners or assayers. Individuals taking physical possession of the metal also have sales taxes, storage, and insurance costs.

The purchaser may arrange to have the dealer (or agent) retain physical possession of the bullion. In this case, evidence of ownership is provided by a *gold deposit certificate* (receipt) issued by the dealer. Since gold certificates are generally nonnegotiable or assignable, there is no loss if it is stolen. The gold deposit certificate method of buying bullion eliminates sales taxes, storage risks (though the dealer will charge a modest storage fee) and the need for assay on resale. It is probably the most convenient way of purchasing gold.

* This "karats" is not to be confused with the "carats" that apply to diamonds.

Gold bullion coins Bullion coins are issued in large number by several governments which guarantee their gold content. They have no numismatic value. The best known gold bullion coins are the U.S. Gold One Ounce, South African Krugerrand, Canadian Maple Leaf, Austrian 100 Corona and the Gold Mexican 50 peso. The first three coins have a pure gold content of one ounce. The Austrian Corona has a gold content of .9802 ounce and the Mexican peso 1.2057 ounces. The premium (cost above the gold value) varies from dealer to dealer. For those who do not want to take physical possession, deposit certificates are available for the coins.

One of the largest bullion dealers is Deak International (212-757-0100) headquartered in New York City. Gold coins can also be purchased at banks where there is generally a very low premium over the gold content value.

Gold stocks The stocks of a number of Canadian and U.S. gold mining companies are traded on the New York (N), American (A) and Over-The-Counter (O) exchanges. Of course, with stocks, the investor is not just buying into gold, but also into the many special problems associated with running a company—production costs, quality of the ore, lifetime of the deposit, etc. However, many gold stocks pay dividends, whereas other gold investments do not pay any return during the holding period.

Some listed stocks are given below:

Agnico-Eagle Mines (O)
Campbell Red Lake Mines (N)
Dome Mines (N)
Sunshine Mining (N)
Homestake Mining Company (N)

A publicly-held New York Stock Exchange closed-end gold fund is ASA Limited. Several mutual funds which invest in gold are given in the mutual fund section of the Almanac (page 364).

South African gold mines are traded on the Over-The-Counter Market by means of ADR (American Depository Receipt). ADR is a claim on foreign stocks (South African gold shares, in this case) held by the foreign branches of large U.S.

banks. Holders of ADRs are entitled to dividends which, in the case of South African gold shares, may be substantial. The ADRs of these companies are listed in *The Wall Street Journal* under the Foreign Securities section, which follows the OTC quotations.

Some major South African gold mining companies are:

Blyvooruitzicht
Buffelsfontein
East Driefontein
Kloof
President Brand
President Steyn
Randfontein
West Dreifontein
Western Deep Levels
Western Holdings

Mutual funds specializing in gold and precious metals A number of mutual funds (see page 364) specialize in gold and precious metals stocks. These funds provide diversification among a number of issues thereby reducing risk associated with any particular stock.

Options on gold stocks Put and call options are available on Homestake Mining (Chicago Options Exchange) and on ASA Limited (American Options Exchange). These options may be used for leveraged speculation or for hedging existing gold holdings. Holders of call options gain if the gold shares increase, while holders of put options benefit if prices decline.

The Philadelphia Stock Exchange trades a gold/silver option based on an index of seven different stocks in the industry.

Options on gold bullion Put and call options on gold bullion are traded on the International Options Market (IOM) of the Montreal Stock Exchange. IOM options are on 10 ounces of gold. Contract months are Feb/May/Aug/Nov.

Monex (Newport Beach, CA) provides put and call options on 32.15 ounces of gold. The Monex options are not tradeable but can be exercized during the option period. Expiration periods are 30, 60, 90, and 185 days. Mocatta Metals (New York) also offers futures contracts.

Since options are paid in full, they are not subject to margin calls or forced liquidation as is the case with futures contracts. At this time, quotations on bullion options are not available in the daily press.

Gold futures contract Gold futures contracts are obligations to buy or sell 100 ounces of gold on or before a specified date at a specified price. Futures contracts must be exercised if held to maturity, while options contracts need not be exercised if held to maturity. Futures contracts are purchased on margin, and hence, are subject to margin call and possible forced liquidation. They are widely quoted in the financial press, and the market is highly organized.

As with options, futures contracts may be used for leveraged speculation or for hedging. Speculators will buy contracts if they anticipate a price increase or sell contracts in anticipation of a price decrease.

Gold futures are traded on the N.Y. Commodity Exchange, the International Monetary Market of the Chicago Mercantile Exchange, and other markets.

Options on Gold Futures Contracts Options on Gold Futures contracts (the right to buy and sell a gold futures contract rather than the metal) are actively traded on the New York Comex. The futures contract underlying the options is for 100 ounces of gold. Contract months are April/Aug./Dec. Gold futures options premiums are reported daily in the *Wall Street Journal.*

Investing in Diamonds

Diamond prices are very volative. For example, they have appreciated on the average of about 12.6% over the ten-year period 1969–1979 (compared to a consumer price index of 6.1% during the same period of time). There have been periods (the recession of 1973—1974 and in 1981) when the price of investment quality diamonds slipped as much as 40%. A major factor stabilizing the market is DeBeers, a South African diamond company which handles as much as 80% of the world's diamonds. While the appreciation of diamonds has been impressive, potential buyers should be aware that prices are not quoted in the daily newspapers; therefore, selling the stones at a profit may be difficult. Quotes are available in the *Rappaport Diamond Report,* 15 West 47 Street, New York, NY 10036, (212) 354-0575. Another good source of information on the diamond industry is the Diamond Registry, 30 West 47 Street, New York, NY 10036, (212) 575-0444. The registry publishes a monthly newsletter which includes price ranges, trends, and forecasts as well as other pertinent material.

To locate reputable gem dealers check with the Diamond Registry (address above) or the

American Gem Society
5901 West 3rd Street
Los Angeles, CA 90036-2898
(213) 936-4367

American Diamond Industry Association
71 West 47 Street
New York, NY 10036
(212) 575-0525

Buyers should only deal with reputable firms, and the stones should be certified by an independent laboratory such as the Gemological Institute of America and International Gemological Institute with offices in New York City.

Diamonds are ranked in terms of the 4 C's—carat (one carat equals 1/142 ounces weight), color, clarity, and cut.

Carat For investment purposes the diamond should be more than .5 carat. However, diamonds of more than 2 carats may be difficult to sell.

Color There are six main categories, each with subdivisions:

D,E,F—Colorless
G,H,I,J—Near colorless
K,L,M—Faint yellow
N,O,P,Q,R—Very light yellow
S,T,U,V,W,X,Y,Z—Light yellow
Fancy yellow stone

Color should be in the range from D to H. However, Fancy Yellow Stones often command very high prices because of their scarcity.

Clarity Although bubbles, lines, and specks (inclusions) are natural to diamonds, they may interfere with the passage of light through the diamond. With a 10X magnification, a professional appraiser can grade the diamond according to the ten clarity grades:

FL—Flawless
IF—Internally flawless
VVS-1, VVS-2—Very, very slight inclusions
VS-1, VS-2—Very slight inclusions
SI-1, SI-2—Slight inclusions
I-1, I-2, I-3—Imperfect

Investment grade stones should be in the range FL to VS-2.

Cut There are several types of cuts—oval, marquise, pear shaped, round brilliant and emerald. Round brilliant stones are preferred for investment purposes. Proportions are important, and the preferred values are:

Depth % (total depth divided by girdle diameter): 57% to 63%.
Table (table diameter divided by girdle diameter): 57% to 66%.
Girdle thickness should be neither very thick nor very thin.

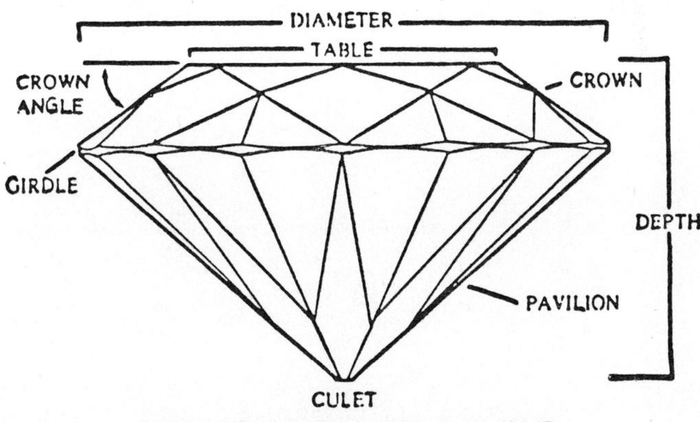

THE ROUND BRILLIANT DIAMOND

Investing in Collectibles

Sotheby's Art Index ®

Category	Weight	July 27	July 13	July 1986	July 1985
Old Master Paintings	17	349	349	303	289
19th Century European Paintings	12	303	303	251	249
Impressionist & Post-Impressionist Paintings	18	661	661	380	356
Modern Paintings (1900-1950)	10	666	666	364	336
American Paintings (1800-pre-WW II)	3	789	789	687	635
Continental Ceramics	3	320	320	290	284
Chinese Ceramics	10	550	550	493	486
English Silver	5	349	349	314	298
Continental Silver	5	201	201	190	178
American Furniture	3	452	452	380	324
French & Continental Furniture	7	319	319	285	273
English Furniture	7	594	594	447	382
Weighted Aggregate		475	475	369	336

Sept. 1975 = 100.

The data reflected in the Sotheby's Art Index are based on results of auction sales by affiliated companies of Sotheby's and other information deemed relevant by Sotheby's. Sotheby's does not warrant the accuracy of the data reflected therein. Nothing in any of the Sotheby's Indices is intended or should be relied upon as investment advice or as a prediction, warranty or guaranty as to future performance or otherwise. All individual prices quoted in this review are aggregate prices, inclusive of the buyer's premium.

Source: Reprinted by courtesy of *Barron's National Business and Financial Weekly,* July 27, 1987 and Sotheby's.

Investing in Real Estate

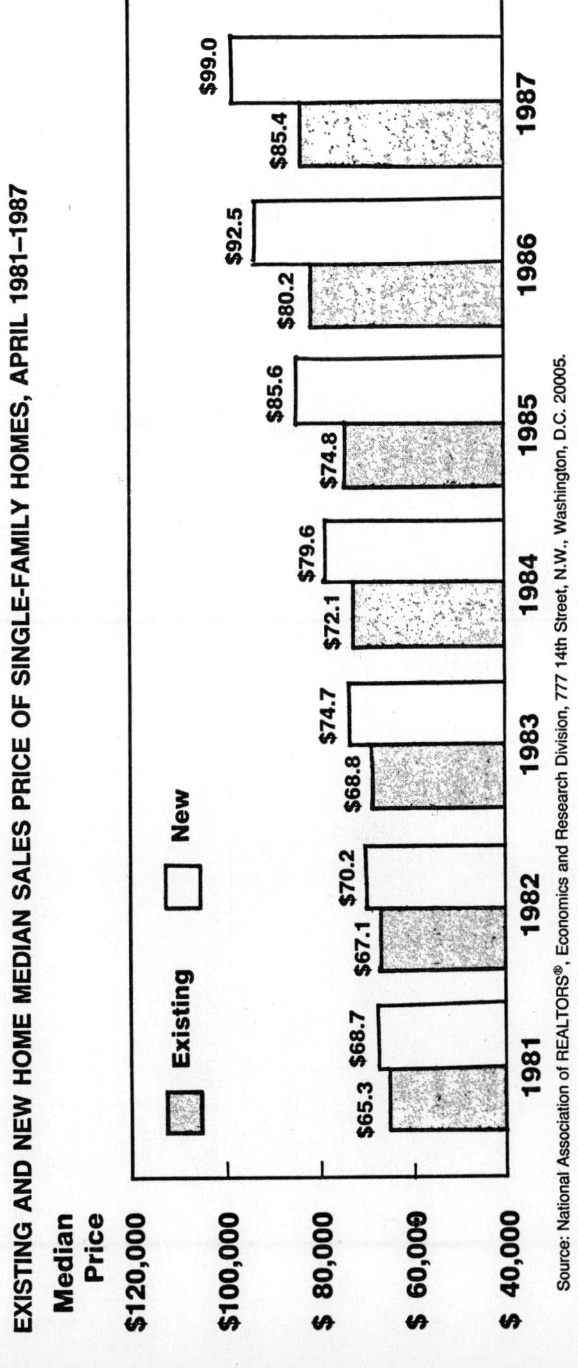

Source: National Association of REALTORS®, Economics and Research Division, 777 14th Street, N.W., Washington, D.C. 20005.

MEDIAN SALES PRICE OF EXISTING SINGLE-FAMILY HOMES FOR METROPOLITAN AREAS* (not seasonally adjusted in thousands of dollars)

Metropolitan Area	Years			Quarters				
	1984	1985	1986	1986				1987
				I	II	III	IV	I^r
Akron	$ 50.4	$ 52.7	$ 56.2	$ 51.1	$ 58.2	$ 56.9	$ 56.7	$ 54.7
Albany/Schenectady/Troy	52.9	60.3	72.7	67.5	73.3	74.4	76.3	80.1
Albuquerque	73.4	76.8	81.6	77.6	79.7	85.4	82.0	83.1
Orange County (Anaheim/Santa Ana MSA**)	133.7	136.2	147.7	138.0	149.4	149.6	152.4	156.1
Baltimore	66.1	72.6	74.0	71.6	72.8	78.0	74.3	81.0
Baton Rouge	73.5	74.6	70.9	73.6	73.3	69.8	68.5	68.3
Birmingham	65.1	64.5	68.3	67.1	69.4	69.6	66.7	67.5
Boston	100.0	134.2	159.2	145.6	156.2	163.0	167.8	170.0
Buffalo/Niagara Falls	44.8	46.7	52.4	49.7	54.0	52.8	53.5	55.6
Charlotte/Gastonia/Rock Hill, NC-SC	66.8	69.4	n/a	70.6	75.9	75.4	n/a	n/a
Chicago	79.5	81.1	86.1	82.0	84.7	86.7	85.8	85.7
Cincinnati	58.9	60.2	n/a	62.1	64.2	64.5	n/a	63.8
Cleveland	62.7	64.4	66.9	62.1	68.0	68.4	65.1	n/a
Columbus	59.9	62.2	65.5	62.6	67.7	66.1	64.0	66.9
Dallas/Ft. Worth	82.2	87.7	92.8	93.4	93.6	92.4	89.8	91.2
Denver	82.7	84.3	86.4	84.6	87.3	87.5	85.8	89.9
Des Moines	52.4	52.5	55.9	52.7	59.0	55.2	55.0	55.9
Detroit	48.5	51.7	58.1	54.0	57.5	59.9	60.1	64.3
El Paso	57.8	57.6	59.0	57.2	60.9	59.6	58.5	58.0
Ft. Lauderdale/Hollywood/Pompano Beach	73.1	74.6	77.7	72.6	75.1	83.4	77.7	76.6
Grand Rapids	42.8	46.7	50.4	48.9	51.6	50.6	49.7	51.7
Hartford	87.4	99.6	129.0	106.4	127.6	132.0	134.6	136.6
Houston	77.6	78.6	69.9	70.4	72.0	70.4	67.6	64.7
Indianapolis	53.1	55.0	59.0	55.7	60.8	59.9	57.5	61.6
Jacksonville	55.7	58.4	62.8	58.9	57.5	65.7	62.7	62.7
Kansas City	59.1	61.4	65.4	65.7	67.0	64.1	65.1	72.9
Las Vegas	76.3	75.1	77.5	74.6	76.9	81.3	78.5	76.1

Los Angeles Area**	115.3	n/a	128.8	120.4	128.7	132.9	130.2	130.1
Louisville	48.9	50.6	51.7	48.1	52.6	53.7	51.9	52.1
Memphis	64.1	64.6	70.6	66.3	71.3	71.5	69.9	70.6
Miami/Hialeah	79.5	80.5	81.1	78.5	85.7	85.5	79.1	74.7
Milwaukee	68.2	67.5	69.9	67.6	71.0	70.8	69.2	67.8
Minneapolis/St. Paul	74.0	75.2	77.9	76.3	79.0	78.1	77.4	80.4
Nashville/Davidson	62.9	66.1	70.8	68.4	71.4	71.2	71.7	73.4
New York/Northern New Jersey/Long Island	105.3	134.0	160.6	147.2	160.0	167.8	167.6	169.4
Oklahoma City	63.9	64.7	63.0	62.8	65.0	62.3	62.9	62.4
Omaha	56.2	58.3	58.8	58.6	62.0	57.8	58.8	57.8
Orlando	70.1	70.3	72.5	70.3	74.5	72.8	72.1	73.6
Philadelphia	65.2	70.8	74.5	72.2	73.6	75.6	77.1	79.8
Phoenix	74.7	74.7	78.4	76.2	78.8	79.1	77.9	78.4
Portland	62.9	61.5	62.6	59.9	63.4	63.1	62.5	62.7
Providence	59.6	67.5	87.6	71.9	84.4	91.9	96.4	101.3
Rochester	59.7	64.2	68.3	66.3	68.3	69.1	69.1	69.5
St. Louis	61.8	65.7	70.9	67.5	72.0	72.0	71.9	71.9
Salt Lake City/Ogden	65.8	66.7	68.5	66.4	67.8	69.9	69.0	68.1
San Antonio	67.5	67.7	69.2	67.0	69.1	69.3	70.2	67.6
San Diego**	100.2	106.4	118.2	110.0	119.9	121.1	118.8	121.1
San Francisco Bay Area	129.9	n/a	n/a	n/a	n/a	164.9	164.8	n/a
Syracuse	50.7	58.8	64.3	59.6	64.9	66.2	66.4	65.2
Tampa/St. Petersburg/Clearwater	58.4	58.4	61.1	56.8	62.1	62.8	62.4	59.8
Toledo, OH	50.7	51.9	56.0	52.1	57.4	60.2	53.2	53.4
Tulsa	67.3	66.7	65.5	66.4	66.8	65.6	63.4	64.1
Washington, D.C.	93.0	97.1	101.2	101.1	102.8	98.9	102.0	107.7
West Palm Beach/Boca Raton/Delray Beach	84.8	88.3	92.6	86.0	94.9	96.6	90.9	96.9

n/a Not Available r Revised

*All areas are metropolitan statistical areas (MSA) as defined by the U.S. Office of Management and Budget. They include the named central city and surrounding suburban areas. ** Provided by the California Association of REALTORS®

Source: National Association of REALTORS®, Economics and Research Division, 777 14th Street, N.W., Washington, D.C. 20005.

HOUSING AFFORDABILITY

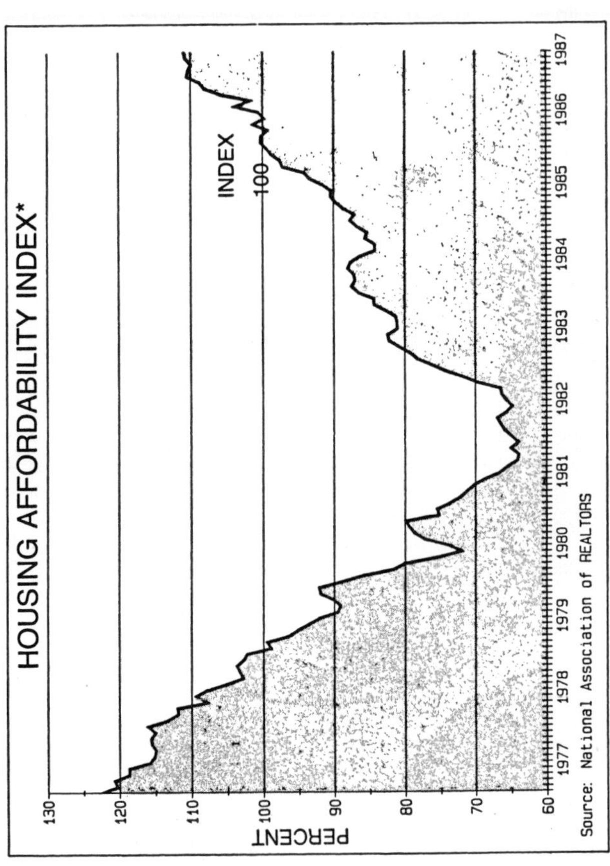

Year	Median-Priced Existing Single-Family Home	Mortgage Rate**	Monthly P & I Payment	Payment as % Income[r]	Median Family Income[r]	Qualifying Income***	Affordability Indexes		
							Composite	Fixed	ARM
1981	$66,400	15.12%	$677	36.3%	$22,388	$32,485	68.9	68.9	68.9
1982	67,800	15.38	702	35.9	23,433	33,713	69.5	69.4	69.7
1983	70,300	12.85	616	30.1	24,580	29,546	83.2	81.7	85.2
1984	72,400	12.49	618	28.2	26,433	29,650	89.1	84.6	92.1
1985	75,500	11.74	609	26.2	27,735	29,243	94.8	89.6	100.6
1986	80,300	10.25	576	23.7	29,200	27,631	105.7	102.8	112.2
1986									
Apr	$80,200	10.37%	$581	24.7%	$28,223	$27,872	101.3	99.6	105.5
May	83,200	10.15	592	25.0	28,345	28,392	99.8	98.6	103.4
Jun	82,600	10.20	590	24.9	28,467	28,305	100.6	99.2	106.5
Jul	79,900	10.26	573	24.1	28,590	27,517	103.9	102.0	111.2
Aug	82,000	10.26	588	24.6	28,712	28,240	101.7	98.9	109.8
Sep	80,300	10.08	568	23.6	28,834	27,243	105.8	102.5	113.2
Oct	79,400	9.97	556	23.0	28,956	26,689	108.5	104.8	117.2
Nov	80,400	9.84	557	23.0	29,078	26,729	108.8	104.8	118.0
Dec	80,800	9.65	551	22.6	29,200	26,430	110.5	106.2	118.8
1987									
Jan	$82,100	9.53%	$554	22.7%	$29,308	$26,578	110.3	107.6	117.6
Feb	85,000	9.21	557	22.7	29,417	26,758	109.9	107.2	116.8
Mar[r]	85,600	9.09	555	22.6	29,525	26,661	110.7	108.5	118.1
Apr[p]	85,400	9.14	557	22.5	29,633	26,717	110.9	109.2	119.2

r Revised

p Preliminary

* Index equals 100 when median family income equals qualifying income.

** Effective rate on loans closed on existing homes—Federal Home Loan Bank Board.

Source: National Association of REALTORS®, Economics and Research Division, 777 14th Street, N.W., Washington, D.C. 20005.

FARM REAL ESTATE VALUES: INDEXES OF THE AVERAGE VALUE PER ACRE OF LAND AND BUILDINGS, BY STATE, GROUPED BY FARM PRODUCTION REGION, FEB. 1, 1980–81; AND APRIL 1, 1982–85; AND FEB. 1, 1987[1]

State	1980	1981	1982	1983	1984	1985	1986	1987	Percent change 1986–87
				1977=100					
Northeast									
Maine[2]	135	143	149	152	162	185	215	234	9
New Hamphire[2]	135	143	149	152	162	185	215	234	9
Vermont[2]	135	143	149	152	162	185	215	234	9
Massachusetts[2]	135	143	149	152	162	185	215	234	9
Rhode Island[2]	135	143	149	152	162	185	215	234	9
Connecticut[2]	135	143	149	152	162	185	215	234	9
New York	119	126	132	129	133	128	131	148	13
New Jersey	120	123	128	125	129	141	157	213	36
Pennsylvania	140	144	133	128	138	127	122	145	19
Delaware	151	158	143	143	146	128	137	138	1
Maryland	166	188	178	160	165	158	142	138	-3
Lake States									
Michigan	138	157	152	141	141	121	108	96	-11
Wisconsin	159	179	174	165	155	126	106	93	-12
Minnesota	154	179	174	155	144	109	81	66	-19
Corn Belt									
Ohio	156	160	137	121	116	90	81	75	-7
Indiana	150	161	140	122	121	96	81	71	-12
Illinois	135	144	131	117	115	84	73	67	-9
Iowa	139	150	139	121	108	77	61	54	-11
Missouri	154	165	153	133	133	102	94	85	-9
Northern Plains									
North Dakota	136	145	149	142	142	116	102	91	-11
South Dakota	141	150	150	140	136	101	87	72	-17
Nebraska	137	151	143	129	114	82	67	62	-8
Kansas	134	137	136	126	122	98	81	71	-12
Appalachian									
Virginia	139	149	143	144	143	140	147	143	-3
West Virginia	150	160	177	177	172	143	139	136	-2
North Carolina	141	155	149	150	158	142	129	125	-3
Kentucky	147	153	154	149	143	129	124	113	-9
Tennessee	136	146	138	131	135	127	128	131	2

State	1980	1981	1982	1983	1984	1985	1986	1987	Percent change 1986-87
				1977=100					
Southeast									
South Carolina	130	137	136	128	125	121	117	107	-9
Georgia	132	139	128	124	122	116	110	113	3
Florida[3]	141	157	149	152	155	147	138	141	2
Alabama	149	176	174	165	162	154	152	146	-4
Delta States									
Mississippi	156	198	189	174	183	163	147	128	-13
Arkansas	163	188	196	174	167	152	126	114	-10
Louisiana	169	200	199	195	195	181	145	106	-27
Southern Plains									
Oklahoma	143	156	164	156	156	126	107	95	-11
Texas	144	158	185	191	208	229	190	169	-11
Mountain States									
Montana	142	148	157	146	149	125	115	94	-18
Idaho	134	144	151	140	140	129	111	98	-12
Wyoming[5]	126	135	140	133	136	122	106	104	-2
Colorado	147	161	164	161	166	154	126	129	2
New Mexico[4,5]	166	178	185	176	180	162	133	121	-9
Arizona[4,5]	167	179	186	177	181	163	142	149	5
Utah[4,5]	169	181	188	179	183	165	153	146	-5
Nevada[4,5]	178	190	198	188	192	173	151	160	6
Pacific States									
Washington	124	146	152	152	157	151	133	118	-11
Oregon	132	144	145	138	137	114	103	95	-8
California	166	201	221	223	223	201	183	159	-13
48 States	145	158	157	148	146	128	112	103	-8
Alaska (1986=100)							100	76	-24

[1] These indexes are based on USDA surveys.

[2] Indexes for 1980–87 were estimated by combining survey data to obtain an average rate of change for these 6 New England States.

[3] Indexes for 1980–82 were estimated using the average of the percentage changes in the Georgia and Alabama indexes.

[4] Index for 1980 was estimated by combining survey data to obtain an average rate of change for these 4 Mountain States.

[5] Indexes for 1981–1985 were estimated using the average of the percentage changes in the Montana, Idaho, and Colorado indexes. 1986 indexes for Arizona and Nevada, based on the average of the percentage change in Montana, Idaho, and Colorado.

Source: *Agriculture Land Values,* Economics Research Service, U.S. Department of Agriculture.

Industrial Real Estate Market: Selected Cities

ATLANTA

METROPOLITAN INDUSTRIAL REAL ESTATE MARKET DATA

ATLANTA

CENTRAL CITY: ATLANTA
SUBURBAN: ATLANTA

INDUSTRIAL MARKET CHARACTERISTICS

	Central City	Suburbs
Total Space	25,000,000 sq. ft.	128,000,000 sq. ft.
Total Vacant	1,200,000 sq. ft.	15,000,000 sq. ft.
Vacancy Rate	4.8 %	11.7 %
Contruction	200,000 sq. ft.	5,000,000 sq. ft.

DOLLAR VOLUME OF SALES AND LEASES COMPARED TO A YEAR AGO

Manufacturing		Warehousing Distribution		High Technology	
Sales	Leases	Sales	Leases	Sales	Leases
SAME	SAME	UP 5 %	SAME	SAME	DOWN 12%

GROSS SALES AND LEASE PRICES OF PRIME INDUSTRIAL BUILDINGS AND SITES

	Central City		Suburbs	
	Per Square Foot	Change From a Year Ago	Per Square Foot	Change From a Year Ago
Building Sales Prices				
Less than 5,000 sq. ft.	$ 35.00- $ 45.00	SAME	$ 40.00- $ 50.00	SAME
5,000-20,000 sq. ft.	$ 25.00- $ 37.00	SAME	$ 25.00- $ 37.00	SAME
20,000-40,000 sq. ft.	$ 20.00- $ 30.00	SAME	$ 23.00- $ 32.00	SAME
40,000-60,000 sq. ft.	$ 18.00- $ 25.00	SAME	$ 20.00- $ 25.00	SAME
60,000-100,000 sq. ft.	$ 17.00- $ 23.00	SAME	$ 18.00- $ 23.00	SAME
100,000 or more sq. ft.	$ 16.00- $ 18.00	SAME	$ 15.00- $ 21.00	SAME
Prime High Technology	$ 50.00- $ 75.00	SAME	$ 70.00- $ 85.00	SAME
Site Sales Prices				
Improved				
Less than 2 acres	$ 2.50- $ 3.25	UP 12 %	$ 2.50- $ 4.00	UP 6 %
2-5 acres	$ 2.25- $ 2.75	UP 13 %	$ 2.25- $ 3.50	UP 6 %
5-10 acres	$ 1.75- $ 2.25	UP 6 %	$ 2.10- $ 3.00	SAME
10 or more acres	$ 1.75- $ 2.00	UP 14 %	$ 1.50- $ 2.75	SAME
Unimproved				
Less than 10 acres	$ 1.75- $ 2.25	UP 14 %	$ 2.00- $ 3.50	UP 6 %
10-100 acres	$ 1.50- $ 2.00	UP 14 %	$ 1.75- $ 3.00	SAME
100 or more acres	$ 1.00- $ 1.50	UP 14 %	$ 1.50- $ 5.50	SAME
Annual Lease Prices				
Less than 5,000 sq. ft.	$ 3.25- $ 5.00	UP 10 %	$ 3.75- $ 5.00	UP 5 %
5,000-20,000 sq. ft.	$ 2.75- $ 3.75	UP 5 %	$ 3.25- $ 4.25	UP 5 %
20,000-40,000 sq. ft.	$ 2.50- $ 3.50	UP 5 %	$ 3.00- $ 4.00	SAME
40,000-60,000 sq. ft.	$ 2.25- $ 3.25	UP 5 %	$ 2.75- $ 3.75	SAME
60,000-100,000 sq. ft.	$ 2.00- $ 3.00	UP 5 %	$ 2.50- $ 3.50	SAME
100,000 or more sq. ft.	$ 1.75- $ 2.75	UP 5 %	$ 2.25- $ 3.25	SAME
Prime High Technology	$ 8.00- $ 12.00	SAME	$ 7.00- $ 10.00	DOWN 1%

CHICAGO

METROPOLITAN INDUSTRIAL REAL ESTATE MARKET DATA

CHICAGO

CENTRAL CITY: CHICAGO
SUBURBAN: ALL CHICAGO METROPOLITAN SUBURBS

INDUSTRIAL MARKET CHARACTERISTICS

	Central City	Suburbs
Total Space	170,000,000 sq. ft.	500,000,000 sq. ft.
Total Vacant	15,500,000 sq. ft.	40,000,000 sq. ft.
Vacancy Rate	11.0 %	8.0 %
Contruction	750,000 sq. ft.	5,000,000 sq. ft.

DOLLAR VOLUME OF SALES AND LEASES COMPARED TO A YEAR AGO

Manufacturing		Warehousing Distribution		High Technology	
Sales	Leases	Sales	Leases	Sales	Leases
UP 10 %	UP 10 %	UP 18 %	UP 18 %	UP 15 %	UP 15 %

GROSS SALES AND LEASE PRICES OF PRIME INDUSTRIAL BUILDINGS AND SITES

	Central City		Suburbs	
	Per Square Foot	Change From a Year Ago	Per Square Foot	Change From a Year Ago
Building Sales Prices				
Less than 5,000 sq. ft.	$ 33.00	UP 10 %	$ 45.00	UP 7 %
5,000-20,000 sq. ft.	$ 27.00	UP 8 %	$ 37.00	UP 6 %
20,000-40,000 sq. ft.	$ 24.00	UP 14 %	$ 31.00	UP 7 %
40,000-60,000 sq. ft.	$ 22.00	UP 10 %	$ 28.00	UP 8 %
60,000-100,000 sq. ft.	$ 18.00	UP 20 %	$ 24.00	UP 4 %
100,000 or more sq. ft.	$ 15.00	UP 15 %	$ 22.00	UP 5 %
Prime High Technology	NA	NA	$ 55.00	UP 4 %
Site Sales Prices				
Improved				
Less than 2 acres	$ 1.50- $ 5.00	SAME	$ 1.50- $ 5.00	SAME
2-5 acres	$ 2.00- $ 4.00	SAME	$ 1.50- $ 5.00	UP 10 %
5-10 acres	$ 1.00- $ 2.75	UP 10 %	$ 1.50- $ 4.00	UP 10 %
10 or more acres	$ 1.00- $ 1.50	UP 10 %	$ 1.00- $ 3.50	UP 10 %
Unimproved				
Less than 10 acres	NA	NA	$ 1.25	UP 20 %
10-100 acres	NA	NA	$ 1.00	UP 20 %
100 or more acres	NA	NA	$ .65	UP 20 %
Annual Lease Prices				
Less than 5,000 sq. ft.	$ 4.50	UP 6 %	$ 5.50	UP 5 %
5,000-20,000 sq. ft.	$ 4.00	UP 23 %	$ 5.00	UP 11 %
20,000-40,000 sq. ft.	$ 3.50	UP 8 %	$ 4.50	UP 13 %
40,000-60,000 sq. ft.	$ 3.25	UP 8 %	$ 4.25	UP 6 %
60,000-100,000 sq. ft.	$ 3.00	UP 20 %	$ 4.00	UP 5 %
100,000 or more sq. ft.	$ 2.50	UP 11 %	$ 3.75	UP 15 %
Prime High Technology	NA	NA	$ 13.00	SAME

HOUSTON

METROPOLITAN INDUSTRIAL REAL ESTATE MARKET DATA

HOUSTON

CENTRAL CITY: HOUSTON
SUBURBAN: HOUSTON

INDUSTRIAL MARKET CHARACTERISTICS

	Central City	Suburbs
Total Space	80,695,000 sq. ft.	126,390,000 sq. ft.
Total Vacant	9,676,000 sq. ft.	24,807,000 sq. ft.
Vacancy Rate	12.0 %	19.6 %
Contruction	0 sq. ft.	140,000 sq. ft.

DOLLAR VOLUME OF SALES AND LEASES COMPARED TO A YEAR AGO

Manufacturing		Warehousing Distribution		High Technology	
Sales	Leases	Sales	Leases	Sales	Leases
DOWN 10%	DOWN 10%	UP 10 %	UP 10 %	UP 10 %	UP 10 %

GROSS SALES AND LEASE PRICES OF PRIME INDUSTRIAL BUILDINGS AND SITES

	Central City		Suburbs	
	Per Square Foot	Change From a Year Ago	Per Square Foot	Change From a Year Ago
Building Sales Prices				
Less than 5,000 sq. ft.	$ 30.00- $ 45.00	DOWN 8%	$ 15.00- $ 50.00	DOWN 8%
5,000-20,000 sq. ft.	$ 30.00- $ 40.00	DOWN 8%	$ 20.00- $ 45.00	DOWN 8%
20,000-40,000 sq. ft.	$ 20.00- $ 35.00	DOWN 8%	$ 15.00- $ 40.00	DOWN 8%
40,000-60,000 sq. ft.	$ 15.00- $ 30.00	DOWN 8%	$ 15.00- $ 35.00	DOWN 8%
60,000-100,000 sq. ft.	$ 10.00- $ 25.00	DOWN 8%	$ 15.00- $ 30.00	DOWN 8%
100,000 or more sq. ft.	$ 10.00- $ 15.00	DOWN 8%	$ 12.00- $ 22.00	DOWN 8%
Prime High Technology	$ 10.00- $ 25.00	DOWN 8%	$ 30.00- $ 60.00	DOWN 8%
Site Sales Prices				
Improved				
Less than 2 acres	$ 3.00- $ 6.00	DOWN 1%	$ 1.50- $ 6.00	DOWN 1%
2-5 acres	$ 2.50- $ 6.00	DOWN 1%	$ 1.50- $ 6.00	DOWN 1%
5-10 acres	$ 2. - $ 5.00	DOWN 1%	$ 1.00- $ 5.00	DOWN 1%
10 or more acres	$ 2.00- $ 5.00	DOWN 1%	$ 1.00- $ 5.00	DOWN 1%
Unimproved				
Less than 10 acres	$ 2.00- $ 6.00	DOWN 1%	$ .50- $ 2.50	DOWN 1%
10-100 acres	NA	NA	$ .30- $ 2.00	DOWN 1%
100 or more acres	NA	NA	$ .10- $ 1.00	DOWN 1%
Annual Lease Prices				
Less than 5,000 sq. ft.	$ 2.40- $ 4.50	SAME	$ 2.40- $ 4.50	SAME
5,000-20,000 sq. ft.	$ 2.40- $ 4.00	SAME	$ 2.40- $ 4.00	SAME
20,000-40,000 sq. ft.	$ 2.00- $ 3.50	SAME	$ 2.00- $ 3.50	SAME
40,000-60,000 sq. ft.	$ 1.50- $ 3.00	SAME	$ 1.50- $ 3.00	SAME
60,000-100,000 sq. ft.	$ 1.25- $ 2.50	SAME	$ 1.50- $ 2.50	SAME
100,000 or more sq. ft.	$ 1.10- $ 2.00	SAME	$ 1.10- $ 2.00	SAME
Prime High Technology	$ 3.50- $ 8.00	SAME	$ 3.50- $ 8.00	SAME

LOS ANGELES—CENTRAL

METROPOLITAN INDUSTRIAL REAL ESTATE MARKET DATA

LOS ANGELES--CENTRAL

CENTRAL CITY: CENTRAL LOS ANGELES, DOWNTOWN LOS ANGELES
SUBURBAN: VERNON, COMMERCE

INDUSTRIAL MARKET CHARACTERISTICS

	Central City	Suburbs
Total Space	NA	NA
Total Vacant	NA	NA
Vacancy Rate	NA	NA
Contruction	NA	NA

DOLLAR VOLUME OF SALES AND LEASES COMPARED TO A YEAR AGO

Manufacturing		Warehousing Distribution		High Technology	
Sales	Leases	Sales	Leases	Sales	Leases
UP 5 %	UP 5 %	UP 10 %	UP 10 %	NA	NA

GROSS SALES AND LEASE PRICES OF PRIME INDUSTRIAL BUILDINGS AND SITES

	Central City		Suburbs	
	Per Square Foot	Change From a Year Ago	Per Square Foot	Change From a Year Ago
Building Sales Prices				
Less than 5,000 sq. ft.	$ 55.00	UP 8 %	$ 45.00	UP 8 %
5,000-20,000 sq. ft.	$ 50.00	NA	$ 40.00	NA
20,000-40,000 sq. ft.	$ 45.00	NA	$ 38.00	NA
40,000-60,000 sq. ft.	$ 42.00	NA	$ 35.00	NA
60,000-100,000 sq. ft.	$ 38.00	NA	$ 35.00	NA
100,000 or more sq. ft.	$ 35.00	NA	$ 32.00	NA
Prime High Technology	NA	NA	NA	NA
Site Sales Prices				
Improved				
Less than 2 acres	$ 15.00- $ 20.00	UP 10 %	$ 8.00- $ 10.00	NA
2-5 acres	$ 12.00	NA	$ 7.00	NA
5-10 acres	$ 10.00	NA	$ 5.00- $ 7.00	NA
10 or more acres	NA	NA	NA	NA
Unimproved				
Less than 10 acres	NA	NA	NA	NA
10-100 acres	NA	NA	NA	NA
100 or more acres	NA	NA	NA	NA
Annual Lease Prices				
Less than 5,000 sq. ft.	$ 6.00	NA	NA	NA
5,000-20,000 sq. ft.	$ 4.80	NA	NA	NA
20,000-40,000 sq. ft.	$ 4.56	NA	NA	NA
40,000-60,000 sq. ft.	$ 4.20	NA	NA	NA
60,000-100,000 sq. ft.	$ 3.84	NA	NA	NA
100,000 or more sq. ft.	$ 3.60	NA	NA	NA
Prime High Technology	NA	NA	NA	NA

NEW YORK—NEW YORK CITY

METROPOLITAN INDUSTRIAL REAL ESTATE MARKET DATA

NEW YORK CITY

CENTRAL CITY: NEW YORK CITY
SUBURBAN:

INDUSTRIAL MARKET CHARACTERISTICS

	Central City	Suburbs
Total Space	400,000,000 sq. ft.	NA
Total Vacant	4,250,000 sq. ft.	NA
Vacancy Rate	1.1 %	NA
Contruction	NA	NA

DOLLAR VOLUME OF SALES AND LEASES COMPARED TO A YEAR AGO

Manufacturing		Warehousing Distribution		High Technology	
Sales	Leases	Sales	Leases	Sales	Leases
UP 20 %	NA	UP 20 %	UP 20 %	NA	NA

GROSS SALES AND LEASE PRICES OF PRIME INDUSTRIAL BUILDINGS AND SITES

	Central City		Suburbs	
	Per Square Foot	Change From a Year Ago	Per Square Foot	Change From a Year Ago
Building Sales Prices				
Less than 5,000 sq. ft.	$ 40.00- $150.00	UP 50 %	NA	NA
5,000-20,000 sq. ft.	$ 35.00- $ 75.00	UP 20 %	NA	NA
20,000-40,000 sq. ft.	$ 35.00- $ 75.00	UP 20 %	NA	NA
40,000-60,000 sq. ft.	$ 32.00- $ 60.00	UP 20 %	NA	NA
60,000-100,000 sq. ft.	$ 30.00- $ 60.00	UP 20 %	NA	NA
100,000 or more sq. ft.	$ 30.00- $ 50.00	UP 15 %	NA	NA
Prime High Technology	NA	NA	NA	NA
Site Sales Prices				
Improved				
Less than 2 acres	$ 10.00- $250.00	UP 150 %	NA	NA
2-5 acres	$ 8.00- $ 40.00	UP 50 %	NA	NA
5-10 acres	$ 7.00- $ 20.00	UP 100 %	NA	NA
10 or more acres	NA	NA	NA	NA
Unimproved				
Less than 10 acres	$ 5.00- $ 15.00	UP 50 %	NA	NA
10-100 acres	NA	NA	NA	NA
100 or more acres	NA	NA	NA	NA
Annual Lease Prices				
Less than 5,000 sq. ft.	$ 6.00- $ 15.00	UP 50 %	NA	NA
5,000-20,000 sq. ft.	$ 4.00- $ 12.00	UP 25 %	NA	NA
20,000-40,000 sq. ft.	$ 4.00- $ 10.00	UP 25 %	NA	NA
40,000-60,000 sq. ft.	$ 4.00- $ 8.00	UP 25 %	NA	NA
60,000-100,000 sq. ft.	$ 4.00- $ 8.00	UP 10 %	NA	NA
100,000 or more sq. ft.	$ 3.75- $ 6.50	SAME	NA	NA
Prime High Technology	NA	NA	NA	NA

Source: *INDUSTRIAL REAL ESTATE MARKET SURVEY, 1986 Review and 1987 Forecast.* Society of Industrial and Office REALTORS® & the Economics and Research Division of the National Association of REALTORS®, 777 14th Street, NW, Suite 400 Washington, DC 20005-3271.

CONVENTIONAL LOANS ON NEW HOMES

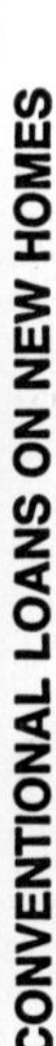

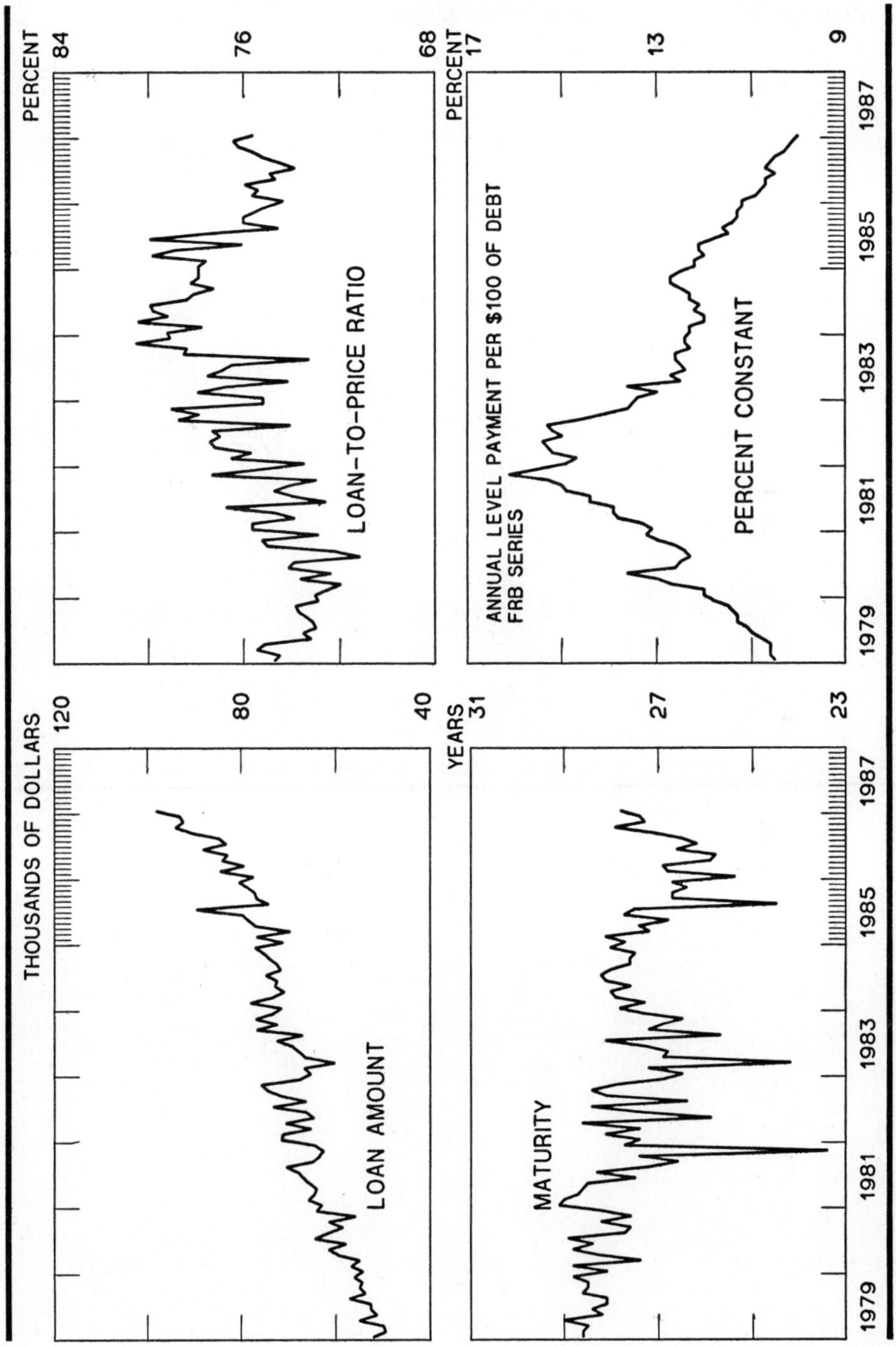

Source: *Federal Reserve Chart Book*, Board of Governors of the Federal Reserve System.

Average Sales Price of Industrial Buildings

Prime Industrial Building. A building in the top 25 percent of overall desirability of the existing inventory. Such buildings are considered to be for *general* purpose uses such as industrial, research, warehouse and/or manufacturing. (*Special* purpose buildings are not to be considered in this category.)

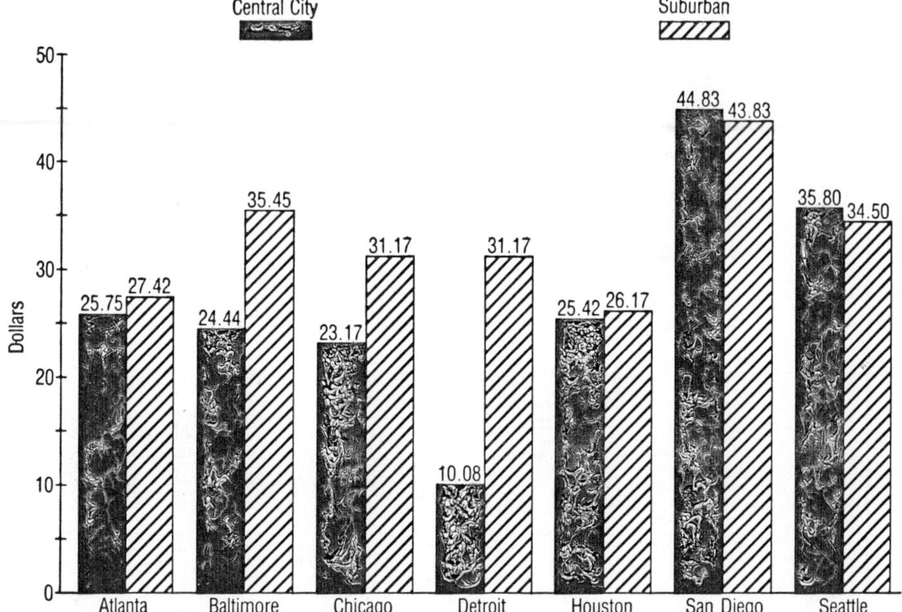

Source: INDUSTRIAL REAL ESTATE MARKET SURVEY: 1986 Review and 1987 Forecast. Society of Industrial and Office REALTORS® and the Research Division of the National Association of REALTORS®, 777 14th Street, NW, Suite 400, Washington, DC 20005–3271.

Average Sales Price of Industrial Buildings

Prime High-Technology Building. Generally, 30 percent or more office, fully air-conditioned, 12–18′ clear, extensive landscaping and parking, architecturally impressive. In some areas of the country where high-tech industries are not prevalent, this building could be used as a showroom or as pure office.

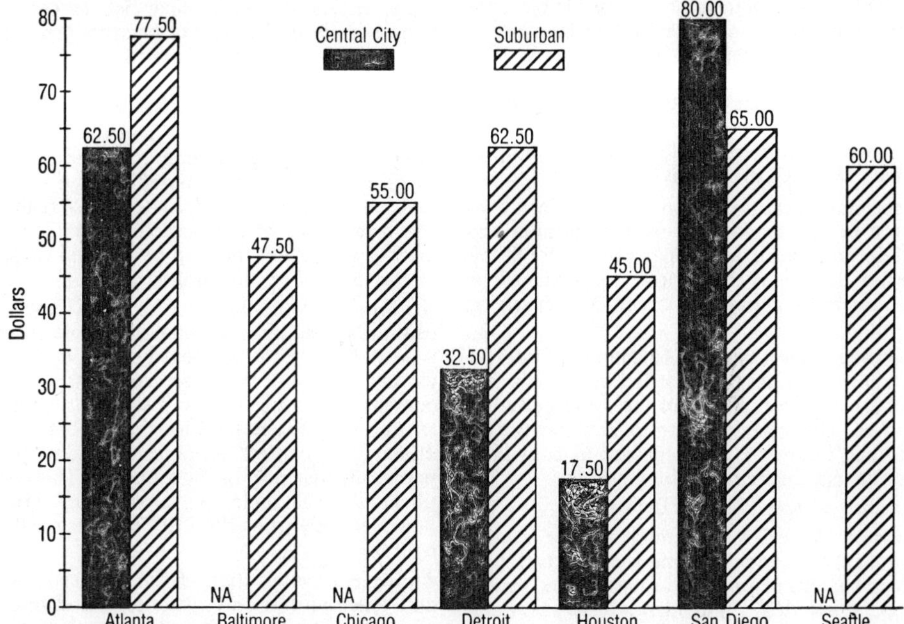

Source: INDUSTRIAL REAL ESTATE MARKET SURVEY: 1986 Review and 1987 Forecast. Society of Industrial and Office REALTORS® and the Research Division of the National Association of REALTORS®, 777 14th Street, NW, Suite 400, Washington, DC 20005–3271.

Glossary of Real Estate and REIT Terms

This glossary of terminology used in conjunction with discussions of real estate investment trusts has been prepared by the Research Department of the National Association of Real Estate Investment Trusts. Credit should be given to Realty Income Trust, a NAREIT member, which produced a glossary of terms upon which NAREIT drew heavily.

Acceleration clause A condition in a loan contract or mortgage note which permits the lender to demand immediate repayment of the entire balance if the contract is breached or conditions for repayment occur, such as sale or demolition.

Accrued interest or rent An amount of interest or rent which has been earned but which may not have been received in the same period as earned. On many short-term first mortgages, accrued interest is not received in cash until permanent financing is obtained.

Acquisition loan See C&D loan.

Advisor A REIT's investment advisor (usually pursuant to a renewable one-year contract) provides analysis of proposed investments, servicing of the portfolio, and other advisory services. Fee limits for advisory services are prescribed by many state securities regulators. Also spelled "adviser."

Amortization The process of retiring debt or recovering a capital investment through scheduled, systematic repayments of principal; that portion of fixed mortgage payment applied to reduction of the principal amount owed.

Anchor Tenant An important tenant, usually with an excellent credit rating (also known as a triple-A tenant), which takes a large amount of space in a shopping center or office building and is usually one of the first tenants to commit to lease. The anchor tenant usually is given lower rent because of the desirability of having that tenant at the property, both because of its credit rating and its ability to generate traffic.

Appraisal An opinion by an expert of the value of a property as of a specified date, supported by the presentation and analysis of relevant data. The appraisal may be arrived at by any or all of three methods: the cost approach (cost to reproduce), the market approach (comparison with other similar properties), or the income approach (capitalization of actual or projected income figures).

Assessed value The value of a property which is assigned to it by a taxing authority for purposes of assessing property taxes; often assessed value bears a fixed relationship by local statute to market value.

Asset swaps See swap program.

Assets Anything of value owned by the company. Assets are either financial, as cash or bonds; or physical, as real or personal property. For REIT tax purposes, more than 75% of the trust's assets must be property owned or securities backed by real estate.

Assumption of mortgage When the responsibility for repaying existing indebtedness secured by property is "assumed" by the second purchaser. In most jurisdictions, this relieves the first owner of the original obligations, at least to the extent that can be satisfied by sale of this asset after foreclosure.

Attribution More than 50% of a REIT's shares cannot be held by fewer than six people (otherwise it becomes a personal holding company for tax purposes). When someone has indirect control over someone else's shares (such as a trustee over shares held for the benefit of another) then "control" for personal holding company purposes may be "attributed." This complicated legal topic of "attribution" arises, however, only when the REIT's shares are held by a few.

Audit An examination of the financial status and operations of an enterprise, based mostly on the books of account, and undertaken to assure conformity to generally accepted accounting principles and to secure information for, or to check the accuracy of, the enterprise's balance sheet, income statement, and/or cash flow statement.

Balloon mortgage A mortgage loan which provides for periodic payments, which may include both interest and principal, but which leaves the loan less than fully ammortized at maturity, requiring a final large payment which is the "balloon." Usually the term does not apply to an "interest only" loan whose full principal is due upon maturity or upon call during its life.

Bankrupt When liabilities exceed assets, Federal laws enable the entity to dissolve in an orderly fashion (Chapter VII), or permit a court officer to restructure the company into a survivor "going business" (Chapter X), or permit existing management to do the same under court supervision (Chapter XI), or to do so despite the preferred position of secured creditors if real property is the only asset of the business (Chapter XII).

Beneficial owner The person who ultimately benefits from ownership of shares or other securities—in contrast to "nominees" (often pseudonyms for control of investment professionals so as to facilitate security transactions without having to track down beneficial owners to participate in each step of the procedures).

Source: National Association of Real Estate Trusts, 1101 Seventeenth Street, N.W., Washington, D.C. 20036.

Blue sky laws State laws regulating conditions of sale of securities of companies, (particularly those just starting out of the "clear blue sky") for the protection of the investing public. National stock exchange rules usually supercede state laws pursuant to a "blue chip" exemption contained in such state laws. The federal securities laws dovetail with state laws and pertain to publicly held companies, primarily as to accounting and disclosure practices.

Bond A debt certificate which (a) represents a loan to a trust, (b) bears interest, and (c) matures on a stated future date. Short term bonds (generally with a maturity of five years or less from the date of issuance) are often called notes. See debentures.

Book value per share Shareholder equity as adjusted to tangible net worth (assets minus liabilities plus paid-in capital) per share outstanding.

Borrower A person or entity who received something of value, ordinarily money, and is obligated to pay it back, as the debtor to the creditor, usually pursuant to a note or "IOU" containing terms and conditions.

Broker A person who is paid to act as an intermediary in connection with a transaction, in contrast to a dealer or principal who buys or sells for his own account. In the REIT world, the term "broker" usually refers to a real estate salesman, although the term is also used for "stockbrokers" too.

Building lien An encumbrance upon the property by the contractor or subcontractors. Also known as a "mechanic's" or "materialman's" lien.

Building permit Written permission by the local municipality (usually through the building inspector or other agent) allowing construction work on a piece of property in accordance with plans which were submitted and conforming to local building codes and regulations.

Business trust An unincorporated business in which assets are given to trustees for management to hold or to sell, as investments. The business trust form was first fully developed in Massachusetts, under common law, and the term "Massachusetts business trust" is sometimes used to describe entities formed in other states. It is a form of business through a trustee or trustees who hold legal title to the property of the business. Capital contributions are made to the trustees by the beneficaries whose equitable title and interest in the property of the trust are evidenced by trust certificates, usually called shares of beneficial interest. The earnings of the trust are paid to them, as dividends are paid to stockholders. The beneficiaries generally enjoy limited liability, as the control and management of the trust rests solely with the trustees, but the trust form or organization can be distinguished from a corporation. Early REIT tax laws relied on this distinction to define eligible real estate operations.

Capital gain The amount by which the net proceeds from resale of a capital item exceed the adjusted cost (or "book value") of the asset. If a capital asset is held for more than twelve months before disposition it is taxed on a more favorable basis than a gain after a shorter period of time.

Capitalization rate The rate of return utilized to value a given cash flow, the sum of a Discount Rate and a Capital Recapture Rate. It is applied to any income stream with a finite term over which the invested principal is to be returned to the investor or lender.

Cash flow The revenue remaining after all cash expenses are paid, i.e., non-cash charges such as depreciation are not included in the calculation.

Cash flow per share. Cash flow divided by the common shares outstanding. Shareholders must make this computation themselves since the SEC has prohibited companies from stating this calculation.

Net cash flow. Generally determined by net income plus depreciation less principal payments on long-term mortgages.

Cash on cash return The "cash flow" from a property expressed as a percentage of the cash "equity" invested in a property.

Chapter X See bankrupt.

Collateral An item of value, such as real estate or securities, which a borrower pledges as security. A mortgage gives the creditor the right to seize the real estate collateral after non-performance of the debtor.

Commitment A promise to make an investment at some time in the future if certain specified conditions are met. A REIT may charge a fee to the borrower at the time of making the commitment. A REIT's level of commitments minus expected repayments can be regarded as an indication of future funding requirements.

"Take-out" commitment is one provided by the anticipated long-term lender, usually with complicated terms and conditions that must be met before the "take out" becomes effective.

"Gap" commitment is an anticipated short-term loan to cover part of the final "take-out" that the long-term lender refuses to advance until certain conditions are met (like 90% rent-up of an apartment after construction is completed). The amount above the "floor" or basic part of the loan is the "gap," and the gap commitment is issued to enable the construction lender to make a construction loan commitment for the full amount of the takeout loan instead of only for the "floor" amount.

"Standby" commitment is one that the lender and borrower doubt will be used. It exists as reassurance to a short-term construction lender that if, after completion of a building, the borrower cannot find adequate long-term "take-out" financing, the construction lender will be repaid.

Compensating balances Money which is sometimes required by banks to be held in checking accounts by borrowers, as part of their loan agreement.

Condominium A form of fee ownership of whole units or separate portions of multi-unit buildings which facilitates the formal filing, recording and financing of a divided interest in real property. The condominium concept may be used for apartments, offices and other professional uses. See cooperatives.

Conduit tax treatment So long as most (if not all) earnings are passed along by an entity, then federal taxation is avoided at the entity's level. REITs, mutual funds, and certain kinds of holding companies are elibible for "conduit tax treatment" under certain conditions.

Constant The agreed-upon periodic (usually monthly) payment to pay the face interest rate, with any residual amount going to amortize the loan.

Construction and development loan (C&D) A short-term loan for the purpose of constructing a building, shopping center, or other improvement upon real estate, or developing a site in preparation for construction. A C&D loan is normally disbursed in increments (called *draws* or *draw-downs*) as building proceeds, rather than in a single disbursement, and is conditioned upon compliance with a variety of factors. It is usually repaid with the proceeds of the permanent loan. A land loan or purchase and development loan is sometimes made for the purpose of acquiring unimproved vacant land, usually as a future building site and for financing improvements to such land (street, sewers, etc.) as a prerequisite to construction of a building upon the site.

Contingent Interest Interest on a loan that is payable only if certain conditions occur, in contrast to interest that becomes an accrued liability (whether or not paid) at a specific time.

Cooperative A form of ownership whereby a structure is owned by a corporation or trust with each individual owner holding stock in the corporation representative of the value of his apartment. Title to the apartment is evidenced by a proprietary lease which often does not qualify as adequate collateral for some lenders.

Cost-to-carry The concept specified by the accounting profession to be used by REITs in computing anticipated interest cost on debt needed to "carry" non-earning or partially-earning assets until they're restored to earning status or sold

Current Liabilities Money owed and due to be paid within one year.

Dealer Someone who buys property with the purpose of selling it at a profit rather than holding it as an investment. A dealer's profits are taxed at the ordinary income rate rather than the capital gains rate regardless of how long the property is held for resale (in contrast to the investor who sells a property after a year and pays at the capital gains rate). A REIT is not permitted to be a dealer unless it is willing to pay a 100% tax on gains from such sales in the year in which it is deemed to be a dealer; sales of foreclosed property do not fall within this definition. See principal.

Debenture An obligation which is secured only by the general credit of the issuing trust, as opposed to being secured by a direct lien on its assets, real estate or otherwise. A debenture is a form of a bond.

Declaration of Trust Similar to articles of incorporation for a corporation, this document contains rules for operation of the trust, selection of its governing trustees, etc., and is the keystone of a REIT.

Deed A legal instrument which conveys title from one to another. It must be (a) made between competent parties (b) have legally sound subject matter (c) correctly state what is being conveyed (d) contain good and valuable consideration (e) be properly executed by the parties involved and (f) be delivered to be valid.

Deed in lieu of foreclosure The device by which title to property is conveyed from the mortgagor (borrower) to the mortgagee (lender) as an alternative to foreclosure. While this procedure can transfer effective control more quickly, many lenders eschew it because undiscovered prior liens (from a workman who was never paid but hadn't gotten around to filing his valid, but late, claim for example) remain enforceable in contrast to the more formal foreclosure procedures which wipe out prior claims after due notice.

Deferred maintenance the amount of repairs that should have been made to keep a property in good running condition, but which have been put off. The term contemplates the desirability of immediate expenditures, although it does not necessarily denote inadequate maintenance in the past.

Deficiency dividend The process of paying an "extra" dividend after the close of the fiscal year so as to comply with REIT tax requirements to pay out more than 90% of income. See dividend.

Depreciation The loss in value of a capital asset, due to wear and tear which cannot be compensated for by ordinary repairs, or an allowance made to allow for the fact that the asset may become obsolete before it wears out. The purpose of a depreciation charge is to write off the original cost of an asset by equitably distributing charges against its operation over its useful life, matching "cost" to the period in which it was used to generate earnings. Depreciation is an optional noncash expense recognizable for tax purposes. If the REIT pays out more than its taxable earnings, then it is distributing a "return of capital" or—as is commonly stated in the industry—"paying out depreciation."

Development loans See Construction and development loan.

Dilution The situation which results when an increase occurs in a company's outstanding securities without a corresponding increase in the company's assets and/or income.

Discount rate An interest rate used to convert a future stream of payments into a single present value. See capitalization rate.

Dividend or distribution The distribution of cash or stock to shareholders of a company which is made periodically as a means of distributing all or a portion of net income or cash flow. Technically, a dividend can be paid only from net taxable income, so many REITs distribute cash and later characterize their distributions as capital gains or a tax-free return of capital if net taxable income is less than the cash paid out.

Dividend or distribution yield The annual dividend or distribution rate for a security expressed as a percent of its market price. For most REITs, the "annualized" rate is the previous quarter's distribution times four, regardless of how the distribution is characterized.

Draw A request from a borrower to obtain partial payment from the lender pursuant to a loan commitment. The lender reassures himself that the borrower has completed the required steps (such as putting in the concrete properly) before advancing money. Often, the borrower submits bills from subcontractors, which are then "paid" by the lender after inspecting the subcontractor's work. In such cases, the check is usually made out to the subcontractor but must be signed by the borrower, too, so that the lender ends up only with one borrower. See construction and development loan.

Effective Borrowing Costs The cost of borrowing after adjustment for compensating balances or fees in lieu of compensating balances, and selling expenses in the case of publicly sold debt.

Encumbrance A legal right or interest in real estate which diminishes its value. Encumbrances can take a number of forms, such as easements, zoning restrictions, mortgages, etc.

Entrepreneur An individual who is responsible for a commercial or real estate activity who takes a certain risk of loss in a transaction for the right to enjoy any profit which may result.

Equity The interest of the shareholders in a company as measured by their paid-in capital and undistributed income. The term is also used to describe (i) the difference between the current market value of a property and the liens or mortgages which encumber it or (ii) the cash which makes up the difference between the mortgage(s) and the construction or sale price.

Equity leveraging The process by which shares are sold at a premium above book value (in anticipation of greater earnings).

Equity participation Usually, the right of an investor to participate to some extent in the increased value of a project by receiving a percentage of the increased income from the project. If a REIT were to participate in a percentage of the net income of a venture (such as the shopping center's owner/lessor), then it could be deemed to be a partner in an active business. Thus, most REIT leases spell out the "equity participation" as a percentage of gross receipts or sales (which is a more stable measure of sales activity, anyway, and one readily identifiable from the lessor's federal income tax statement).

Escrow A deposit of "good faith" money which is entrusted to a third party (often a bank) until fulfillment of certain conditions and agreements, when the escrow may be released or applied as payment for the purchase of property or for services rendered.

Estoppel certificate An instrument used when a mortgage or lease is assigned to another. The certificate sets forth the exact remaining balance of the lease or mortgage as of a certain date and verifies any promises to tenants that may have been made by the first owner for which the second owner may be held accountable.

Exculpatory clause A clause which relieves one of liability for injuries or damages to another. Exculpatory clauses are placed in REIT documents with the intention of eliminating personal liability of its trustees, shareholders and officers.

Expenses The costs which are charges against current operations or earnings of a building, company or other reporting entity. They may have been "paid out" in cash, or accrued to be paid later, or charged as a bookkeeping procedure to reflect the "using up" of assets (as in depreciation) utilized in the production of income during the period of current operations.

Face value The value which is shown on the face of an instrument such as a bond, debenture or stock certificate. The "face rate" of a debt instrument is often known as its "coupon rate."

Fair market value See Market value.

Fee or fee simple Title to a property which is absolute, good and marketable; ownership without condition.

Fiduciary A relationship of trust and confidence between a person charged with the duty of acting for the benefit of another and the person to whom such duty is owed, as in the case of guardian and ward, trustee and beneficiary, executor and heir.

First mortgage That mortgage which has a prior claim over all other liens against real estate. In some jurisdictions, real estate taxes, mechanics liens, court costs, and other involuntary liens may take priority over such a contractual lien: title companies "clear" properties so as to reassure first mortgage lenders (and owners) of their uncontested position and to guarantee them of that position under certain conditions.

Fiscal year The 12-month period selected as a basis for computing and accounting for a business. A fiscal year need not coincide with the calendar year, except for all REITs initially qualifying for special tax treatment after 1976.

Fixed assets Assets, such as land, buildings and machinery, which cannot be quickly converted into cash. For REITs, most "fixed assets" are real property although some (like furniture in an apartment lobby) may be personal property.

Fixed charges Those interest charges, insurance costs, taxes and other expenses which remain relatively constant regardless of revenue. See net lease.

Floating rate A variable interest rate charged for the use of borrowed money. It is determined by charging a specific percentage above a fluctuating base rate, usually the prime rate as announced by a major commercial bank.

Floor loan A portion or portions of a mortgage loan commitment which is less than the full amount of the commitment and which may be funded upon conditions less stringent than those required for funding the full amount, or the "ceiling" of the loan. For example, the floor loan, equal to perhaps 80% of the full amount of the loan, may be funded upon completion of construction without any occupancy requirements, but substantial occupancy of the building may be required for funding the full amount of the loan, which is referred to as the "ceiling." See commitment, gap.

Foreclosure The legal process of enforcing payment of a debt by taking the properties which secure the debt, once the terms of the obligation are not followed. Upon foreclosure, the entire debt might not be fully discharged by transfer and disposition of the property (as determined by the courts). If so, a "deficiency judgment" may be obtained, at which point the lender is like any other creditor in attempting to get the debtor to pay the deficiency. Collection of the deficiency judgment in major real estate transactions is rare, but it becomes a major factor in negotiations if the borrower decides to return to the real estate business in the future.

Fully diluted earnings The hypothetical earnings per share of a company, computed after giving effect to the number of shares which would be outstanding if all convertible debt and warrants were exercised, and also to any reduction in interest payments resulting from such exercise.

Gap commitment See commitment, gap. Also see floor loan.

General lien A lien against the property of an individual or other entity generally, rather than against specific items of realty or personal property.

Ground lease See sale-leaseback.

Holding company A corporation that owns or controls the operations of various other companies. Many REITs were sponsored by bank or insurance holding companies whose subsidiary companies advise and manage REITs, pursuant to contracts with the REIT's trustees.

Independent contractor A firm hired to actively manage property investments. A tax-qualified REIT must hire an independent contractor to manage and operate its property, so as to distinguish itself as an investor rather than an active manager.

Income property Developed real estate, such as office buildings, shopping centers, apartments, hotels and motels, warehouses and some kinds of agricultural or industrial property, which produce a flow of income—in contrast to non-income generating real estate like raw land which would be bought and held for a speculative profit upon resale or development.

Indenture The legal document prepared in connection with, for example, a bond issue, setting forth the terms of the issue, its specific security, remedies in case of default, etc. It may also be called the "deed of trust."

Indentured trustee A trustee, generally the trust department of a major bank, which represents the interest of bondholders under a publicly offered issue.

Insider A person close to a trust who has intimate knowledge of financial developments before they become public knowledge.

Interest rate The percentage rate which an individual pays for the use of borrowed money for a given period of time.

Intermediate-term loan A loan for a term of three to ten years which is usually not fully amortized at maturity. Often, developers will seek interim loans by which to pay off construction financing, in anticipation of obtaining long-term financing at a later date on more favorable terms, either because long-term rates decline generally or because the project can show an established, stable earnings history.

Interim loan A type of loan which is to be repaid out of the proceeds of another loan. Ordinarily, not self-liquidating (amortized), the lender evaluates the risk of obtaining refinancing as much as the period risk. See C&D loans.

Investment advisor See advisor.

Joint venture The entity which is created when two or more persons or corporate entities join together to carry out a specific business transaction of real estate development. A joint venture is usually of limited duration and usually for a specific property; it can be treated as a partnership for tax purposes. The parties have reciprocal and paralleling rights and obligations.

Junior mortgage loan Any mortgage loan in which the lien and the right of repayment is subordinate to that of another mortgage loan or loans. A "second mortgage" is a junior mortgage. "Third, fourth," etc. mortgages are always deemed to be secondary.

Land loan See Construction and development loan.

Land-purchase leaseback See sale-leaseback.

Late charge The charge which is levied against a borrower for a payment which was not made in a timely manner.

Lease A contract between the owner of property (lessor) and a tenant (lessee) setting forth the terms, conditions and consideration for the use of the property for a specified period of time at a specified rental. See sale-leaseback and net lease.

Leasehold improvements The cost of improvements or betterments to property leased for a period of years, often paid for by the tenant. Such improvements ordinarily become the property of the lessor (owner) on expiration of the lease; consequently their cost is normally amortized over the life of the lease if the lessor pays for them.

Leverage The process of borrowing upon one's capital base with the expectation of generating a profit above the cost of borrowing.

Liability management The aspect of the management of a company concerned with the planning and procurement of funds for investment through the sale of equity, public debt and bank borrowings. In the REIT industry, the phrase contrasts to "asset management" or the real estate side of the business.

Line of credit Usually, an agreement between a commercial bank and a borrower under which the bank agrees to provide unsecured credit to the borrower upon certain terms and conditions. Normally, the borrower may draw on all or any part of the credit from time to time.

Limited partnership A partnership which limits certain of the partners' (the limited partners) liability to the amount of their investment. At least one partner (the "general partner") is fully liable for the obligations of the partnership and its operations, usually with the limited partners participating as investors only.

Loan loss reserve A reserve set up to offset asset values in anticipation of losses that are reasonably expected. Initially, REITs had insufficient operating experience to anticipate losses in any one class of investments or for a portfolio as a whole, so tax authorities would not permit substantial contributions toward a reserve as an allowable period expense. When difficulties arose, the conversion of short-term loans to longer-term property holdings required some form of recognition of likely losses in the financial statements. A novel procedure for REITs was devised by requiring, for book purposes, computation of additions to the reserve based in part on the probable cost of sustaining the troubled assets over the longer period of time necessary to "cure" the problem. Also known as "allowance for losses."

Loan run-off The rate at which an existing mortgage portfolio will reduce (or "run-off") to zero if no new loans are added to the portfolio.

Loan swaps See asset swaps.

Long-term mortgage Any financing, whether in the form of a first or junior mortgage, the term of which is ten years or more. It is generally fully amortized.

Loss carry forwards The net operating loss (NOL) incurred in prior years, which may be applied for tax purposes against future earnings, thereby reducing taxable income. For REITs (which must pay out most of their taxable income), NOLs can be carried forward eight years; for non-REIT-taxed companies, NOL can be carried forward for only seven years.

Market value The highest price in terms of money which a property will bring in a competitive and open market under all conditions requisite to a fair sale—the buyer and the seller each acting prudently, knowledgeably, and at arm's length. See appraisal.

Moratorium A period in which payments of debts or other performance of a legal obligation is suspended temporarily, usually because of unforeseen circumstances which make timely payment or performance difficult or impossible. This forebearance can be whole or partial.

Mortgage A publicly recorded lien by which the property is pledged as security for the payment of a debt valid even beyond death ("mort" is death in French). In some states a mortgage is an actual conveyance of the property to the creditor until the terms of the mortgage are satisfied. While there is always a "note" secured by a mortgage document, both the note and mortgage instrument are commonly called "the mortgage." For types, see: first, junior, short-term, long-term, wrap-around and construction and development mortgage definitions.

Mortgage banker A non-depository lender who makes loans secured by real estate and then usually packages and sells those loans in large groups to institutional investors, pursuant to a "long-term commitment" he has negotiated with the life insurance company or other institutional investor. Mortgage bankers frequently arrange to service these mortgages for the out-of-town institutions, collecting regular payments, keeping the lender up to date on the progress of the loan, escrowing payments for taxes and insurance premiums, and, if necessary, administering foreclosure proceedings. Many REITs were sponsored by mortgage bankers.

Mortgage constant The total annual payments of principal and interest (annual debt service) on a mortgage with level-payment amortization schedule, expressed as a percentage of the initial principal amount of the loan.

Mortgagee in possession A lender or one who holds a mortgage who has taken possession of a property in order to protect an interest in the property. Usually, this is done with commercial properties as to which rents, management fees and other disbursements continue even if the mortgage is in default. The possession must be taken with the consent of the mortgagor (or a court, in cases of foreclosure) and the mortgagee must be careful to do only those things to the property that the mortgagor (or court) will agree to accept, should it resume its role as a credit-worthy owner.

Net Income The dollar amount that remains after all expenses, including taxes, are deducted from gross income. For regular companies, it is also called after-tax profit, the "bottom line" figure of how a company has performed with its investors' money. For REITs, it is net taxable income which, if fully distributed, is not taxed.

Net lease A lease, sometimes called a net-net (insurance and taxes) or even a net-net-net lease (insurance, taxes, and maintenance) in which the tenant pays all costs, including insurance, taxes, repairs, upkeep and other expenses, and the rental payments are "net" of all these expenses. See lease and fixed charges.

Net worth The remaining asset value of a property company or other entity after deduction of all liabilities against it.

Non-accrual loans See non-earning investments.

Non-earning investments The category of loans or investments which are not earning the originally anticipated rate of return. Some may be characterized as "partially earning." When interest is recorded as earned rather than as received (accrued interest), "non-accrual investments" are those which management expects not to receive interest as originally contemplated. In the vernacular, nonearning investments are "problem loans" or "troubled properties."

Non-qualified REIT A REIT that was formerly qualified, or conducts its affairs as if it is qualified, but that has elected for the tax year in question to be treated like a normal business corporation for tax purposes. Thus, some restraints (primarily against active management and holding property for sale) are lifted, while REIT conduit tax treatment is lost.

Occupancy rate The amount of space or number of apartments or offices or hotel rooms which are rented as compared with the total amount or number available. The rate is usually expressed as a percentage.

Operating expenses Expenses arising out of or relating to business activity such as interest expense, professional fees, salaries, etc.

Operating income Income received directly from business activity in the normal course, as contrasted with capital gains income, or other extraordinary income.

Option A right to buy or lease property at a certain specified price for specified terms. Consideration is typically given for the option, which is exercisable over a limited time span. If the option is not exercised, the consideration is forfeited. A loan to a developer secured by his option to obtain real estate is considered a "qualified" REIT asset.

Origination The process by which a loan is created, including the search for (or receipt of) the initial plans, the analysis and structuring of the proposed financing, and the review and acceptance procedures by which the commitment to make the investment is finally issued.

Overage income Rental income above a guaranteed minimum depending on a particular level of profit or retail sales volume by the tenant, payable under the terms of a lease.

Participations A lender often "participates out" or sells a portion of his loan to another lender while retaining a portion and managing the investment. REITs buy real estate secured participations as well as originating them.

Par Value The face value assigned to a security when it is issued. The stated par value of a security generally has nothing to do with its market or book value.

Passivity The state of owning investments but not actively managing them (as a property management firm does for the investor) or engaging in trading the securities (like a broker or dealer). This "passivity" test is implicit behind several of the REIT tax requirements.

Pension funds Money which is accumulated in trust to fund pensions for companies or unions and which is frequently invested in part in real estate. A co-mingled real estate pension fund account is managed, usually under contract to a financial institution, much like a REIT except that its shares are not publicly traded but instead sold to other pension funds.

Permanent financing See long-term loan.

Point An amount which represents 1% of the maximum principal amount of an investment. Used in connection with a discount from, or a share of, a principal amount deducted at the time funds are advanced, it represents additional compensation to the lender.

Portfolio The investments of a company, including investments in mortgages and/or ownership of real property. REIT portfolios usually consist of equity in property, short-term mortgages, long-term mortgages and/or subordinated land sale-lease-backs.

Portfolio turnover The average length of time from the funding of investments until they are paid off or sold.

Preferred shares Stocks which have prior claim on distributions (and/or assets in the event of dissolution) up to a certain definite amount before the shares of beneficial interest are entitled to anything. As a form of ownership, preferred shares stand behind senior subordinated and secured debtholders in dissolution, as well as other creditors.

Prepayment penalty The penalty which is imposed on the borrower for payment of the mortgage before it is due. Often a mortgage contains a clause specifying that there is to be no prepayment penalty, or limits the prepayment penalty to only the first few years of the mortgage term.

Price earning ratio A ratio which consists of the market price divided by current annualized earnings per share. Such a computation is now found in most daily stock listings. For REITs, annualization of quarterly earnings is computed by multiplying the most recent distribution by four, regardless of the distribution's later characterization as a dividend, return-of-capital, or capital gains.

Prime lending rate The rate at which commercial banks will lend money from time to time to their most credit-worthy customers, used as a base for most loans to financial intermediaries such as REITs.

Principal The buyer or seller in a real estate transaction as distinguished from an agent.

Principal The sum of money loaned. The amount of money to be repaid on a loan excluding interest charges.

Prior lien A lien or mortgage ranking ahead of some other lien. A prior lien need not itself be a first mortgage.

Pro forma Projected or hypothetical as opposed to actual as related, for example, to a balance sheet or income statement.

Problem investments See nonearning investments.

Prospectus A document describing an investment opportunity; the detailed description of new securities which must be supplied to prospective interstate purchasers under the Securities Act of 1933.

Provision for loan losses Periodic allocation of funds to loan loss reserves in recognition of a decline in the value of a loan or loans in a trust's portfolio due to a default on the part of the borrowers.

Proxy An authorization given by a registered security holder to vote stock at the annual meeting or at a special meeting of security holders.

Purchase and leaseback See sale-leaseback.

Pyramiding In stock market transactions, this term refers to the practice of borrowing against unrealized "paper" profits in securities to make additional purchases. In corporate finance, it refers to the practice of creating a speculative capital structure by a series of holding companies, whereby a relatively small amount of voting stock in the parent company controls a large corporate system. In real estate, it refers to the practice of financing 100% or more of the value of the property.

Qualified assets Assets which meet tax requirements for special REIT tax treatment, i.e. real property. In any tax year, 75% of a REIT's assets must be invested in real property, either through ownership or by securities secured by real estate. A "partially qualified" asset is one that qualifies under the 90% test of being a passive investment in a security, but not under the 75% real estate test.

Qualified income That portion of income which is classified as interest, rents, or other gain from real property, as spelled out in the REIT tax laws.

Raw land Land which has not been developed or improved.

RCA See revolving credit agreement.

Real estate investment trust (REIT, pronounced "reet") A trust established for the benefit of a group of investors which is managed by one or more trustees who hold title to the assets for the trust and control its acquisitions and investments, at least 75% of which are real estate related. A major advantage of a REIT is that no federal income tax need be paid by the trust if certain qualifications are met. Congress enacted these special tax provisions to encourage an assembly method, which is essentially designed to provide for investment in real estate what the mutual provided for investment in securities. The REIT provides the small investor with a means of combining his funds with those of others, and protects him from the double taxation that would be levied against an ordinary corporation or trust.

Revolving credit agreement (or "revolver") A formal credit agreement between a group of banks and a REIT, the terms of which are reviewed periodically when it is "rolled over" or "revolved" or refinanced by a similar agreement. For many trusts, "revolvers" have replaced informal lines of credit extended by individual banks to REITs, thereby providing a uniform (and usually restrictive) approach by all creditors, reassuring each bank that others in the RCA would not be paid off preferentially.

Registration statement The forms filed by a company with the Securities and Exchange Commission in connection with an offering of new securities or the listing of outstanding securities on a national exchange.

Reserves for loss See loan loss reserve.

Return of capital A distribution to shareholders in excess of the trust's earnings and profits, usually consisting of either depreciation or repayment of principal from properties or mortgages held by the trust. Each shareholder receiving such a distribution is required to reduce the tax basis of his shares by the amount of such distribution. For financial accounting purposes, what constitutes a return of capital may differ from that determined under Federal income tax requirements.

Return on equity A figure which consists of net income for the period divided by equity and which is normally expressed as a percentage.

Right of first refusal The right or option granted by a seller to a buyer, to have the first opportunity of acquiring a property.

Rights offering The privilege extended to a shareholder of subscribing to additional stock of the same or another class or to bonds, usually at a price below the market and in an amount proportional to the number of shares already held. Rights must be exercised within a time limit and often may be sold if the holder does not wish to purchase additional shares.

Sale-leaseback A common real estate transaction whereby the investor buys property from and simultaneously leases it back to, the seller. This enables the previous owner (often a developer) to "cash out" on an older property while retaining control.

Land sale-leaseback—this procedure, made common by several REITs that specialize in the transaction, affects only the land under income—producing improvements (such as shopping centers, etc.)—leaving the depreciable improvements in the hands of those who might benefit from the tax consequences. Since the improvements were probably financed with the proceeds of a first mortgage which remains in effect, the rights of the new investor are made second, or junior, to those of the first mortgage holder. Hence the common phrase "subordinated land sale-leaseback." In return for accepting a less secure position, the new investor usually obtains an "overage" clause whereby additional rent is paid anytime gross income of the shopping center (or whatever) exceeds a pre-determined floor.

Seasoned issues Securities of large, established companies which have been known to the investment public for a period of years, covering good times and bad.

Second mortgages See junior mortgage loan.

Secured debt For REITs, senior mortgage debt secured by specific properties. In case of default on "nonrecourse" debt, the lender may assume property ownership but may not pursue other assets of the lender.

Senior mortgage A mortgage which has first priority.

Senior unsecured debt Funds borrowed under open lines without security. Most bank lines to REITs were unsecured.

Shares of beneficial interest Tradable shares in a REIT. Analogous to common stock in a corporation.

Shareholders' equity Primarily money invested by shareholders through purchase of shares, plus the accumulation of that portion of net income that has been reinvested in the business since the commencement of operations.

Short-term mortgage A loan upon real estate for a term of three years or less, bearing interest payable periodically, with principal usually payable in full at maturity.

Sinking fund An arrangement under which a portion of a bond or preferred stock issue is retired periodically, in advance of its fixed maturity. The company may either purchase a stipulated quantity of the issue itself, or supply funds to a trustee or agent for that purpose. Retirement may be made by call at a fixed price, or by inviting tenders, or by purchase in the open market.

Sponsor The entity which initiated the formation of a REIT and usually acts (often via a subsidiary) as investment advisor to the trust thereafter. The sponsor puts the reputation of its institution on the line for the REIT and usually arranges lines of credit, provides support services and, occasionally, compensating balances.

Spread Difference between percentage return on an investment and cost of funds to support the investment.

Standby commitment See commitment, standby.

Standing loan Usually not amortized, the loan is secured by completed property that has not yet been refinanced with a "permanent" long-term mortgage.

Subordinated debt Debt which is junior to secured and unsecured senior debt, it may be convertible into shares of beneficial interest for

REITs. Senior subordinated debt is senior to other subordinated debt.

Subordinated ground lease See sale-leaseback.

Swap Program A procedure for reducing debt (by a troubled REIT) by trading an asset to the creditor in return for cancellation of part of a loan to the REIT. Often a cash premium payment is made in addition to reduction of the debt. The premium may then be distributed to the other creditors pro rata. The amount of the cash premium, or the ratio of cash-to-debt reduction to be applied against the value of the asset, is sometimes determined by a sealed-bid "auction" process as set forth in the "revolving credit agreement" between the creditors and the REIT. See RCA.

Syndicate A group of investors who transact business for a limited period of time and sometimes with a single purpose. It is a short-term partnership.

Take-out commitment See commitment.

Tax shelter The various aspects of an investment which offer relief from income taxes or opportunities to claim deductions from taxable income. Although tax shelters are an important facet of real estate investment, they do not have a direct influence on REIT investment choices because qualified trusts are exempt from income taxes.

Usury The charging of interest rates for the use of money higher than what's allowed by local law.

Warrants Stock purchase warrants or options give the holder rights to purchase shares of stock, generally running for a longer period of time than ordinary subscription rights given shareholders. Warrants are often attached to other securities, but they may be issued separately or detached after issuance.

Working capital Determined by subtracting current liabilities from current assets. It represents the amount available to carry on the day-to-day operation of the business.

Work-out When a borrower has problems, the process undertaken by the lender to help the borrower "work out" of the problems becomes known itself as a "work out." The presumption during a "work out" is that the borrower will eventually resume a more normal debtor's position once problems are solved within (presumably) a reasonably short time.

Wrap-around mortgage A type of junior mortgage used to refinance properties on which there is an existing first mortgage loan. The face amount of the wrap-around loan is equivalent to the unpaid balance on the existing mortgage plus cash advanced to the property owner upon funding. Such loans carry a higher interest rate than the existing mortgage. The wrap-around lender assumes the obligation to maintain payments of principal and interest on the existing mortgage so as to enhance his right to make claim from his secondary position.

Yield In the stock market, the rate of annual distribution or dividend expressed as a percentage of price. Current yield is found by dividing the market price into the distribution rate in dollars. In real estate, the term refers to the effective annual amount of income which is being accrued on an investment expressed as a percentage of its value.

Employee Benefits in Medium and Large Firms*

Plans that permit employees to reduce taxable income by channeling part of their earnings into retirement funds became more common in 1986, according to the U.S. Department of Labor's Bureau of Labor Statistics. These plans, called "salary reduction plans" or "cash or deferred arrangements," are authorized by sections 401(k) and 403(b) of the Internal Revenue Code.

The Bureau's eighth survey of employee benefits shows that salary reduction plans to fund retirement savings were available to 31 percent of full-time workers in 1986, up from 26 percent in 1985. Coverage increased for both white-collar workers (from 37 percent in 1985 to 42 percent in 1986) and blue-collar workers (from 14 to 19 percent). Additionally, 2 percent of employees were covered by plans permitting them to reduce their taxable income by putting profit-sharing distributions into a retirement account.

Salary reduction plans come in a variety of forms. Twenty-one percent of all workers (white- and blue-collar combined) were covered by plans permitting salary reduction contributions to an employer-funded savings and thrift plan and six percent to a profit-sharing plan, while most of the remaining four percent were in free-standing plans (no employer contribution).

The Bureau's survey of employee benefits provides representative data for 21.3 million full-time employees in a cross-section of the nation's private industries in 1986. The survey's scope generally was limited to medium and large establishments employing at least 100 or 250 workers, depending upon the industry.

Flexible Benefits

For the first time, the 1986 survey studied flexible benefits plans and reimbursement accounts. While such plans have attracted much attention recently, the survey showed that their incidence is limited: Eight percent of white-collar workers and two percent of blue-collar workers could participate in one or both of these benefit plans. Five percent of all employees covered by the survey were eligible for reimbursement accounts, which are used to pay for expenses not covered by a company's regular benefits package, such as insurance premiums, child care, or health care deductibles. Two percent of employees were eligible for flexible benefits or cafeteria plans. A flexible benefits plan was defined in the survey as a plan giving employees a choice among two or more types of benefits. Thus, plans that permitted a selection in only one benefit (for example, a choice among several health insurance options or plans) were not classified as flexible benefits plans.

Defined Contribution Plans

Sixty percent of employees participated in one or more defined contribution plans in 1986, up from 53 percent in 1985. These plans, which usually specify the employer's contribution but not the employee's benefit, take a variety of forms. The most common defined contribution plans in 1986 were stock ownership (covering 30 percent of workers), savings and thrift (28 percent), and profit sharing (22 percent). Participation in each increased in 1986, and many employees participated in more than one type of plan.

Most employees in stock ownership plans were in Payroll-Based Stock Ownership Plans—PATSOPs. In these plans, employers receive a tax credit, computed as a percentage of payroll, for amounts they contribute to the PAYSOP. This tax credit expired on December 31, 1986.

For the first time, the survey tabulated the provisions of deferred profit sharing plans and PAYSOPs. Three-fifths of the participants in deferred profit sharing plans had employer contributions determined by a stated formula; the other two-fifths were in plans where contributions were at the discretion of the employer. Profit sharing contributions were nearly always allocated to individual accounts based on each employee's earnings, as were PAYSOP contributions. Eighty-five percent of PAYSOP participants faced stricter with-

---

* Detailed information of the benefit provisions studied are available in a bulletin, "Employee Benefits in Medium and Large Firms, 1986 published by the Bureau of Labor Statistics.

Source: "BLS Reports on Employee Benefits in Medium and Large Firms, 1986," in *News*, March 1987, U.S. Department of Labor, Bureau of Labor Statistics, Washington, DC 20212. For further historical and technical data call 202-523-9444.

FULL-TIME EMPLOYEES PARTICIPATING IN SELECTED EMPLOYEE BENEFIT PROGRAMS, MEDIUM AND LARGE PRIVATE INDUSTRY ESTABLISHMENTS, UNITED STATES,[1] 1985. [In percent]

Employee Benefit Program	All Employees	Professional and Administrative Employees	Technical and Clerical Employees	Production Employees
Paid:				
Holidays	99	99	100	98
Vacations	100	99	100	100
Personal leave	25	33	35	15
Lunch period	10	3	4	17
Rest time	72	58	69	82
Funeral leave	88	87	87	88
Military leave	66	74	72	58
Jury duty leave	93	96	96	90
Sick leave	70	93	93	45
Sickness and accident insurance	49	28	35	69
Long-term disability insurance	48	68	60	30
Health insurance	95	96	94	96
Life insurance	96	97	96	95
Retirement	89	92	92	87
Defined benefit pension	76	78	78	74
Defined contribution plan[2]	47	53	55	40
Capital accumulation[3]	23	31	29	16

[1] The survey excludes data for executives and employees in constant travel status, such as airline pilots, as well as data for Alaska and Hawaii. Benefits paid for entirely by the employee were excluded from this tabulation.

[2] Includes money purchase pension, profit sharing, savings and thrift, stock bonus, and employee stock ownership plans in which employer contributions must remain in the participant's account until retirement age, death, disability, separation from service, age 59½, or hardship.

[3] Includes plans in which employer contributions may be withdrawn from the participant's account without regard to the conditions listed in footnote 2.

drawal policies than the 7-year provision permitted by the tax code.

Defined Benefit Pension Plans

Seventy-six percent of the workers were covered by defined benefit pension plans in 1986, a slight decline from 1985. The plans, which have formulas for determining the employee's annuity are usually paid for in full by the employer. In 1986, 72 percent of the participants had plans relating benefits to earnings; for example, 1-½ percent of earnings times years of service. Such plans, predominant among white-collar workers, often coordinate benefits with those from Social Security. Most other participants—mainly blue-collar workers—received specified dollar amounts of benefits for each year of service, which were rarely coordinated with Social Security benefits.

Sixty-four percent of pension plan participants could retire with full benefits before age 65. The two most common pre-age 65 requirements reported for full retirement benefits were any age, with 30 years service, and age 62, with 10 years' service. Reduced pensions were available at age 55 to two-thirds of participants, with service requirements ranging from none to 20 years.

Health and Life Insurance

Changes in health care plans continued to emphasize less expensive means of delivering medical treatment. Home health care was available to 66 percent of plan participants in 1986, up from 56 percent in 1985; hospice care coverage rose from 23 to 31 percent. In addition, the percentage of participants in plans paying for a second surgical opinion increased from 50 to 57 percent; and those with financial incentives to seek a second opinion rose from 24 to 35 percent. Alternatives to traditional fee-for-service plans are also gaining in acceptance. Fourteen percent of plan participants were enrolled in Health Maintenance or Preferred Provider Organizations, a survey high. (Preferred Provider Organization plans contain incentives for participants to seek treatment from designated health care providers.)

After holding steady in 1985, the proportion of employees contributing to health insurance premiums turned upward in 1986. Forty-one percent were in plans requiring them to pay part of the premiums for their own health care, up from 35 percent the year before. Sixty percent were in plans requiring contributions for family coverage, up from 53 percent. These contributions for single and family coverage averaged $13 and $41 a month, respectively, and represented increases of 6 and 8 percent from 1985. (Medical care costs registered by the Consumer Price Index for All Urban Consumers rose 7.5 percent for 1986.)

Broadened coverage in other health areas was not directly related to cost control. The percentage of participants covered for alcoholism treatment increased from 68 to 70 percent between 1985 and 1986 and, for drug abuse treatment, from 61 to 66 percent. Participation in vision care plans also grew from 35 to 40 percent. Under major medical plans, the most common lifetime maximum benefit was $1 million. Stop-loss coverage, which caps an individual's out-of-pocket outlays for covered medical services, applied to 81 percent of major medical plan participants. This marked the sixth year of steady growth since 1980, when 55 percent were covered. In 1986, outlays for covered expenses were capped at $1,200 or less per year for 3 out of 4 participants with stop-loss provisions.

Indications are that many health insurance plans will be affected by the Consolidated Omnibus Budget Reconciliation Act (COBRA). This Act requires the extension of health plan protection for at least 18 months to terminated or laid-off workers who agree to pay up to 102 percent of premium costs. The 1986 benefits survey, conducted immediately prior to COBRA, reported that 46 percent of participants were in firms which either discontinued insurance immediately upon layoff or had no established policy. Thirty-four percent were eligible for coverage paid at least in part by employers. Most of the remaining participants could continue coverage at their own cost. Regardless of financing, continuation periods were usually 6 months or less. Only 4 percent were in plans which extended health insurance indefinitely.

Group health insurance coverage continued after etirement in plans covering 72 percent of the active employees. Nearly all of these employees were in plans that extended benefits to retirees below age 65. Sixty-five percent of the employees were in plans that covered retirees 65 and over; 38 percent were in plans where retiree premiums were fully paid by the employer, 16 percent were in plans where the cost was financed by both employer and retiree, and 10 percent were in retiree-paid plans. Retirees' benefits were usually the same as those for active workers, though payments were coordinated with Medicare.

Life insurance for 66 percent of the workers covered was based on earnings; most of the remainder were provided flat dollar amounts. Earnings-based formulas, typically paying one or two times annual earnings, applied to over four-fifths of the white-collar workers. Flat amounts were common among blue-collar workers, where they applied to half of the plan participants and provided an average benefit of nearly $10,000. Eleven percent of all 1986 life insurance participants were in plans that also provided monthly income to surviving family members for a limited period, typically 24 months. Seventeen percent received insurance coverage for their dependents.

Paid Time Off

Time off with pay is available to employees in a variety of forms—from daily rest breaks to annual vacations of several weeks. In 1986, paid lunch time (available to a tenth of the workers) averaged 27 minutes a day, while paid rest periods (covering nearly three-fourths of the workers) averaged 26 minutes per day. The number of paid holidays averaged 10.0 days; the amount of vacation, which typically varied by length of service, averaged 8.8 days after 1 year of service, 15.8 days after 10 years, and 20.6 days after 20 years of service. Personal (multipurpose) leave averaged 3.7 per year, funeral leave, 3.2 days per occurrence, and military leave, 11.5 days a year; time off for paid jury duty leave was usually provided as needed.

Disability Income Benefits

In 1986, income continuation during short periods of disability was provided to 94 percent of workers by sick leave, sickness and accident insurance, or both. Protection for lengthy periods of disability was provided by long-term disability insurance which covered 48 percent of the workers, while 37 percent (some with long-term disability insurance) were eligible for immediate disability benefits under their pension plans.

Paid sick leave plans varied greatly in the number of days off available. For example, after 1 year of service, plans specifying a maximum annual benefit allowed an average of 15.2 days off per year with full pay; when days off were specified for each disability, the average was 59.2 days. The number of days of annual sick leave also varied depending on whether the plan was coordinated with sickness and accident insurance benefits and whether it allowed carryover of unused sick leave days from year to year. Sickness and accident insurance pays a portion of an employee's regular earnings, usually for a maximum of 26 weeks.

Long-term disability insurance typically pays 50 or 60 percent of regular earnings when an employee is disabled for a prolonged period. Long-term disability payments usually begin after sick leave and sickness and accident insurance are exhausted and continue as long as the person is disabled or until retirement age. Career-ending disabilities may entitle an employee to an immediate pension, but the pension may be deferred until other forms of income, such as long-term disability insurance, have ceased.

Selected On-Line Business/Financial Data Bases

On-line data bases are collections of computer stored data which are retrievable by remote terminals. The data bases are collected and organized by a so-called *producer*. The latter provides the data base to a *vendor* who distributes the data by means of a telecommunication network to the user. Often a vendor will offer a large number of different data bases. In some instances the producer and vendor are the same.

Using an on-line data base requires: (1) a *terminal* (a typewriter-like device usually equipped with a video display) to receive data and send commands to the vendor's computers, and (2) a *modem* for coupling the terminal to a telephone line. Printouts (hard copy) of the desired information can be obtained with the aid of electronic printers located at the user's terminal or, alternatively, ordered from the vendor.

The user accesses the data base by dialing a telephone number and then typing (on the terminal keyboard) a password provided by the vendor. Searching the data base is done with special commands and procedures peculiar to each base.

The contents of data bases vary. Some provide statistical data only—usually in the form of time series. Other bases provide bibliographic references and, in some instances, abstracts or the full text of articles.

Specifics concerning data base contents, instructions, and prices are available from vendors. Listed below are some major business data bases and vendors. More complete information concerning data bases is available from the sources given below.

ABI Inform

Provides references on all areas of business management with emphasis on "how-to" information.

Producer: Data Courier Inc. (Louisville, KY)

Vendors: BRS, DIALOG, SDC

Accountants Index

Contains reference information on accounting, auditing taxation, management and securities.

Producer: American Institute of Certified Public Accountants (New York, NY)

Vendors: SDC

American Profile

Provides statistical information on U.S. households including population, income, dependents, and also data on types of businesses in an area.

Producer: Donnelley Marketing (Stamford, CT)

Vendors: Business Information Service

Business Credit Service

Provides business credit and financial information.

Producer: TRW, Inc. (Orange, CA)

Vendors: TRW

Canadian Business and Current Affairs

English language business and popular periodicals

Producer: Micromedia Limited (Toronto, Ontario)

Vendor: DIALOG, CISTI

CIS Index

Contains references and abstracts from nearly every publication resulting from Senate and House Committee meetings since 1970.

Producer: Congressional Information Services, Inc. (Washington, DC)

Vendors: Dialog, SDC

Commodities

Contains over 41,000 times series of current commodity prices for the U.S., Canada, U.K., and France.

Producer: Wolff Research (London, U.K.)

Vendor: I. P. Sharp

Compendex (Computerized Engineering Index)

Contains over 1 million citations and abstracts to the world wide engineering literature.

Producer: Engineering Information Inc. (New York)

Vendor: BRS, D-STAR, DIALOG.

CompuServe, Inc.

Provides reference, statistical and full text retrieval of information of personal interest including health, recipes, gardening, financial and investment data including the Compustat and Value Line data bases.

Producer: CompuServe, Inc. (Columbus, OH)

Vendor: CompuServe

Compustat

Provides very extensive financial data on companies.

Producer: Standard And Poor's Compustat Service, Inc. (Englewood, CO)

Vendors: ADP, Business Information Services, CompuServe, Data Resources, Chase Econometrics/Interactive Data Corp.

Disclosure II

Provides extracts of 10K and other reports filed with the Securities and Exchange Commission.

Producer: Disclosure Inc. (Bethesda, Maryland)

Vendors: Business Information Services (Control Data). Dialog, Dow Jones, New York Times Information Services, Mead Data Central.

Dow Jones News/Retrieval Service and Stock Quote Reporters

Contains text of articles appearing in major financial publications including the *Wall Street Journal* and *Barrons*. Quote Service provides quotes on stocks, bonds, mutual funds.

Producer: Dow Jones & Company (New York, NY)

Vendors: BRS, Dow Jones & Company

DRI Capsule/EEI Capsule

Provides over 3700 U.S. social and economic statistical time series such as population, income, money supply data, etc.

Producers: Data Resources, Inc. (Lexington, MA) and Evans Economics Inc. (Washington, DC)

Vendors: Business Information Services, United Telecom Group, I. P. Sharp

Federal Register Abstracts

Provides coverage of federal regulatory agencies as published in the Federal Register.

Producer: Capitol Services (Washington, DC)

Vendors: DIALOG, SDC

GTE Financial System One Quotation Service

Provides current U.S. and Canadian quotations and statistical data on stocks, bonds, options, commodities and other market data.

Producer: GTE Information Systems (Reston, VA)

Vendor: GTE Information Systems, Inc.

The Information Bank

Provides an extensive current affairs data source consisting of abstracts from numerous English language publications.

Producer: The New York Times Information Service

Vendor: The New York Times Information Service

LEXIS

Contains full text references to a wide range of legal information including court decisions, regulations, government statutes.

Producer: Mead Data Central (New York, NY)

Vendor: Mead Data Central

NEXIS

Provides full text business and general news including management, technology, finance, science, politics, religion.

Producer: Mead Data Central (New York, NY)

Vendor: Mead Data Central

PTS Marketing and Advertising Reference Service

Provides citations with abstracts & articles on the marketing and advertising of consumer goods and services.

Producer: Predicast, Inc. (Cleveland, OH)

Vendors: DIALOG, BRS, DATA-STAR

PTS Prompt

Covers world wide business news on new products, market data, etc.

Producer: Predicast, Inc. (Cleveland, OH)

Vendors: ADP, BRS, DIALOG

Quick Quote

Provides current quotations, volume, high-low data for securities of U.S. public corporations.

Producer: CompuServe Inc.

Vendor: CompuServe

Quotron 800

Provides up to the minute quotation and statistics on a broad range of securities such as stocks, bonds, options, commodities.

Producer: Quotron Systems Inc. (Los Angeles, CA)

Vendor: Quotron Systems Inc.

The Source

Covers a broad variety of consumer services business and financial information including travel information, reservations, restaurant reviews etc.

Producer: Source Telecomputing (McLean, VA)

Vendor: Source Telecomputing Corp.

Trinet Company Data Base

Provides data on about 250,000 companies in the U.S.

Producer: Trinet, Inc. (Parsippany, NJ)

Vendors: DRI, DIALOG, Mead Data Central

Value Line II

Provides extensive financial data from the Value Line Investment Survey covering over 1600 major companies.

Producer: Arnold Bernhard & Co. (New York, NY)

Vendors: ADP Service, Chase Econometrics/Interactive Data Corp., CompuServe Data Resources, Inc.

For further information:

A. T. Kruzas and J. Schmittroth, *Encyclopedia of Information Systems,* Gale Research (Book Tower, Detroit, MI 48226) revised periodically.

The North American On Line Directory 1985, R. R. Bowker (New York, NY 10017) annual.

On Line Data Base Services Directory; Gale Research (address above) revised periodically.

The Federal Data Base Finder. A guide to more than 3,000 free and fee based data bases provided by the US Government. Available from Information USA, 1200 Beall Mt. Road, Potomac, MD 20854.

Guidance on Software Maintenance. Superintendent of Documents, Government Printing Office, Washington, DC 20402. Offers advice on maintaining software and suggestions on how to streamline your system.

Introduction to Software Packages. Superintendent of Documents (address given above). Sources of information on available software packages.

Databasics: Your Guide to On Line Business Information, Garland Publishing Co. (New York, NY 10016).

Directory On Line Data Bases, Cuadra/Elsevier Associates, 25 Vanderbilt Avenue, New York, NY 10017. A comprehensive standard reference.

Wall Street Computer Review, 150 Broadway, New York, NY 10038. This periodical covers current developments and contains informative articles.

Data Base Vendors

ADP Network Services, Inc
175 Jackson Plaza
Ann Arbor, MI 48106
313-769-6800

BRS, Inc.
1200 Route 7
Latham, NY 12110
518-783-1161
800-833-4707

Business Information Services
Control Data Corporation
500 West Putnam Avenue
Greenwich, CT 06830
203-622-2000

Chase Econometrics/Interactive Data Corporation
95 Hayden Avenue
Lexington, MA 02173
617-890-8100

CompuServe, Inc.
5000 Arlington Centre Boulevard
Columbus, OH 43220
614-457-8600
800-848-8990

Data Resources, Inc. (DRI)
1750 K Street NW
Washington, DC 20006
202-663-7720

DIALOG Information Services, Inc.
3460 Hillview Avenue
Palo Alto, CA 94304
415-858-3810
800-334-2564

Dow Jones & Company, Inc.
P.O. Box 300
Princeton, NJ 08540
609-452-2000
800-257-5114

General Electric Information Services Company
401 North Washington Street
Rockville, MD 20850
301-294-5405

GTE Information Systems, Inc.
12490 Sunrise Valley
Reston, VA 22046
800-638-4215

Mead Data Central
P.O. Box 933
Dayton, OH 45401
800-227-4908

The New York Times Information Services, Inc.
229 West 43 Street
New York, NY 10036
800-543-6862

Quotron Systems, Inc.
5454 Beethoven Street
Los Angeles, CA 90066
213-398-2761

SDC Search Service/Orbit
1340 Old Chain Bridge Road
McLean, VA 22101
703-442-0000
800-334-7575

I. P. Sharp Associates
Exchange Tower
Toronto, Ontario, Canada M5X IE3
416-364-5361
800-387-1588

Source Telecomputing Corporation
1616 Anderson Road
McLean, VA 22102
703-734-7500X546
800-336-3366

TRW Information Services Division
505 City Parkway West
Orange, CA 92668
714-937-2000

Business Information Directory

Information Sources

GENERAL REFERENCES

The *United States Government Manual* is an annual publication. It describes the organization, purposes, and programs of most government agencies and lists top personnel. Available from the Superintendent of Documents, Government Printing Office, Washington, DC 20402.

Washington Information Directory is an annual publication listing, by topic, organizations and publications which provide information on a wide range of subjects. It also lists congressional committee assignments, regional federal offices, embassies, and state and local officials. Published by the Congressional Quarterly, Inc., 1414 22nd Street NW, Washington, DC 20037.

Statistical Abstracts of the United States, published annually, is the standard summary on the social, political, and economic statistics of the United States. It includes data from both government and private sources. Appendix II gives a comprehensive list of sources. (Available from the Superintendent of Documents, Government Printing Office, Washington, DC 20402)

Business Information Sources by Lorna M. Daniells ranks among the best general guides to business publications. It contains extensive references to U.S. business and economic data, including statistics, U.S. and foreign investment. Published by the University of California Press, Berkeley, CA.

Researcher's Guide to Washington Experts, Washington Researchers, 2612 P Street NW, Washington, D.C. 20007.

Population information on all aspects of national and world population is provided by the Population Reference Bureau, Inc., 2213 M Street NW, Washington, DC 20037, or call 202–785–4664.

The Washington Information Research Service provides reports and guidance to information on a fee basis. Write Washington Researchers, 2612 P Street NW, Washington, DC 20007, or call 202–333–3499.

Information USA is a reference book with leads about how to tap the information mine of the federal government. Published by Penguin Books, 624 Madison Avenue, New York, NY 10022.

FEDfind explains how to get services and publications from the U.S. Government. Published by ICUC Press, P.O. Box 1447-NR, Springfield, VA 22151.

Professional and trade organizations and publications are a major source of contacts and information. Key directories to these sources are listed below:

Encyclopedia of Associations, published by Gale Research Co., Book Tower, Detroit, MI 48226.

The World Guide to Trade Associations gives a comprehensive national and international listing of associations. Published by R. R. Bowker Co., 205 East 42 Street, New York, NY 10017.

Ulrich's International Periodical Directory covers both domestic and foreign periodicals. Published by R. R. Bowker Co., 205 East 42 Street, New York, NY 10017.

Standard Periodical Directory covers U.S. and Canadian periodicals. Published by Oxbridge Communications, Inc., 150 Fifth Avenue, New York, NY 10011.

The 1987 IMS Directory of Publications provides titles of trade newspapers and periodicals. Published by IMS Press, 426 Pennsylvania Avenue, Fort Washington, PA 19034.

Standard Rate and Data Service provides information on periodical circulation and advertising rates. Published by Standard Rates and Data Service, Inc., 5201 Old Orchard Road, Skokie, IL 60077–1021.

Encyclopedia of Information Systems and Services. Descriptions of U.S. organizations (and some foreign) that produce, process, store, and use bibliographic and non-bibliographic information. About 1500 data bases covered. Published by Gale Research Co., Book Tower, Detroit, MI 48226.

National Directory of Addresses and Telephone Numbers. A national business directory that lists all SEC registered companies, major accounting and law firms, banks, and financial institutions, associations, unions, etc. Available from Concord Reference Books, Inc., 830 Third Avenue Street, New York, NY 10022.

Encyclopedia of Business Information, a comprehensive single-volume source, is updated periodically. Available from Gale Research Co., Book Tower, Detroit, MI 48226.

Business Publications Index and Abstracts is a two volume set listing books, transaction proceedings, etc. with abstracts of each entry.

Published by Gale Research Co., Book Tower, Detroit, MI 48226.

National Trade and Professional Associations of the United States. A comprehensive listing of professional trade and labor associations, including addresses, membership size, publications by the associations, and convention schedules. An annual published by Columbia Books, 777 14th Street NW, Washington, DC 20005.

Encyclopedia of Banking and Finance, is a comprehensive source on subjects indicated in title. Bankers Publishing Co., Boston, MA.

Listings of trade directories are given in the following:

Guide to American Directories, published by B. Klein Publications, Inc., P.O. Box 8503, Coral Springs, FL 33065.

Directory of Directories, distributed by Gale Research Co., Book Tower, Detroit, MI 48226.

Directory of Marketing Research Houses and Services is an annual available from the American Marketing Association, 420 Lexington Avenue, New York, NY 10022.

BUSINESS AND ECONOMICS INFORMATION

Government publications referred to below may be obtained from the Government Printing Office (GPO), Washington, DC, 20402, unless other indicated.

Business and economic information is provided by the following key references.

Survey of Current Business is a major publication which is supplemented on a weekly basis with *Current Statistics.* The publication contains articles as well as comprehensive statistics on all aspects of the economy, including data on the GNP, employment, wages, prices, finance, foreign trade, and production by industrial sector. (GPO)

Business Conditions Digest is a monthly with an extensive collection of charts and tables on the national income and products, leading coincident and lagging cyclical indicators, foreign trade, prices, wages, analytical ratios, and international production and stock prices. (GPO)

Economic Indicators is a monthly summary-type publication prepared by the Council of Economic Advisers. It contains charts and tables on natural output, income, spending, employment, unemployment, wages, industrial production, construction, prices, money, credit, federal finance, and international statistics. (GPO)

Federal Reserve Bulletin is a monthly issued by the Federal Reserve System, containing articles and very extensive tabulated data on all aspects of the monetary situation, credit, mortgage markets, interest rates, and stock and bond yields. A monthly *Chart Book* is available which contains charts of financial and monetary data. Both are available from the Board of Governors, Federal Reserve System, Washington, DC 20551.

Monthly Labor Review. This monthly publication provides articles and statistics on employment, productivity, wages, earnings, prices, wage settlements, and work stoppages. (GPO)

U.S. Industrial Outlook is an annual providing evaluations and projections of all major industrial and commercial segments of the domestic economy. (GPO)

Quarterly Financial Report for Manufacturing, Mining, and Trade Corporations is issued by the Bureau of the Census of the U.S. Department of Commerce. It covers corporate financial statistics including sales, profits, assets, and financial ratios, classified by industry group and size. (GPO)

Current Industrial Reports are a series of over 100 monthly, quarterly, semiannual, and annual reports on major products manufactured in the United States. For subscription, contact the Bureau of the Census, U.S. Department of Commerce, Washington, DC 20233. (GPO)

Annual Survey of Manufacturers. General statistics of manufacturing activity for industry groups, individual industries, states, and geographical regions are provided. (GPO)

County Business Patterns is an annual publication on employment and payrolls, which include a separate paperbound report for each state. (GPO)

Foreign Trade is a Bureau of the Census publication giving monthly reports on U.S. foreign trade. (GPO)

Population: Current Report is a series of monthly and annual reports covering population changes and socioeconomic characteristics of the population. (GPO)

Retail Sales: Current Business Report is a weekly report which provides retail statistics. (GPO)

Wholesale Trade, Sales and Inventories: Current Business Report provides a monthly report on wholesale trade. (GPO)

Key Economic Data Service Package provides access to the Department of Commerce Electronic Bulletin Board. The Bulletin Board includes same day postings of data provided by both the Bureau of Labor Statistics and the Bureau of Economic Analysis. Twice a month there are updates from the Bureau of the Census on the principal indicators, monetary statistics and foreign trade. Also provided is the most current *SIC Manual.* Available from the National Technical Information Service, 5285 Port Royal Road, Springfield, VA 22161.

CORPORATE INFORMATION

The major sources of information on publicly held corporations (as well as government and municipal issues) are: *Moody's Investor Services, Inc.*, owned by Dun & Bradstreet, 99 Church Street, New York, NY 10007, and *Standard & Poor's Corp.*, owned by McGraw-Hill, 25 Broadway, New York, NY 10004.

Standard & Poor's *Corporate Records* and Moody's *Manuals* are large multivolume works published annually and kept up to date with daily (for Standard & Poor's) or semiweekly (for Moody's) reports. The services provide extensive coverage of industrials, public utilities, transportation, banks, and financial companies. Also included are municipal and government issues.

In addition, the above corporations provide computerized data services and magnetic tapes. Compustat tapes, containing major corporate financial data, are available from Investor's Management Services, Inc., Denver, CO, a subsidiary of Standard & Poor's. Time-sharing access to Compustat and other financial data bases is available through Interactive Data Corporation, Waltham, MA (617) 890–1234.

DISCLOSURE II, available from Disclosure, Inc., (5161 River Road, Bethesda, MD 20816) provides an on line data base of corporate information for some 10,000 companies. Disclosure II can be used via the Dow Jones Retrieval Service, New York Times Information Service, Lockheed's DIALOG Information Services, Inc., ADP, CompuServe, among others.

Also available from Disclosure is MICRO/SCAN: Disclosure II, a monthly diskette service which provides information on dividends per share, 4-year growth rate in earnings per share, price/book value, etc. For information call 800–638–8076.

The 10-K and other corporate reports are filed with the Securities and Exchange Commission and are available at local SEC offices, investor relations departments of publicly traded companies, as well as various private services, such as Disclosure Inc. which provides a complete microfiche service. *The SEC News Digest*, formerly published by the government, is now available from Disclosure, Inc. (address above). Included in the *Digest* is a daily listing of 8K reports, a daily Acquisitions of Securities Report, as well as information about what's happening inside the SEC.

Disclosure Inc. has two additional services helpful for researching a corporation. Through the *SEC Watch Service* any report filed by a company with the SEC can be retrieved while corporate information such as prospective supplements and tender offers can be retrieved through the *SEC Research Service*.

Betchel Information Service located at 15740 Shady Grove Road, Gaithersburg, MD 20877 is another SEC document retrieval service. The Index of financial documents is updated several times a day.

Major trade directories include the annual *Thomas Register of American Manufacturers* (published by Thomas Publishing Company, 1 Pennsylvania Plaza, New York, NY 10005) and Dun & Bradstreet's *Reference Book of Manufacturers*.

Thomas Register includes in one volume an alphabetical listing of manufacturers, giving address, phone number, product, subsidiaries, plant location, and an indication of assets. Dun & Bradstreet's *Reference Book* covers similar information, including sales and credit. Dun & Bradstreet's *Million Dollar Directory* series provides data on U.S. companies whose net worth is $1,000,000 and up, including information on privately held corporations; also published is a companion volume the *Billion Dollar Directory* which tracks America's corporate families.

Directory of Wall Street Research, an annual published by Nelson Publishing, Rye, NY lists security analysts with a subject specialty, top corporate officers, and brokerage firms researching a given company.

Register of Corporations is published by Standard and Poor's Corp., 345 Hudson Street, New York, NY 10014.

Directory of Corporate Affiliations and International Directory of Corporate Affiliations are references to the structure of major domestic and international corporations. Published by NRPC, 3004 Glen View Road, Wilmette, IL 60091.

Sources of State Information on Corporations, provides information filed by companies with the state governments and also business related data collected by the states. Washington Researchers Publishing, 2612 P Street NW, Washington, DC 20007.

How to Find Information About Companies: The Corporate Intelligence Sourcebook provides information on sources helpful in researching either private or public companies. Available from Washington Researchers Publishing. (See above for the address.)

Ward's Directory of Private Companies supplies data on private companies (and their subsidiaries) with annual sales volume of one half to $11 million that are not publically traded. Available from Ward's Business Directory, 11 Davis Drive, Belmont, CA 94002.

Future earnings projections of listed companies based on surveys by securities analysts are provided by Lynch, Jones, and Ryan, 325 Hudson Street, New York, NY 10013 (212-243-3137).

Information on foreign corporations is available from *World Trade Data Reports,* U.S. Department of Commerce, Washington, D.C. 20230 (202-377-4203).

TRACKING FEDERAL GOVERNMENT DEVELOPMENTS

Commerce Business Daily (*CB*). This daily provides information on contract awards and subcontract opportunities, Defense Department awards, and surplus sales. *CB* is available on-line from: United Communications Group, 8701 Georgia Avenue, Silver Springs, MD 20910; DIALOG Information Services, 3460 Hillview Avenue, Palo Alto, CA 94304; or Data Resources, Inc., 2400 Hartwell Avenue, Lexington, ME 02173. (GPO)*

Federal Register. This daily provides information on federal agency regulations and other legal documents (GPO).*

CQ Weekly Report. This major service follows every important piece of legislation through both houses of Congress and reports on the political and lobbying pressures being applied. Available from the Congressional Quarterly Service, 1414 22nd Street, Washington, DC 20037.

Daily Report for Executives. A daily series of reports giving Washington developments that affect all aspects of business operations. Available from the Bureau of National Affairs, Inc., 1231 25th Street NW, Washington, DC 20037. Call: 301-258-1033.

Two major services, the *Bureau of National Affairs, Inc.* (address above) and the *Commerce Clearing House, Inc.* (4025 West Peterson Avenue, Chicago, IL 60646), publish a large number of valuable weekly looseleaf reports covering developments in all aspects of law, government regulations, and taxation.

* Government Printing Office.

INDEX PUBLICATIONS

Indexes of a wide variety of articles appearing in periodicals, trade presses, and financial services dealing with corporations, industry, and finance are given in the following:

Business Periodicals Index published by H. W. Wilson Co., 950 University Avenue, Bronx, NY.

Funk and Scott Index of Corporations and Industries, published by Predicast, Inc., 11001 Cedar Street, Cleveland, OH 44141.

Major newspaper indexes are:

Wall Street Journal Index published by Dow Jones & Co. Inc., 22 Cortland Street, New York, NY 10007 (monthly).

New York Times Index published by the New York Times Company, 229 W. 43rd Street, New York, NY 10036 (semimonthly, cumulates annually).

TRACKING ECONOMIC INDICATORS

Composite Index of Leading Economic Indicators: Each month the Bureau of Economic Analysis compiles this data from the 12 leading economic indicators. This material appears each month in the *Bureau's Business Conditions Digest* (BCD) available by subscription from:

Superintendent of Documents
Government Printing Office
Washington, DC 20402

Index values are available towards the very end of each month by calling: 202-523-0541.

Consumer Price Index (*CPI*) (changes in cost of goods to customers): For these monthly reports prepared by the Bureau of Labor Statistics write:

Bureau of Labor Statistics
Department of Labor
441 G Street NW
Washington, DC 20212

CPI 24 hour hotline: 202-523-1239.

Producer Price Index (*PPI*) (measures changes in prices received in primary markets by producers). For monthly reports write:

Bureau of Labor Statistics
Department of Labor
441 G Street NW
Washington, DC 20212

PPI 24 hour hotline: 202-523-1765.

Available from the Bureau of Labor Statistics (BLS) are press releases on *State and Metropolitan Area Unemployment* (issued monthly), the *Employment Cost Index* (issued quarterly, and the *Employment Situation Study* (released monthly). For a sample copy call 202-523-1221. To subscribe write:

Bureau of Labor Statistics
Department of Labor
Washington, DC 20230

BLS hotline: 202-523-1239
Major BLS Statistics: 523-9658

Unemployment Insurance Claims Weekly may be obtained by calling or by writing:

Employment and Training Administration
Department of Labor
601 D Street, NW
Washington, DC 20213

Releases on the *Money Supply* (Report H-6, issued weekly) and on *Consumer Credit* (Report G-19, issued monthly) may be obtained from the

Publications Services
Federal Reserve Board
Washington, DC 20551
202-452-3244

Personal Consumption Expenditure Deflator is prepared monthly by the Bureau of Economic Analysis of the Department of Commerce. This information appears in a press release *Personal Income and Outlays* and can be obtained in writing from the

Current Business Analysis
Bureau of Economic Analysis
Department of Commerce
Washington, DC 20230

For information call 202-523-0777.

Monthly Trade Report (index of retail sales and accounts receivable) is compiled by the Bureau of the Census and published in *Current Business Reports* as part of what is known as the BR series. Also available are *Current Business Reports Wholesale Trade* and *Current Business Reports Selected Services.* To subscribe contact the Superintendent of Documents (Address given above). For a sample copy call: 301-763-4100.

Value of New Construction Put in Place is a Census Bureau monthly report (part of the C-30 Series) which charts the dollar amount of new construction. It is available on an annual subscription basis from the Superintendent of Documents, Government Printing Office, Washington, DC 20402. For a sample copy call: 301-763-5717.

Joint Economic Committee of Congress Reports

Reports on the economic issues studied by the Joint Economic Committee are available free of charge from:

Joint Economic Committee of Congress
Dirksen Senate Office Building
Washington, DC 20510
202–224–5321

FEDERAL INFORMATION CENTERS (FICs)

FICs located in key cities throughout the country are a joint venture of the U.S. General Services Administration and the U.S. Civil Services. Each center is a focal point for obtaining information about the federal government and often about state and local governments. A member of the center's staff can either provide information or direct inquiries to an expert who can. Some centers have specialists who speak foreign languages. The coordinator of the FICs is located at 18th and F Streets, NW, Washington, DC 20405. For a list of FICs write to: Consumer Information Center, Pueblo, CO 81009.

TRACKING CONGRESSIONAL ACTION

Congressional action information can be obtained from several sources. The Legis Office will provide information on whether legislation has been introduced, who sponsored it, and its current status. For House or Senate action, call 202–225–1772.

Cloakrooms of both houses will provide details on what is happening on the floor of the chamber. House cloakrooms: Democrat 202–225–7330; Republican 202–225–7350. Senate cloakrooms: Democrat 202–224–4691; Republican 202–224–6391.

ASSISTANCE FROM U.S. GOVERNMENT AGENCIES

The **Office of Business Liaison (OBL)** serves as the focal point for contact between the Department of Commerce and the business community. Through the *Business Assistance Program* individuals and firms are guided through the entire government complex. Other services include dissemination of information and reports such as *Outlook.* Write Office of Business Liaison, U.S. Department of Commerce, Washington, DC 20230. This office is also a focal point for handling inquiries for domestic business information.

OBL telephone numbers:

Office of the Director . . (202) 377-3942
Outreach Program 377-1360
Business Assistance
Program 3176

Industry experts in the International Trade Administration can provide specifics about an industry.

Country experts in the Department of State provide up to date economic and political information on countries throughout the world, as well as background reports on specific countries. For information contact:

Country Desk Officers
U.S. Department of State
2201 C Street NW
Washington, DC 20520
Telephone: 202–647–4000

Major Bureau of Labor Statistics Indicators are available daily from a recorded message at 202–523-9658.

Economic news and highlights of the day are provided by phone from the Department of Commerce. For economic news call 202–393–4100. For news highlights call 202–393–1847.

The Energy Information Center will provide free information on energy and related matters. Write National Energy Information Center, Forrestal Building, 1000 Independence Avenue SW, Washington, DC 20585. Call 202–586–5000.

Industry information statistics and details on specific industries can be obtained from the Department of Commerce, Washington, DC 20230; or call 202–377–4356.

Technical and scientific information is provided by the **National Technical Information Service** of the Department of Commerce, 5285 Port Royal, Springfield, VA 22161, which handles requests about government-sponsored research of all kinds. The basic charge to research a subject is $125. For information call 703–487–4600. For orders call 703–487–4650. For rush orders within the local calling area call 703–487–4700. For rush order outside the local calling area call 800–336–4700.

The **Census Bureau** produces detailed statistical information for the Nation. Information is available on population, housing, agriculture, manufacturing, retail trade, service industries, wholesale trade, foreign trade, mining, transportation, construction, and the revenues and expenditures of state and local governments. The Bureau also produces statistical studies of many foreign countries.

Information Sources in the Bureau of the Census

User Services:

General Information .... (301) 763-4100
Data User Training 763-1510
Geographic Information 763-5270
Product Information (print, map) 763-4100
Map Orders .... (812) 288-3212

Government, Commerce and Industry Subjects:

Agriculture Data .... (301) 763-1113
Business Data (Retail, Wholesale, Services) 763-7564
Construction Statistics 763-7163
Government Data 763-7366
Industry Data 763-7800
Manufacturers Data 763-7666

Population, Housing and Income Subjects:

Housing Data .... (301) 763-2881
International Statistics 763-2870
Neighborhood Statistics (1980 Census) 763-2358
Population Data (age, race, income, education, etc.) 763-5020
Special Demographic Studies 763-7720

Government, Commerce and Civic Relations: .... (301) 763-2436

Regional Assistance:

Atlanta, Georgia .... (404) 347-2274
Boston, Massachusetts .... (617) 223-0226
Charlotte, North Carolina .... (704) 371-6144
Chicago, Illinois .... (312) 353-0980
Dallas, Texas .... (214) 767-0625
Denver, Colorado .... (303) 234-3924
Detroit, Michigan .... (313) 226-7742
Kansas City, Kansas .... (913) 236-3731
Los Angeles, California .... (213) 209-6612
New York, New York .... (212) 264-3860
Philadelphia, Pennsylvania .... (215) 597-8313
Seattle, Washington .... (206) 442-7080

For a detailed telephone contact list .... (301) 763-2436

Source: *Business Services Directory*, U.S. Department of Commerce, Office of Business Liason.

Information Sources in the U.S. Department of Commerce: Quick Reference List

Aeronautical Chart Sales........... (301) 436-6990
Business Assistance...................(202) 377-3176
Commerce Speakers..................(202) 377-1360
Copyright Information*.............. (202) 287-8700
Consumer Information............... (202) 377-5001
District Export Councils............. (202) 377-4767
Energy Related Inventions-
  Evaluation................................(301) 975-4000

Export
  Counseling.............................. (202) 377-3181
  Export Trading Companies ....(202) 377-5131
  License/Application................ (202) 377-4811

Fish Exports/Imports................. (202) 673-5478
Fishery Management Plans........ (202) 673-5263
Foreign Trade Zones.................. (202) 377-2862
Freight Rates** ....(202) 426-5812
Industry/Products
  Information..............................(202) 377-1461
Metric Information .... (202) 377-0944
Micro Computer Information
  Exchange.................................(301) 948-5717
Minority Owned Business...........(202) 377-8015
Nautical Chart Sales .... (301) 436-6990
NTIS Sales Desk.........................(703) 487-4650
Overseas Customer Lists........... (202) 377-3022
Overseas Marketing ....(202) 377-3022
Overseas Trade Fairs................. (202) 377-8220
Patent & Trademark
  Information..............................(703) 557-3080
Productivity Enhancement
  Information..............................(202) 377-0940

Procurement
  Bidder's List............................ (202) 377-3387
  Commerce Buy List................ (202) 377-3387
  MBDA Profile System............. (202) 377-2414
  NOAA Opportunities...............(202) 377-1537
  Small Business........................(202) 377-1472
  Women Owned Business ....(202) 377-1472

Federal Procurement
  Conferences............................ (202) 377-2975

Publications
  "Business America"
    Magazine............................. (202) 377-3251
  Commerce Business Daily...... (202) 377-4868

*Handled by the Library of Congress
**Handled by Maritime Commission

Domestic Economic
  Development.........................(202) 377-5113
NBS Reference Materials .... (301) 975-2012
NTIA Publication
  Information........................... (202) 377-1551
Sea Grant Research ....(301) 443-8923

Small Business
  Assistance...............................(202) 377-3176
  Procurement/Set Asides........ (202) 377-1472

Standards & Codes for
  Products..................................(301) 975-4036

Statistics
  Business Cycles...................... (202) 523-0535
  Capital Investment.................. (202) 523-0874
  Gross National Product.......... (202) 523-0669
  Foreign Travelers to U.S. .... (202) 377-0140
  Housing Starts........................ (301) 763-5731
  Income Data .... (301) 763-5020
  International Trade
    Balance................................(202) 523-0620
  Personal Income by
    County................................ (202) 523-0951
  Population.............................. (301) 763-5020
  Price Indexes.......................... (202) 523-0828
  Retail Trade Data .... (301) 763-4100
  Trade Statistics....................... (202) 377-2185

Technology
  International Joint
    Ventures.............................. (202) 377-0944
  National Joint Ventures...........(202) 377-5914
  Small Business........................(202) 377-8111
  Time of Day............................(303) 499-7111

Travel
  "America, Catch the
    Spirit." .... (202) 377-4752
  Tourism Information
    (Inbound)..............................(202) 377-4752

Weather
  Climate for Farming ....(301) 763-4690
  Forecast—
    U.S. Eastern Cities ....(301) 899-3244
  Forecast—
    U.S. Western Cities ....(301) 899-3249
  Past Conditions.......................(202) 673-5381
  Tide & Water Levels................(301) 443-8441

Women Owned Business............(202) 377-1472

Source: *Business Services Directory,* U.S. Department of Commerce, Office of Business Liason.

Commodities: Sources of Government Information

Information on various commodities may be obtained by calling the following:

Office of Industries
International Trade Commission
Telephone: 292–523–0146

Bureau of Mines
The Bureau uses three basic classifications:

Ferrous Metals
  Telephone: 202–634–1010
Nonferrous Metals
  Telephone: 202–634–1055
Industrial Minerals
  Telephone: 202–634–1202

Crops Branch
Department of Agriculture
Telephone: 202–786–1840

Metals, Minerals and Commodities
Trade Development
Telephone: 202–377–0575

Minerals Industries
Bureau of the Census
Telephone: 202–763–5938

Industry and Commodity Classification
Bureau of the Census
Telephone: 202–763–1935

Available through the Government Printing Office (202–783–3238) are the Bureau of the Census Publications, *U.S. Imports, U.S.A. Commodities by Country* and *U.S. Exports Schedule 13, Commodities by Country.*

Federal and State Government Assistance Available to U.S. Businesses: Center for the Utilization of Federal Technology

Government support of technical innovation is growing rapidly both at the Federal and State levels. A helpful source for information regarding the transfer of Federal technology to the U.S. economy is the **Center for the Utilization of Federal Technology (CUFT)**, which is part of the National Technical Information Service (NTIS) of the U.S. Department of Commerce, 5285 Port Royal Road, Springfield, VA 22161; (703) 487-4838. One of its major roles is to link U.S. businesses with federally developed technologies and resources having commercial or practical application. By working directly with U.S. Government agencies, CUFT has prepared a number of directories and catalogs to alert companies to these valuable Government resources.

Its most recent directory, *Directory of Federal and State Business Assistance–A Guide for New and Growing Companies*, presents full descriptions to financial, management, innovation, and information programs and services established to help both large and small firms in their day-to-day operations. A listing of state services is given on page *609*.

A companion directory, *Directory of Federal Laboratory and Technical Resources–A Guide to Services, Facilities, and Expertise*, provides detailed descriptions of technology-oriented Federal resources. Especially notable are the entries describing 91 technical information centers offering information assistance in focused technology areas.

Also available are the *Federal Technology Catalogs–Guides to New and Practical Technologies* which annually offer full descriptions to more than 1,200 new technologies and R&D developments. Another annual catalog series, *Catalogs of Government Patents*, provides quick access to the more than 1,400 U.S. Government-owned inventions available for licensing (often exclusively).

For further information, write or call CUFT at the address given above or call (703) 487-4838.

Business Assistance Program: Commerce Department

The Business Assistance program is designed to shorten the time it takes a businessperson to track down information within the labyrinth of government bureaus and agencies. Business Assistance Program staffers can provide information or direct inquiries to the proper authority on such subjects as regulatory changes, government programs, services, policies, and even relevant government publications for the business community. For information call 202–377–3176 or write: Business Assistance Program Business Liason Office, Rm 5898-C, Department of Commerce, Washington, DC 20230.

U.S. General Services Administration: Business Service Centers

The Business Service Centers are a one stop, one point of contact for information on General Services Administration and other Government contract programs. The primary function is to provide advice on doing business with the Federal Government. The Centers provide information, assistance, and counseling and sponsor business clinics, procurement conferences, and business opportunity meetings.

Business representatives interested in selling products and services to the Government should contact the nearest Business Service Center given on page 608.

Mailing Address and Telephone	Area of Service
Business Service Center General Services Administration John W. McCormack Post Office and Courthouse Boston, MA 02109 (617) 223–2868	Connecticut, Maine, Massachusetts, New Hampshire, Rhode Island, and Vermont
Business Service Center General Services Administration 26 Federal Plaza New York, NY 10007 (212) 264–1234	New Jersey, New York, Puerto Rico, and Virgin Islands
Business Service Center General Services Administration 7th and D Streets, SW., RM. 1050 Washington, DC 20407 (202) 472–1804	District of Columbia, nearby Maryland, Virginia
Business Service Center General Services Administration 9th and Market Streets Room 1300 Philadelphia, PA 19107 (215) 597–9613	Delaware, Pennsylvania, West Virginia, Maryland, Virginia
Business Service Center General Services Administration Richard B. Russell Federal Building and Court House 75 Spring Street Atlanta, GA 30303 (404) 221–5103	Alabama, Florida, Georgia, Kentucky, Mississippi, North Carolina, South Carolina, and Tennessee
Business Service Center General Services Administration 230 South Dearborn Street Chicago, IL 60604 (312) 353–5383	Illinois, Indiana, Ohio, Michigan, Minnesota, and Wisconsin
Business Service Center General Services Administration 1500 East Bannister Road Kansas City, MO 64131 (816) 926–7203	Iowa, Kansas, Missouri, and Nebraska
Business Service Center General Services Administration 819 Taylor Street Fort Worth, TX 76102 (817) 334–3284	Arkansas, Louisiana, New Mexico, Oklahoma, and Texas
Business Service Center General Services Administration Building 41, Denver Federal Center Denver, CO 80225 (303) 236–7409	Colorado, Montana, North Dakota, South Dakota, Utah, and Wyoming
Business Service Center General Services Administration 525 Market Street San Francisco, CA 94105 (415) 454–9000	California (northern), Hawaii, and Nevada (except Clark County)
Business Service Center General Services Administration 300 North Los Angeles Street Los Angeles, CA 90012 (213) 688–3210	Arizona, Los Angeles, California (southern), and Nevada (Clark County only)
Business Service Center General Services Administration 440 Federal Building 915 Second Avenue Seattle, WA 98174 (206) 442–5556	Alaska, Idaho, Oregon, and Washington

State Information Guide

Regional Directories

Central Atlantic States Manufacturing Directory, T. K. Sanderson Organization, 200 E. 25 Street, Baltimore, MD 21218

Daltons' Greater Philadelphia Industrial Directory, Dalton Corp., 2925 N. Broad Street, Philadelphia, PA 19132

Directory of Central Atlantic States Manufacturers, Manufacturers' News, Inc., 4 E. Huron Street, Chicago, IL 60611; George D. Hall Company, 20 Kilby Street, Boston, MA 02109

Directory of New England Manufacturers, The, George D. Hall Company, 20 Kilby Street, Boston, MA 02109

Eastern Manufacturers' and Industrial Directory, Bell Directory Publishers, Inc., 1995 Broadway, New York, NY 10023

MacRae's Blue Book, The National Industrial Directory, 87 Terminal Drive, Plainview, NY 11803

Midwest Manufacturers' and Industrial Directory, Industrial Directory Publishers, 1002 Park Avenue Building, Detroit, MI 48226

New England Apparel Directory, Register Publication, Inc., 99 Chauncey Street, Boston, MA 02111

New England Industrial Service Directory, George D. Hall Company, 20 Kilby Street, Boston, MA 02109

New England Manufacturers Directory, Manufacturers' News, Inc., 3 E. Huron Street, Chicago, IL 60611

State Executive Directory, Carroll Publishing Company, 1058 Thomas Jefferson NW, Washington, DC 20007

State Sales Guides, Dun & Bradstreet, Inc., 99 Church Street, New York, NY 10007

Survey of Industries in Texarkana (Arkansas-Texas), Texarkana Chamber of Commerce, Box 1468, Texarkana, AK 75501

State Business Assistance Publications

Directory of Incentives for Business Investment and Development in the U.S., The Urban Institute Press, available from UPA, 4720 Boston Way, Lanlam, MD 20706. State by state guide to economic business incentives. Included are descriptions of state assistance and financial assistance programs.

Monthly Checklist of State Publications, Superintendent of Documents. Washington, DC 20402. A monthly list of documents and publications received from the States.

State Administrative Officials Classified by Function, Council of State Governments, Iron Works Pike, P.O. Box 1190, Lexington, KY 40578. Names, titles, telephone numbers and addresses of state officials and administrators.

BUSINESS ASSISTANCE CENTERS BY STATE*

These centers offer assistance in business related matters. Such assistance includes information gathering, location of expert help, and guidance on new technologies. Most of these centers also are able to offer other types of assistance, such as market feasibility, or at least link businesses with appropriate contacts.

Alabama

Alabama Department of Agriculture and Industries, Post Office Box 3336, Montgomery, AL 36193. Contact (205) 261-2650. *Assistance:* Information/Technical

Alabama Department of Economic & Community Affairs–State Planning, 3465 Norman Bridge Road, P.O. Box 2939, Montgomery, AL 36105–0939. Contact Mr. Ned Butler at (205) 284-6706. *Assistance:* Business planning/information/Networking/Technical

Alabama Department of Economic and Community Affairs–Energy Division, 3465 Norman Bridge Road, P.O. Box 2939, Montgomery, AL 36105–0939. Contact Mr. Fred Braswell at (205) 284-8952. *Assistance:* Financial/Information/Networking/Technical

Alabama Department of Environmental Management, 1751 Federal Drive, Montgomery, AL 36130. Contact Ms. Marilyn Elliott at (205) 271-7715. *Assistance:* Information/Networking

Alabama Development Office, c/o State Capital, Montgomery, AL 36130. Contact (205) 263-0048. *Assistance:* Business planning/Financial/Information/Networking/Technical

Alabama High Technology Assistance Center, University of Alabama in Huntsville, 222 Morton Hall, Huntsville, AL 35899. Contact Dr. Edward F. Stafford at (205) 895-

* Source: *Directory of Federal and State Business Assistance: A Guide for New and Growing Companies,* National Technical Information Service, Center for the Utilization of Federal Technology, U.S. Department of Commerce. For further information call 703–487–4838.

6409. *Assistance:* Business planning/Information/Networking/Technical

Alabama International Trade Center, P.O. Box 1996, Patton Building, University, AL 35486. Contact Mr. Nisa Bacon at (205) 348-7621. *Assistance:* Business planning/Information/Networking/Technical

Alabama Small Business Development Consortium, 1717 11th Avenue South, Medical Towers Building, Suite 419, Birmingham, AL 35294. Contact Mrs. Sherry Dilbeck at (205) 934-7260. *Assistance:* Business planning / Financial / Information / Management / Networking / Technical. *Eligibility:* Smaller businesses

Auburn Technical Assistance Center, 202 Langdon Annex, Auburn University, AL 36849. Contact Mr. Henry Burdg at (205) 826-4659. *Assistance:* Management/Technical

Alabama State Department of Revenue, Research and Information Division, Administrative Building, 64 North Union Street, Montgomery, AL 36130. Contact Mr. William E. Crawford at (205) 261-3094 or 3366. *Assistance:* Information/Networking

Center for Economic Development & Business Research, Jacksonville State University, College of Commerce and Business Administration, 114 Merrill Hall, Jacksonville, AL 36265. Contact Ms. Pat W. Shaddix at (205) 435-9820 Ext: 324. *Assistance:* Business planning/Information/Technical

Economic Development Technical Assistance Unit, Tuskegee University Human Resources Development Center, P.O. Box 681, Tuskegee Institute, AL 36088. Contact (205) 727-8764. *Assistance:* Business planning/Information

Management Development Center, Jacksonville State University, Merrill Bldg., Room 113-A, Jacksonville, AL 36265. Contact Mr. David R. Copeland at (205) 435-9820 Ext: 342. *Assistance:* Business planning/Management

Alaska

Agricultural Loan Fund, Alaska Department of Natural Resources, Division of Agriculture, Pouch A, Wasilla, AL 99687. Contact (907) 376-3276. *Assistance:* Financial

Alaska Commercial Fishing and Agriculture Bank, P.O. Box Y-2070, Anchorage, AL 99509. Contact (907) 276-2007. *Assistance:* Financial/Networking/Technical

Alaska Industrial Development Authority, 1577 C Street, Suite 304, Anchorage, AL 99501–5177. Contact (907) 274-1651. *Assistance:* Financial/Networking

Economic Development Center, School of Business and Public Administration, University of Alaska-Juneau, 1108 F Street, Juneau, AK 99801. Contact Dr. Al Borrego at (907) 789-4402. *Assistance:* Business planning/Technical

Loan Fund Programs, Department of Commerce and Economic Development, Division of Investments, Pouch D, Juneau, AL 99811. Contact (907) 465-2510. *Assistance:* Financial

Arizona

Arizona Department of Commerce, 1700 West Washington, 4th Floor, Phoenix, AZ 85007. Contact Ms. Beth S. Jarman at (602) 255-5371. *Assistance:* Business planning/Financial/Information/Technical

Business and Trade Program, Arizona Department of Commerce, 1700 West Washington, 4th Floor, Phoenix, AZ 85007. Contact Ms. Beth S. Jarman at (602) 255-5371. *Assistance:* Business planning/Information/Networking/Technical

Development Finance Program, Arizona Department of Commerce, 1700 West Washington, 4th Floor, Pheonix, AZ 85007. Contact Ms Beth S. Jarman at (602) 255-5371. *Assistance:* Business planning/Financial/Information/Technical

Arkansas

Arkansas Industry Training Program, Education Building-West, #3 Capitol Mall, Little Rock, AR 72201. Contact Mr. Richard Cochran at (501) 371-2165. *Assistance:* Training

Arkansas Science and Technology Authority, 200 Main Street, Suite 201, Little Rock, AR 72201. Contact Dr. John Ahlen at (501) 371-3554. *Assistance:* Financial/Information/Networking/Technical

Business Development Services–University of Arkansas at Little Rock, 5th Floor, Library Building, UALR, 33rd and University Ave., Little Rock, AR 72204. Contact Mr. Paul McGinnis at (501) 371-5535. *Assistance:* Business planning/Financial/Information/Networking/Technical

Center for Technology Transfer–University of Arkansas at Little Rock, Department of Industrial Engineering, 309 Engineering Building, University of Arkansas, Fayetteville, AR 72701. Contact Dr. C. Robert Emerson at (501) 575-3156. *Assistance:* Information/Networking/Technical

Division of Finance–Arkansas Industrial Development Commission, One State Capital Mall, Little Rock, AR 72201. Contact Mr. Larry Patrick at (501) 371-1151. *Assistance:* Financial/Information/Networking/Technical

Energy Division–Arkansas Industrial Development Commission, One State Capitol

Mall, Little Rock, AR 72201. Contact Ms. Cherry Duckett at (501) 371-1370. *Assistance:* Information/Networking/Technical

Marketing Division–Arkansas Industrial Development Commission, One State Capitol Mall, Little Rock, AR 72201. Contact Ms. Maria Haley at (501) 371-7678. *Assistance:* Information/Networking/Technical

Minority Business Division–Arkansas Industrial Development Commission, One State Capitol Mall, Little Rock, AR 72201. Contact Mr. James Hall at (501) 371-1060. *Assistance:* Business planning/Financial/Information/Networking/Technical. *Eligibility:* Minority businesses

California

Economic Adjustment Unit, Department of Commerce, 1121 L Street, Suite 600, Sacramento, CA 95814. Contact (916) 322-1515. *Assistance:* Training/Business planning/Information/Technical

Office of Business Development, Department of Commere, 1121 L Street, Sacramento, CA 95814. Contact (916) 322-5665. *Assistance:* Information

Office of Economic Research, Department of Commerce, 1121 L Street, Sacramento, CA 95814. Contact (916) 322-5853. *Assistance:* Information

Office of Small Business, Department of Commerce, 1121 L Street, Sacramento, CA 95814. Contact (916) 445-6545. *Assistance:* Business planning/Financial/Information/Technical. *Eligibility:* Smaller businesses

Urban University Center, Western Research Application Center, University of Southern California, 3716 South Hope Street, Los Angeles, CA 90007. Contact (213) 743-2371. *Assistance:* Business planning/Information/Technical

Colorado

Business Information Center, Office of Regulatory Reform, 1525 Sherman Street, #110, Denver, CO 80203. Contact (303) 866-3933. *Assistance:* Information

Colorado Housing Finance Authority, Commercial Programs, 500 E. 8th Ave., Denver, CO 80203. Contact (303) 861-8962. *Assistance:* Financial. *Eligibility:* Smaller businesses

Division of Commerce and Development, 1313 Sherman Street, #523, Denver, CO 80203. Contact (303) 866-2205. *Assistance:* Information/Networking/Technical

Minority Business Development Agency, 1525 Sherman Street, 7th Floor, Denver, CO 80203. Contact (303) 866-2077. *Assistance:* Information/Technical. *Eligibility:* Minority businesses

Small Business Assistance Center, 1690 38th Street, #101, Boulder, CO 80301. Contact (303) 444-5723. (800) 521-1243 in Colorado. *Assistance:* Business planning/Information/Technical. *Eligibility:* Smaller businesses

Connecticut

Connecticut Department of Economic Development–Business Services, 210 Washington Street, Hartford, CT 06106. Contact Mr. John J. Carson at (203) 566-3842. *Assistance:* Business planning/Information/Networking/Technical

Connecticut Department of Economic Development–Investment Incentives, 210 Washington Street, Hartford, CT 06106. Contact Mr. John J. Carson at (203) 566-3842. *Assistance:* Financial

Connecticut Department of Economic Development–Technical Assistance, 210 Washington Street, Hartford, CT 06106. Contact Mr. John J. Carson at (203) 566-3842. *Assistance:* Business planning/Information/Networking/Technical

Connecticut Development Authority, 217 Washington Street, Hartford, CT 06106. Contact Mr. Richard L. Higgins at (203) 522-3730. *Assistance:* Financial

Connecticut Product Development Corporation, 93 Oak Street, Hartford, CT 06106. Contact Mr. Jack Frazier at (203) 566-2920. *Assistance:* Financial

Connecticut Technology Assistance Center, Connecticut Department of Economic Development, 210 Washington Street, Hartford, CT 06106. Contact Mr. Eric Ott at (203) 566-4587 or 4862. *Assistance:* Training/Business planning/Financial/Information/Networking/Technical

Delaware

Delaware Development Office, Business Services Unit, 99 Kings Highway, P.O. Box 1401, Dover, DE 19903. Contact (302) 736-4271. *Assistance:* Financial/Information

Delaware Small Business Development Center, Suite 005 Purnell Hall, University of Delaware, Newark, DE 19716. Contact David Park at (302) 451-2747. *Assistance:* Business planning/Information/Management. *Eligibility:* Smaller businesses

District of Columbia

District of Columbia Department of Employment Services, 1350 Pennsylvania Avenue, N.W., Washington, DC 20004. Contact Ms Jackie Threadgill at (202) 639-1179. *Assistance:* Training/Information/Networking

Financial Services Division, Office of Business and Economic Development, 1350 Pennsylvania Avenue, N.W., Washington,

DC 20001. Contact Ms. Pamela Vaughn Cooke Henry at (202) 727-6600. *Assistance:* Financial

Minority Business Opportunity Commission, 613 G Street, N.W., Washington, DC 20001. Contact Mr. William C. Jameson at (202) 727-3817. *Assistance:* Financial/Information/Networking. *Eligibility:* Minority businesses

Technical Services Division, Office of Business and Economic Development, 1350 Pennsylvania Avenue, N.W., Washington, DC 20004. Contact Mr. Kwasi Hulman at (202) 727-6600. *Assistance:* Information/Management/Networking/Technical

Florida

Business Service Program, Bureau of Business Assistance, Florida Department of Commerce, 107 West Gains Street, Tallahassee, FL 32301. Contact Mr. Leonard Elize at (904) 488-9357. *Assistance:* Information/Networking.

Financial Service, Bureau of Business Assistance, Florida Department of Commerce, 107 West Gains Street, Tallahassee, FL 32301. Contact Mr. Leonard Elize at (904) 488-9357. *Assistance:* Financial/Networking

Entrepreneurship Program, Bureau of Business Assistance, Florida Department of Commerce, 107 West Gains Street, Tallahassee, FL 32301. Contact Mr. Leonard Elize at (904) 488-9357. *Assistance:* Information

Florida Economic Development Center, 325 College of Business, Florida State University, Tallahassee, FL 32306-1007. Contact Mr. Roy Thompson at (904) 644-1044. *Assistance:* Business planning/Financial/Information/Networking/Technical

Florida Small Business Development Centers, University of West Florida, Pensacola, FL 32514. Contact Mr. Gregory L. Higgins at (904) 478-2820. *Assistance:* Business planning / Information / Management / Networking / Technical. *Eligibility:* Smaller businesses

NASA/Southern Technology Applications Center, University of Florida, 307 Weil Hall, Gainsville, FL 32611. Contact Mr. J. Ronald Thornton at (904) 392-0854. *Assistance:* Information/Networking/Technical

North Florida Entrepreneurial Network, Room 325, College of Business, Florida State University, Tallahassee, FL 32306–1007. Contact Mr. Greg Cardamone at (904) 644-1044. *Assistance:* Information/Networking/Technical

Production Innovation Center, University of North Florida, 4567 St. Johns Bluff Road, Jacksonville, FL 32216. Contact Mr. Richard L. Christian at (904) 646-2487. *Assistance:* Business planning/Information/Networking/Technical. *Eligibility:* Smaller businesses

Quest for Technology Program at Florida State University, 325 College of Business, Florida State University, Tallahassee, FL 32306–1007. Contact (904) 644-1044. *Assistance:* Business planning/Financial/Information/Networking/Technical

Georgia

Advanced Technology Development Center, 430 Tenth Street, Suite N-116, Atlanta, GA 30318. Contact (404) 894-3575. *Assistance:* Information/Networking/Technical

Georgia Department of Community Affairs, Room 800, 40 Marietta Street, N.W., Small Business Revitalization Program, Atlanta, GA 30303. Contact Mr. Steve Storey at (404) 656-6200. *Assistance:* Financial/Information/Networking/Technical

Georgia Productivity Center, Georgia Institute of Technology, Atlanta, GA 30332. Contact Dr. Bikram Garcha at (404) 658-4000. *Assistance:* Business planning/Information/Networking/Technical

Economic Development Division, Economic Development Laboratory, Georgia Tech Research Institute, Atlanta, GA 30332. Contact Mr. Arthur Brown at (404) 894-3858. *Assistance:* Business planning/Technical

Technical Assistance Center, Atlanta University, Inc., 223 Chestnut Street, S.W., Atlanta, GA 30314. Contact Mr. Thurmond Williams at (404) 681-0251. *Assistance:* Business planning/Technical. *Eligibility:* Minority businesses

The Small Business Development Center, College of Business Administration, Brooks Hall, The University of Georgia, Athens, GA 30601. Contact Mr. Lee Quarterman at (404) 658-3550. *Assistance:* Business planning/Information/Networking.

Financial Assistance Branch, Department of Planning and Economic Development, 250 South King Street, Honolulu, HI 96813. Contact (808) 548-4617. *Assistance:* Financial/Information/Networking. *Eligibility:* Smaller businesses

Hawaii

Department of Agriculture, State of Hawaii, 1428 South King Street, Honolulu, HI 96814. Contact (808) 548-7108. *Assistance:* Financial/Information/Networking/Technical

Industry and Product Promotion, Business Development Branch, Department of Planning and Economic Development, 250 South King Street, Honolulu, HI 96813. Contact (808) 548-3908. *Assistance:* Business planning/Information/Networking

International Services Branch, Department of Planning and Economic Development, 250 South King Street, Honolulu, HI 96813. Contact (808) 548-4621. *Assistance:* Business planning/Information/Networking

Pacific Business Center Program, College of Business Administration, 2404 Maile Way, Honolulu, HI 96822. Contact (808) 948-6286. *Assistance:* Business planning/Management. *Eligibility:* Smaller businesses

Small Business Information Service, Department of Planning and Economic Development, 250 South King Street, Honolulu, HI 96813. Contact (808) 548-7645. *Assistance:* Business planning/Information/Networking

Special Duty Attorney General for Small Business, 335 Merchant Street, Room 241A, Honolulu, HI 96813. Contact (808) 548-6744. *Assistance:* Information/Technical. *Eligibility:* Smaller businesses

Idaho

Idaho Business and Economic Development Center, 1910 University Drive, Boise State University, Boise, ID 83725. Contact Mr. Ronald R. Hall at (208) 385-1640. *Assistance:* Business planning/Information/Management/Networking/Technical

Idaho Department of Commerce, Statehouse, Room 108, Boise, ID 83720. Contact Mr. Jay Engstrom at (208) 334-4719. *Assistance:* Business planning/Financial/Information/Networking/Technical

Idaho Small Business Development Center, 1910 University Drive, Boise State University, Boise, ID 83725. Contact (208) 385-1640. *Assistance:* Business planning/Information/Management/Networking/Technical. *Eligibility:* Smaller businesses

Region District Associations, Idaho Department of Commerce, Statehouse, Room 108, Boise, ID 83720. Contact Mr. Jay Engstrom at (208) 334-4719. *Assistance:* Financial

Illinois

Bond Programs, Illinois Department of Commerce and Community Affairs, 620 East Adams Street, Springfield, IL 62701. Contact (217) 782-6861. For the Chicago area, contact State of Illinois Center, 100 West Randolph Street, Suite 3-400; (312) 917-3133. *Assistance: Financial*

Center for Urban Economic Development, School of Urban Planning and Policy, The University of Illinois at Chicago, Box 4348, Chicago, IL 60680. Contact (312) 996-2178. *Assistance:* Business planning/Information/Technical

Business Expansion Assistance, Illinois Department of Commerce and Community Affairs, 620 East Adams Street, Springfield, IL 62701. Contact (217) 782-6861. For the Chicago area, contact State of Illinois Center, 100 West Randolph Street, Suite 3-400; (312) 917-3133. *Assistance:* Information/Networking

Development Finance Unit, Illinois Department of Commerce and Community Affairs, 620 East Adams Street, Springfield, IL 62701. Contact (217) 782-6861. For the Chicago area, contact State of Illinois Center, 100 West Randolph Street, Suite 3-400; (312) 917-3133. *Assistance:* Technical

Export Assistance, Illinois Department of Commerce and Community Affairs, 620 East Adams Street, Springfield, IL 62701. Contact (217) 782-6861. For the Chicago area, contact State of Illinois Center, 100 West Randolph Street, Suite 3-400; (312) 917-3133. *Assistance:* Information/Networking/Technical

Export Financing, Illinois Department of Commerce and Community Affairs, 620 East Adams Street, Springfield, IL 62701. Contact (217) 782-6861. For the Chicago area, contact State of Illinois Center, 100 West Randolph Street, Suite 3-400; (312) 917-3133.

Illinois Enterprise Zone Program, Illinois Department of Commerce and Community Affairs, 620 East Adams Street, Springfield, IL 62701. Contact (217) 782-6861. For the Chicago area, contact State of Illinois Center, 100 West Randolph Street, Suite 3-400; (312) 917-3133. *Assistance:* Financial

Illinois Inventor's Council, Illinois Department of Commerce and Community Affairs, 620 East Adams Street, Springfield, IL 62701. Contact (217) 782-6861. For the Chicago area, contact State of Illinois Center, 100 West Randolph Street, Suite 3-400; (312) 917-3133. *Assistance:* Networking/Technical

Illinois Resource Network, Illinois Department of Commerce and Community Affairs, 620 East Adams Street, Springfield, IL 62701. Contact (217) 782-6861. For the Chicago area, contact State of Illinois Center, 100 West Randolph Street, Suite 3-400; (312) 917-3133.

Industrial Health and Safety Consultation, Illinois Department of Commerce and Community Affairs, 620 East Adams Street, Springfield, IL 62701. Contact (217) 782-6861. For the Chicago area, contact State of Illinois Center, 100 West Randolph

Street, Suite 3-400; (312) 917-3133. *Assistance:* Technical

Illinois Software Association and Center, Illinois Department of Commerce and Community Affairs, 620 East Adams Street, Springfield, IL 62701. Contact (217) 782-6861. For the Chicago area, contact State of Illinois Center, 100 West Randolph Street, Suite 3-400; (312) 917-3133. *Assistance:* Information/Networking

Large Business Development Program, Illinois Department of Commerce and Community Affairs, 620 East Adams Street, Springfield, IL 62701. Contact (217) 782-6861. For the Chicago area, contact State of Illinois Center, 100 West Randolph Street, Suite 3-400; (312) 917-3133. *Assistance:* Information/Management. *Eligibility:* Minority businesses

Minority Business Assistance, Illinois Department of Commerce and Community Affairs, 620 East Adams Street, Springfield, IL 62701. Contact (217) 782-6861. For the Chicago area, contact State of Illinois Center, 100 West Randolph Street, Suite 3-400; (312) 917-3133. *Assistance:* Information/Management. *Eligibility:* Minority businesses

One-Stop Permit Center, Illinois Department of Commerce and Community Affairs, 620 East Adams Street, Springfield, IL 62701. Contact (217) 782-6861. For the Chicago area, contact State of Illinois Center, 100 West Randolph Street, Suite 3-400; (312) 917-3133. *Assistance:* Information

Procurement Assistance Program, Illinois Department of Commerce and Community Affairs, 620 East Adams Street, Springfield, IL 62701. Contact (217) 782-6861. For the Chicago area, contact State of Illinois Center, 100 West Randolph Street, Suite 3-400; (312) 917-3133. *Assistance:* Technical

Sites, Buildings, and Community Profile Program, Illinois Department of Commerce and Community Affairs, 620 East Adams Street, Springfield, IL 62701. Contact (217) 782-6861. For the Chicago area, contact State of Illinois Center, 100 West Randolph Street, Suite 3-400; (312) 917-3133. *Assistance:* Information

Small Business Development Centers, Illinois Department of Commerce and Community Affairs, 620 East Adams Street, Springfield, IL 62701. Contact (217) 782-6861. For the Chicago area, contact State of Illinois Center, 100 West Randolph Street, Suite 3-400; (312) 917-3133. *Assistance:* Business planning/Information/Networking/Technical. *Eligibility:* Smaller businesses

Small Business Development Program, Illinois Department of Commerce and Community Affairs, 620 East Adams Street, Springfield, IL 62701. Contact (217) 782-6861. For the Chicago area, contact State of Illinois Center, 100 West Randolph Street, Suite 3-400; (312) 917-3133. *Assistance:* Financial. *Eligibility:* Smaller businesses

Small Business Financing Funds, Illinois Department of Commerce and Community Affairs, 620 East Adams Street, Springfield, IL 62701. Contact (217) 782-6861. For the Chicago area, contact State of Illinois Center, 100 West Randolph Street, Suite 3-400; (312) 917-3133. *Assistance:* Financial. *Eligibility:* Smaller businesses

Small Business Growth Corporation, Illinois Department of Commerce and Community Affairs, 620 East Adams Street, Springfield, IL 62701. Contact (217) 782-6861. For the Chicago area, contact State of Illinois Center, 100 West Randolph Street, Suite 3-400; (312) 917-3133. *Assistance:* Financial. *Eligibility:* Smaller businesses

Small Business Hotline, Illinois Department of Commerce and Community Affairs, 620 East Adams Street, Springfield, IL 62701. Contact 800-252-2930. *Assistance:* Information

Small Business Investment Companies, Illinois Department of Commerce and Community Affairs, 620 East Adams Street, Springfield, IL 62701. Contact (217) 782-6861. For the Chicago area, contact State of Illinois Center, 100 West Randolph Street, Suite 3-400; (312) 917-3133. *Assistance:* Financial. *Eligibility:* Smaller businesses

Small Business Energy Audit Assistance, Illinois Department of Commerce and Community Affairs, 620 East Adams Street, Springfield, IL 62701. Contact (217) 782-6861. For the Chicago area, contact State of Illinois Center, 100 West Randolph Street, Suite 3-400; (312) 917-3133. *Assistance:* Technical. *Eligibility:* Smaller businesses

Technology Commercialization Centers, Illinois Department of Commerce and Community Affairs, 620 East Adams Street, Springfield, IL 62701. Contact (217) 782-6861. For the Chicago area, contact State of Illinois Center, 100 West Randolph Street, Suite 3-400; (312) 917-3133. *Assistance:* Information/Networking/Technical

Training Programs, Illinois Department of Commerce and Community Affairs, 620 East Adams Street, Springfield, IL 62701. Contact (217) 782-6861. For the Chicago area, contact State of Illinois Center, 100 West Randolph Street, Suite 3-400; (312) 917-3133. *Assistance:* Training/Financial

Venture Capital and Direct Loan Programs, Illinois Development Finance Authority, Illinois Department of Commerce and Community Affairs, 620 East Adams Street, Springfield, IL 62701. Contact (217) 782-6861. For the Chicago area, contact State of Illinois Center, 100 West Randolph Street, Suite 3-400; (312) 917-3133. *Assistance:* Financial

Indiana

Agricultural Development Corporation, Division of Business and Financial Services, Indiana Department of Commerce, One North Capitol, Suite 700, Indianapolis, IN 46204. Contact (317) 232-8782. *Assistance:* Financial

Basic Industries Retraining Program, Division of Business and Financial Services, Indiana Department of Commerce, One North Capitol, Suite 700, Indianapolis, IN 46204. Contact (317) 232-8782. *Assistance:* Financial

Business and Industrial Development Center, Purdue University, Engineering Administration Building, West Lafayette, IN 47907. Contact (800) 821-8261. *Assistance:* Financial/Networking/Technical

Center for Entrepreneurial Resources and Applied Research, School of Continuing Education, Ball State University, Muncie, IN 47306. Contact (800) 541-9313. *Assistance:* Networking/Technical

Center for Research and Management Services, Indiana State University, School of Business, Terre Haute, IN 47809. Contact (812) 232-3232. *Assistance:* Information/Technical

Commercial/Industrial Liaison, Indiana University, Purdue University Indianapolis, 355 North Lansing, Indianapolis, IN 46202. Contact (317) 264-8285. *Assistance:* Networking

Division of Agriculture, Indiana Department of Commerce, One North Capitol, Suite 700, Indianapolis, IN 46204. Contact (317) 232-8770. *Assistance:* Information/Technical

Disadvantaged Business Enterprise Program, Equal Employment Opportunity Section, Indiana Department of Highways, Room 1313, State Office Building, Indianapolis, IN 46204. Contact (317) 232-5093. *Assistance:* Technical. *Eligibility:* Minority businesses

Division of Continuing Studies and Community Services, Indiana University East, 2325 Chester Blvd., Richmond, IN 47374. Contact (317) 966-82621. *Assistance:* Training/Management

Division of Economic Analysis, Indiana Department of Commerce, One North Capitol, Suite 700, Indianapolis, IN 46204. Contact (317) 232-8959. *Assistance:* Information

Division of Energy Policy, Indiana Department of Commerce, One North Capitol, Suite 700, Indianapolis, IN 46204. Contact (317) 232-8940. *Assistance:* Financial/Information/Technical

Division of Industrial Development, Indiana Department of Commerce, One North Capitol, Suite 700, Indianapolis, IN 46204. Contact (317) 232-888. *Assistance:* Information/Networking

Division of Research, Graduate School of Business, Indiana University, Bloomington, IN 47405. Contact (812) 335-5507. *Assistance:* Information

Economic Development Administration University Center at IUPUI, 611 North Capitol Avenue, Indianapolis, IN 46204. Contact Mr. Frank Bivens at (317) 262-5052. *Assistance:* Business planning/Information/Networking/Technical

Enterprise Zone Program, Division of Business and Financial Services, Indiana Department of Commerce, One North Capitol, Suite 700, Indianapolis, IN 46204. Contact (317) 232-8782. *Assistance:* Financial

Entrepreneur in Residence, School of Business, Indiana University, Room 460A, Bloomington, IN 47405. Contact (812) 335-9200. *Assistance:* Business planning/Management/Networking. *Eligibility:* Smaller businesses

Indiana Contractors Educational Center, Inc., 617 Indiana Avenue, Suite 319, Indianapolis, IN 46204. Contact (317) 635-6364. *Assistance:* Technical. *Eligibility:* Smaller businesses and minority businesses

Innovators Forum, Rose-Hulman Institute of Technology, 5500 Wabash Avenue, Terre Haute, IN 47803. Contact Mr. Jim Eifert at (812) 877-1511. *Assistance:* Networking/Technical

Industrial Development Bond Program, Division of Business and Financial Services, Indiana Department of Commerce, One North Capitol, Suite 700, Indianapolis, IN 46204. Contact (317) 232-8782. *Assistance:* Financial

Indiana Technology Referral Network and Technology 2000 Program, EDA University Center at IUPUI, 611 North Capitol Avenue, Indianapolis, IN 46204. Contact (800) 641-4434. *Assistance:* Information/Networking/Technical

Indiana Regional Minority Suppliers Development Council, 151 N. Delaware, Room 1560, Box 44801, Indianapolis, IN 46224. Contact (317) 634-2586. *Assistance:* Information/Networking. *Eligibility:* Minority businesses

Indiana Employment Development Commerce, Division of Business and Financial Services, Indiana Department of Commerce, One North Capitol, Suite 700, Indianapolis, IN 46204. Contact (317) 232-8782. *Assistance:* Financial

Institute for Molecular and Cellular Biology, Indiana University, Jordan Hall, Bloomington, IN 47405. Contact (812) 335-4183. *Assistance:* Technical

Institute of Transnational Business, College of Business, Ball State University, Muncie, IN 47302. Contact (317) 285-5207. *Assistance:* Information/Technical. *Elligibility:* Smaller businesses

Investment Incentive Program, Division of Business and Financial Services, Indiana Department of Commerce, One North Capitol, Suite 700, Indianapolis, IN 46204. Contact (317) 232-8782. *Assistance:* Financial

Materials Research Institute, Indiana University, Bloomington, IN 47405. Contact (812) 335-9127. *Assistance:* Technical

Inventors and Entrepreneurs Society of Indiana, Purdue University Calumet, Hammond, IN 46323. Contact Daniel Yovich at (219) 844-0520. *Assistance:* Information/Networking

McMillen Productivity and Design Center, Indiana Institute of Technology, 1600 East Washington Blvd., Fort Wayne, IN 46803. Contact (219) 422-5561. *Assistance:* Technical

Office of International Trade, Division of Business Expansion, Indiana Department of Commerce, One North Capitol, Suite 700, Indianapolis, IN 46204. Contact (317) 232-8845. *Assistance:* Information

Office of Industrial Training and Development, Indiana Vocational Technical College, One West 26th Street, P.O. Box 1763, Indianapolis, IN 46206. Contact (317) 929-4772. *Assistance:* Training/Technical

Office of Minority Business Enterprise, Division of Business Expansion, Indiana Department of Commerce, One North Capitol, Suite 700, Indianapolis, IN 46204. Contact (317) 232-8820. *Assistance:* Business planning/Information/Management/Technical. *Eligibility:* Minority businesses

Office of Research and Graduate Development, Indiana University, Bryan Hall 104, Bloomington, IN 47405. Contact (812) 335-9813. *Assistance:* Networking/Technical

Office of the Business Ombudsman, Division of Business Expansion, Indiana Department of Commerce, One North Capitol, Suite 700, Indianapolis, IN 46204. Contact (800) 824-2476. *Assistance:* Technical

SBIR Proposal Assistance, Office of Research, Ball State University, 1825 Riverside Avenue, Muncie, IN 47306. Contact (317) 285-1600. *Assistance:* Technical. *Eligibility:* Smaller businesses

Small Business Development Centers, Indiana Economic Development Council, One North Capitol Street, Suite 200, Indianapolis, IN 46204. Contact (317) 634-6407. *Assistance:* Business planning/Information/Technical. *Eligibility:* Smaller businesses

Task Force on New Technologies, Purdue University Calumet, 2233 17th Street, Hammond, IN 46323. Contact William Robinson at (219) 844-0520. *Assistance:* Information/Networking/Technical

Technology Services Center, Indiana State University, School of Technology, Terre Haute, IN 47809. Contact Mr. Milton Woods at (812) 232-6311. *Assistance:* Technical

Training for Profit Program, Division of Business and Financial Services, Indiana Department of Commerce, One North Capitol, Suite 700, Indianapolis, IN 46204. Contact (317) 232-8782. *Assistance:* Training/Financial

Transportation Rate Service and Ombudsperson Program, Indiana Port Commission, 143 West Market Street, Room 204, Indianapolis, IN 46204. Contact (800) 232-PORT. *Assistance:* Information/Technical

Urban Technology Outreach Program, Purdue University Calumet, 2233 17th Street, Hammond, IN 46323. Contact William Robinson at (219) 844-0520. *Assistance:* Information/Networking/Technical

Vocational Technical Services Center, Indiana State University, Classroom Bldg., Room 206, Terre Haute, IN 47809. Contact (812) 232-6311. *Assistance:* Training

Iowa

Center for Industrial Research & Service, Iowa State University of Science and Technology, Ames, IA 50011. Contact (515) 294-3420. *Assistance:* Information/Management/Networking/Technical

Economic Development Set-Aside Program, Office for Planning and Programming, 523 East 12th Street, Des Moines, IA 50319. Contact (515) 281-3711. *Assistance:* Financial

Golden Circle Loan Guaranty Fund, Small Business Development Center, Drake University, 210 Aliber Hall, Des Moines, IA 50311. Contact (515) 271-2655. *Assistance:* Financial. *Eligibility:* Smaller businesses

Industrial New Jobs Training Program, Iowa

Development Commission, 600 East Court Avenue, Suite A, Des Moines, IA 50309. Contact (515) 281-8329. *Assistance:* Training

Iowa High Technology Council, Iowa Development Commission, 600 E. Court Street, Des Moines, IA 50309. Contact (515) 281-3251. *Assistance:* Financial

Iowa Product Development Corporation, 600 E. Court Ave., Suite C, Des Moines, IA 50309. Contact Mr. Doug Getter at (515) 281-3251. *Assistance:* Financial

Small Business Development Center, Iowa State University, Heady Hall, Ames, IA 50011. Contact Mr. Jan A. DeYoung at (515) 294-8069. *Assistance:* Business planning/Information/Networking/Technical. *Eligibility:* Smaller businesses

Small Business Loan Program, Iowa Finance Authority, 550 Liberty Building, 418 Sixth Avenue, Des Moines, IA 50309. Contact (515) 281-4058. *Assistance:* Financial

Kansas

Center for Entrepreneurship, 130 Clinton Hall, Wichita State University, Wichita, KS 67208. Contact Dr. Fran Jabarra at (316) 689-3000. *Assistance:* Management/Networking

Center for Productivity Enhancement, Room 100, Wallace Hall, Wichita State University, Wichita, KS 67208. Contact Dr. Richard Graham at (316) 689-3402. *Assistance:* Information / Management / Networking / Technical

Engineering Extension, Ward Hall 133, Kansas State University, Manhattan, KS 66506. Contact (913) 532-6026. *Assistance:* Information/Technical

Kansas Advanced Technology Commission, 503 Kansas Avenue, Topeka, KS 66603. Contact Dr. Phillips V. Bradford at (913) 296-5272. *Assistance:* Financial/Information/Networking

Small Business Development Centers, Clinton Hall, Room 021D, Wichita State University, Wichita, KS 67208. Contact Ms. Susan K. Osborne-Howes at (316) 689-3193. *Assistance:* Business planning/Information/Management/Networking. *Eligibility:* Smaller businesses

Kentucky

Center for Business Development, College of Business and Economics, University of Kentucky, Lexington, KY 40506. Contact Mr. James G. Owen at (606) 257-1751. *Assistance:* Business planning

Small Business Development Center, University of Kentucky, 18 Porter Building, Lexington, KY 40506–0205. Contact Mr. Jerry Owen at (606) 257-1751. *Assistance:* Business planning/Information/Technical. *Eligibility:* Smaller businesses

NASA/University of Kentucky Technology Applications Program, University of Kentucky, 109 Kinkead Hall, Lexington, KY 40506–0057. Contact (606) 257-6322. *Assistance:* Information/Technical

Office of Business and Technology, Kentucky Commerce Cabinet, 2400 Capital Plaza Tower, Frankfort, KY 40601. Contact Mr. Cary W. Blankenship at (502) 564-7670. *Assistance:* Business planning/Information/Networking/Technical. *Eligibility:* Smaller businesses

Louisiana

Center for Economic Development, College of Business Administration, University of New Orleans, New Orleans, LA 70122. Contact Dr. Ivan J. Miestochovitz at (504) 283-0663. *Assistance:* Business planning/Management/Technical

Department of Commerce, P.O. Box 94185, Baton Rouge, LA 70804–9185. Contact (504) 342-5361. *Assistance:* Financial/Information/Networking

Xavier University Economic Development Center, P.O. Box 71-B, New Orleans, LA 70126. Contact (504) 483-7675. *Assistance:* Business planning/Management/Technical

Maine

Maine Development Foundation, One Memoria Circle, Augusta, ME 04330. Contact (207) 622-6345. *Assistance:* Business planning/Information/Networking/Technical

Maine Growth Program, State Development Office, 193 State Street, State House Station 59, Augusta, ME 04333. *Contact* (207) 289-2656. *Assistance:* Financial

Maine State Development Office, 193 State Street, State House Station 59, Augusta, ME 04333. Contact (207) 289-5700. *Assistance:* Financial/Information/Networking

Small Business Development Center, Center for Research and Advanced Study, University of Southern Maine, 246 Deering Avenue, Portland, ME 04102. Contact Mr. Warren Purdy at (207) 780-4420. *Assistance:* Business planning/Information/Networking/Technical. *Eligibility:* Smaller businesses

The New Enterprise Institute, Center for Research and Advanced Study, University of Southern Maine, 246 Deering Avenue, Portland, ME 04102. Contact Dr. Richard J. Clarey at (207) 780-4420. *Assistance:* Business planning/Information/Management/Networking/Technical

Maryland

Development Credit Corporation of Maryland, Maryland Department of Economic and Community Development, 45 Calvert Street, Annapolis, MD 21401. Contact 1-800-654-7336. Those outside of Maryland should call (301) 269-3514.

Development Credit Fund, Inc., Maryland Department of Economic and Community Development, 45 Calvert Street, Annapolis, MD 21401. Contact 1-800-654-7336. Those outside of Maryland should call (301) 269-3514. *Assistance:* Financial. *Eligibility:* Minority businesses.

Maryland Energy Financing Administration, Maryland Department of Economic and Community Development, 45 Calvert Street, Annapolis, MD 21401. Contact 1-800-654-7336. Those outside of Maryland should call (301) 269-3514. *Assistance:* Financial

Maryland Business Assistance Center, Maryland Department of Economic and Community Development, 45 Calvert Street, Annapolis, MD 21401. Contact 1-800-654-7336. Those outside of Maryland should call (301) 269-3514. *Assistance:* Financial/Information/Networking

Maryland Office of Business and Industrial Development, Maryland Department of Economic and Community Development, 45 Calvert Street, Annapolis, MD 21401. Contact 1-800-654-7336. Those outside of Maryland should call (301) 269-3514. *Assistance:* Financial

Maryland Industrial Training Program, Maryland Department of Economic and Community Development, 45 Calvert Street, Annapolis, MD 21401. Contact 1-800-654-7336. Those outside of Maryland should call (301) 269-3514. *Assistance:* Technical

Maryland Industrial Development Financing Authority, Maryland Department of Economic and Community Development, 45 Calvert Street, Annapolis, MD 21401. Contact 1-800-654-7336. Those outside of Maryland should call (301) 269-3514. *Assistance:* Financial

Maryland Small Business Development Financing Authority, Maryland Department of Economic and Community Development, 45 Calvert Street, Annapolis, MD 21401. Contact 1-800-654-7336. Those outside of Maryland should call (301) 269-3514. *Assistance:* Financial. *Eligibility:* Smaller businesses

Technology Extension Service, University of Maryland, Engineering Research Center, College Park, MD. Contact Mr. W. Travis Walton at (301) 454-7941. *Assistance:* Information/Networking/Technical

Massachusetts

Center for Economic Development, 203 Hampshire House, University of Massachusetts, Amherst, MA 01003. Contact (413) 549-4930. *Assistance:* Business planning/Information/Networking/Technical

Community Development Finance Corporation, 131 State Street, Suite 600, Boston, MA 02109. Contact Mr. Charles T. Grigsby at (617) 742-0366. *Assistance:* Financial. *Eligibility:* Smaller businesses

Guaranteed Loan Program, Massachusetts Industrial Finance Agency, 400 Atlantic, Boston, MA 02210. Contact (617) 451-2477. *Assistance:* Financial. *Eligibility:* Smaller businesses

Massachusetts Business Development Corporation, One Liberty Square, Boston, MA 02109. Contact Mr. Kenneth J. Smith at (617) 723-7515. *Assistance:* Financial

Massachusetts Technology Development Corporation, 84 State Street, Suite 500, Boston, MA 02109. Contact Mr. John F. Hodgman at (617) 723-4920. *Assistance:* Financial

Massachusetts Industrial Finance Agency, 400 Atlantic, Boston, MA 02210. Contact (617) 451-2477. *Assistance:* Financial

Office of Training and Employment Policy, Executive Office of Economic Affairs, Office of Training & Employment Policy, Charles F. Hurley Bldg., 4th Floor, Government Center, Boston, MA 02114. Contact Ms. Catherine N. Stratton at (617) 727-2252. *Assistance:* Training/Financial

Site Inventory Tracking Exchange, Massachusetts Department of Commerce, 100 Cambridge Street, Boston, MA 02202. Contact (617) 727-3215. *Assistance:* Information

Spirit Line, Massachusetts Department of Commerce, 100 Cambridge Street, Boston, MA 02202. Contact (617) 727-3217 or (In State) 1-800-632-8181. *Assistance:* Information/Networking

Small Business Assistance Division, Massachusetts Department of Commerce, 100 Cambridge Street, Boston, MA 02202. Contact (617) 727-4005. *Assistance:* Business planning/Financial/Information/Networking. *Eligibility:* Smaller businesses

State Office of Minority Business Assistance, Massachusetts Department of Commerce, 100 Cambridge Street, 13th Floor, Boston, MA 02202. Contact (617) 727-8692. *Assistance:* Information/Networking. *Eligibility:* Minority businesses

The Office of Financial Development, Massachusetts Department of Commerce and Development, 100 Cambridge Street, Boston, MA 02202. Contact (617) 727-2932. *Assistance:* Information/Networking

Trade Development Program, Massport Foreign Trade Unite, 99 High Street, Boston, MA 02110. Contact (617) 973-5611. *Assistance:* Business planning/Financial/Information/Networking/Technical

Michigan

Center for Research on Integrated Manufacturing, University of Michigan College of Engineering, Chrysler Center, Ann Arbor, MI 48109. Contact Mr. Robert W. Schneider at (313) 763-5630. *Assistance:* Technical

Environmental Research Institute of Michigan, P.O. Box 8618, Ann Arbor, MI 48107. Contact Mr. George Peace at (313) 994-1200. *Assistance:* Technical

Food Industry Institute, 302 Food Science Building, Michigan State University, East Lansing, MI 48824. Contact Dr. Thayne Dutson at (517) 355-8295 or 355-8474. *Assistance:* Business planning/Information/Technical

Industrial Technology Institute, P.O. Box 1415, Ann Arbor, MI 48106. Contact (313) 769-4000. *Assistance:* Information/Technical

Industrial Development Institute, Michigan State University, 225 Administration Building, East Lansing, MI 48824. Contact Mr. Michael Martin at (517) 355-2180. *Assistance:* Business planning/Information/Networking/Technical

Institute of Science and Technology, The University of Michigan, 2200 Bonisteel Boulevard, Ann Arbor, MI 48109. Contact Mr. Larry R. Crockett at (313) 763-9000. *Assistance:* Business planning/Financial/Information/Networking/Technical

Metropolitan Center for High Technology, 2727 Second Avenue, Wayne State University, Detroit, MI 48201. Contact Mr. Bob Erlandson at (313) 963-0616. *Assistance:* Business planning/Information/Networking/Technical.

Michigan Biotechnology Institute, 276 Bessey Hall, Michigan State University, East Lansing, MI 48824. Contact Dr. Patrick Oriel at (517) 355-2277. *Assistance:* Business planning/Information/Networking/Technical

Michigan Department of Commerce–Technology Transfer Network, Hollister Building, #212, 106 West Allegan, Lansing, MI 48913. Contact (517) 373-7411. *Assistance:* Business planning/Financial/Information Networking/Technical

Michigan Energy and Resource Research Association, 328 Executive Plaza, 1200 Sixth Street, Detroit, MI 48226. Contact Mr. Todd Anuskiewicz at (313) 964-5030. *Assistance:* Information/Networking/Technical

Michigan Molecular Institute, 1910 West St. Andrews Road, Midland, MI 48640. Contact Mr. Gordon B. Carson at (517) 832-5553. *Assistance:* Technical

Michigan Strategic Fund, Michigan Department of Commerce, Hollister Building, #212, Lansing, MI 48913. Contact Mr. Gary Prince at (517) 373-7411. *Assistance:* Financial

Michigan Technology Deployment Service, Michigan Department of Commerce, Hollister Building, 106 West Allegan, Lansing, MI 48913. Contact Dr. Jack Russell at (517) 373-7411. *Assistance:* Financial/Information/Networking/Technical

Office of New Enterprise Services, Michigan Department of Commerce, Hollister Building, #212, 106 West Allegan, Lansing, MI 48913. Contact Mr. Gary Prince at (517) 373-7411. *Assistance:* Financial/Information/Networking

Minnesota

College of St. Thomas Entrepreneurial Enterprise Center, Peavey Center, 11 Peavey Road, Chaska, MN 55318. Contact (612) 448-3534. *Assistance:* Business planning/Information/Networking/Technical

Department of Energy and Economic Development, 900 American Center Building, 150 East Kellogg Boulevard, St. Paul MN 55101. Contact Mr. Mark Dayton at (612) 296-6424. *Assistance:* Business planning/Information/Networking/Technical

Department of Jobs and Training, 390 North Robert Street, St. Paul, MN 55101. Contact (612) 296-2536. *Assistance:* Information

Development Resources Program, 900 American Center Building, 150 East Kellogg Boulevard, St. Paul, MN 55101. Contact Mr. Harry Rosefelt at (612) 296-5010. *Assistance:* Financial/Information

Financial Management Division, Department of Energy and Economic Development Authority, 900 American Center Building, 150 East Kellogg Boulevard, St. Paul, MN 55101. Contact Mr. Edward J. Meyer at (612) 296-6616. *Assistance:* Financial

Inno-Media, 230 Tenth Avenue South, Minneapolis, MN 55415. Contact Mr. Gary Howe at (612) 342-4311. *Assistance:* Business planning/Information/Networking/Technical

Minneapolis Technology Enterprise Center, Inc., 1313 Fifth Street, S.E., Minneapolis,

MN 55414. Contact (612) 623-7774. *Assistance:* Business planning/Information/Networking/Technical. *Eligibility:* Smaller businesses

Minnesota Cooperation Office, 965 Southgate Office Plaza, 5001 West 80th Street, Bloomington, MN 55437. Contact Mr. Theodore A. Johnson at (612) 830-1230. *Assistance:* Business planning/Information/Networking/Technical. *Eligibility:* Smaller businesses

Minnesota Office of Biomedical/Health Systems, 900 American Center Building, 150 East Kellogg Boulevard, St. Paul, MN 55101. Contact Mr. Michael C. O'Donnell at (612) 297-1388. *Assistance:* Information/Networking

Minnesota Project Innovation, 511 11th Avenue South, Minneapolis, MN 55415. Contact (612) 375-8084. *Assistance:* Financial/Information/Networking. *Eligibility:* Smaller businesses

Minnesota Trade Office, 90 West Plato Boulevard, St. Paul, MN 55107. Contact Mr. William C. Dietrich at (612) 296-4222 (Telex: 853610 MTOAG). *Assistance:* Information/Networking

Office of Project Management, 900 American Center Building, 150 East Kellogg Boulevard, St. Paul, MN 55101. Contact (612) 297-1160. *Assistance:* Financial

Office of Software Technology Development, 900 American Center Building, 150 East Kellogg Boulevard, St. Paul, MN 55101. Contact Ms. Rosemary T. Fruehling at (612) 297-1554. *Assistance:* Business planning / Financial / Information / Networking / Technical

Small Business Assistance Office, 900 American Center Building, 150 East Kellogg Boulevard, St. Paul, MN 55101. Contact Mr. Charles A. Schatter at (612) 296-3871. *Assistance:* Business planning/Information. *Eligibility:* Smaller businesses

University Research Consortium, Minneapolis Business and Technology Center, 511 11th Avenue South, Minneapolis, MN 55415. Contract Dr. Ellen Fitzgerald at (612) 341-0422. *Assistance:* Business planning/Information/Networking/Technical

Mississippi

Finance Division Department of Economic Development, P.O. Box 849, Jackson, MS 39205. Contact Mr. E. F. Mitcham at (601) 359-3437. *Assistance:* Financial

Industrial Division Department of Economic Development, P.O. Box 849, Jackson, MS 39205. Contact Mr. James W. Miller at (601) 359-3439. *Assistance:* Information/Networking

Institute for Technology Development, 3825 Ridgewood Rd., Jackson, MS 39211. Contact Neil Yawn at (601) 982-6456. *Assistance:* Information/Networking/Technical

Marketing Division Department of Economic Development, P.O. Box 849, Jackson, MS 39205. Contact Mr. Bill McGinnis at (601) 359-3607. *Assistance:* Technical

Mississippi Research and Development Center, 3825 Ridgewood Rd., Jackson, MS 39211. Contact Ms. Joyce Lewis at (601) 982-6231 (This is a toll free number within the state). *Assistance:* Business planning/Management/Networking/Technical

Missouri

Business and Industry Extension Service, 821 Clark Hall, University of Missouri-Columbia, Columbia, MO 65211. Contact Dr. Tom Henderson at (314) 882-4321. *Assistance:* Business planning/Information/Networking/Technical

Enterprise Zones Program, Missouri Division of Community and Economic Development, P.O. Box 118, Jefferson City, MO 65102. Contact Mr. Bill Blade at (314) 751-4241. *Assistance:* Financial/Technical

Existing Business Assistance, Missouri Division of Community and Economic Development, P.O. Box 118, Jefferson City, MO 65102. Contact Mr. Bill Blade at (314) 751-4241. *Assistance:* Information/Financial

Financial Programs, Missouri Division of Community and Economic Development, P.O. Box 118, Jefferson City, MO 65102. Contact Mr. Bill Blade at (314) 751-4241. *Assistance:* Financial

High Technology Program, Missouri Division of Community and Economic Development, P.O. Box 118, Jefferson City, MO 65102. Contact Mr. Bill Blade at (314) 751-4241. *Assistance:* Information/Technical

Industrial Development Time Deposit Program, Missouri Division of Community and Economic Development, P.O. Box 118, Jefferson City, MO 65102. Contact Mr. Bill Blade at (314) 751-4241. *Assistance:* Financial

Missouri Corporation for Science and Technology, P.O. Box 118, Jefferson City, MO 65102. Contact Mr. Jeffrey Coffey at (314) 751-3906. *Assistance:* Business planning/Financial/Information/Networking/Technical

On-the-Job Training, Division of Employment Security, P.O. Box 59, Jefferson City, MO 65104. Contact Mr. Bruce Carnet at (314) 751-3215. *Assistance:* Training

Montana

Advisory Council on Science & Technology, Department of Commerce, 1424 Ninth Avenue, Helena, MT 59620. Contact Mr.

Frank Culver at (406) 444-5473. *Assistance:* Information/Networking/Technical

Agriculture Marketing Assistance, Department of Agriculture, Sixth & Roberts, Helena, MT 59620. Contact Mr. Steve Kalgaard at (406) 444-2402. *Assistance:* Information/Technical

Business Assistance Division, Department of Commerce, 1424 Ninth Avenue, Helena, MT 59620. Contact Mr. Gary Faulkner at (406) 444-4325. *Assistance:* Business planning/Information/Technical. *Eligibility:* Smaller businesses

Development Finance Technical Assistance, Business Assistance Division, Department of Commerce, 1424 Ninth Avenue, Helena, MT 59620. Contact Mr. Ron Preston at (406) 444-4323. *Assistance:* Business planning/Financial/Technical

Disadvantaged Business Enterprise and Women Business Enterprise, Department of Highways, Capital Station, Helena, MT 59620. Contact Ms Peg M. Dolan at (406) 444-6332. *Assistance:* Technical

Industrial Start-Up Training Program, Job Service and Training Division, Department of Labor & Industry, P.O. Box 1728, Helena, MT 59624. Contact Mr. Gary Curtis at (406) 444-4500. *Assistance:* Training

International Export Assistance, Business Assistance Division, Department of Commerce, 1424 Ninth Avenue, Helena, MT 59620. Contact Mr. John J. Maloney at (406) 444-4380. *Assistance:* Technical. *Eligibility:* Smaller businesses

Product Marketing Assistance, Business Assistance Division, Department of Commerce, 1424 Ninth Avenue, Helena, MT 59620. Contact Mr. Gene Marcille at (406) 444-4392. *Assistance:* Information/Networking. *Eligibility:* Smaller businesses

Renewable Energy and Conservation Program, Grant & Loan Section, Department of Natural Resources & Conservation, 25 South Ewing, Helena, MT 59620. Contact Mr. Greg Mills at (406) 444-6774. *Assistance:* Financial/Information/Technical

Small Business Advocate and Business Licensing Center, Business Assistance Division, Department of Commerce, 1424 Ninth Avenue, Helena, MT 59620. Contact Mr. John W. Balsam at 1-800-221-8015. *Assistance:* Information. *Eligibility:* Smaller businesses

University Center for Business & Management Development, 445 Reid Hall, Montana State University, Bozeman, MT 59717. Contact Mr. Neal Nixon at (406) 994-2057. *Assistance:* Business planning/Information/Technical. *Eligibility:* Smaller businesses

Water Development Loan and Grant Programs, Water Development Bureau, Department of Natural Resources & Conservation, 28 South Rodney, Helena, MT 59620. Contact Ms. Caralee Cheney at (406) 444-6668. *Assistance:* Financial

Nebraska

Nebraska Food Processing Center, 134 Filley Hall, University of Nebraska-Lincoln, East Campus, Lincoln, NE 68583–0919. Contact Dr. Lowell D. Satterlee at (402) 472-2831. *Assistance:* Information/Networking/Technical

Nebraska Technical Assistance Center, W191 Nebraska Hall, University of Nebraska-Lincoln, Lincoln, NE 68588–0535. Contact Mr. Michael W. Riley, Director at (402) 472-5600. *Assistance:* Information/Networking/Technical

Nevada

City of Las Vegas Loan Program, 400 E. Stewart, Las Vegas, NV 89101. Contact Mr. Jack Thomason at (702) 386-6551. *Assistance:* Financial

Commission on Economic Development, Capitol Complex, 600 E. William, Suite 203, Carson City, NV 89710. Contact Mr. Andrew P. Grose at (702) 885-4325. *Assistance:* Financial

Nevada Small Business Development Center, University of Nevada, College of Business Administration, Business Building, Room 411, Reno, NV 89557–0016. Contact Mr. Sam Males at (702) 784-1717. *Assistance:* Business planning / Information / Management / Technical. *Eligibility:* Smaller businesses

State Office of Community Services, Capitol Complex, Carson City, NV 89710. Contact (702) 885-4420. *Assistance:* Financial/Technical

White Pine County Loan Programs, P.O. Box 1002, Ely, NV 89301. Contact Ms. Karen Rajala at (702) 289-8841. *Assistance:* Financial

New Hampshire

New Hampshire Office of Industrial Development, Department of Resources and Economic Development, P.O. Box 856, Concord, NH 03301. Contact Mr. Paul H. Guilderson at (603) 271-2591. *Assistance:* Business planning / Financial / Information / Networking / Technical

New Hampshire Office of Industrial Development-Export Assistance Program, Department of Resources and Economic Development, P.O. Box 856, Concord, NH 03301. Contact Mr. Paul H. Guilderson at (603) 271-2591. *Assistance:* Business planning/Information/Networking/Technical

Office of Small Business Programs, 110 McConnell Hall, University of New Hampshire, Durham, NH 03824. Contact Mr. Craig R. Seymour at (603) 862-3556. *Assistance:* Business planning/Information/ Technical

New Jersey

New Jersey Commission on Science and Technology, 225 W. State Street, CN 542, Trenton, NJ 08625. Contact Mr. Edward Cohen at (609) 984-1671. *Assistance:* Financial. *Eligibility:* Smaller businesses

New Jersey Economic Development Authority, 200 South Warren Street, Capital Place One, CN 990, 6th Floor, Trenton, NJ 08625. Contact Mr. James J. Hughes at (609) 292-1800. *Assistance:* Financial/Technical

New Jersey State Office of Minority Business Enterprise, Department of Commerce and Economic Development, 1 West State Street, Trenton, NJ 08625. Contact Mr. Lee L. Davis at (609) 292-0500. *Assistance:* Business planning/Financial/Information/ Networking. *Eligibility:* Smaller businesses and minority businesses

Office of Business Advocacy, New Jersey Department of Commerce and Economic Development, New Jersey National Bank Building, Room 604, #1 West State Street, CN 823, Trenton, NJ 08625. Contact Paul Krane at (609) 292-0700. *Assistance:* Information/Networking/Technical

Office of Industrial Development, New Jersey Department of Commerce and Economic Development, 1 West State Street, CN 823, Trenton, NJ 08625. Contact Mr. Charles Connell at (609) 292-2462. *Assistance:* Financial/Information/Networking/ Technical

Office of Small Business Assistance, New Jersey Department of Commerce and Economic Development, 1 West State Street, CN 823, Trenton, NJ 08625. Contact (609) 984-4442. *Assistance:* Business planning/ Financial/Information/Networking/Technical. *Eligibility:* Smaller businesses and minority businesses

Rutgers University Technical Assistance Program, Rutgers University, 180 University Avenue, Newark, NJ 07102. Contact Ms. Patricia Johnson at (201) 648-5891. *Assistance:* Business planning/Technical. *Eligibility:* Smaller businesses

New Mexico

Agricultural Marketing Development Office, New Mexico Department of Agriculture, New Mexico State University, P.O. Box 5600, Las Cruces, NM 88003. Contact (505) 646-4929. *Assistance:* Technical

Business Assistance and Resource Center, 1920 Lomas, N.E., Albuquerque, NM 87131. Contact Mr. James T. Ray at (505) 277-3541. *Assistance:* Business planning/ Information/Management/Technical

Center for Business Research and Services, New Mexico State University, Box 3CR, Las Cruces, NM 88003. Contact (505) 646-1434. *Assistance:* Business planning/Information/Technical

Development Training Programs, Economic Development and Tourism Department, Bataan Memorial Building, Santa Fe, NM 87503. Contact (505) 827-6200. *Assistance:* Training

Energy Research and Development Institute, 1220 South Street, Francis Drive #358, Santa Fe, NM 87501. Contact (505) 827-5886. *Assistance:* Financial

Industrial and Agricultural Finance Authority, Economic Development and Tourism Department, Bataan Memorial Building, Santa Fe, NM 87503. Contact (505) 827-6004. *Assistance:* Financial

New Mexico Solar Industry Development Corporation, 5301 Central N.E., Suite 705, Albuquerque, NM 87108. Contact (505) 262-2247. Contact (505) 262-2247. *Assistance:* Information/Networking/Technical

The Economic Incentive Loan Program, Economic Development and Tourism Department, Bataan Memorial Building, Room 201 EDB, Santa Fe, NM 87503. Contact (505) 827-6200.

Technology Innovation Centers, Anderson School of Management, University of New Mexico, Albuquerque, NM 87131. Contact (505) 277-2009. *Assistance:* Business planning / Financial / Information / Networking / Technical

New York

Centers for Advanced Technology Program, New York State Science and Technology Foundation, 99 Washington Avenue, Albany, NY 12210. Contact Mr. William J. Donohue at (518) 474-4347. *Assistance:* Information/Technical

Corporation for Innovation Development Program, New York State Science and Technology Foundation, 99 Washington Avenue, Albany, NY 12210. Contact (518) 474-4349. *Assistance:* Financial

Division for Small Business, New York State Department of Commerce, 320 Park Avenue, New York, NY 10169. Contact Mr. Raymond R. Norat at (212) 309-0400. *Assistance:* Business planning / Financial / Information / Management / Networking / Technical. *Eligibility:* Smaller businesses

Economic Development and Technical Assistance Center, State University of New York, Plattsburg, NY 12901. Contact Steven Hyde at (518) 654-2214. *Assistance:* Business planning/Information/Technical

Industrial Innovation Extension Service, New York State Science and Technology Foundation, 99 Washington Avenue, Albany, NY 12210. Contact Mr. H. Graham Jones at (518) 474-4349. *Assistance:* Information/Networking/Technical

New York State Small Business Development Center, State University of New York, State University Plaza, Albany, NY 12246. Contact Mr. James L. King at (518) 473-5398. *Assistance:* Business planning/Information/Management/Technical. *Eligibility:* Smaller businesses

New York State Small Business Innovation Research (SBIR) Promotion Program, 99 Washington Avenue, Albany, NY 12210. Contact Mr. H. Graham Jones at (518) 474-4349. *Assistance:* Financial/Information. *Eligibility:* Smaller businesses

Regional Technology Development Organization, New York State Science and Technology Foundation, 99 Washington Avenue, Albany, NY 12210. Contact Mr. H. Graham Jones at (518) 474-4349. *Assistance:* Information / Management / Networking / Technical

The Port Authority of New York and New Jersey, Economic Development Department, One World Trade Center-745, New York, NY 10048. Contact (800) 221-5468 or (212) 466-8848. *Assistance:* Financial

North Carolina

Center for Improving Mountain Living, Western Carolina University, Cullowhee, NC 28723. Contact Mr. Tom McClure at (704) 227-7492. *Assistance:* Technical

Minority Business Development Agency, 430 N. Salisbury Street, Raleigh, NC 27611. Contact Mr. Julian Brown at (919) 733-2712. *Assistance:* Business planning/Information/Networking/Technical. *Eligibility:* Minority businesses

National Minority Suppliers Development Council, P.O. Box 9156, Charlotte, NC 28299. Contact (704) 372-8732. *Assistance:* Business planning/Information/Networking/Technical. *Eligibility:* Minority businesses

North Carolina Small Business Development Centers, North Carolina Department of Community College, 20 Education Building, Raleigh, NC 27611. Contact Dr. Jean Overton at (919) 733-6385. *Assistance:* Business planning / Information / Networking / Technical. *Eligibility:* Smaller businesses

North Carolina Technological Development Authority, 430 N. Salisbury Street, Raleigh, NC 27611. Contact Mr. Chilton Rogers at (919) 733-7022. *Assistance:* Financial/Information. *Eligibility:* Smaller businesses

Small Business and Technology Development Center, 820 Clay Street, Raleigh, NC 27605. Contact (919) 733-6343 or 1-800-258-0862. *Assistance:* Business planning/Financial/Technical

Small Business Development Division, North Carolina Department of Commerce, 430 North Salisbury Street, Raleigh, NC 27611. Contact Mr. Lewis Myers at (919) 733-7980. *Assistance:* Business planning/Financial/Information/Networking. *Eligibility:* Smaller businesses

North Dakota

Bank of North Dakota, 700 East Main Avenue, Bismarck, ND 58501. Contact Mr. Herb Thorndal at (701) 224-5602. *Assistance:* Financial

Center for Economic Development, North Dakota State University, Fargo, ND 58102. Contact Dr. Robert L. Sullivan at (701) 237-8873. *Assistance:* Technical. *Eligibility:* Smaller businesses

Center for Innovation and Business Development, University of North Dakota, Engineering Experiment Station, Grand Forks, ND 58202. Contact Mr. Bruce Giovig at (701) 777-3132. *Assistance:* Business planning / Information / Networking / Technical. *Eligibility:* Smaller businesses

North Dakota Economic Development Commission, Liberty Memorial Building, Bismarck, ND 58505. Contact (701) 224-2810. *Assistance:* Financial/Information/Networking/Technical

State Development Credit Corporation, Box 1212, Bismarck, ND 58502. Contact Mr. William Smith at (701) 223-2288. *Assistance: Financial. Eligibility:* Smaller businesses

Ohio

Ohio Technology Transfer Organization, 1712 Neil Avenue, Columbus, OH 43210. Contact Dr. Robert E. Bailey at (614) 422-5485. *Assistance:* Business planning/Information/Networking/Technical

The Thomas Edison Program, P.O. Box 1001, Columbus, OH 43266–0413. Contact Mr. Christopher Coburn at (614) 466-3086. *Assistance:* Financial/Information/Technical

Urban Economic Development Center, Cleveland State University, Euclid Avenue at East 24th Street, Cleveland, OH 44115.

Contact Mr. David Garrison at (216) 687-2134. *Assistance:* Business planning/Management/Networking/Technical

Oklahoma

Oklahoma Small Business Development Center, 517 West University Boulevard, Durant, OK 74701. Contact Mr. Lloyd Miller at (405) 924-0277. *Assistance:* Business planning / Financial / Information / Networking / Technical. *Eligibility:* Smaller businesses

Association of Central Oklahoma Governments, 4801 Classen, Suite 200, Oklahoma City, OK 73118. Contact Mr. Greg Wallace at (405) 848-8961. *Assistance:* Information/Networking/Technical

Central Oklahoma Economic Development District, 400 N. Bell, Shawnee, OK 74801. Contact (405) 273-6410. *Assistance:* Financial/Information

International Trade Services, 440 S. Houston, Room 205, Tulsa, OK 74127. Contact (918) 521-2865. *Assistance:* Information/Networking

Kerr Industrial Applications Center, Southeastern Oklahoma State University, Sta. A, Box 2584, Durant, OK 74701-2584. Contact Dr. Tom J. McRorey at (405) 924-6822. *Assistance:* Information/Technical

Oklahoma Industrial Finance Authority, 4042 N. Lincoln, Oklahoma City, OK 73105. Contact (405) 521-2182. *Assistance:* Financial

Rural Enterprises, 10 Waldron Drive, P.O. Box 1335, Durant, OK 74702-1335. Contact Mr. Lloyd Collins at (405) 924-5094. *Assistance:* Business planning/Financial/Information/Networking/Technical

South Western Oklahoma Development Authority, P.O. Box 569, Building 400, Clinton-Sherman Industrial Air Park, Burns Flats, OK 73624. Contact (405) 562-4884. *Assistance:* Financial/Information/Technical

Technology Transfer Center, 1515 West Main, P.O. Box 1713, Durant, OK 74702–1713. Contact (405) 920-0132. *Assistance:* Information/Networking

Training for Industrial Production Division, Oklahoma Department of Economic Development, State Vo-Tech Department, 4042 N. Lincoln Blvd., Oklahoma City, OK 73105. Contact (405) 521-2195. *Assistance:* Training

University Center of Oklahoma, East Central Oklahoma State University, Ada, OK 74820. Contact Mr. Thomas Beebe at (405) 332-8000. *Assistance:* Technical. *Eligibility:* Smaller businesses

Oregon

Business Information Division, Oregon Economic Development Department, 595 Cottage Street, N.W., Salem, OR 97310. Contact (503) 373-1200. *Assistance:* Financial/Information

The Oregon Productivity Center, School of Industrial and General Engineering, Oregon State University, Corvallis, OR 97331. Contact Dr. James Riggs at (503) 754-4645. *Assistance:* Business planning/Information/Technical

Oregon Small Business Development Network, 1059 Willamette St., Eugene, OR 97401. Contact Mr. Wendell Anderson at (503) 687-9125. *Assistance:* Business planning / Information / Networking / Technical. *Eligibility:* Smaller businesses

International Trade Division, Oregon Economic Development Department, 595 Cottage Street, N.W., Salem, OR 97310. Contact (503) 373-1200. *Assistance:* Business planning/Information

Pennsylvania

Appalachian Regional Commission Program, Department of Commerce, Bureau of Appalachian Development & State Grants, 467 Forum Bldg., Harrisburg, PA 17120. Contact Paul Hallacher at (717) 787-7120. *Assistance:* Financial/Technical

Ben Franklin Partnership–Challenge Grants/Advanced Technology Centers, Department of Commerce, 463 Forum Building, Harrisburg, PA 17120. Contact Mr. Roger Tellefsen at (717) 787-4147. *Assistance:* Business planning / Financial / Information / Networking / Technical

Ben Franklin Partnership-Research "Seed" Grants, Department of Commerce, 463 Forum Building, Harrisburg, PA 17120. Contact Mr. Roger Tellefsen at (717) 787-4147. *Assistance:* Financial. *Eligibility:* Smaller businesses

Ben Franklin Partnership–Small Business Incubator Program, Department of Commerce, 463 Forum Building, Harrisburg, PA 17120. Contact Mr. Roger Tellefsen at (717) 787-4147. *Assistance:* Business planning / Financial / Information / Networking / Technical. *Eligibility:* Smaller businesses

Business Infrastructure Development Program, Department of Commerce, Bureau of Appalachian Development and State Grants, 467 Forum Building, Harrisburg, PA 17120. Contact Mr. William Logan at (717) 787-7120. *Assistance:* Financial

Customized Job Training Program, Department of Education, Bureau of Vocational and Adult Education, 6th Floor, 333 Market Street, Harrisburg, PA 17126-0333.

Contact Mr. Bill Krash at (717) 787-5293. *Assistance:* Financial/Technical

Employee Ownership Assistance Program, Department of Commerce, Bureau of Economic Assistance, 405 Forum Building, Harrisburg, PA 17120. Contact Mr. Alan Welder at (717) 787-1909. *Assistance:* Financial/Technical

Office of Minority Business Enterprise, Department of Commerce, 491 Forum Building, Harrisburg, PA 17120. Contact Mr. Clarence Smith at (717) 783-1301. *Assistance:* Business planning/Financial/Information/Networking. *Eligibility:* Minority businesses

Pennsylvania Capital Loan Fund, Department of Commerce, Bureau of Economic Assistance, Room 405 Forum Building, Harrisburg, PA 17120. Contact: Mr. Alan Welder at (717) 787-1909. *Assistance:* Financial *Eligibility:* Smaller businesses

Pennsylvania Energy Development Authority, Department of Commerce, 462 Forum Building, Harrisburg, PA 17120. Contact Mr. Bill Roth at (717) 787-6554. *Assistance:* Financial

Pennsylvania Industrial Development Authority, Department of Commerce, Bureau of Economic Assistance, 405 Forum Building, Harrisburg, PA 17120. Contact Mr. Gerald Kapp at (717) 787-6245. *Assistance:* Financial

Pennsylvania Technical Assistance Program, The Pennsylvania State University, 501 J Orvis Keller Building, University Park, PA 16802. Contact Mr. Roy Marlow at (814) 865-0427. *Assistance:* Information/Technical

Revenue Bond and Mortgage Program, Department of Commerce, Bureau of Economic Assistance, Room 405 Forum Building, Harrisburg, PA 17120. Contact Mr. Alan Welder at (717) 787-1909. *Assistance:* Financial

Pennsylvania Minority Business Development Authority, Department of Commerce, 405 Forum Building, Harrisburg, PA 17120. Contact Mr. William Peterson at (717) 783-1127. *Assistance:* Business planning/Financial/Technical. *Eligibility:* Minority businesses

Seed "Venture" Capital Fund, Ben Franklin Partnership, Department of Commerce, 463 Forum Building, Harrisburg, PA 17120. Contact Mr. Roger Tellefsen at (717) 787-4147. *Assistance:* Financial

Small Business Action Center, Department of Commerce, 438 Forum Building, Harrisburg, PA 17120. Contact Ms. Jill Morrow at (717) 783-5700. *Assistance:* Business planning/Information/Networking/Technical. *Eligibility:* Smaller businesses

Rhode Island

Brown Venture Forum, Box 1949, Providence, RI 02912. Contact (401) 863-3528. *Assistance:* Business planning/Information/Networking

Export Trade Program, Rhode Island Department of Economic Development, 7 Jackson Walkway, Providence, RI 02903. Contact (401) 277-2601. *Assistance:* Information/Networking/Technical

Federal Procurement Program, Rhode Island Department of Economic Development, 7 Jackson Walkway, Providence, RI 02903. Contact (401) 277-2601. *Assistance:* Financial

Financing Program, Rhode Island Department of Economic Development, 7 Jackson Walkway, Providence, RI 02903. Contact (401) 277-2601. *Assistance:* Financial

Job Development and Training Division, Rhode Island Department of Economic Development, 7 Jackson Walkway, Providence, RI 02903. Contact (401) 277-2090. *Assistance:* Training

Marketing Division, Rhode Island Department of Economic Development, 7 Jackson Walkway, Providence, RI 02903. Contact (401) 277-2601. *Assistance:* Information/Technical

Minority Business Program, Rhode Island Department of Economic Development, 7 Jackson Walkway, Providence, RI 02903. Contact (401) 277-2601. *Assistance:* Information/Networking/Technical. *Eligibility:* Minority businesses

Opportunities Industrialization Center, 1 Hilton Street, Providence, RI 02905. Contact (401) 272-4400. *Assistance:* Financial/Information/Technical

Rhode Island Partnership for Science and Technology, Rhode Island Department of Economic Development, 7 Jackson Walkway, Providence, RI 02903. Contact Mr. Bruce R. Lang at (401) 277-2601. *Assistance:* Financial

Rhode Island Department of Environmental Management, 22 Hayes Street, Providence, RI 02908. Contact (401) 277-2781. *Assistance:* Information

Rhode Island Small Business Development Center, Bryant College, Smithfield, RI 02917. Contact (401) 232-6111. *Assistance:* Business planning/Information/Technical. *Eligibility:* Smaller businesses

University of Rhode Island Business Assistance Programs, University of Rhode Island, Kingston, RI. Contact (401) 792-4320. *Assistance:* Information/Technical

South Carolina

Agriculture Marketing Division, F & V Market News, P.O. Box 13531–0531, State Farmers Market, Columbia, SC 29201. Contact (803) 758–2293. *Assistance:* Information

Business Assistance and Services Information Center, State Development Board, 1301 Gervais Street, P.O. Box 927, Columbia, SC 29202. Contact (803) 758-3046 (or toll free in S.C. 800-922-6684). *Assistance:* Financial/Information/Networking/Technical

Economic Development and Technical Assistance Center, Benedict College, Harden & Blanding Streets, Columbia, SC 29204. Contact (803) 256-4220. *Assistance:* Business planning/Information/Technical

Job Creation Network–Incubators, Business Assistance and Services Information Center, South Carolina State Development Board, P.O. Box 927, Columbia, SC 29202. Contact Mr. P. M. Smurthwaite at (803) 758-3046 or 1-800-922-6684 (in-state). *Assistance:* Business planning/Financial/Information/Networking/Technical

Office of Small and Minority Business Assistance, 1205 Pendleton Street, Suite 305, Columbia, SC 29201. Contact (803) 758-5560. *Assistance:* Business planning/Information/Networking/Technical

Planning and Research Division, S.C. State Development Board, P.O. Box 927, Columbia, SC 29202. Contact (803) 758-2411. *Assistance:* Information

Small Business Development Center, College of Business Administration, University of South Carolina, Columbia, SC 29208. Contact Mr. William F. Littlejohn at (803) 777-4907. *Assistance:* Business planning/Information/Networking/Technical. *Eligibility:* Smaller businesses

The South Carolina Jobs Economic Development Authority, 1203 Gervais Street, Columbia, SC 29201. Contact (803) 758-2094. *Assistance:* Financial/Technical

South Dakota

Division of International Trade, University of South Dakota, School of Business, Vermillion, SD 57069. Contact Mr. John Huminiski at (605) 677-5455. *Assistance:* Information/Networking/Technical

Financing Assistance Program, Department of State Development, 711 Wells, Box 6000, Pierre, SD 57501. Contact (605) 773-5032. *Assistance:* Business planning/Financial/Information/Technical. *Eligibility:* Smaller businesses

Procurement Assistance Program, Department of State Development, 711 Wells, Box 6000, Pierre, SD 57501. Contact (605) 773-5032. *Assistance:* Business planning/Information/Networking/Technical

Tennessee

Office of Minority Business Enterprise, 7th Floor, 320 6th Avenue North, Nashville, TN 37219–5305. Contact (615) 741-2545. *Assistance:* Business planning/Financial/Information/Technical. *Eligibility:* Minority businesses

Regional Economic Development Center, 226 Johnson Hall, Memphis State University, Memphis, TN 38152. Contact (901) 454-2056. *Assistance:* Business planning/Information/Technical

The University of Tennessee Center for Industrial Services, Suite 401, Capitol Boulevard Building, Nashville, TN 37219. Contact (615) 242-2456. *Assistance:* Business planning/Financial/Technical

Tennessee Technology Foundation, P.O. Box 23184, Knoxville, TN 37933. Contact Dr. David A. Patterson at (615) 966-2804. *Assistance:* Financial / Information / Networking / Technical. *Eligibility:* Smaller businesses and minority businesses

Small Business Office, Department of Economic and Community Development, Rachel Jackson Building, 7th Floor, 320 6t Avenue North, Nashville, TN 37219–5308. Contact Mr. John E. Smith at (615) 741-2626. *Assistance:* Financial/Information/Networking/Technical. *Eligibility:* Smaller businesses

Texas

Center for Economic Development, University of Texas at San Antonio, San Antonio, TX 78285. Contact (512) 224-1945. *Assistance:* Business planning/Information/Management/Technical

Economic Development Center, Texas South University, School of Management, 3100 Cleburne Avenue, Houston, TX 77004. Contact (713) 52-7785. *Assistance:* Business planning/Information/Technical. *Eligibility:* Smaller businesses

Center for Technology Development and Transfer, EMS 103, University of Texas, Austin, TX 78712. Contact Dr. Helen Dorsey at (512) 471-7501. *Assistance:* Licensing inventions

Institute for Ventures in New Technology, Texas Engineering Experiment Station, The Texas A&M University System, College Station, TX 77843. Contact Mr. Franklin Sekera at (409) 845-0538. *Assistance:* Financial

Loan Programs, Texas Economic Development Commission, 410 East 5th Street, P.O. Box 12728, Capitol Station, Austin,

TX 78711. Contact (512) 472-5059. *Assistance:* Financial

Small Business Loan Programs, Texas Economic Development Commission, Finance Department, 410 East 5th Street, P.O. Box 12728, Capitol Station, Austin, TX 78711. Contact (512) 472-5059. *Assistance:* Financial. *Eligibility:* Smaller businesses

Technology Training Board, Texas Economic Development Commission, P.O. Box 12728, Capitol Station, Austin, TX 78711. Contact Dr. Helen Dorsey at (512) 472-5059. *Assistance:* Information

Texas Research and Technology Foundation, Suite 345, 8207 Callaghan Road, San Antonio, TX 78230. Contact (512) 342-6063. *Assistance:* Financial/Information/Networking/Technical

Utah

Business Development Program, Utah Business and Economic Development Division, Room 6150, State Office Building, Salt Lake City, UT 84114. Contact (801) 533-5325. *Assistance:* Financial/Information/Networking/Technical. *Eligibility:* Smaller businesses

Utah Business Development Centers, University of Utah, Graduate School of Business, Room 410 BUC, Salt Lake City, UT 84112. Contact Mr. James Bean at (801) 581-7905. *Assistance:* Business planning/Financial/Information/Technical

Utah Innovation Center, 417 Wakara Way, Research Park, Salt Lake City, UT 84108. Contact Dr. Wayne S. Brown at (801) 584-2500. *Assistance:* Business planning/Financial/Information/Networking/Technical

Utah Technology Finance Corporation, 417 Wakara Way, Suite 150, Salt Lake City, UT 84108. Contact Mr. Grant Cannon at (801) 583-8832. *Assistance:* Financial. *Eligibility:* Smaller businesses

Vermont

Entrepreneurship Program, Division of Economic Development, Pavilion Building, 109 State Street, Montpelier, VT 05602. Contact Mr. Curt Carter at (802) 828-3221. *Assistance:* Business planning/Information/Networking/Technical

Export Development Program, Division of Economic Development, Pavilion Building, 109 State Street, Montpelier, VT 05602. Contact Mr. Graene Freeman at (802) 828-3221. *Assistance:* Business planning / Financial / Information / Networking / Technical

Small Business Resource and Referral Service, Division of Economic Development, Pavilion Building, 109 State Street, Montpelier, VT 05602. Contact Ms. Cindy Jones at (802) 828-3221. *Assistance:* Information/Networking. *Eligibility:* Smaller businesses

Vermont Business Expansion Program, Division of Economic Development, Pavilion Building, 109 State Street, Montpelier, VT 05602. Contact Mr. Steve Parsons at (802) 828-3221. *Assistance:* Business planning/Financial/Information/Networking/Technical

Vermont Trading Program, Division of Economic Development, Pavilion Building, 109 State Street, Montpelier, VT 05602. Contact Mr. Lou Dworshak at (802) 828-3221. *Assistance:* Training

Virginia

Center for Innovative Technology, P.O. Box 15373, Herndon, VA 22070–9998. Contact (703) 689-3000. *Assistance:* Financial/Information/Networking

Community Organization for Minority Economic Development, Planning and Community Services, 901 Main Street, Level B, Lynchburg, VA 24504. Contact (804) 846-2778. *Assistance:* Business planning/Management/Technical. *Eligibility:* Minority businesses

Division of Energy, Department of Mines, Minerals, and Energy, 2210 West Broad Street, Richmond, VA 23220. Contact (804) 257-0330. *Assistance:* Information

Export Development–International Marketing Division, Virginia Department of Economic Development, 1000 Washington Bldg., Richmond, VA 23219. Contact (804) 786-3791. *Assistance:* Information/Technical

George Mason Institute, George Mason University, 4400 University Drive, Fairfax, VA 22030. Contact Mr. Tom Ingram at (703) 323-2568. *Assistance:* Business planning/Information/Networking

Hampton University Business Assistance Center, P.O. Box 6148, Hampton, VA 23668. Contact (804) 727-5570. *Assistance:* Business planning/Information/Management/Technical

Norfolk Business Development Center, Plaza One Building, Suite 801, 1 Main Plaza East, Norfolk VA 23510. Contact (804) 627-5254. *Assistance:* Business planning/Information/Management/Technical. *Eligibility:* Minority businesses

Office of Small Business and Financial Services. Virginia Department of Economic Development, 1000 Washington Building, Richmond, VA 23219. Contact Small Business Coordinator at (804) 786-3791. *Assistance:* Financial / Information / Management / Networking / Technical

The Metropolitan Business League, 214 East Clay Street, P.O. Box 26751, Richmond, VA 23261. Contact (804) 649-7473. *Assistance:* Business planning/Technical. *Eligibility:* Minority businesses

Tidewater Regional Minority Purchasing Council, Inc., 142 West York Street, Suite 308, Norfolk, VA 23510. Contact (804) 627-8471. *Assistance:* Information/Networking/ Technical

Virginia Employment Commission, 703 East Main Street, P.O. Box 1358, Richmond, VA 23233. Contact (804) 786-8223. *Assistance:* Information/Technical

Virginia Port Authority, 600 World Trade Center, Norfolk, VA 23510. Contact (804) 623-8000. *Assistance:* Information/Technical

Virginia Regional Minority Supplier Development Council, 1214 Westover Hills Blvd., Suite 208, Richmond, VA 23225. Contact (804) 231-1023. *Assistance:* Technical. *Eligibility:* Minority businesses

Virginia State, Office of Minority Business Enterprise, Ninth Street Office Building, Room 1028, Richmond, VA 23219. Contact (804) 786-5560. *Assistance:* Information/ Technical. *Eligibility:* Minority businesses

Washington

Business and Government Relations, Department of Trade and Economic Development, 101 General Administration Building, AX-13, Olympia, WA 98504. Contact Ms. Sandra Granger at 1-800-237-1233 (Toll free in the state) (206) 753-5634. *Assistance:* Information/Networking

Community Development Finance Program, Department of Community Development, 9th & Columbia Bldg., Olympia, WA 98504. Contact Mr. Chris Barada at 1-800-562-5677. *Assistance:* Financial

Department of Revenue, Department of Revenue, General Administration Building, Olympia, WA 98504. Contact (206) 753-5540. *Assistance:* Financial

Development Loan Fund, Department of Community Development, 9th & Columbia Bldg., Olympia, WA 98504. Contact Ms. Joan Machlis at (206) 754-8976. *Assistance:* Financial

Domestic and International Trade Development, Department of Trade and Economic Development, 312 First Avenue North, Seattle, WA 98109. Contact Mr. Paul Mastilak at (206) 464-6283. *Assistance:* Information/ Networking/Technical

Job Skills Program, Commission for Vocational Education, Building 17, Airdustrial Park, Olympia, WA 98504. Contact Mr. Tom Lopp at 1-800-233-6267 (Toll free within the state) (206) 754-3321. *Assistance:* Training

Job Training Partnership Program, Department of Employment Security, 212 Maple Park, Olympia, WA 98504. Contact Mr. Gary Gallwas at 1-800-233-6267 (Toll free in the state) (206) 754-1024. *Assistance:* Training

License Information Service, Business License Center, Department of Licensing, Eastside Plaza, PB-01, 1300 Quince Street, Olympia, WA 98504. Contact 1-800-562-8203 (Toll free in the state) (206) 753-2784. *Assistance:* Information

Small Business Assistance Program, State Board for Community College Education, 319 East Seventh Avenue, Olympia, WA 98504. Contact Mr. Ron Fowler at (206) 753-2000. *Assistance:* Training. *Eligibility:* Smaller businesses

Small Business Development Center, College of Business and Economics, Pullman, WA 99164–4740. Contact Mr. Lyle M. Anderson at (509) 335-1576. *Assistance:* Business planning / Information / Networking / Technical

Office of Minority and Women's Business Enterprises, FK-11, 406 South Water, Olympia, WA 98504. Contact (206) 753-9693. *Assistance:* Technical. *Eligibility:* Smaller businesses and minority businesses

Small Business Export Finance Assistance Center, Department of Trade and Economic Development, 312 First Avenue North, Seattle, WA 98109. Contact Mr. Robert Sebastian at (206) 464-7123. *Assistance:* Business planning/Financial/Networking

West Virginia

Center for Regional Progress, Marshall University, Huntington, WV 25701. Contact Mr. Byron D. Carpenter at (304) 696-6797 *Assistance:* Business planning/Technical

West Virginia Division of Small Business, Governor's Office of Community and Industrial Development, State Capitol Complex, Charleston, WV 25305. Contact Ms. Eloise Jack at 1-800-225-5982. Those out of state should call (304) 348-2960. *Assistance:* Business planning/Financial/Information/Networking/Technical. *Eligibility:* Smaller businesses

Wisconsin

Bureau of Business Development Services, Department of Development, 123 West Washington Ave., P.O. Box 7970, Madison, WI 53707. Contact Mr. Mim Gruentzel at (608) 266-0165. *Assistance:* Business planning / Information / Networking / Technical

Permit Information Center, Department of Development, 123 West Washington Ave., P.O. Box 7970, Madison, WI 53707. Contact Mr. Phillip Albert at 1-800-435-7287. Those outside the state should call (608) 266-9869. *Assistance:* Information/Networking

Wyoming

Division of Manpower Planning, Barrett Building, 3rd Floor, Cheyenne, WY 82002. Contact Mr. David Griffin at (307) 777-7671. *Assistance:* Training/Financial/Technical

Economic Development and Stabilization Board, Herschler Building, Third Floor, Cheyenne, WY 82002. Contact (307) 777-7285. *Assistance:* Financial/Information/Technical

Wyoming Business Development Center, Casper College, 125 College Drive, Casper, WY 82601. Contact Mr. Mac Bryant at (307) 268-2552. *Assistance:* Business planning / Financial / Information / Management / Networking / Technical. *Eligibility:* Smaller businesses

Wyoming Community Development Authority, P.O. Box 634, Casper, WY 82602. Contact Mr. Mark Peterson at (307) 265-0603. *Assistance:* Financial/Networking/Technical

State Data Center Program of the Bureau of the Census

Access to the many statistical products available from the Bureau of the Census is provided through the services of the joint federal-state cooperative State Data Center Program. Through the Program, the Bureau furnishes statistical products, training in the data access and use, technical assistance, and consultation to states which, in turn, disseminate the products and provide assistance in their use.

Additional information on the State Data Program and a list of the State Data Centers can be obtained by contacting the User Services staff in any of the Bureau's regional offices or by calling the Data User Services Division of the Bureau of the Census at 301-763-1580.

State Information Offices

Alabama*

State Capitol, Montgomery, AL 36130
(205) 261–2500

* For Small Business Administration offices, see page 268.

INFORMATION OFFICES

Commerce/Economic Development
Alabama Development Office
135 S. Union Street
Montgomery, AL 36130

Department of Economic & Community Affairs
3465 Norman Bridge Road
Montgomery, AL 36105

Corporate
Secretary of State
State Office Building
Montgomery, AL 36130

Taxation
Department of Revenue
Administrative Building
64 N. Union Street
Montgomery, AL 36130

State Chamber of Commerce
Alabama Chamber of Commerce
468 S. Perry Street
P.O. Box 76
Montgomery, AL 36101

International Commerce
Department of International Trade
3465 Norman Bridge Road
P.O. Box 2939
Montgomery, AL 36105-0939

Banking
State Banking Department
651 Administrative Building
Montgomery, AL 36130

Securities
Alabama Securities Exchange Commission
100 Commerce Street
First Southern Towers
Montgomery, AL 36130

Labor and Industrial Relations
Department of Industrial Relations
649 Monroe Street
Montgomery, AL 36130

Alabama Department of Labor
Administrative Building
64 N. Union Street
Montgomery, AL 36130

Insurance
Department of Insurance
135 S. Union Street
Montgomery, AL 36130

Uniform Industrial Code
Alabama Development Office
State Capitol
Montgomery, AL 36130

INDUSTRIAL AND BUSINESS DIRECTORIES

Alabama Directory of Mining and Manufacturing, Alabama Development Office, State Capitol, Montgomery, AL 36130

Alabama Industrial Directory, Manufacturers' News, Inc., 3 E. Huron Street, Chicago, IL 60611; State Industrial Directories Corp., 2 Penn Plaza, New York, NY 10001

Alabama International Trade Directory, Office of State Planning and Federal Programs, State Capitol, Montgomery, AL 36130

Birmingham Industrial Directory, Birmingham Chamber of Commerce, 1914 6th Avenue, Birmingham, AL 35203

Alabama Metalworking Directory, Office of State Planning and Federal Programs, State Capitol, Montgomery, AL 36130

Alaska

STATE CAPITOL, JUNEAU, AK 99811
(907) 465–2111

INFORMATION OFFICES

Commerce/Economic Development
Department of Commerce & Economic Development
P.O. Box D
Juneau, AK 99811

Corporate
Department of Commerce & Economic Development
Corporation Section
P.O. Box D
Juneau, AK 99811

Taxation
Department of Revenue
P.O. Box S
Juneau, AK 99811

State Chamber of Commerce
Alaska State Chamber of Commerce
310 2nd Street
Juneau, AK 99801

International Commerce
Division of International Trade
Department of Commerce & Economic Development
3601 C Street
Anchorage, AK 99503

Banking
Division of Banking
Department of Commerce & Economic Development
P.O. Box D
Juneau, AK 99811

Securities
Division of Securities and Corporations
Department of Commerce and Economic Development
P.O. Box D
Juneau, AK 99811

Labor and Industrial Relations
Department of Labor
1111 W. 8th Street
Juneau, AK 99801

Insurance
Division of Insurance
Department of Commerce and Economic Development
P.O. Box D
Juneau, AK 99811

Uniform Industrial Code
Department of Natural Resources
Uniform Commercial Code
3601 C Street
Anchorage, AK 99503

INDUSTRIAL AND BUSINESS DIRECTORIES

Alaska Directory of Commercial Establishments, Manufacturers' News, Inc., 4 E. Huron Street, Chicago, IL 60611; State Industrial Directories Corp., 2 Penn Plaza, New York, NY 10001

Alaska Petroleum and Industrial Directory, 409 W. Northern Lights Boulevard, Anchorage, AK 99603

Arizona

STATE CAPITOL, PHOENIX, AZ 85007
(602) 255–4900

INFORMATION OFFICES

Commerce/Economic Development
Department of Commerce
1700 W. Washington Avenue
Phoenix, AZ 85007

Corporate
Arizona Corporation Commission
P.O. Box 6019
Phoenix, AZ 85005

Taxation
Department of Revenue
State Capitol
1700 W. Washington Avenue
Phoenix, AZ 85007

State Chamber of Commerce
Arizona State Chamber of Commerce
3216 N. Third Street
Phoenix, AZ 85012

Banking
Banking Department
815 Century Plaza
Phoenix, AZ 85012

Insurance
Insurance Department
801 E. Jefferson
Phoenix, AZ 85034

Securities
Arizona Corporation Commission
1200 W. Washington Avenue
Phoenix, AZ 85007

International Commerce
Department of Commerce
1700 W. Washington Avenue
Phoenix, AZ 85007

Labor and Industrial Relations
Industrial Commission
800 W. Washington Street
P.O. Box 19070
Phoenix, AZ 85005

INDUSTRIAL AND BUSINESS DIRECTORIES

Arizona Directory of Industries, Manufacturers' News, 3 E. Huron Street, Chicago, IL 60611

Arizona Directory of Manufacturers, Manufacturers' News, Inc., 3 E. Huron Street, Chicago, IL 60611; State Industrial Directories Corp., 2 Penn Plaza, New York, NY 10001

Arizona USA International Trade Directory, Arizona State Department of Economic Planning and Development, 1700 W. Washington Avenue, Phoenix, AZ 85007

Directory of Arizona Manufacturers, Phoenix Chamber of Commerce, Phoenix, AZ 85001

Arkansas

State Capitol, Little Rock, AR 72201
(501) 371–1010

INFORMATION OFFICES

Commerce/Economic Development
Industrial Development Commission
Big Mac Building
One State Capitol Mall
Little Rock, AR 72201

Corporate
Secretary of State
Corporation Department
State Capitol
Little Rock, AR 72201

Taxation
Division of Revenue Services
Department of Finance and Administration
Joel Y. Ledbetter Building
7th and Wolfe Streets
Little Rock, AR 72201

State Chamber of Commerce
Arkansas State Chamber of Commerce
911 Wallace Building
Little Rock, AR 72201

International Commerce
Industrial Development Commission
Big Mac Building
One State Capitol Mall
Little Rock, AR 72201

Banking
Bank Department
323 Center Street
Little Rock, AR 72201

Securities
Securities Department
Heritage West Building
201 East Markham
Little Rock, AR 72201

Labor and Industrial Relations
Arkansas Department of Labor
1022 High Street
Little Rock, AR 72202

Insurance
Insurance Division
University Towers Building
Little Rock, AR 72204

Ombudsman
State Claims Commission
State Capitol
Little Rock, AR 72201

INDUSTRIAL AND BUSINESS DIRECTORIES

Arkansas Directory of Industries, Manufacturers' News, 3 E. Huron Street, Chicago, IL 60611

Directory of Arkansas Manufacturers, Arkansas Industrial Development Foundation, P.O. Box 1784, Little Rock, AR 72203; State Industrial Directories Corp., 2 Penn Plaza, New York, NY 10001

State and County Economic Data (annual), University of Arkansas Industrial Research Center, University of Arkansas, Little Rock College of Business Administration, 33rd and University Avenue, Little Rock, AR 72204

California

State Capitol, Sacramento, CA 95814
(916) 332–9900

INFORMATION OFFICES

Commerce/Economic Development
Department of Commerce
1121 L Street
Sacramento, CA 95814

Corporate
Secretary of State
1230 "J" Street
Sacramento, CA 95814

Taxation
Board of Equalization
1020 N Street
Sacramento, CA 95808

State Chamber of Commerce
California Chamber of Commerce
1027 10th Street
P.O. Box 1736
Sacramento, CA 95808

International Commerce
California State World Trade Commission
1121 L Street
Sacramento, CA 95814

Banking
State Banking Department
235 Montgomery Street
San Francisco, CA 94104

Securities
Department of Corporations
1025 P Street
Sacramento, CA 95814

Labor and Industrial Relations
Department of Industrial Relations
525 Golden Gate Avenue
P.O. Box 603
San Francisco, CA 94101

Insurance
Department of Insurance
600 S. Commonwealth Avenue
Los Angeles, CA 90005

INDUSTRIAL AND BUSINESS DIRECTORIES

California Handbook, Center for California Public Affairs, 226 W. Foothill Boulevard, Claremont, CA 91711

California International Business Directory, Center for International Business, 333 S. Flower Street, Los Angeles, CA 90071

California Manufacturers Register, Time-Mirror Press, 1115 S. Boyle Avenue, Los Angeles, CA 90023; Manufacturers' News, Inc., 4 E. Huron Street, Chicago, IL 60611; State Industrial Directories Corp., 2 Penn Plaza, New York, NY 10001

Los Angeles Area Chamber of Commerce Southern California Business Directory and Buyers Guide, Los Angeles Chamber of Commerce, 404 S. Bixel Street, Los Angeles, CA 95113

San Francisco Manufacturers Directory, San Francisco Chamber of Commerce, 333 Pine Street, San Francisco, CA 94577

Colorado

State Capitol, Denver, CO 80203
(303) 866–5000

INFORMATION OFFICES

Commerce/Economic Development
Division of Commerce and Development
Department of Local Affairs
Centennial Building
1313 Sherman Street
Denver, CO 80203

Corporate
Secretary of State
Corporation Division
1560 Broadway
Denver, CO 80203

Taxation
Administrative Division
Department of Revenue
1375 Sherman Street
Denver, CO 80261

State Chamber of Commerce
Colorado Association of Commerce and Industry
1390 Logan Street
Denver, CO 80203

International Commerce
Foreign Trade Office
Division of Commerce & Development
1313 Sherman Street
Denver, CO 80203

Banking
Division of Banking
Department of Regulatory Agencies
303 W. Colfax Street
Denver, CO 80202

Securities
Division of Securities
1560 Broadway
Denver, CO 80202

Labor and Industrial Relations
Division of Labor
1313 Sherman Street
Denver, CO 80203

Insurance
Division of Insurance
303 W. Colfax Street
Denver, CO 80204

Uniform Industrial Code
Commercial Recordings Division
1560 Broadway
Denver, CO 80203

Business Ombudsman
Business Information Center
1525 Sherman Street
Denver, CO 80203

INDUSTRIAL AND BUSINESS DIRECTORIES

Directory of Colorado Manufacturers, Business Research Division, Graduate School of Business Administration, Campus Box 420, University of Colorado, Boulder, CO 80309

Connecticut

State Capitol, Hartford, CT 06106
(203) 566–4200

INFORMATION OFFICES

Commerce/Economic Development
Department of Economic Development
210 Washington Street
Hartford, CT 06106

Corporate
Secretary of State
Corporations Division
30 Trinity Street
Hartford, CT 06106

Taxation
Department of Revenue Services
92 Farmington Avenue
Hartford, CT 06106

State Chamber of Commerce
Connecticut Business and Industry Association
370 Asylum Street
Hartford, CT 06103

International Commerce
Department of Economic Development
210 Washington Street
Hartford, CT 06106

Banking
Department of Banking
44 Capitol Avenue
Hartford, CT 06106

Securities
Divisions of Securities & Business Investments
Department of Banking
44 Capitol Avenue
Hartford, CT 06106

Labor and Industrial Relations
Department of Labor
200 Folly Brook Boulevard
Wethersfield, CT 06109

Insurance
Department of Insurance
165 Capitol Avenue
Hartford, CT 06106

Uniform Industrial Code
Department of Economic Development
210 Washington Street
Hartford, CT 06106

Business Ombudsman
Department of Economic Development
210 Washington Street
Hartford, CT 06106

INDUSTRIAL AND BUSINESS DIRECTORIES

Classified Business Directory—State of Connecticut, Connecticut Directory Co., Inc., 322 Main Street, Stamford, CT 06901

Connecticut Classified Business Directory, Connecticut Directory Co., Inc., 322 Main Street, Stamford, CT 06901

Connecticut State Industrial Directory, Manufacturers' News, 3 E. Huron Street, Chicago, IL 60611; State Industrial Directories Corp., 2 Penn Plaza, New York, NY 10001

Directory of Connecticut Manufacturing Establishments, Connecticut Department of Labor, 200 Folly Brook Boulevard, Wethersfield, CT 06109

Delaware

Legislative Hall, Dover, DE 19901
(302) 736–4101

INFORMATION OFFICES

Commerce/Economic Development
Delaware Development Office
99 Kings Highway
P.O. Box 1401
Dover, DE 19903

Corporate
Secretary of State
Corporations Department
P.O. Box 898
Dover, DE 19903

Taxation
Department of Finance
Division of Revenue
Carvel State Office Building
820 N. French Street
Wilmington, DE 19801

International Commerce
99 Kings Highway
P.O. Box 1401
Dover, DE 19903

State Chamber of Commerce
Delaware State Chamber of Commerce, Inc.
One Commerce Center
Wilmington, DE 19801

Banking
State Bank Commission
Collins Building
P.O. Box 1401
Dover, DE 19903

Labor and Industrial Relations
Division of Industrial Affairs
Department of Labor
Carvel State Office Building
820 N. French Street
Wilmington, DE 19801

Insurance
State Insurance Commission
21 The Green
Dover, DE 19901

INDUSTRIAL AND BUSINESS DIRECTORIES

Delaware Directory of Commerce and Industry, Delaware State Chamber of Commerce, One Commerce Center, Wilmington, DE 19801

Delaware State Industrial Directory, State Industrial Directories Corp., 2 Penn Plaza, New York, NY 10001

Florida

STATE CAPITOL, TALLAHASSEE, FL 32301
(904) 488–1234

INFORMATION OFFICES

Commerce/Economic Development
Department of Commerce
Collins Building
107 W. Gaines Street
Tallahassee, FL 32301

Division of Economic Development
Department of Commerce
Collins Building
Tallahassee, FL 32301

Corporate
Secretary of State
Division of Corporations
Capitol Building
Tallahassee, FL 32304

Taxation
Department of Revenue
Carlton Building
Tallahassee, FL 32301

State Chamber of Commerce
Florida State Chamber of Commerce
P.O. Box 11309
Tallahassee, FL 32302

International Commerce
Florida Department of Commerce
Bureau of International Trade
Collins Building
Tallahassee, FL 32301

Banking
Florida Department of Banking & Finance
The Capitol
Tallahassee, FL 32301

Securities
Florida Department of Banking & Finance
Division of Securities
1402 Capitol
Tallahassee, FL 32301

Labor and Industrial Relations
Florida Department of Labor and Employment Security
Atkins Building
1320 Executive Center Drive, East
Tallahassee, FL 32301

Insurance
Florida Department of Insurance
The Capitol
Tallahassee, FL 32301

Uniform Commercial Code
Florida Department of State
Bureau of Uniform Commercial Code
P.O. Box 5588
Tallahassee, FL 32314

Business Ombudsman
Florida Department of Commerce
Bureau of Business and Community Development
Collins Building
Tallahassee, FL 32301

INDUSTRIAL AND BUSINESS DIRECTORIES

Directory of Florida Industries, Manufacturers' News, Inc., 4 E. Huron Street, Chicago, IL 60611; Florida State Chamber of Commerce, P.O. Box 11309, Tallahassee, FL 32302; State Industrial Directories Corp., 2 Penn Plaza, New York, NY 10001

Florida Industries Guide, McHenry Publishing Co., Inc., Box 935, Orlando, FL 32802

Georgia

STATE CAPITOL, ATLANTA, GA 30334
(404) 656–2000

INFORMATION OFFICES

Commerce/Economic Development
Department of Industry and Trade
230 Peachtree Street NW
Atlanta, GA 30303

Corporate
Corporations Division
Secretary of State
2 Martin Luther King Jr. Drive, SE
Atlanta, GA 30334

Taxation
Department of Revenue
270 Washington Street, SW
Atlanta, GA 30334

State Chamber of Commerce
Business Council of Georgia
1280 CNN Center
Atlanta, GA 30303–2705

International Commerce
Department of Industry and Trade
230 Peachtree Street, NW
Atlanta, GA 30303

Banking
Department of Banking and Finance
2990 Brandywine Road
Atlanta, GA 30341

Securities
Securities Division
Secretary of State
2 Martin Luther King Jr. Drive, SE
Atlanta, GA 30334

Labor and Industrial Relations
Department of Labor

254 Washington Street, SW
Atlanta, GA 30334

Insurance
Office of Commissioner of Insurance
2 Martin Luther King Jr. Drive, SE
Atlanta, GA 30334

INDUSTRIAL AND BUSINESS DIRECTORIES

Georgia Manufacturing Directory, Department of Industry and Trade, 230 Peachtree Street, NW, Atlanta, GA 30303

Georgia World Trade Directory, Business Council of Georgia, 575 CNN Center, Atlanta, GA 30303–2705

Industrial Sites in Georgia, Georgia Power Company, Box 4545DJ, Atlanta, GA 30303

Georgia International Trade Directory, Department of Industry and Trade, 230 Peachtree Street NE, Atlanta, GA 30303

Georgia Directory of International Services, World Congress Institute, 1 Park Place S, Fulton Federal Building, Atlanta, GA 30303

International Companies with Facilities in Georgia. Department of Industry and Trade, 230 Peachtree Street, NW, Atlanta, GA 30303

Hawaii

State Capitol, Honolulu, HI 96813
(808) 548–2211

INFORMATION OFFICES

Commerce/Economic Development
Department of Planning and Economic Development
250 S. King Street
Honolulu, HI 96813

Department of Commerce and Consumer Affairs
1010 Richards Street
Honolulu, HI 96813

Corporate
Department of Commerce and Consumer Affairs
Business Registration Division
P.O. Box 40
Honolulu, HI 96810

Taxation
Department of Taxation
830 Punchbowl Street
Honolulu, HI 96813

State Chamber of Commerce
Chamber of Commerce of Hawaii
735 Bishop Street
Dillingham Building
Honolulu, HI 96813

International Commerce
International Services Branch
State Department of Planning and Economic Development
P.O. Box 2359
Honolulu, HI 96804

Hawaii Foreign-Trade Zone No. 9, Pier 2
Honolulu, HI 96813

Banking
Division of Financial Institutions
State Department of Commerce and Consumer Affairs
1010 Richards Street
Honolulu, HI 96813

Securities
Division of Financial Institutions
State Department of Commerce and Consumer Affairs
1010 Richards Street
Honolulu, HI 96813

Labor and Industrial Relations
State Department of Labor and Industrial Relations
830 Punchbowl Street
Honolulu, HI 96813

Insurance
Insurance Division
State Department of Commerce and Consumer Affairs
1010 Richards Street
Honolulu, HI 96813

Business Ombudsman
Office of the Ombudsman
465 S. King Street
Honolulu, HI 96813

INDUSTRIAL AND BUSINESS DIRECTORIES

Directory of Manufacturers, State of Hawaii, Chamber of Commerce of Hawaii, Dillingham Building, 735 Bishop Street, Honolulu, HI 96813

Hawaii Business Directory, Hawaii Business Directory, Inc., 1164 Bishop Street, Honolulu, HI 96813

Hawaii Directory of Manufacturers, Manufacturers' News, Inc., 4 E. Huron Street, Chicago, IL 60611; State Industrial Directories Corp., 2 Penn Plaza, New York, NY 10001

Idaho

State Capitol, Boise, ID 83720
(208) 334–2411

INFORMATION OFFICES

Mailing address for all state offices is:
Statehouse
Boise, ID 83720

Commerce/Economic Development
Department of Commerce
Capitol Building
Boise, ID 83720

Corporate
Secretary of State
State Capitol
Boise, ID 83720

Taxation
Department of Revenue and Taxation
700 W. State Street
Boise, ID 83720

State Chamber of Commerce
Idaho Association of Commerce and Industry
805 West Idaho
Boise, ID 83702

International Commerce
Department of Commerce
Statehouse
Boise, ID 83720

Banking
Department of Finance
700 W. State Street
Boise, ID 83720

Securities
Department of Finance
700 W. State Street
Boise, ID 83720

Labor and Industrial Relations
Department of Labor and Industrial Services
277 N. 6th Street
Boise, ID 83720

Insurance
Department of Insurance
700 W. State Street
Boise, ID 83720

Uniform Industrial Code
Department of Labor and Industrial Services
277 N. 6th Street
Boise, ID 83720

Business Ombudsman
Department of Commerce
Statehouse
Boise, ID 83720

INDUSTRIAL AND BUSINESS DIRECTORIES

Manufacturing Directory of Idaho, Center for Business and Research, University of Idaho, Moscow, ID 83843

Idaho Opportunities, Department of Commerce, Capitol Building, Boise, ID 83720

Illinois

STATE HOUSE, SPRINGFIELD, IL 62706
(217) 782–2000

INFORMATION OFFICES

Commerce/Economic Development
Department of Commerce and Community Affairs
620 E. Adams Street
Springfield, IL 62701

Corporate
Corporate Division
Centennial Building
Springfield, IL 62756

Taxation
Department of Revenue
101 W. Jefferson Street
Springfield, IL 62708

State Chamber of Commerce
Illinois State Chamber of Commerce
20 N. Wacker Drive
Chicago, IL 60606

International Commerce
Department of Commerce & Community Affairs
State of Illinois Center
100 W. Randolph Street
Chicago, IL 60601

Banking
Department of Financial Institutions
100 W. Randolph Street
Chicago, IL 60601

Securities
Secretary of State
840 S. Spring Street
Springfield, IL 62704

Labor and Industrial Relations
Department of Labor
100 N. 1st, Alzina Building
Springfield, IL 62706

Department of Commerce & Community Affairs
620 E. Adams Street
Springfield, IL 62701

Insurance
Department of Insurance
320 W. Washington Street
Springfield, IL 62767

Uniform Industrial Code
Department of Commerce & Community Affairs
620 E. Adams Street
Springfield, IL 62701

Business Ombudsman
Department of Commerce & Community Affairs
620 E. Adams Street
Springfield, IL 62701

INDUSTRIAL AND BUSINESS DIRECTORIES

Chicago Buyers' Guide, Chicago Association of Commerce and Industry, 130 S. Michigan Avenue, Chicago, IL 60603

Chicago Cook County and Illinois Industrial

Directory, National Publishing Corp., 3150 Des Plaines Avenue, Des Plaines, IL 60018

Chicago Geographic Edition, Manufacturers' News, Inc., 4 E. Huron Street, Chicago, IL 60611; State Industrial Directories Corp., 2 Penn Plaza, New York, NY 10001

Illinois Industrial Directory, Illinois Industrial Directories National Publishing Corp., 3150 Des Plaines Avenue, Des Plaines, IL 60018

Illinois Manufacturers Directory, Manufacturers' News, Inc., 3 E. Huron Street, Chicago, IL 60611; State Industrial Directories Corp., 2 Penn Plaza, New York, NY 10001

Illinois Services Directory, Manufacturers' News, Inc., 3 E. Huron Street, Chicago, IL 60611

Business Financing Programs, Department of Commerce and Community Affairs, 620 E. Adams, Springfield, IL 62706

Indiana

STATE HOUSE, INDIANAPOLIS, IN 46204
State Information Center
(317) 232–3140

INFORMATION OFFICES

Commerce/Economic Development
Department of Commerce
1 N. Capitol Avenue
Indianapolis, IN 46204

Corporate
Secretary of State
Corporation Division
State House
Indianapolis, IN 46204

Taxation
Department of Revenue
State Office Building
Indianapolis, IN 46204

State Board of Tax Commissioners
201 State Office Building
Indianapolis, IN 46204

State Chamber of Commerce
Indiana State Chamber of Commerce, Inc.
1 N. Capitol Avenue, Ste 200
Indianapolis, IN 46204

International Commerce
International Trade Division
Indiana Department of Commerce
1 N. Capitol Avenue
Indianapolis, IN 46204-2243

Banking
Department of Financial Institutions
State Office Building
Indianapolis, IN 46204

Securities
Secretary of State
Securities Commission
1 N. Capitol Avenue
Indianapolis, IN 46204-2243

Labor and Industrial Relations
Indiana Industrial Board
State Office Building
100 N. Senate Avenue
Indianapolis, IN 46204

Insurance
Indiana Department of Insurance
State Office Building
100 N. Senate Avenue
Indianapolis, IN 46204

Uniform Industrial Code
Uniform Commercial Code Division
Secretary of State Office
State House
Indianapolis, IN 46204

Business Ombudsman
Office of Regulatory Ombudsman
Indiana Department of Commerce
1 North Capitol Avenue
Indianapolis, IN 46204-2243

INDUSTRIAL AND BUSINESS DIRECTORIES

Indiana Industrial Directory, Harris Publishing Co., 2057–2 Aurora Rd., Twinsburg, OH 44087 Indiana State Chamber of Commerce, 1 N. Capitol Avenue, Ste 200, Indianapolis, IN 46204

Iowa

STATE CAPITOL, DES MOINES, IA 50319
(515) 281–5011

INFORMATION OFFICES

Commerce/Economic Development
Department of Economic Development
200 E. Grand
Des Moines, IA 50309

Corporate
Secretary of State
Corporation Division
Hoover Building
Des Moines, IA 50319

Taxation
Department of Revenue
Hoover Building
Des Moines, IA 50319

International Commerce
Department of Economic Development
200 E. Grand
Des Moines, IA 50309

Banking
Department of Commerce
Banking Division
530 Liberty Building
Des Moines, IA 50309

Iowa Housing Finance Authority
550 Liberty Building
Des Moines, IA 50309
Securities
Department of Commerce
Insurance Division
Securities Bureau
Lucas Building
Des Moines, IA 50319
Labor
Department of Employment Service
Division of Industrial Services
100 E. Grand
Des Moines, IA 50319
Bureau of Labor
100 E. Grand
Des Moines, IA 50319
Insurance
Department of Commerce
Insurance Division
Lucas Building
Des Moines, IA 50319

INDUSTRIAL AND BUSINESS DIRECTORIES

Directory of Iowa Manufacturers, Iowa Department of Economic Development, 200 E. Grand, Des Moines, IA 50309

Doing Business in Iowa, Iowa Department of Economic Development, 200 E. Grand, Des Moines, IA 50309

Kansas

State House, Topeka, KS 66612
(913) 296–0111

INFORMATION OFFICES

Commerce/Economic Development
Department of Economic Development
503 Kansas Avenue
Topeka, KS 66603
Corporate
Secretary of State
State House
Corporation Department
Topeka, KS 66612
Taxation
Department of Revenue
State Office Building
915 Harrison Street
Topeka, KS 66612
State Chamber of Commerce
Kansas Chamber of Commerce and Industry
500 Bank IV Tower
534 Kansas
Topeka, KS 66603-3460
International Commerce
Department of Economic Development
503 Kansas Avenue
Topeka, KS 66603
Banking
Banking Department
700 Jackson Street
Topeka, KS 66603
Securities
Securities Commissioner of Kansas
503 Kansas Avenue
Topeka, KS 66603
Labor and Industrial Relations
Department of Human Resources
512 W 6th Street
Topeka, KS 66603
Insurance
Insurance Department
420 W. 9th Street
Topeka, KS 66612
Business Ombudsman
Department of Economic Development
400 W. 8th Street
Topeka, KS 66603–3957

INDUSTRIAL AND BUSINESS DIRECTORIES

Directory of Kansas Manufacturers and Products, Kansas Department of Economic Development, 400 W. 8th Street, Topeka, KS 66603–3957; State Industrial Directories Corp., 2 Penn Plaza, New York, NY 10001

Directory of Manufacturers, Wichita, Kansas, Wichita Area Chamber of Commerce, 350 West Douglas, Wichita, KS 67202

Kansas Fortune 500 Companies, Kansas Department of Economic Development, 400 W. 8th Street, Topeka, KS 66603–3957

Kansas Manufacturing Firms in Export, Kansas Department of Economic Development, 400 W. 8th Street, Topeka, KS 66603–3957

Kansas Association Directory, Kansas Department of Economic Development, 400 W. 8th Street, Topeka, KS 66603–3957

Kentucky

State Capitol, Frankfort, KY 40601
(502) 564–3130

INFORMATION OFFICES

Commerce/Economic Development
Department of Economic Development
Capitol Plaza Office Tower
Frankfort, KY 40601

Corporate
Office of Secretary of State
Corporation Division
Capitol Building
Frankfort, KY 40601

Taxation
Revenue Cabinet
Capitol Annex
Frankfort, KY 40601

State Chamber of Commerce
Kentucky Chamber of Commerce
Versailles Road
P.O. Box 817
Frankfort, KY 40602

International Commerce
Kentucky Commerce Cabinet
Office of International Marketing
Capitol Plaza Tower
Frankfort, KY 40601

Banking
Kentucky Department of Financial Institutions
Division of Banking and Thrift Institutions
911 Leawood Drive
Frankfort, KY 40601–3392

Securities
Kentucky Department of Financial Institutions
Division of Securities
911 Leawood Drive
Frankfort, KY 40601

Labor Industrial Relations
Kentucky Labor Cabinet
The 127 Building
Frankfort, KY 40601

Insurance
Kentucky Department of Insurance
P.O. Box 517
Frankfort, KY 40602

Uniform Industrial Code
Kentucky Department of Housing, Buildings, and Construction
The 127 Building
Frankfort, KY 40601

Business Ombudsman
Kentucky Department of Economic Development
Capitol Plaza Tower
Frankfort, KY 40601

INDUSTRIAL AND BUSINESS DIRECTORIES

Kentucky International Trade, Kentucky Commerce Cabinet, Capitol Plaza Tower, Frankfort, KY 40601

Kentucky Directory of Manufacturers, Department of Economic Development, Capitol Plaza Tower, Frankfort, KY 40601; and from Manufacturers' News, 4 E. Huron Street, Chicago, IL 60611; State Industrial Directories Corp., 2 Penn Plaza, New York, NY 10001; Harris Publishing Co., 20572 Aurora Road, Twinsburg, OH 44087

Louisiana

STATE CAPITOL, BATON ROUGE, LA 70804
(504) 342–7015

INFORMATION OFFICES

Commerce/Economic Development
Department of Commerce
P.O. Box 94185
Baton Rouge, LA 70804–9185

Corporate
Secretary of State
Division of Corporation
P.O. Box 94125
Baton Rouge, LA 70804–9125

Taxation
Department of Revenue
P.O. Box 3440
Baton Rouge, LA 70823

State Chamber of Commerce
Louisiana Association of Business and Industry
P.O. Box 80258
Baton Rouge, LA 70898

International Commerce
Department of Commerce
Office of International Trade, Finance and Development
P.O. Box 94185
Baton Rouge, LA 70804–9185

Banking
Department of Commerce
Office of Financial Institutions
P.O. Box 94095
Baton Rouge, LA 70804

Securities
Louisiana Securities Commission
315 Louisiana State Office Building
325 Loyola Avenue
New Orleans, LA 70112

Labor and Industrial Relations
Department of Labor
P.O. Box 94094
Baton Rouge, LA 70804–9094

Insurance
Office of Insurance Rating Commission
P.O. Box 94157
Baton Rouge, LA 70804

Uniform Industrial Code
Department of Commerce
P.O. Box 94185
Baton Rouge, LA 70804–9185

Department of Labor
P.O. Box 94094
Baton Rouge, LA 70804–9094

Business Ombudsman
Department of Commerce
P.O. Box 94185
Baton Rouge, LA 70804–9185

INDUSTRIAL AND BUSINESS DIRECTORIES

Louisiana Directory of Manufacturers, Department of Commerce, 101 France Street, Baton Rouge, LA 70802; and from Manufacturers' News, Inc., 4 E. Huron Street, Chicago, IL 60611; State Industrial Directories Corp., 2 Penn Plaza, New York, NY 10001

Louisiana International Trade Directory, World Trade Center, 2 Canal Street, New Orleans, LA 70130

Maine

STATE HOUSE, AUGUSTA, ME 04333
(207) 289–1110

INFORMATION OFFICES

Commerce/Economic Development
State Development Office
193 State Street
State House Station #59
Augusta, ME 04333

Corporate
Department of State
Division of Corporations
Statehouse Station #101
Augusta, ME 04333

Private Development Associations
Maine Development Foundation
1 Memorial Circle
Augusta, ME 04330

Taxation
Bureau of Taxation
Department of Finance and Administration
State House Station #24
Augusta, ME 04333

State Chamber of Commerce
Maine State Chamber of Commerce and Industry
126 Sewall Street
Augusta, ME 04330

International Commerce
State Development Office
193 State Street
State House Station #59
Augusta, ME 04333

Banking
Bureau of Banking
Hallowell Annex
Correspondence to:
State House Station #36
Hallowell, ME 04347

Securities
Bureau of Banking
Securities Division
State House Station #36
Augusta, ME 04333

Labor and Industrial Relations
Department of Labor
20 Union Street
P.O. Box 309
Augusta, ME 04330

Insurance
Bureau of Insurance
Hallowell Annex
Hallowell, ME 04347
Correspondence to:
State House #34
Augusta, ME 04333

Business Ombudsman
State Development Office
State House Station #59
Augusta, ME 04333

INDUSTRIAL AND BUSINESS DIRECTORIES

Maine Marketing Directory, State Development Office, State House Station #59, Augusta, ME 04333

Maine Register, Tower Publishing Company, Portland, ME 04101

Maryland

STATE HOUSE, ANNAPOLIS, MD 21404
(301) 974–2000

INFORMATION OFFICES

Commerce/Economic Development
Department of Economic and Community Development
45 Calvert Street
Annapolis, MD 21401

Corporate
State Department of Assessments and Taxation
301 W. Preston Street
Baltimore, MD 21201

Taxation
Comptroller of the Treasury
Louis L. Goldstein Treasury Building
P.O. Box 466
Annapolis, MD 21404

State Chamber of Commerce
Maryland State Chamber of Commerce
60 West Street
Annapolis, MD 21401

International Commerce
Department of Economic and Community Development
Office of International Trade

World Trade Center
401 East Pratt Street
Baltimore, MD 21202

Maryland Port Administrator
Office of Port Administration
World Trade Center
Baltimore, MD 21202

Banking
State Banking Commission
34 Market Place
Baltimore, MD 21202

Securities
Division of Securities
Office of the Attorney General
7 N. Calvert Street
Baltimore, MD 21202

Labor and Industrial Relations
Division of Labor and Industry
Department of Licensing and Regulations
501 St. Paul Place
Baltimore, MD 21202

Insurance
State Insurance Division
Department of Licensing and Regulation
501 St. Paul Place
Baltimore, MD 21202

Business Ombudsman
Department of Economic and Community Development
Maryland Business Assistance Center
45 Calvert Street
Annapolis, MD 21401

INDUSTRIAL AND BUSINESS DIRECTORIES

Directory of Maryland Manufacturers, Maryland Department of Economic and Community Development, 45 Calvert Street, Annapolis, MD 21401

Maryland State Industrial Directory, State Industrial Directories Corp., 2 Penn Plaza, New York, NY 10001

Maryland High-Tech Directory, Maryland Department of Economic and Community Development, 45 Calvert Street, Annapolis, MD 21401

Massachusetts

State House, Boston, MA 02133
(617) 727–2121

INFORMATION OFFICES

Commerce/Economic Development
Governor's Office of Economic Development
Room 109
State House
Boston, MA 02133

Massachusetts Department of Commerce and Development
Division of Economic Development
100 Cambridge Street
Boston, MA 02202

Executive Office of Economic Affairs
2101 McCormack Building
1 Ashburton Place
Boston, MA 02108

Department of Commerce and Development
Leverett Saltonstall Building
100 Cambridge Street
Boston, MA 02202

Corporate
Secretary of State
1 Ashburton Place
Boston, MA 02108

Taxation
Accounting Bureau
Leverett Saltonstall Building
100 Cambridge Street
Boston, MA 02202

International Commerce
Office of International Trade and Investment
Executive Office of Economic Affairs
1 Ashburton Place
Boston, MA 02208

Banking
Division of Banks and Loan Agencies
100 Cambridge Street
Boston, MA 02202

Securities
Secretary of State
Securities Division
1 Ashburton Place
Boston, MA 02108

Labor and Industrial Relations
Executive Office of Labor
1 Ashburton Place
Boston, MA 02108

Department of Labor and Industries
Executive Office of Economic Affairs
100 Cambridge Street
Boston, MA 02202

Insurance
Division of Insurance
100 Cambridge Street
Boston, MA 02202

INDUSTRIAL AND BUSINESS DIRECTORIES

Directory of Directors in the City of Boston and Vicinity, Bankers Service Co., 14 Beacon Street, Boston, MA 02108

Directory of Massachusetts Manufacturers, George D. Hall Company, 20 Kilby Street, Boston, MA 02109

Massachusetts Directory of Manufacturers,

Manufacturers' News, Inc., 4 E. Huron Street, Chicago, IL 60611

Massachusetts State Industrial Directory, State Industrial Directories Corp., 2 Penn Plaza, New York, NY 10001

Michigan

State Capitol, Lansing, MI 48913
(517) 373–1837

INFORMATION OFFICES

Commerce/Economic Development
Department of Commerce
525 W. Ottawa Street
P.O. Box 30225
Lansing, MI 48909

Corporate
Corporation and Securities Bureau
6546 Mercantile Way
P.O. Box 30054
Lansing, MI 48909

Taxation
Bureau of Collection
Department of Treasury
Treasury Building
Lansing, MI 48922

State Chamber of Commerce
Michigan State Chamber of Commerce
200 N. Washington Square
Lansing, MI 48933

International Commerce
Office of International Development
Department of Commerce
P.O. Box 30105
Lansing, MI 48909

Banking
Financial Institutions Bureau
Department of Commerce
Law Building
P.O. Box 30224
Lansing, MI 48909

Securities
Corporation and Securities Bureau
Department of Commerce
6546 Mercantile Way
P.O. Box 30222
Lansing, MI 48909

Labor and Industrial Relations
Bureau of Labor Relations
Department of Labor
State of Michigan Plaza Building
1200 Sixth Street
Detroit, MI 48226

Department of Labor
Lansing Plaza
309 North Washington
P.O. Box 30015
Lansing, MI 48909

Insurance
Insurance Bureau
Department of Licensing and Regulation
611 West Ottawa
North Ottawa Tower
P.O. Box 30220
Lansing, MI 48909

INDUSTRIAL AND BUSINESS DIRECTORIES

Directory of Michigan Manufacturers, Manufacturers' News, Inc., 4 E. Huron Street, Chicago, IL 60611; Manufacturers Publishing Co., 8543 Puritan Avenue, Detroit, MI 48238

Harris Michigan Marketers Industrial Directory, Harris Publishing Company, 33140 Aurora Road, Cleveland, OH 44139

Michigan State Industrial Directory, State Industrial Directories Corp., 2 Penn Plaza, New York, NY 10001

MacRae's Michigan State Industrial Directory, MacRae Publishing, 817 Broadway, New York, NY 10003

Economic Development Corporations Directory for the State of Michigan, Department of Commerce, Office of Business and Community Development, Lansing, MI 48909

Minnesota

State Capitol, St. Paul, MN 55155
(612) 296–6013

INFORMATION OFFICES

Commerce/Economic Development
Department of Energy and Economic Development
900 American Center Building
St. Paul, MN 55101

Minnesota Department of Commerce
Metro Square Building
7th and Robert Streets
St. Paul, MN 55101

Corporate
Corporation Division
180 State Office Building
St. Paul, MN 55155

Taxation
Department of Revenue
Centennial Office Building
St. Paul, MN 55145

State Chamber of Commerce
Minnesota Association of Commerce and Industry
Hanover Building
480 Cedar Street
St. Paul, MN 55101

International Commerce
Minnesota Trade Office
90 W. Plato Boulevard
St. Paul, MN 55107

Banking
Minnesota Department of Commerce
Banking Division
Metro Square Building
7th & Robert Streets
St. Paul, MN 55101

Securities
Minnesota Department of Commerce
Registration Unit
Metro Square Building
7th & Robert Streets
St. Paul, MN 55101

Labor and Industrial Relations
Minnesota Department of Labor and Industry
444 Lafayette Road
St. Paul, MN 55101

Insurance
Minnesota Department of Commerce
Policy Analysis Division
Metro Square Building
7th & Robert Streets
St. Paul, MN 55101

Business Ombudsman
Department of Energy and Economic Development
900 American Center Building
St. Paul, MN 55101

INDUSTRIAL AND BUSINESS DIRECTORIES

Minnesota Directory of Manufacturers, Manufacturers' News, Inc., 4 E. Huron Street, Chicago, IL 60611; State Industrial Directories Corp., 2 Penn Plaza, New York, NY 10001

Mississippi

New Capitol, Jackson, MS 39205
(601) 359–3100

INFORMATION OFFICES

Commerce/Economic Development
Mississippi Department of Economic Development
P.O. Box 849
Jackson, MS 39205

Department of Agriculture and Commerce
1604 Sillers Building
Jackson, MS 39205

Corporate
Secretary of State
Corporation Division
P.O. Box 136
Jackson, MS 39205

Taxation
Tax Commission
102 Woolfolk Building
Jackson, MS 39201

State Chamber of Commerce
P.O. Box 1849
Jackson, MS 39205-1849

Banking
Department of Banking and Consumer Finance
1206 Woolfolk State Office Building
Jackson, MS 39205

Securities
Department of State
Securities Division
P.O. Box 136
Jackson, MS 39205

Labor and Industrial Relations
1520 W. Capitol Street
Jackson, MS 39205

Insurance
Department of Insurance
1804 Sillers Building
Jackson, MS 39205

INDUSTRIAL AND BUSINESS DIRECTORIES

Mississippi International Trade Directory, Mississippi Marketing Council, Box 849, Sillers State Office Building, Jackson, MS 39205

Mississippi Manufacturers' Directory, Manufacturers' News, Inc., 4 E. Huron Street, Chicago, IL 60611; Public Information Office, Mississippi Research and Development Center, Jackson, MS 39205; State Industrial Directories Corp., 2 Penn Plaza, New York, NY 10001

Missouri

State Capitol, Jefferson City, MO 65101
(314) 751–2151

INFORMATION OFFICES

Commerce/Economic Development
Department of Economic Development
Truman State Office Building
P.O. Box 1157
Jefferson City, MO 65102

Corporate
Secretary of State
Corporations Division
P.O. Box 778
Jefferson City, MO 65102

Taxation
Department of Revenue
Division of Taxation
Truman State Office Building
P.O. Box 629
Jefferson City, MO 65105

State Chamber of Commerce
Missouri Chamber of Commerce
428 East Capitol Avenue
P.O. Box 149
Jefferson City, MO 65102

International Commerce
International Business Development
Economic Development Program
Truman State Office Building
P.O. Box 1157
Jefferson City, MO 65102

Banking
Missouri Division of Finance
Truman State Office Building
P.O. Box 716
Jefferson City, MO 65102

Securities
Office of the Secretary of State
Securities Division
Truman State Office Building
P.O. Box 778
Jefferson City, MO 65102

Labor and Industrial Relations
Missouri Dept. of Labor & Industrial Relations
421 E. Dunklin
Jefferson City, MO 65102

Insurance
Missouri Division of Insurance
Truman State Office Building
P.O. Box 690
Jefferson City, MO 65102

Uniform Industrial Code
Missouri Division of Labor Standards
P.O. Box 449
Jefferson City, MO 65102

Business Ombudsman
Office of the Lieutenant Governor
Missouri State Capitol
P.O. Box 563
Jefferson City, MO 65102

INDUSTRIAL AND BUSINESS DIRECTORY

Contacts Influential: Commerce and Industrial Directory (for Kansas City Area), Contacts Influential, Inc., 6347 Brookside Boulevard, Suite 204, Kansas City, MO 64113

Missouri Directory of Manufacturing and Mining (annual), Informative Data Co., 3546 Watson Road, St. Louis, MO 63139

Montana

State Capitol, Helena, MT 59620
(406) 444–3111

INFORMATION OFFICES

Commerce/Economic Development
Department of Commerce
1424 9th Avenue
Helena, MT 59620

Economic Development and Research
Department of Commerce
1429 9th Avenue
Helena, MT 59620

Census and Economic Information Center
Department of Commerce
1429 9th Avenue
Helena, MT 59620

Corporate
Secretary of State
Corporation Bureau
State Capitol Building
Helena, MT 59620

State Chamber of Commerce
Montana Chamber of Commerce
P.O. Box 1730
Helena, MT 59601

International Commerce
International Export Officer
Montana Department of Commerce
1424 9th Avenue
Helena, MT 59620

Banking
Commissioner of Financial Institutions
Montana Department of Commerce
1424 9th Avenue
Helena, MT 59620

Securities
Securities Division
State Auditor's Office
Sam Mitchell Building
Helena, MT 59620

Labor & Industrial Relations
Commissioner's Office
Montana Department of Labor & Industry
Lockey and Roberts
Helena, MT 59620

Insurance
Insurance Division
State Auditor's Office
Sam Mitchell Building
Helena, MT 59620

Uniform Commercial Code
Secretary of State
Uniform Commercial Code Bureau
State Capitol Building
Capitol Station
Helena, MT 59620

Business Ombudsman
Small Business Advocate
Montana Department of Commerce
1424 9th Avenue
Helena, MT 59620

INDUSTRIAL AND BUSINESS DIRECTORIES

Montana Manufacturers and Products Directory, Department of Commerce, 1424 9th Avenue, Helena, MT 59620

Montana Business & Industrial Location Guide, Department of Commerce, 1424 9th Avenue, Helena, MT 59620

Nebraska

STATE CAPITOL, LINCOLN, NE 68509
(402) 471–3111

INFORMATION OFFICES

Commerce/Economic Development
Department of Economic Development
301 Centennial Mall South
P.O. Box 94666
Lincoln, NE 68509

Corporate
Secretary of State
Corporation Division
State Capitol
Lincoln, NE 68509

Taxation
Department of Revenue
Centennial Mall South
P.O. Box 94818
Lincoln, NE 68509

State Chamber of Commerce
Nebraska Association of Commerce and Industry
P.O. Box 81556
Lincoln, NE 68501

International Commerce
Nebraska Department of Economic Development
International Division
Nebraska State Office Building
Lincoln, NE 68509

Banking
Department of Banking and Finance
Nebraska State Office Building
P.O. Box 95006
Lincoln, NE 68509

Securities
Department of Banking and Finance
Bureau of Securities
Nebraska State Office Building
Lincoln, NE 68509

Labor and Industrial Relations
Nebraska Department of Labor
550 South 16th Street
P.O. Box 94600
Lincoln, NE 68509

Insurance
Department of Insurance
Nebraska State Office Building
Centennial Mall South
Lincoln, NE 68509

Uniform Industrial Code
Uniform Commercial Code Division
Nebraska State Office Building
Lincoln, NE 68509

Business Ombudsman
State Claims Board
Office of Risk Management
Nebraska State Office Building
Lincoln, NE 68509

INDUSTRIAL AND BUSINESS DIRECTORIES

Directory of Nebraska Manufacturers and Their Products, Manufacturers' News, Inc., 4 E. Huron Street, Chicago, IL 60611

Directory of Nebraska Manufacturers and Their Products, Nebraska State Department of Economic Development, Lincoln, NE 68509

Manufacturers and Wholesalers Directory, Lincoln Chamber of Commerce, 200 Lincoln Building, Lincoln, NE 68508

Directory of Manufacturers for the Omaha Metropolitan Area, Omaha Economic Development Council, 1606 Douglas, Omaha, NE 68102.

Directory of Major Employers for the Omaha Area, Omaha Economic Development Council, 1606 Douglas, Omaha, NE 68102.

Nevada

STATE CAPITOL, CARSON CITY, NV 89710
(702) 885–5627

INFORMATION OFFICES

Commerce/Economic Development
Department of Commerce
201 S. Fall Street
Carson City, NV 89710

Department of Economic Development
600 E. William Street
Capitol Complex
Carson City, NV 89710

Corporate
Secretary of State
Capitol Complex
Carson City, NV 89710

Taxation
Department of Taxation
1340 S. Curry Street
Carson City, NV 89710

State Chamber of Commerce
Nevada Chamber of Commerce Association
P.O. Box 2806
Reno, NV 89505

International Commerce
Department of Commerce
201 S. Fall Street
Carson City, NV 89710

Banking
Financial Institutions Division
Department of Commerce
406 E. Second Street
Carson City, NV 89710

Securities
Secretary of State
Capitol Complex
Carson City, NV 89710

Labor and Industrial Relations
Labor Commission
505 E. King Street
Carson City, NV 89710

Department of Industrial Relations
1390 S. Curry Street
Carson City, NV 89710

Insurance
Insurance Division
Department of Commerce
201 S. Fall Street
Carson City, NV 89710

INDUSTRIAL AND BUSINESS DIRECTORIES

Nevada Industrial Directory, Gold Hill Publishings Co., Inc., P.O. Drawer F, Virginia City, NV 89440

Nevada Directory of Business, Manufacturers' News, Inc., 4 E. Huron Street, Chicago, IL 60611

Directory of Nevada Mine Operations, Division of Mine Inspection Department of Industrial Relations, 1380 S. Curry Street, Carson City, NV 89710

New Hampshire

State House, Concord, NH 03301
(603) 271–1110

INFORMATION OFFICES

Commerce/Economic Development
Department of Resources and Economic Development
Division of Economic Development
105 Loudon Road, Building #2
Prescott Park
Concord, NH 03301

Corporate
Secretary of State
Corporations Division
State House Annex
Concord, NH 03301

Taxation
Board of Taxation
61 S. Spring Street
Concord, NH 03301

Department of Revenue Administration
61 S. Spring Street
Concord, NH 03301

State Chamber of Commerce
Business and Industry Association of New Hampshire
23 School Street
Concord, NH 03301

International Commerce
Department of Resources & Economic Development
Division of Economic Development
105 Loudon Road, Building #2
Prescott Park—Concord, NH 03301

Banking
Banking Department
State of New Hampshire
47 N. Main Street
Concord, NH 03301

New Hampshire Banking Association
125 N. Main Street
Concord, NH 03301

Securities
Insurance Department, Securities Division
State of New Hampshire
169 Manchester Street
Concord, NH 03301

Labor and Industrial Relations
Department of Employment Security
State of New Hampshire
32 S. Main Street
Concord, NH 03301

Department of Labor
19 Pillsbury Street
Concord, NH 03301

Insurance
Insurance Department
State of New Hampshire
169 Manchester Street
Concord, NH 03301

Standard Industrial Code
Department of Employment Security
State of New Hampshire
32 S. Main Street
Concord, NH 03301

INDUSTRIAL AND BUSINESS DIRECTORIES

Made in New Hampshire, New Hampshire Office of Industrial Development, Department of Resources, Concord, NH 03301

New Hampshire Register, Tower Publishing Company, 163 Middle Street, Portland, ME 04111

New Jersey

State House, Trenton, NJ 08625
(609) 292–2121

INFORMATION OFFICES

Commerce/Economic Development
Department of Commerce and Economic Development
CN 820, 1 W. State Street
Trenton, NJ 08625

Division of Travel and Tourism
CN 826, 1 West State Street
Trenton, NJ 08625

Economic Development Authority
200 S. Warren Street
CN 990, Capitol Place One
Trenton, NJ 08625

Corporate
Secretary of State
State House
CN 300
Trenton, NJ 08625

Taxation
Department of Treasury
Division of Taxation
CN 240, 50 Barrack Street
Trenton, NJ 08625

State Chamber of Commerce
New Jersey State Chamber of Commerce
240 W. State Street
Trenton, NJ 08625

International Commerce
Division of International Trade
744 Broad Street
Newark, NJ 07102

Banking
Department of Banking
CN 340, 36 W. State Street
Trenton, NJ 08625

Securities
Bureau of Securities
80 Mulberry Street
Newark, NJ 07102

Labor and Labor Relations
Department of Labor and Industry
CN 110, John Fitch Plaza
Trenton, NJ 08625

Insurance
Department of Insurance
CN 325, 201 E. State Street
Trenton, NJ 08625

Business Ombudsman
Department of Public Advocate
25 Market Street, CN 850
Trenton, NJ 08625

INDUSTRIAL AND BUSINESS DIRECTORIES

New Jersey State Industrial Directory, Manufacturers' News, Inc., 4 E. Huron Street, Chicago, IL 60611; State Industrial Directories Corp., 2 Penn Plaza, New York, NY 10001

New Mexico

State Capitol, Sante Fe, NM 87503
(505) 827–4011

INFORMATION OFFICES

Commerce/Economic Development
Economic Development and Tourism
Bataan Memorial Building
Sante Fe, NM 87503

Corporate
State Corporation Commission
P.O. Drawer 1269
Sante Fe, NM 87501

Taxation
Bureau of Revenue
Manuel Lujan Sr. Building
Santa Fe, NM 87501

State Chamber of Commerce
Association of Commerce and Industry of New Mexico
117 Quincy NE
Albuquerque, NM 87108

International Commerce
Department of International Trade
Bataan Memorial Building
Sante Fe, NM 87503

Banking
Lew Wallace Building
Sante Fe, NM 87503

Securities
Lew Wallace Building
Sante Fe, NM 87503

Labor and Industrial Commission
509 Camino de Los Marques
Sante Fe, NM 87501

Insurance
State Corporation Commission
P.O. Box 1269
Sante Fe, NM 87501

INDUSTRIAL AND BUSINESS DIRECTORIES

New Mexico Directory of Manufacturing, Manufacturers' News, Inc., 4 E. Huron Street, Chicago, IL 60611; New Mexico Commerce and Industry Department, Bataan Memorial Building, Santa Fe, NM 87503; State Industrial Directories Corp., 2 Penn Plaza, New York, NY 10001

New York

State Capitol, Albany, NY 12224
(518) 474–8390

INFORMATION OFFICES

Commerce/Economic Development
Department of Commerce
One Commerce Plaza
Albany, NY 12245

Division of Regional Economic Development
One Commerce Plaza
Albany, NY 12245

Corporate
Secretary of State
162 Washington Avenue
Albany, NY 12231

Taxation
State Tax Commission
Department of Taxation and Finance
State Campus Building #9
Albany, NY 12227

State Chamber of Commerce
New York State Business Council
152 Washington Avenue
Albany, NY 12210

Small Business Advisory Board
Division for Small Business
230 Park Avenue
New York, NY 10169

International Commerce
Department of Commerce
230 Park Avenue
New York, NY 10169

Banking
Department of Banking
194 Washington Avenue
New York, NY 12210

Labor and Industrial Relations
Department of Labor
State Campus
Albany, NY 12240

Insurance
Department of Insurance
Empire State Plaza
Agency Building #1
Albany, NY 12257

Business Ombudsman
Department of Commerce
Division for Small Business
230 Park Avenue
New York, NY 10169

INDUSTRIAL AND BUSINESS DIRECTORIES

New York and Surrounding Territory Classified Business Directory, New York Directory Co., Inc., 1440 Broadway, New York, NY 10018

New York Classified Business Directory, New York Directory Co., Inc., 1440 Broadway, New York, NY 10018

MacRae's New York State Industrial Directory, MacRae's Blue Book, Inc., 87 Terminal Drive, Plainview, NY 11803

New York State Industrial Directory, State Industrial Directories Corp., 2 Penn Plaza, New York, NY 10001; Manufacturers' News, Inc., 4 E. Huron Street, Chicago, IL 60611

Directory of Minority and Woman's Business, Minority and Woman's Business Division, New York State Department of Commerce, 230 Park Avenue, New York, NY 10169

North Carolina

State Legislative Building, Raleigh, NC 27611
(919) 733–1110

INFORMATION OFFICES

Commerce/Economic Development
Department of Commerce
430 N. Salisbury Street
Raleigh, NC 27611

Corporate
Secretary of State
Corporation Division
300 N. Salisbury Street
Raleigh, NC 27611

Taxation
Department of Revenue
2 S. Salisbury Street
Raleigh, NC 22760

State Chamber of Commerce
North Carolina Citizens for Business and Industry
P.O. Box 2508
Raleigh, NC 27602

International Commerce
International Development
Department of Commerce
430 N. Salisbury Street
Raleigh, NC 27611

Banking
Banking Commission
Department of Commerce
430 N. Salisbury Street
Raleigh, NC 27611

Securities
Secretary of State
Securities Division
300 N. Salisbury Street
Raleigh, NC 27611

Labor and Industrial Relations
Department of Labor
214 W. Jones Street
Raleigh, NC 27611

Insurance
Department of Insurance
430 N. Salisbury Street
Raleigh, NC 27611

Business Ombudsman
Business Assistance
Department of Commerce
430 N. Salisbury Street
Raleigh, NC 27611

INDUSTRIAL AND BUSINESS DIRECTORIES

Directory of North Carolina Manufacturing Firms, North Carolina Department of Commerce, Raleigh, NC 27611; State Industrial Directories Corp., 2 Penn Plaza,

New York, NY 10001; Manufacturers' News, Inc., 4 E. Huron Street, Chicago, IL 60611

North Dakota

STATE CAPITOL, BISMARCK, ND 58505
(701) 224–2000

INFORMATION OFFICES

Commerce/Economic Development
Economic Development Commission
Liberty Memorial Building
Bismarck, ND 58505

Corporate
Corporation Department
Office of the Secretary of State
Bismarck, ND 58505

Taxation
Tax Department
State Capitol
Bismarck, ND 58505

State Chamber of Commerce
Greater North Dakota Association—State Chamber of Commerce
P.O. Box 2467
Fargo, ND 58102

International Commerce
International Trade Department
Economic Development Commission
Liberty Memorial Building
Bismarck, ND 58505

Banking
State Banking Commission
State Capitol
Bismarck, ND 58505

Securities
Securities Commissioner
State Capitol
Bismarck, ND 58505

Labor and Industrial Relations
State Commissioner of Labor
State Capitol
Bismarck, ND 58505

Insurance
Insurance Commissioner
State Capitol
Bismarck, ND 58505

Uniform Industrial Code
Secretary of State
State Capitol
Bismarck, ND 58505

Business Ombudsman
Economic Development Commission
Liberty Memorial Building
Bismarck, ND 58505

INDUSTRIAL AND BUSINESS DIRECTORIES

North Dakota Manufacturers Directory, Economic Development Commission, Liberty Memorial Building, Bismarck, ND 58505; Manufacturers' News, Inc., 4 E. Huron Street, Chicago, IL 60611; State Industrial Directories Corp., 2 Penn Plaza, New York, NY 10001

Strictly Business, Frontier Directory Co., Inc., 515 E. Main Street, Bismarck, ND 58501

Ohio

STATE HOUSE, COLUMBUS, OH 43215
(614) 466–2000

INFORMATION OFFICES

Commerce/Economic Development
Ohio Department of Development
30 E. Broad Street
Columbus, OH 43266

Corporate
Secretary of State
Corporation Section
30 East Broad Street
Columbus, OH 43266

Taxation
Department of Taxation
30 E. Broad Street
Columbus, OH 43216

State Chamber of Commerce
Ohio Chamber of Commerce
35 E. Gay Street
Columbus, OH 43215

International Commerce
Ohio Department of Development
International Trade Division
30 E. Broad Street
P.O. Box 1001
Columbus, OH 43266

Banking
Ohio Department of Commerce
Division of Banks
Two Nationwide Plaza
Columbus, OH 43266

Securities
Ohio Department of Commerce
Division of Securities
Two Nationwide Plaza
Columbus, OH 43266

Labor and Industrial Relations
Ohio Department of Industrial Relations
2323 W. Fifth Avenue
P.O. Box 825
Columbus, OH 43266

Office of Collective Bargaining

Insurance
Ohio Department of Insurance
2100 Stella Court
Columbus, OH 43266

Uniform Industrial Code
Industrial Commission of Ohio

Division of Safety and Hygiene
246 N. High Street
Columbus, OH 43266

Business Ombudsman
Ohio Department of Development
Small and Developing Business Division
Minority Business Development Division
P.O. Box 1001
Columbus, OH 43266

INDUSTRIAL AND BUSINESS DIRECTORIES

Akron, Ohio Membership Directory and Buyers Guide, Akron Area Chamber of Commerce, P.O. Box 436, Crystal Lake, IL 60014

Directory of Manufacturers in the Toledo Area, Toledo Area Chamber of Commerce, 218 Huron Street, Toledo, OH 43604

Directory of Ohio Manufacturers, Harris Publishing Co., 2057–2 Aurora Road, Twinsburg, OH 44087; Manufacturers' News, Inc., 4 E. Huron Street, Chicago, IL 60611

Manufacturers Directory, Columbus Area Chamber of Commerce, 37 North High Street, Columbus, OH 43215

Ohio and International Trade, Division of International Trade, Department of Development, P.O. Box 1001, Columbus, OH 43266

Oklahoma

State Capitol, Oklahoma City, OK 73105
(405) 521–1601

INFORMATION OFFICES

Commerce/Economic Development
Department of Commerce
6601 Broadway Extension
Oklahoma City, OK 73116

Corporate
Secretary of State
State Capitol
Oklahoma City, OK 73105

Taxation
Tax Commission
M. C. Connors Building
Oklahoma City, OK 73105

State Chamber of Commerce
Oklahoma State Chamber of Commerce & Industry
4020 North Lincoln
Oklahoma City, OK 73105

International Commerce
International Trade Division
Department of Commerce
6601 Broadway Extension
Oklahoma City, OK 73116

Banking
Oklahoma Banking Services
4100 Lincoln Boulevard
Oklahoma City, OK 73105

Securities
Oklahoma Securities Commission
2915 Lincoln Boulevard
Oklahoma City, OK 73152

Labor and Industrial Relations
Oklahoma Labor Department
State Capitol
Oklahoma City, OK 73105

Insurance
Insurance Commission
408 Will Rogers Memorial Office Building
Oklahoma City, OK 73105

Uniform Industrial Code
Universal Commercial Code Division
County Clerk's Office
County Court House
Oklahoma City, OK 73102

INDUSTRIAL AND BUSINESS DIRECTORIES

Oklahoma Directory of Manufacturers and Products, Media/Marketing & Advertising, Department of Commerce, 6601 Broadway Extension, Oklahoma City, OK 73116

Oregon

State Capitol, Salem, OR 97310
(503) 378–3131

INFORMATION OFFICES

Commerce/Economic Development
Department of Economic Development
595 Cottage Street, N.E.
Salem, OR 97310

Corporate
Corporation Commission
Commerce Building
158 12th Street N.E.
Salem, OR 97310

Taxation
Department of Revenue
Revenue Building
955 Center Street
Salem, OR 97310

International Commerce
Economic Development Department
International Trade Division
921 S.W. Washington
Portland, OR 97205

Banking
Department of Commerce
Banking Division
280 Court Street N.E.
Salem, OR 97310

Securities
Department of Commerce
Corporation Division—Securities Section
Commerce Building
158 12th Street N.E.
Salem, OR 97310
Labor and Industrial Relations
Bureau of Labor and Industries
1400 S.W. 5th Avenue
Portland, OR 97201
Insurance
Department of Commerce
Insurance Division
Commerce Building
158 12th Street N.E.
Salem, OR 97310
Uniform Industrial Code
Department of Commerce
Building Codes Division
401 Labor and Industries Building
Salem, OR 97310

INDUSTRIAL AND BUSINESS DIRECTORIES

Oregon Manufacturers Directory, Department of Economic Development, 595 Cottage Street, N.E., Salem, OR 97310; State Industrial Directories Corp., 2 Penn Plaza, New York, NY 10001; Manufacturers' News, Inc., 4 E. Huron Street, Chicago, IL 60611

Pennsylvania

Main Capitol Building, Harrisburg, PA 17120
(717) 787–2121

INFORMATION OFFICES

Department of Commerce
Department of Commerce
433 Forum Building
Harrisburg, PA 17120

Bureau of Domestic and International Commerce
Department of Commerce
453 Forum Building
Harrisburg, PA 17120

Bureau of International Commerce
Department of Commerce
450 Forum Building
Harrisburg, PA 17120

Bureau of Economic Assistance
Department of Commerce
405 Forum Building
Harrisburg, PA 17120

Small Business Action Center
Department of Commerce
494 Forum Building
Harrisburg, PA 17120
Corporate
Department of State
Bureau of Corporations
North Office Building
Harrisburg, PA 17120
Taxation
Department of Revenue
Strawberry Square
Harrisburg, PA 17127
State Chamber of Commerce
Pennsylvania Chamber of Commerce
222 N. Third Street
Harrisburg, PA 17101
Banking
Banking
333 Market Street
Harristown II
Harrisburg, PA 17101-2290
Securities
Securities Commission
333 Market Street, Harristown II,
Harrisburg, PA 17101
Labor and Industrial Relations
Department of Labor & Industry
Labor & Industry Building
7th & Forster Streets
Harrisburg, PA 17120
Insurance
Insurance
Strawberry Square
Harrisburg, PA 17120

INDUSTRIAL AND BUSINESS DIRECTORIES

Industrial Directory of the Commonwealth of Pennsylvania, Department of General Services, Harris Publishing Company, 2057-2 Aurora Road, Twinsburg, OH 44087

Rhode Island

State House, Providence, RI 02903
(401) 277–2000

INFORMATION OFFICES

Commerce/Economic Development
Department of Economic Development
7 Jackson Walkway
Providence, RI 02903
Taxation
Division of Taxation
Department of Administration
289 Promenade Street
CIC Complex
Providence, RI 02908
Corporate
Secretary of State
Corporation Department

270 Westminster Street
Providence, RI 02903

State Chamber of Commerce
Rhode Island Chamber of Commerce
91 Park Street
Providence, RI 02908

International Commerce
Rhode Island Department of Economic Development
European Office
Meir 24
2000 Antwerp
Belgium

Banking
Department of Business Regulation
Banking Division
100 N. Main Street
Providence, RI 02903

Securities
Department of Business Regulation
Banking Division
100 N. Main Street
Providence, RI 02903

Labor and Industrial Relations
Department of Labor
220 Elmwood Avenue
Providence, RI 02907

Insurance
Department of Business Regulation
Insurance Division
100 N. Main Street
Providence, RI 02903

Uniform Industrial Code
Department of Labor
220 Elmwood Avenue
Providence, RI 02907

Business Ombudsman
Business Action Center
Department of Economic Development
7 Jackson Walkway
Providence, RI 02903

INDUSTRIAL AND BUSINESS DIRECTORIES

Rhode Island Directory of Manufacturers, Department of Economic Development, 7 Jackson Walkway, Providence, RI 02903

Rhode Island State Industrial Directory, State Industrial Directories Corp., 2 Penn Plaza, New York, NY 10001

South Carolina

State House, Columbia, SC 29211
(803) 734–9818

INFORMATION OFFICES

Commerce/Economic Development
South Carolina State Development Board
P.O. Box 927
1301 Gervais Street
Columbia, SC 29202

Taxation
Tax Commission
P.O. Box 125
Columbia Mill Building
Columbia, SC 29201

Corporate
Secretary of State
P.O. Box 11350
Columbia, SC 29211

State Chamber of Commerce
South Carolina Chamber of Commerce
1301 Gervais Street
Columbia, SC 29202

International Commerce
South Carolina State Development Board
1301 Gervais Street
P.O. Box 927
Columbia, SC 29202

Labor and Industrial Relations
South Carolina Labor Department
Landmark Center, 3600 Forest Drive
P.O. Box 11329
Columbia, SC 29211

Insurance
South Carolina Department of Insurance
1612 Marion Street
P.O. Box 100105
Columbia, SC 29202–3105

Business Ombudsman
South Carolina State Development Board
1301 Gervais Street
P.O. Box 927
Columbia, SC 29202

INDUSTRIAL AND BUSINESS DIRECTORIES

Industrial Directory of South Carolina, South Carolina State Development Board, P.O. Box 927, 1301 Gervais Street, Columbia, SC 29202

South Dakota

State Capitol, Pierre, SD 57501
(605) 773–3011

INFORMATION OFFICES

Commerce/Economic Development
Governor's Office of Economic Development
711 Wells Avenue
Capitol Lake Plaza
Pierre, SD 57501

Department of Commerce and Regulation
910 E. Sioux
Pierre, SD 57501

Corporate
Secretary of State
Corporation Division
Capitol Building
Pierre, SD 57501

Taxation
Department of Revenue
Kniep Building
Pierre, SD 57501

State Chamber of Commerce
Industry & Commerce Association of South Dakota
300 S. Highland
P.O. Box 548
Pierre, SD 57501

International Commerce
Governor's Office of Economic Development
P.O. Box 6000
Pierre, SD 57501

Banking
Department of Commerce and Regulation
Division of Banking
105 S. Euclid
Pierre, SD 57501

Securities
Department of Commerce and Regulation
Division of Securities
910 E. Sioux
Pierre, SD 57501

Labor and Industrial Relations
Department of Labor
Division of Labor and Management
Kneip Building
Pierre, SD 57501

Insurance
Department of Commerce and Regulation
Division of Insurance
910 E. Sioux
Pierre, SD 57501

INDUSTRIAL AND BUSINESS DIRECTORIES

Directory of South Dakota Industries, Manufacturers' News, Inc., 4 E. Huron Street, Chicago, IL 60611

South Dakota Manufacturers and Processors Directory, Governor's Office of Economic Development, 711 Well Avenue, Capitol Lake Plaza, Pierre, SD 57501; State Industrial Directories Corp., 2 Penn Plaza, New York, NY 10001

South Dakota Export Directory, Governor's Office of Economic Development, 711 Well Avenue, Capitol Lake Plaza, Pierre, SD 57501

Tennessee

State Capitol, Nashville, TN 37219
(615) 741–2001

INFORMATION OFFICES

Commerce/Economic Development
Department of Economic and Community Development
Rachel Jackson Building
320 6th Avenue North
Nashville, TN 37219

Corporate
Secretary of State
Records Division
James K. Polk Building
Nashville, TN 37219

Taxation
Department of Revenue
927 Andrew Jackson Building
500 Deaderick Street
Nashville, TN 37242

State Chamber of Commerce
State Chamber Division of the Tennessee Taxpayers Association
242 Doctors Building
Nashville, TN 37203

International Commerce
Department of Economic & Community Development
International Sales & Marketing
Rachel Jackson Building
320 6th Avenue North
Nashville, TN 37219

Banking
Department of Financial Institutions
James K. Polk State Office Building
505 Deaderick Street
Nashville, TN 37219

Securities
Department of Commerce & Insurance
Securities Division
614 Tennessee Building
Nashville, TN 37219

Labor and Industrial Relations
Department of Labor
501 Union Building
Nashville, TN 37219

Insurance
Department of Commerce & Insurance
Insurance Division
State Office Building
Nashville, TN 37219

Business Ombudsman
Department of Economic & Community Development
Business & Industry Services Division
Rachel Jackson Building
320 6th Avenue North
Nashville, TN 37219–5308

INDUSTRIAL AND BUSINESS DIRECTORIES

Directory of Tennessee Industries, Manufacturers' News, Inc., 4 E. Huron Street, Chicago, IL 60611; State Industrial Directories Corp., 2 Penn Plaza, New York, NY 10001

Texas

State Capitol, Austin, TX 78701
State Information: (512) 463–4630

INFORMATION OFFICES

Commerce/Economic Development
Texas Economic Development Commission
410 East 5th Street
Austin, TX 78711
Corporate
Secretary of State
P.O. Box 13601
Sam Houston Building
Austin, TX 78711
Taxation
Comptroller of Public Accounts
104 LBJ State Office Building
Austin, TX 78774
State Chamber of Commerce
Texas State Chamber of Commerce
206 W. 13th Street
Austin, TX 78752

Tourism Department
P.O. Box 12008
Austin, TX 78711

Lower Rio Grand Valley Chamber of Commerce
P.O. Box 1499
Weslaco, TX 78596

South Texas Chamber of Commerce
300 W. 15th Street
Austin, TX 78101

East Texas Chamber of Commerce
P.O. Box 1592
Longview, TX 75606

West Texas Chamber of Commerce
P.O. Box 1561
Abilene, TX 79604
International Commerce
International Division
Texas Economic Development Commission
P.O. Box 12728, Capitol Station
Austin, TX 78711
Banking
Texas Department of Banking
2601 North Lamar
Austin, TX 78705
Securities
Securities Board
P.O. Box 367, Capitol Station
1800 San Jacinto St.
Austin, TX 78711–3169
Labor and Industrial Relations
Texas Department of Labor and Standards
P.O. Box 12157, Capitol Station
Austin, TX 78711
Insurance
Texas State Board of Insurance
State Insurance Building
1110 San Jacinto
Austin, TX 78701–1998
Uniform Industrial Code
Uniform Commercial Code Section
Secretary of State's Office
P.O. Box 12887, Capitol Station
Austin, TX 78711
Business Ombudsman
Texas Economic Department Commission
410 E. 5th Street
P.O. Box 12728
Austin, TX 78711

INDUSTRIAL AND BUSINESS DIRECTORIES

Dallas Business Guide, Dallas Chamber of Commerce, Fidelity Tower, Dallas, TX 75201

Directory of Texas Manufacturers, Bureau of Business Research, University of Texas, Austin, TX 78712; State Industrial Directories Corp., 2 Penn Plaza, New York, NY 10001

Fort Worth Directory of Manufacturers, Fort Worth Area Chamber of Commerce, 700 Throckmorton Street, Fort Worth, TX 76102

Texas Exporter-Importer Directory, Gulf International Trades, Box 52717, Houston, TX 77052

Texas Manufacturers Directory, Manufacturers' News, Inc., 4 E. Huron Street, Chicago, IL 60611

Utah

State Capitol, Salt Lake City, UT 84114
(801) 533–4000

INFORMATION OFFICES

Commerce/Economic Development
Department of Business Regulation
160 East 300 South Street
Salt Lake City, UT 84111-5802

Department of Community and Economic Development
6290 State Office Building
Salt Lake City, UT 84114

Office of Planning & Budget
Data Resources Section
116 Capitol Building
Salt Lake City, UT 84114
Corporate
Division of Corporations
Heber M. Wells Building
160 E. 300 South
Salt Lake City, UT 84111–5802
Taxation
Department of State Tax Commission
Heber M. Wells Building

160 E. 300 South
Salt Lake City, UT 84134–4000

International Commerce
International Business Development
Division of Economic & Business Development
6150 State Office Building
Salt Lake City, UT 84114

Banking
Department of Financial Institutions
Heber M. Wells Building
160 E. 300 South
P.O. Box 89
Salt Lake City, UT 84110-5802

Securities
Division of Securities
Heber M. Wells Building
160 E. 300 South
P.O. Box 89
Salt Lake City, UT 84110–5802

Labor and Industrial Relations
Industrial Commission of Utah
Heber M. Wells Building
160 E. 300 South
Salt Lake City, UT 84110-5800

Insurance
Department of Insurance
Heber M. Wells Building
160 E. 300 South
Salt Lake City, UT 84110-5803

Uniform Industrial Code
Employment Security/Job Service
174 Social Hall Avenue
Salt Lake City, UT 84147

INDUSTRIAL AND BUSINESS DIRECTORIES

Directory of Utah Manufacturers, Manufacturers' News, Inc., 4 E. Huron Street, Chicago, IL 60611; Department of Employment Security, 1234 S. Main Street, Salt Lake City, UT 84147

Vermont

State House, Montpelier, VT 05602
(802) 828–2228

INFORMATION OFFICES

Commerce/Economic Development
Agency of Development and Community Affairs
Department of Economic Development
109 State Street
Montpelier, VT 05602

Corporate
Secretary of State
Corporation Department
26 Terrace Street
Montpelier, VT 05602

Taxation
Department of Taxes
Agency of Administration
109 State Street
Montpelier, VT 05602

State Chamber of Commerce
Vermont State Chamber of Commerce
P.O. Box 37
Montpelier, VT 05602

Insurance
Department of Banking and Insurance
120 State Street
Montpelier, VT 05602

Banking
Department of Banking and Insurance
120 State Street
Montpelier, VT 05602

Securities
Department of Banking and Insurance
120 State Street
Montpelier, VT 05602

Labor and Industrial Relations
Department of Labor and Industry
120 State Street
Montpelier, VT 05602

Uniform Commercial Code
Department of Banking and Insurance
120 State Street
Montpelier, VT 05602

Business Ombudsman
Agency Development and Community Affair
Department of Economic Development
109 State Stree
Montpelier, VT 05602

INDUSTRIAL AND BUSINESS DIRECTORIES

Vermont Directory of Manufacturers, Vermont Agency of Development and Community Affairs, Montpelier, VT 05602

Vermont State Industrial Directory, Manufacturers' News, Inc., 4 E. Huron Street, Chicago, IL 60611; State Industrial Directories Corp., 2 Penn Plaza, New York, NY 10001

Vermont Yearbook, The National Survey, Chester, VT 05143

Virginia

State Capitol, Richmond, VA 23219
(804) 786–0000

INFORMATION OFFICES

Commerce/Economic Development
Department of Economic Development
1000 Washington Building
Richmond, VA 23219

Department of Conservation and Historic Resources
1100 Washington Building
Richmond, VA 23219

Corporate
State Corporation Commission
1220 Bank Street
Richmond, VA 23209

Taxation
Department of Taxation
2200 W. Broad Street
P.O. Box 6-L
Richmond, VA 23282

State Chamber of Commerce
Virginia State Chamber of Commerce
611 E. Franklin Street
Richmond, VA 23219

International Commerce
Department of Economic Development
1000 Washington Building
Richmond, VA 23219

Banking
State Corporation Commission
Bureau of Financial Institutions
701 E. Byrd Street
P.O. Box 2AE
Richmond, VA 23205

Securities
State Corporation Commission
Division of Securities and Retail Franchising
11 S. 12th Street
Richmond, VA 23219

Labor and Industrial Relations
Department of Labor and Industry
205 N. 4th Street
P.O. Box 12064
Richmond, VA 23241

Insurance
State Corporation Commission
Bureau of Insurance
1220 Bank Street
Richmond, VA 23209

Uniform Industrial Code
Virginia Employment Commission
Research and Analysis Division
703 E. Main Street
Richmond, VA 23211

Business Ombudsman
Department of Agriculture and Consumer Services
Office of Consumer Affairs
1100 Bank Street
Richmond, VA 23219

INDUSTRIAL AND BUSINESS DIRECTORIES

Industrial Directory of Virginia, Chamber of Commerce, 611 E. Franklin Street, Richmond, VA 23219

Virginia Industrial Directory, Manufacturers' News, Inc., 4 E. Huron Street, Chicago, IL 60611; State Industrial Directories Corp., 2 Penn Plaza, New York, NY 10001

Washington

101 General Administration Building,
Olympia, WA 98504
(206) 753–5630

INFORMATION OFFICES

Commerce/Economic Development
Department of Trade and Economic Development
101 General Administration Building
Olympia, WA 98504

Corporate
Secretary of State
Corporate Division
Legislative Building
Olympia, WA 98504

Taxation
Department of Revenue
412 General Administration Building
Olympia, WA 98504

State Chamber of Commerce
Association of Washington Business
1414 S. Cherry Street
Olympia, WA 98501

Small Business Development Centers
441 Todd Hall
Washington State University
Pullman, WA 99164–4740

180 Nickerson
Seattle, WA 98109

1000 Plum SE
Olympia, WA 98504

303 E. D Street
Yakima, WA 98901

Freeway Plaza Building
Spokane, WA 99204

Western Washington University
Park Hall
Bellingham, WA 98225

International Commerce
Department of Trade & Economic Development
Domestic & International Trade Dursion
312 First Avenue North
Seattle, WA 98109

Banking
General Administration Building
Banking & Consumer Finance
218 General Administration Building
Olympia, WA 98504

Securities
Department of Licensing Building
Att: Securities Division
1300 Quince Street SE
Olympia, WA 98504

Labor and Industrial Relations
Department of Labor & Industries
Employment Standards—Apprenticeship
Crime Victims Division
925 Plum Street SE
Olympia, WA 98504

Insurance
Insurance Commissioner's Office
Insurance Building
Olympia, WA 98504

Uniform Commercial Code
Department of Licensing
Business License Centre
405 Black Lake Place
Olympia, WA 98502

Business Ombudsman
Department of Trade & Economic Development
Office of Small Business
101 General Administration Building
Olympia, WA 98504

INDUSTRIAL AND BUSINESS DIRECTORIES

1986 Directory of Advanced Technology Industries in Washington State, Economic Development Partnership for Washington State, 18000 Pacific Highway South, Seattle, WA 98188

Business Assistance in Washington State, Washington State International Trade Directory, Department of Trade and Economic Development, 101 General Administration Building, Olympia, WA 98504

Minority Women Business Enterprises, Office of Minority Women Business Enterprises, 406 S. Water Street, Olympia, WA 98504

Washington Manufacturers Register, Times Mirror Press, 1115 S. Boyle, Los Angeles, CA 90023

MacRae's Washington State Industrial Directory, 87 Terminal Drive, Plainview, NY 11803

Washington Forest Industry Mill Directory, Department of Natural Resources, 1065 S. Capitol Way, Olympia, WA 98504

Directory of Washington Mining Operations, Department of Natural Resources, Olympia, WA 98504

West Virginia

State Capitol, Charleston, WV 25305
(304) 348–3456

INFORMATION OFFICES

Commerce/Economic Development
Governor's Office of Community and Industrial Development
1900 Washington Street East
Building I
Charleston, WV 25305

Corporate
Secretary of State
Corporate Division
1900 Washington Street East
Building 1
Charleston, WV 25305

Taxation
Tax Department
1900 Washington Street East
Building 1
Charleston, WV 25305

State Chamber of Commerce
P.O. Box 2789
1101 Kanawha Valley Building
Charleston, WV 25330

International Commerce
Governor's Office of Community and Industrial Development
1900 Washington Street East
Building 6
Charleston, WV 25305

Banking
Department of Banking
1900 Washington Street East
Building 5
Charleston, WV 25305

Securities
Auditor's Office
1900 Washington Street East
Building 1
Charleston, WV 25305

Labor & Industrial Relations
Governor's Office of Community and Industrial Development
1900 Washington Street East
Building 6
Charleston, WV 25305

Insurance
Insurance Department
2100 Washington Street East
Charleston, WV 25305

Uniform Industrial Code
Governor's Office of the Secretary of State
1900 Washington Street East
Building 1
Charleston, WV 25305

Business Ombudsman
Governor's Office of Community and Industrial Development East
Building 6
Charleston, WV 25305

INDUSTRIAL AND BUSINESS DIRECTORIES

West Virginia Manufacturing Directory, Harris Publishing Company, Inc., 2057–2 Aurora Road, Twinsburg, OH 44087; State Industrial Directories Corp., 2 Penn Plaza, New York, NY 10001

Wisconsin

State Capitol, Madison, WI 53702
(608) 266–2211

INFORMATION OFFICES

Commerce/Economic Development
Department of Trade Development
123 W. Washington Avenue
Madison, WI 53702
Corporate
Secretary of State
Corporate Division
201 E. Washington Avenue
Madison, WI 53707
Taxation
Department of Revenue
125 S. Webster Avenue
P.O. Box 5933
Madison, WI 53708
State Chamber of Commerce
Wisconsin Association of Manufacturers and Commerce
111 E. Wisconsin Avenue
Milwaukee, WI 53202
International Commerce
International Business Services
Department of Development
123 W. Washington Avenue
Madison, WI 53702
Banking
Banking, Office of the Commissioner
123 West Washington Avenue
P.O. Box 7876
Madison, WI 53707
Securities
Securities—Office of the Commissioner
111 West Wilson Avenue
Madison, WI 53703
Labor and Industrial Relations
Department of Industry, Labor, and Human Relations
201 E. Washington Avenue
P.O. Box 7946
Madison, WI 53707
Insurance
Office of the Commissioner of Insurance
123 West Washington Avenue
Madison, WI 53702
Uniform Industrial Code
Department of Industry, Labor and Human Relations
201 E. Washington Avenue
Madison, WI 53702
Business Ombudsman
Small Business Ombudsman
Department of Development
123 W. Washington Avenue
Madison, WI 53702

INDUSTRIAL AND BUSINESS DIRECTORIES

Classified Directory of Wisconsin Manufacturers, Wisconsin Association of Manufacturers and Commerce, 111 E. Wisconsin Avenue, Milwaukee, WI 53202; State Industrial Directories Corp., 2 Penn Plaza, New York, NY 10001
Wisconsin Manufacturers Directory, Manufacturers' News, Inc., 4 E. Huron Street, Chicago, IL 60611
Wisconsin Local Development Organizations (annual), Wisconsin Department of Development, 123 W. Washington Avenue, Madison, WI 53702

Wyoming

State Capitol, Cheyenne, WY 82002
(307) 777–7011

INFORMATION OFFICES

Commerce/Economic Development
Economic Development and Stabilization Board
Herschler Building
Cheyenne, WY 82002
Wyoming Small Business Development Center
130 N. Ash
Casper, WY 82601
Corporate
Secretary of State
Corporate Division
State Capitol
Cheyenne, WY 82002
Taxation
Department of Revenue and Taxation
Herschler Building
Cheyenne, WY 82002
International Commerce
International Trade Office
State Planning Coordinator
Herschler Building
Cheyenne, WY 82002
Banking
State Examiner
Herschler Building
Cheyenne, WY 82002
Securities
Secretary of State
Securities Division
State Capitol
Cheyenne, WY 82002
Labor and Industrial Relations
Department of Labor and Statistics
Herschler Building
Cheyenne, WY 82002
Insurance
Insurance Commission

Herschler Building
Cheyenne, WY 82002

Uniform Industrial Code

Industrial Siting Administration
Barrett Building
2301 Central
Cheyenne, WY 82002

Industrial Development Division
Economic Planning Development and Stabilization Board
Herschler Building
Cheyenne, WY 82002

INDUSTRIAL AND BUSINESS DIRECTORIES

Wyoming Directory of Manufacturing and Mining, Manufacturers' News, Inc., 4 E. Huron Street, Chicago, IL 60611; Economic Development and Stabilization Board, Herschler Building, Cheyenne, WY 82002; State Industrial Directories Corp. 2 Penn Plaza, New York, NY 10001

Puerto Rico

CAPITOL, SAN JUAN, PR 00901
(809) 724–6040 (House of Representatives)
(809) 724-2030 (Senate)

INFORMATION OFFICES

Commerce/Economic Development

Puerto Rico Department of Commerce
P.O. Box S 4275
San Juan, PR 00905

Puerto Rico Economic Development Administration
G.P.O. Box 2350
San Juan, PR 00936

Puerto Rico Planning Board
P.O. Box 41119
San Juan, PR 00940

Government Development Bank
P.O. Box 42001
Minillas Station
Santurce, PR 00940

Economic Development Bank
P.O. Box 5009
Hato Rey, PR 00929–5009

Taxation

Puerto Rico Department of Treasury
P.O. Box S-4515
San Juan, PR 00901

Office of Industrial Tax Exemption
P.O. Box 2121
Hato Rey, PR 00918–2121

Chamber of Commerce

Chamber of Commerce of Puerto Rico
P.O. Box 3789
San Juan, PR 00904

Puerto Rico Manufacturers Association

P.O. Box 2410
Hato Rey, PR 00919

Securities

Office of the Commissioner of Financial Institutions
P.O. Box 4515
San Juan, PR 00905

Labor and Industrial Relations

Puerto Rico Labor Relations Board
P.O. Box 4048
San Juan, PR 00905
National Labor Relations Board
Federal Building
Charlos E. Chardon Street
Hato Rey, PR 00918

Insurance

Office of the Insurance Commissioner
P.O. Box 8330, Fdez Juncos Station
Santurce, PR 00910

Puerto Rico Insurance Companies Association, Inc.
Housing Investment Building
San Juan, PR 00918

Uniform Industrial Code

Department of Labor and Human Resources
505 Muñoz Rivera Avenue
Prudencio Rivera Martínez Building
Hato Rey, PR 00918

Business Ombudsman

Ombudsman Office
1205 Ponce de León Avenue
Banco de San Juan
Santurce, PR 00907–3995

International Commerce

Puerto Rico Department of Commerce
External Trade Promotion Program
P.O. Box S 4275
San Juan, PR 00905

US Department of Commerce
International Trade Administration
Charlos E. Chardon Street
Federal Building
Hato Rey, PR 00918

Puerto Rico Chamber of Commerce
International Trade Division
P.O. Box 3789
San Juan, PR 00904

Banking

Puerto Rico Bankers Association
Banco Popular Center
Hato Rey, PR 00918

INDUSTRIAL AND BUSINESS DIRECTORIES

Puerto Rico Official Industrial and Trade Directory, Witcom Group, Inc., P.O. Box 2310, San Juan, PR 00902

The Businessman's Guide to Puerto Rico, Puerto Rico Almanacs, Inc., P.O. Box 9582, Santurce, Puerto Rico 00908

International Information Sources

Foreign Trade Information

Business people seeking information about foreign commercial opportunities or sources of business contacts have available a number of government and private services that are described in this and subsequent sections. The extensive nature of these services is not always fully appreciated by members of the business community. Some of the most helpful services are provided by the International Trade Administration (ITA) 202–377–3808 of the Department of Commerce, described below. This agency is particularly helpful in establishing initial contacts and in evaluating foreign markets.

Foreign credit information sources are provided at the end of this section.

DEPARTMENT OF COMMERCE

Address: Constitution and 14th Street NW, Washington, DC 20230. Information phone: 202–377–2000.

The central export information source within the Department of Commerce is the **International Trade Administration** (ITA), which promotes the growth of U.S. industry and commerce, both foreign and domestic. The four units with functions relevant to exporters are:

- U.S. and Foreign Commercial Service (US&FCS)—the framework within which ITA gathers accurate and timely commercial information, distributes it through a worldwide network of trade specialists, and provides in-depth counseling, assistance, and support to the business community (below).
- International Economic Policy (IEP)—the office organized on a country and regional basis which gives market-specific counsel to American business (page 662).
- Trade Development (TD)—the industry unit responsible for formulating trade policy and promotion activities (page 662).
- Trade Administration (TA)—the office responsible for safeguarding the national interest through effective administration of U.S. trade laws (page 663).

Sources: Excerpted from *Business America, A Basic Guide to Exporting*, and other U.S. Department of Commerce sources.

U.S. and Foreign Commercial Service (US&FCS)

The U.S. and Foreign Commercial Service (US&FCS), the only federal agency with a global network of international trade professionals, is charged with the nuts-and-bolts work of improving the ability of U.S. business to compete overseas. US&FCS collects marketing information at overseas posts and makes it available to U.S. companies at district offices and branch offices.

The US&FCS emphasizes practical advice and information help U.S. exporters in very specific ways. A company can find out which countries have the best market potential for its products and can then find out who to contact overseas.

Through the US&FCS, U.S. firms have direct access to more than 95 percent of the global marketplace for goods and services. Such access can be a big advantage for American firms, particularly small- and medium-sized businesses that lack export departments and overseas representation.

District office trade specialists, drawing from a large commercial data base fed by overseas commercial officers, provide individualized marketing packages for U.S. companies on their specific products and services and offer one-on-one export counseling. Beginners and experienced exporters both are eligible.

The district offices arrange export seminars, conferences, and workshops. To multiply the effects of their efforts, they coordinate activities with state and local governments, trade associations, world trade clubs, banks, local chambers of commerce, small business development centers, and colleges and universities. More than 900 of these organizations are termed "associate offices"; they distribute information to areas where no US&FCS district offices are located. The district offices give U.S. companies direct contact with seasoned exporters through District Export Councils (DECs) comprised of experienced business people.

Commercial officers attached to U.S. embassies and consulates search for sales leads, qualified agents, and distributors; make appointments with key buyers and government officials; and counsel firms frustrated by trade barriers.

The US&FCS's new Commercial Information Management System (CIMS) makes it possible to transmit information electronically from overseas posts to the district offices. Thus, U.S. exporters have quick and easy access to information on:

Market statistics dealing with exports, imports, consumption, production or infrastructure;

Tariff and non-tariff trade barriers, import regulations, policies, and product standards;

Domestic and foreign competition, individual competitor firms and competitive factors;

Distribution practices;

End users; and

How to promote products in the market.

The US&FCS has several programs geared toward helping companies make contact with potential agents, distributors, buyers, or joint-venture partners, including:

Agent Distributor Service—This customized search for interested and qualified foreign representatives will identify up to six foreign prospects who have examined a company's product literature and have expressed interest in representing its product.

Commercial News USA—This monthly magazine will promote a company's product or service to more than 90,000 overseas agents, distributors, government officials, and end-users. A black-and-white photo and brief description will highlight a product or service and give a firm an opportunity to search for its best markets worldwide or to focus on a particular region.

In *Commerce Business Daily,* US&FCS publicizes proposed foreign government procurement actions and foreign trade leads, as well as information on U.S. Government procurement actions. For a sample, write US&FCS, U.S. Department of Commerce, Washington, D.C. 20230. To subscribe, call the Superintendent of Documents, U.S. Government Printing Office, Washington, D.C. 20402, on 202-783-3238.

Comparison Shopping—This custom-tailored service can provide a firm with key marketing and foreign representation information about its specific product. US&FCS staff conduct on-the-spot interviews in certain overseas countries to determine nine key marketing facts about the product, including sales potential in the market, comparable products, distribution channels, price, competitive factors, and qualified buyers.

Foreign Buyer Program—Without the expense of traveling overseas, an exporter can meet qualified foreign buyers for his product or service at selected trade shows in the United States. The US&FCS promotes these shows worldwide to attract foreign buyer delegations, manages an International Business Center, counsels U.S. firms, and brings together buyer and seller.

Trade Opportunities Program—This program can provide a firm with current sales leads from overseas firms seeking to buy or represent its product or service. These leads are available electronically or printed. Trade opportunity information is available in two forms:

1. *TOP Notice* daily searches the TOP computer and automatically sends only the leads for those products and services for which the subscriber is registered.

2. *TOP Bulletin* is a weekly publication of all the leads received the previous week for all products from all countries.

Export Mailing List Services (EMLs) are mailing lists of prospective overseas customers from the Commerce Department's automated worldwide file of foreign firms. EMLs identify manufacturers, agents, retailers, service firms, government agencies, and other one-to-one contacts. EMLs information is available in three forms:

1. *Export Mailing Lists* are on-line, custom retrievals based on the market criteria specified by the exporter.

2. *Trade Lists* provide listings for all the companies in the computer for a single country across all product sectors, or all the companies in a single industry across all countries.

3. Access to the Commerce Department's worldwide file of foreign firms is also available at a local Commerce Department District Office, or from the private sector DIALOG database.

World Traders Data Report—The US&FCS prepares these custom reports to assist a company in evaluating its potential trading partners. The service includes background information, standing in the local business community, creditworthiness, and overall reliability.

Trade events constitute another major type of US&FCS export assistance. A company can do as little as sending a product catalog overseas or as much as fully participating in trade missions or major international exhibitions. US&FCS programs include:

Catalog and Video-Catalog Shows—A firm can gain market exposure for its product or service without the cost of traveling overseas by participating in a catalog or video-catalog show. The firm provides its product literature or promotional video, and the US&FCS will send an industry expert to display this material to select foreign audiences in several countries.

Trade Missions—Participating in a trade mission will give an exporter an opportunity to confer directly, on-the-spot, with targeted foreign business and government representatives. US&FCS staff provides complete logistical and promotional support to the missions. They will identify and arrange a full schedule of appointments for an exporter in each country that he visits.

Trade Fairs—Trade fairs are one of the most popular ways of promoting goods and services overseas because they not only give the seller an opportunity to meet customers face-to-face but also to assess the competition. US&FCS supports U.S. participation in international trade fairs, making it easier for U.S. firms to exhibit and gain international recognition. US&FCS selects certain international trade fairs for special endorsement, called certification. As a result of this cooperation with private show organizers, U.S. exhibitors receive special services designed to enhance their market promotion efforts.

The best way for a U.S. exporter to make use of these services is to visit the closest US&FCS district office.

Useful US&FCS Telephone Numbers:

Headquarters	(202) 377–5777
Caribbean Basin Business Information Center	377–2527
Domestic Operations	377–4767
Export Counseling	377–3181
Export Promotion Services:	
Foreign Market Analysis and Contact Programs	377–1468
Trade Event Programs	377–4231
Foreign Operations	377–1599
Public Affairs	377–3808

International Economic Policy (IEP)

International Economic Policy (IEP) identifies and analyzes foreign commercial barriers and opportunities, offers a range of counseling services to U.S. businesses, and participates in bilateral and multilateral consultations and negotiations.

IEP is organized by region and country; it has four regional groups: Africa, the Near East, and South Asia; East Asia and the Pacific; Europe; and the Western Hemisphere. IEP's Office of Policy Coordination complements the individual efforts of the regional units by coordinating projects and initiatives affecting countries in more than one region.

The regional groups are staffed by country specialists who counsel U.S. businesses on foreign market conditions, business practices, and government regulations; develop specific information on promising commercial opportunities; identify foreign trade and investment barriers and devise strategies to remove them; and support the efforts of senior U.S. government policymakers to improve U.S. commercial opportunities worldwide. The unit's country specialists publish periodic reports on foreign market conditions and requirements *(Overseas Business Reports* and *Foreign Economic Trends)* and numerous special studies.

Overseas Business Reports (OBR) include current and detailed marketing information, trade outlooks, statistics, regulations, and market profiles. They are available from the Superintendent of Documents, U.S. Government Printing Office, Washington, DC 20402.

Foreign Economic Trends (FET) present current business and economic developments and the latest economic indicators in more than 100 countries. They are prepared on an annual or semiannual basis by the U.S. Foreign Service and U.S. Foreign Commerical Service. Available from the Superintendent of Documents, U.S. Government Printing Office, Washington, D.C. 20402.

Through its Office of Multilateral Affairs, IEP coordinates the Department's involvement in U.S. government efforts to strengthen the world trading system and improve U.S. commercial opportunities through multilateral agencies, such as the General Agreement on Tariffs and Trade (GATT).

The office also develops and coordinates departmental positions on several issue areas affecting multilateral trade policy. These include the U.S. Generalized System of Preferences (GSP) program and Section 301 of the Trade Act of 1974, which provides redress from unfair foreign trade practices.

IEP also works to ensure that foreign governments meet their obligations under existing multilateral agreements, such as the GATT non-tariff codes negotiated during the last major trade round.

Useful IEP Telephone Numbers

Headquarters	(202) 377–3022
GATT Division	377–3681
International Organizations	377–3227
U.S. Trade by Region	
Africa	377–2175
Canada	377–3643 or 0849
Caribbean Basin & Mexico	377–2527
Eastern Europe	377–2645
European Community	377–5276
Israel Information Center	377–4652
Japan	377–4527
Near East	377–4441
Pacific Basin	377–3875
Peoples Republic of China and Hong Kong	377–3583
South America	377–2436
South Asia	377–2954
U.S.S.R.	377–4655
Western Europe	377–5341

Trade Development

Trade Development's analysis, policy development, and export promotion capability is designed to enhance the efforts of businesses of all sizes to increase market share at home and abroad.

Of TD's nine operating units, seven specialize in specific industrial sectors—Science and Electronics, Capital Goods and International Construction, Automotive Affairs and Consumer Goods, Textiles and Apparel, Aerospace, Services, and Basic Industries. An eighth unit is Trade Information and Analysis, which addresses international debt and currency questions and other issues that affect all sectors and coordinates TD policy recommendations on issues that cut across industry sectors. The ninth unit is Trade Adjustment Assistance, which provides technical assistance to firms and industries injured by import competition.

TD industry sector analysts monitor significant developments affecting their industries, especially those relating to efforts by foreign competitors. The Trade Information and Analysis unit follows important trends that affect overall U.S. industry and identify cross-cutting issues that, while of primary concern to one sector, have potential for affecting others.

Each year, TD publishes two major publications. *The U.S. Trade Performance and Outlook* analyzes the factors that influence the U.S. trade balance. The *U.S. Industrial Outlook* contains analyses and forecasts of domestic and international trends for more than 350 U.S. manufacturing and service industries.

TD conducts a two-part analytical program. The first measures overall U.S. and foreign competitive performance, using indicators such as productivity and growth rates, and assesses the effectiveness of various measures of competitiveness. The second produces a series of published *Competitive Assessments,* which include in-depth analyses of individual industries and detailed discussions of their specific position in the international arena.

TRADE PROMOTION

TD helps U.S. businesses in specific export efforts. Analysts identify industries with high export potential and work with the U.S. and Foreign Commercial Service to assist exporters.

Each year, TD organizes dozens of seminars to introduce U.S. producers to export markets. TD recruits companies for trade missions, helps participants in meetings with prospective customers and foreign officials, and assists with trade shows.

TD also organizes "Foreign Buyer" groups to visit U.S. trade shows; administers the Export Trading Company Act program to help companies pool their export efforts, and offers technical assistance to import-injured companies under the Trade Adjustment Assistance program.

Even firms in those U.S. industries unaffected by increased foreign competition need to redouble their efforts to secure their market position. The Trade Development unit can give them some good pointers.

Useful TD Telephone Numbers

Headquarters	202–377–1461
Trade Reference Room (trade statistics)	377–4211
Science and Electronics	377–3548
Capital Goods and International Construction	377–5023
Automotive Affairs and Consumer Goods	377–0823
Textiles and Apparel	377–3737
Aerospace	377–8228
Services	377–5261
Basic Industries	377–0614
Trade Information and Analysis	377–1316
Trade Adjustment Assistance	377–0150

Trade Administration (TA)

The Trade Administration (TA) unit of ITA is speeding up the necessary process of national security export licensing and is seeking to make the control process a less intimidating experience for uninitiated exporters.

In 1985, the unit put the Export Control Automated Support System into operation. To meet exporter demand for information on the status of licenses, it put on line the System for Tracking Export License Applications (STELA), a new automated voice response system which is available to exporters 16 hours a day on weekdays and eight hours on Saturdays.

SEMINAR PROGRAMS

In its effort to make applying for an export license less intimidating, TA conducts seminars on export controls and licensing all over the nation as well as overseas.

Learning about export controls and licensing is a must for most U.S. businesses, particularly for high-technology firms most subject to national security controls. The TA seminars are aimed at providing the knowledge that exporters must have.

Licensing officers and export administration specialists from the Commerce Department teach the courses that are usually co-sponsored by District Export Councils and other not-for-profit trade organizations in conjunction with US&FCS district offices. For information call: 202–377–8731.

The basic program in the TA seminars focuses on export control fundamentals. Attendees learn about general, special, and individual validated licenses, the Commodity Control List, how to fill out the 622P Application for an export license, and what documentation is needed, depending on commodity and country destination. They receive hands-on instruction in the use of the regulations. In the advanced seminar, attendees receive more in-depth explanations and analyses of the regulations, requirements of supporting documentation, the interagency review process, and distribution license control requirements.

ADDITIONAL TA PROGRAMS AND SERVICES

To assist the exporter, the following programs are available:

Counseling for Exporters: Assistance for exporters is available from the Exporters Assistance Division at a walk-in Counseling Service in Room 10990 at the 14th Street and Pennsylvania Avenue entrance of the Department of Commerce.

Publication Program: For information on booklets/brochures for the business community call 202-377-8731. Recent publications include: *Export Licensing Information and Assistance* (telephone referral), *Introduction to the Export Administration Regulations, The Quick Reference Guide to the Export Administration Regulations,* and an updated copy of the *Denial Orders Currently Affecting Export Privileges.*

Computer Systems Parameters: To assist the exporter in completing the required forms for export of electronic computers and related equipment to Bloc Country Groups call 202-377-4145 for assistance.

Technical Advisory Committees (TACs): The TACs are a voluntary joint industry-government mechanism through which the concerns of various industries can be discussed. For information, call 202-377-2583.

Useful TA Telephone Numbers

Headquarters	(202) 377–1455
Export Administration	377–5491
Emergency Licensing Requests	377–2752 or 4811
License Status (STELA)	377–2752
Publications	377–8731
Seminars	377–8731
Trade Fair Licenses	377–4811
Regulations and Policy Information	377–4811
Export Enforcement	377–8252
Anti-Boycott Compliance	377–2381
Field Offices:	
California—Los Angeles	(818) 904–6019
California—San Jose	(408) 466–4204
New York—New York	(212) 264–3950
Virginia—Springfield	(703) 487–4950
Import Administration	(202) 377–1780

SELECTED INTERNATIONAL TRADE ADMINISTRATION PUBLICATIONS AND SERVICES

In addition to the previously mentioned publications there are others to help exporters reach and expand foreign markets. The foremost of these is *Business America,* which is Commerce Department's principal periodical for domestic and international business news and covers a wide range of topics. Subscriptions are available from the Superintendent of Documents, General Printing Office, Washington, DC 20402. Other publications include:

A Basic Guide to Exporting: This publication takes a step-by-step approach to exporting especially designed for firms with little or no export experience. Assessment of export potential is treated first, along with sources of export counseling and education. Other topics include: selecting markets, export strategies, pricing, financing, shipment, methods of payment, export documentation, and government regulations. A glossary of export terms and list of export-assistance groups is provided. Available from the Superintendent of Documents, General Printing Office, Washington, DC 20402.

A Summary of U.S. Export Administration Regulations, prepared by thc International Trade Administration, provides a brief introduction to export control licensing provisions contained in the Commerce Department's *Export Administration Regulations.*

Expand Overseas Sales With Commerce Department Help describes the various types of assistance available from the Commerce Department for small businesses seeking foreign markets. Available from International Trade Administration.

The U.S. Department of Commerce has discontinued publication of the *Export Promotion Calendar* due to budget cutbacks. However, the same information (e.g., listings of Commerce Department supported trade events in the U.S. and overseas, etc.) that was in the printed publication is now on-line at Department of Commerce District Offices around the country.

Other services available to exporters include the following.

Custom Statistical Service (CSS) is a tailored set of tables of U.S. export or import statistics. The custom service allows an exporter to obtain data for specific products or countries of interest, or for ones which may not appear in the standard ESP country and product rankings. Data can be supplied in other formats such as quantity, unit quantity, unit value and percentages.

New Product Information Service (NPIS)

This program provides worldwide publicity for new U.S. products available for immediate export. Promotional descriptions are published in *Commercial News USA* magazine. Information on selected NPIS products is also broadcast overseas by the U.S. Information Agency's "Voice of America" radio shows. For an application, contact a Trade Specialist at the nearest ITA District Office or write the Director, New Product Information Service, US&FCS, Room 2106, U.S. Department of Commerce, Washington, D.C. 20230.

Industry-Organized Government-Approved (IOGA) Trade Missions

Trade missions of this type are export-oriented events planned and organized by nonfederal government groups such as local and state governments, industry trade associations, and chambers of commerce. For information, contact: Export Promotion Services, US&FCS, U.S. Department of Commerce, Washington, D.C. 20230; telephone: 202-377-4231.

U.S. FOREIGN-TRADE ZONES (FTZs)

Firms involved in certain operations subject to significant customs duties should consider using Foreign Trade Zones (FTZs), which are now available in more than 100 port of entry communities throughout the United States. Among the advantages of using an FTZ are the following:

1. Foreign and domestic merchandise may be moved into an FTZ for storage, exhibition, assembly, manufacture, or other processing free of duties and quotas;
2. Duties are payable and quotas are applied if and when the merchandise enters the U.S. market;
3. Domestic goods entering the FTZ for export are considered exported when they enter the zone.

Information on FTZs is available from the Office of Service Industries, ITA, Department of Commerce, Washington, D.C. 20230; telephone: 202-377-3575.

DEPARTMENT OF AGRICULTURE

The U.S. Department of Agriculture's (USDA) export promotion efforts are centered in the Foreign Agricultural Service (FAS), but other USDA agencies also offer services to the U.S. exporter of agricultural products. For information on the promotion of U.S. farm products in foreign markets, services of commodity and marketing specialists in Washington, D.C., trade fair exhibits, publications and information services, and financing programs contact the Director of Export Programs Division, FAS, U.S. Department of Agriculture, Washington, D.C. Telephone: (202) 477-6343.

Department of Commerce International Trade Administration District Offices

District Office Assistance

†Alabama, Birmingham	(205) 254-1331
Alaska, Anchorage	(907) 271-5041
Arizona, Phoenix	(602) 261-3285
Arkansas, Little Rock	(501) 378-5794
California, Los Angeles	(213) 209-6707
˙California, Santa Ana	(714) 836-2461
˙California, San Diego	(619) 293-5395
†California, San Francisco	(415) 566-5860
†Colorado, Denver	(303) 844-3246
†Connecticut, Hartford	(203) 722-3530
Florida, Miami	(305) 350-5267
˙Florida, Clearwater	(813) 461-0011
˙Florida, Jacksonville	(904) 791-2796
˙Florida, Orlando	(305) 425-1247
˙Florida, Talahassee	(904) 488-6469
Georgia, Atlanta	(404) 881-7000
Georgia, Savannah	(912) 944-4204
Hawaii, Honolulu	(808) 546-8694
˙Idaho, Boise	(208) 334-2470
Illinois, Chicago	(312) 353-4550
˙Illinois, Palantine	(312) 397-3000 Ext. 532
˙Illinois, Rockford	(815) 987-8100
Indiana, Indianapolis	(317) 269-6214
Iowa, Des Moines	(515) 284-4222
˙Kansas, Wichita	(316) 269-6160
Kentucky, Louisville	(502) 582-5066
Louisiana, New Orleans	(504) 589-6546
˙Maine, Augusta	(207) 622-8249
Maryland, Balitmore	(301) 962-3560
˙Maryland, Rockville	(301) 251-2345
Massachusetts, Boston	(617) 223-2312
Michigan, Detroit	(313) 226-3650
˙Michigan, Grand Rapids	(616) 456-2411
Minnesota, Minneapolis	(612) 349-3338
Mississippi, Jackson	(601) 960-4388
†Missouri, Kansas City	(816) 374-3142
Missouri, St. Louis	(314) 425-3302
Nebraska, Omaha	(402) 221-3664
Nevada, Reno	(702) 784-5203
†New Jersey, Trenton	(609) 896-4222
New Mexico, Albuquerque	(505) 766-2386
New York, Buffalo	(716) 846-4191
New York, New York	(212) 264-0634
˙New York, Rochester	(716) 263-6480
†North Carolina, Greensboro	(919) 378-5345

†Ohio, Cincinnati	(513) 684-2944
Ohio, Cleveland	(216) 522-4750
Oklahoma, Oklahoma City	(405) 231-5302
*Oklahoma, Tulsa	(918) 581-7650
Oregon, Portland	(503) 221-3001
Pennsylvania, Philadelphia	(215) 597-2866
Pennsylvania, Pittsburgh	(412) 644-2850
Puerto Rico, San Juan	(809) 753-4555
*Rhode Island, Providence	(401) 528-5104 Ext. 22
South Carolina, Columbia	(803) 765-5345
*South Carolina, Charleston	(803) 724-4361
*South Carolina, Greenville	(803) 235-5919
*Tennessee, Memphis	(901) 521-4137
Tennessee, Nashville	(615) 251-5161
*Texas, Austin	(512) 472-5059
†Texas, Dallas	(214) 767-0542
Texas, Houston	(713) 229-2578
Utah, Salt Lake City	(801) 524-5116
Virginia, Richmond	(804) 771-4557
Washington, Seattle	(206) 442-5616
*Washington, Spokane	(509) 456-4557
West Virginia, Charleston	(304) 347-5123
Wisconsin, Milwaukee	(414) 291-3473

†Regional Offices
*Denotes Branch Office

Financing Exports*

Many sources of financial assistance are available to exporters. In addition to your own working capital or bank line of credit, the following are brief descriptions of some important sources of export financing assistance.

COMMERCIAL BANKS

A logical first step in choosing financing is to approach a local commercial bank for advice. If a company finds that its bank does not have an international department, then a good bank can be recommended by several sources:

- The US&FCS District Office.
- Eximbank or The Small Business Administration.
- The company's current bank.
- The company's freight forwarder.
- An experienced exporter referred by the local District Export Council or World Trade Club.

Most of these sources can also discuss financing needs and make helpful suggestions.

If a company is new to exporting or is a small or medium-sized business, it is important to select a bank that not only has an international department, but that also is sincerely interested in serving businesses of similar type or size. Of the many thousands of banks in the United States, several hundred have international departments, about half of which find it profitable to serve small- or medium-sized exporters.

When selecting a bank, the exporter should ask the following questions:

- How big is the bank's international department?
- Does it have foreign branches or correspondent banks? Where are they located?
- What are charges for confirming a letter of credit, processing drafts, and collecting payment?
- Can the bank provide buyer credit reports? Free or at what cost?
- Does it have experience with U.S. and State government financing programs that support small business export transactions? If not, is it willing to participate in these programs?
- What other services can it provide (trade leads, etc.)?

TYPES OF BANK FINANCING

The same type of commercial loans that finance domestic activities—including loans for working capital and revolving lines of credit—are available to finance export sales until payment is received. However, most banks do not usually extend credit solely on the basis of an order; thus these loans can tie up assets that must be used as collateral and can use up limited credit lines that may be needed for other transactions.

In many cases, Federal and State small business export finance programs can help reduce the need for collateral and extend the amount of credit available. There are also ways to avoid normal commercial loans altogether by requesting banker's acceptance financing.

If an export transaction is paid by using letters of credit or trade drafts, banker's acceptance financing can be used to provide immediate payment to the exporter. This follows even though the letter of credit or draft calls for payment from the buyer up to 180 days in the future.

When a letter of credit or draft is formally approved for payment (through endorsement by a bank or by the buyer), it is called an "acceptance." This document can either be kept by the exporter until the stated terms of credit have expired and then be presented for payment, or it can usually be sold immediately to a U.S. bank at a discount. In the

* Source: Excerpted from *A Basic Guide to Exporting*, U.S. Department of Commerce and other sources.

case of an irrevocable letter of credit, payment is guaranteed by a foreign bank, and the U.S. bank will not require collateral or other proof of ability to pay from the exporter. With a trade draft, such proof may be required since the bank must come to the exporter for repayment if the buyer defaults.

The advantages of banker's acceptance financing, especially when a letter of credit is used, are the following:

- The exporter receives immediate payment in contrast to commerical loans where the cost of goods is financed but profit is not realized until payment is received.
- Less of the exporter's capital and credit line is tied up in financing (none if a letter of credit is used).
- The total interest charges and fees are usually lower—thus costs are lower for both buyer and seller.

As with any type of export financing, it should be noted that finance charges for banker's acceptances may be passed through to the buyer as part of the terms of sale (made clear in the quotation and invoice as part of the price or an added charge). For more information on this type of financing, contact one of the sources of advice listed earlier in this chapter.

FEDERAL GOVERNMENT EXPORT FINANCING PROGRAMS

A bank with a good international department experienced with government export finance programs can often advise an exporter on the different programs available. Most of the programs described below—including State programs—are intended to work through a commercial bank. Banks that participate in these programs are the agents that apply on the exporter's behalf for program benefits. The exporter need not become an expert, yet knowing the existence of these financing opportunities can be quite valuable.

Even if a bank that is currently being used by an exporter has had no experience with government export financing programs, this bank may still be used if it is willing to follow program guidelines. If assistance is needed in locating a bank that uses any of these programs, contact the appropriate Federal or State agency. The descriptions below provide a basic overview. More information can be had from the government agency listed, from banks, and also from the Department of Commerce publication *A Guide to Financing Exports*, available from US&FCS District Offices. The Department of Commerce operates no financing programs but can help exporters choose among programs that exist: Contact a local US&FCS District Office or the Office of Trade Finance, International Trade Administration, in Washington, DC. Telephone: (202) 377-3277.

EXPORT-IMPORT BANK

Address: 811 Vermont Avenue NW, Washington, DC 20571. Phone: 202–566–8990. Public Affairs Phone: 202–566–8860

Small Business Advisory Hotline Service

800−424–5201

The Export-Import Bank (Eximbank) of the United States offers direct loans for large projects and equipment sales that usually require long-term financing; it guarantees loans made by cooperating U.S. and foreign commercial banks to U.S. exporters and to foreign buyers of U.S. products and services; and, through a private insurance association, the Foreign Credit Insurance Association (FCIA) (see page 668), it provides insurance to U.S. exporters enabling them to extend credit to their overseas buyers.

In all cases, Eximbank must find a "reasonable assurance of repayment" as a precondition of participating in the transaction. However, because the bank offers loan guarantees and credit insurance, a major effect of using Eximbank programs is to reduce the amount of collateral required to finance a loan and to generally make financing more available than would be the case without its support.

Among Eximbank's array of loan, guarantee, and insurance programs are four that are especially helpful to small companies and those that are new to exporting:

- Working Capital Guarantee Program.
- Export Credit Insurance.
- Commercial Bank Guarantees.
- Small Business Credit Program.

Details on these programs are available from Eximbank.

Eximbank and FCIA also provide other credit programs for medium and long-term financing. Long-term financing (5 years and longer) is generally for export of capital equipment and large-scale installations. This financing takes the form either of a direct credit to an overseas buyer or a financial guarantee assuring repayment of a private bank credit. Eximbank often blends these two forms of support into a single financing package. The chart on page 668 gives a brief guide to the use of different programs. In the chart, exports are divided into three categories, and for each category there are two or more program options.

EXIMBANK/FCIA
Program Selection Chart

Exports	Appropriate Programs
Short-Term (up to 180 days)	
Consumable	Export Credit Insurance
Small manufactured items	Working Capital Guarantee
Spare Parts	
Raw Materials	
Medium-Term (181 days to 5 years)	
Mining and refining equipment	Export Credit Insurance
Construction equipment	Commercial Bank Guarantees
Agricultural equipment	Small Business Credit Program
General aviation aircraft	Medium-Term Credit
Planning/feasibility studies	Working Capital Guarantee
Long-Term (5 years and longer)	
Power plants	Direct Loans
LPG & gas producing plants	Financial Guarantees
Other major projects	
Commercial jet aircraft or locomotives	
Other heavy capital goods	

For complete information on the above programs contact the Export-Import Bank at the phone numbers given above. Detailed information on Eximbank and FCIA programs and services is provided in the brochure *The Export-Import Bank: Financing for American Experts—Support for American Jobs.* For a free copy write: Office of Public Affairs, Export-Import Bank, Washington, D.C. 20571.

FOREIGN CREDIT INSURANCE ASSOCIATION (FCIA)

Address: 40 Rector Street, New York, NY 10006. Phone: 212–306–5000.

The export credit insurance offered by FCIA provides three basic incentives for American exporters when they do offer competitive terms to buyers. It enables them to (1) protect corporate assets as credit is extended; (2) maximize the rate of plant utilization as overseas competition is matched and orders won; and (3) improve corporate liquidity when insured foreign receivables are financed.

FCIA administers the U.S. export credit insurance program on behalf of its member insurance companies and the Export-Import Bank, an agency of the U.S. Government. The private insurers cover the normal commercial credit risks, primarily the insolvency of or protracted payment default by overseas buyers.

U.S. SMALL BUSINESS ADMINISTRATION [SBA]

Answer desk: 800–368–5855
Business publications: 202-653-6365

Through financial assistance programs, the SBA can promote small business participation in international trade by making funds available for export-oriented activities.

Funds may be used to purchase machinery, equipment, facilities, supplies, or materials needed to manufacture or sell products overseas, as well as for working capital. Working capital loans may be used to defray the costs of developing or penetrating foreign markets. Specifically, this can include costs for professional foreign marketing advice and services, foreign business travel, shipping sample merchandise abroad, shopping foreign markets, participating in overseas trade center shows and international fairs, foreign advertising and preparation of promotional materials, and other related purposes.

For information on the SBA financial assistance programs, policies and requirements, contact the nearest SBA field office (see page 268).

PRIVATE EXPORT FUNDING CORPORATION (PEFCO)

Address: 280 Park Avenue, New York, NY 10017. Telephone: 212–557–3100.

PEFCO, owned by 62 investors (mostly commercial banks), lends only to finance export of goods and services of U.S. manufacture and origin. PEFCO's loans generally have maturities in the medium-term area and all are unconditionally guaranteed by Eximbank as to payment of interest and repayment of principal. PEFCO's funds supplement the financing of U.S. exports available through commercial banks and Eximbank.

Before contacting PEFCO, the potential borrower (a foreign buyer) or the U.S. exporter should obtain an indication from Eximbank that its board will issue a Financial Guarantee for part of the required financing. Exporters or foreign buyers with no experience in using Eximbank or PEFCO funding should first approach an experienced commercial bank; the bank will then determine whether a PEFCO loan would be a reasonable supplement to the funds provided by other sources.

OVERSEAS PRIVATE INVESTMENT CORPORATION (OPIC)

Address: 1129 20th Street NW, Washington, DC. 20521. Information phone: 800–424–OPIC; in DC: 202–653–2800.

OPIC, established in 1971, is an independent agency of the U.S. government with the mission of reducing or eliminating private investment risks in the developing countries. OPIC insures U.S. investors against political risks of expropriation, inconvertability of local currency holdings, and damage from war, revolution, or insurrection. The agency offers lenders protection by guaranteeing payment of principal, interest, and loans.

The corporation offers investment information and counseling to business and participates in the cost of locating and developing projects.

DEPARTMENT OF AGRICULTURE

The Foreign Agricultural Service (FAS) of the U.S. Department of Agriculture provides financial support for U.S. agricultural exports through the Food for Peace program and the Commodity Credit Corporation. Under the Food for Peace program, Title I of the Agricultural Trade Development and Assistance Act of 1954 (Public Law 480, as amended) authorizes U.S. Government financing of sales of U.S. agricultural commodities to friendly countries on concessional credit terms. Sales are made by private business firms usually by bids. FAS administers agreements under this program.

Through the Commodity Credit Corporation (CCC), FAS provides U.S. exporters with short-term, commercial export financing support under two programs: The Export Credit Guarantee Program and the Blended Credit Program.

For additional information contact: General Sales Manager, Export Credits, Foreign Agricultural Service, 14th Street and Independence Ave., S.W., Washington, DC 20250. Telephone: (202) 447-3224.

STATE AND LOCAL EXPORT FINANCE PROGRAMS

As of January 1, 1985, 15 State governments have authority to operate export financing programs. Some of these programs allow a State development agency to act as a delivery agent for Eximbank programs. Other programs include State funded loan guarantee programs. Exporters should contact the State's economic development agency for more information (see page 629).

Export Trading Companies and Export Management Companies

Many export trading companies (ETC's) and export management companies (EMC's) can help finance export sales in addition to acting as export representatives. However, this is true mainly for larger companies. Large ETC's may of course be able to purchase goods for export on-the-spot and thus eliminate the need for financing and other risks. When this is not the case, trading companies in a few instances may provide short-term financing themselves, but more significantly, they are also offering established contacts to make it easier for their exporter clients to obtain credit and credit insurance. Moreover, several trading companies are large enough to arrange countertrade transactions, in which trading and financing would be inseparable.

EXPORT MANAGEMENT COMPANIES (EMCs)

Export management companies (EMCs) will not only act as your export representative but, in some cases, will carry the financing for your export sale, assuring you of immediate payment and removing from your firm any foreign credit risk. EMCs solicit and transact business in the name of the manufacturers they represent for a commission, salary, or retainer plus commission. Many EMCs will also carry the financing for export sales, ensuring immediate payment for the manufacturer's products.

An agreement with an EMC can be an especially advantageous arrangement for smaller firms that do not have the time, personnel, or money to develop foreign markets, but wish nonetheless to establish a corporate and product identity overseas. For a description of services rendered to exporters by EMCs (and suggestions for choosing an appropriate firm) request Commerce's pamphlet, *"The EMC—Your Export Department."* Commerce also publishes a *"U.S. Export Management Companies Directory"* listing the names, addresses, and industry specialties of more than 1,100 EMCs in the United States. A copy of the first publication may be requested from the Publications Sales

Branch, International Trade Administration, U.S. Department of Commerce, Washington, D.C. 20230. The "EMC Directory" can be purchased from: Superintendent of Documents, U.S. Government Printing Office, Washington, D.C. 20402.

The Foreign Trade Market Place, edited by George J. Schults, contains a listing of export management companies with sections on export opportunities, trade shows, financing, etc. Published by Gale Research, Book Tower, Detroit, MI 48226.

Exporters Directory, U.S. Buyers Guide, The Journal of Commerce, 445 Marshall Street, Phillipsburg, 08865. Lists export firms, including export managers, export merchants, manufacturers (as well as products exports) and trade association.

Export Trading Companies

The Office of Export Trading Company Affairs (OETCA) promotes the formation of export trading companies and is responsible for administering the antitrust preclearance program set up by the Export Trading Company Act of 1982.

OETCA is also responsible for the Contact Facilitation Service, a clearinghouse for matching U.S. suppliers of exportable goods and services with firms that provide trade facilitation services. To register for this service, contact the nearest Commerce Department District Office. The *Contact Facilitation Service Directory*, giving the names of registered firms and their products and services.

The *Export Trading Company Guidebook*, published by the Department of Commerce, explains the Export Trading Company Act and the Certificate of Review program and offers guidance in setting up and operating various types of export trading companies.

For further information contact OETCA at 202-377-5131.

Other Private Sources

FACTORING HOUSES

Certain companies, known as "factoring houses" or simply "factors" will purchase your export receivables (i.e., your invoices to foreign buyers) for a somewhat discounted price, perhaps 2 to 4 percent less than their face value. The actual amount of the discount will depend on the factoring house, the kind of product(s) involved, the customer, and the country. Factors offer two important advantages: (1) They enable you to receive immediate payment for your goods, freeing cash that could otherwise be tied up for months. (2) They relieve you of the burden of collection.

Arrangements with factoring houses are made either with or without "recourse." Arrangements "with recourse" leave you, the exporter, ultimately liable for repaying the factor if the foreign buyer defaults or other problems prevent payment within a reasonable period. Arrangements "without recourse" free you from this responsibility. Naturally, factors that accept export receivables "without recourse" generally require a large discount.

CONFIRMING

Designed to help exporters and importers expand their markets, improve cash flow, and create greater profit leverage, "confirming" is a financial service in which an independent company confirms an export order in the vendor's own country and makes payment for the goods in the currency of that country. This service can pay for and finance on terms the following items: The goods themselves, transportation (ocean or air), inland transportation at both ends, forwarding fees, customs brokerage fees, duties, etc. For the U.S. exporter, this means that the entire export transaction, from factory to end-user, can be fully coordinated and paid for with terms. Though common in Europe, confirming is still in its infancy in the United States. There are, however, U.S. firms that will provide such assistance. For further information, contact: Director, Office of Export Marketing Assistance, International Trade Administration, U.S. Department of Commerce, Washington, D.C. 20230.

Foreign Sales Corporation (FSC)*

A Foreign Sales Corporation (FSC) is a foreign chartered corporation through which exports can be made. A portion of the foreign income thus generated will be exempt from Federal taxation as of 1985.

In order to qualify as a FSC certain criteria must be met with respect to the management of the FSC and the exports made through it. Among the requirements are:

- The FSC must be incorporated and have its main office in a qualified foreign country or U.S. possession.
- The FSC must not have more than 25 shareholders.

* Source: International Trade Administration, U.S. Department of Commerce.

- A statement of election to be treated as a FSC must be filed with the Internal Revenue Service.
- A bank account must be maintained in a foreign bank and accounting records kept in a foreign office.

There are two exceptions for small exporters. (1) Small exporters may use the FSC without meeting some of the export activities test or (2) small exporters may maintain their DISC (Domestic International Sales Corporation) by paying an annual interest charge on the DISC deferred tax liability.

Further information can be obtained by calling 202–377–4471.

Export Assistance from State Governments

State development agencies, departments of commerce, and other departments within State governments often provide valuable assistance to exporters within the State. These groups may provide assistance in marketing, market development, and in arranging for trade shows and trade missions. The agencies in each state responsible for international trade and export assistance to local firms are given under each state in the State Information Guide section of the *Almanac*, page 629. Information is also obtainable from the National Association of State Development Agencies (NASDA), 444 N. Capitol Street, Washington, DC 20001. Telephone: 202–624–5411.

Private and Government Information Sources: International Commerce†

ASEAN-U.S. Business Council (U.S. Section)[1]
Phone: (202) 463–5486

Academy of International Business
World Trade Education Center
Cleveland State University
Cleveland, OH 44115
Phone: (216) 687–3733

Advisory Council on Japan-U.S. Economic Relations (U.S. Section)[1]
Phone: (202) 463–5489

Affiliated Advertising Agencies International
World Headquarters
1393 East Iliff Avenue
Aurora, CO 80014
Phone: (303) 750–1231

American Arbitration Association
140 West 51st Street
New York, NY 10020
Phone: (212) 484–4000

American Association of Exporters and Importers
30th Floor, 11 West 42nd Street
New York, NY 10036
Phone: (212) 944–2230

American Enterprise Institute for Public Policy Research
1150 17th Street, NW., Suite 1200
Washington, DC 20036
Phone: (202) 862–58001

American Importers Association
11 West 42nd Street
New York, NY 10036
Phone: (212) 944–2230

American Institute of Marine Underwriters
14 Wall Street, 21st Floor
New York, NY 10005
Phone: (212) 233–0550

American Management Association
440 1st Street, NW.
Washington, DC 20001
Phone: (202) 347–3092

American National Metric Council
1010 Vermont Avenue, NW.
Washington, DC 20005
Phone: (202) 628–5757

American Society of International Executives
1777 Walton, Suite 419
Blue Bell, PA 19422
Phone: (215) 643–3040

American Society of International Law
2223 Massachusetts Avenue, NW.
Washington, DC 20008
Phone: (202) 265–4313

Bankers Association for Foreign Trade
1101 16th Street, NW., Suite 501
Washington, DC 20036
Phone: (202) 833–3060

† Source: *Basic Guide to Exporting*, International Trade Administration, U.S. Department of Commerce.

[1] Address: Chamber of Commerce of the United States, International Division, 1615 H Street NW, Washington, DC 20062.

Brazil-U.S. Business Council (U.S. Section)[1]
Phone: (202) 463–5485

Brookings Institution (The)
1775 Massachusetts Avenue, NW.
Washington, DC 20036
Phone: (202) 797–6000

Bulgarian-U.S. Economic Council (U.S. Section)[1]
Phone: (202) 463–5482

Carribbean Central American Action
1333 New Hampshire Avenue, NW.
Washington, DC 20036
Phone: (202) 466–7464

Caribbean Council
2016 O Street, NW.
Washington, DC 20036
Phone: (202) 775–1136

Chamber of Commerce of the United States
1615 H Street, NW.
Washington, DC 20062
Phone: (202) 659–6000

Coalition for Employment Through Exports, Inc.
1801 K Street, NW.
Washington, DC 20006
Phone: (202) 296–6107

Committee for Economic Development
1700 K Street, NW
Washington, DC 20006
Phone: (202) 296–5860

Committee on Canada-United States Relations (U.S. Section)[1]
Phone: (202) 463–5488

Conference Board (The)
845 Third Avenue
New York, NY 10022
Phone: (212) 759–09001

Council of the Americas
680 Park Avenue
New York, NY 10021
Phone: (212) 628–3200

Council on Foreign Relations, Inc.
58 East 68th Street
New York, NY 10021
Phone: (212) 734–0400

Customs and International Trade Bar Association
% 40 Siegel Mandell and Davidson
1 Whitehall Street
New York, NY 10004
Phone: (212) 425–0060

Czechoslovak-U.S. Economic Council (U.S. Section)[1]
Phone: (202) 463–5482

Egypt-U.S. Business Council (U.S. Section)[1]
Phone: (202) 463–5487

Emergency Committee for American Trade
1211 Connecticut Avenue, Suite 801
Washington, DC 20036
Phone: (202) 659–5147

Foreign Credit Interchange Bureau—National Assoc. of Credit Managers
475 Park Avenue South
New York, NY 10016
Phone: (212) 578–4410

Foreign Policy Association
205 Lexington Avenue
New York, NY 10016
Phone: (212) 481–8450

Fund for Multi-National Management Education (FMME)
680 Park Avenue
New York, NY 10021
Phone: (212) 535–9386

Hungarian-U.S. Economic Council (U.S. Section)[1]
Phone: (202) 463–5482

Ibero American Chamber of Commerce
2100 M Street, NW., Suite 607
Washington, DC 20037
Phone: (202) 296–0335

India-U.S. Business Council (U.S. Section)[1]
Phone: (202) 463–5492

Institute for International Development
354 Maple Avenue West
Vienna, VA 22108
Phone: (703) 281–5040

International Advertising Association
475 Fifth Avenue
New York, NY 10077
Phone: (212) 684–1583

International Airforwarders and Agents Association
Box 627
Rockville Center, NY 11571
Phone: (516) 536–6229

International Bank for Reconstruction and Development
1818 H Street, NW.
Washington, DC 20006
Phone: (202) 477–1234

International Cargo Gear Bureau
17 Battery Place
New York, NY 10004
Phone: (212) 425–27501

International Economic Policy Association
1625 Eye Street, NW.
Washington, DC 20006
Phone: (202) 331–1974

International Executives Association, Inc.
114 East 32nd Street
New York, NY 10016
Phone: (212) 683–9755

International Finance Corporation
1818 H Street, NW.
Washington, DC 20433
Phone: (202) 477–1234

International Insurance Advisory Council (U.S. Section)[1]
Phone: (202) 463–5480

International Trade Council
750 13th Street, SE.
Washington, DC 20003
Phone: (202) 547–1727

Israel-U.S. Business Council (U.S. Section)[1]
Phone: (202) 463–5478

National Association of Export Management Companies, Inc.
200 Madison Ave.
New York, NY 10016
Phone: (212) 561–2025

National Association of Manufacturers
1776 F Street, NW.
Washington, DC 20006
Phone: (202) 626–3700

National Association of State Development Agencies
Hall of State, Suite 345
444 North Capitol, NW.
Washington, DC 20001
Phone: (202) 624–5411

National Committee on International Trade Documentation (The)
350 Broadway
New York, NY 10013
Phone: (212) 925–1400

National Council for U.S. China Trade (The)
1050 17th Street, NW.
Washington, DC 20036
Phone: (202) 429–0340

National Customs Brokers and Forwarders Association of America
One World Trade Center
New York, NY 10048
Phone: (212) 432–0050

National Export Traffic League
234 Fifth Avenue
New York, NY 10001
Phone: (212) 697–5895

National Foreign Trade Council
11 West 42nd Street
New York, NY 10036
Phone: (212) 944–2230

National Industrial Council
1776 F Street, NW.
Washington, DC 20006
Phone: (202) 626–3853

Nigeria-U.S. Economic Council (U.S. Section)[1]
Phone: (202) 463–5734

Organization of American States
19th & Constitution Avenue, NW.
Washington, DC 20006
Phone: (202) 789–3000

Overseas Development Council
1717 Massachusetts Avenue, NW
Suite 501
Washington, DC 20036
Phone: (202) 234–8701

Pan American Development Fund
1889 F Street, NW.
Washington, DC 20006
Phone: (202) 789–3969

Partners of the Americas
1424 K Street, NW.
Washington, DC 20005
Phone: (202) 628–3300

Partnership for Productivity International
2441 18th Street, NW.
Washington, DC 20009
Phone: (202) 234–0340

Polish-U.S. Economic Council (U.S. Section)[1]
Phone: (202) 463–5482

Private Export Funding Corporation
280 Park Avenue
New York, NY 10017
Phone: (202) 557–3100

Romanian-U.S. Economic Council (U.S. Section)[1]
Phone: (202) 463–5482

Sudan-U.S. Business Council (U.S. Section)[1]
Washington, D.C. 20062
Phone: (202) 463–5487

Trade Relations Council of the United States, Inc.
1001 Connecticut Avenue, NW.
Washington, DC 20036
Phone: (202) 785–4194

The U.S.-U.S.S.R. Trade and Economic Council
New York, NY 10022
Phone: (202) 644–4550

The U.S.-Yugoslav Economic Council, Inc.
1511 K Street, NW.
Washington, DC 20005
Phone: (202) 737–9652

The U.S.A.-Republic of China Economic Council
200 Main Street
Crystal Lake, IL 60014
Phone: (815) 459–5875

United States of America Business and Industry Advisory Committee
1212 Avenue of the Americas
New York, NY 10036
Phone: (212) 354–4480

Washington Agribusiness Promotion Council
14th & Independence Avenue
Auditors Building
Washington, DC 20250
Phone: (202) 382–8006

World Trade Institute
1 World Trade Center 55 West
New York, NY 10048
Phone: (212) 466–4044

DUN & BRADSTREET

Address: 99 Church Street, New York, NY. 10007 Phone: 212–312–6500.

Dun & Bradstreet provides a number of valuable services and publications in the area of international business, i.e., international credit reports on companies, international marketing guides and services, and directories of foreign firms. Dun & Bradstreet publishes the comprehensive annual, *Exporters Encyclopedia*, with monthly supplements. It details the rules and regulations in over 220 world markets and is arranged alphabetically by country and market area. *Principal International Businesses* is a useful marketing publication providing addresses, lines of business, sales figures, and other information on nearly 50,000 foreign firms.

INTERNATIONAL REPORTS

Address: 200 Park Avenue South, New York, NY 10003 Phone: 212–477–0003

International Reports publishes reports on sources of worldwide export credit insurance, foreign investment guarantees, and export financing under the title of *Insurance in International Finance*.

It also publishes the monthly *International Commercial Finance Service*, containing extensive information and data on financing and interest rates, surveys of credit ratings, and foreign payment records of individual countries.

BUSINESS INTERNATIONAL

Address: One Dag Hammarskjold Plaza, New York, NY 10017. Phone: 212–750–6300.

Business International publishes a series of weekly reports: *Business International* (a global view of business); *Business Europe; Business Latin America; Business Asia; Eastern Europe Report; Business China* (People's Republic); *Business International Money Report; Investing, Licensing, Trading Report;* and *Financing Foreign Operations.* It publishes a multivolume series, *Doing Business with Eastern Europe.*

COMMERCE CLEARING HOUSE

Address: 4025 West Peterson Avenue, Chicago, IL 60646. Phone 312–583–8500.

Commerce Clearing House publishes a number of widely used looseleaf series updated on a weekly or monthly basis. In the international field these include: *Euromarket News; Doing Business in Europe; Balance of Payment Reports; Common Market Reports;* and *Income Taxes World Wide.* It also publishes a number of detailed tax and legal guides for specific countries, i.e., Canada, Mexico, Australia, England, and Germany.

U.S. DEPARTMENT OF STATE

Address: New State Building, 2201 C Street, NW, Washington, DC 20520.

Information: 202–632–9884.

Publications

Background Notes of the Countries of the World gives profiles of foreign countries.

Key Officers of Foreign Service Posts lists the addresses and phone numbers of all American embassies and consulates and their key personnel.

Department of State Bulletin is a weekly publication devoted to the latest developments in international politics and trade agreements.

THE LIBRARY OF CONGRESS

The Library of Congress's international divisions provide overseas free research assistance on social, economic, and political topics. Call:

African and Middle East Division	202–287–7937
Asian Division	202–287–5420
European Division	202–287–5413
Hispanic Division	202–287–5400

Write: Library of Congress, 10 First Street SE, Washington, D.C. 20540.

UNITED STATES INTERNATIONAL TRADE COMMISSION*

Address: 701 E Street NW, Washington, DC 20436. Information phone: 202–523–0161.

Formerly the U.S. Tariff Commission, the name was changed to the U.S. International Trade Commission in 1974.

> The commission is given broad powers of investigation relating to the customs laws of the United States and foreign countries, the volume of importation in comparison with domestic production and consumption, the conditions, causes, and effects relating to competition of foreign industries with those of the United States and all other factors affecting competition between articles of the United States and imported articles.

Businesspersons who believe they have been injured by unfair trade methods from abroad may file a complaint with this commission.

Summaries of trade and tariff information may be obtained directly from the commission.

Sources of International Credit Information

International Trade Administration, U.S. Department of Commerce, Washington, DC.

Dun & Bradstreet, 99 Church Street, New York, NY 10007.

FCIB-NACM Corp., 520 8th Avenue South, New York, NY 10018.

Major Commercial Banks

U.S. Department of Agriculture, U.S. Foreign Agriculture Service, Export Credit Sales Program, Washington, DC 20250.

* Source: *U.S. Government Organization Manual.*

International Organizations

UNITED NATIONS (UN)

Address: New York, NY 10017. Information phone: 212–754–1234.

The UN and its affiliated organizations publish a large number of reports and statistical tables covering all member nations. Publications may be obtained by writing: Sales Section, United Nations Publications, New York, NY 10017. A periodic check list of UN publications is available on request.

PUBLICATIONS

Economic Survey of Europe.

Journal of Development Planning.

Guidelines for Contracting for Industrial Projects in Developing Countries.

World Economic Survey.

Annual Bulletin of Exports of Chemical Products.

Annual Bulletin of Coal Statistics for Europe.

Statistics of World Trade in Steel.

Annual Bulletin of Gas Statistics for Europe.

Annual Bulletin of Electric Energy Statistics for Europe.

Economic Bulletin for Europe.

Economic Bulletin for Asia and the Pacific.

Economic Bulletin for Africa.

Economic Bulletin for Latin America.

Quarterly Bulletin of Statistics for Asia and the Pacific.

Statistical Yearbook for Asia and the Pacific.

Demographic Yearbook.

Yearbook of International Trade Statistics Vol. I: Trade by Country; Vol. II: Trade by Commodity.

Monthly Bulletin of Statistics provides monthly statistics on 70 subjects from more than 200 countries and territories together with special tables illustrating important economic developments. Quarterly data for significant world and regional aggregates are also prepared regularly for the bulletin.

Statistical Yearbook is a comprehensive compilation of international statistics relating to: population and manpower; agricultural, mineral, and manufacturing production; construction; energy; trade; transport; communications; consumption; balance of payments; wages and prices; national accounts; finance; development assistance; health; housing; education; science and technology; and culture.

Population and Vital Statistics Reports (quarterly).

Yearbook of National Accounts Statistics.

Yearbook of International Trade Statistics.

Yearbook of Construction Statistics.

Commodity Trade Statistics (quarterly).

World Trade Annual.

The Growth of World Industry: Vol. I General Industrial Statistics; Vol. II Commodities Production Data.

INTERNATIONAL MONETARY FUND (IMF)

Address: 19th and H Streets NW, Washington, DC 20431. Phone: 202–623–7061.

The IMF was organized in 1945 with the purpose of promoting international monetary cooperation and consultation. The fund also seeks to facilitate the expansion of international trade and currency exchange stability. The fund issues Special Drawing Rights (SDR), a form of reserve currency used by central banks for settling balance of payment obligations.

PUBLICATIONS

The IMF issues a broad range of publications (some in conjunction with the World Bank Group) of interest to the business community.

Foreign Trade Statistics. Series A. This monthly bulletin provides a breakdown of overall trade by main commodity categories and available indices of foreign trade unit values and volumes. *Series B. Trade by Commodities. Analytical Abstracts* (quarterly). *Series C. Trade by Commodities. Market Summaries* (yearly).

Provisional Oil Statistics (quarterly).

The Annual Report of the Executive Directors reviews the funds' activities, policies, organization, and administration and surveys the world economy, with special emphasis on international liquidity, payments problems, exchange rates, and world trade.

Annual Report on Exchange Restrictions reviews developments in exchange controls and restrictions and other measures that may have direct implications for the balance of payments of member countries.

International Financial Statistics (monthly) reports for most countries of the world current data needed for analyzing problems of international payments and inflation and deflation, i.e., data on exchange rates, international liquidity, money and banking, international trade, prices, production, government finance, interest rates, and other items. Information is presented in country tables for each country and in tables with area and world aggregates. Charts on each country page show recent changes in important series.

Balance of Payments Yearbook presents statistics in a standard form, expressed in a common unit of account, for countries that report information to the fund on their balance of payments transactions. In the tables that are designated as "standard presentations," these transactions are classified in terms of objective criteria; in the tables designated as "analytic presentations," they are regrouped to facilitate further analysis and certain cumulative balances are drawn.

Direction of Trade Statistics is published jointly by the International Monetary Fund and the International Bank for Reconstruction and Development. The monthly issues provide the latest available information on each country's direction of trade, with comparative data for the corresponding period of the preceding year.

The *IMF Survey* is a topical report of the fund's activities (including all press releases, texts of communiques and major statements, SDR valuations, and exchange rates) presented in the broader context of developments in national economics and international finance.

ORGANIZATION FOR ECONOMIC COOPERATION AND DEVELOPMENT (OECD)

Address: 2 Rue Andre Pascal 75775 Paris CEDEX16, France.

1750 Pennsylvania Avenue NW, Washington, DC 20026. Phone: 202–724–1857.

The OECD, established in 1961, is an outgrowth of the Organization for European Economic Cooperation, set up under the Marshall Plan in 1948. It consists of 24 developed countries: Canada, United States, Japan, Australia, New Zealand, Austria, Belgium, Denmark, England, Finland, France, West Germany, Greece, Iceland, Italy, Luxembourg, Netherlands, Norway, Portugal, Spain, Sweden, Turkey, Switzerland, and Yugoslavia.

PUBLICATIONS

OECD Observer is intended for people who are interested in and concerned with economic and social planning in the broadest sense and who want to have relevant information in the most succinct form possible. It presents in readable fashion the entire range of OECD's work—in economic affairs, trade, manpower, social affairs, science and education, the environment, financial affairs, and development assistance. (Published bimonthly.)

The *OECD Economic Outlook* is a twice yearly, detailed survey of economic trends and prospects for the immediate future.

OECD Financial Statistics supplies complete, up-to-date, authoritative information on financial markets in 24 European countries, the United States, Canada, and Japan. (Published yearly with bimonthly supplements.)

OECD Economic Surveys is an annual analysis of the economic policy of each OECD country as seen by the others.

Main Economic Indicators, a monthly publication, is an essential source of statistics for the student of the international business cycle.

Indicators of Industrial Activity is a quarterly publication that provides an overall view of short-term economic developments in different industries for all OECD member countries.

Monthly Statistics of Foreign Trade includes a detailed regional analysis of trade of the main country groupings in the OECD area. Series are shown non-adjusted and seasonally adjusted.

Foreign Trade by Commodities is an annual publication with matrix tables showing trade between OECD countries and partner countries of commodity groups defined at 1- and 2-digit levels of the Standard International Trade Classification. Separate volumes are published for exports and imports.

GENERAL AGREEMENT ON TRADE AND TARIFFS (GATT)

Address: Centre William Rappard, 154 Rue de Lausanne, Geneva, Switzerland.

GATT is a multilateral trade treaty (entered into force in 1948) among 83 countries providing for the reduction of tariffs and other trade barriers, standardization of trade procedures, and the resolution of trade disputes. GATT publishes *Compilations of Basic Information on Export Markets; Guide to Sources of Foreign Trade Information; Analytical Bibliography: A Compendium of Sources: International Trade Statistics;* and *World Directory of Industry and Trade Associations.*

Selected Bibliography

A. Market Identification and Assessment

Addresses to AID Missions Overseas, Office of Small and Disadvantaged Business Utilization/Minority Business Center, Agency for International Development, Washington, DC 20523. Free.

AID Commodity Eligibility Listing, Office of Small and Disadvantaged Business Utilization/Minority Resource Center, Agency for International Development, Washington, DC 20523, 1984 revised. Lists groups of commodities, presents the Agency for International Development (AID) commodity eligibility list, gives eligibility requirements for certain commodities and describes commodities that are not eligible for financing by the agency. Free.

AID Regulation 1, Office of Small and Disadvantaged Business Utilization/Minority Resource Center, Agency for International Development, Washington, DC 20523. This tells what transactions are eligible for financing by the Agency for International Development (AID), and the responsibilities of importers, as well as the bid procedures. Free.

AID Financed Export Opportunities, Office of Small and Disadvantaged Business Utilization/Minority Resource Center, Agency for International Development, Washington, DC 20523. Fact sheets also referred to as "Small Business Circulars", they present procurement data about proposed foreign purchases. Free.

American Bulletin of International Technology Transfer, International Advancement, P.O. Box 75537, Los Angeles, CA 90057. Bimonthly. A comprehensive listing of product and service opportunities offered and wanted for licensing and joint ventures agreements in the United States and overseas.

Annual Worldwide Industry Reviews (AWIR).[3] Provide a combination of country by country market assessments, export trends, and a 5-year statistical table of U.S. Exports for a single industry integrated into one report and quickly show an industry's performance for the most recent year in most countries. Each report covers 8 to 18 countries.

Big Business Blunders: Mistakes in Multinational Marketing, 1982, David A. Ricks,

Source: Excerpted from *A Basic Guide to Exporting*, International Trade Administration, U.S. Department of Commerce

1. Prices are not given in this section.
2. To order: Superintendent of Documents, General Printing Office, Washington, DC 20402.
3. For information: Export Promotion Office, U.S. Department of Commerce, P.O. Box 14207, Washington, DC 20044. Telephone: 202–377–2432.
4. For information: U.S. Department of Agriculture, Foreign Agricultural Services, Washington, DC 20250. Telephone: 202–477–7937.
5. Contact Local U.S. & FC District Office (page 665) or call 202–377–2432.

Doug Jones-Irwin, Homewood, IL 60430. 200 pp. $13.95.

Business America.[2] International Trade Administration, U.S. Department of Commerce. Principle Commerce Department publication for presenting domestic and international business news and news of the application of technology to business and industrial problems.

Catalogo de Publicaciones de la OPS, Pan American Health Organization/World Health Organization, 525 23rd Street, NW., Washington, DC 20037. A free guide of publications, many of which are in English. This catalog is published in Spanish.

Country Market Surveys (CMS).[3] This report series offers short summaries of International Market Research (IMR) geared to the needs of the busy executive. Highlight market size, trends and prospects in an easy to read format.

Country Trade Statistics (CTS).[3] A set of four key tables that indicate which U.S. products are in the greatest demand in a specific country over the most recent five-year period. Indicate which U.S. industries look best for export to a particular country and the export performance of single industries. Tables highlight top U.S. exports, those with the largest market share, the fastest growing, and those which are the primary U.S. market.

Custom Statistical Service.[3] Individually tailored tables of U.S. exports or imports. The custom service provides data for specific products or countries of interest, or for ones which may not appear in the standard ESP country and product rankings for a chosen industry. With Custom Statistics one can also obtain data in other formats such as quantity, unit quantity, unit value and percentages. Custom orders are priced by the number of products, countries, or other data desired.

Developments in International Trade Policy, International Monetary Fund, Publications Unit, 700 19th Street, NW., Washington, DC 20431. This paper focuses on the main current issues in trade policies of the major trading nations.

Direction of Trade Statistics, International Monetary Fund, Publications Unit, 700 19th Street, NW., Washington, DC 20431. This monthly publication provides data on the country and area distribution of countries' exports and imports as reported by themselves or their partners. A yearbook is published annually which gives seven years of data for 157 countries and two sets of world and area summaries.

Directory of Leading U.S. Export Management Companies, 1984, Bergamo Book Co., 15 Ketchum Street, Westport, CT 06881.

Economic and Social Survey for Asia and the Pacific, UNIPUB, P.O. Box 1222, Ann Arbor, MI 48106. Tel: (800) 521–8110. Analyzes recent economic and social developments in the region in the context of current trends. Examines agriculture, food, industry, transport, public finance, wages and prices, and external trade sectors.

Element of Export Marketing, John Stapleton, 1984, Woodhead-Faulkner, Dover, NH.

Entry Strategies for Foreign Markets—From Domestic to International Business, Franklin R. Root, American Management Association, 1977.

EXIM Bank Information Kit, Public Affairs Office, Export-Import Bank of the United States, 811 Vermont Avenue, NW., Washington, DC 20571. Includes the Bank's annual report, which provides information on interest rates and the Foreign Credit Insurance Association.

Export Development Strategies: U.S. Promotion Policy, Michael R. Czinkota and George Tasar, Praeger, New York, NY, 1982.

Export Directory.[4] Describes the principle functions of the Foreign Agricultural Service and lists agricultural attaches. Free.

Export Directory: Buying Guide, biennial, Journal of Commerce, 110 Wall Street, New York, NY 10005.

Export-Import Bank: Financing for American Exports—Support for American Jobs, Export-Import Bank of the United States, 1980. Free.

Export Statistics Profiles (ESP).[3] Tables of U.S. exports for a specific industry help identify the best export markets and analyze the industry's exports product-by-product, country-by-country over each of the last five years to date. Data is rank-ordered by dollar value.

Export Strategies: Markets and Competition, Nigel Percy, 1982, Allen & Unwin, Winchester, MA 01890.

Exporter's Encyclopedia, annual with semimonthly updates, Dun & Bradstreet International, One Exchange Plaza, Suite 715, Jersey City, NJ 07302. Provides a comprehensive, country-by-country coverage of 220 world markets. It contains an examination of each country's communications and transportation facilities, customs and trade regulations, documentation, key contacts, and unusual conditions that may affect operations. Financing and Credit abroad are also examined.

Exporting: A Practical Manual for Developing Export Markets and Dealing with Foreign Customs, 2nd Edition, Earnst Y. Maitland, 1982, Self-Counsel Press.

Exporting from the U.S.A.: How to Develop Export Markets and Cope with Foreign Customs, A.B. Marring, 1981, Self-Counsel Press.

Exporting to Japan, American Chamber of Commerce in Japan, 1982, A.M. Newman.

FAS Commodity Report.[4] These reports provide information on foreign agricultural production in 22 commodity areas.

FATUS: Foreign Agricultural Trade of the United States.[4] This report of trends in U.S. agricultural trade by commodity and country and of events affecting this trade is published six times a year with two supplements.

Findex: The Directory of Market Research Reports, Studies and Surveys, FIND/SVP, The Information Clearinghouse, 500 Fifth Avenue, New York, NY 10036. Tel: (212) 354–2424. Over 10,000 listings.

Foreign Agriculture.[4] A monthly publication containing information on overseas markets and buying trends, new competitors and products, trade policy developments and overseas promotional activities.

Foreign Agriculture Circulars.[4] Individual circulars report on the supply and demand for commodities around the world. Products covered include: diary, livestock, poultry, grains, coffee, and wood products.

Foreign Commerce Handbook, Chamber of Commerce of the United States, 1615 H Street, NW., Washington, DC 20062. Lists organizations of assistance to U.S. exporters, as well as up-to-date published information on all important phases of international trade and investment.

Foreign Economic Trends (FET), Superintendent of Documents, U.S. Government Printing Office, Washington, DC 20402. Prepared by the U.S. and Foreign Commercial Service. Presents current business and economic developments and the latest economic indications in more than 100 countries. Available from ITA Publications Distribution, Rm. 1617D, U.S. Department of Commerce, Washington, DC 20230.

Foreign Market Entry Strategies, Franklin R. Root, 1982, AMACOM, New York, NY 10020.

General Economic Problems, OECD Publications and Information Center, Suite 1207, 1750 Pennsylvania Avenue, NW., Washington, DC 20006–4582. Tel: (202) 724–1859. Contains the latest monographs on: Economic policies and forecasts; growth; inflation; national accounts; international trade and payments; capital markets; interest rates; taxation; and energy, industrial and agricultural policies.

Glossary of International Terms, International Trade Institute, Inc., 5055 N. Main Street, Dayton, OH 45415. Tel: (800) 543–2453.

A Guide to Export Marketing, International Trade Institute, Inc., 5055 North Main Street, Dayton, OH 45415. Tel: (800) 453–2453.

Handbook of International Statistics, UNIPUB, P.O. Box 1222, Ann Arbor, MI 48106. Tel: (800) 521–8110. Examines structural trends in 70 developing and developed countries.

Highlights of U.S. Import and Export Trade.[2] Statistical book of U.S. imports and exports.

How to Build an Export Business: An International Marketing Guide for Minority-Owned Businesses.[2]

International Development, OECD Publications and Information Center, Suite 1207, 1750 Pennsylvania Avenue, NW., Washington, DC 20006–4582. Tel: (202) 724–1857. Contains the latest monographs on: Financial Resources and aid policies, general problems of development, industrialization, transfer of technology, rural development, employment, human resources, imigration, and demography.

International Financial Statistics, International Monetary Fund, Publications Unit, 700 19th Street, NW., Washington, DC 20431. Monthly publication is a standard source of international statistics on all aspects of international and domestic finance.

International Market Research (IMR) Reports.[3] This is an in-depth industry sector analysis for those who want the complete data for one industry in one country.

International Market Information (IMI).[3] These are special "bulletins" that point out unique market situations and new opportunities to U.S. exporters in specific markets.

International Marketing, 5th edition, 1983, Philip R. Cateora, Irwin, Homewood, IL 60430.

International Marketing, Raul Kahler, 1983, Southwestern Publishing Co., Cincinnati, OH 45227.

International Marketing, 3rd edition, Vern Terpstra, 1983, Dryden Press, Hinsdale, IL 60521.

International Marketing, Revised Edition, Hans Thorelli & Helmut Becker, eds., 1980, Pergamon Press, Elmsford, NY 10523.

International Marketing, 2nd edition, 1981, L. S. Walsh, International Ideas, Philadelphia, PA 19103.

International Marketing: An Annotated Bibliography, 1983, S. T. Cavusgil & John R. Nevin, eds., American Marketing Association.

International Marketing Handbook, 1985, 3 Vols., Frank S. Bair, ed., Gale Research Co., Detroit, MI 48226, 3,637.

International Marketing Research, 1983, Susan P. Douglas & C. Samual Craig, Prentice-Hall, Englewood Cliffs, NJ 07632.

International Monetary Fund: Publications Catalog, International Monetary Fund, Publications Unit, 700 19th Street, NW., Washington, DC 20431. Free.

International Trade Operations . . . A Managerial Approach, R. Duane Hall, Unz & Co., 190 Baldwin Ave., Jersey City, NJ 07303.

Local Chambers of Commerce Which Maintain Foreign Trade Services, 1983. International Division, Chamber of Commerce of the United States, 1615 H Street, NW., Washington, DC 20062. A list of chambers of commerce that have programs to aid exporters. Free.

Market Shares Reports, National Technical Information Services, U.S. Department of Commerce, Box 1553, Springfield, VA 22161. These are reports for over 88 countries. They provide basic data needed by exporters to evaluate overall trends in the size of markets for manufacturers.

Marketing Aspects of International Business, 1983, Gerald M. Hampton & Aart Van Gent, Klewer-Nijhoff Publishing, Bingham, MA.

Marketing High-Technology, William L. Shanklin & John K. Ryans, Jr., DC Heath & Co., 125 Spring Street, Lexington, MA 02173.

Marketing in Europe, Economic Intelligence Unit, Ltd., 10 Rockefeller Plaza, New York, NY 10020, monthly. Journal provides detailed analysis of the European market for consumer goods. The issues are published in three subject groups: Food, drink and tobacco; clothing, furniture and consumer goods; and chemists' goods such as pharmaceuticals and toiletries.

Marketing in the Third World, Erdener Kaynak, Praeger, New York, NY 10175, 302 pp., $29.95.

Metric Laws and Practices in International Trade—Handbook for U.S. Exporters, 1982.[2]

Monthly World Crop Production.[4] Report provides estimates on the projection of wheat, rice, coarse grains, oilseeds, and cotton in selected regions and countries around the world.

The Multinational Marketing and Employment Directory, 8th edition, World Trade Academy Press, Inc., 50 East 42nd Street, New York, NY 10017, 1982, two volumes. This directory lists more than 7,500 American corporations operating in the United States and overseas. The directory is recognized as an outstanding marketing source for products, skills and services in the United States and abroad.

Multinational Marketing Management, 3rd edition, 1984, Warren J. Keegan, Prentice Hall, Englewood Cliffs, NJ 07632.

OECD Publications, OECD Publications and Information Center, Suite 1207, 1750 Pennsylvania Avenue, NW., Washington, DC 20006–4582. Tel: (202) 724–4582. Free.

Outlook for U.S. Agricultural Exports.[4] This report analyzes current developments and forecasts U.S. farm exports in coming months by commodity and region. Country and regional highlights discuss the reasons why sales of major commodities are likely to rise or fall in those areas.

Overseas Business Reports (OBR).[2] Reports include current-marketing information, trade forecasts, statistics, regulations, and marketing profiles. Available from ITA Publications, Rm. 1617D, U.S. Department of Commerce, Washington, DC 20230.

Product/Country Market Profiles.[3] These products are tailor-made, single product/multi-country; or single country/multi-product reports. They include trade contacts, specific opportunities, and statistical analyses.

Profitable Export Marketing: A Strategy for U.S. Business, Maria Ortiz-Buonafina, Prentice-Hall, Englewood Cliffs, NJ 07632.

Reference Book for World Traders, Annual, Croner Publications, Inc., 211 Jamaica Avenue, Queens Village, NY 11428. A loose-leaf reference book for traders. Gives information about export documentation, steamship lines and airlines, free trade zones, credit and similar matters.

Source Book . . . The "How to" Guide for Exporters and Importers, Unz & Co., 190 Baldwin Avenue, Jersey City, NJ 07036.

Trade and Development Report, UNIPUB, P.O. Box 1222, Ann Arbor, MI 48106. Tel: (800) 521–8110. This report reviews current economic issues and longer run development in international trade.

Trade Directories of the World, Annual, Croner Publications, Inc., 211 Jamaica Avenue, Queens Village, NY 11428.

Trends in World Production and Trade, UNIPUB, P.O. Box 1222, Ann Arbor, MI 48106. Tel: (800) 521–8110. Report discusses the structural change in world output, industrial growth patterns since 1960, changes in the pattern of agricultural output, and changes in patterns in trade in goods and services. Product groups and commodity groups are defined according to SITC criteria.

United Nations Publications, United Nations and Information Center, 1889 F Street, NW., Washington, DC 20006. Free.

U.S. Export Sales.[4] A weekly report of agricultural export sales based on reports provided by private exporters. Free.

U.S. Export Weekly—International Trade Reporter, Bureau of National Affairs, Inc.

U.S. Farmers Export Arm.[4] 1980. Free.

Weekly Roundup of World Production and Trade.[4] Provides a summary of the week's important events in agricultural foreign trade and world production. Free.

World Agriculture.[4] Provides production information, data and analyses by commodity and country, along with a review of recent economic conditions and changes in food and trade policies.

World Agriculture Regional Supplements.[4] Provides a look by region at agricultural developments during the previous year and the outlook for the year ahead.

The World Bank Catalog of Publications, World Bank Publications, P.O. Box 37525, Washington, DC 200013. Free.

World Economic Outlook: A Survey by the Staff of the International Monetary Fund, International Monetary Fund, Publications Unit, 700 19th Street, NW., Washington, DC 20431. This yearly report provides a comprehensive picture of the international situation and prospects. Highlights the imbalances that persist in the world economy and their effects on inflation, unemployment, real rates of interest and exchange rates.

World Economic Survey, UNIPUB, P.O. Box 1222, Ann Arbor, MI 48106. Tel: (800) 521–8110. Assesses the world economy. It provides an overview of developments in global economics for the past year and provides an outlook for the future.

Yearbook of International Trade Statistics, UNIPUB, P.O. Box 1222, Ann Arbor, MI 48106. Tel: (800) 521–8110. Offers international coverage of foreign trade statistics. Tables are provided for overall trade by regions and countries. Vol. I: Trade by Commodity. Vol. II: Commodity Matrix Tables.

B. Selling & Sales Contacts

American Export Register, Thomas Publishing Co., 1 Penn Plaza, 250 N. 34th Street, New York, NY 10010, 1984. This book is designed for persons searching for U.S. suppliers, for foreign manufacturers seeking U.S. buyers or representatives for their products. Contains product lists in four languages, an advertiser's index, information about and a list of U.S. Chambers of Commerce abroad, and a list of banks with international services and shipping, financing and insurance information.

Background Notes.[2] Four to twelve page summaries on the economy, people, history, culture and government of about 160 countries.

A Business Guide to the Near East and North Africa, 1981.[2] Designed to provide U.S. business with information on the nature of these markets, how to do business in these areas, and how the Department of Commerce can help in penetrating these markets.

Commercial News USA (CN), Monthly export promotion magazine circulated only overseas, listing specific products and services of U.S. firms. Applications for participation in the magazine are available from the District Offices of the U.S. and Foreign Commercial Service, U.S. Department of Commerce.

Directory of American Firms Operating in Foreign Countries, 10th Edition, 1984, World Trade Academy Press, 50 E. 42nd Street, New York, NY 10017. Contains the most recent data on more than 4,200 American corporations controlling and operating more than 16,500 foreign business enterprises. Lists every American firm under the country in which it has subsidiaries or branches, together with their home office branch in the United States. Gives the names and addresses of their subsidiaries or branches, products manufactured or distributed.

Export Mailing List Service (EMLS).[3] Targeted mailing lists of prospective overseas customers from the Commerce Department's automated worldwide file of foreign firms. EMLs identify manufacturers, agents, retailers, service firms, government agencies and other one-to-one contacts. Information includes name and address, cable and telephone numbers, name and title of a key official, product/service interests, and additional date.

How to Get the Most from Overseas Exhibitions, International Trade Administration, Publications Distribution, Room 1617D, U.S. Department of Commerce, Washington, DC 20230.

Japan: Business Obstacles and Opportunities, 1983, McKinney & Co., John Wiley, NY.

Management of International Advertising: A Marketing Approach, 1984, Dean M. Peeples & John K. Ryans. Allyn & Bacon, Boston, MA 02159.

Service Industries and Economic Development: Case Studies in Technology Transfer. Praeger Publishers, New York, NY 10175. 1984.

Top Bulletin.[3] Weekly publication of trade opportunities received each week from overseas embassies and consulates. Also available on computer tape.

Trade Lists.[3] Preprinted trade lists are comprehensive directories listing all the companies in a country across all product sectors, or all the companies in a single industry across all countries.

World Traders Data Reports (WTDRs).[3] Service provides background reports on individual foreign firms. WTDRs are designed to help U.S. firms evaluate potential foreign customers before making a business commitment.

C. Financing Exports

Chase World Guide for Exporters, Export Credit Reports, Chase World Information Corporation, One World Trade Center, Suite 4533, New York, NY 10048. The *Guide,* covering 180 countries, contains current export financing methods, collection experiences and charges, foreign import and exchange regulations and related subjects. Supplementary bulletins keep the guide up to date throughout the year. The *Reports,* issued quarterly, specify credit terms granted for shipment to all the principal world markets. The reports show the credit terms offered by the industry groups as a whole, thereby enabling the reader to determine whether his or her terms are more liberal or conservative than the average for specific commodity groups.

FCIB International Bulletin, FCIB-NACM Corp., 475 Park Avenue South, New York, NY 10016, twice monthly. The Bulletin presents export information and review of conditions and regulations in overseas markets.

Financing and Insuring Exports: A User's Guide to Eximbank and FCIA Programs, Export-Import Bank of the United States, User's Guide, 811 Vermont Avenue, NW., Washington, DC 20571. A 350 page guide which covers Eximbank's working capital guarantees, credit risk protection (guarantees and insurance), medium-term and long-term lending programs. Includes free updates during calendar year in which the guide is purchased.

Financial Institutions and Markets in the Far East, Morgan Guarantee Trust Company of New York, 23 Wall Street, New York, NY 10015. Discusses export letters of credit, drafts, and other methods of payment and regulations of exports and imports.

A Guide to Checking International Credit, International Trade Institute, Inc., 5055 North Main Street, Suite 270, Dayton, OH 45415.

A Guide to Financing Exports, U.S. and Foreign Commercial Service, International Trade Administration Publications Distribution, Room 1617D, U.S. Department of Commerce, Washington, DC 20230, 1985. Brochure.

A Guide to Understanding Drafts, International Trade Institute, Inc., 5055 N. Main Street, Dayton, OH 45415. Tel: (800) 543–2455, 64 pp.

A Guide to Understanding Letters of Credit, International Trade Institute, Inc., 5055 N. Main Street, Dayton, OH 45415.

A Handbook on Financing U.S. Exports, Machinery and Allied Products Institute, 1200 18th Street, NW., Washington, DC 20036.

Official U.S. and International Financing Institutions: A Guide for Exporters and Investors, International Trade Administration, U.S. Department of Commerce. Available from the Superintendent of Documents, U.S. Government Printing Office, Washington, DC 20402.

Specifics on Commercial Letters of Credit and Bankers Acceptances, James A. Harrington, 1979 UNZ & Co., Division of Scott Printing Corp., 190 Baldwin Avenue, Jersey City, NJ 07036, 1979.

D. Laws and Regulations

Customs Regulations of the United States.[2]

Distribution License, 1985 Office of Export Administration, Room 1620, U.S. Department of Commerce, Washington, DC 20230 free.

Export Administration Regulations.[2] Covers U.S. export control regulations and policies, with instructions, interpretations and explanatory material. Last revised Oct 1, 1984.

Export Marketing of Capital Goods to the Socialist Countries of Eastern Europe, 1978, M. R. Hill, Gower Publishing Company.

Manual for the Handling of Applications for Patents, Designs and Trademarks Throughout the World, Ocrooibureau Los En Stigter B.V., Amsterdam, the Netherlands.

Summary of U.S. Export Regulations, 1985, Office of Export Administration, Room 1620, Department of Commerce, Washington, DC 20230.

Technology and East-West Trade, 1983, Summarizes the major provisions of the Export Administration Act of 1979 and its implications in East-West trade, Office of Technology Assessment, U.S. Department of Commerce, Washington, DC 20230.

E. Shipping and Logistics

Export Documentation Handbook, 1984 Edition, Dun & Bradstreet International, 49 Old Bloomfield Avenue, Mt. Lakes, NJ 07046. Compiled by Ruth E. Hurd, Dun's Marketing Services.

Export-Import Traffic Management and Forwarding, 6th edition, 1979. Alfred Murr, Cornell Maritime Press, Box 456, Centerville, MD 21617. Presents the diverse functions and varied services concerned with the entire range of ocean traffic management.

Export Shipping Manual, Indexed, looseleaf reference binder. Detailed current information on shipping and import regulations for all areas of the world. Bureau of National Affairs, 1231 25th Street, NW., Washington, DC 20037.

Guide to Canadian Documentation, International Trade Institute, Inc., 5055 N. Main Street, Dayton, OH 45415.

Guide to Documentary Credit Operations, ICC Publishing Corporation, New York, NY 1985.

Guide to Export Documentation, International Trade Institute, Inc., 5055 N. Main Street, Dayton, OH 45415.

Guide to International Ocean Freight Shipping, International Trade Institute, 5055 N. Main Street, Dayton, OH 45415.

Guide to Selecting the Freight Forwarder, International Trade Institute, Inc., 5055 North Main Street, Suite 270, Dayton, OH 45415.

Journal of Commerce Export Bulletin, 110 Wall Street, New York, NY 10005. A weekly newspaper that reports port and shipping developments. Lists products shipped from New York and ships and cargoes departing from 25 other U.S. ports. A "trade prospects" column lists merchandise offered and merchandise wanted.

Shipping Digest, Geyer-McAllister Publications, Inc., 51 Madison Avenue, New York, NY 10010. A weekly which contains cargo sailing schedules from every U.S. port to every foreign port, as well as international air and sea commerce news.

F. Licensing

Foreign Business Practices . . . Material on Practical Aspects of Exporting, International Licensing and Investment, 1981.[2]

American Bulletin of International Technology Transfer, International Advancement, P.O. Box 75537, Los Angeles, CA 90057, bimonthly. Comprehensive listing of product and service opportunities offered and sought for licensing and joint ventures agreements in the United States and overseas.

International Technology Licensing: Competition, Costs, and Negotiation, 1981, J. Farok Contractor, Lexington Books, Lexington, MA 02173.

Investing, Licensing, and Trading Conditions Abroad, Business International Corporation, base volume with monthly updates.

Sources for Market Research

Product/Industry Data Resources

Export Statistics Profiles (ESP).[5] Analyzes exports for a single industry—product-by-product, country-by-country—over each of the last 5 years to date. Data are often rank-ordered by dollar value to identify quickly the leading products and industries. The basic element of the ESP consists of tables showing the sales of each product in the industry to each country, as well as competitive information, growth, and future trends. Each ESP also includes an Export Market Brief—a narrative analysis highlighting the industry's prospects, performance, and leading products. ESP's are currently available for 35 industries.

Custom Statistical Service.[5] This service offers data on products not covered in one of the standard ESP industries. In addition, this service allows the exporter to tailor data to meet his or her specific needs. Data are available in formats different from those contained in the standard ESP, such as quantity and unit value and percentages, as well as for imports of products.

Foreign Trade Report, FT 410.[2] Monthly FT 410 provides a statistical record of shipments of all merchandise from the United States to foreign countries, including both the quantity and dollar value of exports to each country during the month covered by the report. Also contains cumulative export statistics from the first of the calendar year. Report FT 410 (monthly and cumulative for U.S. Exports, Schedule E Commodity by Country) is available by subscription. The reports may also be available at US&FCS District Offices and many large libraries.

International Market Research (IMR).[5] These reports are in-depth analyses for those who want a more complete picture for one industry in one country. A report includes information such as market size and outlook, end-user analysis, distribution channels, cultural characteristics, business customs and practices, competitive situation, trade barriers, and trade contacts.

Country Market Surveys (CMS).[5] Surveys are 8- to 12-page summaries of IMR reports on industry themes. They highlight market size, trends, and prospects in an easy-to-read format.

Competitive Assessments. The U.S. Department of Commerce has published over 20 industry studies that examine the present and future international competitiveness of each industry. Industries examined range from solid wood products to fiber optics. Topics usually include industry performance, recent foreign competition (and foreign government assistance), U.S. Government assistance, trends, and an assessment of future international competitiveness. Contact local US&FCS District Office or Office of Trade Information and Analysis, Industrial Analysis Division, Room 4881, U.S. Department of Commerce, Washington, DC 20230. Tel: (202) 377–4944.

Annual Worldwide Industry Reviews (AWIR).[5] This product is a combination of country-by-country market assessments, export trends, and 5-year statistical tables of U.S. exports for a single industry integrated into a report of one to three volumes. They show an industry's performance for the most recent year in many countries. Each volume covers 9–20 countries.

Product Market Profiles (PMP).[5] A PMP is a single product, multicountry report that includes trade contacts, specific trade leads, and statistical analysis.

Comparison Shopping Service. Service provides a custom-tailored export market research survey on a U.S. client firm's specific product in a single country. The survey covers key marketing factors in the target country, including overall marketability, names of competitors, comparative prices, entry and distribution channels, and names of potential sales representatives or licensees. The survey is conducted on-site by U.S. commercial officers and is available for standard off-the-shelf products (no custom or specialty items) in selected countries.

Market Share Reports. Provides basic data to evaluate overall trends in the size of markets for exporters. Also measures changes in the import demand for specific products and compares the competitive position of U.S. and foreign exporters. Contact the National Technical Information Service, U.S. Department of Commerce, Box 1553, Springfield, VA 22161. Telephone: (202) 487–4630.

Export Information System (XIS) Data Reports. Available from the U.S. Small Business Administration (SBA) for approximately 1700 product categories, the XIS Data Reports provide to a small business a list of the 25 largest importing markets for its product, the 10 best markets for U.S. exporters of that product, the trends within those markets and the major sources of foreign competition, based on Department of Commerce and United Nations data. There is no charge to small businesses for this service. Contact the local SBA Field Office.

FINDEX: The Directory of Market Research Reports, Studies and Surveys. Publication contains over 10,000 listings of market research reports, studies, and surveys. Contact FIND/SVP The Information Clearinghouse, 500 Fifth Avenue, New York, NY 10036. Telephone: (212) 354–2424.

Country Data Resources:

Country Market Profiles (CMP).[5] Single country, multi-industry reports that include relevant trade statistics, economic and market analysis, and trade contacts in a single report.

Country Trade Statistics (CTS).[5] Each CTS gives details of all U.S. exports to a single country over the most recent 5 year period. They show the exporter which U.S. industries look best for export to a particular country. Each country report contains four key statistical tables showing the leading and fastest growing U.S. exports of about 200 product categories to the country.

Foreign Economic Trends (FET).[5] FET's present current business and economic developments and the latest economic indicators for more than 100 countries. FET's are prepared either annually or semiannually depending on the country.

International Market Information (IMI).[5] These special bulletins point out unique market situations and new opportunities to U.S. exporters in specific markets.

Overseas Business Reports (OBR's).[2] Reports provide background statistics and information on specific countries useful to exporters. They present economic and commercial profiles, issue semiannual outlooks for U.S. trade, and publish selected statistical reports on the direction, volume, and nature of U.S. foreign trade with the country.

Background Notes.[2] This series surveys a country's people, geography, economy, government, and foreign policy. Prepared by the Department of State, it includes important national economic and trade information, including major trading partners.

U.S. Agency for International Development's Congressional Presentations. Provide country-by-country data on nations to which the agency will provide funds in the coming year. Also provide detailed information on past funding activities in each individual country. In addition, the publications list projects and their locations that the agency desires to fund in the upcoming year (i.e. a hydroelectrical project in Egypt). Since these projects require U.S. goods and services, the *Congressional Presentations* can give U.S. exporters an opportunity to plan ahead by allowing an early look at potential projects. For ordering information, contact the U.S. Agency for International Development (AID), Department of State, Washington, DC 20523. Telephone: (703) 235–1840.

Trade and Development Program's Congressional Presentation. This publication reports the dollar amount spent by the agency by industry in specific countries around the world for the past several years. For ordering information about Trade and Development's *Congressional Presentation,* contact Trade and Development Program, U.S. Department of State, Washington, DC 20523. Telephone: (703) 235–3663.

Exporters Encyclopedia. An extensive handbook on exporting, this publication contains market information on over 220 world markets, which are individually covered. Contact Dun's Marketing Services, Three Century Drive, Parsippany, NJ 07054. Telephone: (800) 526–0651 (toll free).

Doing Business in Foreign Countries. A series on doing business in most foreign countries, these individual guides are often provided to clients or interested parties by some large or international accounting firms, banks, or other service firms. These publications provide information on specific countries and include demographic and cultural backgrounds, economic climates, restrictions and incentives to trade, duties, documentation requirements, tax structure, and other useful information.

Worldwide Background Data

Statistical Yearbook. This international trade information on products is provided by the United Nations. Information on importing countries and, to help assess competition, exports by country are included. Order by calling 800–521–8110.

World Population. The U.S. Bureau of the Census collects and analyzes worldwide demographic data that can assist exporters in identifying potential markets for their products. Information on each country—total population, fertility, mortality, urban population, growth rate, and life expectancy—is updated every 2 years. Also published are detailed demographic profiles (including analysis of labor force structure, infant mortality, etc.) of individual countries (price and availability varies). *World Population* is free. Contact the Center for International Research, Room 407, Scuderi Building, U.S. Bureau of the Census, Washington, DC 20233.

International Economic Indicators. These are quarterly reports providing basic data (for years and quarters) on the economies of the United States and seven principal industrial countries. Include statistics on gross national product, industrial production, trade, prices, finance, and labor; they also measure changes in key competitive indicators. Reports can provide an overall view of international trends or a basis for more detailed analyses of the economic situation. Annual subscription is available through: ITA Publications Sales Branch, Room 1617D, U.S. Department of Commerce, Washington, DC 20230.

International Financial Statistics. A monthly publication produced by the International Monetary Fund. It presents statistics on exchange rates, money and banking, production, government finance, interest rates, and other subjects. Available from the International Monetary Fund, Publications Unit, 700 19th Street, NW., Washington, DC 20431. Telephone: (202) 473–7430.

World Bank Atlas. Published by the World Bank, this publication presents population, gross domestic product, and average growth rates for every country. Available from World Bank Publications, P.O. Box 37525, Washington, DC 20013.

OTHER PUBLICATIONS

Europa Year Book is an annual two-volume work covering a wide range of commercial, economic, and political statistics and information about every country in the world. Volume I deals with international organizations and the countries of Europe, while Volume II covers Africa, the Americas, Asia, and Australia. It is published by Europe Publications, Ltd., 18 Bedford Square, London, England.

Jane's Major Companies of Europe is an annual providing extensive information about all major European companies. It is available from Jane's Yearbooks, 8 Shepherdess, London N1 7LW, England.

Foreign Commerce Handbook provides information on international trade and foreign markets. Included are addresses and phone numbers of organizations involved with foreign trade, a glossary of foreign commercial terms and a bibliography of indexes and periodicals. Available from the Chamber of Commerce of the United States, 1615 H Street NW, Washington, DC 20062.

International Directory of Marketing Research Houses and Services (the "Green Book") is a directory of marketing research organizations in some 50 countries and includes descriptions of services, contact people, phone numbers, and addresses. Available from: American Marketing Association, 420 Lexington Avenue, New York, NY 10170.

Lambert's World Government Directory identifies government officials in 168 countries as well as officials in Inter-Governmental organizations. Published by International Executive Reports, 115 Massachusetts Avenue NW, Washington, DC 20005.

Country Experts in the Federal Government is a guide to U.S. government analysts for almost all countries. Published by Washington Researchers, 2612 P Street, NW, Washington, DC 20007.

International Research Center Directory edited by Anthony F. Kruzas and Kay Gill identifies 15,000 university-related, independent and government research organizations throughout the world. Available from Gale Research Company.

Croner's Reference Book for World Traders is a three volume work covering basic data and hard-to-locate information for international traders and market researchers. Available from Croner Publications, 211–05 Jamaica Avenue, Queens Village, New York, 11428.

Incoterms is a booklet providing a set of international rules for interpreting the main terms used in foreign trade contracts. Available from the U.S. Council of the International Chamber of Commerce, Inc. 1212 Avenue of the Americas, New York, NY 10036. Also publishes other useful material.

Revised American Foreign Trade Definitions, is a compilation from the National Council of Importers, the Chamber of Commerce of the U.S., and the National Foreign Trade Council. Available from the National Foreign Trade Council at 100 E. 42nd Street, New York, NY 10017.

European Markets: A Guide to Company and Industry Information Sources is a three volume resource for accessing information on European companies and markets. Available from Washington Researchers, 2612 P Street NW, Washington, DC 20007.

Exporters' Encyclopaedia, Dun & Bradstreet International, 99 Church Street, New York, NY 10007. Gives country by country coverage of 220 world markets.

International Information Available in the U.S. by Country

This section lists helpful addresses in the United States for those doing business with countries where business practices may present certain problems.

JAPAN

Exporters and importers generally find it essential to use the services of the Japanese trading companies, which offer a wide range of services including negotiation of overseas deals, transportation, storage, finance, and marketing. The largest trading companies are listed below. The small exporter will often do better using smaller trading companies that specialize in one or two types of products. Exporters seeking an appropriate trading company should contact a local JETRO Office (Japan External Trade Office):

Bank of America Tower*
555 S. Flower Street
Los Angeles, CA 90071
Telephone: 213–626–5700

360 Post Street
San Francisco, CA 94108
Telephone: 415–392–1333

229 Peachtree Street, NE
Atlanta, GA 30303
Telephone: 404–681–0600

230 N. Michigan Avenue
Chicago, IL 60601
Telephone: 312–527–9000

1221 Avenue of the Americas
New York, NY 10020
Telephone: 212–997–0400

One World Trade Center
2100 Stemmons Freeway
Dallas, TX 75258
Telephone: 214–651–0839

1221 McKinney Street
One Houston Center
Houston, TX 77010
Telephone: 713–759–9595

P.O. Box 3356
Marina Station
Mayaguez, PR 00708
Telephone: Mayaquez 832–0861

When U.S. firms encounter difficulty doing business with Japanese companies because of Japanese regulations contact the Japan desk of the International Trade Administration at 202–377–4527.

MAJOR TRADING COMPANIES (NEW YORK OFFICES)

Mitsubishi International Corporation
520 Madison Avenue
New York, NY 10022

Mitsui & Company
200 Park Avenue
New York, NY 10017

Marubeni America Corporation
200 Park Avenue
New York, NY 10066

C. Itoh & Co. (America), Inc.
335 Madison Avenue
New York, NY 10017

Sumitomo Corporation of America
345 Park Avenue
New York, NY 10154

Toyo Menka (America), Inc.
One World Trade Center
New York, NY 10048

Kanematsu-Gosho (USA), Inc.
1133 Avenue of the Americas
New York, NY 10036

Nichimen America, Inc.
1185 Avenue of the Americas
New York, NY 10036

PUBLICATIONS ON TRADING WITH JAPAN

Country Market Profiles—Japan contains statistics on exports, information on some seven industries with export potential to Japan, developments in bilateral trade, and much more. Prepaid, this book is available from the Office of Trade Information Services, Department of Commerce, P.O. Box 14207, Washington, DC 20044.

How to Find Information about Japanese Companies and Industries is an extensive guide to information sources both here and abroad helpful for doing business with Japan. Available from Washington Researchers Publishing, 2612 P Street NW, Washington, DC 20007.

THE PEOPLE'S REPUBLIC OF CHINA (PRC)

For information or advice on contacting the Chinese on commercial matters, call or write to:

U.S. Department of Commerce
International Trade Administration Office of PRC and Hong Kong
Washington, DC 20230
Telephone: 202–377–3583/4681

Commercial Office
Embassy of the People's Republic of China
2300 Connecticut Avenue, N.W.
Washington, DC 20008

For free publications on trade with China call 202–328–2520

Doing Business with China, prepared by the International Trade Administration (Department of Commerce) is available from the:

Superintendent of Documents
Government Printing Office
Washington, D.C. 20402

THE NATIONAL COUNCIL FOR U.S.-CHINA TRADE

Address: 1818 N Street NW, Suite 500. Washington, DC 20220. Phone: 202–429–0340.

The Council, a nonprofit, private organization maintaining close liaison with the U.S. government, serves as a forum for the discussion of trade policy and issues. It also serves as a focal point for business contact and the dissemination of information on marketing in the PRC. The council maintains a business counseling service; it also publishes the *China Business Review* bimonthly. The council facilitates the reciprocal arrangements of trade missions and trade exhibitions in the United States and China.

USSR AND EASTERN EUROPE*

USSR

USSR Affairs Division, International Economic Policy (202–377–4655). This division collects, analyzes, and disseminates current information on economic, commercial, and other developments in the USSR and estimates their impact on the U.S. business community. The division develops policy guidance in our commercial relationship with the Soviet Union and provides staff support to and representation on the Joint Commer-

* Source: Excerpted from Department of Commerce Overseas Reports, "Trading with the USSR" and other Department of Commerce sources.

cial Commission. It also maintains close contact with the U.S. Commercial Office in Moscow and with USSR commercial officials in the United States in order to initiate and pursue official representations on behalf of the American business community.

Within the U.S. Department of Commerce there are several helpful sources. Among them are:

U.S.S.R. Division: 202–377–4655
Export Administration: 202–377–5497
Export Counseling Center: 202–377–3181

It may be to the company's advantage to touch base with the following USSR commercial organizations in the United States to try to obtain some indication of Soviet interest and to identify contacts in the Soviet Union:

The Trade Representation of the USSR in the U.S.A., 2001 Connecticut Avenue NW, Washington, DC 20008, telephone: 202–232–5988.

The Amtorg Trading Corporation, 750 Third Avenue, New York, NY 10017, telephone: 212–972–1220.

The staffs of both Amtorg and the Trade Representation include representatives of individual foreign trade organizations (FTOs).

The USSR Consulate General, 2790 Green Street, San Francisco, CA 94123, telephone: 415–922–6642, may have information conveniently available for companies on the West Coast.

U.S.-U.S.S.R. Trade and Economic Council, 805 Third Avenue, New York, NY 10022, telephone: 212–644–4550.

For a list of U.S. Business representatives, consultants and trading companies doing business with the U.S.S.R. call 202–377–4655.

EASTERN EUROPE

Commercial transactions with Bulgaria, Czechoslovakia, East Germany, Hungary, Poland, and Romania are similar to those with the USSR. Contracts are negotiated with the appropriate Foreign Trade Organization. For detailed information about trade shows, missions, export licenses, and FTOs, contact the Office of East-West Trade, Department of Commerce in Washington, or the Commerce Department Offices at the district level. Another key source of information is the U.S. East-West Trade Development Office in Vienna.

BULGARIA

Bulgarian Embassy
2100 16th Street NW
Washington, DC 20009

Bulgarian Commercial Counselor
121 E. 62nd Street
New York, NY 10021

CZECHOSLOVAKIA

Czechoslovakian Embassy
3900 Linnean Avenue NW
Washington, DC 20008

Office of the Czechoslovakian Commercial Counselor
292 Madison Avenue
New York, NY 10016

EAST GERMANY
(German Democratic Republic)

Embassy of the German Democratic Republic
1717 Massachusetts Avenue NW
Washington, DC 20036

Permanent Mission of German Democratic Republic to the United Nations
58 Park Avenue
New York, NY 10016

U.S. banks with offices in Berlin
Citibank, New York NY

HUNGARY

Embassy of Hungary to the United States
2437 15th Street NW
Washington, DC 20009

Office of the Commercial Counselor of the Embassy of Hungary
2401 Calvert Street
Washington, DC 20008

Hungarian Consulate
8 E. 75th Street
New York, NY 10021

POLAND

Economic Counselor's Office
Embassy of the Polish People's Republic
2540 16th Street NW
Washington, DC 20008

Polish Consulate General
233 Madison Avenue
New York, NY 10016

Polish Commercial Counselor's Office
1 Daghammarskjold Plaza
New York, NY 10017

Office of Polish Commercial Consul
333 E. Ontario Street
Chicago, IL 60611

Polish Chamber of Foreign Trade
44 Montgomery Street
San Francisco, CA 94104

U.S. banks with offices in Warsaw
First National Bank, Chicago

ROMANIA

Romanian Embassy
1607 23rd Street NW
Washington, DC 20008

Romanian Office of the Economic Counselor
200 E. 38th Street
New York, NY 10016

Romanian Foreign Trade Promotion Office
100 W. Monroe Street
Chicago, IL 60603

Romanian Foreign Trade Promotion Office
22 Battery Street
San Francisco, CA 94111

U.S. banks with offices in Bucharest
Manufacturer's Hanover Trust, New York, NY

NEAR EAST AND NORTH AFRICA*

The Office of the Near East (Telephone: 202–377–4441) within the International Trade Administration serves as the focal point for the U.S. Department of Commerce response to the changing economic situation and significant business opportunities in the Near East and North Africa. The group assembles, analyzes, and disseminates to the U.S. business community information on economic conditions and new opportunities in the area, provides counseling for and makes representations on behalf of U.S. exporters, and plans promotional programs to assist U.S. firms to take advantage of the expanded commercial potential.

To take advantage of these programs call:

Israel	202–377–4652
Arab States	377–5767
Iran	377–5545
North Africa	377–4652 or 5737

For information on major projects in Trade Development call 202–377–4441.

ALGERIA

Embassy of Algeria
2118 Kalorama Road NW
Washington, DC 20008
Telephone: 202–328–5300

BAHRAIN

Embassy of Bahrain
3502 International Drive NW
Washington, DC 20008
Telephone: 202–342–0741

* Source: *A Business Guide to the Near East & North Africa*, International Trade Administration, U.S. Department of Commerce.

ARAB REPUBLIC OF EGYPT

Embassy of the Arab Republic of Egypt
2310 Decatur Place NW
Washington, DC 20008
Telephone: 202–232–5400

Commercial and Economic Office
2232 Connecticut Avenue NW
Washington, DC 20008
Telephone: 202–234–1414

Egyptian Commercial Office
20 E. 46th Street
New York, NY 10017
Telephone: 212–286–0060

Permanent Economic Mission
500 Fifth Avenue
New York, NY 1010
Telephone: 212–398–9130

Consulate of the Arab Republic of Egypt
1110 Second Avenue
New York, NY 10022
Telephone: 212–759–7120

Consulate of the Arab Republic of Egypt
3001 Pacific Avenue
San Francisco, CA 94115
Telephone: 415–346–9700

IRAQ

Iraqi Interests Section
Indian Embassy
1801 P Street NW
Washington, DC 20008
Telephone: 202–483–7500

ISRAEL

Embassy of Israel
3514 International Drive NW
Washington, DC 20008
Telephone: 202–364–5500

Israel Consulates General
Atlanta, Boston, Chicago, Houston, Los Angeles, New York City, Philadelphia, and San Francisco

Investment Authority and Branches:
350 Fifth Avenue
New York, NY 10001
Telephone: 212–560–0610

174 N. Michigan Avenue
Chicago, IL 60601
Telephone: 312–332–2160

Israel Trade Center
350 Fifth Avenue
New York, NY 10001
Telephone: 212–560–0660

Israel Supply Mission
350 Fifth Avenue
New York, NY 10001
Telephone: 212–560–0680

6380 Wilshire Boulevard
Los Angeles, CA 90048
Telephone: 213–651–5700

JORDAN (HASHEMITE KINGDOM OF)

Embassy of Jordan
2319 Wyoming Avenue, NW
Washington, DC 20008
Telephone: 202–265–1606

Consulate General
866 U.N. Plaza
New York, NY 10017
Telephone: 212–752–0135

Consulates are also located in Houston, Chicago, Scottsdale, and Palm Beach.

STATE OF KUWAIT

Embassy of Kuwait
2940 Tilden Street NW
Washington, DC 20008
Telephone: 202–966–0702

LEBANON

Embassy of Lebanon
2560 28th Street NW
Washington, DC 20008
Telephone: 202–462–8600

Consulate General
9 E. 76th Street
New York, NY 10021
Telephone: 212–744–7905

Consulate General
1300 Lafayette East
Detroit, Michigan 48207
Telephone: 313–963–0233

MOROCCO

Embassy of Morocco
1601 21st Street NW
Washington, DC 20009
Telephone: 202–462–7979/82

Consulate General
437 Fifth Avenue
New York, NY 10016
Telephone: 212–683–3062

OMAN

Embassy of the Sultanate of Oman
2342 Massachusetts Avenue NW
Washington, DC 20008
Telephone: 202–387–1980

Combined Consulate and Permanent Mission to the United Nations
605 Third Avenue
Room 3304
New York, NY 10016
Telephone: 202–682–0447

QATAR

Embassy of Qatar
600 New Hampshire Avenue NW
Washington, DC 20037
Telephone: 202–338–0111

SAUDI ARABIA

Saudi Arabian Embassy
1520 18th Street NW
Washington, DC 20036
Telephone: 202–483–2100

Consulate General
866 United Nations Plaza
New York, NY 10017
Telephone: 212–752–2740

Consulate
5433 West Heimer, Suite 825
Houston, Texas 77056
Telephone: (713) 961–3351

Commercial Attache
1155 15th Street NW
Washington, DC 20005
Telephone: 202–331–0422

SYRIAN ARAB REPUBLIC

Embassy of the Syrian Arab Republic
2215 Wyoming Avenue NW
Washington, DC 20008
Telephone: 202–232–6313

TUNISIA

Embassy of Tunisia
2408 Massachusetts Avenue NW
Washington, DC 20008
Telephone: 202–234–6644

Tunisian Investment Promotion Agency
Tunisian National Tourist Office
2408 Massachusetts Avenue NW
Washington, DC 20008
Telephone: 202–234–6644

UNITED ARAB EMIRATES

Embassy of the United Arab Emirates
Suite 740
600 New Hampshire Avenue, N.W.
Washington, DC 20037
Telephone: 202–338–6500

YEMEN ARAB REPUBLIC

Embassy of the Yemen Arab Republic
600 New Hampshire Avenue, NW
Suite 860
Washington, DC 20037
Telephone: 202–965–4760

Consulate of the Yemen Arab Republic
211 East 43rd Street
Room 2402
New York, NY 10017
Telephone: 212–986–0990

FAST MATCH

A quick, easy way to match your international business requirements to the appropriate Government programs or services designed to satisfy those needs

IF YOU ARE SEEKING INFORMATION REGARDING →

USE ↓

	Potential Markets	Market Research *	Direct Sales Leads	Agents/Distributors	Licenses	Credit Analysis	Financial Assistance	Risk Insurance	Tax Incentives
Foreign Trade Statistics (FT-410)	•								
Global Market Surveys	•	•							
Foreign Market Reports	•	•							
Market Share Reports	•	•							
Foreign Economic Trends	•	•							
Business America	•	•	•	•	•				
Commercial Exhibitions	**	**	•	•	•				
Overseas Business Reports (OBR)		•							
Overseas Private Investment Corp.		•					•	•	
Commerce Business Daily			•						
New Product Information Service			•	•	•				
Trade Opportunity Program (TOP)			•	•	•				
Industry Trade Lists			•	•	•				
Special Trade Lists			•	•	•				
Export Mailing List Service (EMLS)			•	•	•				
Agent/Distributor Service (ADS)				•					
World Traders Data Reports (WTDR)						•			
Export—Import Bank							•	•	
Foreign Credit Insurance Assoc. (FCIA)								•	
Domestic Int'l. Sales Corp. (DISC)							•		•

* Foreign Trade Outlook Market Profiles; Industry Trends; Distribution and Sales Channels; Transportation Facilities; Local Business Practices and Customs; Investment Criteria; Import Procedures and Trade Regulations; and Industrial Property Rights.

** Research material developed regarding a planned exhibition and released to support promotional activities.

Cost of services may be obtained from Commerce District Offices.

Source: Industry and Trade Administration, U.S. Department of Commerce.

Index